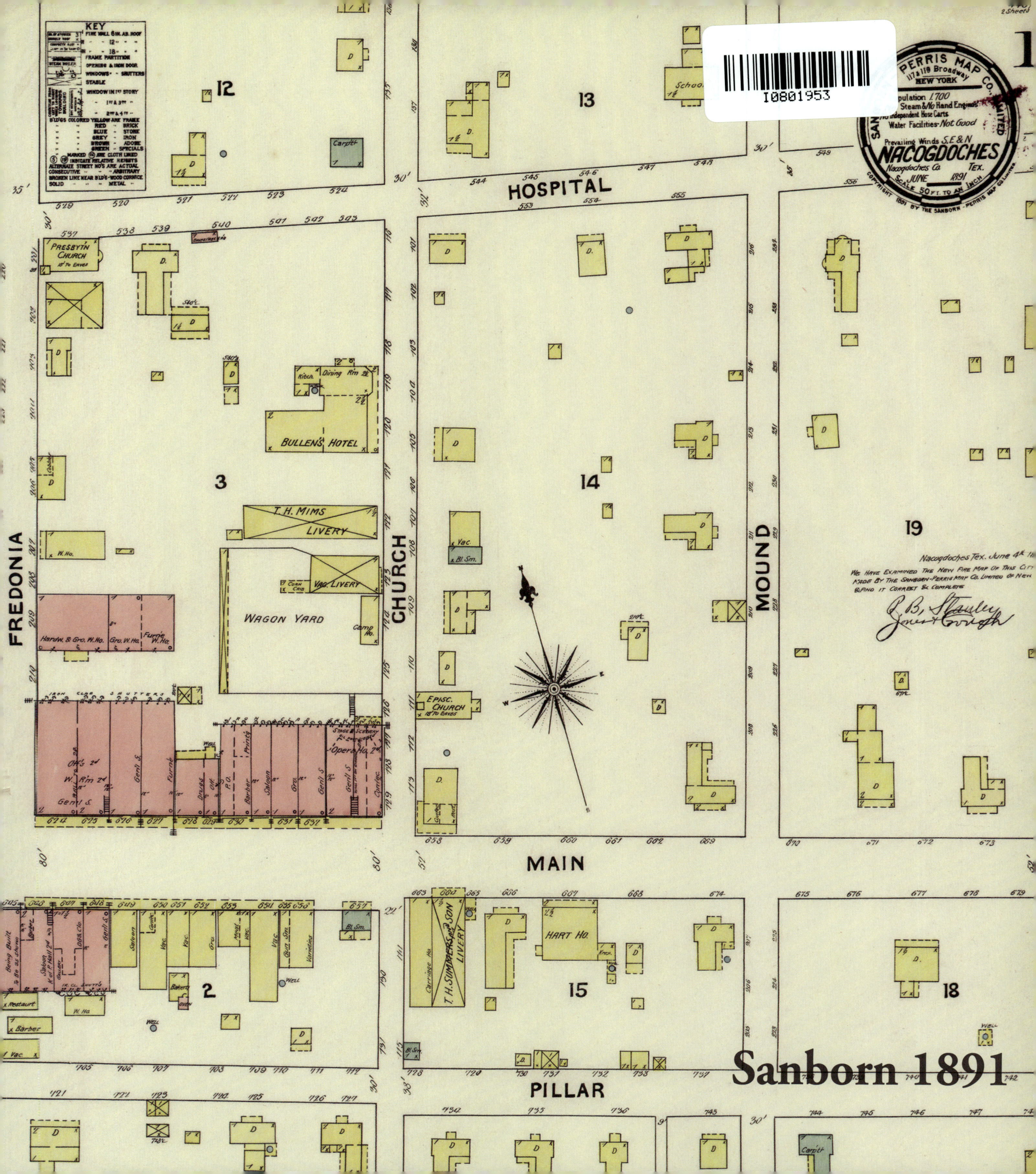

Sanborn 1891

Diedrich Rulfs

Designing Modern Nacogdoches

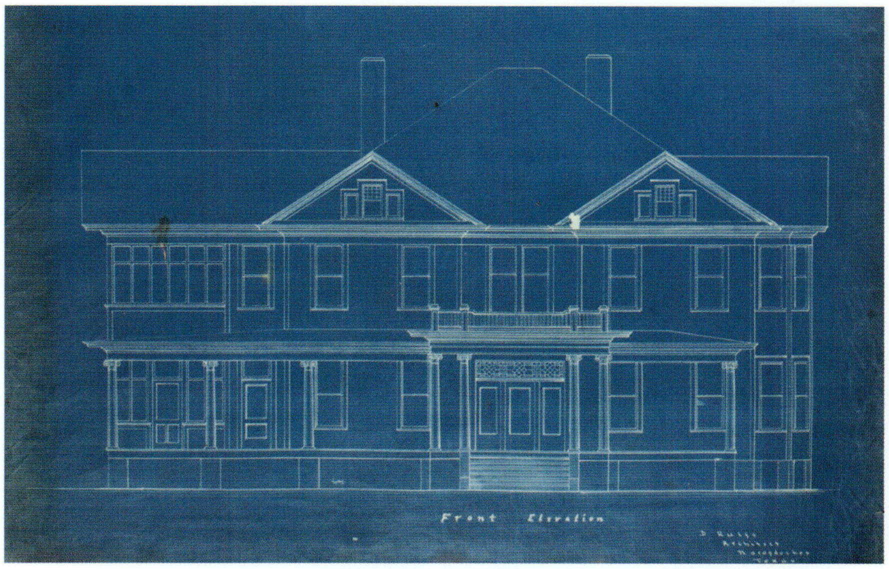

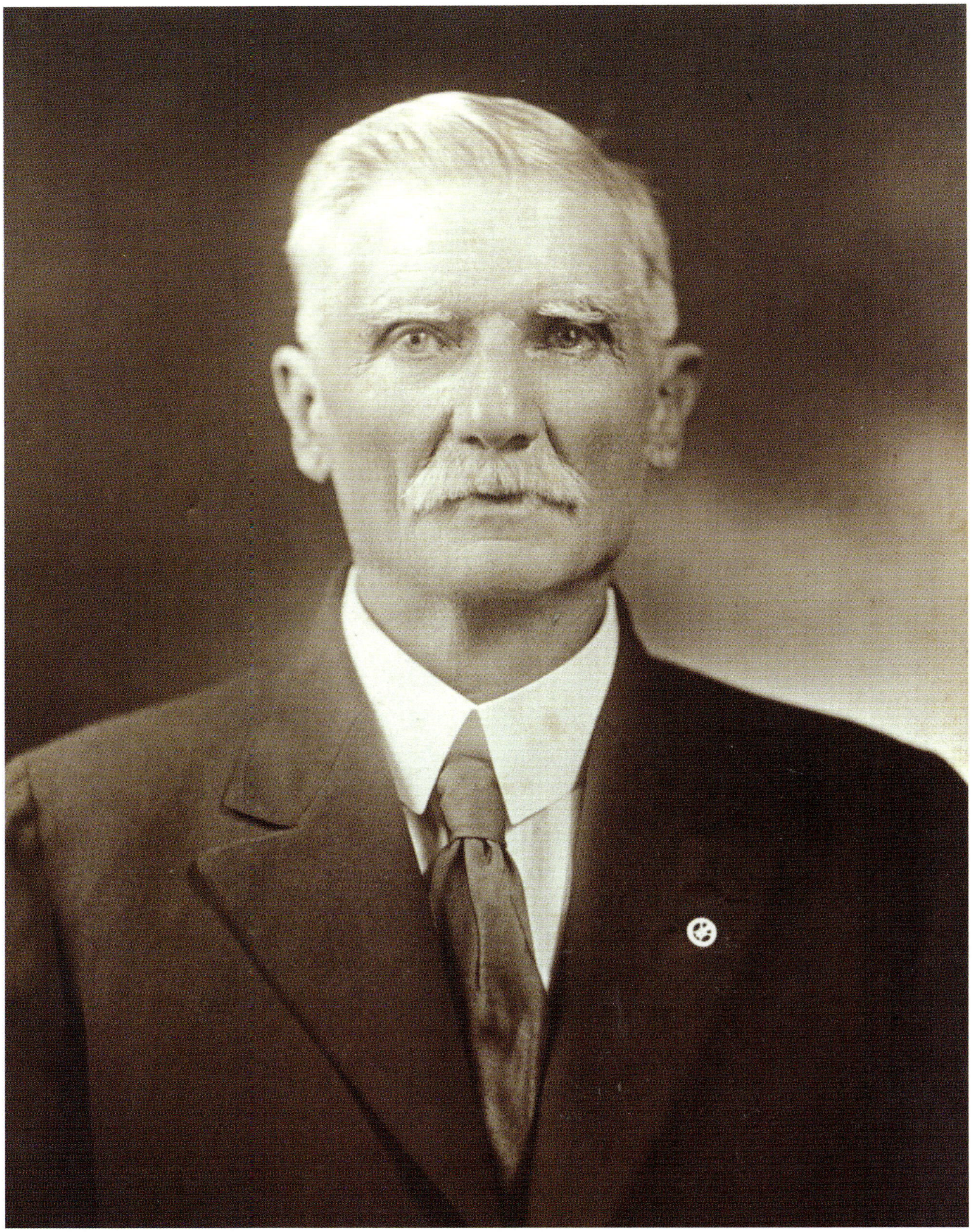

Diedrich Anton Wilhelm Rulfs
1848-1926

Diedrich Rulfs

Designing Modern Nacogdoches

Jere Langdon Jackson
Color Photography by Christopher Talbot

Faculty, Stephen F. Austin State University

Stephen F. Austin State University Press
Nacogdoches, Texas

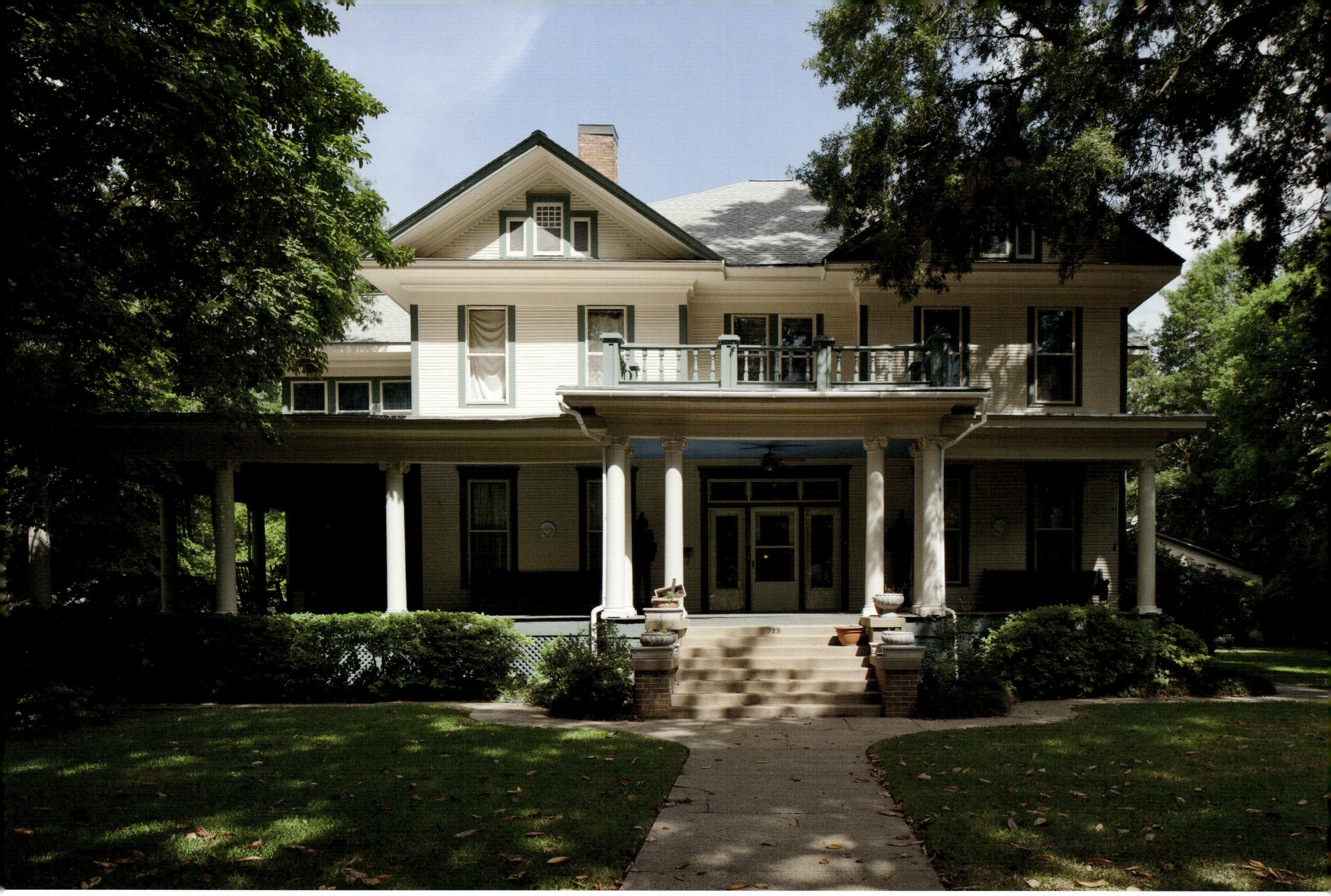

D. K. Cason House, Logansport Street (1914)

Manufactured in China by Everbest Printing Co.
Four Colour Imports

First edition
The paper used in this book meets the minimum requirements of the American National Standard for Permanence of Paper for Printed Library Materials,

z39.48-1984. Binding materials have been chosen for durability.

The views and opinions expressed in this text belong solely to the author and do not necessarily reflect those of SFA Press or Stephen F. Austin State University.

LIBRARY OF CONGRESS
CATALOGING-IN-PUBLICATION DATA
Jackson, Jere Langdon, 1941-
Diedrich Rulfs: Designing Modern Nacogdoches/ Jere Langdon Jackson;
Principal photography by Christopher Talbot. – 1st ed.
Includes bibliographical references and index.

ISBN-13: 978-1-936205-17-2 (cloth: alk. paper)
1. Rulfs, Diedrich Anton Wilhelm, 1848-1926---Criticism and Interpretation. 2. Architecture, Domestic-Texas-Nacogdoches. 3. Architecture-Texas-Nacogdoches-19th and 20th century. 4. Eclecticism in architecture-Texas-Nacogdoches. 5. Nacogdoches (Tex.)-Buildings, structures, etc.

I. Talbot, Christopher. II. Title.

CONTENTS

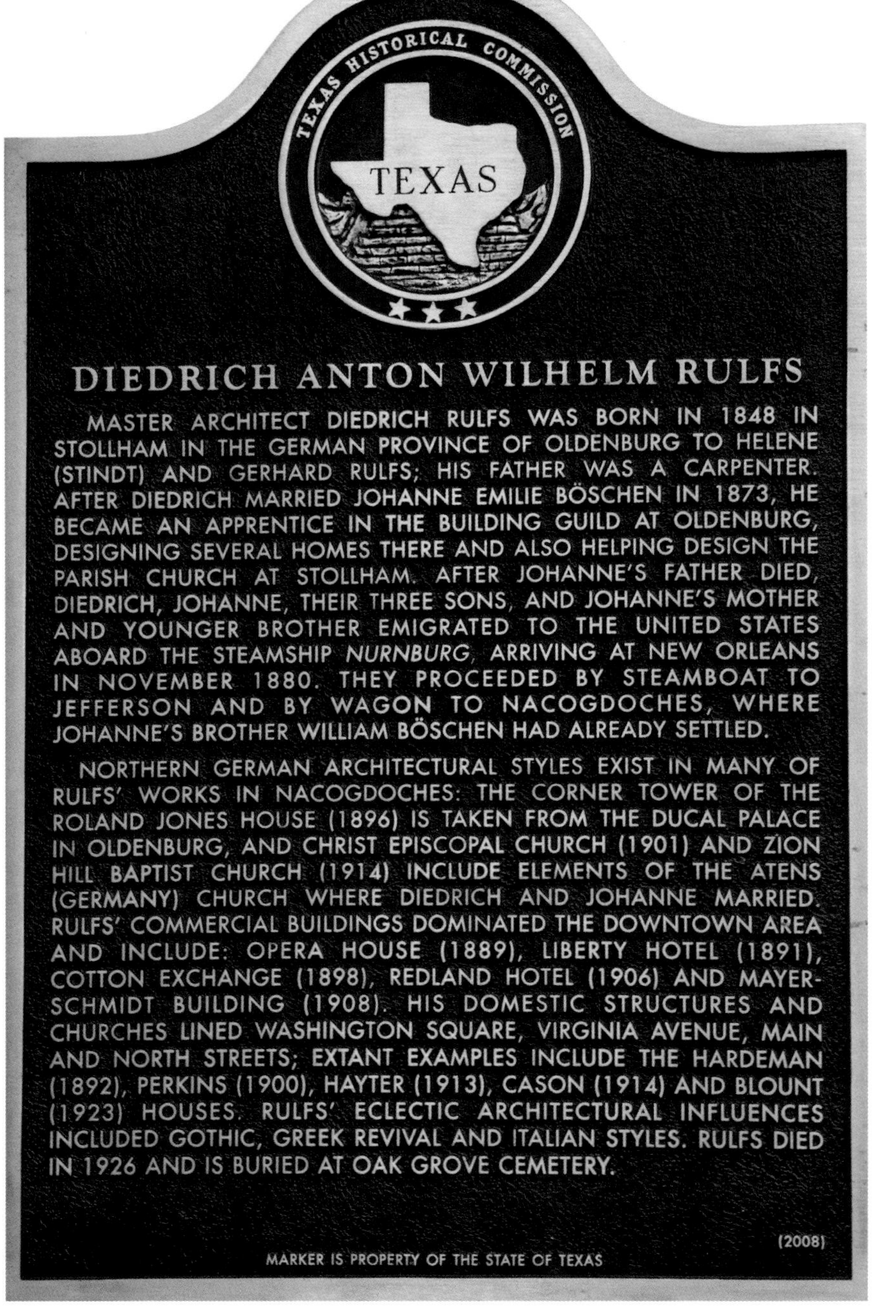
TEXAS HISTORICAL COMMISSION
TEXAS
DIEDRICH ANTON WILHELM RULFS
MASTER ARCHITECT DIEDRICH RULFS WAS BORN IN 1848 IN STOLLHAM IN THE GERMAN PROVINCE OF OLDENBURG TO HELENE (STINDT) AND GERHARD RULFS; HIS FATHER WAS A CARPENTER. AFTER DIEDRICH MARRIED JOHANNE EMILIE BÖSCHEN IN 1873, HE BECAME AN APPRENTICE IN THE BUILDING GUILD AT OLDENBURG, DESIGNING SEVERAL HOMES THERE AND ALSO HELPING DESIGN THE PARISH CHURCH AT STOLLHAM. AFTER JOHANNE'S FATHER DIED, DIEDRICH, JOHANNE, THEIR THREE SONS, AND JOHANNE'S MOTHER AND YOUNGER BROTHER EMIGRATED TO THE UNITED STATES ABOARD THE STEAMSHIP NURNBURG, ARRIVING AT NEW ORLEANS IN NOVEMBER 1880. THEY PROCEEDED BY STEAMBOAT TO JEFFERSON AND BY WAGON TO NACOGDOCHES, WHERE JOHANNE'S BROTHER WILLIAM BÖSCHEN HAD ALREADY SETTLED.
NORTHERN GERMAN ARCHITECTURAL STYLES EXIST IN MANY OF RULFS' WORKS IN NACOGDOCHES: THE CORNER TOWER OF THE ROLAND JONES HOUSE (1896) IS TAKEN FROM THE DUCAL PALACE IN OLDENBURG, AND CHRIST EPISCOPAL CHURCH (1901) AND ZION HILL BAPTIST CHURCH (1914) INCLUDE ELEMENTS OF THE ATENS (GERMANY) CHURCH WHERE DIEDRICH AND JOHANNE MARRIED. RULFS' COMMERCIAL BUILDINGS DOMINATED THE DOWNTOWN AREA AND INCLUDE: OPERA HOUSE (1889), LIBERTY HOTEL (1891), COTTON EXCHANGE (1898), REDLAND HOTEL (1906) AND MAYER-SCHMIDT BUILDING (1908). HIS DOMESTIC STRUCTURES AND CHURCHES LINED WASHINGTON SQUARE, VIRGINIA AVENUE, MAIN AND NORTH STREETS; EXTANT EXAMPLES INCLUDE THE HARDEMAN (1892), PERKINS (1900), HAYTER (1913), CASON (1914) AND BLOUNT (1923) HOUSES. RULFS' ECLECTIC ARCHITECTURAL INFLUENCES INCLUDED GOTHIC, GREEK REVIVAL AND ITALIAN STYLES. RULFS DIED IN 1926 AND IS BURIED AT OAK GROVE CEMETERY.
(2008)
MARKER IS PROPERTY OF THE STATE OF TEXAS

DEDICATION

With love, to the women in my life

Sarah Elizabeth Ragland Jackson

Rebecca Margaret Elizabeth • Mary Catherine Lois

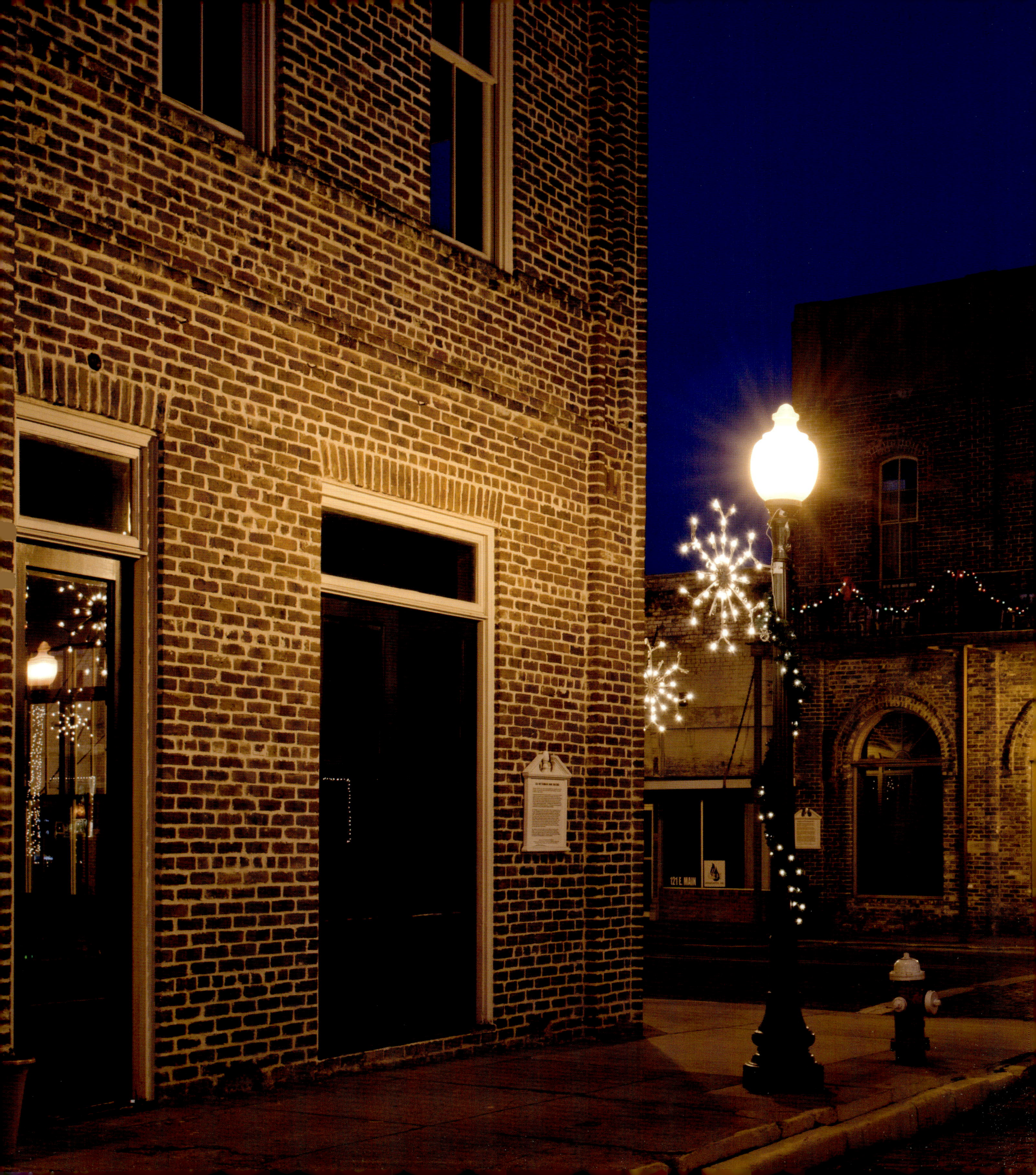
121 E MAIN

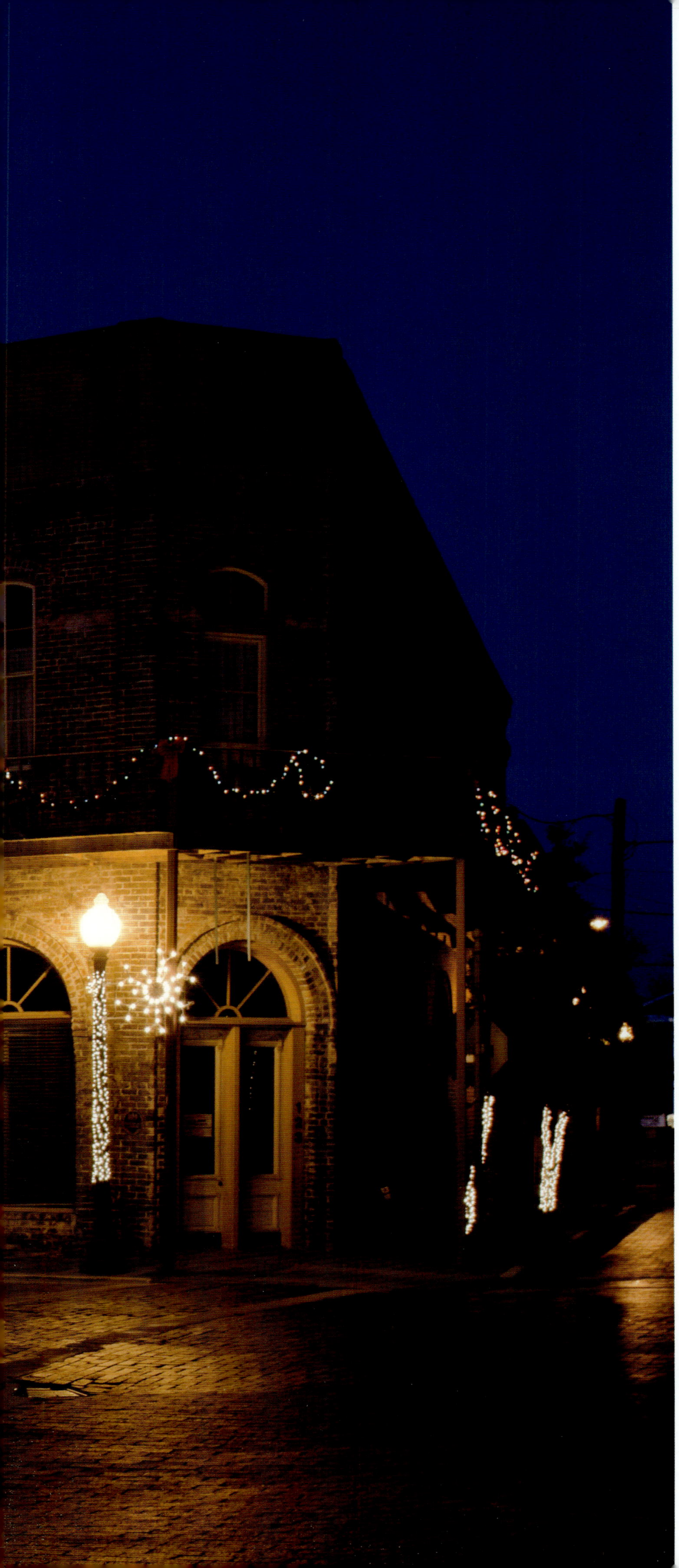

A special thanks to the following patrons who helped make the publication of this book possible.

Charles Bradbury

Ed & Gwen Cole Annuity Fund

Friends of Historic Nacogdoches

Joseph & Mary Devine

Robert & Jo Ellen Carlson Grubel

Morris Jackson

Mike & Marianne Keller
In memory of Earl & Mary Ellis Elliot and Kelso & Myrtis Woodward

LindaMcKinney

Tom McKinney

Craig Stripling

Barbara Stump

Larry & DianaWalker

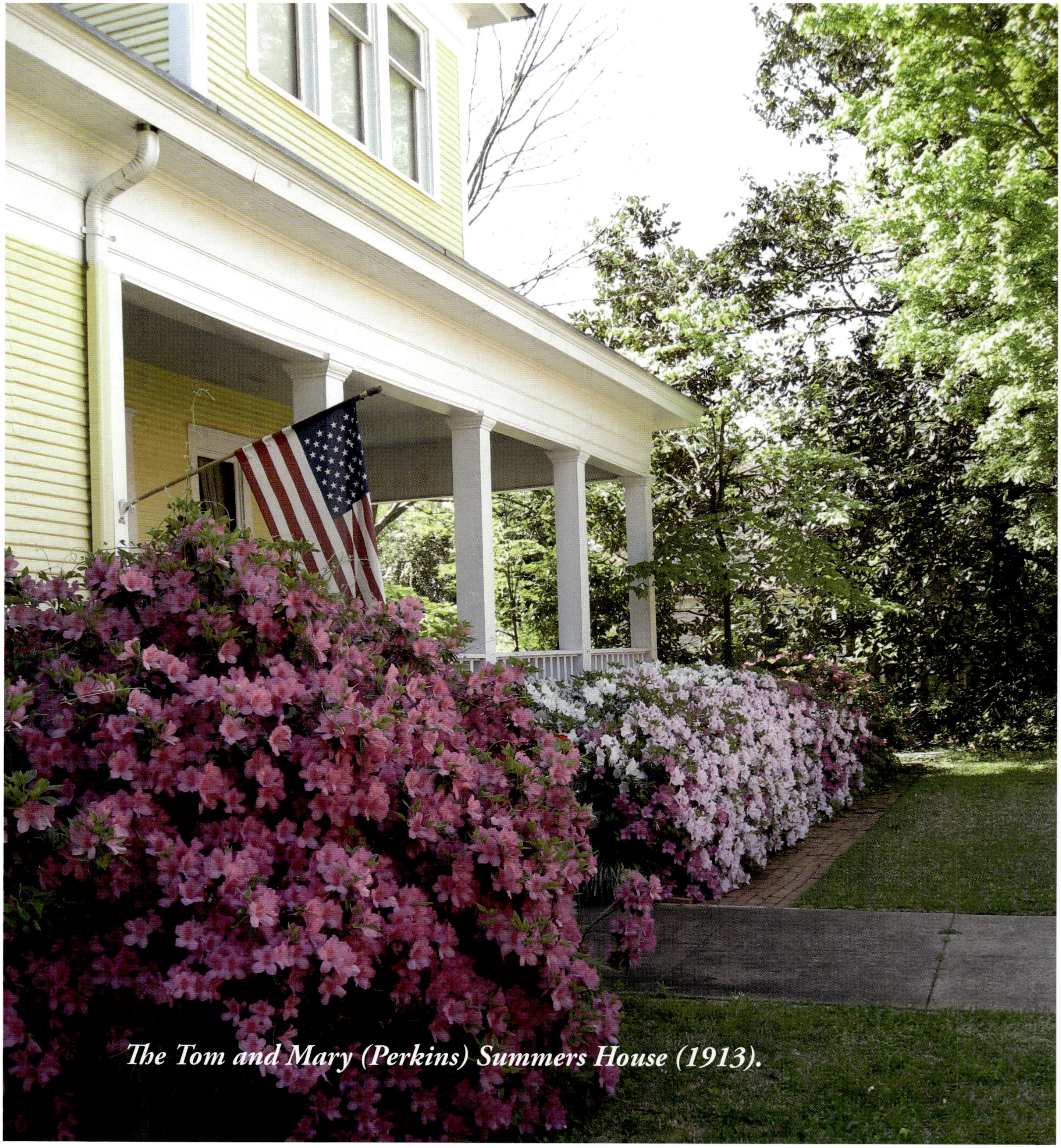

The Tom and Mary (Perkins) Summers House (1913).

PREFACE

I am a professional historian and a resolute tourist. Very early in my education I encountered a statement attributed to St. Augustine, "The world is a great book of which they who never stir from home read only a page." I took the quotation to heart and grabbed every opportunity to travel. I went into the field of history in part to experience travel through time intellectually. As I travelled, I always sought to penetrate the visible experiences by looking into their historical development. I live in one of the most historically distinguished towns in Texas – Nacogdoches, where so much of the story of the state begins. Yet, Nacogdoches is one of the best kept tourist secrets in the nation. One main reason for this is, the visual experience of visiting Nacogdoches is so vastly different from the image of the town one experiences in textbooks. Historically, the glory days of Nacogdoches ended sometime in the mid-nineteenth century. Visually, however, Nacogdoches is a late nineteenth century town–and a very interesting one in my opinion. This book seeks to bridge the disconnect one experiences in visiting modern Nacogdoches by telling the story of an extraordinary journey through time by a very distinguished town and a North German architect. Their journey together began in 1880 when Diedrich Anton Wilhelm Rulfs traveled with his family from Oldenburg, Germany, to the late pioneer town of Nacogdoches, and it ends in 1926 as the new city of Nacogdoches, forever marked by this talented architect, embarks on yet another journey as the home of Stephen F. Austin State Teachers College.

My journey to understand the German-immigrant Rulfs began in 1970 in St. Paul, Minnesota. I was at that time teaching at Macalester College and had just accepted a position in the History Department at Stephen F. Austin State University. In planning to move my family, I subscribed to the Nacogdoches *Daily Sentinel* for several months to scan the classified advertisements for a house. One intriguingly worded listing caught my attention:

"LARGE ANTIQUE, 100x150."

The realtor recommended by my new chairman did not hold this listing. After touring several of the houses on her list, I asked to see the "Large Antique." Reluctantly, she complied. When we pulled up in front of 304 North Church Street, I stepped out and exclaimed, "This is it!" My mother poked me in the ribs and whispered, "Keep your mouth shut, or they will raise the price!" The realtor, however, did not like antiques, was frightened even to go through the house, and knew that the asking price would not produce much of a commission, anyway. The asking price was $21,000. As my friend John Lester always used to advise me, "Jere, it depends on whether you are looking down or up on the price of something." Coming, as I was, from prices in the St. Paul-Minneapolis area, I was looking down. But, even looking up, it was a good buy! Sarah, my wife, and I bought the house that same day.

Back in 1913, Tom and Mary (Perkins) Summers had commissioned Diedrich Rulfs to remodel one of his earlier houses for them; they wanted to move "into town from the country" so that their children could grow up near the public school on Washington Square. (They lived one mile north on Starr Street!) I purchased the house shortly after Mrs. Summers died. Several pieces of outside cypress furniture, designed by D. Rulfs and constructed by his brother William Henry, came with the house. While not fully appreciated at the time, architectural specifications written by Rulfs himself also came with the house. F. I. Tucker, the lawyer for the Summers family and a colorful local historian, prepared at my request a detailed abstract of the property. Fortunately, a lifetime friendship with Florence Patton (granddaughter of Mary and Tom Summers) and other members of her family also came with the house. The house came with a neighborhood of cordial Nacogdoches families. Across Edwards Street to the south, Fran and Ed Moore, with their delightful young children, were restoring a home pre-dating mine. On the north in the same block lived Miss Gladys Hardeman, herself a local historian and a descendant of a famous Texas family. Across the street lived Gene and Mary Sanders, who had just refurbished her mother's home on the corner of Church and Arnold Street. Miss Mamie Middlebrook lived south of the Moores, and Dr. Stewart and Hollis (Mast) Barron had the property to the east. Mrs. Barron had lived across Mound Street as a child.

While we were undertaking our initial steps to rework the Summers house's plumbing and electricity, even before we ever took up residence, the Moores and their cousins Chuck and Ann Phillips introduced Sarah and me to Old Washington Square and the history of Old Nacogdoches University. As we began to walk our English bulldog around the area and to admire the many lovely old houses, Miss Gladys told us stories about the houses and the neighborhood; her uncle had built in the next block. Mrs. Julia Taylor, another charming neighbor, operated an antique shop in the

Tolbert Hardeman House. Sarah and I made frequent visits to that wonderful house as we looked for furniture. We soon became friends with Earl and Mary Ellis Elliott; my daughter Becky and Elliott Anderson, their only granddaughter, soon became lifelong friends. One day, Mr. Adlai Mast, Jr., who always drove home up Church Street on his way home for lunch, stopped to meet the person who had purchased the old Summers place. Mr. Mast took a great interest in the way I was rearranging the iron ore rocks in my landscaping efforts. Gene Sanders, the neighbor across Church Street, joined us. Mr. Sanders, then one of the owners of Cason-Monk Hardware Company, had as many questions about me as I did about the neighborhood. Both men wanted to know where my family resided and where I had attended high school and college. Playing off the fact that I had Minnesota license plates, I told them my family and my wife's family lived "up north." Adlai said, "I knew it!" I hesitated a moment before I added, "Longview, Gregg County." We had a good laugh. I began to feel comfortable calling on the deep memories surrounding me in the area.

None of these people, however, could answer my growing questions about the architect, whose signed specifications I had on my house. Interestingly, however, they all remembered him or knew many things about him. They also knew members of the Rulfs family still living in Nacogdoches, but no one knew how extensively he had changed Nacogdoches. Ann Phillips had some personal memories. As a child, Ann was an attendant in the wedding of Wilhelmina Thompson, the daughter of William Henry Rulfs; but even Ann and Chuck Phillips knew only bits and pieces about the houses Rulfs designed in town (even though they lived in one). Adlai Mast knew that Rulfs had constructed his father's house, but never really thought much about it. Miss Gladys knew that Rulfs had built her home, had remodeled the house in 1912, and had built houses and buildings for both of her uncles. As she casually stated, "He did most of the houses in town." Interestingly, when she had led a tour of the Tolbert Hardeman House in 1960, she did not think it was important to mention the architect and builder. To Miss Hardeman, her uncle had "built" the house. I repeatedly ran into that double meaning. Miss Mamie knew Rulfs had done her father's house on Irion Hill.

After cursory research, I realized that none of the tours of homes from the 1930s onward, none of the articles discussing the tearing down of important houses, none of the architectural books, and almost none of the casual conversations with homeowners – ever mentioned the name of the architect Diedrich Rulfs. The single newspaper reference to Rulfs within recent memory, I discovered later, came from the late 1930s when architect Hal Tucker, who apprenticed with Rulfs, mentioned to the *Daily Sentinel* that he was using Mr. Rulfs's original plans (since disappeared) when reconstructing the Christ Episcopal Church at the time of its move from Washington Square to the corner of Mound and Starr streets where it now stands.

When the Moores and the Phillipses asked me to join their group on the Nacogdoches County Historical Survey Committee in 1972, I did so with pleasure. I undertook to help Chuck do research to request a Texas Historic Landmark status for the Roland Jones House. In the process of interviewing the Ashford Joneses, I got to know another neighborhood family. At the dedication of the Jones House marker in 1973, I produced a history of the house and delivered the speech at the dedication. It was my first speech on Diedrich Rulfs.[1] The program chairman of the local chapter of the Daughters of the American Revolution, asked me to speak at one of their upcoming meetings. For their meeting, I put together a mimeographed booklet entitled "A Walk Around Old Washington Square," which I handed out to everyone. At that DAR luncheon, I met Anna Kathryn Rulfs Holbrook, the granddaughter of the architect. I recently found a copy of my mimeographed walking tour in the scrapbook she kept on her grandfather; it was the initial item in the memorabilia. Mrs. Holbrook, a lifetime resident of San Augustine, was subsequently very helpful and generous with her time. Unfortunately, her grandfather kept few documents. She shared with me several important documents she had acquired about her family's German roots. Mrs. Holbrook, however, knew more family information than she did specific details about the architecture of D. Rulfs.[2]

Shortly thereafter, Anna Kathryn introduced me to her cousin Mrs. Mary Stewart Duncan. Mrs. Duncan was the architect's niece on his wife's side; her father, William (Böschen) Stewart, had encouraged the Rulfs to immigrate to Texas. She was 89 years old at the time I met her. As part of my research, I interviewed Mrs. Duncan extensively; she helped both her second cousin Anna Kathryn and me to understand the extent to which Rulfs had transformed the town. She toured around with us in a car and pointed out families she knew had used her uncle's skills and services. She helped us to construct crude maps of these structures. She also helped Chuck Phillips to establish the family homes along the distance of Pilar Street.

In short, within two years of beginning my living-journey through Nacogdoches history, I had acquired new friends, a detailed set of architectural plans, a new itinerary of my neighborhood, a new interesting legacy to explore, and a new topic on which to indulge the historian's urge to collect information and documents. Victor Fain, the editor of the *Daily Sentinel*, asked me to join the newly established Nacogdoches Zoning Board which he chaired. Shortly thereafter, I drafted a set of historic preservation ordinances, which the Members of the Historical Survey Committee then recommended to the City. The ordinances called for the establishment of a Landmark Preservation Committee, which was done. In 1975, when the Texas Historical Commission asked Chuck Phillips and me to assist them with the first systematic survey of neighborhoods in Nacogdoches for the purpose of historic preservation, Chuck took the early years; and I did the late nineteenth century onward. This survey, incorporated into the Victor and Victor Survey in the 1980s, became the basis for the Historical Commission's later nominations for the National Register. As the author of the architectural resources for Nacogdoches wrote, "Although everyone provided much useful information, Dr. Jere Jackson was particularly helpful."[3] When Jerry Baker asked me in 1976 to contribute to the *The Bicentennial Commemorative History of Nacogdoches,* my chapter reviewed the architectural history of Nacogdoches. The article, entitled "Nacogdoches' Visible Past," focused mainly on extant structures. The heart of the article focused primarily on the contributions of D. Rulfs.[4]

I made my first trip to Oldenburg to seek background on Diedrich Rulfs in 1980. Since I had no car, I took a taxi from Nordenham to Stollhamm. After visiting the family church and having lunch at the nice hotel next door, I caught a ride with a local in the hotel to the family village of Stollhammerwisch. I walked from house to house, but there was not much to see but farmland. I stopped to rest by sitting on a milk can at the gate of one farm. When the farmer came out to see who was perched on his milk can, we struck up a conversation. After telling him my quest, he graciously secured me a ride on the milk truck that came to pick up his milk.

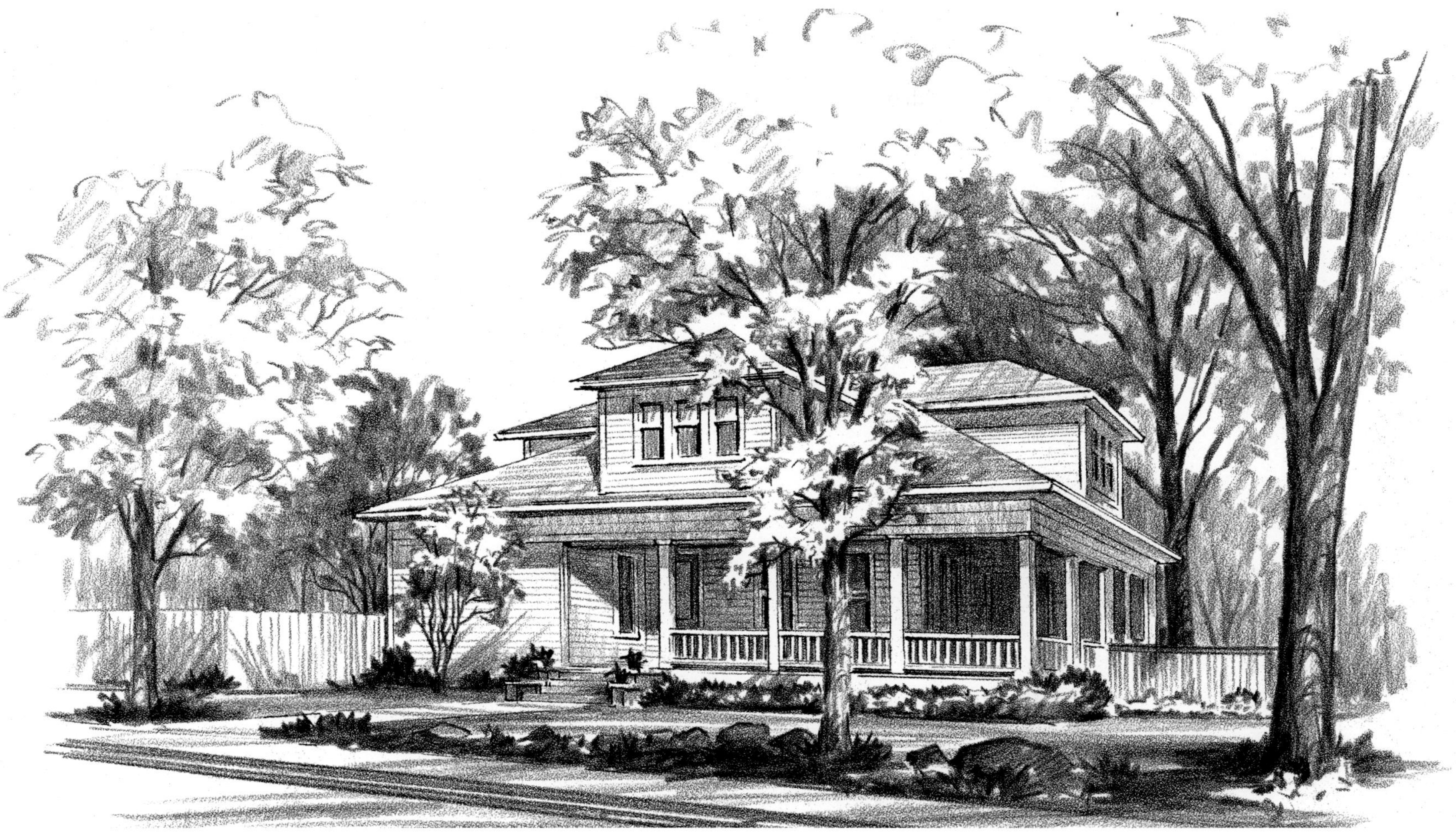

FIGURE (Preface) 2. Drawing of 304 North Church Street by Reese Kennedy in 1972. Commissioned by Jere and Sarah Jackson.

On the way back into Nordenham, making stops at every farm, the driver and I became friends. Back in town, he introduced me to one of his friends who bore the surname Rulfs. Although we could never establish a direct connection with the D. Rulfs family (after one hundred years!), we enjoyed a beer together in their favorite *stube* and spent an hour or so discussing the continued existence of Rulfs and Böschen families in the area, which we confirmed by looking in the telephone book. On my return to the area in 2010, I rented a car and enjoyed all of the province, especially the churches along the north of the peninsula such as Blexen where Edward Diedrich Rulfs was born just before the family departed for their trip to Texas.

Over the years I have continued to make public many segments of my research. I have written appeals for preservation, such as for the Eugene Blount House or Zion Hill Baptist Church or the Stephen Blount House; I have written applications for grants from the National Endowment for the Arts; I have written endless Texas historical marker applications for structures and surveys; I undertook research for the Nacogdoches Heritage Club (at Florence Patton's request) on a grant from the Texas Historical Commission to document many of the buildings in the downtown area; I delivered presentations for the East Texas Historical Association and the Texas Preservation Association; I have written numerous articles for the *Daily Sentinel*; and I have given countless speeches to organizations, such as the Daughters of the American Revolution, the Daughters of the Republic of Texas, the Rotary Club, the East Texas Historical Association, and others on the transformation of Nacogdoches in the early modern period.

The present book is a continuation of my travel journals through the life and times of this creative architect as he changed the context in which I now live. It has given me some useful excuses to travel, this time to northern Germany–Oldenburg, in particular. As Rulfs gave concreteness to the ideas of his patrons, I hope to give concreteness to the legacy of Diedrich Rulfs to Nacogdoches by placing his creations into the social, economic, and spatial contexts of their time. The book, written primarily for a local audience, is an educational travel book through the forgotten recent history of Nacogdoches – a context in which we all still live. Preservation begins with appreciation. To drive a visual literacy of his works home to local readers unfamiliar with his works, there is a purposeful repetition of images, especially in the last chapter, which is reflective. As a side advantage, I hope visitors to Nacogdoches will look at the visible artifacts of the recent past presented in this book as proof of the continued vitality of this historic town.

I must disclaim from the beginning any desire to overstate the case for Rulfs by making assertions that cannot be substantiated. There is no need to do that, for there is overwhelming evidence for the work attributed to him in this book. Throughout the documentation and contacts, there are multiple construction arrangements in both commercial and domestic buildings. Where there are questions, they frequently stem from how to define the term '*a building by Rulfs.*' First, Rulfs designed and then constructed many buildings and houses. Second, he frequently designed the house or building, and others constructed the building from his plans. Third, he remodeled many older homes in the town. More often than not, he revisited many of his earlier buildings in order to update them. Fourth, he rebuilt buildings that were damaged by fire, sometimes having to replace them completely with a new building. Fifth, in at least one known case, his construction firm built a house designed by another architect; and in two other instances, Rulfs served as the supervising architect on buildings designed by another architectural firm. Finally, his family continued to work in construction for years after the architect was dead, thus producing a Rulfs house, but not a D. Rulfs house. Nomenclature is also a big problem when using public and even private sources. The newspaper is likely to use phrases such as 'Blount built,' 'Perkins constructed,' or even 'Schmidt planned a new building;' but these men were active businessmen, who hired other professionals to *design or build* anything in a true architectural or contractual sense. The leaders of Nacogdoches conceived and paid for what they wanted, usually by engaging the professional and skilled services of D. Rulfs.

As late as 1970, the architect Diedrich Rulfs remained unmentioned; in press terms, the architect was anonymous. The present book is part of a long-range aim to rescue Mr. Rulfs from the anonymity that has cloaked his singular contributions to designing modern Nacogdoches. The historian who freezes his thoughts into print, however, must humbly acknowledge that history is always "under construction" as more information becomes available. There are, *no doubt*, houses in Nacogdoches by D. Rulfs not mentioned in this work. This book will also have mistakes. However, the task of preserving the architect's legacy has suffered from a lack of published research, as opposed to published statements, on the subject. The various surveys of Nacogdoches conducted by the Texas Historical Commission and the historians of the National Register of Historic Places have mistakes, some imparted to them by me. For instance, in 1972 we listed the name of the architect as "Dietrich Antone Gerard Rulfs"; and this misinformation made its way into permanent historical markers on the Roland Jones House and Christ Episcopal Church.[5] The various surveys, especially their details, are also works in progress. While this work cites the various surveys, I will not always agree with the material found therein due to more extensive later research. As reminded recently, however, the preservation of the legacy of the past is always a challenge, nowhere more so than in protecting a practical art such as architecture.[6] This book, above all, is a contribution to the local history of a distinguished town.

A great description of writing any lengthy work comes from Winston Churchill; my dissertation advisor Dr. James Godfrey recommended it to me. "Writing a book is an adventure. To begin with, it is a toy and an amusement; then it becomes a mistress, and then it becomes a master, and then a tyrant. The last phase is that just as you are about to be reconciled to your servitude, you kill the monster, and fling him out to the public."[7]

Acknowledgments

One of the most pleasurable undertakings in a book is thanking those who helped in the collaboration. Contributors who are omitted, but who should not be, haunt every author.

To my wife, Sarah, my companion in everything worthwhile in the last fifty years, I owe my most fundamental thanks. Sarah steadfastly supported the project from the beginning. As a bonus, Sarah is an accomplished writer who was generous with her time and suggestions.

Collaboration with Christopher Talbot has made this book one of the more enjoyable experiences of my academic career. His photographic and development skills are amazing. His eager commitment and professional approach to this project have made the book visually a treat for the reader. His color photographs will constitute a major contribution to historic preservation in Nacogdoches. There are reasons why professional photographers snap dozens of shots from every angle. Chris supported my knowledge of the buildings and town with just the right shots.

This portrait of Rulfs and his times owes many debts: to those in the past who felt an obligation to write impressions on paper, to those who transmitted memories through oral traditions, to those who preserved their family homes and buildings, and to lovers of beautiful things, who preserved the buildings and drawings once they passed into other hands.

I am particularly beholden to early contacts. The Summers family loved and lived in my home from 1913 until I purchased it in 1970. My first document by Rulfs came from their family records. One of my longest friendships in Nacogdoches is with Florence Patton, granddaughter of Tom and Mary Summers. From neighbors, who were preservationists before the concept became popular, I collected my first general information through conversations: Gladys Hardeman, Mamie Middlebrook, Mary and Gene Sanders, Chuck and Ann Phillips, Fran and Ed Moore, Ashford and May Ervin Jones and friends such as Adlai Mast, Jr., Mary Ellis Elliott, Bryan Davis, Langston and Virginia Nelson, and Nell Cason.

I owe specific thanks to certain members of the Rulfs family. The architect's nieces, Mary Stewart Duncan and Wilhelmina Thompson, shared their deep memories with the author in the 1970s. Granddaughter, Anna Kathryn Holbrook, graciously supplied me with family pictures and documents. Other members of the Rulfs family, such as his great granddaughter Henrianna Pierce, have offered access to the remaining family photographs and documents. John D. Rulfs, Jr., grandson of William Henry Rulfs, shared his family memories with me. A German genealogist, Hans-Rudolf Mengers, supplied me a complete family lineage before their 1880 departure for Texas. I am most grateful to him.

Scholarship is a cumulative endeavor. It gives great pleasure to admit standing on the shoulders of others. This book owes a special thanks to the scholarship of Carolyn Reeves Ericson. Without Carolyn's works, in particular her biographical dictionaries (*Gateway II*, *Gateway III*, and *Nacogdoches County Families*), this work would have drifted all over the landscape. Carolyn has also offered many oral suggestions on numerous occasions. Other friends, scholars, and local colleagues whose work provided insights are: Francis Abernethy, Jimmy Partin, Bryan Davis, and Gary Borders. Many friends have passed away: Joe Ericson, Chuck Phillips, Robert Maxwell, Charlotte Montgomery, Archie P. McDonald, and Victor and Lucille Fain. Working with Bob Brinkman and others at the Texas Historical Commission has also produced enlightening resources: surveys, national register nominations, historical markers, and other collaborative publications. Designated staffs at the City of Nacogdoches have amassed impressive data mines for the city's historical districts and preservation. Scott Ingles and Brian Bray have overseen that process admirably. In conjunction with the Center for Regional Heritage Research, under the direction of Mark Barringer, the City has placed substantial information online. The staff at the East Texas Research Center, where the vast majority of documents and photographs are housed, has made endless contributions to this work: Linda Reynolds, Jennifer Brancato, and Kyle Ainsworth on the current staff; earlier, there were many others.

Among the many people who shared their private collections of documents and photographs, I am grateful to the following: Delbert Teutsch shared his collection with the author in the early years (much of it is now in the ETRC). Campbell Cox, Cecil Sparks, Edward Blount (Jerry) Baker [for the Baker-Montgomery archive], Linda Greer, the Fire Department, City Archive, and Charles Bright have sizable collections of general and specific family photographs. Craig Stripling and Pam Thorstenson shared their large collections of photographs relative to their families and houses. Others who generously shared photographs and information with the author are: Tom and Enid Davison (in the 1970s), Jim and Beth Kingham, Bob and Ruth Carroll, Tom and Henry Middlebrook, Leland and Dianne House, David Alford, Richard and Cherry Baker, John and Travis Mast, Judy Buckingham, Carol Willis, Cole Sessom, Bill and Mary Whitten, Bill Patton, Reagan Patton, Florence Patton, Jeff Abt, Jimmy Partin, Mike Bay, Molly Smith, Mary Ann Bussa and Libby Bussa Duggar, Anita Farr, J.R. and Jill Ornelas, Paul Davis, Penny (Jones) Holcomb, Susie Lower, Lera Millard Thomas, Tom McKinney, First United Methodist Church, David and Ann Norton, Claudette Sutton, Barbara Stump, Richard Orton, Birdie Wade, and Joan Cason who presented the author with the D. K. Cason Papers (now in the ETRC).

Numerous friends supplied more than documents and pictures; they provided insights, knowledge, and time. Among those I would include Ann Phillips, Jerry Baker, Brian Davis, Charles Bright, Campbell Cox, Ab Abernethy, Craig Stripling, Florence Patton, Jerry Sutton, John Anderson, and Tom McKinney.

I am indebted to Stephen F. Austin State University for allowing me to work on this project. Both President Baker Pattillo and Provost Richard Berry encouraged the work from the beginning. They were particularly keen on the collaborative undertaking between the School of Art and the History Department. Several deans over the years provided support, including the present Dean Brian Murphy. James Standley understood the time involved in researching and writing a complicated work. Kimberly Verhines of the SFA University Press was one of the first people to commit to and encourage the book's publication. Kim has endured many postponements at my insistence and suffered these delays with grace. Kim also engaged Dianne House to undertake the reading and proofing of the drafts of the manuscript. Dianne's knowledge of Nacogdoches has proved very helpful. While all of my colleagues in the History Department have given encouragement, in particular, I wish to thank John Dahmus, Deanne Malpass, Bobby Johnson, Robert Mathis, Sylvia McGrath, Calvin Hines, and Perky Beisel. Coworkers associated in the Center for East Texas Studies include Meredith May, a very competent student assistant for several years; Tom McKinney, Mary Devine, and Jeff Roth, while working on tangential projects, each contributed material for the project. Later, as we worked with Florence Patton and the Heritage Club to place markers on the commercial buildings in the downtown area, Tom McKinney, Dan Rankin, and Melissa Darlington helped to untangle the difficult property records. In addition, Melissa kept us organized and in line grammatically. Sue Terry, who worked during the period of heavy lifting on the book in recent years, did invaluable research as well as tedious proofreading on various drafts of the manuscript. A special thanks to Mary Devine and Shirley Luna for their work on checking the galley proofs. My sincerest thanks to all of these coworkers.

The houses of D. Rulfs in Nacogdoches are large art objects – favorite subjects of local and visiting artists. Sometimes, drawings and paintings preserve the mood better than photographs. A special thanks to my colleague Reese Kennedy, who worked with the author in the 1970s to document the houses of Rulfs. I want to thank Losie Sutton Jenkins and Rebecca Stanly for sharing their art to help illustrate this book.

Last, but not least, I want to thank the owners of the various properties by Rulfs for allowing their possessions to be photographed and documented. Diedrich Rulfs, a humble man in every way, would blush at the esteem in which his creations are held in Nacogdoches.

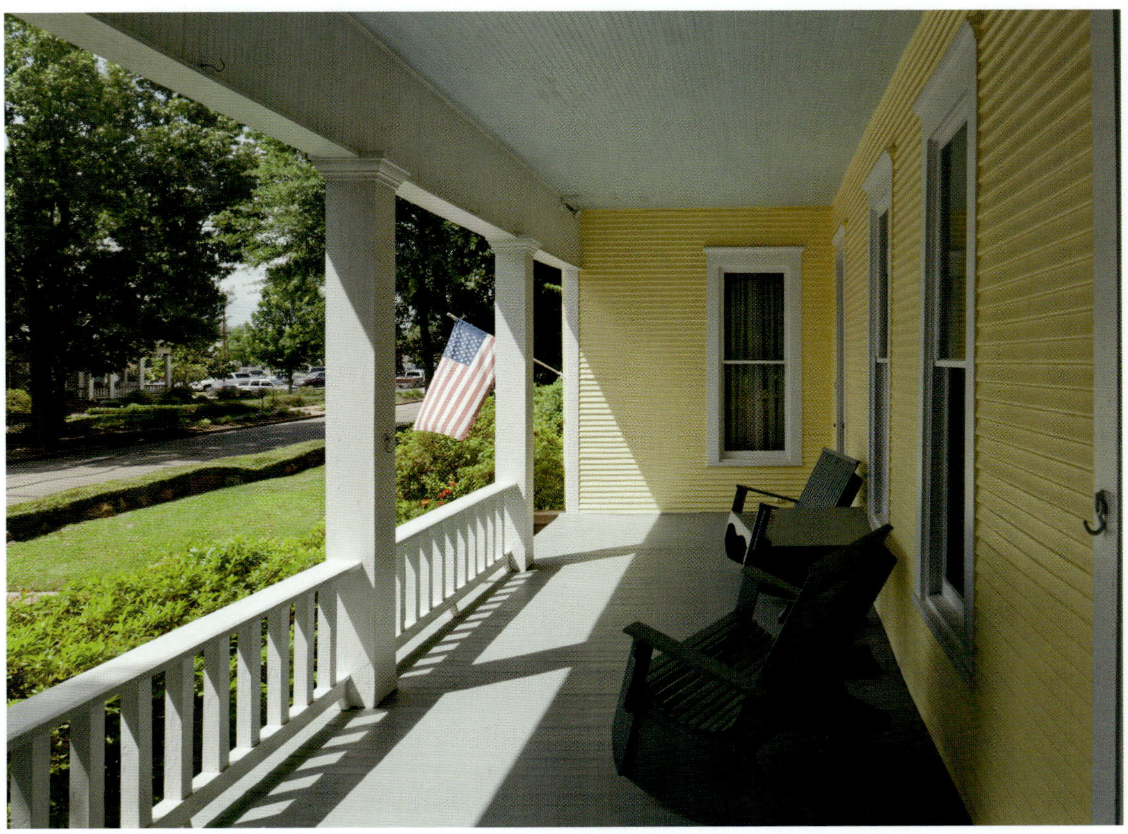

FIGURE (Preface) 3. Summers House Porch
The front porch of the Summers House, incorporated under the main hipped roof of the house, wraps from the living room aound the old parlor to the new screened sleeping porch on the southeast of the house. Mr. Rulfs designed and made the cypress furniture shown in the photograph for the house.

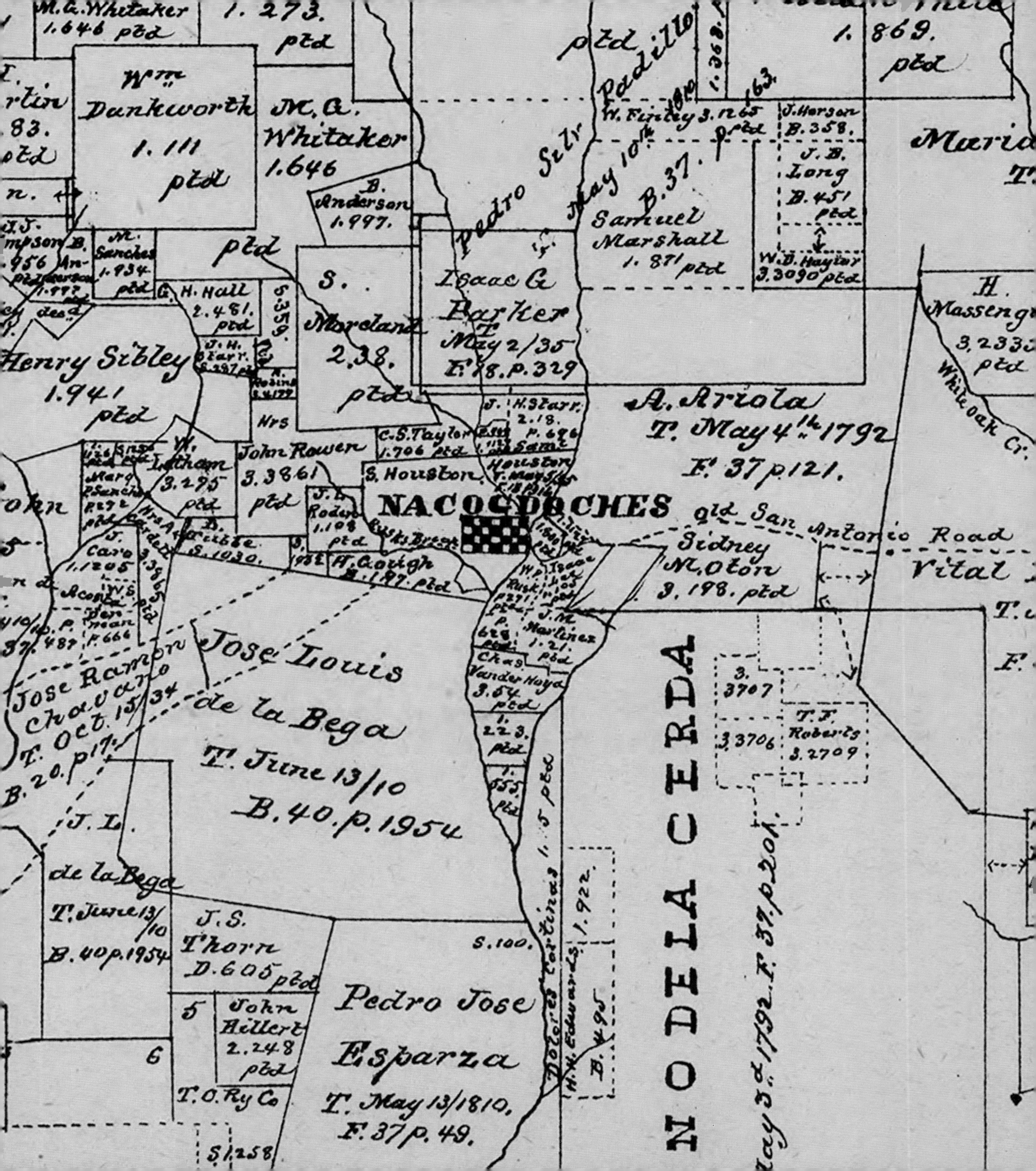
NACOGDOCHES
Wm Dankworth 1.111 ptd
M. A. Whitaker 1.646
B. Anderson 1.997
S. Morland 2.38. ptd
Isaac G Barker T. May 2/35 F. 18. p. 329
Pedro Sil'r
Padillo
Samuel Marshall 1.871 ptd
J. B. Long B. 451 ptd
A. Ariola T. May 4th 1792 F. 37 p. 121.
Old San Antonio Road
Sidney N. Oton 3.198. ptd
Henry Sibley 1.941 ptd
W. Latham 3.295 ptd
John Rowen 3.3861 ptd
S. Houston
C. S. Taylor 1.706 ptd
H. Gough
Jose Louis de la Bega T. June 13/10 B. 40. p. 1954
Jose Ramon Chavano T. Oct. 15/34 B. 20. p 171.
J. M. Martinez 1.21 ptd
Chas. Vander Hoya 3.54 ptd
NODELA CERDA
T. F. Roberts 3.2709
J. S. Thorn D. 605 ptd
John Hillert 2.248 ptd
Pedro Jose Esparza T. May 13/1810. F. 37 p. 49.
Dolores Cortinas
T. O. Ry Co
H. Massengill 3.233 ptd
White oak Cr.
Vital

INTRODUCTION

"Now, Nacogdoches has a soul, a spirit, an atmosphere. She is no raw product of today or yesterday. There are ghosts on her streets .... Gentle Franciscan fathers and curious, credulous redmen; lordly Mexican alcaldes and courtly French adventurers.... stubborn, spirited, courageous American Empres arios; ...men like Rusk, ...Crockett, ...Houston ...Travis." Karle Wilson. *Daily Sentinel,* 1907.

Nacogdoches styles itself the "Oldest Town in Texas." Yet, what really distinguishes a town is not age. It is the importance of the people who lived there, the history that was made there, and the continuation of vitality there. Nacogdoches is a distinguished town, historically one of the most interesting towns in the state of Texas. Of the important characteristics most travelers associate with Texas—*oil, cattle, wheeler-dealers, Sam Houston, independent nation status*—they all started in Nacogdoches. No one can write an early history of Texas without writing about Nacogdoches. This book is about the continuing vitality of Nacogdoches, specifically focusing on the young German architect responsible for the design of the modern city. The book is the first of two works on the renaissance of Nacogdoches in the late nineteenth and twentieth centuries. The sequel will discuss the history of Stephen F. Austin State University that dominates the Nacogdoches story from the 1920s to the present.

In 1880 a young architect named Diedrich Anton Wilhelm Rulfs migrated to Nacogdoches from Oldenburg, Germany. Rulfs found a frontier town, an anachronism even for that time, and before he died, he had assisted others in transforming it into a proud city with hundreds of buildings now listed on the National Register of Historic Places. The arrival of the railroad triggered the revival of Nacogdoches economically, but the man who molded the new wealth into a visually significant reality was the master builder D. Rulfs. His contribution, obvious to his contemporaries, has receded since his death and needs new attention. The editor of the *Nacogdoches Chronicle* concluded in 1897: "With his advent among us dates the real beginning of improvements in our city."[1] Yet, in the extensive tours of his homes during the 1960s, there was not one mention of the architect who designed the houses. In his four decades of work in Nacogdoches, Rulfs reordered the downtown commercial district, *twice*; he drew the plans for six churches, two public schools, the city hall, and several hotels; and, if these accomplishments were not enough, he redefined the city's domestic living spaces by creating most of the important residences constructed during his lifetime. The outside architects who practiced in Nacogdoches were the exception, not the rule. Rulfs's career was truly remarkable, perhaps singularly unique in the State of Texas.

In 1907 Karle Wilson Baker, another notable newcomer who adopted Nacogdoches, expressed sentiments that capture something both she and her friend D. Rulfs felt about Nacogdoches. "Sometimes a stranger, coming into a new place, is more sensitive to the atmosphere of that place than are the residents themselves."[2] Baker's creative medium was words, and she advanced to become a famous poetess and an important Texas woman of letters. (Incidentally, Baker lived and wrote in two houses designed by Rulfs.) Architecture was the creative medium of Diedrich Rulfs. The creative legacies of these two adoptive citizens made Nacogdoches as rich a place historically as did the deeds of earlier adoptive citizen-patriots, such as Sam Houston and Thomas J. Rusk. Diedrich Rulfs and Karle Wilson Baker are now part of the "ghosts" who enhance the atmosphere of historic Nacogdoches. The town as it grew, did not save much visual evidence from its illustrious Spanish and Revolutionary past. In 1902, the town stood by and watched a leading citizen tear down its most visible link to its colonial past—the Old Stone Fort. Fortunately, much of Rulfs's legacy can still be seen and enjoyed. Will the town protect this visual feast? This book is being written with the premise in mind that awareness must precede concrete steps.

FIGURE. 1. Introduction. (Across) Detail, Map of Nacogdoches County, 1881, Published by W. C. Walsh Commissioner General Land Office State of Texas. Texas General Land Office.

This map clearly shows the original square mile of the Old Town of Nacogdoches; the city lots to this day start from this designation of the "Old Town."

The Divisions of the Book

Part One of the book surveys the antecedents–Nacogdoches before Rulfs and Rulfs before Nacogdoches. Except for the brief survey at the end of this introduction, the book makes no attempt to trace the impressive early history of the town. In 1880 Nacogdoches was definitely a frontier town in both appearance and attitude. Its buildings were wooden, its streets were muddy, its attitude was parochial, and its population depleted–"a sad relic of past glory."[3] The objective in the first chapter is to explore in words and images the condition of Nacogdoches in the year the Rulfs family arrived. In a parallel chapter, the emphasis will shift to the background of Rulfs in Lower Saxony, from his birth in 1848 to his journey from Bremen to Nacogdoches in 1880.

Part Two of the work concentrates on the architect's work in the nineteenth century. The initial chapter focuses on his work in transforming the wooden business district into bricks and mortar. In the following three companion chapters in part two, the architect's redefinition of the domestic contexts in Nacogdoches will center on both extinct and extant structures in three main areas: Downtown and North Street, Washington Square, and finally Forbes and Irion Hills (Virginia Avenue and West Main).

Part Three begins with a transitional chapter. Nacogdoches experienced an identity crisis in the period after the turn of the twentieth century and before the First World War. A discussion of the plights that befell the town will help to set the middle phase of the architect's career. The following chapters, as before, begin with his commercial commissions, continue with a chapter devoted to his churches and civic buildings, and finally, two chapters exploring his eclectic architecture in the period before the World War.

Part Four opens with the dramatic events of 1917, the year in which Nacogdoches exhibited its modern transformation and charted a new direction. As the town dedicated itself to a more focused future, it reviewed the remarkable contributions of Diedrich Rulfs. Although Rulfs by then was seventy years of age, he was not ready for retirement. The buildings he designed after World War I still visually dominate the Square, East Main Street, and the entrance to the new college which would preoccupy its future as a city. The final chapter will reflect over the career of Diedrich Rulfs, reviewing and highlighting his legacy to Nacogdoches.

A Brief History of Nacogdoches

Before launching into an analysis of Nacogdoches in 1880, it is perhaps useful to summarize briefly the history of the community and its place in the history of Texas. The architect had to confront all of the implications of this past.

Pre-Historic Nacogdoches. Paleolithic settlement of Nacogdoches began about 10,000 B. C. with early ceramic evidence starting about 2,000 B.C. The area of the downtown, between the Lanana and the Banita Creeks, became a Caddoan site somewhere around 700 B.C. From around 1250 to 1450 A.D., a distinct development associated with Caddoan architectural traditions established a large nuclear village with attendant structural and mortuary mounds, supported by maize agriculture and a wide trade in exotic goods. A civic ceremonial center developed (in the plaza area now known as Washington Square) and large burial mounds were built. The Spanish first discovered these mounds in the sixteenth century. The Nacogdoches Indians were friendly, and their word for friend was "tejas"– or Texas. Local legend has it that the Indian town was founded when a Caddo chief on the Sabine River sent one of his twin sons three days to the west and the other three days to the east. The settlements they established were Nacogdoches, Texas, and Natchitoches, Louisiana, using Spanish and French spellings of the same tribal names.

Colonial Nacogdoches. While the Spanish explored the interior of Texas in 1528, maps do not show the explorers in the Nacogdoches area before the 1540s. The first descriptions of the area date from the French explorers in 1685. Alonso De León attempted the first colonization of the area in his series of reconnaissance expeditions between 1686 and 1690. The whole of East Texas was little more than a pawn in the French and Spanish imperial rivalries at this time. To quell French interest, the Spanish established a permanent settlement in 1716 named *Nuestra Señora del Pilar de Nacogdoches.*[4] The Spanish also established a series of missions in the vicinity. *Nuestra Senora de Guadalupe de los Nacogdoches* was located in the town, and *Mission Concepción,* which originally stood considerably outside the town, later moved to its present site when San Antonio was established in 1731. The most famous road across the state, and one of the oldest highways in the United States, *El Camino Real* (the King's Highway), had Nacogdoches as one of its main eastern terminals.[5] Inside the town, the Royal Road split into two streets, Main and Pilar Streets. When the Spanish lieutenant governor, Don Antonio Gil Y'Barbo, laid out the streets of the town in 1779 and built his Stone House, he established what became the province's first courthouse and first public square, *Plaza Principal.* By configuring the streets for defensive reasons, according to Spanish practice, Y'Barbo bequeathed to the town its unique layout–and many future problems for surveyors. Nacogdoches remained an important Spanish and Mexican colonial outpost, the capital of East Texas, until the Texas Revolution. The state eventually carved a total of twenty-six Texas counties from Sabine to Dallas out of the Nacogdoches colonial province.

Republican Nacogdoches. The city gave birth to three independent republics before the Lone Star Republic. The city today proudly flies nine flags, not six like the rest of Texas: the colonial flags of the Spanish, French, and Mexican; the independent republics of Gutierrez-Magee, Long Republic, Fredonia Republic; and, finally, the modern flags of the Lone Star Republic and State of Texas, the banner of the Confederate States of America, and the national Stars and Stripes of the United States of America.[6]

In 1832 the Battle of Nacogdoches was one of the opening salvos of the Texas Revolution. A combined force of Mexican and Anglo citizens attacked the fortified Mexican garrison in the center of town. The area around the Stone House and *Plaza Principal*, however, formed a natural fortress on three sides. Only after Adolphus Sterne showed the newly arrived Redlanders from San Augustine a way to out-flank the Mexicans, by going through the area of Washington Square and coming down the peninsula, did the garrison fall. The Battle of Nacogdoches cleared East Texas of Mexican troops and made the movement for Texas independence much less dangerous.[7]

The citizens of Nacogdoches led the fight for Texas independence. Sam Houston made Nacogdoches his first home in Texas.[8] Four signers of the Texas Declaration of Independence, among them Houston's second in command Thomas J. Rusk, were locals. Other citizens of Nacogdoches, led by Adolphus Sterne and Henry Raguet, recruited and outfitted volunteers who fought for Texas Independence. Many of these died in the Battle of the Alamo.[9] While President of the Republic, Houston still thought of Nacogdoches as his home.[10] Later, both of the state's first United States Senators, Houston and Rusk, had roots in Nacogdoches. What a historic legacy!

At the time of the Texas Revolution, Nacogdoches had a population of approximately 3,500 people; many more temporarily lived in Nacogdoches as they passed through. While the state was still agricultural, the town was full of merchants and lawyers who made their living by supplying the needs of the thousands of travelers and settlers entering through this Gateway to Texas. Main Street was lined with general merchandise stores, restaurants, saloons, and hotels.

Mid-Nineteenth Century Nacogdoches. In the period before the Civil War, Nacogdoches seemed to be on a steady course, albeit one downwardly adjusted. The town constructed a new courthouse in 1856. Nacogdoches University, chartered by the Republic in 1845, moved into a magnificent new headquarter in 1859—a long dream come true.[11] In 1861, Lyne Taliaferro (Tol) Barret drilled the first producing oil well in the state just outside town. Unfortunately, a lack of financial resources and the unavailability of appropriate transportation to exploit the oil, when coupled with the demands of the War, dashed whatever dreams there were for continued prosperity. The university's building became a Confederate hospital and later a headquarters for occupying Union forces. A period of stagnation ensued and lasted for at least two decades. Isolated by a lack of transportation, the Nacogdoches Port of Pattonia briefly gave hope that river traffic on the Angelina River might address the need, but the effort proved impractical. In 1880 the population of the town had fallen to around 500 people. The editor of the local newspaper noted that the town was a shadow of its former self.

Modern Nacogdoches. The arrival of the railroad in the city in 1883 changed everything and led to decades of near revolutionary modifications to Nacogdoches. The railroad transformed the economy by making all of the rich resources in the East Texas region available to the rest of the nation and world. Farmers could send their products to far-away markets, immigrants could easily find their way into the area, and local citizens could just as easily travel to the rest of the nation. The new booming economy rested on exploiting cotton, timber, and, to a lesser extent tobacco. Nacogdoches again became a hub for general merchandising. Many of the leaders who recognized and took advantage of the new opportunities in Nacogdoches came from outside, many from Germany. The impact of this prosperity on the architecture of the town is a main subject of this book.

In the early twentieth century, the economic boom slowed as it did across the nation. When the railroad and the automobile shifted the town's axis from east/west to north/south, Nacogdoches found itself limited to regional traffic within the state. Nacogdoches became, once again, isolated as it was before the coming of the railroad in 1883. In the north, the new major highways entering the state went to service cities such as Dallas and Fort Worth; in the south, the new arteries across the state went to Houston and San Antonio. When the Old University closed its doors in 1900, East Texas had no institution of higher education. The search for a replacement took two decades. Not until Nacogdoches was named as the location for Stephen F. Austin State Teachers College in 1917 did the town recapture its old dreams of being the educational center of East Texas. The Great Depression and World War II, however, then snatched away most of the advantages. Nacogdoches had to wait until the returning veterans in the fall of 1945 and, later, their offspring in the 1960s, before the town experienced another economy boom comparable to what it witnessed in the 1890s.

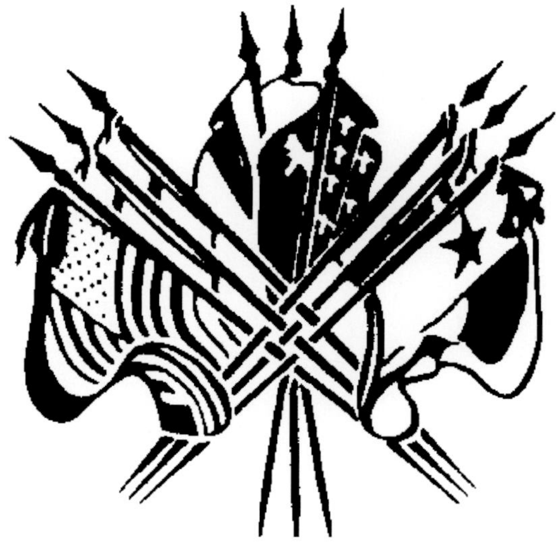

FIGURE. 2. Introduction. Nacogdoches Nine Flags Logo.

Shortly after beginning to promote the town as serving under nine flags rather than the standard Texas collection of six, the author designed this logo that the City of Nacogdoches now uses. In 2008 the Texas Historical Commission approved a subject marker for the "Nine Flags of Nacogdoches."

THE NINE FLAGS OF NACOGDOCHES

Throughout the storied history of Nacogdoches, nine different flags have flown over the region. The six flags of Texas are well known, but three others have also been raised. The traditional six flags include those for Spain (1519 – 1685; 1690 – 1821), France (1685 – 1690), Mexico (1821 – 1836), the Republic of Texas (1836 – 1845), the United States of America (1845 – 1861; 1865 – present), and the Confederate States of America (1861 – 1865).

The earliest of the other flags was an emerald banner for the Gutiérrez-Magee Expedition (1812 – 1813). Lt. Augustus Magee and Col. Bernardo Gutiérrez organized an army which controlled territory east of San Antonio. However, Gutiérrez lost support, a Mexican force regained San Antonio, and the army disbanded. Another flag contained red and white stripes with one white star on a red field, representing the Long Republic (1819). Col. James Long set up a government from Nacogdoches, which fell to Spanish forces; he was later captured and killed. The final of the three flags was red and white, and inscribed with the words, "Independence, Freedom and Justice." It belonged to Republic of Fredonia (1826 – 1827). Empresario Haden H. Edwards proclaimed a new republic following the Mexican revocation of his colonial charter. When he failed to enlist aid, Edwards fled, ending the rebellion.

Nacogdoches has been a Gateway to Texas for hundreds of years, not only for settlers but also for ideals. The Nine Flags of Nacogdoches represent revolutionary activity that was essential to the Spirit of Texas. In 1997, residents began celebrating the Nine Flags Festival, which commemorates the city's importance as a center of freedom and a community vital to Texas history. (2008)

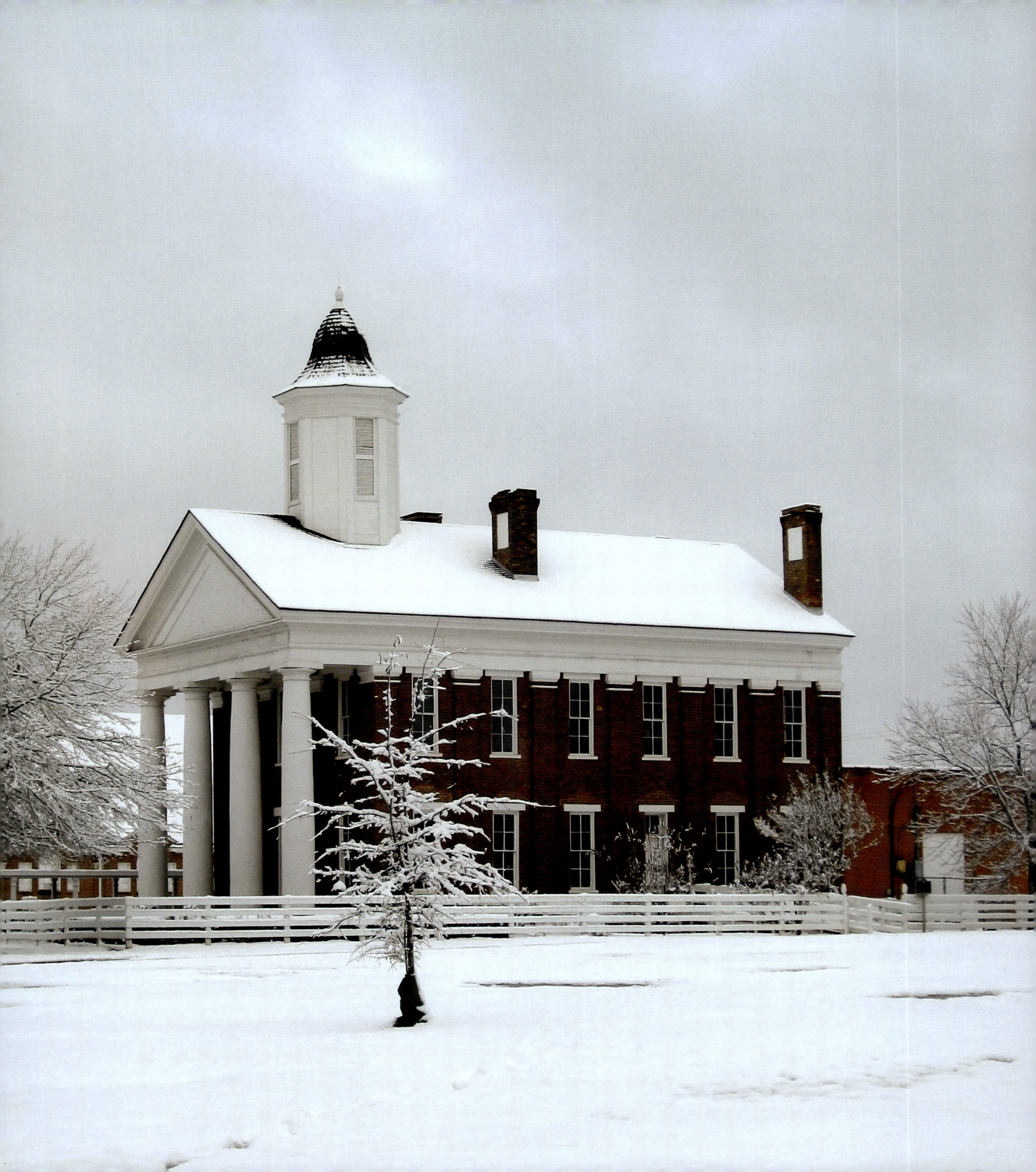

CHAPTER I

Nacogdoches Before Rulfs

A Portrait of Nacogdoches in 1880

"The town, as it now exists, is by no means equal to what it has been in the past, either as to population, wealth, or importance.... Nacogdoches is now a town of about 500 inhabitants .... [on the] same footing with ordinary county sites, save in point of history, a somewhat sad relic of past glory." Richard W. Haltom, *Nacogdoches* (1880).

In 1880 Nacogdoches was a pioneer community with great expectations. It was at a turning point in its history. Most people knew the expected arrival of a railroad in town would change everything; there was too much evidence from other cities to think otherwise. Interestingly, many of the people who were to shape the future of Nacogdoches were just arriving, and many of them came from outside the town. Some, such as W. U. Perkins, E. A. Blount, Ira Link Sturdevant, and Richard W. Haltom, came from nearby counties. Others, such as D. K. Cason, Roland Jones, and Karle Wilson Baker, came from nearby states. Others, for instance, John Schmidt and Abraham Mayer, came from Germany. Reiterating what Karle Wilson (Baker) wrote in 1907, "Sometimes a stranger, coming into a new place, is more sensitive to the atmosphere of that place than are the residents themselves. They are accustomed to it; to a stranger it is new and delightful. Genuine lovers of travel roam over the world not so much to see buildings and monuments, as to detect and enjoy this spirit, this personality or soul, of the places they visit."[1]

The greatest migration in world history occurred in the latter part of the nineteenth century, when almost sixty million immigrants left Europe. Lured by the boundless opportunities in the United States, half of these traveled to North America.[2] Nacogdoches itself received new immigrants from many countries, including England, Ireland, Germany, France, Italy, and Switzerland. Among the immigrants who were to have a significant impact on the economy and the visible history of Nacogdoches, the Germans were perhaps the most influential.[3] Together, they started major new businesses and rebuilt the wooden frontier town into a modern city of bricks and mortar. The present chapter discusses not only the mood of Nacogdoches around 1880—the problems, the leaders, the thought patterns, the opportunities—but also, the look and feel of the frontier town before the arrival of an unknown architect and builder named Diedrich Rulfs from Northern Germany.

FIGURE 1.1. (Opposite) Old University Building in 2010.
The Old Nacogdoches University celebrated its 150th anniversary in 2009. The building has changed little since it was built. It has fallen into disrepair often, but having survived a crisis in 1904, it received enough attention to keep it stable. In the 1960s, when major restoration was undertaken by the Nacogdoches Historical Society, they restored the chimneys, which earlier efforts had removed. The building belongs to the NISD and is under the care of the Nacogdoches Federation of Women's Clubs. Photograph by the author.

New Immigrants Arrive

Among the millions of immigrants to America, two Germans from the Rhineland, Abraham Mayer (1856-1911) and John Schmidt (1856-1934), migrated to East Texas.[4] The two young men were born in the same year, were playmates in youth and students together, and set out as young men on careers at the same time. In 1874, they sailed to New York City to seek their fortunes. For a while, they worked as "salary boys" in various odd jobs. Mayer, through a contact in Texas, accepted a job in Henderson, Texas, in 1876. A year later, Schmidt followed his friend to East Texas. Both men were to become close friends with the legendary editors of Nacogdoches newspapers—Richard W. (Bill) Haltom (1857-1907) and Giles Haltom (1867-1951)[5] —and were to relate their life stories to the Haltom brothers. The Haltoms, for their part, felt the stories historically important enough to document and repeat often.[6] The account of the events in 1878, as recounted in a 1928 Special Edition of the *Daily Sentinel* by Giles Haltom, is very much in line with what his older brother, Richard, published earlier:

> The two friends worked hard at their respective jobs during the day and spent their evenings together in the lobby of the hotel [in Henderson] where they boarded, listening to the stories told by the various traveling men and drummers who came in from day to day and each seemed to vie with the other in telling big stories about the various localities through which they had traveled. In those days the drummers carried several trunks and traveled by surrey, pulled by two big horses....
>
> Much of the talk of the drummers was about the town of Nacogdoches, which they said was 45 miles south of Henderson, directly in the path of the railroad building northward from Houston, the center of a vast cotton and timber area, and no doubt destined one day to be the emporium of all the East Texas country.
>
> Abe Mayer and John Schmidt, listening to the various stories about the Nacogdoches country, decided that the sooner they arrived on the spot the better their opportunities would be to develop the business they had in mind—a great mercantile business. A pool of their resources showed that they had $700 in money, two suits of clothes each, and one billion dollars in optimism and reserve energy. This was certainly capital of sufficient volume to undertake anything worthwhile, and so the youngsters moved to Nacogdoches.[7]

Abe Mayer and John Schmidt were twenty-one years of age when they decided to visit Nacogdoches for the first time. Transportation, however, was a problem. Nacogdoches was isolated, and this isolation was keeping the county from sharing in the prosperity then exploding all over Texas. Although the distance between Henderson and Nacogdoches was roughly 45 miles, the trip for Mayer and Schmidt by surrey took 18 hours.

Haltom continues: "It was past midnight in the early part of February and in the year 1878, when a two-horse surrey stopped in front of the old Hyde House, which was at that time a popular hostelry in the town of Nacogdoches." The Hyde House was a pioneer residence on Hospital Street turned into a hotel. In reflecting on the difficulties facing any visitor at the time, Haltom observed, "There was not a real good road in Nacogdoches County nor a graded street in the town of Nacogdoches. It is a matter of difficulty for people of the present generation, surrounded by all conveniences to visualize the situation or conditions that prevailed."[8] There was no running water, no indoor toilets, no gas or electric lights, no telephones, no drainage for streets, no city services whatsoever, not even a volunteer fire department in a wooden town.

As Schmidt and his friend Mayer began to survey the town the next morning, the first man they met was another German immigrant, Francis Rusche (1823-1901),[9] who had arrived in Nacogdoches before the Civil War. Rusche's house sat across Hospital Street from the Hyde House, where the Fredonia Hotel stands today. He offered to show the two visitors around the town, translating when necessary. They walked down Fredonia Street to visit the Old Stone House (or Stone Fort), where Rusche explained the building's history. As the story goes, Rusche also "told of the wonderful undeveloped resources of this new and splendid land, and especially did he grow eloquent when he told of the railroad that was being built northward from Houston." Although Rusche conceded that the town was "little more than a village" at the time, he added there were many "distinguished families" in the town. He emphasized how many of the immigrant families came from Germany: the Hoyas, Shindlers, Hillenkamps, Müllers, Böschens, Eichels, and Voigts.[10] While German immigrants are central to this book, there were important immigrants from other ethnic backgrounds who were to play major roles. [Among the descendants of English heritage, they would meet and become close friends with W. U. Perkins (1856-1940).[11]] Perkins had come to Nacogdoches on horseback from Laneville (near Henderson) in Rusk County. Will Perkins was among the first businessmen to become close friends and partners with the German immigrants in the next few decades as they developed Nacogdoches.[12]

Haltom says that Schmidt and Mayer "met practically all the businessmen of Nacogdoches on their trip during that eventful day." Many of those introduced became lifelong friends, men such as "John P. Davidson, R. C. Shindler, Fritz Hoya, Lawrence Taylor, X. W. Pressley and John H. Cox."[13] Haltom compares Mayer and Schmidt to Jason in Homer's *Iliad;* they "had come to the historic town in the west, in search of Golden Fleece."[14] Impressed by their reconnaissance run and encouraged by their Henderson sponsor, Schmidt and Mayer immediately leased space on the west side of the Nacogdoches Square from Frederick Voigt (1825-1880).[15] (Voigt, an earlier German immigrant from Westphalia, had come to the United States back in 1846. He had commanded the Nacogdoches Volunteers during the Civil War and now ran a bakery on the west side of the square next to the building he had leased to Schmidt.) Under their combined names, Mayer & Schmidt, they opened a small grocery business with goods brought down from Henderson on wagons. Within a year, they purchased the rented property.[16] The decision to make Nacogdoches their permanent home manifested itself in other ways. John Schmidt married Miss Elizabeth K. Voigt, Frederick's daughter, on January 13, 1880, in the Christ Episcopal Church. At the time of the 1880 Federal Census, Abe Mayer lived and boarded with the Schmidts.[17]

Haltom on Nacogdoches in 1880

Historians endlessly debate whether history makes men or men make history. The *story* lies in the interplay of men and circumstances, as Shakespeare observed in discussing Julius Caesar's crossing of the Rubicon:

> There is a tide in the affairs of men
> Which taken at the flood, leads on to fortune;
> Omitted, all the voyage of their life
> Is bound in shallows and in miseries.[18]

The great leaders of Nacogdoches in the past, such as Sam Houston, Henry Raguet, Adolphus Sterne, and Thomas J. Rusk—all newcomers to the frontier town—had all passed from the scene.[19] In the late 1870s, the question John Schmidt pondered was whether Nacogdoches would have the leaders to seize the tide "at the flood" or whether the town would continue to be "bound in shallows and in miseries" as had been the case since the Civil War. Schmidt thought Nacogdoches needed new immigrants. In the person of R. W. (Bill) Haltom, Schmidt found not only a very sympathetic ear, but also a cohort with a megaphone—a newspaper.

Over the years Bill Haltom ran a succession of local newspapers.[20] An unabashed promoter of local interests, Haltom had long desired to publish a book on the history of Nacogdoches as a way to promote the town. He hated the scant coverage given to Nacogdoches in recent histories. He felt editors in Dallas and Houston, especially, were giving biased and incorrect coverage in order to promote their cities.[21] Schmidt encouraged Haltom in his desire to have an easily available history to help promote the town, and Haltom warmly endorsed Schmidt's idea of making a plea for new citizen-leaders. With financial support from the new citizen-businessmen Mayer and Schmidt, in April of 1880 Haltom published a small book entitled *A History and Description of Nacogdoches County Texas*.[22] The book was a catalogue of the assets and history of Nacogdoches, wrapped in a direct appeal for outsiders to migrate to Nacogdoches. Since Schmidt also sponsored the passage of Diedrich Rulfs to Nacogdoches, it is distinctly possible that Diedrich Rulfs was one of the first recruits attracted by Haltom's little book geared to immigrants interested in East Texas.[23] Haltom's optimistic little playbook would have helped Rulfs to review the evidence and the options before uprooting his entire family for relocation. The book has passages that jump to one's attention and have meaning when considering immigrants such as the Rulfs. As discussed in the next chapter, however, Rulfs did not actually need a primer to get the message. In recruiting Rulfs, Schmidt had a much more direct way of enticing the young architect to Texas and of telling him the advantages awaiting him in East Texas. William Henry Stewart, (1841-1915),[24] Rulfs's brother-in-law and himself one of Schmidt's recruits, was already in Nacogdoches at the time. Before launching into that story, however, a consideration of Haltom's work might prove enlightening.

Modern historians have found Haltom's book invaluable. His history broke new ground. Economic historians have found his catalog of resources interesting and his conclusions sound. One historian, expanding on Haltom's idea that Nacogdoches was poor despite the vast resources around them, extended this to all of East Texas. The region, wrote James Reese, was "consistently poor" and never really shared in the prosperity of the other regions of Texas, albeit seldom in want.[25] Haltom later republished his own book and found ways to recycle parts of the work in later years.[26] Haltom's descriptions of Nacogdoches as the gateway to Texas inspired the poet Karle Wilson Baker to write the poem "Nacogdoches Speaks" (1936).[27] Also, Haltom's lamentation about the lack of a decent system of transportation led to a very good book by Robert Maxwell entitled *Whistle in the Piney Woods*. In his book, Haltom provides tantalizing asides about the townscape of Nacogdoches—descriptions of buildings now lost or

FIGURE 1.2. The Old Stone Fort, ca. 1880.
The northeast corner of the Square about the time John Schmidt, Abe Mayer, and W. U. Perkins arrived in Nacogdoches. Fredonia Street separates the Old Stone Fort and Shindler's General Store. Courtesy of ETRC.

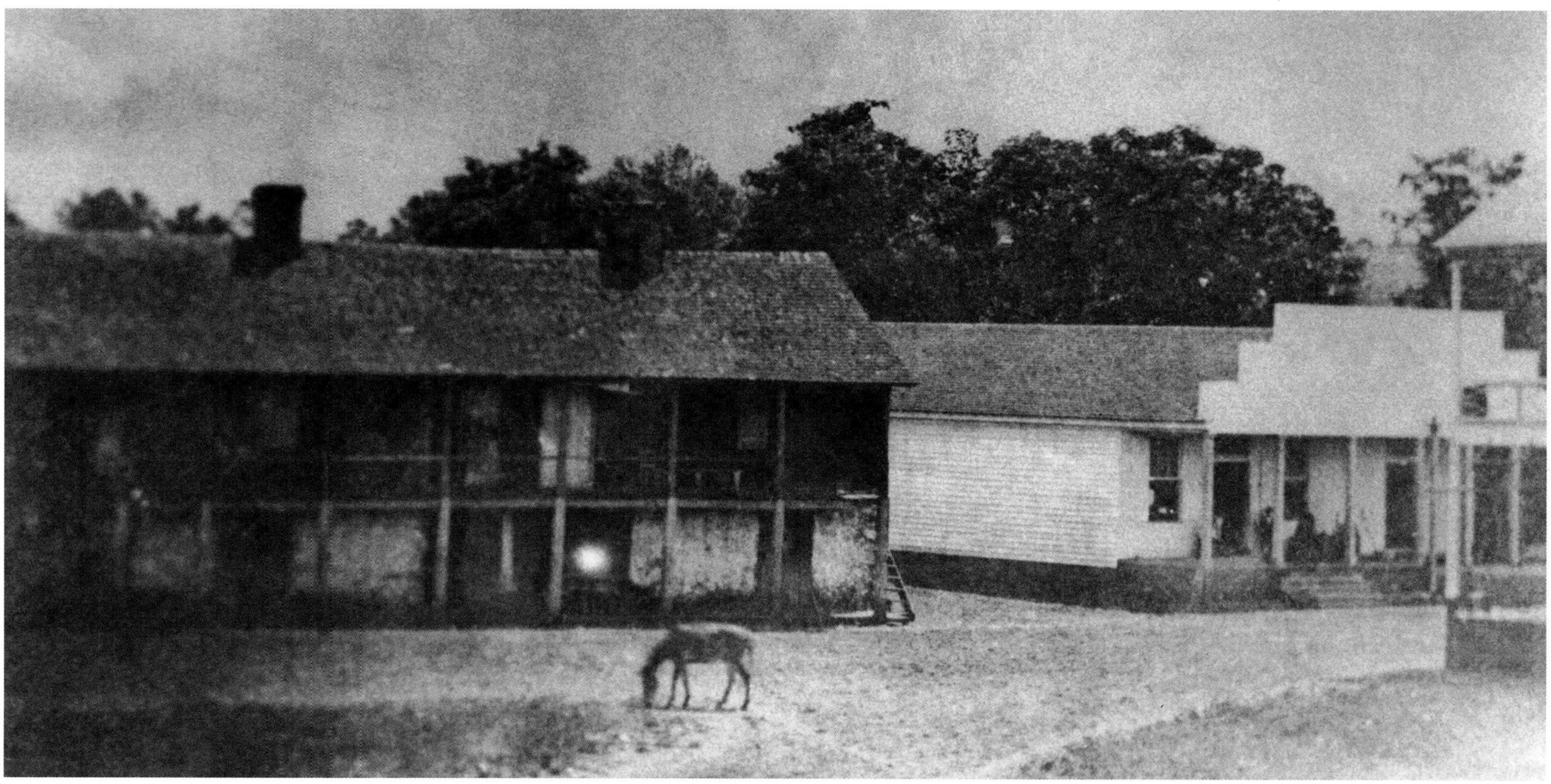

forgotten. For instance, he clearly describes the County Courthouse built in the Greek Revival style on the south side of the Square in 1856, of which no images exist.[28]

Haltom's book resembles an almanac more than a history. As such, the author hides all warts and exaggerates the merits of the town, painting, primarily, a lovely picture of the town for the visitor, immigrant, and businessman.

Haltom's description of the public square is worth quoting in full:

> The main public square, or plaza, as it is called in Mexican style, is smaller than usual in American towns. It is not square, nor is it regularly laid out, though it might so appear to the casual observer. It is surrounded, partly so, at least, by business houses, after the usual style, and being almost level, it is quite pretty. In the center is a public well, shelter, shaded, and fenced in a tasty manner. The streets are more or less irregular, being in some instance not parallel, in others not straight, and again intercepted by buildings and off-sets, or having other similar defects. But, with all this, the streets are sufficiently regular and level as to greatly beautify the town, some of them being almost unsurpassed for attractive features, and in a general way, the visitor who sees the town for the first time, is charmed with its beauty. The peculiar irregularities in the streets and plaza are Mexicanisms that are at once recognized by those familiar with such things.[29]

Any architect or businessman looking at his sections on timber, industries, potential transportation facilities, and the tax structure, would have found Nacogdoches a most promising place to relocate. Also, most families would have found the catalog of religions, politics, schools, society, and healthy environment equally appealing. As with any promotional work, one must take care to note the omissions. While an average of temperatures in Nacogdoches might elicit a statement such as this: "To sum up the temperature, it is on the whole, quite pleasant."[30] (No visitor to Nacogdoches from June 15 to September 15 would agree that this rosy statement was indicative of the whole truth.) Haltom also totally ignored the abysmal state of race relations and played down distinctions between classes with this platitude: "There are very few distinctions or classes of society, generally but two, the best and not the best."

Haltom's appeal to immigrants took a variety of forms. Some were generic: "There is lots of room here. The county is not crowded.... Lands are cheap and fertile, timber and water of the very best kind.... [An easy place to have a home] well worth the consideration of the immigrant." Some of Haltom's arguments were more specific:

> The people of the county . . . are glad to welcome new comers of the right kind into their neighborhood, whether from the north or from Europe, whether Yankees, Jews, or Germans or any other nationality, regardless of race, color or previous condition. . . . Immigrants, who seek and select homes here, no matter whence they come, are the most welcomed.
>
> The town, as it now exists, is by no means equal to what it has been in the past, either as to population, wealth, or importance. This will be understood when we take into consideration the comparative standing that it had in the early history of the State. It was not only one of the very earliest settled towns in Texas, but was an intermediate point, or a regular gate of entrance and exit, on the main overland route between Texas and the other States.... It was a prominent and much frequented town.... a place of much business, furnishing supplies and merchandise, not only for transient customers and to residents of the immediate town and vicinity, but also to an extensive scope of country around in every direction. Fortunes were thus rapidly made and wealth accumulated here. As a natural consequence aristocracy arose, and people had classes of society peculiar to such places and occasions, there was no small degree of pretension to refinement.[31]

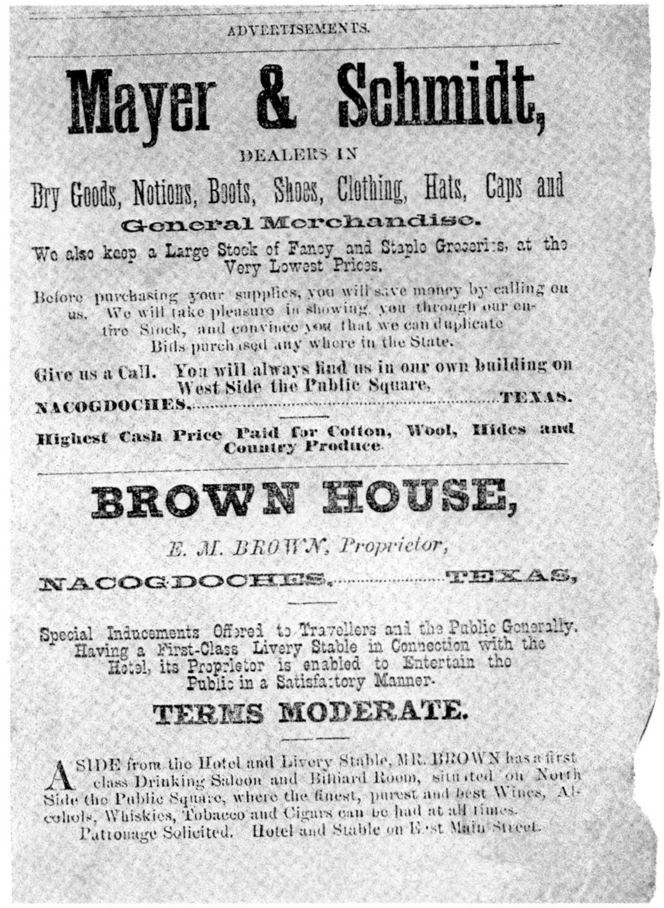

FIGURE 1.3. 1880 Advertisement Mayer & Schmidt Company, in Haltom's History.

The Mayer & Schmidt Company (M&S) opened on the west side of the Square in 1878. In Haltom's History of Nacogdoches (1880), there were only two sponsors, M&S and E. M. Brown's Hotel. In addition to selling groceries and general merchandise, M&S bought and sold cotton even at this early date; they would turn these trades into major East Texas businesses.

Haltom drew a stark contrast between 1834 and 1880. He estimated the population of the municipality in 1834 at 3,500 and, in 1880, about 500.[32] By 1880, when he was writing, he thought Nacogdoches was "*save in point of history, a somewhat sad relic of past glory* [Italics Added]." Without transportation, the town had no way to exploit its advantages. The nearest railroad in 1880 was sixty miles away in Crockett. Nacogdoches did not even have a bank and was "no longer one of the centers of the events that are celebrated in the history of Texas." In addressing the town's prospects for a railroad line, Haltom always emphasized the positive—*always*: "Nacogdoches has good prospects . . . at no very distant day. Our strongest hope lies with the Houston East & West Texas Narrow Gage road." While admitting the disadvantages of noise and complexity, he predicted the railroad's arrival would herald "a grand epoch in the life of this county, a new page in its history, a change that will strain every nerve, a regeneration."[33]

In summation, Haltom's 1880 book is not only an interesting work of history, but it is also a unique catalog of the condition of the resources of the county: timber and cotton, mercantile trade, value of property, soil conditions, weather, building resources, business climate, schools, churches, and even people. His insights are invaluable, as long as one corrects for his willful optimism. Since the present book is on architecture, a discussion of the look and feel of Nacogdoches in 1880 will help to set a context for D. Rulfs's contributions.

The Townscape

Haltom did not have the technology at hand in Nacogdoches in 1880 to include pictures in his book. In order to give the reader an idea of what Nacogdoches looked like in 1880, beyond Haltom's words, the following pages attempt to create a suitable visual framework by using pictures outside his book. While some of these photographs have appeared in other books, all too frequently they appear without spatial or architectural analysis.

D. B. Alexander, in his review of architectural traditions of Texas, has distinguished six major periods in the state's development: Spanish Colonial, Pioneer Settlement (1820-1870), Greek Revival (1840-1870), Victorian (1870-1900), Eclectic Revival (1900-1940), and Twentieth Century Modern (1950 to date).[34] Using these categories, the author below will review what Nacogdoches looked like in 1880. (Although Nacogdoches was an important Indian center, only mounds from their culture in the Washington Square area were extant in 1880.)

Nacogdoches in 1880

Colonial Influence. Only a few buildings survived to 1880 from the long period of Spanish Colonial dominance. The climate, and not just cultural or historical explanations, helps to give meaning to this fact. East Texas weather proved unfavorable for traditional Spanish building methods; the humidity is too severe for the use of adobe or even flat roofs. Other building materials, for instance, huge stands of timber and an abundance of rocks, existed in East Texas. Additionally, Spanish traditions were not the only colonial model felt in Nacogdoches in the Eighteenth Century. French provinces were very close. Of the two major colonial buildings extant on or close to the Square in 1880, the Old Stone House (Old Stone Fort) and the Red House, neither was architecturally typically Spanish. With their use of internal chimneys, rocks, and hipped and gable roofs, these colonial buildings owed their inspiration to French influences.[35]

There was a most persistent and lingering Spanish influence in Nacogdoches, however, as Haltom correctly noted: the *layout* of the town. In his quaint way, Haltom observed that neither the Square (*Plaza Principal*) nor anything else in the downtown area was very *square*. He attributed the "irregularities" to the Mexicans. The formulae used by Spanish colonials, which sometimes seem haphazard to moderns, dated from the Middle Ages and not from Mexican influences. The Spanish selected sites for strategic reasons. They chose the downtown area of Nacogdoches because it was a natural fortress, the high ground above the confluence of two streams, the crossroad of major trails, and the site with visual perspectives in every direction.[36] Neither the style, the locations, or the uses of these remaining Spanish buildings were to fit very well into the development plans of Nacogdoches after 1880, so it seems. The assumptions used by the Spanish in laying out the organization of downtown Nacogdoches are still viable today.

Pioneer Settlements. Architecture from Anglo-American settlers, who migrated into Texas between 1800 and 1870, existed in abundance in 1880. These buildings dominated the architectural look of the town. The pioneers from various parts of the United States brought with them the typical architecture of their native regions. From Tennessee and Kentucky came the log cabin and the frame house; from the Deep South came an interest in more classical Greek and Roman forms. The merger of these styles into what has been termed "the East Texas House" gave the whole East Texas area an unusually rich architectural heritage. Fine examples of this pioneer architecture existed in downtown Nacogdoches in 1880 and certain houses still exist. The Adolphus Sterne House and the Acosta-Taylor House still stand on their original sites in the downtown area; the Millard-Lee House, a prominent residence which once stood just off the southeast corner of the Square, now survives at Millard's Crossing—carefully moved and restored in the early 1970s by Congresswoman Lera Millard Thomas. Many small houses from the Texas Revolutionary period still existed in 1880. Several of the larger houses of the period, shown here in pictures, served Nacogdoches as hotels: the Red House (the Dunson, later the Goeff Hotel), the John Roberts House (Bullock Hotel), the early Frost Thorn, later Durst House (The Hart Hotel), and the second Frost Thorn House (the Mitchell Hotel).

Greek Revival. The whole Greek Revival architectural period came at an awkward moment for Nacogdoches. In 1834, Nacogdoches was one of the largest towns in the state. As the rest of Texas became available for immigrants, Nacogdoches simply serviced the new pioneers with supplies. Nacogdoches, therefore, at the height of the Greek Revival era, found itself with an over abundance of houses and commercial buildings. Very little construction of any kind took place in Nacogdoches during the mid-nineteenth century. Immigrants who entered Texas through the Nacogdoches gateway moved to the less settled interior sections of the state. As the railroad entered the state, new gateway cities began to supplant Nacogdoches as points of entry. True, as this author has argued elsewhere,[37] the town never had the good fortune during the 1830-40s to have an important resident Greek Revival architect comparable to Augustus Phelps in San Augustine. Even if an architect had lived here, the townspeople had limited wealth to squander on new and expensive domestic architecture. Wealthy merchant Frost Thorn did build two large houses in downtown Nacogdoches, the latter of which did have some Greek influences, but this house was the exception and not the rule. Small stylistic adaptations of Greek elements existed all over Nacogdoches County.[38] For example, while Greek Revival

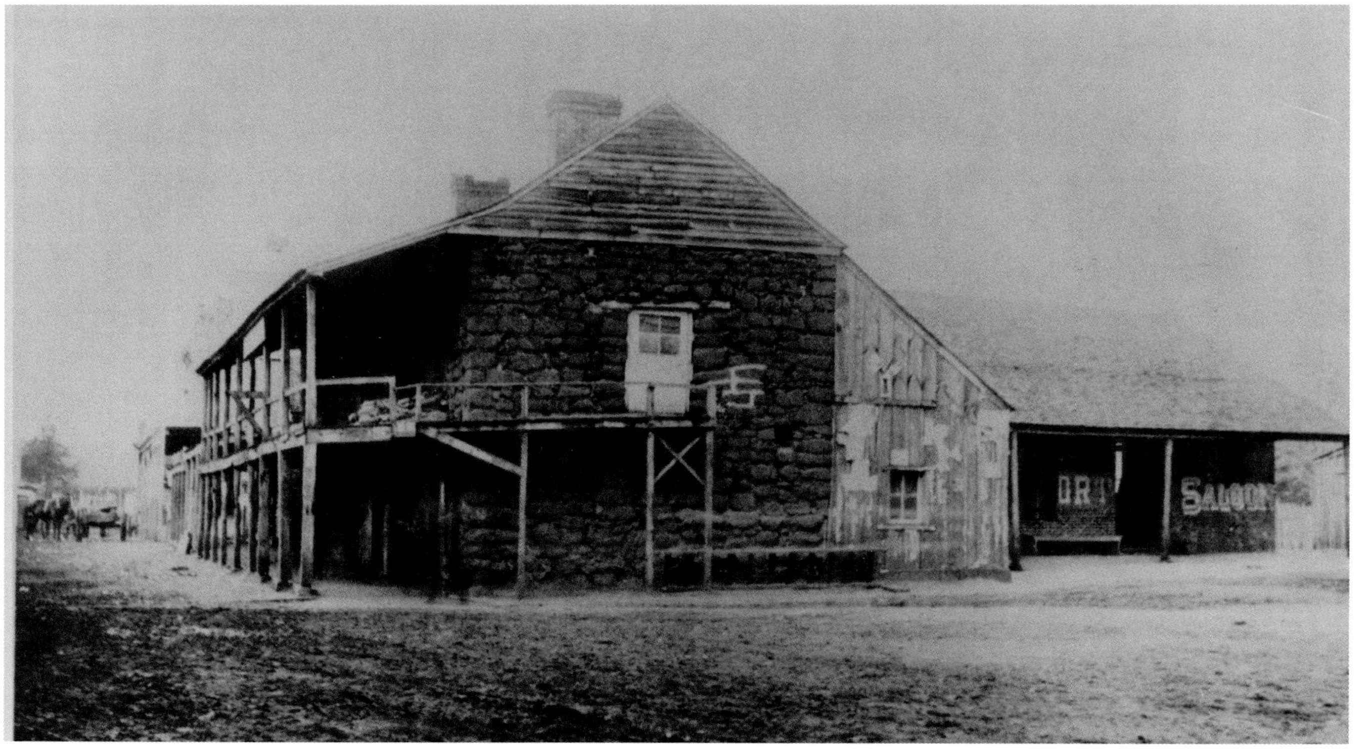

FIGURE 1.4. A View of the Old Stone Fort, ca. 1880.

This view of the Old Stone Fort from the east captures what the visitor arriving in Nacogdoches from Natchitoches and Shreveport (La) would have seen. Notice the condition of the streets at the corner of Fredonia and the Square. Courtesy of ETRC.

architecture in urban settings across the nation appealed to banks and wealthy merchants, Nacogdoches did not even have a bank in 1880.

Nacogdoches did undertake two impressive public buildings in the Greek Revival style in the 1850s and both of these were extant in 1880—a new County Courthouse (1856) and the Nacogdoches University Building (1859). The Greek Revival courthouse has completely escaped the attention of most modern commentators. Haltom, however, gave an interesting description of the temple-like courthouse. First, he noted that it replaced a courthouse that stood in the center of the square—a forgotten bit of local history. Second, he said the building cost $12,000 to build and was, in his words, "a two-story brick building, with gable front and extended roof, supported by large columns, giving it an inviting appearance, quite different from the average Texas courthouse."[39] The Sanborn Fire Map of 1885 confirms the shape, size, and location of this building, even showing the columns.[40]

The University Building (1859) is the only building from the period to have survived into the twenty-first century. This building, well known by modern generations and recently having celebrated its one hundred-fifty year anniversary,[41] is Greek Revival at its best. It is easily the most important structure from that period still standing in East Texas, a gracious example of the taste and general wealth that could be mustered in the town when the cause was recognized as necessary. The public Court House and the private University suggest that the Nacogdoches community was more vibrant and possibly wealthier than previously thought on the eve of the Civil War. It was the war itself that accelerated the downward spiral of the town. Architecturally, as well as economically, Nacogdoches by 1880 was an anachronism–*out of place in time.*

Across the nation after the Civil War, architecture began to reflect the arrival of a new healthier economy and new wealthier patrons. As other communities in Texas began to move into the more ornate and flamboyant styles of the late Victorian era, the economic isolation of Nacogdoches forced people to accept less. They continued to modify existing houses and perhaps to add some more elaborate elements.[42] Not until after the arrival of the railroad in 1883 did Nacogdoches have an opportunity to follow these national trends. Even so, the citizens of Nacogdoches were extremely conservative in their tastes. Throughout the 1880s, patrons limited stylistic elements to turned posts on the porch, more elaborate balustrades, jigsaw ornamentation, and the projection of the "room-on-the-porch" of earlier times into a forward room or sometimes a bay. The Henry Millard House at Millard's Crossing and the Charles Hoya House are good examples. It was very easy to "update" the typical house by adding gingerbread between the posts or making the window sizes larger and taller. Many interesting houses were thus created.[43] The prosperity of Nacogdoches in the last two decades of the century, made possible by the railroad and the commercial tapping of the agricultural products and natural resources of East Texas, eventually produced a new class in town with enough wealth and self-assurance to demand fashionable residences. The second and third parts of this book will analyze the process.

The commercial core of Nacogdoches in 1880, as represented in the illustrations, consisted of vernacular wooden buildings serving a variety of needs. Businesses and residences stood side by side. Some commercial establishments, following long European traditions,[44] served mixed business/domestic purposes. The boarding houses and hotels were, in fact, located in former homes. None of the so-called hotels in town at the time was built for that purpose, but were larger pioneer residences turned into hotels, sometimes retaining the word "house" as part of their name. "The Hyde House," where Mayer and Schmidt first stayed in 1878, was simply the former Hyde home on Hospital Street, relabeled and transformed into the "Hyde House" hotel. The John S. Roberts home on the square became the Bullock Hotel, the Frost Thorn home (later the Durst home) became the long surviving Hart Hotel, and a later Thorn home became the Mitchell Hotel—all extant and in use in 1880.

No plan or unity characterized these small merchant establishments. Unlike the freestanding, Federal style urban buildings in New England, linked as they were by masonry walls and chimneys end to end and their roofs parallel to the streets, the buildings in pioneer Nacogdoches stood gables-forward to the street. In an era before electricity, the windows down the sides of buildings helped to provide light for the interiors. The construction, however, caused drainage problems for neighboring establishments, and the space between buildings caused severe security problems. Most buildings had porches on the front to allow the shopping public to move from building to building with minimal exposure to the weather. The merchants bridged the gap between buildings with boardwalks, but these linking boardwalks, uncovered and frequently at different elevations, caused awkward transitions. The captions under the illustrations expand these statements.

The development of townscape of Nacogdoches in the last two decades of the nineteenth century has escaped modern historians. The dates placed on photographs are misleading or incorrect, and the identifications of whole blocks have received incorrect placement. As a result, no systematic study of the correlation of the existing photographs with existing maps has resulted. The remaining chapters undertake to fill many of these gaps in research.

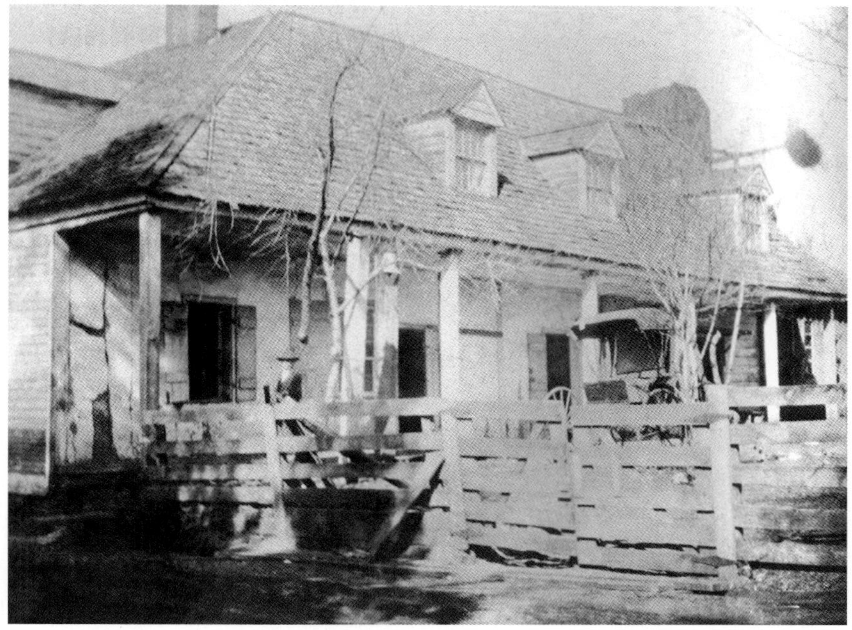

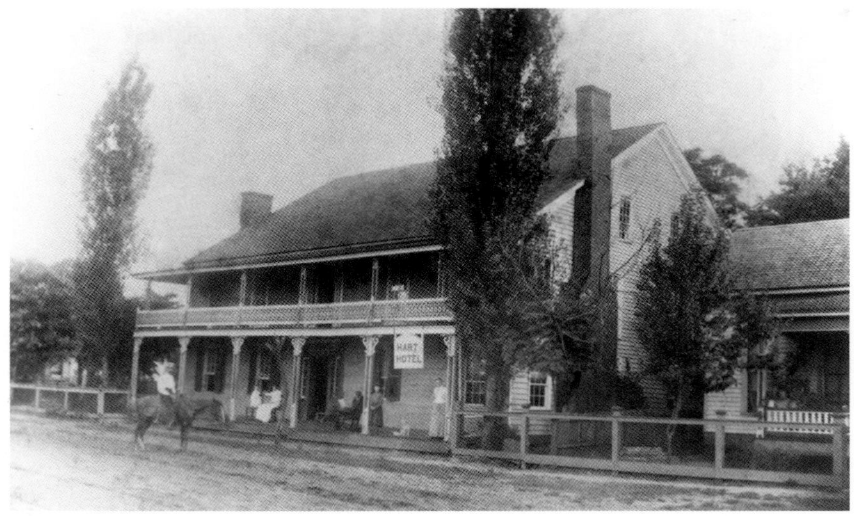

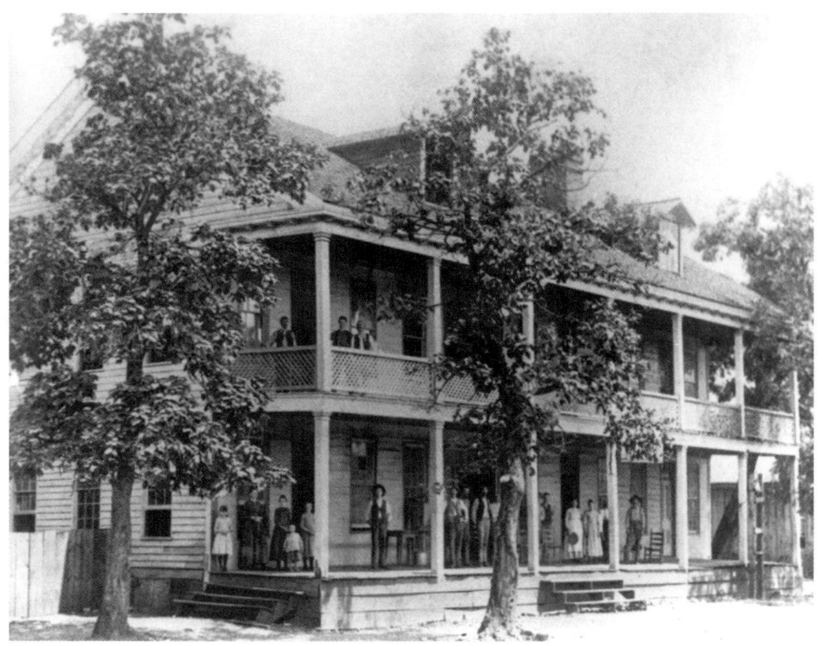

FIGURE 1.5. (Top Right) The Red House on West Pilar Street, ca. 1880.
The Red House, of French colonial design, sat to the southwest of the Square on the main residential street of the town, Pilar. At the time of the Battle of Nacogdoches, colonial Mexican troops lived in the Red House. The house was the second most famous colonial structure in Nacogdoches in 1880. The house, owned by Thomas J. Rusk, became the first home of the Nacogdoches University. Courtesy of ETRC.

FIGURE 1.6. (Right) The Hart Hotel, East Main Street, ca. 1880.
The first Frost Thorn House became the Hart Hotel. It was a popular stop for travelers arriving from the east. It burned after 1900. Courtesy of ETRC.

FIGURE 1.7. (Lower Right) The Mitchell Hotel, ca. 1880.
A later Frost Thorn House became the Mitchell Hotel. While this picture ca. 1880 shows the house in a rather dilapidated state, the structure of Greek Revival detailing was a grand structure for the period. It was more imposing and important than the earlier house (above), which became the Hart Hotel. Courtesy of ETRC.

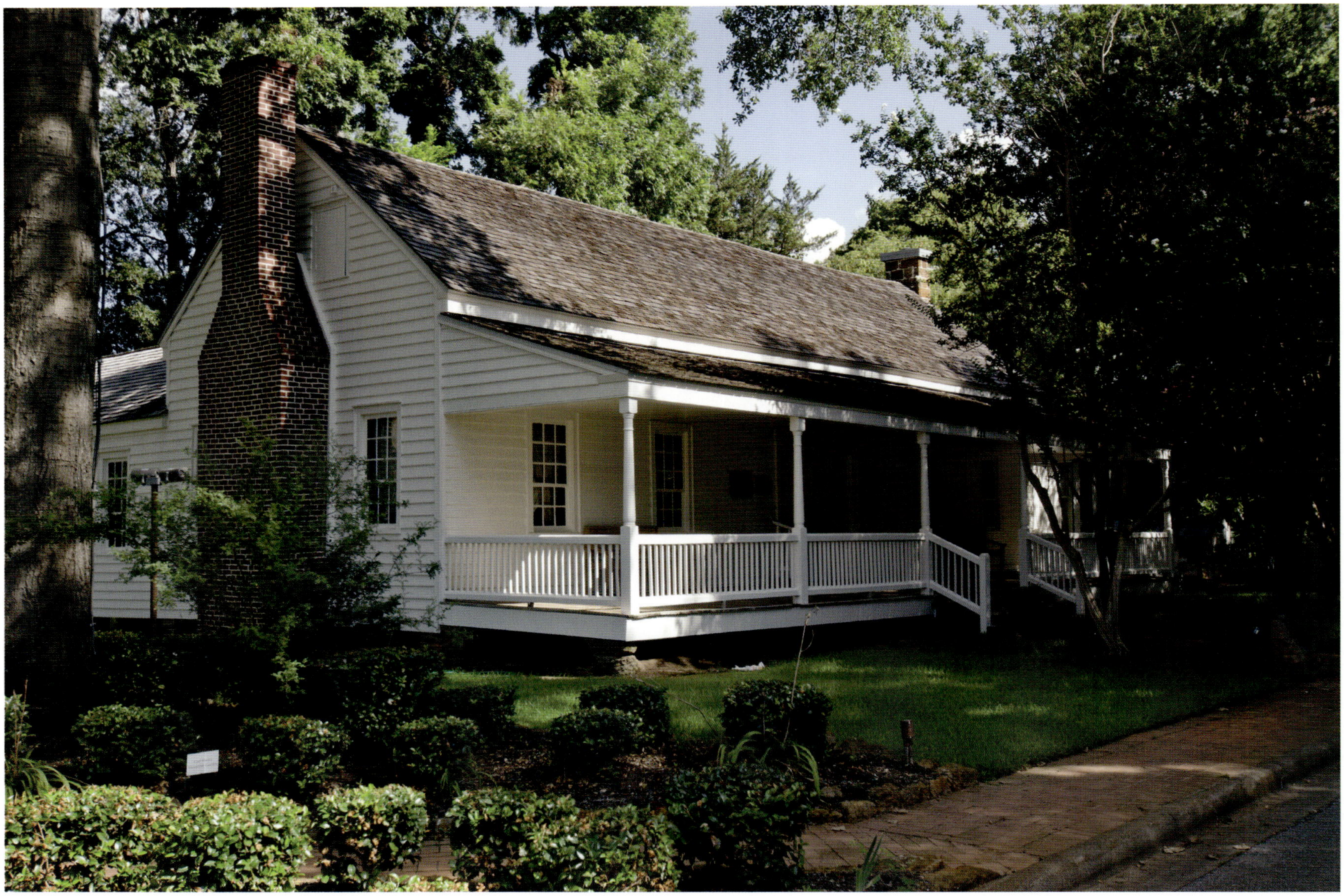

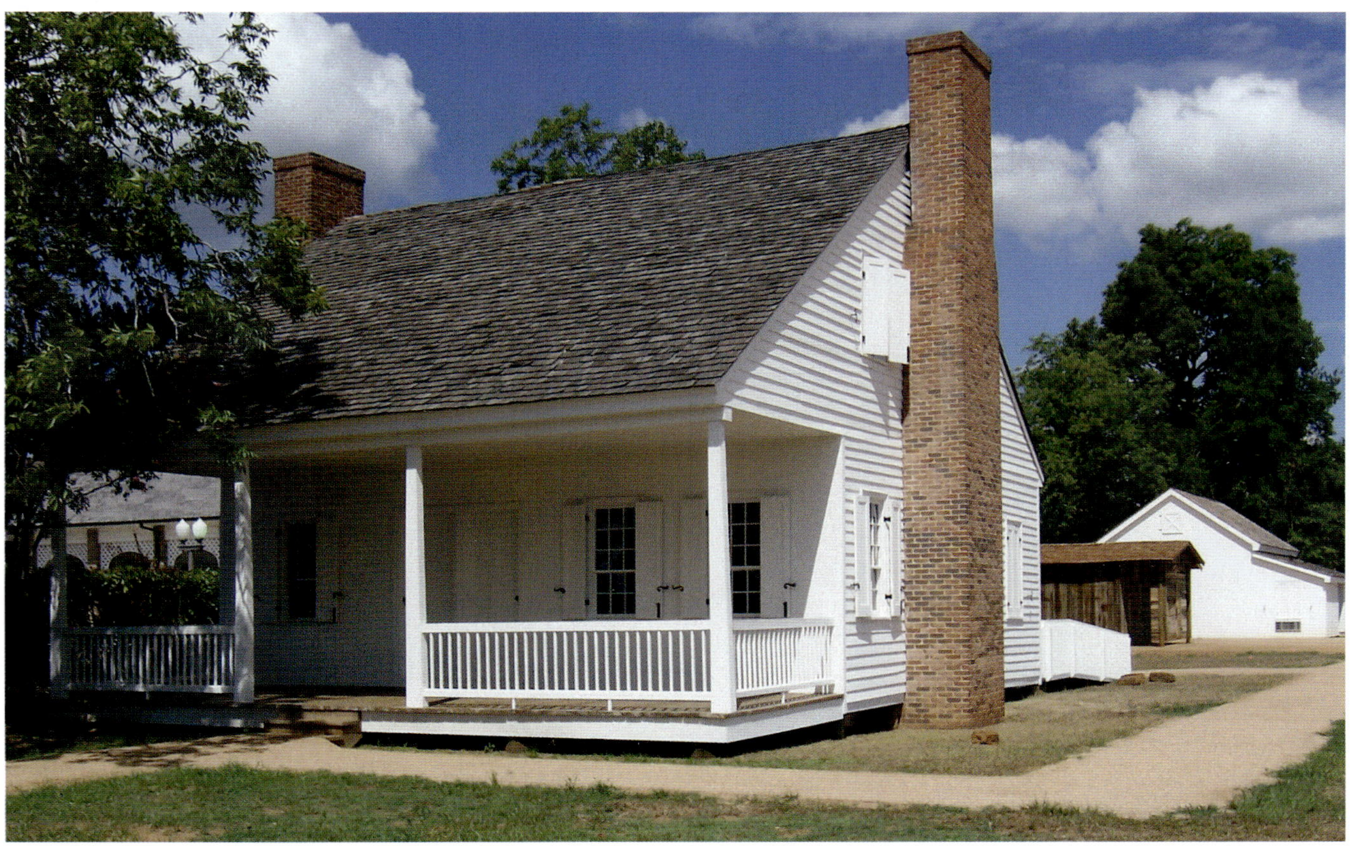

FIGURE 1.8. (Above) The Adolphus Sterne Home (c1830) still stands on its original location, east of downtown Nacogdoches.

FIGURE 1.9. (Left) The Durst-Taylor House (c1827), on North Street, stands on its original lot.

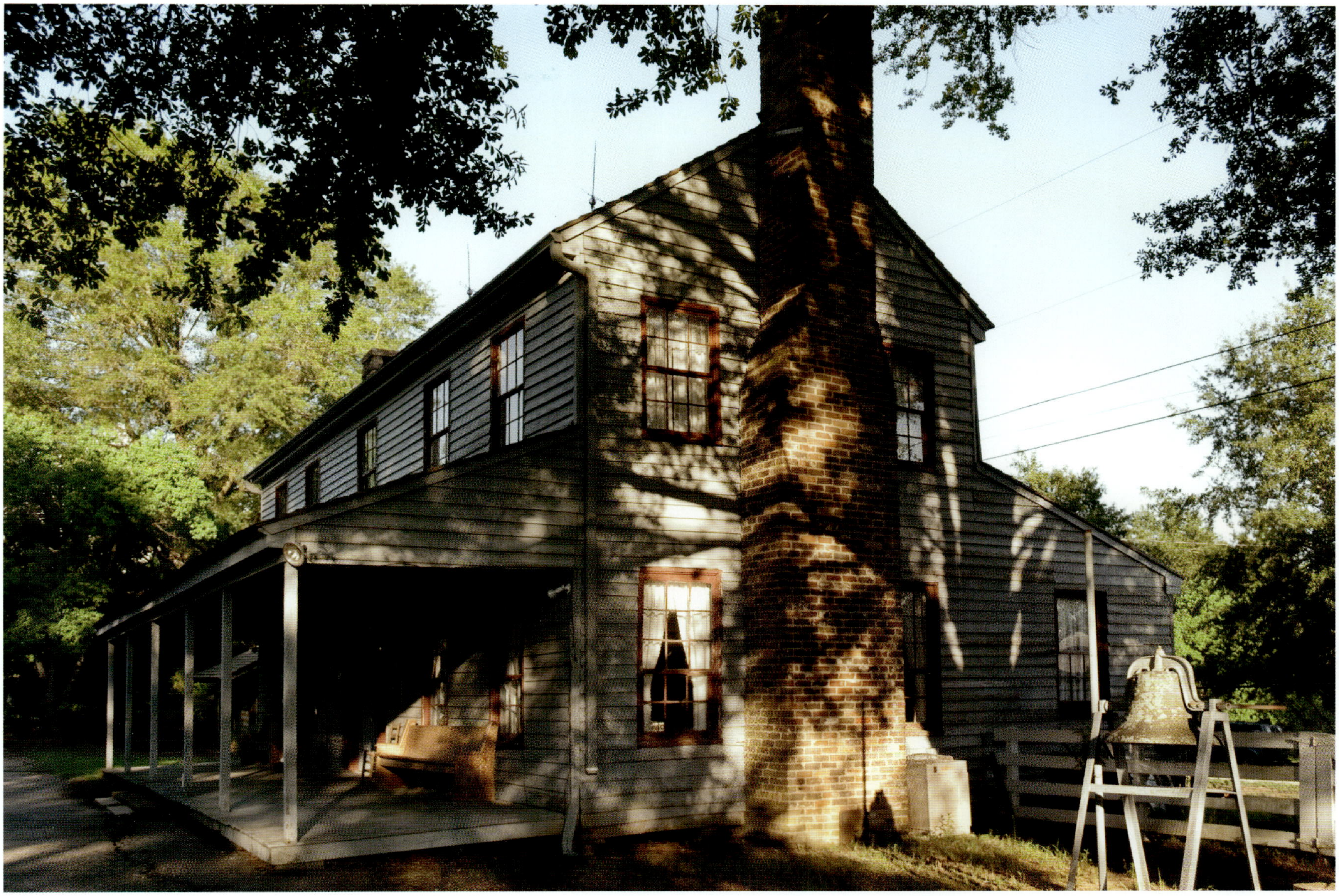

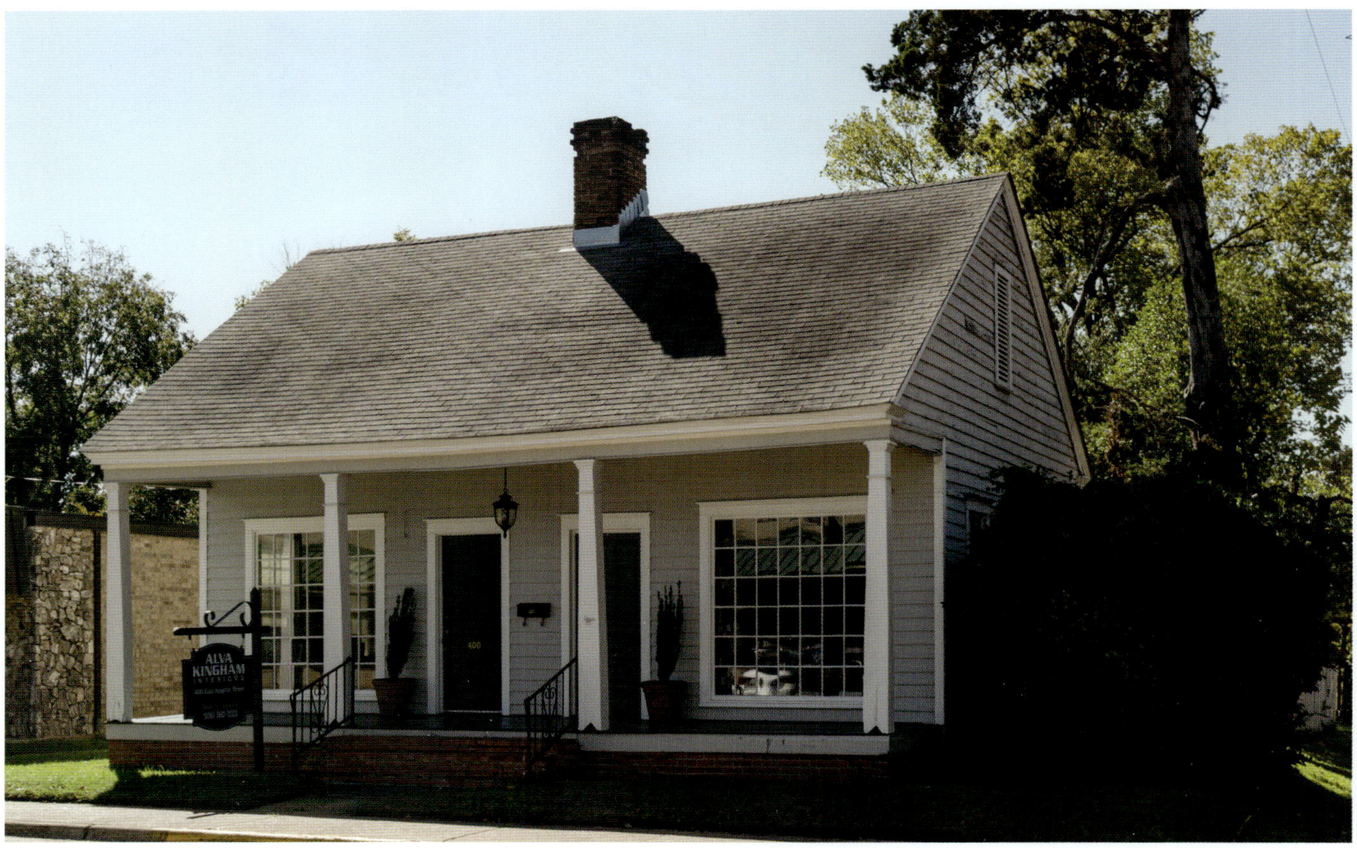

FIGURE 1.10. (Above) The Millard-Lee House (ca. 1835), moved from the town square in the 1970s, now sits at Millard's Crossing Restoration Village on U. S. 59 north of Nacogdoches.

FIGURE 1.11. (Right) The Christ Church Rectory (ca. 1856), on the corner of Hospital and North Church Street, stands on its original location.

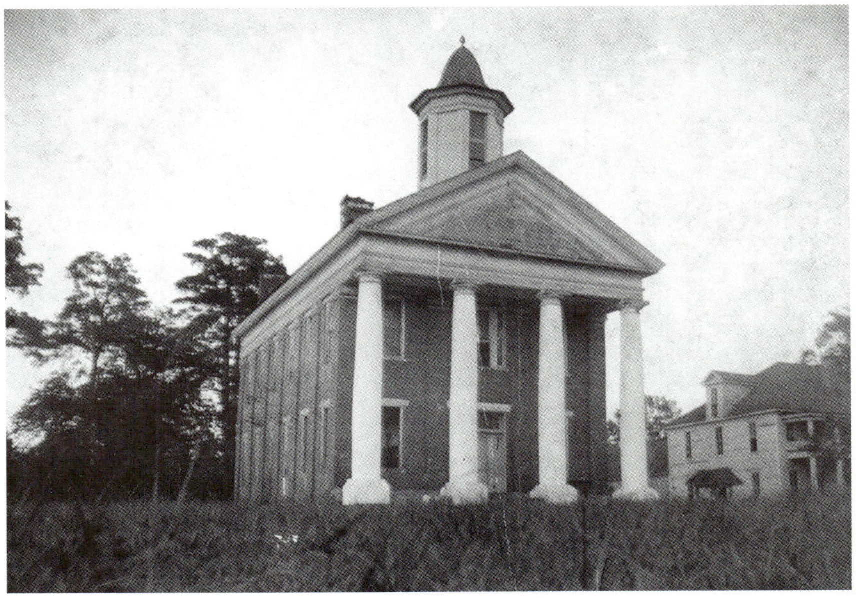

FIGURE 1.12. Old University Building, ca. 1890.

The Nacogdoches University Building, constructed in 1859, appears in this 1890s photograph as it looked about the time D. Rulfs arrived in Nacogdoches. The large wooden structure to the right was the dormitory and boarding facilities for women. This wooden structure, although marked unused, still existed as late as the 1906 Sanborn map. The Old University Building became part of the NISD after 1900. Courtesy of ETRC.

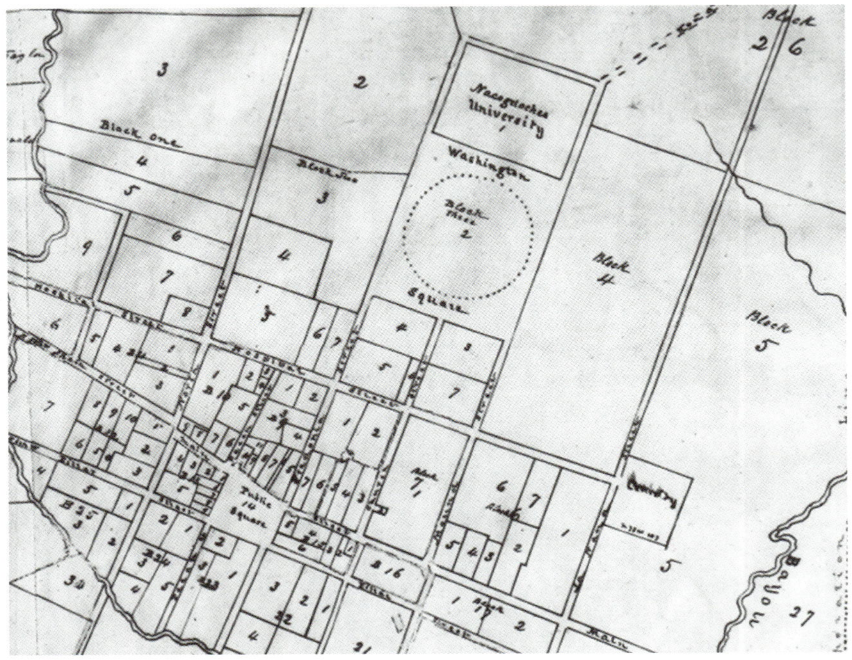

FIGURE 1.13. Detail, Plan of the City of Nacogdoches, by John Forbes. Map 44, 1846.

The Forbes Map is one of the earliest maps to show the whole of the town of Nacogdoches. The map shows block numbers, possibly for the first time, and clearly designates the Public Square and important streets, such as Main, North, Pillar (spelled with two lls), Fredonia, Hospital, and Church. The future home of Nacogdoches University and Washington Square are already on the map. Courtesy of ETRC.

FIGURE 1.14. (Below) City of Nacogdoches Plat No. 1. Map 209, 1856.

While the earlier map (1846) showed the layout for the whole town, this 1856 map below is greatly enlarged and, for instance, identifies the location of the new 1856 Court House on the south side of the Public Square. The source of this map is not indicated on the credits in the ETRC. Since the map only designates lots associated with the Thorn and Edwards families and the title indicates it is associated with another document, the map probably came from County Deed Records and probably had to do with the disposition of property in the Thorn family. Although Church Street appears on the earlier 1846 map above, this plat specifically shows the location of Christ Episcopal Church just north of East Main Street, a lot that Frost and Susan Thorn gave to the church in 1851. Frost Thorn (1793-1854), Texas' first millionaire, had died just before this map was drawn. His wife Susan Edwards Thorn (1799-1891) was on the eve of a second marriage to her husband's nephew James F. Thorn. The Thorn homestead, with Susan's name prominently displayed, is indicated in Block 16. Other lots belonging to Susan, Susan's father (Hayden Edwards), and her lawyer (H. C. Hancock) are shown in Block 12. Courtesy of ETRC.

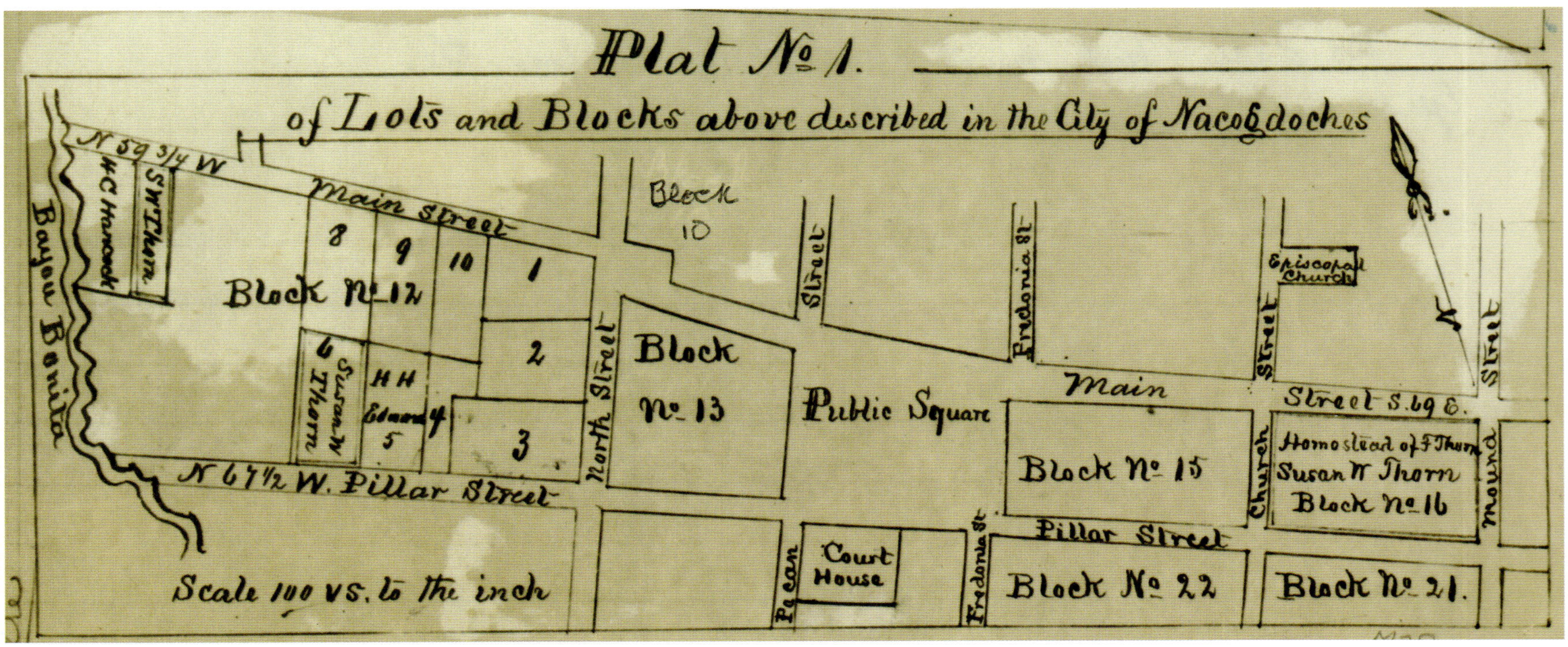

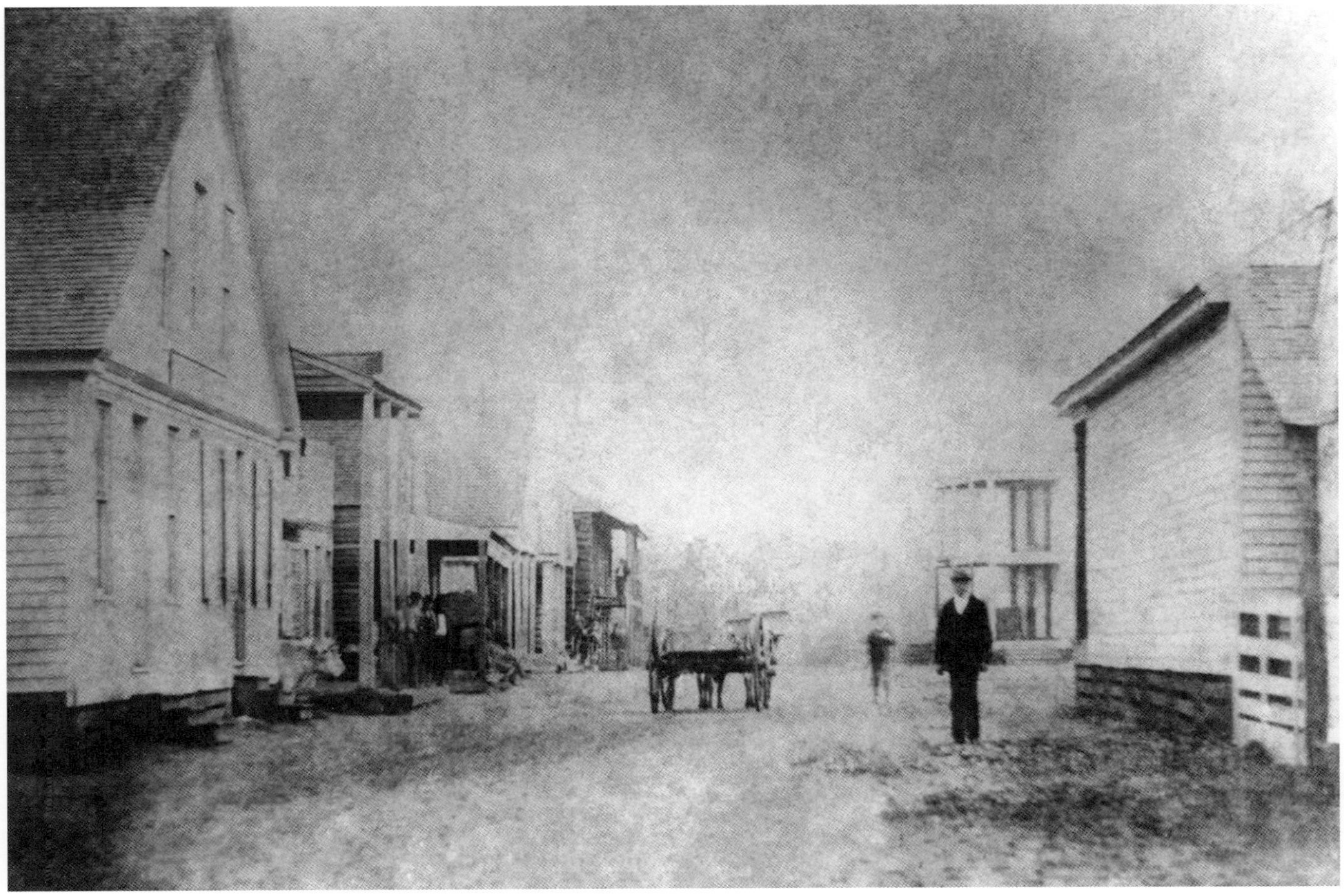

FIGURE 1.15. Main Street, Looking East from North Street to the Square, 1880.

In the photograph left, looking east on Main Street in 1880, one can see many of the elements described in the previous paragraphs: unpaved streets and wooden buildings. The perspective, from the middle of Main Street in front of the S. M. Orton House, is between North Street and the Square. This block would have carried the name "West Main" in 1880; all directions emanated from the Square. In 1926, in a speech given by Giles Haltom and later published in the newspaper, the editor of the Daily Sentinel gave a description of this block, possibly even as he looked at this photograph: "[On the left, stood a] big story and a half building with a side room occupied by John Cox for general merchandising. Cox used a side room for a warehouse and the up-stairs as a residence for his family. The side room was also used as the first business quarters for Perkins and Garrison, Druggists."

Out of the picture to the left of this building would have stood a large barn that, according to Haltom, was "used for the stage lines and mail carrying outfits." The wagon in the middle of the street is approximately where Pecan Street (then Elm) entered the Square. Continuing down the left of the picture, one can see the structures along the north side of the square and make out the porch of the Old Stone House. Across the street from the Stone House on the distant right of the picture, a two-story wooden building stands on the east side of the Square where Regions Bank (the former Stone Fort National Bank) today occupies the corner. The man in the street in the foreground on the right, as if placed there to give depth perception, is most likely R. W. Haltom. The figure is standing by the wooden building housing the G. D. Boger store, on the south side of Main and Pecan where the Wettermark Bank would stand after 1896. The fence to the extreme right of the picture is approximately where the Sam Hayter Building stands today. Courtesy of ETRC.

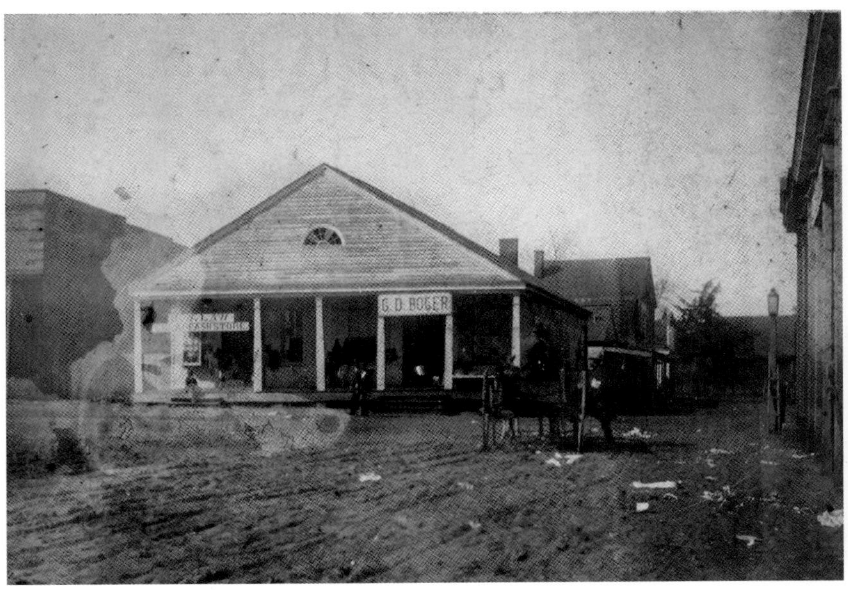

FIGURE 1.16. Main Street, Looking West, ca. 1885.

This view of Main Street from the Square is the opposition of the view in FIGURE 1.15 above. The G. D. Boger General Store, facing the Square, sat on the south side of Main Street. Behind the Boger store stands the two-story brick S. M. Orton House. Courtesy of ETRC.

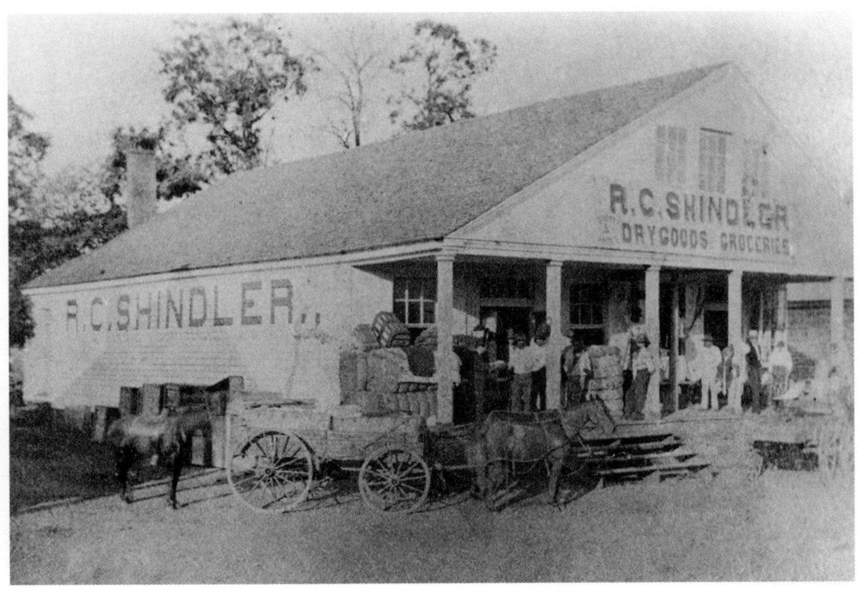

FIGURE 1.17. (Above) Shindler General Store, East Main at Fredonia Street.

In 1884, R. C. Shindler's General Store moved into a new brick building. In 1888, this corner became the permanent home for the Mayer & Schmidt Company. Courtesy of ETRC.

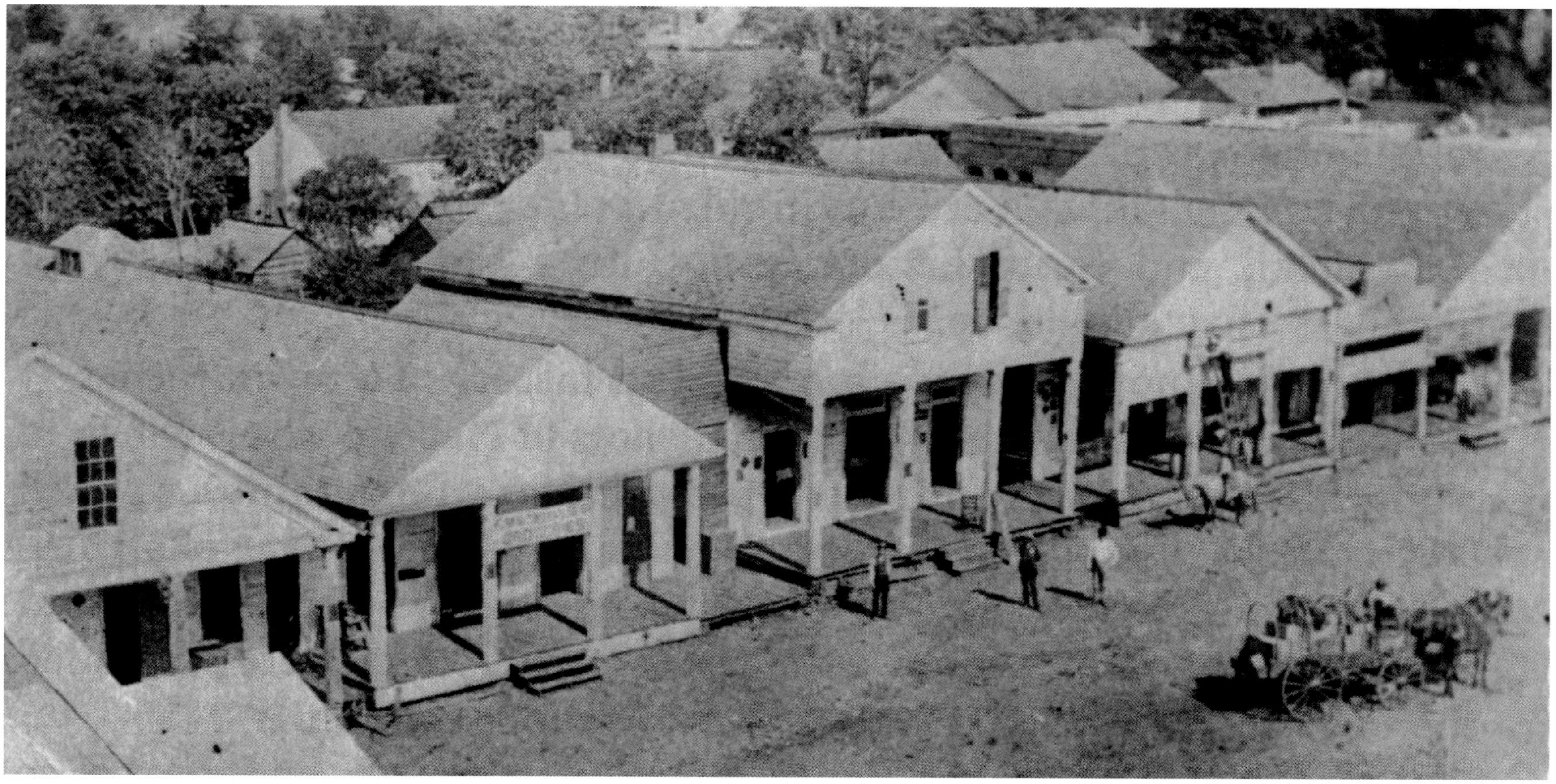

FIGURE 1.18. West Side of the Square, ca. 1880-1884.

This photograph, taken from the roof of the 1856 Court House, illustrates how the West Square looked when Rulfs arrived in town. The vernacular buildings stood with their gables toward the street. The gables, extending to create a porch, formed an almost continuous covered walk along the street side. The gaps between buildings had boardwalks or steps, depending on the elevations. In comparing the photograph to the Sanborn Insurance map of 1885, the first two buildings on the left, owned by the Joseph von der Hoya family, contained a general store and a hardware store. (Behind them on Pilar Street stood the Old Red House.) The 1½ story building in the center of the photograph and the one next to it were the storefronts owned by Fritz Voigt for his bakery. According to Giles Haltom in 1928, and confirmed by the map, "In the rear of one of these buildings was a small two story brick building that had been put for a bakery. I can't realize how these brothers ever raked up the courage enough to build a bakery in Nacogdoches at that time. If they had sold all the bread and pies used by all the people for a radius of fifty miles, they would not have had as much business as Fred Feasell has within the incorporated limits of Nacogdoches today." The next building to the right of Voigt's Bakery was the general store that Mayer and Schmidt purchased from Voigt and opened their grocery business in 1878. Schmidt replaced this building in 1885 with the first brick building on the West Square. North of the M&S building is a small, unknown building. The last building on the upper right housed a general merchandise store, run by G. D. Boger, as shown in FIGURE 1.16. Courtesy of ETRC.

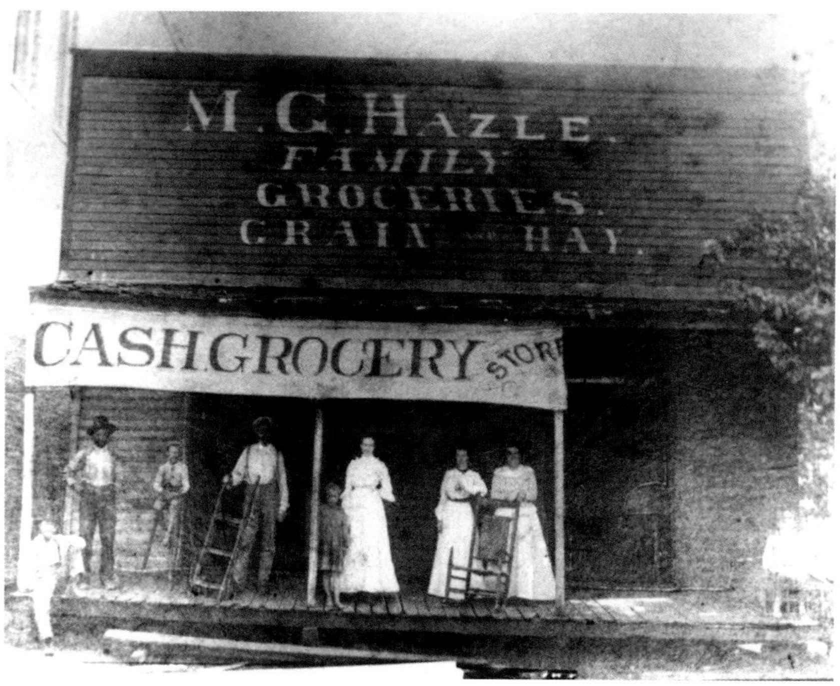

FIGURE 1.19. (Left) Hazle Grocery, Main at Church Street, ca. 1880.

The wooden building housing the Hazle family grocery business would continue to stand at this location until 1901. Courtesy of ETRC.

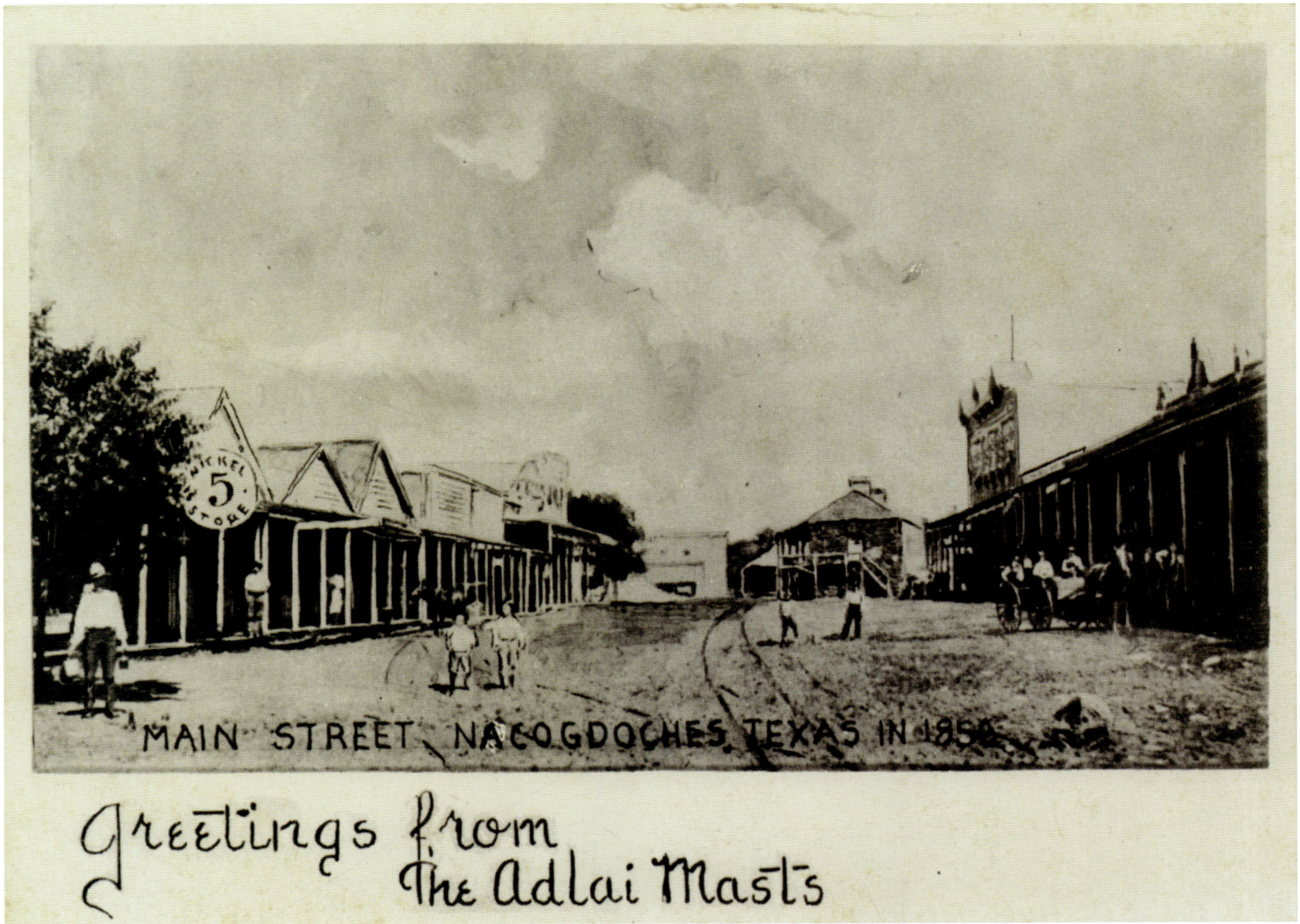

FIGURE 1.20. East Main Street Between Church Street and the Square.

This townscape postcard is a fair representation of the approach to the town square from the east, as one would have experienced Nacogdoches if arriving from San Augustine or Louisiana. This image, however, has misled many who have looked at it or used it in publications. The date placed on the image, "Main Street Nacogdoches, Texas in 1858," is thirty years incorrect! Most probably, the person who labeled it simply transposed the last two numbers, but even the date 1885 is too early. The image depicts East Main Street from the intersection of Church and Main Streets looking west from around 1890, not 1858. If a picture is worth a thousand words, the imprecise dating added to this one conveys a false message.

On close inspection, one can see the Old Stone Fort, projecting into the middle of East Main. The Spanish carefully sighted their main building to occupy the center of the geographical setting, with excellent views in all directions. On the left side of the image, one gets a good impression of late pioneer Nacogdoches—all of wood. Harry H. Cooper, a shoe salesman later to be postmaster, had just opened his "5¢ Store" in 1890 in one of the old buildings; his coin sign can be seen in the left foreground on East Main. In the center and on the right side of the image, one has a good impression of the emerging modern town of Nacogdoches, as designed by D. Rulfs from 1880 onward. To the immediate left of the Old Stone Fort, in the distance on the West Square, stands the Mayer & Schmidt building constructed in 1885, with its characteristic portholes in view. To the right of the Stone House, on the corner of East Main and Fredonia, is the 1888-1889, two-story building, the third home of the Mayer & Schmidt Company. (The new Opera House, not in the picture, sat to the immediate right foreground.) To summarize, the image (c.1890) above represents the old pioneer wooden town of Nacogdoches on the left side of East Main, the emerging new brick buildings of modern Nacogdoches on the right, and dead center between these two perspectives is the Old Stone Fort.

Burke's Texas Almanac (1881) lists "ten general mercantile establishments, one drug store, two saloons, two family groceries, a restaurant, two blacksmith shops…a jeweler's shop, a shoemaker, a saddle and harness maker, three hotels, a livery stable, and several woodwork shops…several land agents and surveyors…(and) nine or ten attorneys, and four doctors." [Partin, Nacogdoches, 108-09]. Mast Greeting Card Courtesy of ETRC.

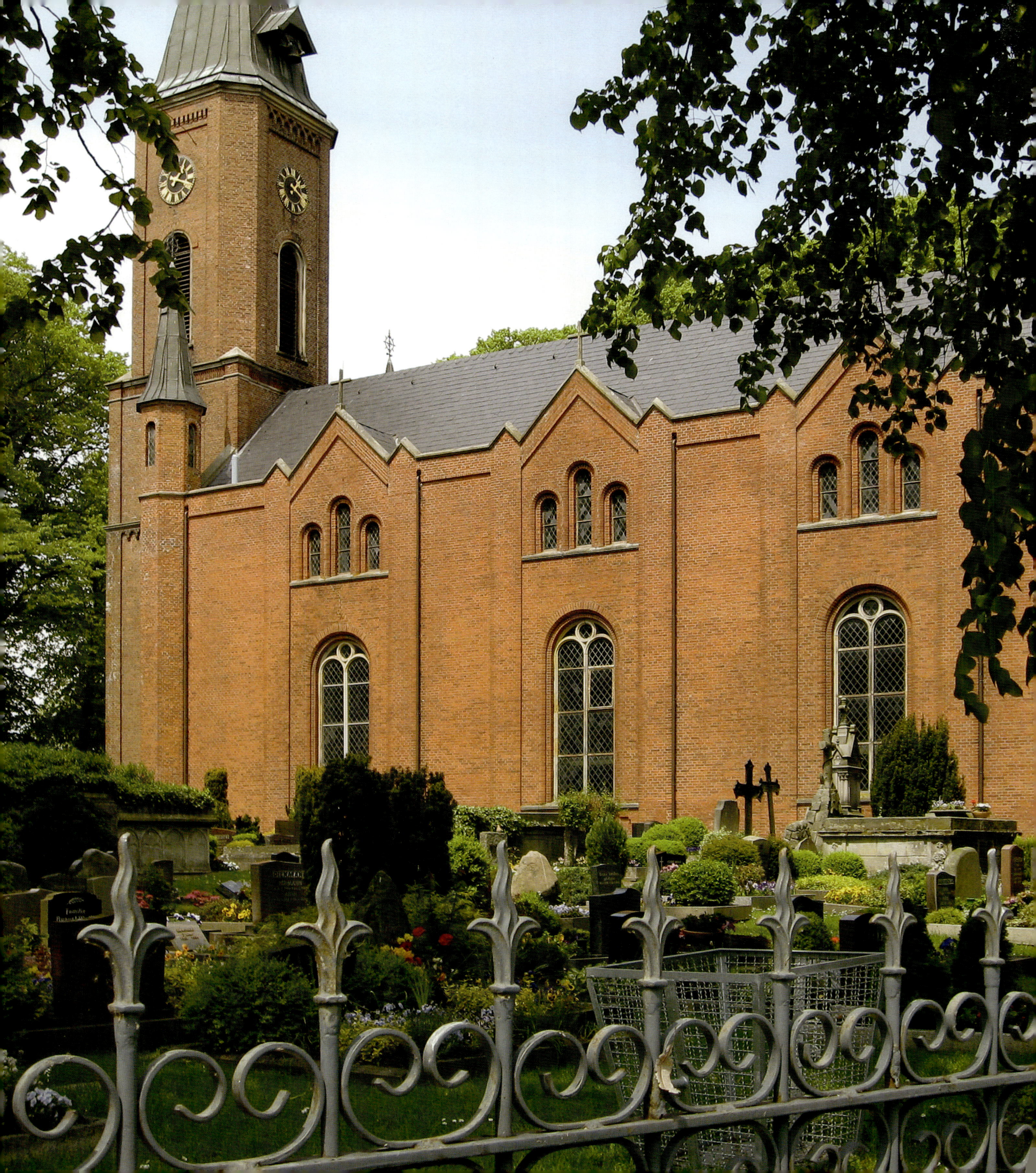

CHAPTER II

Rulfs Before Nacogdoches

Diedrich Rulfs in Oldenburg, Germany, 1848-1880

"The architect was a changeling whose four fathers – the builder, engineer, artist, and archeologist – denied responsibility, and only reluctantly admitted any relationship whatever. In contrast to his contemporaries in England and France, the German architect enjoyed neither a definite social position nor a specific function in public life." Dr. Paul Zucker, *Journal of Architectural Historians.*

Diedrich Rulfs and his family emigrated from Germany to the United States in 1880. It is extremely difficult for a person in the modern world to imagine how difficult and risky an undertaking this must have been. Rulfs was thirty-two years of age at the time, married with three children—the youngest two months old. The party that immigrated to Texas consisted of the five members of his immediate family and two extended family members, his mother-in-law, Helene Böschen, and brother-in-law, Anton Böschen. This chapter will discuss the Rulfs and Böschen family heritages, the state of Oldenburg where Diedrich grew up, his education, and the architectural heritage that he brought with him from northern Europe. The chapter organizes this information around the series of towns in which Rulfs lived and worked and around specific questions: the Butjadingen Peninsula, where he grew to manhood; the ancient town of Atens, where he worked and married; Oldenburg (Stadt), the capital of the province where he worked and trained; and finally, Blexen, where he lived before departing for the United States. The questions addressed in each of these locations will try to determine what influences, historical trends, buildings, and styles current at the time might have shaped his thoughts. Specifically, what did Rulfs bring from his years of preparation in Germany that might have determined his contributions to Nacogdoches? Did he know how to respond to both good and bad economic conditions? Could he respond to both wealthy patrons and to patrons with modest means?

FIGURE 2.1. (Opposite) St. Nicklas Church, Stollhamm, Germany.
The Parish Church and Cemetery where the Rulfs family worshiped and were buried in North Germany. Photograph by author.

A Spelling Problem

Since Mr. Rulfs had trouble with the spelling of his first name throughout his life, perhaps a word of explanation might be helpful. At the time of his christening, in the church records at Stollhamm, his full name was recorded as DIEDERICH ANTON WILHELM RULFS.[1] This spelling of his first name is identical to that of his maternal grandfather (DIEDERICH HERMANN STINDT) who, no doubt, was present at the ceremony. Later, when Rulfs married in Atens, however, *he* signed the nuptial documents as DIEDRICH, dropping the second internal "E." When he attended the christening of his new son in Blexen, Rulfs again spelled his name without the second "E"—DIEDRICH; and he repeated this spelling on the shipping forms when he officially entered the United States in 1880.[2] He repeatedly used this spelling in official documents in this county.

The US Census Records used anything from DERICK to DEDRICK to DEDRELL. Finally in the 1920 Census, the surveyors gave up, as Rulfs himself did in his business advertisements, and simply reduced his first name to an initial—"D. RULFS."[3] Locals even then spelled this letter as "DEE"! While DIEDRICH is the preferred family spelling,[4] on his tombstone, the family at that time placed *only* his initials on the headstone: "D. A. W. RULFS."

The misspelling of his name in Texas came from a pronunciation problem. In German, the combination "IE" is always pronounced as an "E"; the syllable break after the internal "D" would make its pronunciation that of a "T." (In articles, the present author has contributed to this spelling confusion because local sources spelled it with the "T".)[5] Based on the way the name sounded when spoken in German, Anglicized spellings have ranged from "Dietrich" to "Deitrich" and even "Detrich." The most amusing spelling error appears on his naturalization certificate, where the Nacogdoches judge totally transformed his first name into "DANIEL." As Rulfs later explained to his son, he simply bowed to the localization and only forced the judge to add the initials "A. W." in between the "Daniel" and last name to make sure the overall initials would signify only him: "Daniel (A. W.) Rulfs."[6] Rulfs told his son later that the official who signed the documents repeatedly called him "DAVE."[7] (See Figure 2.5 Naturalization Papers of D. Rulfs.) One can see why Diedrich's descendants have bowed to modern conventions and refused to stick with the German spelling. Their English spellings are, interestingly, varied.[8]

The Rulfs Family Heritage

Diedrich Anton Wilhelm Rulfs was born at home in Stollhammerwisch, a rural community about two miles northeast of Stollhamm on the Butjadingen Peninsula, in the Grand Duchy of Oldenburg. He was christened in the family parish Church of Saint Nickolas (*Die St. Nikolai Kirche*) in Stollhamm on March 6, 1848, where for generations his family had worshiped, christened their children, and buried their dead.

Rulfs's paternal grandparents were Wilhelm Rulfs (1791-1839) and Anna Katharine (née Dieckmann) Rulfs (1796-1848); his parents were Gerhard Wilhelm Rulfs (1821-1874) and Helene Margaretha Katharinea (née Stindt) Rulfs (1819-1854).[9] While the grandparents made their home in the nearby community of Iffens (two miles north of Stollhamm) and the parents owned a farm in nearby Stollhammerwisch (two miles northeast), they were *all* christened in Stollhamm and went to the St. Nickolas Church there. Diedrich had a brother born in 1850, but the child died soon after birth.[10] Diedrich's mother, Helene, died in 1854 when he was six. Two years later, his father Gerhard remarried; his second wife, Anna Margarete (née Rosentreter) was from Esenshammer Altendeich, six miles south of Stollhamm. Gerhard and Anna were to have eight children, all born at home in Stollhammerwisch. Several of these half siblings did not survive to adulthood, however.[11] One of Diedrich's half-brothers, Anton Gerhard Rulfs, accidentally drowned at the age of four in the canal near the family home in 1867. Diedrich was close to these siblings and paid for two of them, Heinrich Wilhelm Rulfs (1860-1919) and Sophie Rebecka Rulfs (1862-1940), to join him in Texas in July of 1884; both are buried in Oak Grove Cemetery in Nacogdoches.[12]

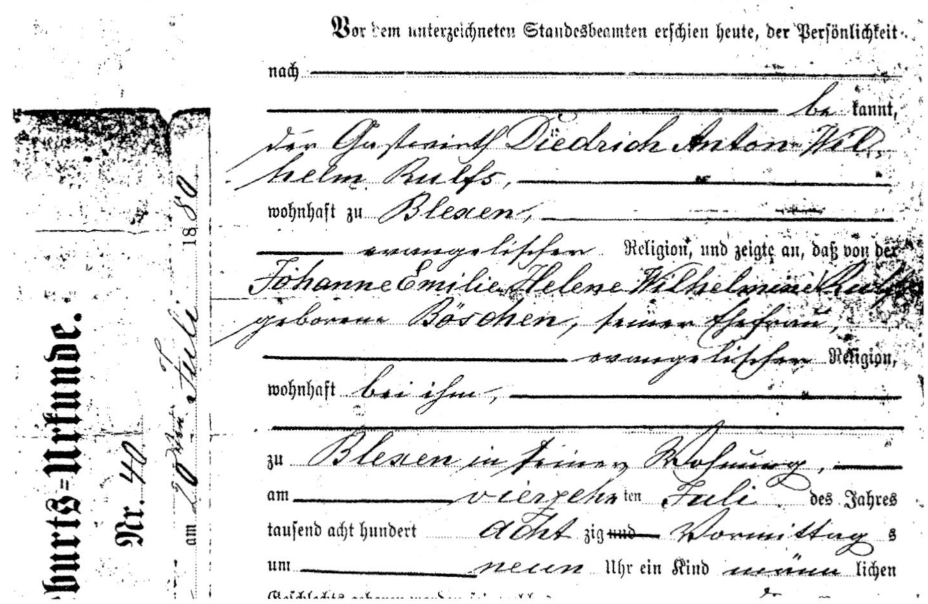

Geburts-Urkunde. Nr. 40. am 20ten Juli 1880

Vor dem unterzeichneten Standesbeamten erschien heute, der Persönlichkeit nach bekannt, der Gastwirth Diedrich Anton Wilhelm Rulfs, wohnhaft zu Blexen, evangelischer Religion, und zeigte an, daß von der Johanne Emilie Helene Wilhelmine Rulfs geborene Böschen, seiner Ehefrau, evangelischer Religion, wohnhaft bei ihm, zu Blexen in seiner Wohnung, am vierzehnten Juli des Jahres tausend acht hundert achtzig Vormittags um neun Uhr ein Kind männlichen

FIGURE 2.2. (Above) Blexen Birth Certificate of Edward Diedrich Rulfs, July 1880.

The name "Diedrich" is spelled twice on this birth certificate of their fourth child, born shortly before the Rulfs sailed for the United States: once in the father's name and once in the son's name. Access to this record shared with the author by Anna Kathryn Holbrook.

FIGURES 2.3 and 2.4. (Below) Rulfs, New Orleans Passenger Lists, 1820-1945.

The two images below show the name of Diedrich Rulfs as they appear in the ship-ping records from the New Orleans Passenger Lists. The one at the top is the printed information supplied by ancestry.com, and the second, a detail of the actual records.

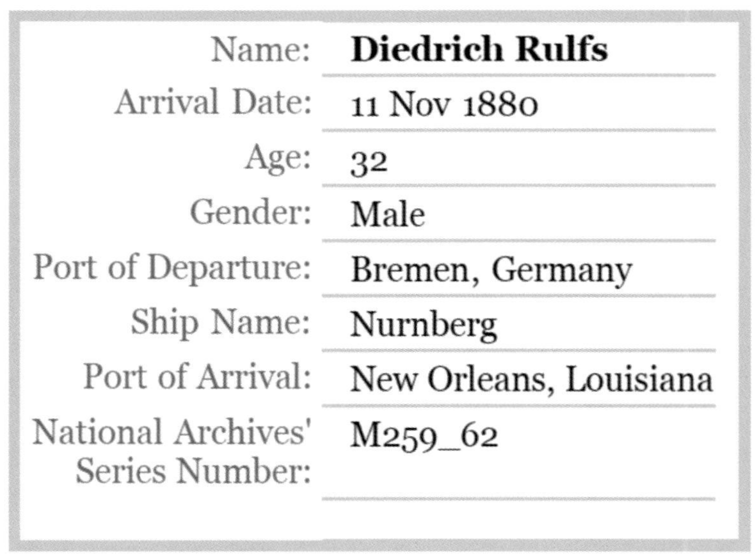

Name:	**Diedrich Rulfs**
Arrival Date:	11 Nov 1880
Age:	32
Gender:	Male
Port of Departure:	Bremen, Germany
Ship Name:	Nurnberg
Port of Arrival:	New Orleans, Louisiana
National Archives' Series Number:	M259_62

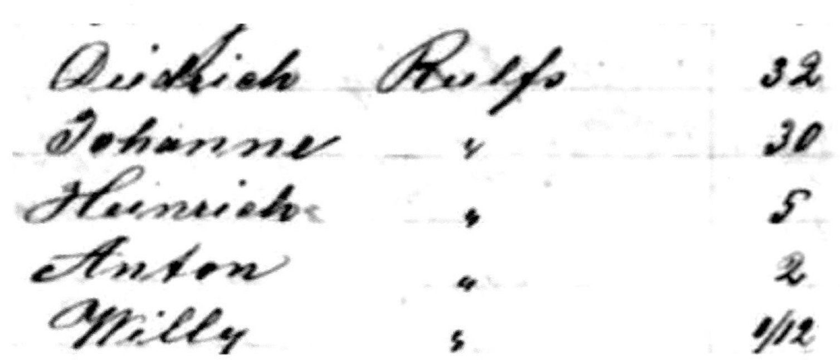

Diedrich	Rulfs	32
Johanne	"	30
Heinrich	"	5
Anton	"	2
Willy	"	1/12

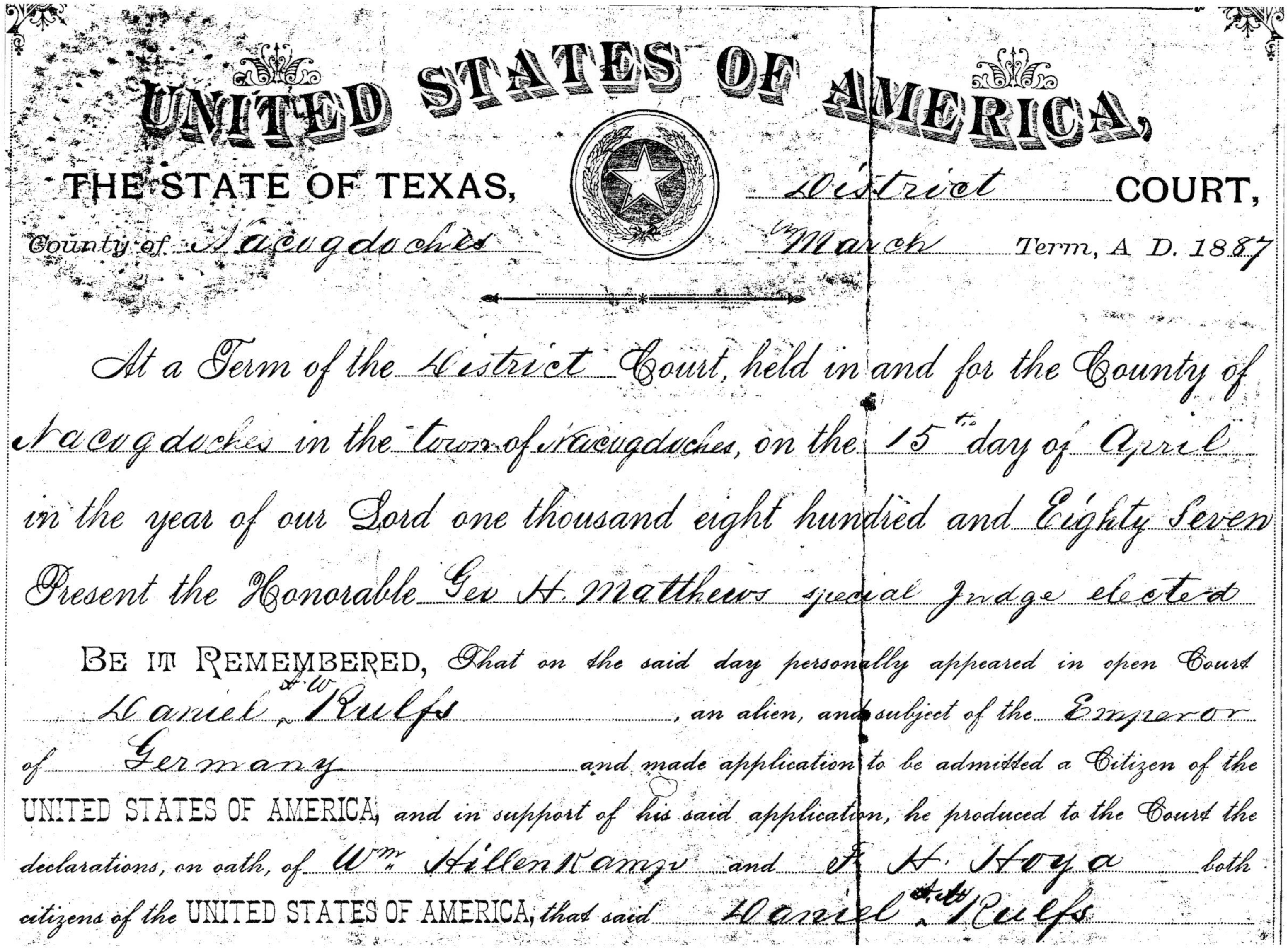

UNITED STATES OF AMERICA,

THE STATE OF TEXAS, District COURT,

County of Nacogdoches March Term, A. D. 1887

At a Term of the District Court, held in and for the County of Nacogdoches in the town of Nacogdoches, on the 15th day of April in the year of our Lord one thousand eight hundred and Eighty Seven Present the Honorable Geo H. Matthews special Judge elected

BE IT REMEMBERED, That on the said day personally appeared in open Court Daniel A.W. Rulfs, an alien, and subject of the Emperor of Germany and made application to be admitted a Citizen of the UNITED STATES OF AMERICA, and in support of his said application, he produced to the Court the declarations, on oath, of Wm. Hillenkamp and F. H. Hoya both citizens of the UNITED STATES OF AMERICA, that said Daniel A.W. Rulfs

FIGURE 2.5. Diedrich Rulfs, Naturalization Certificate, 1887, Detail. *"Daniel," the name assigned to Rulfs in his naturalization document, is clearly visible here. The "A. W." that he had the official write in between the two names, is also visible. Access to this record shared with the author by Anna Kathryn Holbrook.*

Diedrich came from a family of hard-working craftsmen, imbued with the Protestant work ethic, as were their distant relatives the Dutch. While the Rulfs family was very familiar with the rhythm of the agricultural region where they lived, their occupation was non-agricultural. The Rulfs were builders. They owned farmland, but they primarily used it for extra income and for food for the family. Diedrich's grandfather appears on census roles as a "barrel binder." Gerhard Wilhelm, Diedrich's father, appeared in local records at first as a laborer, then as a carpenter (*zimmermann*), and by the census of 1866, as a Master Builder (*Meister*) in both Stollhammerwisch and Geestemunde (a part of Bremen).[13] *Meister* (master builder) was the most important classification in Germany for a person certified to design and construct buildings in an era before professional architecture schools. The Rulfs lived among the people for whom they built and were very much a part of the community. They knew the things their neighbors valued. They appreciated, instinctively, the human desire to have something different and unique without standing out—creature comforts without pretensions. The domestic structures around them were practical, utilitarian, and soundly constructed with attention to the conditions of the weather. The only house in the Stollhamm area that Diedrich Rulfs personally owned and built carries the date 1869.[14] It is quite possible he never lived in this house, but instead built the house to lease for income—a practice he would also employ in Texas. The house has, for it still exists, a hip-on-gable roof which was widely used in Northern Germany, but which Rulfs never used in Texas; the house does have window and brick details, however, which the architect did employ in his work in Nacogdoches.

Perhaps the first lesson learned by any builder in the North Sea coastal areas was the importance of foundations and the exploitation of natural elevations. In the coastal areas of Lower Saxony, where the water table determined everything, churches and homes had to be constructed on the few existing high-ground areas or on carefully built-up mounds. Either way, the foundation and the water table determined the success or failure of buildings. For instance, his home church, St. Nicklas Church in Stollhamm, was successful because it stood on the first naturally elevated ground from the coastline.[15] Most early bell towers along the coast had problems because of soft foundational footings; they had to be constructed separate from the sanctuaries, not unlike the campaniles in Italy (there, due to earthquakes), to accommodate their frequent collapse.

Diedrich Rulfs internalized lessons learned at his father's side: the importance of working with available and native resources, the decorative as well as structural uses of brick patterns, and the frugal importance of adaptive use of existing structures and materials. From his keen observation of his native region, he also became infatuated with church towers, and he

*The Rulfs Family**

Wilhelm Rulfs m. Anna Katharine Dieckmann
(1791-1839) (1796-1848)

Gerhard Wilhelm Rulfs m. (1) Helene Margaretha Katharine Stindt (1819-1854) (2) Anna Margarete Rosentreter (1832-1874)
(1821-1876)

(1):
Diedrich Anton Wilhelm Rulfs
(March 6, 1848 - February 15,1926)
Male Infant (1850)

(2):
Anna Helene Rulfs, (1857-1865)
Heinrich Wilhelm Rulfs (1860-1919)
[Buried in Oak Grove, Nacogdoches]
Sophie Rebecka Rulfs (1862-1940)
[Buried in Oak Grove, Nacogdoches]
Anton Gerhard Rulfs (1863-1867)
Johann Elise Gerhardine Rulfs (1865-1866)
Anna Helene Katharine Rulfs (1868-)
Heinrich Gerhard Wilhelm Rulfs (1870-1877)
Anna Helene Wilhelmine Rulfs (1874-)

* Source: "Genealogy of Gerhard Wilhelm Rulfs, Meister in Stollhammerwisch," Hans-Rudolf Mengers, correspondences with the author, June 21, 2010.

Figure 2.xx The Böschen-Rulfs Family*

Johann Anton Böschen m. Conradine Sophie Wilhelmine Morisee

Diedrich Anton Wilhelm Rulfs (1848-1926) m. Johanne Emilie Helene Wilhelmine Böschen (1849-1918)

Born in Germany: Gerhard William (1875-1943)
Emilie Helene (1877)
Carl Henry (1878-1955)
Edward Anton (1880-1948)
Born in Texas: Mary (1882-1948)
John (1885-1955)

* Source: Anna Kathryn Holbrook, *Nacogdoches County Families*, 580.

FIGURES 2.6 and 2.7. Genealogy of the Rulfs Family.

later would attempt to turn Nacogdoches into a town of spires. While the historic need for church towers as watchtowers against the danger of invaders was no longer necessary in the Germany of his childhood, everywhere he witnessed an active building program of church and tower replacement.[16] Rulfs grasped how important church buildings were as a focus for civic as well as religious pride. He understood that the towers on churches served not only an aesthetic purpose, but also the utilitarian purpose of spatial and visual orientation in a landscape.

The German Context

Oldenburg. Diedrich Rulfs was twenty-two before he became a subject of the Emperor of Germany. The Rulfs, like their neighbors, would have thought of themselves as Lower Saxons *(Niedersachen)* or perhaps Frisians, the ancient name for their area. They were subjects of the Grand Duke Augustus I (reign, 1829-1853), the ruler of the Grand Duchy of Oldenburg.[17] Due to its feudal history, this northwestern part of Europe on the North Sea had developed politically and linguistically as independent states. At the time Rulfs was born in 1848, Oldenburg, Schleswig-Holstein, Hamburg, Mecklenburg, Bremen, Brandenburg, Hesse, North Rhine-Westphalia, and the Kingdom of the Netherlands, were all separate entities.[18] Rulfs was eighteen in 1866 when Prussian Chancellor Otto von Bismarck manipulated the nearby Schleswig-Holstein border conflict into a war with Austria and, in the process, created the North German Confederation. He was twenty-two when Germany formally came into being. The soldiers of Oldenburg helped to win the war against France in 1870-71, and the Grand Duke helped to elect King Wilhelm as Emperor of Germany. The prosperity that followed, however, was politically and economically complicated, albeit exciting.

While Oldenburg remained an "autonomous" state within the new Empire, Oldenburgers had mixed feelings as they experienced the growing power of Prussia, their nearby competitor. With assimilation, they lost control over their own affairs. The tide, however, was too strong to resist. Almost everyone welcomed the opening of new windows onto the wider European economic markets; but, unfortunately, the chills and illnesses that accompanied these new breezes were not as happily received. If Germany caught a cold, Oldenburg sneezed, too, as became evident in the mid 1870s.

Historically, the new state in the Empire was the tenth largest state in Germany. In present day Germany, the much-enlarged federal state of Lower Saxony is second in area and fourth in population among the sixteen states of Germany. The physical description in the 1891 *Encyclopaedia Britannica* is interesting:

> It is almost entirely flat, with a slight inclination towards the sea. In respect of its soil it is divided broadly into two parts, the higher and inland-lying "Geest," consisting of sandy plains intermixed with extensive heaths and moors, and the "marsh lands" along the Coast, consisting of rich but somewhat swampy alluvial soil. The latter, which compose about one-fifth of the duchy, are protected against the inroads of the sea by dykes as in Holland; and beyond these are the so-called "watten," generally covered at high tide, but at many points being gradually reclaimed. The climate is temperate and humid; the mean temperature of the coldest month at the town of Oldenburg is 26º Fahrenheit; of the warmest 66º. Storms are numerous and somewhat violent, owing to the almost entire absence of trees; and fogs and ague [chills] are prevalent in the marsh lands.[19]

The Butjadingen Peninsula. Within the Duchy of Oldenburg, the regional area where Rulfs grew to maturity lies directly on the North Sea. The Butjadingen Peninsula lies between the River Weser on the east with its great commercial port of Bremerhaven and the Bay of Jadebusen on the west with its great German naval port of Wilhelmshaven.[20] Historically, this peninsula changed hands many times–sometimes linked with Bremen and Denmark, but, ultimately an independent entity. While settlements date back to the 2nd Century AD, great flood tides continually wiped out all settlements until the first dikes were built in the 11th century. Disaster remained ever-present if the dikes fell into disrepair. One surge by the North Sea wiped out a third of the population. Like the Dutch, the Frisians (as the Angles, Jutes, and Saxons in the area called themselves) were dependent on a carefully constructed infrastructure: dikes, windmills, drainage ditches along every field, barrier beaches, dredged canals to avoid silting, limited bridges, planted trees, and built-up mounds on which to construct homes.[21] It was in one of the ubiquitous drainage ditches near their home in Stollhammerwisch, as mentioned earlier, that Diedrich's younger half-brother Gerhard Anton drowned in 1867.

The wealth of Oldenburg, in general, lay not in natural resources like minerals or timber, but in livestock. According to the classic 1911 *Encyclopaedia Britannica*, "The ratio of cattle, sheep and horses to the population is one of the highest among the German states. There are few large estates, and the ground is mostly in the hands of small farmers, who enjoy the right of fishing and shooting on their holdings. Game is scarce, but fishing fairly productive."[22] The grassland economy made Oldenburg famous across the continent for its horse market and for its regional cloth, in English known as Osnaburg fabric.[23] From the river harbors, such as Brake and Elsfleth, regional agricultural products were "exported to Scandinavia, Russia, England and the United States, in return for colonial goods and manufactures."[24]

Stollhamm. The agricultural communities of Stollhamm and the smaller Stollhammerwisch were isolated. Most economic activity, except for local products, had to transpire on canals. No major roads appear on the map of 1812. The first road connecting the east river port of Brake to Burhaven over Stollhamm did not appear on a map until 1863. Roads in the area had to be built along the tops of old dikes; the trees planted along these roads existed not to shade the traveler, but to add strength to the dike. The main North Sea dike in the nineteenth century now supports a regional road and has "dike" in its name – Stollhammerdeich Highway (K197). The massive North Sea dike which protects the peninsula today was not there in the years Rulfs lived there. The first railway did not reach Brake, on the river side of the peninsula, until 1873 and was not extended to Nordenham until 1875.[25] (These dates closely parallel the development of rail transportation in the isolated region of East Texas; the first rail service reached Nacogdoches in 1883.) Rulfs departed for the United States before rail service made its way to his hometown, but he clearly understood that economic activity depended on transportation.

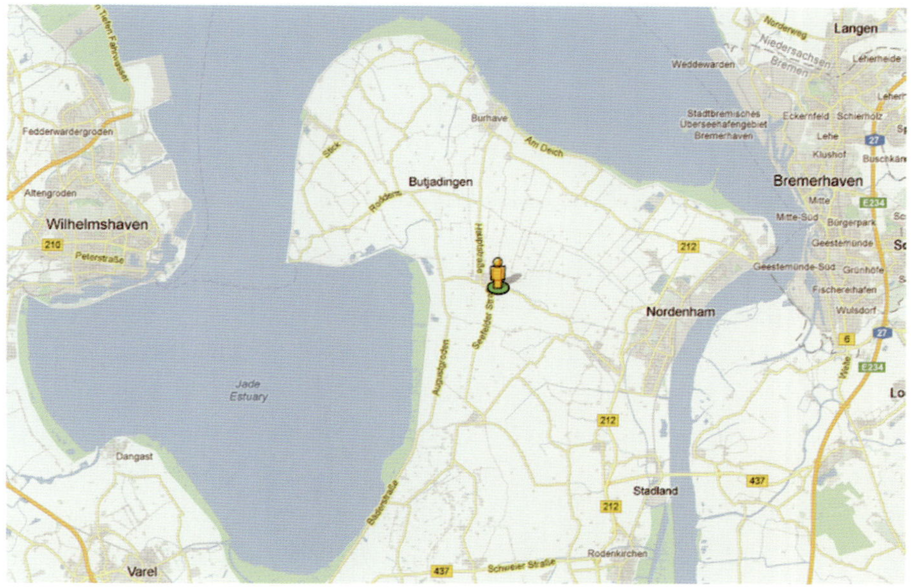

FIGURE 2.9. (Above) Detail, Map of Butjadingen Peninsula.
This detail shows the great North Sea ports of Wilhelmshaven on the left and the port of Bremerhaven on the right. The Weser River, which forms the eastern side of the peninsula, connects the Hanseatic City of Bremen to the North Sea, making Bremen a major port from the Middle Ages to the present. As ships got larger, the new port of Bremerhaven became more important. The small FIGURE indicates Stollhamm. Map from Google Earth.

FIGURE 2.8. (Right) 19th Century Painting by Georg Müller vom Siel (1865–1939).
Windmühle bei Dötlingen, Oldenburger Landesmuseum für Kunst-und Kulturgeschichte.

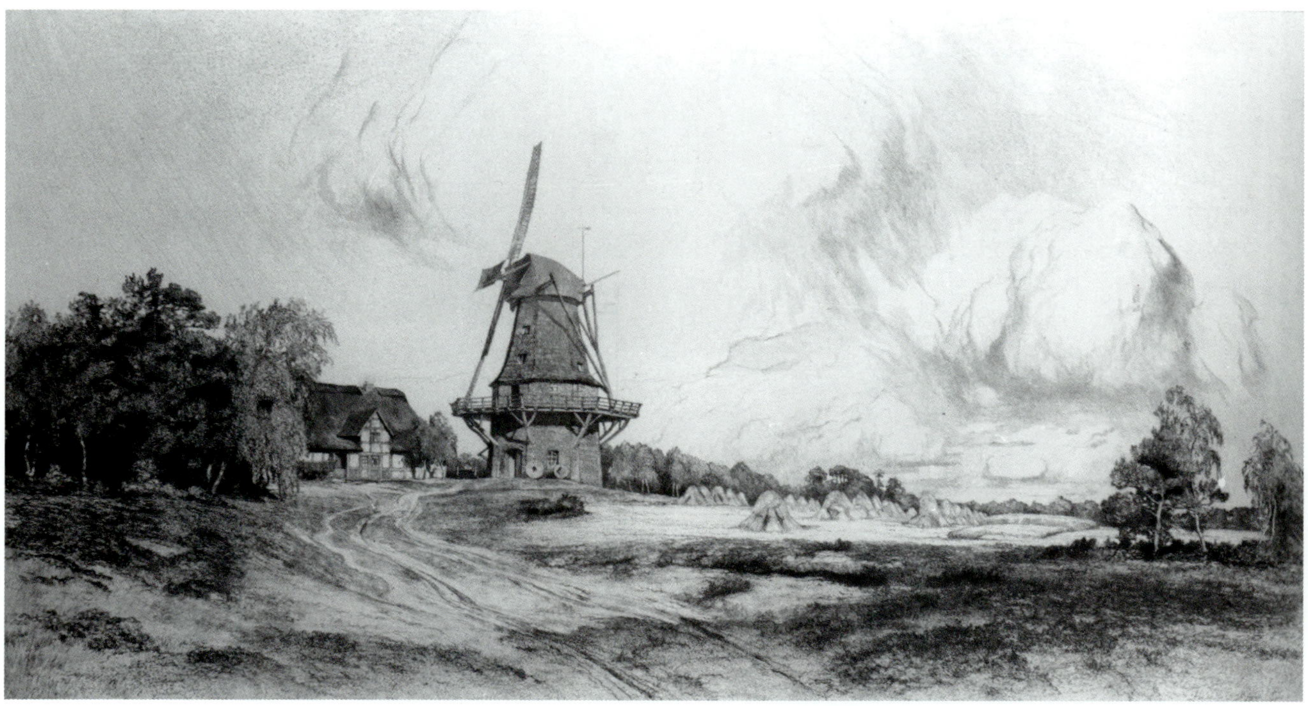

Map of Germany, 1870

Detail

Duchy of Oldenburg

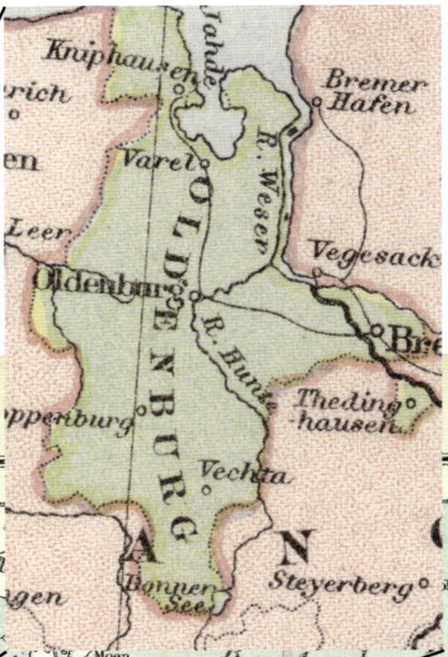

FIGURES 2.10 and 2.11. Map and Detail of Germany in 1870. *Map of the German Empire, published in 1870 by J. Bartholomew. Map in the collection of the author.*

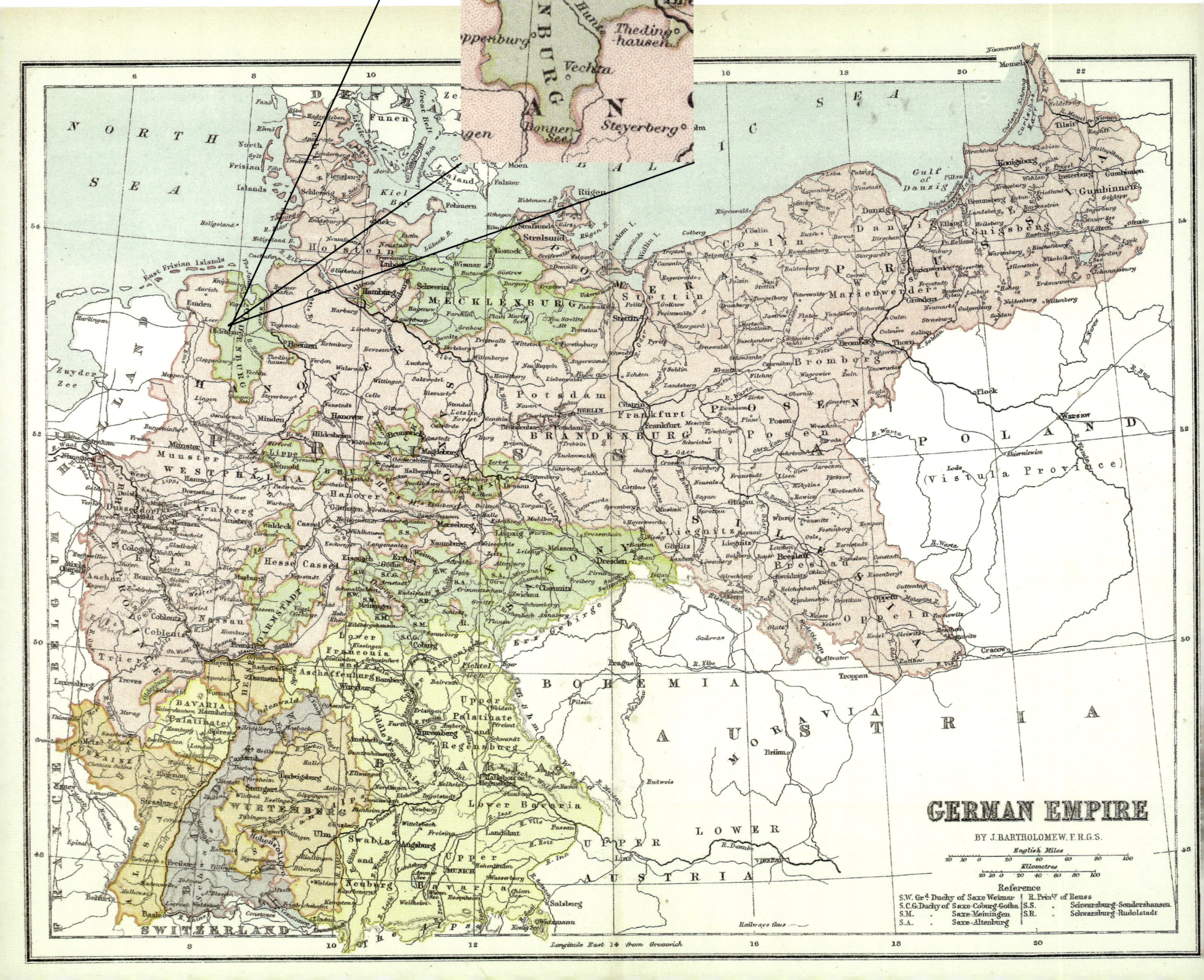

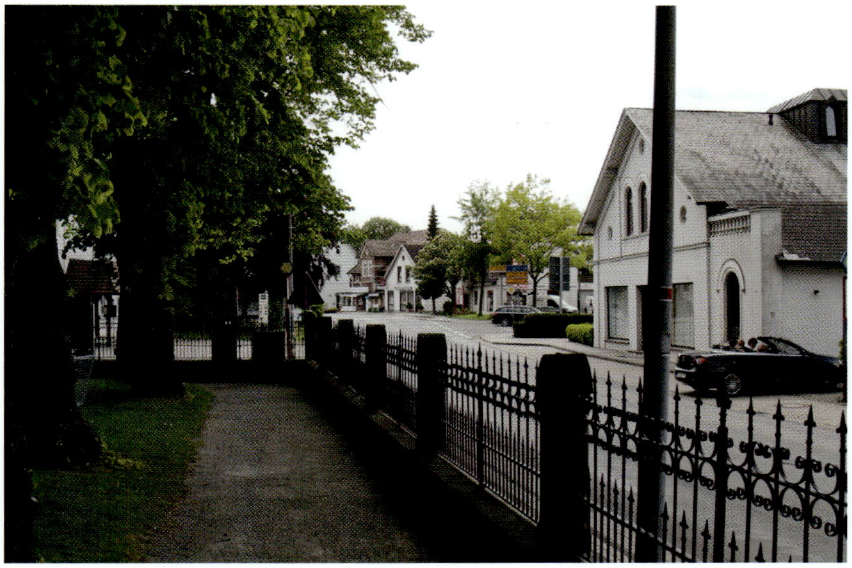

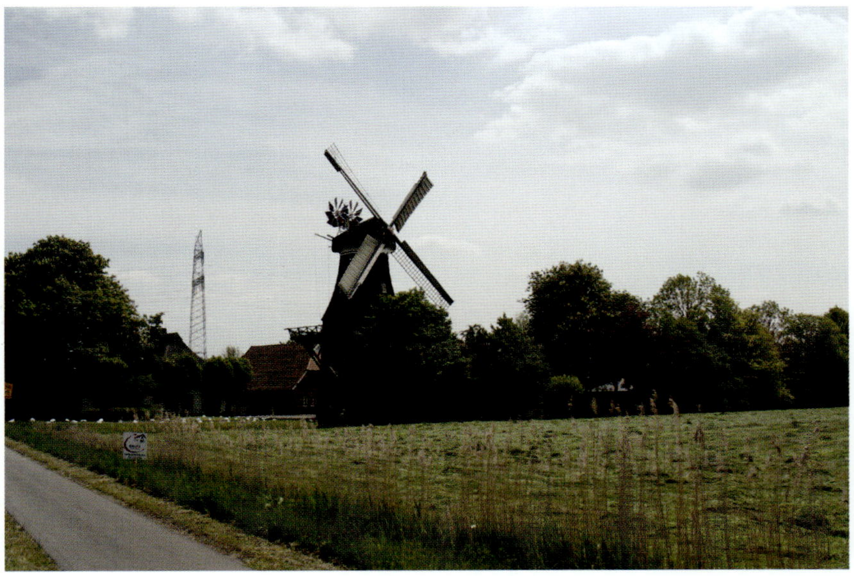

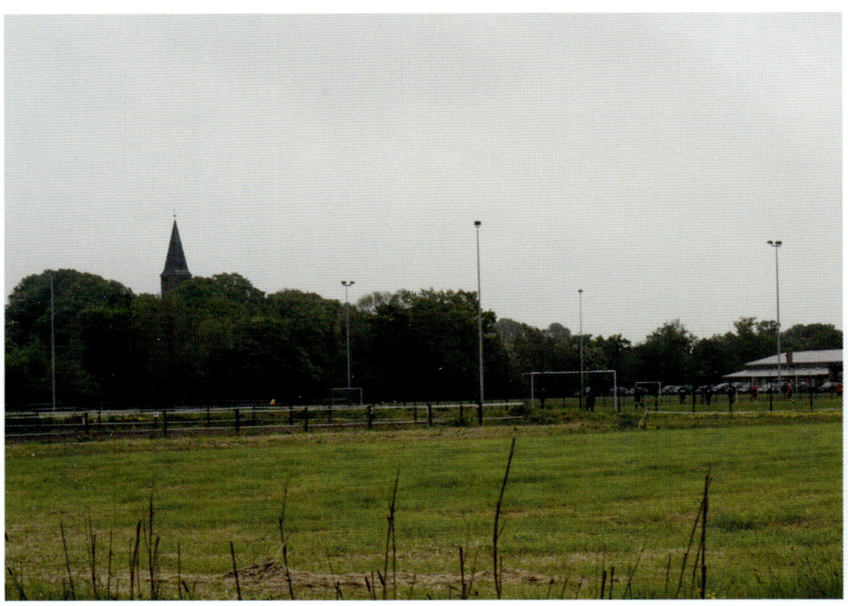

Stollhamm, Germany

FIGURES 2.12 - 2.14. (Left) Scenes of Stollhamm, 2010.
(Top) The Main Street of Stollhamm from the Churchyard. (Middle) Windmill near Stollhamm on the road to Nordenham. (Bottom) Church Tower from the playing field of the school. Photographs by the author.

FIGURE 2.15. (Below) House by D. Rulfs in Stollhammerwisch.
Diedrich Rulfs built and owned this house in Stollhammerwisch, a village outside Stollhamm. It stands on Abbeyhausen Road Nr. 5. The house originally at that location burned in 1857. In 1869 D. A. W. Rulfs bought the property and built the house. It is doubtful whether he ever lived in the house; the dates seem wrong. He probably built the house as a speculation. Certainly this would fit into the chronology of his life established in this work. Soon after building the house, we find him on his way to Oldenburg (Stadt) via Atens. He sold the house in 1873, most likely to finance his wedding to Johanna and their move to the capital.

The house is utilitarian in nature, with few frills except in the detailed brickwork. Stollhamm and the surrounding villages, like Stollhammerwisch, were agricultural communities. The house is characteristic of the broad footing all houses and barns had to have in this north German peninsula. Note the tilting windows on the house. Rulfs used tilting and pivoting windows in several structures in Nacogdoches: the First Methodist and Zion Hill Churches, and on the Hollis Mast House. The clipped gable roof, where the gable has a half-hipped roof instead of a point, was and is very popular in northern Germany. Rulfs did not use this predominantly rural feature in Nacogdoches. There are no classical details to the house; he learned classical styles in Oldenburg during his training there. Photograph compliments of Hans-Rudolf Mengers in Germany.

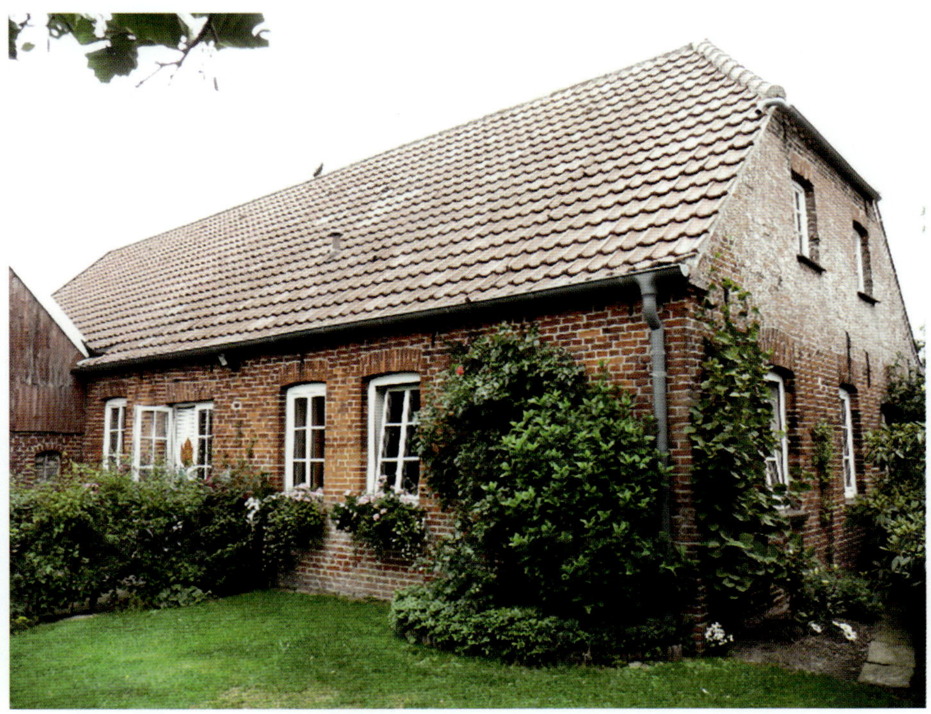

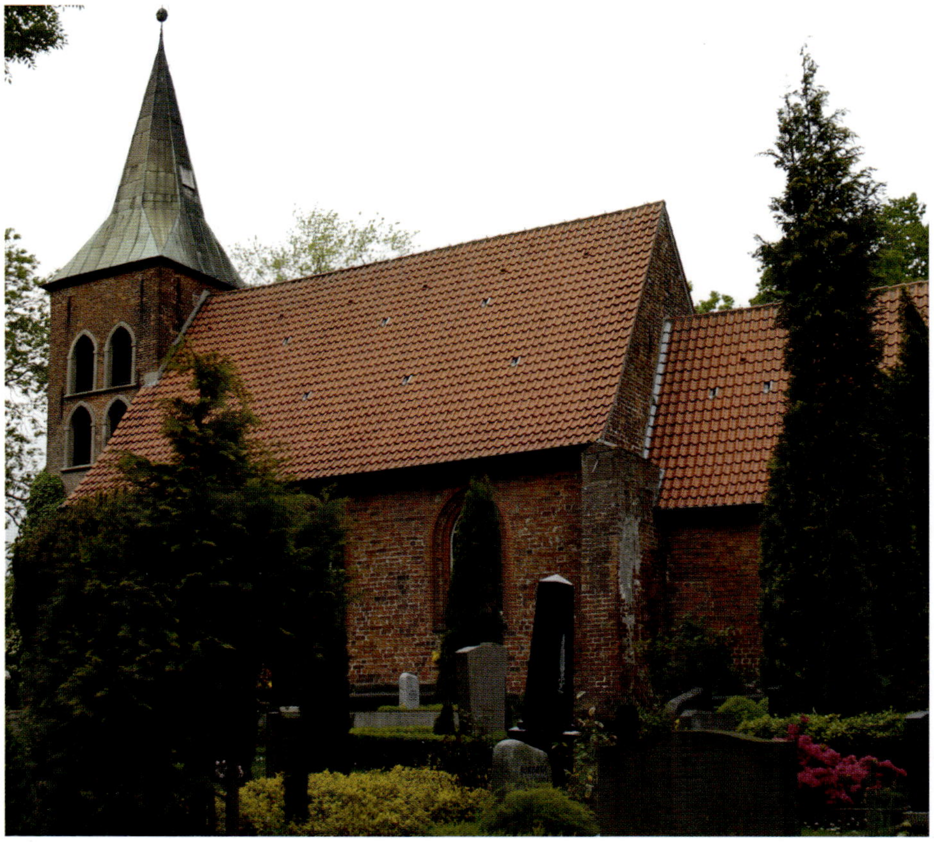

FIGURE 2.16. The Church of St. Mary (St. Marien Kirche) in Atens, Germany in 2010.

Today, the Church of St. Mary is encased within the main city cemetery of Nordenham. While the entire cemetery complex is lovely, the most idyllic part, the inner sanctum or core of the cemetery, surrounds the site of the late medieval former Carmelite Cloister of St. Mary. After the Reformation, the monastery ceased to exist. Now, the chapel is all that remains. The chapel itself needed extensive rebuilding in 1606, and due to poor repairs at that time, the bell tower, as well as the facade of the building, had to be rebuilt a third time a century later. Thick walls and a stepped saddle type roof dominate the church itself. The square tower, topped by a high conical, octagon metal steeple roof is distinctively north German. [Because of the relevance of this structure to architectural examples in Nacogdoches, reference to this church will appear elsewhere in this book.] The interior of St. Mary's still has the chalice-shaped sandstone baptismal font from which Helene would have been christened. The font bears the inscription from Mark 16, v 5: "He who believes and is baptized shall enter the Kingdom of Heaven." There are still Böschens being buried in the cemetery at St. Mary's in Atens today. Photograph taken by the author.

The Church of St. Mary in Atens

Atens and Marriage

In 1870 Diedrich Rulfs moved to the old town of Atens, the German spelling for "Athens." Atens was approximately seven miles east of Stollhamm and was the premier town on this Weser River side of the peninsula. Its ancient status and importance rested on its location on higher ground than most of the other towns; it was less threatened by the North Sea. Atens is today a suburb of Nordenham, an encompassing industrial city that did not even exist in the nineteenth century.[26]

Rulfs took up residence in Atens to expand his apprenticeship experience to someone other than his father. Family tradition holds that his father, a known master builder in the area, helped him secure a position with a friend.[27] However, he did not stay long. To participate in the building boom that had begun to engulf the former Duchy after the Unification of Germany, the young apprentice migrated to the capital city rather quickly. Atens, nonetheless, was a very important part of his life. While working in Atens, he met his future wife Johanne Emilie Helene Wilhelmine Böschen.[28] (They possibly could have met earlier, for she had relatives in Stollhamm.) Johanne was born in Atens on September 26, 1849, and was baptized on October 23 of the same year at the Church of St. Mary *(St. Marien Kirche)* in Atens. According to one document, her father, Johann Anton Böschen, was "a driver" in the building trade in Atens; her mother was Conradine Sophie Wilhelmine (née Morisee).[29]

On June 29, 1873, Diedrich Rulfs married Johanne Böschen in the Church of St. Mary in Atens. Documents show him at the time to be a resident of Oldenburg (Stadt) and list him as a "carpenter."[30] He was twenty-five, and she was twenty-four. To finance his new responsibilities, he sold his rental house in the Stollhammwisch in 1873.[31] The newly wedded couple then took up residence in Oldenburg (Stadt) where he was in training.[32] Diedrich knew the capital was the place for career and educational opportunities. It is tempting to think they traveled down the beautiful, tree lined *Butjadingen Strasse* of today in Oldenburg; but, no matter how romantic, a trip by wagon or coach from Atens would have taken much longer and would not have been very pleasant. Most probably, they made the journey to Oldenburg (Stadt) by riverboat on the Weser River since there was no railroad service. It is at least possible, however, that they could have traveled from the new railroad connection at Brake.

Oldenburg (Stadt)

The 1870s were a period of explosive growth in the capital of the Duchy, Oldenburg (Stadt). The dramatic transformation of the capital came after the arrival of the railroad in 1866 and the closely related connection of the capital to the North Sea by a new canal. In 1848, the year Rulfs was born, the city had approximately 10,000 inhabitants; by the early 1870s, when Rulfs moved there, the population was approximately 13,928; by 1880, the year Rulfs departed for the United States, the population of the city had jumped to 20,575.[33] These developments parallel what happened in Nacogdoches after the arrival of the railroad in 1883. Both cities witnessed massive migrations and development as transportation opened them to wider economic opportunities.

The reasons it took so long to connect Oldenburg by rail to the rest of Europe are complicated. One argument is that this sparsely populated region, which was relatively poor in natural resources, could not financially underwrite the cost of constructing such a railway. While costs no doubt played a role, there is also the fact that the neighboring states of Hanover and Prussia conspired to keep railway projects from coming to fruition in Oldenburg.[34] While treaties were signed early, it was not until Prussia *needed* a railroad connection to service its proposed port in Wilhelmshaven that the money seemed to be forthcoming. Oldenburg's population then exploded. Oldenburg's entry into the North German Confederation changed

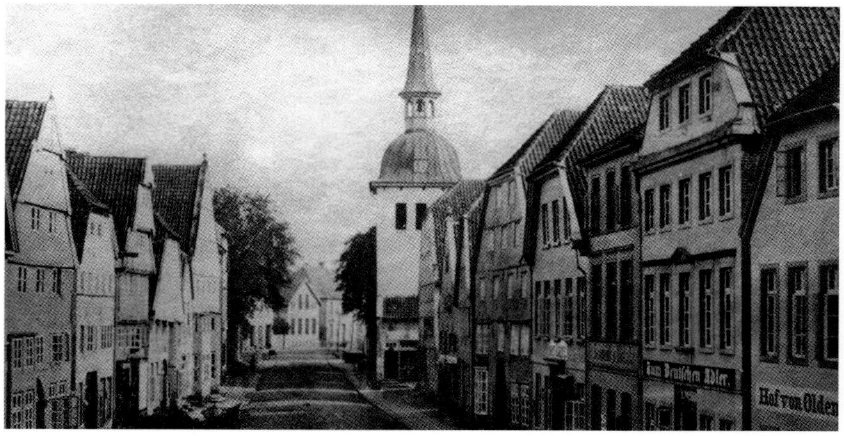

FIGURE 2.17. (Above) Leffers-Eck bis Lappan, Oldenburg, 1875.

The historic photograph of the Lappan and the corner of Renfort (Wall Street) shows the many guesthouses in Oldenburg, which accommodated travelers. Inns with names like "The Court of Oldenburg," "The German Eagle," and "Schmitt's Hotel" are shown in the image. Historical photographs from the "Old Oldenburg ... Join Us" website, http://www.alt-oldenburg.de.

FIGURE 2.18. (Below) Eckhaus, 1880.

The Eckhaus (Corner House) on Eighth Street was constructed after the great city fire in 1676. Postcards of these images are readily available in the stands around Oldenburg today. Photograph from http://www.alt-oldenburg.de.

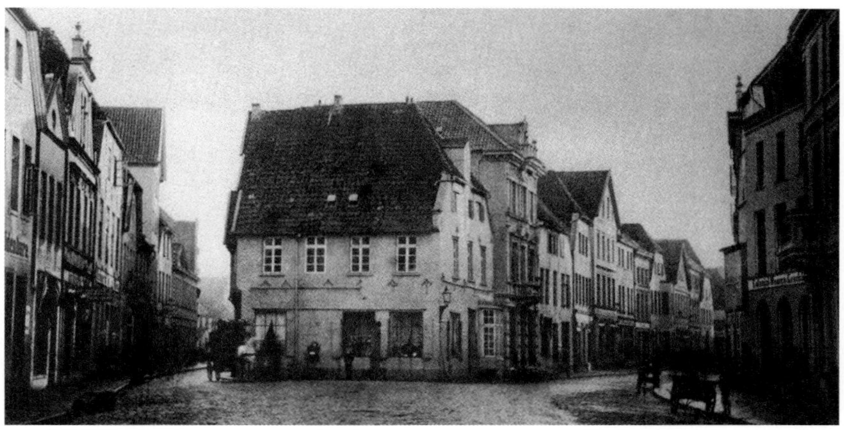

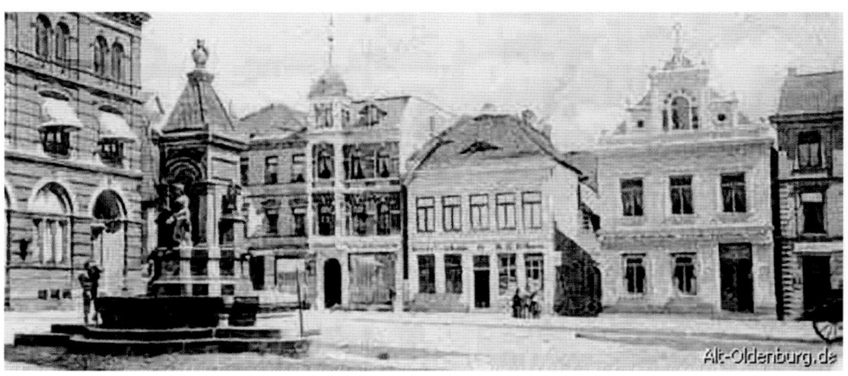

FIGURE 2.19. (Above) Old Market Square, 1880.

A period photograph of the Market Square at the time Rulfs lived in Oldenburg. Everything in this picture is now gone. There are step gables, Palladian windows, arched windows, towers, and other architectural features, which he would use in Nacogdoches.

its political orientation and widened its economic opportunities. It became more attractive to investors and immigrants; but, even so, much of the great infusion of money came from the French war reparations. The city began filling in its smaller canals, replacing its massive protective walls with thoroughfares, creating suburban areas, expanding and building new business establishments, and marshalling its full economic resources to meet the demands and opportunities created by the arrival of the railroads and the new hungry port in Wilhelmshaven. The orientation of the city changed also.[35] The new prosperity in Oldenburg, however, was soon threatened by the onset of the German Depression of 1873.

The Study of Architecture in Germany

While addressing German architectural education in the nineteenth century, Dr. Paul Zucker, a German-American scholar writing for *The Journal of the American Society of Architectural Historians,* noted how unorganized and in transition the study of architecture was in Germany.[36] There were no schools of architecture in Germany until the creation of the Berlin Institute of Technology in 1879, when the older Building Academy (1799) was merged with the Vocational Academy (1829). In Oldenburg, there was "an ample supply of primary, secondary, and special schools," but there was no school of architecture, or, for that matter, even a university. The great university centers of Germany were elsewhere.

The United States and Texas at the time were in a similar state of development, what one author has called a transitional generation. They had universities, but they like Germany had no schools of architecture. For instance, the F. E. and Oscar Ruffini Brothers, who were prominent in nineteenth-century Texas architecture, also trained through apprenticeships and identified themselves not as mechanics or craftsmen, but as professional architects and businessmen.[37] As Dr. Zucker notes, the great German building masters, going back for centuries, had placed all of their emphasis on experience; they spoke disparagingly about the academics who only read about architecture. "Training their apprentices in their craft, they left the academies and all the other educational institutions to the rationalizing classicists." In the late eighteenth century, there was a further revolt against traditional academicism in the movement of romanticism and its ally German nationalism. "Civil architecture," addressing practical functions, was the preference of nineteenth century "architectural workshops," sometimes called "Master Classes," which were conducted in the private offices of the master builders. At the time, architectural artisans were trained in "certain kinds of craftsmanship," with students being more or less apprentices until they were certified as "Masters." While this system later gave rise to the technical high schools in architecture, the emphasis of these early prototypes was more concerned with training civil servants and engineers rather than academic architects.[38]

Diedrich Rulfs fell between these evolving systems, as did his counterparts in the United States. His father had become a Master Builder under the older, pre-institutionalized, practical system of training; he was listed in the 1866 census as such. He would have encouraged his son to follow this same route to professional status; it was a route financially open to a builder's son. Work, not an academic curriculum, was the entry credential into such apprenticeships. Since the demand for skilled craftsmen was very strong, Rulfs would have found any number of master builders who would

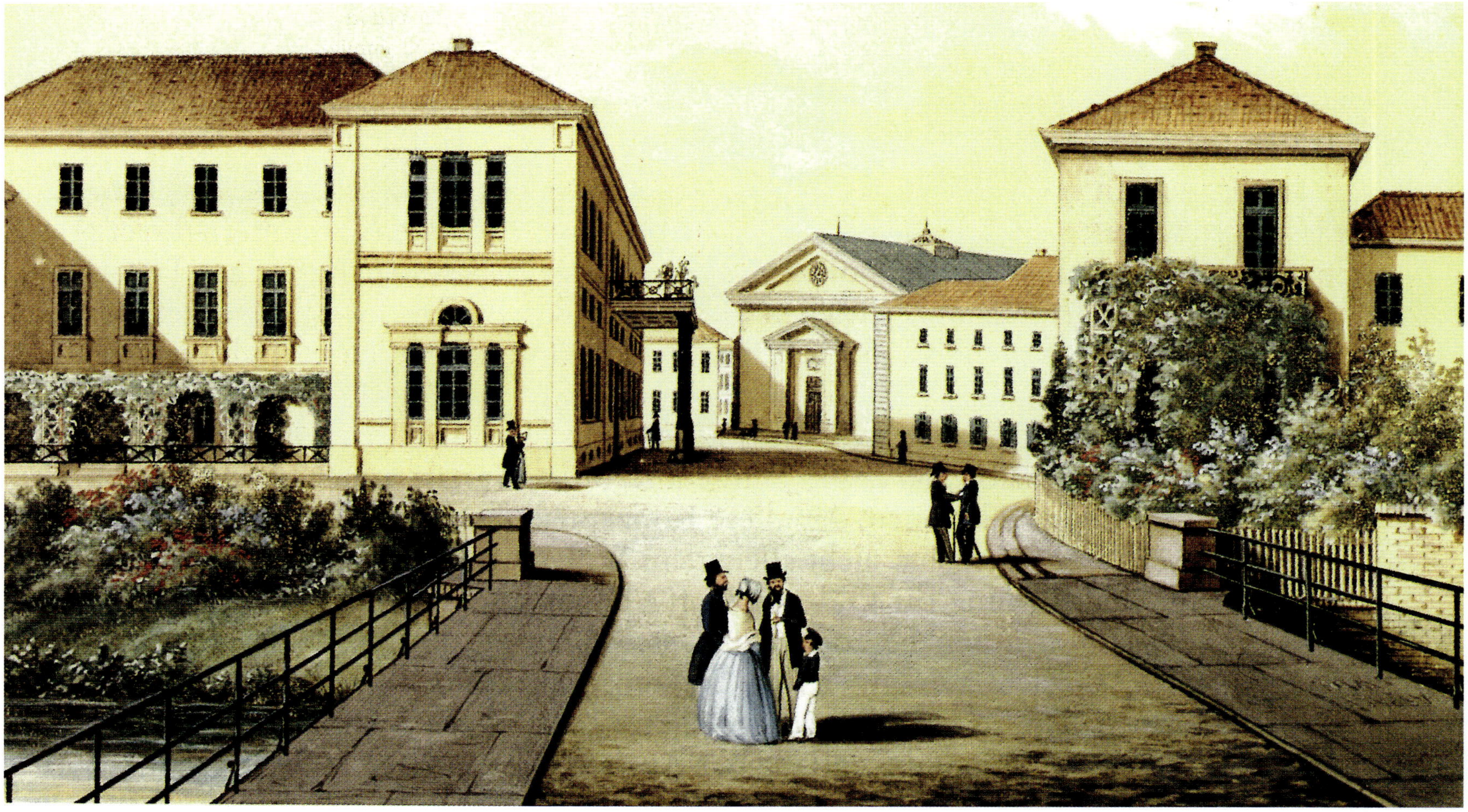

FIGURE 2.20. Gouache of the Everstentor, 1848.
This historic image of the Everstentor from an exhibition on the Kasinoplatze is a gouache by Thomas Presuhn (1848). It is in the Stadtmuseum Oldenburg. Image from the Geschichte Der Stadt Oldenburg, (Isensee Verlag, Oldenburg).

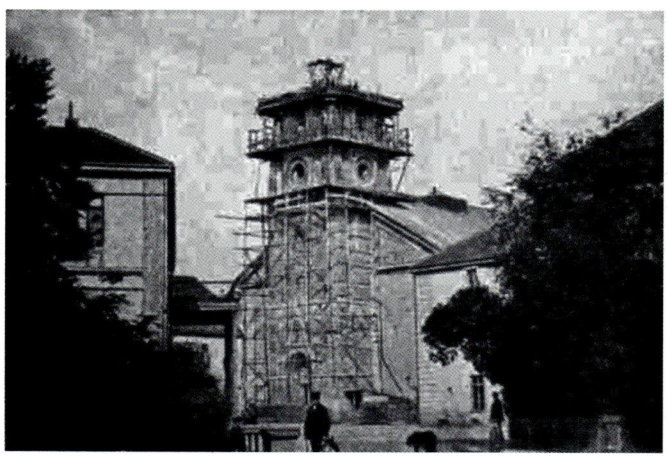

FIGURE 2.21. Construction of the Main Tower of St. Lambert.
The main tower of St. Lambert dates to 1874-7 at the time Rulfs was studying in the Capital City. The interior of the church, rebuilt in 1790, has a classical rotunda resting on Doric columns. The exterior, in stark contrast, is neo-Gothic in red brick and has a collection of towers. These towers and facade were being added to the exterior of the Cathedral during the years that Rulfs lived in Oldenburg (Stadt). Photograph from http://www..alt.Oldenburg.de

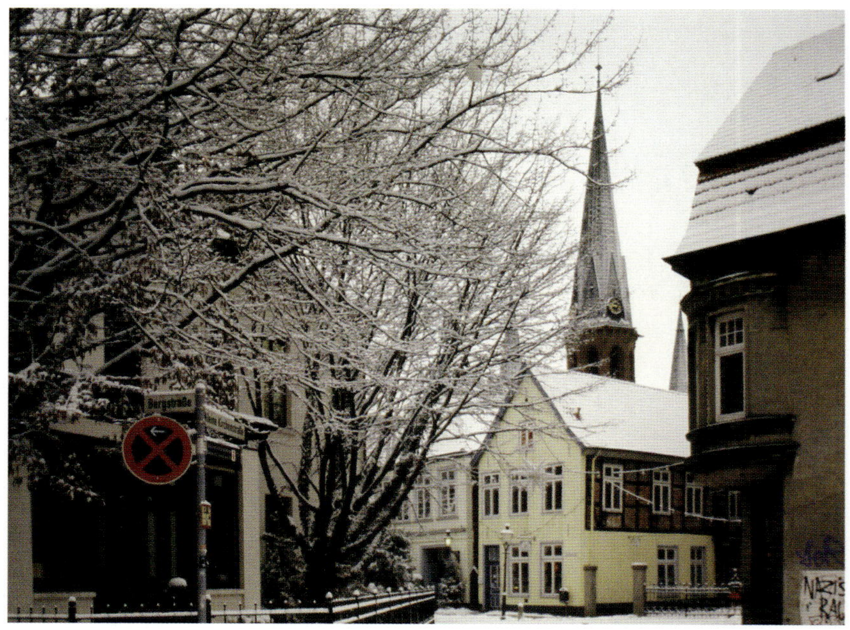

FIGURE 2.22. The Small Church Street.
Not far off the main church square, there is a delightful small street that still imparts the mood of the Oldenburg inner city at the time Rulfs lived there. The view from Church Street shows the sense of orientation which church towers give a city. Photograph from Claus Hammer's Oldenburg: Bilder Einer Stadt, 10.

have accepted him for tutelage. According to family traditions, Diedrich apprenticed with masters in both Atens and Oldenburg. The technical school, which eventually evolved into the School of Architecture in Oldenburg today, was in the process of being established during the years Rulfs studied in the city, but whether he attended the new *Hochschule* while in Oldenburg is unknown. What is certain, however, is that the architecture of the buildings completed during the time he was in Oldenburg inspired his later work in Texas. He was known to have worked in the suburbs in the areas close to these buildings developing in the mid-1870s.[39]

Rulfs's practical education at the hands of a Master Builder, someone who was actively busy in the various kinds of craftsmanship that were popular with contemporary clients, fits the style of the professional career pattern Rulfs developed in Nacogdoches. His technical knowledge and his draftsmanship as an architect testify to his advanced proficiency. The domestic styles being used in Oldenburg at the time were eclectic and ranged from classical to modern. Romanesque, Gothic, and Renaissance Revival styles were among the most requested and made their way into churches, public buildings, and domestic structures. Rulfs was in Oldenburg when the neo-Gothic towers were being added to the St. Lambert Church and the Old Gymnasium was built, as well as the suburban quarters of Haarentor and Dobben along the New Haaren Canal. According to building archives, Rulfs did build several houses in Oldenburg in the mid-1870s, but the start of the "Great Depression" in German finally enveloped Oldenburg, causing a collapse in its housing market.[40] His advancement towards Master Status was cut short.

The Retreat to Stollhamm

Around 1878, Rulfs finally had to retreat to Stollhamm to live with his family. According to family tradition, he trekked around the whole peninsula looking for work and even helped with several church projects that were then under construction or renovation.[41] While the current church history from Stollhamm is not detailed enough to give confirmation to this family tradition, what is certain is that a new parish church building in Stollhamm dates to the period of the young architect's return to the village.[42] Independent confirmation of the building activities in other towns where Rulfs lived temporarily (Burhaven and Blexen) can easily be verified.[43] Whether he helped to plan or to build the Church of St. Nicholas in Stollhamm (*St.-Nikolai-Kirche)* is not as important as the influence the architecture of his home parish church had on his thinking. Rulfs brought design elements from Stollhamm and nearby churches with him to Texas. Perhaps, some of this influence came through his family, many of whom were interested in building and design. His father worshipped in St. Nicholas for many years after Diedrich departed from Germany. The younger half-brother, William Henry, who was also in the building trade and emigrated to Texas in 1884, most certainly would have discussed their family church with him at length. The window treatment of the St. Nicholas Church—a modified Palladian treatment using three arched windows like the Arch of Constantine in Rome—becomes a signature for Rulfs in Nacogdoches. This is more than coincidental. Just as he used other architectural elements from churches where he worshipped, Rulfs brought the memories with him to Nacogdoches.

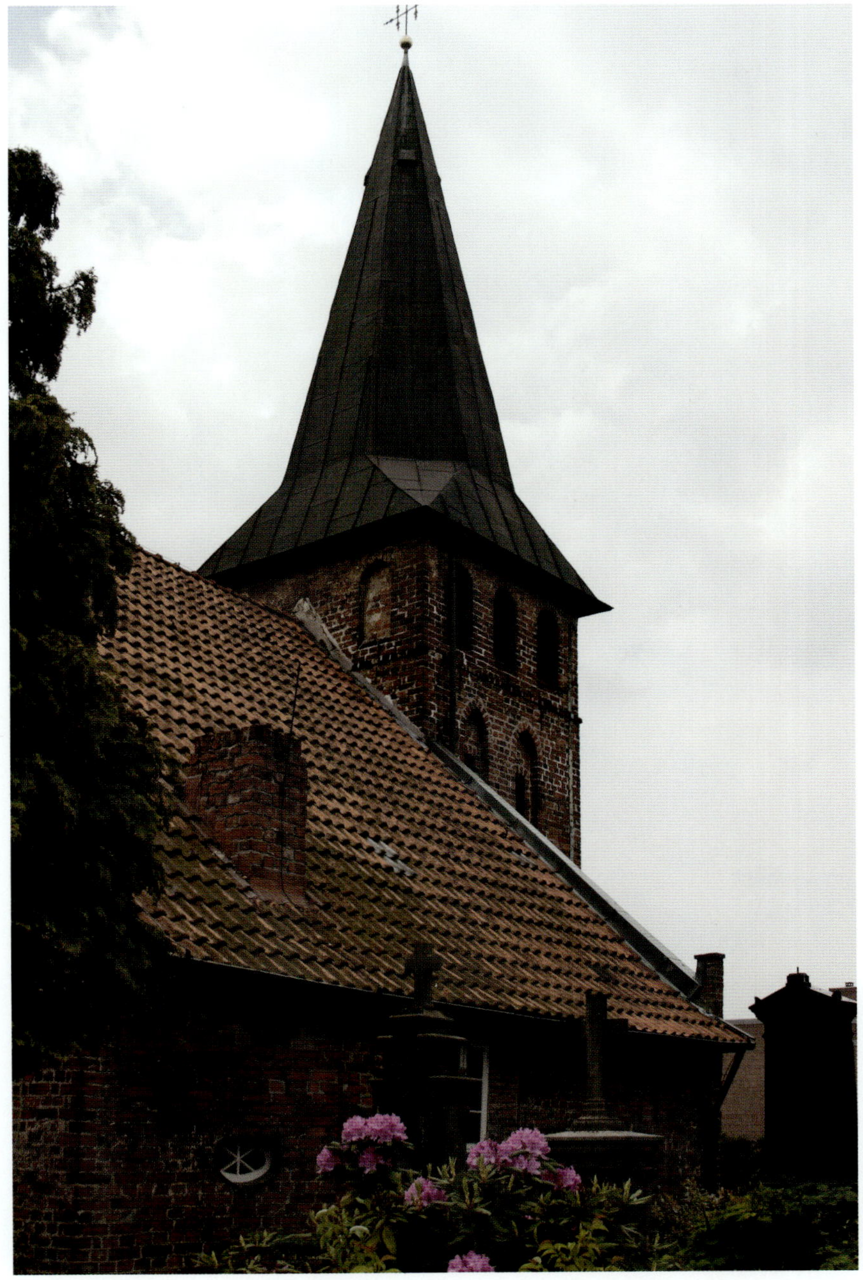

FIGURE 2.23. Chapel of St. Gertrude in Oldenburg. Photograph by author, 2010.

The Chapel of St. Gertrude is the oldest and only surviving medieval religious building in the city of Oldenburg. It dates to the 13th century. It stands at the north entrance of the city at the corner of Nadorster and Alexander Streets. Once part of a medieval infirmary, it stands at the entrance to the city's main cemetery. In the 18th century, the Dukes of Oldenburg built their family mausoleum at the north end of the cemetery; it was the first neo-classical building in Oldenburg. Every student in the city knew these buildings; every tourist book today includes these buildings. Also located in the cemetery is a prominent monument to the fallen in the Franco-Prussian War of 1870-1871.

The square tower on the Gertrude Chapel has a roof that transitions into a an octagon steeple, a common pattern used throughout Lower Saxony. Architect D. Rulfs used this configuration on the towers of Zion Hill Baptist Church and the Main Street Presbyterian Church in Nacogdoches.

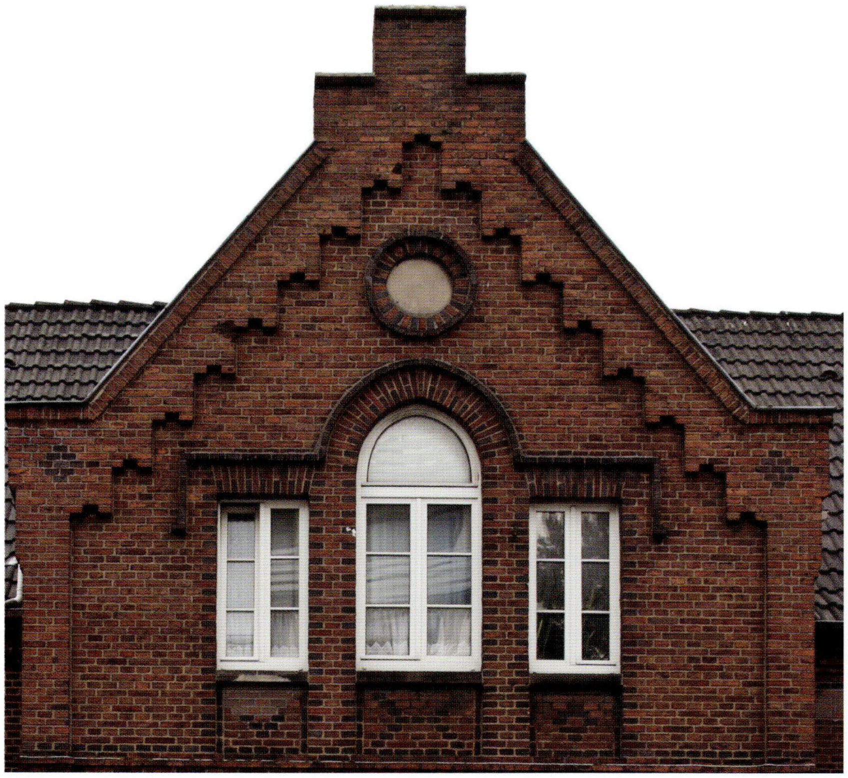

FIGURE 2.24. House on the North Road.
Step gable, hooded window treatments, decorative brickwork, and Palladian windows were common features used by D. Rulfs in Nacogdoches. Photograph by author.

FIGURE 2.25. (Below) Portholes and Hoods.
The Mayer & Schmidt Building on the West Square in Nacogdoches had similar design elements to this building in north Oldenburg. Photograph by author.

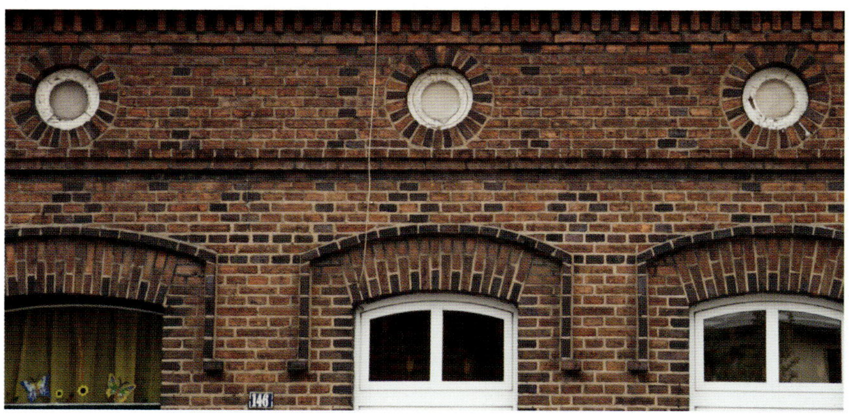

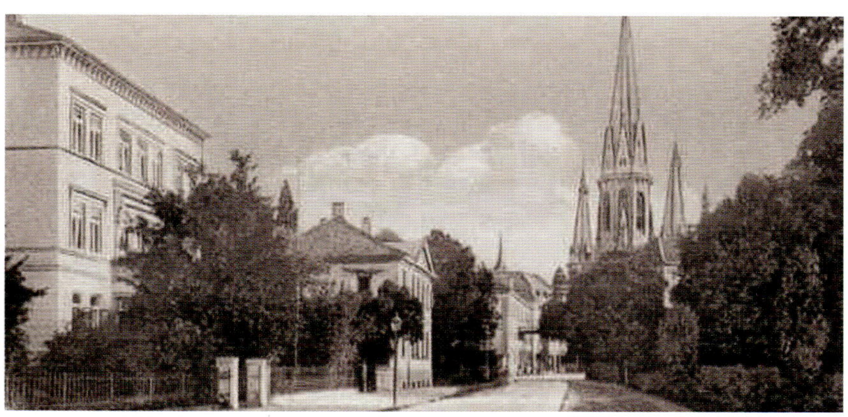

Scenes of Oldenburg

The buildings on these pages are typical of the structures one sees today when driving around the city. Many of these buildings existed during the period D. Rulfs lived in the City of Oldenburg. Most of these buildings are outside the old city walls in the newer areas. While there is no way to know which of these buildings influenced Rulfs, they are typical of the last quarter of the 19th century. What is certain is that Rulfs brought memories of such design elements with him to Texas: elaborate brick work on parapets, the Palladian motifs, stepped gables, hooded arches, Baroque-shaped parapets, and pilasters to separate the divisions of buildings.

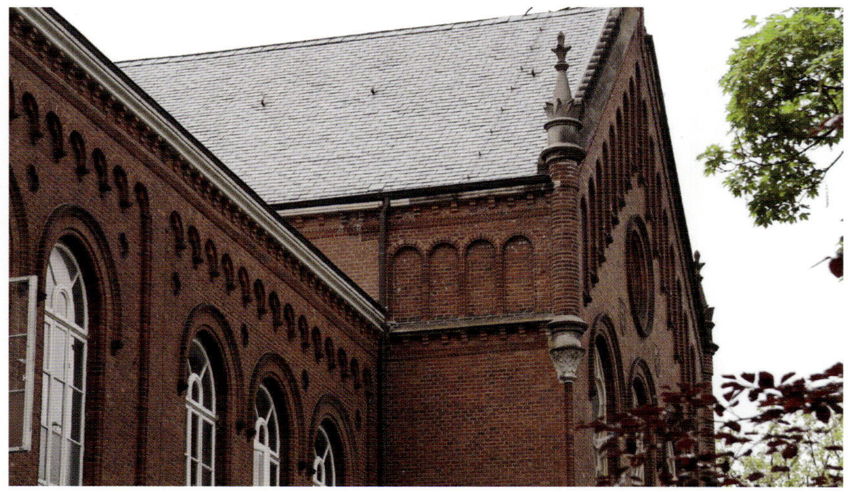

FIGURE 2.26. The Gymnasium (1878). *Photograph by author.*

FIGURE 2.27. (Below) The Old Armory (Built, 1862).
The Old Armory now houses the Jade University School of Architecture in Oldenburg. Photograph by author.

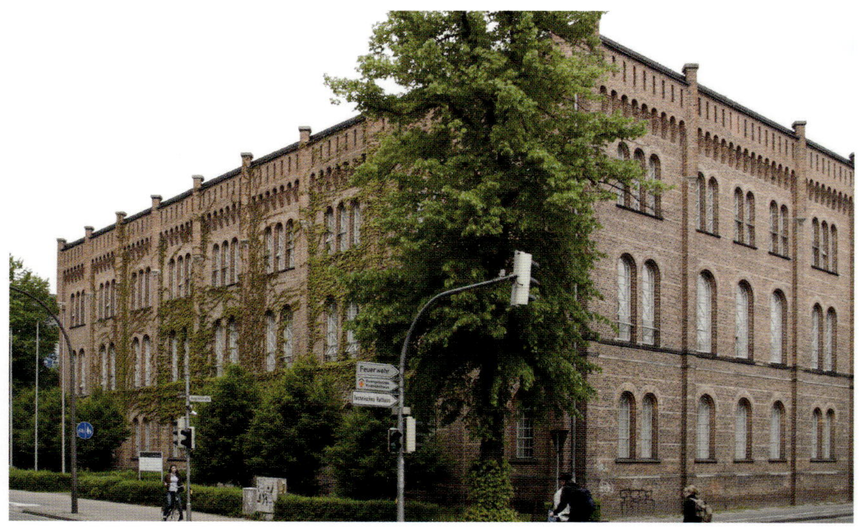

FIGURE 2.28. (Left) Gartenstrasse in Oldenburg.
This historic postcard dated 1903 of the Gartenstrasse in Oldenburg shows the towers of the St. Lambert Church at the end of the street. Card from http://www.alt.Oldenburg.de.

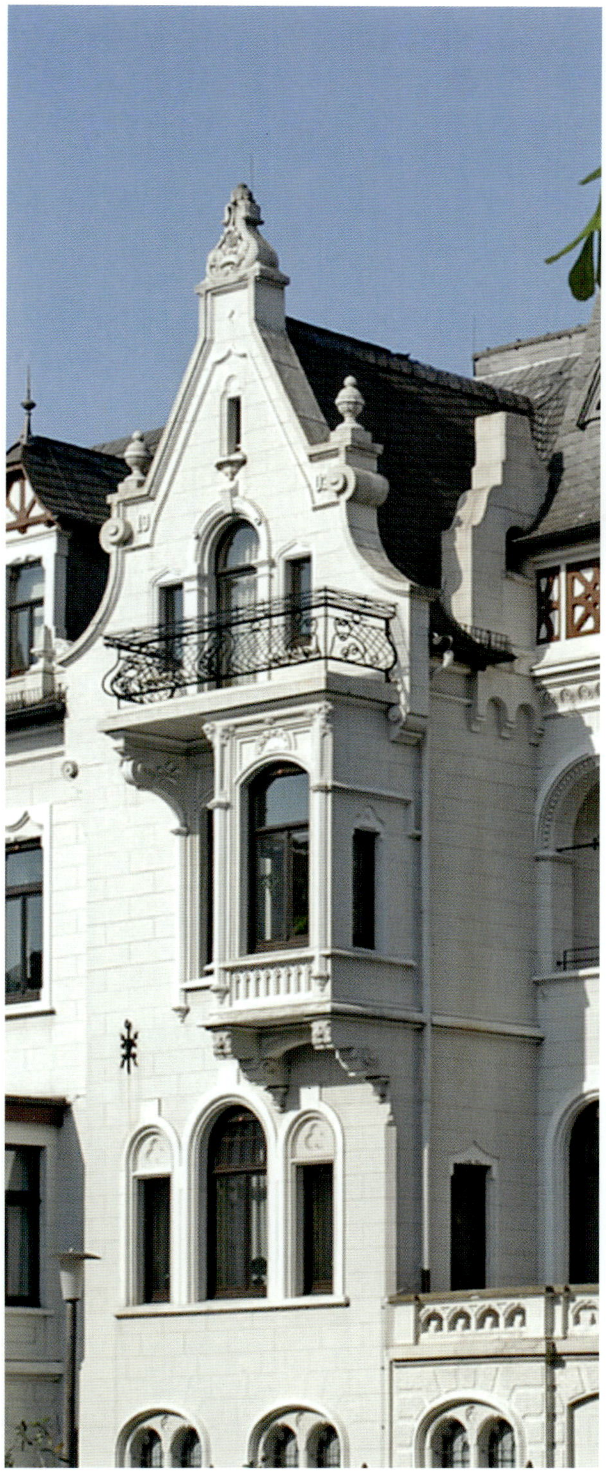

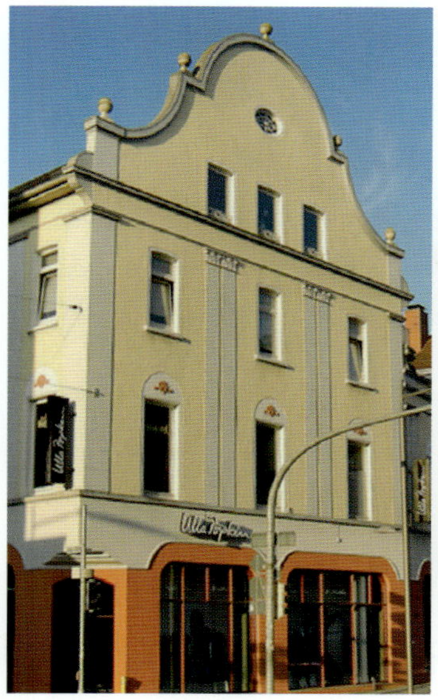

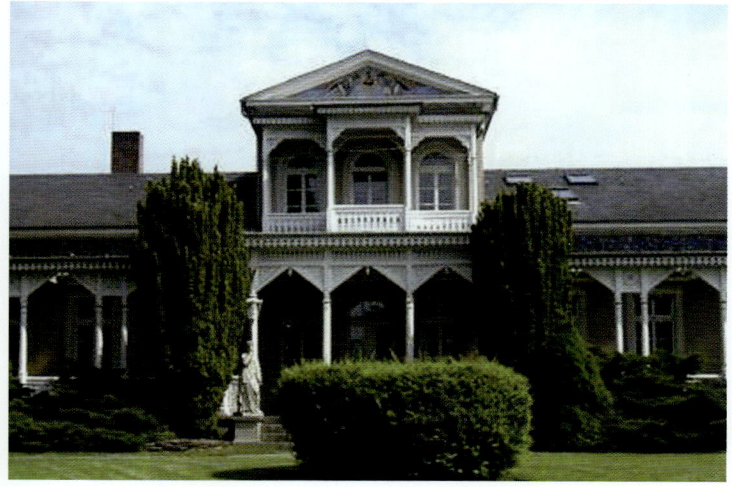

FIGURE 2.29. The Villa Kragge, South of Oldenburg (Stadt) at Wildeshausen, Lower Saxony. *Photograph by author.*

FIGURE 2.30. (Above) Wine Merchant, Oldenburg.
The façade of this wine merchant building has a step-parapet similar to one used by Rulfs in Nacogdoches on the Davidson Apartments. Photograph by the author.

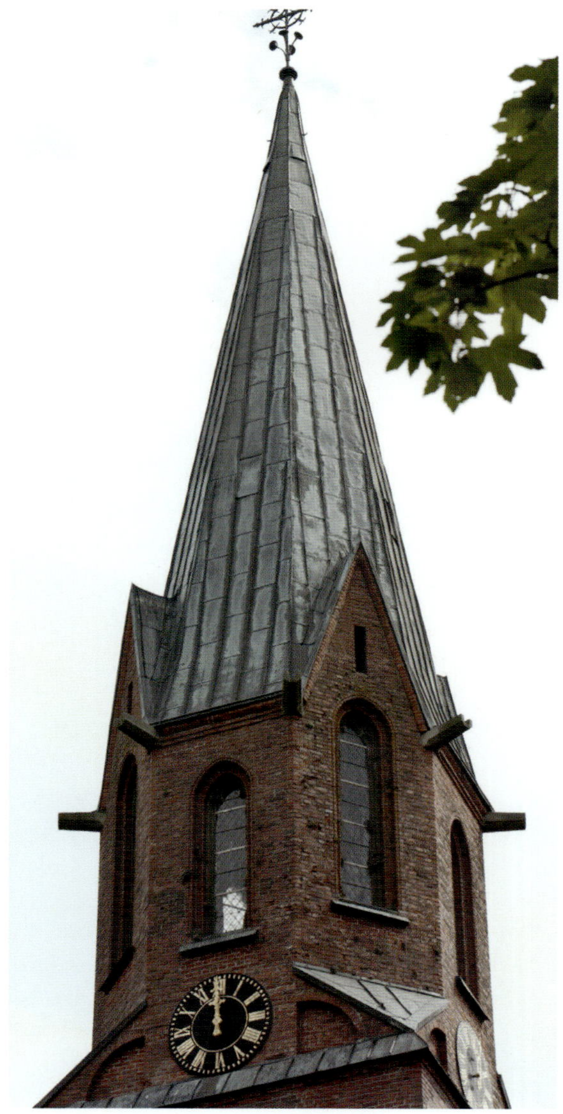

FIGURE 2.31 (Right) St. Petri-Kirche in Burhave.
The Evangelical-Lutheran Church of St. Peter in Burhave was in the process of replacing its 14th century building in years Rulfs was back in the area, between 1878-1880. Its architect was Xavier Lütz. The neo-Gothic structure has many of the same features Rulfs used in the Christ Episcopal Church in Nacogdoches. The treatment around the stained glass windows and the configuration of the steeple are very similar. Photograph by the author.

FIGURE 2.32. (Above) House on Gartenstrasse.
This house is characteristic of the way architectural influences from the past were mixed at the time. The front facade has neo-Gothic influences. This view of the east side has both types of Palladian motifs, which Rulfs used so frequently in Nacogdoches. Photograph by the author.

The Invitation from Texas

In order to explain why Diedrich and Johanne decided to immigrate to the United States in 1880, the narrative must flash back for a moment to the life of another immigrant—William Henry Böschen (1841-1915), Johanne Rulfs's older brother. Johann Anton Böschen, their father, did not want his son to enter a career in the military; therefore, he encouraged the young man to immigrate to the United States around 1860. The young man boarded the *SS Prescott,* which sailed to Baltimore via England and Ireland. Evidently, however, the young man really did want a career in the military. When Böschen landed in the United States, just as the American Civil War was brewing, he volunteered for the Union navy and served for two years under his German name Böschen. Later, when he reenlisted, an official who could not spell his German name, simply signed him up under the name of William Henry Stewart. Five years later, when Stewart was discharged from the navy, he volunteered for a tour of duty with the army. The army sent him to Texas where he was serving at the time of his discharge. Stewart, then in his mid-thirties, found work with the Bremond Railroad Company, which was building a line through East Texas. Some time around 1878, Stewart met a fellow German, John Schmidt, and the two men embarked on a long and interesting friendship. Schmidt recruited Stewart to join him in settling in Nacogdoches. Stewart spent the rest of his life in Nacogdoches: he married Nellie Delilah Miller on December 22, 1881, had two children here, and now rests in Oak Grove Cemetery.[44]

Stewart had lost contact with his family after coming to the United States. Schmidt encouraged him to write home. When he did, Stewart discovered that his father had died. Mother Böschen, who had been "worried sick," according to her granddaughter, wrote him that his sister Johanne had married, had three children (two living), and was expecting a fourth. Her husband, an architect and builder named Diedrich Rulfs, was without steady employment. Stewart encouraged them all to come to Texas. Schmidt said he would sponsor the undertaking. (It is possible that Stewart sent R. W. Haltom's *History and Description of Nacogdoches County,* but this is not possible to document.) Stewart told his newly discovered brother-in-law that Schmidt felt Nacogdoches needed the services of a trained master builder to help guide the expansion of the town, which he thought was inevitable once the railroad arrived.[45] The Rulfs family, including Mother Böschen and her youngest son Anton, immediately began contemplating their eventual action to emigrate from Germany.

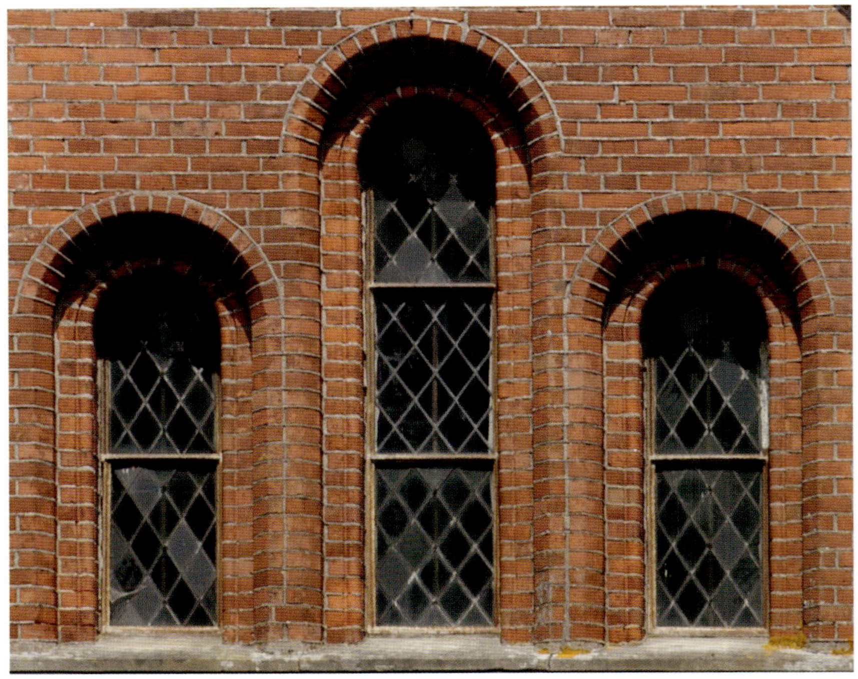

FIGURE 2.34. St. Nicklai Church, Stollhamm in 2010.

The Church of St. Nicklas, the home parish church of the Rulfs family for generations, was rebuilt in 1880. By family tradition, Rulfs helped with the plans for this reconstruction; documents have eluded the author in confirming this family memory. In any case, the Constantine windows (detail above) on the parish church influenced the architect in his work in Nacogdoches. A historic postcard of the St. Nicklas Church exists in the family memorabilia. Even without this evidence, D. Rulfs would have known of the architecture of the building from his brother who came to Texas four years later. His use of this architectural detail, like so many other North German elements, made their way into his work in East Texas. Photographs taken by the author.

FIGURE 2.33. (Right) The Parish Church in Blexen

The Rulfs family, after the death of Baby Emily, lived in Blexen in the north of the peninsula (now a suburb of Nordenham). The Lutheran Church of St. Hippolyt in Blexen is one of the most interesting in the area. Although on the only hill in the area, it still has sustained serious damage from the sea over the years and has been rebuilt several times. Whether Rulfs worked on the church, as family tradition has it, is unknown, but they lived their last two years in Blexen. Their fourth child, Edward Diedrich, was born in the town and christened in the church there. (For the birth certificate, see FIGURE 2.2 earlier in the chapter.) Photograph by the author.

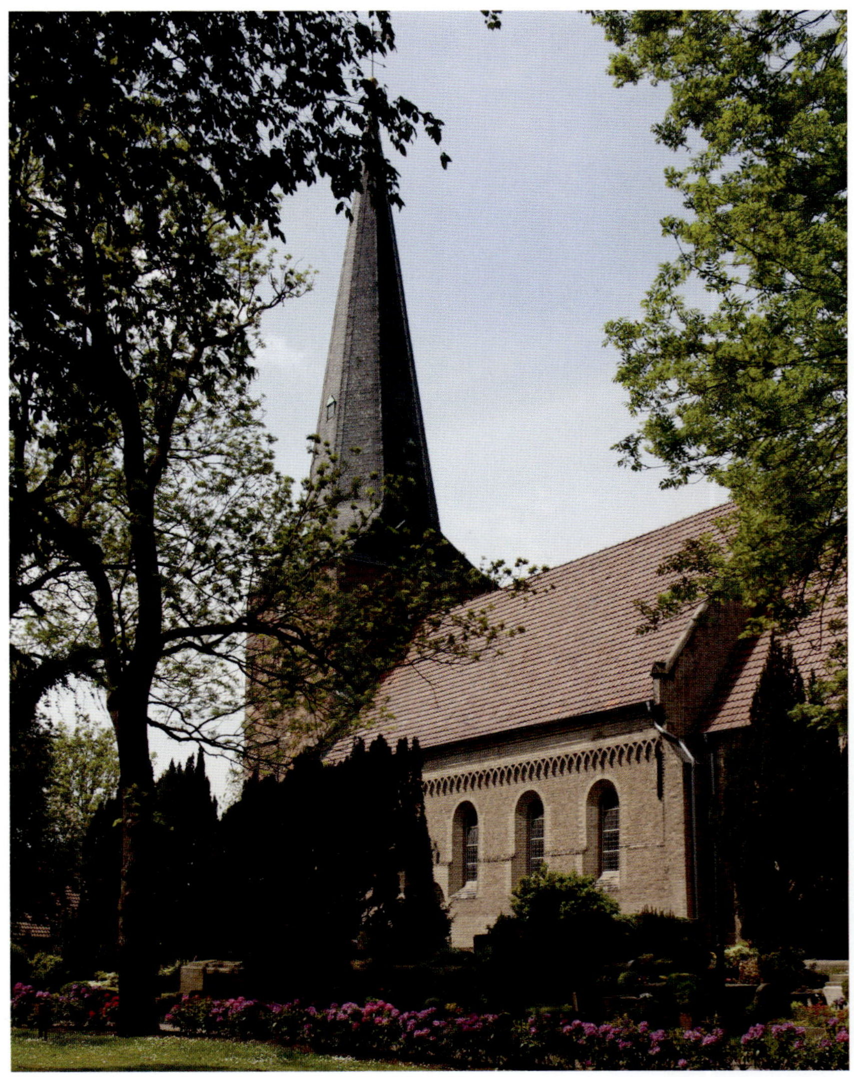

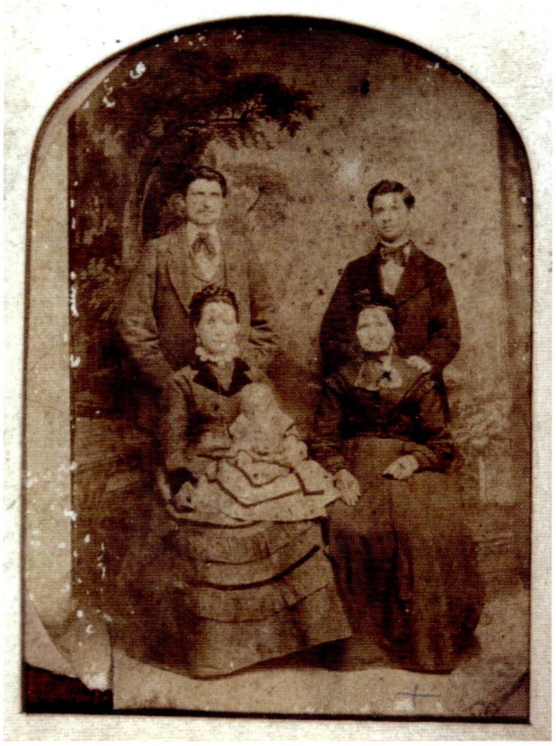

FIGURE 2.35. Rulfs-Böschen Family Portrait, 1877.

Standing: Diedrich Rulfs and Anton Böschen (Brother to Johanne). Seated: Johanne Böschen Rulfs, holding Emily Rulfs, and Sophie Morrisse Böschen (Johanne and Anton's Mother.).

This family photograph dates to 1877. The photograph, most likely, documents the christening of Emily. At the time of Emily's birth, Grandfather Böschen was dead; Grandmother and Anton represented the family at the christening. Since it was Emily's day, the other two children of the Rulfs were not pictured. Sadly, baby Emily lived for only a few months, which would account for why the picture was so treasured by Johanne. Before heading to Texas, the Rulfs would have one more child: Edward Anton (born in 1880) in Blexen.

A machine-generated book, entitled *The Rulfs Name in History*, exists. It is part of the "Our Name in History" series available on any family name from Ancestry.com. Relying mostly on time lines of world events and generalized statistics, these books are generated and sold to encourage genealogical research and contain a limited amount of material on specific individuals. For instance, only one specific fact about the family of Diedrich A. W. Rulfs could the author find in this book, that his son Anton Diedrich was the youngest Rulfs to immigrate in the period covered.[46] There are some general statistics, however, of interest. Of the ports from which the Rulfs families departed, Hamburg ranks as the greatest (95), with Bremen second (44). Overwhelmingly, the Rulfs clans were departing from North West Germany, in particular, Lower Saxony (from Hamburg and Bremen, Bremerhaven, Wilhelmshaven, Hanover, Oldenburg, etc), albeit there were four individuals from Italy and two from Ireland. The largest number of immigrants (238) arrived in New York and the largest concentrations of these remained in the New York area. The peak year was 1936. By comparison, only 13 of the immigrants arrived in New Orleans. [Seven of these were from the D. Rulfs family.] Of the seventeen draft registrants during World War I, most were from New York, but two came from Harris County and one from San Augustine. In the year 2000, there were seven Rulfs families in New York and seven in Texas.[47]

Family memories are hard sometimes to reconcile with concrete documents. According to family memories, the whole group traveled at one time in 1880,[48] which was probably *not* the case. The inclusion of Anton Böschen, the twenty-one year old brother of Mrs. Rulfs, within the family unit that came to Texas causes a problem. According to the passenger lists in New Orleans, Anton Böschen arrived the year before on board the ship *Hanover* on October 10, 1879.[49] It makes perfect sense that Stewart and his mother would have encouraged the young man to do an exploratory run before the family, with a wide range of ages, undertook a journey of this revolutionary nature to a new world. Further proof lies in the fact that the records in 1880 do not include Anton.[50]

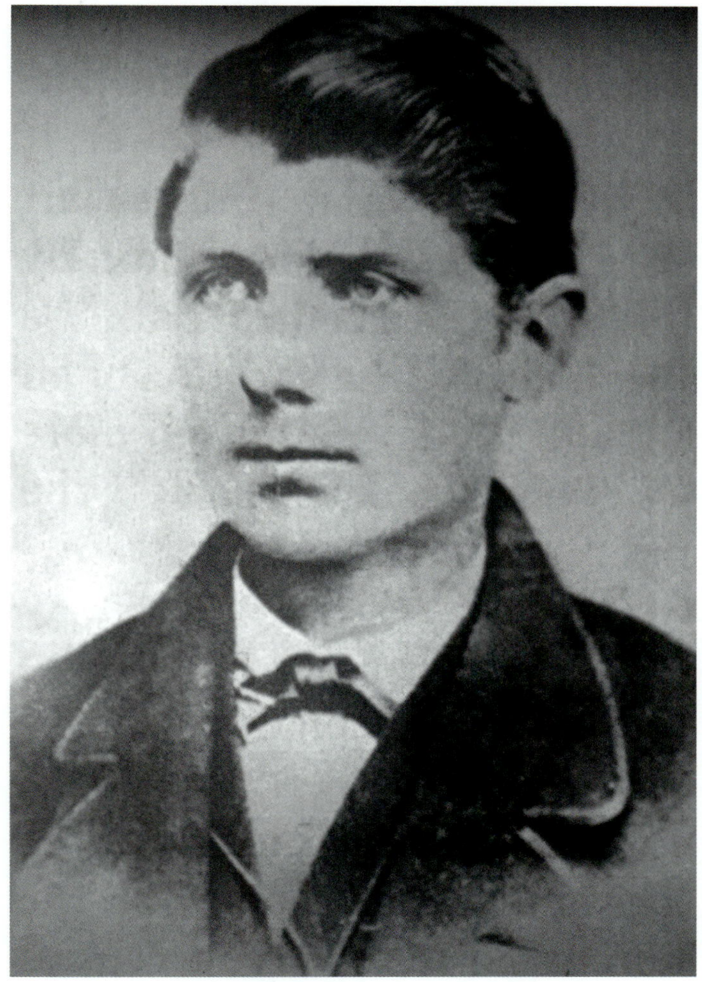

FIGURE 2.36. Diedrich Rulfs, ca. 1880-1881.

This photograph of Rulfs, around the time of his immigration to Texas, was lent to the author by his granddaughter, Anna Kathryn Holbrook.

Diedrich Rulfs and his family sailed from nearby Bremen in 1880 on the steamship *Nurnberg*. After stopping in New York, the ship then proceeded to New Orleans. (This would place them passing through New York Harbor before the placement of the Statue of Liberty there in 1886.) *The New Orleans Passenger Lists* have the Rulfs arriving on November 11, 1880: Diedrich (age 32), his wife Johanne (age 30), his son Gerhard William (age 5), his son Carl Henry (age 2), and his infant son Edward Diedrich Anton (age 1 month).[51] Accompanying them, her name listed as part of the unit, was Mother Böschen. From New Orleans, the family traveled by steamboat to Jefferson, Texas, where they were met by William Henry (Böschen) Stewart and his friend John Schmidt. The group traveled overland to Nacogdoches in two wagons.[52]

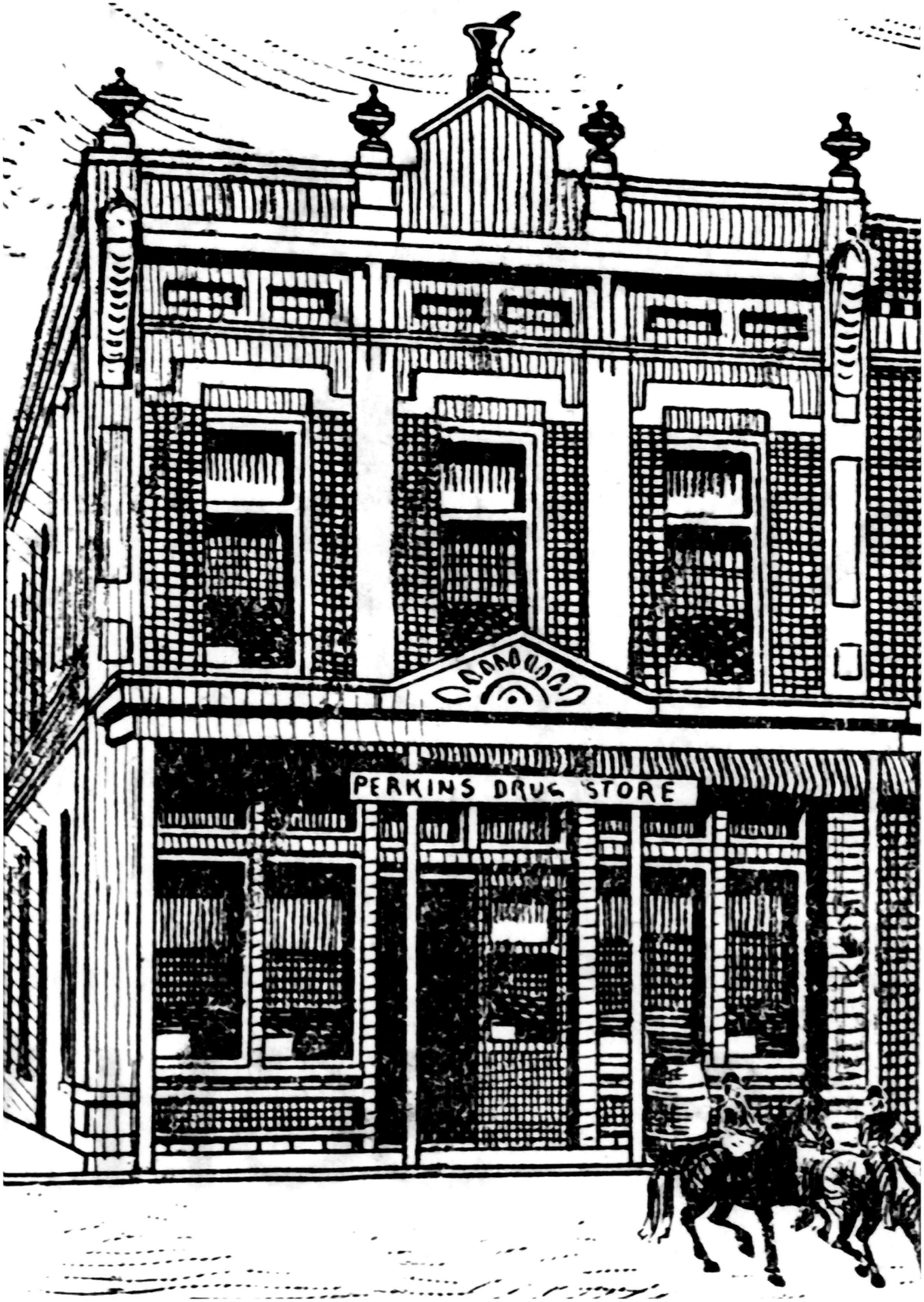
PERKINS DRUG STORE

CHAPTER III

Transforming the Business District

From Wood to Bricks, 1880-1897

"With his advent among us dates the real beginning of improvements in our city." Richard Haltom, *Nacogdoches Chronicle,* 1897.

Three brick structures existed in the frontier town of Nacogdoches in 1880 when Diedrich Rulfs arrived: the Courthouse (1856), the Nacogdoches University Building (1859), and the Orton House (1840s). In his first two decades of work, the architect redesigned the buildings of the central business district, replacing the wooden structures of the frontier town with brick-and-mortar houses of commerce. The process of updating the central business district began on the Square, spread east and west along Main Street, and finally north on the side streets toward Hospital Street. Prominent among the businessmen who participated in the modernization of the frontier town were such men as John Schmidt, Abe Mayer, E. A. Blount, W. U. Perkins, John H. Cox, J. H. Davidson, Benjamin Wettermark, I. L. Sturdevant, D. K. Cason, the Hardeman Brothers (B. F., Lee, and Tolbert), J. H. Summers, Charles Hoya, and, of course, their cheerleader and editor of the newspaper, R. W. Haltom. After 1900, they would be joined by a host of others. To give form to their ideas, these businessmen relied almost exclusively on the talents of the newly arrived German architect—D. Rulfs.

By 1890, after just one decade, outside observers recognized the metamorphosis that was taking place in Nacogdoches. The *Galveston Daily News*, albeit mistakenly condensing the process into two years, accurately assessed the revolutionary nature of the visible changes and identified the watershed event that enabled the explosive burst of activity—the arrival of the railroad:

> Nacogdoches is situated on the line of the Houston East and West Texas road, and is the largest city on that line with the exception of Houston.... Improvements of a substantial character have taken place within the past two years and frame business houses have been supplanted with brick structures, fully twenty have been erected within that time. Six new mercantile houses have established themselves here within two years, all of them carrying good stocks, while numerous other concerns of minor importance have located. The business streets are well laid out and the city presents a metropolitan appearance. The residence portion has been greatly improved by the recent erection of some forty structures from latest designs.[1]

The editor of the local *Nacogdoches Chronicle,* knowing the scene in Nacogdoches better than the outside reporter from Galveston, attributed the changes more specifically to the German-born immigrant architect—D. Rulfs. In a special edition of his newspaper, which will be used throughout this chapter, R. W. Haltom noted over and over the man who deserved the credit for the changes.[2]

FIGURE 3.1. (Opposite) Enlarged Detail of Drawing, The Perkins Brothers Drug Store (1884). *Nacogdoches Chronicle*, September 30, 1897, Courtesy of ETRC.

The Importance of the Square

In most cities, "The Square" and "Main Street" have historical, psychological, and mystical connotations beyond their geography.[3] In Nacogdoches, the Public Square (or *Plaza Principal,* as the Spanish called it) has not only historical connotations, but it also occupies a strategic geographic location as well—the southern end of a long peninsula formed by the Banita and Lanana Creeks. The Spanish, conforming to the ancient patterns of the native Indians, chose the site of the town for defensive reasons. The official Spanish seat of government, the Stone House built by their representative Antonio Gil Y'Barbo, stood at the epicenter of this strategic confluence of streams, roads, and hills. The vistas from the location of the Stone House, on the corner of Main and Fredonia Streets, where Commercial Bank stands today, were critical: up Orton Hill to the east, up Irion Hill to the west, and down Fredonia Street to the south. *Plaza Principal* was the navel of Nacogdoches and virtually impossible to circumvent—the axis where the historic east-west and north-south corridors met and easily the most important intersection in East Texas.[4] In legal terms, all directions emanated from the Square. West Main and West Pilar streets started *at the square*, not as they do today from North and South Street. Likewise, the city originally numbered all its lots from the Square.[5] All of the important early buildings in Nacogdoches—government buildings, quarters of the official militia (the Red House), religious establishments, houses of the leading citizens—sat on or near the Square.[6]

The new businessmen flocking to Nacogdoches in the early 1880s reasoned that the railroad would change not only the importance of the town, but also its orientation. The most valuable commercial properties in Nacogdoches before 1883 were on the Square and along East Main Street, where most people from the other states in the Union entered Nacogdoches. On the west, Pilar Street was the primary entrance and exit; it had the superior ford and later got the first bridges. Pilar was the town's main residential street.[7] By 1878, everyone knew the right-of-way for the new railroad lay along the Banita Creek and knew the designated location for the depot was between Pilar and Main to the west of the Square. While traffic from the east would continue, the newcomers reasoned that the railroad would shift the most frequent arrival point for most travelers to the west. Main Street, in the age of the railroad, would become as important as Pilar had been during the age of the wagon. In 1878, for this reason, Mayer and Schmidt purchased their location between the two streets on the West Square, but they soon began to question whether their original choice had the visibility they needed.

Professor Robert Maxwell, in his book *Whistle in the Piney Woods,* has described the anticipation, the elation at the arrival, and the immediate impact of the railroad in 1883.[8] While never doubted by Haltom, the railroad had many alternative routes. Its arrival was never a sure thing. Everyone seemed to be making bets; the newspapers note rampant speculation on the new railroad's impact on property values. Until the railroad actually arrived, however, few entrepreneurs invested in real estate. They mainly sketched contingency plans.

The Houston East & West Texas Railroad reached the Nacogdoches County line in 1882, and the first train arrived in town in 1883. As Maxwell writes:

> When the HE&WT finally made its way into Nacogdoches it was an occasion for civic celebrations, speeches, and banquets. The Houston press announced a new schedule to the railroad's new terminal: the express left Houston at 9:40 A.M. and arrived in Nacogdoches at 7:10 P. M. The return left at 8:00 A.M. and reached Houston at 5:30 P. M.... As might be expected, Nacogdoches experienced a boom.[9]

Many of the economic changes brought about by the arrival of the railroad have received attention in other works.[10] What remains to explore is the impact of these changes on the physical and visual townscape of the Nacogdoches business district as it replaced its wooden structures with brick and mortar.

Rulfs arrived three years before the railroad. In his own country, he had recently experienced the impact of the railroad's arrival on the provincial capital of Oldenburg. The architect arrived not only with ideas, but after his experiences in the German Depression, he also harbored more than a passing amount of cautiousness. Rulfs knew the advantages and disadvantages that would accompany urbanization—the sudden urban changes wrought by a great influx of money, people, and speculation. He had even experienced the complications of an economic depression after a boom. The young architect immediately recognized that frontier Nacogdoches was insensitive to the extent it was wasting valuable commercial assets. Its stand-alone wooden buildings were inefficient, maintenance nightmares, vulnerable to burglary and fire, and less-than-conducive to a good shopping experience. He immediately began to argue for concentrating different business functions into a single complex with common-walls construction, unified façades, and rear alleyways. These things, however, were a radical departure for the late frontier town.

Even though Rulfs was an extremely perceptive planner, he was at a disadvantage because he had only a minimal command of the English language. Of course, the presence of so many fellow Germans in Nacogdoches helped to alleviate this problem in part, but Rulfs followed very dutifully the unwritten rule among the German community in Nacogdoches: SPEAK ONLY ENGLISH IN PUBLIC. This rule, according to his niece, was a conscious way the German immigrants honored their new homeland. While Rulfs never wrote English very well,[11] he, no doubt, covered his language deficiency in oral conversations by honoring his contacts by being a good listener. He experienced few problems at first for another reason: he only had to sell his ideas to two other people: fellow Germans Abe Mayer and John Schmidt. He could always explain some complicated concepts in private to these immediate patrons and wait for them to convince others. Because of his sound ideas, Rulfs immediately became a trusted business associate of Mayer and Schmidt and other businessmen. His stellar career is testimony to their confidence.

The First Brick Block in Nacogdoches (1884)

When Abe Mayer and John Schmidt first bought their location on the west side of the Square, they did so because the site was between the two important entry streets of Main and Pilar from the new railroad depot. Rulfs argued differently. He thought the West Square would have no visibility to visitors entering from the depot. Since M&S were already having difficulty convincing the adjacent property owners of Rulfs's idea of consolidating their businesses into a single complex, the three men began to look elsewhere for a location to put their ideas into practice. For their first modern brick commercial development, they shifted their sights to the north side of the Square, at the intersection of Pecan and Main Streets (where Kennedy's Jewelry long stood). Their first recruit, another newcomer to Nacogdoches, albeit an East Texan, was W. U. (Will) Perkins (1856-1940).[12] Perkins and his brother-in-law (George P. Garrison) had just opened a drugstore business in a leased building between the Square and North Street (to the west of the proposed brick block site).[13] To get Perkins on board with the new idea, M&S agreed that Perkins would have the premier location on the corner, and they would take the second 'stand', as business locations were called at the time. Besides Perkins and M&S, the third owner in the new venture was T. J. Caraway, a newspaperman who purchased the *Nacogdoches Sun-News* from the Haltoms.[14] No matter how rational and simple the plan sounded, the execution was more complex.

No one anticipated how difficult it would be to overcome the tangled legacy of property ownership and lot descriptions in frontier Nacogdoches. The entire downtown area in the Old Spanish town was a surveyor's nightmare. Since the Spanish conducted their land surveys by sight and used existing landmarks, such as trees, marker stones, or sometimes iron stakes, the measurements on all the lots were less-than-accurate, and the shapes were irregular. Overall, the Spanish system worked in its time; but when inches mattered, as they would with shared walls, the old system presented enormous difficulties. Consolidating the lots on the north side of the Square, among the oldest privately owned lots in Texas, proved particularly complicated, so much so that their lawyers had to put a special plat map in the county deed records to provide a visual aid in addition to their descriptive legal statements.[15] (In 2010, these lots were continuing to give trouble to modern owners.[16])

For the Perkins Drugstore, Rulfs used the latest in Italianate commercial architecture. He placed a pediment over the entrance, a device he specified regularly in houses and businesses. The bands of stone over the windows and the stylized pilasters gave contrast to the brick. The tripartite segments, the variations in brick, and the ornaments on the parapet (reminiscent of the jars regularly used in apothecary shops in Oldenburg and the mortise and pestle at the crest) gave the Perkins Building a unique status even in a uniform commercial consolidation. The functionality of the grouping, therefore, did not lessen the decorative elements if the owner so desired. The new block not only started the transformation of the townscape of the pioneer town to brick, but it also turned heads and helped the businesses to prosper.

Even before the buildings were completed, Bill Haltom christened the newest departure as "the brick block."[17] As other buildings joined the movement to bricks and mortar, the editor of the paper clarified the name by calling the complex "the First Brick Block." After M&S moved their main operations to East Main in 1888 and sold their stand to Hardeman Brothers in 1894, the paper sometimes referred to the block as "the Perkins Block," the only original owner left by that time. Nacogdoches's newest buildings occupied the west end of the North Square. Ironically, the town's oldest building, the Stone House or Old Stone Fort, occupied the east end. The uneasy juxtaposition of these two symbolic structures would prove troublesome in time.

A Second Brick Block on East Main Joins the Transformation

As the North Square plans were maturing, Schmidt shifted his attention to East Main Street, to the northeast corner of Fredonia and Main, immediately across Fredonia Street from the Old Stone House. This was the best business location on the east side of town and even had good visibility from the square. R. C. Shindler, a friend and fellow German immigrant, owned the property and ran a general merchandise-drugstore there. While he did not have the funds to replace his building with a brick one, Shindler had also heard Rulfs talk about the advantages of consolidation. When two merchants from Galveston, Julius Kauffman and Julius Runge, expressed a wish to establish a presence in Nacogdoches, John Schmidt brokered a deal which allowed Shindler a stand in a new brick block in return for selling the corner.[18] John P. Davidson, who owned the adjacent property, also joined this group. Rulfs drew up some plans. The out-of-town mercantile company, unsure they could rent an upper floor and afraid to speculate, asked Rulfs to cut the design to a row of single-story buildings. Rulfs thought this was a mistake. Thinking the buildings should have a second story, the architect convinced them to prepare the foundations so that a second story could be added later—a tactic the architect found useful and used over and over in these years.[19] In order to make the building seem more imposing, Rulfs expanded the parapet on the front walls high above the level of the roof and made it very decorative as he had done on the Perkins Drugstore. To make the businesses more secure, he suggested ironclad metal shutters on the backside of the buildings, as he had done on the First Brick Block. Although these one-story buildings are clearly marked on the first Sanborn Insurance Maps of Nacogdoches in 1885, no pictures of this second brick block survive because it only lasted four years, as discussed below.[20]

The Mayer & Schmidt Building, West Side of the Square (1885)

The owners of the adjacent lots to M&S's original store in the middle of the west Square disliked intensely the concept of the block construction, thinking the concept too novel and too restrictive on the individual property owner's rights.[21] Without this opposition, the west side would have been the *first* of the brick blocks, rather than the north side of the Square. In late 1885, M&S decided they would wait no longer to convert their property into bricks and mortar. *Inadvertently*, however, the delay had provided M&S with a new business formula for Nacogdoches: adding new functions or departments in different buildings owned by the same firm. M&S later would have as many as eight locations in town, utilizing many buildings that they leased but did not own. The process allowed the company to expand and establish a presence in a different part of town without becoming prisoners of specific property owners or investing heavily in both real estate and business function at the same time. Retaining part ownership, but releasing control of the managements, Abe Mayer and John Schmidt would oftentimes spin-off their departments into independent entities. Using these tactics, their company accumulated one of the largest economic empires in East Texas—or to use their advertising phrase, "The Hercules of Nacogdoches' Business Houses."[22]

Quite possibly, the brick structure Rulfs designed to replace M&S's original wooden building on the West Square was the first commercial building the architect ever designed for Nacogdoches. Originally contemplated as part of a brick complex of buildings, the building as built had to be freestanding. The one-and-a-half story edifice was totally unique for Nacogdoches. To add architectural interest, Rulfs used North German design elements, which were unusual in East Texas—three porthole windows for light on the upper half-story and quoins (decorative rectangles) of bricks at the corners of the building. He may have added the reinforced corners once the building had to stand alone, for he did not use these corners when he designed the adjoining buildings later in 1890. The building, easily recognizable in early photographs of Nacogdoches, caught the traveler's eye when approaching the Square from the east.

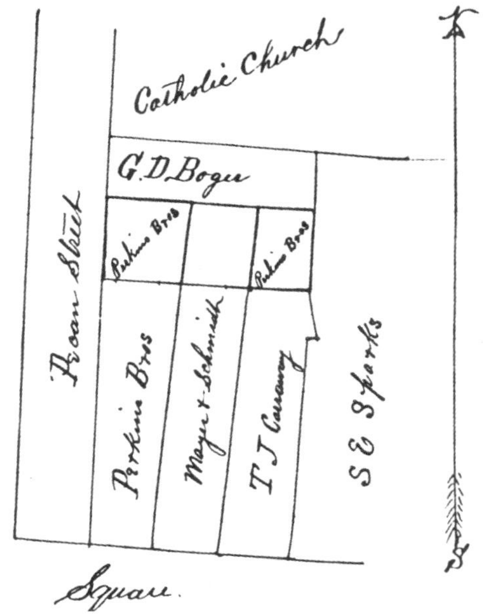

FIGURE 3.3. A Plat Map, 1886. First Brick Block.

The legal and survey work for consolidating property into common-wall construction on the North Square was so difficult that their legal advisors had to place a special plat map into the County Deed Records. Starting on the left along Pecan Street, the Perkins Brothers purchased the first tract, M&S the second, and T. J Carraway the third. On the tract of land owned by S. E. Sparks (at the time of the plat), a fourth building would later complete the First Brick Block. The plat, north of the Brick Block on Pecan Street, also shows the original location of the Sacred Heart Catholic Church dating from 1846. Nacogdoches County Deed Records.

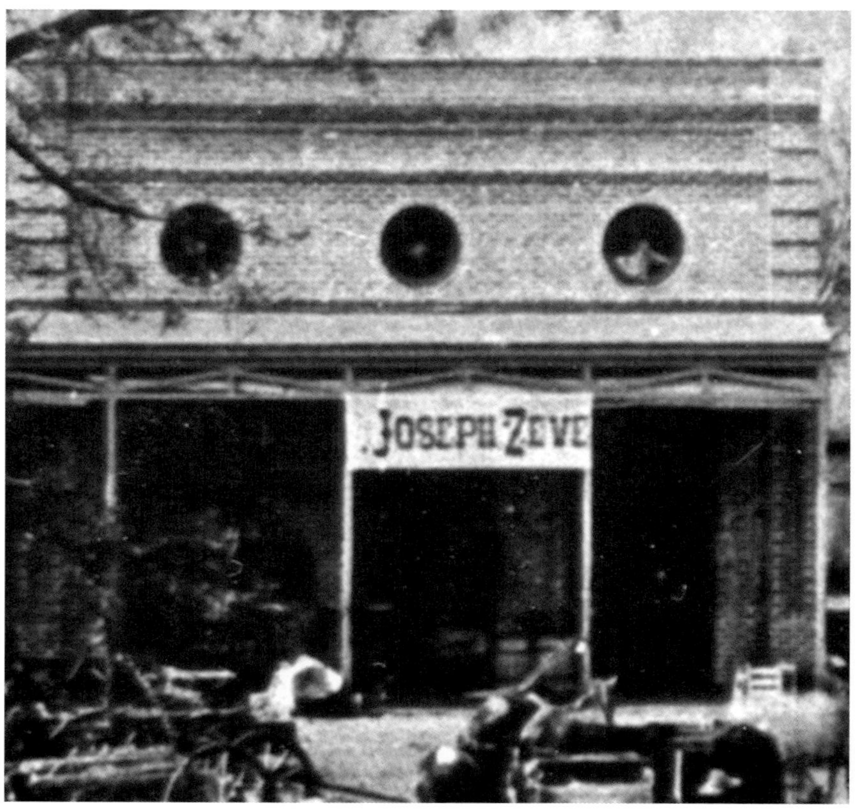

FIGURE 3.5. (Above) Mayer & Schmidt Building, West Square.

This building, built in late 1885, was the first commercial building designed by Rulfs. It was not built, however, until after the "First Brick Block." Designs using portholes were very characteristic of Northern Germany. The photograph, mislabeled to 1882, dates to ca. 1892, by which time Schmidt's associate, Joseph Zeve, was operating an establishment under Mayer & Schmidt's direction in the building. See FIGURE 3.8 for the full image. Courtesy of ETRC.

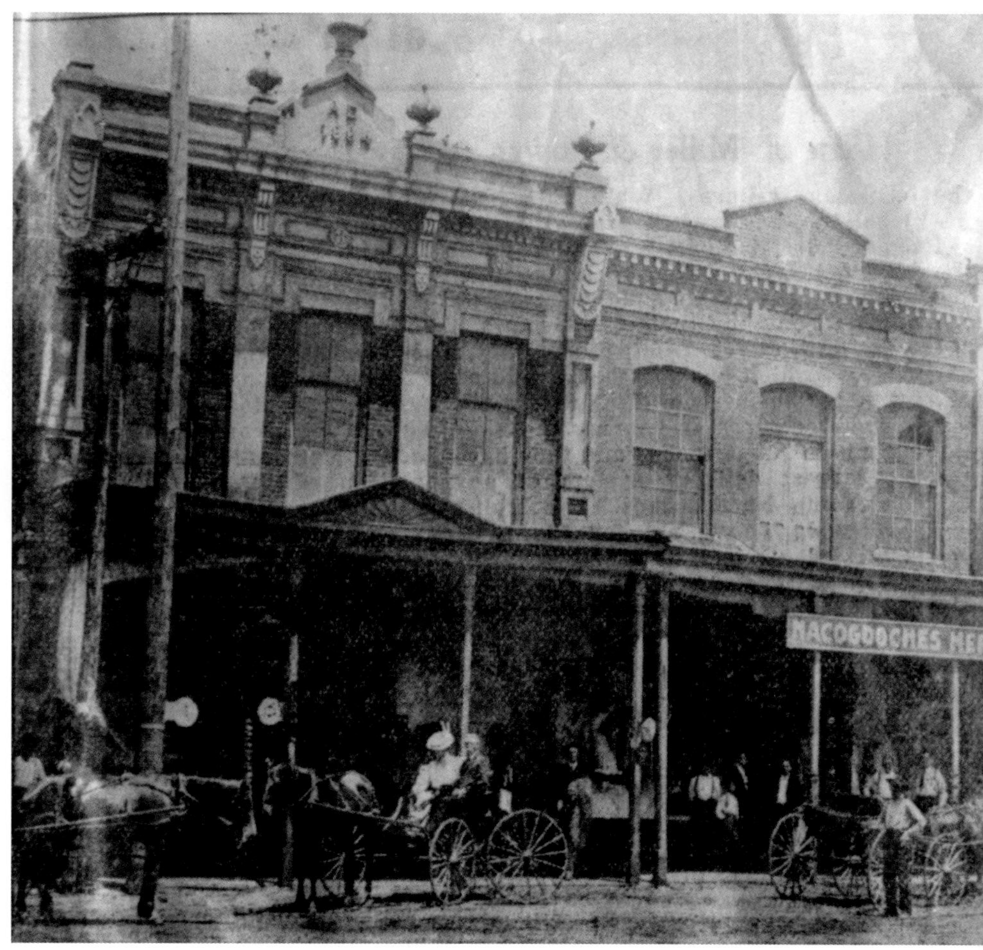

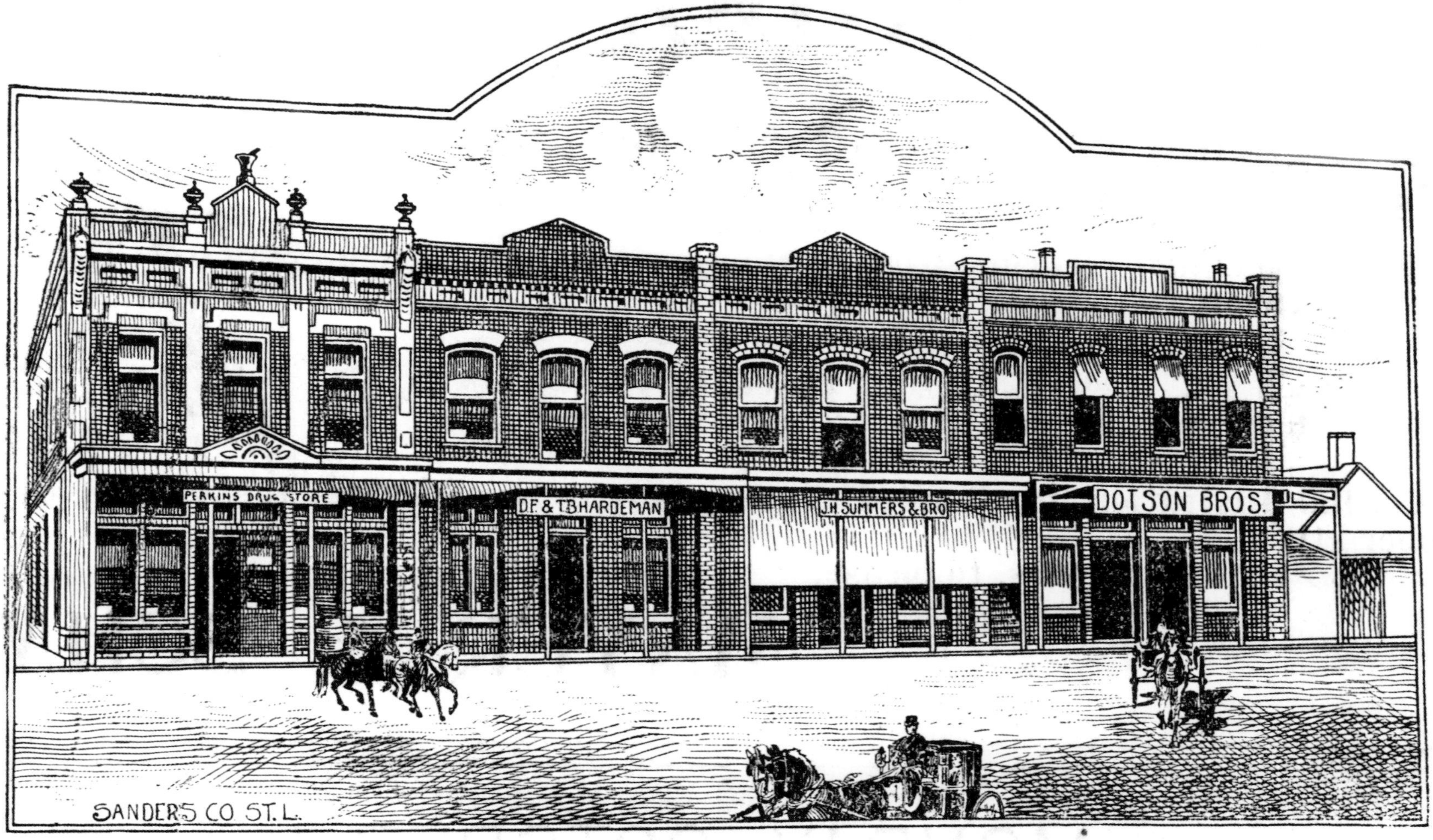

BRICK BLOCK, NORTH SIDE PUBLIC SQUARE.

FIGURE 3.2. (Above) Sanders & CO. Drawing (1897) of The First Brick Block.

This image from the 1897 Nacogdoches Chronicle *shows the four buildings (or "stands") of the First Brick Block, begun in 1884. The decision to consolidate proved an extremely profitable one. From left to right, Perkins Brothers Drugstore remained on the corner of Main and Pecan for two decades before moving. Mayer & Schmidt took the second stand in the original block of 1884, but as their business quickly outgrew the space, they had sold the second stand to the Hardeman Brothers (B. F. and T. B.) in 1888 (Nacogdoches Star, May 11, 1888). The third stand at first housed the printing business of T. J. Caraway, as shown on the plat below; by 1897 Jesse Summers and Sons assumed the location. A fourth unit, built for the Dotson Brothers in 1892, completed the complex as shown in the drawing above.*

Architecturally, the design Rulfs employed for the "First Brick Block" not only utilized space differently, but it also introduced high commercial style to the frontier town, that is, at least in the case of the Perkins Drugstore. The other partners in this overall collective project, whether unprepared to accept the stylistic additions or unwilling to pay for the added expense, did not allow Rulfs to unify the façade across the first three storefronts. Only the building heights were relatively uniform. Perkins was certainly the most confident of the owners and consistently accepted more tasteful suggestions than others. (As will be seen in the next chapter, Perkins allowed Rulfs to design a pace-setting private residence for him, twice, in the coming years.)

Photolithography, available in the 1890s, was not possible in the printing facilities in Nacogdoches. Haltom and others would send their photographs to the Sanders Company in Saint Louis. The Sanders Company would then hire an artist to replicate the image as a line drawing, and then transfer it to a copper plate that the newspaper in Nacogdoches could print. It was an expensive process. Fortunately, in several cases, both the original photograph and the drawings still exist today to allow for comparisons. Nacogdoches Chronicle, 1897, courtesy of ETRC.

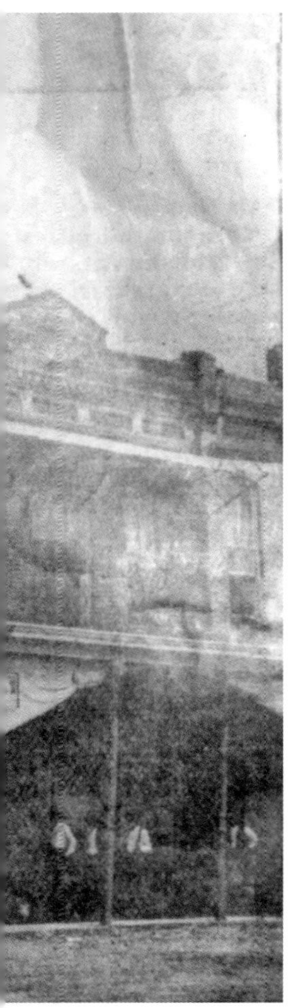

FIGURE 3.4. (Left) Photograph of the First Brick Block, ca. 1897.

This photograph, or one like it, was sent to St. Louis to secure the drawing in FIGURE 3.2. While the surreys are in the drawing, notice that the artist removed the unsightly electrical pole in front of the Perkins Drugstore in the drawing. Photograph courtesy of Campbell Cox.

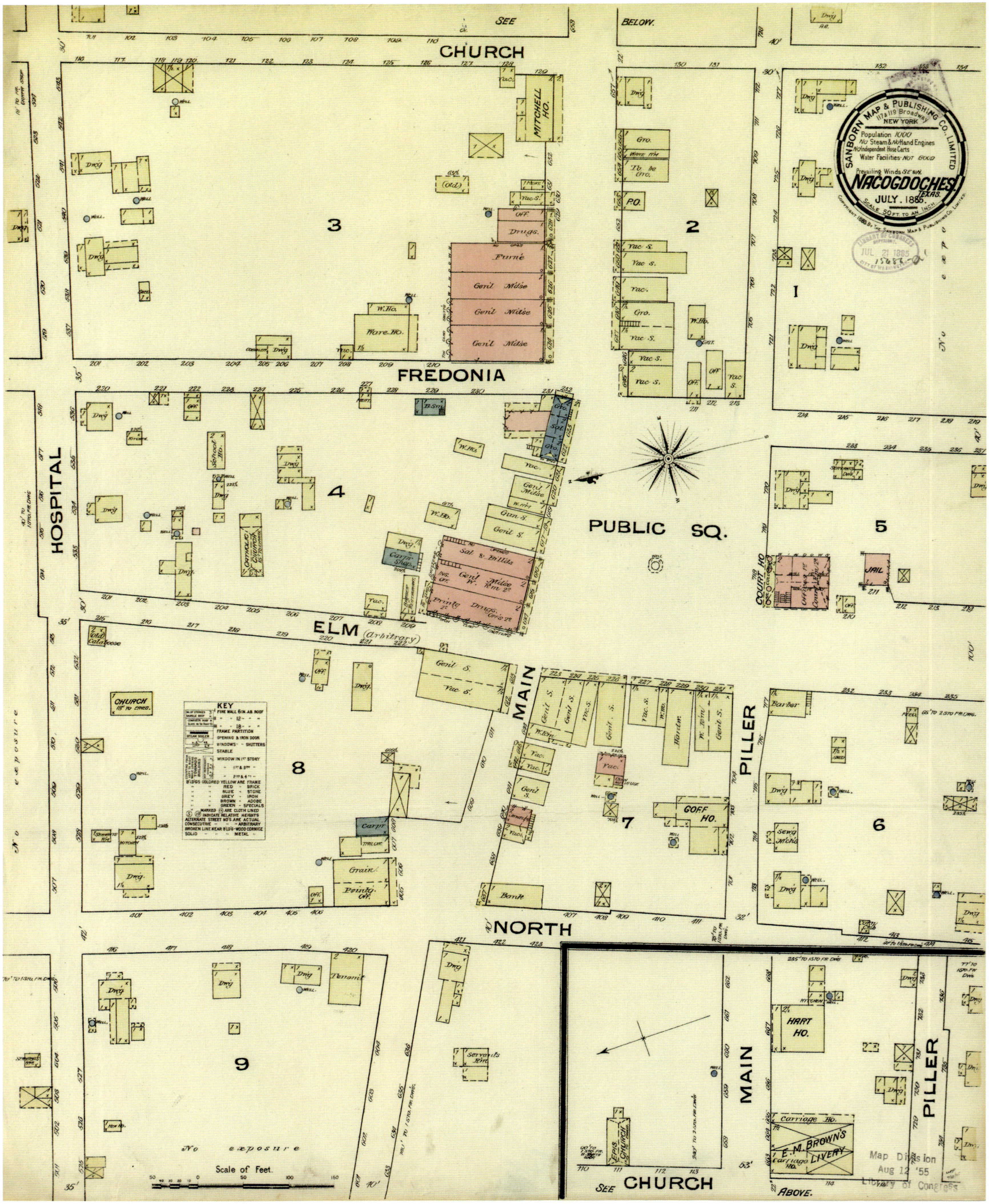
SANBORN MAP & PUBLISHING CO. LIMITED
117 & 119 Broadway
NEW YORK
Population 1000
No Steam & No Hand Engines
No Independent Hose Carts
Water Facilities Not Good
Prevailing Winds
NACOGDOCHES
TEXAS.
JULY. 1885.
Scale 50 FT. TO AN INCH.
CHURCH
FREDONIA
ELM (Arbitrary)
NORTH
HOSPITAL
MAIN
PILLER
PUBLIC SQ.
MITCHELL HO.
GOFF HO.
HART HO.
COURT HO.
JAIL
CATHOLIC CHURCH
CHURCH
EPIS. CHURCH
E.M. BROWN'S LIVERY
Carriage Ho.
School Ho.
Bank
No exposure
Scale of Feet.
SEE BELOW.
SEE ABOVE.
KEY
1
2
3
4
5
6
7
8
9

FIGURE 3.6. (Opposite) The Sanborn Insurance Map, Nacogdoches, 1885.

This map signaled the coming of age of the modern town of Nacogdoches. The famous national Sanborn Company only allotted Nacogdoches one page in that year; by 1891, the town got two pages.

(To maintain orientation, look at the compass symbol above the words "Public Sq." Later maps place north at the top of the pages, which is more natural.)

The three buildings of the First Brick Block of 1884 (in pink, the Old Stone Fort (in purple), and the Second Brick Block starting at Fredonia Street are clearly indicated. The 1856 Courthouse, one of the few brick structures in town when D. Rulfs arrived, and its accompanying Jail sat on the South Square. The new Heiner-designed courthouse replaced this building in 1887.

Notice that there are no brick buildings on the West Square. The Mayer & Schmidt Building discussed in this chapter dates to late 1885, after the completion of the map. By the second mapping period, 1891, there were more brick buildings. John Schmidt by that time had overseen the completion of brick buildings along the north side of East Main Street, between Fredonia and Church, from the Mayer & Schmidt main store to the Opera House. The inset, at the right bottom of the map, shows the Christ Episcopal Church, the Hart Hotel, and E. M. Brown's Livery Stable. Sanborn Maps, University of Texas, Nacogdoches, (1885).

FIGURE 3.7. (Below) The New Courthouse (1887)

Designed by Eugene T. Heiner of Houston. This drawing of Heiner's courthouse on the South Square appeared in the Nacogdoches Chronicle, September 30, 1897. Courtesy of ETRC.

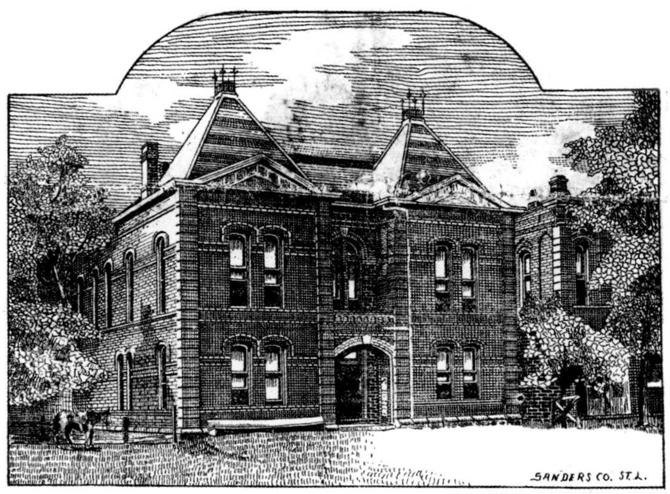

A New Courthouse (1887)

At the time Rulfs arrived in Nacogdoches, the Greek Revival Courthouse of 1856 was the most prominent building on the Square. According to Haltom, who describes the building in detail in his history, the condition of the building was not good.[23] The building's actual condition in 1886, however, is difficult to assess. Whenever locals want something new, they always declare the previous one dangerous. In 1886, the construction of a new courthouse was part of a power struggle between local factions—within the town and between the town and county. In late 1886, the County Court charged a committee of local citizens to look into building a replacement and to determine "its location, probable cost, style, dimensions, materials out of which it shall be built, whether of Wood, Brick or Stone and upon every thing connected with the matter of the cost of construction."[24] Rather quickly, the County announced that they had accepted plans for a new structure by architect Eugene T. Heiner of Houston, a man who had a reputation "as a designer of county courthouses and jails."[25] There is no evidence the committee considered plans from anyone else. The committee met for the first time on December 22; they accepted Heiner's plans by February 18, 1887; and let the bid to the D. N. Darling Company of Palestine for the sum of $11,995 on March 12.[26] The committee had insisted the building cost no more than the 1856 Courthouse it was replacing. The contractor obliged and bid five dollars less.

Based on existing documentation, the committee did not consider D. Rulfs for the project. While one can only speculate as to the reasons, some facts suggest an answer. Champions of county interests, as opposed to promoters of town business interests, were frequently at odds. Both city and county officials held a residue of lingering resentments from the construction of the 1856 building because the town had refused to allow the county to build in the middle of the Square.[27] The committee took sides in the tensions caused by the new brick commercial blocks being advocated in the city at the time.[28] The composition of the committee, and no doubt their decision to go outside of the town for an architect, reflected the resistance of the old forces in town to the changes being promoted by new entrepreneurs, such as Mayer, Schmidt, and Perkins. In the newspapers of the period, Haltom and other progressives reciprocated by omitting any mention of the courthouse's construction, praise for its design, or even an acknowledgement of its existence.[29] While Rulfs certainly benefited from his association with Schmidt, sometimes he lost design contracts because of local reactions to the growing importance of the Schmidt's empire. In the long run, Rulfs's talents and achievements eventually brought his critics around; but by the end of 1886, he had not yet produced a large-scale public building the size of the Courthouse. Another plausible reason for bypassing Rulfs was that the county (always sensitive to keeping pace with other counties) might have chosen Heiner because he was a known architect of courthouses. Heiner, on the other hand, must have thought positively of Rulfs's design work. His new courthouse was similar to the design elements Rulfs had already introduced into the Square. In materials, components, and style, Heiner's design complemented Rulfs's work as represented in the First Brick Block, the Shindler-Kauffman-Runge corner, and the recently completed M&S building. Rulfs reciprocated when he later designed the Davidson Building that stood next to the Courthouse in 1891.

The reputation of the Heiner courthouse, leaving aside any consideration of exterior design, did not fare well or prove lasting in Nacogdoches. Heiner's name, while perhaps known in the nineteenth century, did not survive in local texts or newspapers as the architect for this building and only resurfaced on the state level after a recent study of his over-all career.[30] The Heiner courthouse had, evidently, serious structural defects. The unreasonable cost-restrictions more or less guaranteed the contractor would have to cut corners. Neither the architect nor the contractor had taken into consideration the weakness of the sandy soil on which the building rested, and the Courthouse began to slide off its foundations within a decade of its construction. By the turn of the twentieth century, the officials who inhabited the structure began to appeal for structural reinforcements or a replacement. Some argued that a new jail abutting the Heiner structure on the south would keep the Courthouse from sliding down the hill. The county tried to replace the building in 1902 and again in 1907, but the bond issues failed, victims of the crisis of public confidence discussed in Chapter VII.

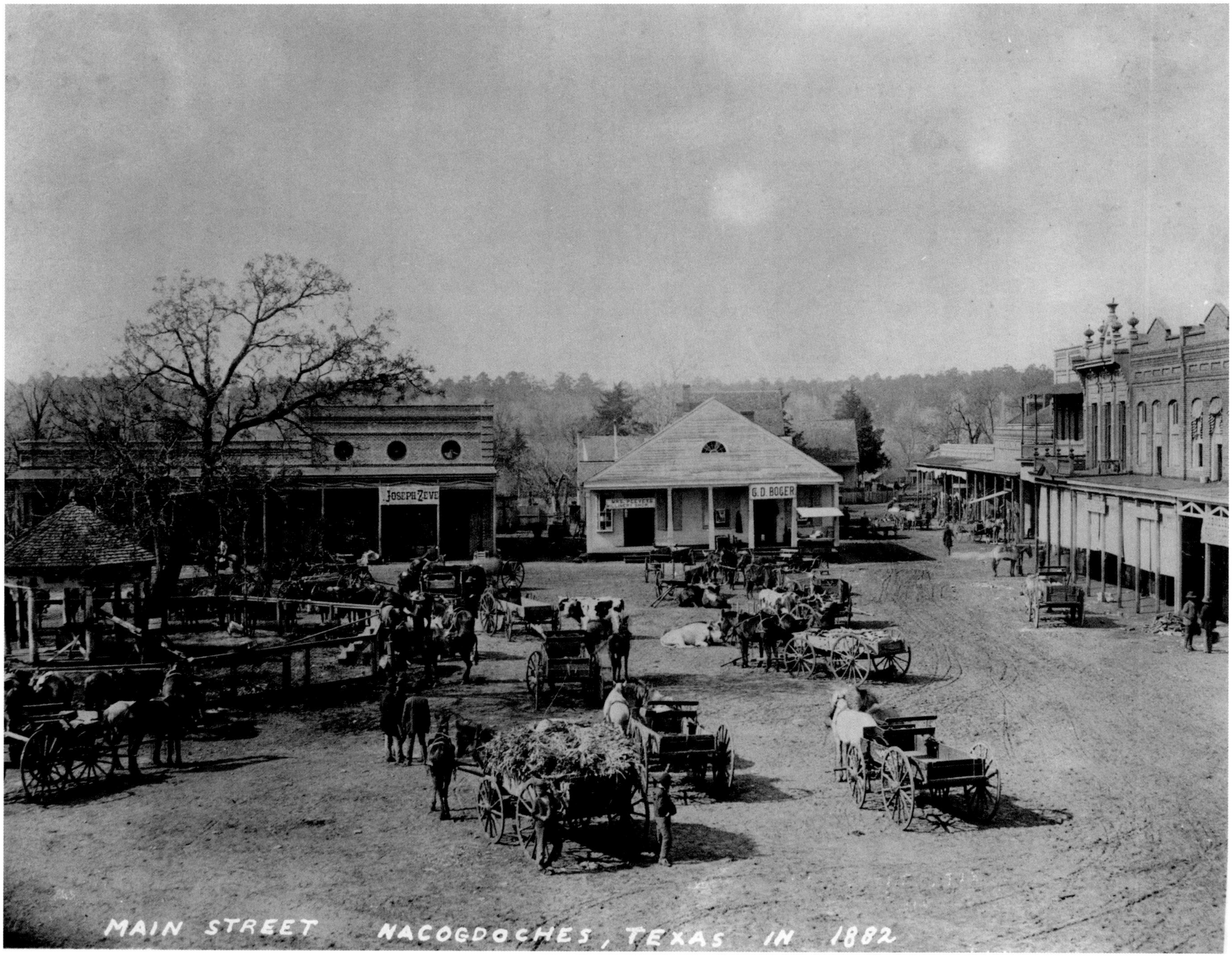

FIGURE 3.8. The Square, Looking West, ca. 1892.

The caption, written on this photograph in white ink, reads "Main Street Nacogdoches, Texas in 1882." The date introduced by this caption is the source of most misinterpretations of the image. The date on the picture is incorrect by almost a decade. The perspective, taken from the second story of the John H. Cox Building (Regions Bank today), is the first indication of the mistake. The John Cox Building on the east of the Square was not built until late 1891. Except for the wooden building in the center housing the G. D. Boger store, all of the buildings in this photograph date between 1884 and 1891 and are the designs of D. Rulfs. Later, in 1896, the architect would replace the Boger store with the Wettermark Bank Building. The completion of the west side of the square, outside the picture to the south, came in 1900 when Fritz Hoya asked Rulfs to build the last two buildings at the south end of Pecan Street.

Moving from left to right: 1) in the foreground, the gazebo and town well pre-date 1880; 2) directly behind the well stands the First National Bank (1890); 3) behind the tree, the Stephen Price & Richard Asa Moore Building (1890); 4) the building with the three portholes is the Mayer & Schmidt Building (1885), only used by the company as their headquarters for a short time [by the time of the picture occupied by Joseph Zeve, an associate in the M&S complex of companies]; 5) the gable front wooden building on the corner of Main Street houses G. D. Boger's store; it is the only building in the picture dating before 1882; 6) the north side of Main Street between the Square and North Street dates to 1888-1890; 7) while North Pecan Street cannot be seen, the balcony of the Cox Building (1888) on the corner of Pecan Street and Main Streets is visible; 8) the First Brick Block (1884), starting with the Perkins Drugstore (easily identified with the apothecary urns on top of the parapet), next the Mayer & Schmidt stand (later the Hardeman Brothers), and only partially visible, the Summers Building (where the two men are talking on the right). Photograph [P70A _8(1)] courtesy of ETRC.

The John H. Cox Building (1888)

The new wealth accompanying the railroad's arrival was not necessarily evenly spread. Newcomers were benefiting more than native businessmen. Were the old timers unable to seize business opportunities, or were the new buildings the reason for the new profits? While the new brick buildings did set new standards of design and functionality, the profitability of both the M&S and Perkins Brothers companies was due only in part to location and buildings. The business acumen of John Schmidt, and to a lesser extent, Abe Mayer, in everything from property, groceries, money lending, and buildings acted like a magnet to attract associates to his side. Likewise, Perkins Brothers created a profitable retail emporium, but they also created wealth in other ways, such as real estate, exploiting cotton by-products (cotton-seed oil), and lending money. As other businessmen undertook to emulate these successes, there was a frenzied rush to consolidate wooden offices and stands into more efficient brick groupings. All called on architect D. Rulfs to replace their late pioneer structures with modern brick and mortar establishments. John H. Cox, who owned the lots directly west of the compellingly successful First Brick Block, was the next to jump into the modernization process.

In late 1887, John H. Cox commissioned Rulfs to draw plans for a two-story brick building at the northwest corner of Pecan and Main. The building would become the anchor for six new buildings in a brick commercial complex to the west. The opportunity to design for Cox presented a number of challenges. Up to this time, Rulfs had not had to cope *visually* with the strange configuration of the Public Square. Albeit at a strange angle, the First Brick Block as a unit faced the Square, as the other brick buildings. Cox naturally wanted as much exposure on the Square as possible; however, a façade totally parallel with Main Street would not only cut off visual access to the Perkins corner drugstore, but it would also create a sharp angle when viewed from the Square. Rulfs solved the problem by using a primary entrance at a 45-degree angle. "Chamfering," as it is called, was a very popular design element employed regularly in Oldenburg and in French Empire architecture all over Europe. It became one of the architect's most frequently employed devices to turn the odd angles of Spanish streets into assets. For instance, Rulfs used chamfered entrances on another building for John H. Cox across the square at the corner of Fredonia and Main (now Regions Bank today), on the Wettermark Bank Building (1896), and the Chronicle Building (1897). He also used the design component in many of his houses.[31]

The Cox Building at the corner of Main and Pecan eventually housed a series of general merchandise and hardware establishments over the years. The Cox family leased the building in 1894 to its first hardware client, Cason, Richardson, & Co. By 1900, the prosperity of the Cason, Richardson, & Co. necessitated more space. They doubled their first-floor space by cutting archways between the corner building and the adjacent one-story building to the west.[32] As discussed in Chapter VIII, Cason had Rulfs design an expansion building directly behind the main store on Pecan Street for his expanding furniture business.[33] The dissolution of the Cason-Richardson and the formation of Cason, Monk & Company in 1906 took the company in a different direction. The first floor of the Cox Building remained essentially a hardware store from 1894 to 1988: after Cason-Richardson moved, Tucker-Sitton Hardware occupied the space from 1910 to 1926; and Branch-Patton Hardware followed from 1926 to 1988.[34] The 1891 Sanborn maps showed the second floor used for offices, but later maps show a variety of uses from residential to a funeral parlor.

Historical discussions concerning the northwest corner of the Square—the area from the middle of the west side of the Square, the corner of Main and Pecan streets, and the First Brick Block—are frequently mistaken in their dating. This has come about because of an interesting, but misdated, photograph. The photograph, which is in the East Texas Research Center, as well as private collections, is discussed at length under FIGURE 3.8.[35]

Collaboration and Circumstances in 1888

In many aspects, one is struck by the extent to which this was a period of collaborations. While human beings are social animals and have to co-operate to survive, this is not always the case when it comes to rival tribes, clans, and businesses. By 1888, Nacogdoches was clearly witnessing a new business model in the Mayer & Schmidt Company: a cooperative business model and a partnership with vision. Without question, Schmidt was the driving force. Since Abe Mayer was a very private man, it is sometimes difficult to know how much leadership to attribute to him. According to Haltom, however, Mayer's contributions were as essential to the team's success as Schmidt's, but not as public. Schmidt evidently thought very highly of Mayer's abilities; he placed Mayer's name first in their partnership and continued to do so for decades.[36] An abundance of public sources exist on John Schmidt. He was an *entrepreneur extraordinaire.* He knew how to get associates to work for and with him. He guided his employees to become managers and oftentimes turned his managers into partners. His sharp eye for trade and marketing opportunities allowed him to create businesses effortlessly and spin them off into independent entities just as effortlessly. He partnered with everyone, and numerous protégés benefited from his largess.

In an immodest, but admittedly accurate description in an 1895 advertisement, John Schmidt referred to the M&S partnership as "the Hercules of Nacogdoches' Business Houses." Many admired the M&S successes, but their self-promoting arrogance irritated other merchants. By saying they were the "leading spirits in almost every worthy local enterprise," by implying they were the only entrepreneurs to hold the public confidence, by claiming that their business was the only one to stretch to expand beyond the limits of Nacogdoches,[37] they undermined their own exceptional network of investments and partnerships. After the turn of the century, when the rising waters of prosperity were not lifting all boats, and the business community began to separate into clans (usually along the line of separate banking constituencies), the headstrong and successful ways of the M&S empire would run into more opposition in Nacogdoches.

Diedrich Rulfs, while not a partner in their primary business, was very much a business partner with Abe Mayer and John Schmidt. It was M&S who gave Rulfs the opportunity to make his reputation as an architect in Nacogdoches. Rulfs depended heavily on the patronage of Schmidt throughout his entire career and benefited from Schmidt's large network of associates. Schmidt recommended Rulfs to everyone. The architect's early commercial commissions came directly from Schmidt, and he entered the residential market by building a house for Schmidt. Later, he received commissions for hotels, schools, and churches because of Schmidt. What is crystal clear is that Schmidt and Mayer had total trust in and reliance on

FIGURE 3.9. John H. Cox Building, Drawing by Sanders Company, *Nacogdoches Chronicle*, 1897.

The Cox Building, the anchor to a new brick block on the north side of East Main between the Square and North Street, still stands much as it did in 1888 when it was built. The Victorian commercial structure has interesting brickwork at the top, a double frame awning and porch around the south and east façades, and a chamfered corner entry on the square. At the time Rulfs designed the buildings to the west of the Cox building, their facing bricks were all red; many of these buildings have received modern facelifts. Rulfs used chamfered or corner entrances across Main Street on the Wettermark Bank Building and across the Square on the Cox Building (now Regions Bank).

Notice that the newpaper in 1897 labeled the address as West Main. All street directions at that time emanated from the Square; today the dividing point is North Street. Courtesy of ETRC.

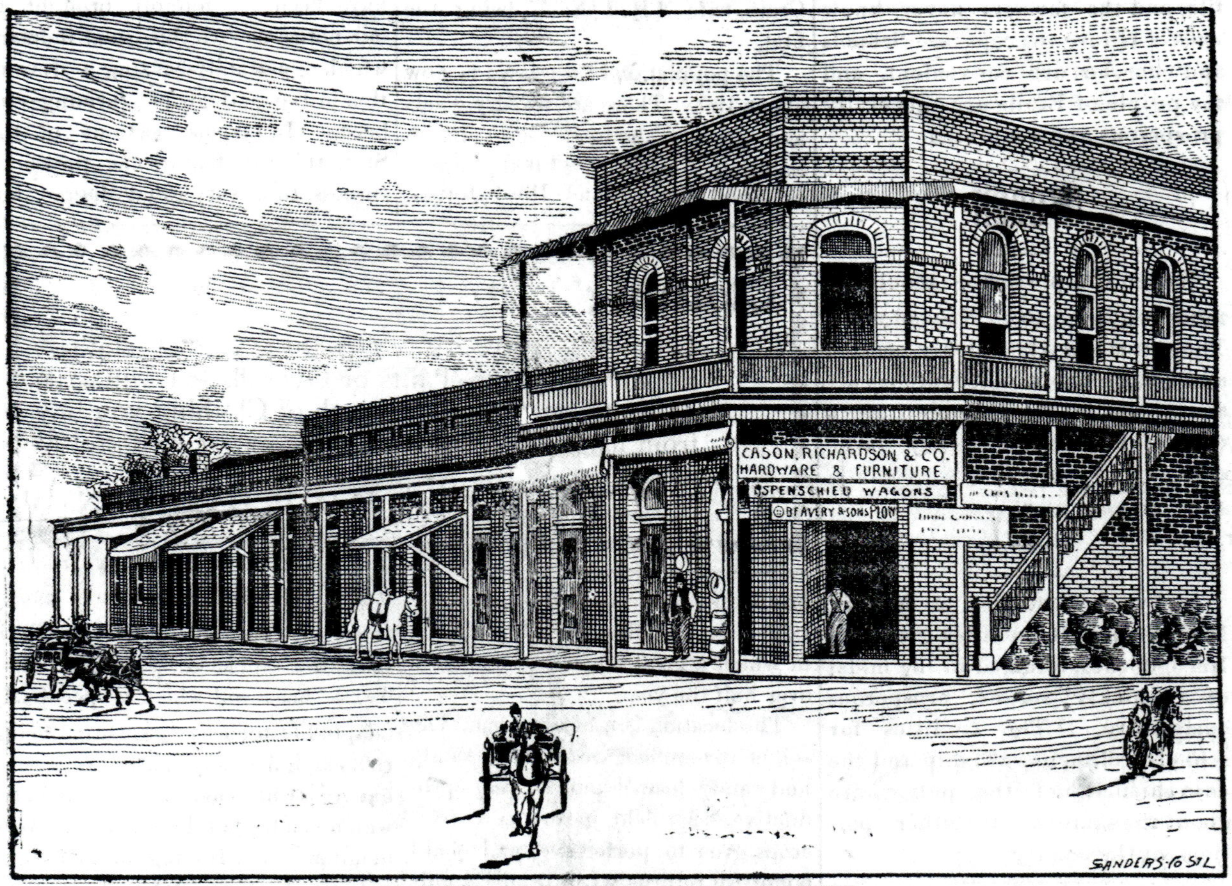

NORTH SIDE WEST MAIN STREET.

FIGURE 3.10. The John H. Cox Building, Northwest Corner of the Square, 2011.

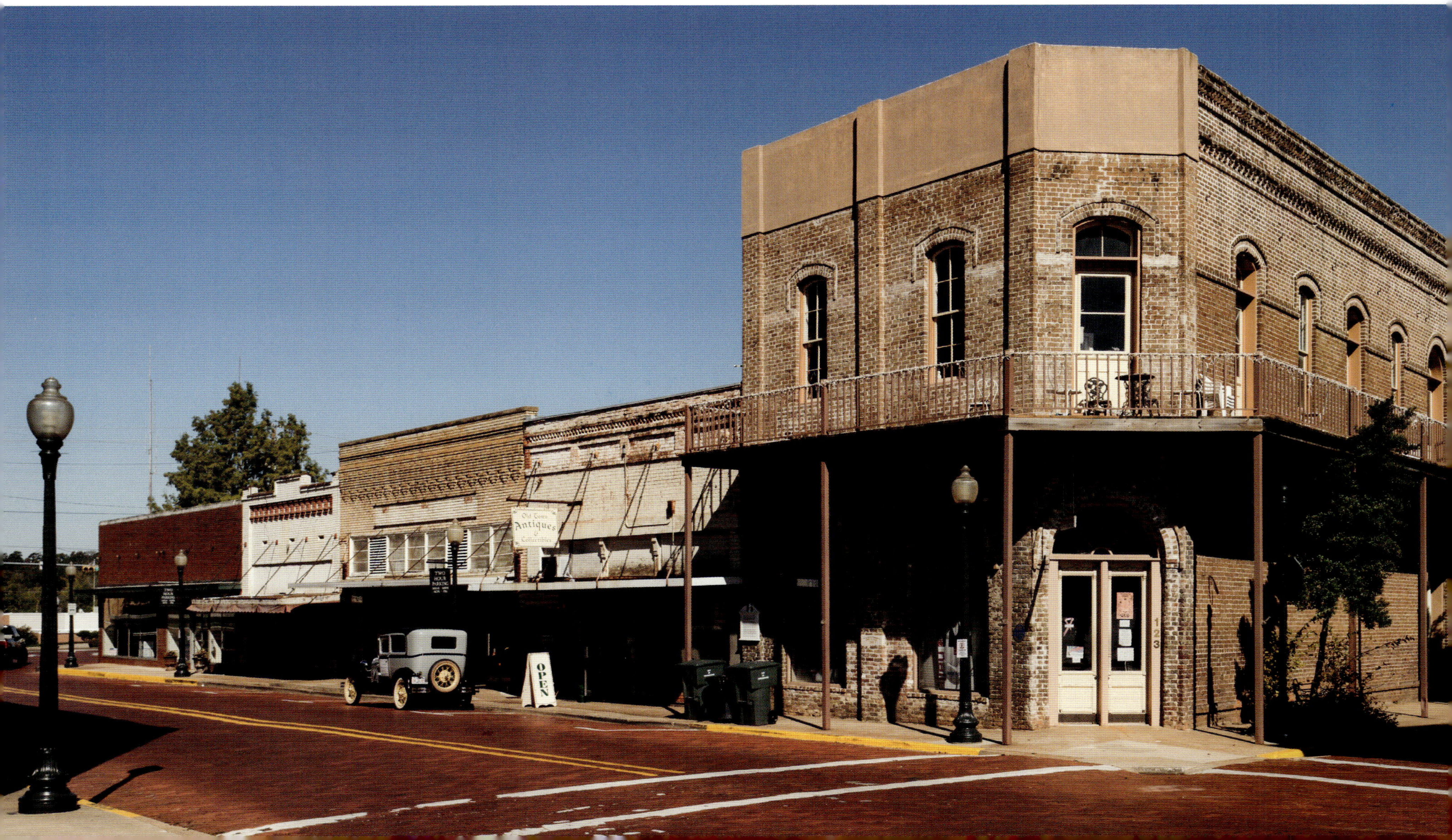

Rulfs's ability to give three-dimensional form to their dreams. He was not only useful to the partners, but he was also essential to their planning process as they calculated their moves. Haltom clearly links the success of M&S with the talents of Diedrich Rulfs. The architect's role in designing modern Nacogdoches was growing with every passing year. Already impressive by 1888, the demands for the services of the architect exploded after this year as he moved from success to success by offering his patrons structures that were durable, functional, and pleasing to the eye.

The Mayer & Schmidt Building on East Main (1888-1889)

In early 1888, Kauffman & Runge, the Galveston merchants, decided to pull out of Nacogdoches. Whether overextended or just displeased with their investment, their departure brought the northeast corner of Main and Fredonia suddenly back onto the market.[38] This development put R. C. Shindler's business and his new home at risk. M&S, well on their way to becoming the most successful merchants and developers in town, immediately saw another great business opportunity. They immediately bought out the Galveston investors and decided to make a strategic move to consolidate their main business operations in the area east of the Old Stone House. They purchased not only the Fredonia-Main corner, but also a warehouse space behind it to provide backup space for inventory. (Eventually, they would concentrate their retail trade, their grocery business, their cotton and hardware business in this location by creating Commerce Street.) At one stroke, their action salvaged Shindler's business and new home and created a powerful new engine of development for the east side of town.

M&S's next move shocked everyone. In an act of true bravado, they expanded the concept of massing brick buildings together all the way down to Church Street. Having learned from their experience on the West Square, where everything moved at a snail's pace, they released plans for redeveloping the whole north side of East Main. They purchased the old Mitchell Hotel and announced their intention to build an entertainment complex on the corner of Main and Church streets. The effect was to put a squeeze on the property owners in between: either cooperate in the modernization process or get out of the way. Years later, in reviewing their actions, Giles Haltom reflected on M&S's strategy:

> Nacogdoches developed rapidly into the commercial emporium. The population doubled, trebled and even quadrupled in a few years. Old ideas, and ideals gave way to the spirit of modern progress, business vim and industrial energy. It was in very truth the beginning of a real renaissance, in all things and along all lines that pertained to industrial development, and among the great figures that acted in a worthy way during these stirring days was the firm of Mayer & Schmidt which had by this time become one of the important factors in the material development of the country.[39]

Rulfs embarked immediately on remodeling the one-story buildings at the corner of Fredonia and Main as the new home for the Mayer & Schmidt Company. He added the second floor, already anticipated, and expanded the warehouse capacities of the buildings on Commerce Street.[40] At the opposite end of the block, at the corner of Main and Church Streets, Rulfs designed a new Opera House to increase the draw of people to the east end of town. Since the Opera House would replace the Old Mitchell Hotel, the partners assured the public they had thought of this, too, by announcing a new hotel to take up the slack and serve the east business district. (The transformation of a former boarding house just north on Church Street into the high-end Bullen Hotel for Nacogdoches is part of Chapter IV.)

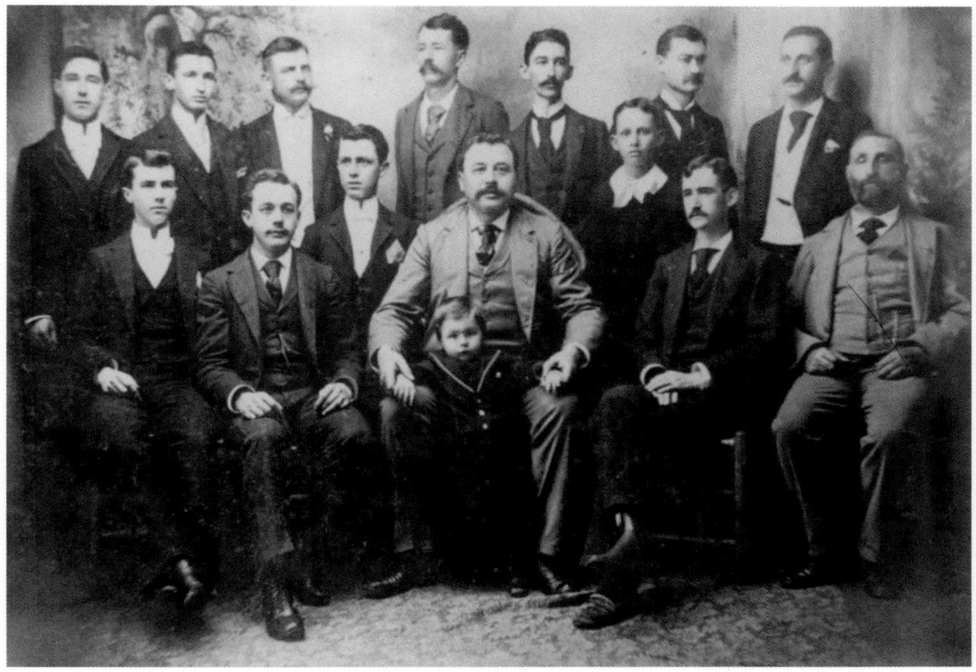

FIGURE 3.11. John Schmidt and Associates, ca. 1893.
Front Row, sitting from left to right: 1) Fritz F. Ingraham (assistant bookkeeper); 2) Jacob Schmidt (partner); 3) John Schmidt (Senior Partner and General Manager) with Herbert Schmidt, his son, between his knees; 4) Jule Smith (Bookkeeper), and 5) Mr. L. Zeve (Cotton Buyer). Center Row: 1) McNeil Chapman (Shoes); 2) Simon Zeve (delivery). Back Row, left to right: 1) John J. Baker; 2) Max Mayer 3) Roland Jones; 4) Henry W. Rusche (Hardware); 5) Robert C. Monk (Groceries); 6) A. Y. Donegan. 5) Sigmund Bruck. Courtesy of ETRC.

The Nacogdoches Opera House (1889)

As part of his scheme to rework the East Main business district, John Schmidt had D. Rulfs design and build new entertainment facilities. Schmidt wanted to induce theatrical companies to stop over as they traveled between engagements in Shreveport and Houston. To build the theater, they had to tear down the Mitchell Hotel, a stagecoach inn originally built ca. 1831 as the home of Frost Thorn. The new Nacogdoches Opera House was a two-story building with a ticket office and businesses on the ground floor (at first general merchandise and a confectionery), with a theater on the second floor. A wide staircase led to the second floor. The height of the ceiling in the theater permitted the existence of a gallery around the south end. At the north end of the theater floor, the stage was flanked by dressing rooms and had an outside stairway, providing access for actors and scenery. From early accounts, the stage was very small and could not accommodate all productions. The front of the building had an open gallery over the sidewalk on which people could stand during intermissions.

While the theater hosted a few opera performances, most of the touring shows were plays, melodramas, occasional burlesques, and magic shows. After the touring season, the theater became a favorite site for community recitals, benefits, town meetings, and dances. The *Daily Sentinel* in 1907, for instance, reported that: "a large crowd of dancers and several chaperones enjoyed a pleasant dance at the opera house. . . . The weather was cool, the music good, floor in good condition, and everything was favorable for good dancing." The Nacogdoches Civic League and the Nacogdoches Fire Department were both organized at this theater in 1907.[41] The Marx Brothers first developed their improvisational style of comedy in the Nacogdoches Opera House. During their act around 1907, a disturbance on Main Street caused most of the audience to run to see what was happening. Accounts differ, but either a runaway horse or mule kicked a cart to pieces and dragged it down the street. The Marx Brothers, angered by the loss of their audience, began to race about the stage in a frenzy of comic behavior. Their parody of their own burlesque and their antics on stage brought the audience back and launched a new direction in their comic careers. According to Groucho Marx, this performance even spawned the first Groucho-ism: "Nacogdoches is full of roaches." He and his brothers were also arrested shortly thereafter for playing euchre, a popular card game, on the porch of the Redland Hotel—a Rulfs Building across the street from the Opera House.[42]

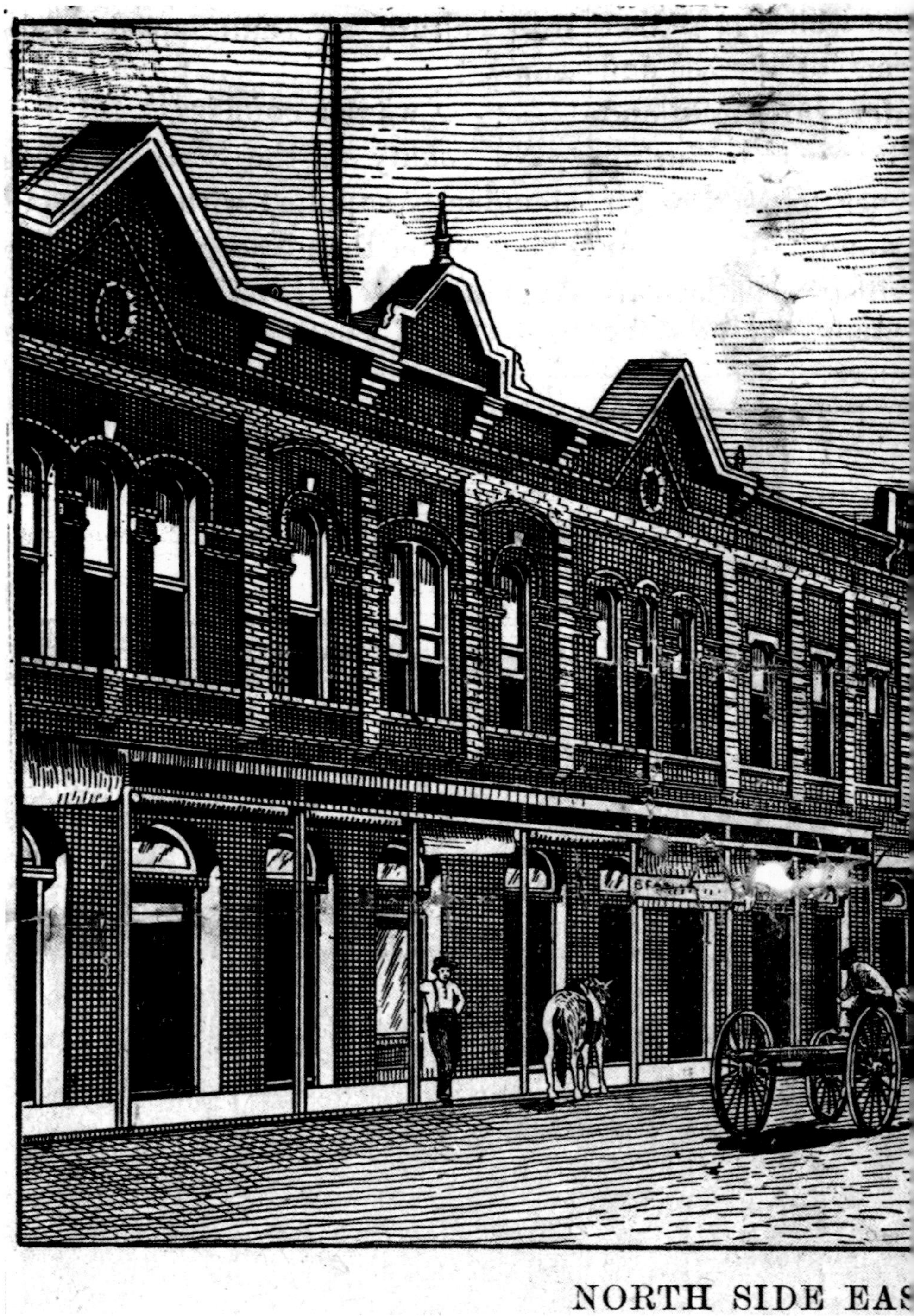

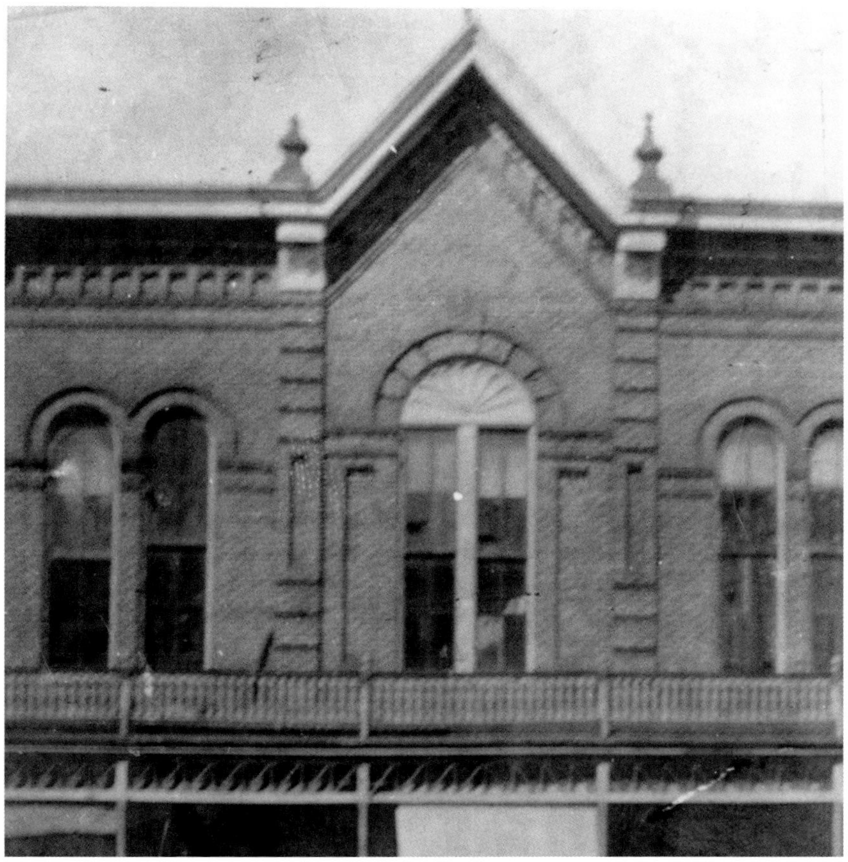

FIGURE 3.12. The Nacogdoches Opera House, ca. 1900.

The east anchor of Schmidt's new north side of East Main block was the Nacogdoches Opera House. The design of the Opera House, planned in 1888 and built in 1889, is very reminiscent of the Mayer & Schmidt Building at the other end of the block. The Italianate design included arched windows and a Palladian motif in the center between quoined pilasters, all beneath a highly patterned cornice. All these elements were in current use in the capitol city of Oldenburg when Rulfs studied there.

Rulfs designed the new building so that the ground story could house retail establishments to pay the rent in-between the performances. Traveling companies on their way to either Houston or Shreveport comprised the main groups who booked the house. Courtesy of ETRC.

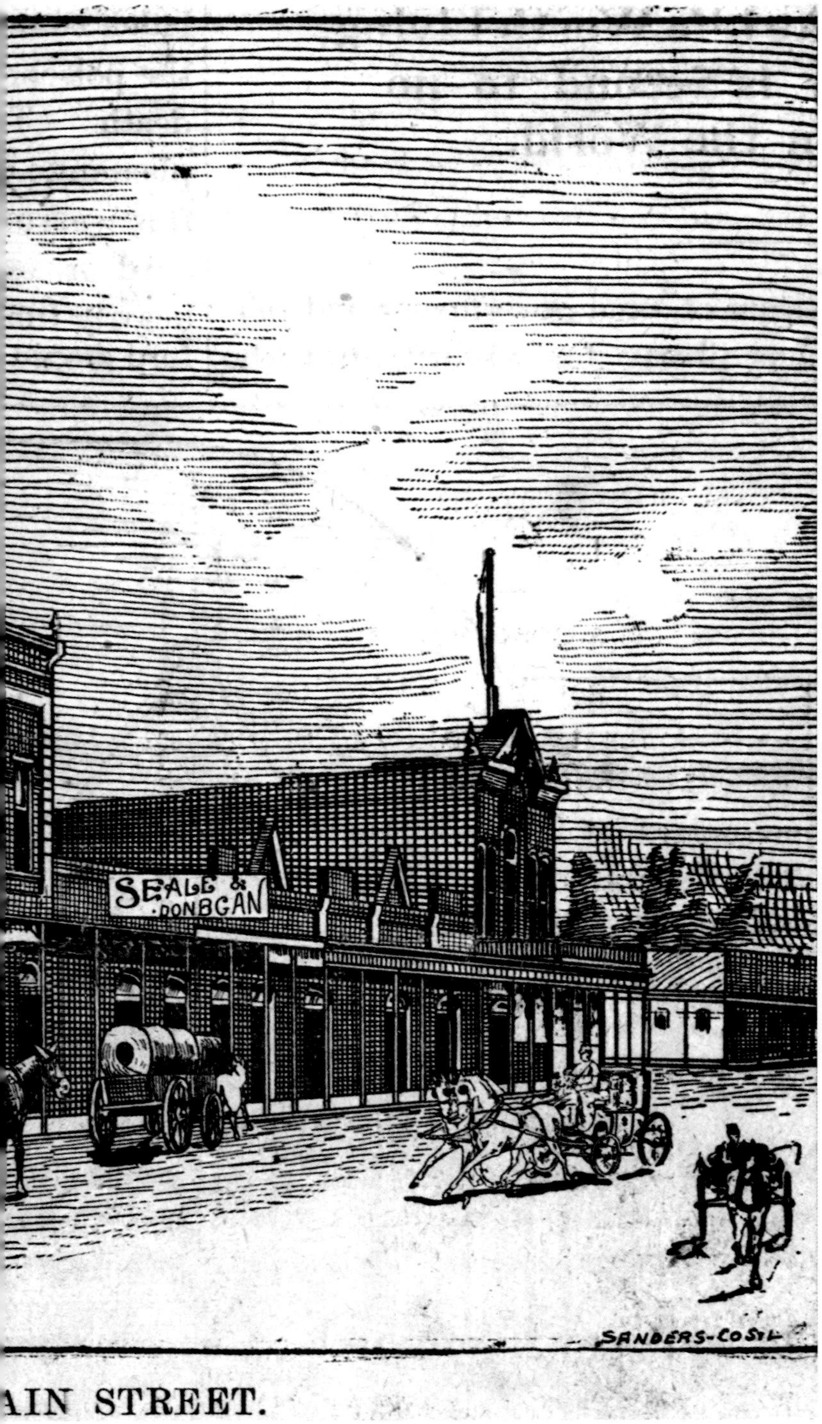

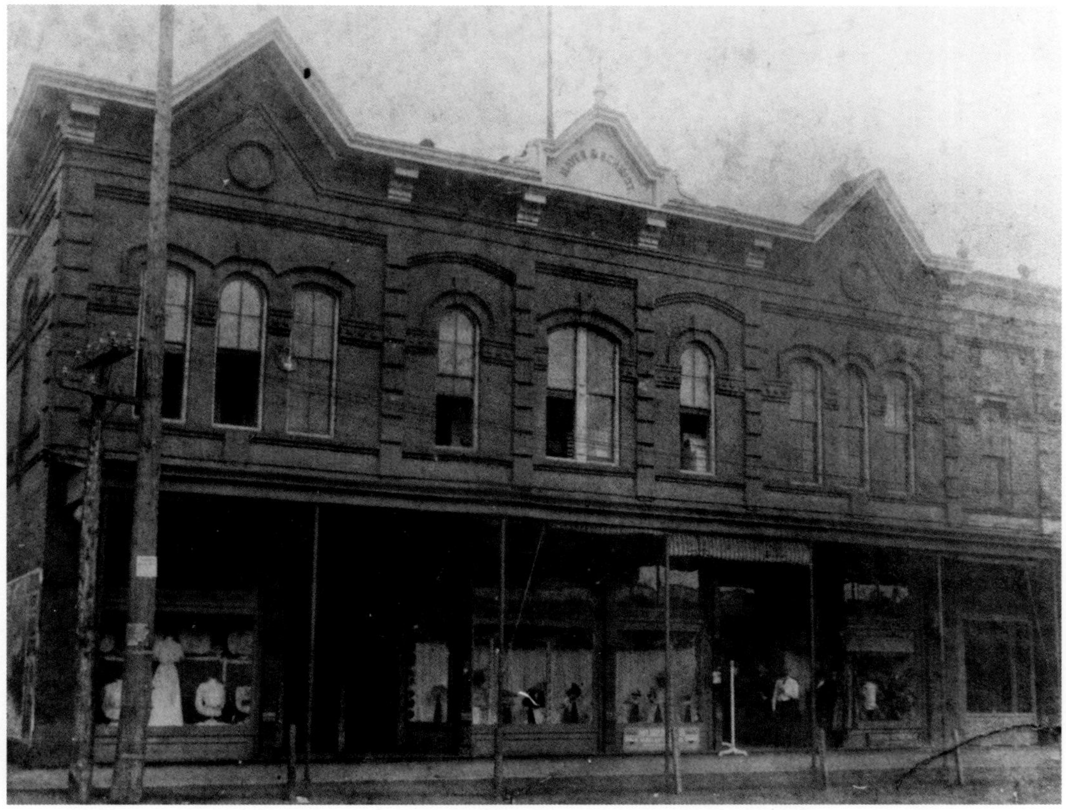

FIGURE 3.14. (Above) The Mayer & Schmidt Building, ca. 1897.

In the facade of the Mayer & Schmidt Building, Rulfs used extensive Italianate styling. The upper story, added four years after the ground floor in 1888, had a complicated and elaborate design of windows (both arched and segmented) with a running hood molding. The building had three divisions, with decorative quoins as pilasters between the segments as well as at the corners. There were belt courses of bricks under the windows, inset panels of corbelled bricks, and a high parapet with a dramatic cornice supported by large eave brackets and moldings. While there were gables at each end of the building, the center segment had a Palladian motif and a crown over the large center window. The name of Mayer & Schmidt formed an arch in the center. Photograph courtesy of Campbell Cox.

FIGURE 3.13. (Above) Sanders Drawing, The North Side of East Main.

This drawing, which appeared in the 1897 Special Edition of the Nacogdoches Chronicle, is another in a series of photographs turned into drawings by the Sanders Company in Saint Louis. Shown in the left foreground of the drawing is the Mayer & Schmidt Building –"The Hercules of Nacogdoches' Business Houses." The M&S Building had decorative arched windows, three gabled parapets with porthole decorations on each end, and a flagpole. Adjoining M&S on the right was the John P. Davidson Building (1888). The façades of the M&S and the Davidson Building were complementary, not identical.

The Opera House (1889) is the two-story building in the distance. It had similar architectural features to the M&S Building and also had a flagpole. In between there were several small buildings, where the Cason-Monk Hardware would stand after 1906. At the end of the drawing is a small wooden building where the Hazle family still had their grocery business in 1897. (The large, two-story Hazle Building, which today occupies the location was yet to come in 1901.) Courtesy of ETRC.

Additions to the Square in the Early 1890s

The First National Bank and the Moore Buildings (1890). The success of the Cox and associated buildings, plus the death of a key opponent to the idea of consolidation (Asa Moore), finally allowed property owners in the middle of the West Square to join the brick revolution. In 1890, Asa Moore's sons, Richard and Stephen Price Moore, finally gave Rulfs the green light to design replacements for their two wooden buildings immediately south of the M&S store.[43] Rulfs made the new buildings to match the original M&S stand in depth and placed on them protective awnings which covered the sidewalk in front. The Moore names are etched in the metal plates, which defined the front steps of their building.[44] These three buildings, although having undergone many modifications and façade changes over the years, stand today in the middle of the West Square. The Moore heirs made money, while the buildings were under construction in 1890, by selling off the southern building to a new group of investors who were establishing a new bank under the name of the First National Bank of Nacogdoches.

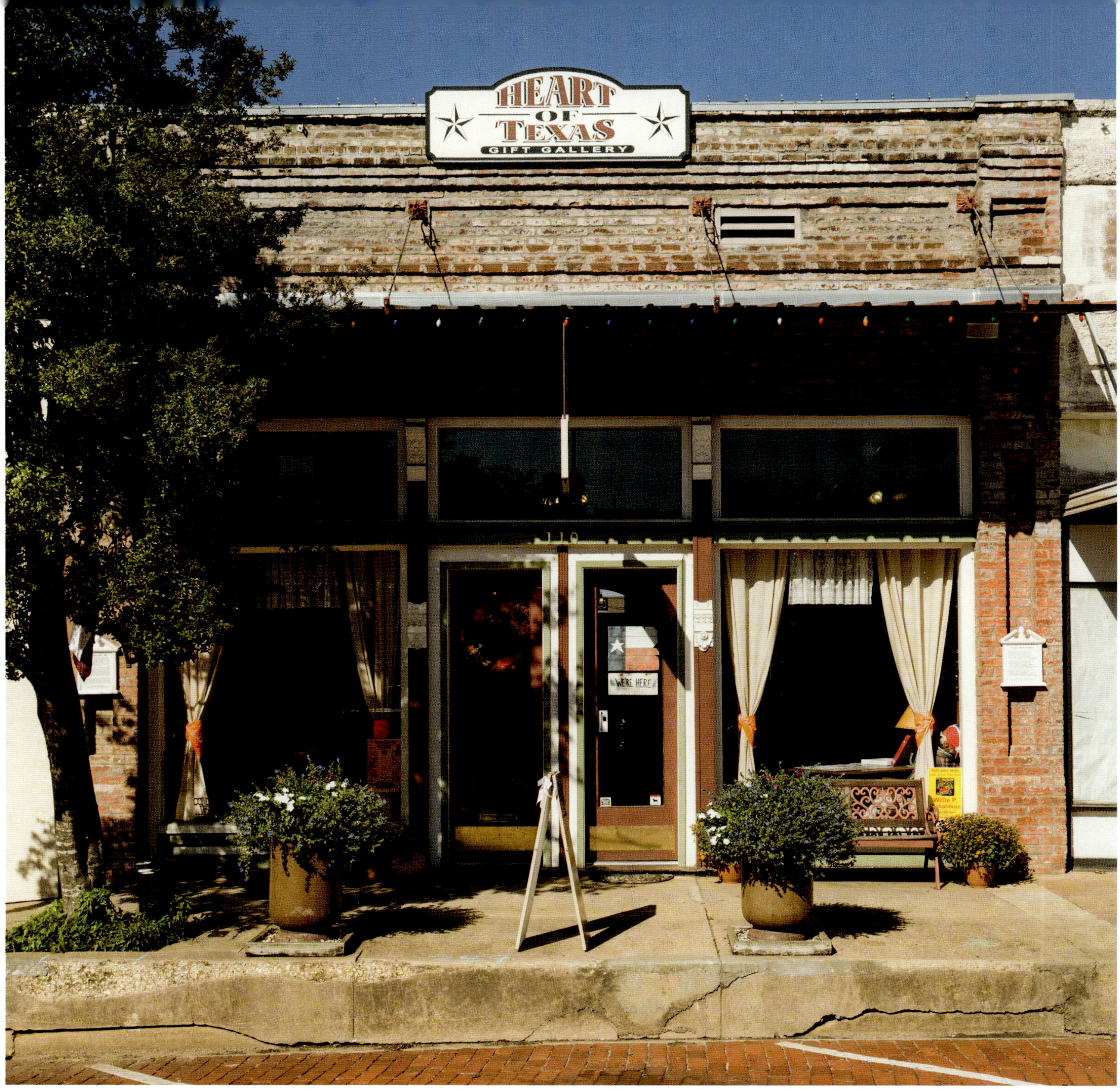

FIGURE 3.15. The Heart of Texas Building, 2011.
While being constructed in 1890, the newly created First National Bank purchased the structure and conducted business there until 1899.

The group had Rulfs modify the façade during construction to fit their new enterprise. While not the first bank in Nacogdoches, First National was the first bank in town to have a national charter (August 1890), the first to have a brick building in which to conduct business, and the first to have a capitalization of $50,000. John P. Davidson, a native of Alabama who came with his brother George to Texas around 1850, organized the bank. Other stockholders included J. W. Shipman, James P. Sutphen, Gus Levy, Paul M. Richardson, and J. E. Mayfield. The new venture itself lasted only a decade and closed its doors at the end of 1899, leaving the private Wettermark Bank once again the only bank operating in Nacogdoches.[45]

The former First National Bank Building served a variety of businesses over the years, among them the Royal Theater, barbershops, Western Union, and the Unity Church of Christianity. Currently, the building at 110 South Pecan is The Heart of Texas Shop; the Moore Brothers Building next door was the long-time home of Jenkins Seed Store.[46]

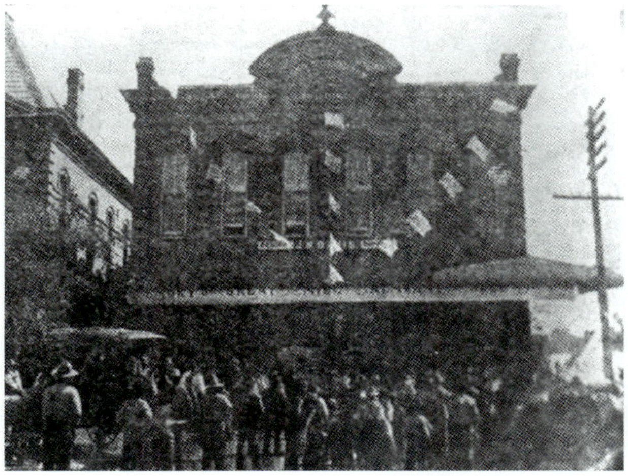

FIGURE 3.16. The John P. Davidson Building (1891).
Now the City Hall of Nacogdoches, the Davidson Building's Italianate cornices, arched windows, and raised parapet have all disappeared in subsequent remodelings.

The John P. Davidson Building (1891). Nacogdoches businessman and financier John P. Davidson owned the property on the corner of Pilar and Pecan, on the south side of the Square, immediately west of the 1887 Courthouse. The corner has an illustrious history. John Forbes, General Sam Houston's Commissary General at the Battle of San Jacinto, built the first house on the property in 1836. Houston later purchased the house. This history has recently received attention by the Texas Historical Commission in a marker entitled, "Sam Houston's First Home in Texas."[47] Davidson bought the property in 1878; by that time, the Houston house was gone. In 1891, Davidson contracted architect D. Rulfs to erect a two-story brick commercial building on the land. It was the architect's fourth opportunity to work for Davidson. While there are photographs of this building, none of them are very good. The façade of the Rulfs building complemented the design of the 1887 Courthouse in some of its details, but with its raised parapet, it looked more like the M&S Building or the Opera House on East Main.[48] In 1908, Davidson's building served as the temporary home of the Mayer & Schmidt Company after their building was destroyed by fire.

The Davidson building, many façades and annexes later, including a third-story addition, stands today and serves Nacogdoches as its Municipal Offices. From the 1920s, a series of hotels occupied the building: Inn Hotel (1924), then the Sam Houston Hotel (1926), and finally the Liberty Hotel (1929). On the 1929 Sanborn Maps, the Liberty Hotel name and the Hotel Annex existed.[49] Frank Hathcock purchased the Liberty in the late 1930s, and Mrs. Hathcock ran the hotel while her husband served in World War II. After the war, in 1947, the Hathcocks remodeled the hotel and announced the re-opening in the *Daily Sentinel*.[50] In the 1950s it became the home of Oliver Beauty College. In 1987, the city acquired all the buildings and renovated them, thereby keeping the city government on the south side of the Square. The old Davidson Building now bears the name the Gladys Hampton Building.[51]

The John H. Cox Building, East Square (1891). Because of the Old Stone Fort's protrusion into East Main Street, the East side of the Square between Main and Pilar is shorter than the other three sides. The only prominent brick building to occupy the East Square is still there. The building, the second major building on the Square designed by Rulfs for John H. Cox, was built in 1891; it replaced a two-story wooden building that had occupied the lot for many years. The footprint of the building has not really changed since its construction, despite the many façades and interior alterations over the decades. The chamfered corner betrays the original configuration. The second floor, at the time of construction, housed the lodge of the Knights of Pythias, a fraternal order of which Mr. Rulfs was an active member. Later, the second floor became the offices of the W. T. Wilson Grain Company. When Farmers and Merchants Bank organized in 1908, they were first in the building next door but moved into the Cox Building in 1909. When Farmers and Merchants merged with Stone Fort National Bank in 1919, the new entity, under the Stone Fort name, occupied the structure. Rulfs reworked the façade in 1919, but the Cox family did not sell the building to the bank until 1929 after John H. Cox's death. The building received makeovers and extensions in 1935, 1956, and 1966. Since 2003, Regions Bank has owned the building.[52]

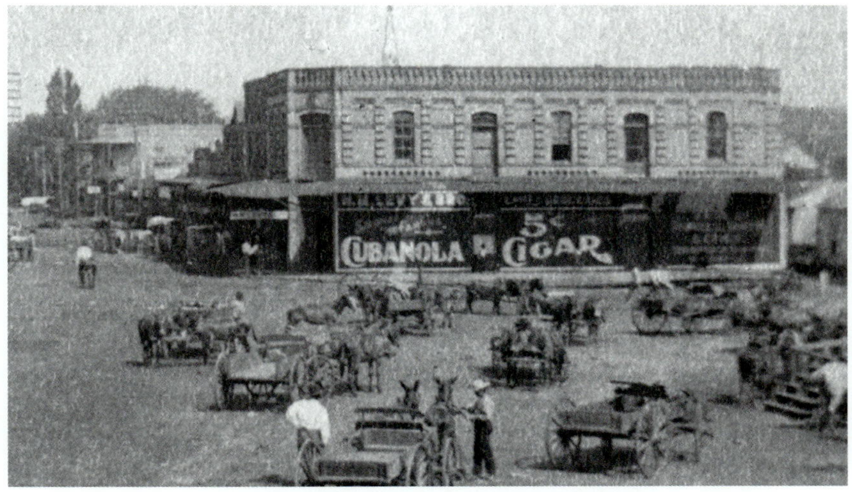

FIGURE 3.17. The Cox Building (1891), East Side of the Square.
The 1891 Sanborn Map shows the Cox building under construction. In his second commercial building design for Cox', Rulfs also used a chamfered corner entrance. The Italianate features of this structure, however, are more restrained than those on the buildings for Schmidt and Davidson. The quoin pilasters are there, but the roofline of the parapet is straight and the cornice tailored and accomplished through brick designs rather than brackets and irregular shapes. In 1919, Rulfs redesigned the façade of this building, simplifying the lines even more. See Chapter XII. The core of Regions Bank today is still this 1891 building, many facelifts later. Courtesy of ETRC.

FIGURE 3.18. (Below) South Side of Main Street at the Square, 1891.
This 1891 Sanborn Map shows the Cox Building, corner of Fredonia and East Main, being built. The building in 1909 became the home of Farmers and Merchants Bank and in 1919 Stone Fort National Bank.

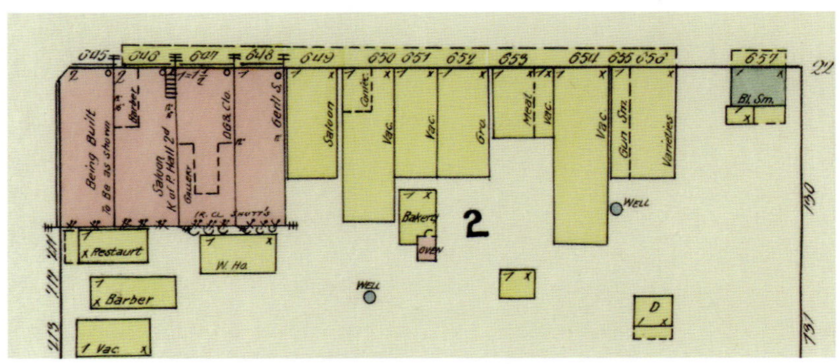

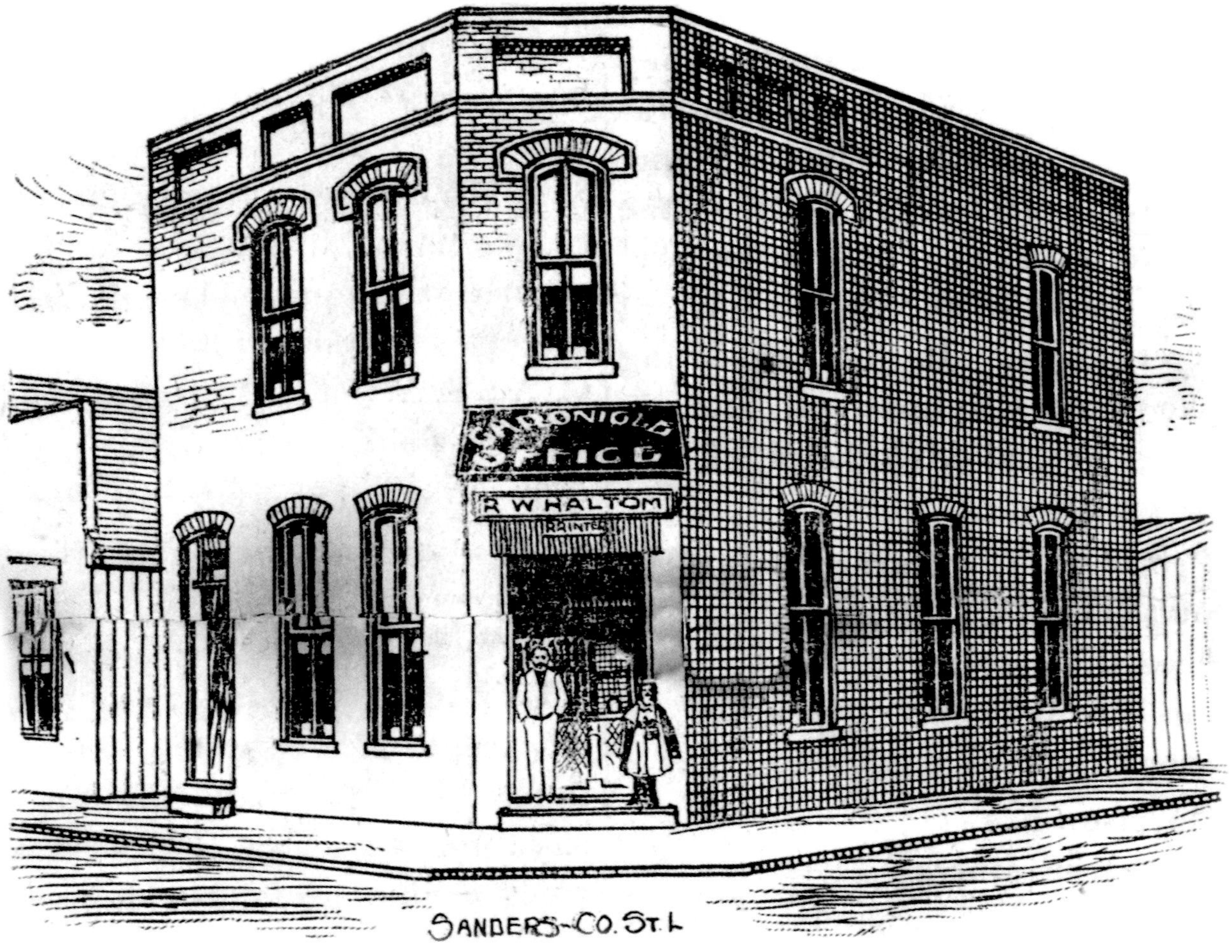

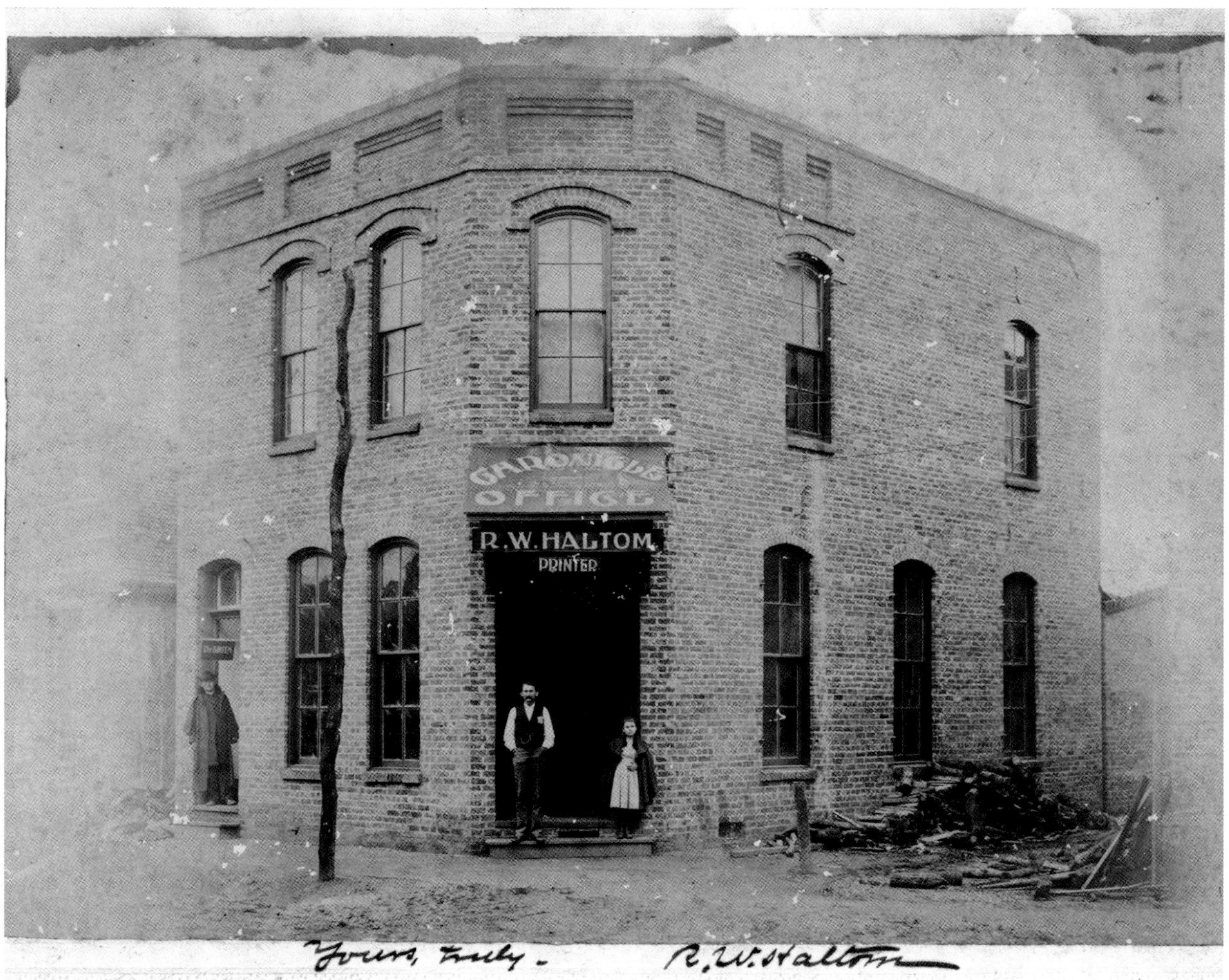

FIGURE 3.19. (Left) Nacogdoches Chronicle Office, 1897.

This drawing by Sanders Company, Saint Louis, appeared in the Nacogdoches Chronicle, *September 30, 1897. Courtesy of ETRC.*

FIGURE 3.20. (Below) Photograph of the Chronicle Office, ca. 1896.

The printing facilities in Nacogdoches could not reproduce photographs directly. As noted before, the newspaper would take a picture, send their photograph to the Sanders Company in Saint Louis, where an artist would replicate the image as a line drawing, place it on a copper plate, and return the plate to Nacogdoches for printing. While several examples still exist and allow for comparisons, none is better than the example of the Chronicle Office, which is signed by R. W. Haltom.

In both the photograph and drawing opposite, Bill Haltom is standing on the front steps of the new Chronicle Building with his daughter Ruby. The sign over the door states: "Chronicle Office. R. W. Haltom, Printer." In the photograph, a man stands in the door to the left, and the sign reads "Dr. Smith" (Dr. W. I. M. Smith), who had an office on the second floor. There is a vertical pole to the left of the entrance and in the alley to the right a stack of firewood necessary to heat the building. Barely visible in the photograph are the wooden buildings right and left.

The Sanders Company's artist has produced a remarkably accurate line drawing, but he has edited the photograph. The architectural details of the building have received clear treatment. But, he has eliminated the man entering the side stairs in the left of the photograph, cleaned up the alleyway between the office and the Perkins Brothers Drugstore by removing the firewood, and has removed the odd pole or tree trunk (no doubt left from the construction phase) to the left of the doorway where Haltom stands. Most interestingly, the Saint Louis artist has added a bit of urban class to the picture by inserting a sidewalk and curb to the building that it did not have in the 1890s or later. Courtesy of ETRC.

The Nacogdoches Chronicle *Office (1892)*

One of the main families promoting the modernization of Nacogdoches was that of Colonel R. D. Orton and his nephews, R. W. (Bill) and Giles Haltom.[53] The family owned several papers over the years: the *Nacogdoches News* (1875); the *Nacogdoches Star* (1877); the *Nacogdoches Star-News* (1887); the revived *Nacogdoches Chronicle* (1890); and, finally, in partnership with W. H. Harris, the town's first daily newspaper, *The Daily Sentinel* (1899).[54] R. W. Haltom was the driving force in the newspapers until 1904 when he became a Member of the Texas House of Representative; thereafter, Giles Haltom, Bill's younger brother, edited and published the *The Daily Sentinel*. R. W. died in 1907 and Giles in 1951.

In 1892, Will Perkins asked Rulfs to design and build a building on Pecan Street, just north of the First Brick Block. The tenant for the building was to be Haltom's weekly *Nacogdoches Chronicle*. (The newspaper leased this building until the family's successor newspaper *The Daily Sentinel* opened in a new home on the east side of town in 1900.) The *Chronicle* office could be seen from Main Street and stood across a small alleyway behind the Perkins Brothers Drugstore. The modest two-story building had a chamfered doorway, detailed brickwork like the commercial buildings along Main Street nearby, and decorative brick hoodmolds over the windows. An exterior door on the north side provided access to the second floor, where a Dr. W. I. M. Smith had his first office. (See the line drawing and photograph in this chapter, Figures 3.19 and 3.20.

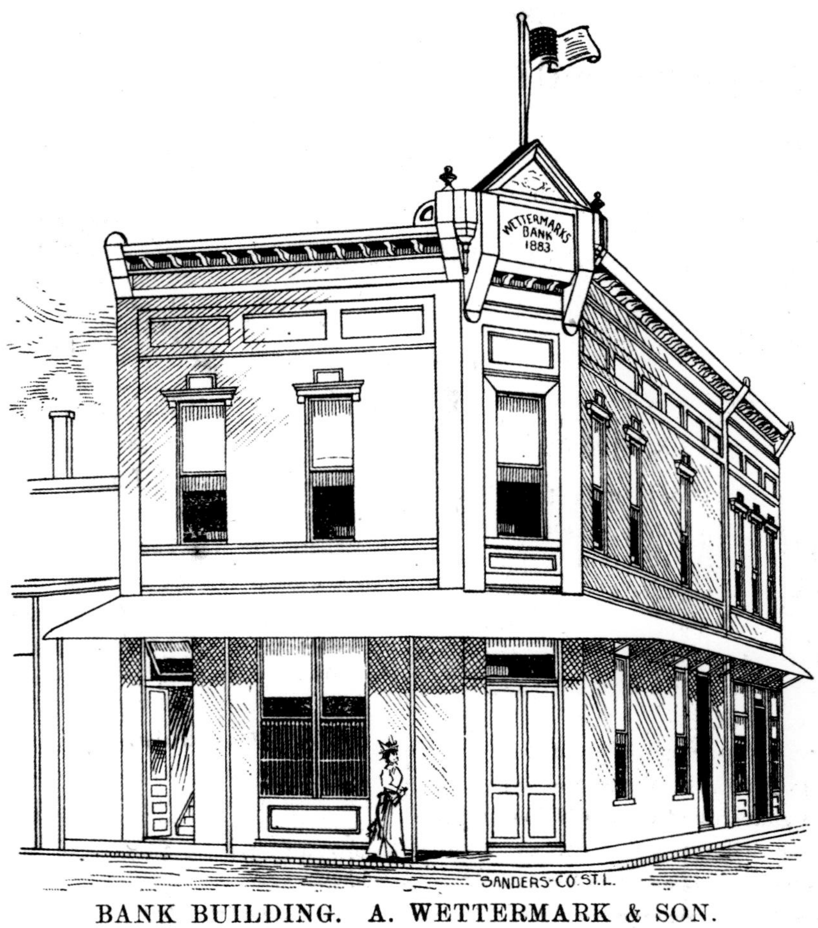

The Wettermark Bank Building (1896)

Rulfs undertook the design and construction of the Wettermark Bank Building in 1896. As mentioned, the replacement of the wooden buildings with brick and mortar on the west side of the Square developed from the center outward: the Mayer and Schmidt Building (1885) started the transformation, which continued with the buildings immediately to the south in 1890. On March 31,1896, the A. Wettermark & Son Bank purchased the north corner of block 13 at the intersection of Main. The Wettermarks paid an eyebrow-raising price of $2,500 and announced their intention to build a new building.[55] The bank, a private company based in Henderson, Texas, was the oldest bank in town dating to 1883; their first building had been on the corner of Main and North Street across from the present-day County Courthouse. Rulfs frequently shared what he was doing with the mappers from the Sanborn Map Company. The 1896 Sanborn Map clearly established the date of the bank building; on the map it was labeled as "being built."[56] Benjamin S. Wettermark, the son of the founder and the principal in charge of the Nacogdoches branch of the family bank, was one of the most prominent leaders in Nacogdoches at the time. Wettermark invested in most of the partnerships in town, sat on many company boards, and took a leading role in sponsoring most major infrastructure improvements. As the nineteenth century ended and the twentieth century began,

FIGURE 3.21. (Left) Drawing, Wettermark Bank (1896)
Nacogdoches Chronicle, September 30, 1897. Courtesy of ETRC.

FIGURE 3.22. (Below) The Wettermark Bank, ca. 1900.
Courtesy of David Alford.

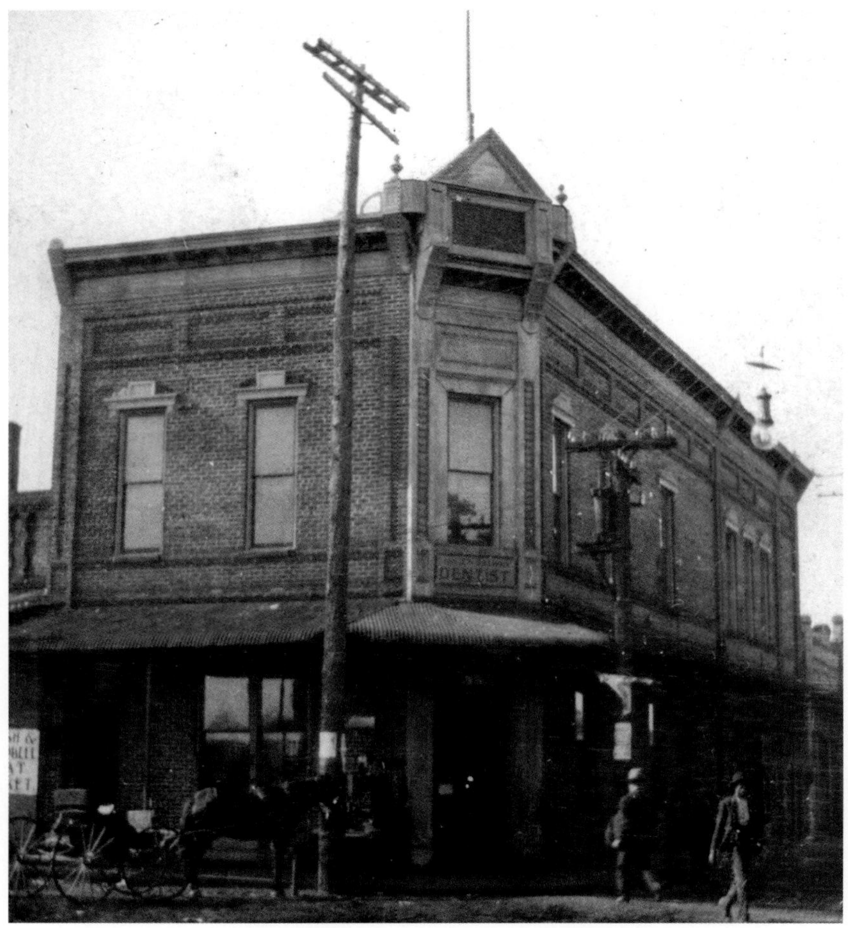

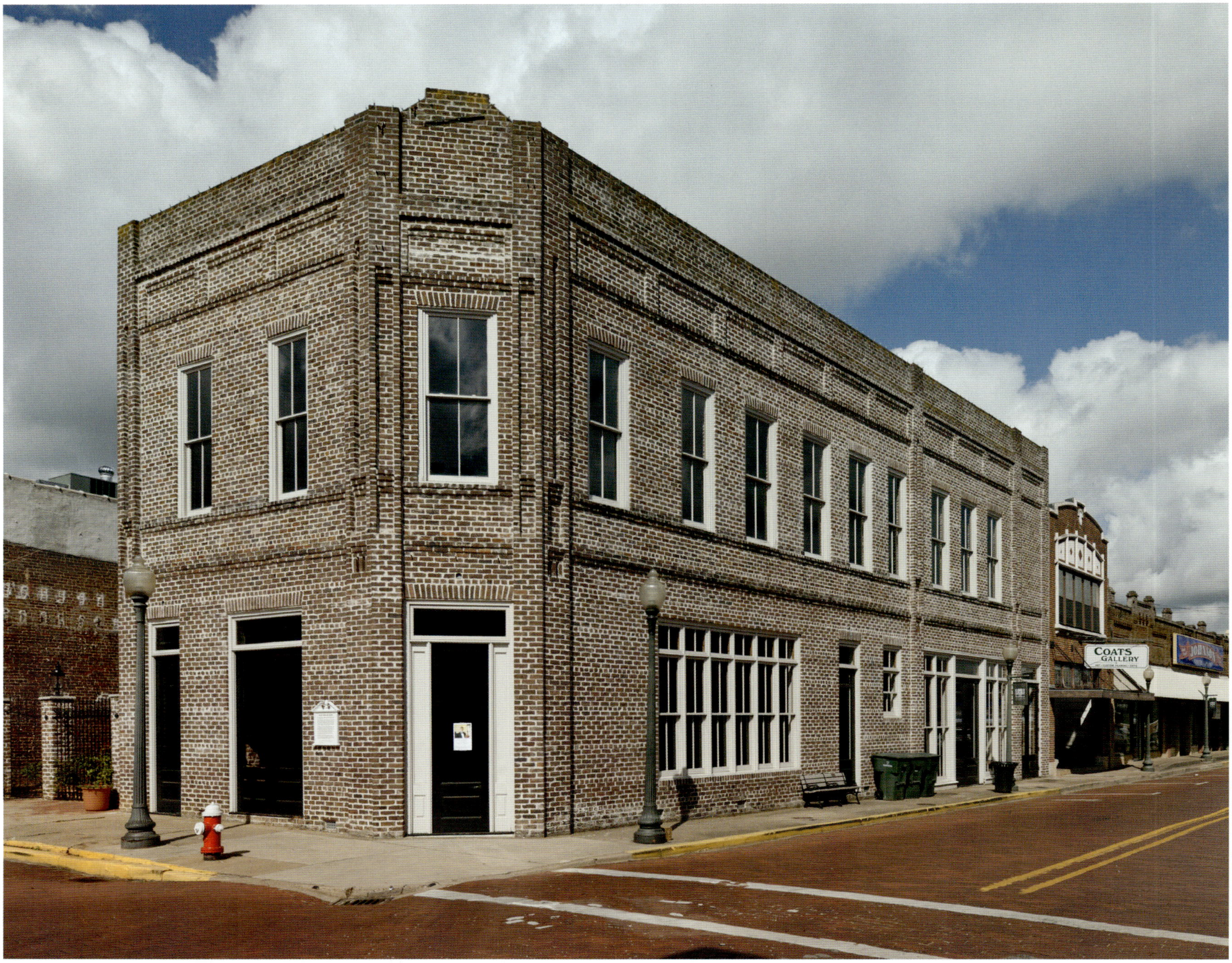

Figure 3.23. Wettermark Bank Building in 2011.

Ben Wettermark became the Mayor of Nacogdoches and would move into a large residence on North Street designed for him by D. Rulfs. (See Chapter IV.)

The Wettermark Bank structure still stands today on its original site. Shortly after completion, the *Henderson Times* described it as "an imposing bank in a magnificent two-story edifice."[57] Fortunately, Haltom wanted to feature the building in his 1897 special edition of the Chronicle. A drawing by the Sanders Company of Saint Louis, when placed by early pictures of the bank, give a very good representation of the original building. Some of the exterior ornamentations have disappeared over the years, such as the elaborate cornices, the bank-signage and flagpole over the doorway, and the awnings. On the other hand, much of the original façade still remains: elaborate brickwork, the inset panels, and the two-story pilasters on either side of the main chamfered doorway, the banding between floors, and an impressive façade along Main Street. Later occupants of the building include: another bank (Stone Fort National Bank opened in the building), pool halls, clothing, barbershops, cobblers, Western Union, and Pool-Perkins Pharmacy (a long-term tenant). In the 1990s, Reese Andrews purchased the building and undertook to restore the structure with assistance from the Nacogdoches Landmark Restoration Fund.[58]

The Banita Hotel (1896)

In 1895, when the Bullen Hotel burned to the ground, the accommodations for high and mid-level travelers in Nacogdoches suffered a serious blow. The construction of the Bullen and the Opera House earlier in 1888-89 had replaced two hostelries, the Mitchell and Hyde House. Elsewhere in the downtown, there were older converted residences being used as hotels, such as the Bullock Hotel and the venerable Hart Hotel. These establishments were less-than-modern. The gap in the east end of the town would take years to fill. In 1895, Rulfs received a commission to design a new hotel near the railway station. The request came from Norvell Green Wade, a wealthy farmer from the Liberty Community.[59] The architect's construction agenda in 1895-96, which included several large houses such as the Harris and Jones residences, did not permit him to build the hotel; he simply drew the plans. One of the Sanders Company (Saint Louis) photo-engraving sketches of the Banita appeared in the 1897 *Nacogdoches Chronicle* with the following caption: "N. G. Wade, Proprietor, D. Rulfs, Architect, Ireson Brothers, Builders.[60]

Giles Haltom, in his 1906 Special Edition of the *Daily Sentinel*, recycled the drawing and the descriptions of his brother, albeit he misdates the structure by five years by calling it fifteen years old:

> Nacogdoches is particularly fortunate in possessing excellent hotel facilities and they have done a great deal toward making the town popular with the traveling public and are a matter of pride to the citizenship of the city. The Banita Hotel, a photo-engraving of which is given in this edition, is one of the large hostelries in East Texas and has afforded accommodations to the traveling public for the past fifteen [sic] years, which is sufficient evidence of its popularity.
>
> The Banita is a two-story structure located on the beautiful Banita creek, from which it derives its name. It contains all modern improvements, is nicely furnished throughout, and in every respect is a modern up-to-date hotel that would do credit to a town of double the population of Nacogdoches. The building contains forty large airy rooms, a large spacious dining room and lobby. The menu is of the highest order, well prepared and wholesome. Polite attendants are maintained in all departments and the service in every respect is all that could be desired.[61]

The two-story Banita Hotel, described aptly in one source, as "similar to resort hotels on the East Coast," had thirty-two rooms originally. In 1901, Rulfs designed, and his brother William Henry Rulfs built, a ten-room addition to the east. The addition had long galleries on two levels and "a number of conveniences and comforts to be found in up-to-date hotels."[62]

In an interview in December of 1980, Wade's grandson R. W. McKinney said the rooms were furnished with marble top stands with a water pitcher, and had wood stoves for heat.[63] McKinney said the hotel was first painted "brown with white trim;" later accounts cite other colors. The front corner section housed the office, the lobby, and living quarters for the proprietor. There was also a huge attic. The west wing along Banita Creek housed the kitchen, and behind the kitchen there was a large woodpile. Because of the heat of the kitchen, the rooms above it were used for storage. For 'drummers' (salesmen), the hotel supplied rented showrooms on the Square to show their wares. Both rooms and meals cost 50 cents each.

Ownership of the Banita stayed in the Wade family after the death of Wade himself, at first under the management of Mrs. Wade and, later, under the ownership of her son-in-law John Richard McKinney (1876-1951).[64] Because Mrs. Wade was an excellent cook, the hotel was a popular "gathering place for locals" during the Wade-McKinney management.[65] Zeno Cox, another son-in-law and third owner of the hotel, turned the hotel in 1920 into the East and West Banita Apartments. Cox called on Rulfs to provide him with direction. Although the plans by Rulfs remain missing, the detailed specifications drawn up by the architect still exist. They show how thorough Rulfs was in assessing the needs of the move and how frugal he was in calling for a reuse of all available doors, windows, bricks, and timber from the old building in the new. Rulfs specified additional construction and changes when necessary to give strength or to update the look of the buildings.[66] In 1926 a fire, in which two people were killed, destroyed the west apartments. The old east wing from 1901, remodeled in 1920, still survives at 210 West Pillar as the Ford Photography Studio.[67]

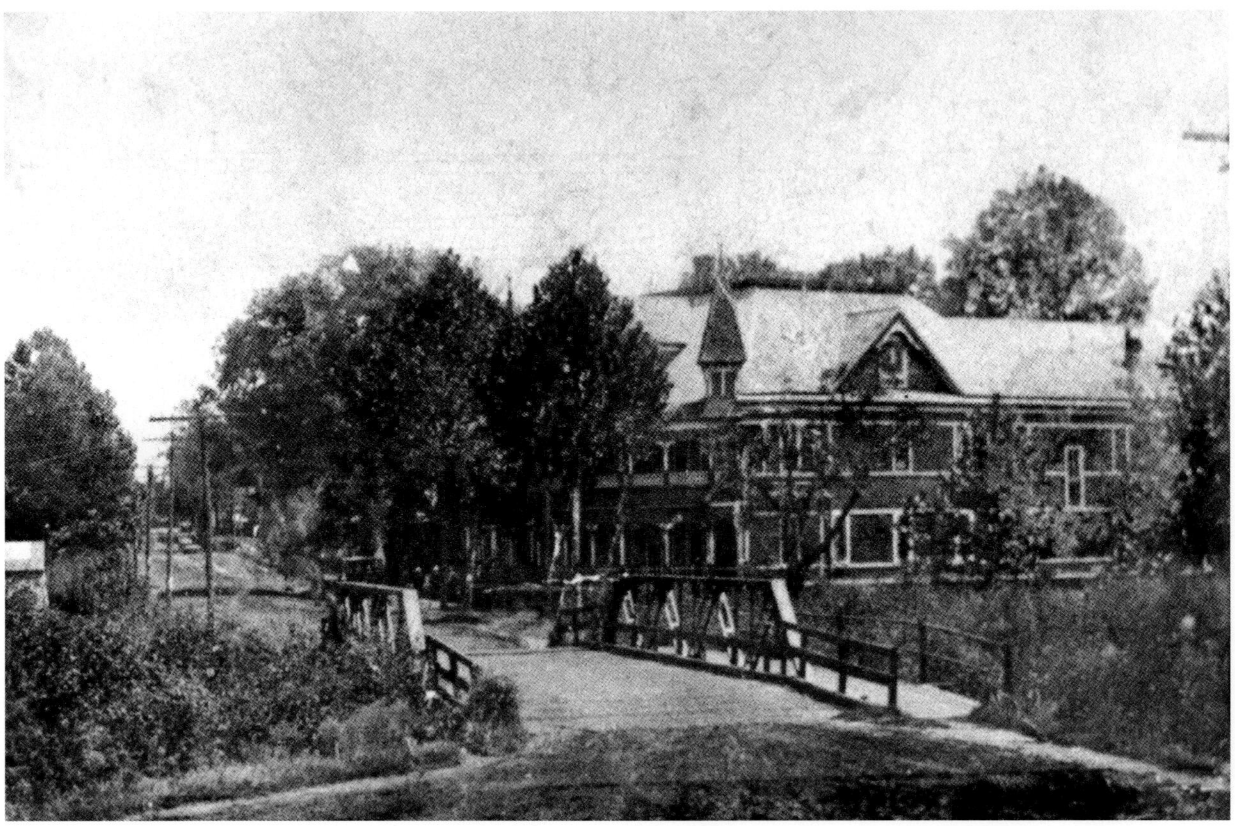

FIGURE 3.24. Banita Hotel from across Banita Creek. *Courtesy of ETRC.*

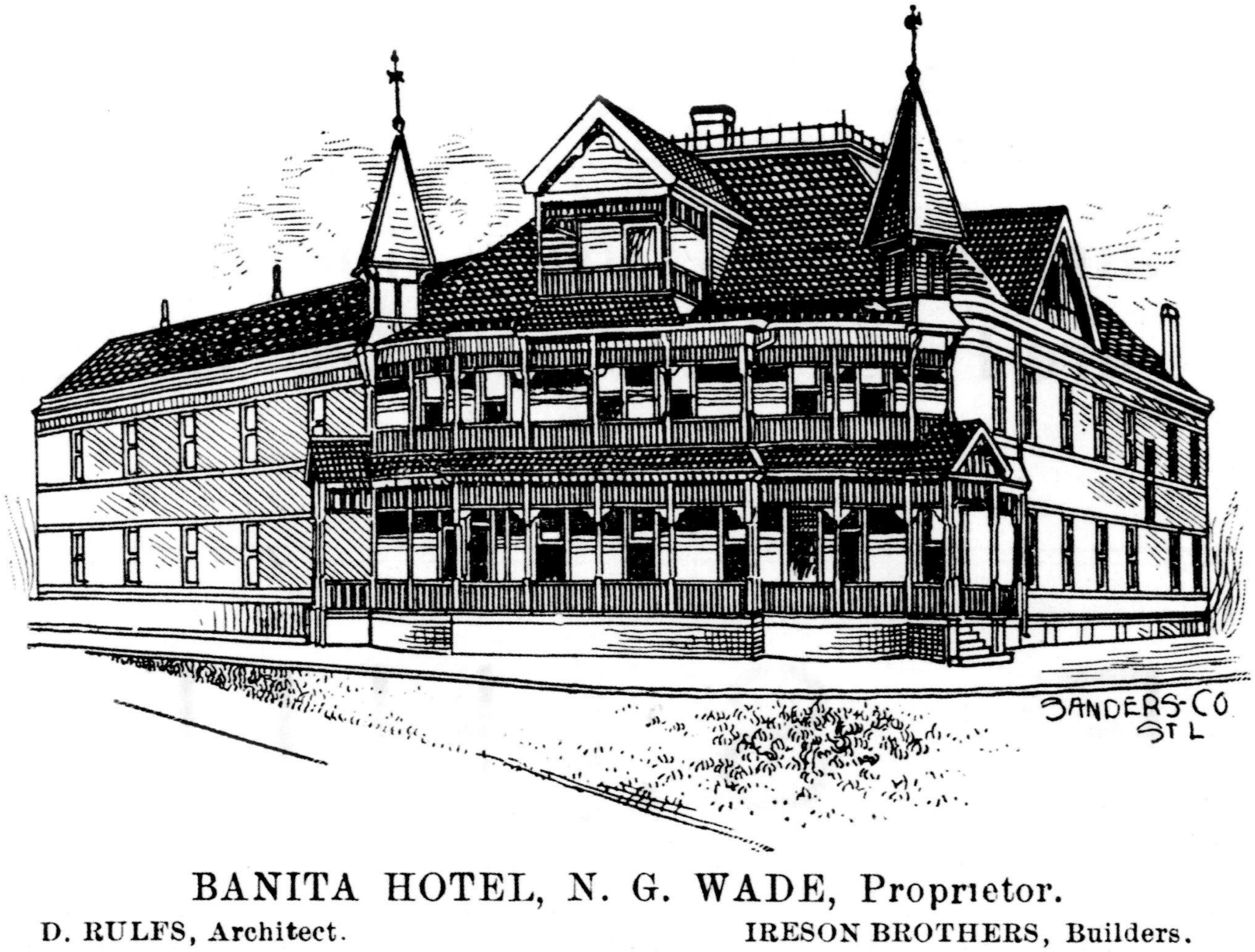

FIGURE 3.25 and 3.26. (Left) A Line Drawing of the Banita Hotel. (Below) The Photograph of the Banita in 1897.

The drawing by the Sanders Company of St. Louis appeared in the Nacogdoches Chronicle, *September 30, 1897. Both the newspaper and the photograph are in the East Texas Research Center and used by their permission.*

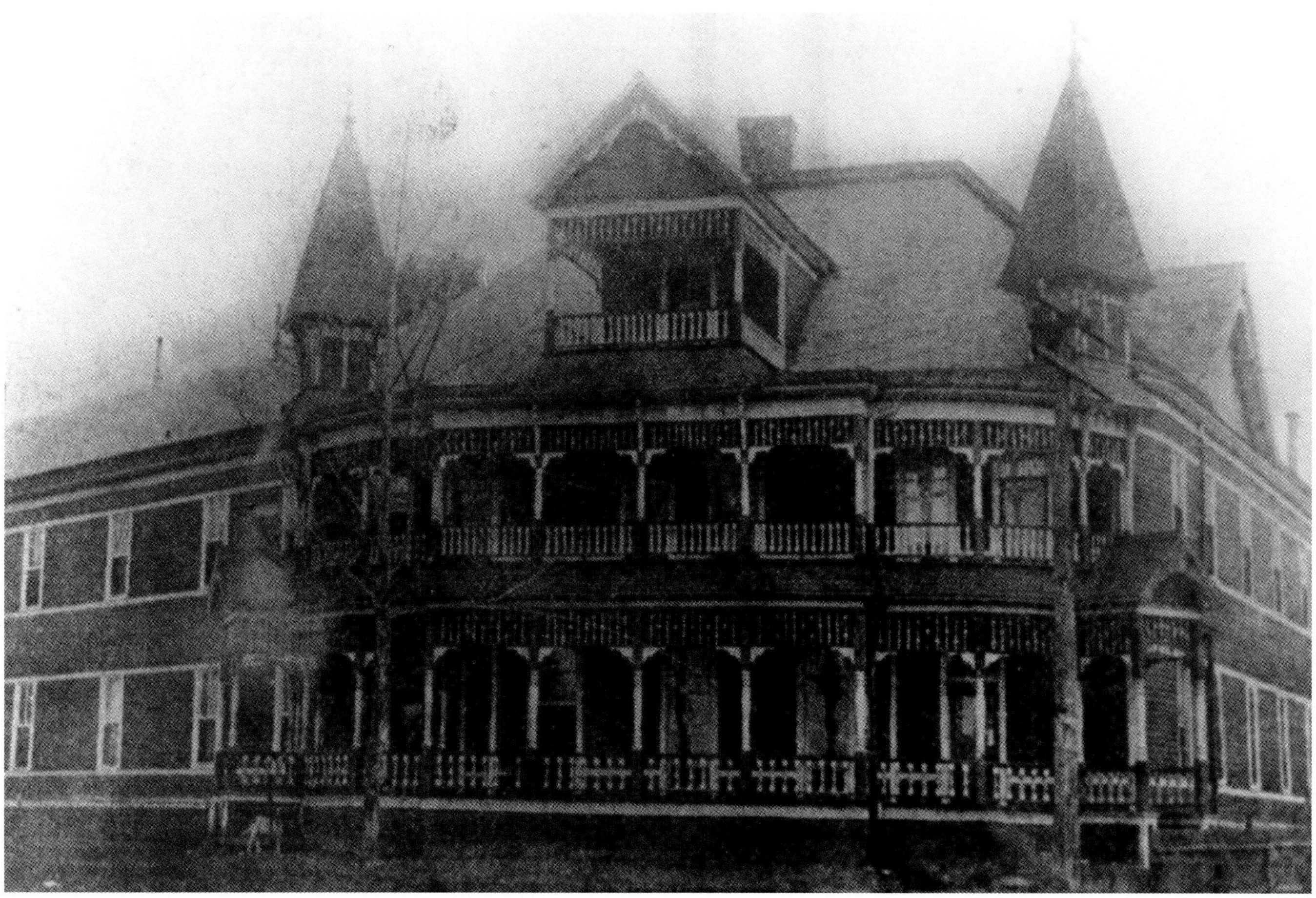

The George Ingraham Building (1897)

The building at 210 East Pilar on the south side of the Square, built after the 1896 Sanborn Map was drawn, was the property of County Judge George F. Ingraham (1842-1920). Ingraham purchased the property in 1896 and erected the building about 1897. At the time, the 1887 County Court House stood next door to the west. Ingraham used the second story as his law office and leased the first floor to commercial concerns. Novell G. Bright purchased the building in 1917 and ran a grocery and feed store there until 1937.[68] Ingraham's grandson, lawyer and local historian F. I. Tucker, practiced law in the building until his death in 1973. Charles Bright, the present owner, lived in the building as a child. In his restoration of the building, Bright restored the porch for the second story that appeared in the period photographs.[69]

At the time the Nacogdoches County Historical Commission applied for Recorded Texas Historic Landmark status for the Ingraham Building in the late 1890s, nothing was stated about who the architect of the building might be.[70] At the time, the author had not done research on the houses done by Rulfs on North Street, or discovered other similar buildings in the downtown area with the same architectural features (because they were gone). The interconnected contacts between Rulfs and Ingraham were strong, as were those with the other families, such as the E. A. Blounts or the F. H. Tuckers. Rulfs built houses and buildings for almost all of Blount's associates in Commercial Bank, such as Schmidt, Tucker, Ingraham, Pearson, and Stripling. While no specific document has yet been found to prove Rulfs did the Ingraham Building, the author is certain that Rulfs designed the building. At the time it was built, Rulfs was remodeling the Ingraham home on North Street, as discussed in Chapter IV. Rulfs also built several buildings of similar commercial design (with second story porches) in the downtown area: the Tucker-Hardeman Building and the H. A. Huntley Buildings on East Main (1898, both destroyed by fire in 1903), the E. D. Williams Building (1901), the B. F. Hardeman Building (1904), and the very prominent E. A. Blount Buildings on the north side of the square (built 1901, destroyed by fire in 1906). Rulfs worked with Ingraham on the buildings of the First Methodist Church (1887 and 1909-10), on Ingraham's daughter's home on Mound Street (she married F. H. Tucker), and on the design of the Masonic Lodge quarters in the Fritz Hoya Building (1900) on the Square.

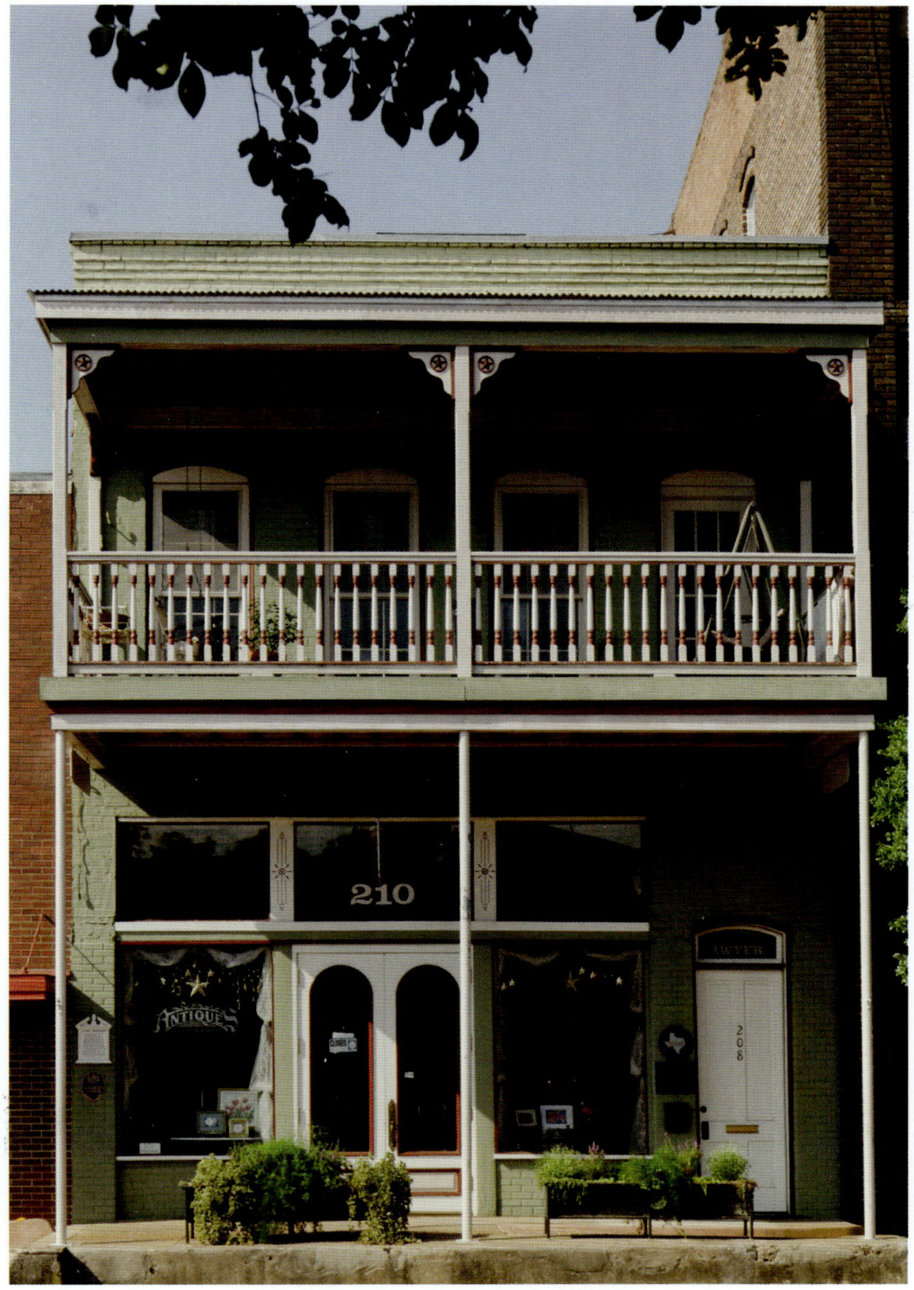

FIGURE 3.28. George Ingraham Office Building (1897).

The Ingraham Office Building is a Recorded Texas Historic Landmark. At the time the structure received this designation, it was not known for sure whether Rulfs had designed the building or not. Since then, research on houses on North Street has confirmed the design done by Rulfs for the Ingraham House at the time of this building on the Square. The design is also very similar to another building Rulfs designed for E. A. Blount on the north side of the Square. With these findings, the author can say with certainty that the architect also designed this building. A later chapter discusses Ingraham's house and the Blount Building in detail.

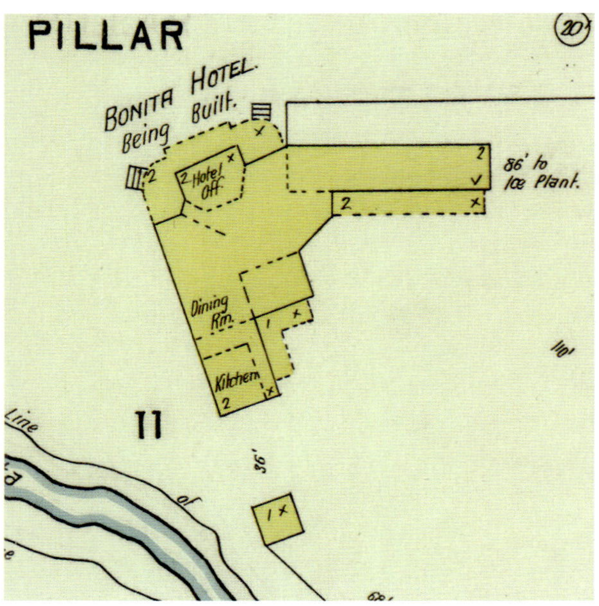

FIGURE 3.27. Banita Hotel. Sanborn Map, 1896.

The map of 1896 shows the Banita Hotel "Being Built." The kitchen and dining room, indicated along the building's west side, are by Banita Creek. Sanborn Maps, UT, Nacogdoches, 1896.

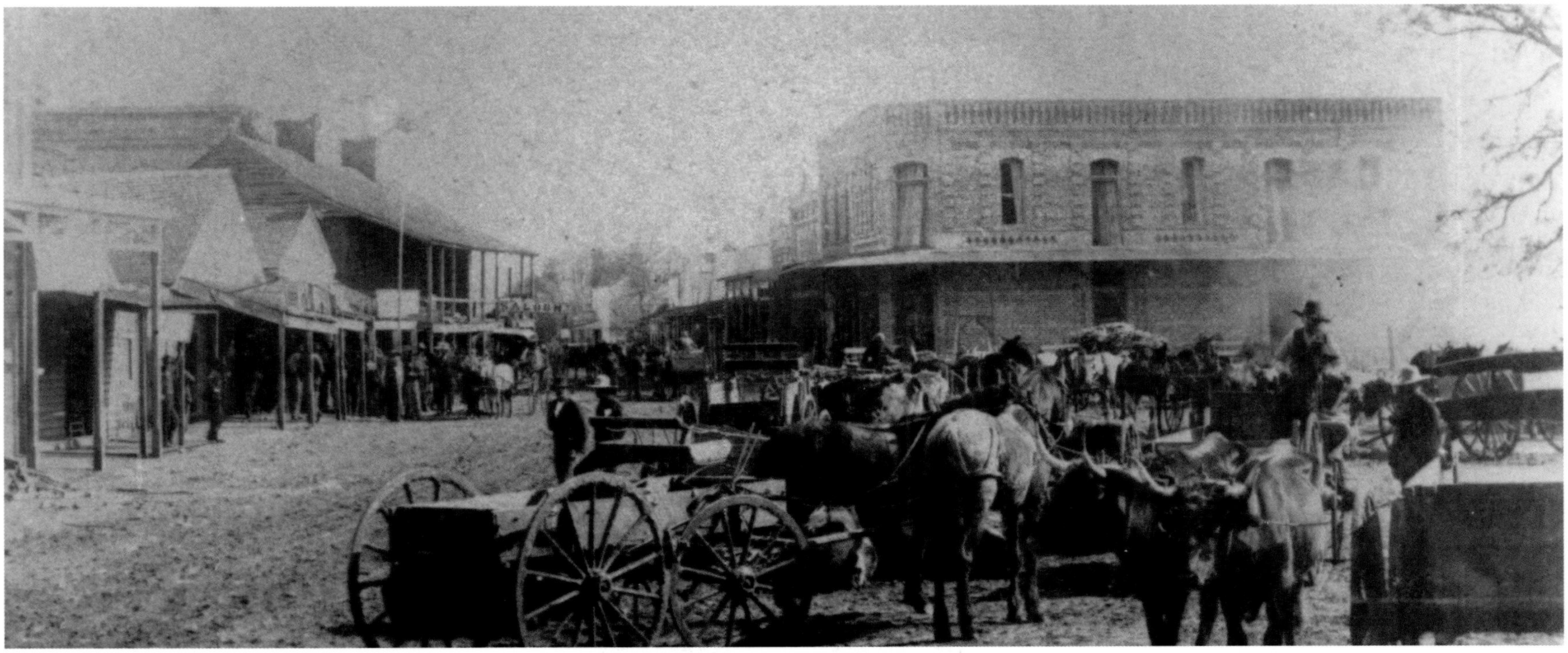

FIGURE 3.29. Main Street at the Square, Looking East. ca. 1899. *Courtesy of ETRC.*

Judgments and Perspectives

The dramatic changes in the Nacogdoches townscape between 1880 and 1900, as it went from wood to bricks, placed Nacogdoches foursquare in line with broad national trends. To allow the reader to sample how differently contemporaries looked upon this transformation process, the opinions of several writers might prove enlightening.

In 1895, a brief thirty-two page promotional pamphlet appeared in Nacogdoches: *City of Nacogdoches, Nacogdoches County*. No author signed the work, but because Spradley & Hutt Printers published the pamphlet, it is reasonable to assume that Sheriff A. J. Spradley, or someone commissioned by him, wrote the piece. Spradley in the mid-1890s published a weekly newspaper entitled the *Plaindealer*. The sponsors of the pamphlet were the Mayer & Schmidt Company (always eager to support booster publications) and the Law Offices of George Ingraham and W. G. Ratcliff. (Not to be outdone, Spradley's rival, R. W. Haltom, quickly responded by reprinting his own 1880 *History*.) The 1895 pamphlet listed the assets for the community: a population of about 3,000, a major railroad line with another on the way, a modern courthouse, a substantial jail, many churches, prosperous businesses, and other attractions. Placing the recent changes into perspective, the pamphlet concluded that Nacogdoches was a near-perfect mixture of old and new: "The principal object of interest to the visitor or stranger in the town of Nacogdoches is the famous "Old Stone Fort." . . . . The old and the new are here combined in unique contrast and proportion, and the combination makes a town so rare and genial that no observant visitor can fail to mark it and admire it." The writer concludes that the town had a proud past and a bight future. "With the possible exception of San Antonio, Nacogdoches is—from the romantic and historical point of view—the most interesting city in Texas."[71]

In dramatic contrast to the above view, another *unknown author*—a traveler who published his thoughts on Nacogdoches in the *New York Sun* in 1896—reached radically different conclusions. While, for the most part, the author lifted observations from Haltom's 1880 *History*, he added a few modern twists and reached, more or less, the same conclusions Haltom had sixteen years earlier. The writer's statement that Nacogdoches had "ceased to occupy an important place among the towns of the state or to exercise the slightest influence upon its politics" and that it was "a sleepy old-century town"—echoed Haltom's earlier work exactly. But, the travel-writer's conclusion that sixteen years later Nacogdoches was still little more than a quaint anachronism, stands as interesting testimony to how conclusions reached in one era seem so radical when repeated in another era: "If anything it is sleepier and rustier now than it ever was." Rugged and uneven streets, pioneer houses "tumbling about the ears of their occupants," and "immigrants continue to pass it by."

The visitor's observation that the courthouse "looks like a ruin," seems oddly out of place when directed at Heiner's 1887 courthouse. The writer probably lifted this comment from Haltom's verdict on the 1856 courthouse. The central focus of the derogatory statements, however, fell not on the courthouse but on the north side of the Square:

> But the sorriest looking place in town is an old stone building facing the public square, and commonly known as the 'old stone fort.' Its walls are rough and yellow with age and they would probably have fallen down long ago were it not for their remarkable solidity. Its builders evidently put the walls there to stay, for they are about thirteen feet thick. The stone were put together without much regard for the rules of masonry, but they were welded solidly with mortar. Nothing less than a cannonade could batter them down. When this old fort was built there is no means of determining, but there are various traditions concerning its origin and history.[72]

The principal object of interest to the visitor or stranger in the town of Nacogdoches is the famous 'Old Stone Fort.' **Plaindealer, 1895**

. . . the sorriest looking place in town is an old stone building facing the public square. **New York Sun, 1896**

City of Nacogdoches, Nacogdoches County **(Nacogdoches: Spradley & Hutt Printers, 1895).**

The principal object of interest to the visitor or stranger in the town of Nacogdoches is the famous "Old Stone Fort." This structure is about sixty feet in length, twenty feet high and twenty feet in width, as to a certainty, the exact date at which the Stone Fort was built, is conjecture....

The old and the new are here combined in unique contrast and proportion, and the combination makes a town so rare and genial that no observant visitor can fail to mark it and admire it. But it is not with old Nacogdoches as the Nacogdoches is to day the brisk modern business city, proud of her historic past, and certain of her bright and prosperous future....

The business section of the city is mostly around the square, and on Main street, east and west. The business section is, for the most part, built up with handsome brick blocks of modern design, and all businesses practiced in modern towns, are represented here and there, and several large jobbing houses which draw trade from a number of surrounding counties. In addition there is a steam gin, an iron foundry, grist mill, two soda water factories, an ice factory and the usual minor industrial works, found in the smaller cities....

With the possible exception of San Antonio, Nacogdoches is—from the romantic and historical point of view—the most interesting city in Texas.

"In Old Nacogdoches," ***Houston Daily Post*****, Sunday, December 13, 1896, reprint from the** ***New York Sun*****, 1896.**

When the time comes to write the history of Texas, for Texas has a history of singular interest, the historian will find abundant material in the quaint old town of Nacogdoches. Little is heard today about old Nacogdoches. The tide of immigration has swept over it to the prairie lands, to the west and southwest. Although Nacogdoches is said to be the oldest town in the state, even older than the ancient mission town of San Antonio, it has long since ceased to occupy an important place among the towns of the State or to exercise the slightest influence upon its politics. . . .

Nacogdoches ...[once] the most important trading post west of New Orleans, gradually lost is prestige and became what it is now –a sleepy old country town. If anything it is sleepier and rustier now than it ever was ....

The streets are rugged and uneven, the old log houses built by the pioneers are tumbling about the ears of their occupants, and the logs are rotting away. Even the old brick court house, which was built not more than fifty years ago, looks like a ruin.

But the sorriest looking place in town is an old stone building facing the public square, and commonly known as the "old stone fort." Its walls are rough and yellow with age and they would probably have fallen down long ago were it not for their remarkable solidity. Its builders evidently put the walls there to stay, for they are about thirteen feet thick. The stones were put together without much regard for the rules of masonry, but they were welded solidly with mortar. Nothing less than a cannonade could batter them down. When this old fort was built there is no means of determining, but there are various traditions concerning its origin and history."[69]

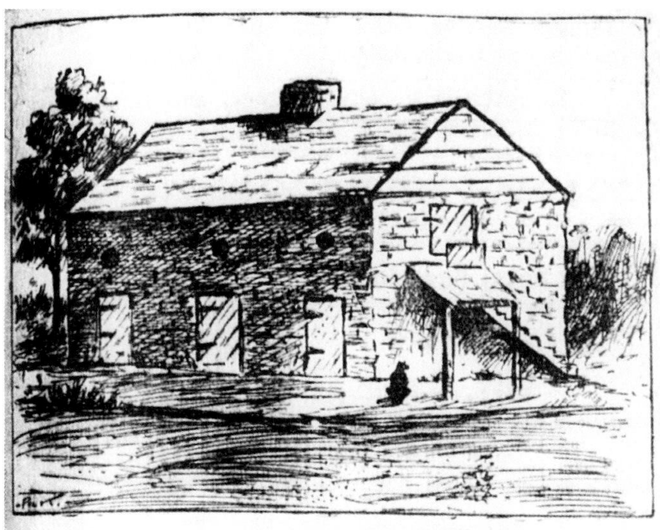

OLD STONE FORT AT NACOGDOCHES.

FIGURE 3.30. Drawing, *Houston Daily Post,* June 2, 1901.

This totally unrealistic drawing of the Old Stone Fort appeared in the Houston Daily Post *as an illustration to accompany one of the articles dealing with the Nacogdoches landmark. This drawing alone would have irritated local Nacogdoches boosters.*

Why, one might ask, is it relevant to cite the outdated opinions expressed in an obscure article in a New York newspaper? It could easily be ignored had the *Houston Daily Post*, which arrived in Nacogdoches regularly the same or next day after being published, not reprinted the *Sun* article in their Sunday edition of December 13, 1896. An obscure New York publication might be over-looked, but the restatement of these criticisms in the leading regional newspaper of Texas caused a furor in Nacogdoches. Townspeople immediately began to besiege the *Post* with letters of protest. One respondent, who gave only his initials as "R. D. C.," accused the travel writer of being either drunk or of confusing Nacogdoches with some other town: "Our streets are as good as any similar town. We have two or three old houses in the town that are occupied. Our courthouse is a good, well-arranged court house and not very old. Nacogdoches has more new residences and storehouses than any town in the State to its population. Within the last five years it can boast of more than $100,000 worth of house building and repairing, all of home capital." The rebuff continued by pointing out that "North street alone is one mile long and thickly settled with mostly new houses," that the population was near 2,000, that the city had electric lights, educational facilities, and "the largest wagon cotton market in the world to its population."[73]

Edward A. Blount, particularly incensed at the charge that the town looked "rustier" than ever, wrote to the *Post*:

> Please let your readers know that it is some other Nacogdoches you speak of, and not our bright growing town, proud of her history, proud of her former illustrious citizens, occupying the prettiest location in East Texas, with two banks, an ice factory, electric lights, bottling works and annual cotton receipts of from 14,000 to 20,000. E. A. Blount."[74]

Haltom's Response: A Special Edition of the Nacogdoches Chronicle

The article in the *Houston Daily Post* immediately provoked R. W. Haltom into compiling a defense for Nacogdoches. His rebuttal came in the form of a special edition of the *Nacogdoches Chronicle* touting the accomplishments of the town. It took many months to research and assemble. The edition did not appear until September 30, 1897. Haltom not only collected information on the leading companies and personalities of the town, but he also had to send off all of the pictures he wanted to use to the Sanders Engraving Company in St. Louis to turn the images into drawings. (See the caption for Figure 3.2) The considerable expense of this edition shows how important he thought the edition was to combat the critics who said Nacogdoches was behind the times. Possibly his first, special editions such as this one become hallmarks of the Haltom's successor newspaper, the *Daily Sentinel*.[75]

The 1897 *Nacogdoches Chronicle Special Edition* contained articles on history, on the array of modern facilities in town, and on leading merchants and houses of business. Pertinent for the present work, the centerpiece of the edition was an article reviewing the first seventeen years of the accomplishments of architect Diedrich Rulfs. There would be other reviews in coming years; in fact, whenever the town wanted to illustrate its transformation in the modern period, it turned to the work of this German immigrant. Haltom's tribute to Rulfs on this occasion, in which he carefully outlined the way D. Rulfs had changed Nacogdoches in the late nineteenth century, is quite remarkable.[76] (See Inset Opposite: "D. Rulfs. Architect, Builder, Contractor.")

There are several examples to indicate that the *Houston Daily Post* regretted having embarrassed Nacogdoches in the way it did. As if to re-emphasize Haltom's judgment and as a way to introduce the Twentieth Century, on May 3, 1899, the *Post* informatively commented on the building boom in Nacogdoches and named those involved:

> NEW BUILDINGS FOR NACOGDOCHES.
>
> Stores, Residences, and a Fine Church Contracted For.
>
> Nacogdoches, Texas. May 1. Contracts for five brick stores, four one-story buildings and one two-story were let today to Mr. H. L. Austin and Mr. William Rulf[s], D. Rulf[s] architect.
>
> The contract for the new Baptist church was let to Mr. D. Rulf[s], he agreeing to erect same for the sum of $6000. The foundation is being laid on the lot where the old church stood. The building will be of frame work and the plans show an elegant church.[77]

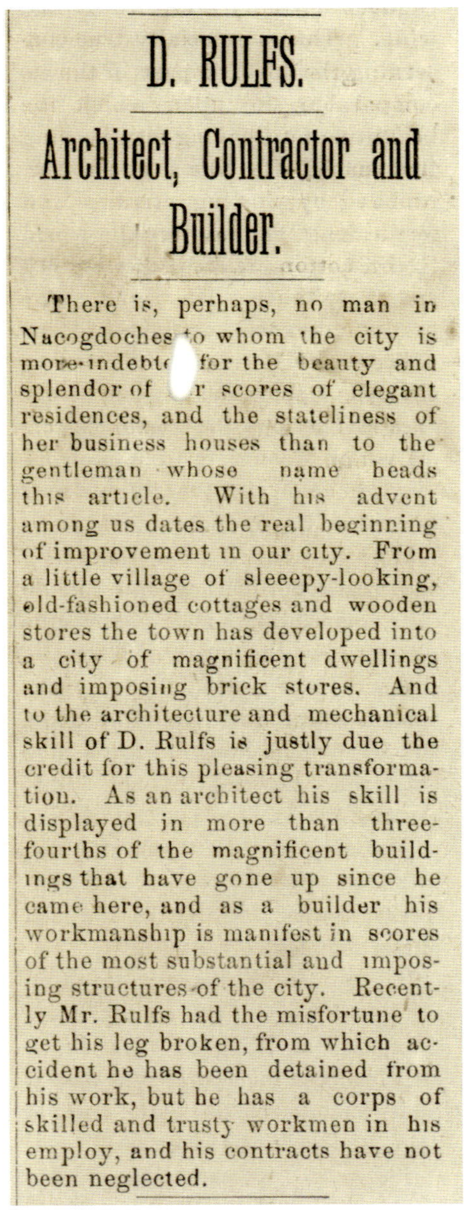

D. RULFS.

Architect, Contractor and Builder.

There is, perhaps, no man in Nacogdoches to whom the city is more indebt[illegible] for the beauty and splendor of [illegible]r scores of elegant residences, and the stateliness of her business houses than to the gentleman whose name heads this article. With his advent among us dates the real beginning of improvement in our city. From a little village of sleeepy-looking, old-fashioned cottages and wooden stores the town has developed into a city of magnificent dwellings and imposing brick stores. And to the architecture and mechanical skill of D. Rulfs is justly due the credit for this pleasing transformation. As an architect his skill is displayed in more than three-fourths of the magnificent buildings that have gone up since he came here, and as a builder his workmanship is manifest in scores of the most substantial and imposing structures of the city. Recently Mr. Rulfs had the misfortune to get his leg broken, from which accident he has been detained from his work, but he has a corps of skilled and trusty workmen in his employ, and his contracts have not been neglected.

FIGURE 3.31. Column, *Nacogdoches Chronicle,* September 30, 1897.

In initial research on Rulfs, the author found this column and had the pleasure of calling it to the attention of Anna Kathryn Holbrook, granddaughter of D. Rulfs. She published it in the volume, Nacogdoches County Families, *edited by Carolyn Ericson.*

Newspaper courtesy of ETRC.

D. RULFS.

ARCHITECT, BUILDER, AND CONTRACTOR.

There is, perhaps, no man in Nacogdoches to whom the city is more indebted for the beauty and splendor of her scores of elegant residences, and the stateliness of her business houses than to the gentleman whose name heads this article. With his advent among us dates the real beginning of improvements in our city. From a little village of sleepy looking, old-fashioned cottages and wooden stores the town has developed into a city of magnificent dwellings and imposing brick stores. And to the architecture and mechanical skill of D. Rulfs is justly due the credit for this pleasing transformation. As an architect his skill is displayed in more than three fourths of the magnificent buildings that have gone up since he came here, and as a builder his workmanship is manifest in scores of the most substantial and imposing structures of the city. Recently Mr. Rulfs had the misfortune to get his leg broken, from which accident he has been detained from his work, but he has a corps of skilled and trusty workmen in his employ, and his contracts have not been neglected. [*Nacogdoches Chronicle,* September 30, 1897.]

With his advent among us dates the real beginning of improvements in our city.

FIGURE 3.32. The Wettermark Bank and the Cox Building, 2012.

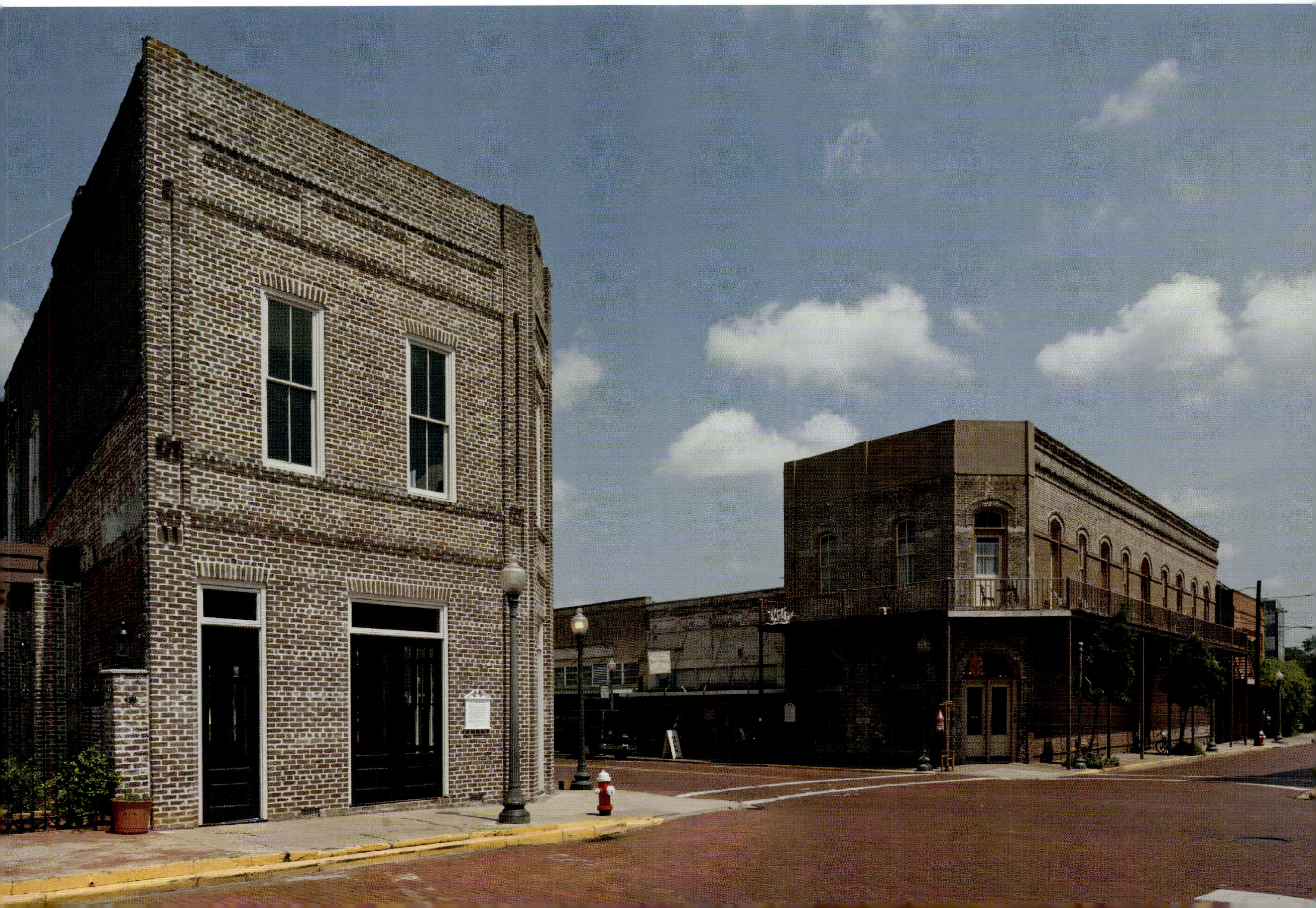

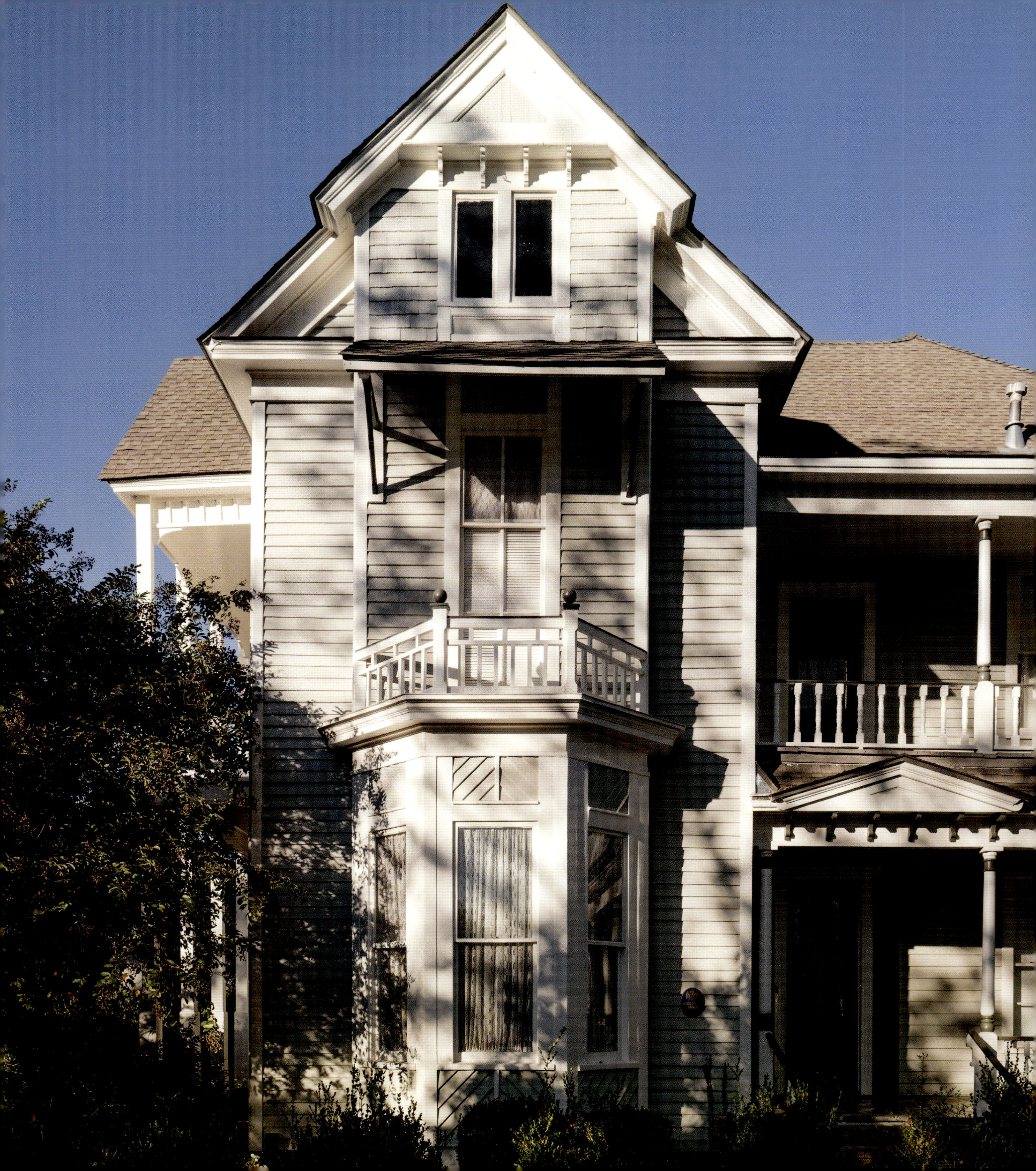

CHAPTER IV

Redefining Domestic Contexts

Downtown and North Street: Phase I

"The residence portion has been greatly improved by the recent erection of some forty structures from latest designs." (*Galveston Daily News,* 1890.)

"From a sleepy village of cottages, etc. . . the town has developed into a city of magnificent dwellings .... And to the architecture and mechanical skill of D. Rulfs is justly due the credit for this pleasing transformation." (Richard Haltom, *Nacogdoches Chronicle,* 1897)

Diedrich Rulfs came to the United States to help in the design and development of Nacogdoches as it responded to the challenges surrounding the anticipated arrival of the railroad. In explaining the development of the town architecturally, however, the commercial buildings did not exist in a vacuum. The domestic contexts of these business owners—their houses, neighbors, and neighborhoods—were as dynamic and interconnected as their commercial relationships. D. Rulfs had as much impact on the designing of modern Nacogdoches in its domestic contexts as he did on the design of the commercial district. Nevertheless, having said this, the success of his *career* in the 1880s rested first and foremost on his commercial projects. He did not cross the Atlantic to build domestic housing. In sharp contrast, the architect's *reputation today* rests primarily on his exceptional legacy of residential homes. While many of Rulfs's commercial structures still exist, unfortunately they are visually concealed behind modern façades and sometimes distorted by awkward makeovers. On the other hand, a surprisingly large number of his domestic structures continue to be part of our visible heritage—many relatively unchanged. Although some are at risk today (sometimes by individuals trying to 'save' them), some of his finest houses still stand on their original sites and are being enjoyed as they were at the time of their creation.

FIGURE 4.1. (Opposite) The Edwards House (1889).
The Minnie Arnold Edwards House, built on Main Street, now sits along Lanana Street, on the back of its original lot. The Main Street footage sold for commercial uses.

Surveys of Nacogdoches architecture, such as those done by the Nacogdoches and the Texas Historical Commissions over the years,[1] are generally organized geographically rather than chronologically. Their objective, to freeze a moment in time for preservation purposes, differs from this study. While referencing these studies, it would distort a discussion of Rulfs's achievements to discuss only buildings that can be photographed today. Sadly, some of his more creative and influential domestic structures are now gone, especially on the most prestigious residential street during the architect's lifetime—North Street.

The National Register of Historic Places (hereafter cited, National Register) identifies five districts in Nacogdoches. In some cases these designations pivot around historic landmark structures that predate Rulfs's arrival in town, such as the Adolphus Sterne House or the Old Nacogdoches University. Briefly, here are districts designated by the National Register in Nacogdoches:

1. *The Sterne-Hoya Historic District*—"a significant collection of domestic buildings erected from the 1830s to the 1910s."

2. *The Downtown Historic District*—"the core of its historic commercial quarter and a portion of its former industrial sector."

3. *Washington Square Historic District*—"one of the most affluent and prestigious neighborhoods in the city. Many of the houses are among the grandest in Nacogdoches."

4. *Zion Hill Historic District* –"a cohesive grouping of modestly detailed domestic buildings.... [whose] focal point of the district is Zion Hill Baptist Church, a monumental institutional building with Gothic Revival stylistic features erected in 1914."

5. *Virginia Avenue Historic District* [Irion Hill]– "a small collection of domestic buildings, most of which date from the late 19th and early 20th centuries."[2]

City maps of these districts are also available.[3]

The domestic architecture of Rulfs is difficult to divide into chapters. In order to avoid confusion, the references of his domestic architecture will flow within the framework established by the surveys of Nacogdoches; these will be cited in the endnotes. Unfortunately, the major examples of pre-1880 architecture had disappeared by the time the surveys began. The Nacogdoches National Register districts, therefore, exist in large part because of the architectural works of Diedrich Rulfs. Removal of his structures would decimate the districts. The next three chapters follow the architect's work as he transforms the domestic contexts in Nacogdoches in the nineteenth century: first, in the downtown and North Street; then Washington Square; and, finally, Irion and Forbes Hills. As in the previous chapter on commercial building, these next chapters will show what a unique and remarkable affinity developed between Rulfs and Nacogdoches, an affinity for each other that lasted more than four decades and crossed over to younger generations of the same families in the twentieth century.

Domestic Architecture in the 1880s

In the mid-1970s, when first discussing Rulfs, the present author incorrectly linked two facts, and unfortunately others have repeated the mistake. Diedrich Rulfs did come to Nacogdoches "at the invitation of Mr. John Schmidt," but he did not come "in order to design and build the latter's house (now gone) on North Street."[4] When Mary Stewart Duncan, Rulfs's niece, stated that one of her uncle's first domestic structures was a home for John Schmidt, the author jumped to the conclusion she meant Schmidt's big mansion on North Street. The 1892 Schmidt House, the big one discussed below in detail, was the only Schmidt home anyone living at the time could remember. The architect did build one of his first domestic structures for Schmidt, but this modest domestic home (now gone) sat in "Germantown," east of downtown. Rulfs built domestic structures for over a decade before he was able to allow his creativity to soar as in the grand houses of the 1890s.

After further research, the idea that Rulfs came to Nacogdoches to build residential structures for *anyone* now seems absurd. In 1880, Nacogdoches did not have the wealth to support an abundance of residential contracts. A case in point, John Schmidt was not a wealthy man when he arrived in Nacogdoches. He was recruiting leaders who could seize the opportunities offered by the arrival of the railroad. Entrepreneurs such as Schmidt, who were to change the face of Nacogdoches, had to *make* their fortunes before they could lavish money on impressive domestic showplaces. The large, single-family mansions all date to the 1890s, with perhaps one exception, the Edwards House, which really was a remodeling job.

The community Rulfs joined in 1880 was deeply conservative and traditional. Nacogdoches stood untouched by architectural sophistication, with the exception of the 1856 Court House, the Old University Building, and perhaps the houses of John Forbes. Vernacular architecture dominated the entire town; even the larger houses seldom rose to the level of being fashionable. Nacogdoches citizens in 1880 had little money with which to dabble in current architectural styles, even if they had so desired. Rulfs was familiar and comfortable with both rural and urban architectural settings in Germany. To succeed, the young master builder knew he would have to give the town the architecture that it expected. Rulfs probably had more problems adjusting to the demands of the East Texas weather and climate than he did to the region's aesthetic norms. Tastes were constantly evolving, but the intense Texas heat was a new reality for Rulfs. Porches, ceiling levels, manipulation of air currents, size and placement of windows, preservation and use of different types of lumber, etc. caused him to adjust. The weather tested his creativity throughout his career. As Haltom had promised in his 1880 *History and Description*, Rulfs found many talented craftsmen in the building trades; great building products and ready availability of these; and most importantly, a booming economy after 1883. All of his friends in northern Germany would have envied this.

Rulfs as a Residential Architect

Many daunting questions must have faced the young German architect when he first arrived in Nacogdoches in 1880. What was the nature of the community he was joining? How long would it take him to absorb the norms and rhythms of life in East Texas? How much creative freedom would he have? What rules and customs must he follow? Could a rural town support the career of an architect or would he have to move to a large city? What skills and materials would he find? What economic resources would his clients possess?

Rulfs and his chosen community were extremely compatible from the beginning. His architectural background in rural Germany fit perfectly the needs of Nacogdoches. He was not trained as an egotistical star, one who demanded the spotlight at all times. Rulfs, known to be very modest, shy, and extremely reserved, came from a tradition that trained its professionals in competent anonymity. Historically, even the architects of the great medieval cathedrals of Europe often remained personally unnamed and unsung. As a professional, Rulfs knew how to focus on his clients' needs rather than on his own creative wishes, but he also knew how to supply attractive options. Rulfs took his place alongside other professionals in Nacogdoches as a stalwart provider of services. Like his mentor, John Schmidt, Rulfs was a good merchant and knew how to market architectural products. He followed the national trends and tastes, but he knew how to localize them as well. In particular, Rulfs offered his clients unique and creative remodeling services. He led the Nacogdoches community by anticipating their needs and blending these with the current trends without becoming a slave to fads. Rulfs became an indispensable figure in an exceptional generation of men who transformed Nacogdoches into a modern city. As he had helped the businesses of Nacogdoches to prosper through their new, more efficient commercial buildings, Rulfs began to bring to their domestic contexts an awareness of how architecture could enhance and satisfy their desire for a fuller life.

From the beginning, however, Rulfs attracted attention and turned heads in Nacogdoches. First and foremost, he provided quality structures. To this, he added just enough style and decoration to satisfy his clients. If they wanted more, he could and would provide it. Of one of his early houses (now gone), on the corner of Pilar and South Church, the newspaper editor commented:

> Col. Tom R. Jennings has almost completed his new residence on Pilar Street, which when finished will be a marvel of beauty. It is especially constructed with a view to comfort and convenience. The light and the breezes can enter from all sides, making it a healthy, happy home. The outside painting is an artistic combination of the brightest and best colors to give it a gay and attractive appearance.[5]

Rulfs had to wait almost a decade before Nacogdoches was ready to splurge on grander residences with high style. He was, in the meantime, designing commercial buildings for patrons who would call on him later to do their residences.

Most of the architect's pre-1890 houses have vanished. Many of the early houses stood close to downtown and did not survive the expansion of the commercial areas, although fire probably destroyed more of the early wooden structures than creeping commercialization. (Nacogdoches had neither a fire department nor hydrants in the nineteenth century, as Carolyn Ericson has documented.)[6] There is another important consideration: some of the architect's early houses no longer look like early houses. Rulfs extended the life of many of his early structures by updating their façades, modernizing their features, and adding new rooms.[7] His first homes were not only modest, but they were also careful studies in architectural accommodation to the living patterns of Nacogdoches. Rulfs correctly sensed that in the 1880s Nacogdoches was not prepared for originality in its domestic architecture. When early clients, such as Charles Hoya, needed or desired new houses, they wanted neither revolutionary floor plans nor radical exterior decorations. Instead, they wanted their conservative lifestyles updated, with perhaps the addition of a modicum of style, character, and charm; but they were not desirous of being modern or trendy or ostentatious. Had Rulfs come to Nacogdoches with a modernist mindset, determined to upend traditional architectural patterns of domestic life, his career would not have lasted very long. By aiming for the center of local expectations and offering something distinctive, but non-threatening, Rulfs provided a real contribution to the context of domestic lives in Nacogdoches. Rulfs suppressed his own creative urges in favor of becoming the *best* architect, contractor, and builder in Nacogdoches. By the end of the 1880s, when his patrons began to demand more, he was ready to accommodate. It is important to remember, however, that his patrons prized his dedication to quality long before they began to clamor for his flawless taste in what constituted style at any moment.

The totality of Rulfs's involvement with certain projects is sometimes difficult to determine. It is unfortunate, but not uncommon at the turn of the twentieth century, for the architect and the builder to be invisible in the general references to a structure. When the newspaper, for instance, reported that 'John Schmidt is building a home on North Street,' the editor does not use the word *building* to mean Schmidt did so with his own hands or even oversaw the tedious details of construction, but that he 'commissioned' the job. Rulfs, trained in the master builder system of Germany in the 1870s, would have accepted that euphemistic use of the term as proper. He trained in a system where the architect was a servant, not a star. The credits for Mr. Rulfs are sometimes hard to determine. Some families have retained detailed records of their domestic projects, but most people have not. The evidence varies from house to house. The descendants of the Harris-Davison family have kept an 1895 drawing by Rulfs for aesthetic reasons. D. K. Cason kept documents by Rulfs as part of his personal and business archives; he kept drawings and specifications on multiple commercial and residential projects—for business reasons, not aesthetic reasons. The daughters of Charles Hoya kept the blueprints of their 1914 houses, and the Price Estate also kept the architectural drawings from their remodeling job.[8] Most often, modern attributions depend on what the newspaper or public records have recorded, on the memory of individuals, or on what architectural continuity exists among the various buildings.

As the *de facto* architect for the city between 1880 and 1925, D. Rulfs wore many architectural hats. In one of his earliest advertisements in the newspapers in 1888, Rulfs styled himself as "D. RULFS: ARCHITECT, CARPENTER. AND CONTRACTOR OF BUILDINGS."[9] As an architect, Rulfs drew sketches of concepts, elevations, floor plans, detailed foundations, cross sections of critical elements, such as stairs and decorative areas—everything one would expect from an architect today. He attached to these drawings detailed specifications for the materials, instructions for the sub-contractors, and quality controls for everything. In the early years, however, the client did not expect many of these detailed instructions. Since the first of his extant residential drawings and specifications dates to 1895, there are several explanations for the lack of drawings before this time. First and foremost, Rulfs himself did not keep an archive of his work; this had not been part of his training. There were no ready means of duplication for drawings until the invention of blueprints. In addition, when he first started working in Nacogdoches, he worked primarily for John Schmidt or Schmidt's business partners. The bond and the cooperation between these two men made formal documentation unnecessary. Schmidt totally trusted Rulfs's skills and integrity. Even with other patrons in the period before 1895, handshakes were more binding than in later years. Evidently, neither Rulfs nor his patrons found it necessary to formalize everything into comprehensive legal documents and contracts, at least ones that were recorded in the public records. Also, as long as he personally selected the building materials, oversaw the details, maintained quality control, supervised the workers, and was aided by his well-trained younger half-brother, William Henry Rulfs, formal documents were less necessary. Formal contracts start appearing in 1895, but even deep into the twentieth century, most residences did not require such documentation. In general, across the nation in the late nineteenth century, the codification of architectural habits by the profession was still in the process of being written.[10] As houses and buildings became more expensive and complicated, as in the case with the June Harris House and Roland Jones House, plans by Rulfs became more extensive and common.[11] However, even after saying this, the lack of documents frequently rested on whether the descendants of the original patron found the retention of such materials convenient or desirable. (Heirs frequently toss the house plans and pictures, keeping only cash, bonds, and deed records.)

Rulfs did not have his own construction firm at first. Only in 1888 did he begin to advertise as a contractor. From the beginning, however, whether he advertised as a formal contractor or not, he mostly built the houses he designed. Numerous sources report his practice of visiting the sites under construction almost daily, constantly giving advice, and sketching on the spot additions and corrections. His brother worked by his side as the project manager or contractor at most of the sites. The two men undertook both new and remodeling assignments. The fees for the architect, as opposed to the construction costs, were almost never recorded in the public records. By the turn of the century, many construction contracts, even those between a patron and Rulfs's brother, William Henry, stated that the work had to be completed as laid out in the drawings and specifications by D. Rulfs.[12] Rulfs *regularly* executed designs and specified plans that other contractors built, as in the example of the Banita Hotel. In one known instance, at a particularly difficult time, Rulfs's construction firm built a domestic design drawn by another architect. He also served as the supervising architect on the 1910 Court House, albeit not the design architect. Along with his brother, Rulfs also undertook various kinds of carpentry and cabinetwork. D. Rulfs, a very modest man, *never* felt declassed or demeaned when someone called him a carpenter or grouped him with carpenters. His German training, with its emphasis on professional craftsmanship, meant that he was popular and respected by the people who worked for and with him. At one juncture, when he found himself faced with a strike, the carpenter's union made it clear that their complaints were not directed at Rulfs as an architect or contractor.[13]

The advertisements Rulfs placed in various newspapers are interesting. In the early weekly newspapers, the ads were sometimes only a sentence long. Even when offset, his standard statements were just text. His basic advertisement simply declared: "D. Rulfs. Architect, Carpenter, and Contractor of Buildings. Nacogdoches, Texas;" sometimes, it was "Architect, Contractor, and Builder."[14] In one of his ads in the *Nacogdoches Chronicle* in 1892, he elaborated by saying: "Will make bids, furnish plans, estimates, etc. Has a well equipped carpenter shop at east end of Pillar St. where he keeps a full supply of well assorted dry lumber on hand for sale."[15] By 1900, when Rulfs knew that townspeople were seriously interested in design, he would include stylistic elements.[16] In one ad, he declared what had become *locally obvious* in Nacogdoches: "My work in Nacogdoches speaks for itself."[17]

The Rulfs Homestead

Before discussing the details of his work for others, it seems appropriate to discuss how and where Rulfs solved his own housing needs. Upon arrival in Nacogdoches, Rulfs leased "a farm three and a half miles from Nacogdoches, where Shawnee Road crosses Eggnog Branch."[18] The idea of combining farming with a career in building, as his father had done in Germany, was part of his heritage; but, as his niece Mary Stewart Duncan recounted, commuting three miles by horse every day to Nacogdoches soon convinced Rulfs this was not really practical or necessary. Very soon, he moved his family closer into town. Mrs. Duncan related to the author that the family lived for a time in the Old Orton House on Orton Hill. Most probably, however, this meant a house on Orton Hill overlooking the city rather than actually in the Orton House.[19] A member of the Orton family, Bryan Holt Davis—a person very knowledgeable about Nacogdoches history and Orton family heritage, doubted that the Old Orton House was ever available in the early 1880s for lease. Rulfs, as an immigrant from the flat landscape of northern Oldenburg, would have found any location on Orton Hill very appealing because of the wonderful view overlooking the area between the two creeks. In Oldenburg, only families with great wealth and tradition had access to hilltop vistas. He later would encourage patrons to build on Forbes and Irion Hills overlooking the town. Diedrich and Johanne had six children. Their daughter Mary Rulfs (1882-1953) was born while they lived on Orton Hill.[20]

According to family tradition, once construction began on his commercial designs on the Square in 1884, Rulfs deemed it necessary to make yet another move to the town-side bank of the Lanana Creek. Since the Lanana Creek had no bridge, his daily ride on horseback to the center of town was frequently unpredictable. His family also found advantages to living closer into town. They were active in Christ Episcopal Church and attended various educational classes in town. Their son John Rulfs (1885-1955) was born in town, presumably in a leased house.[21]

No doubt Rulfs had a philosophical reason for gravitating to the new location where he purchased his homestead property, between East Main and Pilar streets on the west side of the Lanana Creek. He valued the chance to become a neighbor of the Joseph von der Hoya family, earlier German immigrants from the Grand Duchy of Oldenburg.[22] The Hoyas had gravitated to the area for the same reason—they purchased the homestead of Adolphus Sterne, a German from Cologne and a famous Texas patriot. In fact, so many German immigrants flocked to the area east of town it could easily have carried the nickname "Germantown." Rulfs lived near, worked with, and built houses for most of the German-descended citizens of Nacogdoches, such as Schmidt, Müller, Hoya, Shindler, Mast, Rusche, and Helpenstill, to name a few. Interestingly, however, they consciously endeavored to avoid creating a linguistic and cultural enclave. According to Rulfs's niece, there was an unwritten rule among the Germans: "they always spoke English in public in honor of their newly adopted country."[23]

In 1888, Rulfs purchased his homestead property from Zachary Taylor Mast and his wife Martha (Teutsch) Mast. The deed states: "Lot bounded by Main Street on North, by Pillar Street on the South, by Lanana Street on West, and Lanana Bayou on the East."[24] (The Masts, however, probably never lived on the property; they had owned the land only since 1884. According to census records, they maintained a continuous residence in Melrose from 1880 to 1900.[25]) A house must have existed on the property, however, since Rulfs paid $1,200 for it—more than the going rate for such lots. It is possible the Rulfs had rented and lived in the small house on the property, which later became his office. Rulfs eventually built five structures on his East Main property: his residence and three rental houses faced Main, and an office which faced South Lanana. He built the tenant houses to provide income between commissions. He had done this in Germany, too, and found it useful. By rotating his carpenters to keep them employed while idle between other jobs, he constructed the rental properties without excessive expense. He frequently used lumber left over from jobs to construct the houses. He sometimes made one of these houses available to members of his family. In his will he bequeathed one of these houses to his niece Mary Stewart Duncan, who was already living in the house.[26]

Rulfs did not design and build a larger residence for his own family until some time in the early 1890s. No pictures of this residence have come to the author's attention. This house was demolished in the 1960s to install a car-wash. In interviews in 1974, Mary Stewart Duncan described the Rulfs home as "unique, not looking like anything else in town."[27] The house had a two-story tower in the center, a Second Empire-style Mansard roof, a front porch with intricate detailing that wrapped around from the north to the east, a chamfered front door, and a complicated and untraditional floor plan. Rulfs possibly built the house to foster or encourage interest in current styles; and while his effort did not produce a trend, he used certain elements of the house in a variety of other houses across town.[28]

The Office of D. Rulfs

Only one of the original structures on the Rulfs homestead survives: his office. The little house at 113 South Lanana at the east end of Pilar Street, which served as his office, most probably served as the residence of the Rulfs family as a home for a time until he constructed a larger residence to the east. Rulfs did not advertise the building as his office and workshop until 1892, which leads one to assume he possibly used the house as his family residence from 1888 to 1892. In an advertisement in the *Nacogdoches Chronicle* in 1892, he described it as "a well equipped carpenter shop at the east end of Pillar St. where he keeps a full supply of well assorted dry lumber on hand for sale."[29] The structure itself was a very modest Victorian cottage, constructed, interestingly, from bits and pieces of wood from other houses he was building, such as the Charles Hoya House across the street. In remodeling the house recently, the current owners Kristen Lunsford and Thomas Tracy, found the interior walls composed of various types of wood, bits and pieces of timber with both pegs and square nails, and shaped pieces of lumber.[30] A carpenter, especially a traditional one, would want to waste nothing that was still useful. Whereas a client might find this recycling objectionable, a carpenter knew the value of the seasoned wood salvaged from other sites.

The construction business is a continuous juggling act. While Rulfs seemed to have very little problem quickly drawing and specifying a building, the supervision and staging of a construction team became a greater and greater problem as his commissions increased. At first, as long as the domestic construction was close to the downtown commercial areas along Main Street, Rulfs could easily manage both commercial and residential commissions with his workers. In fact, he used the modest houses of the 1880s to cycle the work of his carpenters and bricklayers to keep his men working efficiently. Most craftsmen were already familiar with domestic construction tasks. Rulfs could concentrate on quality control and invest only a limited time in training. Throughout his life, down even to his last house in 1923, Rulfs attempted to visit every building site on a daily basis.[31] William Henry Rulfs, Diedrich's younger half-brother, became his trusted construction manager in the 1890s and continued as the architect's right arm until Henry's death on December 11, 1919.[32]

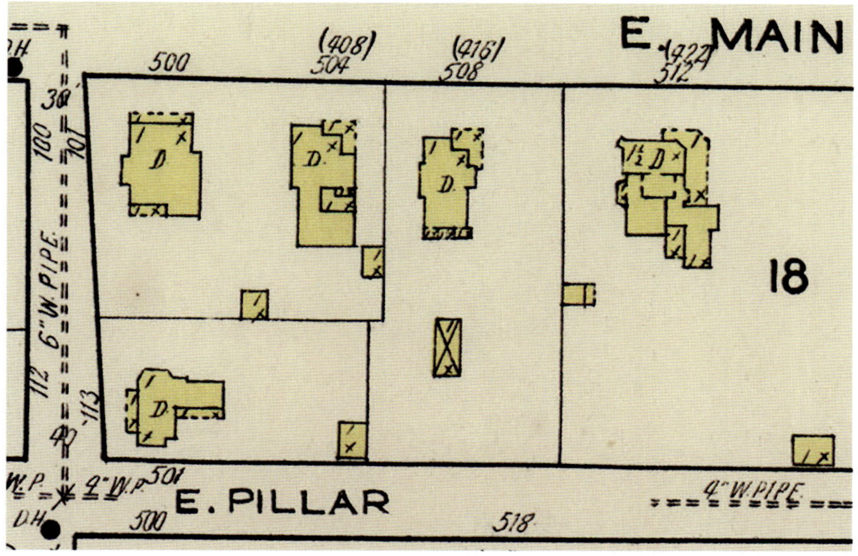

FIGURE 4.2. The Rulfs Homestead, Sanborn Map, 1922.

This detail from the 1922 Sanborn Map (the corner of East Main, South Lanana, and East Pilar Streets) shows the homestead of D. Rulfs as it existed toward the end of his life. Left to right, the first three houses facing Main Street were rental property. The large house by the number "18," the block designation, is the private home of the family. In the second row, facing South Lanana on the corner of Pilar is the office of the architect, the only one of the five houses still in existence. The street east of the homestead property today is "Rulfs Street," named after the architect.

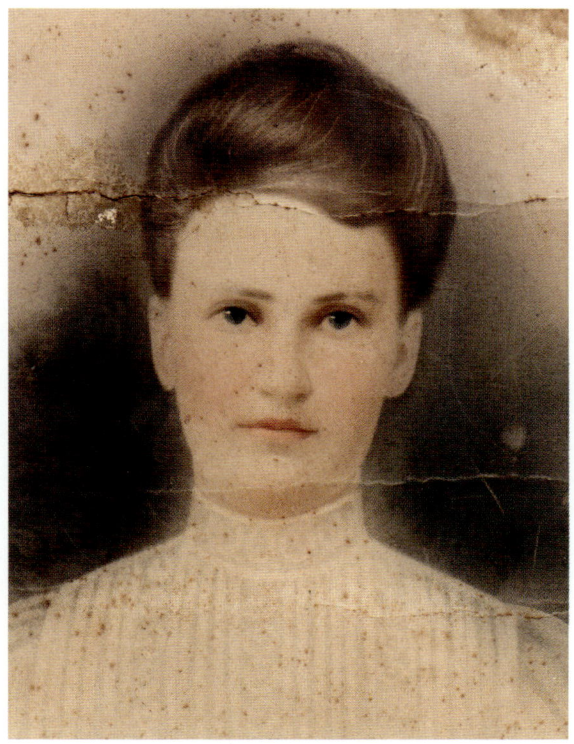

FIGURE 4.3. Mary Stewart (Duncan), ca. 1902.

Mary Stewart, born February 3, 1883, died on August 25, 1986, at the age of 103. The interviews with Mrs. Duncan by the author in the 1970s constitute a major source of information for this book. Picture from the First United Methodist Church Archives.

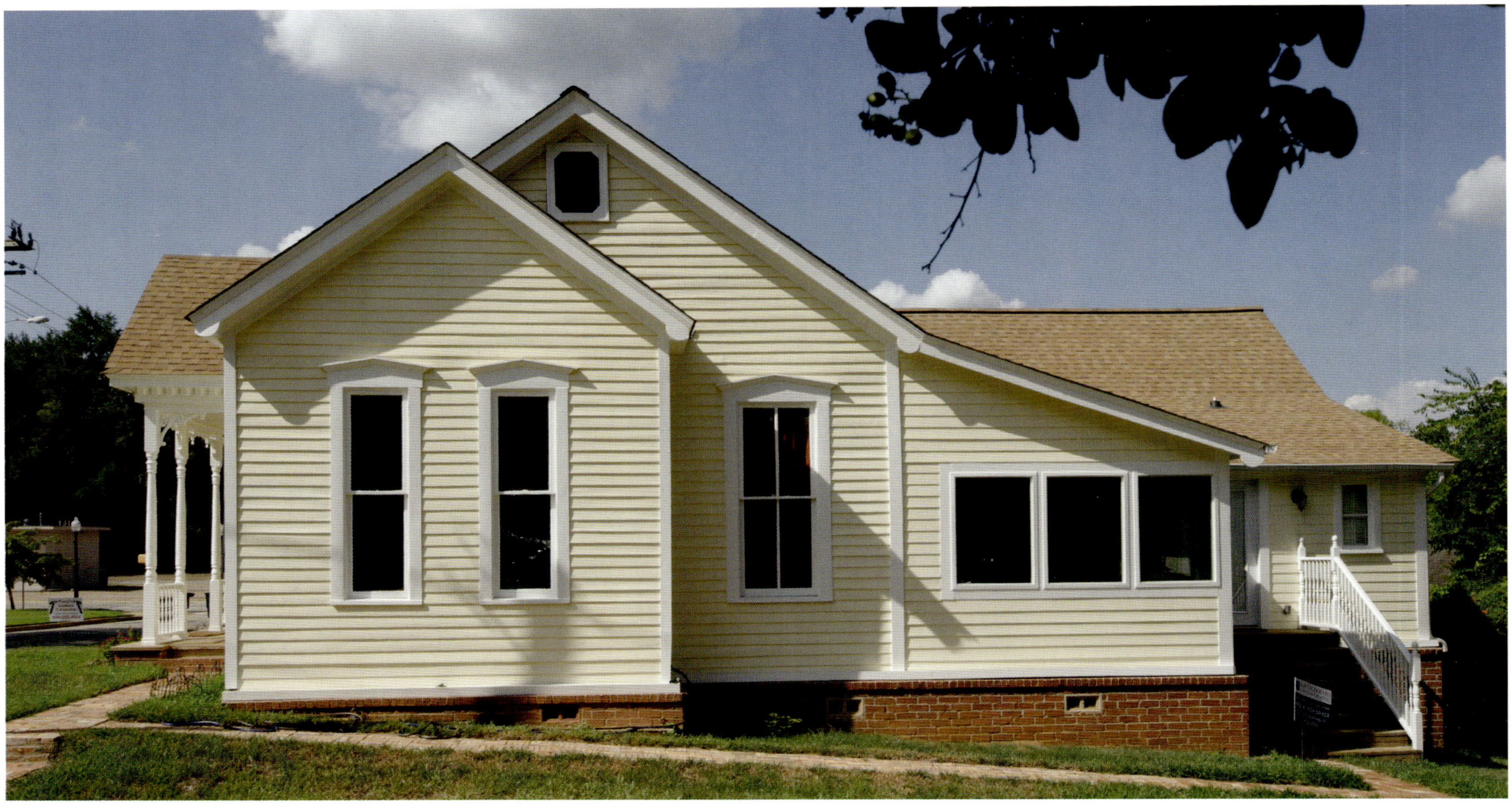

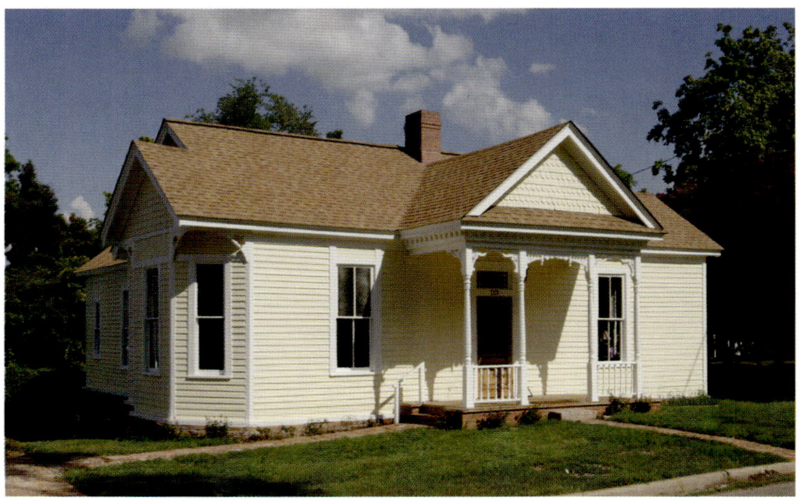

FIGURE 4.4. (Above) The Rulfs Office, Pilar Street Elevation.
Kristen Lunsford and Thomas Tracy have recently restored the office of D. Rulfs.

FIGURE 4.5. (Left) The Office, 113 South Lanana Street.
The porch of the Office has a pediment over the entry and Eastlake detailing. There is a gable and bay window on the north.

FIGURE 4.6. (Below, left). Home of Mary Stewart Duncan.
Two of the small Victorian houses, which Rulfs built for rental income, still existed in the 1980s at the time the author took this picture. Mrs. Mary Stewart Duncan (1883-1986), the architect's niece on his wife's side, lived in this 1898 house at the time the author interviewed her. The pediment of the house is similar to the design Rulfs used in the Harris House portico. Mrs. Holbrook, the granddaughter of Rulfs, took the houses down after the death of Mrs. Duncan and moved her own home from San Augustine onto the property. It was also built by Rulfs.

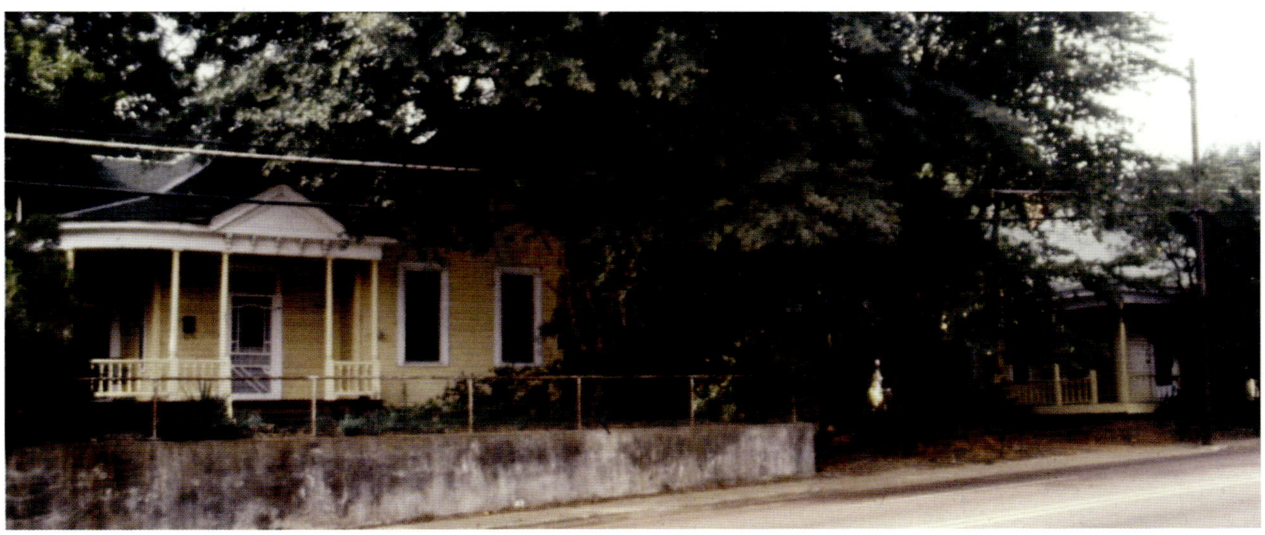

The Charles Hoya House (1888)

The Charles Hoya House on South Lanana Street is an example of the domestic architecture that Rulfs undertook in his first decade of work in Nacogdoches. Rulfs understood the reigning social system. His perceptions, in large part, accounted for his success. Charles Hoya was twelve when his family purchased the Adolphus Sterne House from Sterne's widow.[33] He was thirty-nine when he married Frances "Fanny" Meisenheimer in 1887. The new couple was still living in the Sterne House when their first daughter, Jennie, was born. Whether it was Joseph, Charles, or Fanny who insisted on the change, they asked their neighbor D. Rulfs in 1888 to design and build them a home across the street in Sterne's orchard. The new house, a pleasant upgrade, was similar to the Sterne House, nothing radical or revolutionary. The 1-1/2 story wood frame house (essentially four rooms divided by a central hall downstairs) had lapped siding, a porch across the entire front, and chimneys at both ends. Because of later changes, it is difficult to say with certainty how much porch decoration the structure originally had, but it was most likely similar to what remains on the north end of the porch today, except with turned spindles. By placing the structure on rather high brick foundation piers, the architect differentiated the house from its neighbors and made it more imposing without making it pretentious. The social needs of the new Hoya couple were not great, for they were known to follow rather than set trends. However, when the town had changed and their daughter was coming of age and needed a more genteel setting to receive prospective young men callers, Charles Hoya had Rulfs add a front parlor (circa 1900) in the form of a projecting bay. Rulfs at that time inserted a chamfered entry door and an arch in the hall to give the interior more charm. He adjusted the porch and stairs to match.[34]

Later non-Rulfs extensions off the back of the house, a dining room and kitchen, which came after the arrival of city water, were not built well. Clara Hoya Gray blamed this on the choice of an inferior construction firm.[35] Rulfs enjoyed a long and congenial relationship with the Hoyas. At the time he adjusted the house in 1900, he designed and constructed two buildings for the Hoyas on the West Square. Charles and Fanny Hoya lived in this house until the 1920s. In the period before and after the First World War, Rulfs designed and built more houses for Charles Hoya and his daughters in the Washington Square area. By that time, the Hoyas had learned to allow Rulfs to lead them in constructing more stylish abodes in line with national trends. (See Chapter XI)

The Hoyas, as most clients in the 1880s, wanted value, not radical new living patterns or design innovations. Because it worked, Rulfs continued to use the Hoya formula repeatedly in subsequent years—giving clients quality construction and meeting their expectations in style. Architectural creations that enhanced, changed, or challenged the context of domestic living in Nacogdoches would have to wait for more adventurous patrons. The reward for the architect/builder, in the meantime, was a reputation. He steadily established his credentials as *the* man to engage for architectural services, from conception to finish. Truly, as he later would state in his advertisements, his work in Nacogdoches began to speak for itself.[36]

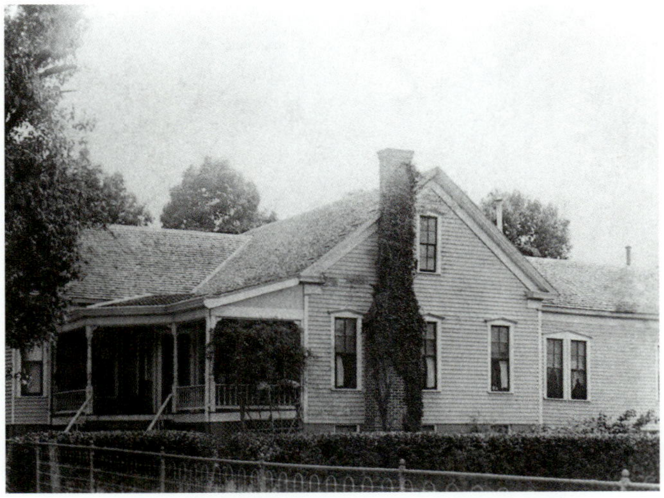

FIGURE 4.7. The Charles and Fanny Hoya House, ca. 1930
Courtesy of ETRC.

FIGURE 4.8. The Charles and Fanny Hoya House, 2011.

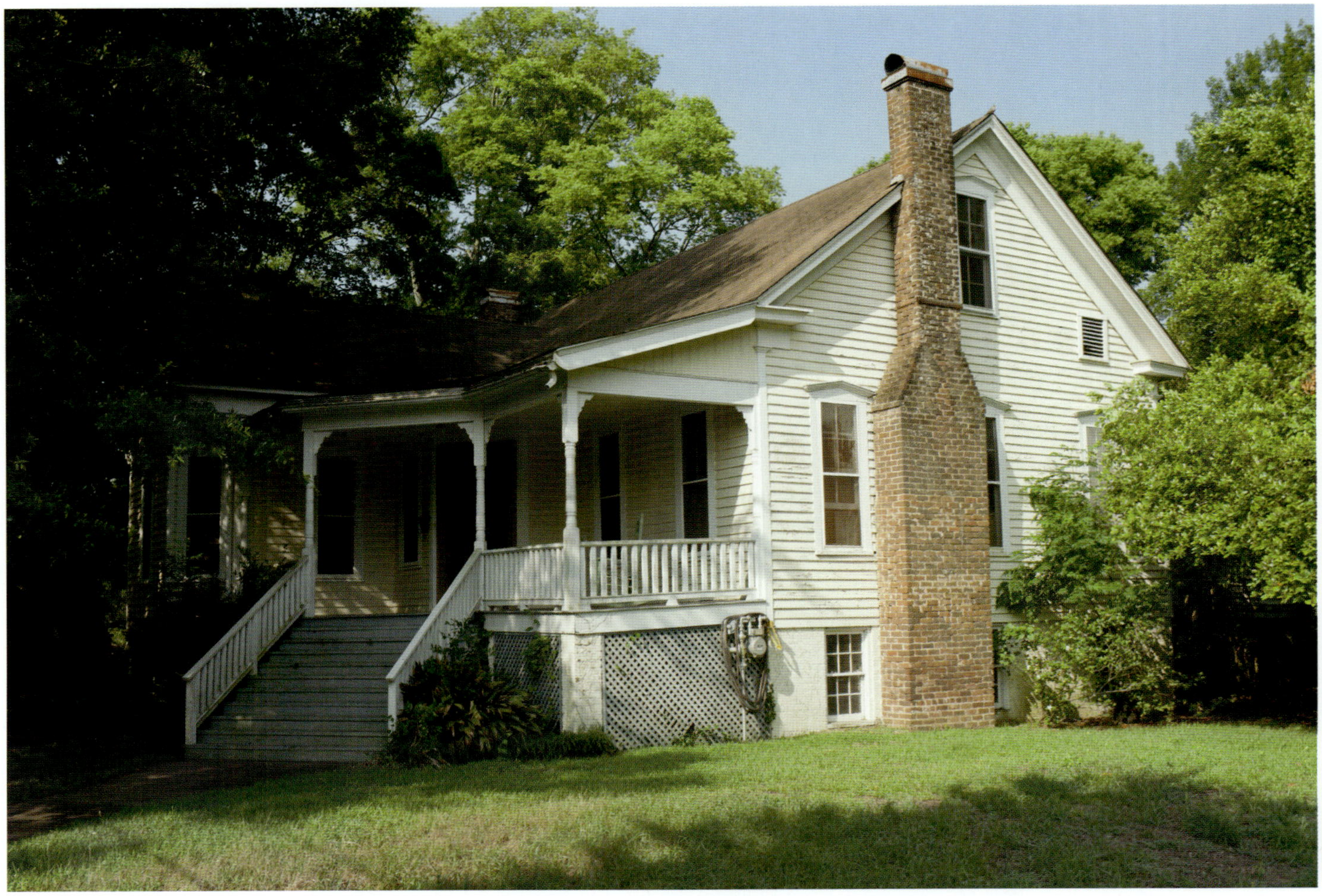

A Mixed Commercial / Domestic Structure—The Bullen Hotel (1888)

As the era of the railroad began to change Nacogdoches, social patterns came up for revision. Everything was fluid: where people met, where they lived, where visitors slept or ate, where everyone worked, went to church, took their entertainment. As previously discussed, the functions of commercial and residential neighborhoods were not well defined in the pioneer town. Nacogdoches did not adopt the fixed type of coding system characteristic of a modern city—zoning—until the 1970s. In the late nineteenth century, what coding existed was determined by tradition, not law. Commercial and residential designations were ill defined, as were even the names and shapes of streets before paving, guttering, and sidewalks.

Church Street, one of the oldest named streets in town, ran only one block between Main and Hospital Street at first. It took its name from its oldest building, the original Christ Episcopal Church (1852-1900). The Old Hyde House anchored the north end of the street, and at the southern end stood the Mitchell Hotel on Main. In 1888, when John Schmidt and Rulfs replaced the Mitchell Hotel with the Opera House, they did so with new facilities in mind. Working with the newcomer Henry Pratt Matthews (1846-1901), who had purchased a former boarding house on Church Street north of the new Opera House, Schmidt and Rulfs planned a new hotel to answer all their needs.[37] Matthews wanted an income property in which he could live and help his recently divorced daughter, Mrs. Esme Bullen,[38] to establish a new life for herself and her young daughter, Genevieve. Schmidt wanted housing for the visitors to his emporium and entertainment center in the east end of town. Rulfs undertook the commission to enlarge the structure in 1888.

The discussion of a hotel in this chapter might seem odd, especially since this hotel would burn in 1895. The Bullen Hotel, however, was not only Rulfs's first hotel in Nacogdoches, but the design and function of the Bullen Hotel also directly influenced several important domestic structures and helped to redefine the domestic contexts in the town. The reworking of the Bullen Hotel established Rulfs's reputation as a makeover artist, and was the direct precursor to the remodeling of the Edwards House on East Main Street in 1888 and the W. U. Perkins house on North Street (1890). Two years later, it influenced the building of the significant Schmidt House on North Street. Of course, the main influence of the Bullen came in 1895 when the owners demanded a replacement, which was a similar structure, the Roland Jones House.

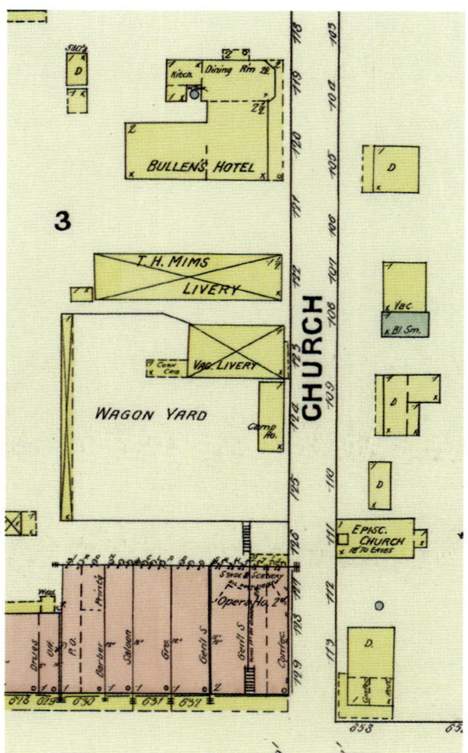

FIGURE 4.9. Bullen Hotel, Sanborn Map Detail, 1891.

On this 1891 map, the development of the Church Street area can be followed. The Christ Episcopal Church (1851) gave the street its name. On Main Street, below the church location, is the M. G. Hazle family general store. The brick block of buildings on the corner of Main and Church, built between 1888 and 1891, include the Opera House, which replaced the Mitchell Hotel. The Bullen Hotel, north of the Wagon Yard and Mims Livery, shows the additions made from the 1885 map.

In his redefinition of the Matthews's property, Rulfs added a large wing to the north (public rooms for dining and entertaining) and a new kitchen off the back to service these. He then doubled the newly-enlarged footprint by adding a second story over the entire structure. Facing Church Street, the new 2-½-story façade included elaborate Queen Anne architectural elements—a bay window, double galleries, and stylish ornamentation. The expansion of the boarding house to make the hotel necessitated tearing down the old Hyde House in order to provide the "requisite out houses for the Bullen Hotel." The loss of the Hyde, a favorite meeting place, caused some angst to the editor of the *Nacogdoches Star*: "This lovely, attractive place has been so long a feature of beauty in our town, that it looks almost like an act of vandalism to disturb any portion of the premise."[39]

The new Bullen Hotel very quickly became the scene of large social gatherings and public events held in Nacogdoches in the early 1890s.[40] Mrs. Esme Bullen, who ran the hotel, was a gracious hostess and enjoyed using the setting the building provided for social functions. In 1888, citizens were willing to consider commercial properties of this size, but they were unwilling to think of purely residential structures of such grandeur. Esme Bullen met her future husband Roland Jones while he was a guest in the Bullen Hotel. In 1893, Esme married Roland Jones in Christ Church (across Church Street in the same block) and held the reception, an event of notice, at the hotel. The effect on others was immediate. Once having tasted such a grand setting, a feeling of deprivation compelled others to demand the same kind of space.

The Minnie Arnold Edwards House (1889)

The old Edwards homestead, across Main Street from the Rulfs homestead, started its existence as a log house and had several makeovers before Rulfs arrived in Nacogdoches. For instance, a neighbor, Adolphus Sterne, commented on one of these remodelings in his famous *Diary*.[41] Payton Forbes Edwards, a descendant of two of the oldest and most important families in the county, transferred this family homestead to his second wife, Minnie Arnold, in 1886. (The Arnolds themselves were an important family.[42]) After seeing the transformation of the Bullen Hotel, Minnie decided her house was insufficient for entertaining and asked Rulfs to remodel the old house once again. Unlike the Hoyas across the street, Minnie's desire to have something beyond the ordinary gave Rulfs a great opening to demonstrate what he could do when given an opportunity.[43]

Rulfs created a pace-setting masterwork out of the old homestead and used elements he would repeat in later houses. He doubled the size of the box-like older house by adding an entirely new wing to the west along Lanana Street. The new wing had a front gable facing Main Street, giving needed verticality to the structure. The window in the attic of the gable

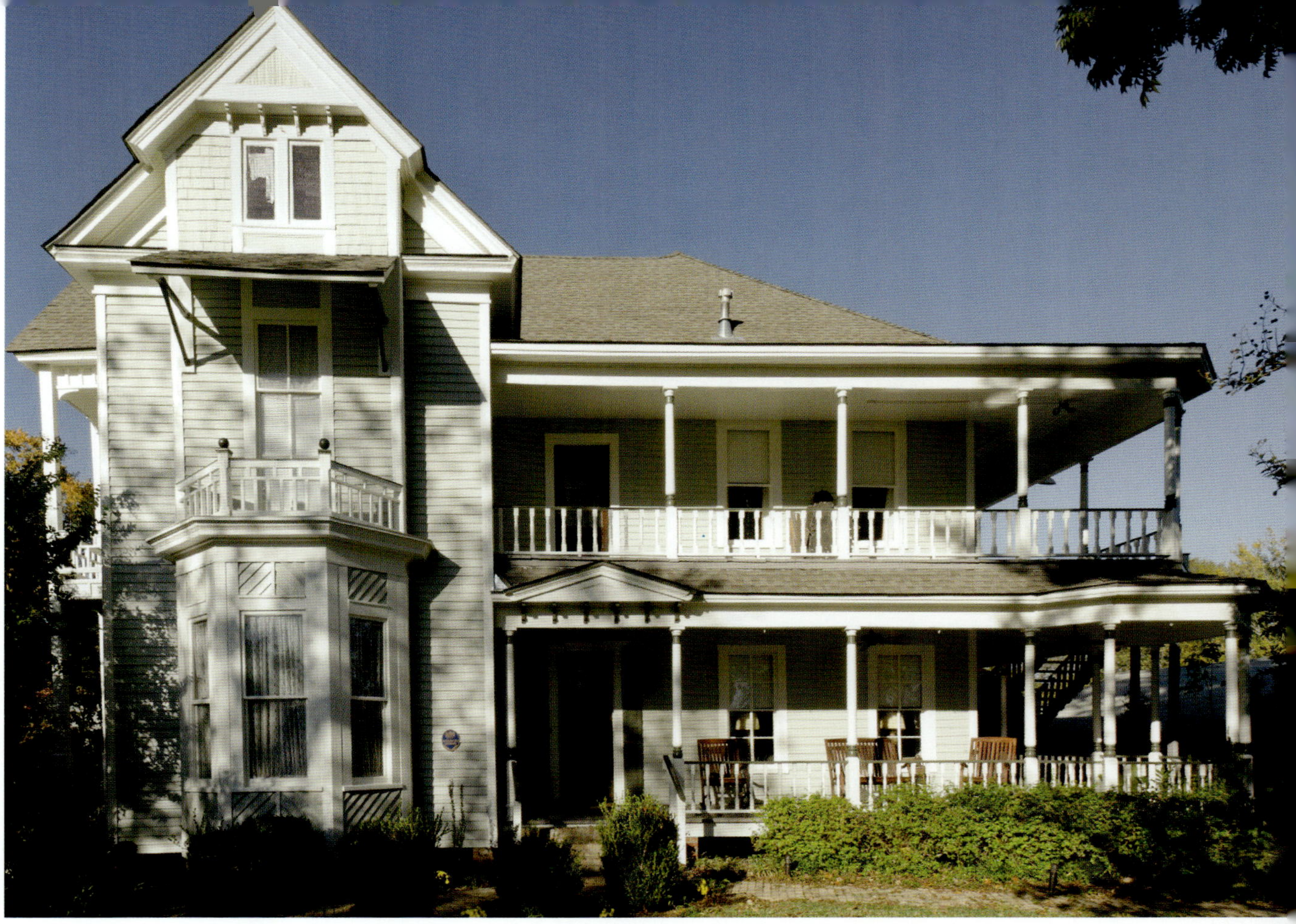

FIGURE 4.10 - 4.11. The South (Right) and West (Below) Façades of the Minnie Arnold Edwards House

On the East Main Street façade, Rulfs used a feature that would become a favorite of his decorative elements–a Juliet window. By topping the first floor bay window with a balustrade and giving the upstairs bedroom a window that doubled as a door, the combination gave the house a romantic effect. (Rulfs used this again on the John Schmidt House and later on the Tolbert Hardeman House on Mound Street.) Rulfs became very fond of using windows that doubled as doors and used them in many houses. By using windows, which extended down to the finished floor level and could be opened by pushing them up into the walls, Rulfs gave enormous flexibility to rooms by allowing access to the porches and balconies. He tied the hip roof of the older section into the new wing by extending the ridgeline into a second gable for the west side. The west gable, with its elegant two-story portico and balcony supported by brackets, gave the house a second façade on Lanana Street. To unify the whole, he re-sided the entire structure with lapped board siding and added interest, under and above the windows, by arranging the siding diagonally. [Also see, Figure 4.1 at the beginning of this chapter.]

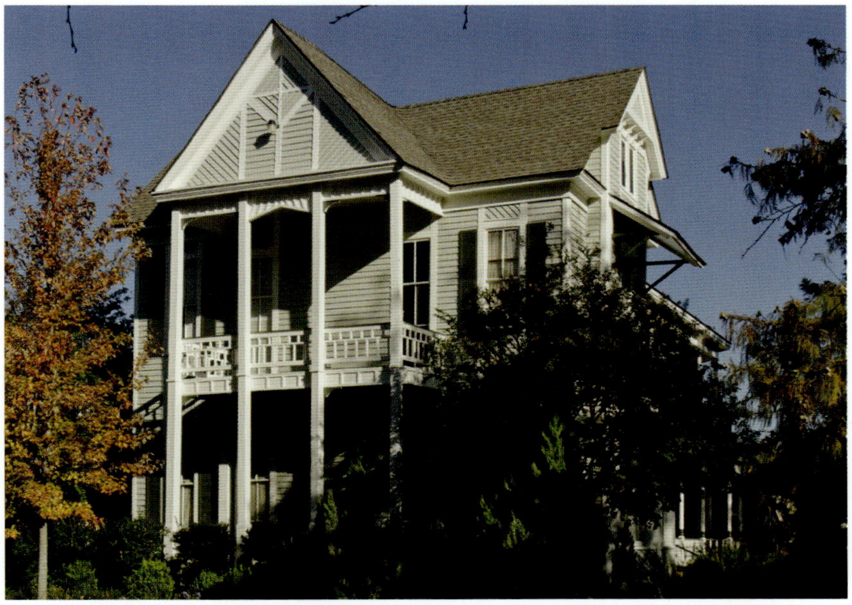

even suggested yet another floor. Around the existing house on the south and east, he wrapped a double gallery—the architect's way of coping with the excessive East Texas heat. In the new wing, he introduced stylish new elements, such as new window sizes, large sliding doors, back-to-back fireplaces, decorative mantles, patterned floors (diagonal board arrangements), popular new millwork, and bay windows. He unified the old and new exteriors by re-siding the entire house (sometimes arranged in patterns), new window sizes, balconies, and combining both hip and gable roof elements. Almost every room in the house has access to the outside from the two-story galleries. A pediment accented the entrance. The chamfered bay window on the southwest corner of the house supported a Juliet balcony off the second story bedroom. On the new west side, a full-height portico, supported by boxed wood columns, gave the side a classical appearance. By decoratively arranging the siding in a diagonal pattern, as inside the pediment, Rulfs gave interest without much expense. A small Stick-style balcony on the west side, supported by brackets and not attached to the box columns, gave another romantic element to the house. The slip-head windows, which extended down to the floor, pushed up into the walls when fully raised and allowed access to the various balconies and porches as doors. Undoubtedly, they also helped to ventilate the large home.

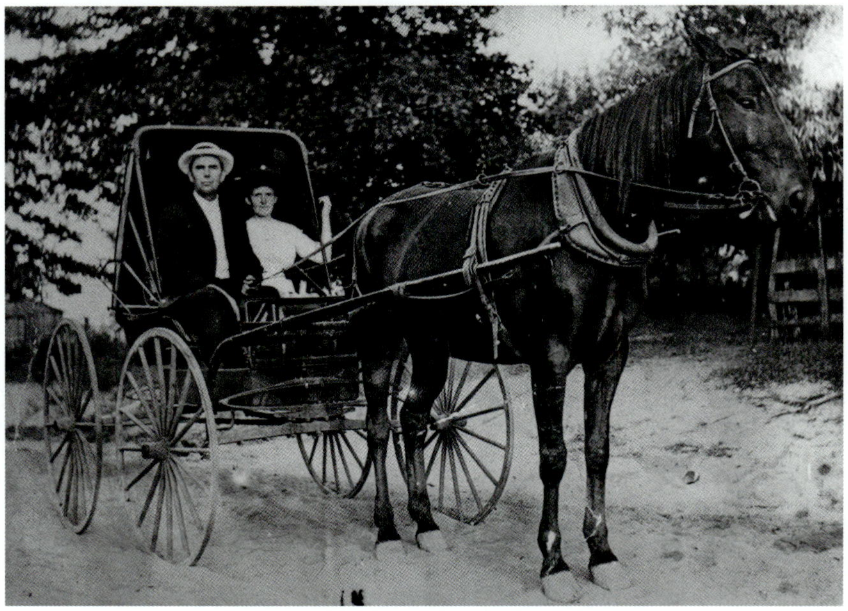

FIGURE 4.12. (Right) Dr. Felix and Molly Tucker, ca.1900

Dr. "Fee" and Miss Molly bought the Edwards House in 1899. They operated what amounts to an early hospital out of the house, using the convenient slip-head windows as patient access to the extensive porch system. The Tuckers sold the house to Luther Swift family in 1905. Courtesy of ETRC.

The Jesse Summers House (ca. 1896)

On April 16, 1887, Jesse Holloway Summers (1848-1933) and his wife, Emma, purchased a lot on Main Street and paid $250 for it.[44] According to an affidavit given later, they erected a residence on the lot shortly after purchasing it and lived there until their deaths (Emma in 1918 and Jesse in 1933). By the time they decided to build their house, the Summers had six of their ten children.[45] The first child born in the house was Sallie Talitha (19 July 1888). The house appears on the Sanborn Map for 1891 for the first time: a one-story, L-shaped domestic structure with a short porch across the front and a long porch along the north extension.[46] (No picture of this first house exists.) From the start, with a family that large, Emma Summers needed more space. Around 1896, the Summers decided to enlarge the house.

Concerning the first house, there is no evidence that Rulfs designed or built the structure—even though he was designing and constructing houses for other neighbors nearby his homestead on East Main (for example, for Schmidt and Hoya). From the pictures of the 1896 remodeled house, however, it is safe to say Rulfs re-designed and enlarged the house: his architectural fingerprints are all over it. Summers, who was in the lumber business, quite possibly oversaw the construction work himself. An argument in crediting the whole remodeling to Rulfs, however, is the fact that Rulfs built all of the children's houses, as discussed in Chapter XI. From a design perspective, the remodeled house follows the examples close by in the same period: the Bullen Hotel, Edwards House, and Charles Hoya House.

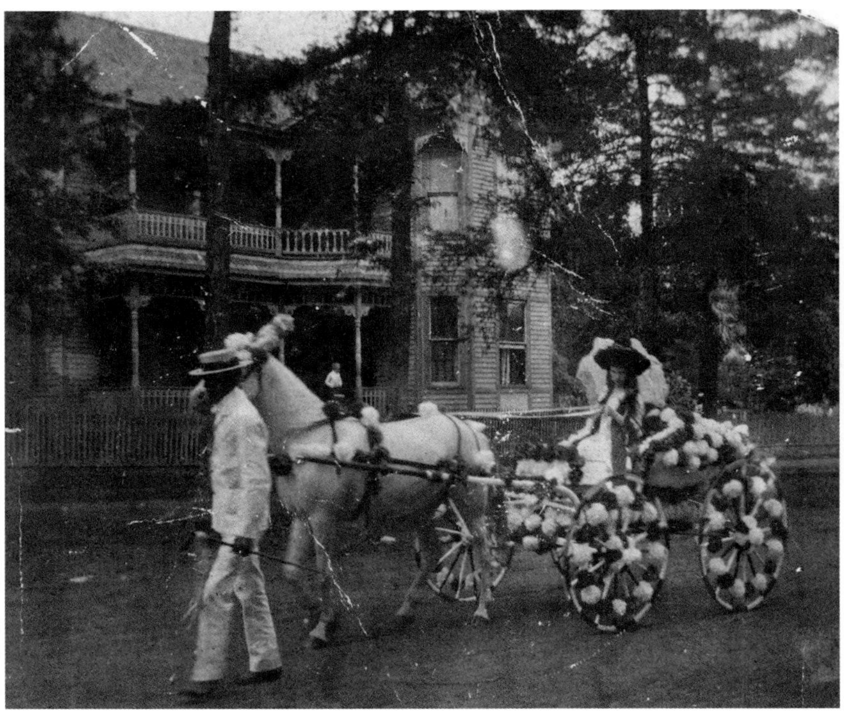

FIGURE 4.13. Summers House on Main Street, ca. 1900.

The photograph, with the house in the background, shows Sallie Talitha Summers and one of her younger brothers headed to a parade in downtown Nacogdoches. Picture courtesy of Henry Middlebrook.

As usual, Rulfs creatively worked around the existing floor plan. First, he doubled the front part of the old house. Second, he projected to the south a new two-story chamfered bay wing to establish a stylish new character for the older house. Third, he reorganized the rear of the house to make it more efficient: he enclosed the former porch, making it into a long hall; enlarged the kitchen-dining area; and added a new porch off the east room. The new fashionable, asymmetrical façade included a gable with a Palladian window and bargeboards, an entrance with pediment and steps at a 45º angle, and a two-story front gallery. The new windows updating the front elevation included the popular slip-head windows, which gave complete access to the new porches. The frieze and the spandrels were standard usage for the period, as can be seen today on the Laura Blount Chapman and Harry Cooper House, but the intricately cut balusters are unique to this house. The Summers House was demolished in 1941.[47]

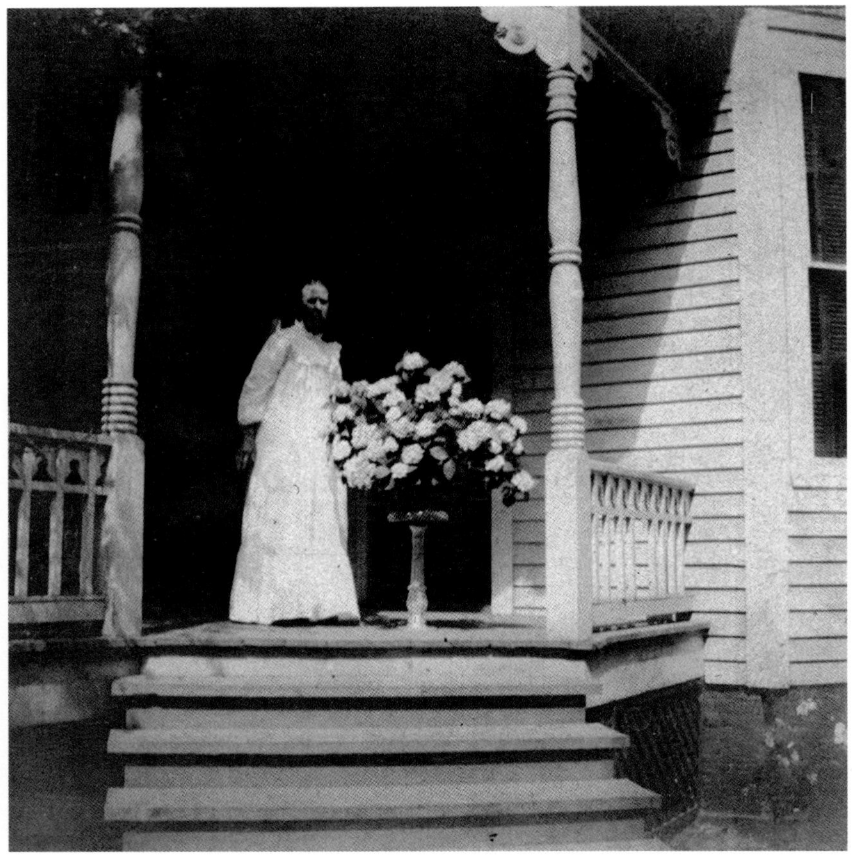

FIGURE 4.14. Emma Summers, Front Porch, Summers Home, East Main Street, ca. 1900.

Occasion unknown. Rulfs frequently used chamfered entrances in the period, as he did while remodeling the Charles Hoya House nearby. Photograph courtesy of Emma Summers' grandson, Henry Middlebrook.

FIGURE 4.15. The Robert C. Shindler House.

Rulfs built the house for Shindler in 1888. In conducting his research on the regional architecture of East Texas, Professor Elliot Evans photographed the Shindler home in 1948. The house was one of the charming variations, which Evans located in Nacogdoches. Photograph from the Evans Collection, ETRC.

In 1955, on its front page, the Daily Sentinel ran a headline and picture of this house: "Landmark Comes Down." The newspaper, while lamenting its destruction, readily accepted Mr. Carl Monk, Sr.'s decision to tear it down "to make way for business growth." Monk, however, admitted, "there are no immediate plans for the lot except to clear it." Such was the state of awareness of preservation in Nacogdoches at the time. As per the times, Rulfs was not mentioned in the 1955 article.

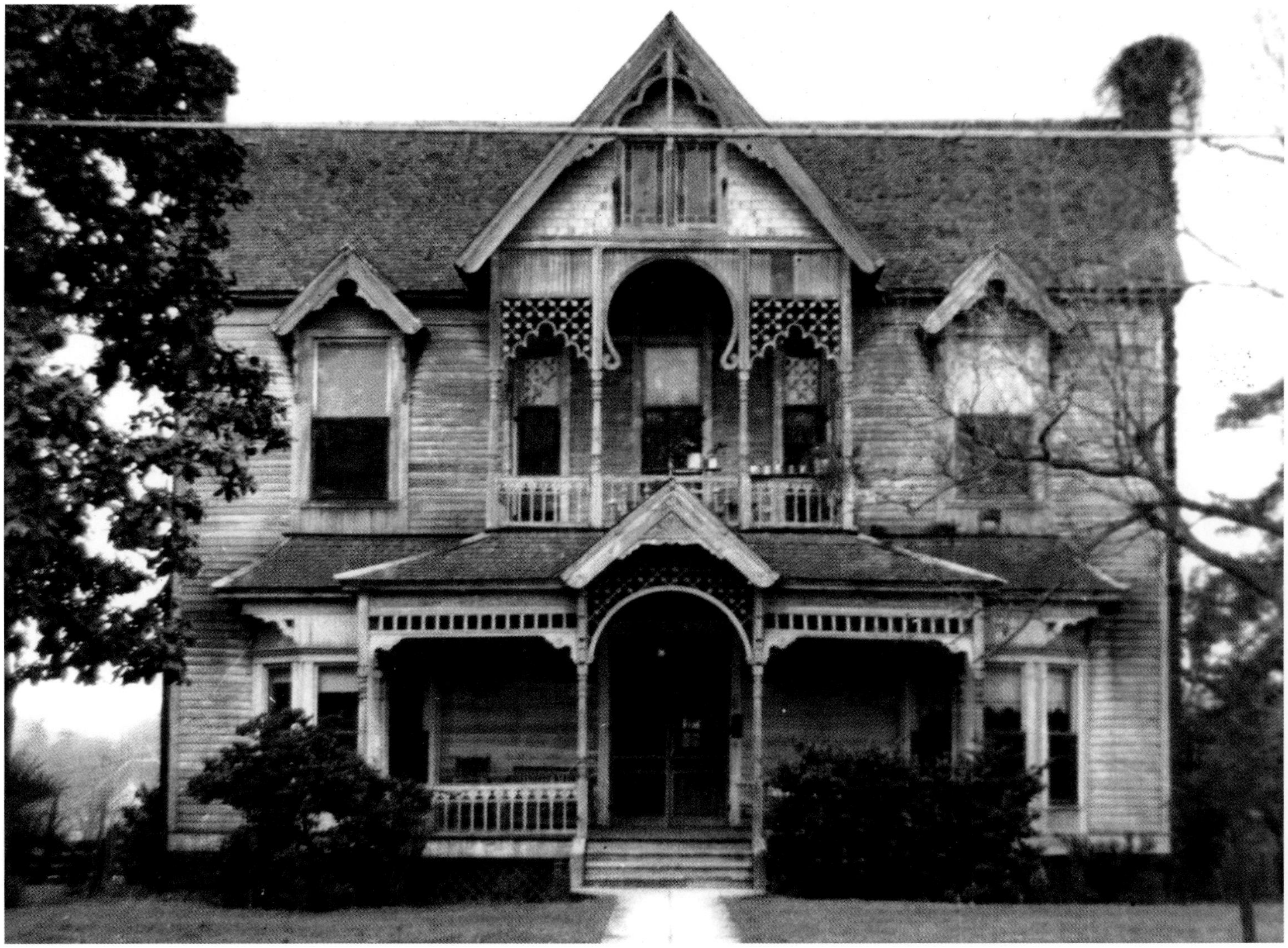

North Street

In describing the residential districts at the turn of the century, the architectural historians of the National Registry Division of the Texas Historical Commission have written:

> The influx of residents to Nacogdoches during the late 1800s and early 1900s not only spurred economic development, [but] it also resulted in a residential construction boom. Early development of the town occurred in a piecemeal fashion and Sanborn maps from the late 19th century indicated that most dwellings were near the public square on Pilar, Hospital, Fredonia, Mound, Main and Lanana streets. As the population expanded, residential growth took place directly north of the downtown along North, N. Fredonia, and N. Mound streets. The more affluent and prominent families built houses on North and N. Mound streets with middle-class families residing on N. Fredonia Street.[48]

While Pilar, East Main, and Hospital Streets continued to be important residential streets for a time after Rulfs arrived, the most important new residential street during the architect's lifetime was North Street. Today's commercial nature of the street should not obscure that fact. If the houses Rulfs designed for North Street still existed, less attention perhaps would accrue to the houses in the areas of Washington Square and Irion Hill. The dominance of North Street lasted until the expansion of SFASU in the 1960-70s. North Street received the first paving and was the home of the bankers and the state senator, and the first hospital. [For a wonderful picture of North Street, see Chapter IX.]

The Shindler House (1888)

When the *Galveston Daily News* in 1890 commented that "the residence portion [of Nacogdoches] has been greatly improved by the recent erection of some forty structures from latest designs," no doubt the R. C. Shindler House on North Street (now gone) was one of the houses that caught the reporter's eye. The Shindler House certainly caught the eye of a later observer, Professor Elliot A. P. Evans, head of the SFA Art Department in 1948, who undertook a survey of houses in East Texas. Evans photographed 175 houses and collected information on 28 houses with the aid of Lois Foster Blount and Mildred Wyatt. Some of his photographs were returned to the SFA Library in 1985 and can be viewed online.[49] In 1952, when Elliot was Chairman of the Art Department at Santa Barbara College of the University of California, he published an article entitled "The East Texas House."[50] In describing the architectural traditions, Evans wrote that the basic plan was symmetrical, consisting of either one or two rooms on either side of a central hall, sometimes two-stories, with a porch across the front, and chimneys at both ends.[51] The Millard-Lee House, which stood just off the square when Rulfs arrived and now stands at Millard's Crossing, is one of the examples the author cited as this type of house. (See Chapter I.) Although the Evans collection of photographs includes four examples of houses by D. Rulfs, Evans attributed *none* of these houses to the German architect, not even the Roland Jones House. The other Rulfs houses include the Shindler House, the Charles Perkins (Steamboat House), and the Kate Powers Samuels House. The Shindler House is a good example of how

Rulfs accepted regional traditions in architecture and gradually moved his patrons, who would accept more current designs, away from the ordinary into something more stylish.

Robert C. Shindler, a druggist of German heritage, who had a business across Fredonia Street from the Old Stone House, became one of Rulfs's earliest friends in Nacogdoches. His wife, Anna Mary Shindler, was the daughter of one of the most important families in Nacogdoches. Her father, Judge Charles S. Taylor (1808-1865),[52] had signed the Texas Declaration of Independence. The Shindler's property lay on the west side of North Street, across the street from the Taylor Homestead, on land transferred to Anna Mary by her father.

The floor plan Rulfs used for the house was very traditional, not unlike the one for Charles Hoya, except it was a full two-story version. The front was essentially an I-House form (two rooms wide and one room deep) with chimneys in the gables at both ends, and an L-shaped addition off the northwest side. A later one-story addition filled in the L to make it seem more of a massed plan. Unlike the Hoyas, however, the Shindlers allowed Rulfs to add several important stylistic elements to enhance the façade and make it more current, such as bay windows in both front rooms. Most pioneer houses, with their porches from end to end, looked overwhelmingly horizontal. For the Shindler House, Rulfs broke up the horizontal elements by adding bay windows; a gallery, which did not completely traverse the first floor; a second-story gallery over the entrance in a forward gable; and decorative elements (brackets, bargeboards, braces, balustrades, and cut-outs). The house certainly qualified for the newspaper's observation as a structure "from latest designs." Overall, the result was one of the most charming houses in Nacogdoches at the time. Of the three Shindler children who grew up in this house–Anna, Rosine, and Robert–they all later commissioned residences from Rulfs.

Shortly after the house was completed, Shindler unexpectedly ran a small ad in the *Nacogdoches Star*: "FOR SALE. My residence on North Street together with about 12 acres of land and all appurtenances. For price and terms apply to R. C. Shindler."[53] From the comments and letters in the newspaper, this horrified many people. R. W. Haltom in an editorial comment in the same edition called for someone to stop this action: "Mr. Shindler's advertisement of his beautiful home for sale, has the sound of desperate earnestness. Is it possible that he wants to change off this place for Tyler? We can't allow him to ever think of leaving us. A guardian of our public interests must take the matter in hand, and not permit the very best men to have to leave here."[54]

The house may have cost more than Shindler anticipated, but the reason for his troubles was downtown. When the Galveston firm who shared his new Brick Block on East Main pulled out, Shindler's whole financial future became uncertain. John Schmidt became the "guardian" who stepped in and saved not only the downtown block, but also the Shindler home as well. The shocks for the Shindler family did not end there. Mrs. Shindler lived in the house only one year. She died from complications resulting from the birth of her daughter Julia, who herself died six days later.[55] After the turn of the century, Shindler sold this house to the Joseph P. Clevenger family who lived there until it was torn down. In 1955, on its front page, the *Daily Sentinel* ran a headline and picture of this house: "LANDMARK COMES DOWN." The newspaper, while lamenting its destruction, readily accepted Mr. Carl Monk, Sr.'s decision to tear it down "to make way for business growth." Monk, however, admitted "there are no immediate plans for the lot except to clear it."[56] Such was the state of awareness of preservation in Nacogdoches at the time. Rulfs was not mentioned in the 1955 article.

One of the houses Rulfs built for the Shindlers was for Robert (Bob) Taylor Shindler (son of R. C.), a very popular young man in town and soon to be elected mayor. This house, which sat west of his father's home on Taylor Avenue, no longer exists. No pictures of the house have survived, but Giles Haltom called it "one of the prettiest homes in town."[57] The reason for mentioning the house at this point in the narrative is that, at the completion of the house, Haltom wrote an interesting news article about it. Upon completion of the job, Rulfs threw one of his German-inspired "pine top" celebrations. Haltom, who loved these celebrations and mentioned them frequently, wrote about this one in some detail. Entitled "Bob's Blow Out," the article in the *Daily Sentinel*, January 16, 1900, stated:

> It is probable that when for the first time in Nacogdoches, in obedience to a time honored custom of the Fatherland, Mr. D. Rulfs 'hoisted a Pine' from the summit of a building nearing completion; some curiosity was aroused as to its meaning, but that time is passed.
>
> In consequence of the evergreen floating over the new residence of Mr. R. T. Shindler as proudly as if it bore the Stars and Stripes or the proud German colors, at 3 o'clock Saturday afternoon this new home on Taylor Avenue was thronged with persons who were congratulating themselves on the existence of such a custom and on the fact that they were Architects, Carpenters, or friends of the hospitable Bob Shindler. A few brief speeches were then in order. Mr. R. C. Shindler spoke for everybody; Mr. Rulfs spoke for the workmen; Mr. Partin spoke for five minutes, and apropos to the occasion Mr. R. T. Shindler had already spoken for a keg of—not nails surely, and this speech more than any other made everyone feel at home and resolve to do justice to the occasion. And they did. That keg, unlike the cruse of oil mentioned in the scripture, eventually failed, and while its down fall was popularly attributed to the fierce onslaughts of one or two veterans, yet the praise should be more evenly distributed as every man did gallant service. For two hours the conflict raged; and then, after a silent survey of the inanimate foe despoiled of its precious possession, the victorious band returned to their respective duties.
>
> Long live the good old German custom![58]

The custom of hoisting a pine continued until Nacogdoches went dry in 1905. In a recent interview, Ann Phillips added an amusing postscript. Ann's family (the Coxes) lived near William Henry Rulfs in an area south of downtown known as "The Flats," a local name given to the high ground south of the Banita Creek along South Fredonia Street. Her uncle and other overgrown young men loved to get a hint from their neighbors whenever the Rulfs brothers were about to have a pine raising so they could mingle with the older celebrants, *at a sanctioned event,* in order to get a taste of beer.[59]

The Blackstone Franklin Hardeman House (ca. 1889)

Another family for whom Rulfs did considerable work was the Hardemans. The family, one of the most illustrious in Texas history, had among its members a signer of the Texas Declaration of Independence, and a Secretary of the Treasury under President Burnet, and even had a Texas county named for them. Dr. Blackstone Hardeman, the first of three Blackstones to live in the county, brought his family to Texas in 1838 and established a Hardeman community, which later became Chireno. His son, Blackstone Hardeman, Jr., who owned and operated a mercantile business in Melrose, moved late in life to Nacogdoches and was buried in Oak Grove Cemetery.[60] Three of his sixteen children became important participants in the development of Nacogdoches in the late nineteenth century: Blackstone Franklin Hardeman (1854-1933), Tolbert Barrett Hardeman (1858-1927), and Robert Lee Hardeman (1864-1943).[61] The Hardeman brothers would commission a series of houses and commercial buildings by the architect Rulfs.[62]

B. F. Hardeman, the first of the brothers to move from Melrose to Nacogdoches (1888), purchased a lot on North Street next to the First Baptist Church. Shortly thereafter, according to his niece, he had Rulfs design and build a residence for him.[63] This was the first of the three houses designed for the Hardeman brothers; the two extant houses appear in other chapters. There is not a good, straightforward photograph of the B. F. Hardeman house; but it is partially visible in the several photographs.[64] The house as shown was a bourgeois cottage with a projected gable on the north side, with corner brackets over the chamfered bay windows, and a short porch south of the bay window along the parlor. There were turned posts, gentle arches of ball-and-dowel spindlework, and rather standard turned balusters under the handrails. Although the Baptists purchased the house sometime in the 1930s, after the death of Mr. Hardeman, and would later remove it to expand their educational facilities, the house was still on the 1948 map prepared by the State for widening North Street.[65]

FIGURE 4.16. Prize-Winning Float, 1899.

The B. F. Hardeman House on North Street was the backdrop for the picture. The Hardemans entered the prize-winning float in the 1899 downtown parade. In the carriage are Addie Hardeman and Mrs. Mary "Hattie" Clark Hardeman. On the porch are Julia and Anna Clark, and Mr. B. F. Hardeman. Courtesy of ETRC.

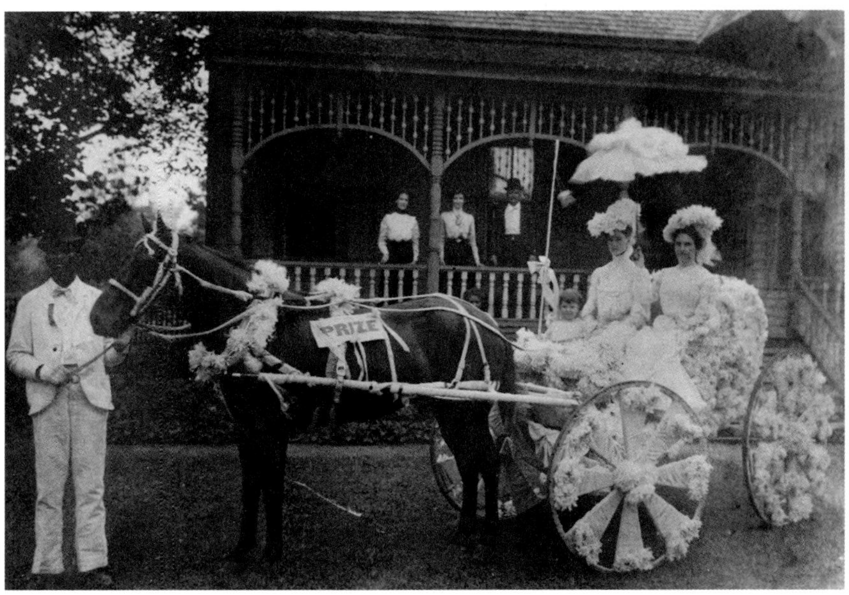

The John T. and Lelia Orton Lucas House (ca. 1890)

Another house, which still exists, typical of the same period, was the home built by Rulfs for the John T. Lucas family. At the time of his marriage, John was thirty years of age and well on his way to being a successful merchant in the hardware business; he had already begun to speculate in land. (The land was part of the Amanda (Voigt) and Fred Müller homestead.) Although John had the land, it was Lelia's father, John Greer Orton, who probably commissioned the house. Orton was a wealthy landowner on the east side of town for whom Orton Hill was named. Orton built homes for all of his children.[66]

The house is configured as the Charles Hoya House and the R. C. Shindler House. All three had chimneys at both ends of north-south oriented houses, porches extending across the front facades, and lapped board siding. Even the treatment of the windows places the house in the same years: the trim on the windows, like on his own office and the Lee Hardeman House, consisted of a simple pediment created out of a shaped board and crown molding. In the inevitable replacement of porches in East Texas, later owners probably boxed in the turned posts and balusters that most probably graced the house originally. The boxed columns, however, give the house a very distinctive appearance. The other feature that is unique to the house and period is the Palladian window in the dormer over the entrance. It is the first known use of this signature feature by Rulfs, several years before he placed them on the Jones House and the Stephen Blount House.

The Lucas family sold the house when they moved to the Tolivar's Crossing in 1903 to found the town of Sacul, Lucas spelled backward. (John and Lelia were the grandparents of Beth (Lucas) Kingham.) The

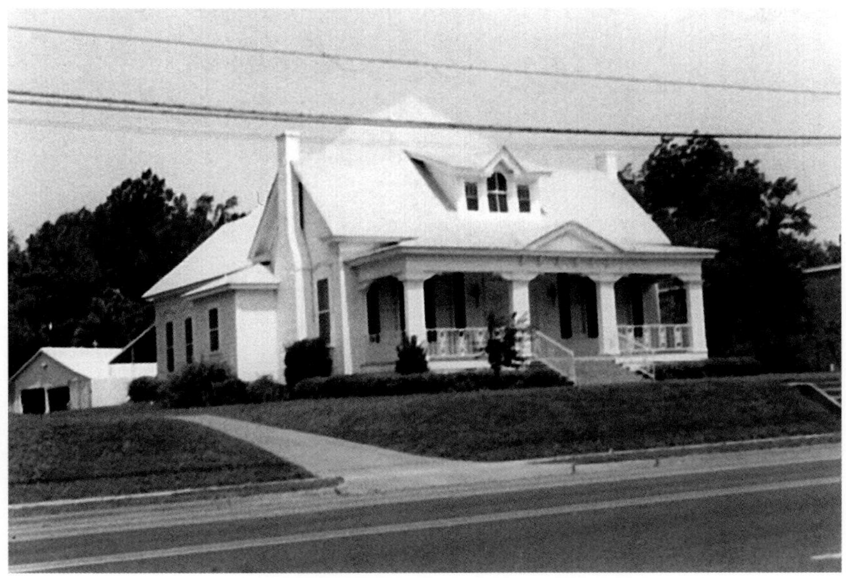

FIGURE 4.17. The Lucas-Floyd-Emmons House, ca. 1952. Courtesy of ETRC.

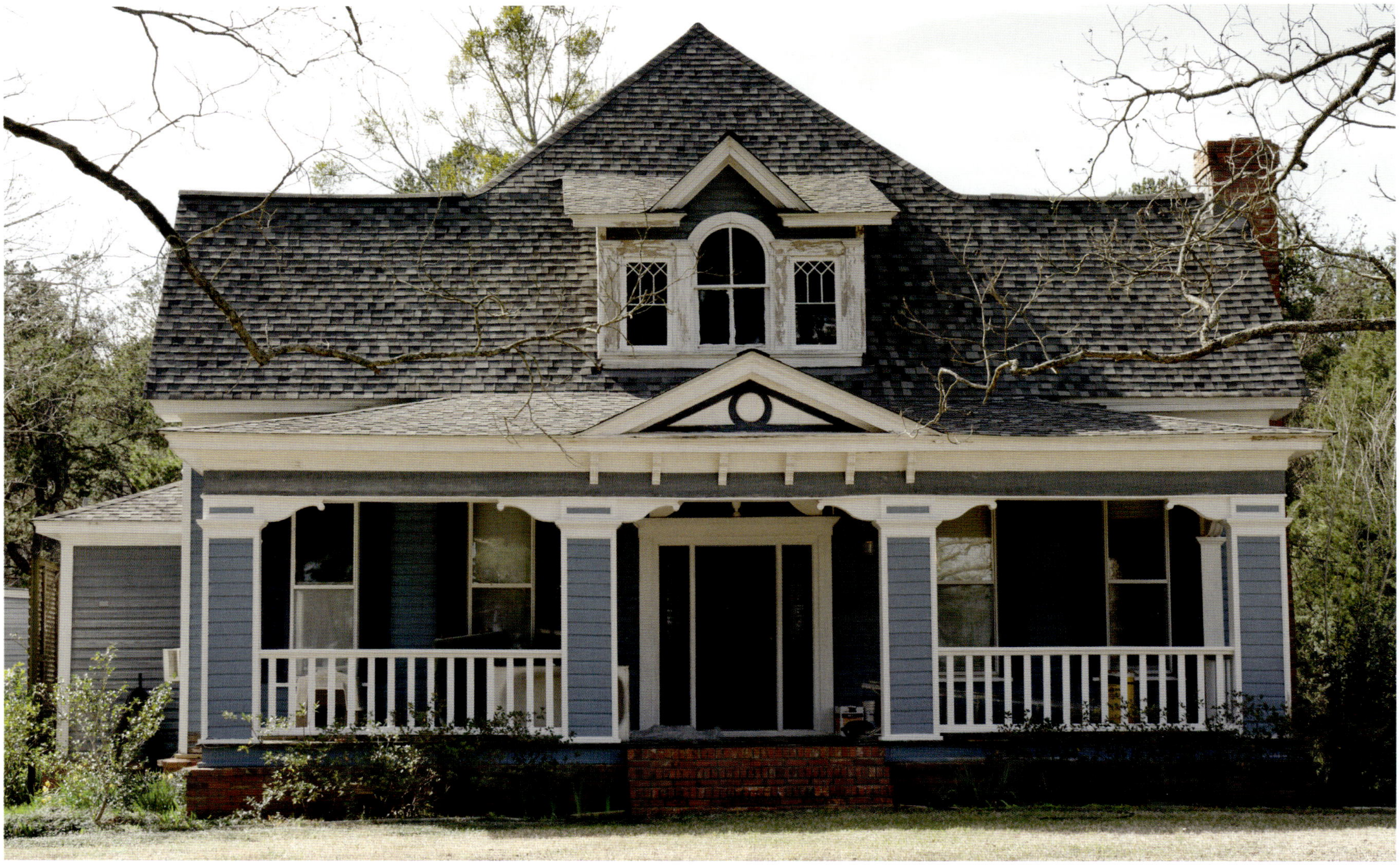

FIGURE 4.18. The Reagan Patton Home, 2012.

family of Luther Wade were the second family to live in the house. The third owners, John F. Floyd and his daughter, Mary Floyd Emmons, owned the house for several decades. Mrs. Bonnie Haskins owned the house in the 1940s until Orland and Alice Patton purchased it in 1977. Decades later, when the Patton family enlarged their commercial buildings, Reagan Patton moved the Lucas House and restored it in a beautiful setting north of Nacogdoches.[67]

The Dominant Houses of North Street

The homes discussed so far did not upend the domestic building standards in Nacogdoches. While, in general, the families who lived on North Street in the late nineteenth and early twentieth centuries reads like a list of who's who in Nacogdoches, three families in particular stand out as having established the standards by which other people in town measured their own domestic contexts.[68] First, there was the Perkins family. The older house that Rulfs remodeled for W. U. Perkins in 1890 confirmed the architect's brilliance as a master of adaptive use and started the stampede to North Street. After a second remodeling by Rulfs in 1910, the family and their house helped to confirm the pre-eminence of the street. Second, there was the John Schmidt family. The house for Schmidt in 1892 set the gold standard for new construction and elegance in Nacogdoches for decades. Friends, relatives, and associates of Schmidt clamored to live nearby their patron. Third, there was the family of E. A. Blount (1849-1914). Blount was the most important banker in town before his death in 1914. The Blount family commissioned Rulfs to do a series of houses, starting with E. A. Blount's own home in 1894 that sealed the dominance of North Street as the premier residential artery. Between 1894 and 1923, D. Rulfs designed no fewer than five houses on North Street for members of the Blount family. In the Blount houses, Rulfs illustrated his command over both large and small houses and eventually over widely divergent styles. Another large house on North Street, done in the mid-1890s but which no longer exists, was the house Rulfs designed and built for John Pickney Davidson (1843-1932). The house, one of several buildings done by the architect for Davidson, sat south of the First Baptist Church and north of the Sturdevant House.

Of all the houses mentioned in the discussion below, only very few remain. With a preservation plan and functional alternatives (such as University Drive), Nacogdoches might have prevented or at least lessened the destruction of homes along North Street that accompanied the expansion of Stephen F. Austin State College in the years between 1948-1973.

The W. U. Perkins House, Phase I (1890)

William Usery Perkins (1856-1940), a very important businessman in the transformation of Nacogdoches in the period after 1880, was the druggist and entrepreneur who joined John Schmidt in hiring Rulfs to build the "First Brick Block" in 1883-84. Looking back at those early days, Perkins reflected, "The hardest working period of his long business career in Nacogdoches was the decade following the location of the firm in the brick building at Pecan and Main Street." He also added that it was one of his most rewarding: "Friendships and business acquaintances were formed there at that time with its vicissitudes have not effaced." Haltom observed that Perkins had a "keen business [sense] and ability and personality."[69] Perkins Brothers, his company, became a household name in East Texas in the late nineteenth century. At first with his brother-in-law, then his brother, Dr. Sam, later with his younger brother, Charles, and finally a nephew, John, Will Perkins turned the drugstore business into a general store that introduced many innovations to Nacogdoches (including ceiling fans and screen doors). Perkins was the scion of a wealthy landowning family from Rusk County near Laneville, but he became wealthy in his own right by his professional skills and his astute investments.[70] Will Perkins and his younger brother, Charles, were also important in real estate, the lending of money (later banking), and in the all-important cotton industry, especially the Cotton Seed Oil Mill.

When Will Perkins married Annie Kemper in 1889, he was thirty-three. Like Charles Hoya, he needed a house of his own in which to begin his married life. In 1890, Perkins purchased the Judge W. G. Ratcliff home, which stood where Tipton Ford Motor Company now stands. The location had the same advantages of all the lots on the west side of North Street: the property went all the way down the hill to Banita Creek. This allowed plenty of room for the requisite livestock (horses, cows for milk, chickens if desired, etc.), and, in addition, enough room on which to build houses for family retainers.

Perkins asked Rulfs to remodel and enlarge the Ratcliff home. Commenting on this house, from pictures she had seen, Will's oldest daughter, Louise Perkins Wilson, said later: "I dimly remember that house. It was a small house; and looked more like the houses in the north. It was built by Judge Ratcliff, I think. They [Will and Annie] added on to it in the Victorian era and then made another still bigger change later."[71]

Without detailed pictures of the original house and the absence of Sanborn Maps for North Street before 1929, it is difficult to know exactly what additions Rulfs made to the original floor plan. According to descriptions from family members and friends and one single photograph, the most likely changes consisted of the following: the addition of a wing to the north of the original house; then a second story over the whole first floor, such as the architect had successfully done on the Edwards House and the Bullen Hotel. Will's daughter, Virginia Perkins Nelson, said, "It worked." She said the house had a narrow front gallery with lots of "gingerbread" and a "little tower."[72] Mrs. Nelson continued, "Possibly the whole of the Ratcliff house was incorporated in the present structure, but the building has been so skillfully done that . . . [I am] unable to say just which part of the Perkins home was a part of the Ratcliff home." The bay window and the ornate porch along the side of the south parlor can partially be seen in the one extant photograph of the house. The porch on the 1890 house was only a single story, unlike the similar entrance treatment used later on the Stephen Blount House, which was a two-story version. (The Perkins House most people remember, the one demolished in 1967, contained the 1890 house,

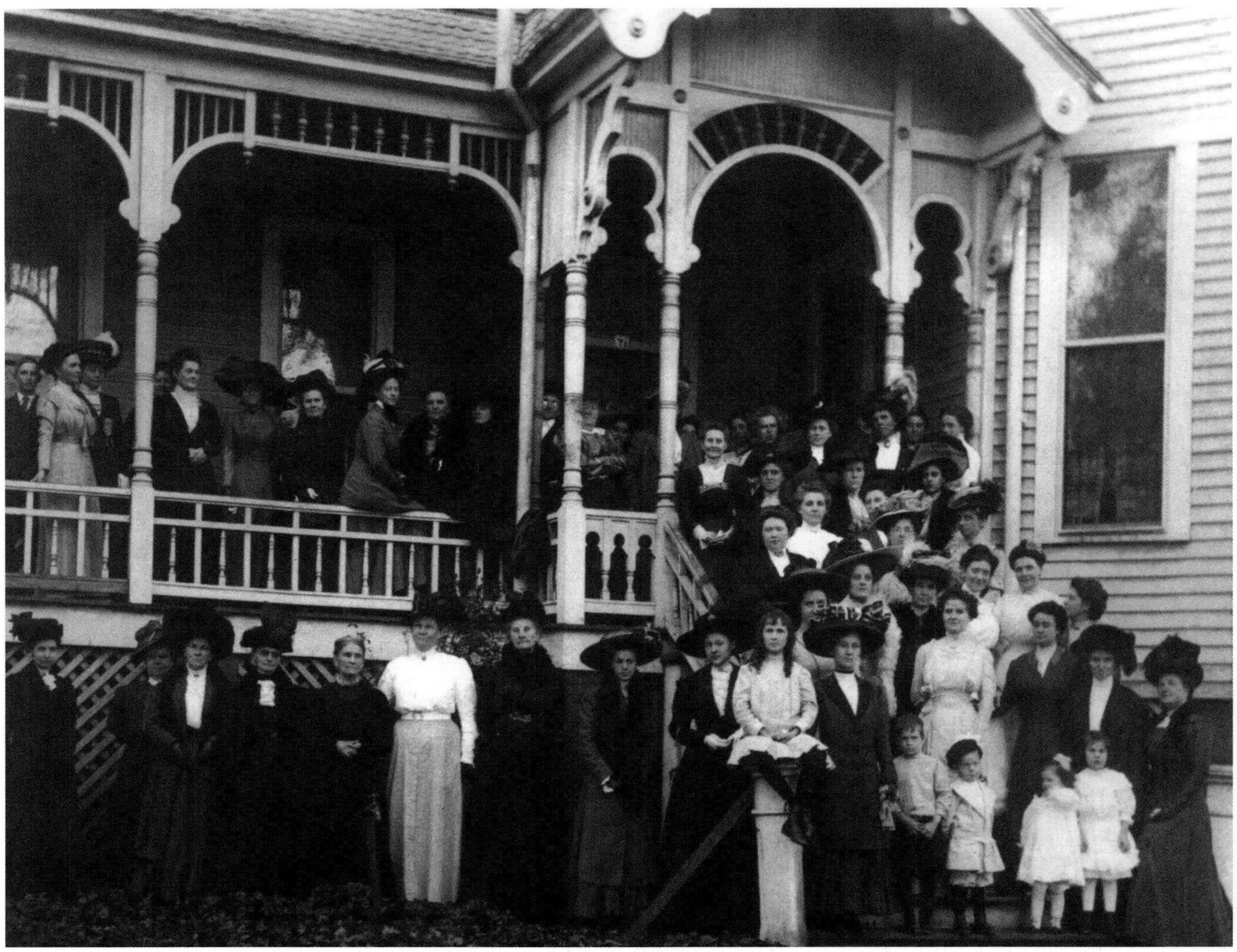

FIGURE 4.19. The Will and Annie Kemper Perkins House.

Perkins House on North Street. It is also probable that the Perkins themselves moved to North Street because the First Baptist Church had purchased land there in 1886. Frequently, after church in the evening and before other church meetings, Baptists gathered at the Perkins' home for tea or ice cream. While many Baptists tended to gravitate to the North Street area, especially after their big church was built in 1899, the Methodists in a similar religious-affiliation created a neighborhood in the Washington Square area. Rulfs built houses and churches for them all. (The churches are discussed in Chapter Nine.

but the look on the exterior was quite different. The updated 1910 house was significant, also, and will come up for further discussion in Chapter 10.

According to descriptions of the 1890 house from friends, there was a parlor on one side and an enormous living room on either side of a generous entrance hall. The entry hall was actually more of a welcoming room. While, as one would expect for the period, fireplaces existed in all of the major rooms, the Perkins House included a fireplace in the entrance hall—a first for Nacogdoches. Later patrons who used the services of the architect demanded the same. The landing of the majestic U-shaped staircase at the rear of the hall extended across the entire width of the hall. Under the landing an arched doorway led to the service areas of the house and kitchen at the rear of the house.[73] A small parlor, to the south of the entrance hall, was probably the former parlor for the Ratcliff house. In the north addition, added by Rulfs, the large new formal drawing room (25' x 36') had an equally large dining room, arranged perpendicular to it, to the west.[74] Between both parlors and the hall, and also between the drawing and the dining room, Rulfs specified oversized double-pocket doors, similar to the ones discussed later in the Roland Jones House. When opened, these doors created an enormous space for entertaining. The Perkins family frequently entertained groups from the First Baptist Church, such as the one on the steps in the photograph, Figure 4.19. Shortly after the completion of the Perkins's home, Haltom wrote in the *Nacogdoches Star-News*: "The improvements being made here are of such a solid permanent character that it gives confidence. Business houses are solid brick. The residences are as neat and tasty and as well arranged as any that can be found in any other city."[75]

The members of the Perkins family *were* trendsetters in two different generations. It was not just a social thing; they used status for their business advantage. Will and Charles Perkins were keenly involved in real estate development along North Street. Their decision to purchase land along North Street, much of it from the Charles Taylor heirs, was followed by recruiting their friends and relatives to locate on the street. Two of Will's early recruits to North Street, shortly after his own move, were his own parents who moved from Rusk County in 1893.[76] A cousin, Dr. Joel Barham, who was a popular physician with a large and successful practice, also decided to live nearby. The house Rulfs designed for Barham is now gone. The first telephone in Nacogdoches connected the Perkins Brothers Drug Store to the home of Dr. Barham.[77] Charles Perkins even built speculative houses. The Steamboat House, discussed in detail later in the chapter, is an example.

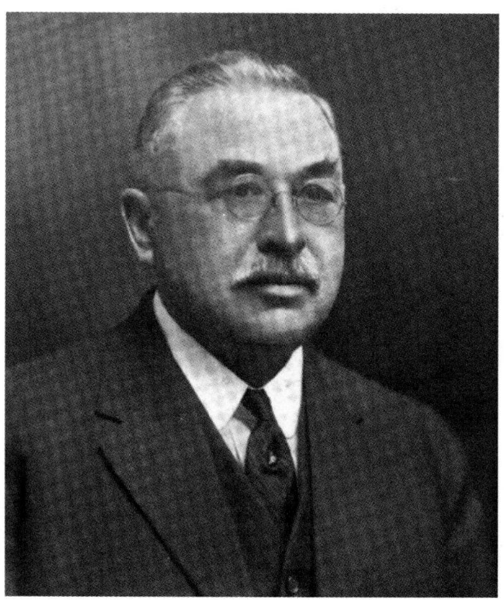

FIGURE 4.20. Portrait of John Schmidt, ca. 1916.

John Schmidt's portrait appeared in the 1916 edition of Frank Johnson's History of Texas and Texans, *Vol. 4.*

John Schmidt and Nacogdoches

Among the first to follow the Perkins to North Street was John Schmidt. Shortly after he purchased the property, Perkins sold the old Charles S. Taylor homestead to Schmidt. The John Schmidt House on North Street (on the south side of Mims Street) was to be a trend-setting event. As it was being built, the newspaper commented on its significance. "John Schmidt's fine residence now being built on the old Curl [Taylor] place is beginning to show it is going to be something very important."[78]

Schmidt loved to turn heads. He instinctively understood the importance of symbolism. He understood the part that social standards played into the overall business world. As in so many other ways in the period after 1878, Schmidt led the citizens of Nacogdoches into new business investments, and now in 1892, he used the talents of his recruited architect even to outdo Perkins in defining the new standards for domestic refinements in Nacogdoches. Architecturally, Nacogdoches had never seen such a display of wealth. Quite possibly, Schmidt selected North Street because Will Perkins had done so before him, but there were other reasons too. North Street was increasingly becoming the new entrance into Nacogdoches. The north-south axis of the town had gained prominence since the coming of the railroad. Houston and Shreveport were replacing Austin and Natchitoches in terms of trade. It was additionally important to Schmidt that the property he purchased was a historic piece of property. The old Taylor-Curl place he chose to tear down to build his home was the homestead and house of Charles S. Taylor, a signer of the Texas Declaration of Independence. The original grant backed up on Washington Square and once included part of the land given in 1845 as the future home of Nacogdoches University.

Architecturally, Schmidt's domestic arrangements in the "Germantown" area were no longer commensurate with his leadership role in the town's economy. The functionality and grandeur of the Bullen Hotel no doubt inspired him, but after seeing the impressive work by Rulfs on any number of houses, such as the Edwards, Shindler, and Perkins houses, Schmidt was impressed anew with the residential skills of his recruited German architect. Schmidt, however, was not about to settle for half measures. He did not want to be known or remembered as living in a hand-me-down house, even one of a famous early patriot such as Charles S. Taylor. A makeover might appeal to an old Southern family like the Perkinses, but John Schmidt sought to be the arbiter of taste and style in Nacogdoches. Schmidt aspired to the leading social role in town. (Interestingly, this was almost the opposite of Diedrich Rulfs, whose personality, training, and careless attitude about keeping documentation on his accomplishments, indicated a man who shunned the spotlight.) Nevertheless, Rulfs the architect could provide the new domestic stage that Schmidt needed for his performances. Because Schmidt was such a strong patron of the architect, a more extensive coverage of Schmidt the man seems appropriate.

Schmidt was, without a doubt, the most prominent entrepreneur in Nacogdoches in the period between 1880 and 1920 and after that, a substantial businessman in Texas in general. The number of business enterprises he initiated, inspired, underwrote, sustained, spun off, and joined is truly impressive.[79] From a small grocery business, Schmidt and his partner, Abe Mayer, re-made the business environment in Nacogdoches, inspirationally as well as physically, in terms of their buildings. At one point Schmidt had as many as eight different establishments around the downtown area. His

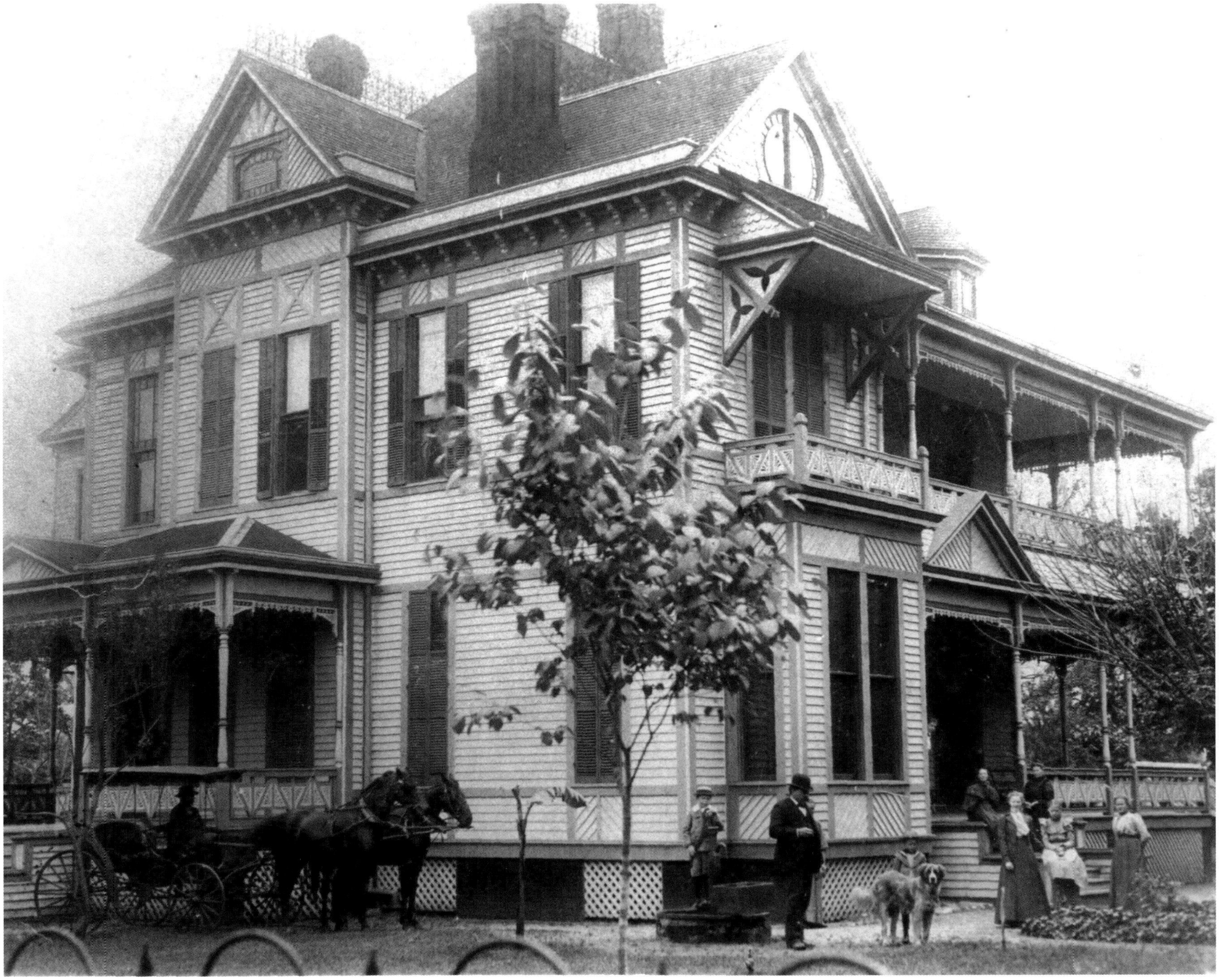

FIGURE 4.21. The John Schmidt House, North Street, 1892.

In this photograph, taken shortly after the house was completed, John Schmidt is in the center; his wife, children, and retainers are gathered around him, even the family dog and carriage. The exterior of the Schmidt House, reminiscent of the Edwards House, had a 2-½-story gable on the northwest front side, a large square bay with a Juliet porch in front of the second story bedroom, and a large double gallery that wrapped to the south. The roof was predominantly a hipped construction with gable projections from the central core. In the front gable, there was an unusual stained glass window composed of two vertical semicircles, lined by tinted glass. Instead of using turned balusters under the handrails, Rulfs used pierced ones, which gave the porches a very custom look. No other house in Nacogdoches ever went to this expense, for while turned spindles could be easily found in the lumberyards and catalogues, the pierced ones were rare. (These can be more clearly seen on the porch off the north side of the house.) The house had built-in shutters, popular in Europe, which could be closed to seal off the house to help keep it cool in the summers. For heating, there were fireplaces in each room and in the entrance hall. Some of the chimneys supported as many as five flues. While standard lapped siding was used, the patterns created a sense of movement in the façade when caught by the light. Rulfs placed a pediment over the front door, a shed roof over the Juliet balcony, and inset panels on the brickwork of the chimneys. Supporting the water collection gutter just below the edge of the roof, Rulfs created an entablature by using banding timbers, patterned siding, brackets, and dentil molding to give the house additional detail. Courtesy of ETRC.

initial company, Mayer & Schmidt, became a powerful nucleus for establishing Nacogdoches as a major retail center for this part of the state. Their use of hyperbole, calling their company "the Hercules of Nacogdoches' business houses," came closer to reality than most at the time or since have admitted. Schmidt launched many important Nacogdoches families into wealth and provided sustenance for many sons, sons-in-laws, and nephews in various businesses.[80] He came to Nacogdoches at an important moment, but he had the sure business instincts to recognize and take advantage of the opportunities at hand. These are not just the present author's thoughts, but also the testaments of people at the time.[81] After his bankruptcy and death in the 1934, John Schmidt's contributions have been forgotten.

Many townspeople recognized that along with his showmanship, Schmidt was a reliable, progressive, and creative businessman. There were few large commercial and industrial activities with which he was not in some way connected. He was highly intelligent, practical, cosmopolitan, and connected. He traveled extensively and visited Germany yearly. He was also deeply involved in Democratic politics. He served as a delegate to the Democratic National Convention when Cleveland was nominated for his second term. He was a supporter of William Jennings Bryan and was responsible for bringing him to Nacogdoches to speak in 1908. Schmidt served as an Alderman in the city on several occasions, City Clerk, School Board Trustee at the time of the dissolution of the Old University, a Mason, and chairman of the first committee to acquire Stephen F. Austin State Teachers College for Nacogdoches. Schmidt was also famous for his oratory. While a Lutheran in his youth, he joined the Christ Episcopal Church in Nacogdoches. He was devoutly religious and contributed to civic ventures, which included the building of the first Opera House, an interest free loan for the construction of Zion Hill Baptist Church, and a donation of land for the Catholic Church across Mims Street.[82]

The John Schmidt House (1892)

The house Rulfs designed and built for John Schmidt was enormous. Its thirteen rooms, a local first at the time, had as much presence on Mims Street as it did on North Street. The house had a basement, where Schmidt kept his imported wines (as did the old German Adolphus Sterne), and the ceilings were 14' high (lowered in later years in order to efficiently heat the structure). Curly-pine graced the structure throughout in wainscoting and doorframes. The doors themselves were of even more exotic and varied woods. The hinged doors were three feet wide, and the pocket doors between the public rooms were fitted to ten-foot openings. According to an article at the time of its destruction, the curly pine molding at the top of the walls next to the ceiling was "approximately eighteen inches wide.[83] The millwork alone would have made the house exemplary. The woods for this house, carefully selected by Rulfs, showcased the best East Texas had to offer. He used a cornucopia of sylvan products: curly-pine, cypress, birch, cedar, walnut, and hickory. To the materials locally available, Rulfs added imported dark woods from Germany to outline each room with a border to add contrast to the flooring. All the mantles came from Europe as well.

The house represented Rulfs at his best. Evidently, Schmidt set no limitations on the architect in realizing the house. While there are no pictures of the interiors, only descriptions, the large pocket doors that the architect used throughout the first floor would have permitted the house to have a very open feeling and to offer complete flexibility for entertaining. Other examples built shortly thereafter and in emulation of the Schmidt House (such as the Roland Jones House) had similar floor plans. In many ways, the house reflected the earlier Bullen Hotel.

The interior innovations in the house also set new standards in Nacogdoches. The house had the first indoor plumbing system in the city. Since the city did not have water distribution at the time, an ingenious rainwater collection system in the attic supplied water for utilitarian purposes throughout the house. For the drinking water, the plans specified a well built into the back kitchen porch. Since this was before the appearance of electricity and natural gas in Nacogdoches, the house had an acetylene power system connected to all rooms of the house. The first house in Nacogdoches to have brilliantly lighted chandeliers and wall sconces, these were later converted to use electricity when that convenience arrived at the end of the decade.

The Blount Family Houses

Two Blount brothers, Edward Augustus (1849-1914) and Stephen William, Jr. (1854-1928), migrated to Nacogdoches in the 1890s to take advantage of the economic boom that followed the railroad's arrival.[84] Their father, Colonel Stephen William Blount, settled in San Augustine in 1835, was a signer of the Texas Declaration of Independence, and represented San Augustine in the Texas Constitutional Convention. The family had extensive land holdings.[85] After their father's death in 1890, the older Blount brothers decided to move west. E. A. Blount probably arrived in Nacogdoches earlier than his younger brother, Stephen, but both were here by the mid-1890s. E. A. Blount was to become the leading banker in Nacogdoches before his death in 1914; he also sat on the board of the Stone Fort National Bank. While associated primarily with the Commercial National Bank, Blount did not purchase controlling interest in the bank until January of 1902.[86]

The Blounts developed a close relationship with D. Rulfs. Their families were both active in the Christ Episcopal Church. Rulfs designed and built many houses and commercial buildings for the Blounts.[87] Rulfs designed and built two houses for E. A. Blount in 1894-95.[88] The larger of the two, Blount's own home, stood just north of the present-day Westminster Presbyterian Church on the west side of North Street. A much smaller house built for Blount's daughter, Laura Blount Chapman, on the occasion of her marriage, still stands on the corner of North and Power Streets.

In 1945, when Blount's house burned in a spectacular explosion and fire, the newspaper referred to it as "the grandest mansion in Nacogdoches."[89]

Gala Held at the Blount House, 1905

The Federation of Women's Clubs in Texas met in Nacogdoches in 1905. According to the *Galveston Daily News,* May 14, in a section entitled, "Texas Society," Mr. & Mrs. E. A. Blount entertained the Federation Club delegates at a gala reception attended by 250 guests. Each room of the large house had a different color scheme with colored imported roses. The paper called it "a fitting background for the beautifully gowned and jeweled ladies with their escorts, who thronged the lovely rooms." The paper called the reception for the statewide guests "one of the largest and most brilliant social affairs ever given in Nacogdoches."

While it is doubtful the house was more opulent than John Schmidt's, the house was very important and was for many years a center of social gatherings in Nacogdoches.[90] The house was a two-story Queen Anne style structure with an asymmetrical façade, a hip-and-gable roof, wrap-around galleries from the north to the south, upstairs balconies with shed roofs, and turned posts with spindle work in between.

Without very close inspection, all Victorian houses look somewhat similar, especially Queen Anne houses with towers. One recent author, Margaret Culbertson, in writing about mail-order house plans in her book *Texas Houses Built by the Book*, suggests that the E. A. Blount House was built from a catalogue of designs by George F. Barker, as was a house in Crockett.[91] There are similarities between the house in Crockett and the Blount House, but the conclusions are based on very poor photographic evidence and outside the chronology of the career of the Nacogdoches architect. While Rulfs undoubtedly drew on many resources for his inspiration and certainly could have drawn on the ideas of Barber, there are readily identifiable differences between the plan suggested as the model and the Blount House: in the porches, the floor plan, and the ornamentation.[92] Culbertson readily admitted: "Most of Barber's early designs consisted of eclectic interpretations and combinations of late Victorian styles." More pertinent, however, is the fact that the Blount House follows the plan and influence of the D. K. Cason House on Church Street. Also, neither E. A. Blount was the type of client who would have sanctioned a canned plan, nor Rulfs the type of architect to need such a crutch. Long relationships are not built on prefabricated ideas, and Rulfs had a long and friendly relationship with two generations in the Blount family, lasting from the mid-1890s to 1923. He designed both commercial and residential properties for them. Blount valued the quality Rulfs could supply and wanted an architect who could not only supervise and guarantee construction, but who could also make changes as the process was underway. After remodeling the Bullen Hotel, the Edwards House, the Perkins House, and also designing and building the Schmidt House, the thought that Rulfs needed a do-it-yourself kit is just not credible.

FIGURE 4.22. The Edward A. Blount House, date unknown.

The Blount daughters and their friends stand in front of the Blount House. Judging from the dress of the young ladies, white dresses with bows in their hair, the occasion was rather formal, perhaps a music recital or Sunday School presentation ceremony. The tower of the house is hidden behind the magnolia tree on the left. Courtesy of ETRC.

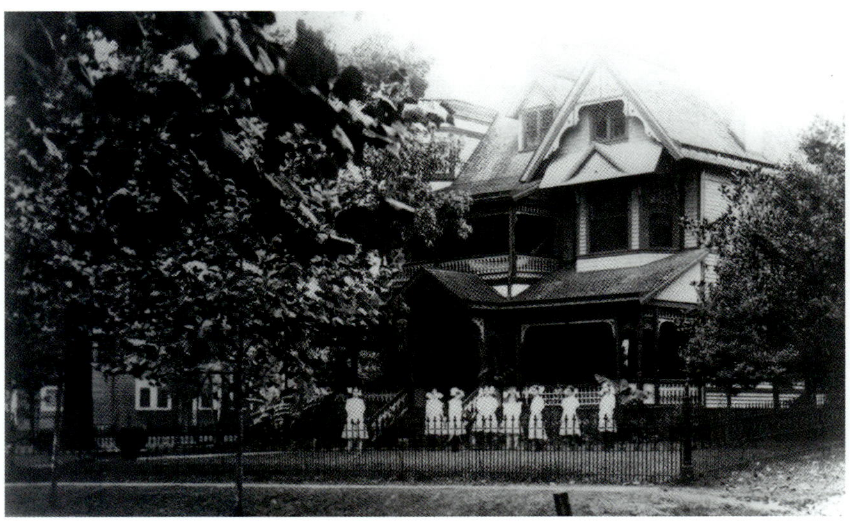

The question of whether Rulfs ever used ideas from books and magazines is relevant. Rulfs, like architects through the ages, most certainly borrowed ideas from the past and from current publications. Plans and ideas were readily available at the time.[93] Also, clients brought ideas to him as they do to most architects. There are many elements in pattern books that fit this or that house by Rulfs. Which examples he used, where he gleaned ideas, how he mixed patterns with his own ideas, cannot be documented since he left no library or archive. Certainly, his houses incorporated many of the typical Queen Anne features of the period—steeply-pitched roofs, dormers, gables, bay windows of every variety, towers, gable ornaments, textured shingles, etc. Architects across the nation drew from a readily available pool of publications. Of the common features that he favored and used in most of his houses, the origins of these influences can as easily be documented to his North German heritage as to plan books: for instance, his signature use of endless versions of three windows grouped together (Palladian windows). He also visited Houston and Galveston often. From various catalogues, he saw and used prefabricated elements readily available in the industrial age: mantles, hardware, doors, specialty moldings, windows, and columns. He, or perhaps his brother and partners, sometimes saved money by re-using plans he had successfully used before, but these resulted in varying degrees of success.[94] By flipping the floor plan, changing the trim, or altering the way the porches wrapped around the house, he could prevent the house from looking like a duplicate. No one complained, at least no one that can be documented.

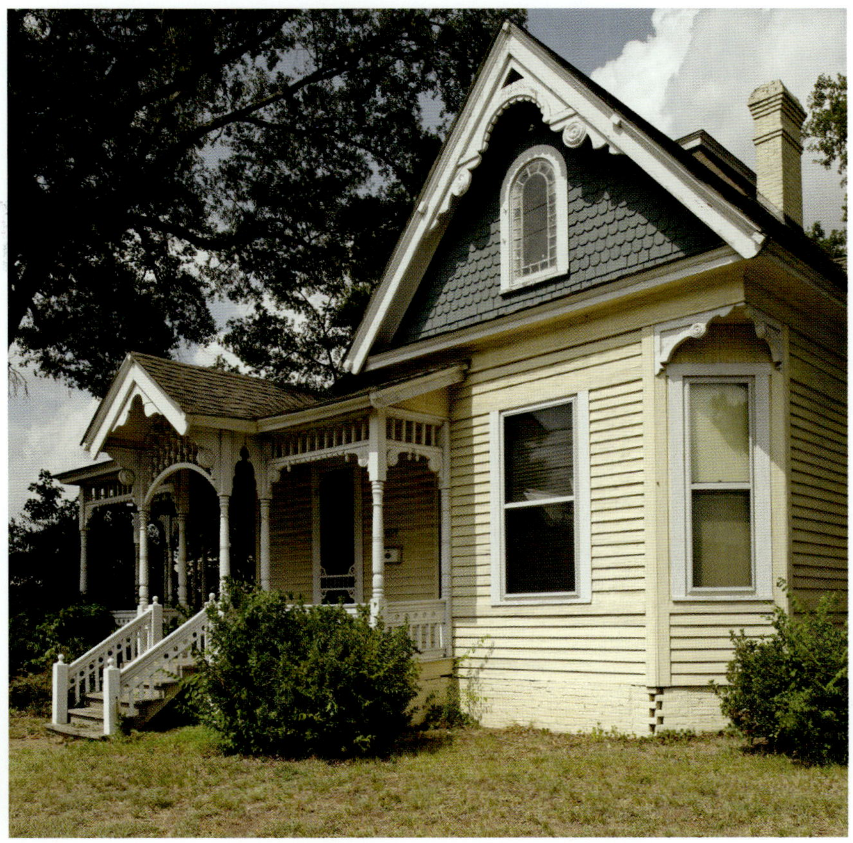

FIGURE 4.26. The Laura Blount Chapman House (1894).

The charming house built by E. A Blount for his daughter, Laura, is now the Henry Clifford Rudisill Trust House in 2011.

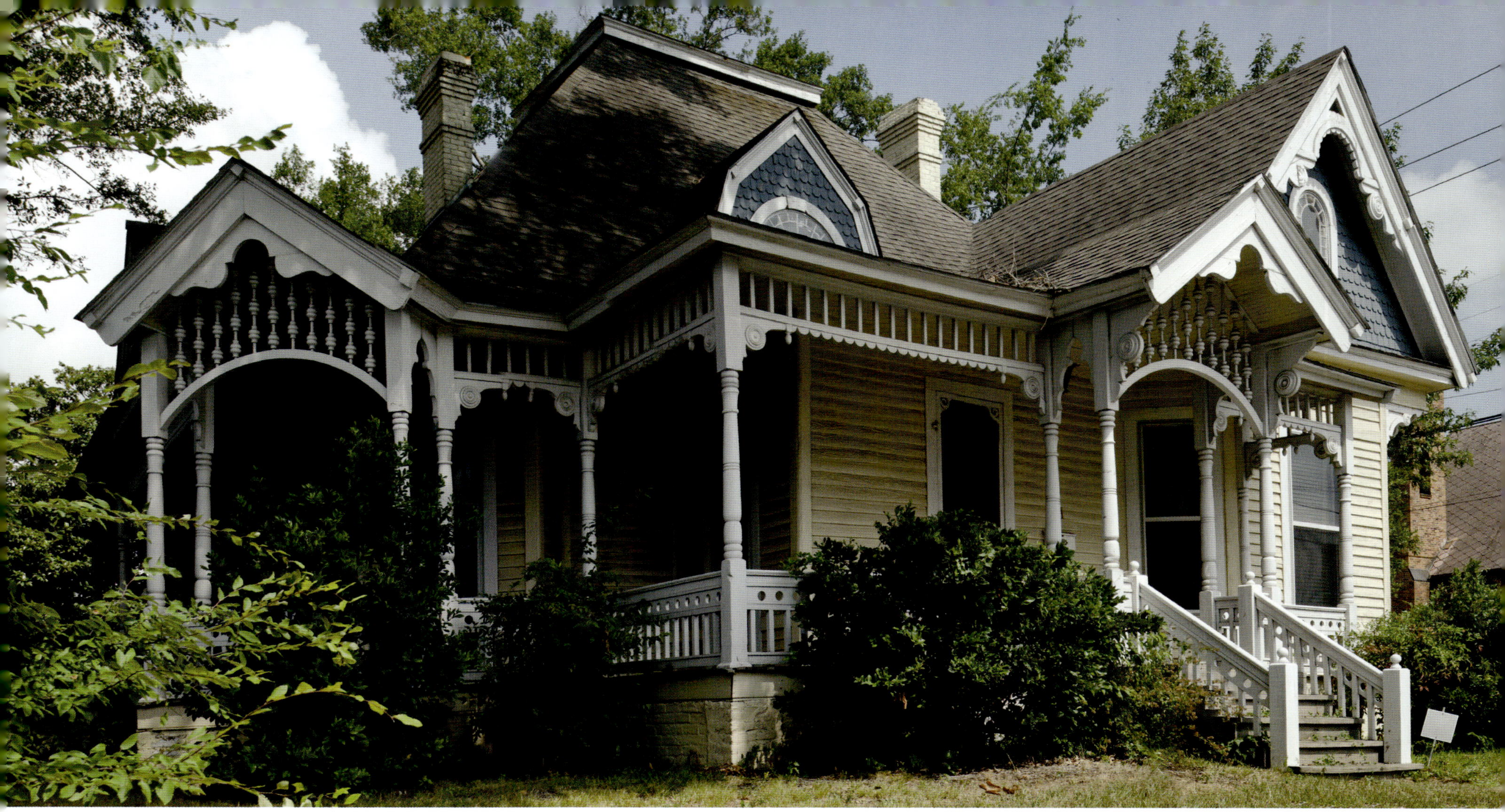

FIGURE 4.19. The Blount-Chapman House, now isolated on North Street by commercial development, is a wonderful example of a Queen Anne cottage by Rulfs. North Street was a pleasant residential street in Nacogdoches until the 1960s.

The Laura (Blount) Chapman House (ca. 1894)

At 821 North Street, on the corner of Power Street, still stands the charming house which Rulfs designed for E. A. Blount as a gift to his daughter Laura Adelaide on her marriage to W. McNeil Chapman on October 10, 1894.[95] The modest house is another good example of how comfortably and quickly Rulfs moved away from the basic "East Texas House" when the client gave approval. The Laura Blount Chapman House has a more sophisticated roof line than the other small houses he had done up to this time. The steeply pitched hip-and-gable roof in this house is a diminutive version of the E. A. Blount House. At the culmination of the roof, Rulfs capped the truncated crest with a faux-widow's walk of decorative iron. He would use this same treatment on the Roland Jones, Stephen Blount, and Benjamin Wettermark Houses. He chose to pierce the massive front part of the roof with a gambrel dormer, featuring a semi-circular (fanlight) window in the center, to give light to the enormous attic space; the arched windows in the front and side gables also served this purpose. (Gambrel roofs were all over his part of North Germany.)

The east or street-side façade was asymmetrical with a gable on the north and a porch that wrapped around the east and south side of the house. The upper part of the gable had a single arched window lined with stained glass panes. In the gable, he used fish-scale shingles and an ornately carved gable ornament, which framed the window below. The gable, which overhung the chamfered corners of the bedroom below, had decorative brackets supporting the overhang. The architect accentuated the main entrance by placing a pediment at the roof line, composed of an arch and ball-and-dowel detailing. The spandrels were neat and tailored, however, their brackets were modest. The occupants of these nineteenth-century houses used their porches as essential living spaces. At the southeast corner of the Laura Blount porch, the direction from which friends would arrive from town, Rulfs pulled out the corner of the porch to create a pergola-like space for a swing. He had used this for the first time on the Edwards House, but he later employed this strategy on several other houses.[96] The grandchildren of later owners fondly remember visiting the house and spending many hours on this porch watching traffic come and go on the street.[97]

Along the porch, Rulfs used slip-head windows. These windows, similar to later triple-hung windows, allowed the check rail to be located above the midpoint of the opening so that when the lower sash was in the fully raised position, people could walk through the opening as if it were a door. Rulfs specified slip-head windows in many houses. Such windows allowed the front hall, the living room, and the dining room to open onto the porch. Later, when screen doors were coupled with slip-head windows and the high interior ceilings, the openings made for a well-ventilated house. Rulfs used these windows on many houses.[98]

In 1896, Laura Chapman unexpectedly died following childbirth.[99] The grandparents, Mr. and Mrs. E. A. Blount, brought up the child, Laura Blount Chapman. In memory of their much-loved daughter, the Blounts dedicated two Tiffany windows in the new Christ Episcopal Church (Rulfs, 1901). For years, E. A. Blount could not bring himself to sell the house; instead he rented the house to various people, for instance the Sam Stripling family. (See Chapter X.) After Blount's death, the estate sold the house to the Henry Clifford Rudisill family. The Rudisill family loved the house and lived in it for the rest of the century, which accounts for its remarkable condition. A Rudisill Family Trust, established by a grandson, Clifford Rudisill, owns and maintains the house today, with plans to give it to the City of Nacogdoches.[100]

The Judge Ingraham House (ca. 1896)

George Frances Ingraham was a prominent lawyer in Nacogdoches; the Bar Association, in a 1920 tribute, labeled him "among the best lawyers in Texas."[101] He served Nacogdoches as county treasurer, County and District Judge, and a State Representative; he was also a Mason and a staunch supporter of the First United Methodist Church. Rulfs worked with Ingraham on many projects: among them were Ingraham's home, office, daughter's house, and, as chairman of the building committee, which erected the 1910 building for the First Methodist Church.[102] In 1888, Ingraham had purchased a house on North Street, where Gound Chevrolet stands today, and lived there for the rest of his life.[103] It is quite possible that E. A. Blount decided to build where he did, just south of the Ingrahams, because the two families were related. Shortly after Blount built, ca. 1896 Rulfs did one of his famous remodeling jobs for Ingraham to enlarge his house; the Ingrahams had a large family (nine children).[104] While the Ingraham House has not survived, the office which Rulfs designed for Judge Ingraham in 1897 still stands at 210 Pilar Street on the south side of the Square.

FIGURE 4.20. The George Ingraham House.

This unsatisfactory photograph is the only one the author could locate of the Ingraham House. Rulfs used the pattern he had employed on the Edwards and Perkins houses. He took a traditional two-story, north-south gable house and added a cross gable wing to the north of the original house. On the front of the new gable, he placed a square bay window with a Juliet porch and duplicated this same treatment on the old south end of the house. He tied the old double galleries of the front into the new wing with slip-head windows on both floors, and replaced the trim and balusters to update it. The new internal chimney at the juncture of new and old wings supported six flues and was very decorative above the roof level. Because he was working with an existing porch, this is one of the few houses on which the architect failed to accentuate the front door with a pediment. Courtesy of ETRC.

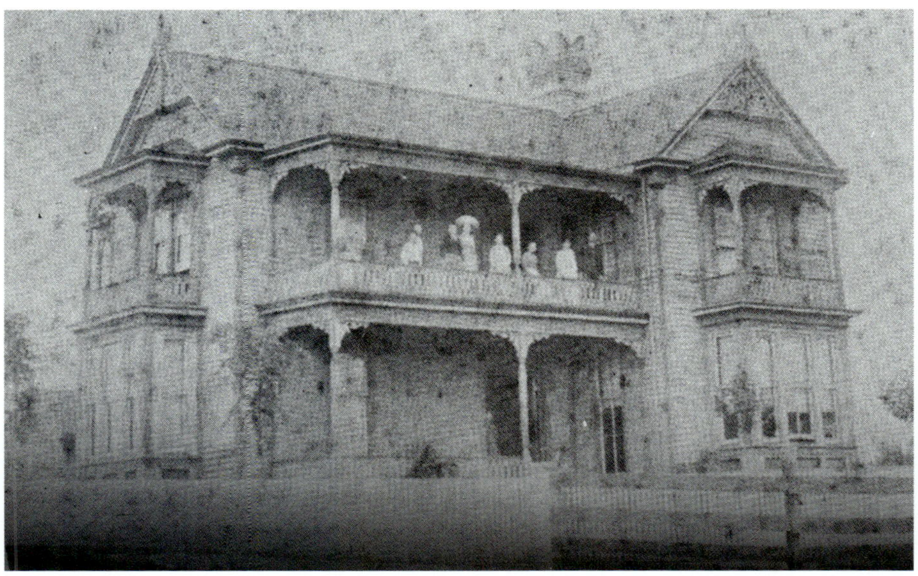

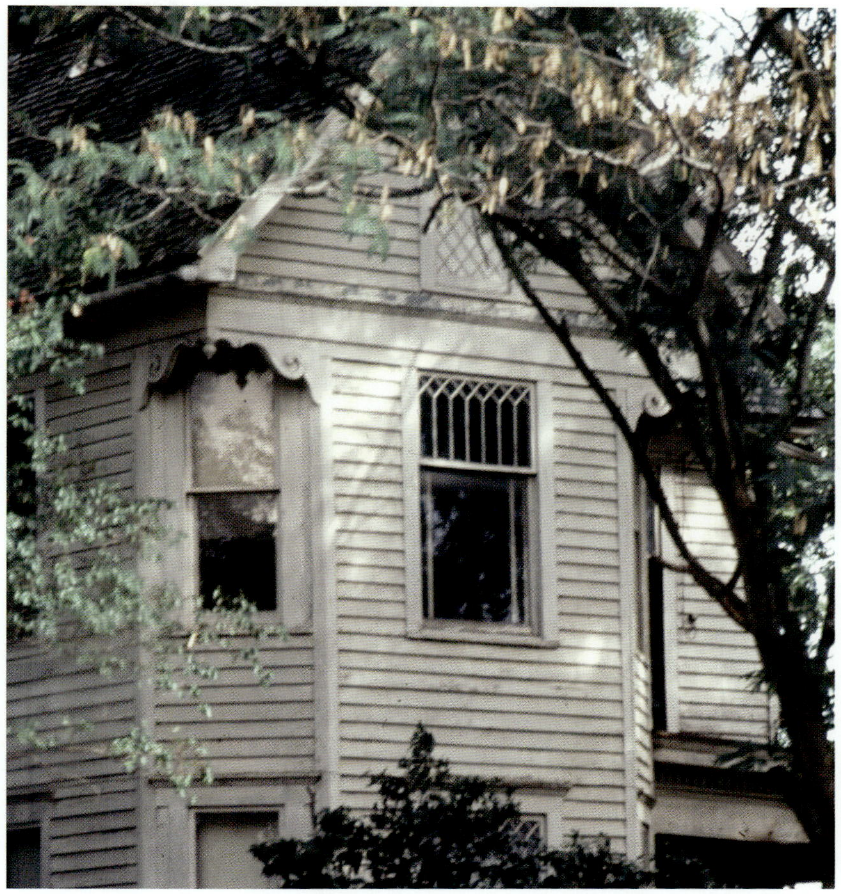

FIGURE 4.21. The John J. Baker House (ca. 1898), Front Bay, 1975.

The details on this house were put together with care. Since the house was a remodel of an earlier structure, Rulfs completely changed the mood and arrangement of the house. Photograph by the author.

The John J. Baker House (ca. 1898)

Another example that illustrates Rulfs's ability to remodel houses was the home on North Street of John J. Baker and his wife, Lelia Levy Baker. Baker worked for John Schmidt at Mayer & Schmidt. In 1896, the Bakers bought a lot from the Charles S. Taylor heirs, Julia Curl and Anna M. Shindler for $1,250; the lot had an existing house, originally a log house, that had been remodeled several times like the Edwards House.[105] Baker secured extra acreage from Beatrice Mims. The house stood just three lots north of the Mims Street, on the east side of North Street. (For information on the Sam Stripling house of 1905 that sat in-between the Mims and the Baker houses, see Chapter X.)

The Baker - Weaver house was one of the favorite houses of Mrs. Mary Stewart Duncan, Rulfs's niece. As Mrs. Duncan discussed her uncle's work, the little Baker House came to her attention anew because it was up for sale in the early 1970s. During the time the house was listed, the author took her suggestion to tour the house and took the unprofessional pictures shown on these pages. Duncan knew the history of the house, and just as she promised, in the middle of the house the log walls were still visible in the back of an added closet.

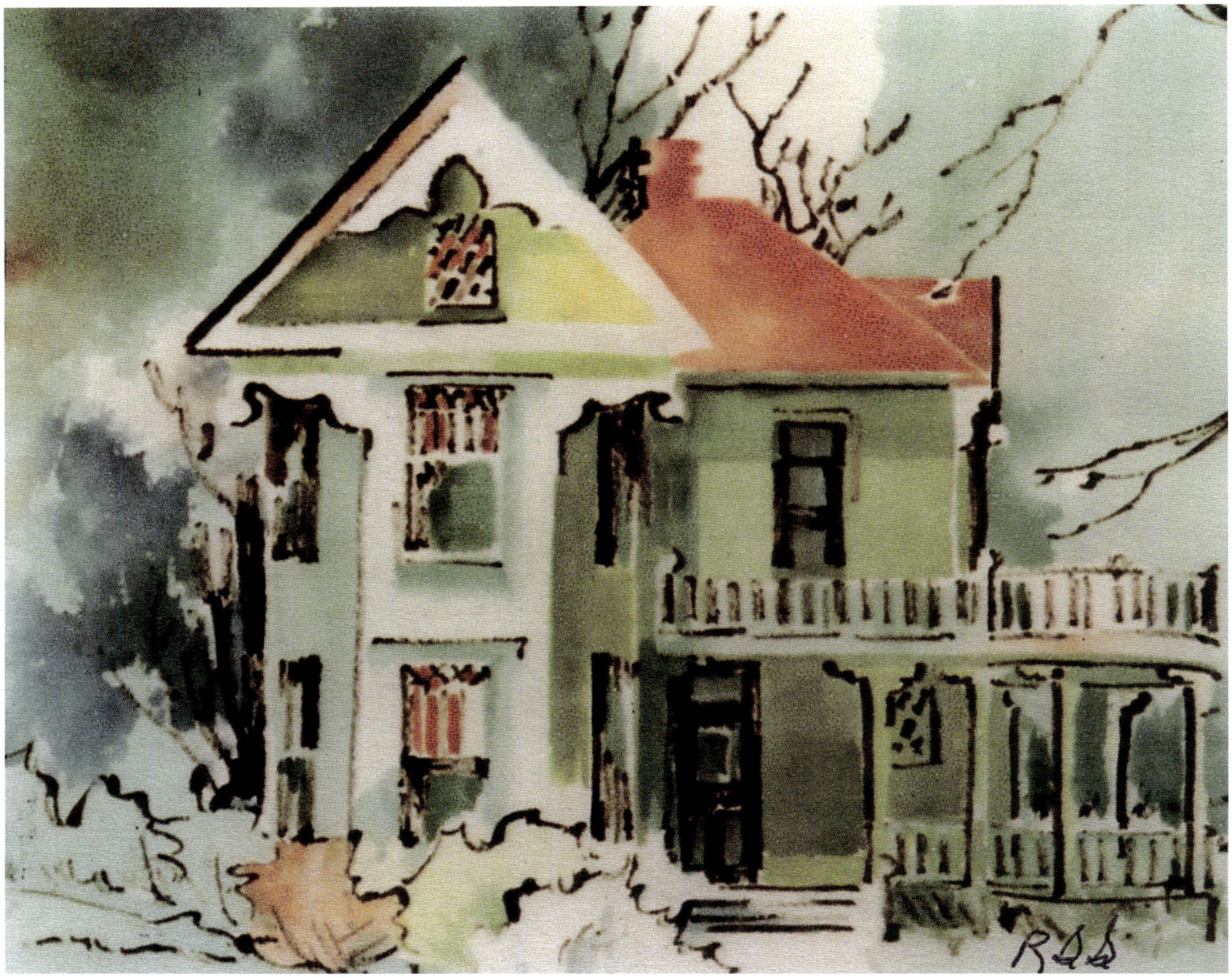

FIGURE 4.22. The Baker House by Artist Rebecca Stanly, ca. 1975. *Drawing compliments of Rebecca Stanly.*

FIGURE 4.23. (Below) Baker House, North Street in 1975.

In this photograph, taken by the author, the front porch has extensive damage from rot. When porches rot, as they invariably do exposed to the weather, people think the whole house is falling down. A contractor, who looked at this house with the author, said the porch was the only unsound part of this structure. Those interested, however, could find no one to undertake saving this charming structure by moving it at the time.

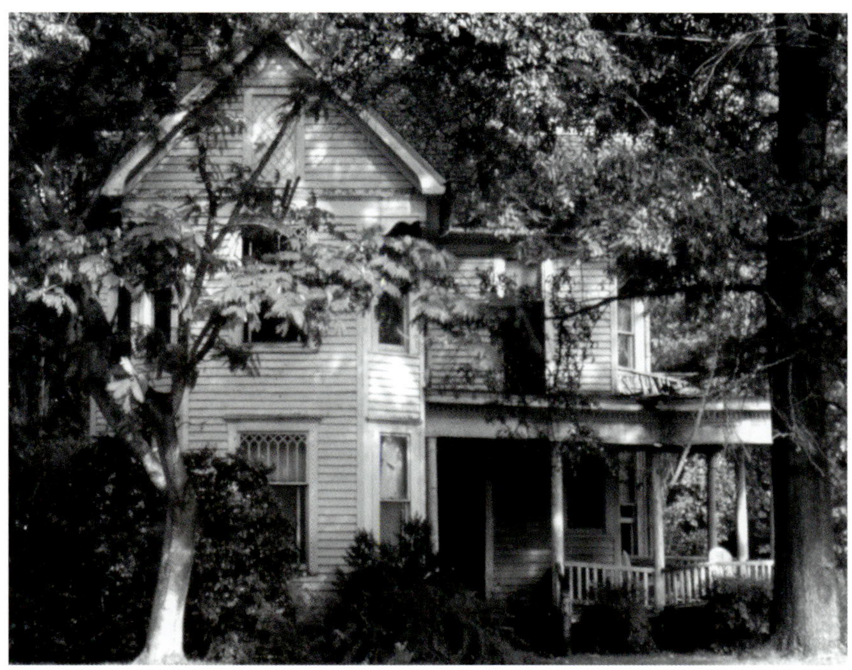

Rulfs designed not only grand houses, but also many charming smaller houses–as one of my colleagues aptly named them, "baby grands."[106] The Baker House was one of his most compact undertakings. Sometime before Rulfs arrived in Nacogdoches, the owners had encased the original log house into an L-shaped structure with two rooms across a hall from the log room.[107] In his makeover, Rulfs added a living room with a bay to the west front, placed a mirror second story over the entire house, and added a new entrance hall and stairway in front of the old hallway. From the new entrance around to the log room, he wrapped a new porch supported by Tuscan columns. At the corner of the porch, he placed a gazebo-like rounded projection, also supported by Tuscan columns, that was mirrored above with a balcony with rails and balustrades. The effect was less heavy than the porches on the larger houses of the era and kept the structure from looking either boxy or dull. The Sam Stripling House (1905), which sat next door, was another of the architect's "baby grands." At the time the Baker House was for sale in the 1970s, the house primarily needed paint and porch repair. Porches in East Texas rot off while one is sitting on them; but, unfortunately, in the vernacular of East Texas, this made most people view the structure as "falling down." It is a pity, in the opinion of the author, that someone could not see past the porch to salvage this small jewel as was done in the case of the Steamboat House discussed below. It would now be equally famous.

The Charles Perkins ("Steamboat") House on North Street (1898)

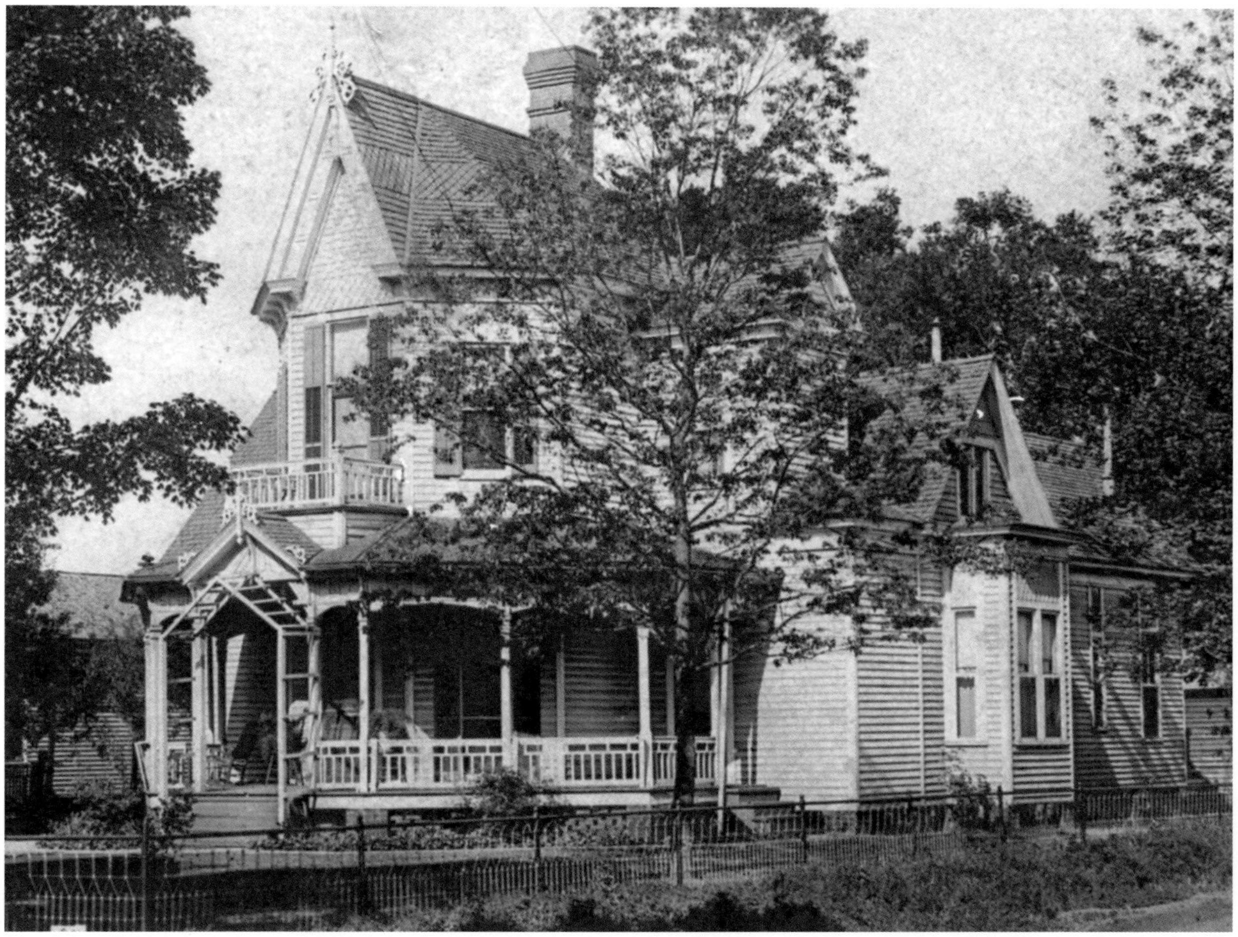

FIGURE 4.24. The Home of Tom and Karle Wilson Baker, ca. 1910.

The Charles Perkins House became the home of Tom and Karle Wilson Baker in 1907. The house sat on North Street throughout the Bakers' tenure to 1916. In the 1940s, the owners pulled it back on the lot and reoriented it to face Baxter Duncan Street in the 1940s. Photograph courtesy of Edward B. (Jerry) Baker.

The house which Rulfs designed and built for Charles Perkins in 1898 is one of the architect's most popular creations, which possibly accounts for why it still exists today after two moves. The "Steamboat House," as locals have christened the house, originally sat on North Street, then on Baxter Duncan Street, and now on Texas Street.[108] Charles Perkins, the younger brother of Will Perkins, was heavily involved in the real estate part of the Perkins Brothers empire; Charles's interests in speculating in land started in the 1880s when he and his brother purchased substantial property on both sides of North Street from the Charles S. Taylor heirs. The brothers bought and sold property all over Nacogdoches. In the next chapter, their decision to build a home for their sister Sarah Richardson is discussed. According to the family historian, Charles did not decide to settle down to become a partner with his brother as a pharmacist until around 1900.[109] Haltom, the editor of the *Daily Sentinel*, thought the sale of the Steamboat house important enough to mention it in his daily column: "Chas. Perkins has sold his pretty little place on North street to Lloyd Bowers. Mr. Perkins will erect a handsome residence on Mound street at once. We are constantly widening and improving and furnishing homes for good people, who are welcomed as desirable citizens.[110]

Architecturally, the Steamboat House demonstrates the creative fun Rulfs must have had combining his favorite elements to produce different outcomes. The front part of the house is a two-story projected chamfered bay room, which houses an entrance hall on the first floor and a bedroom on the second. Around the entrance hall wraps an elegant porch with tailored Stick-style balusters, arched solid wood spandrels linking the chamfered posts, and an arched pediment over the front door. The hip-and-gable roof is complicated. By placing a separate gable with an open bottom over the upper center window of the bay, Rulfs created a dramatically steep triangle over the whole entryway. The Italianate eaves of the upper roof line have decorative support brackets. Instead of using bargeboards, the architect encased the sides of the gable and used cornice returns. The gables on either side of the house were more traditional. Rulfs used a small chamfered bay window on one and a boxed bay in the other, with patterned shingles and bargeboards to give texture. For heating, the house had a central internal chimney with multiple flues; and for cooling, the much-favored slip-head windows gave flexibility and access to the porches.

FIGURE 4.25. (Below) The Weatherly Home 1948.

This photograph, part of the study of East Texas architecture conducted by Professor Elliot Evans while chairman of the Art Department at Stephen F. Austin State College, shows the house facing Baxter Duncan Street where it stood until 1988. Photograph from the Evans Collection, ETRC.

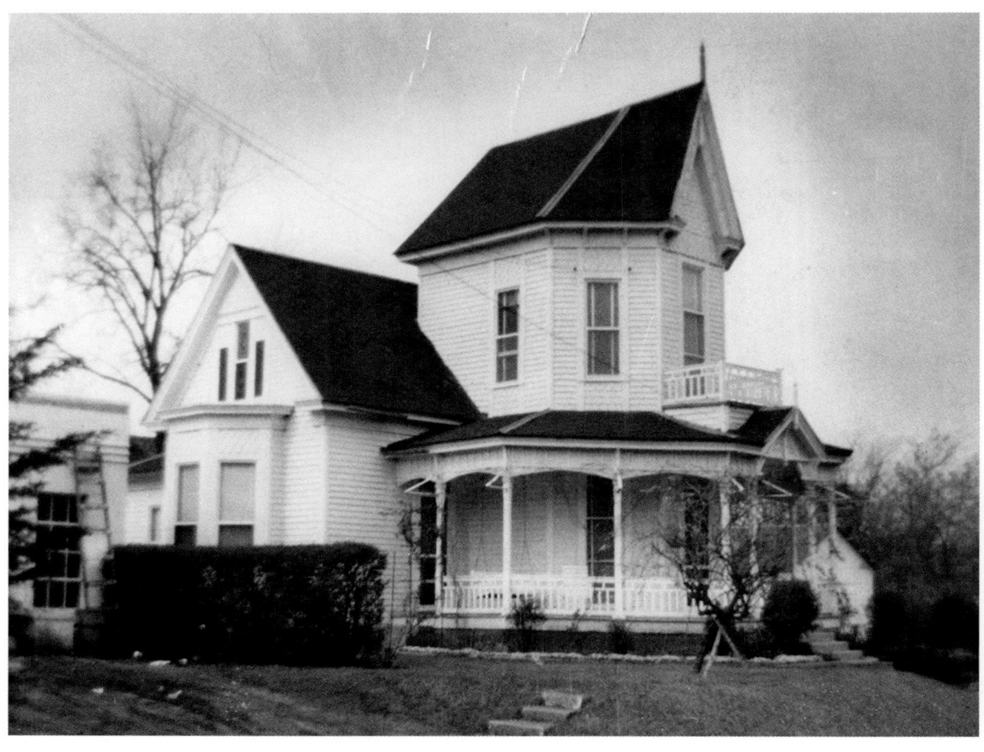

Charles Perkins, Rulfs, or possibly the two of them, used the plans of the Steamboat House three additional times in Nacogdoches. All three houses, however, in the author's opinion, did not produce houses with the same charm and sustained charisma that has accompanied the Steamboat house. The reason was that they tried to use the plans to build less expensive, single-story houses. Without the second story over the entrance hall, the wrap-around porch and projecting roof necessitated an odd and unpleasant roof configuration.[111] Not every success could lead to a profitable trend.

Thomas Ellis Baker, shortly after his marriage to Karle Wilson in 1907, bought the Steamboat House and made it their first home. As both of the Bakers were lovers of nature, they used the front upstairs balcony off their bedroom to study the stars at night. Karle wrote her poem "Altair" in *Blue Smoke,* recording her impressions of the stars, while they lived in this house.[112] In 1916, after the death of Karle's parents, the Bakers moved to Tanglewood, another Rulfs house, on Mound Street (discussed in Chapter XI).

After Bernie Weatherly purchased the house in 1928, he moved the house back and turned it to face Baxter Duncan Street in order to make room for a new gas station on North Street. Burt and Mary Jo Baxter later owned the house for some years. In 1988, former Athletic Director at SFA, Travis "Shorty" Hughes and his wife, Florence, moved the house to 809 Texas Street and lovingly restored it in 1988. They had to cut the house into nine sections and move it at night to meet city standards.[113] The house is now the home of George Ann and John Leonard.

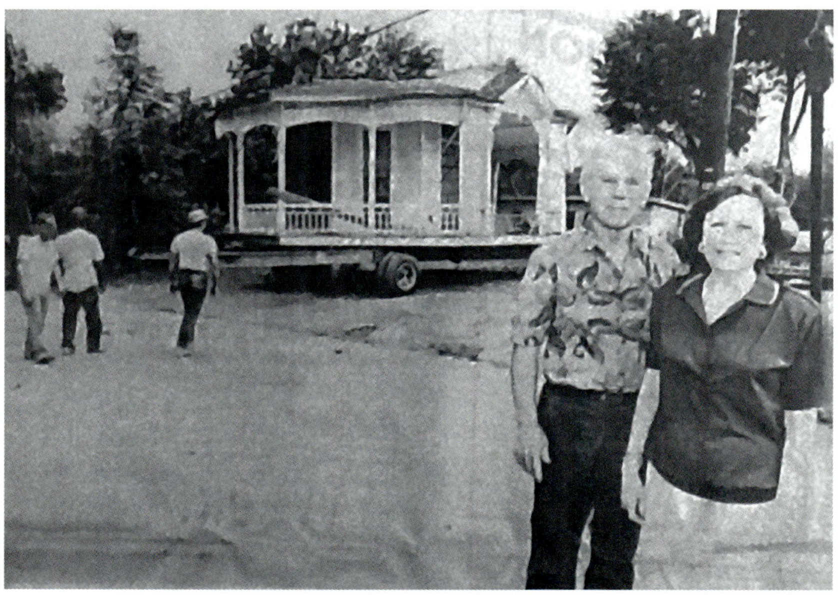

FIGURE 4.26 The "Steamboat" House Being Moved, 1988.

As this picture from the newspaper shows, Shorty and Florence Hughes (front right) are talking to the reporter as the front porch of the house in being moved onto its new location on Texas Street. The move necessitated the house being cut in nine sections. Picture from the Daily Sentinel, July 17, 1988.

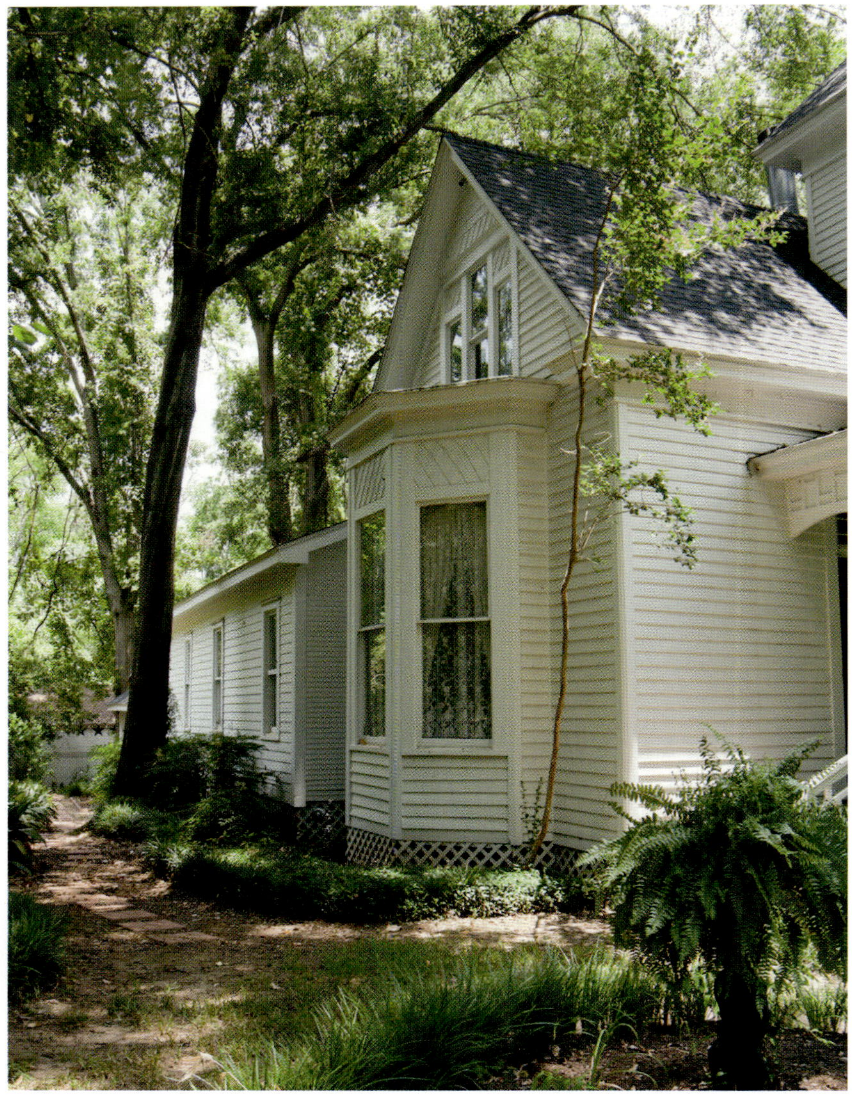

FIGURE 4.27. West Side of the George Ann and John Leonard Home, 2012.

Rulfs used a modified Palladian arrangement for the upstairs gable and a small bay beneath; the opposite side of the house used a square bay.

FIGURES 4.28 (Across)- 4.29. (Below) The Leonard Home, 2011.

The forward upper center of the house was a bedroom, shown below. The center window had a pocket into which it slipped to create a full door to the balcony.

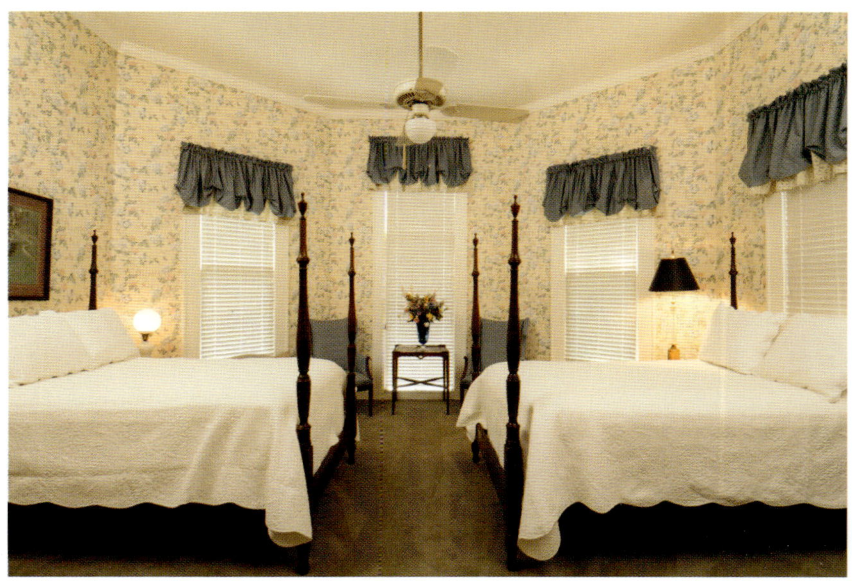

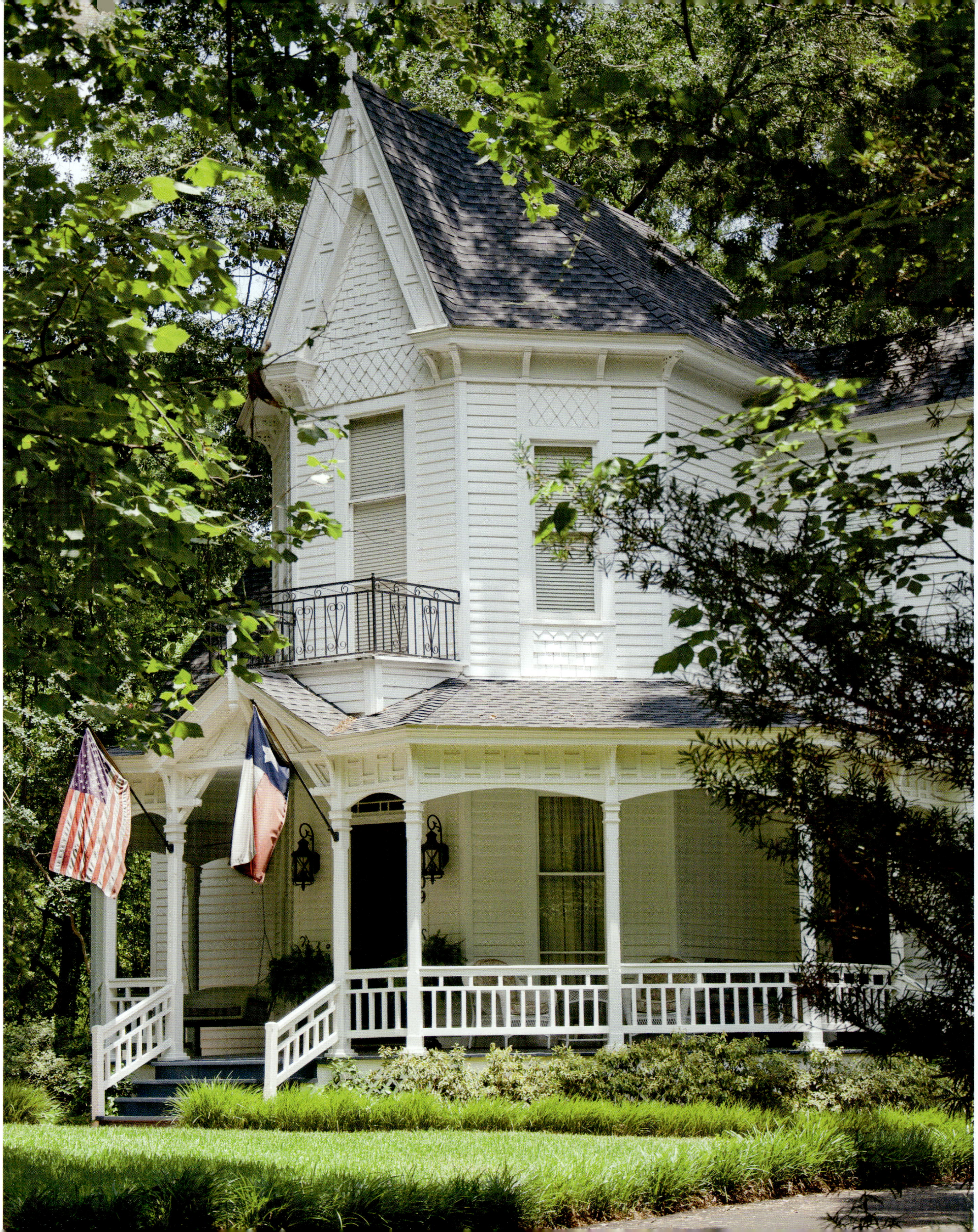

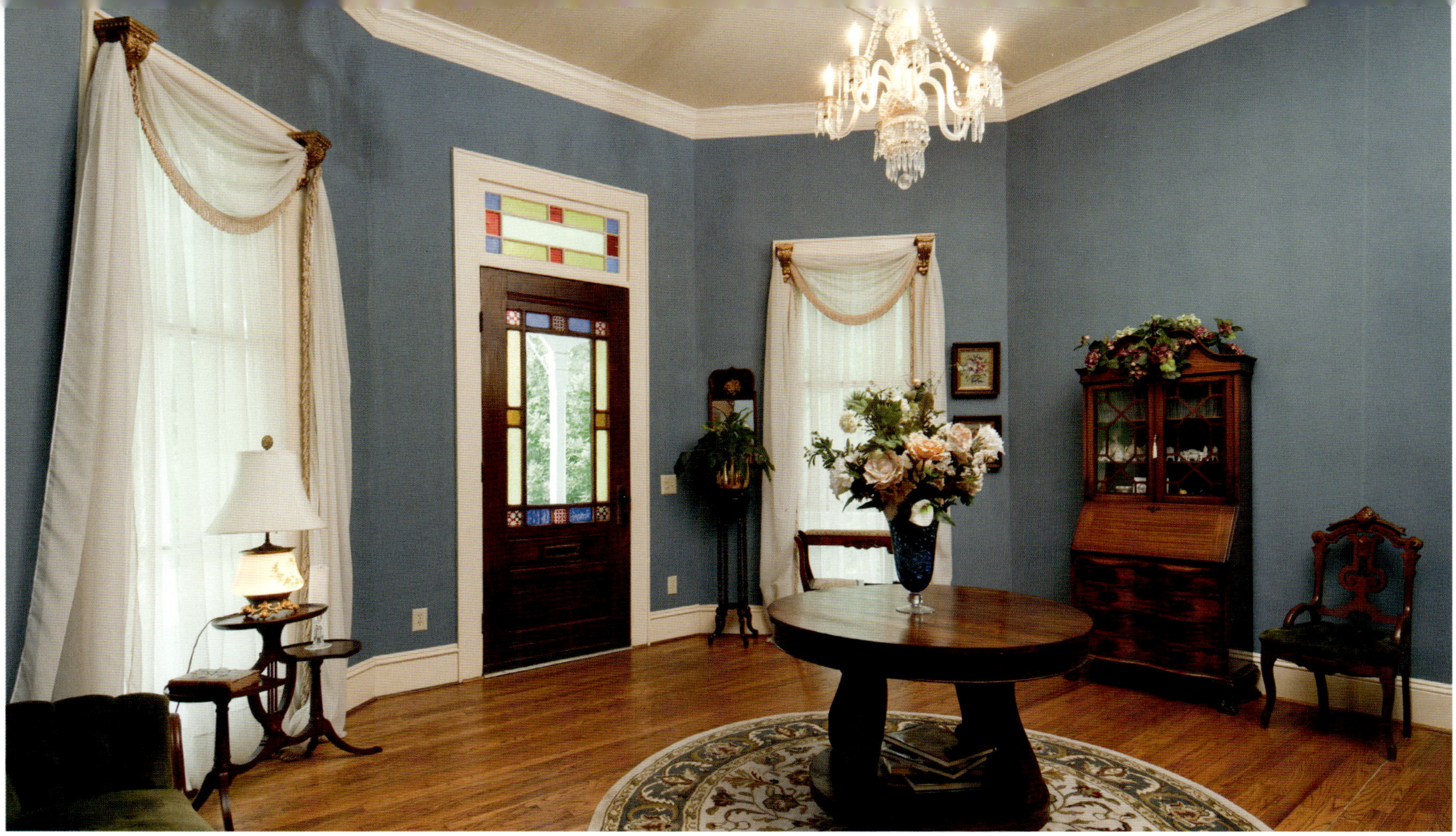

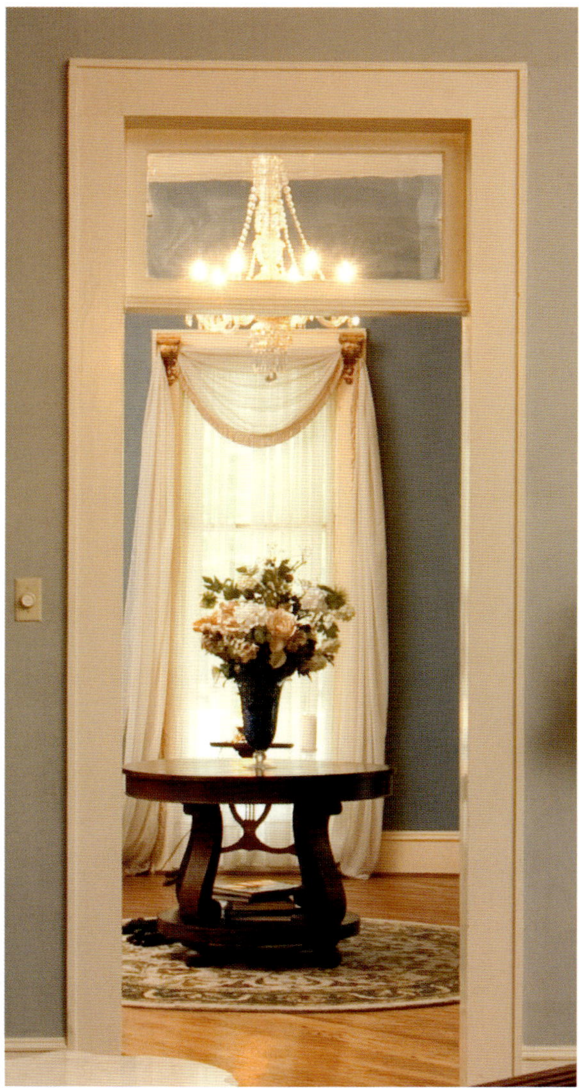

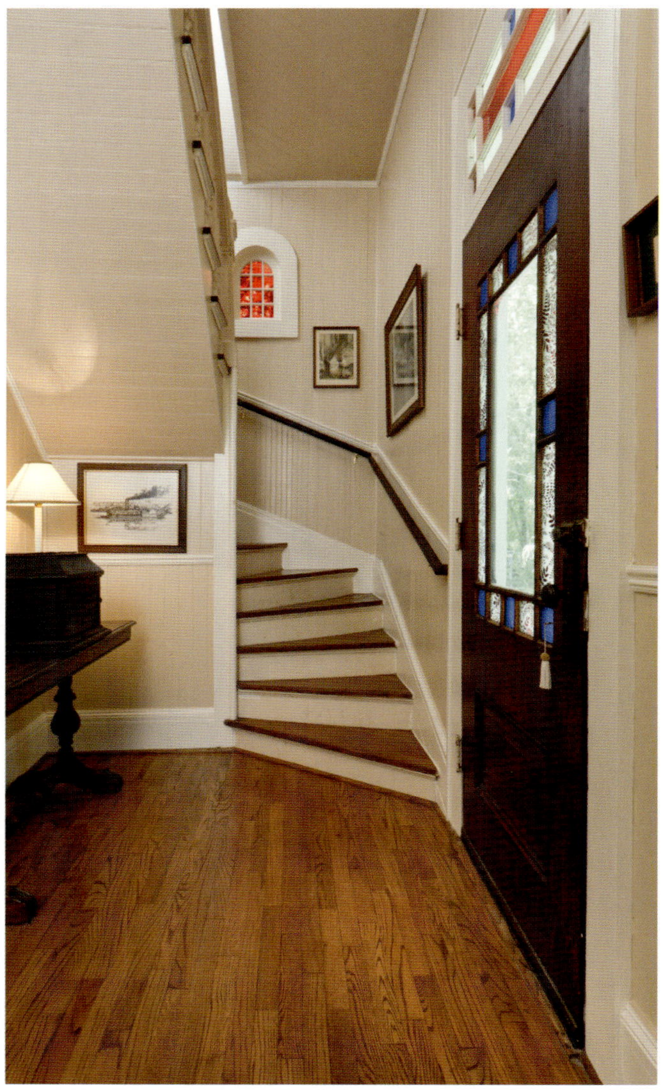

FIGURES 4.30 - 4.32. Interiors, Leonard Home.

When the expansion of the First Baptist Church endangered the Steamboat House in the mid-1980s, Shorty and Florence Hughes moved the house to 809 Texas Street, off Logansport Street, where it stands today. George Ann and John Leonard now own the house.

Entrance hall (above), doorway from the living room to entrance hall (far left), and stairwell (left).

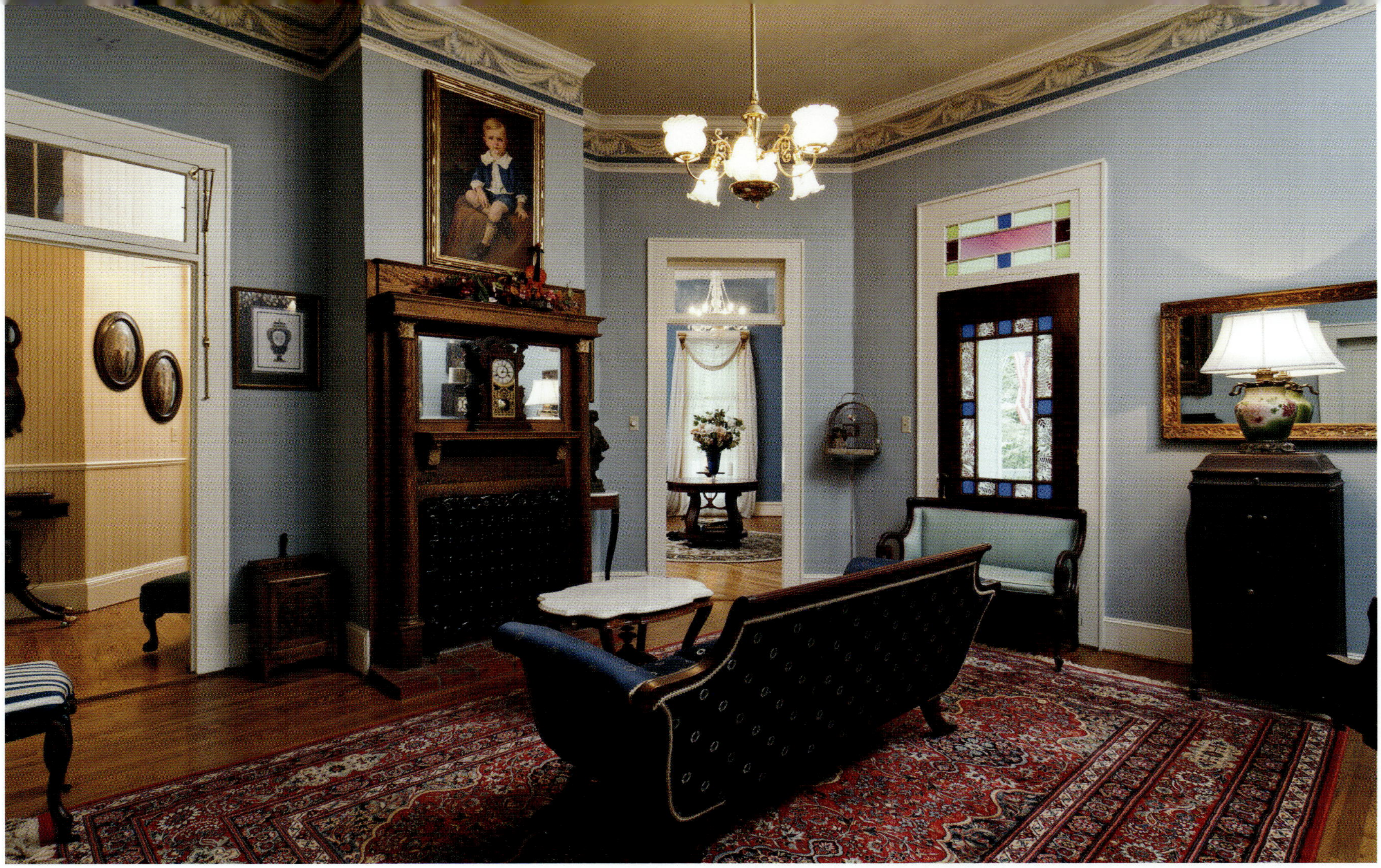

FIGURES 4.33 - 4.34. Two views of the Living Room, George Ann and John Leonard Home, 2011.

The exterior door gives access to the front porch. The exterior of the bay in the living room is shown in FIGURE 4.27.

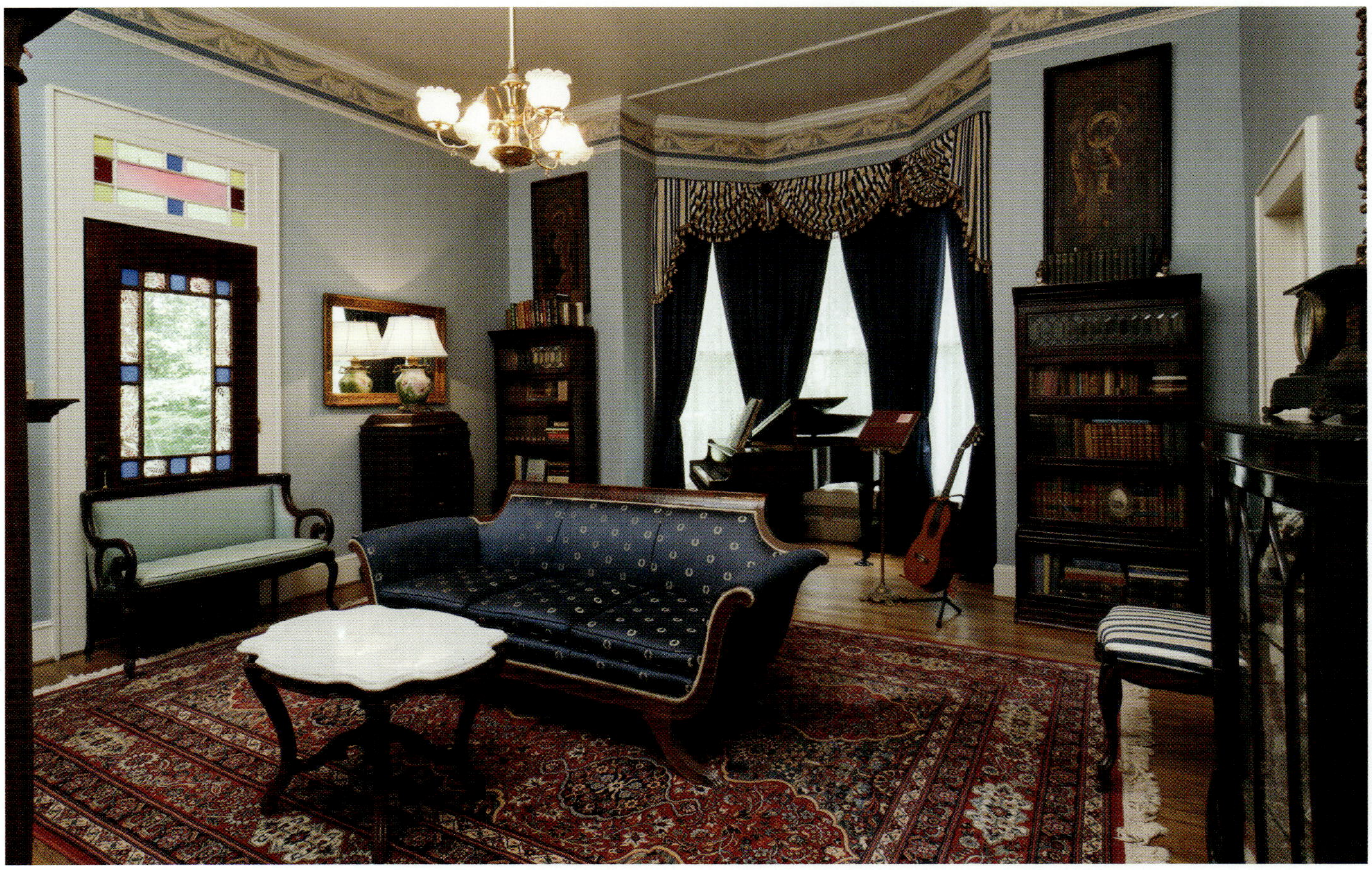

Robert Lindsey House on North Street (1898)

Robert Lindsey (1870-1958) and his wife, Emma, purchased the lot on North Street in 1898 and paid $500 for it. The lot was just south of the old Thomas J. Rusk homestead, which was still standing at the time (directly across from SFASU today). Lindsey was a twenty-seven year old dry goods salesman at the time; his wife played the piano for the First Baptist Church and taught music lessons in town. The Lindseys had no children; however, according to the 1900 Census, Robert's younger sister lived with them.[114] Lindsey and Rulfs undertook several projects together, this house being possibly the first. When Lindsey sold this house on North Street two years later, he immediately had Rulfs build another house for him on Virginia Avenue (discussed in Chapter VI).

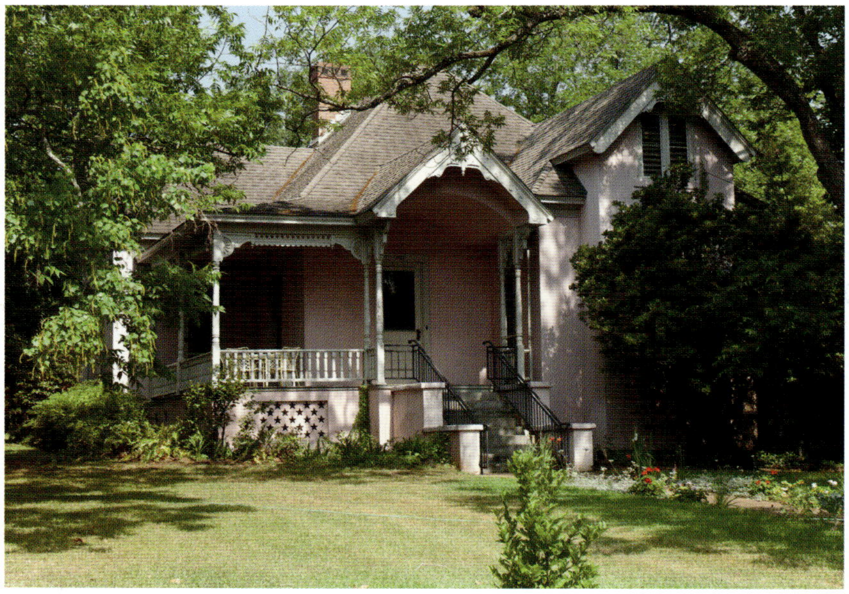

FIGURE 4.35. The Lindsey-Gintz-Montgomery House, 2011.

FIGURE 4.36. (Below) The Living Room of the Montgomery Home, ca. 1998. *Charlotte Baker Montgomery, Dianne Baker, and the author in discussions about the Lindsey-Montgomery House. Photograph by Edward B. (Jerry) Baker.*

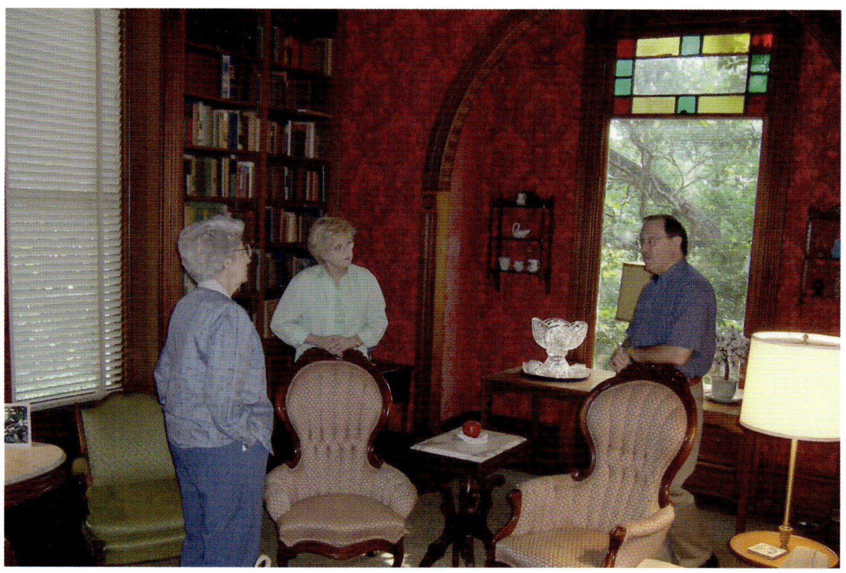

While Rulfs frequently experimented with new materials, it is possible but unlikely that the stucco, which now covers the exterior walls of this house, was original to the house at the time of construction. Records show the house cost around $2,500.[115] Rulfs incorporated many of his signature elements in the house: the slip-head windows on the porch, a squared bay in the front living room, the hip-and-gable roof, a pediment over the entrance (with a barrel ceiling like the 1897 Stephen Blount House), some mantles made in Nacogdoches, and an arch at the end of the front parlor (like he used in many houses). Some pictures show the house without rails and balusters along the porch, but it had these from the beginning.[116]

Subsequent owners included J. J. Lilly (1900), Giles Haltom (1913), the Walter Gintz family (1919), and the Baker-Montgomery family (1952). Gintz, a son-in-law to John Schmidt, extended the house to the west, made changes to the porch, with some modifications to the interior (the placement of the kitchen), and also added some outbuildings.[117]

The Woolam Ira M. Smith House (1898)

One of the many doctors who moved to Nacogdoches in the boom of the 1890s was Dr. Woolam Ira M. Smith (1860-1937), originally from Sabine County. He had a wide background. After attending the University of Virginia, he did medical work at Tulane and ultimately graduated from Atlanta Medical College in Atlanta Georgia; he later did post-graduate work in New Orleans, New York, and Chicago.[118] He started his practice of medicine in 1884 in Chireno, where he continued to maintain an office even in later years, but he practiced all over Nacogdoches County. The lure of the boom years in Nacogdoches, however, drew him steadily into the county seat. In 1897, Smith moved his main office and home to Nacogdoches. He leased office space from W. U. Perkins in the Nacogdoches Chronicle Building on Pecan Street. (See Figure 3.20) Smith's homestead was on the west side of North Street, south of Müller Street, approximately across from where Hughes Street enters North Street.[119] In 1898, Rulfs built a large, two-story house for Smith. He used a rounded bay window on the front forward gable room similar to the one he placed on the Stephen W. Blount House on Mound Street the year before. Unlike the Blount House, however, the L-shaped porch, which wrapped from the side of the forward room around to the back of the house, was in severe contrast to the Blount House; it was very limited in its use of ornamentation. Full-length Tuscan columns supported the single-story porch; because of its flat roof and upper balustrade, the porch formed a continuous balcony for the second story.[120] The roof was hipped with cross gables. The house, larger than it was distinguished, had a second life as Nacogdoches' first modern hospital, as discussed in Chapter IX.

The William H. Crouch House (1898)

William Hill Crouch moved to Nacogdoches from Chireno when the railroad arrived. He joined the Methodist Church shortly thereafter and became a very prominent member. At first, he operated a saddle shop in the Old Stone Fort, then served for four years as Deputy County Clerk. Around 1889, he entered the fire insurance and commission business, which proved very lucrative. He married Leona Thomas in 1891. In 1894, the couple

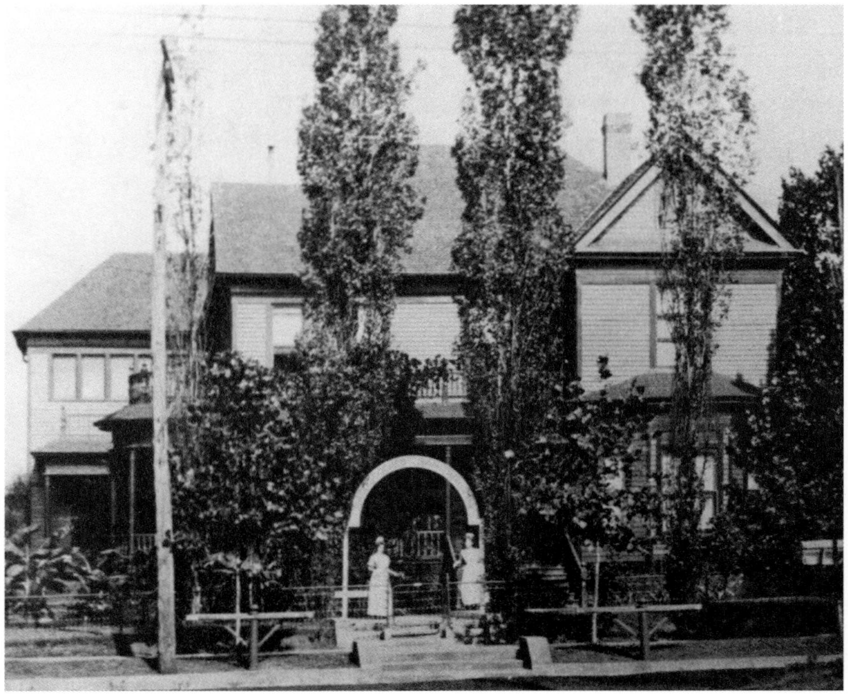

FIGURE 4.37. The Woolam Ira M. Smith House (1898).
This photograph of the Smith House dates to 1911 after its conversion to the Nacogdoches Sanitarium. Courtesy of ETRC.

had twin boys, Willie and Walter. To accommodate his growing family, he asked Rulfs to design a house for him on North Street in 1898, just south of the Laura Blount Chapman House. In design, the structure was similar to the house built later for Emma and Robert Lindsey on Virginia Avenue. The Crouches lived in the house only a few years, selling it in 1905 to T. J. Williams, the founder of the Commercial Bank and president of the Nacogdoches Show Case and Manufacturing Company.[121] Since there are no pictures of this house dating to the period of the Crouch ownership, and since the Nacogdoches community thinks of this house as the Sam Stripling House, a more thorough treatment appears in Chapter X.

The Ira Link Sturdevant House (1898)

Ira Link Sturdevant (1857-1953), another outsider who came to Nacogdoches in 1883 to take advantage of the arrival of the railroad, said that he arrived "with more ambition than money." He put his assets at $32. He was born in Anderson County, albeit at the time he came to Nacogdoches, he moved from Henderson as a buyer and shipper of cotton for the Crow and Baldwin Company.[122] Because there was no depot at the time, Sturdevant and the station master shared a box car as their offices. Sturdevant quickly bought out his employer's interest in the Nacogdoches cotton trade and established his own Cotton Shed and Yard on West Main Street.[123] After he helped to organize the Stone Fort Rifles in 1887, everyone called him "Captain," or, more correctly, "Cap'n." Sturdevant was one of the leading new entrepreneurial pioneers of the 1880s who made modern Nacogdoches.[124] In 1897, Sturdevant became the general manager of the newly created Nacogdoches Compress Company.[125] The Cap'n partnered with a lawyer named E. C. Branch (1860-1919)[126] to organize Nacogdoches' first utilities (the telephone exchange, the water system, and the light plant). In 1903, he organized and was the major stockholder in the new Stone Fort National Bank.[127] At first, he served as a cashier; but in 1906, he became president of the bank and held that position until 1941 when he became chairman of the board of directors.[128]

By the time of his wedding in 1898, Link Sturdevant was forty-one and a very successful businessman. As a wedding present for his new bride, Carrie May Baker, Sturdevant gave her a new Rulfs-designed home on North Street. The house sat on the west side of North Street about two lots above Hospital Street. There were two compelling reasons why Sturdevant selected a lot closer into the old town than most of the other houses discussed thus far. First, the location was close to the owner's cotton yards; in fact, he could see the cotton yard from the back of the house. Second, the location was within a block of the First Methodist Church. Both of the Sturdevants were dedicated Methodists. Another advantage, which came into reality a few years later, was that the house sat within easy walking distance to the town Square, where the future Stone Fort National Bank would conduct business.

Mrs. Carrie Baker Sturdevant (1873-1957) presided over the music *aficionados* [enthusiasts] in Nacogdoches. She played the piano at the Methodist Church, and Sturdevant played the flute; they both sang in the choir on other occasions. The Sturdevant home, built to accommodate their musical interests, had a large music room adjacent to the parlor; two grand pianos graced this room. The Symphony Club almost always met in their home.[129] Carrie's brother, Thomas Ellis Baker and his wife Karle Wilson, lived within easy walking distance up North Street in the Steamboat House.

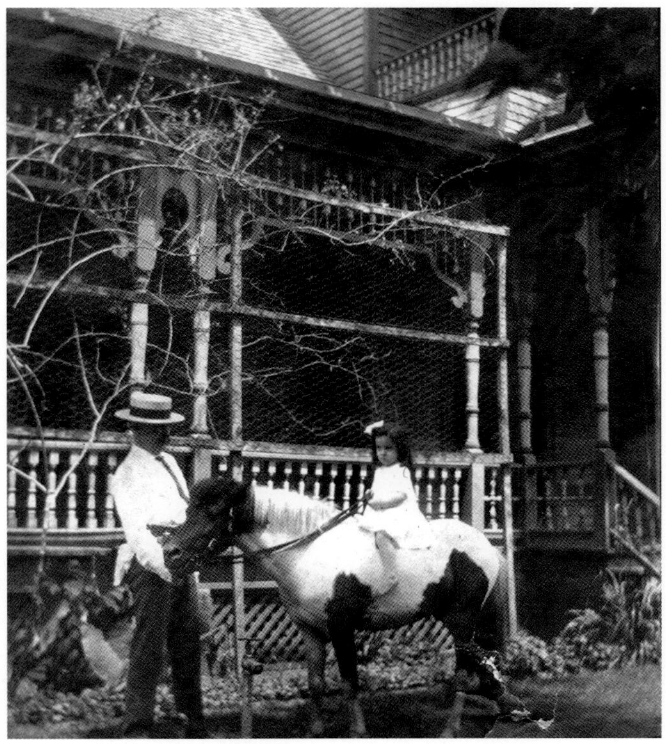

FIGURE 4.38. Room for a Pony.
The Sturdevant House, like all of the houses on the west side of North Street, had enormous tracts of land which sloped down toward Banita Creek. Almost all had barns and outbuildings that were useful to shelter milk cows, horses, and ponies for the children. Carolyn Sturdevant is the young lady on the horse; her attendant is unknown. Photograph courtesy of Carol Willis, granddaughter of the Sturdevants.

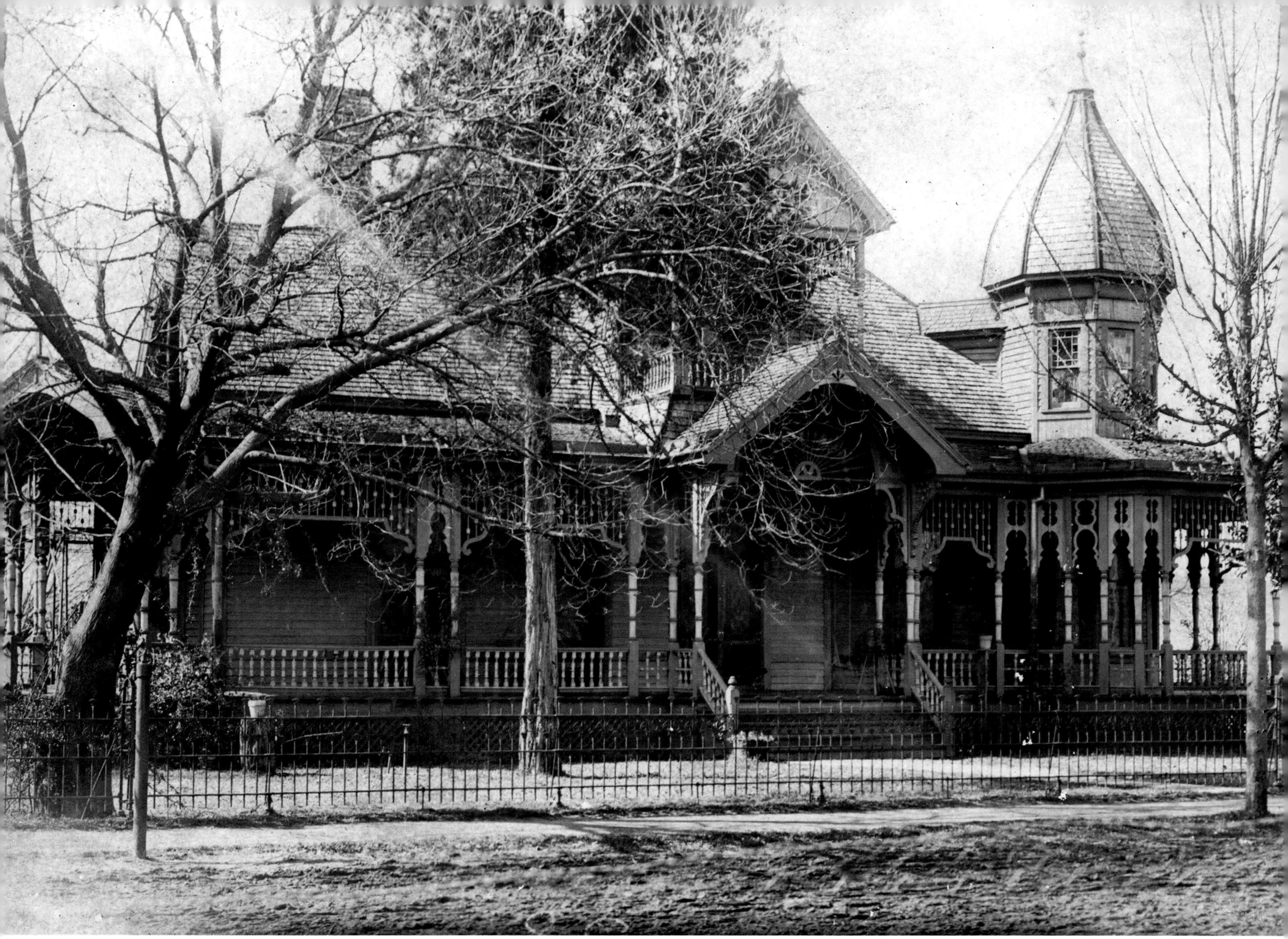

FIGURE 4.39. The Sturdevant House, North Street (1898).
Photograph courtesy of Carol Willis, granddaughter of the Sturdevants.

FIGURE 4.40. (Right) The 1912 Updating of the House.
Cap'n Sturdevant, his wife Carrie, and daughter Margaret survey roof damage after a storm. Photograph courtesy of Carol Willis, granddaughter of the Sturdevants.

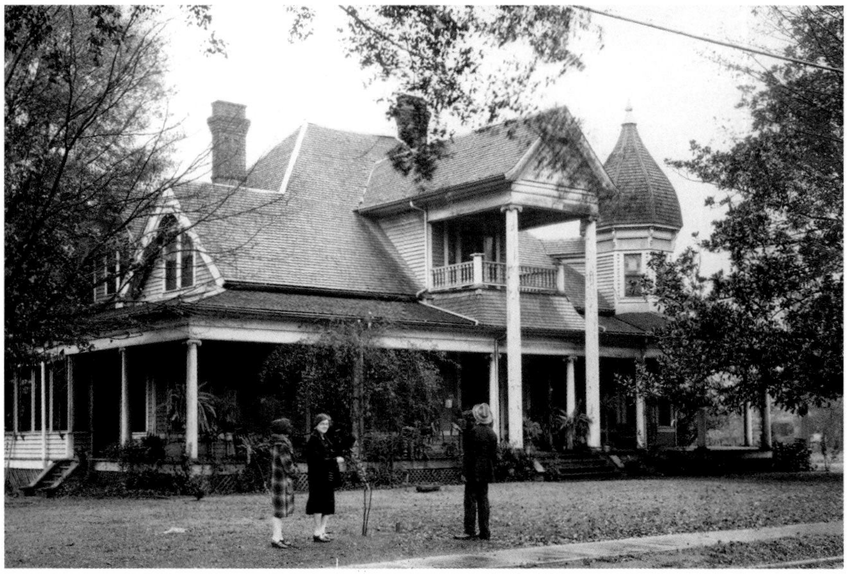

Around 1910, when Will Perkins started a craze for everyone to update their 1890s houses, Rulfs modified the Sturdevant House by stripping off all the fretwork, the spindle balustrades, the original hood pediments over the entrance, and all hints of the exotic influences (except the onion dome on the tower), and streamlined the porch with the placement of unfluted Ionic columns. He extended the gable over the upper front balcony to cover the front entrance and supported this with a pair of two-story Ironic columns, thus leaving the full-width porch below intact. (See Figure 4.40.) Unlike the classical makeover of the Perkins House in 1910, discussed in later chapters, the attempt to give the Sturdevant House a neoclassical appearance did not work overall. The proportions of the new full-height pediment made the thin Ionic columns appear as sticks. Rulfs got it right on the Richardson House in 1915 by re-supporting the porch with boxed columns at the porch level and omitting the upper portion.

Both the Sturdevants and their relatives, the Tom Baker family, were strong advocates in the movement to bring a new college to Nacogdoches. Both families in the late 1920s followed the examples of Eugene Blount and built new residences across from the new Stephen F. Austin State College. Sturdevant tore the 1898 house down at that time.

The Benjamin Wettermark House (1900)

In 1900, Benjamin Wettermark became the new Mayor of Nacogdoches. Wettermark was a leading businessman in town, the owner of the town's first bank. Rulfs remodeled a house for Wettermark in the early 1890s, and this was, by local standards, a lovely place. Abruptly, however, in one of his daily columns, Bill Haltom in the *Daily Sentinel* noted that Wettermark had sold his "beautiful" house on North Street (at Hughes) in order to "build again on a larger scale."[130] Evidently, the earlier house no longer sufficed. Reading between the lines, it appears that the new and grander houses in town (especially the houses for Schmidt, Blount, Harris, and Jones) were pinching Wettermark socially and psychologically, for he was a promoter and a showman.

The new house Rulfs prepared for Mayor Wettermark was, indeed, grand. It continued the new luxurious pace that had started in the early 1890s. The two-and-a-half story mansion had a steep hip-and-gable roof with two large ribbed chimneys in the center, surrounded by a widow's walk balustrade. A large dormer, as on the Harris house, projected from the front roof. In the gables over large two-story bays on both the north and south, Rulfs used his signature – Palladian windows. The entrance had a pediment over the front door and Tuscan columns resting on plinth bases, again like the original plans for the Harris House and used on the Tolbert Hardeman House on Mound. The refined interior, according to one account, had a ballroom for entertaining. The Wettermark House, which predates the new State Teachers College and the Eugene Blount House by twenty-three years, established a new outer limit for residential construction in the city.[131] (The present day Wettermark Street north of the SFASU campus was originally the driveway for the new house.

As the town entered a new century, the mood was most confident and optimistic. Nacogdoches was enjoying the fruits of its new prosperity, which its leading businessmen exhibited in gracious homes along its now famous North Street. Mayor Wettermark was also overseeing a number of other construction projects, among them rental houses and a new bridge. In the "pine top" celebrations, the Rulfs brothers became the subjects of more attention:

> COL. WETTERMARK AND THE CITY COUNCIL DO THE HONORS.
>
> The carpenters who are at work on the three new residences of Col. B. S. Wettermark near the ice factory together with a number of invited friends, enjoyed one of the swellest banquets Saturday evening at Joe's Place, that has ever been set up to the knights of the saw and hammer in Nacogdoches. A table 20 feet long fairly groaned under the weight of roast beef, pork, switzer cheese, salads, pickles, sliced tomatoes, rye bread. etc., while two kegs of beer, fresh and cold, were on tap. Col. Wettermark was present at the beginning and gave the boys an appropriate toast and had them eat as hard as they worked and drink as heartily as they received their pay. It is needless to add that the boys obeyed to the letter Col. Wettermark's injunction and did ample justice to the banquet. Messrs. D. and Will Rulfs, who are the contractors, were present to see that the boys had the same proper attention that is shown them while at work.
>
> It was an enjoyable occasion, and the invited guests seemed to relish the bill of fare as much as the crowd for whose special benefit the spread was given. Mr. Edler, the cigar man was present and "Blue Ribbons" were the brand of cigars used. Another spread, though not so elaborate, was equally as much enjoyed by the bridge gang that have just completed the splendid bridge across the Banita at the depot. The bridge was finished Saturday and the conventional pine top made its appearance which meant a "hoss" on the city council. The result was the city dads "come thru," and the boys had a splendid "blow out."[132]

FIGURE 4.41. North Street, Nacogdoches. The Benjamin Wettermark House, ca. 1910.

By the time of this postcard, the Wettermarks no longer owned the structure. The next family to occupy the house was that of J. J. Hayter. The image gives a good idea of how lonely the house was when built in 1900. The house set at the crest of a hill, just north of the present day campus of SFASU. The driveway of the house was to become Wettermark Street. Courtesy of ETRC.

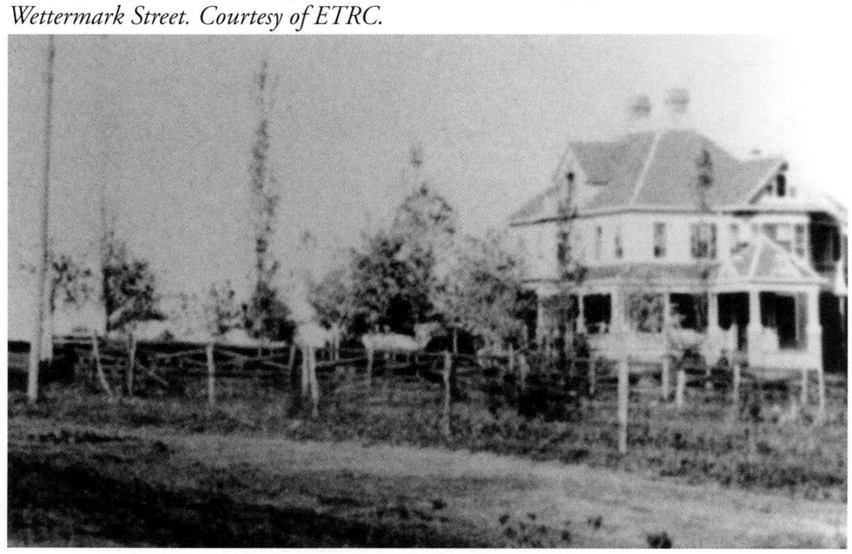

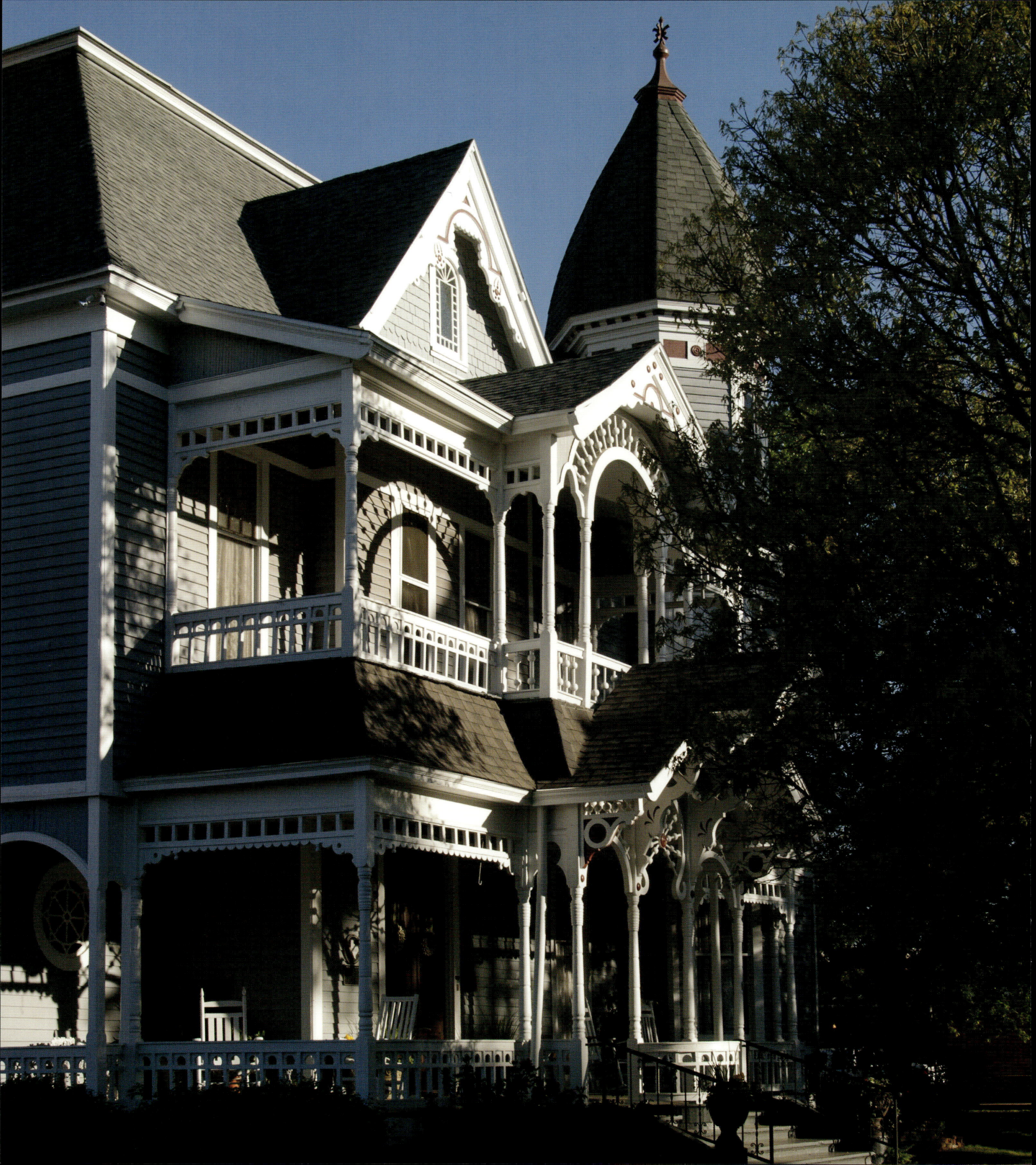

CHAPTER V

Redefining Domestic Contexts

Washington Square, 1890-1900

"The Washington Square Historic District is noteworthy because it is the most intact grouping of late 19th and early 20th century residential architecture. Some of the city's finest examples of Queen Anne, Classical Revival, Tudor Revival, and Bungalow/Craftsman architecture are found within its confines. Many of the residences were designed by noted local architect Dietrich [Sic] Rulfs whose considerable design skills are clearly demonstrated in these buildings." National Register of Historic Places, *Texas Historic Sites Atlas, 1987.*

About Washington Square

In 1845, three citizens, J. R. Arnold, Haden Edwards, and Charles S. Taylor, gave 20½ acres of land north of downtown to create a campus for the newly chartered Nacogdoches University. When laying out the land for the institution's use, the town named the area Washington Square.[1] The university did not move to Washington Square until 1859. The next year, the town designated an unusually wide (sixty-foot) street to lead up to the university from Hospital Street and named it College Boulevard. Interestingly, however, despite the presence of the Old University Building, when the Sanborn Fire Insurance Map Company first illustrated the town in 1885, everything north of Hospital Street was considered *in the country.* The early homes along both sides of Hospital are on the map; it was a major residential area from the days of the Republic with important families, such as the Nelsons, Rusches, Dursts, Hydes, and Voigts, living there.[2] Although new residential development in the Washington Square area began in 1890, the new additions do not appear on the Sanborn Maps until after the completion of the new Central School in 1904. There was a fifteen to twenty year gap between the building of a house and its appearance on the Sanborn Maps.[3] This chapter will cover the initial phase of development on Washington Square to the completion of the Charles Perkins House; a second phase will be covered in Chapter XI.

FIGURE 5.1. (Across) The Roland Jones House (1896-1897).

The town's resumption of the local administration and financing of the Nacogdoches University triggered the initial development in the Washington Square area. In order to raise money, the trustees of Nacogdoches University in 1889 decided to sell off the south end of Washington Square for residential development (the area between present-day Arnold and Edwards Streets). In order to make the lots larger, the town leaders decided to reduce the width of College Boulevard and to rename it Church Street, of which it was really an extension. The new street had an unhindered view of the front of the Old University Building to the north, and this vista gave it great appeal.[4] As people rushed to buy these great lots and to build in this close-in residential area, Diedrich Rulfs immediately received requests for residential designs. In the Washington Square area, his first house was in the 300 block of the new upper Church Street; his second, nearby on Mound Street. Many of his houses from the 1890s in this area still stand, albeit their original characteristics no longer exist because of later makeovers, which give them the look and feel of 20th century residential designs.

Four Houses on North Church Street

In 1890, Rulfs designed the first house on Washington Square property for Sarah Stanley Bagley, a widow who had moved to Nacogdoches in 1889 along with her brother and his wife. A very active Methodist, Mrs. Bagley became the founding president of the "The Ladies Aid Society" of the First United Methodist Church that same year.[5] She chose the location for her house because it was close to her church. The house suited her status as a widow without children.[6] The basic plan of the house at 304 North Church (corner of Arnold at the time) had a central hall with a parlor on the south side, two bedrooms on the north, with a kitchen and service porches at the rear. The front bedroom on the north was part of a chamfered bay projection. A short Victorian porch ran to the south along the parlor. According to the next-door neighbor, Miss Gladys Hardeman, the porch had a pediment over the front door and modest Victorian detailing between the posts that supported the roof. Because Nacogdoches had no water distribution in the town at the time, the house had no indoor bathroom facilities, but it did have a well built into the back porch—an innovation that allowed one to draw water comfortably in all types of weather.[7] The remodeling of this house and the next one by Rulfs will be covered in Chapter XI.

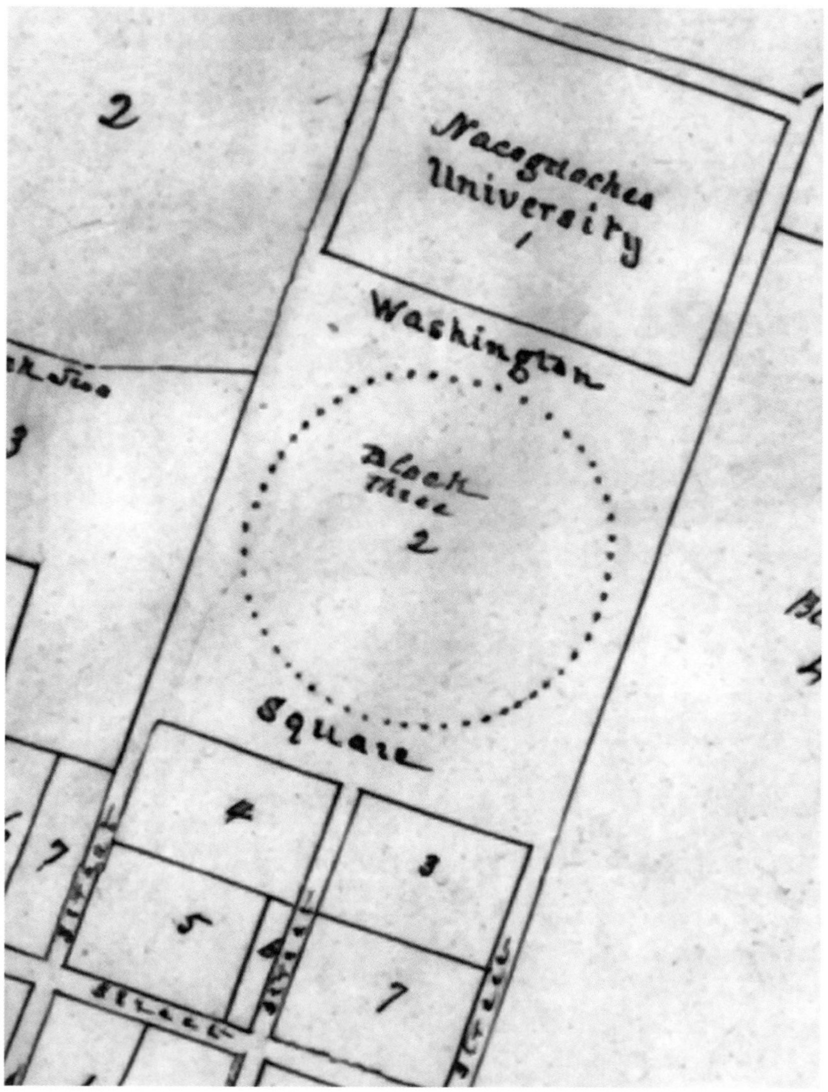

In 1892, Rulfs undertook a second commission on the square at 316 North Church for Robert Lee Hardeman. Hardeman, originally from Melrose and one of three Hardeman brothers to come to Nacogdoches,[8] had joined Mayer & Schmidt's grocery business in 1890 as a salesman.[9] Lee and his wife, Ida Hardeman, were also active members of the nearby First Methodist Church, where Ida served on both the Parsonage Committee and the Home Mission Society Board.[10] John Schmidt encouraged all of his associates to work with Rulfs, but in this case, Lee did not need the suggestion; Rulfs had already designed and constructed a house on North Street for his brother. The Hardemans' first child, Homer, was born in Melrose; but their daughter, Gladys, was born in this one-story house in 1893. Gladys Hardeman lived in the house until her death in 1980.[11] She remembered very well the enlargement of the house by Rulfs in 1913, discussed later.

Although the Hardeman and Bagley houses looked similar, Lee Hardeman's home was larger. Both houses faced west, had short porches outside their parlors, turned posts, fretwork trim, and hipped roofs. The size differences were even more delineated after the houses were remodeled in the period before the First World War.

In 1892-93, Rulfs built the third house on Washington Square for Dick Kendall Cason (1869-1932). The house, which no longer exists, faced east and was directly across Church Street from Sarah Bagley's house (where the Oak Terrace extension of the Fredonia Hotel now stands). Cason, a recruit from Tennessee, had moved to Nacogdoches in 1890 at the suggestion of his cousin W. U. (Will) Perkins. At first, Dick Cason worked as a salesman for George H. Davidson; but within a few years, he purchased the hardware business of H. P. Mims and merged this business into a partnership with another Perkins cousin, Charlie Richardson. After Cason married Willie Maude Nance in April of 1892, he commissioned the house on Church Street for his new bride. They were in the house in January of 1893 when their first child, a daughter named Willie Maud, was born.[12]

The Cason home on Church Street was fully twice the size of the Hardeman home and three times larger than Bagley's small home.[13] The structure, two-stories in some parts, had porches that wrapped around the east and south sides, two balconies, and projecting bays on both the north and south sides of the house. Although a very poor picture of this house has come to the author's attention, Gladys Hardeman carefully described the house in detail. She visited there many times; after the Casons moved out of the neighborhood in 1914, she frequently ate at the boarding house that occupied the structure. The Casons and the Hardemans were both very active Methodists. The house, which appears on the Sanborn maps through the 1946 edition, survived until the building of the Fredonia Hotel in the 1950s.[14] The Cason House anticipated the house Rulfs constructed

FIGURE 5.2. Washington Square Detail, John Forbes Map of Nacogdoches, 1846.

In 1845, the Republic of Texas chartered Nacogdoches University before joining the United States as the 28th state. Local notables J. R. Arnold, Haden Edwards, and Charles S. Taylor gave 20½ acres as the future site for the new university. The designated area appears on this 1846 map with the name Washington Square. Courtesy of ETRC.

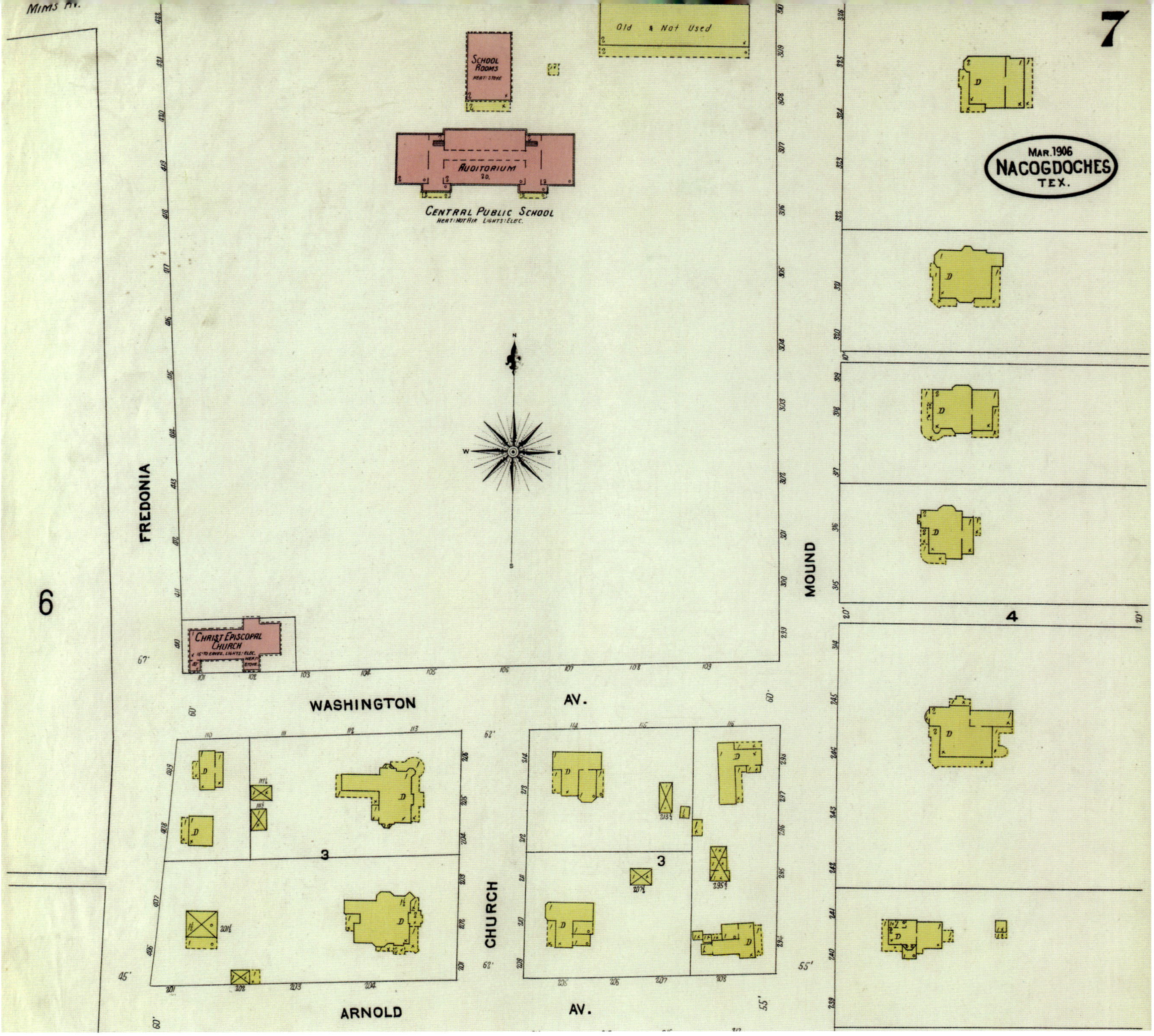

FIGURE 5.3. Detail, Sanborn Map of Nacogdoches, 1906.

The first Sanborn Map to show the streets and houses in the Washington Square Area came in 1906. While earlier maps had shown selective houses (the Tol Hardeman, Garrison, Tucker, and Charles Perkins houses), the building of the new Central School (1904) in front of the Old University (1859) and Christ Episcopal Church (1901) cemented the mappers' attention on the area. Notice that the street names in the area have changed over time. In order to name a street after the original contributors of the land for the Old University, sometime between 1906 and 1912, Washington Avenue (on this map) was renamed Arnold Street, and the former Arnold Avenue was renamed Edwards Street after Haden Edwards.

The four houses facing (North) Church Street discussed in this chapter appear at the bottom center of this map. In order of construction, the Sarah Bagley House dates to 1890; the Lee Hardeman House (north of Bagley) dates to 1892; the Dick Cason House (across from Bagley) dates to late 1892-93 and is the largest house in the grouping; and the Sarah Perkins Richardson House (above Cason) dates to 1897.

On Mound Street, starting with the Schmidt-Price House (1890) in the lower right, moving upward, the Stephen W. Blount House (1897), the Tol Hardeman (1899), the Garrison (1900), Tucker (1900), and Charles Perkins (1900).

The only major house included in the chapter, but not on this map, is the Roland Jones House (1896-97) on the corner of Hospital and Church streets. Chronologically and architecturally, the Jones house belongs in the Washington Square Historical District; geographically, it is included in the Downtown Historical District. Sanborn Maps, UT, Nacogdoches, (1906).

in 1894 for E. A. Blount on North Street, although the Blount House was even larger still.

The bond between D. K. Cason and D. Rulfs endured for decades. Before having Rulfs build his home, Cason had opened his first business partnership, Cason, Richardson & Company, in the building Rulfs had done for J. H. Cox on the corner of Pecan and Main. The house Rulfs designed for Cason on Church Street initiated a series of projects between the two men—domestic, commercial, and public. For instance, Cason commissioned Rulfs to redesign the buildings on Main Street for his newly-formed hardware firm of Cason-Monk & Company in 1906. The architect designed and built a house for his son, a new sanctuary for the Methodist Church (1910), where the Casons worshipped, and later another home for the Casons on Logansport Street in 1914. In 1923, when Cason purchased an older Rulfs building (the Opera House), he initially tried to get the architect to modernize the building for him. Rulfs, aged 75 by then, declined the commission in favor of his young protégé Hal Tucker.[15]

The churches in Nacogdoches played a paramount role, not only in the spiritual life but also in the social life of the community. The location of the churches, therefore, influenced housing development. The North Church Street homes of the Bagley, Hardeman, and Cason families mentioned earlier were conveniently located only a block from the Methodist church, where they were members. A few years later, fellow Methodists, John Garrison, Tolbert Hardeman, and F. H. Tucker, built their houses one block over on Mound Street, and the Sturdevants built close by on North Street. Baptists, such as Will Perkins and George Matthews, also chose to build along or just off North Street to be near their church. John Schmidt, although not far from the original location of Christ Church, proved instrumental in getting his church relocated in 1901 to Washington Square, immediately to the east of his home. The Jones family at first lived across the street from Christ Church and later only two blocks away.

In 1897, Rulfs designed the fourth house on North Church Street for Sarah Alice Richardson; the house at 315 North Church stands immediately north of the Cason home.[16] Sarah Richardson was part of a closely-knit family group who regularly employed D. Rulfs. She was the recently widowed sister of W. U. and Charles Perkins, a cousin to the Casons next door and the Joel Barham family.[17] (Her son, Charlie, became a partner in Cason's hardware business). The Perkins brothers simply assisted their sister and generally oversaw the construction for her; she had her own money. Neither brother was the type to build anything, except in a supervisory sense. It is also highly unlikely, as suggested in one of the city's surveys, that either of the Perkins brothers ever lived in the house, unless Will lived with his sister in 1910 during the remodeling of his home on North Street.[18] Both Will and Charles Perkins understandably enjoyed the concreteness that Rulfs consistently gave their ideas. Rulfs built the Perkins Brothers commercial building in the early 1880s, remodeled a house for Will Perkins in 1890, and remodeled it again in 1910; he built the house for Sarah Perkins Richardson in 1897; he designed and built the Steamboat House for Charles in 1898, several other houses for Charles on North Street by 1899, and then Charles's own home on Mound Street in 1900. D. Rulfs even built houses for other members of the Perkins family in other East Texas towns.[19]

Descriptions of the Sarah Richardson home as it existed between 1897 and 1915 are somewhat sketchy. Gladys Hardeman described the house to the author in 1973 and substantiated her description by a snapshot of herself in a highchair in her own yard with the Richardson house in the background,[20] but this photograph has now disappeared. The house was a one-and-a-half story Queen Anne style domicile with hip-and-gable roof, a balcony over the front door, a gazebo-like feature on the northeast corner, and fretwork detailing along the porch. Miss Hardeman described the house as "similar to the [Roland] Jones and [Stephen] Blount houses" nearby on Church and Mound Streets, but possibly a better comparison would be the Sturdevant House on North Street built about the same time. (See Figure 4.39) The nineteenth-century look of Sarah Richardson's house was lost in a fire around 1915, which (quite fortunately) consumed only the upper portion of the house. The Rulfs plan for the remodeling and updating of this house will appear in a later chapter.

The Schmidt-Price House (1890)

The railroad's arrival and the resultant prosperity speculations, in general, signaled the breakup of the old land-grant properties around the town of Nacogdoches. The deed records for the 200 block of North Mound Street are very interesting. The east side were part of Spanish and later Mexican government grants to Haden Edwards, sometime in surveyor terms as being part of the "Old Town of Nacogdoches." Edwards' daughter, Elizabeth, inherited the land and held it until 1883. The deep acreage, which extended to Lanana Street, was ripe for development and large enough to accommodate a subdivision (which later happened). A series of developers, including John Durst, traded the land at the end of the decade.[21] In 1890, Richard A. Hall (1862-1931) and his wife, Effie, purchased the land with the intention of making it their homestead. While there is no way to verify this, Rulfs quite possibly informed his mentor John Schmidt of Hall's plans; Rulfs was working on the Bagley House, a half a block away, at the time. Schmidt was looking for a house for his nephew Jacob Schmidt, who had recently arrived from Germany. If the old Edwards property became a homestead, access to the eastern portions would get cut off. Since John Schmidt and Abe Mayer owned land in the Zion Hill area, they immediately became concerned. Schmidt offered Hall a quick return on the investment on lower Mound Street and brokered a deal to give Hall another tract of land at the north end of Mound Street, leaving the development of the old Edwards property to Schmidt.[22]

D. Rulfs worked with Schmidt to design and build the house at 222 North Mound Street between April and December of 1890. The house, which followed the Bagley House, was the architect's first house on Mound Street. When Schmidt secured the Charles S. Taylor property on North Street for his own home, he lost interest in the Mound Street property and sold the house and property outright to Jacob Schmidt and his wife, Anna. In 1896, the Schmidts moved and sold the house in 1896 to William Franklin Price (1859-1933) and his wife, Missouri Garrett Price (1884-1947).[23] The house belonged to the Prices for most of the twentieth century. Because the house received a thorough makeover in 1925 after a fire, most observers do not recognize the Schmidt-Price House as being older than the Stephen W. Blount, Jr. House that stands next door. The Prices actually recruited the Blounts to Mound Street and sold them their lot.[24] Mary Blount was Price's sister. Price's occupancy of the House at 222 Mound will receive additional coverage in Chapter XII.

Without a photograph of the original house, the house Rulfs built for Schmidt can only in part be described. A long-time neighbor, Miss Gladys Hardeman, described the house as similar to her uncle's house on North Street, built the year before; the single level porch that covered the entire front and wrapped around the south side had extensive "Victorian gingerbread" detailing.[25] The house does not appear on the Sanborn Maps until 1906. Its footprint indicates a main floor more extensive than its second story; the four front rooms were double, but the east and south extensions were not. A chamfered bay window existed on the second-story over the south wing. While the offset to the east may have been added by the Prices some time between 1896 and 1906, the house as it exists today dates to 1925.[26]

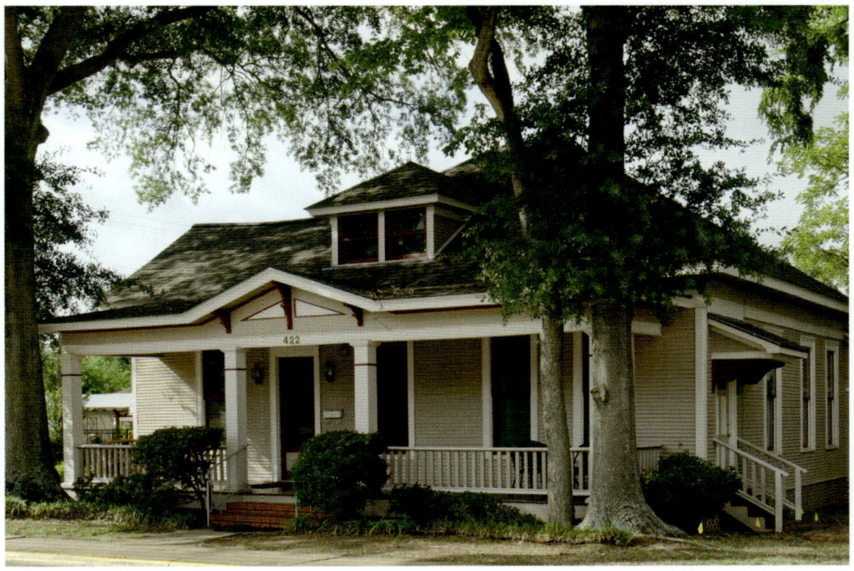

FIGURE 5.5. The June Harris House, Hospital Street, 2011.

The June Harris House on Hospital Street (1893)

Another house, which belongs to the early 1890s, still stands on the southwest corner of Hospital and Mound Streets. Because of its difficult architectural history, however, this house is hard to place and will simply be mentioned here. June Harris (1861-1941), a lawyer, purchased a house on this site in the 1880s. Harris had five children by 1893, when he asked Rulfs to enlarge the house for him. The modest house, shown on the 1891 Sanborn Map, appears considerably enlarged on the 1896 map, with the addition of a projected bay on the front and additional bedrooms. When one of his children was stricken with what then was called "sleeping sickness," Harris moved his family to Forbes Hill, high above the downtown area – covered extensively in the next chapter. As to the house on Hospital Street, it is impossible to trace all of the changes and uses over the years. Will Perkins, who by the time of World War I was the owner, had D. Rulfs to rework the house yet again. The architect removed the front bay room, which had received damage in a fire, changed the roofline with the addition of a dormer, squared the posts into columns, and removed any Victorian vestiges–as he had done with the other houses on Church Street and Perkins' own home. After World War II, the house became the office of Dr. Langston Nelson, who rented the building from the Perkins estate, to which his wife was an heir.[27]

The Roland Jones House (1896-1897)

The Roland Jones House, although not technically on W ashington Square, fits into the narrative of this book more naturally at this point. In the evolution of Rulfs' domestic architecture, both chronologically and stylistically, this magnificent Queen Anne structure belongs with the opening up of the Washington Square residential area as do all the big houses along Mound Street discussed below.

In nominating the Jones House for the National Register of Historic Places, the survey states:

> The Roland Jones House arguably is Nacogdoches' finest example of Queen Anne-styled architecture and is nominated to the National Register under Criterion C. Its asymmetrical and complex massing, intricate detailing and woodwork and unaltered condition distinguish it from other similarly detailed houses in the city....
>
> Completed in 1897, the Jones House featured Queen Anne style detailing that was immensely popular both locally and statewide during the late 19th century. Although many similarly detailed residences were built in Nacogdoches, few displayed such noteworthy ornamentation and craftsmanship. Many of these houses subsequently have been razed making the Jones House all the more significant in local architectural history.[28]

Roland Jones, Jr. (1862-1931), son of a District Judge in Shreveport, Louisiana, was a civil engineer and had served as superintendent of track on the New Orleans, Pacific & Mississippi Valley Railroad before moving to Nacogdoches in 1890. As with so many other young men in Nacogdoches, Jones made a name for himself as an agent for the ever-expanding Mayer & Schmidt Company. At first, Jones was a classer and shipper of cotton. Later Schmidt promoted him to become a buyer in his own right. He also served for six years as a public weigher of cotton.[29] When John Schmidt (Secretary-Treasurer), B. S. Wettermark, Herman Loeb (President), G. H. Davidson, W. U. Perkins, I. L. Sturdevant, and E. A. Blount (Vice-President) decided in 1897 to set up a proper cotton compress operation, Jones became a stockholder. Later, Jones followed Capt. Sturdevant as general manager. After Loeb sold his shares to Jones, the latter assumed the position of president as well as general manager in 1906.[30] Already mentioned in the discussion of the Bullen Hotel (Chapter IV), Jones met his future wife, Lillie Esme Matthews Bullen, while he was living in the hotel; after their marriage, the couple continued to make the hotel their home. When the Bullen Hotel burned to the ground in 1895, the Matthews and Jones families faced a tough decision: Should they rebuild the hotel or use the lot for something else?

Since Roland's work for John Schmidt had by the mid-decade reordered the family's resources, the family was no longer dependent on income from the hotel. Although a good location for a commercial establishment, the lot posed problems for a residence. Some families in the mid-1890s were not comfortable with the downtown environment as a place for domestic living. Some, such as their neighbor June Harris, had decided to move to the more pastoral area of Virginia Avenue, where there was enough space around their homes for livestock and gardens. The Joneses, however, were town dwellers. Esme Jones liked the central location.[31] Her church,

Christ Episcopal Church, was still across the street. She knew and liked the old neighbors, the Francis Rusche family; she approved and liked the new neighbors a block away to the north on Church Street—the Casons. She also knew that the Stephen W. Blount, Jr. family was working with Rulfs at the time on a design for a house on nearby Mound Street. The Joneses finally decided to build a completely new residence on their existing lot. The house would face Church Street, as had the hotel; but since the house was started before clearing the hotel debris, they had Rulfs place the house closer to Hospital Street.[32]

Accounts vary as to who wanted the Queen Anne styling. According to an interview with Genevieve Bullen Patterson, both Roland Jones and her grandfather Matthews "preferred a colonial type house, but their architect, Mr. Dietrich [sic] Rulfs, persuaded them to go for the new style of gingerbread Victorian."[33] This confirms what Patterson told the author, but in a newspaper account, the reporter reversed the influences.[34] Actually, it was Esme Jones, in collaboration with Rulfs, who carried the day. Mrs. Jones desired a more fashionable structure, similar to those in New Orleans, other parts of the nation, and Europe, where she had lived.[35] She wanted a combination of what Rulfs had done for the Bullen Hotel, which Perkins and Schmidt copied to North Street, and the innovations he had introduced there in the meantime. She insisted on the same general distribution of public rooms on the main floor and the relegation of all bedrooms to the upper floor, as in the hotel. While Greek Revival was still very much in vogue in Louisiana, where Roland Jones lived before Nacogdoches, the elites in Nacogdoches always called it "the old style." Roland Jones continued to champion Greek Revival in 1901, when he tried to sway the Vestry on the style for the proposed Christ Episcopal Church. What Rulfs liked was the flexibility the Queen Anne style offered the architect in developing a floor plan. He could have complete freedom to satisfy differing personal and individual needs by planning the house from the inside out. He could add bays, wings, and projections of any kind and proceed to unify the whole by using exterior decorations.

The Jones House, in other ways, followed the innovations that Rulfs had introduced into the Perkins and Schmidt residences on North Street, for example, a fireplace in the entrance hall and an acetylene lighting system. The arrangement of the parlor and living room in the Jones House, however, was less traditional. The formal parlor, which in the other two houses was across the hall from the living room, in this house was located immediately in front of the living room. Because Rulfs placed double pocket doors between the rooms–the entrance hall, parlor, living room, and dining room–the plan created one continuous space for entertaining, dining, and dancing. This change allowed the Jones House to accommodate crowds in an even more comfortable way than either the Schmidt or Perkins residences. Later occupants of the house tried to use the downstairs for bedrooms, but reported that the size of the rooms, their configuration, and their location on a business street, made them feel as if they were "sleeping in a gold-fish bowl."[36]

Rulfs' design for the exterior employs a mixture of elements: a very tall hip-and-gable roof, capped by intricate cast-iron cresting (removed in the 1950s), and two-story galleries on the front with turned posts, beads, and spindles. The exotic Moorish influences, utilized by Rulfs on the front porches and then effectively repeated in an impressive keyhole arch separating the entrance hall from the main stairwell, came from suggestions by Mrs. Jones who had seen them in Natchez, Mississippi. (Rulfs successfully utilized these same elements three years later in the Sturdevant House on North Street; see Figure 3.39.) Rulfs separated the steps leading to the front entrance by a small pulpit-like bay. Encouraged by Mrs. Jones, he incorporated European features. The tower on the northeast corner, topped by an onion dome, is reminiscent of many buildings in Oldenburg, where Rulfs studied and sketched. Rulfs unified the exterior with a series of horizontal and vertical boards arranged and painted for a half-timbered Renaissance effect. The house was a tribute to Rulfs' creative abilities, but it was also part of an evolutionary progression, starting with the Bullen Hotel to the Edwards, Perkins, Schmidt, and Blount houses on North Street, and then back to the Jones House. As the architectural historians of the National Register acknowledge, had the other houses on North Street survived, the Jones House might not stand out so dramatically to modern observers. And yet, after careful study of the other houses, the Jones House holds a special place among the architect's other creations; it is the first house for which we have his specifications.

A description of the house, from its National Register nomination, is presented on page 100.[37]

The notes accompanying the application for Texas Recorded Landmark status are very enlightening and show that in the fall of 1972, the Texas Historical Commission did not know anything about Rulfs. They were asking about the spelling of his name, whether he was an architect or builder or contractor, and "information about where his architectural firm was located."[38] While the historical researchers in Austin had questions, they knew without a doubt who designed the house. They had a set of specifications, which now can be found only in their archives: "Specifications for Residence of Roland Jones, Nacogdoches, Texas, 1896-7." The first line of the document reads: 'Specification of a two (2) story Residence to be erected at Nacogdoches, Texas, for Mr. Roland Jones, according to the Plans prepared by Mr. D. Rulfs, Architect, Nacogdoches, Texas."[39] The specifications called repeatedly for the " best" in lumber and workmanship, even for non-visible areas, such as sills and joists. The instructions for the stairway and wainscoting include very detailed uses of cypress and curly pine. Rulfs knew woods and knew that different types of wood, such as those with wavy wood fibers, would reflect the light in certain ways. The wainscoting also alternated smooth and grooved wood. The mantles upstairs were to be constructed on site and the ones for the main rooms to be furnished by the owner. The extensive set of drawings that accompanied these specifications are now missing, unfortunately; but throughout the document the architect refers his craftsmen to "plans" and "drawings."

In 1953, the *Dallas Morning News* ran a feature article on the house. May Irvin and Ashford Jones discussed how the expansion of the business district in Nacogdoches was threatening the house. They were reacting to the building of the new Fredonia Hotel across the street. The article pointed out that the house was an annual feature on the city's tour of historic buildings, but Mrs. Jones was obviously worried: "If it should ever be necessary to tear the old place down, I think the entire family would want to move out of town during the razing operation." The article did not mention Rulfs by name: "The house was designed by a German architect who insisted that nothing but heart timber, free from knots, be used in its construction. It has a towering cupola and 'gingerbread' ornamentation that reflects the architectural trend of the nineties."[40] Fortunately, the Jones family remained in

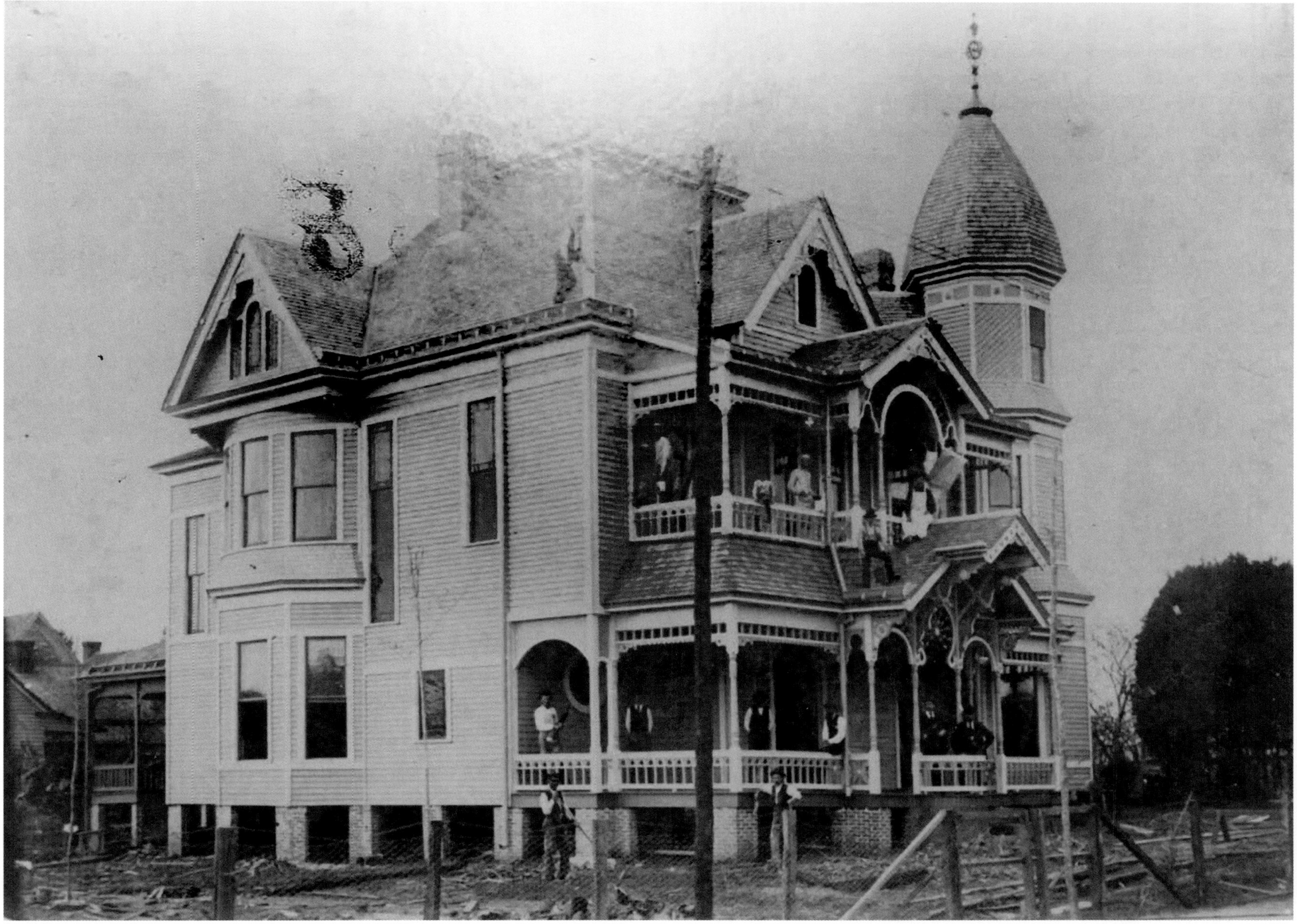

FIGURE 5.6. The Roland Jones House, Under Construction, 1896.

This photograph of the Jones House under construction shows roofers, carpenters on the upper and lower porch. The picture, taken before the front steps were added, has two formally dressed figures standing in the pastor's bay. It seems possible that Jones and Rulfs might be the figures. Photograph courtesy of Penny Jones Holcomb, granddaughter of Esme and Roland Jones.

the house for another twenty years. In 1972, Ashford and Mae Irvin Jones sold the house to Dr. John H. Thomas.[41] John Thomas, a local physician, also valued the house. He, for the first time in the house's history, enclosed the enormous attic as a playroom for his children. His decision to re-floor the main level, which was necessary, became controversial when he did so with a broad-board pattern which did not match the age of the house. He also replaced a Palladian window on the south to put in vents for his air-conditioner exhaust ducts and created an exterior door in place of the north window of the parlor, with a semi-circular roof on the exterior, to give access for his patients, but none of these changes threatened the overall integrity of the house or its exceptional exterior.[42] When he told the author he planned to remove all the pocket doors between the living room and the parlor and dining room, however, he had crossed the line–the character of the interior was truly at stake. When offered an alternative, Thomas agreed to leave the doors in place. He built his new office space within the parameters of the old living room and preserved the doors and the appearance of house. Interestingly, Thomas built an office in the north bay, a hall, and two examining rooms within the confines of the old original living room. These were subsequently very easy to remove.

It was not until the 1980s, when the Fredonia Hotel was desperately in need of restoration, that the town began to realize that their push for renewed tourism necessitated the preservation of houses such as the Roland Jones House and other houses around Washington Square. When Adlai Mast, Jr. purchased the Jones House, he definitely was thinking that restoration and preservation went hand in hand with tourism.[43] The town owes the Mast family, who have deep roots in East Texas, for the preservation of this great nineteenth century architectural gem.[44] A new generation, Karen and John Mast, have continued this interest in the Jones House. Karen, who oversees a bed-and-breakfast concern in the house, sponsored the Texas Historical Commission's subject marker for Diedrich Rulfs on the property.[45]

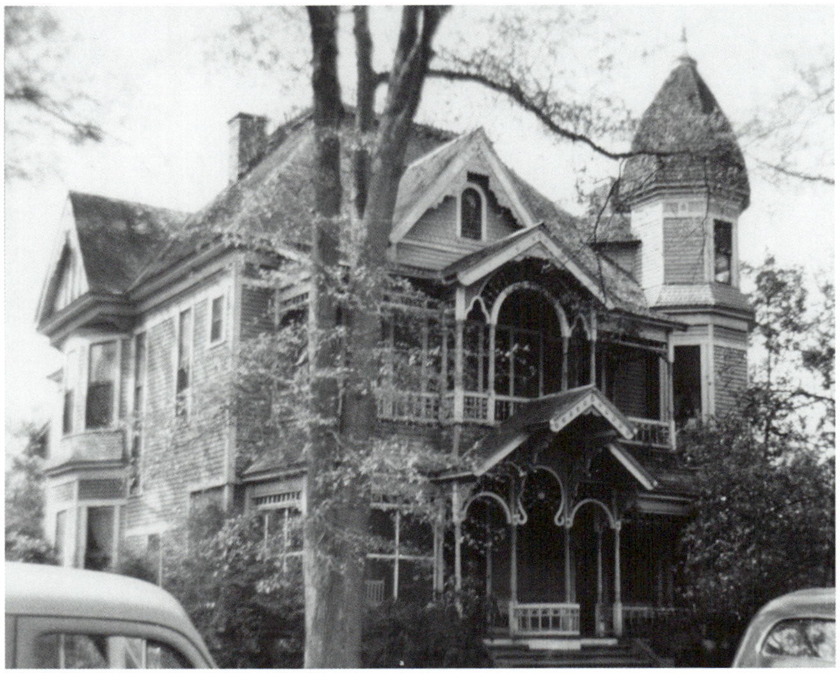

FIGURE 5.7. The Ashford Jones Home, 1948.
The photograph, part of the survey of East Texas houses done by Professor Elliot Evans from SFASC in 1948, did not identify the Roland Jones House as a design of D. Rulfs. Courtesy of ETRC.

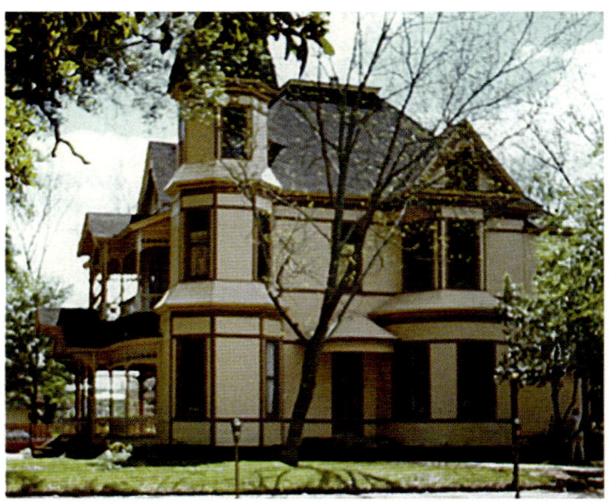

FIGURE 5.8. The Jones House, 1970s.
The house when the Jones family lived there was a shade of chartreuse. In the 1970s, Dr. John Thomas painted it tan with brown trim, highlighted with touches of yellow on the front porch details.

The Roland Jones House is an opulent 2 1/2-story domestic building with Queen Anne styled detailing. The dwelling, which has an asymmetrical plan, utilizes wood frame construction and rests on a pier-and-beam foundation. Its walls are sheathed with weatherboard siding and wood shingles. The residence has a 3-story corner tower with a conical roof and a 2-story front porch with a three-part gabled portico. The Jones House is about two blocks north of the public square in a transitional area between historic neighborhoods and the central business district. Formerly a private residence, the dwelling is now used as an office [and bed-and-breakfast hostelry].

... The front has a two-tiered porch with turned-wood columns, and spindled friezes and balustrades on both floors. A gabled portico with carved and jigsaw wood detailing marks the primary entrance. To enter the house, however, one must go on either side of a curved bay in the middle of the entrance bay. The gabled end of the portico has an intricate spindled frieze with turned wood spheres that appear as if they are suspended in air. Similar motifs are used in the second-floor portico. A third gable extends from the truncated hip roof and is set back directly behind the other porticoes. The tower, which extends from the northeast corner of the house, has a steeply pitched conical roof with eight sides. Wood-shingled pent roofs mark the first and second floors. The house is detached and freestanding, and no outbuildings are on the lot. The Jones House is in good condition with few alterations.

The Roland Jones House arguably is Nacogdoches' finest example of Queen Anne-styled architecture and is nominated to the National Register under Criterion C. Its asymmetrical and complex massing, intricate detailing and woodwork and unaltered condition distinguish it from other similarly detailed houses in the city. The Jones House reflects late 19th-century growth and prosperity in Nacogdoches and, therefore, is associated with Community Planning and Development in Nacogdoches: 1830-1940.

National Register Nomination

FIGURE 5.9. (Opposite) Jones House, East Elevation, 2011.

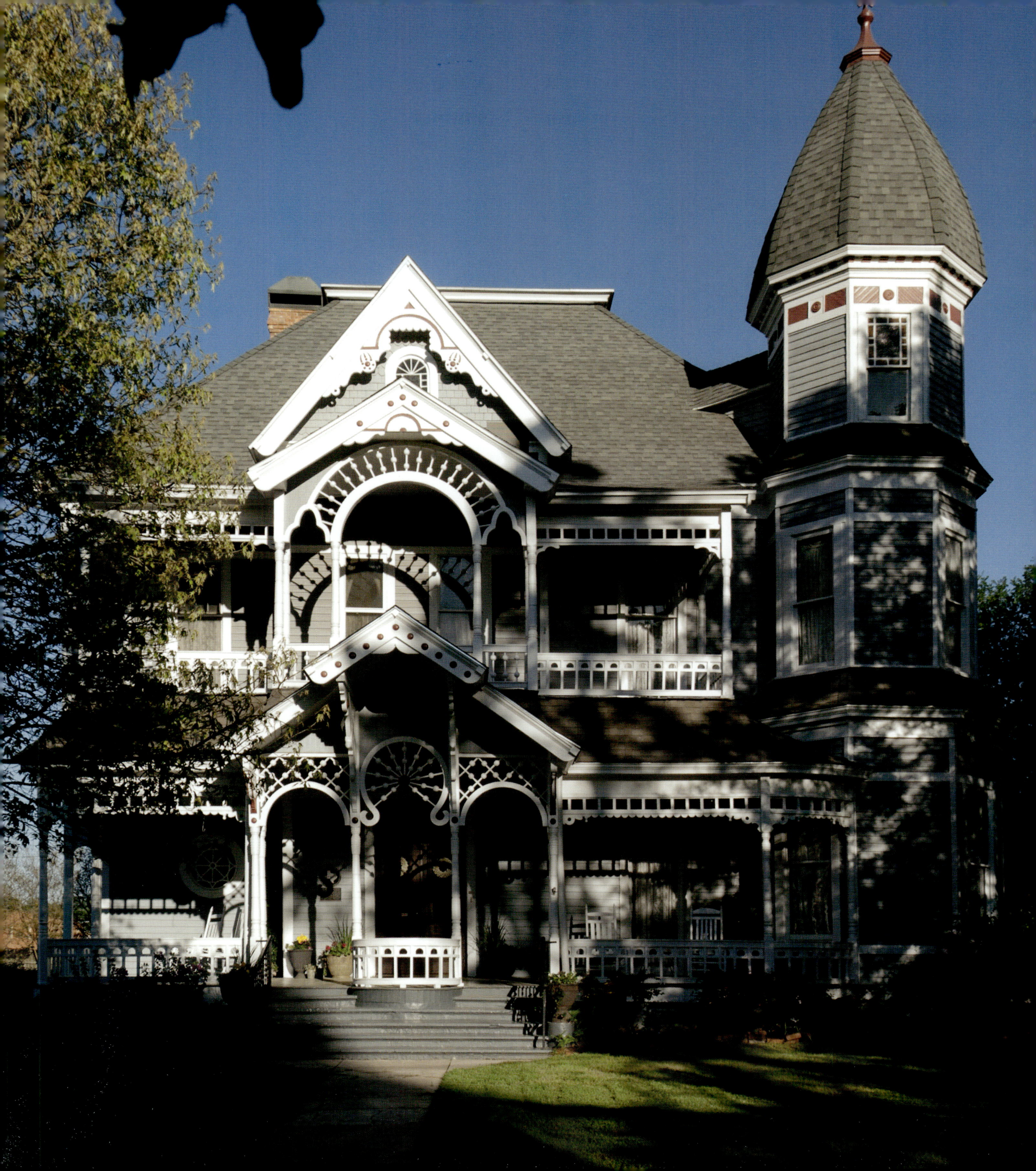

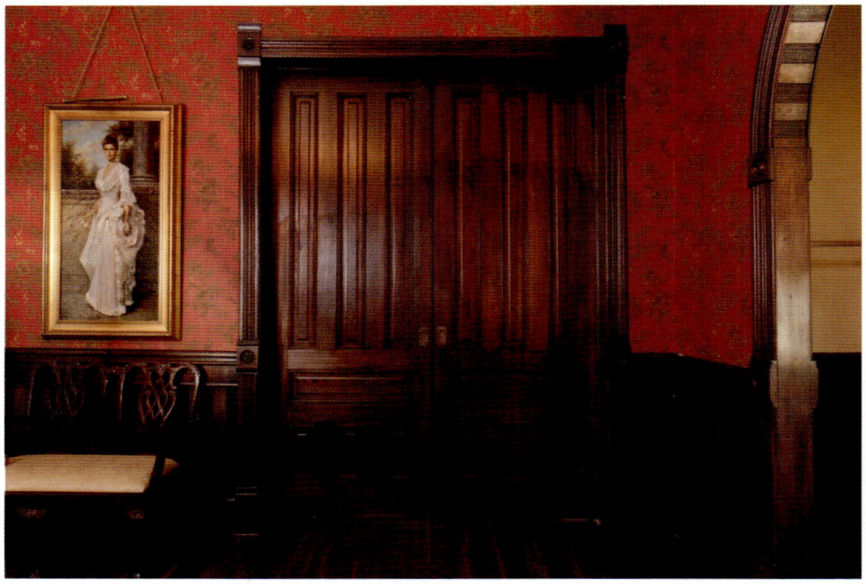

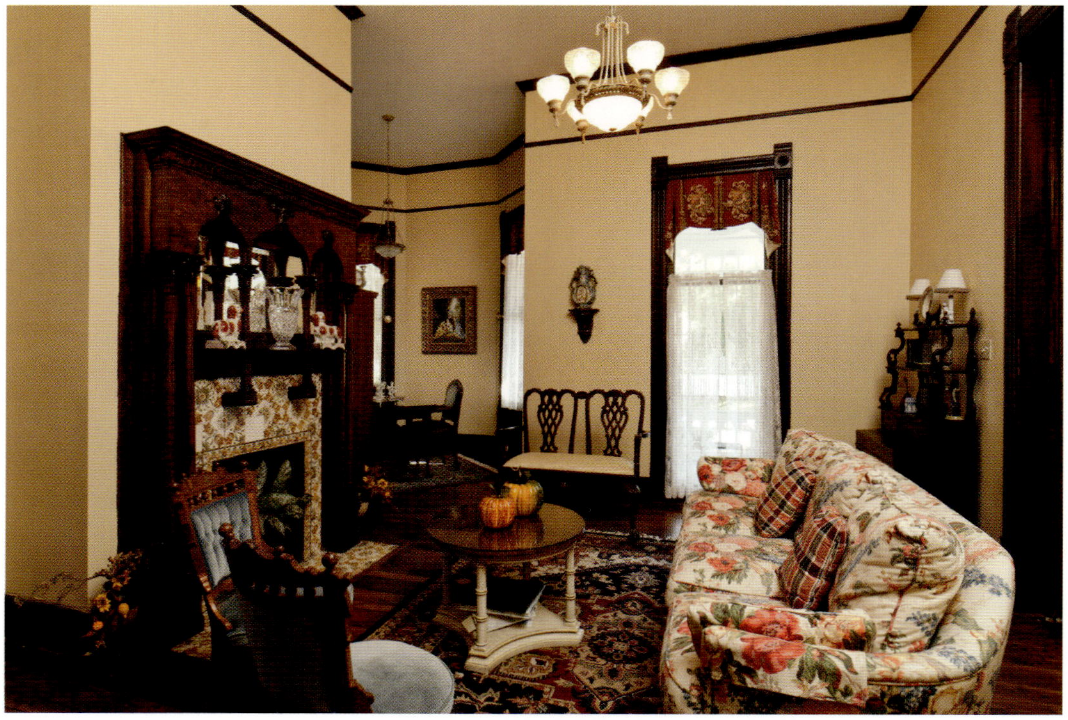

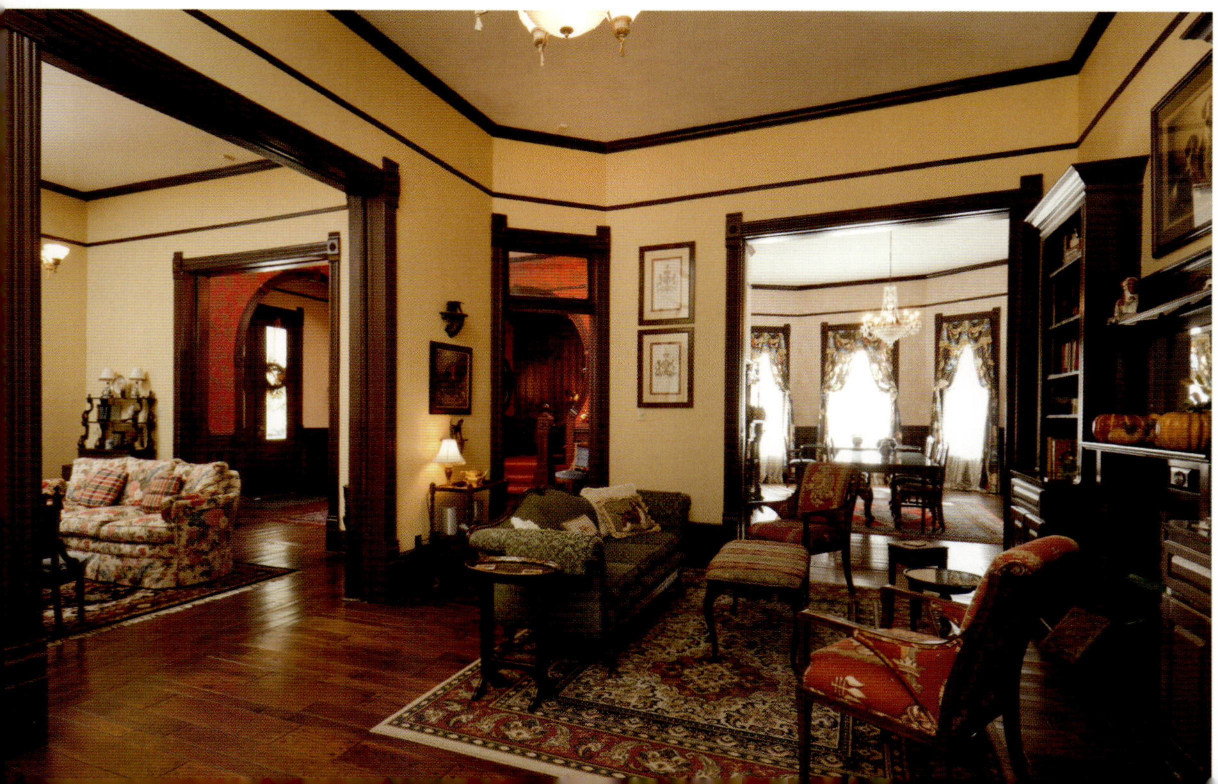

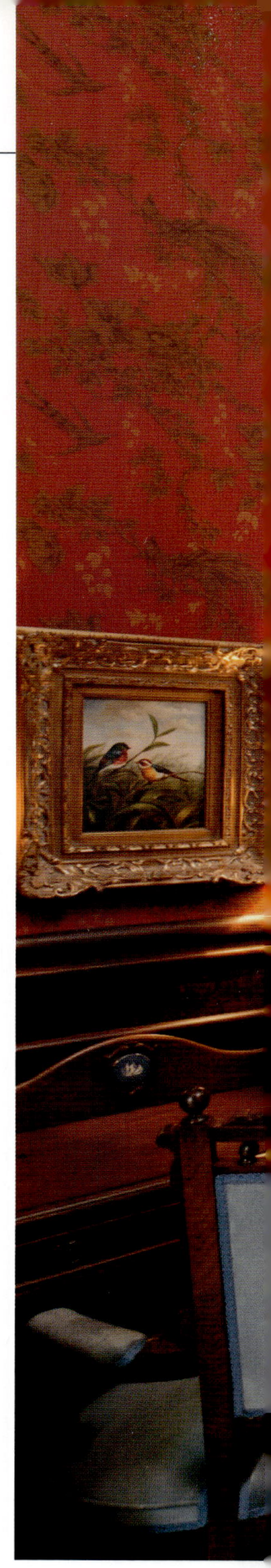

FIGURE 5.10. (Top Left) The Pocket Doors to the Parlor.

FIGURE 5.11. (Middle Left) The Parlor, with its Tower Room.

FIGURE 5.12. (Below Left) The Public Rooms. *Living Room, Parlor, Entrance, and Dining Room.*

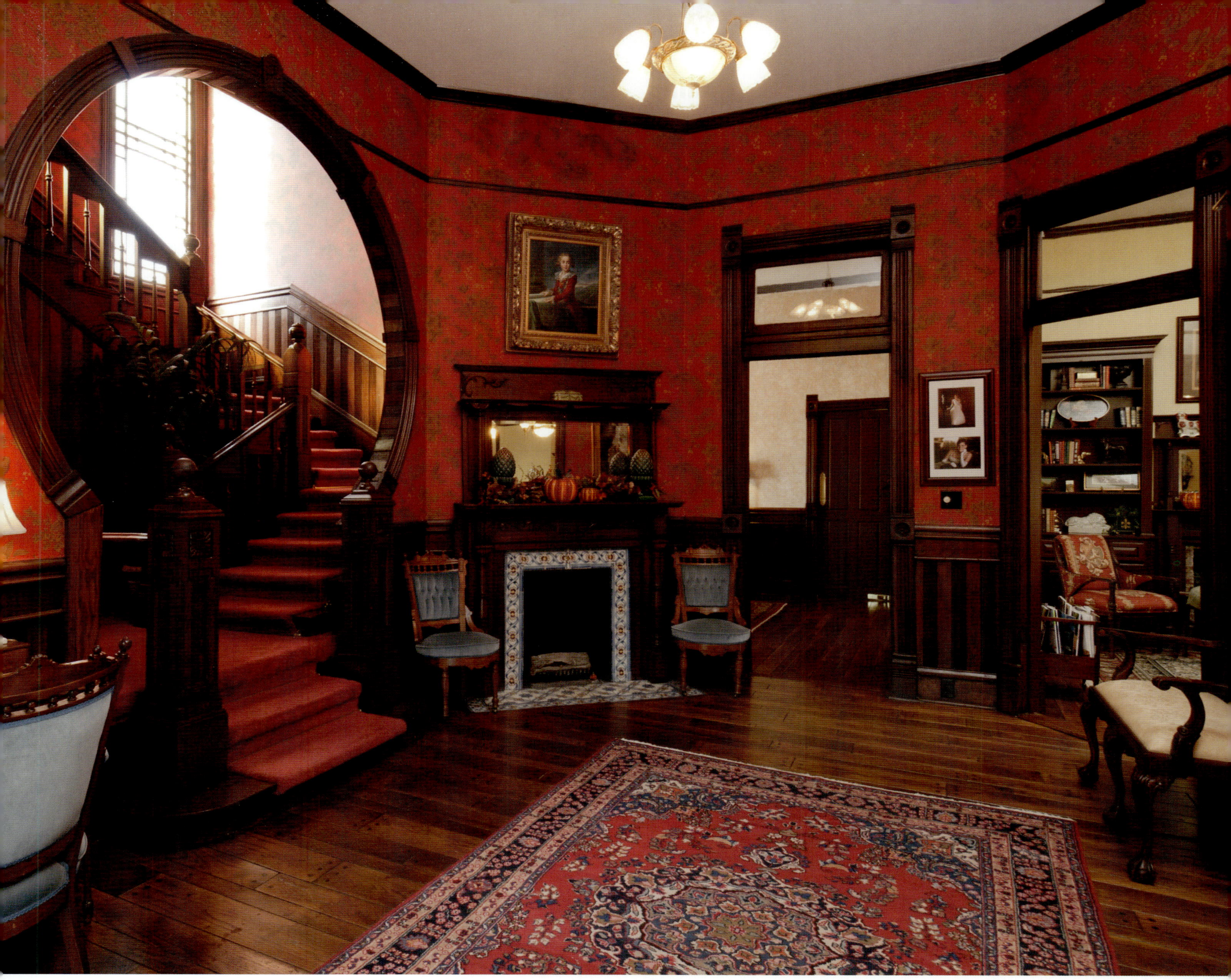

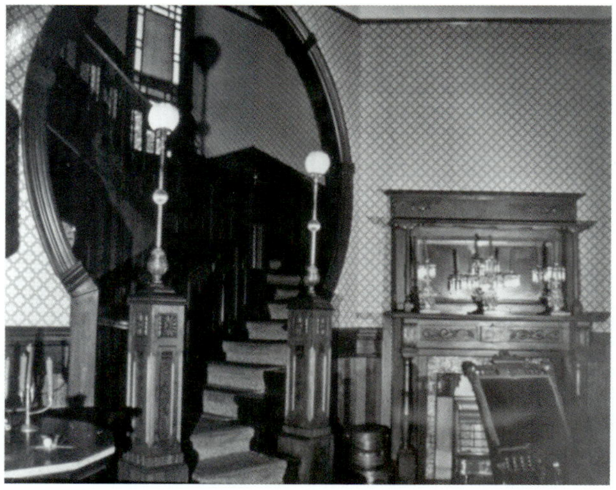

FIGURE 5.13. (Above) Jones House Entrance Hall, 2011.
The dining room is straight ahead, the living room to the right, and the parlor's double-pocket doors are immediately out of the picture to the right. The stairwell is illuminated by art glass.

FIGURE 5.14. (Left) The Stairwell and Entrance, 1930s.
Photograph given to the author in 1972 by Mrs. Ashford Jones.

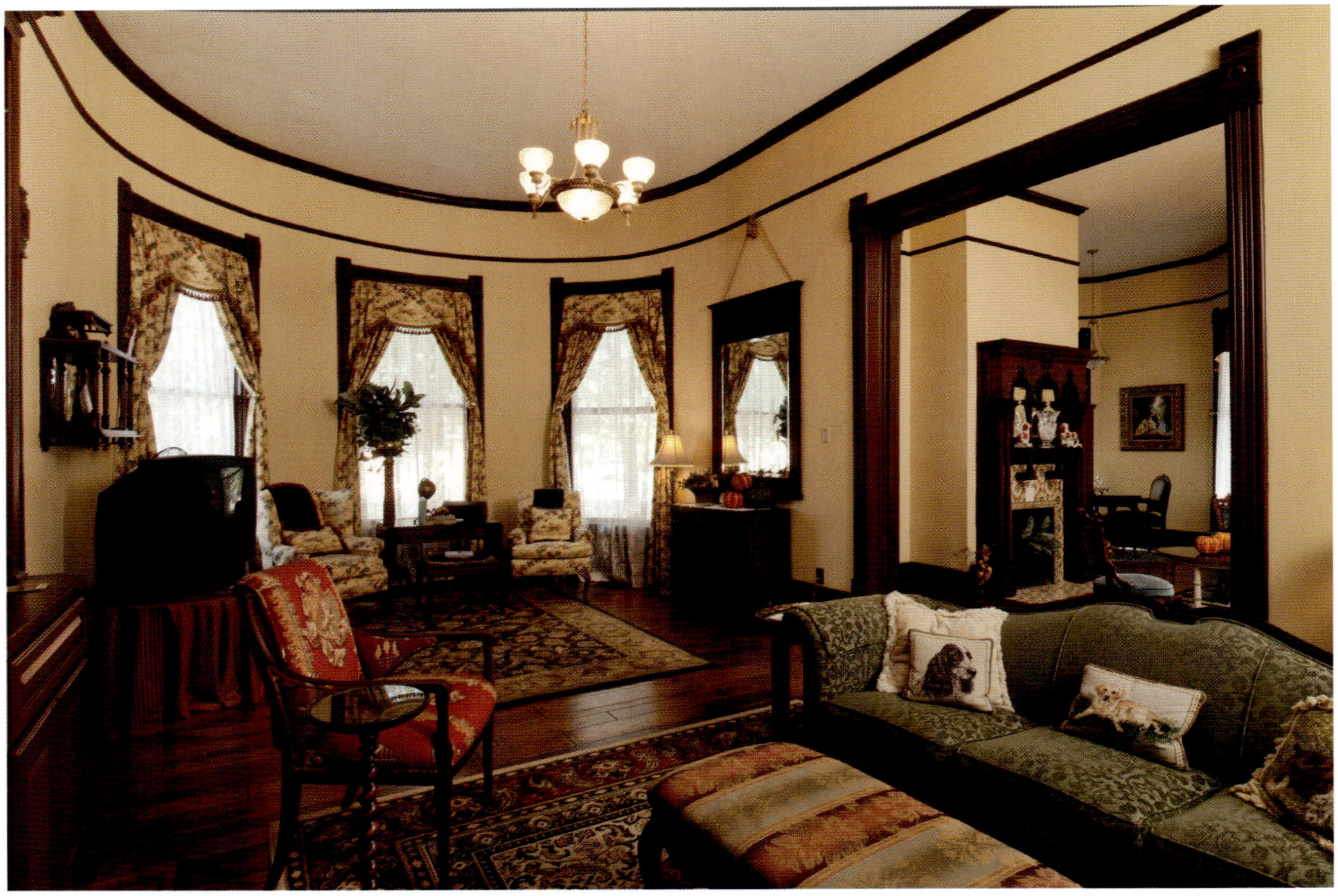

FIGURE 5.15. (Left) Living Room and Parlor.

Between the two rooms, and between the living room and the dining room below, very large pocket doors made possible the sectioning off of smaller spaces.

FIGURE 5.16. (Below) Dining Room

Each of the great rooms on the first floor, including the entrance hall, had fire places with imported mantle pieces.

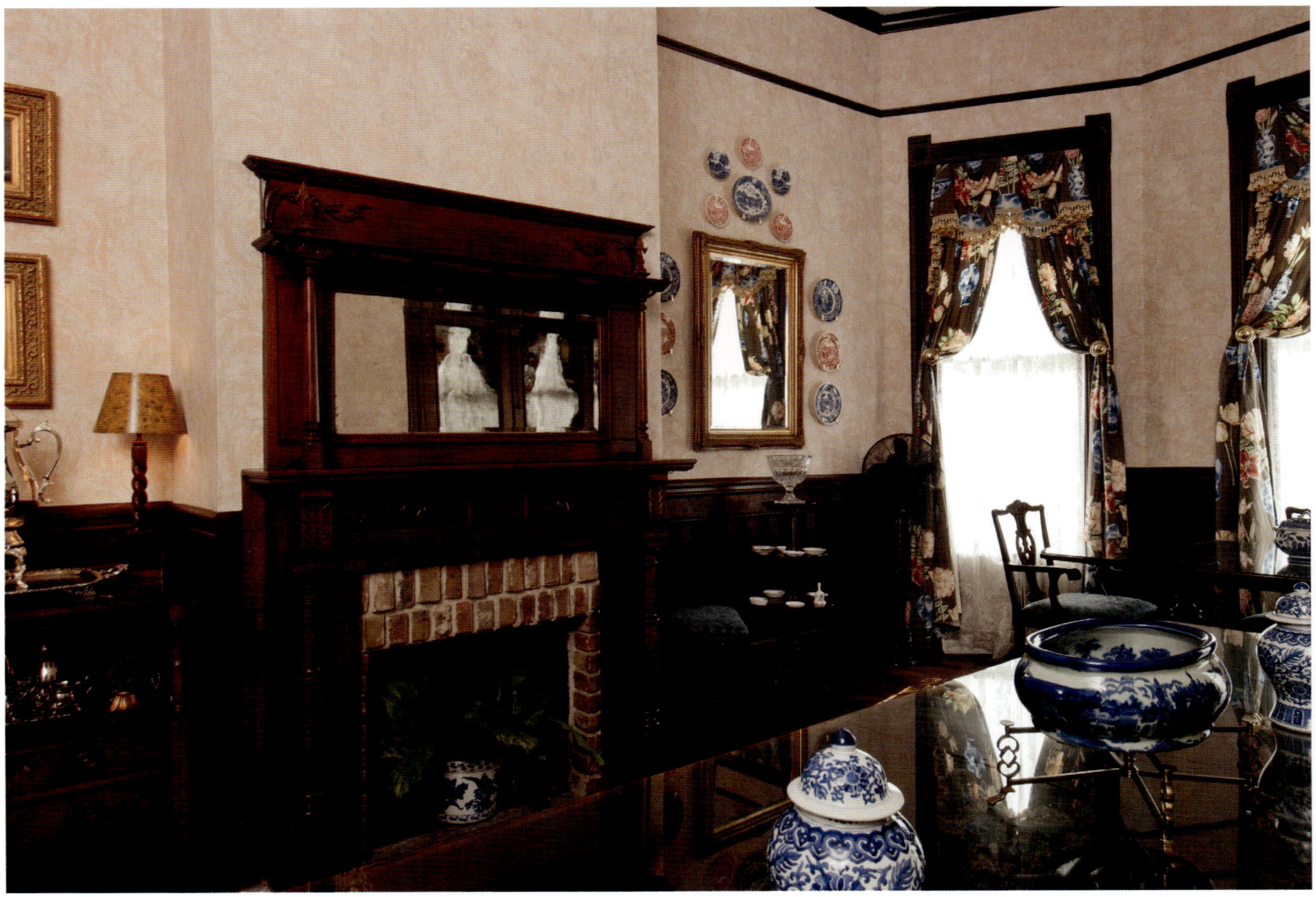

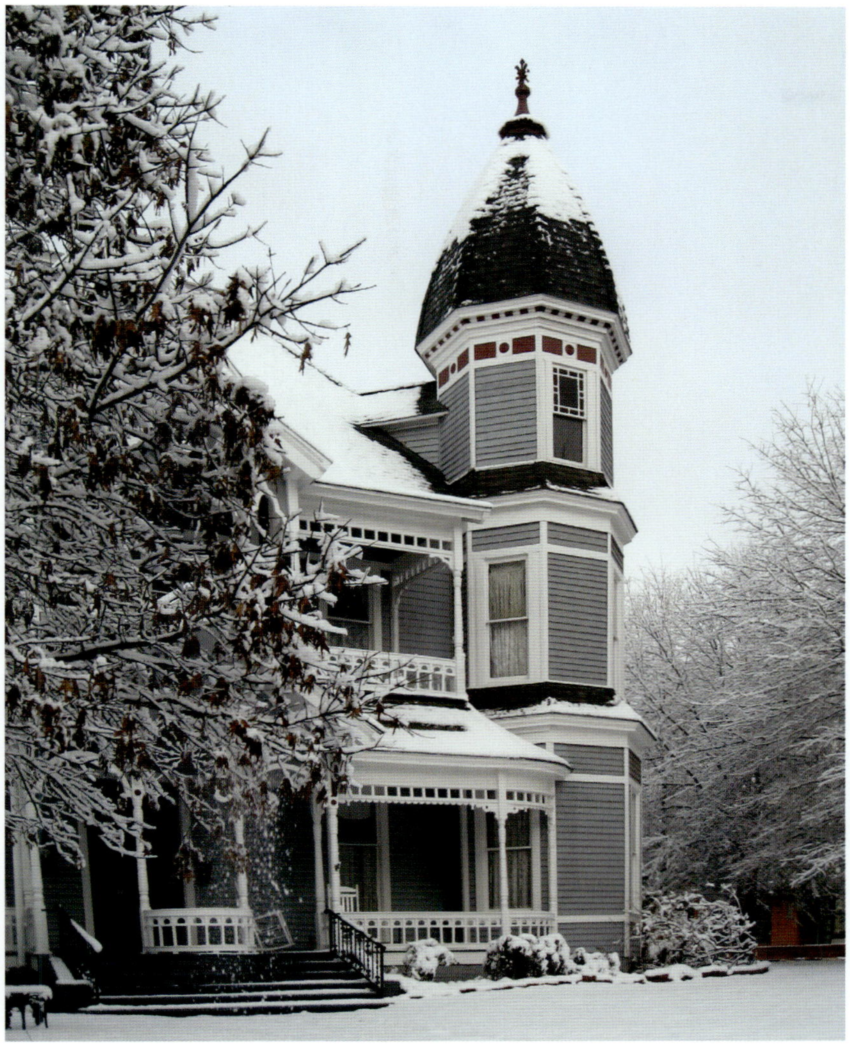

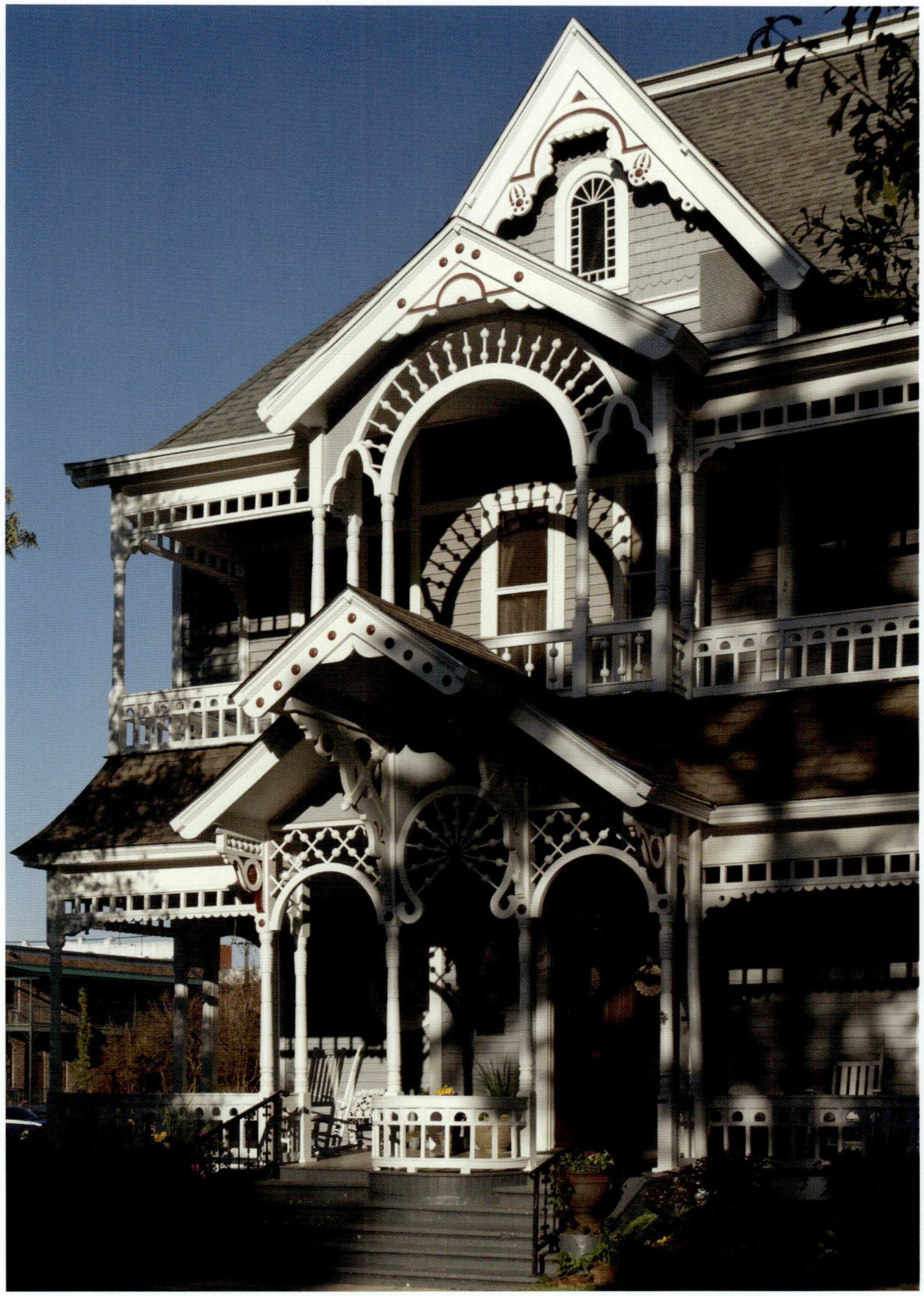

FIGURE 5.17. Photograph by the author, winter of 2010.

FIGURE 5.18. (Right) Roland Jones House, 2011.

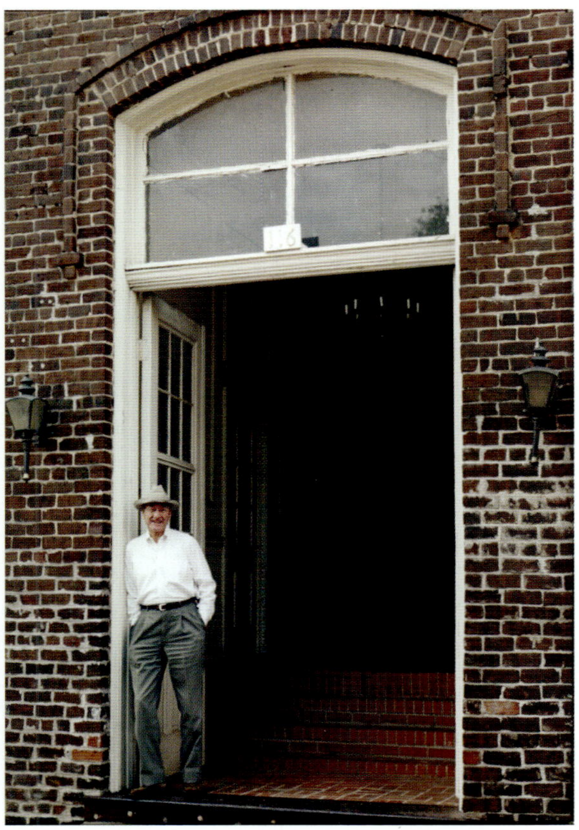

FIGURE 5.19. Adlai T. Mast, Jr.

Posterity owes a major debt to Adlai T. Mast, Jr. for guaranteeing the continued existence, viability, and integrity of the Roland Jones House in the face of surrounding commercialization. Mast, a descendent of a distinguished pioneer family, exhibited a particular affinity for the house, but he also recognized the important part it played in the promotion of tourism for Nacogdoches. As one of the leading advocates for the restoration of the Hotel Fredonia and the addition of a convention center, Mast knew that these interests made preservation of Washington Square, more or less, a necessity. As the National Register noted, the hotel stands in "the most architecturally significant [district] in the city because the neighborhood includes the best and the most intact historic houses in the city."

Mr. Mast is standing in the doorway to his office in the Cotton Exchange Building—an important Rulfs commercial structure nearby in the same city block. Courtesy of John Mast.

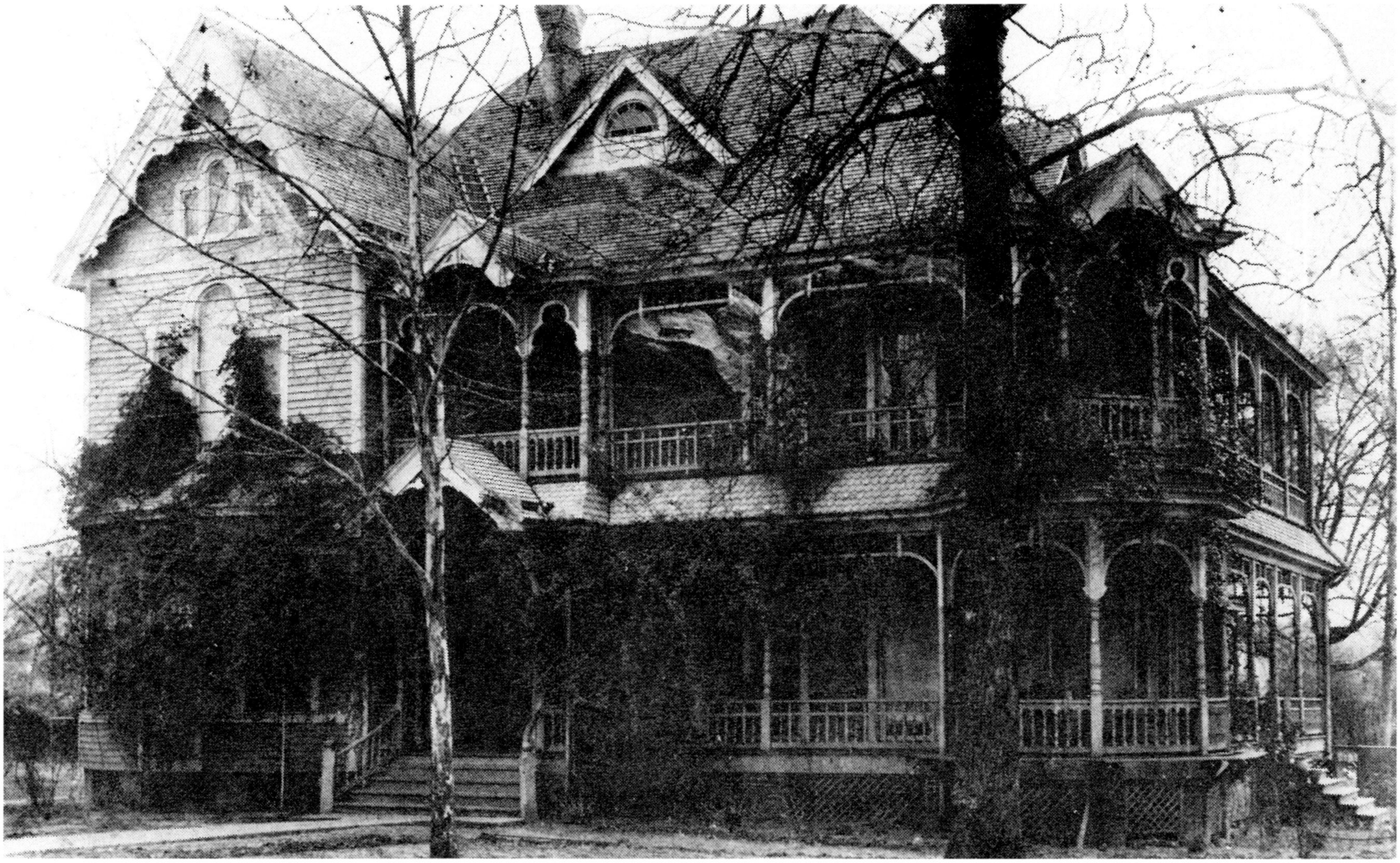

FIGURE 5.20. The Stephen Blount House, 1930s.
Photograph courtesy of Mrs. Earl Huffor, as published in Martha Anne Turner's Old Nacogdoches in the Jazz Age, *8.*

The Mary Price and Stephen William Blount, Jr. House (1897)

In 1991, the National Register deemed the Stephen Blount House one of the most outstanding examples of Queen Anne style architecture in the city–"a significant architectural landmark in both the historic Washington Square neighborhood and the city of Nacogdoches.[46] Because of the architectural importance of this house to the legacy of the architect and to the city's attempt to protect its historical heritage, a somewhat more detailed description seems warranted–for posterity.

Stephen William Blount, Jr. (1854-1928),[47] the younger of the two brothers who migrated to Nacogdoches in the 1890s to take advantage of the economic boom, was known as Judge Blount–quite possibly an honorary title bestowed by his contemporaries on an extremely competent lawyer. His father, Colonel Stephen William Blount, settled in San Augustine in 1835, was a signer of the Texas Declaration of Independence, and represented San Augustine in the Texas Constitutional Convention.[48] The family had extensive land holdings, which Stephen as well as his brother inherited and managed.[49] According to information researched by one of the author's graduate students, Blount "served in the 18th session (1885) of the Texas Legislature. Here, he acted as chairman of the Public Debt Committee and was a member of the Judiciary Committee."[50] Pam Thorstensen, who along with her husband, Lyle, owned the Blount House from 1988 to 2001 and prepared the National Register nomination for the house, wrote: "Judge Blount served . . . on many state and national committees and commissions. One of the most notable is his appointment by Governor Neff to the Historical Board. Started in 1923, the Historical Board became the Historical Survey Committee in 1953, and in 1973, it became the Texas Historical Commission."[51] Blount and his law partner, Beeman Strong,[52] practiced law in an office on the second floor of his brother's building on the Square–designed by Rulfs (1901)–over the Stripling, Haselwood, & Company Drugstore.

While Blount had conducted an active business in buying and selling land in Nacogdoches, it was only after William F. Price, his brother-in-law, decided to make his home at 222 North Mound Street that the Blounts decided to build a house in Nacogdoches. The Blounts completed the new house at 310 Mound before they even transferred the title to the land.[53] The house stayed in the Blount family until Mary Blount's death in 1943, at which time they sold the house to Branch-Patton Hardware for

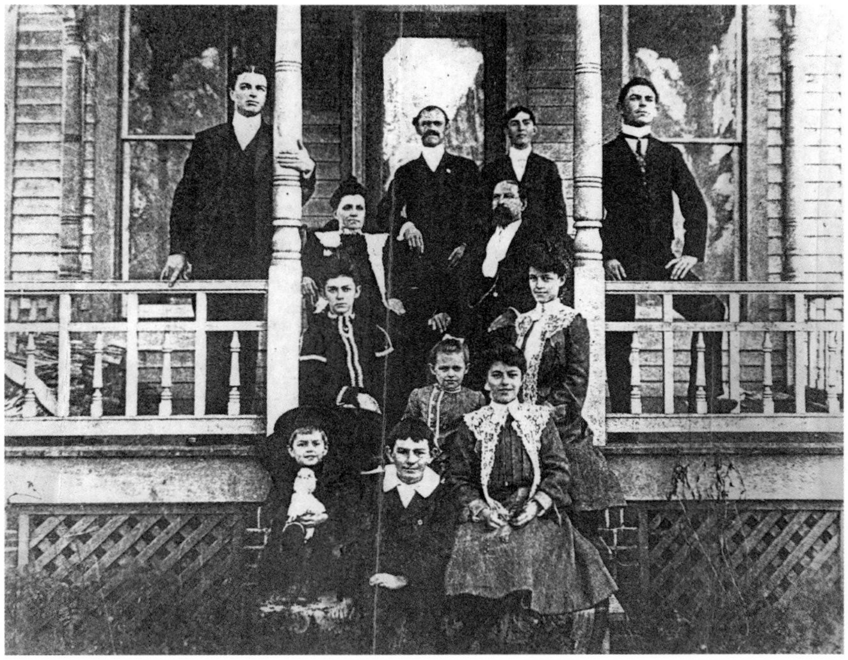

FIGURE 5.21. The Blount Family, ca. 1905.
This portrait of the Stephen and Mary Blount (seated in the center of the picture) was taken on the north porch of the house, the entrance to Judge Blount's Office. The Blounts had eleven children. Photograph courtesy of Pam Thorstenson.

FIGURE 5.22. (Middle) Screened Gazebo on the Front Porch, ca. 1900.
This photograph, which includes Mary Blount's pride and joy–the south garden, confirms that the Blounts even had the octagon gazebo on the front corner screened at one time. Photograph courtesy of Pam Thorstenson.

FIGURE 5.23. (Bottom) Giant Oak Falls in the Garden.
This documentation of the disaster of the oak, which destroyed most of the rose garden, offers the only extant image of the south elevation of the house. Courtesy of ETRC.

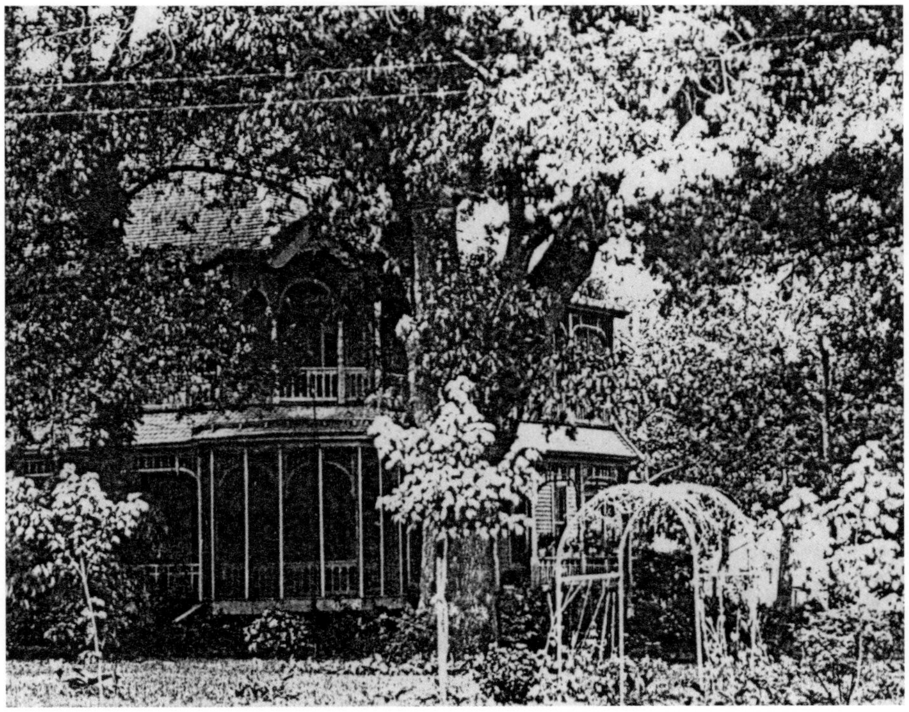

their funeral parlor. Two years later, in 1945, when Cason-Monk Funeral Company sold their location to the First Baptist Church, they purchased the Branch-Patton funeral business and the Blount House and moved the business to Mound Street.[54]

Blount approached Rulfs about plans while the Jones House was still under construction. As a lumberman with family experience in managing land and timber, Stephen Blount (in fact, all of the Blounts) took a keen interest in the types of woods being used in their residences. Since neither he nor his wife and family moved to Nacogdoches before the completion of the house in 1897, Blount's interest quite possibly consisted of selecting the quality and types of woods, not in overseeing construction. Unfortunately, no drawings or specifications survive to document this house, as was the case with the Roland Jones, Tom Summers, or D. K. Cason houses. Testimonies abound, however, about the involvement of the Rulfs brothers in the designing and construction of the house. Because of its unique qualities, everyone interviewed seemed to contribute different information about this particular structure. In the memory of William Henry Rulfs, the architect's brother, the house held a special status. Wilhelmina Rulfs Thompson, while saying that her father was proud of both houses, said he held up the Stephen Blount House as the zenith of his work as a carpenter–his masterpiece. The

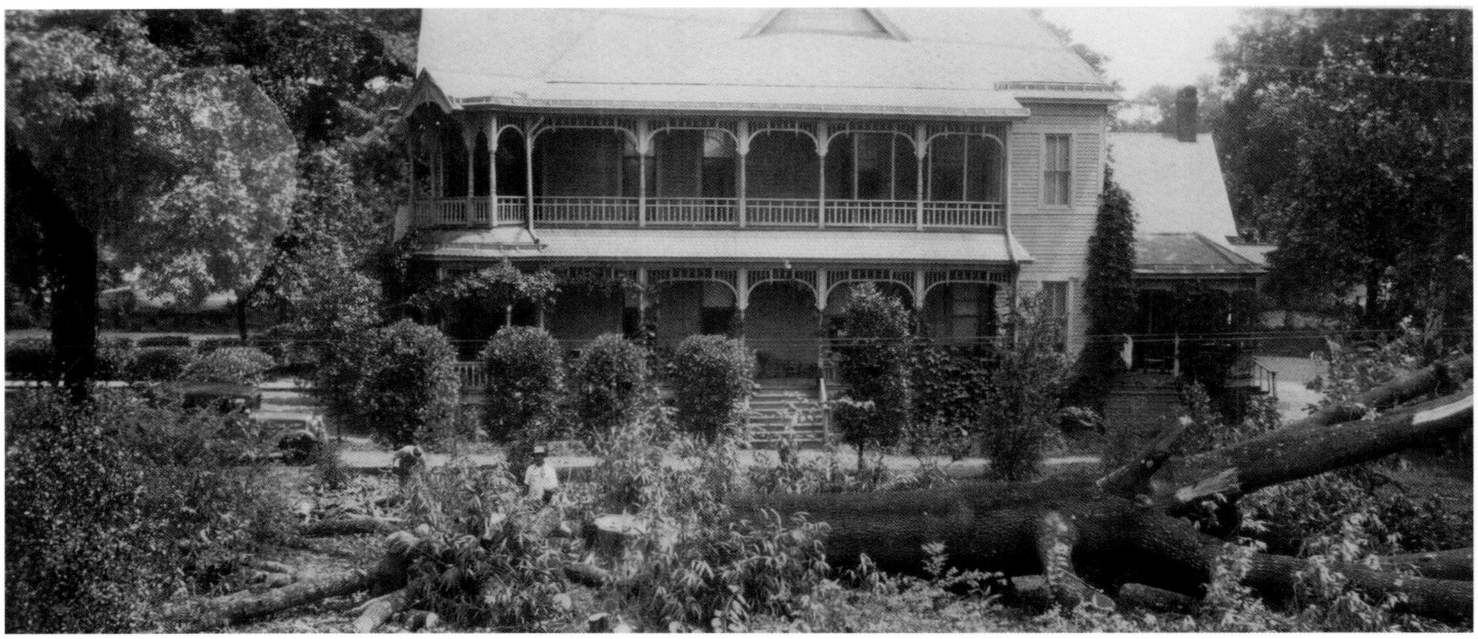

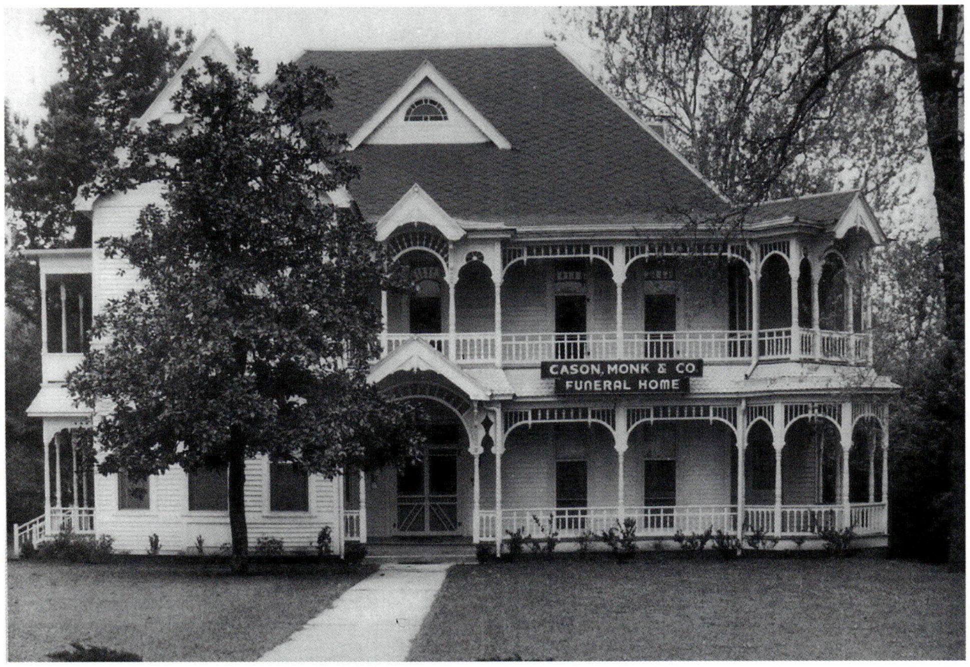

FIGURE 5.24. Cason-Monk Funeral Home, 1945-1980s.
Courtesy of the ETRC.

FIGURE 5.25. The Blount House with the Funeral Chapel Attached, ca. 1985.
Photograph courtesy of Pam Thorstenson.

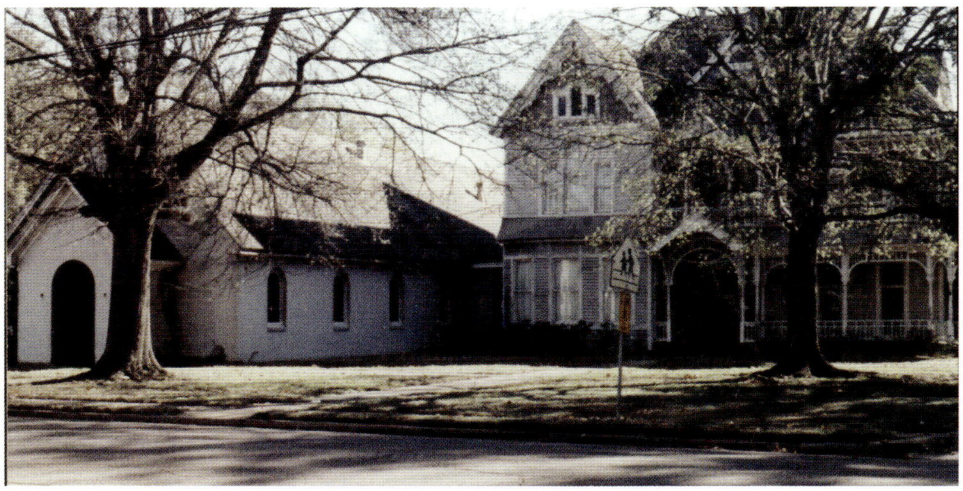

Blount House required more intricate carpentry work on the exterior, because the galleries were more extensive. The stories and the difficulties got more involved as William Henry would retell the details of the great porch system.[55] Mary Stewart Duncan, another niece, remembered more about the family and the social gatherings surrounding the house.

The Architecture

The National Register's description of the house, as it stood in the mid 1990s, is a good place to begin a discussion of the architecture of the house.[56] (See the quote in the next column.)

> *The Blount House was built in 1897 and is an example of the Queen Anne Eastlake style. The wood frame is supported by a brick foundation. Lapped wood siding covers the wall surfaces and decorative shingles and bargeboards fill the gables. The intersecting hip and gable roof is covered with composition shingles [now]. The west façade faces the street and has a highly ornate asymmetrical two-story gallery, which spans from a projecting bay at the north end of the house to the south corner and wraps around to the south façade. The southwest corner of the gallery forms a projecting partial octagon on the lower level and a projecting rectangle on the upper level, capped by an open gable with decorative barge-board and pendant. The gallery incorporates slender Eastlake style turned wooden columns with knobs, molded brackets, pendants, and arched spans between the columns, with a delicate ball and spindle motif along the porch frieze and low spindle and spool-like balusters. The entrance of the porch features an archway accented by a ball and spindle frieze under a pediment. This treatment is repeated on the second floor gallery above the main entrance and on the southwest corner. Both levels of the gallery are divided into three sections. The first section of the first floor is the entry with its Palladian motif, the second is a two bay run along the length of the porch, and the final section is the octagonal projection with its single bay per face. The first section of the second floor is a Palladian motif capped by an open gable with bargeboard and pendant. The second section of the second floor is an evenly divided two-bay run and the third section has a projecting rectangular Palladian motif capped identically to the first section. The entry to the house has double wood doors with raised ornamentation and narrow glass lights with chamfered corners. Four other doors open onto the first floor gallery.*
>
> *The windows are 1/1 wood double-hung with continuous wood trim above. The gabled dormer on the west façade above the gallery has a stained glass fan-shaped Queen Anne style window. Of special note are the Palladian-style windows at the second floor and the attic on the projecting bay of the west façade. The smaller of these two windows in the attic gable is surrounded by fish-scale shingles and an ornate scroll-like bargeboard with paired knobs and a collar tie. The three-part window motif is carried over to the pedimented entryways on the first and second floors of the gallery. On the first floor, the front wall of the projecting bay is slightly bowed with vertical siding above the windows.*
>
> National Register Nomination

The Façade and the Porches

From the view of a tourist, façades are the most important features of a historic structure, since many may never get an opportunity to visit inside a private structure. Most Queen Anne structures are asymmetrical. The front of this structure has two great defining features: a great front-facing projecting gable on the north and a two-story system of galleries, which wrap from this gable to the southeast corner of the house. The front gable is Rulfs at his best–one of his master works. Not only did he represent his favorite Palladian motifs three ways on the gable, but he also incorporated variations into the design of the porch.

No feature of Queen Anne architecture defines the style as much as the porches. Adjusting to the need for porches was one of the big adaptations

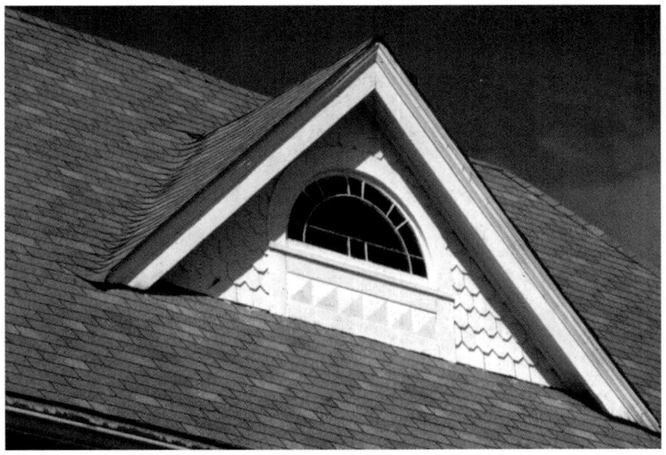

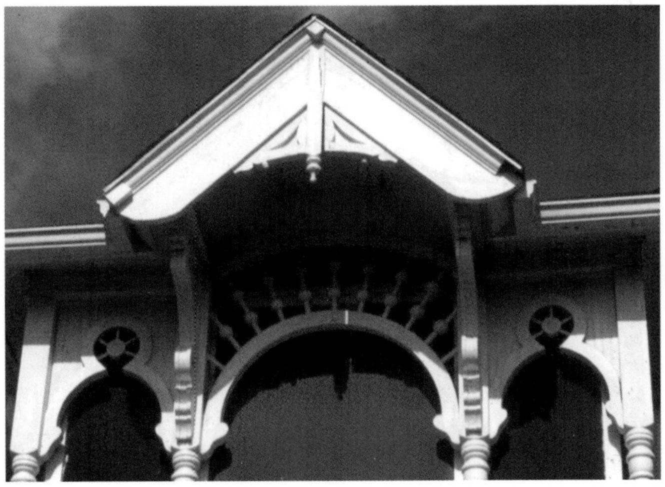

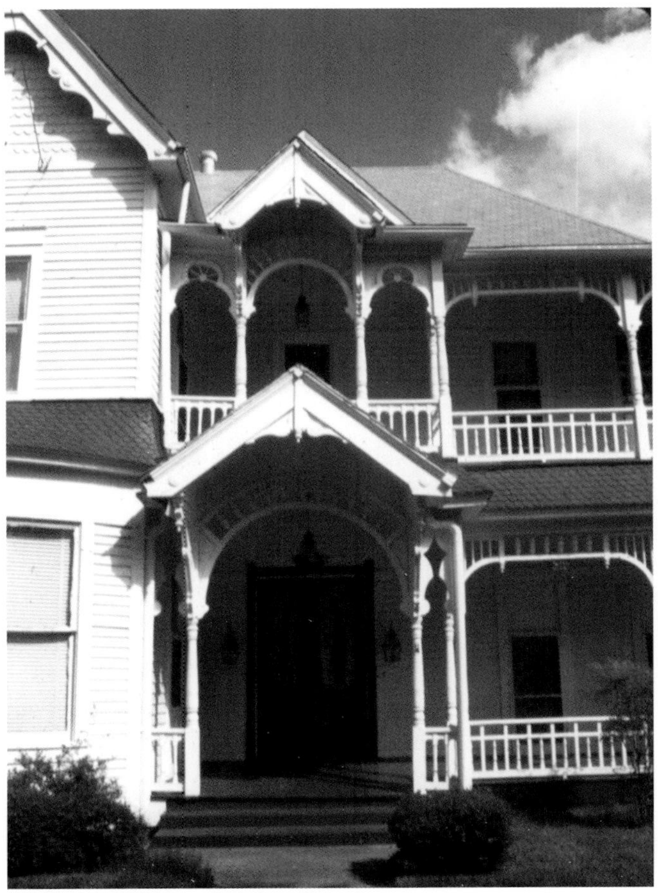

FIGURES 5.26 to 5.30.
Details, West Façade, 1970s.
(Left Top) Gable Roof Projection, with Fan-shaped Window.
(Left Center) Palladian Detail on Upper Porch.
(Left Bottom) Entrance Pediment. Tiered Palladian Motifs.
(Right Top) Detail, Eastlake Spandrels.
(Right) Tower at the Southwest Corner of the Front Porch.
Photographs by the author, 1970s.

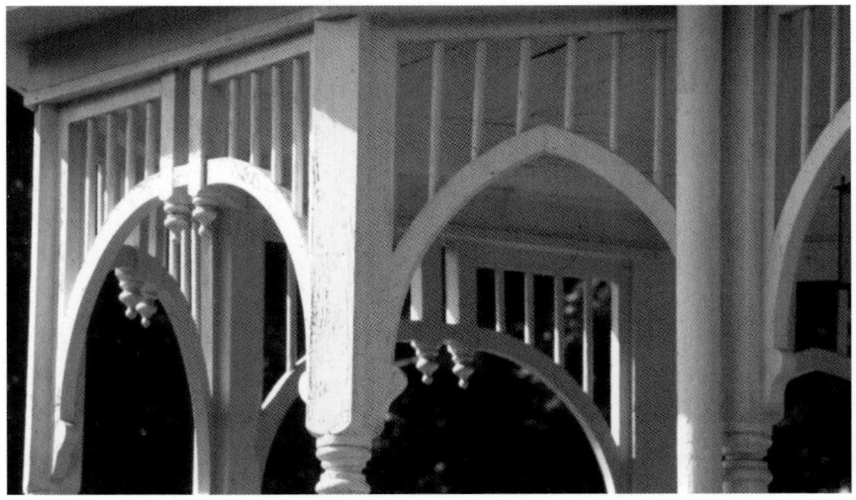

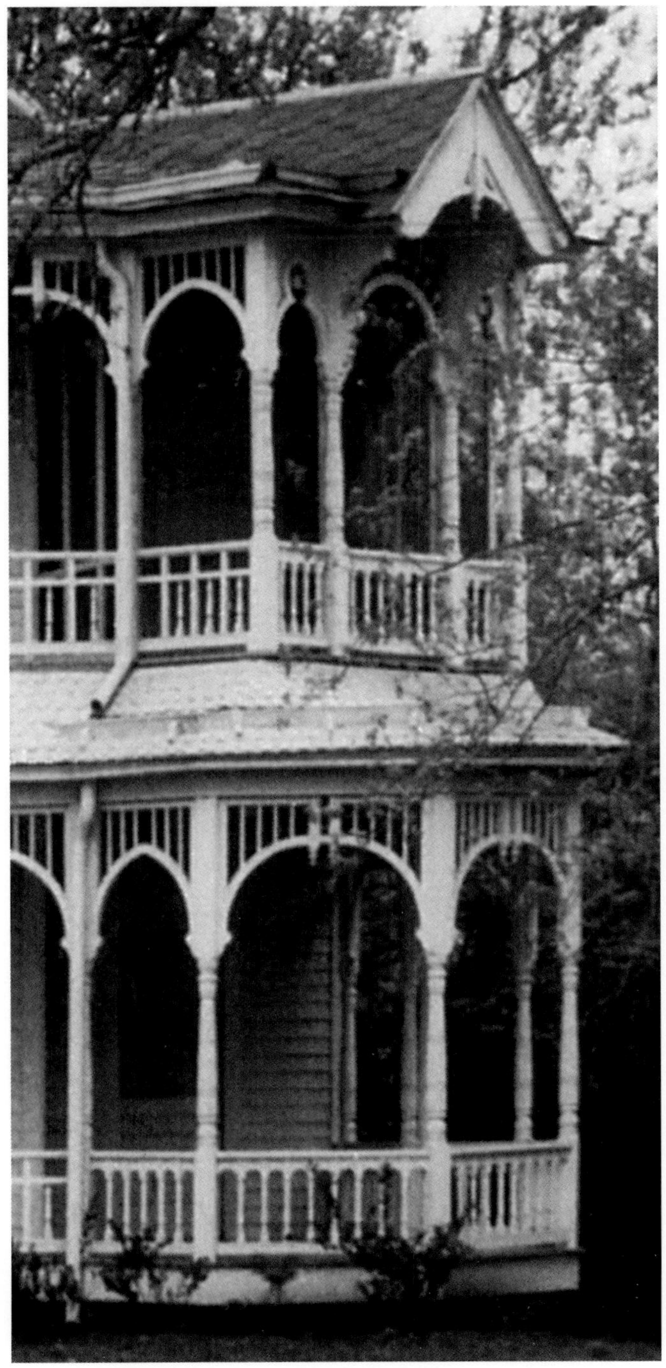

imposed on D. Rulfs by the East Texas region. Few houses in Northern Germany would have had porches; they may have had covered entrances, but the weather precluded outdoor living most of the year. Not so in East Texas. Because the porch in East Texas provided the essential transitional space between being "indoors" and being "outdoors," porches quickly became defining features of the houses designed in Nacogdoches by the architect. He not only gave access to the porches from most rooms through the use of slip-head windows, but he also constantly grappled with the problem of turning this utilitarian necessity into something aesthetic. His endless porch interpretations–a fascinating feature to follow on his houses–almost always define the overall historic character of his houses.

To see what happened to a fine house when the porches ceased to play their defining role, read the discussion in Chapter VI of the June Harris House (1895). When porches fall into disrepair, East Texans usually refer to the *house* as "falling down," whereas, in truth, the judgment applies mainly to the porch. For another example of this, reference the discussion of the J. J. Baker House in Chapter IV.

It is primarily the west and south façades that establish the Stephen Blount House as a masterpiece. Rulfs offset the weight of the great north bay with the airy-laciness of the south galleries. Instead of using a tower, as in the Jones House, Rulfs incorporated a two-story, attached gazebo into the southwest corner of the porches and then continued the double galleries across the entire south façade of the house. On two levels, the south porches offered vistas over the extensive south gardens; Mary Price Blount, an avid gardener, no doubt requested this feature. The gardens connected her house with that of her brother to the south. Mary Stewart Duncan, in relating information on the Stephen Blount House, had very little to say about the technical considerations of constructing this house, but she always thought the house was glamorous–especially the parties in the lovely gardens to the south (where the apartments now stand). The Blounts sometimes strung lanterns over the south garden for parties. Mrs. Duncan, impressed by the size of the family, related how much activity seemed to be around the house.[57] Others have told similar stories.

From the carpenter's point of view, the Blount House galleries were challenging–more difficult to execute than the enclosed tower on the Jones House. First, Rulfs did not design the two levels of the porch as identical, which he had done in a similar porch on the Edwards House. To fit the demands of the steps on the south façade, even the arched spandrels were not uniform. According to Wilhelmina Rulfs Thompson, her father William Henry Rulfs said the construction of the Blount House came at a time when the brothers had an unusually large number of commissions under various stages of completion. The intricacies of the carpentry work on the Blount project, however, could not be delegated.

The house very likely had screen doors from the beginning, but if not, shortly thereafter. These innovations had come to Nacogdoches through the ingenuity of Perkins Brothers Drug Store.[58] Since the Blount House predates the appearance of sheet screening suitable for creating sleeping porches, the enclosure of a portion of the upstairs with screening was the first change to the porches. An early photograph shows the upper south porch screened; later photographs show screening on the southwest octagon on the main floor. By 1910, Rulfs was regularly incorporating sleeping porches into his houses. (The W. U. Perkins House had them added in 1910, as did the residences for Hollis Mast and Tom Summers from their inception.)

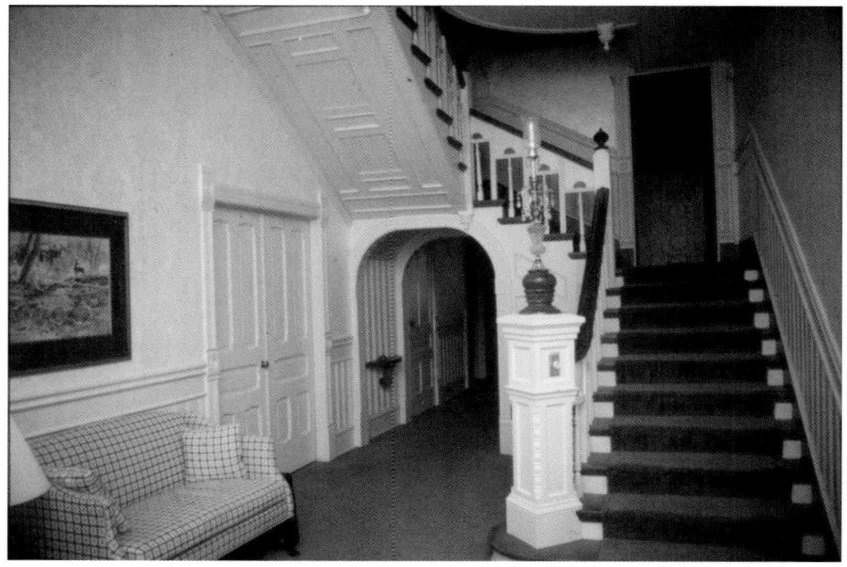

FIGURE 5.31. Entrance Hall, ca. 1980. *Photograph courtesy of Pam Thorstenson.*

Over the years, Rulfs varied the styles of his porches; but as long as porches were necessary, which they were until the arrival of ceiling and attic fans made them less essential, the architect paid extremely close attention to them. Because of their vulnerability to the high humidity of East Texas, porches frequently need attention, even replacements. In the period after 1910, when Rulfs undertook to redesign many of his earlier houses in order to meet changes in taste and technology (electricity and bathrooms), the architect often replaced the original porches and thus altered the look of the structures. Without exception, these changes involved *simplification* of the designs rather than additional elaborations; see the discussion of the Perkins House in Chapter X. The Blount and Jones families, however, refused to tamper with their unique Queen Anne treasures.

The Blount House has received many alterations since the Blounts sold it. The funeral home transformed the living and dining rooms into a chapel and then, after adding an external chapel, reordered them again. The rear of the house funeral home and the south porches underwent extensive remodeling; the second floor had numerous changes as part of the living quarters for the funeral director. In general, the woodwork in the Blount House, while fine, did not set any standards in Nacogdoches as had the Schmidt House. Fortunately, the entrance hall, one of the architect's finest, has escaped extensive changes and today is the most original room in the interior. Modest by comparison to the Perkins, Schmidt, and Jones houses, the entrance hall has no fireplace, no dramatic key-hole entrance to the stairwell, no multiple sets of sliding doors, no dramatic inlaid floors, no original shape. The Blount entrance hall is less intimidating than the others, more human in its proportions: the flights of steps easily manageable and the woodwork intricate but not oppressive. Rulfs loved staircases, and this is one of his masterworks.[59]

After the Blount House ceased to be a funeral home, in 1988 Dr. Lyle Thorstenson and his wife Pam (chairperson of the Landmark Preservation Committee at the time) began the restoration of the great house. Working

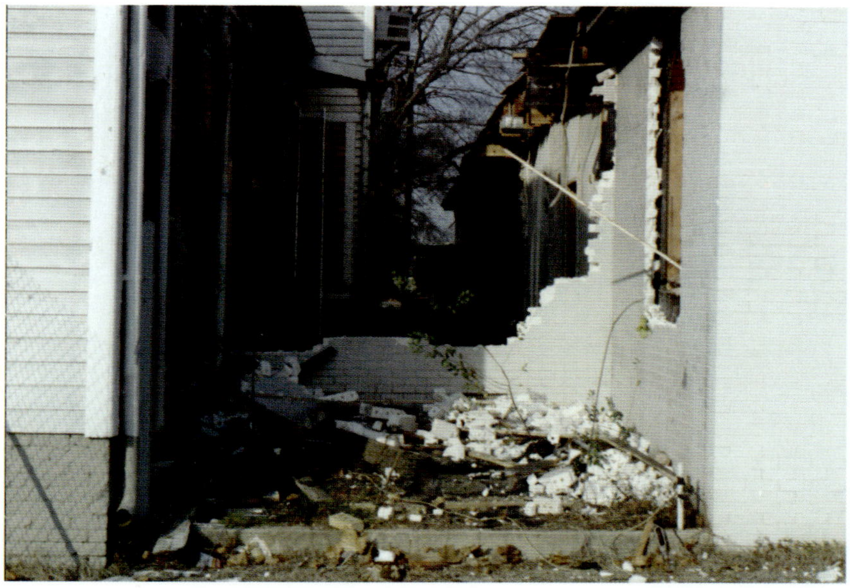

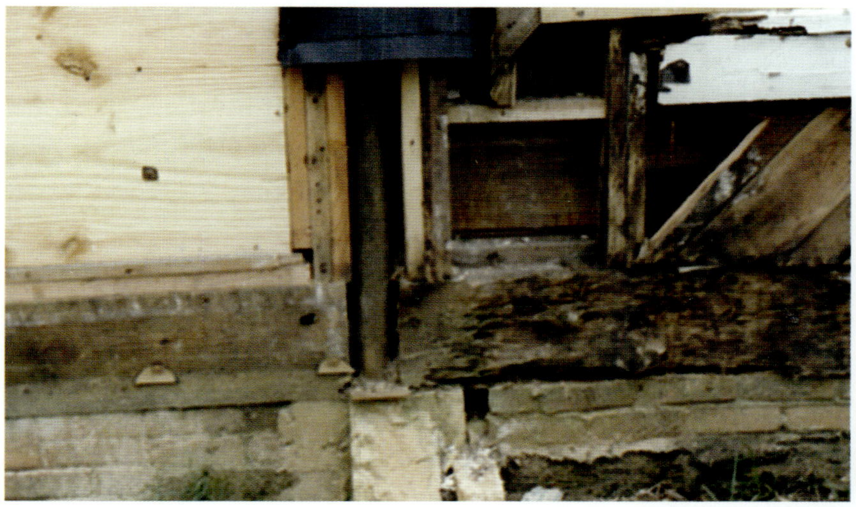

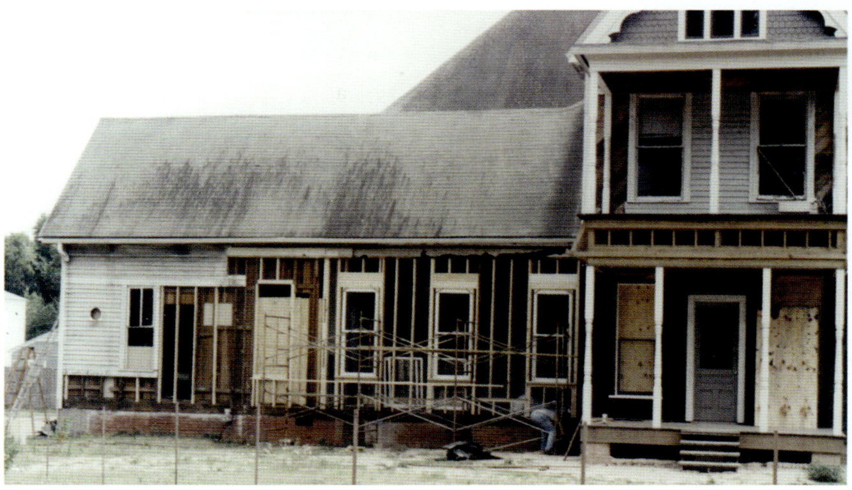

FIGURES 5.32 - 5.34. The Restoration of North Elevation.
(Top) The removal of the external chapel, ca. 1991.
(Middle) The removal of the chapel exposed severe damage on the original house's foundation. ca. 1991.
(Below) The extent of the restoration necessary after the removal of the chapel in the 1990s was monumental: windows, framing, sills, roofing, and replacement of the double-level north porch. Photographs courtesy of Pam Thorstenson.

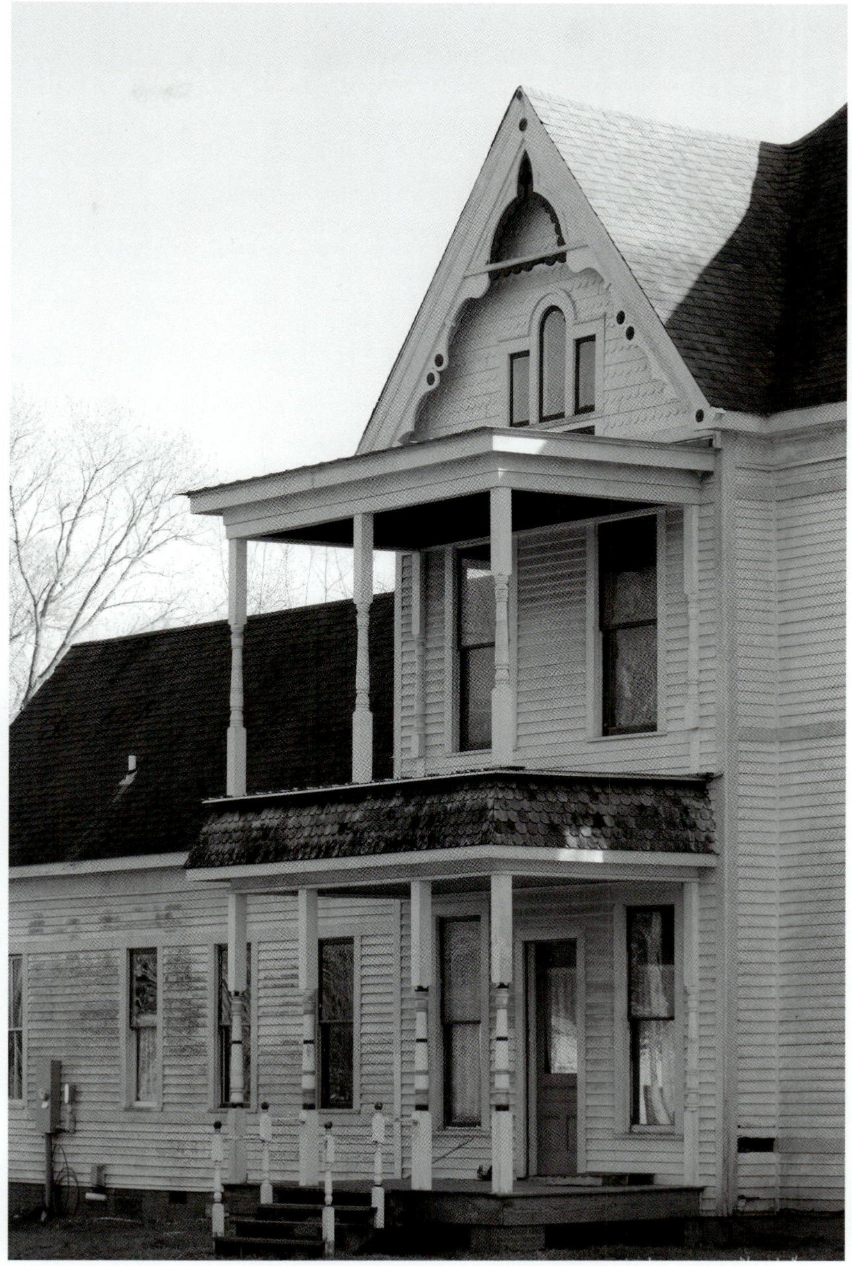

FIGURE 5.35. The North Elevation as Completed, 2010.

in close collaboration with the architectural division of the Texas Historical Commission, the Thorstensons removed the external brick chapel, cleared away rot, and re-supported the living room and other north rooms, rebuilt the north porch and the entire north elevation, added a new roof, removed many of the interior partitions introduced after 1945, and planned a complete restoration of the west porch by ordering extensive millwork out of Houston. Some of the saga of this work appears in photographs on these pages. Having achieved their goal of stabilizing the house, the Thorstensons sold the structure.[60] Several owners afterwards attempted to continue the restoration, but the undertaking proved overwhelming for them.[61]

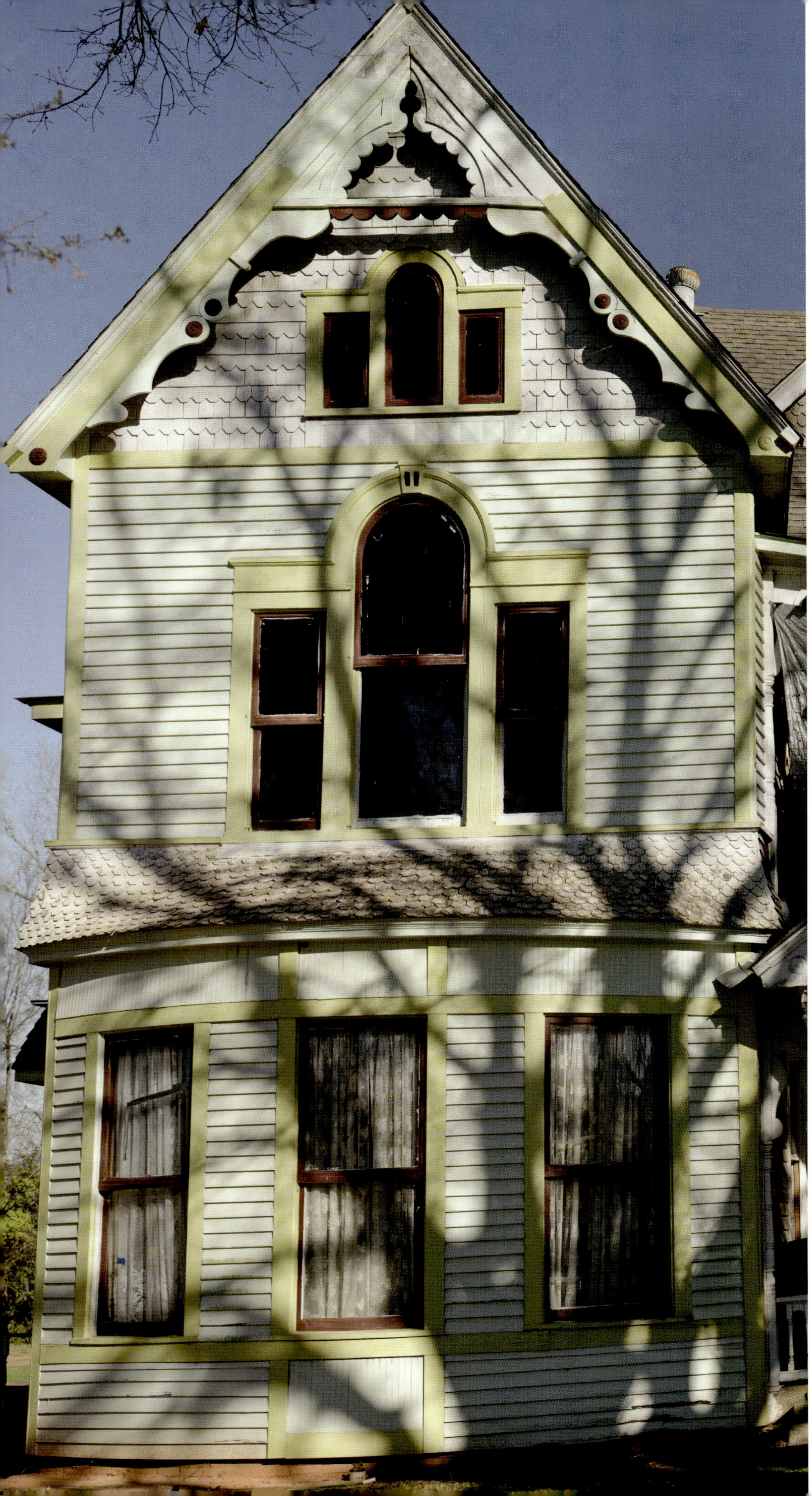

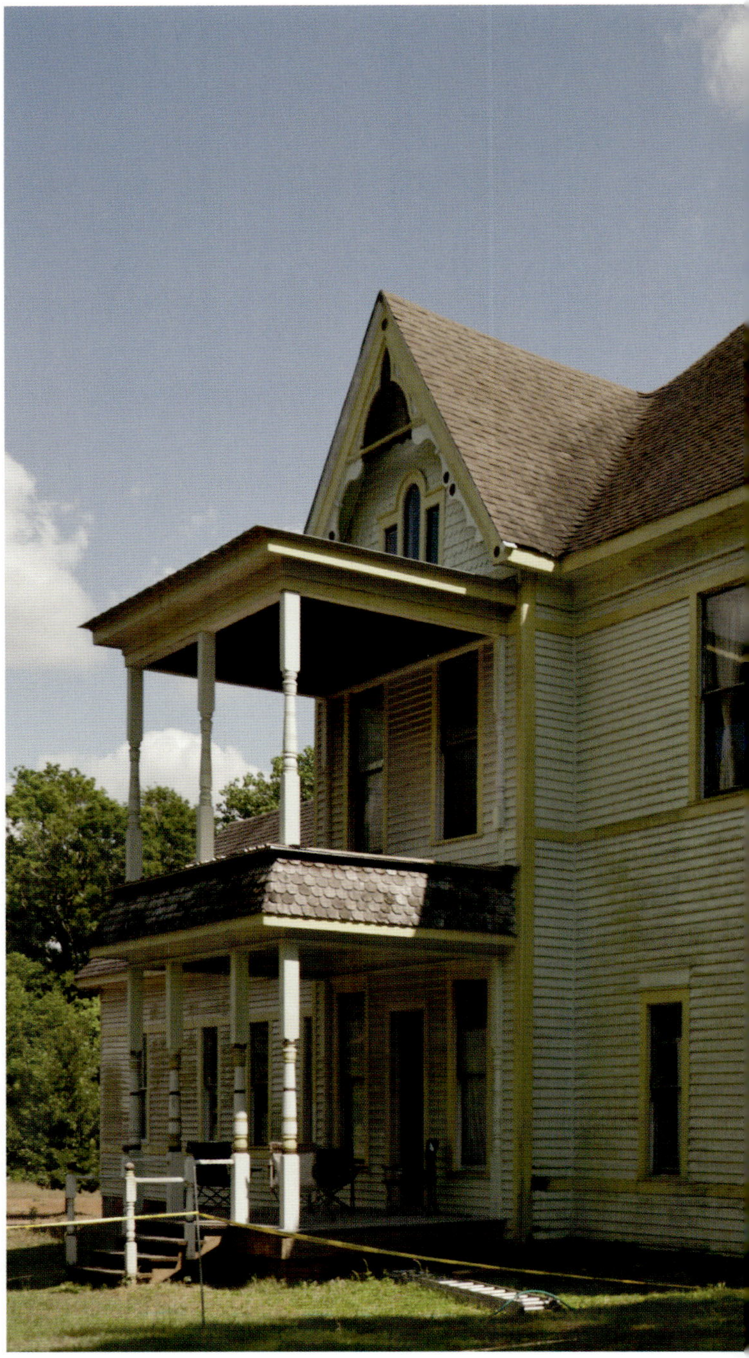

FIGURE 5.36. (Left) The Great Forward-Gable.

The west-front gable of the S. W. Blount House is one of the best designs of D. Rulfs and the best carpentry work of his brother, William Henry Rulfs. The stacked configuration has three levels of triple windows: a large bow window on the ground level, an oversized Palladian configuration of the second level, and a less dramatic Palladian configuration in the tympanum, which is also reflected in the gable ornament.

FIGURE 5.37. (Above) Northwest Corner, Blount House.

FIGURE 5.37b. (Right) Drawing of Proposed Additions.

The area marked in yellow designate the requested changes. The drawing is from the public records in the City Landmark Papers.

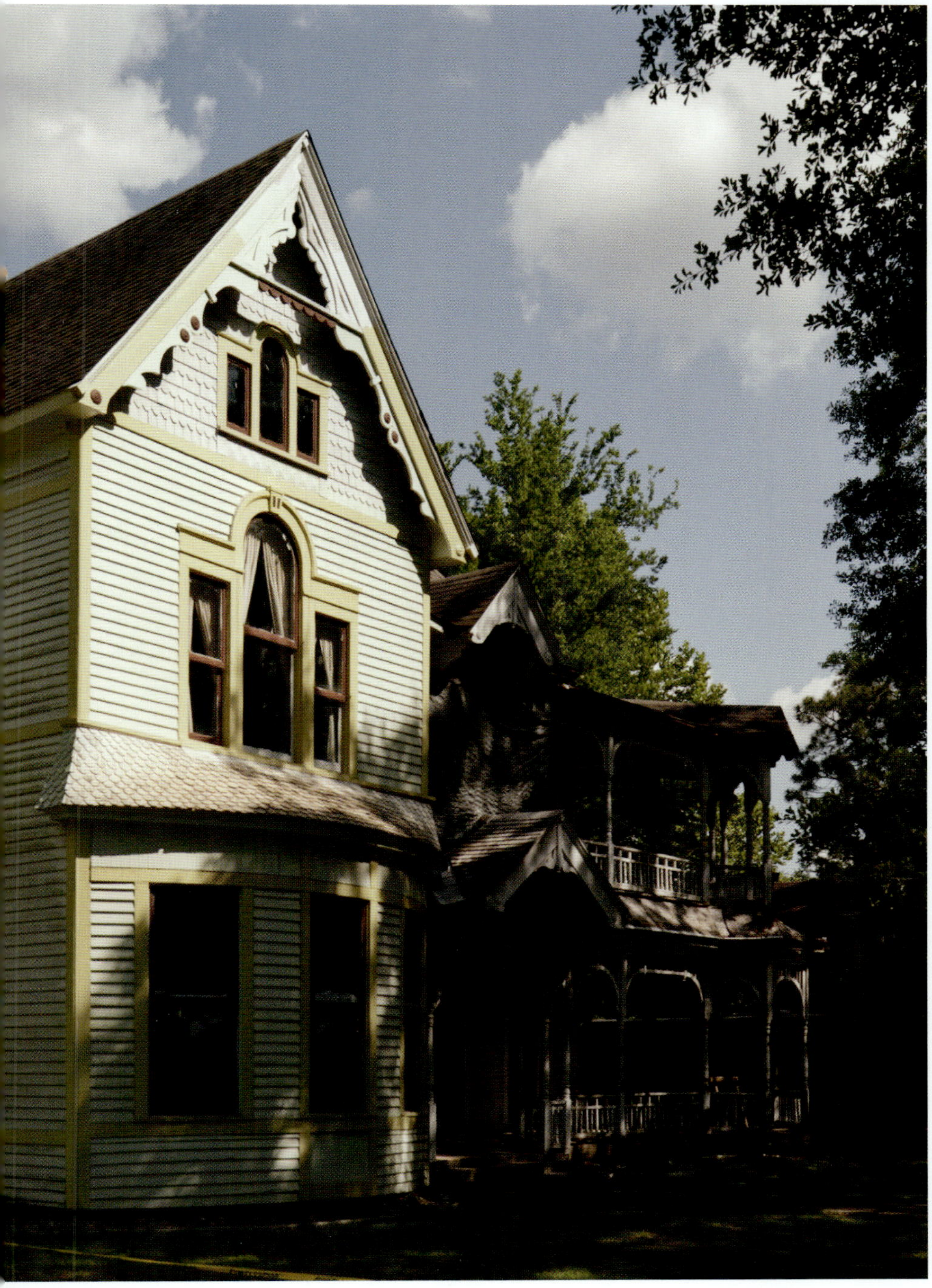

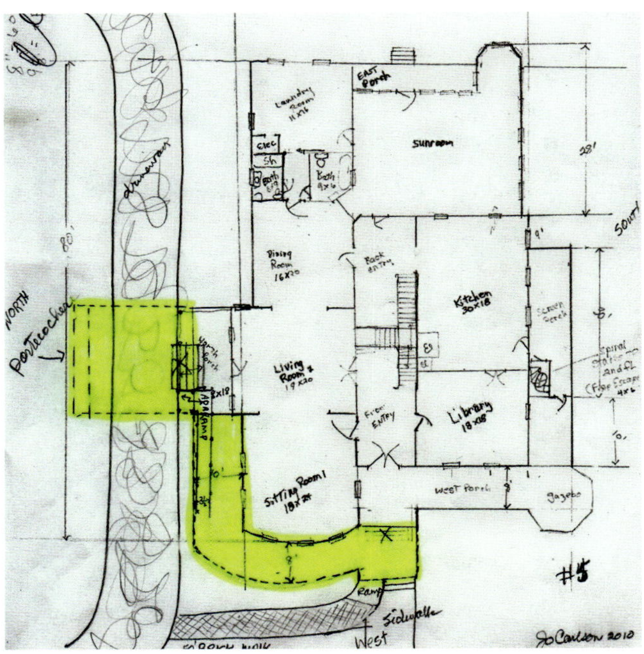

In 2009, a new chapter in the history of the Stephen Blount House began when Dr. Robert Gruebel and Jo Ellen Carlson-Gruebel purchased the property. They possessed the means to arrest further deterioration and enhance the property by making it their homestead. However, no one expected them to reverse the exterior alterations made to the rear of the property by the funeral home. Working with the Nacogdoches Historic Landmark Preservation Committee, the owners asked for and received approval for virtually all of their proposed changes to the sides of the house and the rear. (The ordinances in force at the time were primarily façade ordinances, having nothing to do with interior changes.)

A controversy arose in 2010, however, when the new owners announced their intention to alter the configuration of the front façade. The proposal, illustrated in Figure 5.37b, called for an extension of the front portico and a new porch to wrap around the front gable, bow window, and north side to provide access to individuals with mobility impairments. The NHLPC centered its concern for the integrity of the west, main façade, in particular, the unique three-tiered Palladian treatment in the front gable, its bow window, and the stacked pediments over the front entrance as these specific architectural designs were the only ones left standing in Nacogdoches.

When the NHLPC denied the requested additions, the applicants appealed to the Nacogdoches City Commission. The City Commission returned the application to the NHLPC for a second reading. The re-examination request failed, too. A host of local preservationists, including the author, former owners, and members of the Blount family supported the denial. After being contacted by a concerned member of the Nacogdoches County Historical Commission regarding the proposed changes to the Stephen William and Mary Price Blount House, the preservation architects at The Texas Historic Commission recommended against the alterations, stating that:

> Even though this property is listed in the National Register, the THC has no review authority in this particular case since the building is privately owned and the project is privately financed with no Federal funding involved. Our comments on this matter were requested and are offered as recommendations. . . .
>
> Based on our interpretation of the Standards it is our informal determination that the proposed project does not meet the Standards, and that the location of the new addition is inappropriate.[62]

In a letter to the editor published by the *Daily Sentinel* under the title "A Case for the Landmark Committee," I argued for preservation of the front façade and warned that an exemption could cost the city its credibility because future buyers will not have confidence in the city's historic zoning protection.[63] (For a full text, see Endnote 63.)

In March 2011, the City Commission granted Dr. and Mrs. Gruebel an exemption for their proposed project, and expansion of the porch system around the northwest corner of the house began in 2013.

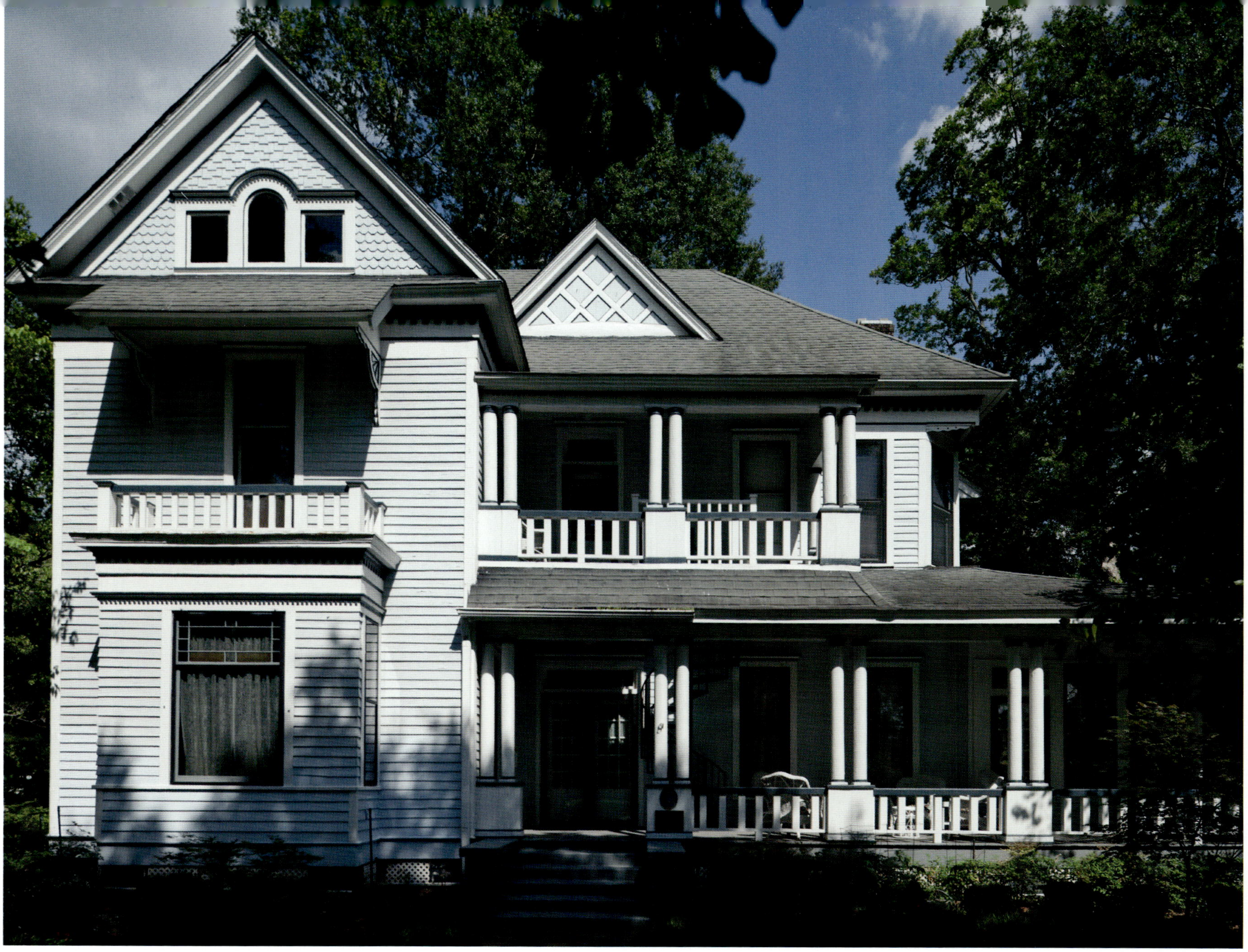

The Tolbert B. Hardeman House (1899)

The third Hardeman brother to join in the development of Nacogdoches in the 1890s was Tolbert (Tol) Barrett Hardeman (1858-1927).[64] While the brothers had family funds and invested in many projects, including real estate, Tol became associated with his younger brother, Lee Hardeman, in working as a manager for John Schmidt in the grocery business–the original enterprise of Mayer & Schmidt. When Schmidt expanded his wholesale grocery interests, Lee and Tol invested and became partners in the Nacogdoches Wholesale Grocery Company. Schmidt eventually sold his controlling interest in the company to the Hardeman brothers.

The house Rulfs designed for Tol Hardeman still stands at 408 North Mound just north of the Stephen Blount House. According to Tol's niece, Gladys Hardeman, the site chosen for the house was on the northernmost edge of the downtown: "No other houses were to the north, but construction of other homes followed soon thereafter. As if standing guard on the south side was one of the largest and oldest oak trees in Nacogdoches." For some time, the site had been associated with the Old Nacogdoches University and was the home of "a very large park where tournaments were held on patriotic holidays when the winner crowned his queen."[65] The last tournaments occurred in 1898.

In 1963 when Miss Gladys wrote about her uncle's house for the *Daily Sentinel*, the house was part of a tour of homes sponsored by the local chapter of the Colonial Dames of America.[66] Intriguingly, she never mentioned the name Diedrich Rulfs in her information on the house, nor, for that matter, did any of the Colonial Dames brochures of the 1960s mention him, albeit most of the houses on the tours were designed by Mr. Rulfs.[67] When asked in an interview about this omission, Miss Gladys confessed that she had never really thought about it: "Of course, I knew Mr. Rulfs well and knew many members of the family. Wilhelmina Rulfs [Diedrich's niece, Wilhemina Thompson] has been one of my best friends all my life. I just never really thought much about it. Mr. Rulfs designed and built most of the houses in town, and I guess we all just assumed that everyone knew this."[68] Other interviewees have said exactly the same thing, simply taking for granted what was common knowledge and obvious to everyone at the time. Had Mr. Rulfs worked out of Dallas or Houston, he would have been recognized as an architectural genius. An authority is someone who travels from at least seventy-five miles away to render his advice.

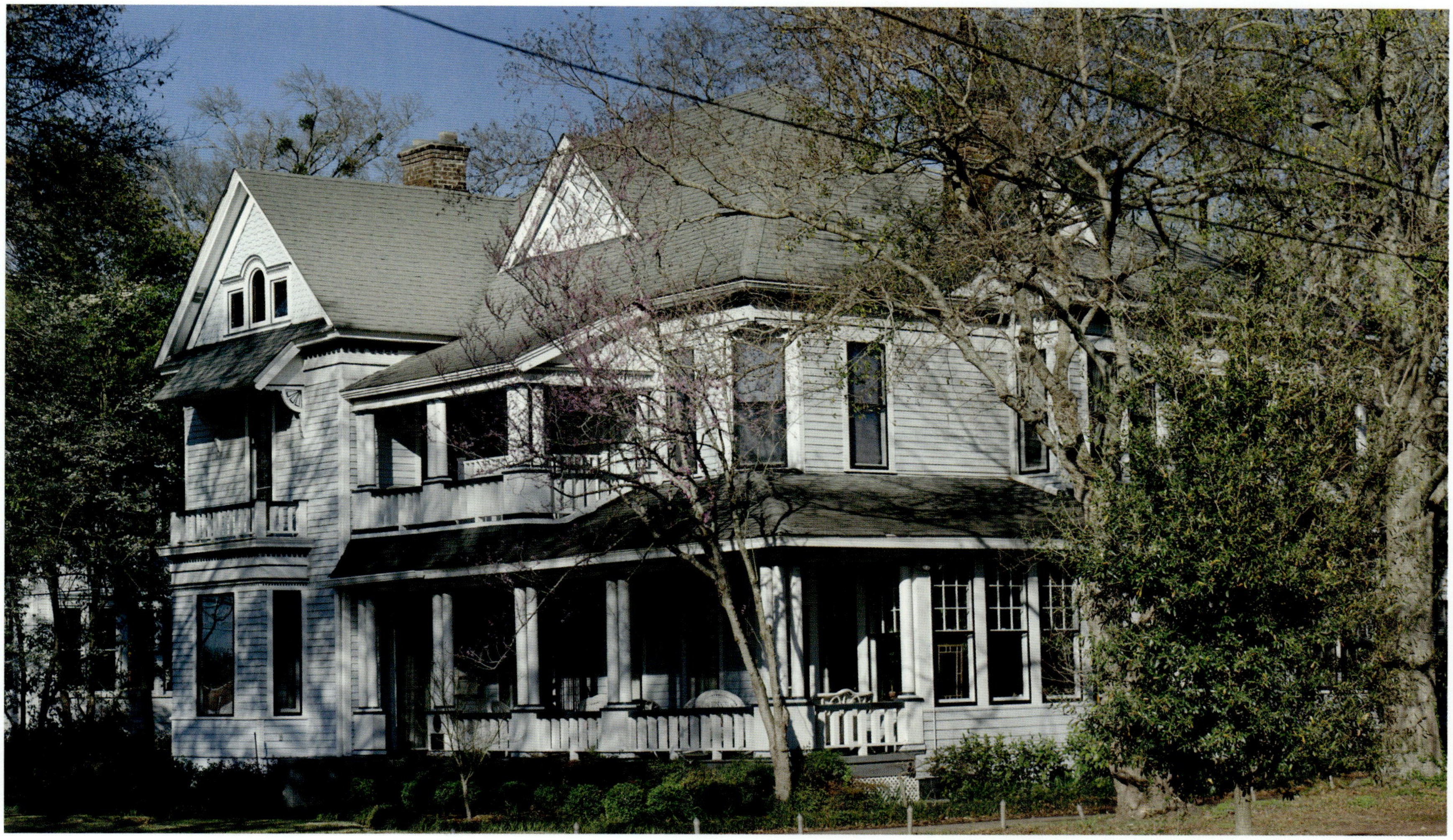

FIGURES 5.38 and 5.39. (Across and Above) Two Views of the Tol Hardeman House.

These two views of the Tol Hardeman House from different angles show the special architectural features of this 1899 house. Rulfs combined many of his favorite features on this house: front-facing gables, bay windows, Palladian windows, slip-head win-dows, wide entablatures, paired Tuscan columns on plinth bases, and a second story half-gallery.

On the façade of this house, Rulfs utilized some of his favorite architectural features. The architect had specified in his drawing the use of paired Tuscan columns on plinth bases for the Harris House in 1895, but he did not actually use them; full length columns were more readily available. (See Chapter 6). By the time of the Tol Hardeman House, Rulfs returned to the idea and placed them on both the main porch and the second story half-porch. The gable front of this house is a variation on the ones employed in the Edwards, Schmidt, and Ingraham houses: a projecting square bay window with a second floor balcony, slip-head window, shed roof, and the quintessential Palladian window at the attic level. Additional decorative elements on this house are particularly nice: the gable projecting from the roof with its cross-timbered paneling and the use of dentil molding.

The house originally had a more traditional interior arrangement: a central hall, parlor to the south, living room to the north with the dining room east between the living room and kitchen. After the Lamar Acker family purchased the house in 1915, they 'modernized' the house by joining the entrance hall and the parlor into one room, took out the double sliding doors, removed the stained glass windows, introduced clear glass doors with glass transoms, enclosed the central staircase into a middle hall, and replaced the pine floors with oak. In an interview, Miss Gladys Hardeman admitted she was not sure whether these changes were under the hand of Rulfs or not. She associated the changes with the arrival of gas heating.[69] This would put the changes in the late 1920s when the gas pipeline arrived. Martin and Julia Taylor, who owned the house in the period after World War II, redecorated the house and used the front rooms as an antique shop, but they did not make any structural changes. William (Bill) and Sue Brophy purchased the house in the 1970s, but they also made few changes. In 1995, the house became the property of Mary Elizabeth and Chappell Jordan, Jr.[70] Since the house served as a bed-and-breakfast for some years, the owners introduced the circular stairs on the front porch to meet ordinance requirements. In the last decade, the Jordans have returned the house to a single-family dwelling and have carefully preserved the charm of this turn-of-the-century landmark. How fortunate tourists are to have the integrity of the Washington Square area preserved in such a manner.

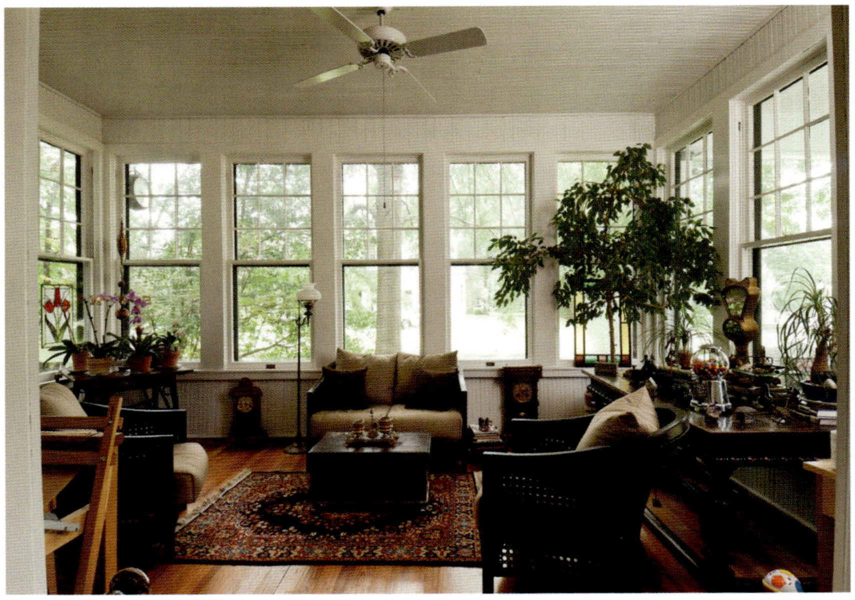

FIGURE 5.40. (Above Left) The Sunroom.

The sunroom of the house, an enclosure of part of the wrap-around porch, was created in 1915.

FIGURE 5.41. (Center) The Living Room Today.

FIGURE 5.42. (Below) The Parlor and the Front Bay Window.

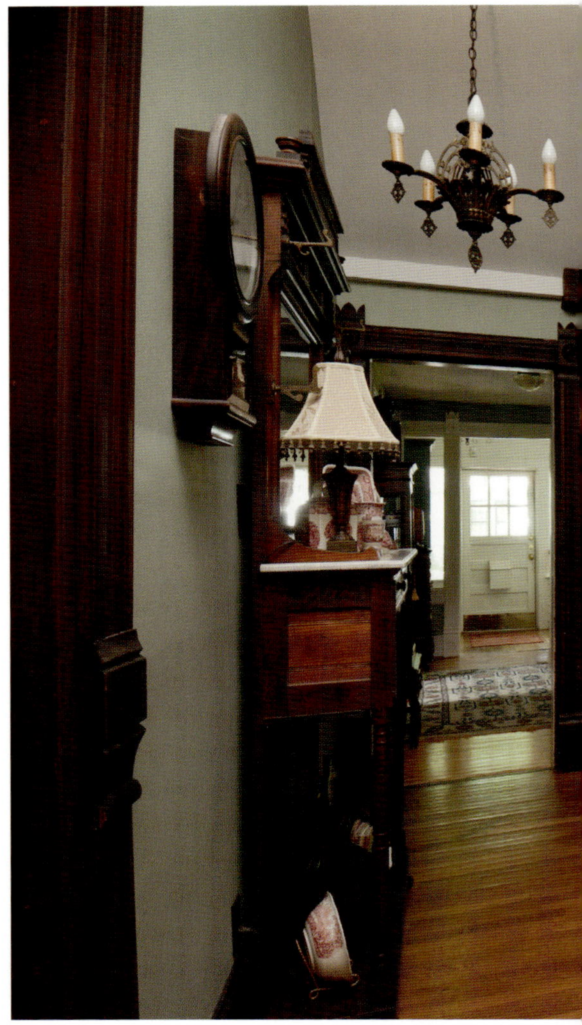

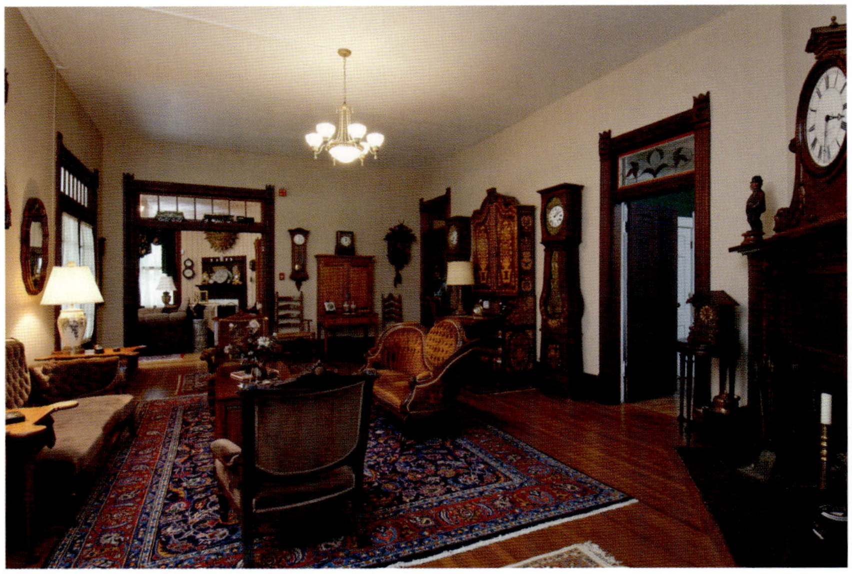

FIGURE 5.43. (Right) The Inner Hall and Stairway.

FIGURE 5.44. (Below, Right) The Dining Room.

The Dining Room, located within the large north bay, has a built-in china cabinet as did the Jones, Blount, and Tucker-Branch houses. Originally, the floors were pine. Lamar Acker introduced the lovely oak flooring some time after 1915 when he refitted the house with natural gas.

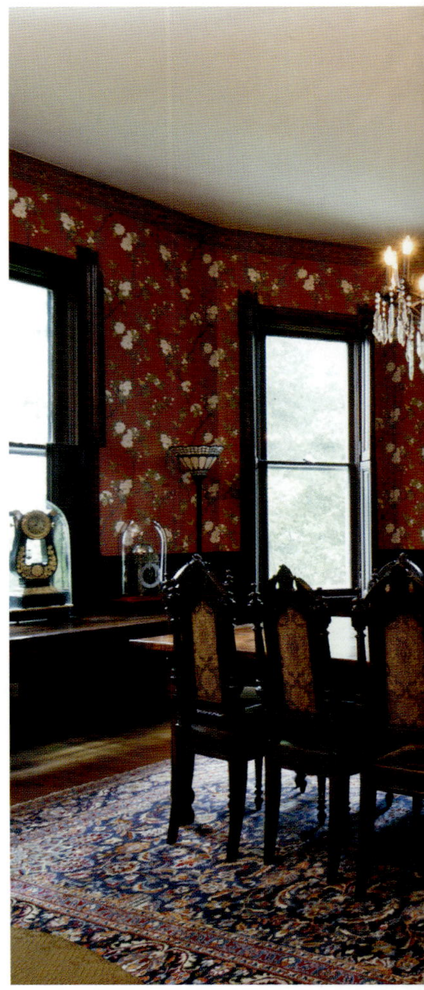

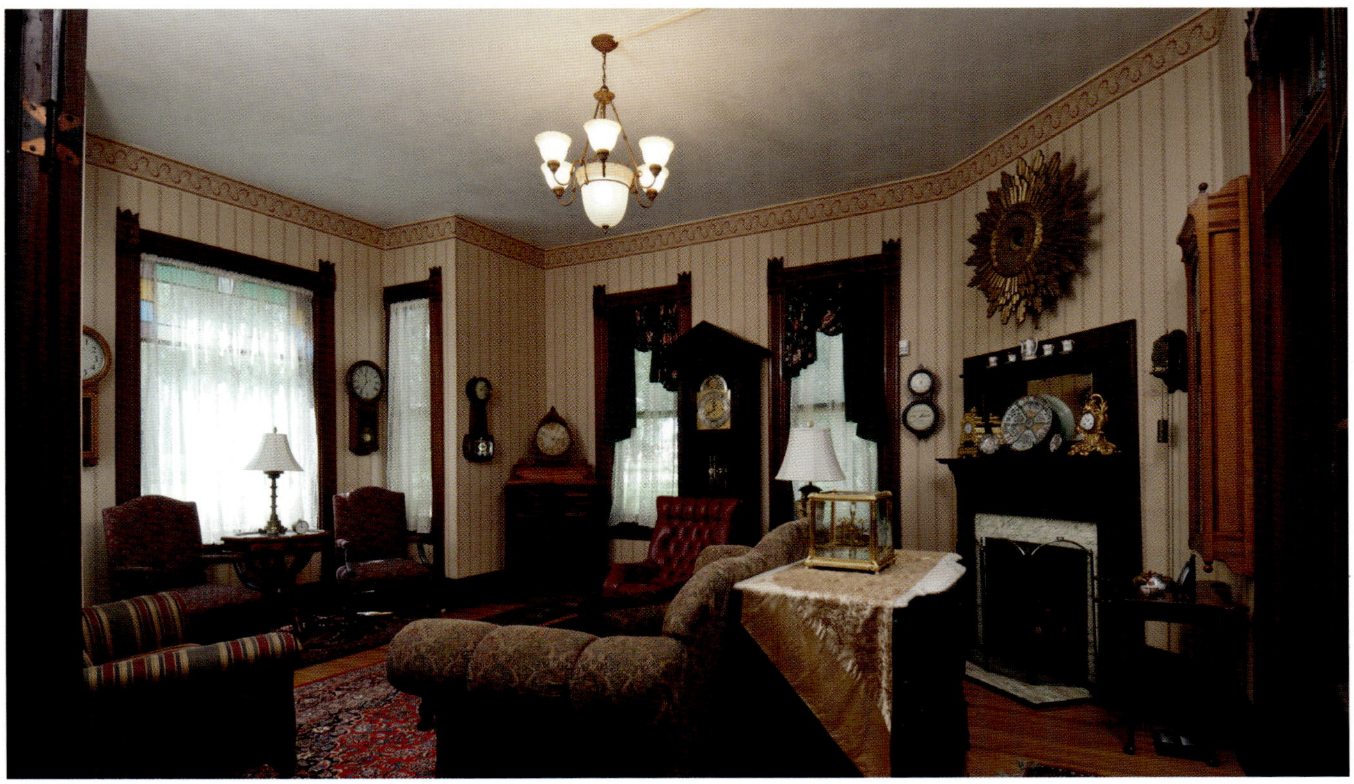

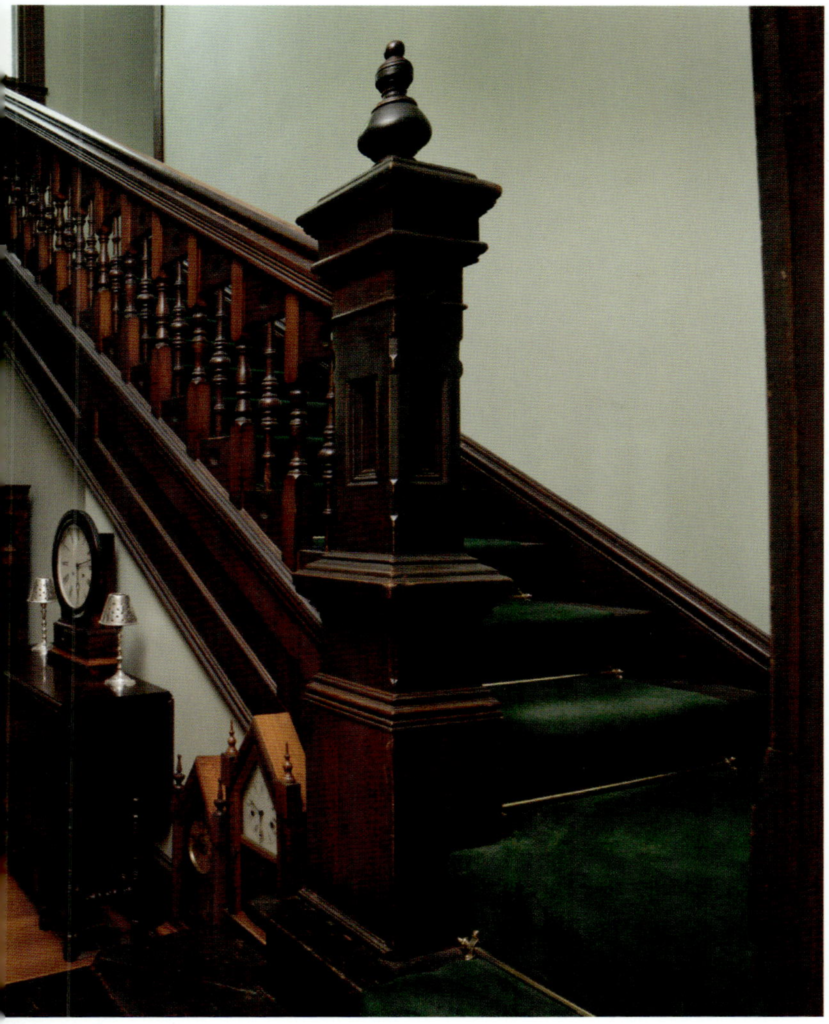

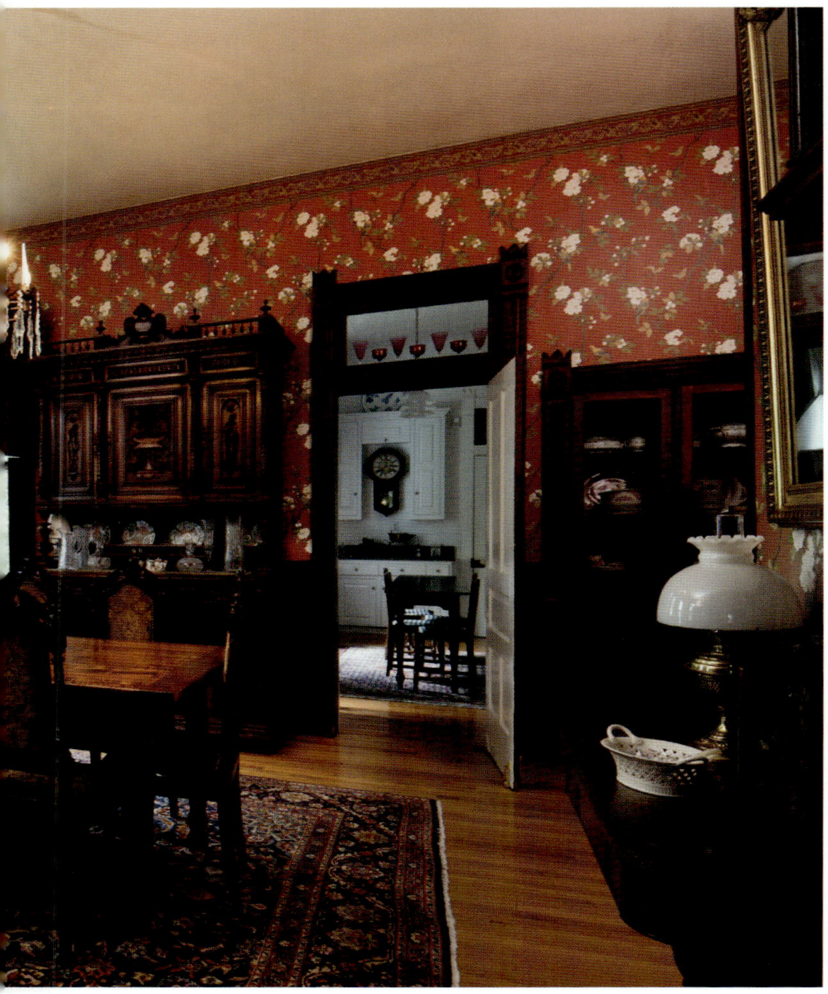

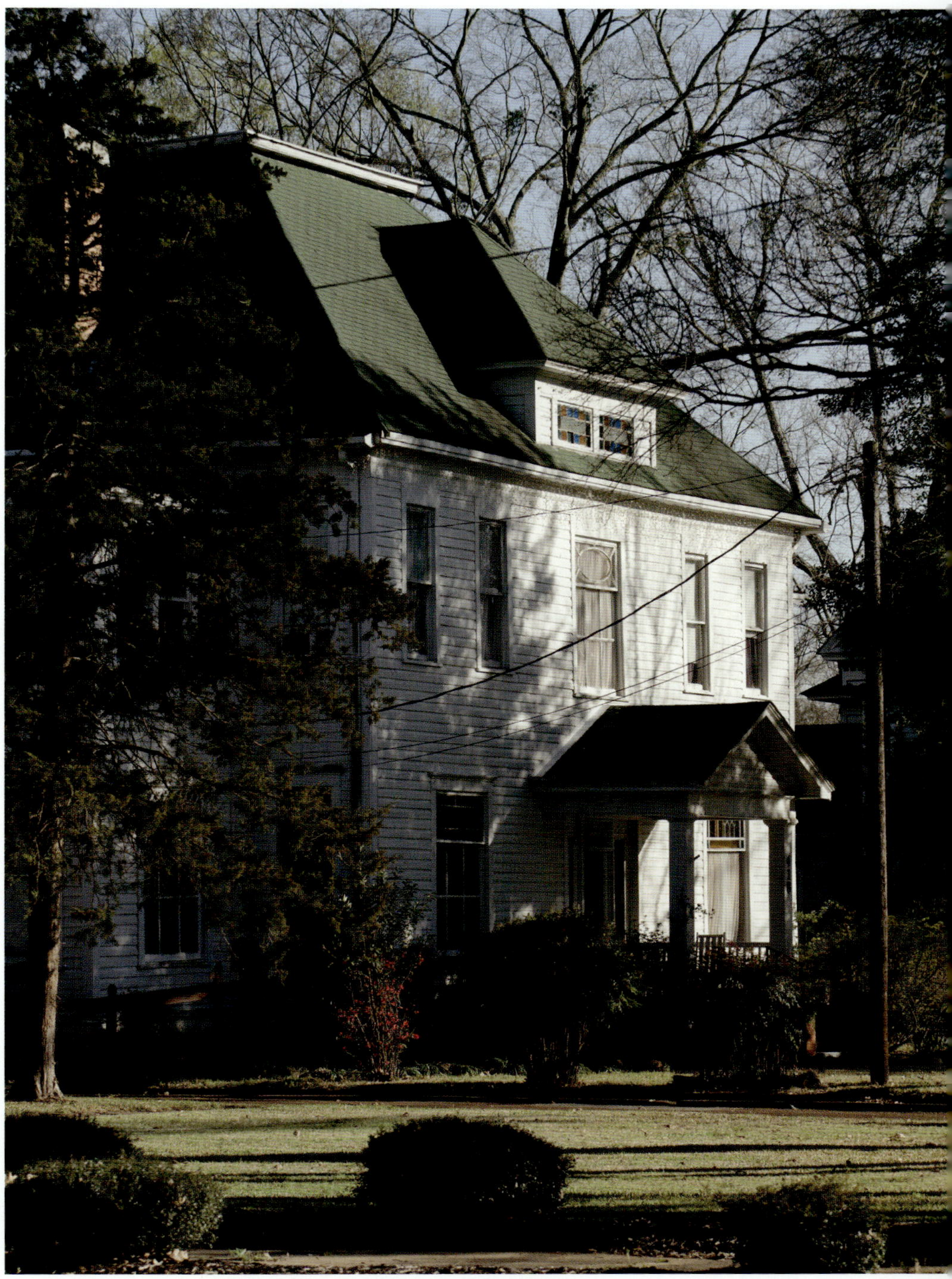

FIGURE 5.45. (Above) The John Garrison House in 2011.

The John Garrison House (1900)

The construction of the John Garrison House at 418 North Mound Street, because of its similarity in design to another house (the Matthews House on North Street), was thought at one time to date to the year 1905, but this is incorrect.[71] Garrison, a lawyer in Nacogdoches, purchased the lot in 1899, and the *1900 United States Census* (June) already shows John, his wife Minta, and their two daughters living at the Mound Street address. The Census interestingly indicates that F. H. (Hal) Tucker (30) and Rosa Ingraham Tucker (24) were living with the Garrisons as boarders, presumably while their own house was being completed next door.[72] The building activity was so quick and intense in the area that the Sanborn Map

Company decided to put in a special insert in their survey completed in October 1900. The insert did not even include the already existing houses, such as the Stephen Blount House or the Tol Hardeman House, just the new houses for the Garrisons, the Tuckers, and the Perkinses. As the only architect and an important builder in town, Rulfs often consulted with the field men who created the Sanborn Maps, and the maps frequently included his works under construction. In 1900, for instance, the Sanborn Map indicated that the Charles Perkins House was drawn "from plans."[73]

The Garrisons may have planned from the beginning to supplement their income with renting out rooms–a common practice at the time. The market for rooms was especially strong for young unmarried professionals, such as school teachers. As mentioned, there were boarders in 1900 when the house first appears on the census records. After the sale of the house in 1910 to the J. B. Stripling family, the house actually became known thereafter as the Stripling Apartments.[74] The apartments were very popular with public school teachers and, in the 1920s, when Stephen F. Austin State Teachers College opened across the street on the Washington Square campus, with college instructors as well.

The Garrison House has had many makeovers. The house as originally built had an extensive porch system across the front façade, which wrapped on the south side to a chamfered bay window. The center of the porch over the front door was two-story which, gave accessibility to the exterior from the upper hall. This device, which Rulfs used rather frequently, gave a strong verticality to the building.[75] He placed a large hip-roof dormer at the attic level over this porch. The house must have looked similar to the Matthews House on North Street. (See Figure 10.20.) He used upper windows of stained glass and "diamond and prism paned glass." The porches were removed in the 1930s, and a new small entry porch with simple columns and pediment were added.[76] Susan Pack Reents now owns the house.

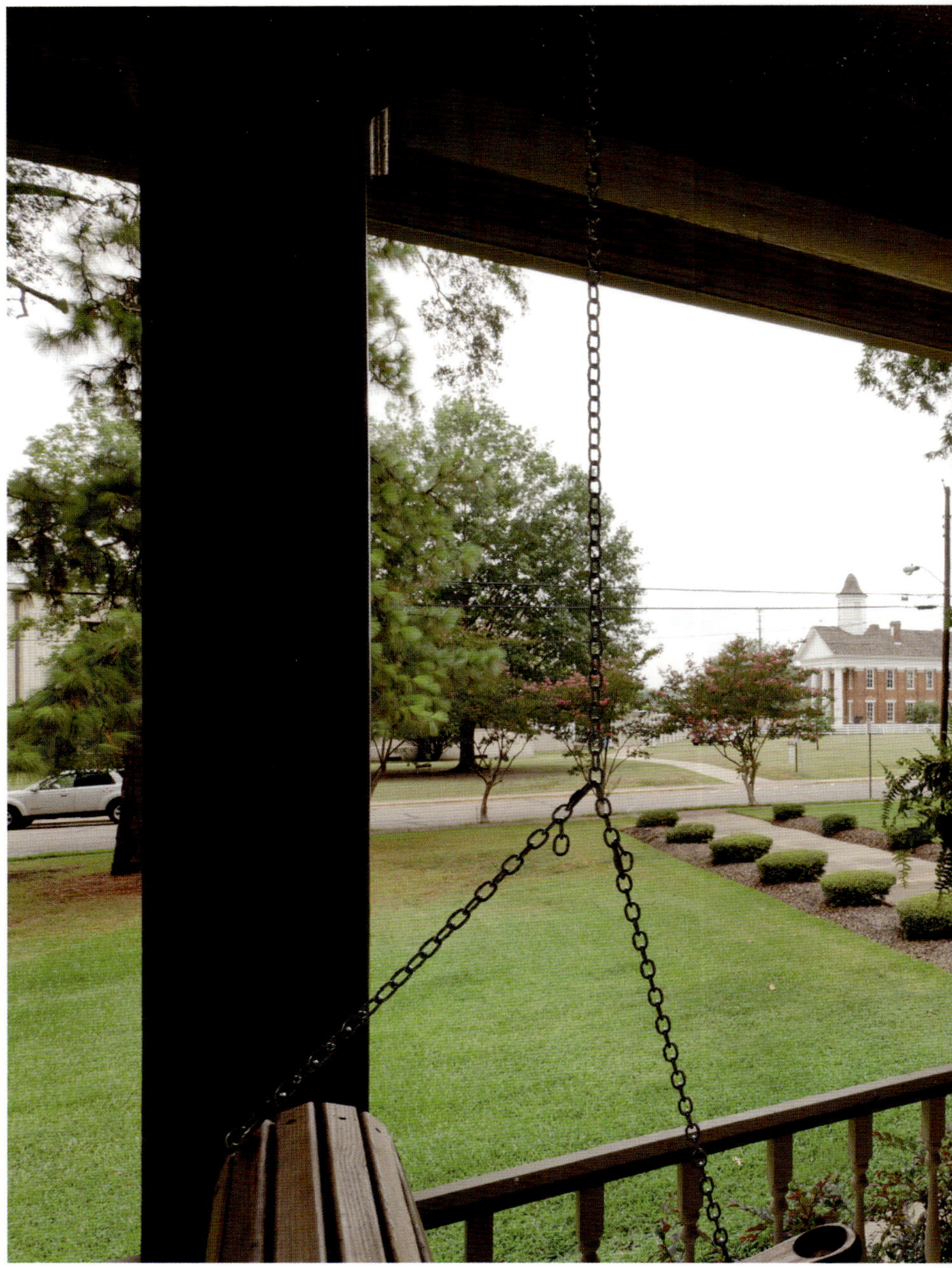

FIGURE 5.47. (Above) The Old Nacogdoches University Building.

From the front porch of the Tucker-Branch House, the view of the Old University still gives an idea of the appealing reason why patrons asked D. Rulfs to build houses for them on Washington Square. The Hardeman, Garrison, Tucker, and Perkins houses all shared this same view when they were built. The Central School, which obstructed this view was not built until 1904.

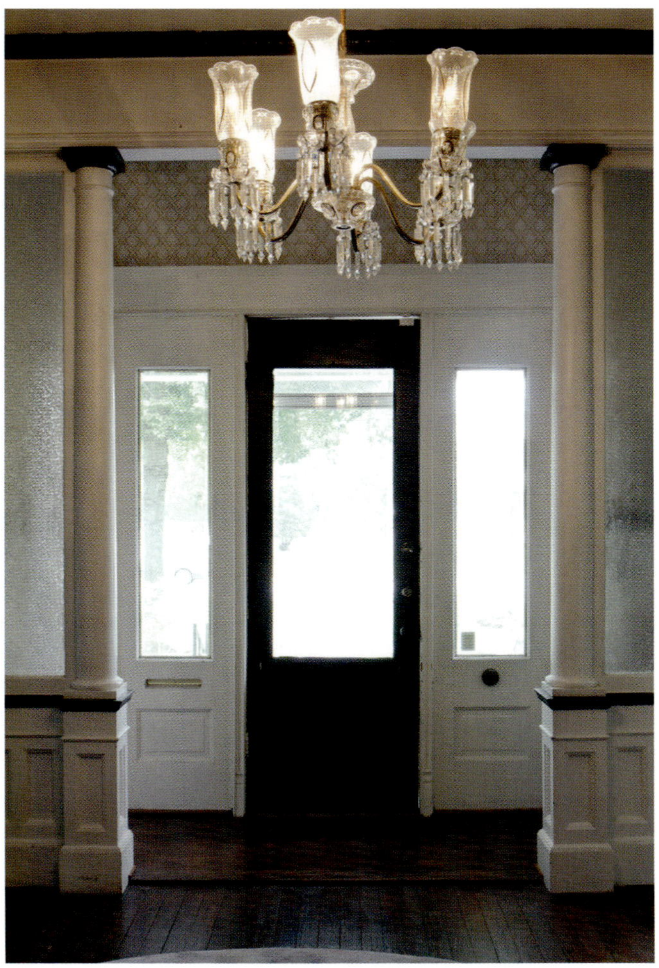

FIGURE 5.46. (Left) The Alcove in the Entrance Hall.

The Tuscan columns on the interior of the Garrison House are the only ones that now remain. The exterior originally had Tuscan columns and balustrades on a large wrap-around porch.

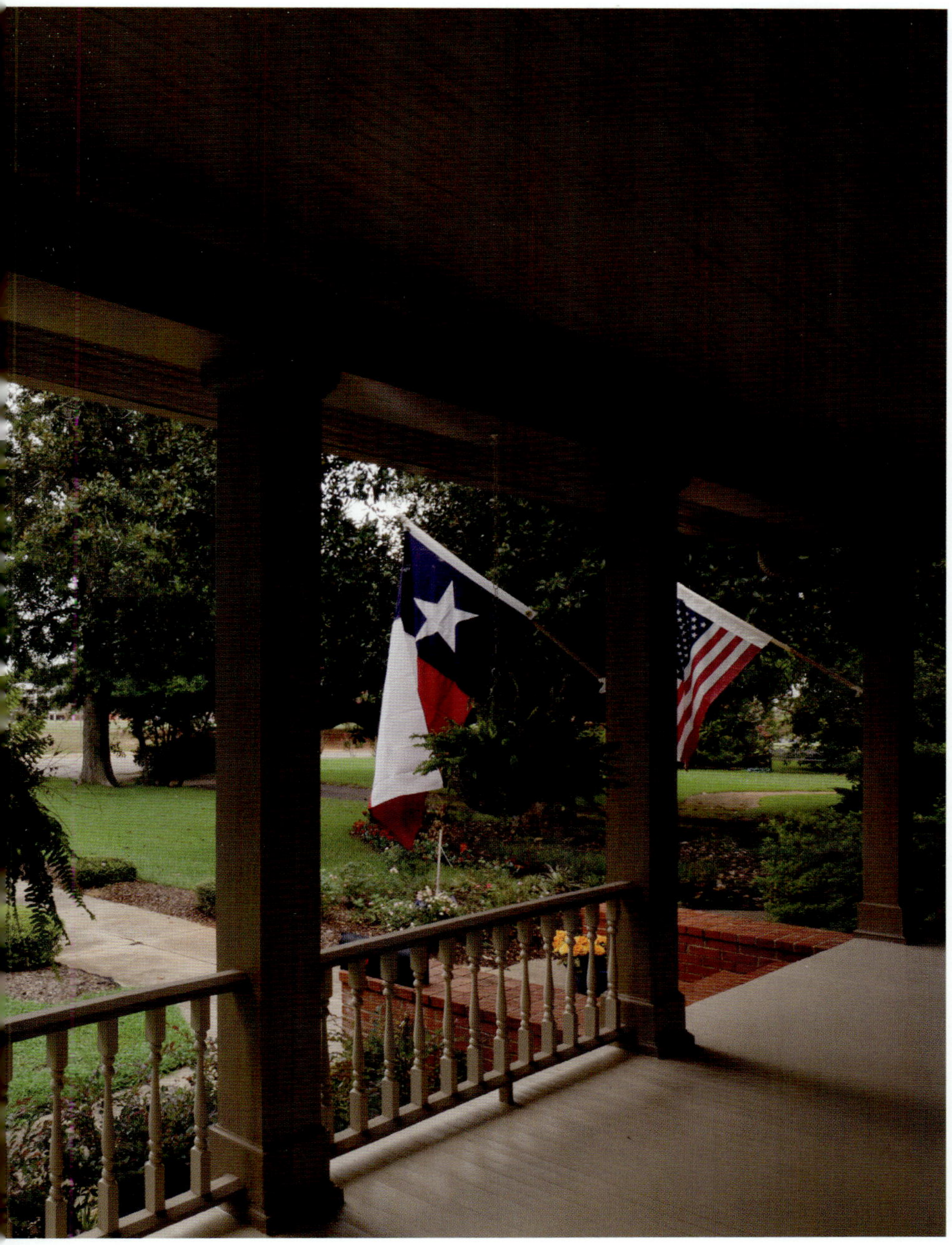

The Tucker-Branch House (1900)

Francis Harrison Tucker (1869-1941), known as Hal, purchased the lot at 504 North Mound Street in 1899, one month before his marriage to Rosa Ingraham. Rosa's father, George F. Ingraham, sold the lot to Tucker for $700.00.[77] The newly-weds may have planned the house immediately, but they did not move into the house until after October of 1900. When the US Census was taken in June of that year, the Tuckers were leasing rooms in the Garrison home next door. Hal Tucker was a cashier at the Commercial Bank and named one of his children Edward Blount, after the bank's president, E. A. Blount.[78] The couple were one of the Methodist families who wanted to live near their church; the subsequent occupants of the house were also Methodist. Although Rulfs built several houses for members of the large Tucker family in Nacogdoches, this is the only one extant.

Most people in Nacogdoches think of this house as belonging to the K. P. Branch family, but the Branches bought the house later. In 1908, when Rosa Tucker died after delivering her fifth child, Hal Tucker no longer wanted to remain in the house and sold it immediately to George and Lollie King. The Kings resold the house in 1913 to Florence "Flossie" and Kline Polk Branch.[79] Branch was a partner in the Branch-Patton Hardware Company. The Branches had a son, Raymond, who was listed in the 1920 census (age 12), but subsequent records could not be found on him.[80] When Flossie Branch's two nieces, Myrtis and Mary Ellis Bryan, lost their mother in 1924, the girls came to live with their aunt; the Branches adopted the two girls and brought them up as their own in Nacogdoches in this house.[81] Mary Ellis and husband, Earl Elliott, made the house their home after 1956. Their daughter Marianne Elliott Keller and her husband, Michael, now own the house. The unusually good condition of the house can be attributed to its long lineage within one related family group.

The house, as originally designed by Rulfs, had thin Tuscan columns on the porch, tailored trim, turned balusters, and a projecting gable extension at the southwest corner of the porch. Rulfs used this same feature on other houses built in the same period, before and after the Tucker House.[82] When the Branches moved into the house, they had Rulfs modernize the porch as was fashionable in the period after 1910 by adding the boxed columns and removing the gable on the corner of the porch.[83]

The roof of the house is a standard hip-and-gable, used by Rulfs on many domestic structures. The two very harmonious gables, which are dominant features on the front of this house, give the house a much more symmetrical appearance than the Laura Blount House. Cross gables emerge from the hip roof over the middle of the house on the north and south sides. Under three of these gables in the living room, the dining room, and the south bedroom, there are chamfered bay windows. Rulfs's use of an oversized central window in each of these bays (a new feature at the time) gave the bays an entirely different feeling. To tie all of the windows of the house together, the architect used diamond-patterned mullions: over the bay windows, around the lights of the front door, in the charming corner windows on the porch, and in the attic level windows in the gables. His decision to recess the front door behind an elliptical arch, supported on slender wood columns, further enhanced the sophisticated refinements of this house. To add to these refinements of this modest-sized house, Rulfs used intricate patterns of shingles in the gables, carved bargeboards, decorative chimneys, and iron roof cresting to complete the complex roof structure. While the first floor porch at the rear of the house is original, the second floor rooms and porch on the east and south were added after the nieces moved into the house in the late 1920s.[84]

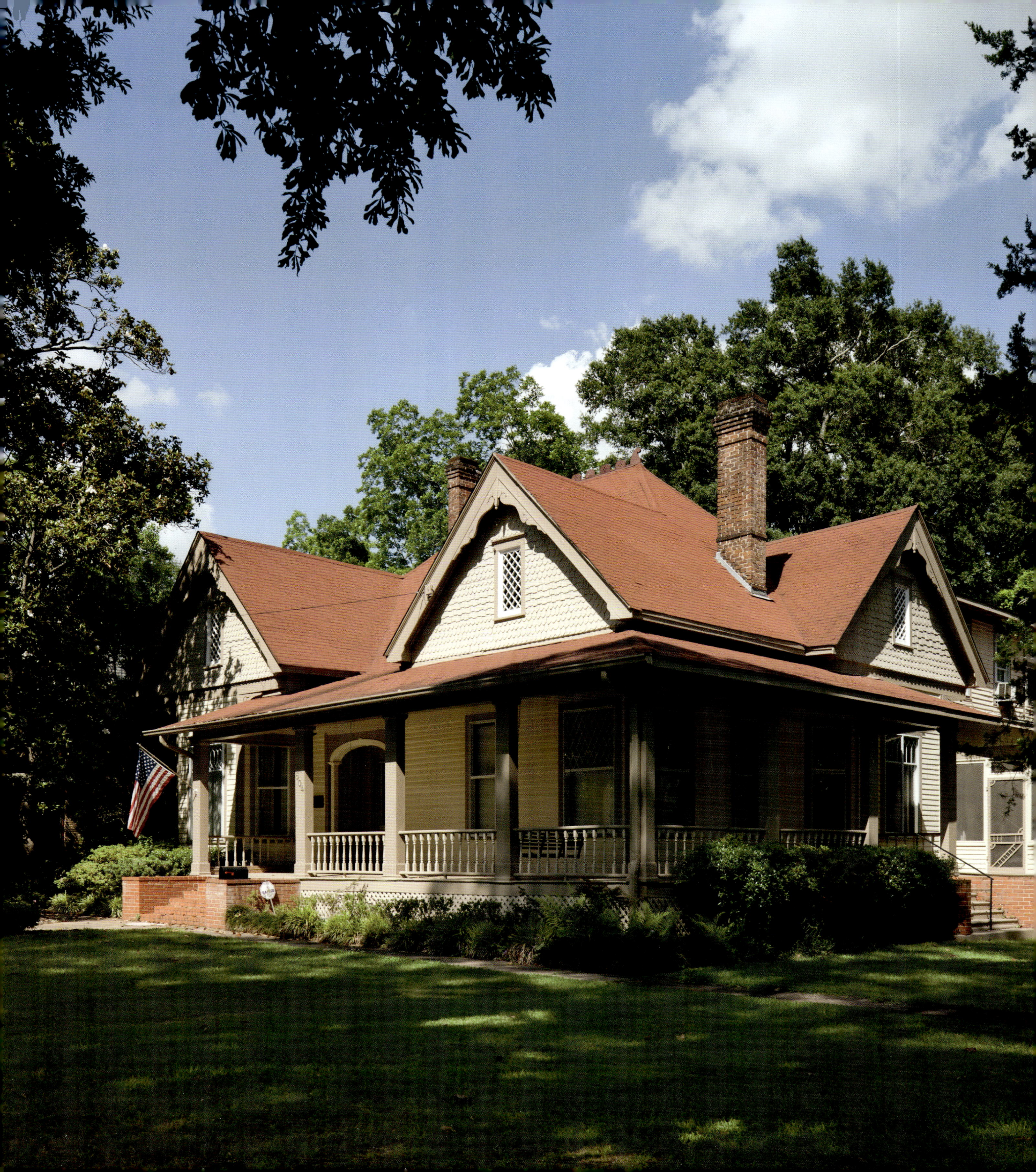

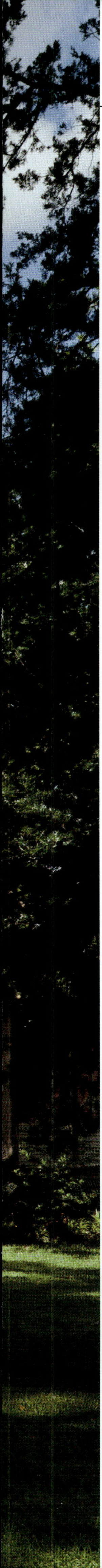

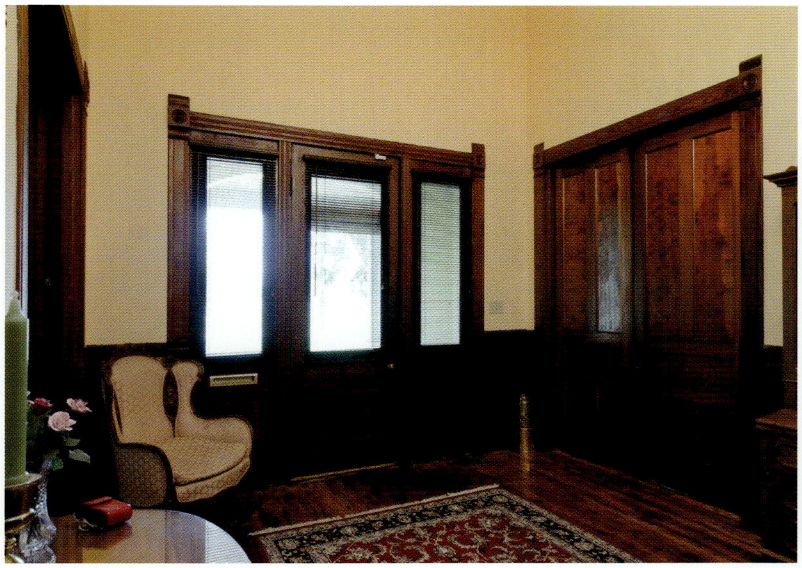

FIGURE 5.48. (Above) The Entrance Hall.
There are three sets of double pocket doors in the house, which create generous flow in the structure.

The Francis Harrison Tucker House

Home of Marianne Elliott and Michael Keller

504 North Mound Street

FIGURE 5.49. (Left) Tucker-Branch House, 2011.

FIGURE 5.50. (Below) Details on the Tucker House.
The details of the Tucker House include: hipped roof with front gable, fish scale shingles, diamond window panes, decorative bargeboards, elaborate chimney stack, and iron roof cresting.

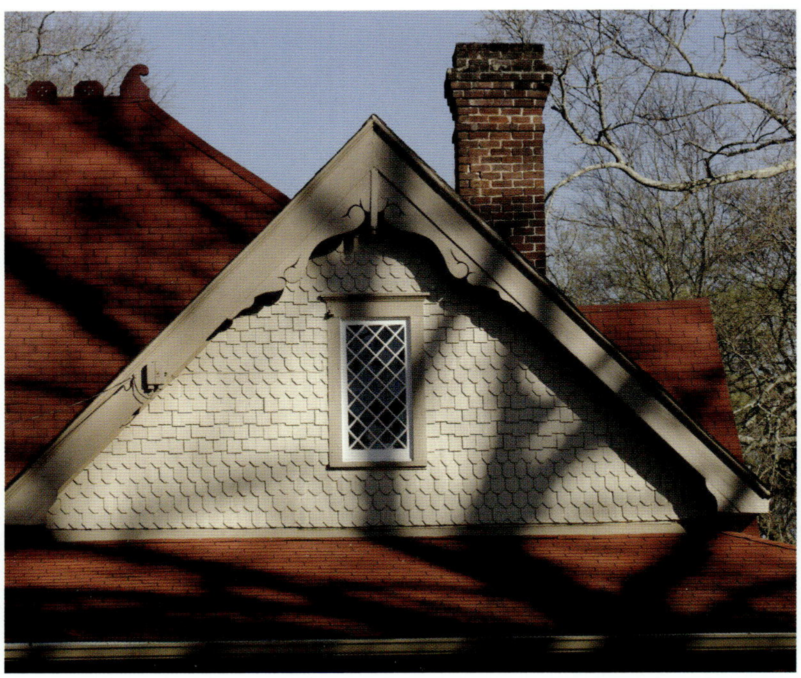

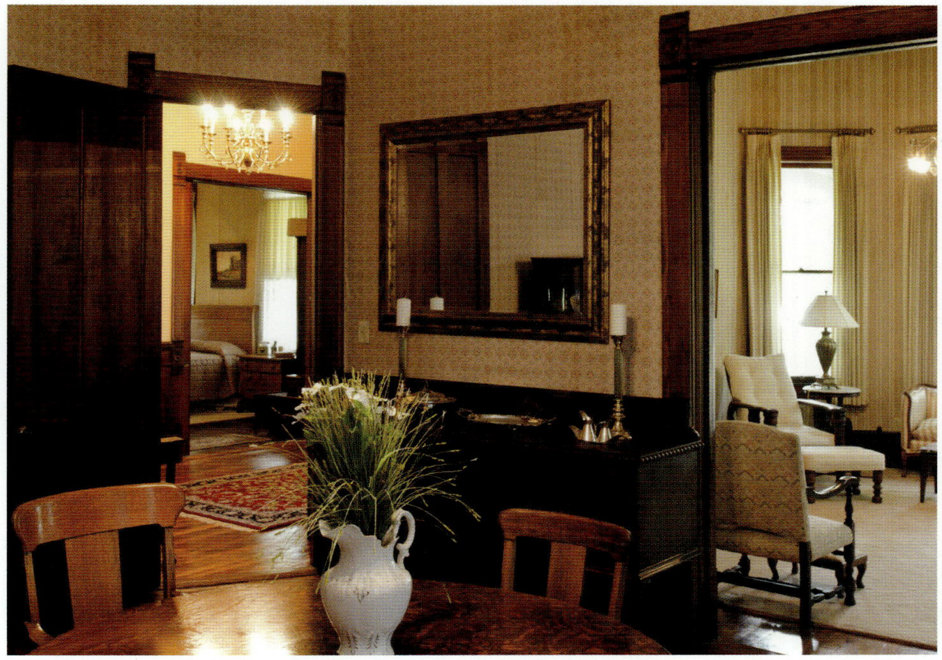

FIGURE 5.51. Perspectives and Flow.
This picture from the dining room of the Tucker House gives a good indication of the openness of the views in the house. The living room has two sets of double-pocket doors, between the dining room and the entrance hall; and the library, now a guest room across the entrance hall, has another set of pocket doors.

FIGURE 5.52. (Below) Family Room.
The window in the center of this photograph, part of the chamfered bay at the end of the family room, is an example of how Rulfs utilized slip-head windows in many houses. Although the door-window has today has been replaced by a door, the function of access to the front porch remains.

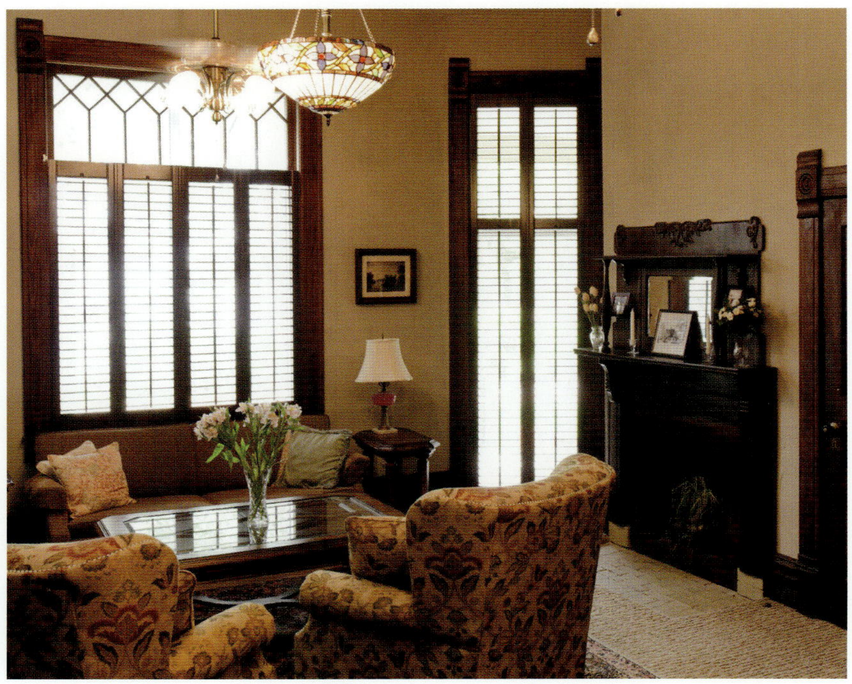

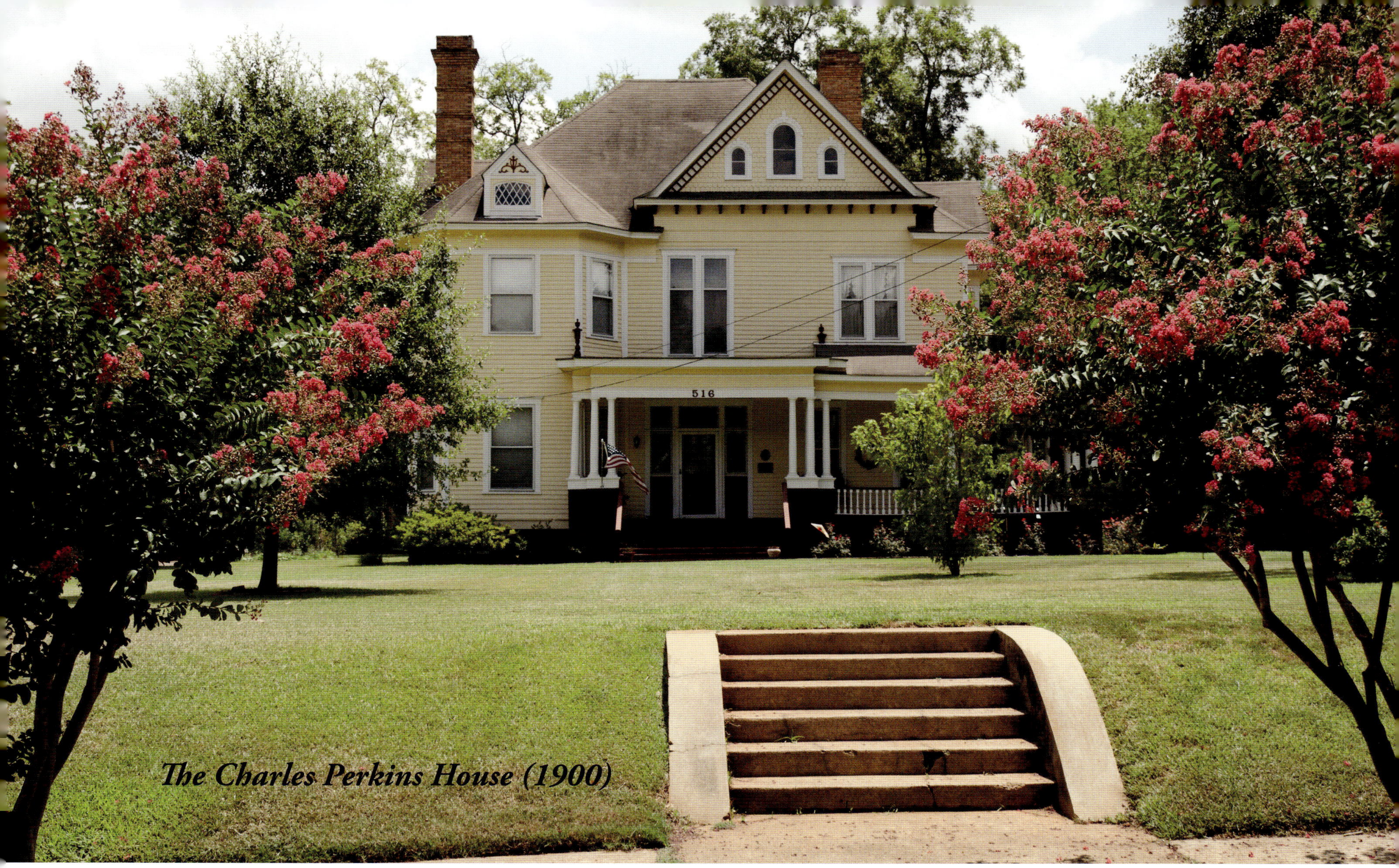

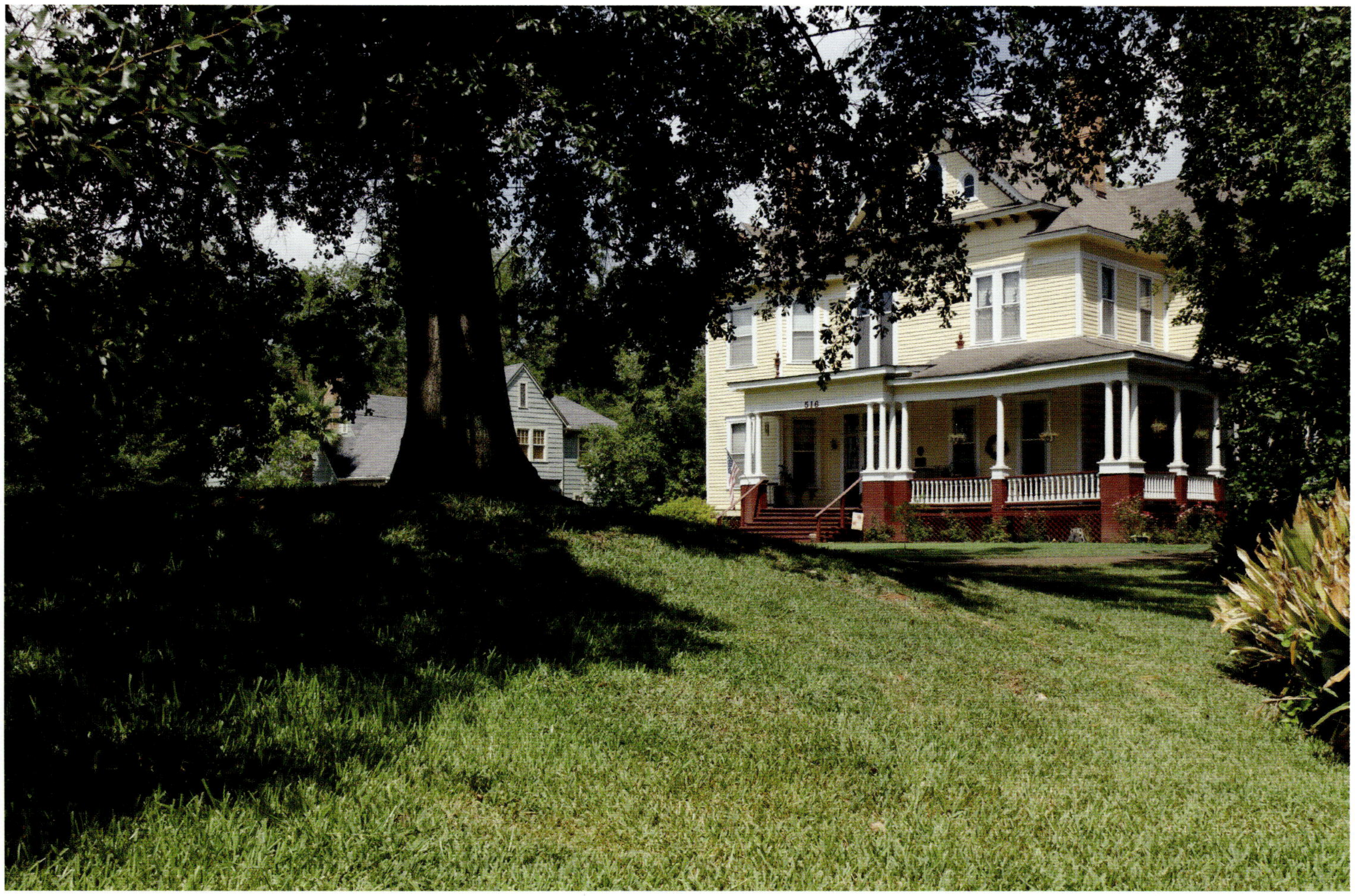

FIGURE 5.53. Front Elevation from Mound Street, 2011.

FIGURE 5.54. (Left) The Historic Caddoan Indian Mound.

Of the many Indian Ceremonial Burial Mounds, which gave the name to the street, only the one in front of the Perkins House still survives. The story of the excavation of the mound can be studied from the artifacts at Stephen F. Austin State University..

The Charles Perkins House (1900)

Charles Perkins (1860-1926) was the younger brother of W. U. (Will) Perkins. When Perkins Brothers opened their drug store in 1880, the brothers involved were W. U. (Will) Perkins and his older brother, Dr. Sam Perkins. Although Sam Perkins died of typhoid in 1883, their youngest brother, Charles Perkins, did not join the successful family druggist firm until much later in 1900. There is some speculation that he trained as a doctor; but as late as 1900, Charles Perkins listed himself in the census of that year as a merchant in the clothing business in Melrose.[85] The Perkins family, however, like the Schmidts and the Blounts, invested in many different types of Nacogdoches enterprises. Charles, it seems, managed the family's investments in land and town real estate. He may have dabbled in several endeavors, trying to establish his independence before joining his successful older brother. Charles's decision to join Will in the drugstore as a pharmacist is closely tied to the arrival of his fourth child and his need to settle into a more steady employment.

As mentioned in the discussion of the Steamboat House on North Street, Charles Perkins "sold his pretty little place on North Street" in early 1900 and commissioned Rulfs to undertake a more major residence on Mound Street.[86] Although interested in real estate development, Charles knew nothing about designing or building in a technical sense. He oversaw the construction of his sister's house on Church Street; but he, as his brother Will, relied heavily on the professional skills of D. Rulfs to give shape to their ideas. By June of 1900, when Rulfs showed the floor plans to the Sanborn mappers, they had completed their collaboration.[87]

The setting chosen for the house is particularly grand. The panoramic view is exceptional. The house occupies the highest elevation on Washington Square, sits further away from the street than neighboring houses (offering important space for the historic Caddoan Indian burial mound on the southwest corner), and rests on a higher set of piers than surrounding houses. Throughout his career, Rulfs enjoyed enhancing his designs with these preconditions.

The Charles Perkins House at 516 North Mound is a large 2-1/2 story late Victorian mansion, the same size as the Jones and Blount houses to the south, but the house is decidedly different. There is no double porch; and although there was a balcony over the front entrance originally, there was no pediment as in both of the other houses; the Queen Anne massed plan is less elaborate than the other two houses. The Tuscan columns–single, double, and grouped at the corners–give the house a very different appearance than the other houses on Washington Square, for example the Stephen Blount or Tol Hardeman houses. The monumental chimneys on this house are some of the finest in Nacogdoches. In place of a tower, Rulfs designed a two-story chamfered bay rooms covered by a hip rather than a gable roof and surrounded by flared, boxed eaves. The single dormer over this enormous forward bay is one of the most decorative features of the house. The diamond-patterned light of this dormer is reflected in the elaborate series of lead-glass lights surrounding the front door. Like the Cooper House on Irion Hill just a few years earlier, the Charles Perkins House had a forward facing gable in line with the main façade. In the large central gable, Rulfs placed three arched windows, more widely spaced than normal, instead of the more traditional Palladian forms utilized down the street.

Perkins owned the house until 1923; both he and his wife died in 1926.[88] While Henry R. Mast owned the house between 1923 and 1930, he and his wife never lived in the house, according to his grandsons Henry and Tom Middlebrook.[89] The mid-century owners of the house, from 1930 to 1977, were Mr. and Mrs. Thomas Reavley.[90] For a time, Reavley operated a potato chip factory on the property; according to locals, the smell drove the students at the high school across Mound Street to distraction. Dr. Robert and Ruth Carroll purchased the house in 1977 and have lived there the last 35 years. Dr. Carroll has turned the front office-pharmacy of Charles Perkins, with its slip-head access to the porch, into a collection of artifacts associated with both early medicine and pharmacy.[91]

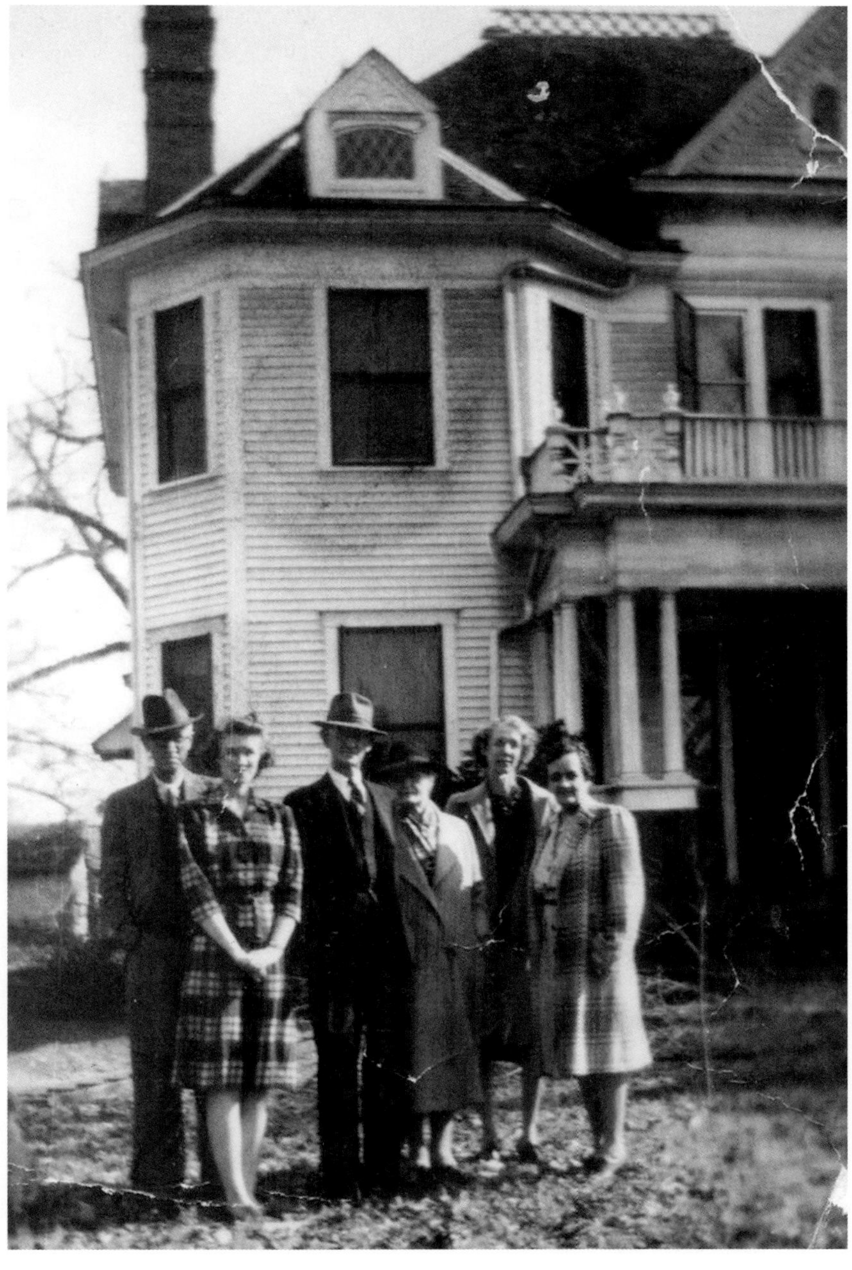

FIGURE 5.55. Members of the Charles Perkins Family.

This picture, date unknown, shows two features of the Perkins House now gone: the roof cresting and the balustrades over the entry. If one looks closely at the elevation opposite, the return-posts of the balustrade are still visible on current pictures. Photograph compliments of Ruth Carroll.

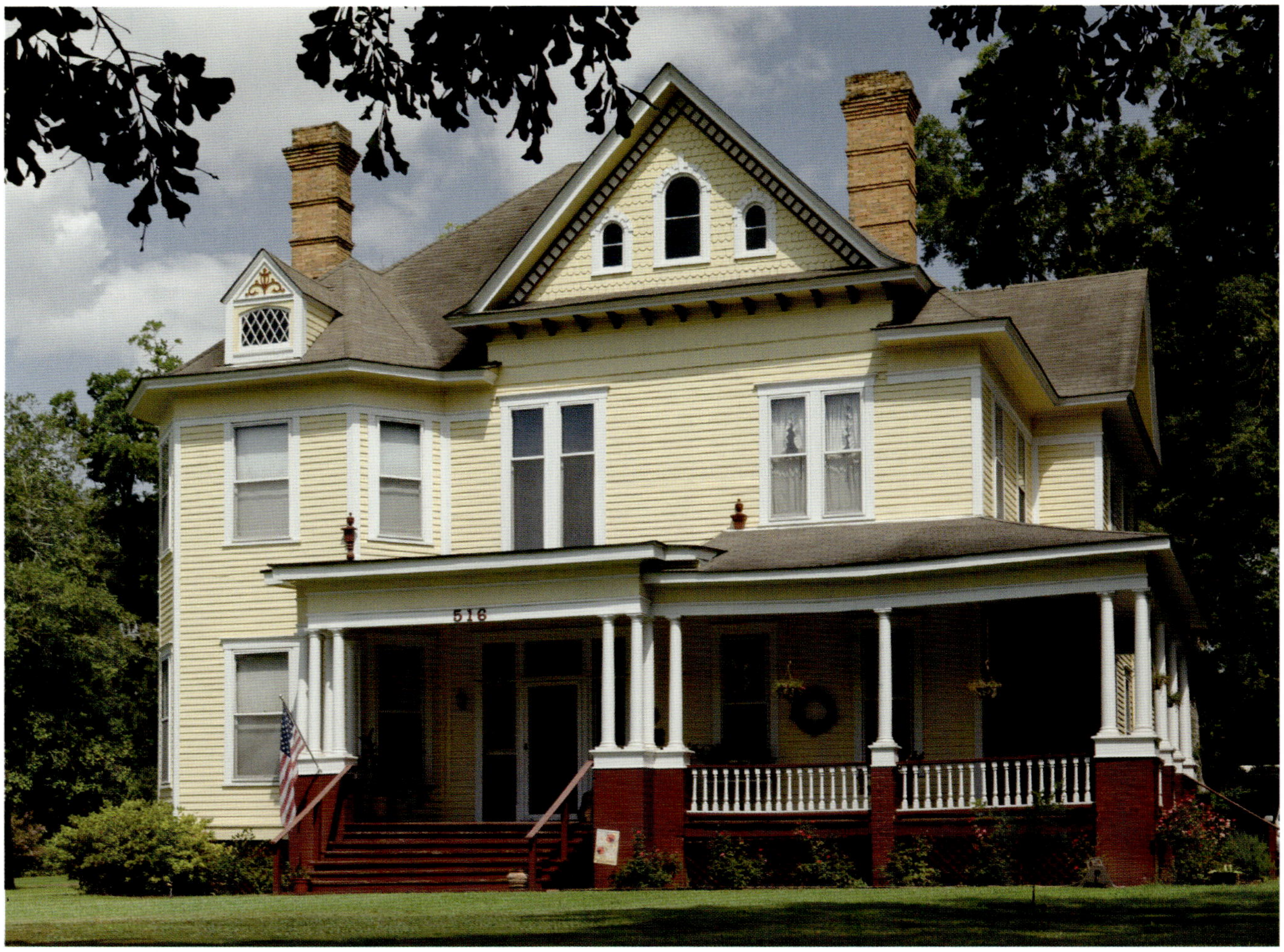

FIGURE 5.56. The Robert and Ruth Carroll Home, 2011.

FIGURE 5.57. The Porch of the Perkins House. *The porch has a commanding view of Washington Square.*

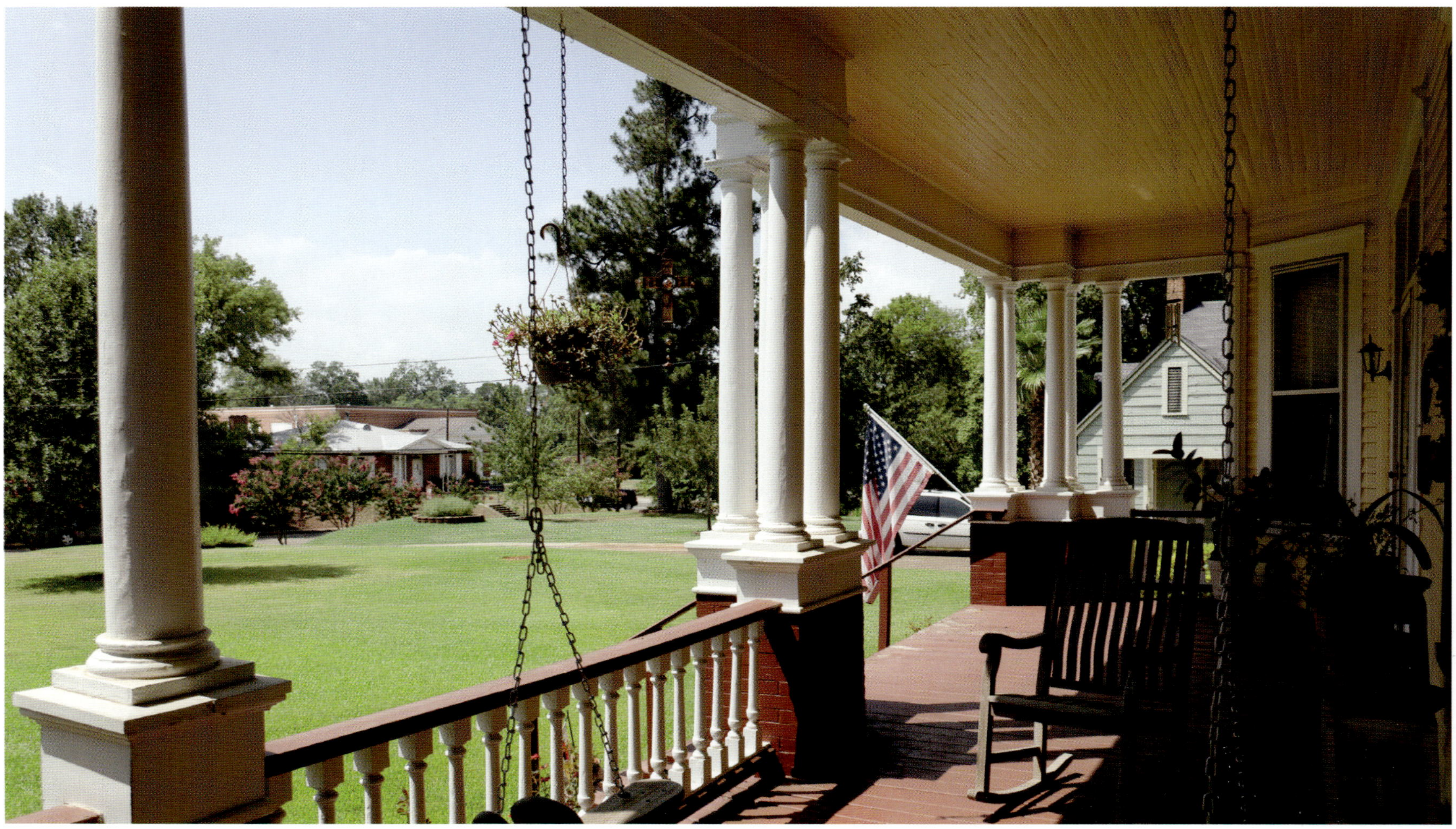

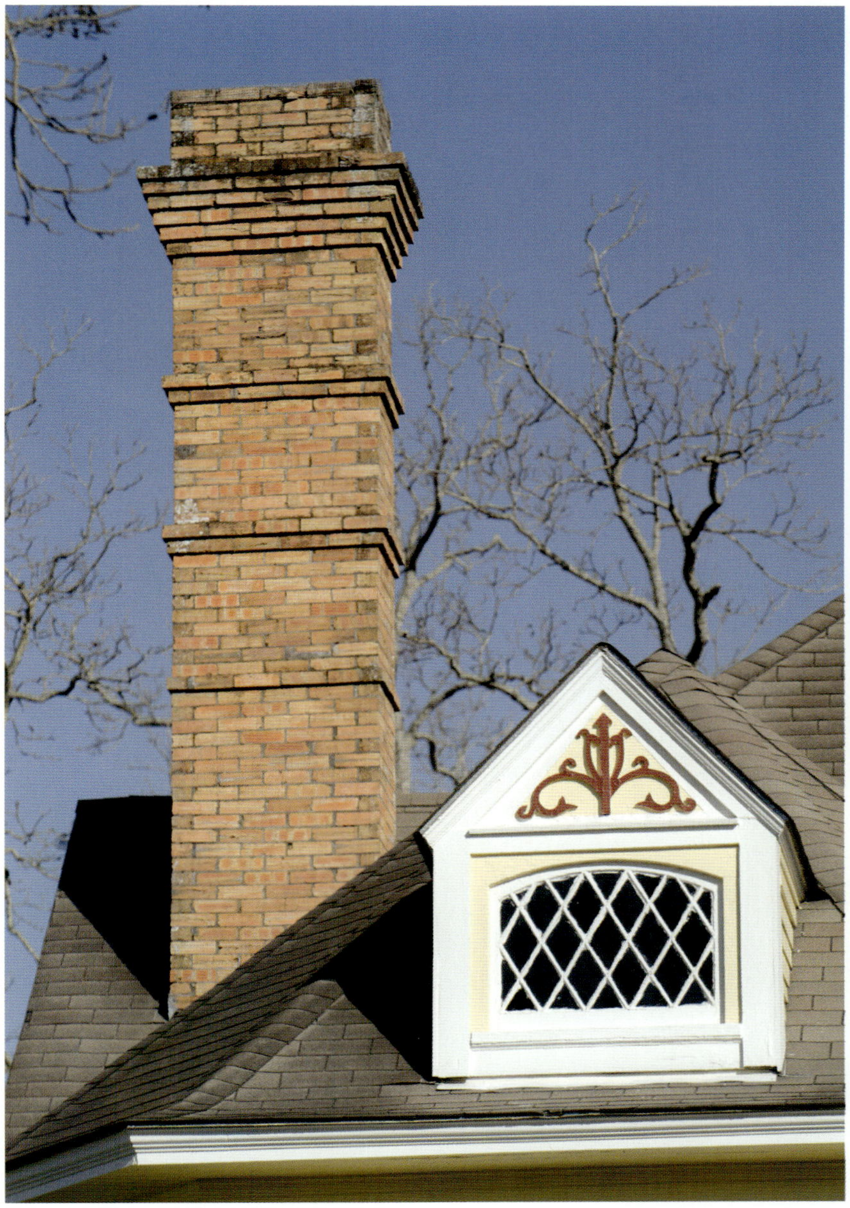

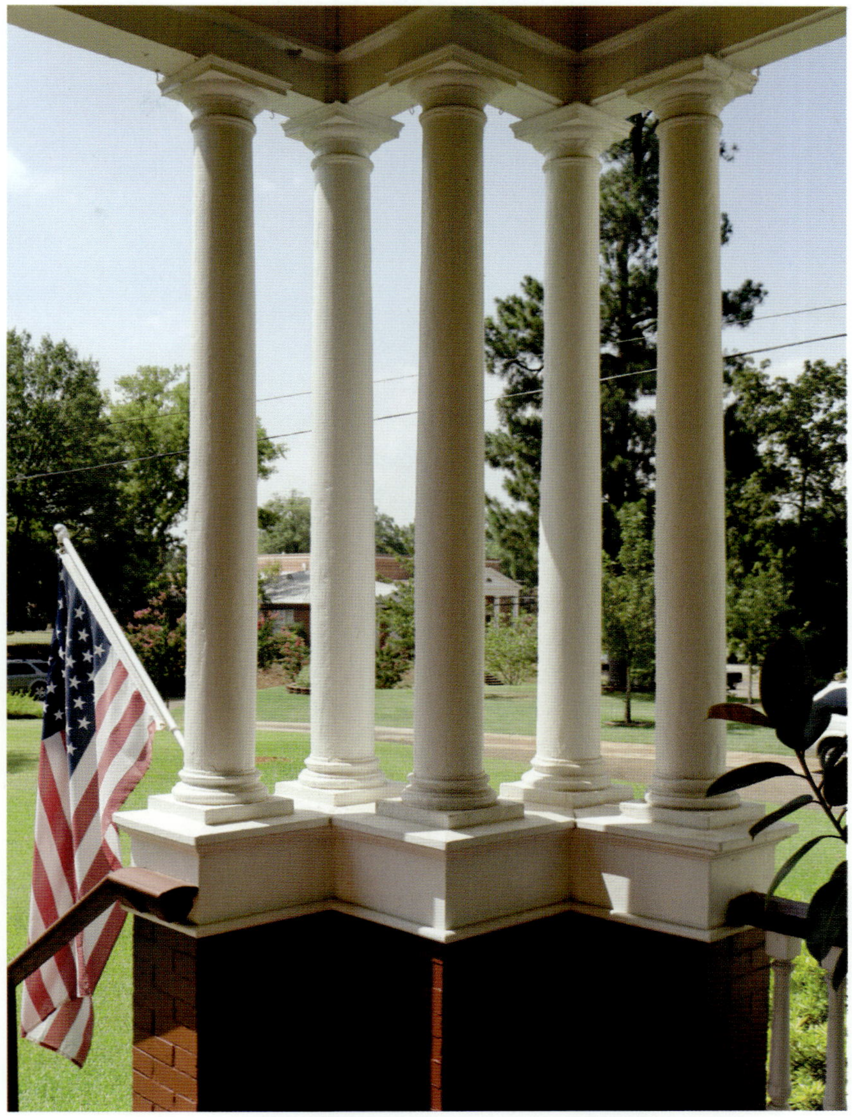

FIGURE 5.61. Grouped Tuscan Columns, Northwest Corner of the Front Porch.

FIGURE 5.58. Dormer and Chimney, Perkins House.

FIGURE 5.59. (Right) Local and National Landmark Designations

.

The National Register of Historic Places established the "Washington Square Historic District" in 1989. The Charles Perkins House by Rulfs proudly displays landmark plaques by both the National Register and the Local Historic Landmark Commission.

FIGURE 5.60. (Far Right) Watercolor by James Syder hangs in the living room.

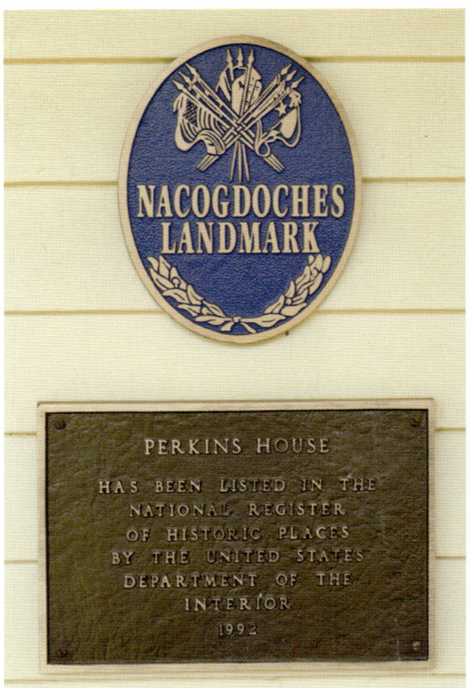

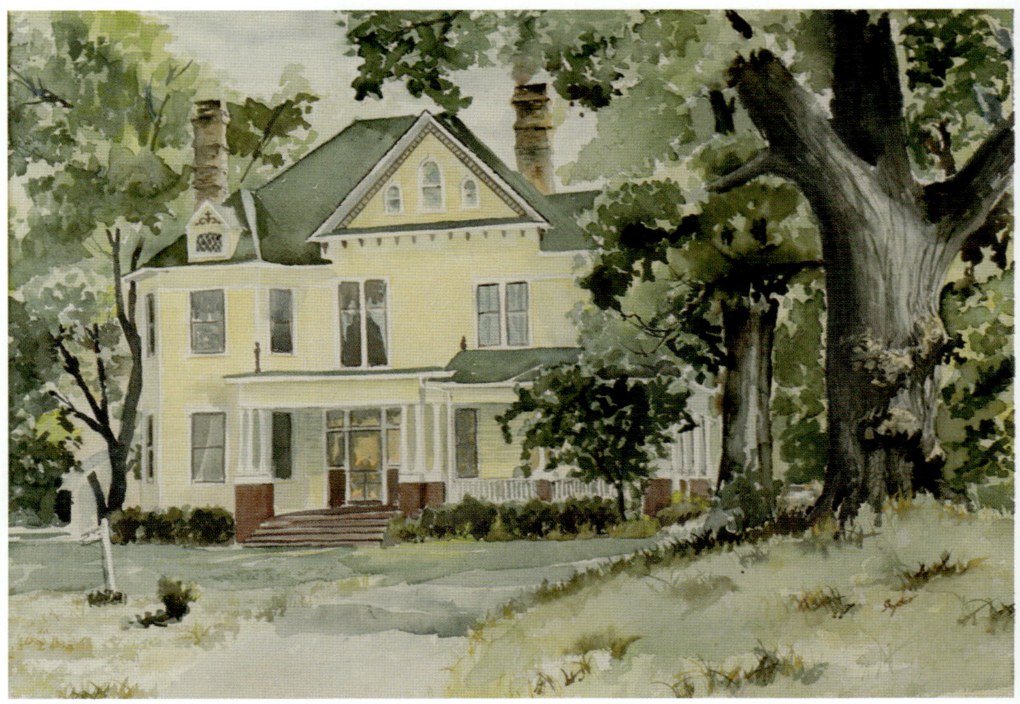

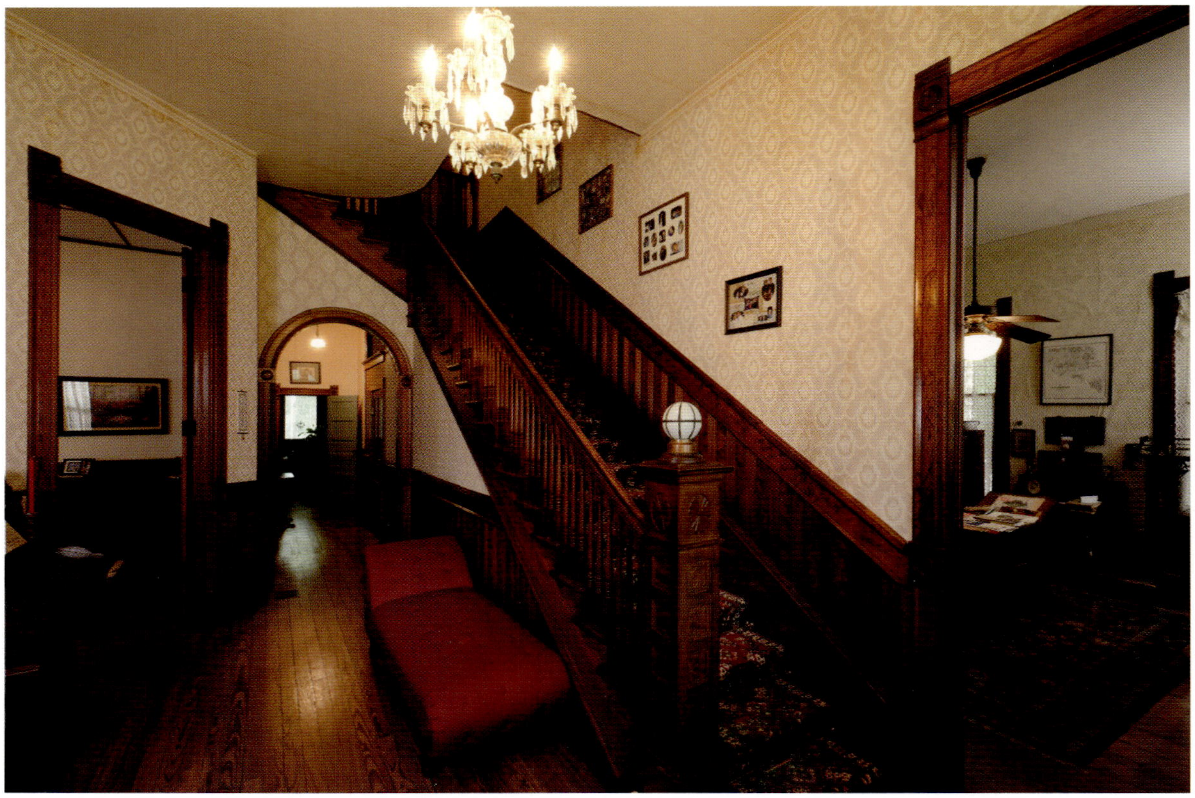

FIGURE 5.62. Entrance Hall, Dining Room Door (Left), Office Door (Right). The arch separated the front and back halls.

FIGURE 5.63. (Below) The Entrance Door.

The entrance door, with its three-part transom and side panels of leaded glass, is one of the important features of the house. The hardware and the woods were also elements of richness in the completion of this house. The door to the left belongs to the office and the doors to the right to the parlor-living room.

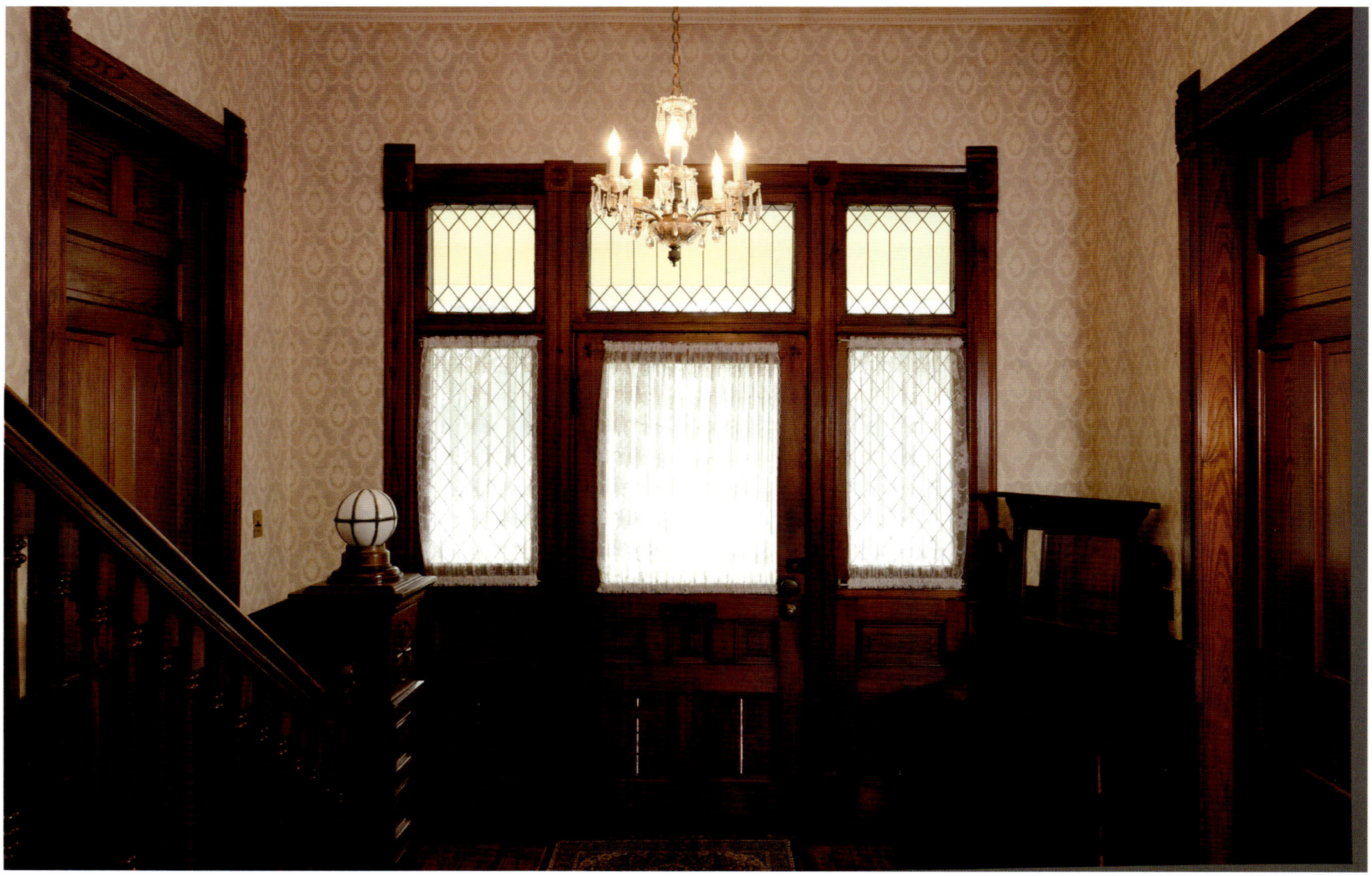

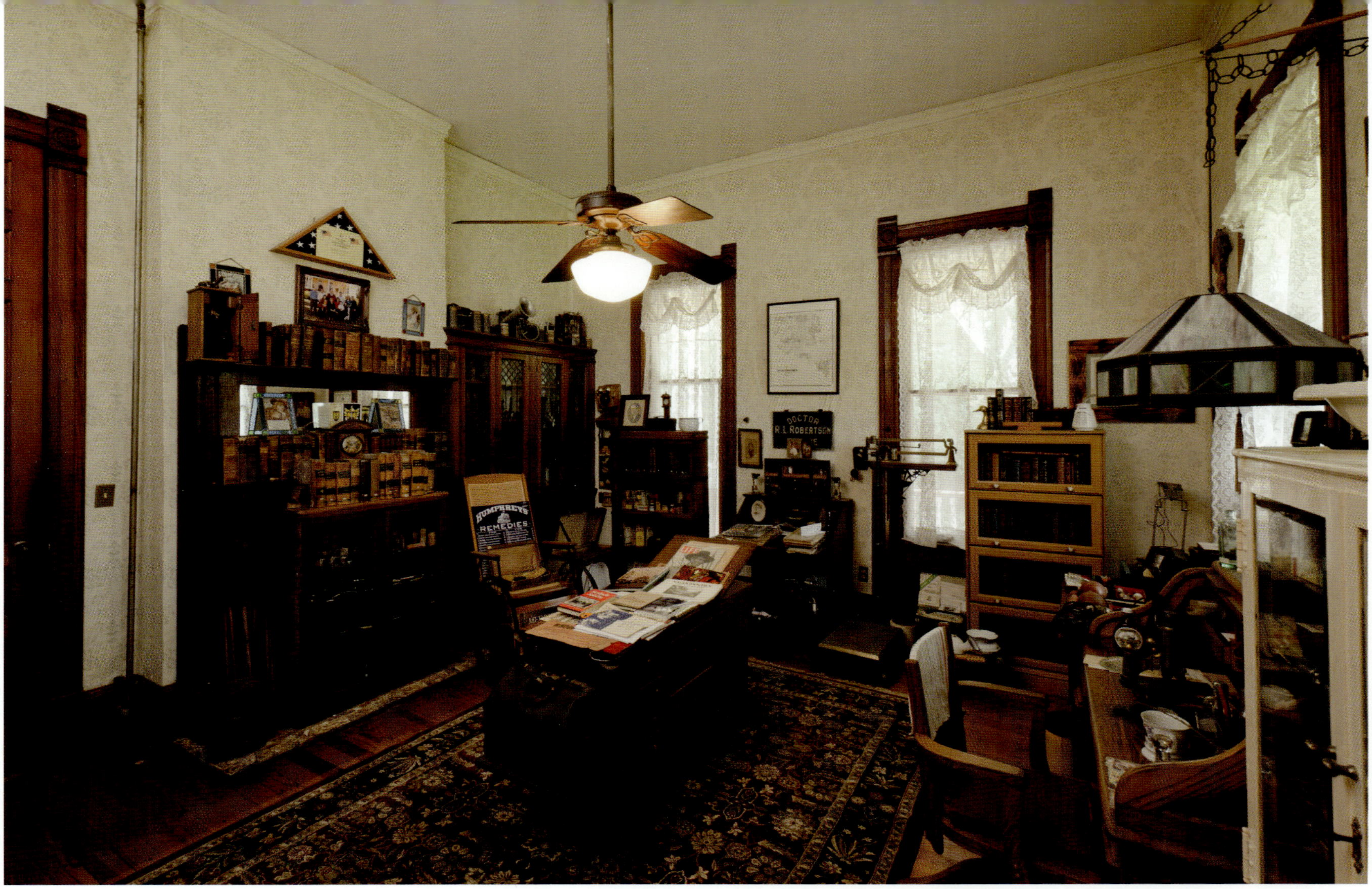

FIGURE 5.64. (Above) Dr. Robert Carroll's Office.

Charles Perkins used this room as his after-hours pharmacy. He stored his pharmaceuticals in the leaded-glass cabinet built into the wall (far corner of the room). The slip-head window next to the cabinet, sometimes called a doctor's window, allowed patients to access the office without coming into the private rooms of the house. Dr. Carroll has an extensive collection of artifacts from early medical history in the room today. (There is a cabinet/bookcase in front of the unused fireplace's mantel.)

FIGURE 5.65 (Below) The South Front Porch.

The south side of the wrap-around front porch had a set of steps and a slip-head window to provide access to the pharmany office.

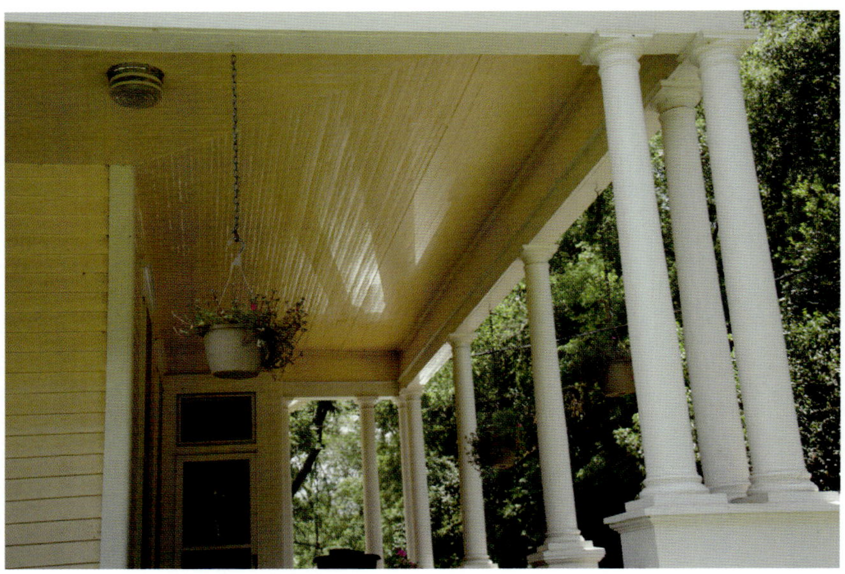

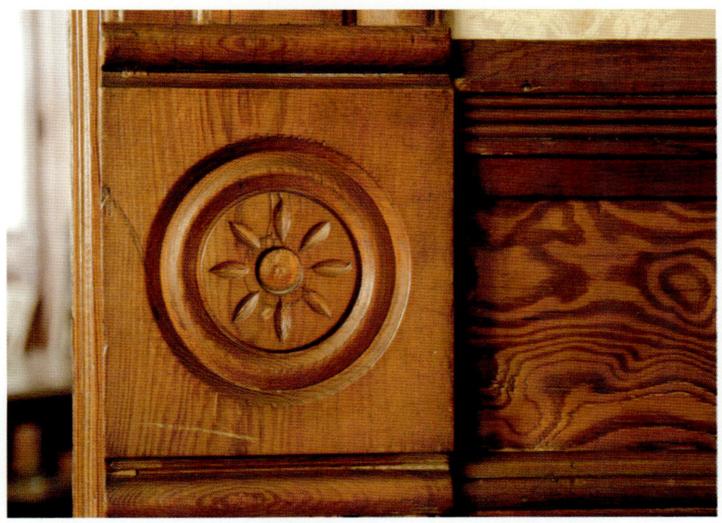

FIGURE 5.66. Woodwork Detail.

The finish work on the Rulfs houses was as important as the overall design. Many of the great Queen Anne houses, such as the houses for Roland Jones, Stephen Blount, and Charles Perkins, had elaborate door surrounds with decorative block inserts and crests. The curly pine, seen in this picture, topped elaborate wainscot combinations of millwork.

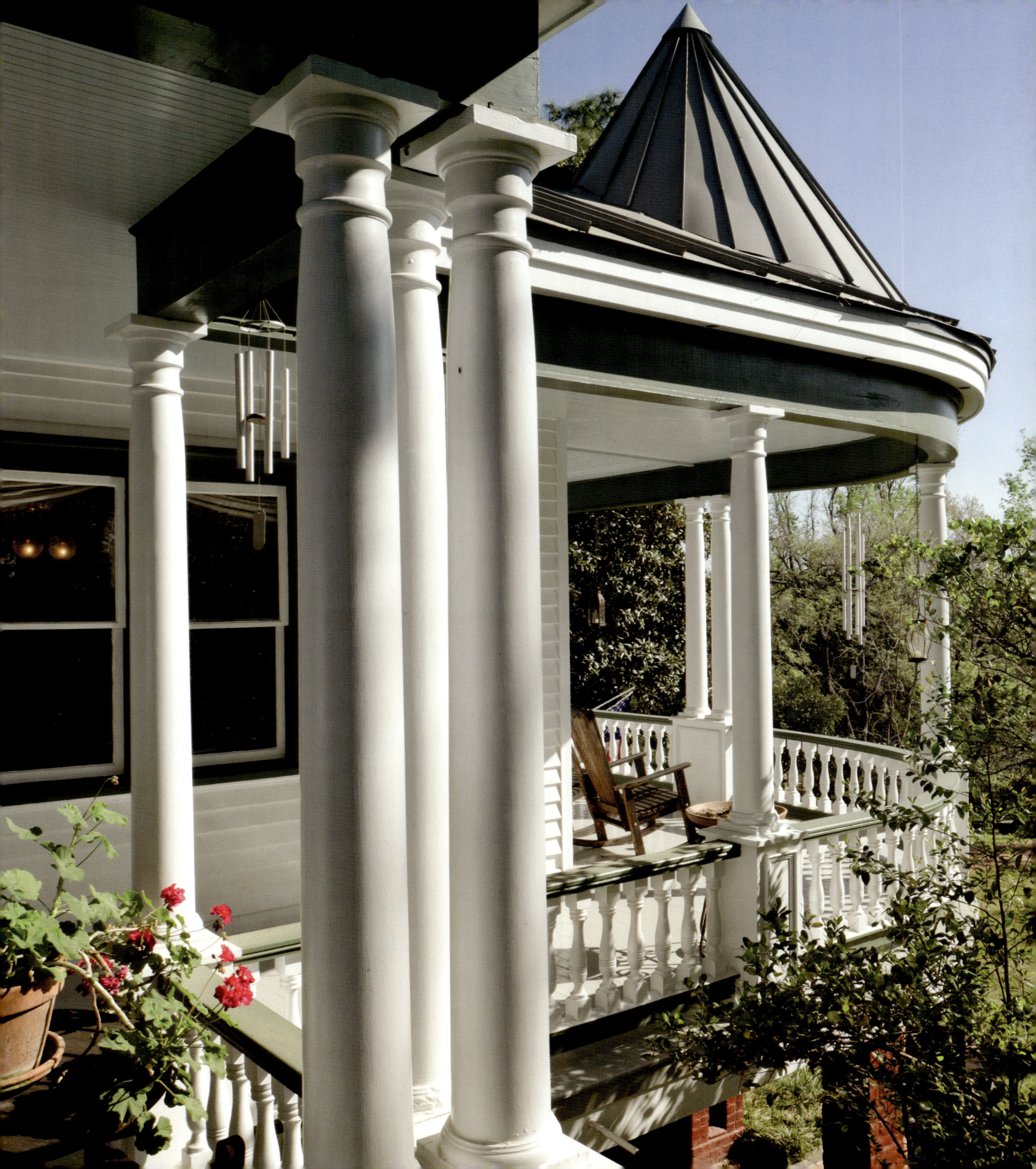

CHAPTER VI

Redefining Domestic Contexts

Irion and Forbes Hills

"Several prominent citizens of Nacogdoches were attracted to the elevated topography on the western bluff of Irion Hill overlooking the city, and they subsequently erected elaborate dwellings . . . . among the finest examples in the city." "Historic and Architectural Resources of Nacogdoches," *National Register.*

Three strategic elevations surround downtown Nacogdoches: Orton Hill to the east, Irion Hill (and Forbes Hill) to the west, and Fredonia Hill to the south. The Spanish, who worried about defending the interior of Texas from further intrusions by the French from the east, saw Irion Hill as the most important of the three—the last stronghold protecting the interior of Texas. They immediately established a presence on Irion Hill in the eighteenth century. In the center of this defensive location, between the two creeks, stood the Old Stone House on the Square. Immediately after Texas Independence, the leaders of Nacogdoches divided the city, including Irion Hill, into blocks and lots as shown on the city maps of 1837 and 1846. (See Figures 1.13 & 1.14.) Considering their population of 3500 at the time, perhaps they had every right to believe that they were being realistic. Their optimistic projections, however, never materialized. While there may have been many reasons for this, the main explanation remains that subsequent pioneer immigrants into Texas looked upon Nacogdoches as a gateway to the interior of the new state. Land in Nacogdoches was either already claimed or too expensive. While Nacogdoches prospered in the decade immediately following the Revolution, the population steadily declined. The Civil War completed the town's slip into marginal status.

FIGURE 6.1. (Opposite) East Porch Detail, June Harris House (1895); restored by Dr. Richard and Cherry Baker.

At the turn of the twentieth century, people in Nacogdoches would have distinguished between Irion Hill (at the top of West Main Street) and Forbes Hill (the name used by old timers for the southern bluffs, now along Virginia Avenue). In drawing the Virginia Avenue National Register District (Forbes Hill), the houses that Rulfs did on Irion Hill were not included. From the point of view of discussing the architect's work west of downtown, however, this is not useful. The drive to occupy the town-side crests of the western bluffs was part of a particular movement in town. The movement commenced with the building of the June Harris House in 1895, and with perhaps a few exceptions, ended after the completion of the West End School (now Nettie Marshall Elementary). Rulfs completed this work on both Irion and Forbes hills within a decade, unlike the development of residences along North Street and around the Washington Square area—both of which have distinct phases on both sides of the date 1900.

A number of reasons determined why development of the hills on both east and west sides of downtown remained a dream from colonial times forward. The height of the hills themselves and the poor accommodations for crossing the creeks limited the appeal of the trans-creek areas as building sites. The only domestic structures on Irion hill were farmhouse dwellings, most of which sat on or just off the old highways (Durst Street and West

Main) that ran to Douglass. The old Dorsey homestead is a good example.[1] Even the expansion of residential areas along East Main and North Street after the arrival of the railroad did not have an immediate impact along the crest of Irion or Forbes hills. The development of property along the Banita Creek at the foot of Irion Hill consisted mainly of industrial and commercial concerns that needed to be close to the railroad. The building of hotels, such as the Banita Hotel, or boarding houses made sense also. The idea of developing residential property to the west of the downtown grew out of the initial building activity in the Washington Square area. The study made by the Texas Historical Commission in the mid-1990s, is correct in observing that "several prominent citizens of Nacogdoches were attracted to the elevated topography on the western bluff of Irion Hill overlooking the city, and they subsequently erected elaborate dwellings."[2]

The triggering event seems to have been the decision by Junius (June) Clark Harris (1861-1941), a prominent lawyer in town, to move his family from the congestion of Hospital Street to Forbes Hill (what eventually became Virginia Avenue) in order to secure a better environment for his growing family.[3] June Harris and Diedrich Rulfs had worked together on a house on the corner of Hospital and Mound, as mentioned in the previous chapter. When one of Harris' children became extremely ill, Harris wanted to move to the country straight away. He quickly purchased a thirty-acre tract of undeveloped farmland on Forbes Hill as the site for his new homestead. Rulfs, having spent his first thirty years in a part of Germany almost totally devoid of hills, readily took up the challenge of creating a residence that would take advantage of the elevated location. Harris's eventual decision to create a real estate company to promote the Forbes/Irion hill area also offered new opportunities for the architect. Harris supplied the land; his new real estate partner, Robert Lindsey, supplied the legwork and promotion; and Rulfs supplied the designs and frequently the construction. Oftentimes, Henry Austin was one of the players on this team. They constituted an effective team.

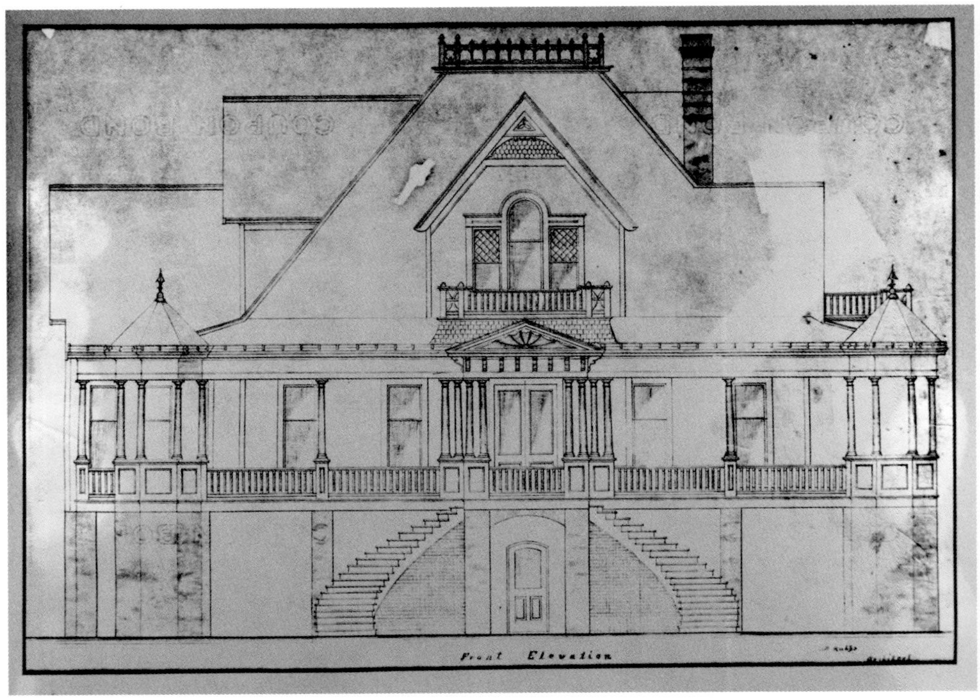

FIGURE 6.2. (Above) "Front Elevation, D. Rulfs." Facsimile of the Drawing of the Harris House (1895).

While the original drawing has color added, this copy, given by the descendants to Dr. and Mrs. Richard Baker, demonstrates the great attention to detail for which the architect was noted. Facsimile courtesy of Dr. Richard Baker

FIGURE 6.3. (Across) Detail of Drawing by Rulfs.

The author photographed the original colored drawing of the front elevation of the Harris House in 1974. The drawing still exists in the possession of the Harris-Davison heirs.

The June Harris House (1895)

The house Rulfs designed for the June Harris family was one of his most spectacular designs. Fortunately, it still stands at 612 Virginia Avenue.[4] The architect's houses on North Street from the early 1890s (for Will Perkins, John Schmidt, and E. A. Blount) had redefined the standards for wealthy patrons in Nacogdoches. Unfortunately, these houses did not survive the commercial development of North Street in the 1960-70s. No one even offered to save them by moving them off North Street. Because both Washington Square and the hills west of town were not as suitable for commercial development, anyone interested in seeing fine examples of domestic architecture by Rulfs can still experience them in these two areas. June Harris was an attorney with an impressive reputation and an important list of patrons. In addition, he had a large following of young men in town who wanted to read law under his tutelage.[5] Later in Harris' career, Texas Governor Pat Neff asked the Nacogdoches lawyer to work with a commission charged with re-codifying the laws of the State of Texas. Because his law practice demanded constant access to the County Courthouse, his office was on the Square, and his first home at the southwest corner of Hospital and Mound Streets was within convenient walking distance.[6] Harris' downtown residence, remodeled by Rulfs in 1892, would most likely have become too cramped for the growing Harris family (eventually ten children). According to family tradition, however, the main reason for his abrupt decision to relocate his family to the country was something else: "Two of the children, Margaret and Audley, contracted what they called 'slow fever' [sleeping sickness]. It was thought it was probably typhoid fever and the cause the quality of the water."[7] Harris not only wanted a deep and fresh source of water, but he also wanted his children to have more play space and room for ponies. For quality-of-life reasons, he purchased a thirty-acre farm on Forbes Hill, just half a mile from the town center. While Harris eventually developed his property into a formal subdivision, almost immediately he sold off some portions of the property to promote the movement of prominent families to the area.[8]

Rulfs' original drawing, labeled "Front Elevation," has survived for the Harris House. (See Figure 6.03) The Harris front elevation demonstrates clearly the great attention to detail and proportions that characterized the architect's buildings.

The Harris project challenged Rulfs in a number of ways. While the architect frequently lifted houses off the ground in order give them a more imposing presence (as in the Charles Hoya House), the east façade of this

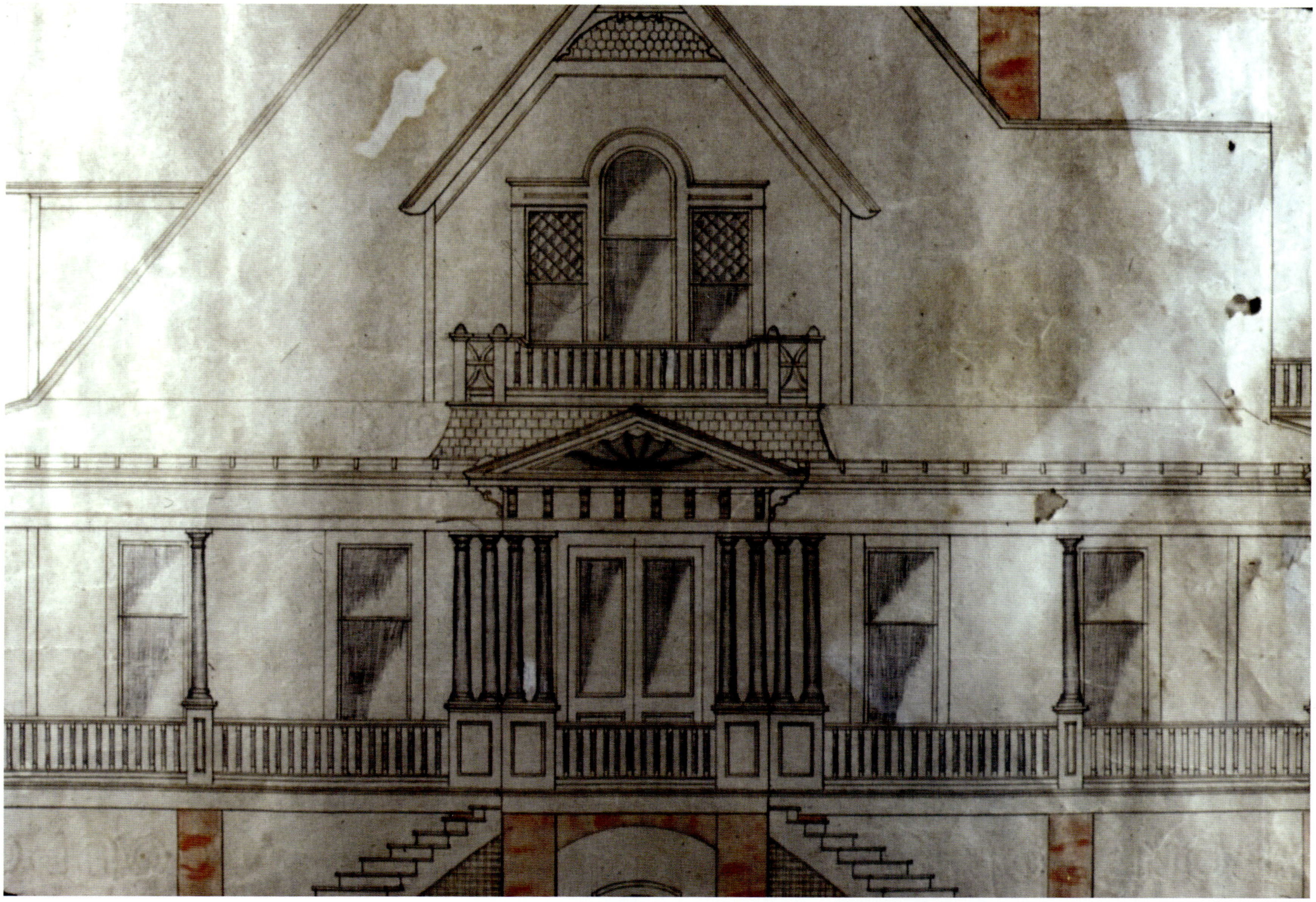

The June C. Harris House (1895)

house is his most striking use of this device. The decision to establish the crest of the hill as the base line for the house meant that the east façade, as shown in the elevation, had to rest on massive structural support-piers to compensate for the hill's slope. The result, a raised cottage, was not done to protect the house from groundwater as was done in houses in southern Louisiana, but to meet Harris' demand for outdoor living spaces and vistas, much like modern houses have attached decks to overlook some distinctive landscape. Every room on the main floor had access to the great porches that wrapped around the house on three sides. To the south on Sunset Street, there was a wing of bedrooms.[9] The impression of the galleries along the entire east façade was dramatic, but overwhelmingly horizontal. To break this, Rulfs projected a centralized grand portico, from which twin stairs descended gracefully to the front lawn, and over which he placed a dormer-room with a Palladian window. The high-pitched hip roof had large gables on the north and the south and iron cresting at the top. The drawing demonstrates how effectively Rulfs could encase the demands of his patron within a conceptual design of enduring appeal. The result is not just another Victorian house with a wrap-around gallery or even another typical Southern raised cottage with a hip roof, but a truly ingenious work of synthesis.

The east stairs, while giving the house its distinctive appearance, were never practical as an entrance for guests and were mostly an architectural device. While they gave the family, especially children then and now, access to the front yard, the utilitarian entrance to the public rooms was through the lower arched entryway. The entrance hall to the house was at ground level through the brick archway beneath the portico and grand steps. At the back of the entrance hall, an indoor stairway ascended to the main floor central hall. On the west side of the house, the family had a variety of entrances. They could access the main floor from the galleries that wrapped around three sides of the house or through the ground level service rooms. Harris built a large barn, which according to one family member, "stood in the back yard along with the smoke houses and servants' quarters. . . . The barn housed the horses, carriages, and the surrey with the fringe on top. The family enjoyed having their huge Christmas tree in the barn occasionally."[10]

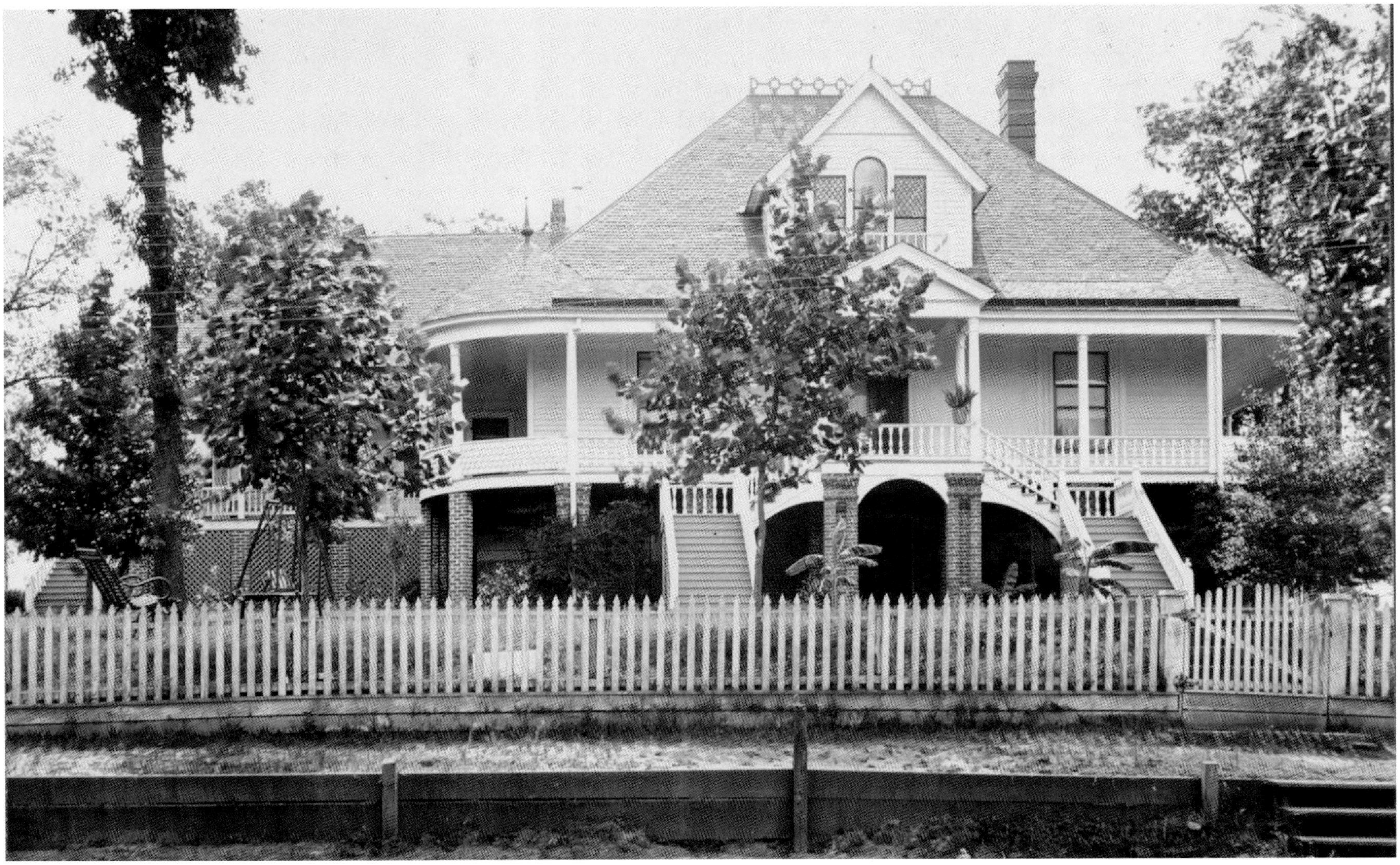

FIGURE 6.4. The June Harris House, ca. 1900

The east elevation of the Harris House indicates three floors. The rusticated ground floor contained service rooms. The second story or noble floor of the house, with the public rooms and bedrooms, had two entrances, from the exterior via the grand staircase through the portico to the impressive porch system, and from the brick entryway on the ground level through a reception hall to the main internal stairway. The third floor, suggested by the dormer-room, was never closed in for normal use until the Bakers did so in the 2000s. Photograph courtesy of Dr. & Mrs. Richard Baker.

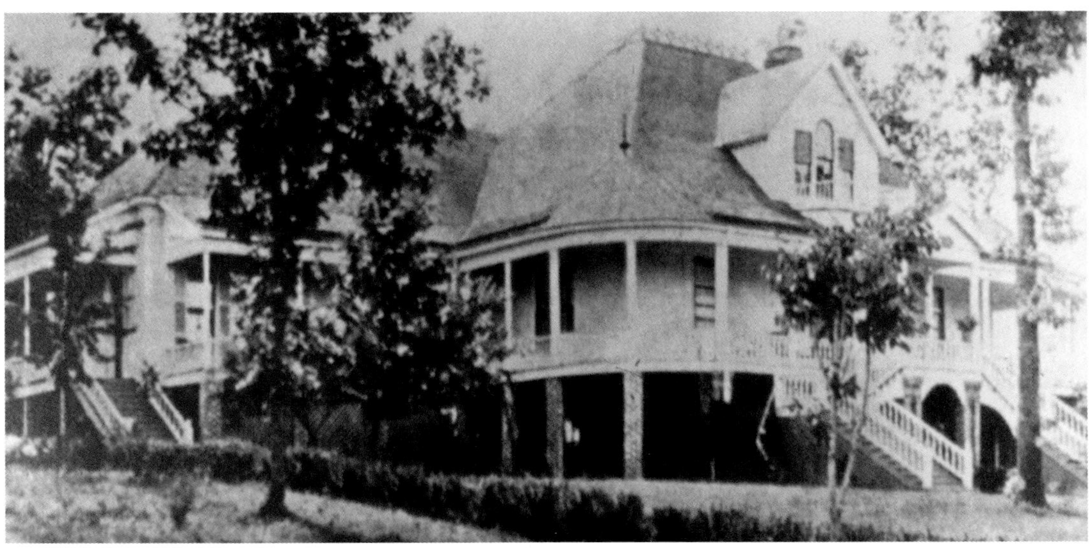

FIGURE 6.5. View from Southeast, ca. 1910.

The south wing of the Harris House is rarely seen. The porches of the house wrapped around the south, too, with stairs to the front and back. This wing of the house, removed in the 1930s, became another house down Sunset Street.

FIGURE 6.6. (Across) The Tom and Enid Davidson Home in 1976.

The author took this picture at the time of the interviews with Tom and Enid Davisons. Without the great porch system, the Harris House looks radically different.

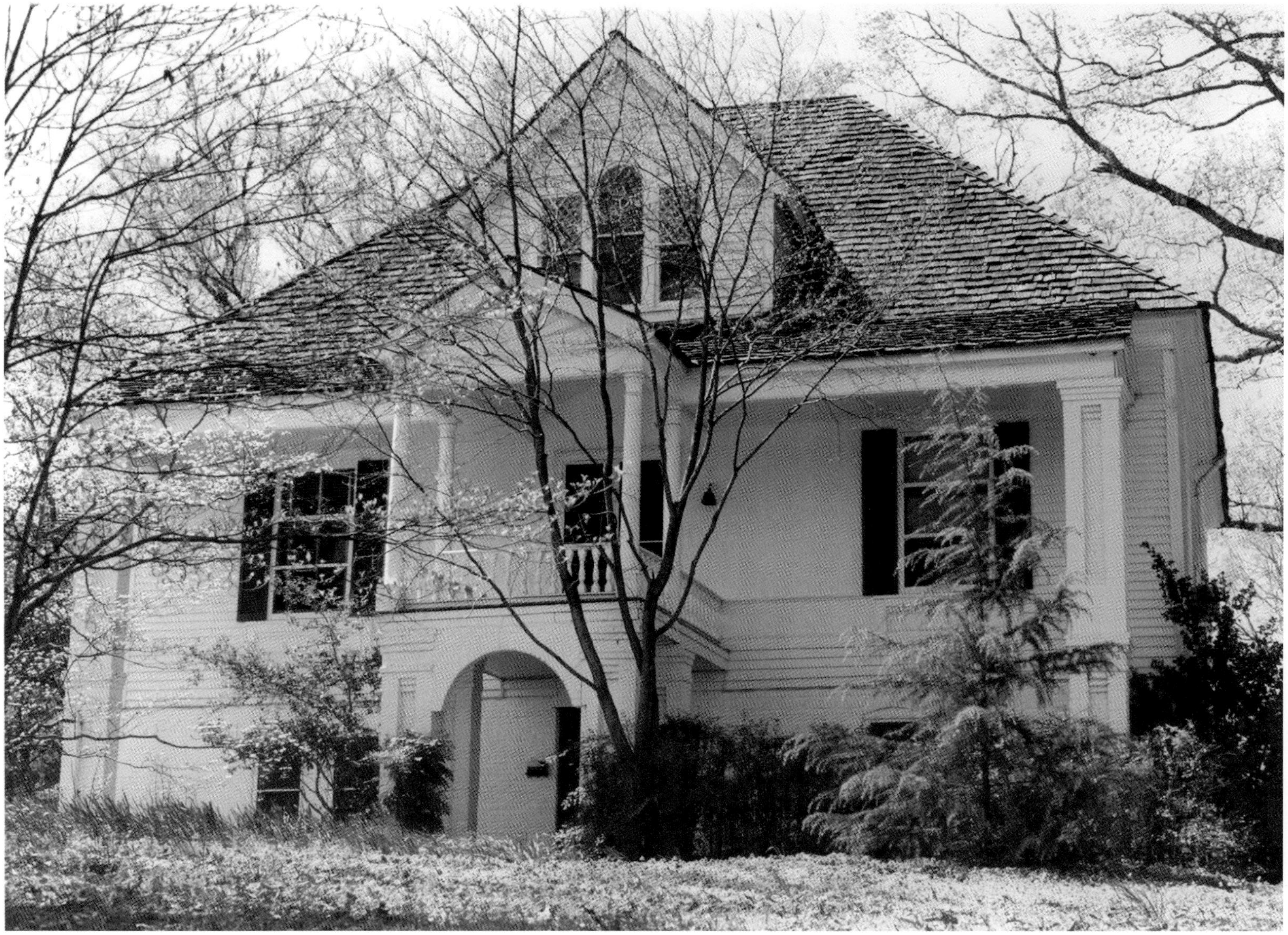

The evolution of the Harris house, even during Rulfs' lifetime, is fascinating and well documented in pictures and family interviews.[11] First, the house as built does not match Rulfs' own original drawing. As construction started, Rulfs was unable to secure the prefabricated columns he had initially envisioned. Therefore, he worked with the full-length Tuscan columns he could secure. He later transferred the idea of paired columns on a plinth base to designs he did for the Crouch House on North Street and the Tolbert Hardeman House on Washington Square, both done within a few years. Second, he modified the curved stairways– difficult to construct and support – into straight designs with a ninety-degree landing in the middle. Third, the house as built included only the enclosed entrance hall, a kitchen, and utility space in the basement. On Forbes Hill the view enticed Rulfs to place all the family quarters on the upper floor – not fear of ground or rising water, as in Louisiana raised cottages. Rulfs provided porches to exploit the view and give every room access to plenty of fresh air. Rulfs frequently anticipated and offered his clients the possibility of expanding their houses; the need for this was almost immediate for Harris. While he did not take in the attic's gable space immediately, in 1898, Rulfs expanded the ground floor under the main living quarters. The spaces between the great piers were incorporated within the enclosed area of the house to accommodate a shop, an office, and a pantry.[12] (The huge third floor remained unfinished until after 2003.)[13]

In the 1930s, to cope with the constrictions of the Depression, the Harris descendants moved their formal living quarters to the basement floor, lowered the ceilings on the original main floor to facilitate heating, detached the south wing entirely (moving it down Sunset Street to create a complete house for rental income), and removed entirely the grand but rotten porches and stairs on the east façade.[14] In this form, looking nothing like the original, the building survived until the early 2000s. Richard and Cherry Baker purchased the house and soon undertook major steps to restore it. (Charles Bright, who had undertaken similar work on the Lindsey House down Virginia Avenue, aided and encouraged them in their work.) In their restoration efforts, since an original Rulfs drawing existed, the Bakers chose to approximate Rulfs' original drawing of the porch, using Tuscan columns on raised plinth bases rather than the full-length single columns as built in 1895.[15] The Bakers chose not to go back to the curved staircases of the drawing, but to use the solution Rulfs used of a landing midway to keep the stairs manageable.

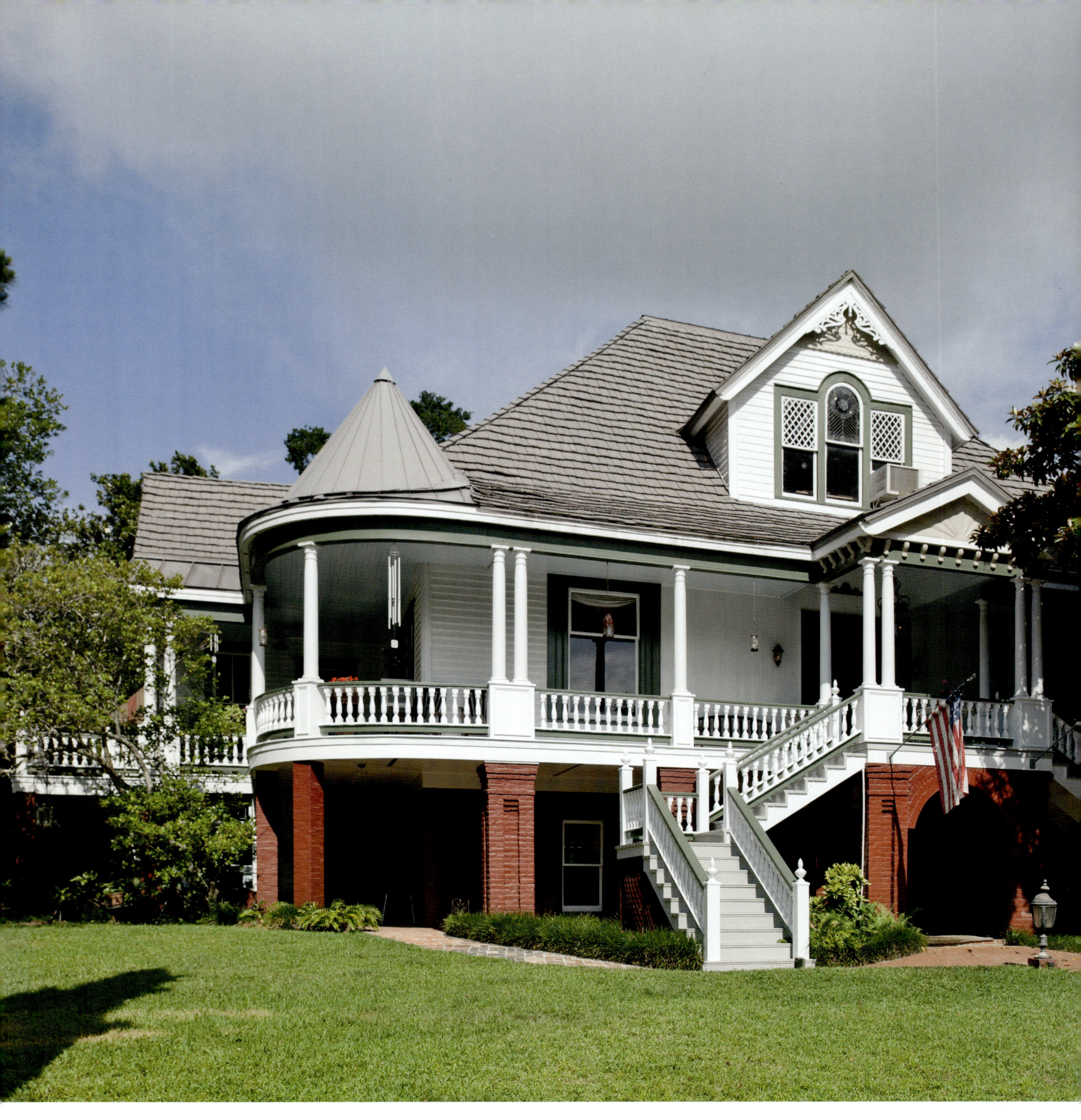

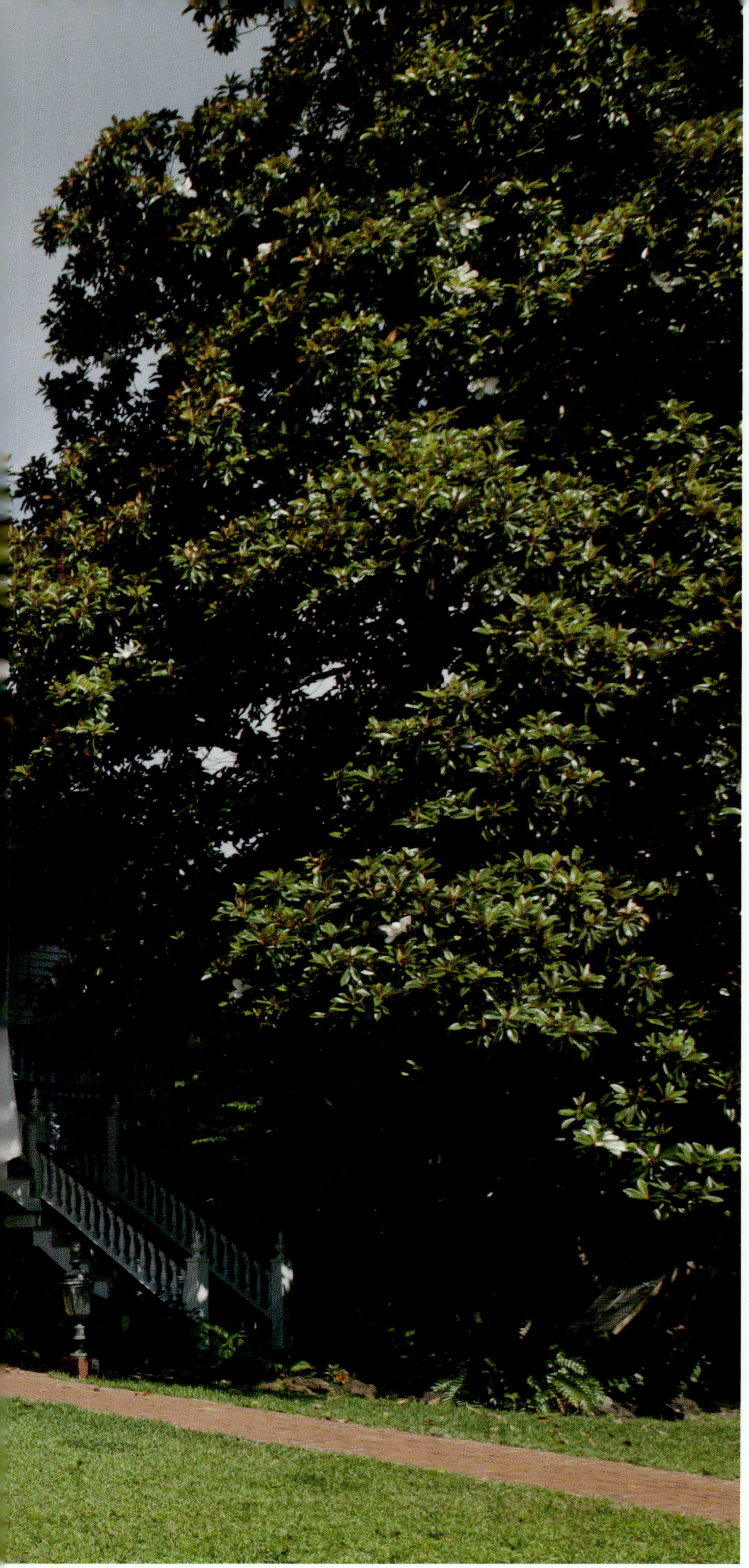

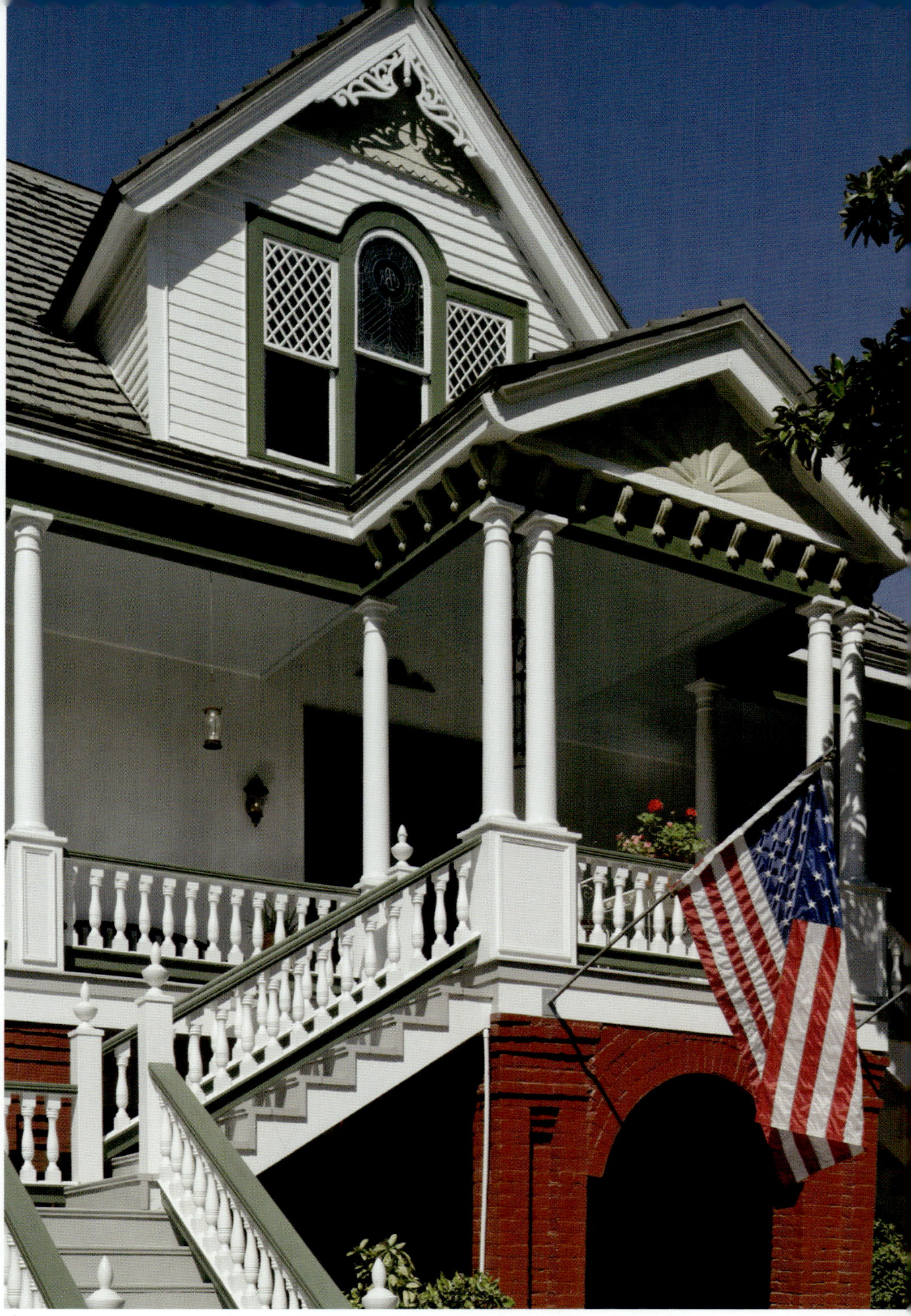

FIGURE 6.7. (Left) The Baker Home in 2011.
FIGURE 6.8. (Above and Below) Details, East Façade and Porch.

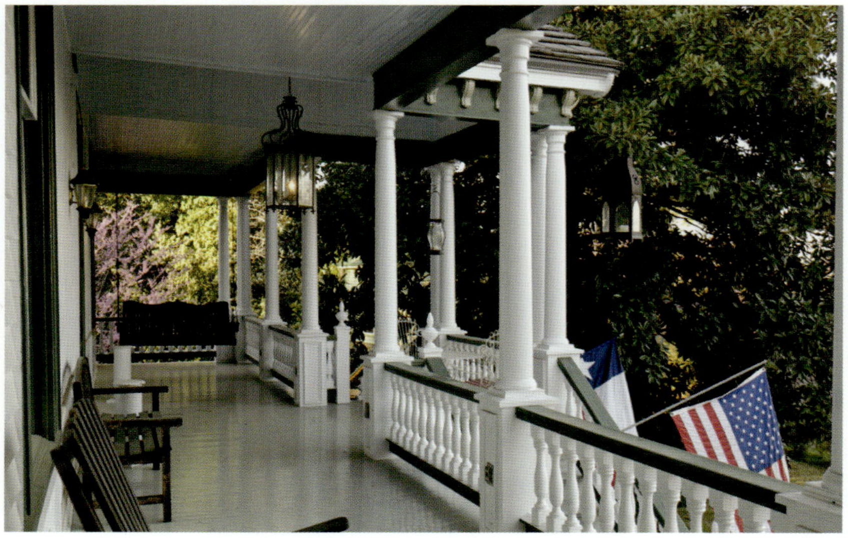

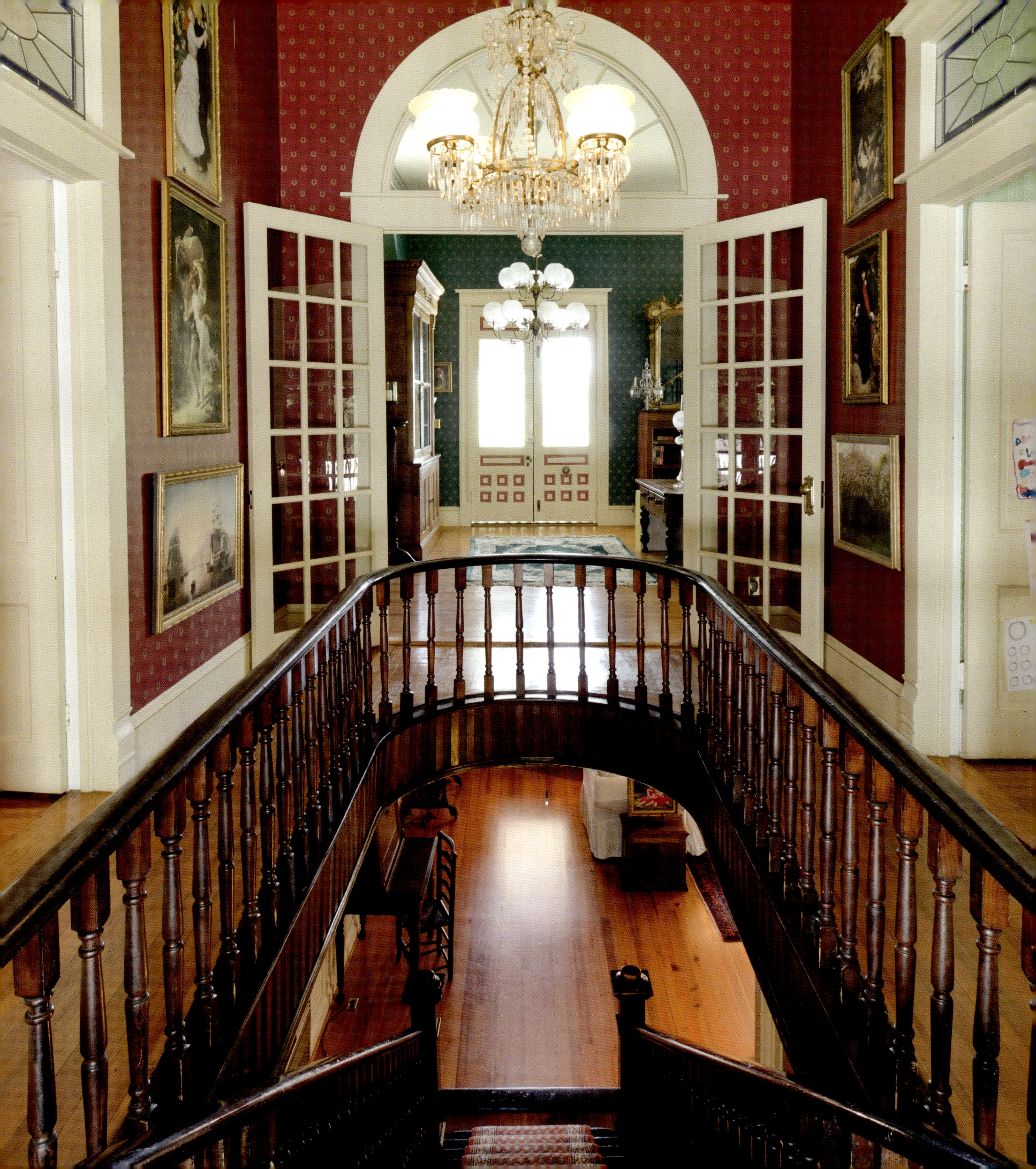

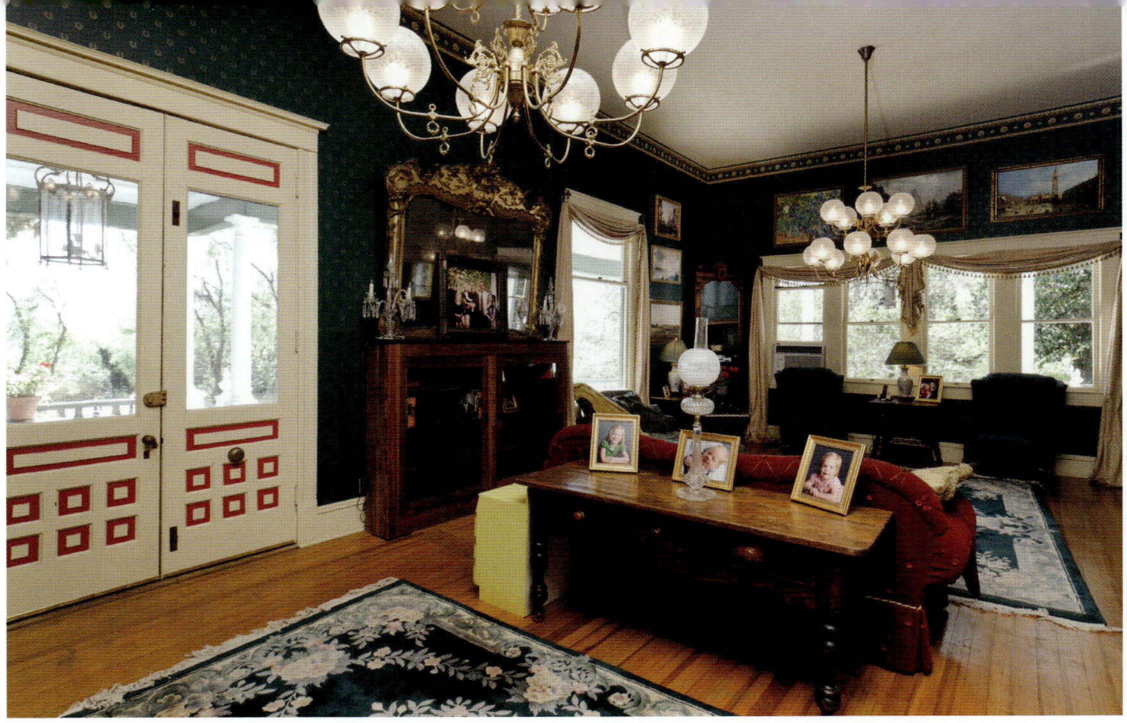

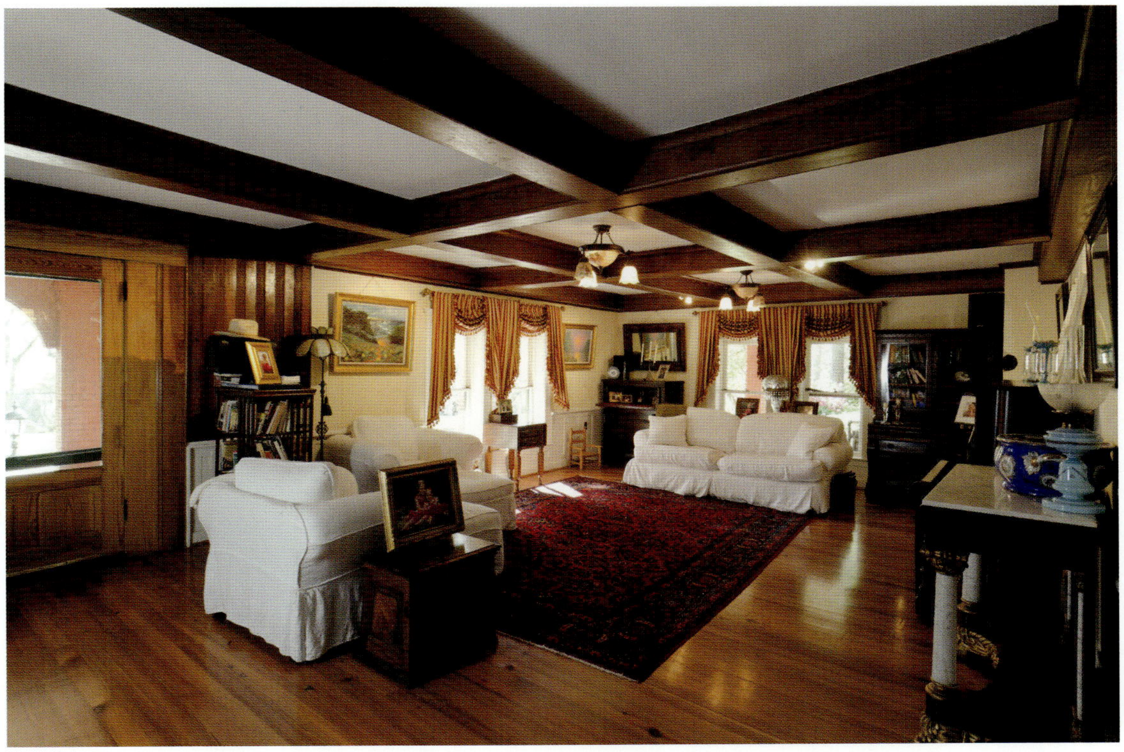

FIGURE 6.09. (Opposite) Upper and Lower Entrances.

This picture, taken from the west side of the interior, shows the noble level of the house with the living room and entrance off the east portico. Down the stairs is the lower lobby and ground floor entryway from Virginia Avenue, now part of the lower family room.

FIGURE 6.10. (Top Right) Living Room.

FIGURE 6.11. (Middle Right) Family Room, on the ground floor.

FIGURE 6.12. (Lower Right) Guest Bedroom, northeast front of the house, off the main living room.

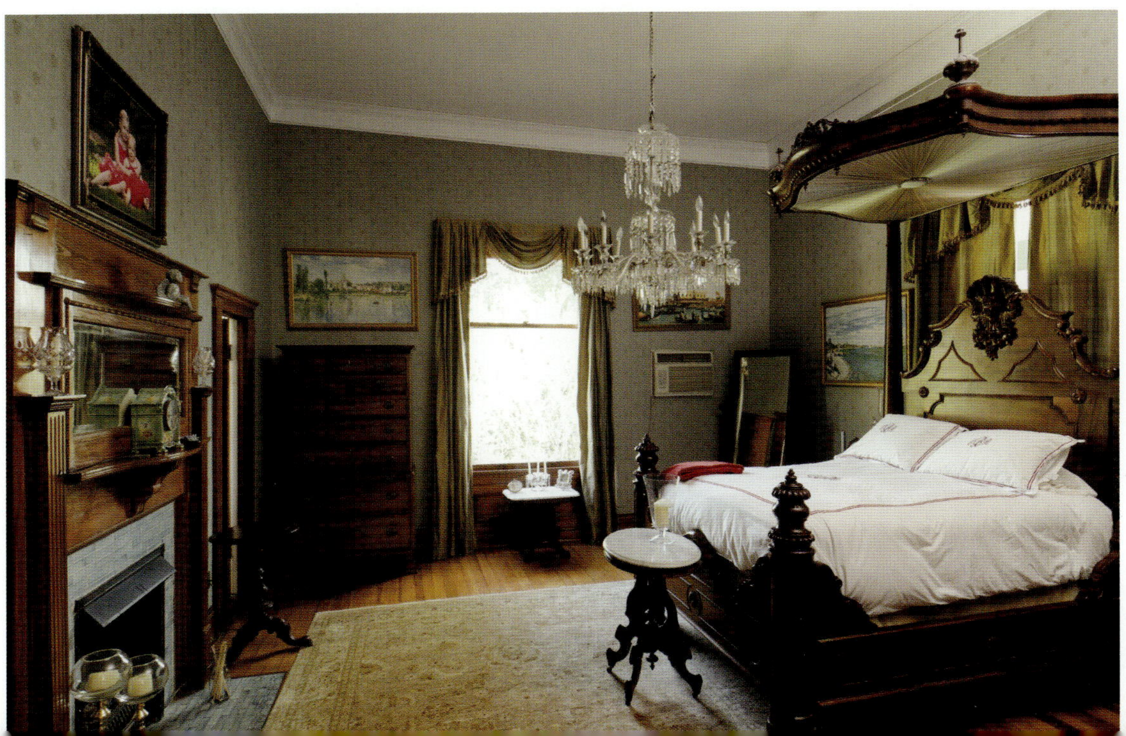

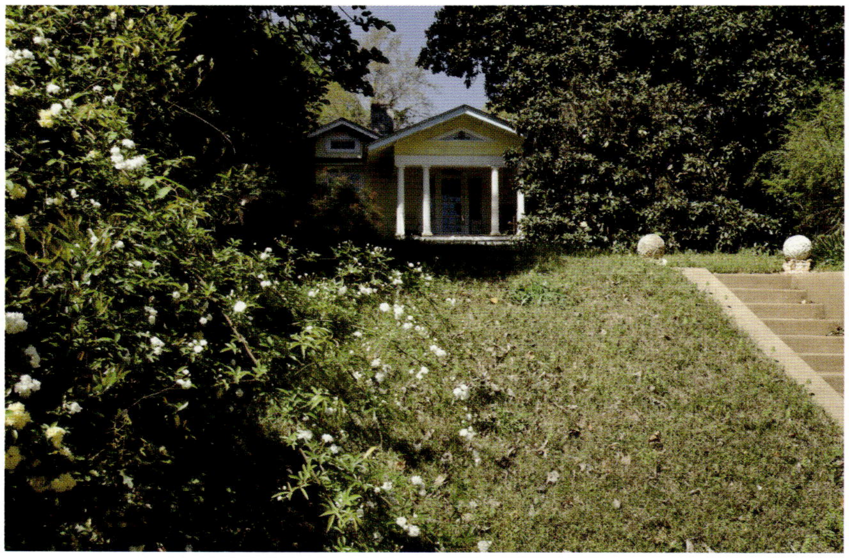

FIGURES 6.13 and 6.14. The Ezell-Davison Cottage from Virginia Avenue and Detail of Façade.

The Ezell-Davison Cottage (1916)

While the inclusions of a discussion of the house at 602 Virginia Avenue is out of any reasonable stylistic or chronological sequence here, the house's intimate relationship to the great Harris House next door warrants overlooking these considerations.

Clytie Augusta Harris, the eldest of June Harris' daughters, was born on March 2, 1882. She was in her mid-teens when the family moved to Forbes Hill. She was the first of the children to marry. After her marriage to Edwin J. Ezell, Jr., and the birth of their daughter in 1913, the grand-parents began the process of attracting the couple to live nearby on Forbes Hill. Harris asked Rulfs to draw plans for a house to build next door–a gift cottage. In 1915, the Harrises transferred the property at 602 Virginia Avenue; it was the north side of his homestead, where their children had played earlier. The house, built by H. T. Crain, was completed in March of 1916.[16] For some unknown reason, the Ezells only lived in the house for three years. In 1919, they moved to Harris, Texas, and sold the house to Clytie's younger sister, Elliece, and her husband, Thomas Scipio Davison, an insurance salesman. Since the public records indicate an evaluation of $3400 at the time of sale to the Davisons, that is not unreasonable to

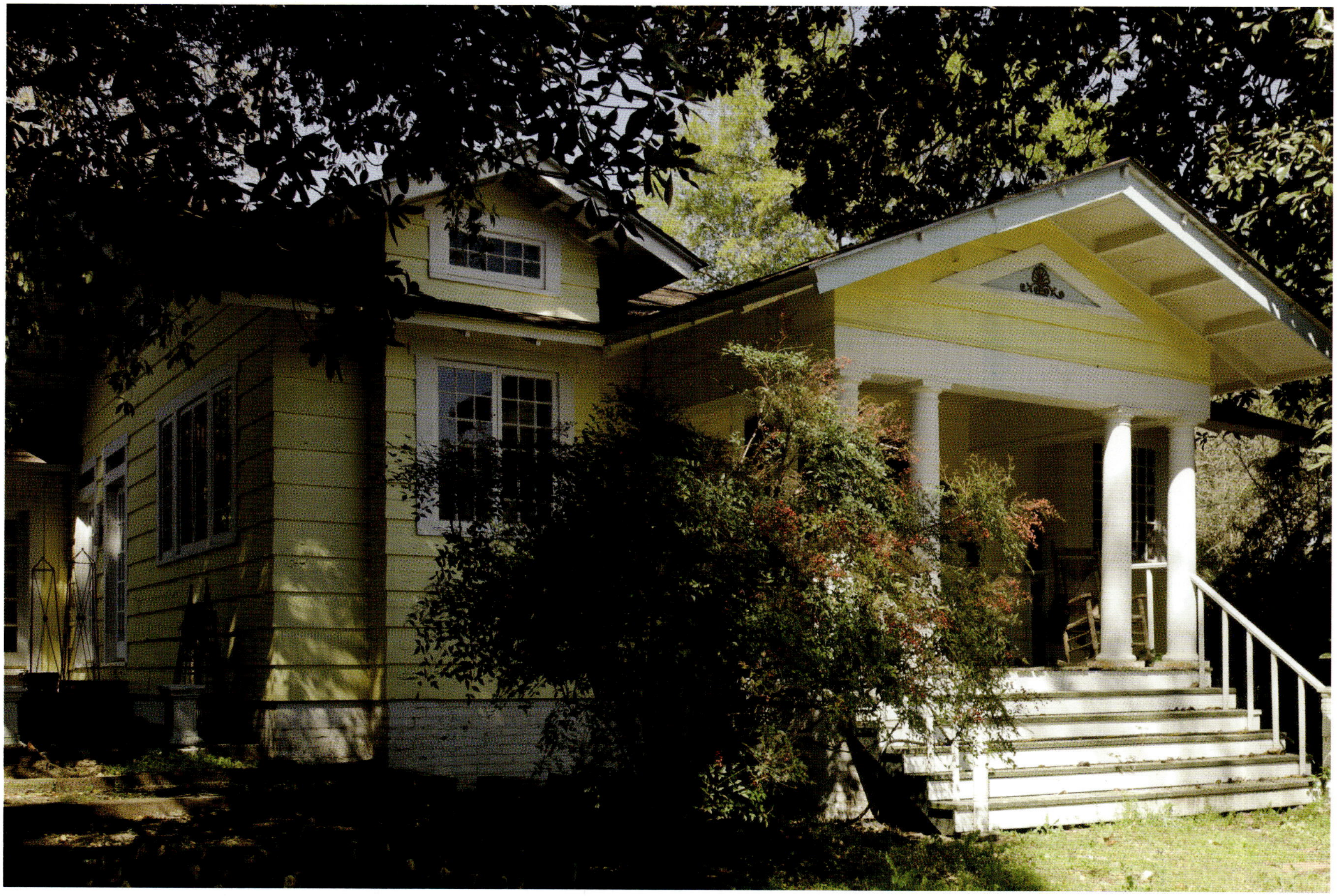

conclude that was near the value in 1916 at the time of construction.[17] The Davisons were in their new home at the time of the 1920 Census.[18]

In an interview with the author in 1976, Tom Davison said that both he and his sister, Emily, were born in the Harris House. Concerning the plans for the cottage by Rulfs, Tom said his grandfather kept the original plans and that, unfortunately, he (Tom) had misplaced them somewhere in the attic. The story Davison told was that June Harris was much chagrined that the cottage, due to inflation in the last twenty years, cost more than his own large house next door.[19] When June Harris and his wife later moved to Austin, the Davisons moved into the big Harris home next door and sold the cottage.[20]

The Ezell-Davison Cottage is typical of the eclectic way Rulfs used elements that were popular in the nation. This house has elements that reflect the shingle-style houses of the late Queen Anne period as well as elements of the Prairie and Bungalow Styles that emerged from the older Arts & Crafts movement. Rulfs had used side gables on many of his early houses, but the use here on the Davison cottage with the low-pitched roof and large overhanging eaves with exposed rafters, seems to be more in line with the Bungalow Style he used with the house designed for Robert Cason about the same time. (See Chapter XII) The architect, however, used certain unique features on this house: oversized cypress siding, projecting square bays with dormers overhead in the roof, a siding-enclosed porch, and windows banked into a Palladian configuration. The large boards of the siding wrap around the corners of the house and projecting bays without vertical interruption. This Rulfs used on no other house. The porch, as originally built, had siding all the way up to the height of the balustrade, short square columns, and wooden benches built into the porch on either side of the door. Since the siding on the entire house was stained very dark or had weathered that way, the appearance of the porch was very heavy. The house in general with this dark siding looked as if it were a mountain lodge or retreat. In order to lighten the effect, Dr. Elizabeth Deanne Malpass, who purchased the house in the 1970s, did what Rulfs had done on many of the houses in town: she inserted a classical element with four Tuscan columns. This cleared away the weightiness of the front portico. Because Rulfs designed the two front dormers as extensions of bay windows below, their windows reflected light into the interior, giving the main front rooms a very airy feeling.

In comparing her home, which cost more, to the Harris House, Dr. Malpass amusingly refers to her house as "a baby grand."

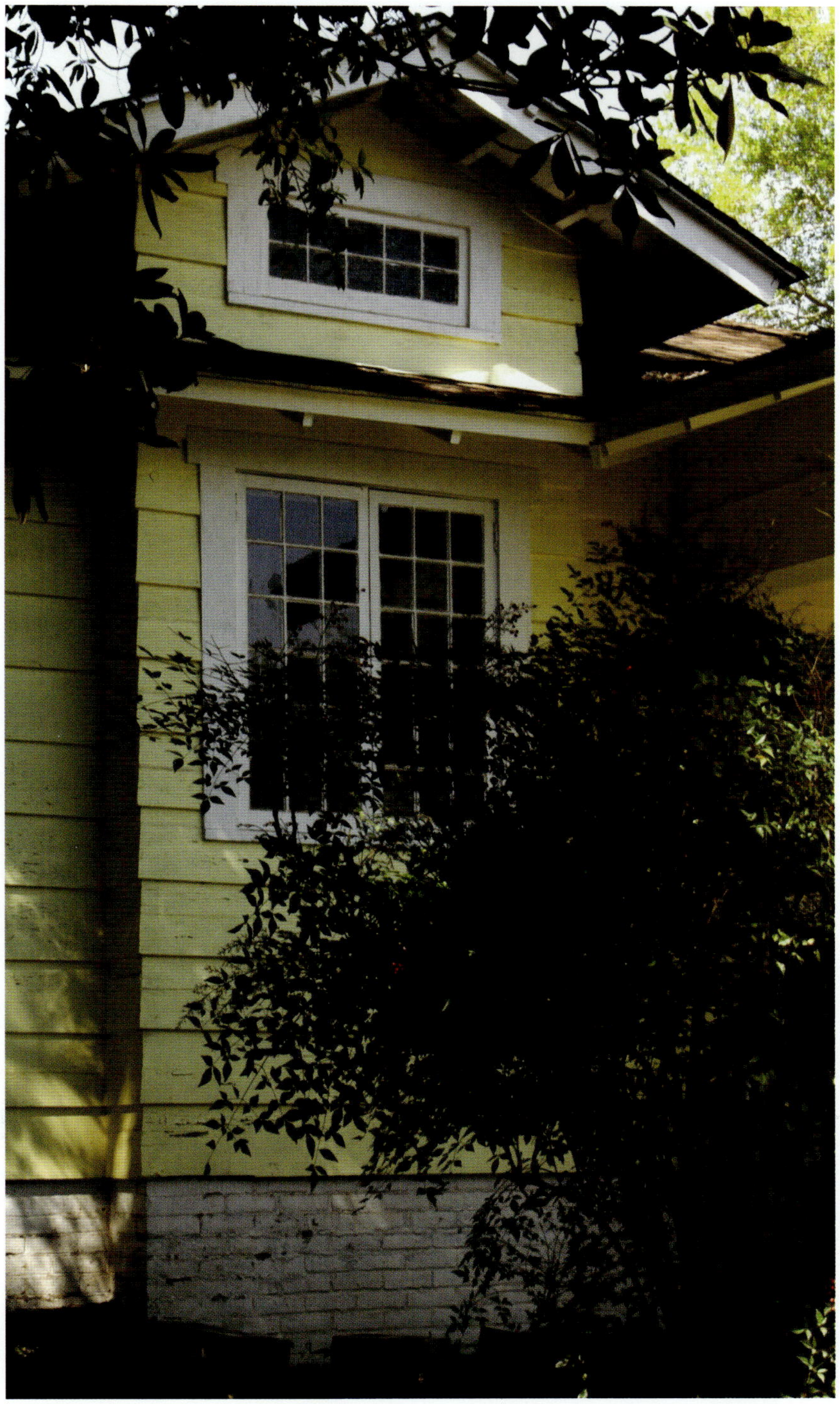

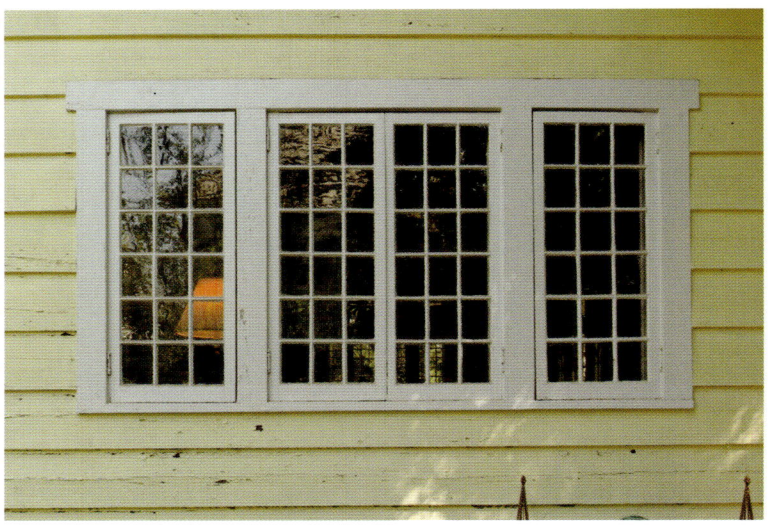

FIGURE 6.15. (Above) Bay-Dormer, Living Room.
The unusual bay-dormers on the east façade of the Ezell-Davison Cottage are clad in large oversized cypress boards, which have no vertical distinctions at the corner. The dormer's window gave added light to both the living room and dining rooms.

FIGURE 6.16. (Left) South Windows, Living Room.

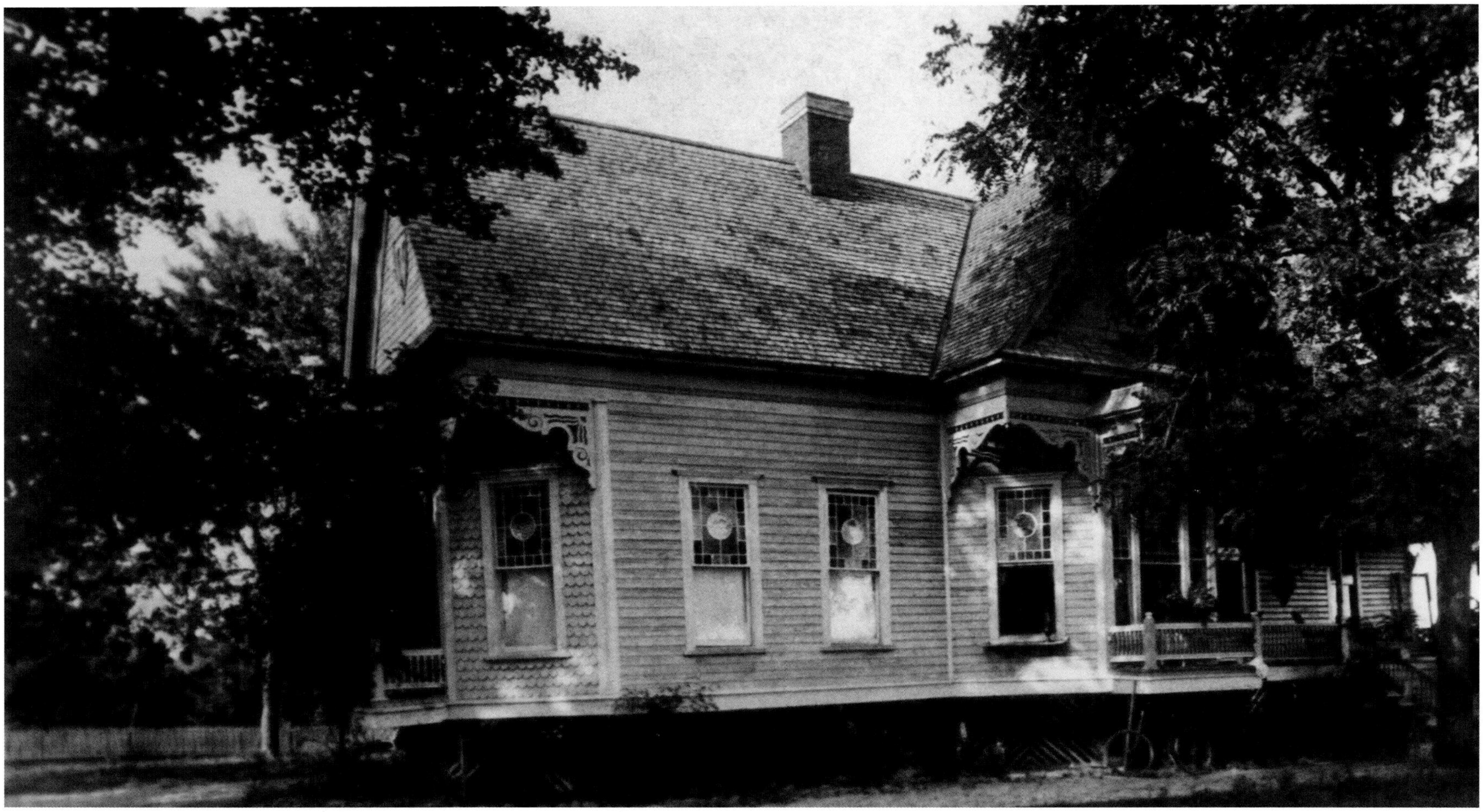

FIGURE 6.17. The Monk House on Cox Street, ca. 1900
Courtesy of the ETRC.

The Robert Monk House (1898)

Robert Columbus Monk (1866-1933), who moved to Nacogdoches in 1890, was one of the young men who made his mark in town by being part of the Mayer & Schmidt Company.[16] At the time of the 1893 staff portrait, Monk was in charge of the grocery department. (See Figure 3.11). Robert and Mamie Monk were one of the first families to join Harris in the move to Forbes Hill.[17] By 1898, at the time he built his home up the street from Harris, Monk had migrated to the hardware department of Mayer & Schmidt. Later, when Schmidt spun off his hardware department into a new entity in 1906, R. C. Monk joined with D. K. Cason, John E. and W. L. Gaston, and Schmidt to form Cason-Monk and Company.[18] (See Chapter VIII.) Schmidt was the vice-president, with Cason serving as president.

At the time the Monks purchased their lot on Cox Street in 1897, they had five children. Emery Monk, the sixth of their ten children, later said he was the first of the siblings to be born in the new house. The town's projected plans to build an elementary school on the west side of the town, which Harris and his real estate partner Robert Lindsey heavily promoted, greatly influenced Monk's decision to move to the west end hills. Emery Monk said all of his siblings attended the school across the street from his home—the West End School, known later as Nettie Marshall.[19] While it was commonplace for those associated with Schmidt to use Rulfs as their architect, Monk and Rulfs were also fraternal brothers in the Knights of Pythias.

Rulfs undertook the design and construction of the Monk House in 1898. To designate the front of the house, Rulfs placed a pediment over the front door on Cox Street. In reality, however, the design took full advantage of the corner lot to give the house two fronts and views down the slopes to the east of the valley below. Prominent steps existed at both ends of the wrap-around porch, as well as sidewalks and inset concrete steps at the curb on both streets. On the north, the porch started from a projecting chamfered bay room and wrapped around to another chamfered bay on the south. The upper part of the one-over-one windows had leaded glass, with decorative circular centers. In 1898, the Tax Office set an evaluation of $1000 on the house; on the 1907 rolls it was valued at $1500.[20] Some time around World War I, the Monks replaced the turned posts supporting the original porch roof with boxed columns to update.[21]

The R. C. Monk House, while moved out of the Virginia Avenue District in 1991, still exists and now stands on County Road 211 off Appleby Sand Road. The present owners of the house are Patrick and Mary Beth Kuhns,[22] who graciously allowed us to take pictures of the house in its lovely new country setting.

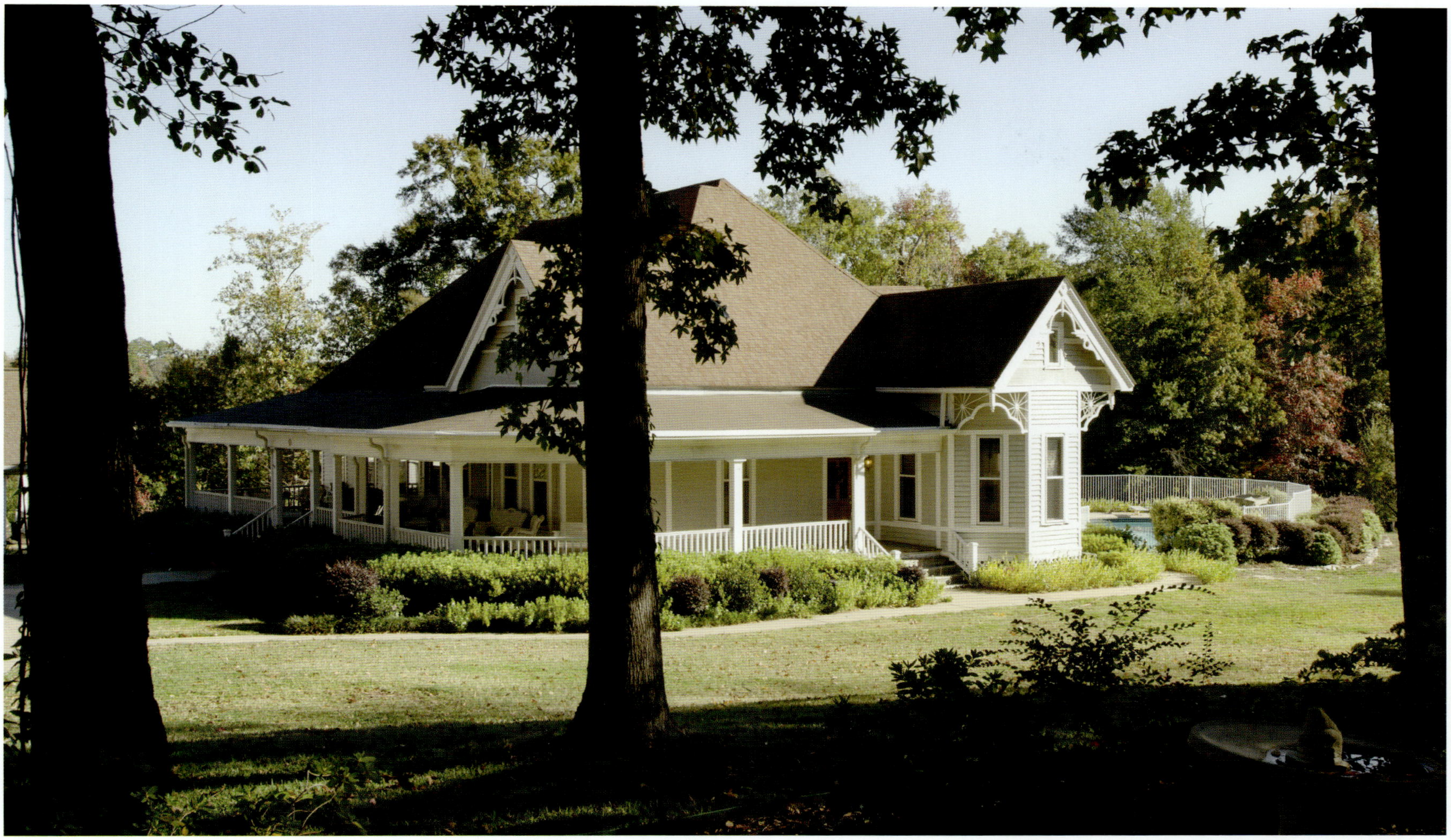

FIGURE 6.18. (Above) The Patrick & Mary Beth Kuhns Home in 2012.

The 19th century look of the Monk House, with its turned posts and balustrades, changed around 1912: the turned posts and balustrades became boxed columns and straight balusters. When the house was moved to the country in the 1990s, the owners widened and extended the west porch and used the east porch to overlook a new pool.

FIGURE 6.19. (Right) The Monk House, 2012, Detail.

The Monk House had a chamfered bay room on the Cox Street side and one on the east side. The tympanum of the front gable had a glass-tinted window, a decorative ornament, and elaborate supporting brackets, which after the move were changed.

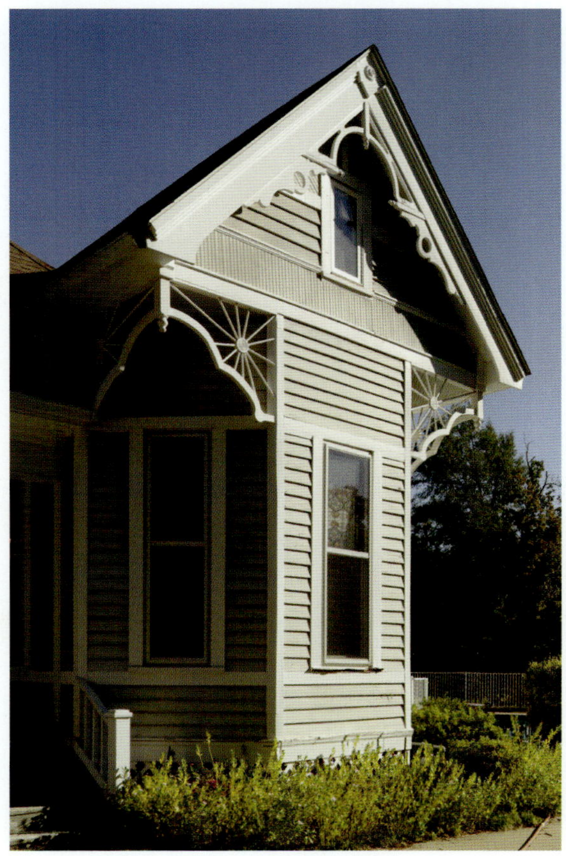

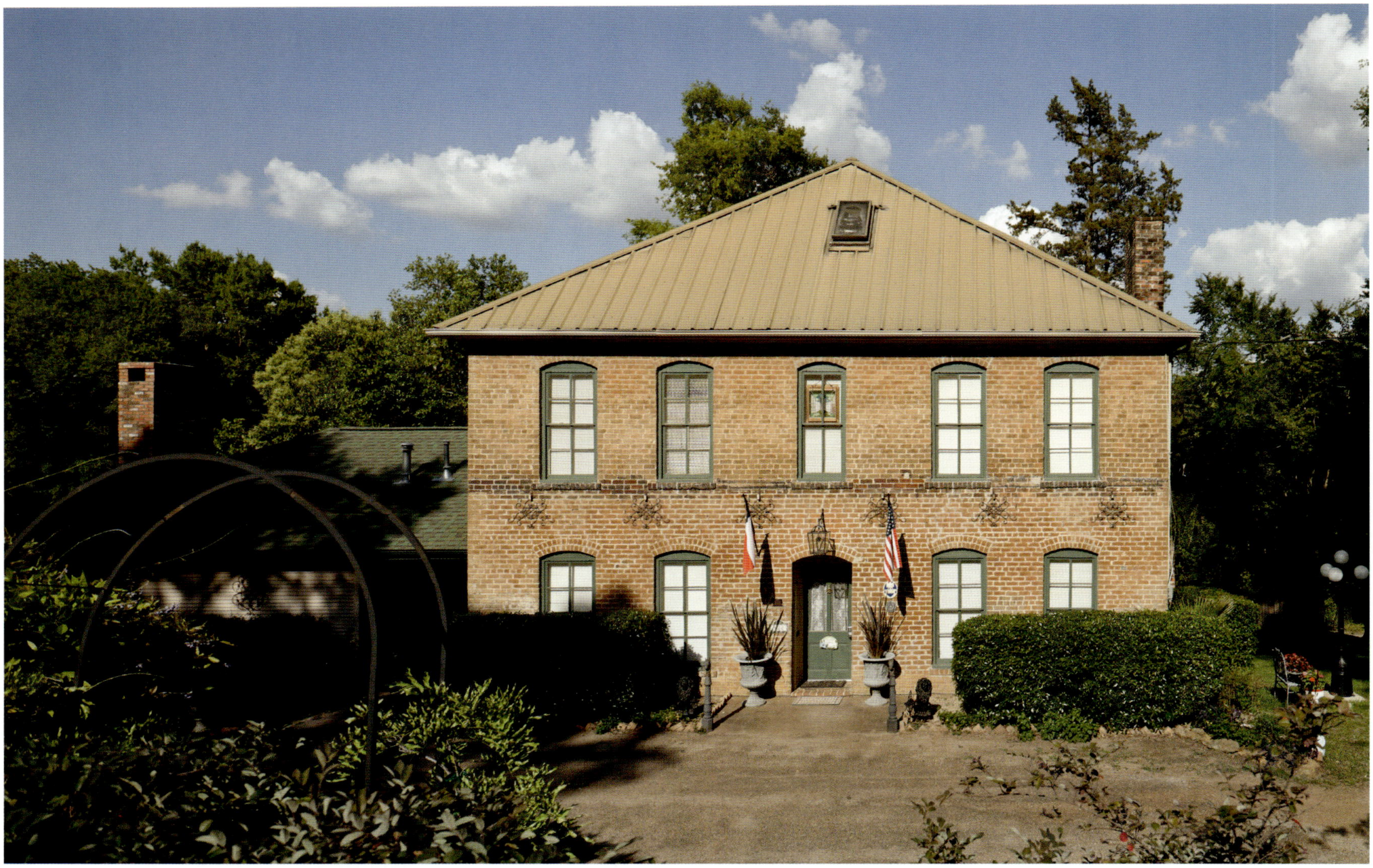

FIGURE 6.20. West Façade of the Henry Austin House, 2011.

The Austin House, now the Brick House Bed & Breakfast, is essentially a two-story square brick house. It has the same window and door arrangements on both the east and west sides. The Sanborn Maps indicate there was no upstairs porch on the west side; the west side possibly included a large screened addition originally. In the 1970s, the Andersons added the extension to the left in this picture.

The Henry L. Austin House (c. 1898)

Henry Austin, a brick-maker and contractor, often worked with Rulfs. There are contracts, newspaper statements, and specifications that testify to their collaborations.[23] Austin received most of his commission as the brick man who helped Rulfs transform the central business district of Nacogdoches from wood into brick. He was part of a triumvirate: Rulfs designed and established the specifications for the buildings; a construc-tion firm, frequently the Rulfs construction firm under the supervision of William Henry Rulfs, supplied the labor and other building materials; and Austin supplied the bricks and masonry materials.[24] (See the section on the First Baptist Church in Chapter 9). The Henry Austin House, however, is an anomaly. It set no trends in Nacogdoches or in Rulfs' architecture.

The Austin House, thought at one time to date to 1886,[25] dates to 1898-99. Austin's ownership of the property is contemporaneous with the second stage of the June Harris House. In order to get the basement-level rooms expanded, Harris offered Austin two lots and $250 for the latter's services and brickwork "as may be desired."[26] Since the brick contractor sold the house at 522 Virginia Avenue rather quickly, Austin probably built the house in order to take advantage of the intense demand for houses, not as a residence for his own family. Certainly, Charles Perkins and Robert Lindsey speculated on North Street in the same way, and Lindsey and Harris later did the same on Irion Hill. Rulfs partnered with all of these men.

As noted earlier, when Rulfs arrived in Nacogdoches, there was only one private brick residence in town—the Orton House on Main between the Square and North Street. The Ortons owned the main brick company in town. Austin, who purchased the Orton firm, is responsible for the second brick residence in town. Both families, no doubt, felt it obligatory to encourage the residential use of bricks.

Rulfs designed the Austin House, like the Harris House, to take advantage of the east view over the Banita Valley and downtown. On the main east front elevation, a large one-story gallery wrapped around the entire south, east, and north sides of the house and virtually doubled the size of the living area of the square brick house. To accentuate the main east

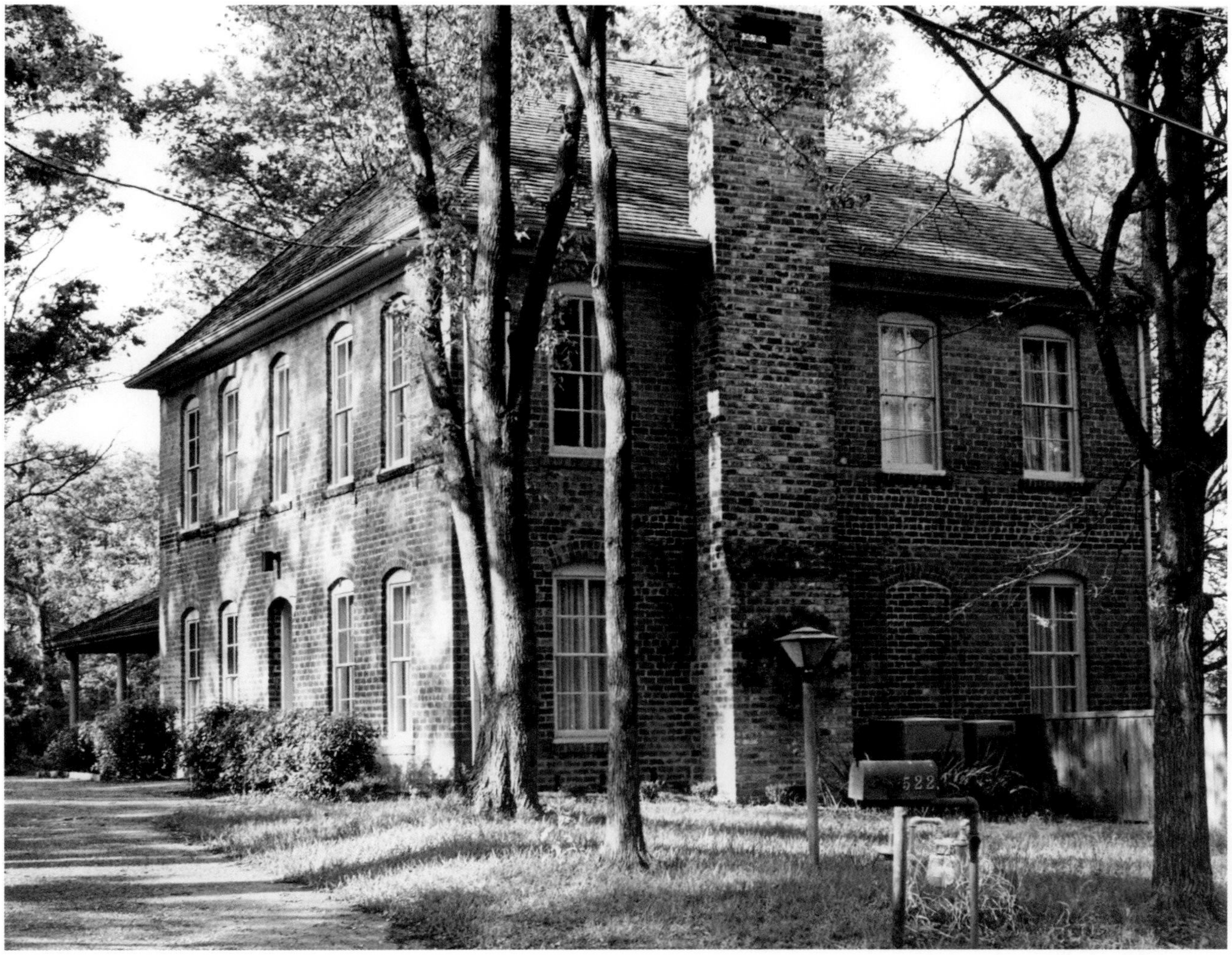

FIGURE 6.21. The Anderson Home in 1976.
Photograph by the author.

FIGURE 6.22. East Façade, Austin House, ca. 1920.
This image, a detail from a much larger photograph, shows how the porches wrapped around the south, east, and north sides of the house. The observation porch over the east entrance, no doubt, offered one of the best views of downtown Nacogdoches of any of the hilltop houses. Photograph courtesy of David and Anne Norton, current owners.

entrance, Rulfs pulled the porch forward on the main east porch level, as he would do later on several other houses, and then placed a pedimented gallery on the second floor. This gave the upper bedrooms access to the same wonderful outdoor view of the valley. (After the removal of the porches, later owners added a wrought iron balcony to offer access to the same view from the upper hall.) While Rulfs regularly used Austin's firm for brick foundations, Rulfs did not normally specify load-bearing masonry walls except in commercial construction, and probably did it this time because Austin wanted to build the house himself. For others, this option was not attractive in an area where wood was so available, inexpensive, and flexible. For the most part, construction of homes with brick veneers did not begin until a decade later.

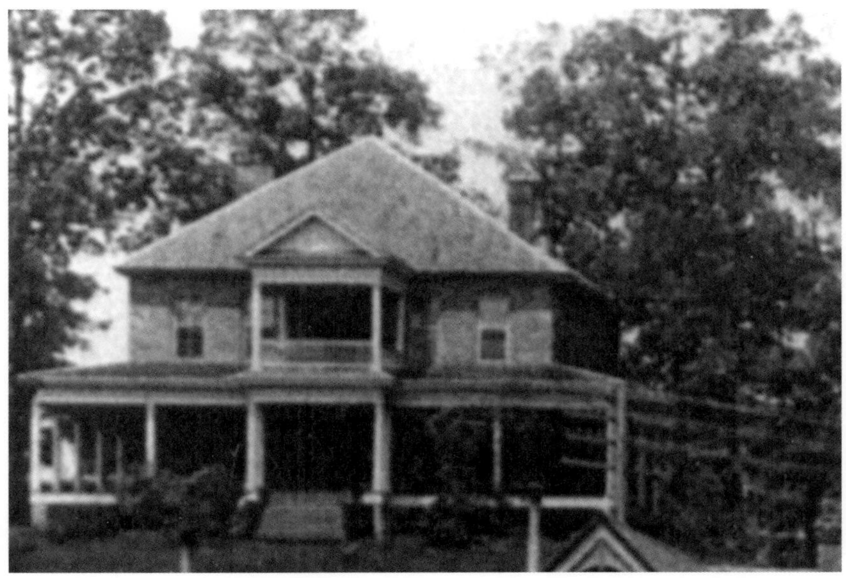

The house may have been built for Bridwell in the first place, much as R. A. Hall had constructed the Schmidt (later Price) House on Mound Street. According to the survey information on the house, "T. F. Bridwell occupied the structure from 1900 to 1910 and was followed by Arthur Marshall, the manager for Nacogdoches Ice & Cold Storage Company, who lived there for the next 19 years. It was the home for Claude M. Barrett, the son of Tol Barrett, until 1961."[27] John and Florence Anderson undertook extensive work on the house in the 1970s to preserve the house. The house today is a popular bed and breakfast owned by Anne and David Norton.[28]

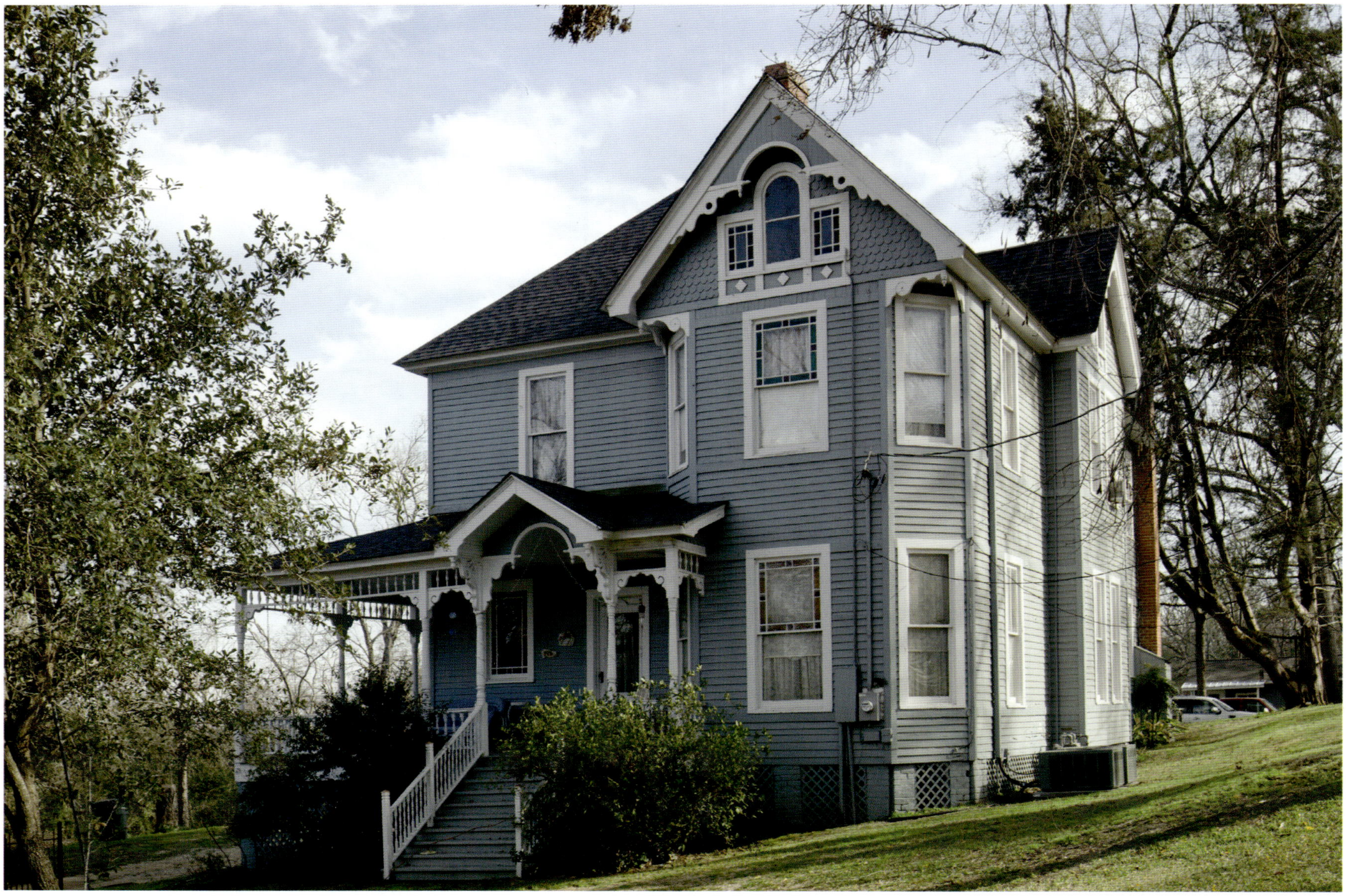

FIGURE 6.23. The Vernon E. Middlebrook House (1898).
Rulfs used the Palladian motifs on the porch pediment and in the tympanum of the north front gable on this house, as he had done on the Stephen Blount House the year before. The house today is the home of Fred and Kay Hooper.

The Judge Vernon E. Middlebrook House (1898)

Judge Vernon Eugene Middlebrook (1865-1930), a lawyer in Nacogdoches who became the County Judge and later a Judge on the Court of Civil Appeals,[29] purchased his homestead on West Main on August 21, 1897.[30] Although the land was not purchased from the Harris-Lindsey property, it was part of the same land speculation that accompanied the rush to the hills west of town (as was the Cooper House across the street). W. U. Perkins at one time considered moving to the high lots overlooking the city and owned this lot.[31] Unfortunately, the Sanborn Maps do not take in the West Main houses until 1922—when the house appears for the first time. The date of the Middlebrook House is not difficult to determine, however. The Judge bought the property in 1897; and his daughter, Miss Mamie Middlebrook (1899-1989), said she was born in the house (January 19, 1899) shortly after it was finished.[32] In discussions with the author, Miss Mamie also confirmed that Rulfs was the architect who designed and oversaw the construction of the house. She, like Miss Gladys Hardeman, was good friends with Wilhelmina Rulfs Thompson.[33] (The author was fortunate enough to be Miss Mamie's neighbor on Church Street from 1970 to her death in 1989.) When the Middlebrook family decided to sell the property in 1969, an affidavit of ownership documenting the family's ownership was necessary because the parents had died intestate.[34] One reason the house is in such good condition is that it has only had three owners: the Middlebrooks (1898-1969), Dick and Suzie Lower (1969-1983), and Fred and Kay Hooper after 1983.[35]

According to Suzie Lower, who purchased the house from the Middlebrook heirs, the sunrises, sunsets, and night views are exceptional from the northeast porch. It was their favorite place for parties.[36]

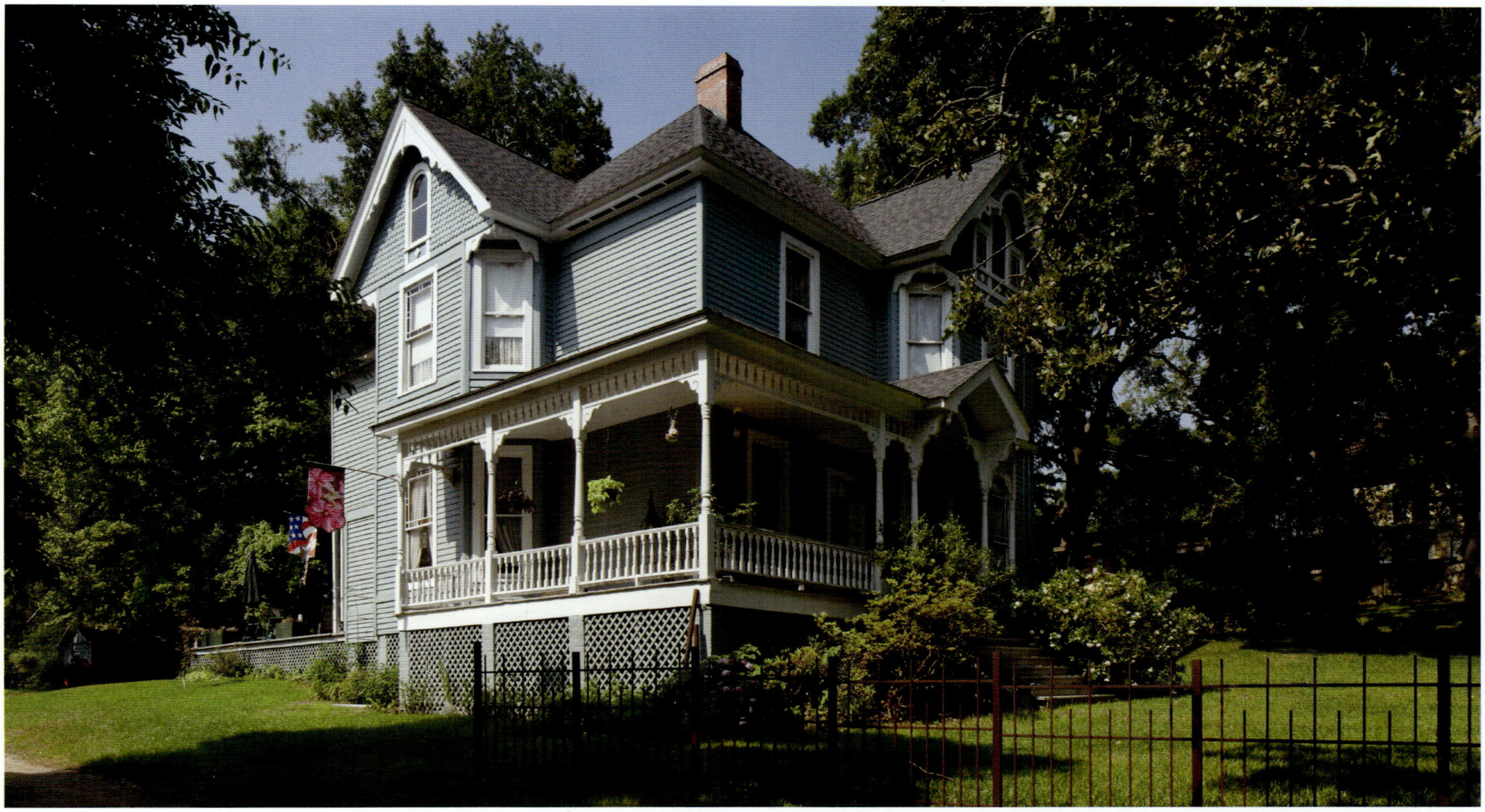

FIGURE 6.24. The Northeast Corner of the Middlebrook House.
The house has a steep hipped roof with several gable projections. Between the two-story chamfered bay gable on the north and the east, the architect wrapped a porch around the northeast corner of the house. The front porch thus took advantage of the special view over the downtown area. By comparison to the Stephen Blount House of the previous year, the architect used restrained Queen Anne elements on this house.

FIGURE 6.25. (Below) The Suzie and Dick Lower Home.
The Lowers' daughter, Sarah, born in 1967, is running across the front yard. The 1970 photograph is courtesy of Suzie Lower.

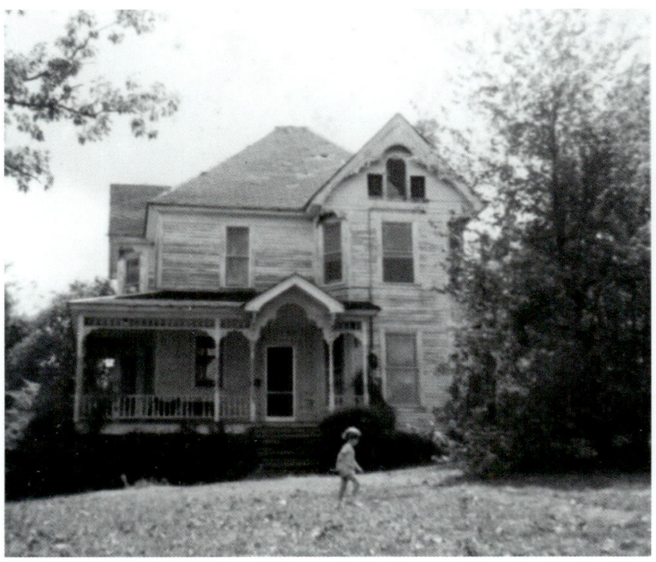

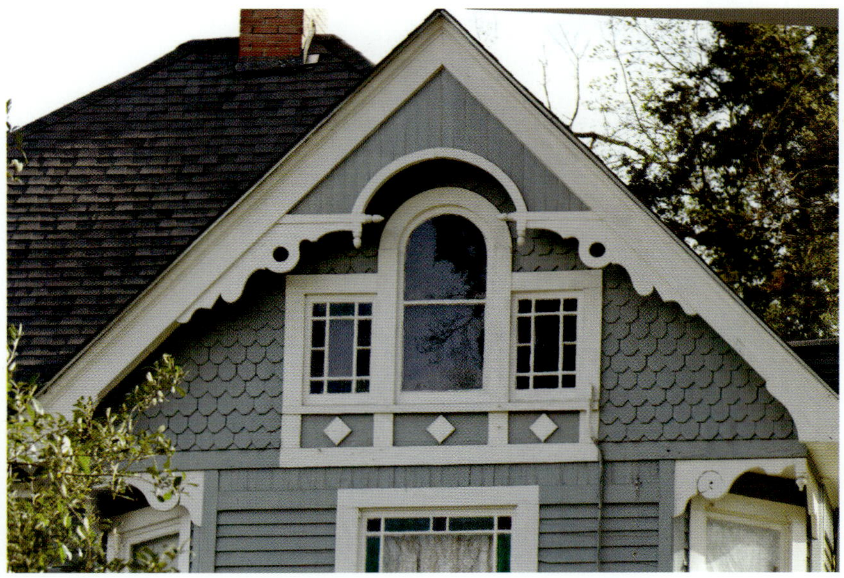

FIGURE 6.26. Palladian Window, North Gable
The tympanum, which overhangs the chamfered or cutaway windows below, has many decorative elements in addition to the Palladian window: brackets, fish-scale shingles, and graceful bargeboards with an arched ornament at the crest. The windows on this north front are lined with art glass of various colors. These elements stand out as a result of the contrasts in paint.

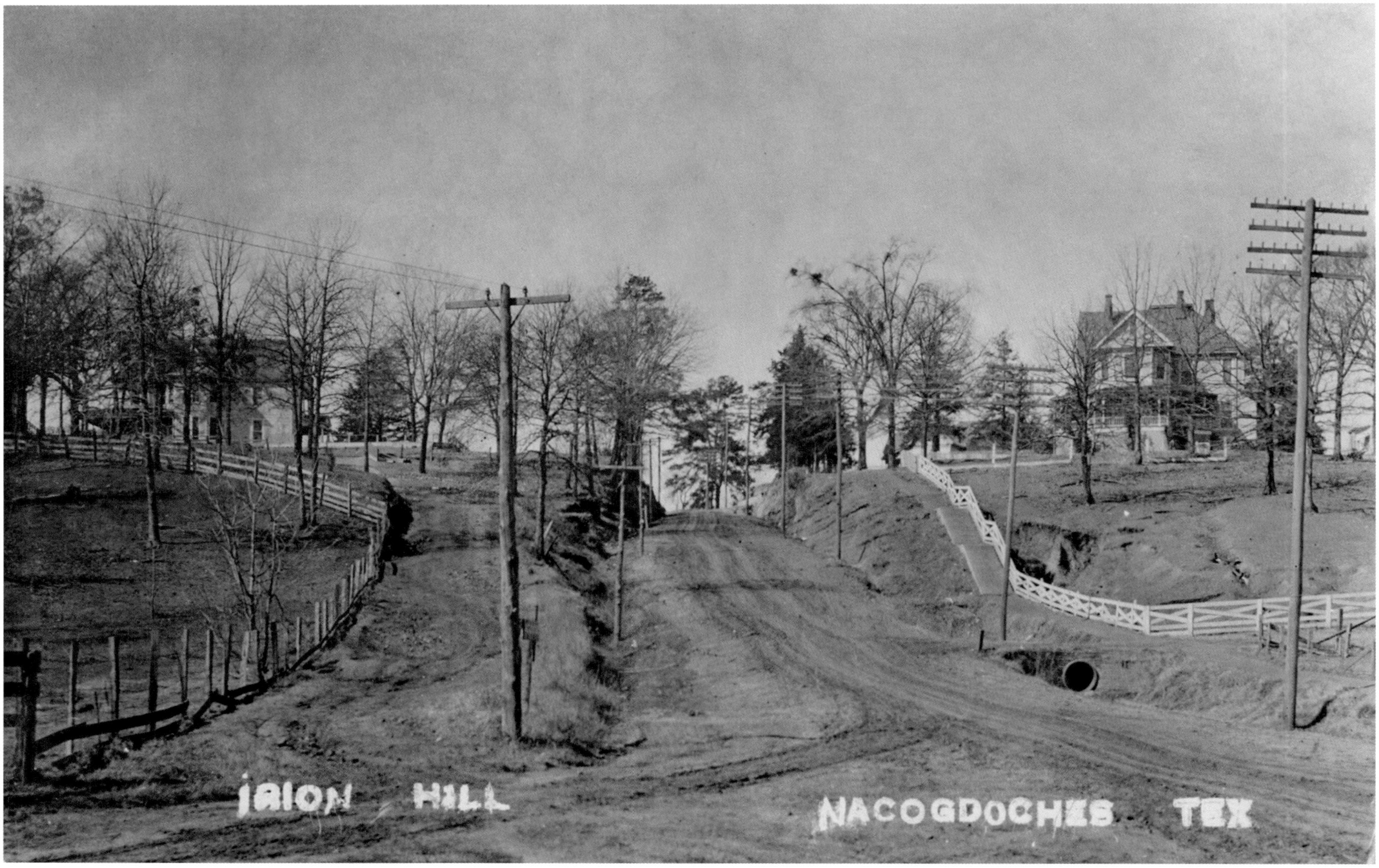

FIGURE 6.27. Irion Hill–West Main Street, ca. 1910.

This postcard picture of West Main Street and Irion Hill shows three Rulfs houses. On the left, virtually out of the picture, is the Judge Vernon Middlebrook House (1898); only the steps are showing. The most visible house on the left is the Phillip Sanders House (1901). On the right, the Harry H. Cooper House (1898). All of these houses had wonderful views of downtown Nacogdoches; today trees obscure much of the view. Courtesy of ETRC.

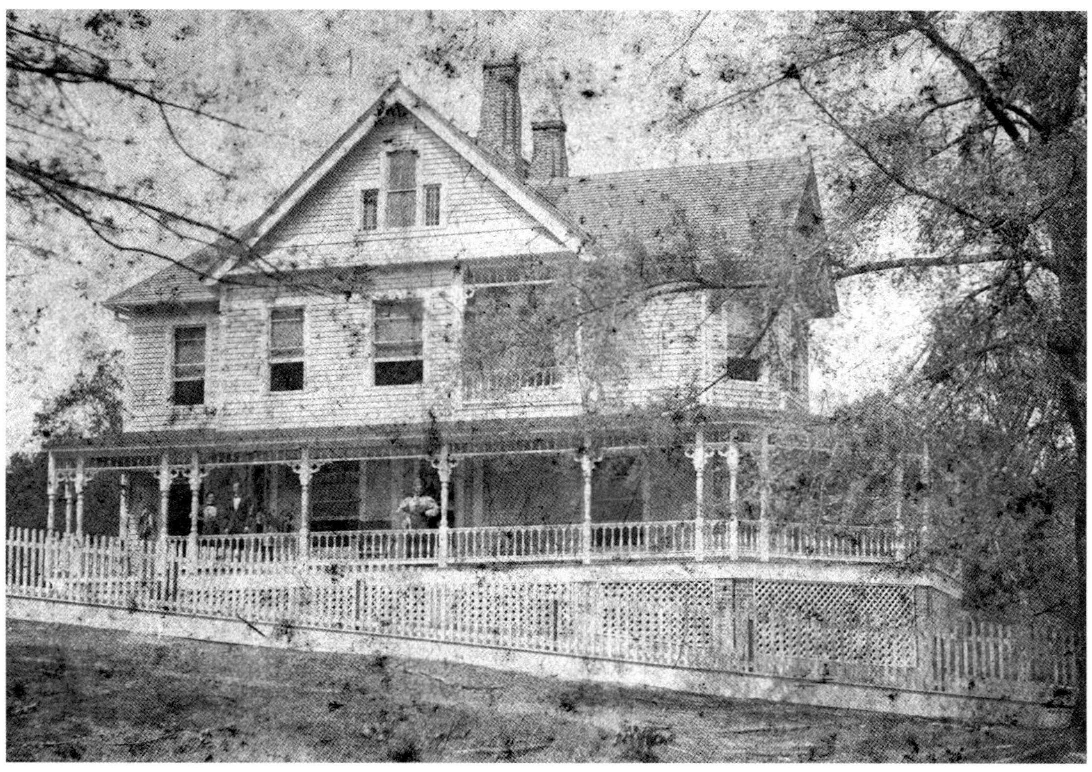

FIGURE 6.28. The Harry Cooper House, ca. 1899.

This commemorative photograph of the Cooper House, taken shortly after completion, shows the first inhabitants of the house on the front porch: Harry and Catherine Cooper and Mary Hoffman. Although degraded, the photograph is being used because it shows the original relationship of the house to West Main Street. The fence at the edge of the property also shows the degree of the slope. The street, lowered more than twenty five feet in subsequent decades, now has the house isolated on a lonely hill. Photograph compliments of Cole Sessom, present owner of the house.

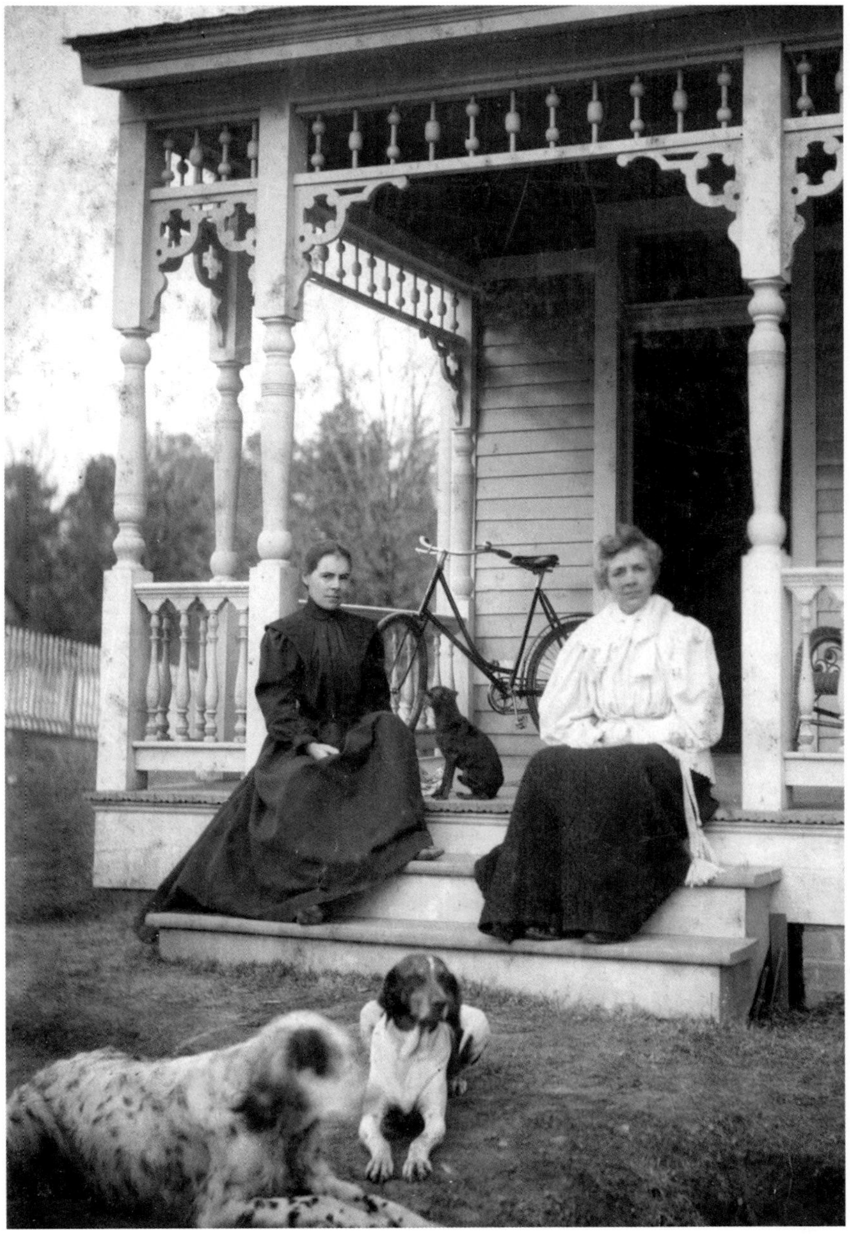

The Harry H. Cooper House (1898)

Harry Hunsecker Cooper (1859-1939) was a young Pennsylvanian who came to Nacogdoches around 1890 as a salesman for the Clark Shoe Company. He liked the town and decided to stay, opening a business called the "5¢ Store" on East Main. (See Figure 1.20). Shortly after his arrival in town, in 1892 the local Stone Fort Rifle Volunteers elected Cooper as their second Captain, a signal honor for a newly arrived "Yankee."[37]

With the idea of getting in on the rush to the hills started by June Harris, Cooper bought property on Irion Hill in 1896.[38] 1897 was a big year in Cooper's life. First, at age thirty-eight, he became a Major in the Third Regiment, Texas Volunteer Infantry.[39] Second, he began his first term as the United States Postmaster in Nacogdoches (1897-1913); he would serve a second term from 1923 to 1927.[40] Third, he borrowed money from the Wettermark Bank to get a new house under way.[41] Fourth, he returned in late 1897 to Pennsylvania to marry his childhood sweetheart Catherine Hofmann.[42] Cooper brought Catherine and her unmarried sister, Mary Hofmann, back to Texas; they all lived at the Banita Hotel while the house was being built.[43] This house has only had three owners: the Coopers (1898-1944); Colonel William B. and Mary Bates (1944-1995); Cole and Sidney Sessom (1995-present).[44]

The architect's affinity for the hillsides can be seen in this house. The owner and Rulfs arranged the house to take full advantage of the views and the downward slope of the hill, as Rulfs earlier did with the Harris House. However, Main Street, unlike Virginia Avenue, does not parallel Irion Hill. Because Cooper as the new postmaster wanted a Main Street address, Rulfs designed a plan that was less formal. On the street façade, he placed the entrance off-center at the west end. This eliminated the need for dramatic front steps or two-level entries. Rulfs reserved the slope of the hill and the views for the east porches and rooms. The Cooper solution required only two risers to enter the front porch and front door.

FIGURE 6.29. Catherine Cooper (On the right) and Mary Hoffmann (Her Sister), ca. 1900.

When built, the entrance steps to the Cooper House were on Main Street. Later when the engineers lowered the elevation of the street, the Coopers added steps at the west end of the porch and changed the address to Cooper Street, as seen in the photograph below. Photograph compliments of Cole Sessom.

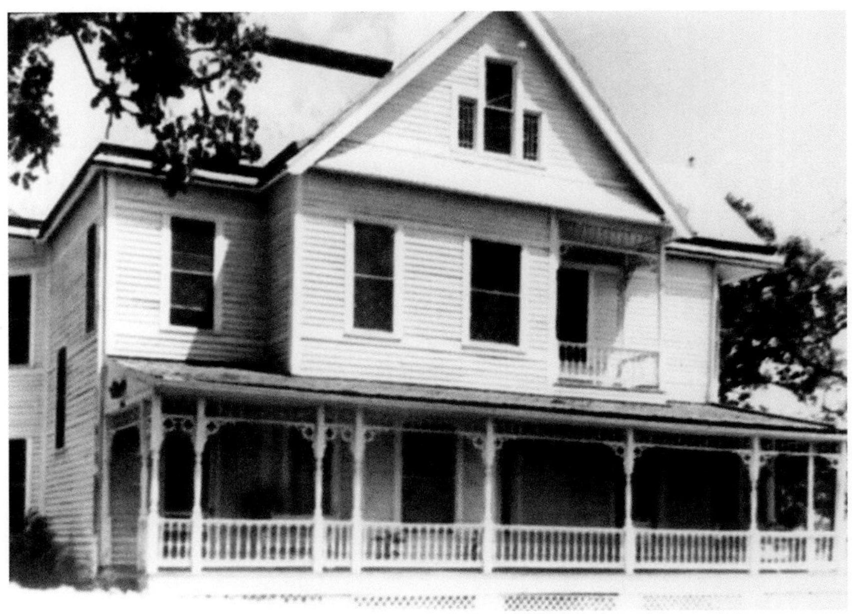

FIGURE 6.30. (Right) Archival Picture of the Cooper House.

This picture of the Cooper House, date unknown, shows the Palladian window in the large gable before its replacement by louvers for the attic fan. The porch entrance in this picture is on the west end. The pocket-porch off the second story sitting room is more clearly visible in this picture. Courtesy of ETRC.

The Cooper House is more like a modern, panoramic lodge house at a mountain retreat than a private home. Its main feature was the east-facing gable wing, with two-story chamfered bay rooms, overlooking downtown Nacogdoches. (See FIGURES 6.27-6.28) The whole center of the main floor was oriented to take part in the view. A small entrance hall, more a place for coats and umbrellas than reception, opened immediately into a suite-like space consisting of a generous living room and dining room, around which wrapped additional living spaces in the form of enveloping porches. Since there were no steps descending from these porches, their perspectives were their reasons for existence. The formal nature of the interior divisions–Ionic wood columns on plinth bases, seem to the modern eye almost out of character with the outward orientation of the rooms and the lodge-like treatment of the fireplace. The mixture seem to reflect the compromises that both Rulfs and Cooper (northerners living in southern climates) found themselves adjusting to in many areas of their lives. The paneling in the stairwell is noteworthy. According to Mary Bates, Cooper took a particular interest in the stairs, making sure they were built along Masonic principles; he was a very active Mason.[45] Rulfs used a similar image of this house's gable front to design the Phillip Sanders House directly across West Main Street.

The presence of a sister-in-law in the house from the beginning may have led Cooper to configure the upstairs bedrooms into suites. The master bedroom, a large chamber in the east bay, had its own dressing room and private upstairs balcony (later closed in). The photographs showing the house at the turn of the century indicate few large trees downhill from the house. The views of the downtown, no doubt spectacular in 1900, are still impressive and, according to the present owner, wonderful when the town holds fireworks displays.[46] Although the east side of the house had great height for the purpose of storage, Cooper brought his Pennsylvanian traditions with him to East Texas and insisted on having a basement dug under the house as a place to store his wine. Because of the depth needed to reach ground water for a well, Cooper had a large cistern built under the house to collect rainwater for use on the property.

The most dramatic change in the house's appearance today has nothing to do with the architect, but to the fact that the level of West Main Street has changed so dramatically. When built, as shown in photographs on these pages, the front entrance was only slightly higher than the grade of the dirt roadway. Mary Stewart Duncan, the niece of Rulfs, first pointed out this important circumstance to the author in discussing the house in the 1970s.[47] The address was always on Main Street, as was the Sanders House across the street, until the grade level forced the use of the side streets as the entrance. The removal of a small span of porch rail made this reorientation complete; the entrance was always at the crest of the property.

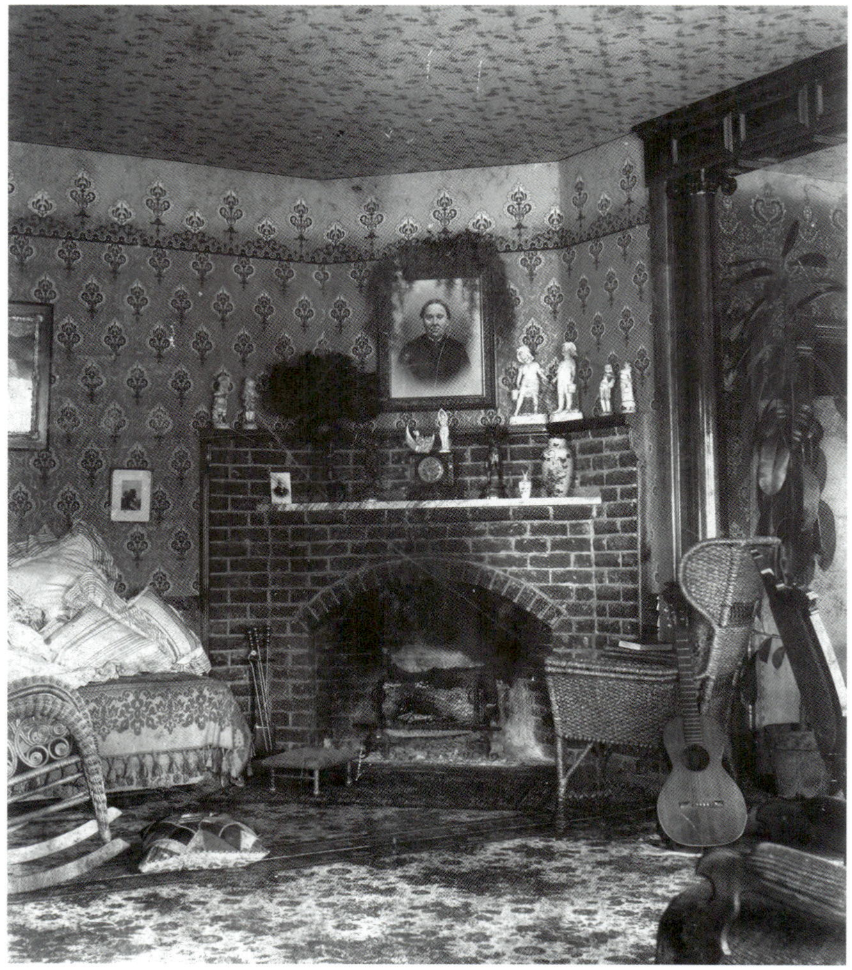

FIGURE 6.31. (Above) Living Room, ca. 1910.
This period photograph of the Cooper living room shows the Ionic columns between the living and dining rooms. The design of the corner fireplace, with a wooden mantel was more characteristic of Cooper's Pennsylvanian heritage than the work of D. Rulfs. The room is decorated for a holiday with greenery draped over the picture of probably one of their parents. A favorite guitar leans up against the wicker chair. Photograph compliments of Cole Sessom.

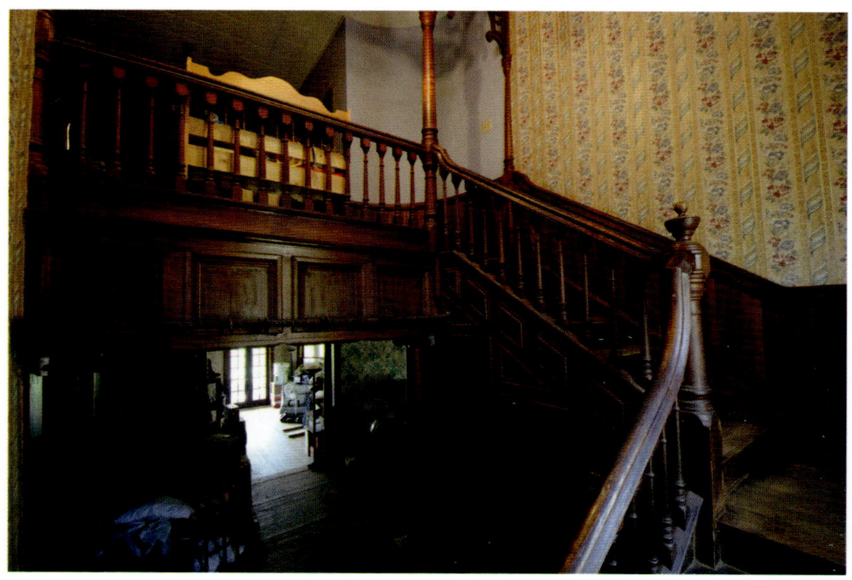

FIGURE 6.32. (Right) Stairwell, Cooper House.
This picture of the stairwell looks through the living room, with the fireplace on the left, to the dining room. The dining room, completely surrounded by the great porch system, had fantastic views of downtown Nacogdoches. Both the staircase and the entrance to the dining room have unfluted Ionic columns on plinth bases.

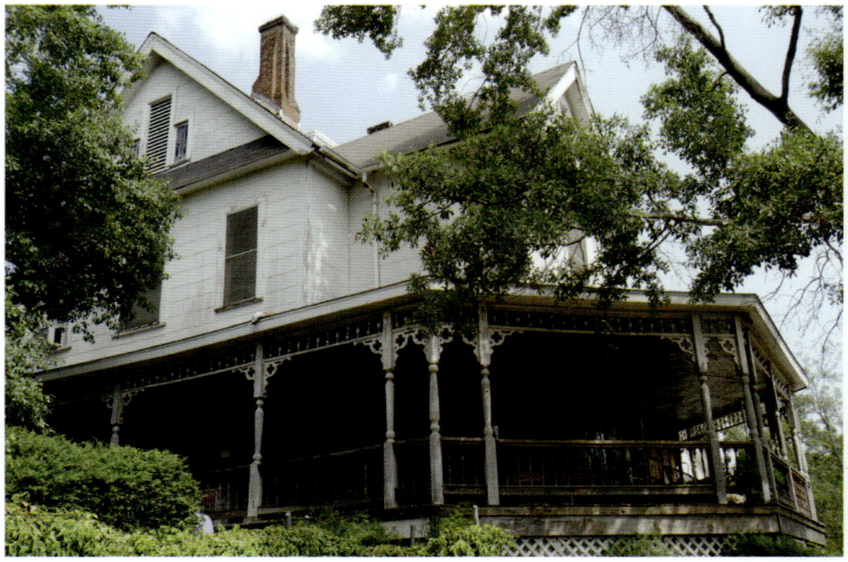

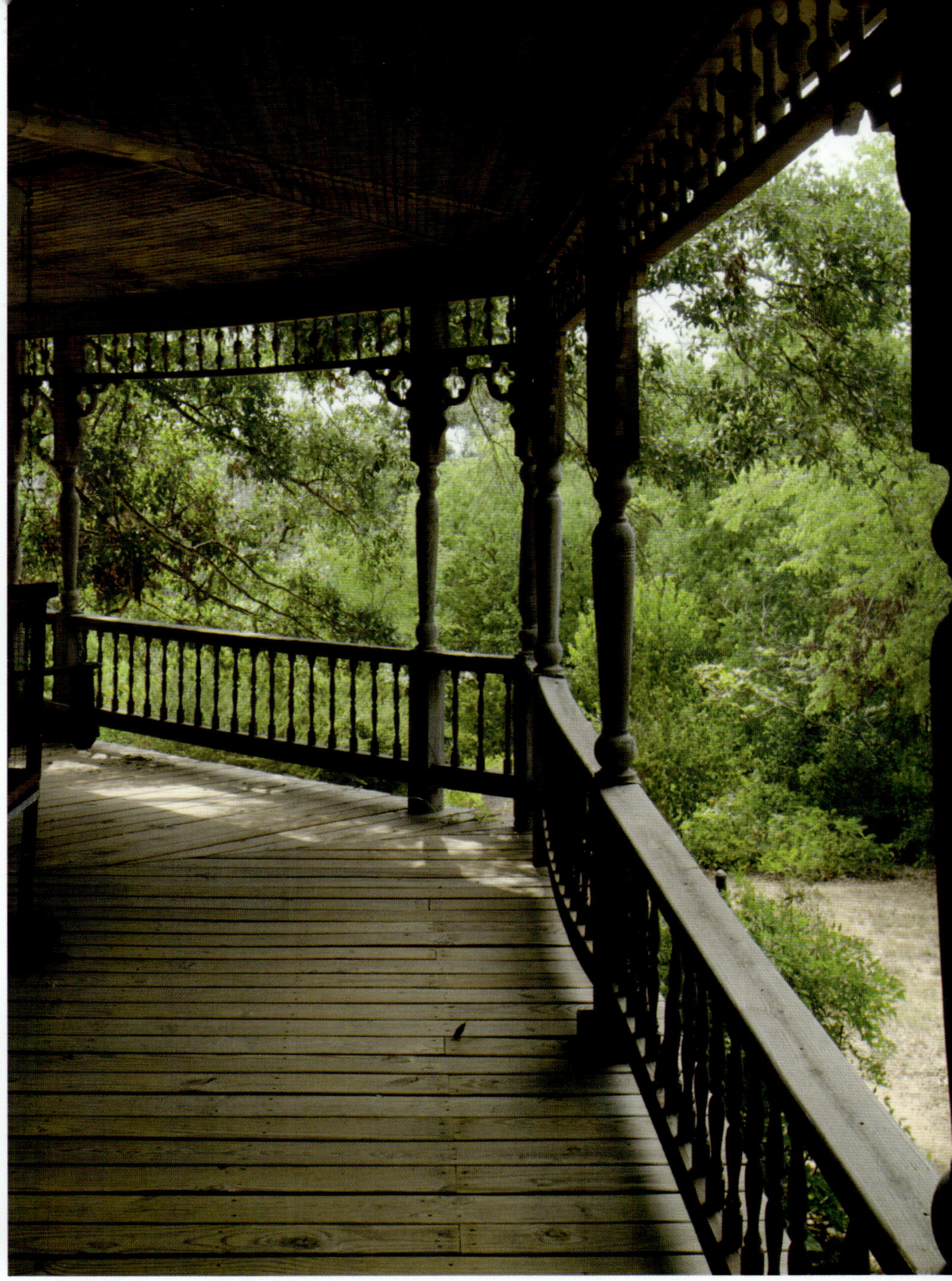

FIGURES 6.33 to 6.35. (Above, Below and Right) The Southeast Porch of the Harry Cooper House and Bracket Detail.

The defining feature of the Cooper House was its system of porches. One continuous porch wrapped from the west, along the entire south façade, and around the east bay of the house. The portion around the dining room in the east bay was the main outdoor living room of the house. To make it more comfortable, at one time, the owners screened the entire eastern portion of the gallery.

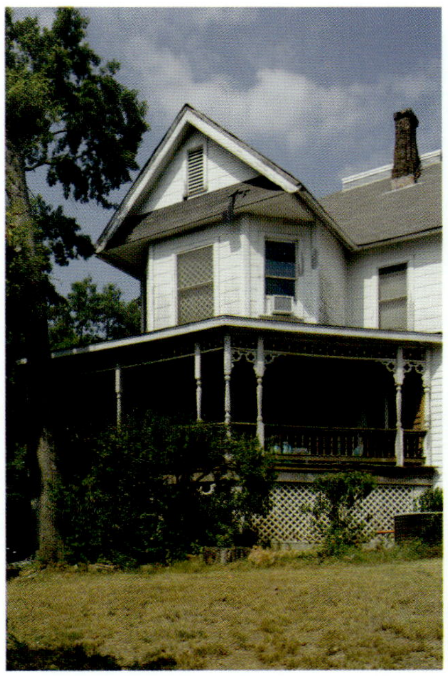

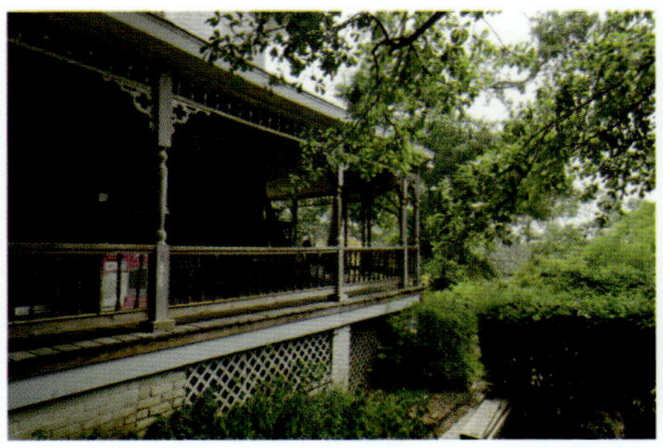

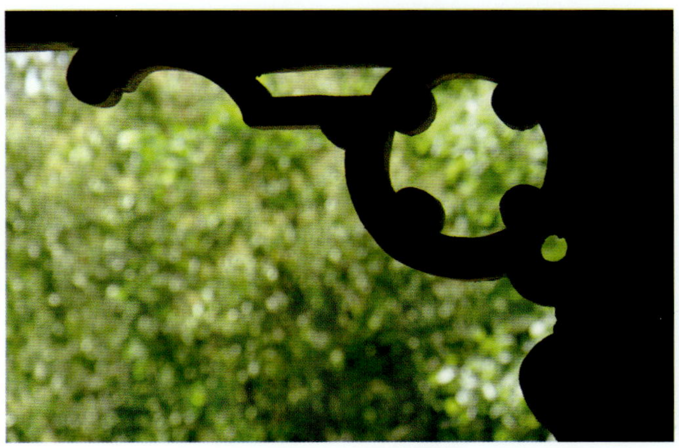

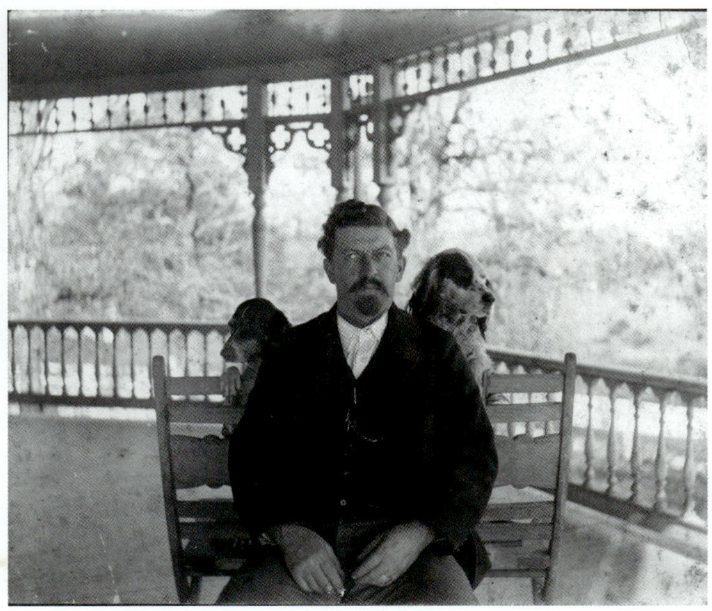

FIGURE 6.36. (Right) Harry Cooper, ca. 1900.

This period photograph, taken not long after his house was finished, shows Cooper and his beloved dogs on the chairs behind him at the southeast corner of the porch. Photograph compliments of Cole Sessom.

The William and Amanda Sanders House (1898)

When Phillip D. Sanders (1815-1890) moved from Alabama to Nacogdoches County in 1850, he already had one son, William Toombs (1849-1898); his second son, Phillip Monroe (1850-1921) was born in Texas in 1850.[48] The family originally lived in the Douglass area. As Nacogdoches opened up to trade in agricultural products after the arrival of the railroad, the two sons, Will and Phillip ("Dode"), became involved in facilitating the movement of cotton from the farms to the railroad. A rail car would hold about fifty bales of cotton; but if the bales were compressed, it would hold over three times as many. The establishment of the Cotton Compress Company in 1897 made the cotton trade more profitable for everyone; the Sanders brothers' contacts in the county suddenly became much more valuable. They built a large brick warehouse near the railroad tracks and purchased the Summers Building on the North Square in Rulfs' First Brick Block.[49]

Both Will and Phillip purchased land on Irion Hill[50] and made attempts to sell lots, but it was not until after Harris began the rush to the hills and talk of an elementary school commenced that sales began to become realistic. Will's homestead was on the west side of South Sanders Street. His property was relatively level; and, therefore, more marketable, but it would be the next generation who would sell the lots.[51] Will's land was more suitable for building; Phillip had more extensive holdings, but much of it was not suitable for building and never worked as a subdivision. The 1922 Sanborn Map was the first to show the houses on Irion Hill.[52]

D. Rulfs built houses for both of the Sanders brothers on Irion Hill. The Will Sanders House is the older of the two. The house most likely dates to the first part of 1898. After the house was started, Will died suddenly in October and left Amanda to complete the house. She had seven children living with her, ranging in ages from three to sixteen.[53] Their oldest child, Anna Virginia (Virgie), would become a formidable woman.[54] She not only helped her mother, Amanda, carry on with Will's investments and partnership with Phillip, but she also helped to develop a subdivision with the family's land holdings—the A. V. Sanders Subdivision.[55] To keep things running, Miss Virgie rented rooms in her family home. Garland Roark, the novelist, was one of her tenants.[56] Miss Virgie founded the Nacogdoches Historical Society and led the drive in 1936 to get the State to reconstruct a Replica of the Old Stone Fort. She kept her family home in good condition and lived there until her death in 1966. R. J. and Audrey Quick purchased the house the next year.[57]

The Sanders House at 220 South Sanders Street has undergone many renovations. While the basic outlines of the front porch are the same, the current owners added the concrete floor and changed the balustrades. The two-story porch system at the back of the house was later completely enclosed. The brick skirt, as with most houses, came later as a way to eliminate drafts and facilitate heating. Rulfs probably used this same plan and same window arrangement for the Butt House on East Main. Rulfs would have enjoyed the irony of placing similar houses on the top of both hills. The oval front door and sidelights are somewhat unusual for Rulfs, but he did use similar doors on the E. C. Branch House on Virginia and in a house in Garrison; they were readily available in the catalogues to order. The placement of the windows across the front, the use of horizontal banding over the windows, and the decorative gable-dormer, piercing the massive hip roof, are common for the architect during the period.[58]

The original floor plan was very standard for Rulfs: an entrance hall with a staircase, large pocket doors for access to the parlor, a dining room (also with large pocket doors) and kitchen to the west, and four rooms upstairs. The parlor and dining room, as well as the upstairs bedrooms on the north have corner fireplaces—all four of them. The dining room, with its north square bay and its attractive corner fireplace and mantel, is one of the nicest rooms in the house. The other interior rooms of the house have received considerable alterations over the years.

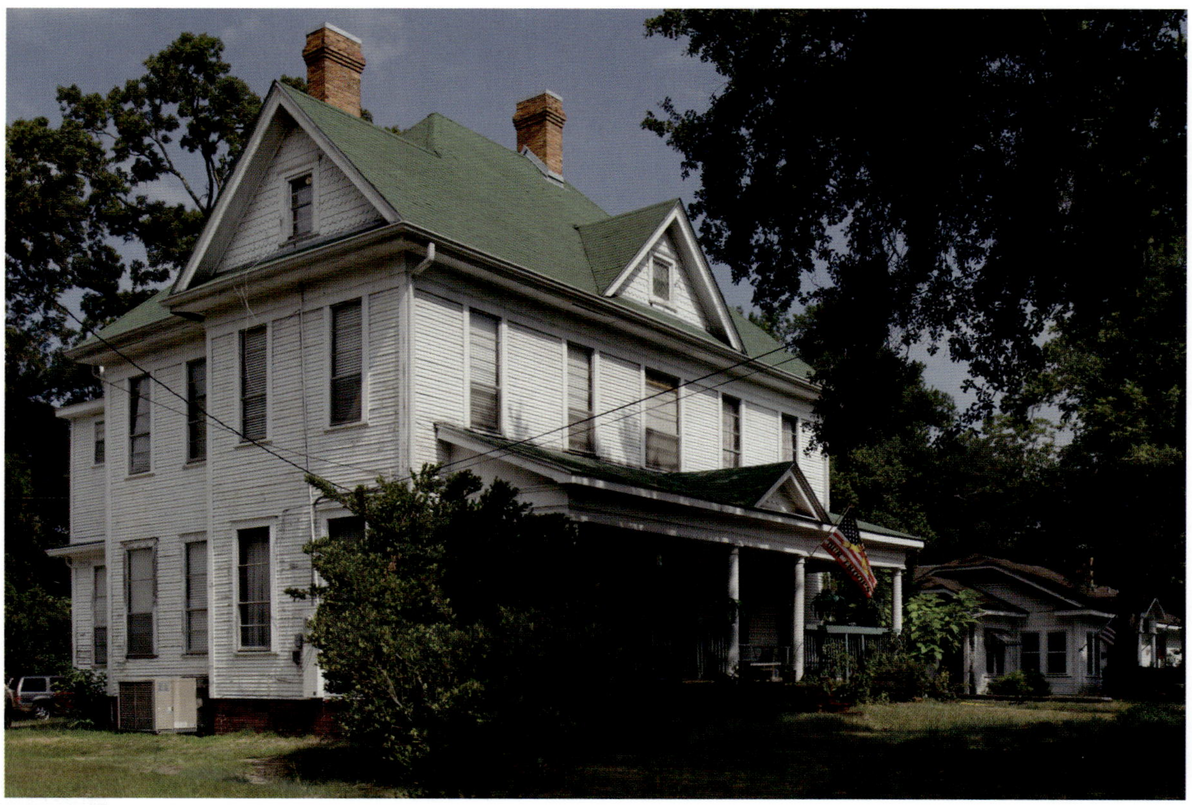

FIGURE 6.37. The William and Amanda Sanders House (1898), now the R. J. and Audrey Quick Home, 2011.

The porches on the William Sanders House have undergone several renovations over the years. Later owners enclosed the two-story porches at the back of the house. The front porch, once wood, is now concrete. While the columns that remain are probably original, their numbers are reduced and the balustrades totally new. Rulfs used a simi-lar floor plan in building the Charles Butts House on the east side of town.

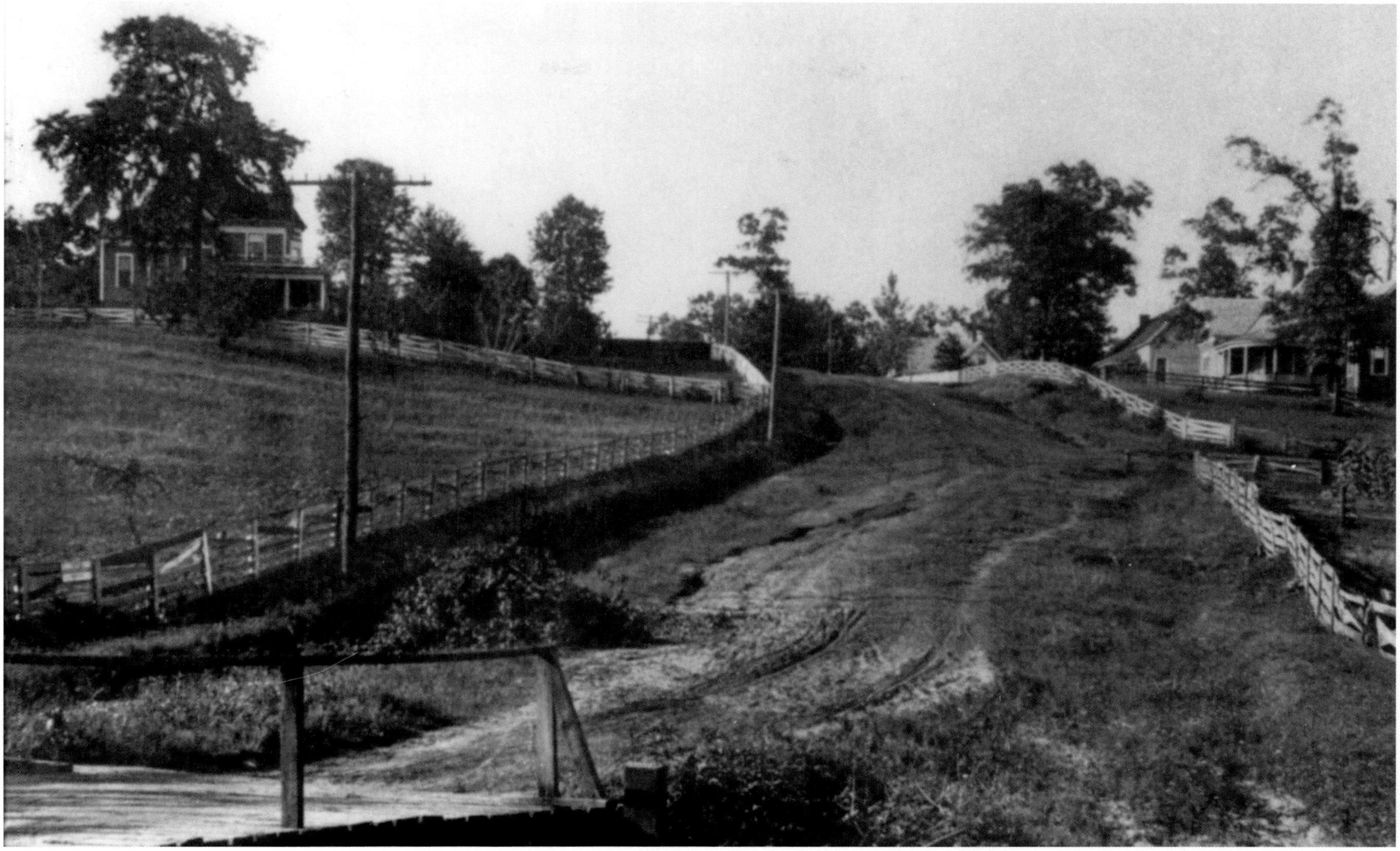

FIGURE 6.38. Virginia Avenue (looking north) ca. 1905.

The large house on the left at the crest of the hill is the Emma and Robert Lindsey House. Access to Virginia Avenue in the era of horses and buggies was a dilemma. The southern approach, shown in this photograph, allowed the residents of Virginia Avenue to take the hill in two stages. The nearest access from town, Cox Street, was extremely steep. It was difficult in good weather and impossible in bad. (Today, Cox Street is no longer used to access Forbes Hill; the abandoned roadway, however, is still visible and is used for utility lines.) Photograph courtesy of Mr. Charles Bright.

FIGURE 6.39. (Right) Line Drawing of the Lindsey House, 1992.

Many artists have found the Robert Lindsey house inspiring. Shortly after the restoration of the second story balustrades, Rebecca Stanly did several drawings and water colors of the house. Drawing used by permission of Rebecca Stanly.

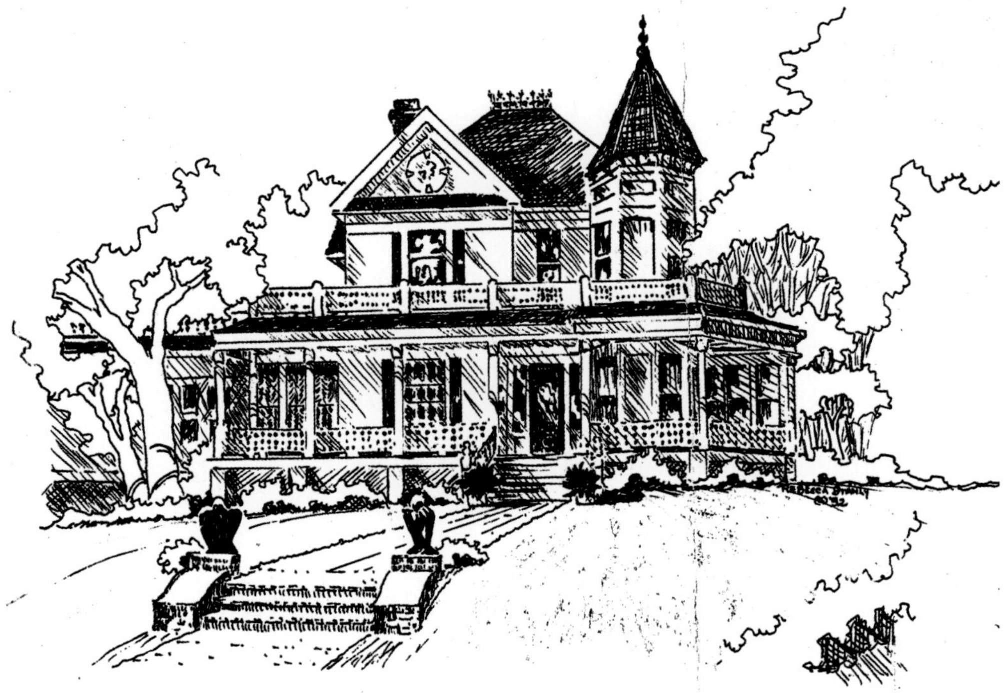

The Robert and Emma Lindsey House

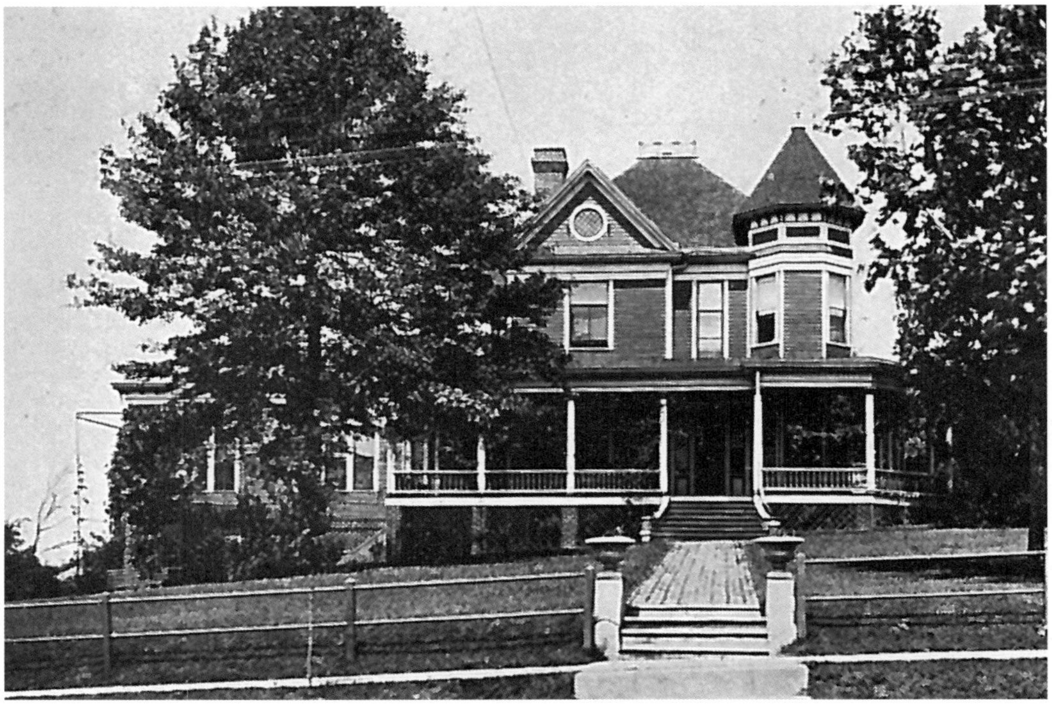

FIGURE 6.40. (Left) The Lindsey House in 1917.
Photograph from the Pamphlet, "The Twenty-Three Reasons Why." Author's personal copy.

The Robert and Emma Lindsey House (1900-1901)

The Robert and Emma Lindsey House is one of the grand houses on Virginia Avenue, one of the cornerstones of the Virginia Avenue National Register Historical District. Before building the house at 706 Virginia, the Lindseys had lived in a house designed and built by Rulfs for them on North Street, as discussed in Chapter IV. In the United States Census of 1900, Lindsey recorded his occupation as a dry goods salesman; in the 1910 census, he would list himself as being in real estate.[59] The booming nature of the real estate market in Nacogdoches and the quick sale of his first home on North Street no doubt enticed him into the new occupation. The offer of a business partnership with June Harris to promote the property on Forbes Hill, however, cemented his transition. *The Daily Sentinel* reported in 1901 that Harris and Lindsey were moving their real estate offices into the new Hazle Building.[60] Unlike the Harrises who moved to a larger home because of a growing family, the Lindseys, who had no children, wanted a larger house to give Emma more space for her music students and their recitals and receptions. She was the pianist at the First Baptist Church and taught private lessons to a large number of young people in the town. Lindsey was an original volunteer in the Nacogdoches Fire Department, took part in the opening of Aqua Vita Park, worked on recruiting a college for the town, and hosted many of the festivities at the time of the opening of Stephen F. Austin State Teachers College in 1923.

For the Lindsey House, Rulfs employed an asymmetrical façade, consisting of an octagon tower on the north side and a prominent front-facing gable on the south. The house has some of the general characteristics used on the E. A. Blount House (1894) and the Crouch-Stripling House (1898) House on North Street: asymmetrical façades, corner towers, dominant front-facing gables, hip-and-gable roofs, overhanging eaves with corbel supports, and wrap-around front porches. The Blount House, the earliest of the three houses, was the largest, finest, and most elaborate. The Lindsey House and the Crouch-Stripling House were the most alike, but the floor plans were reversed. Rulfs may have applied this technique to keep Lindsey's expenses down. In both houses, Rulfs abandoned the Victorian ornamentation in favor of more tailored, classical elements. Columns rather than posts supported their more generous verandas. In the case of the Lindsey House, the use of full-height Tuscan columns follows the pattern of the Harris House. All three houses, however, are highly eclectic and did not rely on any particular set of architectural patterns. On the other hand, these latter houses reflect a trend in Rulfs' taste: his growing preference for more classical details and for less ornamentation.[61] (After the carpentry-intensive effort of the porch on the Stephen Blount House (1897), neither Diedrich nor his brother William Henry was ready to take on such a project again. See Chapter V.)

The slope of Forbes Hill determined the architecture of the Lindsey House in a different way from the Harris House up the street. In many ways, the architect had faced this same problem with the Cooper House (1898) on West Main: the main entrances to this house had to be at one end of the house because of the slope of the hill. The everyday entrances to the Lindsey house, such as the kitchen and side porch, were on the north side: low and accessible. This allowed the front door to be mainly ceremonial, yet because it was on the uphill side of the asymmetrical street façade, it was still manageable. Rulfs successfully achieved for Lindsey's house the main objectives of all the Forbes Hill houses—to use the hillside elevations to capture views and better air—by maximizing, in this case, the vistas to the east and southeast. Since Forbes Hill to the east of the house was essentially a bald pasture when the house was built, the elevated south porch allowed for wonderful vistas. Lindsey must have had a very easy time selling real estate from these porches on three sides of his new home. When Lindsey later extended the house by adding a large music room on the south, in order to be level with the main floor of the house, the addition had to be two-story. The ground floor became a storage place for carriages and, later, automobiles.[62]

The south music room, built to facilitate Emma Lindsey's expanding musical activities, could accommodate more than 100 guests. It also served as a ballroom. The most important years for the enjoyment of the house by the Lindseys came in the first two decades of the twentieth century. They hosted grand musical and poetry *soirees* in the house. As one interviewee commented, it became a meeting place for music lovers in the town.[63] Emma sent elaborate, hand drawn invitations to her guests.[64]

FIGURE 6.41. (Right) The Guy and Penelope Anderson Home, 1976.

The author took this photograph at the time of the interviews with the Andersons. The remodeling done in the previous decade had removed the upper balustrade and the circular window in the gables, which have now been restored by Charles Bright.

FIGURE 6.42. (Below) Steps of the Lindsey House, ca. 1906.

A Gathering of Ladies from the First Baptist Church, Front Steps of the Lindsey House. Image courtesy of James Partin.

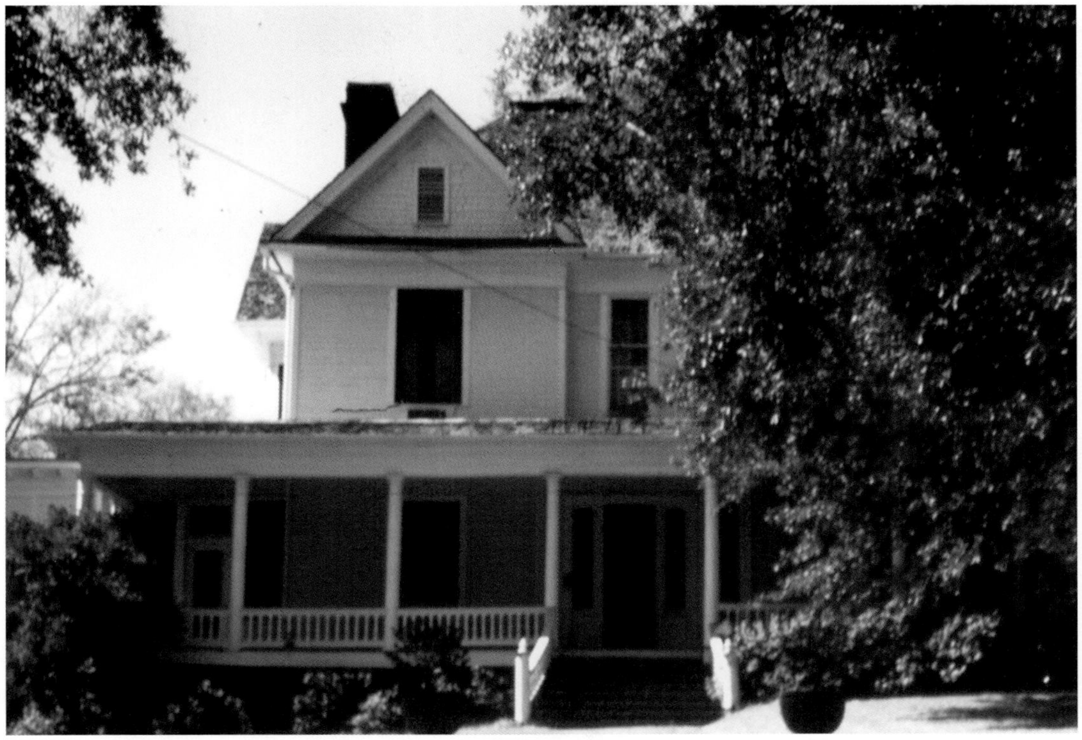

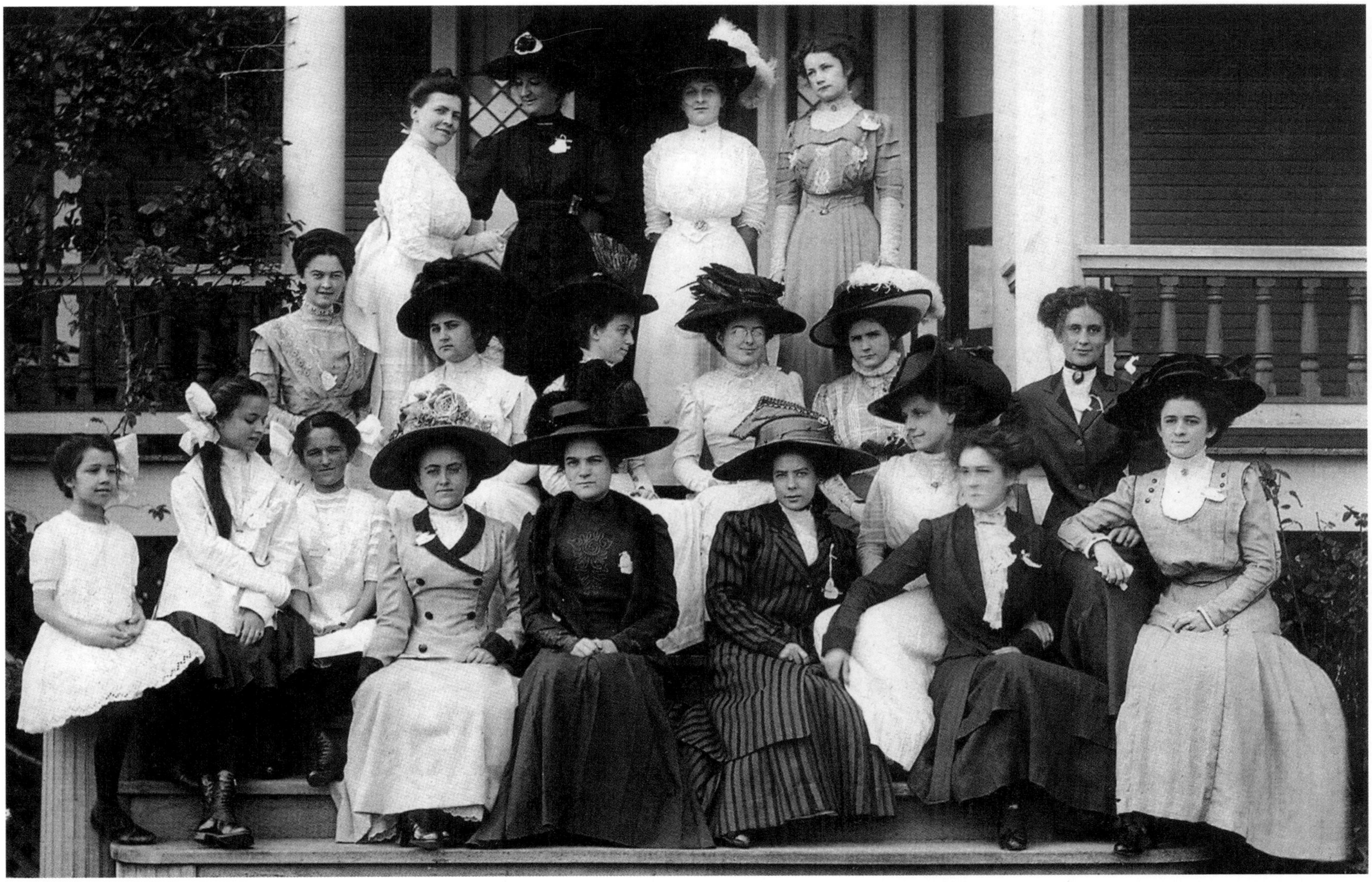

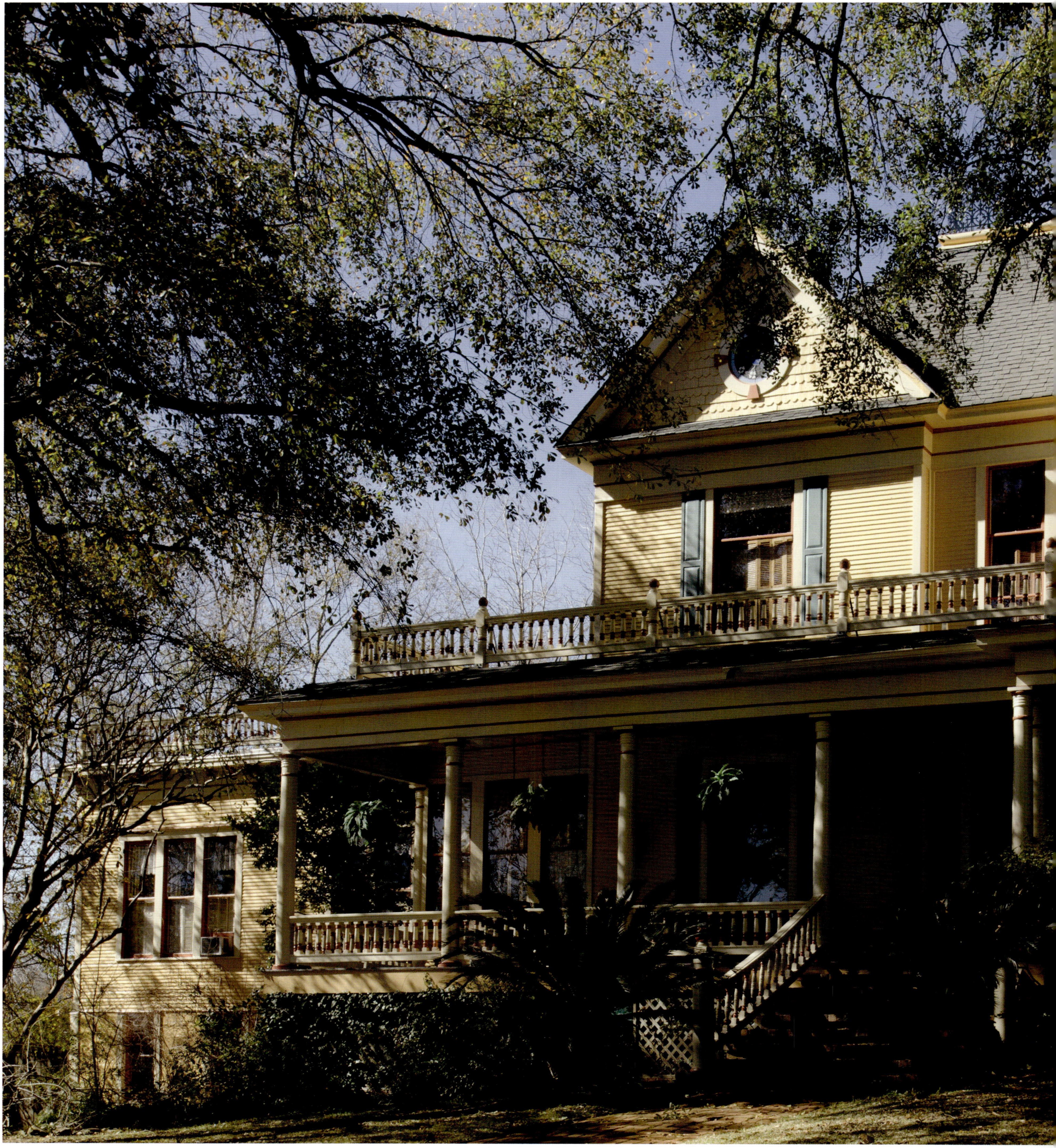

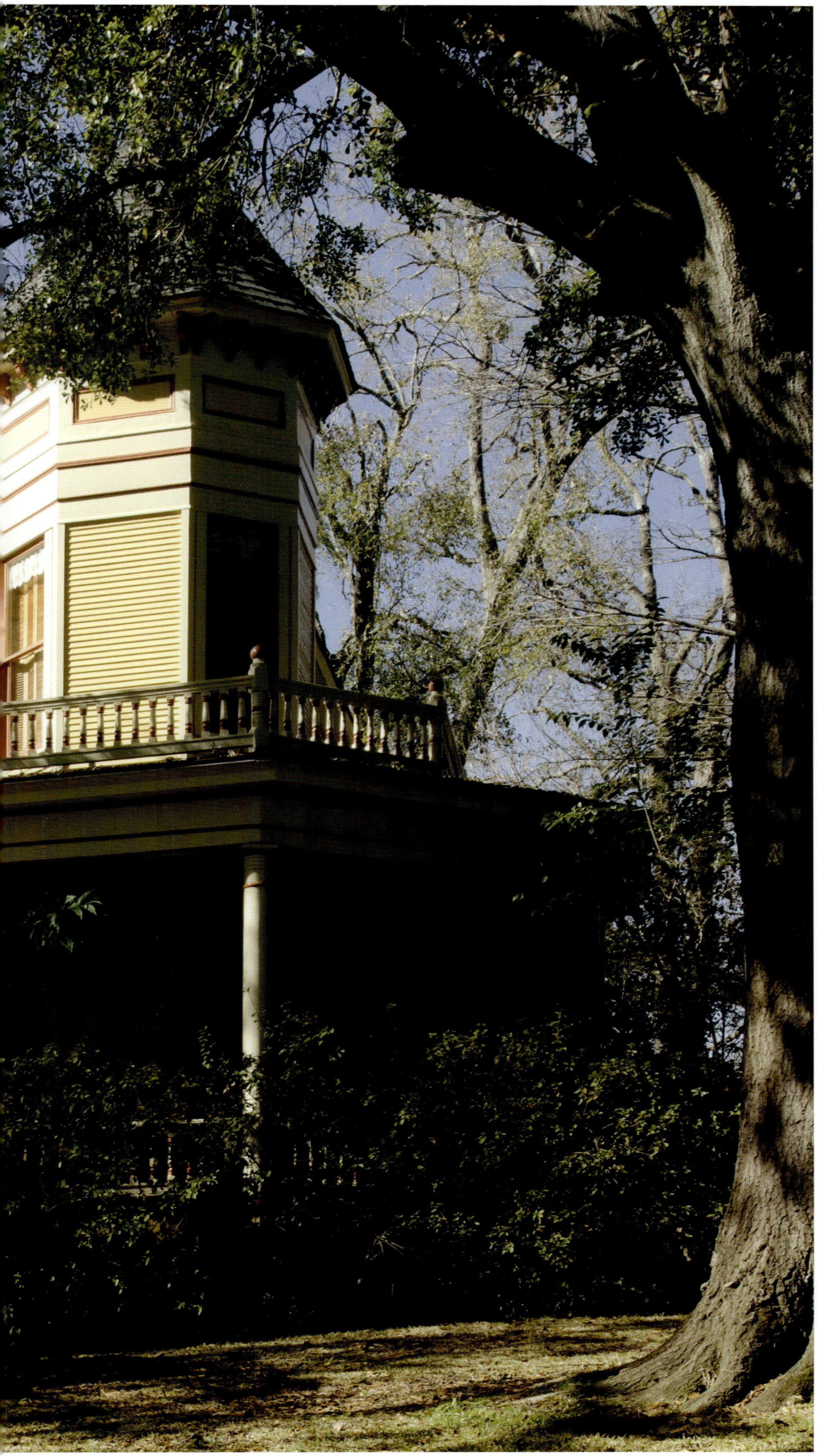

The Lindsey House (1900-1901)

Home of Charles and Carolyn Bright

Virginia Avenue National Register District

FIGURE 6.43. The Bright Home.

By the time of the Great Depression, however, the maintenance of the house became a burden. The Lindseys downsized to a nearby house and sold the big house to Sam Hayter for his daughter Mary Elizabeth and her husband, Kelly Bell. "Baby Sis," as she was known in the family, enjoyed the house, according to friends. When she developed severe allergies, she and her husband moved to Midland. Sam Hayter then gave the house to another daughter, Penelope, and her husband, Guy Anderson.[65] The Andersons hired noted Texas architect Rayford Stripling to direct a complete renovation of this house in the 1950s. Stripling made three bedrooms out of the large music room; closed in some of the porch spaces on the north and south sides of the main floor to create sun rooms; added shutters throughout the house on both floors; and, renovated the kitchen and bathroom.[66] The paneling and the classical mantel were added at that time.

Charles and Lois Marie Bright purchased the house in 1998 and undertook an impressive and complete restoration effort. They restored the balustrades to the roof of the front porch, reinstalled the ornamental ironwork-cresting atop the complex hip-and-gable roof, introduced art glass to the decorative port hole window in the front gable, and restored the finial to the roof of the octagonal tower. Unlike other houses that have endured extensive and inappropriate interpretations, the Lindsey House had the good fortune to be purchased by a family such as the Brights, who did everything possible to maintain the integrity of the original façade of the house while updating its interior in needed ways. All people who appreciate architecture and beautiful things owe them a great debt for their painstaking efforts, as will be obvious from the photographs displayed within these pages.

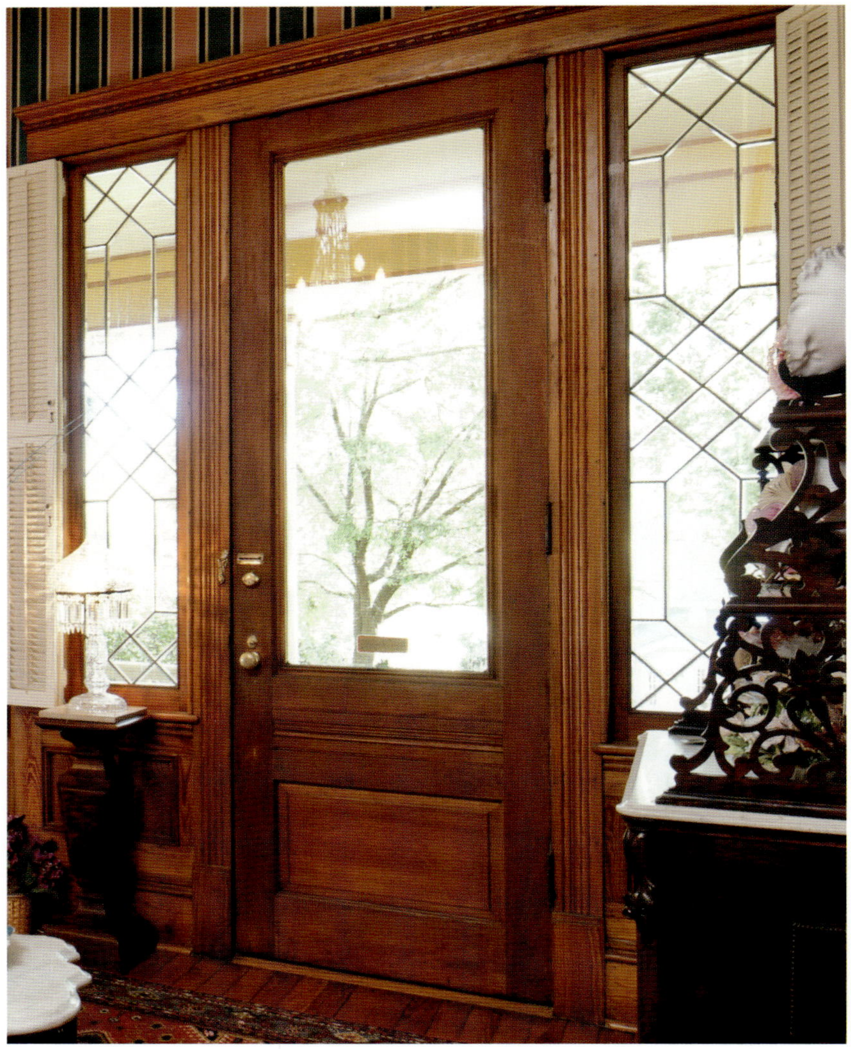

FIGURE 6.45. (Above) Interior Photograph of the Front Door, 2011.

FIGURE 6.46. (Across) Azalea Time.

FIGURE 6.47. (Below) Charles Bright in His Living Room.

The picture on the table in the foreground is of Lois Marie (Gibbs) Bright, now deceased. Mr. Bright did not want his photograph taken, but sometimes an author must override such requests. The devotion of the Brights to preservation and beautification in Nacogdoches must be acknowledged in more than a thank you note.

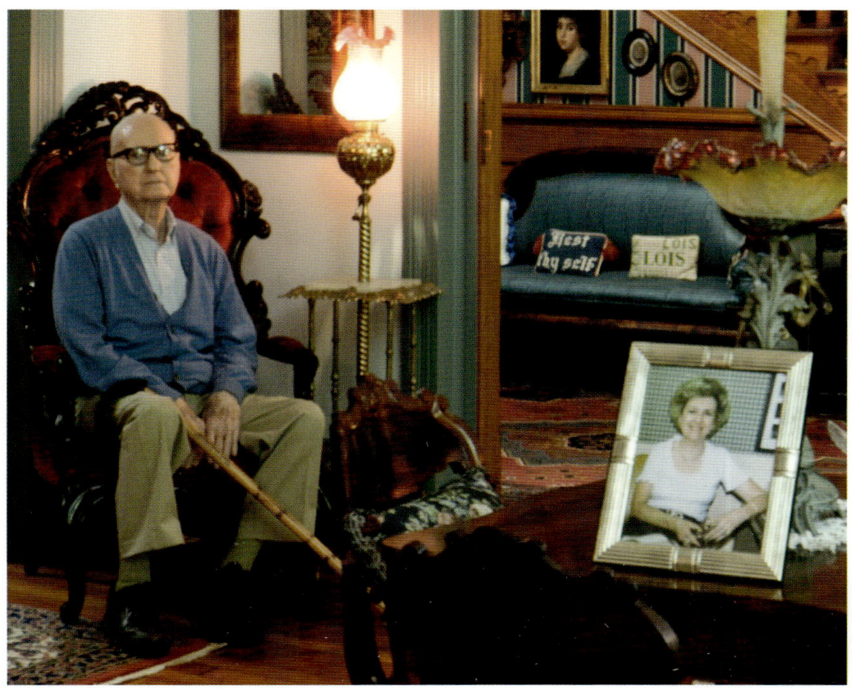

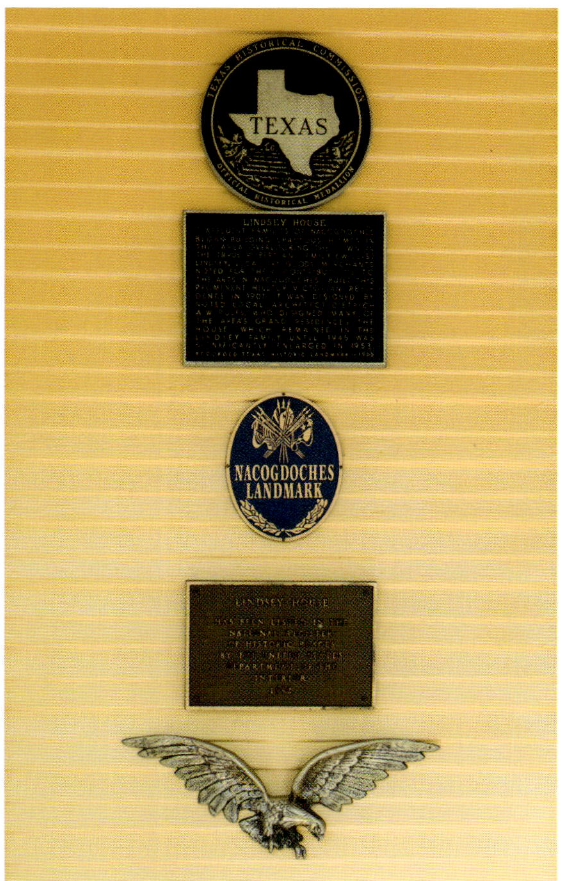

FIGURE 6.44. Accolades for the Lindsey House.

The various accolades offered in tribute to the house: a Texas Historic Landmark, a Nacogdoches Landmark, and a National Register Landmark.

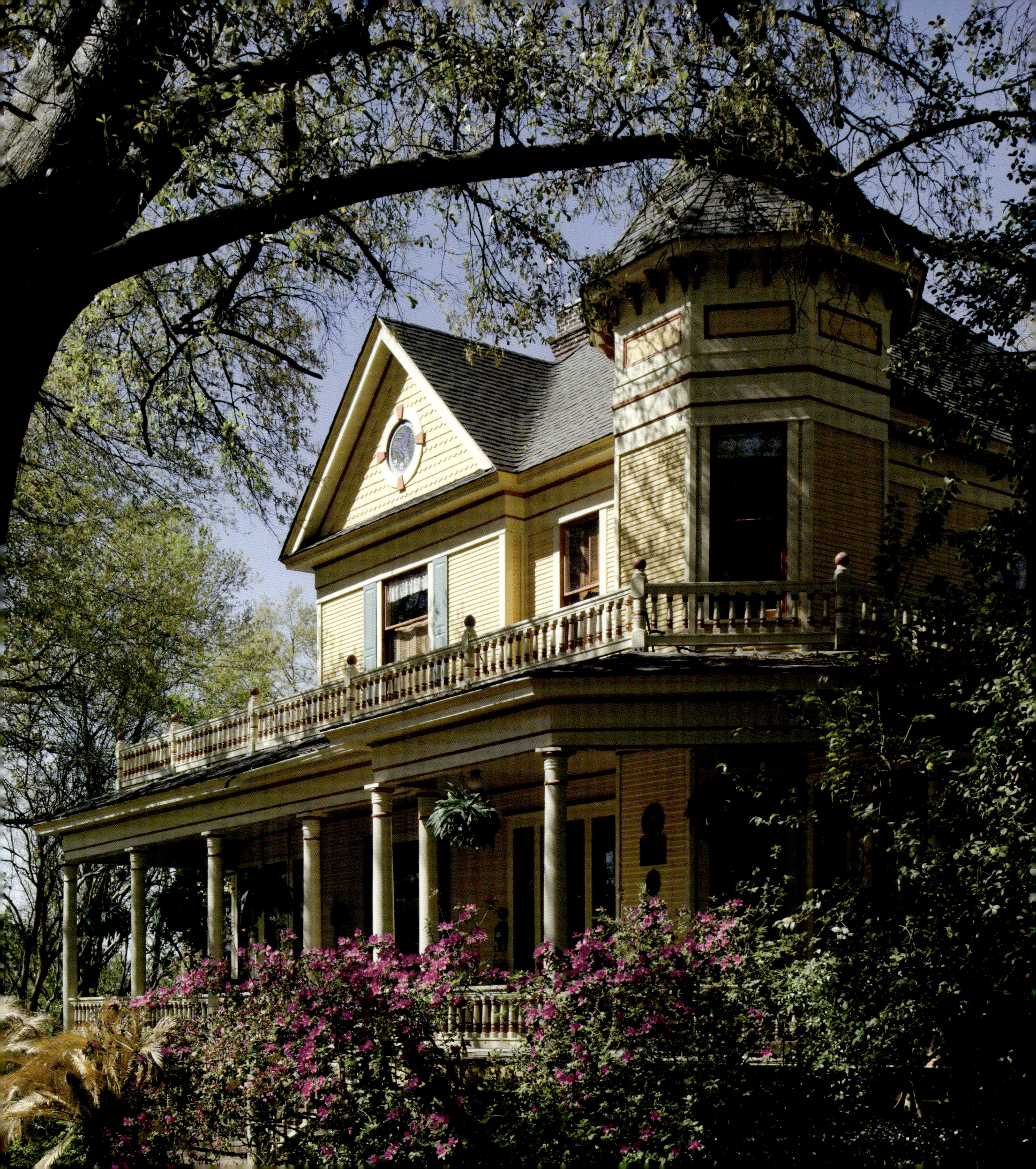

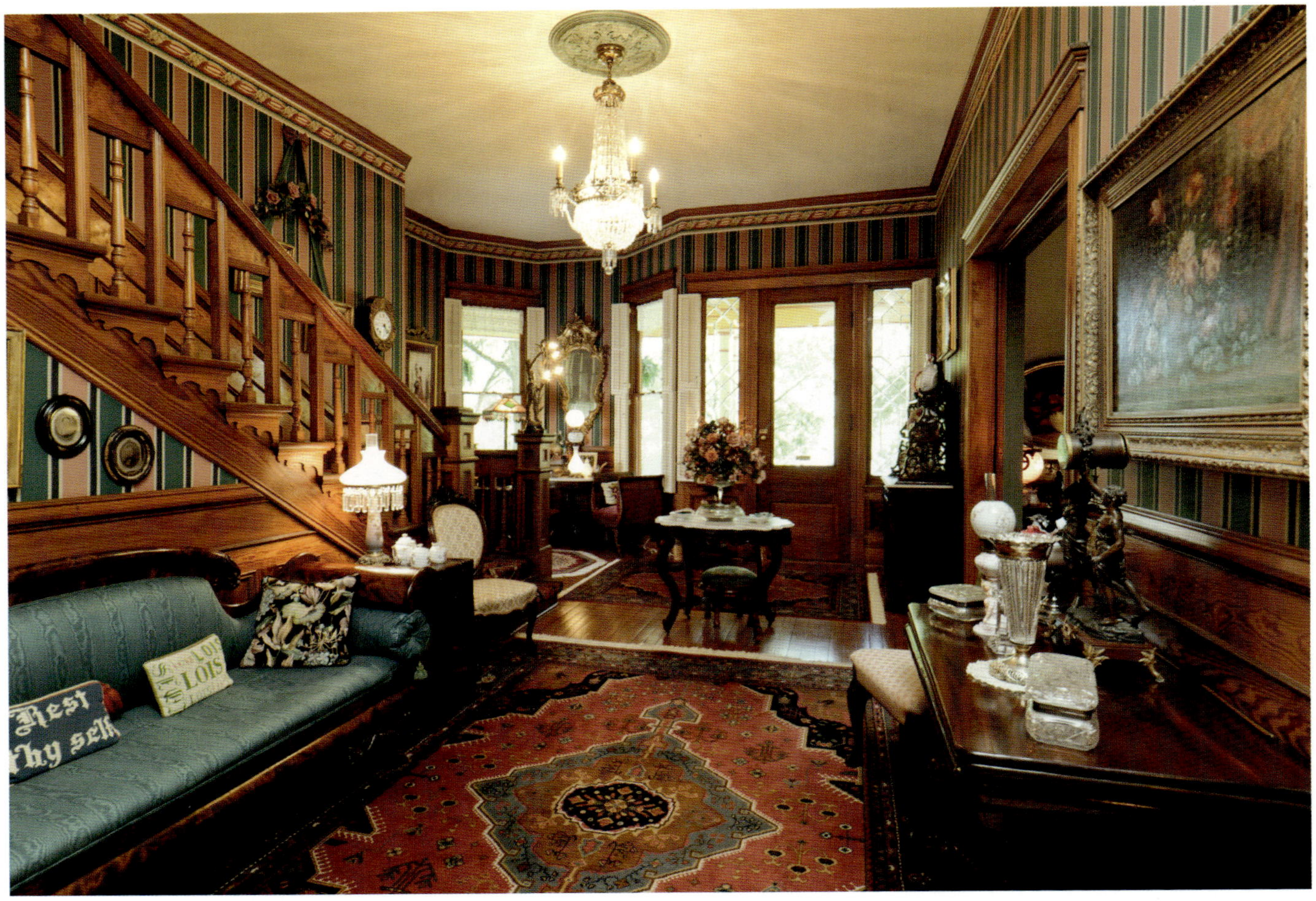

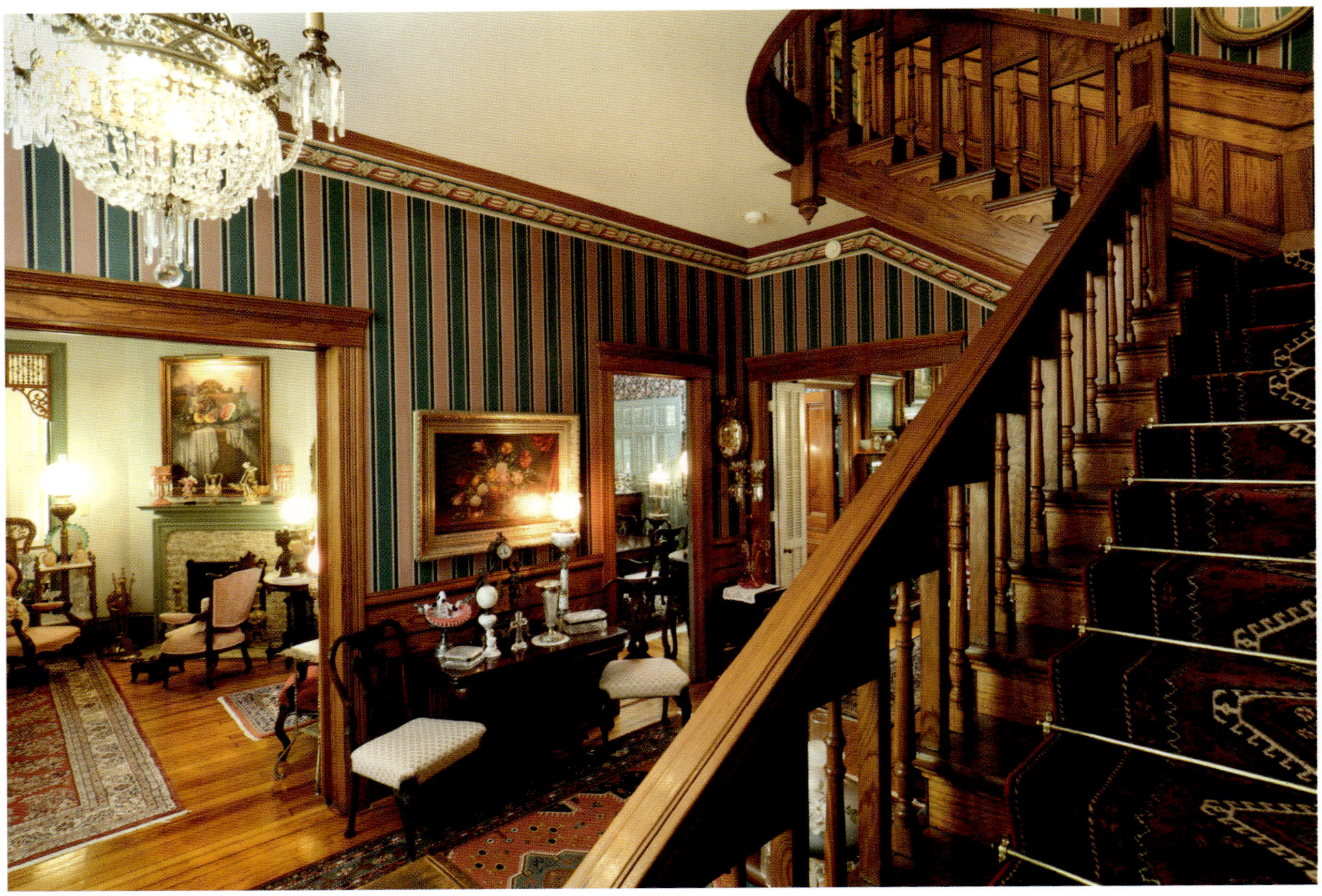

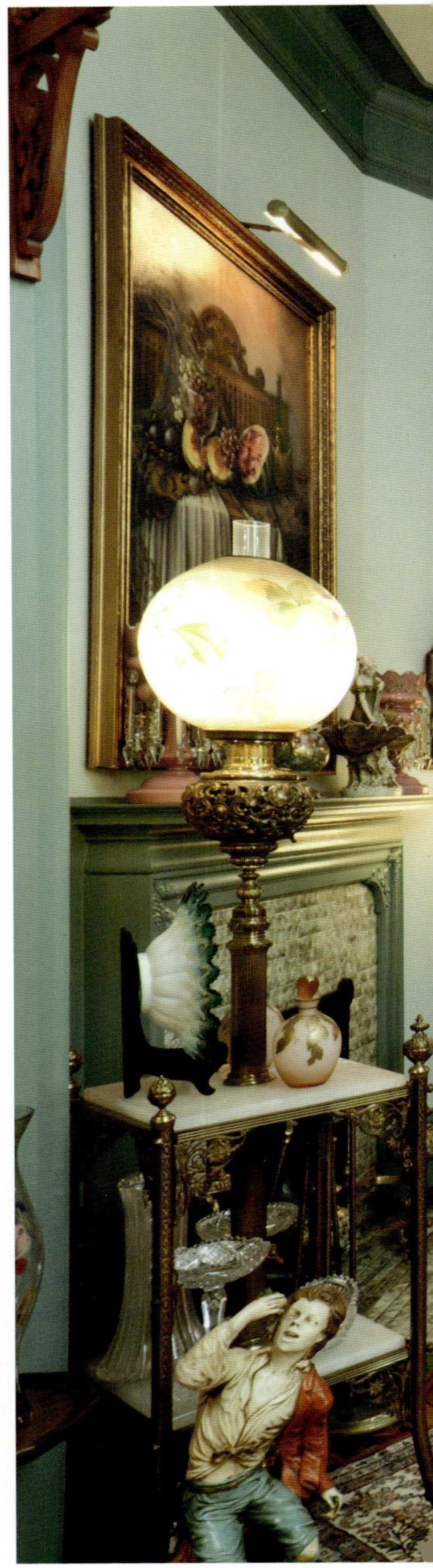

FIGURES 6.48 - 6.50. Entrance hall and the parlor of the of the Charles Bright Home.

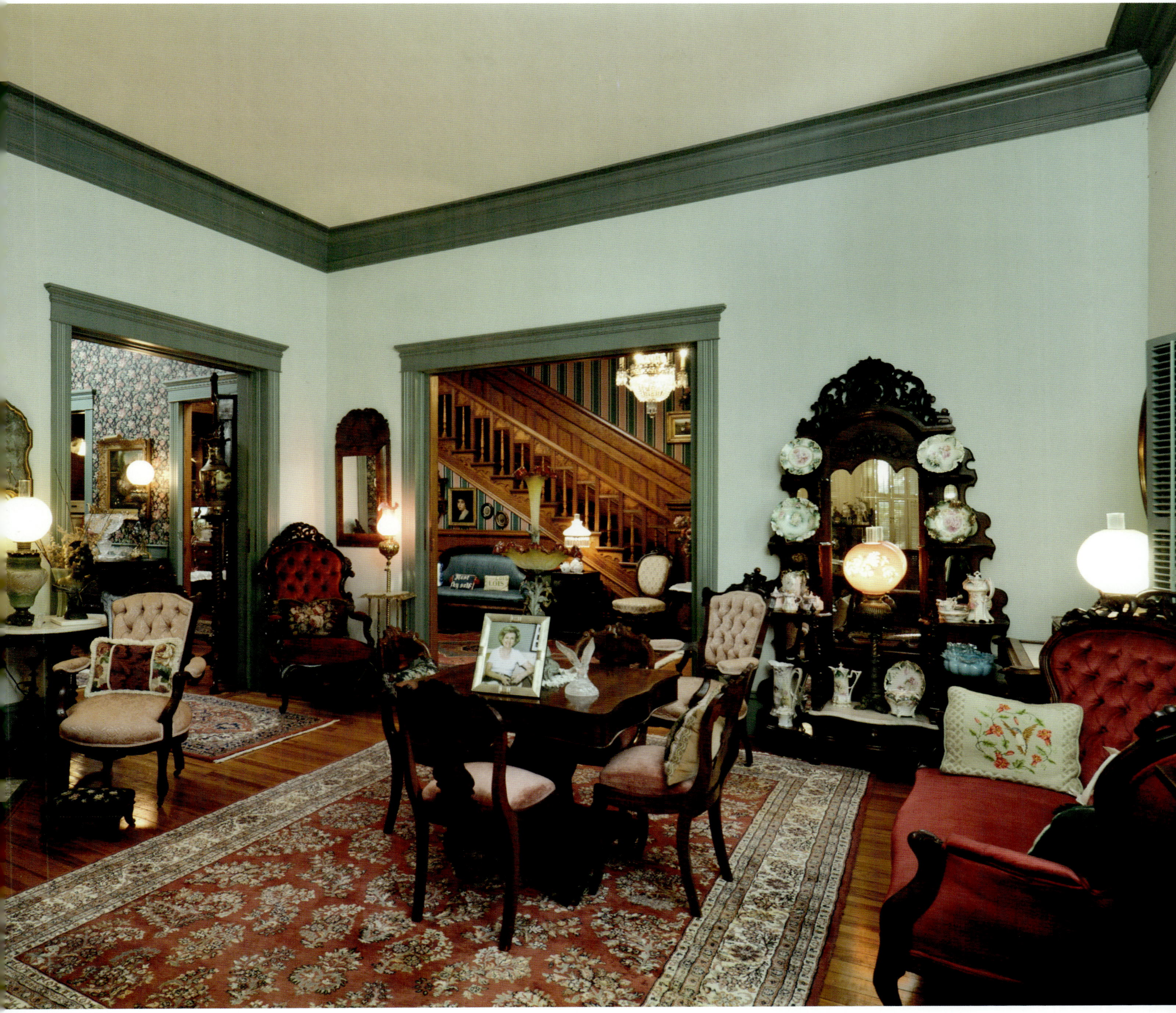

The Lindsey-Anderson-Bright House

Virginia Avenue National Register District

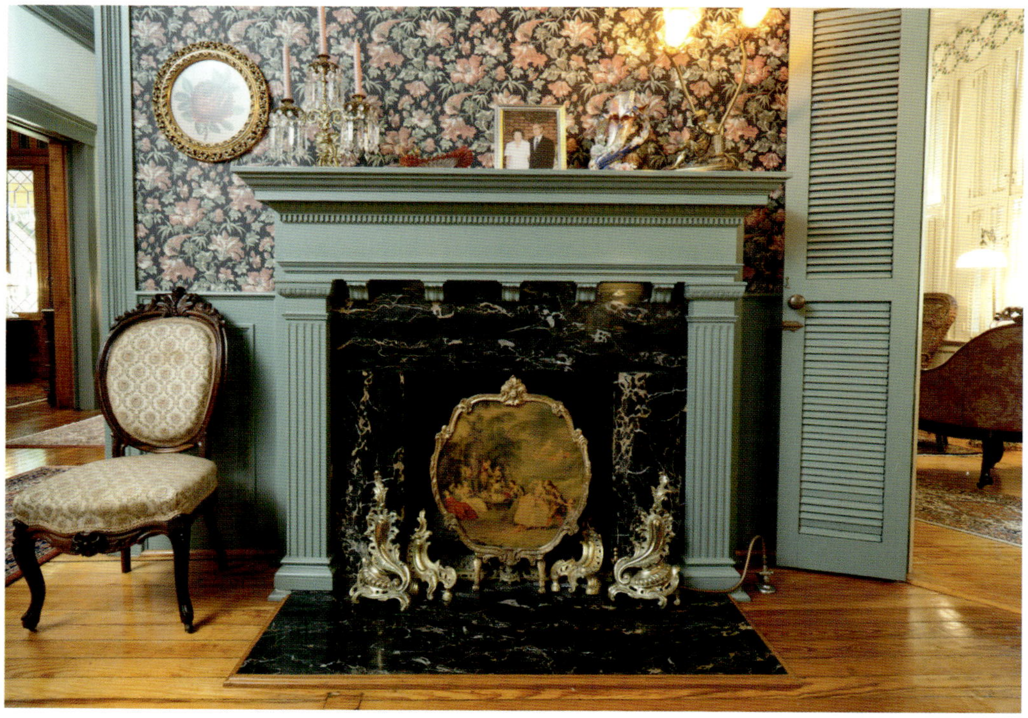

FIGURE 6.51. The Dining Room Fireplace, 1950s.
Designed by Architect Rayford Stripling for the Andersons.

FIGURE 6.52. The Dining Room.
The wainscoting in the dining room dates to the 1950s and the Stripling remodeling job. The dining room furniture once belonged to the Kurth family in Lufkin.

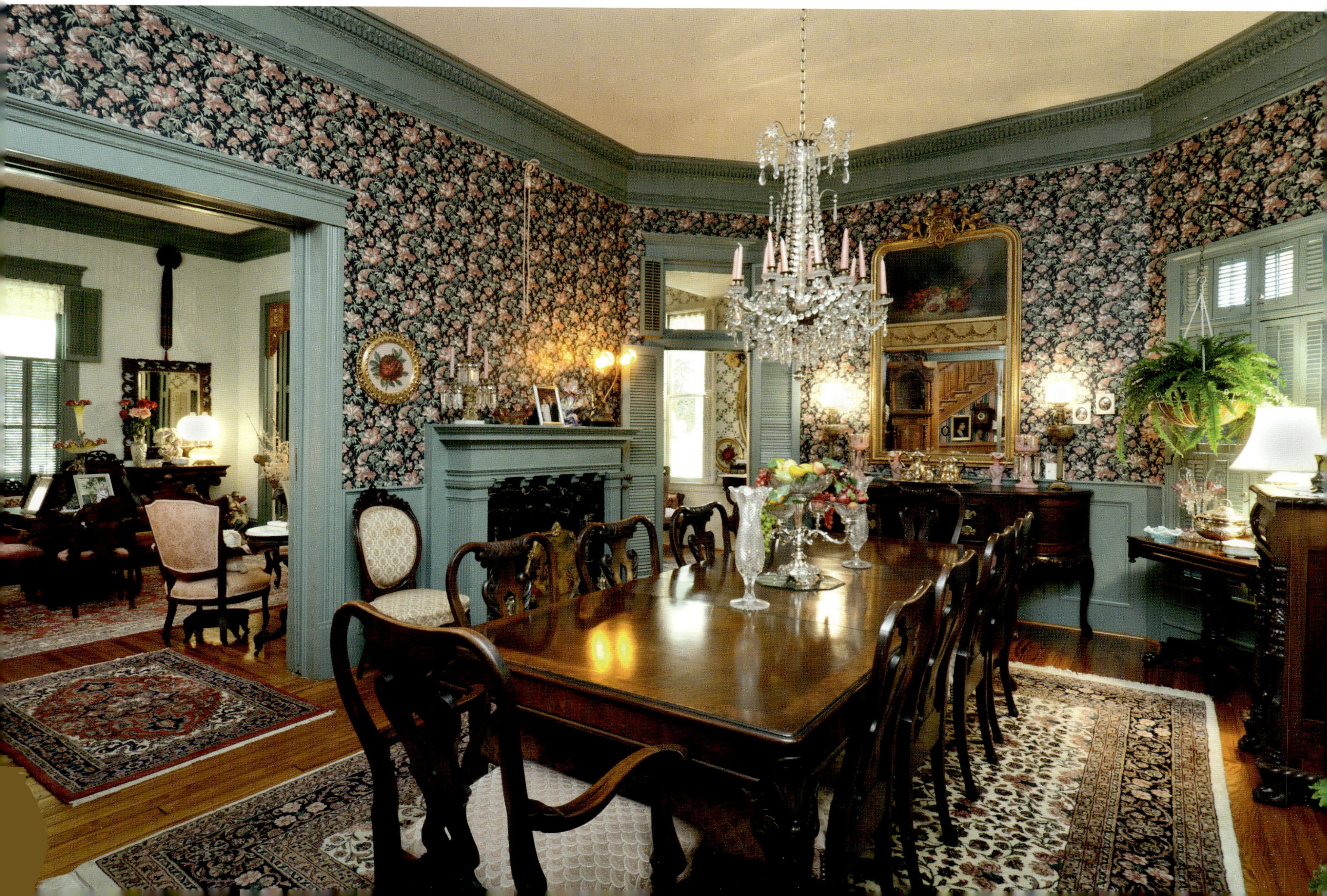

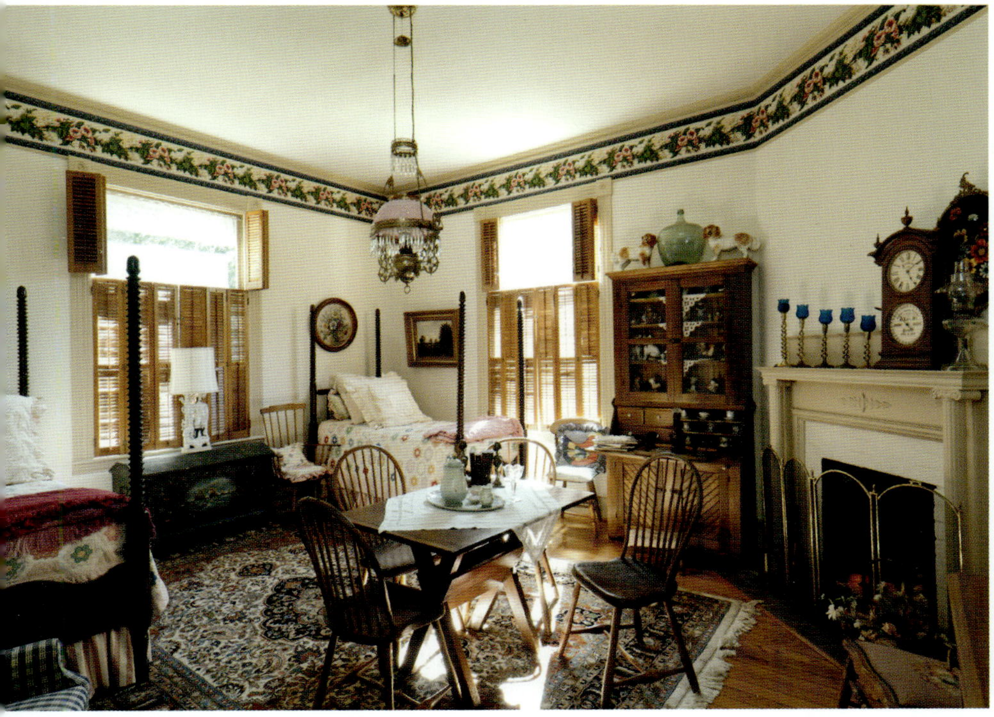

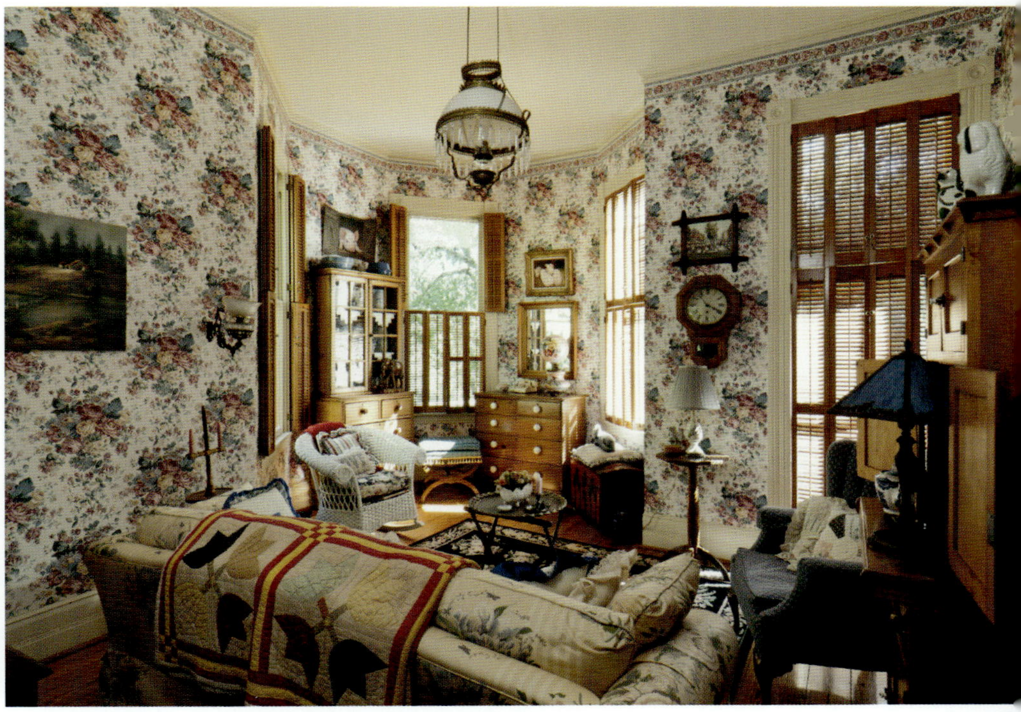

FIGURES 6.53 - 6.55. Upstairs at the Bright Home.
(Left) Southeast Bedroom.
(Above) Northeast Tower-Sitting Room.
(Below) The Bedroom in the South Bay.

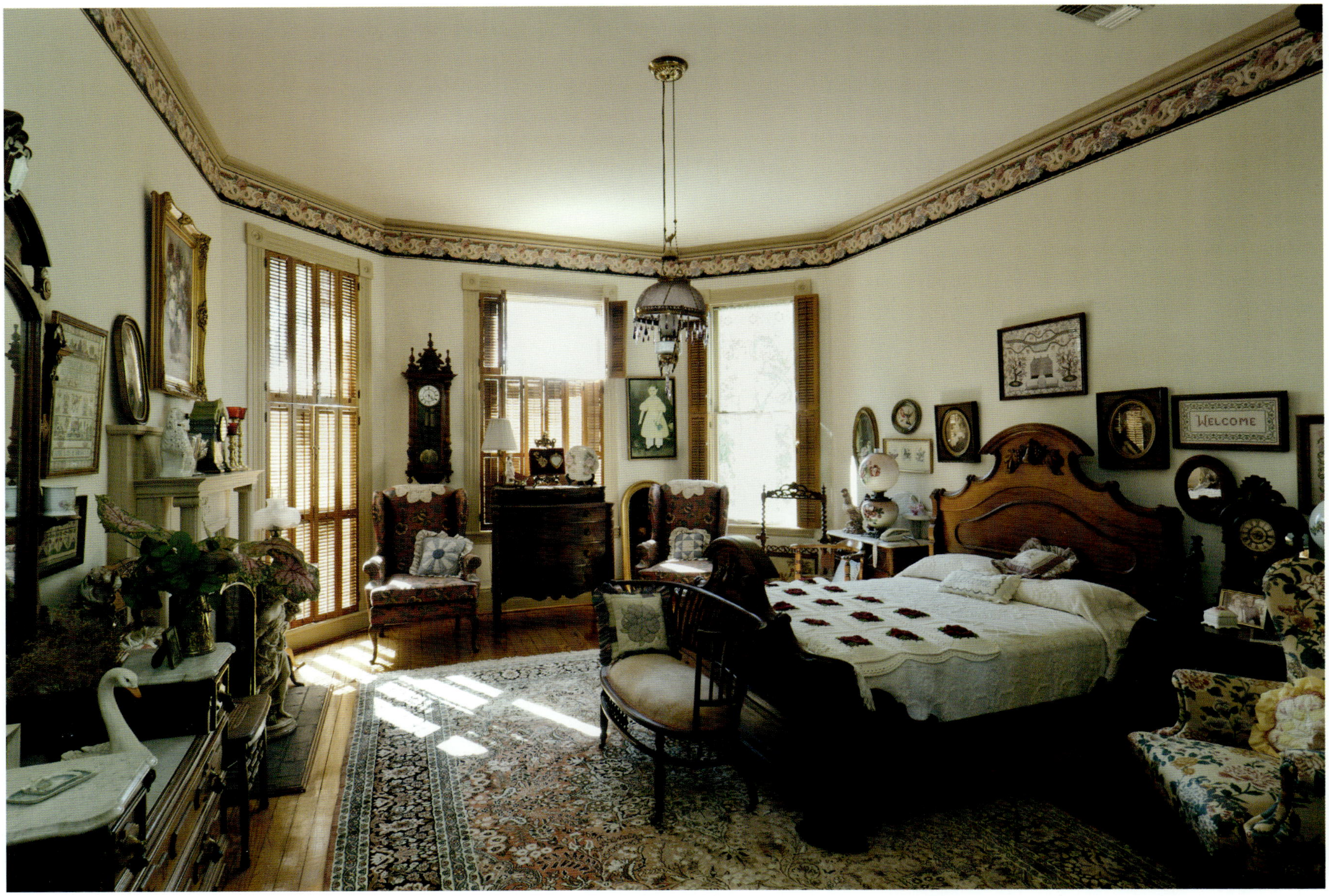

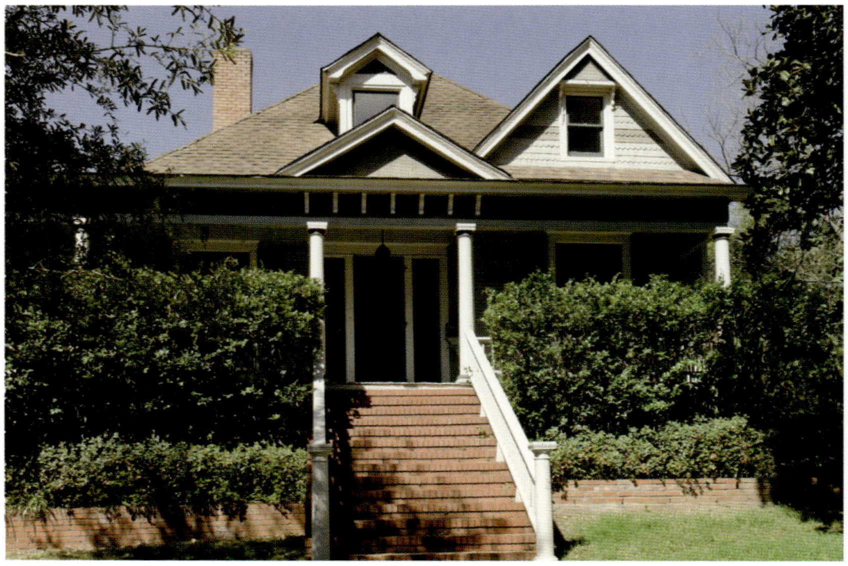

FIGURE 6.56. The Branch-McKinney House.

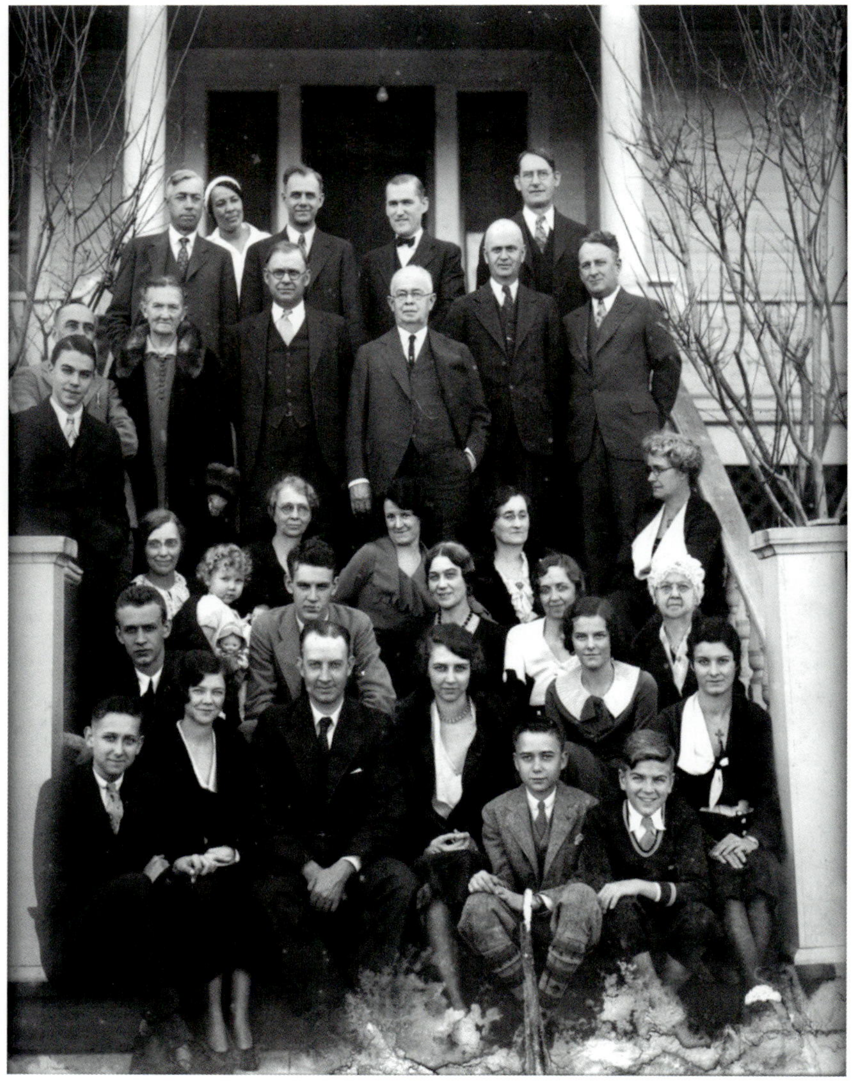

FIGURE 6.57. (Right) McKinney-Wade Reunion, 1932.
In 1932, on the steps of the Branch-McKinney House, the family members gathered for a commemorative photograph. In the center of the next-to-top row, with his hand in his pocket, is Frank Aikman, long-time friend of the family. This book discusses Aikman in Chapter XII. Photograph compliments of Libby Bussa Duggar, great-great granddaughter of J. R. and Laura McKinney.

The Branch-McKinney House (1900)

Elbert Clinton Branch (1860-1919) was a prominent lawyer in Nacogdoches. He and his wife, Jessie Beeson Branch, appear in Nacogdoches public records for the first time in the tax roles of 1890. Branch joined Link Sturdevant as the co-founder of the town's utilities: electricity, telephone service, and waterworks. Branch also financed his younger brother K. P. Branch and Orland Patton when they entered the hardware business.[67] In the 1890s, the Branches lived for a time at 216 North Church Street;[68] but by the time of the 1900 Census, they had sold this house and were living temporarily as boarders with the Roland Jones family while their house was being built on Irion Hill.[69] In 1900, Branch joined his good friend June Harris on Irion Hill and purchased the lot between Harris and Lindsey, and asked Rulfs to design a residence for him. (The small road in between the Harris and Lindsey houses had not at the time become Sunset Street.)

The Branch House at 704 Virginia Avenue is a less complicated house than either of its neighbors on the north or south: no full second story, no towers, and no dramatic raised galleries. The façade of the house had standard Rulfs elements: a hip-and-gable roof, a forward facing gable on the right front, a dormer and pediment over the entrance, and a porch across the east front, which wrapped around the south side of the house to take advantage of the good southern view down the street. The house is similar to the houses Rulfs designed for the Mayfields on East Main and the Woodalls on North Street in 1901. The house had no entrance hall, combining the parlor and entrance. This is an arrangement Rulfs had in his own home and would use in the modern houses, such as the Guy Blount House on North Street. Large double pocket doors opened the parlor to the living room and the living room to the dining room. On the north side of the Branch House, there is a large chamfered bay window in the dining room. From early photographs, one can discern that the front steps and the balustrades have been modified, but because so much shrubbery has always existed around the house, it is difficult to tell how much change has taken place. The unusually large double-hung windows are dramatic when seen from the interior of the house. These large windows were popular in the houses Rulfs designed for Washington Square. Rulfs continued to use the new types of molding introduced in the Lindsey House, but the uses of the new egg-and-dart moldings are less elaborate than in the Phillip Sanders House the next year.

Marcus Comer Smith and his wife (from Longview) were living in the house at the time of the 1910 census; they later purchased the house from the Branches in 1912. In 1918, when John Richard McKinney and his wife, Laura Wade McKinney, sold the Banita Hotel to their brother-in-law, Zeno Cox, the McKinneys purchased the Branch House from the Smiths for $4500.[70] McKinney had given up his management of the Banita Hotel in favor of working with Frank Speir Aikman's Mahdeen Company (makers of hair tonic).[71] McKinney was an officer and manager of the company. Aikman, a bachelor, was a frequent visitor to the McKinney household on

Virginia Avenue.[72] (See Figure 6.57). The McKinneys lived in the house for forty-one years. After McKinney's death in 1951, Laura Wade McKinney remained in this house for some years and then sold it in 1959 to B. H. and Mattie Moore.[73] When the author first interviewed the Moores in the 1970s, they were particularly fond of the house; their sojourn there lasted for thirty-seven years. When Edward A. and Susan C. Conley purchased the house in 1996, they undertook extensive renovations. The main exterior changes were to stabilize elements like the porch, which had deteriorated over the years—as they inevitably do in the humidity of East Texas. The house is currently owned by Linda Lindsey, who graciously gave us permission to photograph the house.[74]

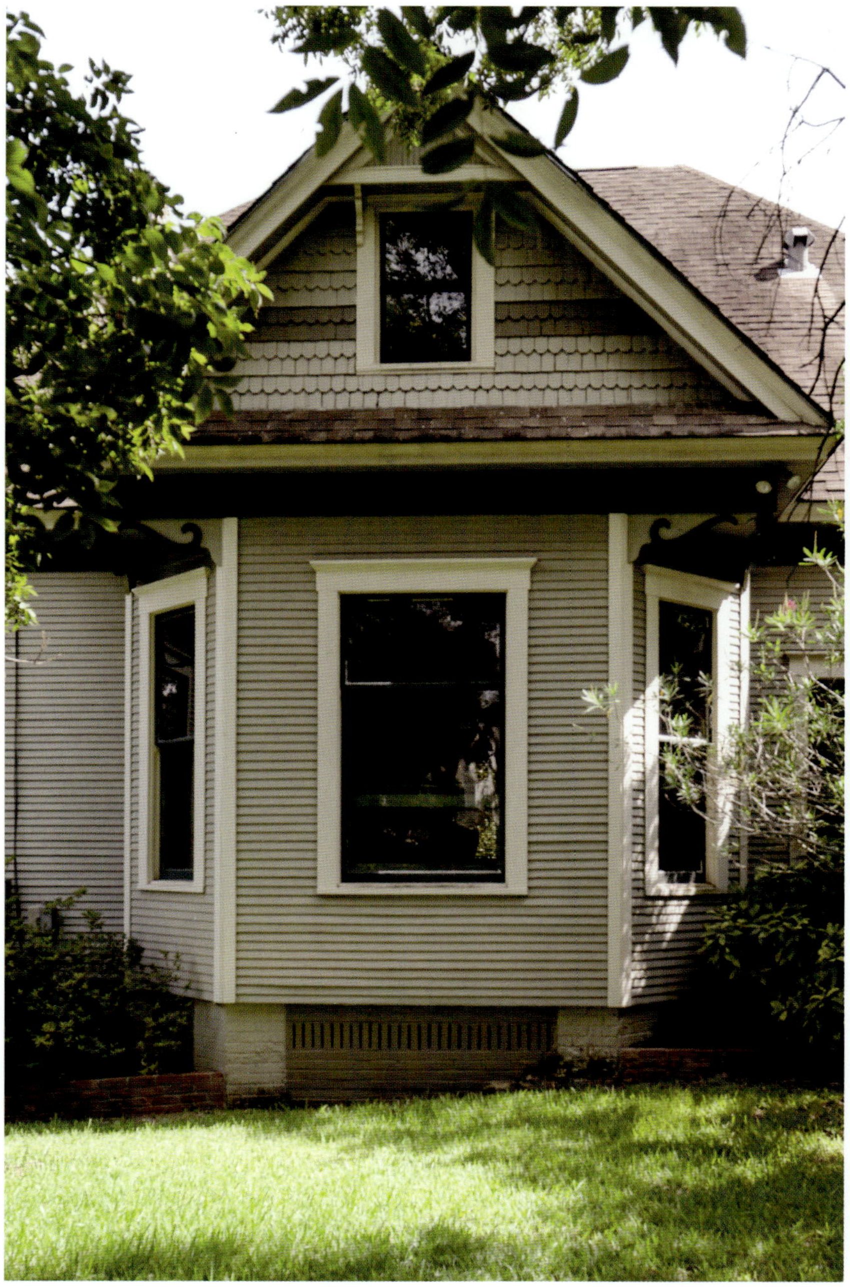

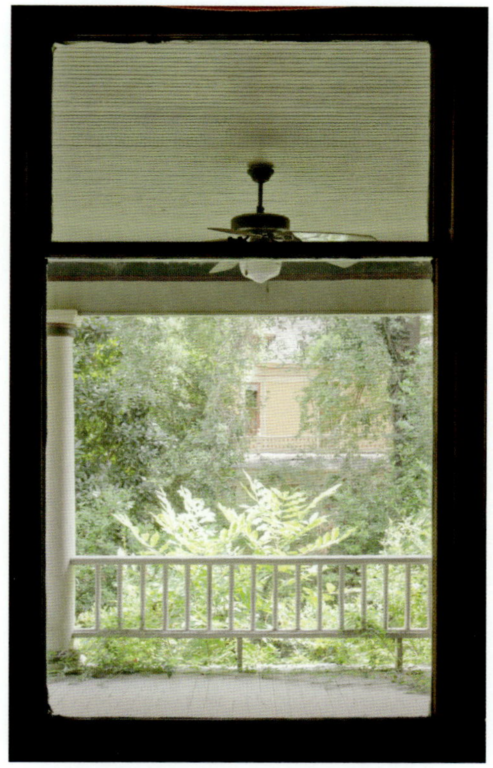

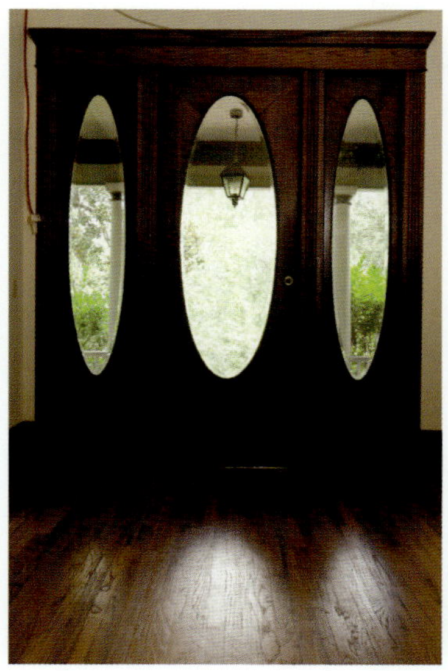

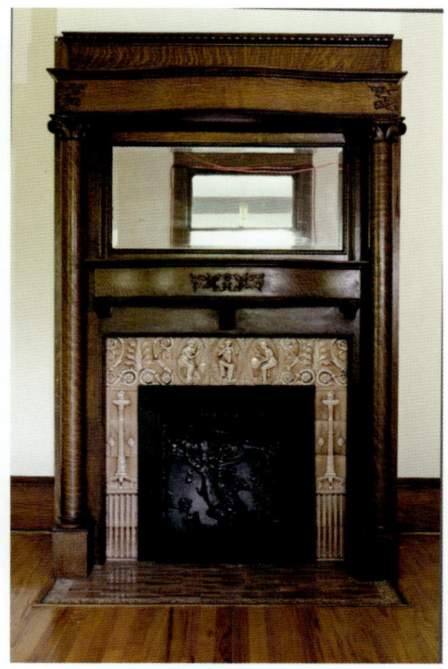

FIGURE 6.58. (Left) The North Gable, Dining Room.

FIGURE 6.59. (Top) Window in the Living Room
Oversized windows with a fixed upper sash were considered more fashionable in the period after 1900.

FIGURES 6.60 and 6.61. (Above) Front Door and Living Room Mantle.
Mantles and front doors such as these were available from catalogs in 1900 when this house was built.

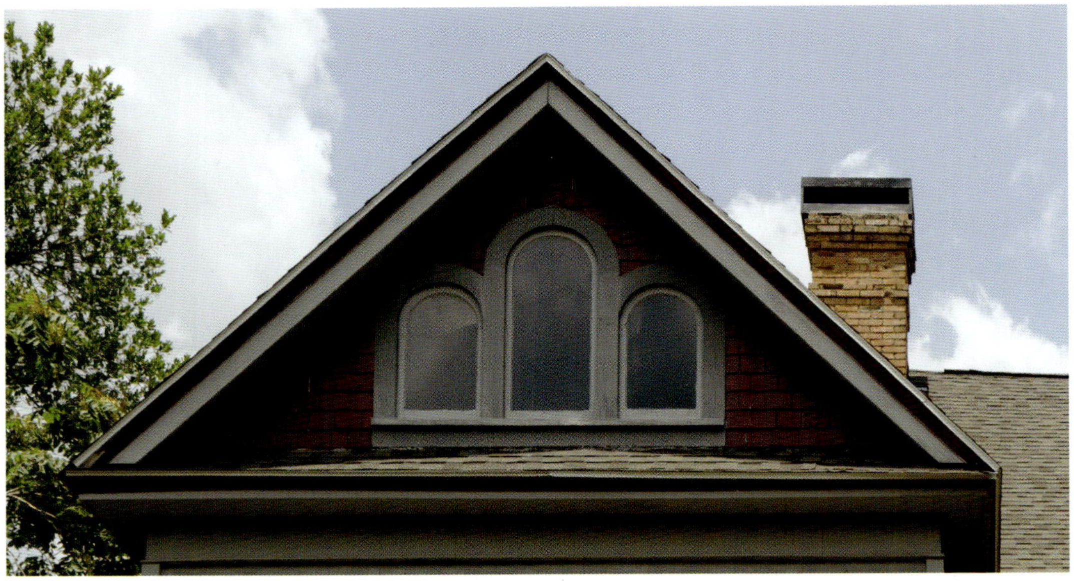

FIGURE 6.62. Three-arch Palladian Window, Tympana, Pearson House (1900).

While Rulfs utilized several varieties of Palladian motifs on the Pearson House, this three-arch version occupies the tympana of all the prominent gables that extend from the hip roof. The inspiration for this version comes from the Rulfs family church in Stollhamm, Germany. Rulfs used this Constantine Arch version in several of his Nacogdoches designs, for instance, the Charles Perkins House on Mound Street.

The Pearson-Spradley House (1900)

The most impressive house on West Main Street is the house at 904—designed by Rulfs for the William Brown Pearson family. Since the family of Duncan S. Spradley owned the house from 1915 to 2001 and saved it, the name Pearson-Spradley seems appropriate for clarity. Mrs. Elizabeth Spradley Bauman, the baby of ten children and four years old when her father bought the house, lived in the home for eighty-three years.[75]

William Pearson (1861-1943) came to Nacogdoches from Nashville, Tennessee. He was a very active member of the community in the 1890s and was the Postmaster from 1893-1897, just before H. H. Cooper, soon to be his neighbor on Irion Hill.[76] Before becoming an officer in Commercial Bank, he worked as a bookkeeper for the Mayer & Schmidt Company. Pearson was a dedicated Mason: active in Tennessee, the local Milam Lodge No. 2 in Nacogdoches, and in the Grand Lodge of Texas, where he held certificates to teach and the title of Grand Secretary Emeritus for life. The Masonic history said of him: "His life as a man and a Mason and his character were unexcelled."[77] Pearson purchased the property at the top of Irion Hill on West Main in 1899,[78] not long after the birth of his son, Joel Barham Pearson, (named after the doctor who delivered him) on Christmas Eve, 1898. Evidence that the Pearson family needed a larger house is clear from the Federal Census of June 1900. Pearson at age thirty-nine and his wife, Lydia, at thirty-eight, already had eight children, ranging in ages from one to eighteen. When Pearson approached the Harris-Lindsey real estate partnership for help in building a new home for his family, he found that Rulfs and Lindsey had several sketches and ideas for houses in advanced stages of development.[79] By the end of November that year, when their ninth child arrived, the Pearsons were in their new house.[80]

Rulfs evidently had great fun incorporating his unique architectural interests in the designs of this house. Rulfs employed the usual period prerequisites—a steeply pitched hipped roof with cross gable projections, a wrap-around porch with a pediment to accentuate the entrance, internal chimneys with multiple flues, double sliding doors between the hall and living room and between the living room and dining room, decorative shingle siding for accent in the gables, corner brackets, and Tuscan columns. In addition, the architect decided to indulge his affinity for Palladian motifs on the exterior. In the tympana of all the gables (front and sides), he placed the three arched-windows version utilized in his home church in Stollhamm. For the focal point of the upper gallery, he pulled forward a small gable dormer; the barreled arch within the gable, when coupled with the support posts and balustrades for the gallery, created a stylish Palladian-inspired motif on the upper façade. The large entablature gave the porch a very formal appearance. In the entrance hall, Rulfs used a staircase very much like the Stephen Blount House and repeated the idea of an entry fireplace, such as in the Perkins, Schmidt, and Jones houses. The house had seven fireplaces, four downstairs and three on the second floor. Upstairs and down, Rulfs used his favorite slip-head windows to afford complete access to the porches. He also reinforced the ceiling of the front porch for a large swing in the southeast corner.[81]

Because the Pearson's twenty-fifth wedding anniversary was reported in *The Daily Sentinel*, there exists a description of a large party in the house in 1908. The Pearson children and friends gave a rather formal reception in the house. Among the ladies who assisted in the party, the following also lived in Rulfs houses: Perkins, Harris, Blount, Middlebrook, Matthews, Branch, Jones, Schmidt. Individual *petits fours* with monograms and punch were on the dining table for the guests. "The home was most artistically and appropriately decorated for this notable occasion, the graceful southern smilax, draping doorways, framing windows and pictures and wreathing the stairway, while luxuriant ferns and stately palms everywhere lent their beauty to the rooms."[82]

In 1915, the Pearsons sold the house to Duncan S. Spradley (1865-1944) and his wife, Freddie Houston Spradley. (Duncan was a brother to the well-known Nacogdoches Sheriff Andrew John Spradley.) During their ownership of eighty-six years, which lasted until the year 2001, the Spradleys added several outbuildings[83] and enclosed the back porch for a sunroom, but they made no major changes and maintained the integrity of the house. In an era before air conditioning, the attention Rulfs gave to ventilation and outdoor living paid dividends. In the childhood memories of Duncan's granddaughter, Dianne House, the time spent in the outdoor living spaces impressed her:

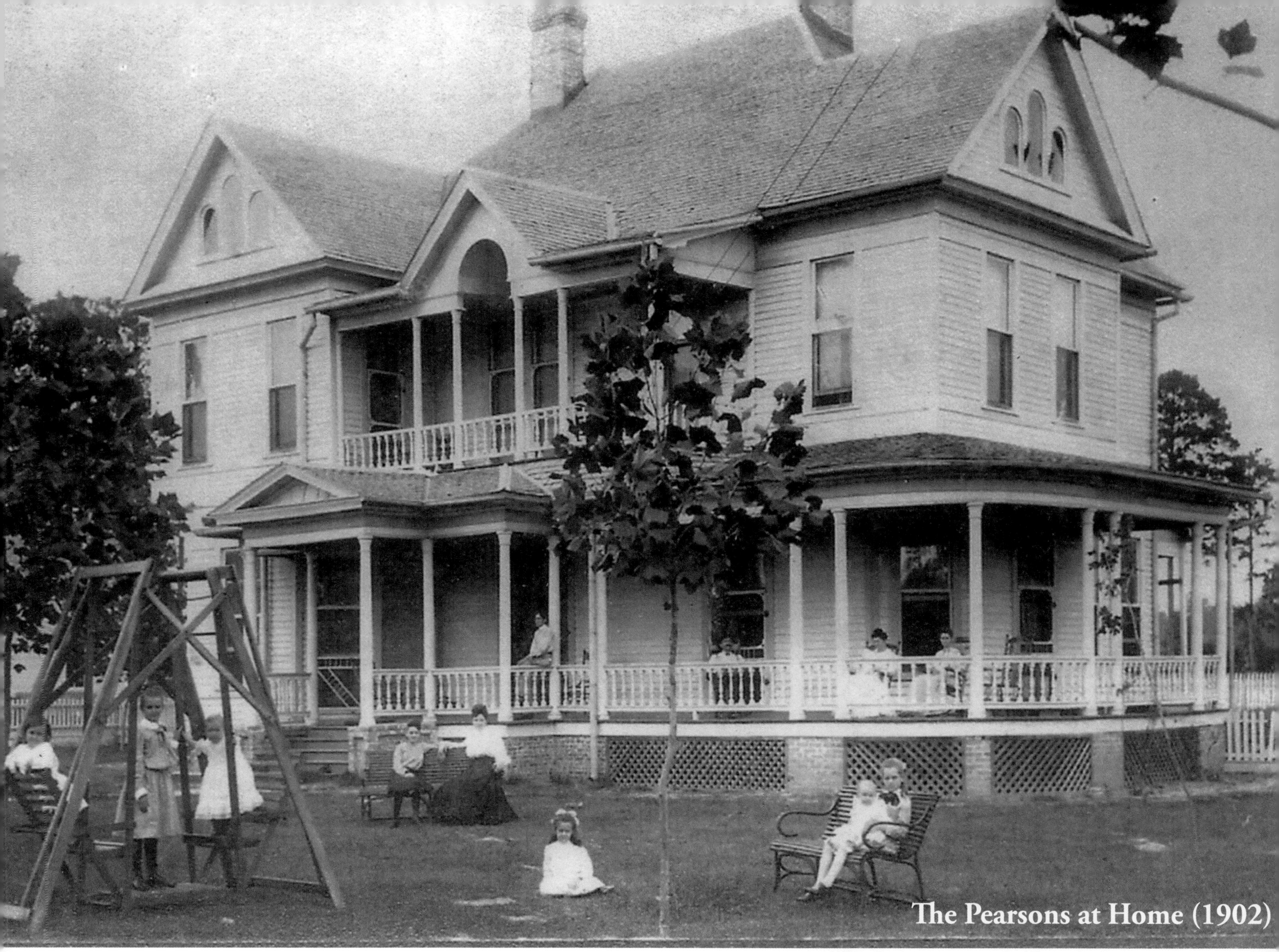

FIGURE 6.63. (Above) Front Yard Scene, ca. 1902.

The Pearsons had eleven children, but only nine of these were to survive. In this picture, there are ten children. The two older sons and the parents are on the porch, the eldest daughter on the center settee, and the rest positioned in front of their new home. From estimating the age of the baby in the lap of her sister (born in June of 1902), the picture most likely dates to the fall of 1902. The Sycamore trees, which were a distinctive feature of the house, are saplings in the picture.

The Pearson House is a textbook example of the architectural features used by Rulfs in this period: Palladian motifs, slip-head windows that opened on the porches, slim Tuscan columns, a wrap-around porch on the main level and a half-porch on the second, a classical pediment over the entrance, and latticework between the piers of the foundation.

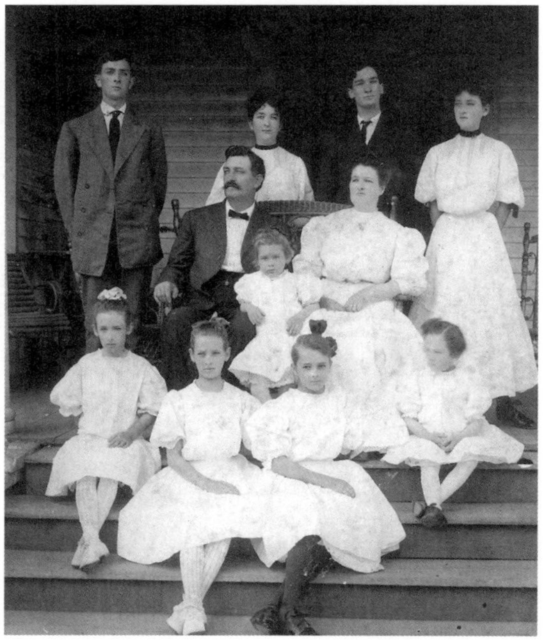

FIGURE 6.64. (Right) Pearson Family, ca. 1908.

This Pearson family portrait, taken on the twenty-fifth wedding anniversary of the parents, includes all of their living children. The two youngest girls, Lucy and Mildred, were born in this house.

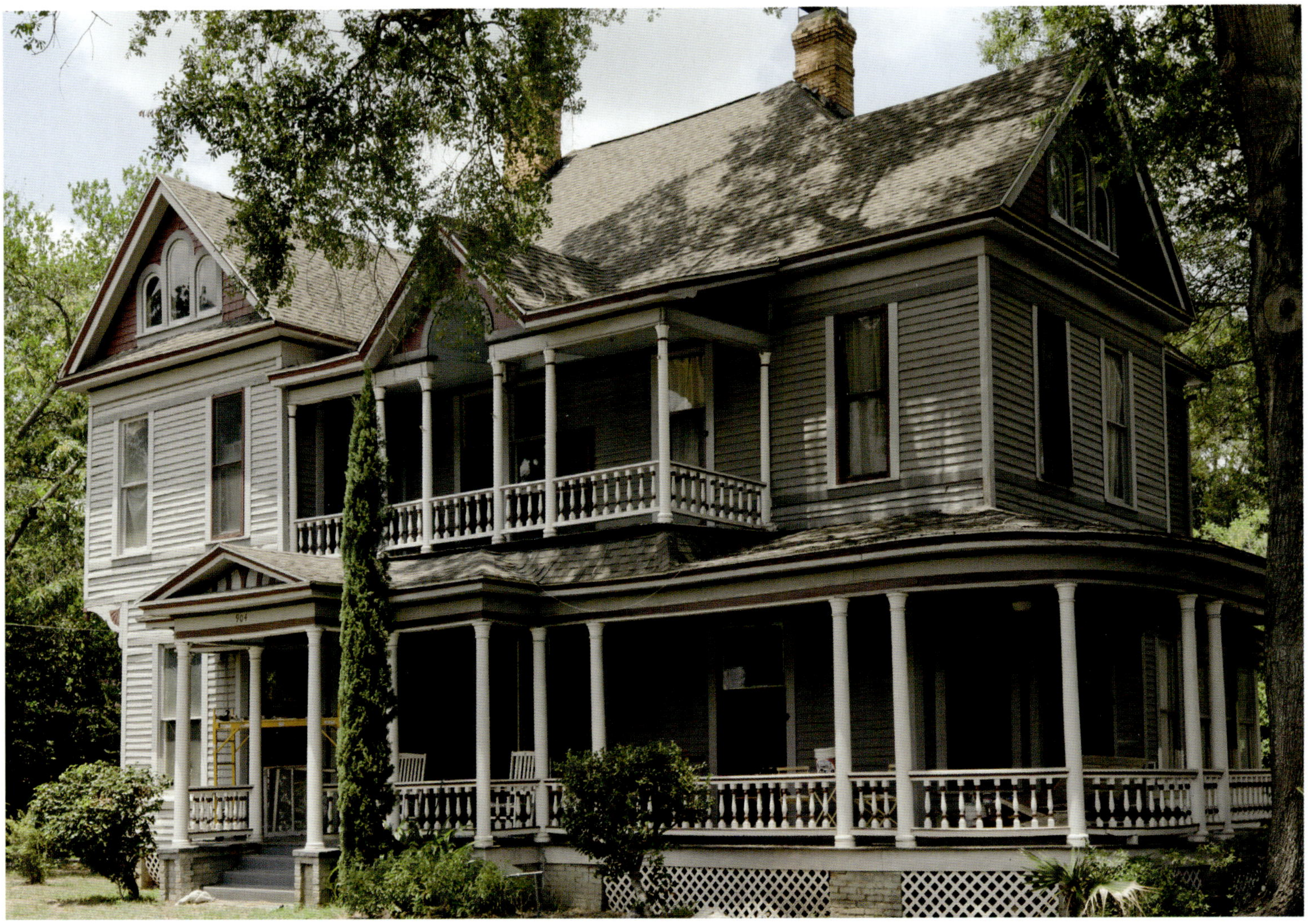

FIGURE 6.65. The Mary and Robert Whitten Home, 2012.

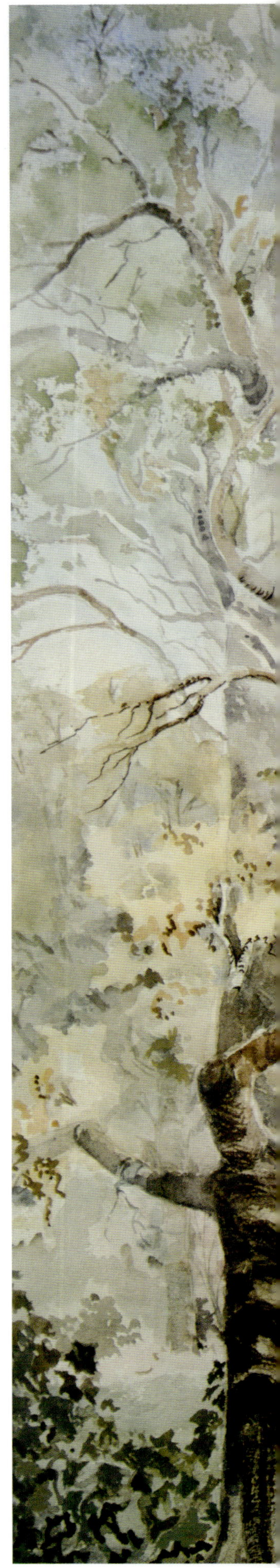

FIGURE 6.66. (Right) Watercolor of the Spradley Home by Rebecca Stanly, 1983.

Watercolor compliments of Dianne and Leland House. Dianne's grandfather Spradley owned the house after 1915.

> Of course, there was a wonderful swing in the curve of the front porch. The steps on the east side of the front porch bring back fond memories of my cousins and me eating watermelon brought from my grandparents' Big Loco farm, now on Lake Nacogdoches. The children were never allowed to eat the melons in the house. I can't imagine why!
>
> An interesting note about the trees that used to be in a double row completely around the front and east of the house: they were giant sycamores. Many were cut down when Highway 21 was widened.[84]

In additional correspondence with the author, Dianne continued:

> Papa Spradley bought this beautiful house to accommodate his large family of ten children and to provide better medical services and schooling for the younger children. The older children attended the Douglass schools and were driven in the surrey by one of the workers on the Big Loco farm to school and back each day.[85]

Robert and Mary Whitten, the current owners, have pledged themselves to "accurate and sensitive restoration and preservation." They appreciate the historic and aesthetic value of the architecture of this unique house. They have completed their first phase of stabilization of the grand old structure by stemming the damages of time to the porch, by bringing the wiring and plumbing up to code, and by weatherizing the exterior—all major and expensive undertakings.

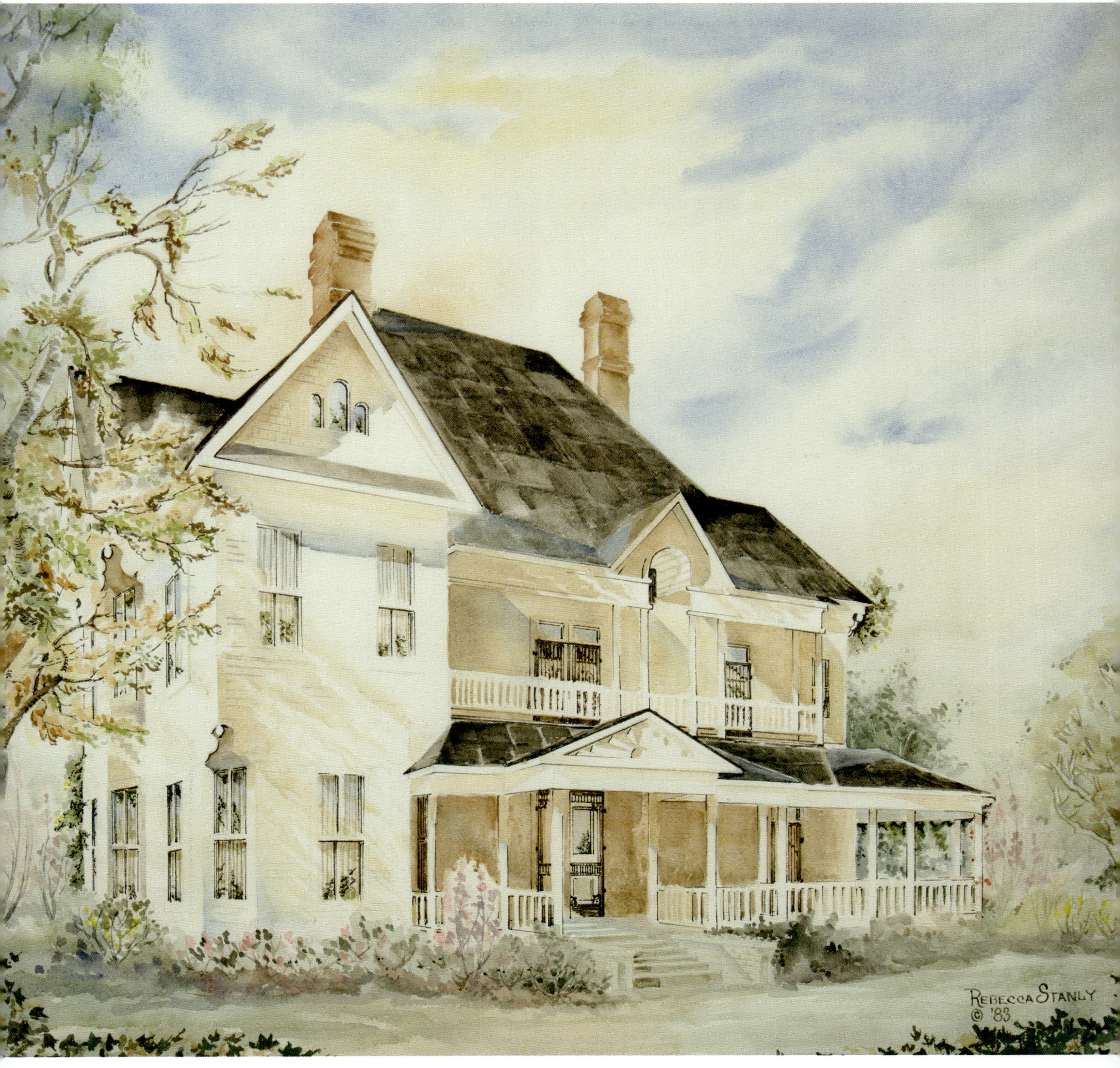
REBECCA STANLY
© '83

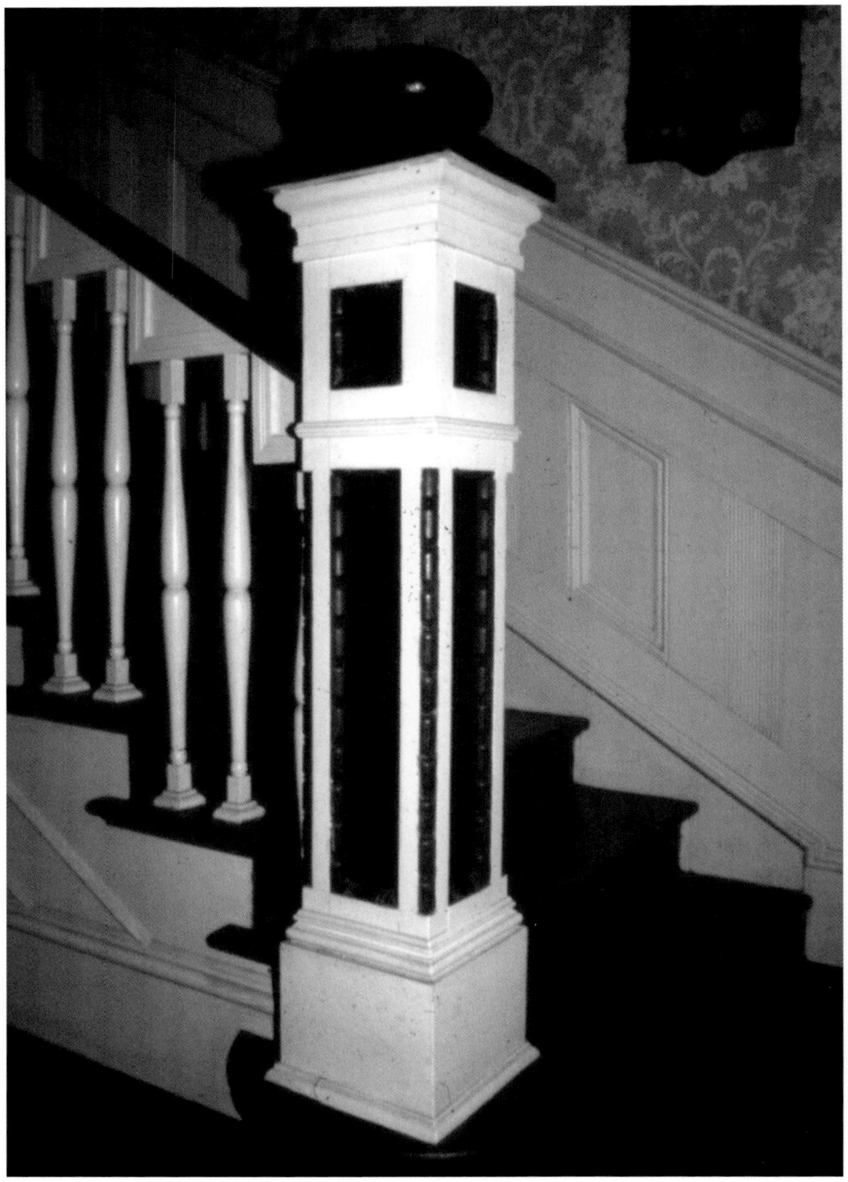

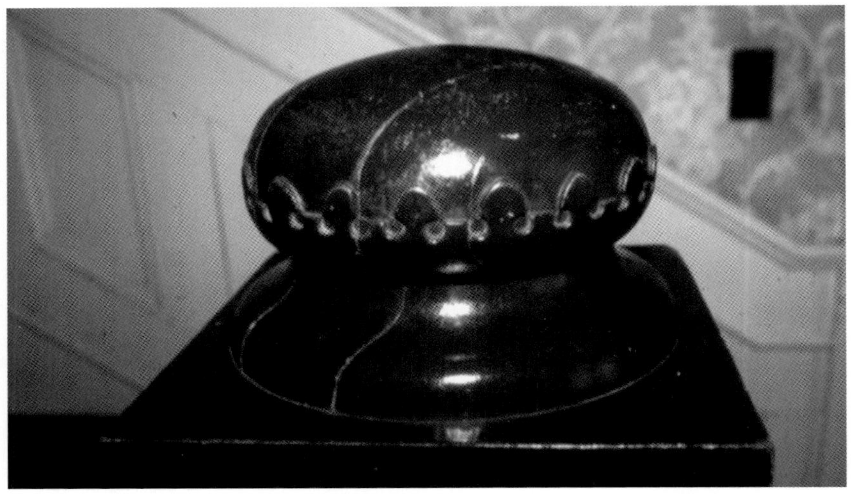

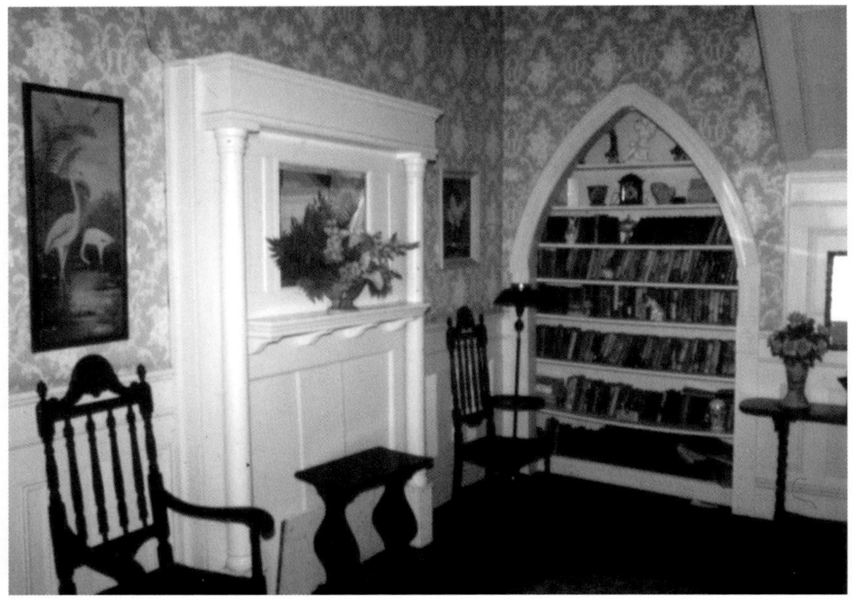

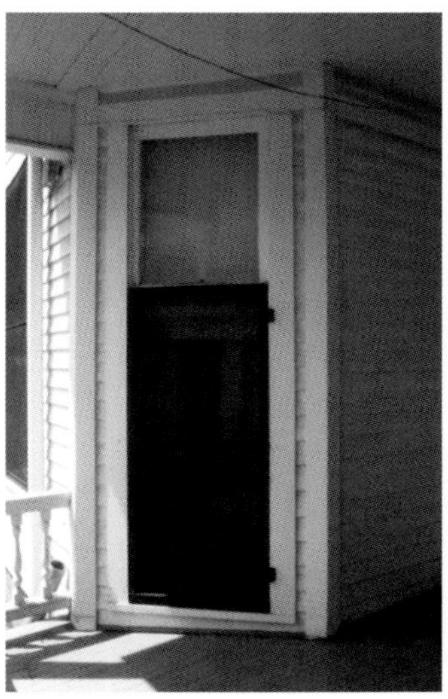

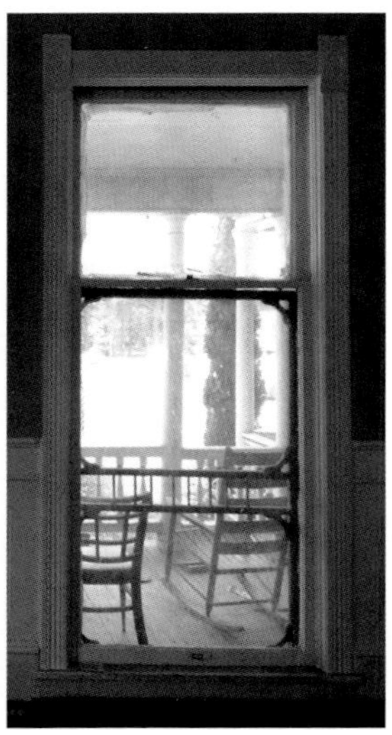

FIGURES 6.67 and 6.68. (Above) Slip-head Windows.

Examples of the slip-head windows used extensively in the Pearson-Spradley House. The lower sash disappeared into the wall when raised and the hinged screen door allowed for protection from the mosquitoes. Photographs by the author.

FIGURES 6.69 - 6.70. (Top and Above) Entrance Hall of Pearson-Spradley House, ca. 1976.

When the author first visited the Pearson-Spradley House in the mid-1970s and took these pictures, the Gothic-arched passageway to the back hall was a bookcase and the fireplace was sealed off. Photographs by the author.

FIGURES 6.71 - 6.72 (Below) Entrance Hall, c2001.

The two pictures below, provided to the author by the Whittens, date from the period after Elizabeth Spradley Bauman sold the house. The extensive paneling and wainscoting are particularly nice in this chamber.

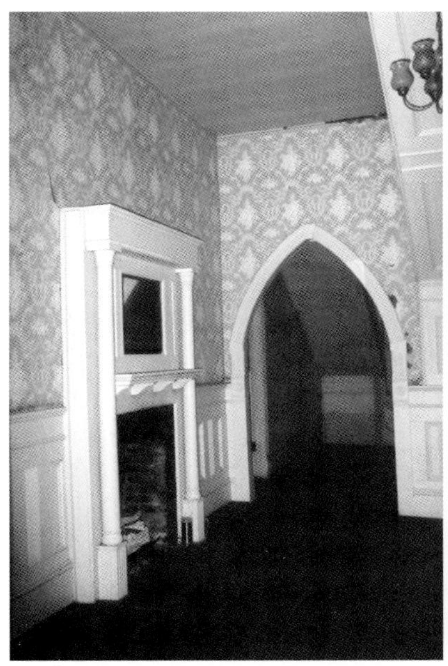

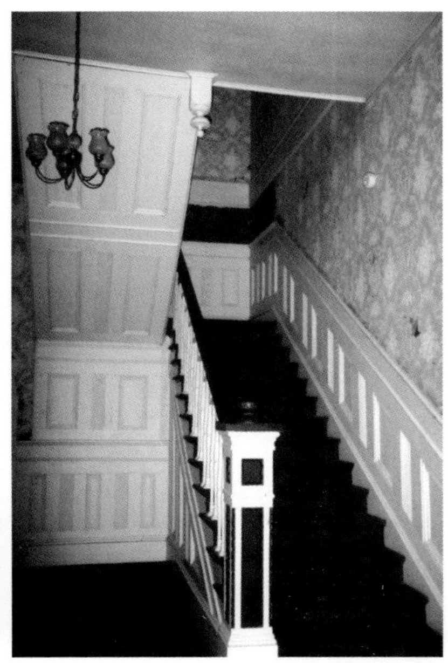

The Phillip Monroe Sanders House (1901-1902)

Although Phillip Sanders owned the land on West Main at Sanders Street from 1891, the house he built dates to 1901 or 1902.[86] According to the 1900 US Census, the Phillip Sanders family was living on the Looneyville Road–a ten member household, which included five children ranging from nine to eighteen, and three boarders. By the next census in 1910, the parents and three unmarried children (ages 19-26) are living on Main Street. The Sanborn Maps are fairly useless for the development of the houses on Irion Hill, since they do not take in the West Main area until 1922. Many tax collection records are missing; the first available for the house are from 1907. Any doubt about the date of the house, however, does not extend to a question of whether Rulfs built the house for Sanders. In interviews with the author, both Rulfs' niece, Mary Stewart Duncan, and Phillip Sanders' cousin, James Eugene Sanders, the author's neighbor, confirmed the architect's involvement.[87]

Architecturally, the house fits into the years between 1901 and 1903. The eclectic elements employed by Rulfs in these years abound on this house. The architect's favorite elements—pediments over the front door, Tuscan columns (both full and half length), Palladian windows (both arched and square), and chamfered corners, as well as horizontal and vertical banding—help to confirm his design involvement, but do not help with a date. He used all of these elements from the early 1890s to the early 1910s. His preference for plain entablatures after 1900 helps somewhat; the house has no fretwork friezes, but he used turned balusters until 1905 because they were readily available. His use of both narrow and wide 1/1 windows, for example, places the house around 1900 when the wide windows became available in the local catalogues. He used the same narrow 1/1 windows used on the Will Sanders House; however, on this house he paired the windows. (On other houses with the paired windows, as in the Tom Summers house later, he usually grouped older windows as he remodeled a house.) The cutaway upper balcony Rulfs designed is like the house across the street (albeit the Cooper upper gallery was enclosed later.) It is interesting that he did not use slip-head windows here, but doors on both the lower and upper porches. Unlike the Cooper and Middlebrook homes, the front wrap-around porch and the pocket porch both face the well-established top-of-the-hill neighborhood.

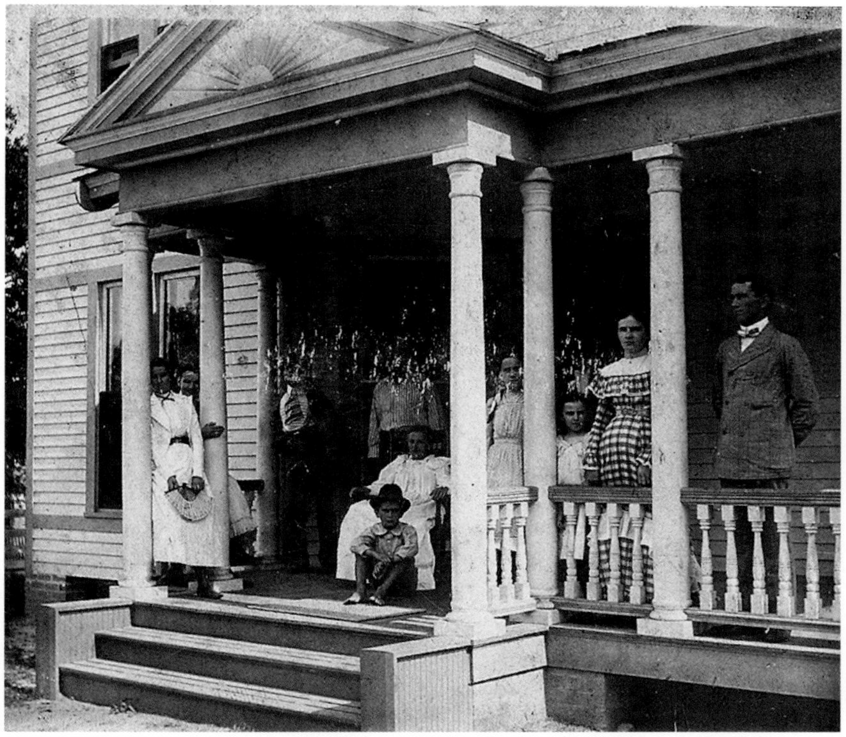

FIGURE 6.73. (Above) The Sanders Family, Porch of the Phillip Sanders House, Date Unknown, ca. 1906. *Photograph compliments of Barbara Stump.*

FIGURE 6.74 (Below) The Philip Sanders House, Irion Hill, 2011.

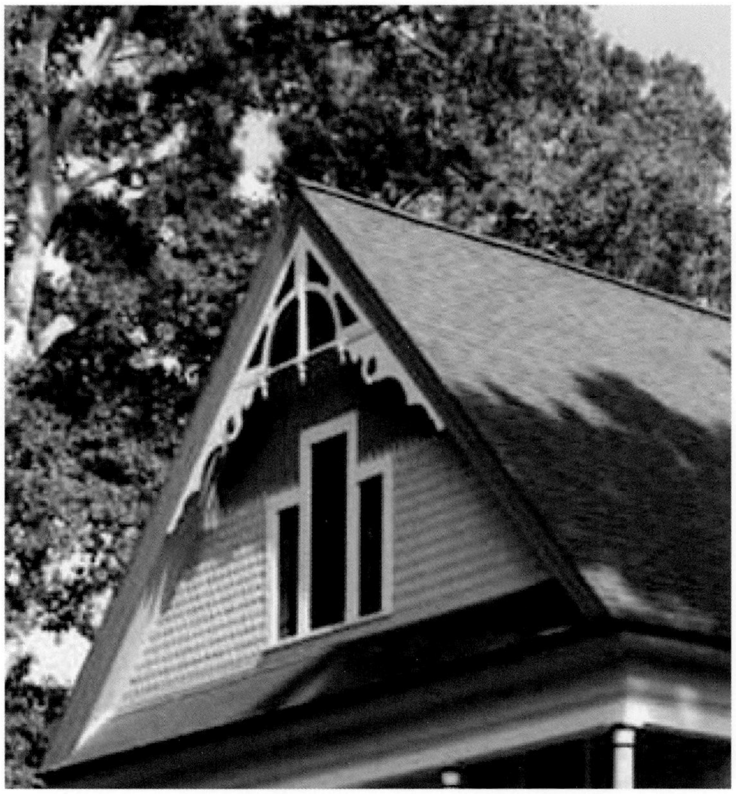

There are several unique features to this house. The full-width front gable façade, for instance, is not part of a complex asymmetrical façade as in the Cooper house across West Main, but a defining feature of the house. Also, while the house does have a hipped roof in the rear, it is different from his standard hip-and-gable roofs, such as the one he used on the Will Sanders or Pearson homes. The lower roofs of the cross gables on the west and east of the house tie into the larger main front gable of the house. The tympana have only restrained ornaments; the encasing bargeboards are perfectly straight. Even the bracket supports on the cut-away bays on each side of the house are restrained. The Palladian group in the center was composed of an ordinary, narrow 1/1 window with two multi-colored side lights. (The Middlebrook and Cooper Houses have similar Palladian motifs using stained glass.) The ventilation louvers in the center of the grouping, as on the Cooper home across the street, were a later addition. The horizontal elements on this house keep the vertical elements well-balanced.

Michael and Barbara Stump, who purchased the house in 2002,[88] have done a wonderful job of restoration on the house. The carefully chosen colors for the exterior help to emphasize the many architectural details: the horizontal banding boards, the gable ornament, the pediment over the door, and the collars on the columns.

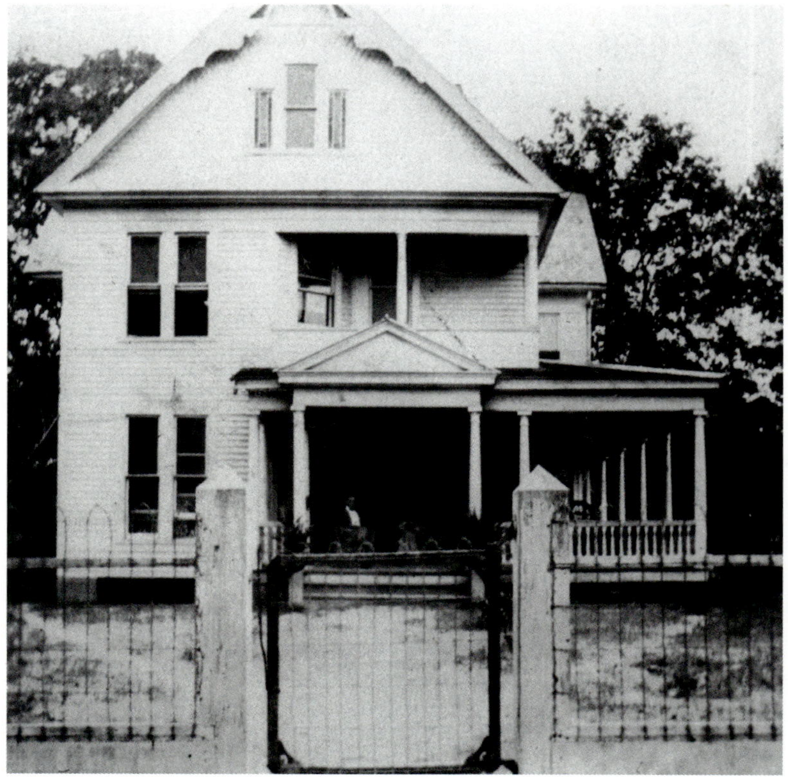

FIGURE 6.75. (Above) The Phillip Monroe Sanders House, ca. 1903.

As this photograph (ca. 1903) of the Phillip Sanders House shows, the entrance gate to the house stood on West Main Street. After the great excavation work was done to lower the slope of Main Street, the owners changed its address to Sanders Street sometime after 2002. Courtesy of ETRC.

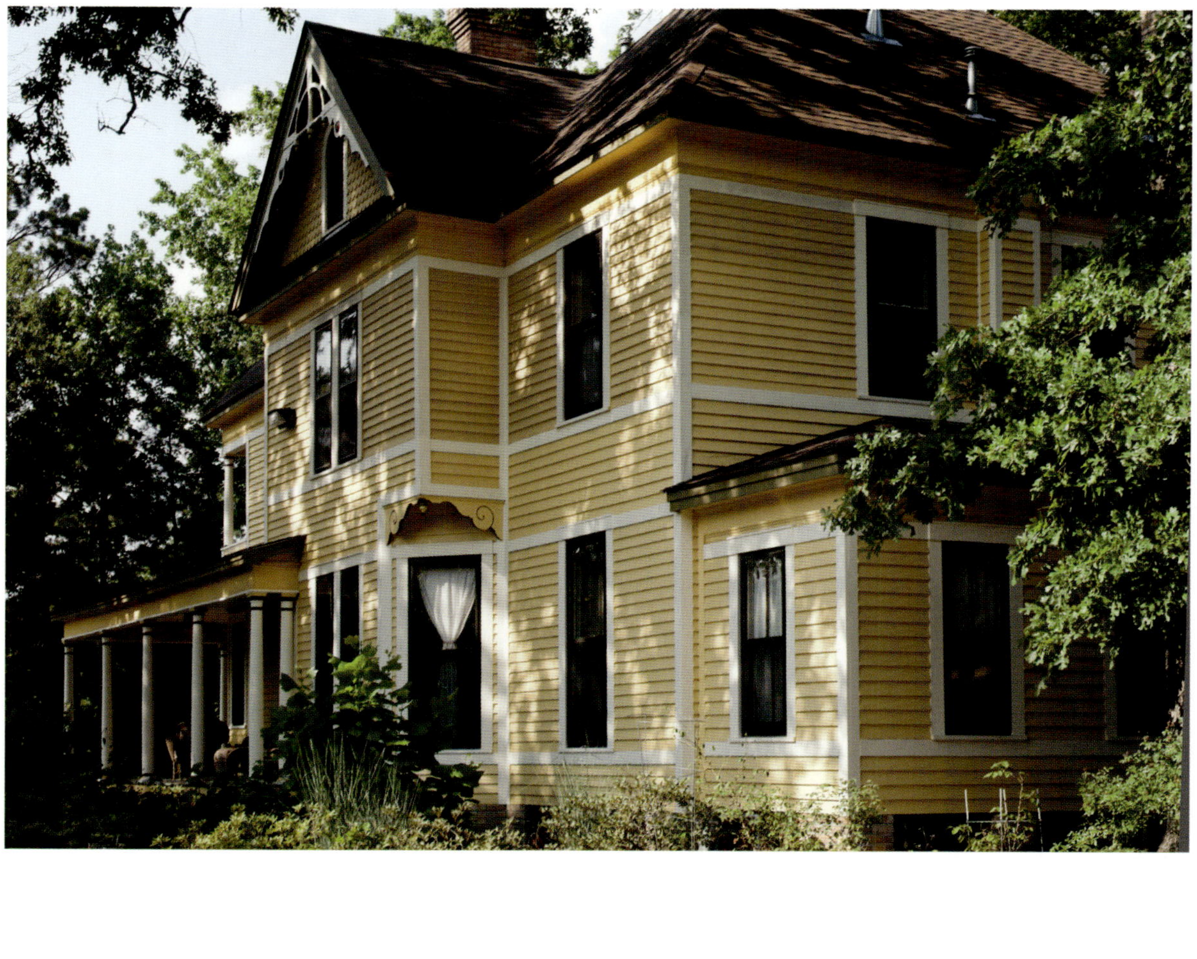

FIGURE 6.76. (Left) The West Side of the Stump Home.

The Sanders House, unlike the Cooper and Middlebrook houses, did not have the same dramatic views of the downtown, although the second floor pocket porch off the front did have such a view. The distance of the house from Sanders Street on this west side, however, allowed for an important pastorial vista and a view of the Pearson House across Main Street.

FIGURE 6.77. (Right) North Elevation, Stump Home.

The Phillip Monroe Sanders House faces Main Street. Michael and Barbara Stump, who owned the house after 2002, created a new drive-way entrance on Sanders Street; creating a new entrance on Main Street would have been too dangerous, given the 5-way intersection at the top on the hill. By incorporating their western property into the approach to the house, the Stumps made the new approach seem completely natural.

They also enhanced the architectural details of the exterior in a most admirable way due by their selections of paint.

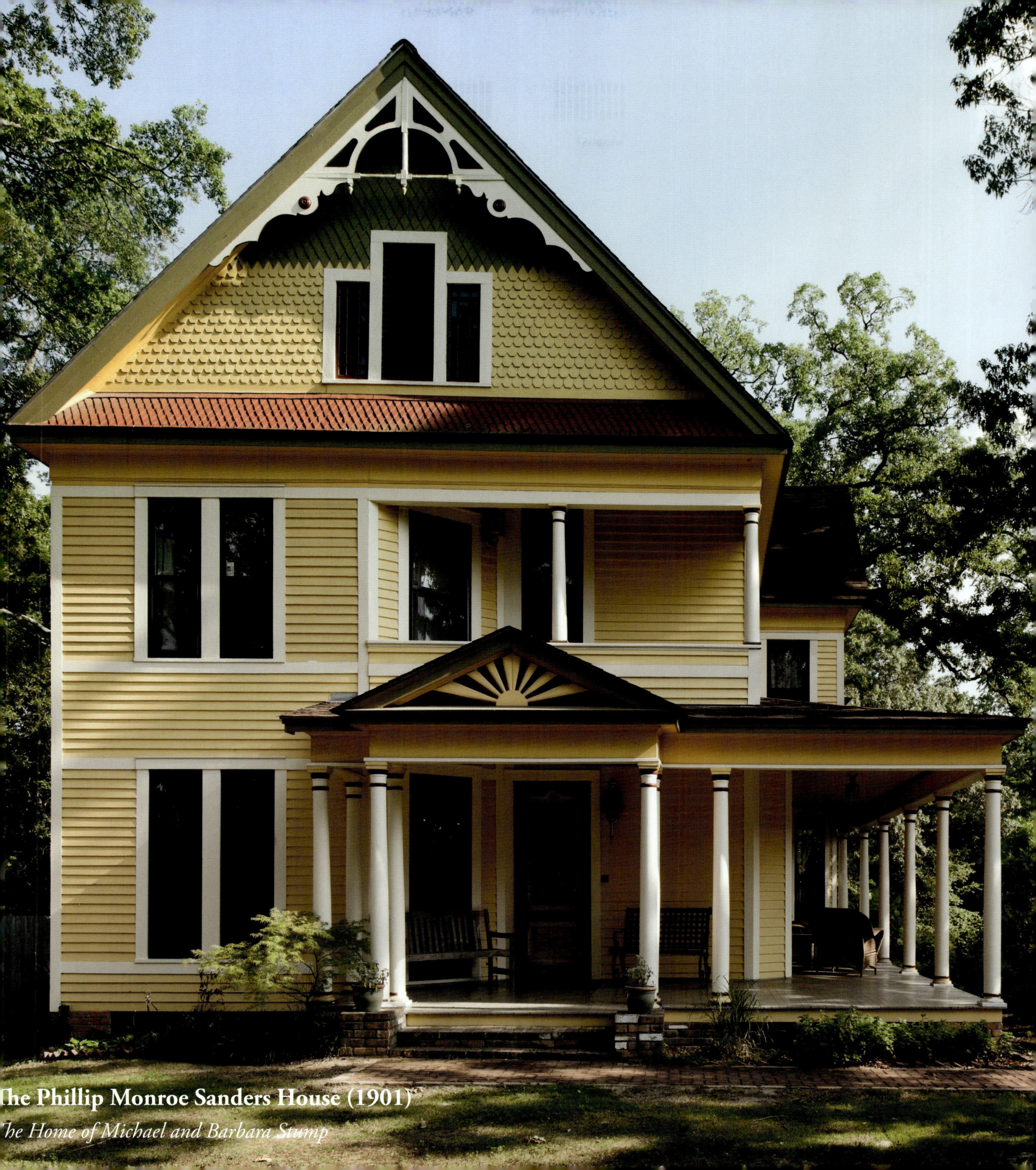

The Phillip Monroe Sanders House (1901)

The Home of Michael and Barbara Stump

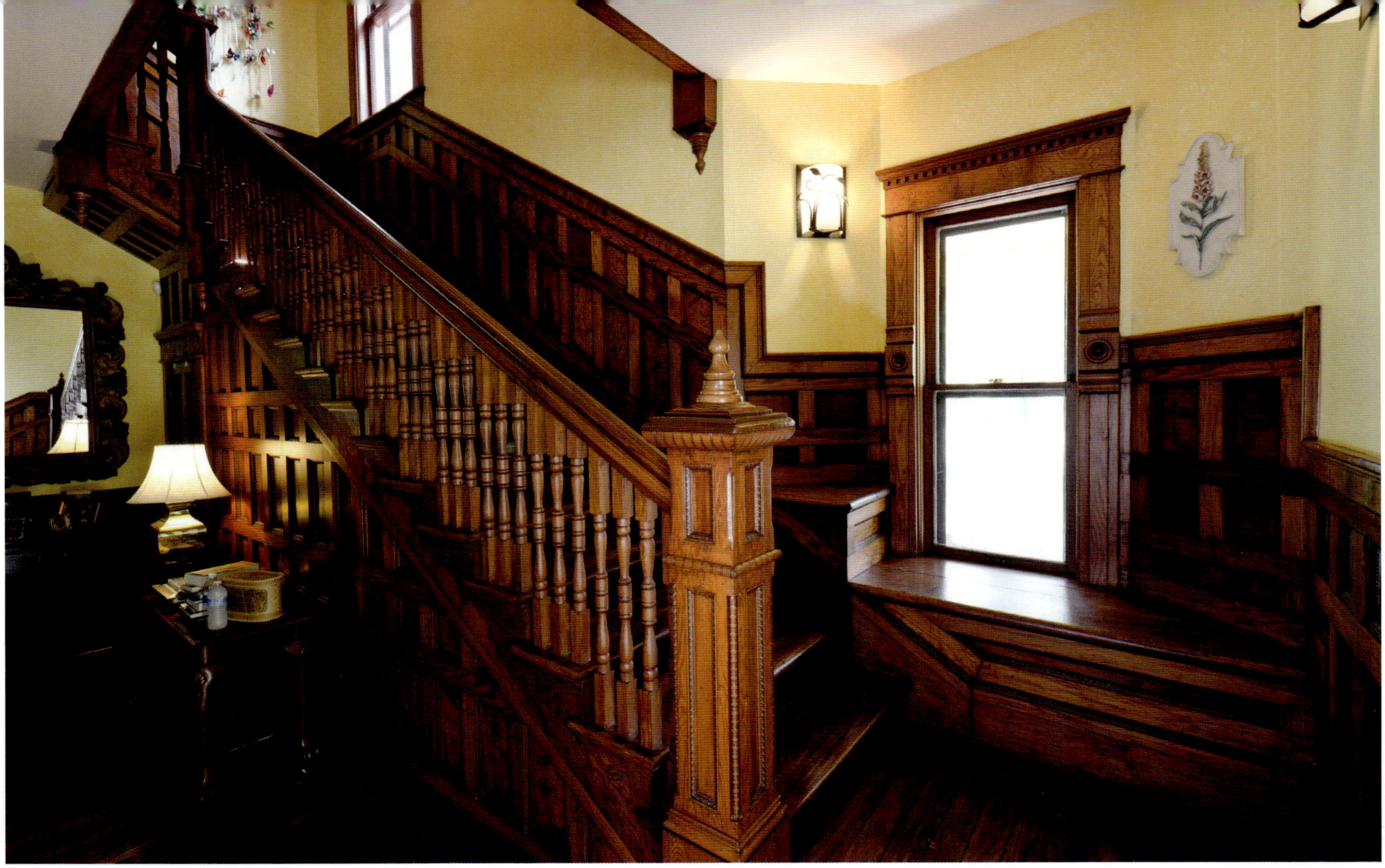

FIGURES 6.78 - 6.80. The Staircase at the Sanders House.

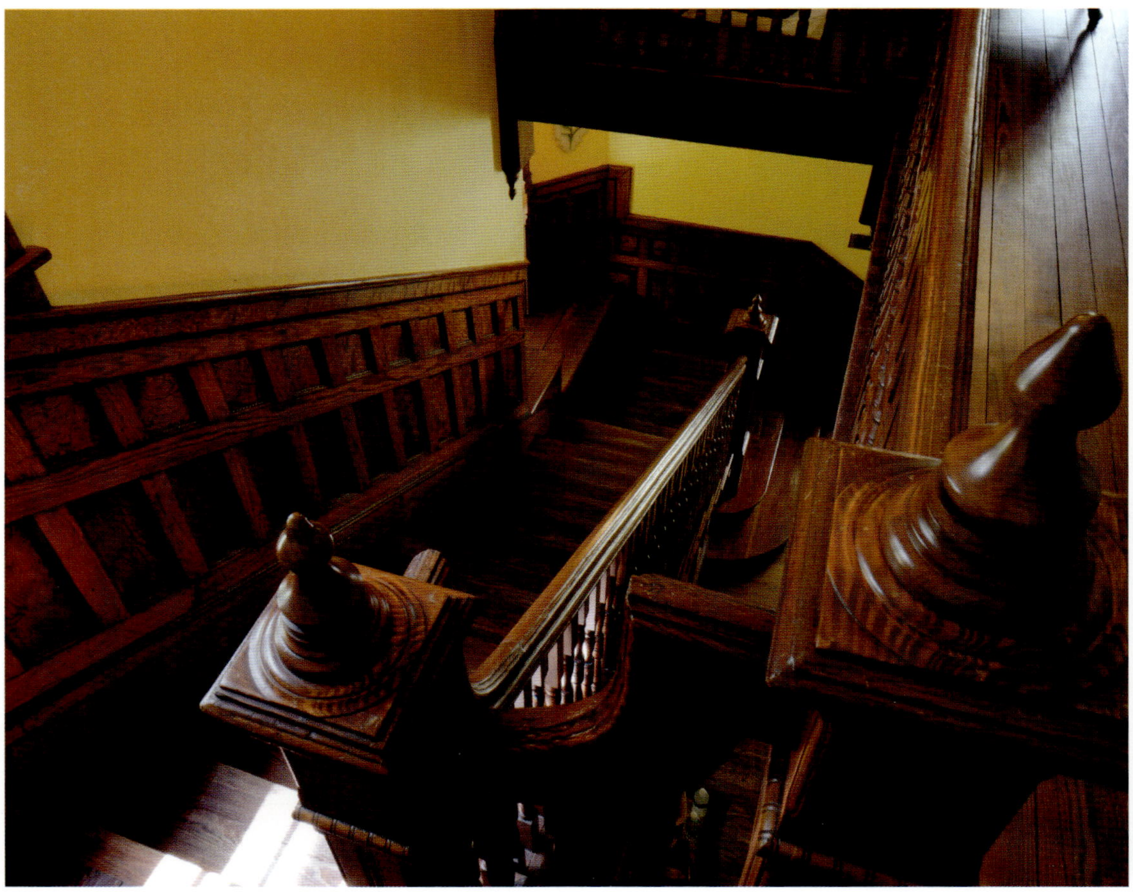

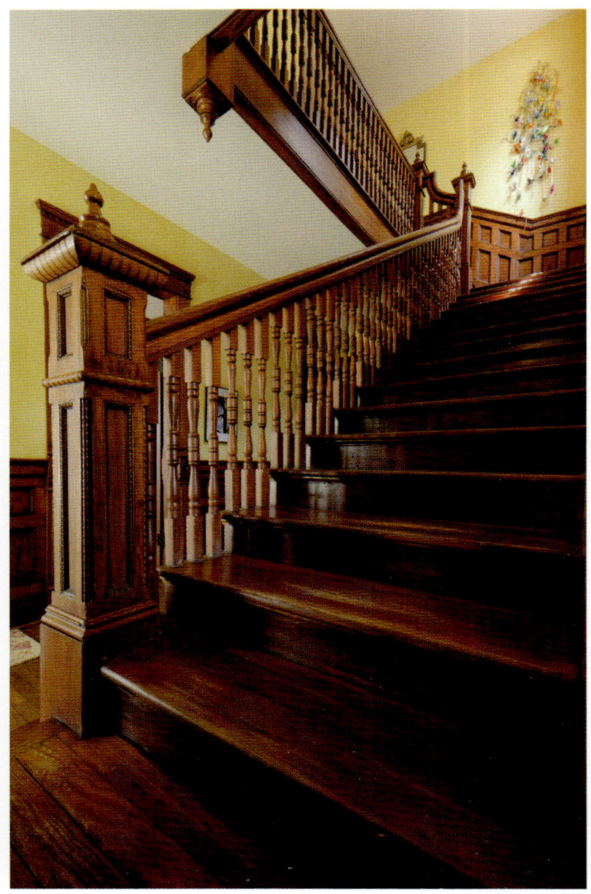

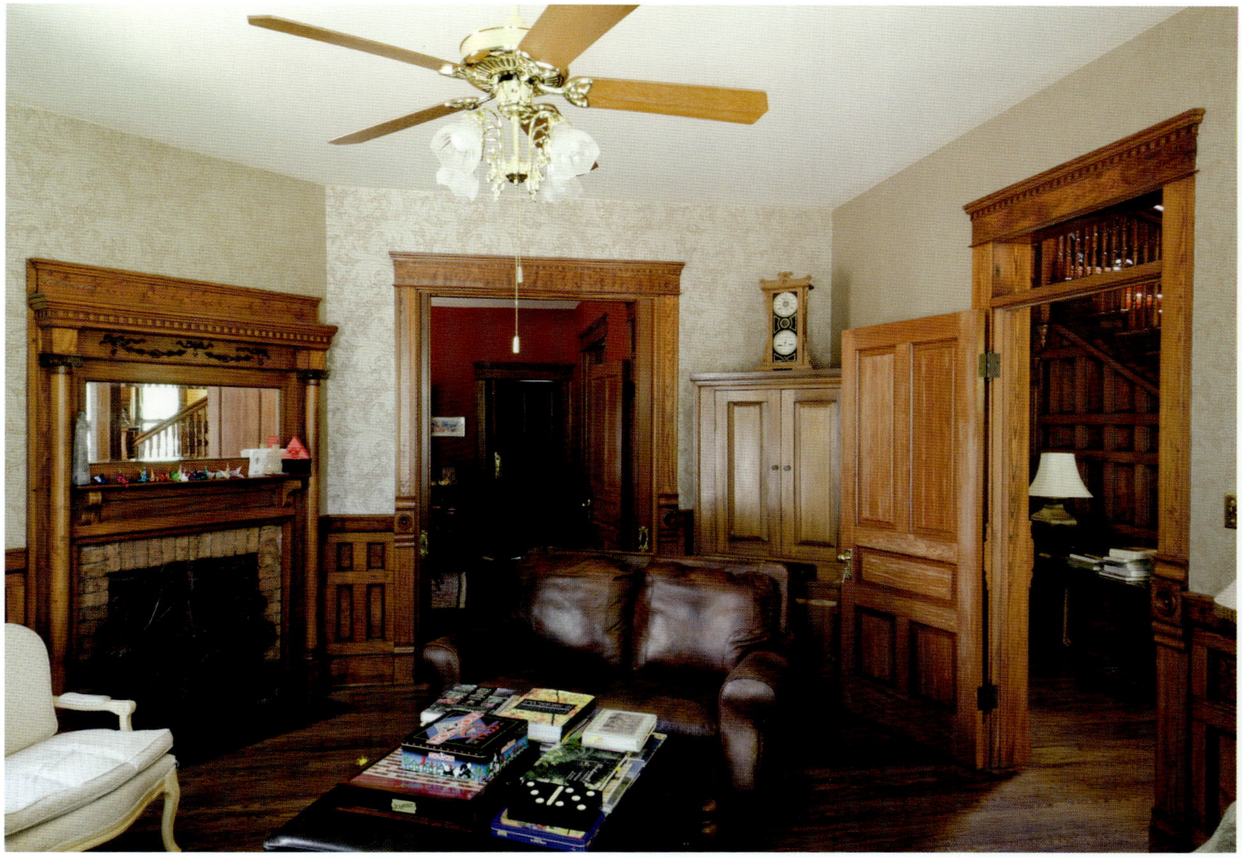

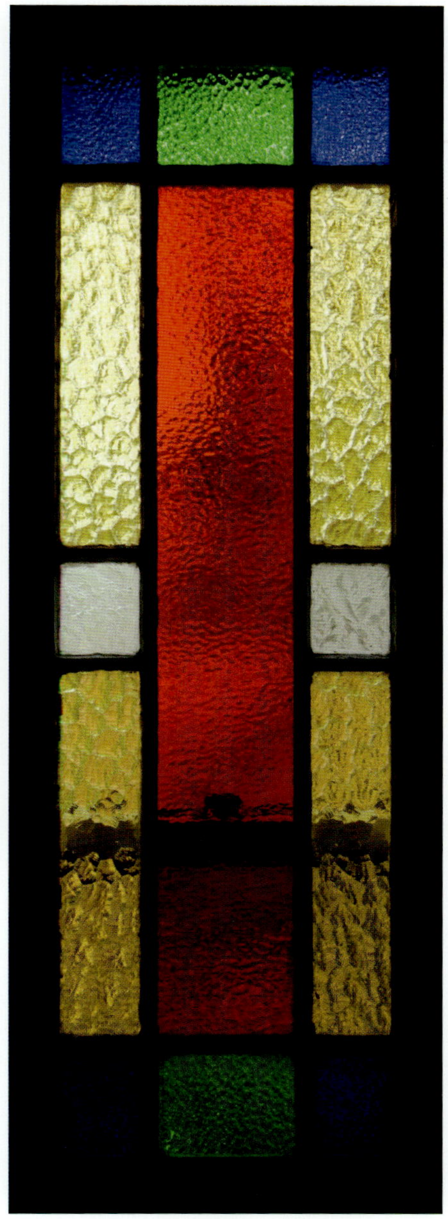

FIGURE 6.81. Parlor, The Stump Home.

FIGURES 6.82 (Right) and 6.83. (Below, Right) Colored Glass Sashes.
Rulfs used stained or colored glass windows in many of his houses. These would have appeared in catalogues for order. Some windows at the turn of the Twentieth Century had clear central panes surrounded by colored glass. This sash, salvaged from the side of the Palladian grouping in the front gable (below, right) in 2003, has a crimson center panel framed with small colored panes. Before the replacement with louvers, the central window in this configuration was a simple double hung window with two clear sashes to provide light to the attic.

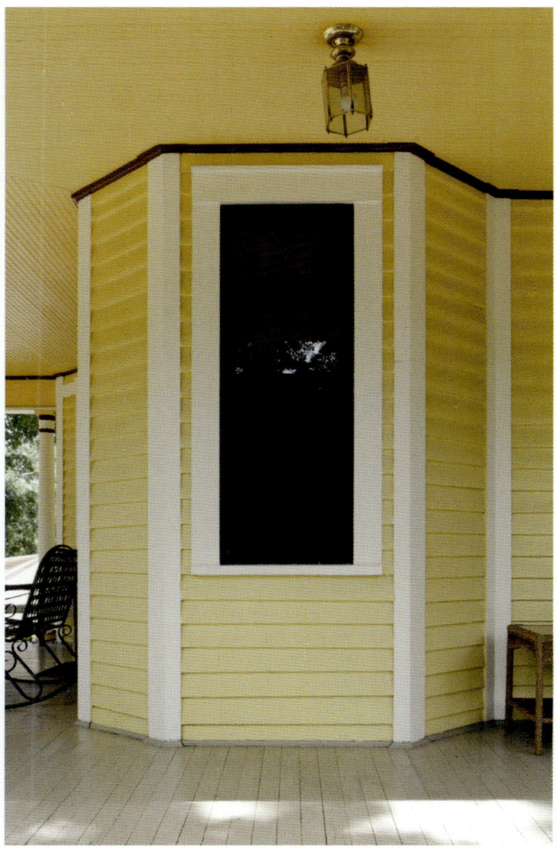

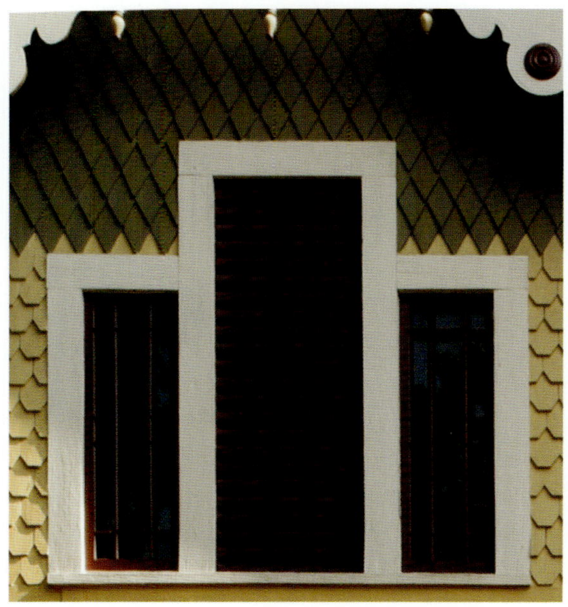

FIGURE 6.84. (Left) Exterior of the Seat and Window on the Staircase.
The inclusion of the seat and window on the interior required a bay configuration on the porch.

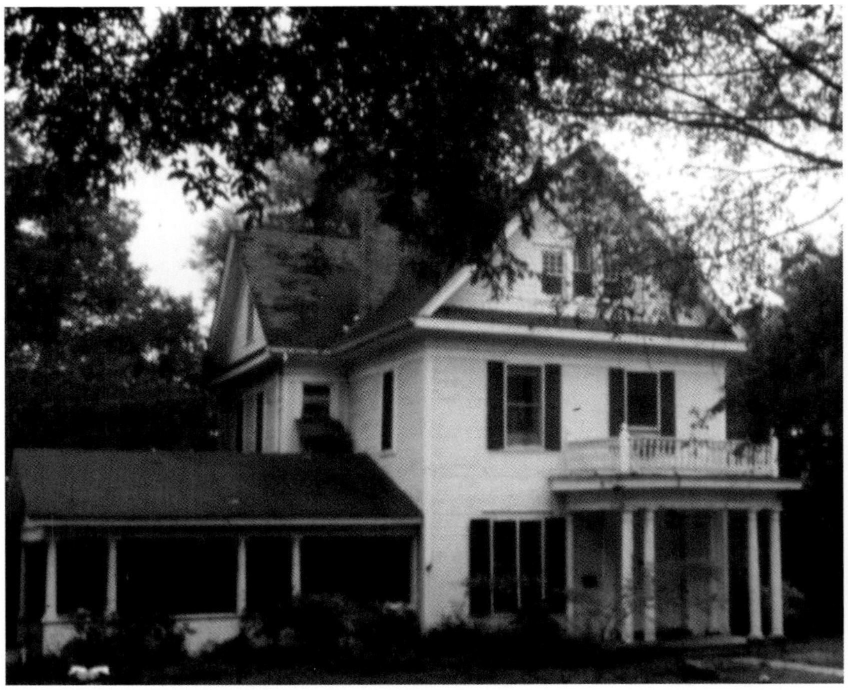

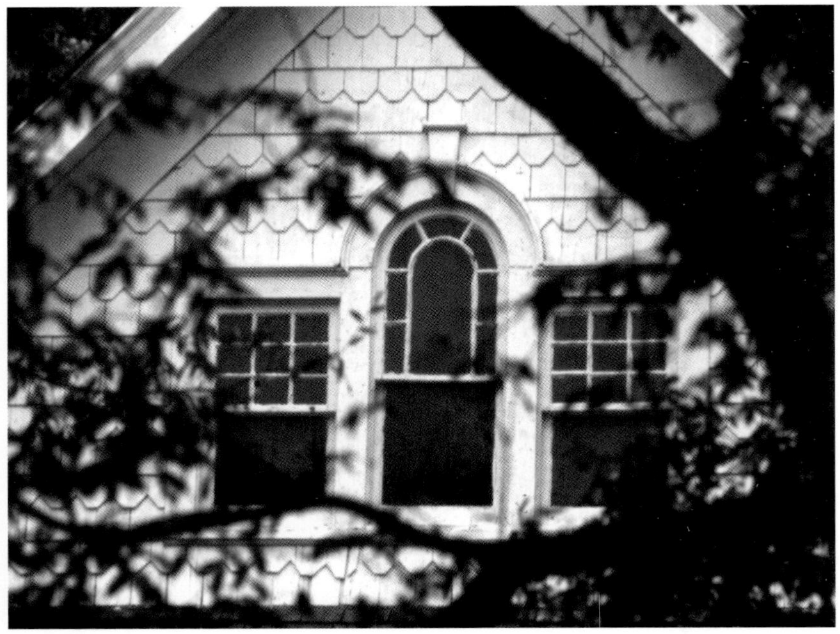

FIGURES 6.85 and 6.86. William Harrington House, 1976.
Photographs by the author in 1976.

The William H. Harrington House (c1910-1911)

The house at 703 Virginia Avenue, subjected to less research that many of the houses on Virginia Avenue, is most likely a Rulfs house. Confirmation of this does not rest with direct testimony or documentation like so many of the other houses in the area. The niece of the architect, when she interviewed with the author, was more interested in the houses on the west side of Virginia and said nothing about this house. The Victor and Victor Survey and the National Register Nomination for the district have the house dated to 1904, but this is surely incorrect. June Harris did sell the land to his partner Robert Lindsey in 1904 for $600.00,[89] but it took four years for Lindsey to find a buyer. In 1908 he sold the land to William H. Harrington for $900.00; at that price, it would not have included a house. The Harringtons are in the 1910 Census, but they are not at this location until the 1920 federal survey.[90] By using census records, the house could date any time between 1910 and 1920. The property remained in the Harrington family until 1943, when O. F. Baxter purchased the house and lot. The attribution of the house to the Baxter family is surely incorrect.[91]

The first Sanborn Map to document the area of Virginia Avenue is 1922.[92] The Harrington House is definitely on the map at that time, but this does not mean the house was built that late. Even the Harris House (1895) does not appear on a map until 1922. The house's footprint remains the same from 1922 to 1946. (See FIGURE 6.87 Sanborn Map.) It is a two-story, T-shaped house that has a predominant front gable and cross gables along the back (or east side). The original porch—always one-story—wrapped around the entire front wing of the house; there were doors at the ends of both the north and south sides.

Why attribute the house to Rulfs? The first and most obvious clue is the use of the Palladian window in the tympanum of the front gable. The fact that the seller of the lot was Lindsey also argues for Rulfs being the architect. The two men collaborated on a number of houses. Using Rulfs was a measure of importance Lindsey would have suggested to his new neighbors. Additionally, the house is very similar to another house on Irion Hill. The predominant front gable, reminds one of the Phillip Sanders House at 100 South Sanders, with the exception that the porch on the Harrington-Baxter House went around both sides of the front gable, instead of just one half. Both houses have cross gables, which form a T at their rear. (Rulfs had used this also on the Steamboat House and the Slay House on North Street.) Across the entire east side of the house, overlooking the city, there was a two-story gallery—the great selling point of all the Irion-Forbes houses.

The Sanborn Maps do not indicate a pediment, or at lease one that projected from the line of the porch. The Harrington House had symmetry because the porches wrapped the entire front. Since the entrance was not in the middle of the house, Rulfs possibly did not have a pediment over the front door; that would have emphasized the asymmetrical nature of this fact. Of course, the entrance of the Phillip Sanders House was not in the middle of the house, but the porch to the west made it seem so. It is reasonable to think the house had Tuscan columns (the preference of Rulfs) across the entire front gallery. When the Baxters removed the front porch from the house, they most likely used some of columns to support the new entry porch and used the rest for the carport, which was added to the north side.

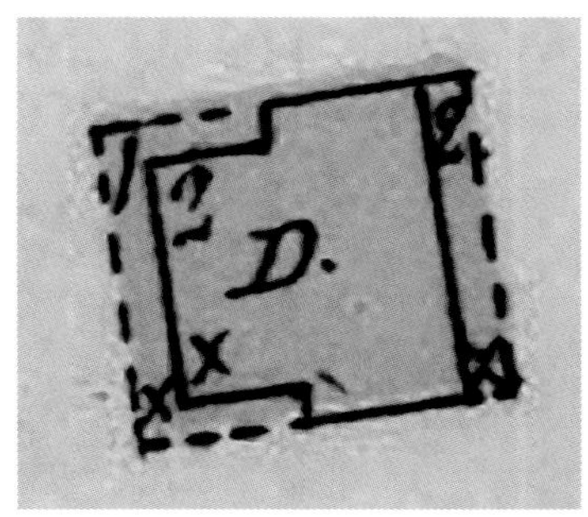

FIGURE 6.87. Harrington House, 1922 Sanborn Map
This drawing of the Harrington House gives the footprint of the house before the wrap-around front porch was removed.

The Evolution of the North Square, Between 1885-1900

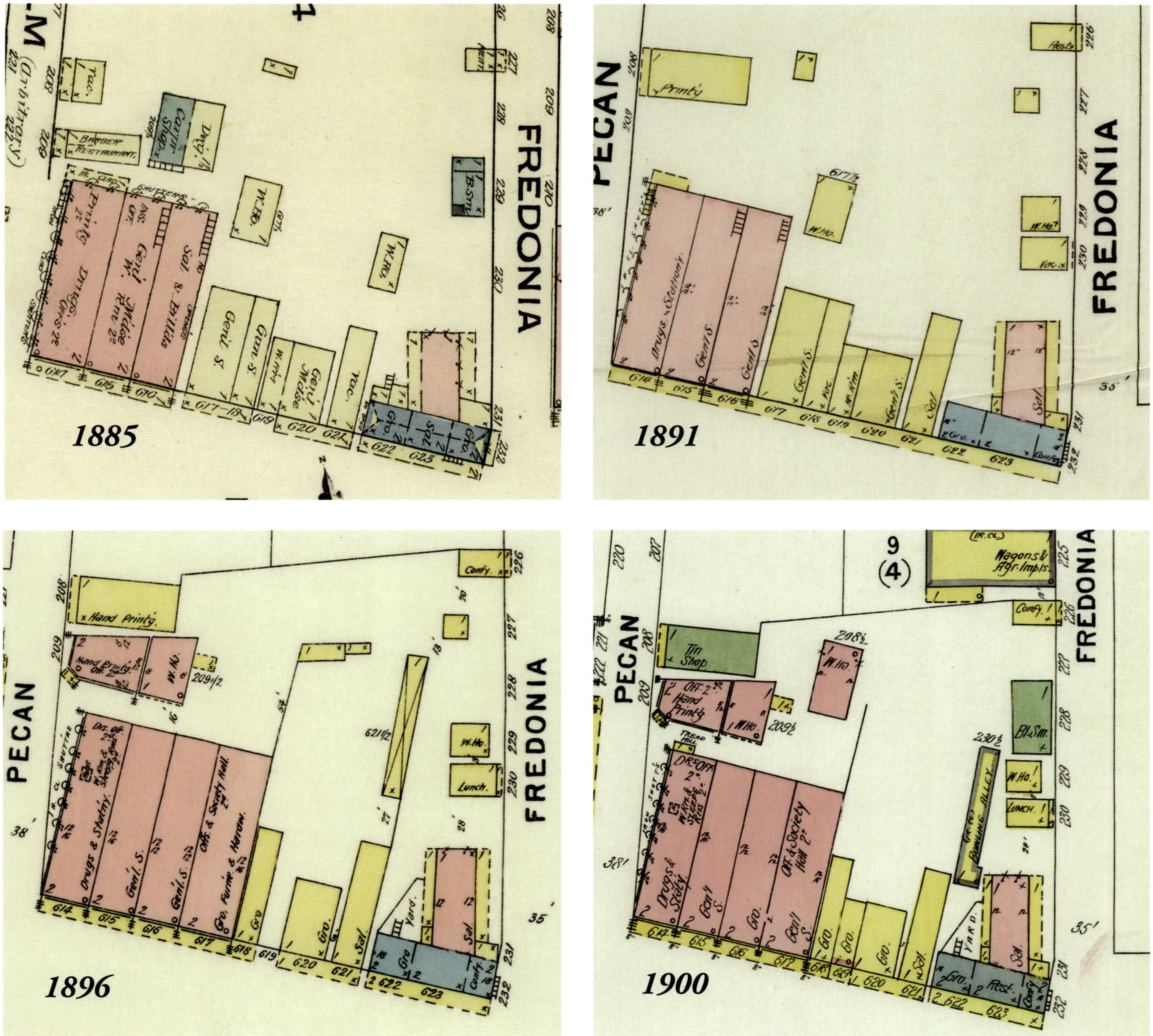

FIGURES 6.88 - 6.91. Details of the North Side of the Square, Sanborn Maps 1885-1900.

As a close survey of these maps of Main Street along the North Square shows, the only constant landmark on the maps is the Old Stone House (Stone Fort) shown in blue to indicate stone. The first brick block by Rulfs shows an enlargement between 1891 and 1896, with a fourth unit. Before the next visit by the Sanborn cartographers, this would change.

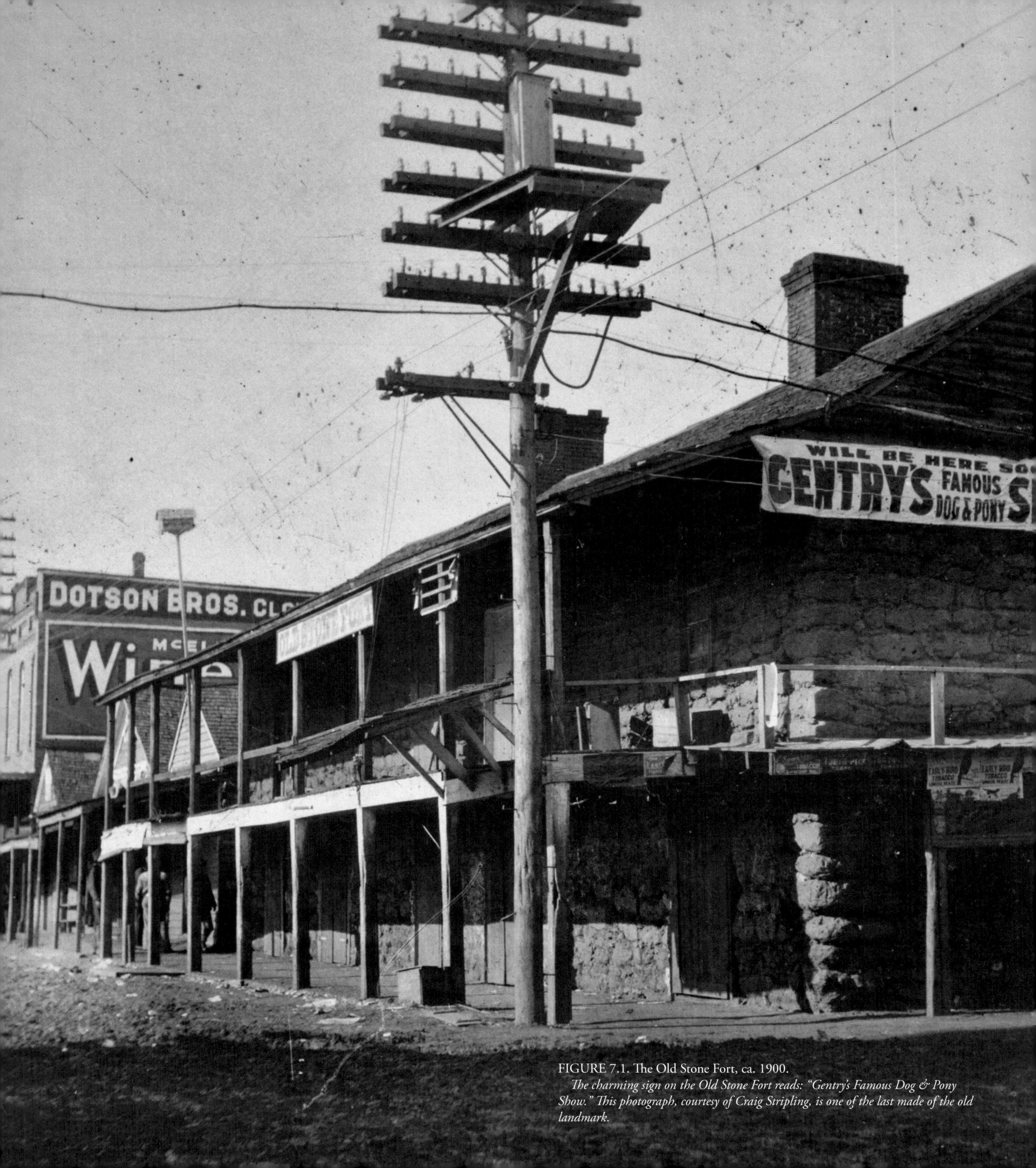

FIGURE 7.1. The Old Stone Fort, ca. 1900.

The charming sign on the Old Stone Fort reads: "Gentry's Famous Dog & Pony Show." This photograph, courtesy of Craig Stripling, is one of the last made of the old landmark.

CHAPTER VII

The Crises

Transition to a New Century, 1900-1909

"When sorrows come, they come not single spies, but in battalions." Shakespeare, *Hamlet.*

> It was wrapped in tradition as in a garment, permeated—not to say–drugged–by the perfume of its past. Yet the tradition was vague and nebulous; it was almost impossible for the inquiring newcomer to put his finger on a fact .... Nacogdoches, sitting beside her dusty streets, beneath her immemorial trees, was so proud of being "historic" that she had forgotten her history. Karle Wilson Baker on Nacogdoches in 1900.

The past is a puzzle, and by turning and focusing on the different shapes of the pieces, historians eventually hope to fit the puzzle together. A clearer picture of the past sometimes emerges only by taking a second look at the same material or, as in the case with this book, looking at the material through a different prism or lens while adding new research findings. The main purpose of this chapter is to establish a context, a mood for the subsequent chapters. Diedrich Rulfs is *not* the main actor in the dramatic events discussed in this chapter. His work in transforming the town, however, did not happen in a vacuum. This chapter focuses on the angst Nacogdoches experienced after the turn of the century.

Perhaps convenient, but the turn of every new century seems to trigger reassessments. Reassessments can inspire confidence or apprehension. In almost all cases, the process proves transforming. By 1900, Nacogdoches had spent two decades catching up with the modern world: its population had increased from 500 to nearly 2000; its downtown had become a profitable center of business. The town had clothed itself in the garment of new commercial and residential buildings. With remarkably few controversies challenging the overall direction of events, most leaders anticipated the new century with pride and confidence, bordering on self-satisfaction. Nacogdoches had weathered the national economic downturn in 1893 without incident. The consolidation of the rail lines, under the new ownership of the Southern Pacific Line in 1899,[1] seemed just the stimulus to ensure economic prosperity. Inevitably, however, unforeseen events have a way of intervening.

Reconciling the past, the present, and the future is a perennial problem. In reflection, one can sense that the changes of the last two decades of the previous century had interrupted the stability of Nacogdoches. The result was an identity crisis. Is stability built on materialistic considerations, or is stability as much related to non-materialistic measurements? By 1900, competing visions emerged. How would Nacogdoches define itself? Once defined, how could the answer be manifest and translated into the future? What signature image would the town project to the rest of the state and nation? Of course, all towns go through identity crises from time to time, but few have gone through one as dramatic as the one Nacogdoches experienced in the opening years of the new century. As the champions of modernization prepared to steam ahead full throttle, each year of the new century seemed to bring one or more new sorrows to challenge the charted course.

While law enforcement, the main service provided by the County of Nacogdoches, continued to be a problem between the town and the county, new unforeseen challenges began to plague the town as it emerged from its sleepy, rural pioneer past. With change came the need for new restrictions. Questions abounded, some practical, others more philosophical, but all with important implications. What services should the town provide? Could the town have closely grouped buildings without fire codes and a fire department? How would the absence of services affect the emerging city's safety, development, and appeal to outside businesses and potential residents? Could the town claim to be modern without paved streets, a water and electrical system, sewage, and drainage? Always a central question, should these services be provided privately or publicly? Perhaps all ages struggle with combinations of these questions, but they all seemed to hit Nacogdoches at one time because of the rapid changes in the prior decades.

One contemporary barometer of trouble was R. W. Haltom's newly established *Daily Sentinel.* Whenever Nacogdoches was criticized, whenever the image of the town came up for discussion, whenever troubles threatened, Haltom assembled a special edition to boost the town's morale and to reassure the public that everything was on track. "God's in his heaven: all's right with the world!" in the words of Robert Browning.[2] Of course, Haltom wanted to make sure he helped to direct the course of the town in line with the way advocated by the establishment he served. To Haltom, the leaders of the town had everything under control. There is an irony that must be noted at this point: while noting Haltom's perennial boosterism and propaganda in favor of his supporters and advertisers, the historian is very much dependent on Haltom's *Daily Sentinel*–as the instrument of record–to observe the events of the time.

Several histories of the town at the turn of the twentieth century have come out in recent years. In *Nacogdoches: The History of Texas' Oldest City,* Jimmy Partin, Carolyn and Joe Ericson, and Archie McDonald discuss the national and regional patterns into which Nacogdoches fits. The town, like the country, was in an uneasy transition from its rural, frontier status into a more modern, urban one. Inertia confronted every change.[3] From 1880 onward, however, Nacogdoches had overwhelmingly embraced change over inertia. The prosperity brought by the coming of the railroad made this transition easy to accept. The town seemed to welcome the arrival of new industries. The new luxuries, such as telephones and electricity, quickly became necessities. On the other hand, as Carolyn Ericson documents in *Fires and Firemen of Nacogdoches,* the town was in denial that it could have a modern, urban existence without public services, such as a fire department, waterworks, permanent bridges, paved roads, and public schools. It would take a breakdown before the need for these things came into focus. In the book *A Hanging in Nacogdoches: Murder, Race, and Polemics in Texas's Oldest Town,* Gary Borders, a former editor of the *Daily Sentinel,* confirms the conflict between rural and urban elements and discusses some of the internal frictions between the past and the present. Nacogdoches wanted to move out of its pre-industrial past, but it clung tenaciously to contradictory traditions from the pre-modern past. Built environments, such as buildings, are more easily modernized than thought patterns and habits. (A century later, Americans would make similar comments about third-world countries.) While Nacogdoches clung to its pre-Civil War attitudes and Wild West traditions well into the twentieth century (especially in political and race relations), the town resented the unfavorable impressions these attitudes generated throughout the state and nation and began to fear the impact that these negative attitudes might have on the town as a center for tourists. Because uneasiness is hard to measure, most books ignore the subject. The closing of the Old University, for instance, is a subject most histories push off until the period of the First World War when Nacogdoches finally got around to doing something about the town's loss.[4]

The Role of Education in the Emerging City: The Death of the Old University.

Day one of the new century brought heartbreak to many Nacogdoches citizens. On January 1, 1900, the charter of the Old Nacogdoches University expired. For years, citizens had realized that Nacogdoches University was ill and perhaps dying. They had tried outsourcing its care to the Catholic Church, the Masons, and Keachi College; but, by the mid-1890s, all of these had failed. The resumption of local responsibility made the building the focal point of public education, but local control did not arrest its slide. Lois Foster Blount, the first faculty member hired at Stephen F. Austin State Teachers College, writes, "It had become clear that a university could not be maintained and the charter was not renewed."[5] Oftentimes, the finality of a long illness does not register on the conscious mind until one witnesses a coffin being lowered into the ground.

The non-renewal of the charter, the ultimate failure of Nacogdoches University, was more of a blow to the town's self-image than to its material interests in 1900. In writing about the Old University, Lois Blount posed some serious questions: "In our present understanding of the term [the] school was never a university. It was a preparatory school although some college subjects were included in the curriculum."[6] The benefits and the place of the university in the scheme of things had always been somewhat unclear. After the arrival of the railroad, the arguments for its economic benefits were questioned. Some people supported the university idea because their forefathers had established the institution. Questions abounded. While the university's presence was comforting, were the people of the region willing to underwrite the institution with bond issues and taxation? Just because one had played in the shadows of its old building or even attended classes there, were these non-material reasons for the institution enough to warrant restoring it? On the other hand, as some hoped, perhaps the state would somehow assume and satisfy the educational needs formerly assigned to the university. Can one separate the essential and the ephemeral in the subject of education? Can modernization continue without destruction? How can progress be reconciled with tradition?

When the charter expired, the members of the Board of Trustees of the Nacogdoches University were the same champions of entrepreneurial progress who had just remade the downtown business district. John Schmidt chaired the board, and members included E. A. Blount, W. U. Perkins, F. C. Ford, George Matthews, Jesse H. Summers, T. B. Hardeman, J. H. Thomas, D. K. Cason, John Orton, L. Zeve, and June C. Harris. The Board petitioned the Court for power to dispose of the remaining property held by the University. After selling the external assets, such as land, the board transferred the Washington Square campus to the newly-formed Nacogdoches Independent School District. They immediately began planning a bond election to replace the Old University Building, and no one challenged them. They most certainly would have torn the old building down had events discussed below not intervened. Furthermore, had the town's economic conditions not deteriorated in coming years, they might never have united to seek a replacement for the institution. When the first

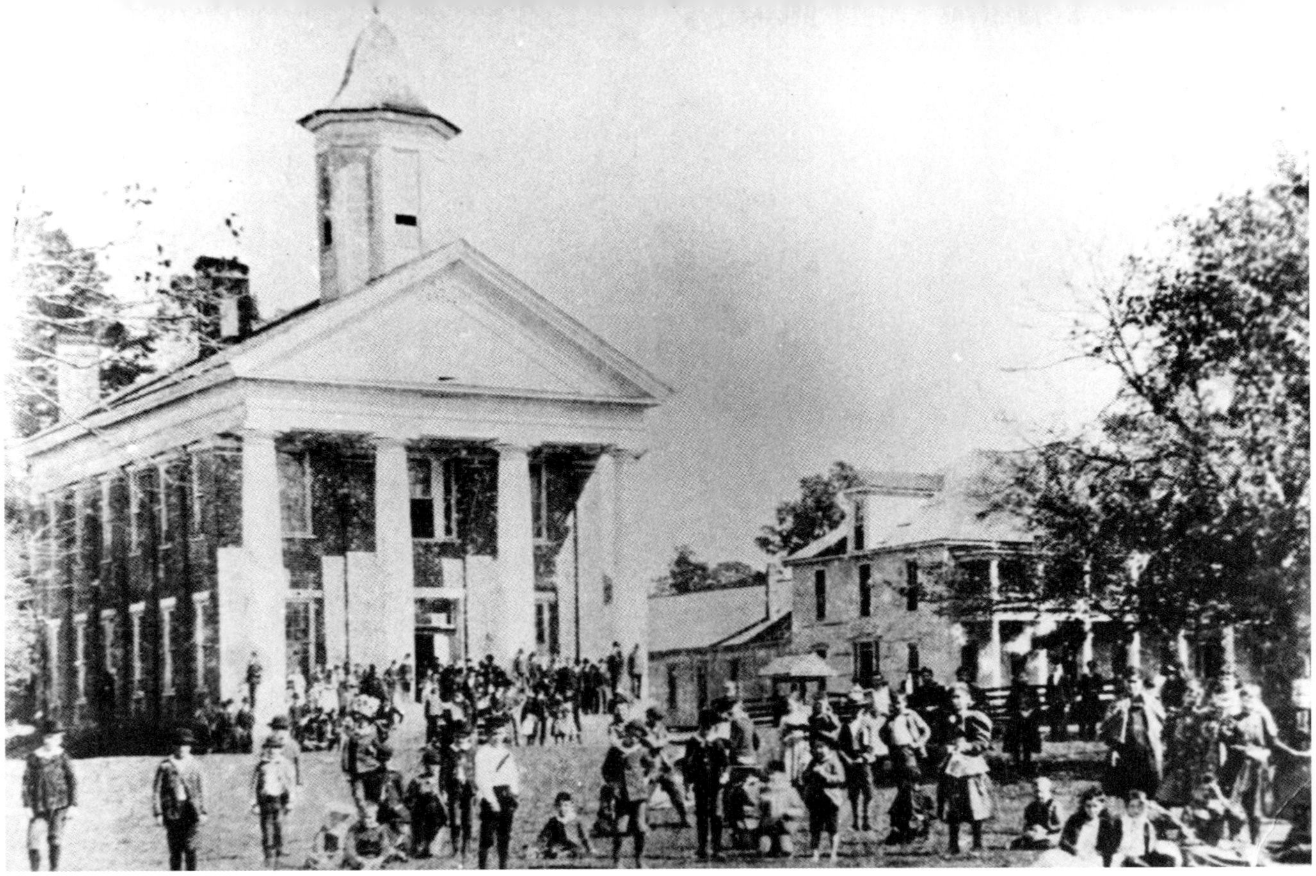

FIGURE 7.2. The Old University, ca. 1890.

Nacogdoches University was the focal point of many activities in Nacogdoches: assemblies, plays, concerts, picnics, sports activities, and speeches. Sam Houston spoke from the steps when running for governor. In the picture, families gathered to celebrate graduation rituals. The building to the right of the Old University housed additional classrooms and dormitory space for women students; behind that an adjoining facility for serving food to the students.

opportunities presented themselves, Nacogdoches found the competition stiff. East Texas Baptist College in 1904 went elsewhere; another opportunity passed by in 1907.[7] The educational aspirations of the town were difficult to replace.

The Role of History in the Emerging City: The Destruction of the Old Stone House

The demise of the Old University had raised the question of the role of education in the town's self-image. Equally important was the role of history. In later years, reflecting on Nacogdoches around 1900, Karle Wilson Baker, the famous Nacogdoches poet and writer, eloquently addresses the irony facing Nacogdoches:

> It was wrapped in tradition as in a garment, permeated—not to say–drugged–by the perfume of its past. Yet the tradition was vague and nebulous; it was almost impossible for the inquiring newcomer to put his finger on a fact .... *Nacogdoches, sitting beside her dusty streets, beneath her immemorial trees, was so proud of being "historic" that she had forgotten her history.* [Italics added][8]

Some citizens, while not overtly contemptuous, saw history as an obstacle to "progress" as they defined it: Nacogdoches had to choose to live in the past or in the future. Some argued if Nacogdoches wanted to be modern, it had to replace everything old with something new. They offered no definition of "progress" to accommodate tradition. At the same time, these very leaders were eager to promote Nacogdoches as a tourist destination *because* of its long history.

Before 1900, the replacement of relatively recent wooden buildings with modern brick stores did not seem to violate much history. Occasionally, as mentioned previously, someone would lament the passing of an old building (as in the case of the Hyde House). This lament, however, was not for the passing of something historical. It was more like the passing of something familiar, the nostalgia felt as the passing of one's youth. Thus, the firestorm that was about to sweep both city and state over the fate of the Old Stone Fort caught Nacogdoches completely unprepared.

Very early in the efforts to update Nacogdoches, the Old Stone House became a bone of contention between the advocates and opponents of change. In 1884, just after the construction of the Brick Block, Charley Sterne, son of Adolphus Sterne, contributed an editorial to suggest that Nacogdoches should "let nothing mar the beauty of your town or obstruct the demands of trade." Instead, Sterne suggested, Nacogdoches should build a monument and "let the old fort go."[9] Later, in 1896, when the *New York Sun* published its travel article on Nacogdoches, the most negative comments in the article fell once again on the Old Stone House, calling it "the sorriest looking place in town."[10]

By republishing the article in a state newspaper, the *Houston Daily Post,* embarrassed local citizens more than the fact that some Yankee traveler had disparaged their town. The positive parts of the article were overshadowed by the slights: "a sleepy old century town," as "uninviting as ever," one that "immigrants continue to pass," a town that had "ceased to occupy an important place among the towns of the state or to exercise the slightest influence upon its politics." Those who responded mainly focused on the town's recent economic progress, its new commercial and domestic structures, and its enormously profitable cotton market. Mr. E. A. Blount, while the only defender of the town's visible history, sandwiched it into a sentence with praise of its material progress:

> Please let your readers know that it is some other Nacogdoches you speak of, and not our bright growing town, proud of her history, proud of her former illustrious citizens, occupying the prettiest location in East Texas, with two banks, an ice factory, electric lights, bottling works and annual cotton receipts of from 14,000 to 20,000.[11]

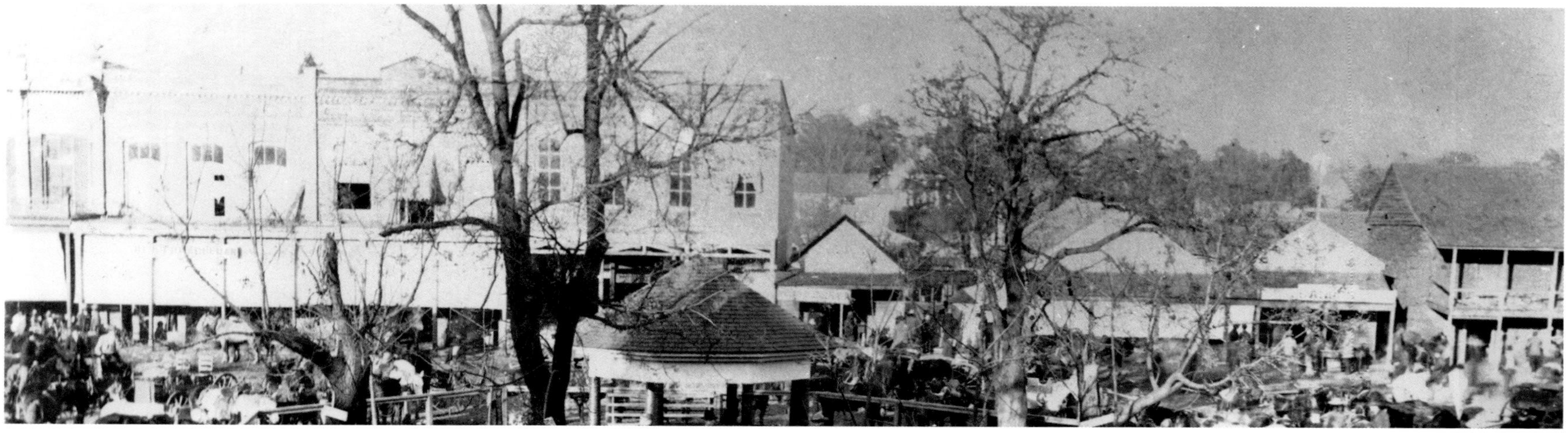

FIGURE 7.3. (Above) Detail of the North Square in 1900.
This photograph of the Square, used often to illustrate the use of the square by wagons and cattle around the old Well, is rarely examined closely for the buildings in the background. The left side of the picture is consumed by the First Brick Block by Rulfs with the fourth building in place since 1894. The middle of the North Square, composed of frame buildings with street-facing gables, would soon be replaced by the Blount Buildings in 1901 and 1902. To the extreme right stands the Old Stone Fort. Courtesy of ETRC.

Debates about the place of history in the new progressive Nacogdoches raged on, but the Old Stone House stood its ground, protected by its historical aura and ownership in the hands of the pioneering Roberts family. John S. Roberts was a signer of the Texas Declaration of Independence; his pioneer home still sat on the southeast corner of the Nacogdoches Public Square. On June 5, 1901, however, the following advertisement appeared in *The Daily Sentinel* and excited everyone's interest:

> For Sale.
>
> The Old Stone Fort property, consisting of the Old Stone Fort and lot, with several wooden buildings. Lot fronts 70 feet on public square and 237 feet on Fredonia street. Property rents at $100.00 per month. For particular address
>
> E. C. Roberts, 1015 Mckee Street, Houston, Texas.[12]

Before anyone had time to think, just ten days later, a second notice appeared in the paper that the landmark had sold to Perkins Brothers.[13] (Charles Perkins, a real estate developer, had just joined his older brother, William U. Perkins (age 45), in the family's pharmacy business.) The brothers announced that they planned to tear down the Old Stone House and replace it with a modern home for their drugstore and with office space to rent upstairs.

Instantly, Nacogdoches became the focus of a statewide hue and cry. The *Jacksonville Banner* asked, "What has become of Nacogdoches' patriotism?"[14] Haltom, the editor of *The Daily Sentinel,* was ambiguous and "vacillated over what should be done."[15] Haltom was, after all, one of the leading promoters of modernization. On the other hand, he was also a strong advocate of the town's history. Rather than taking sides, Haltom

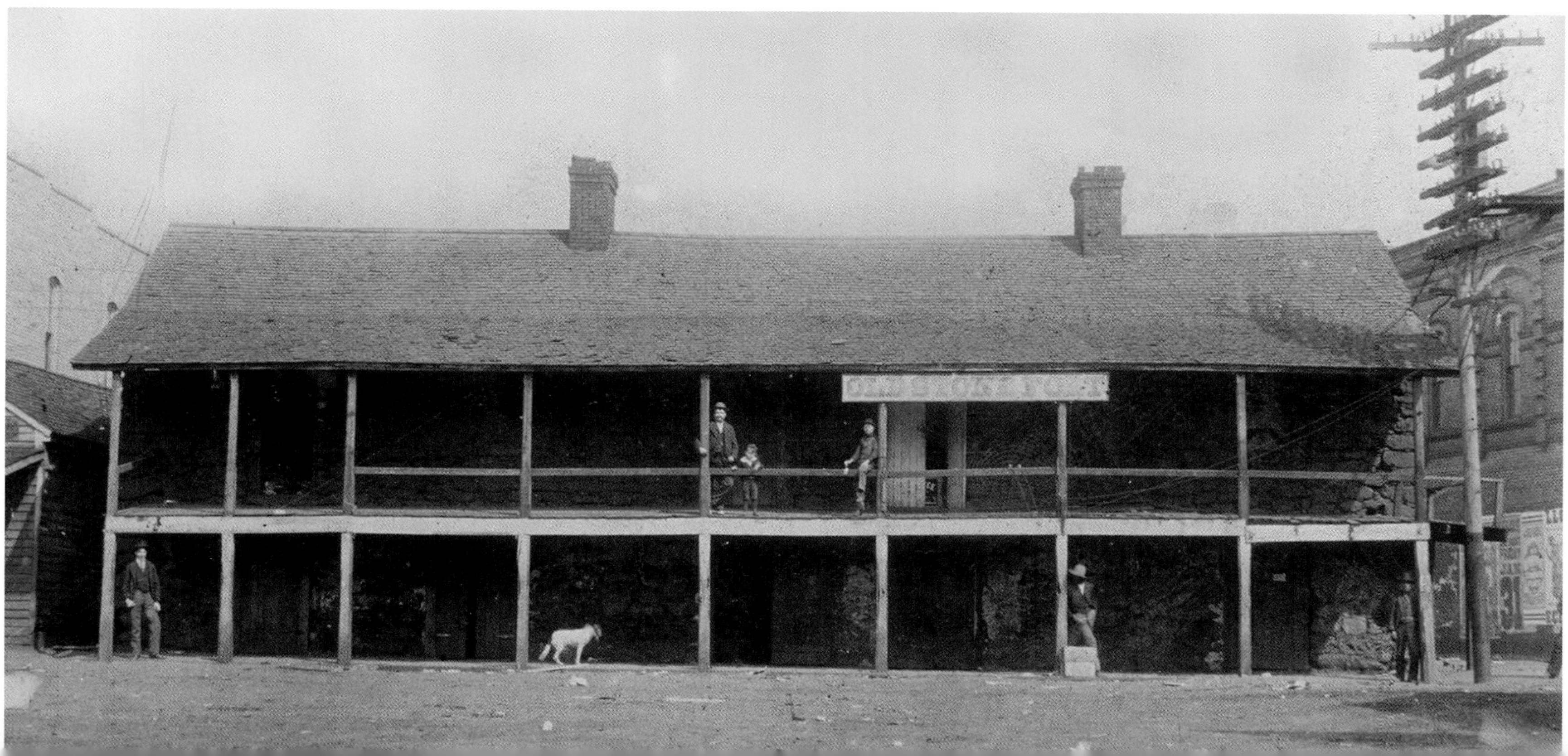

FIGURE 7.4. (Below) The Old Stone Fort Saloon, Late 1901.
This ground level view of the Old Stone Fort is another late photograph of the building. Two of the pre-1800 wooden buildings in photograph 7.3 above are gone. The Dial's Saloon remains. To the right of the Old Stone Fort Saloon stands the large building done by Rulfs for the Mayer & Schmidt Company, across Fredonia Street. Notice the posters and notices on the side of the M&S Building. Courtesy ETRC.

Instantly, Nacogdoches became the focus of a statewide hue and cry.

used the old newspaper ruse of republishing an article from another newspaper (which he had just criticized the *Houston Daily Post* for doing). It was a trial balloon, a position with which he agreed but for which he did not have to take responsibility. From the *Timpson Herald,* on June 15, came this lamentation:

> We regret to hear this. While it requires a great deal of patriotism on the part of one family to lose the use of what might be otherwise a more valuable investment simply because it is an historic relic valuable to posterity, there should be patriotism enough in a town or locality to buy and care for so interesting a building. Nacogdoches now possesses the only historic building in this part of the State and an effort should be made to preserve it.[16]

Haltom's support for the Stone Fort was abstruse and complex. On the 24th of June, Haltom published summaries of the notoriety coming from across the State. "The question of tearing down the old Stone Fort has aroused the interest of patriotic people and the press of Texas, and it is probable that move will be set on foot to buy it and preserve it at any price. The State would probably appropriate ten thousand dollars toward that end. The Daughters of the Republic will take the lead in the undertaking."[17] In another piece:

> Let our cities, towns and villages call meetings, discuss the situation and a committee or committees be appointed to raise the necessary money and pay to the late purchasers the amount of purchase, in that Texas shall not bear the obloquy and shame incident to the tearing down of the Old Stone Fort. A prompt and speedy appeal to the people of Texas at this juncture will meet with a prompt and material response. The state should have purchased this property long ago, but it seems the Legislature thought that the price was too exorbitant. Money should not weigh against patriotism.[18]

A letter in the *Houston Daily Post*, March 7, 1902, stated: "Marble and granite are well enough when it is the best we have, but in this case we do not want them. The old fort appeals to our hearts and our senses in manner that no art of language can approach—one is the substance, the other the shadow."[19]

Nothing had prepared Nacogdoches for the very public, statewide nature of this debate. Only political or racial differences had ever generated such heat; the modernization of Nacogdoches up to this point, had elicited few negative comments, to say nothing of *protests*. The sources of the criticisms were coming from women and from outsiders. This made the men furious. The Perkins brothers were not only unprepared, but they were also incensed.[20] The issue seemed to divide the town; quickly, everyone took sides. Haltom also took sides, sometimes against himself. At one point, he suggested the relocation of the Old House, but then added, the replacement would not be genuine. Citing the building's last use as a saloon, the supporters of the temperance movement joined in the call for its destruction as a "den of iniquity," obviously overlooking the fact that the structure did not lease itself.[21] Those who favored the building's replacement cried that progress was in danger, that private enterprise was being undermined, that the reactionaries were marching against everything modern. Calls for public mindedness were derided: "Patriotism is scarce when you go after it through a fellow's pocket book."[22] George Ingraham, a lawyer in town, even suggested the old Roman recipe for Carthage after its defeat, *salt the earth:* "I may be willing that the Old Stone Fort, (from whose hoary walls has oozed a continuous stream of 'calamity water' ever since 1854 and for how much longer I don't know) should be torn down, and the ground upon which it stood plowed up and sowed in salt, and the rocks of which it is composed pulverized...."[23]

In an application for a Texas Historical Subject Marker to commemorate the Old Stone House (Fort), the present curator at the Stone Fort Museum, Carolyn Spears, has written:

> While most were content with expressing their opinion publicly, the material efforts to preserve the building arose from a variety of women's clubs in Nacogdoches and across the state. The *Houston Herald* described a meeting dedicated to the preservation of the Fort at the residence of Mrs. Mary Jane Briscoe. The groups in attendance included the Daughters of the American Revolution, the Daughters of the Republic of Texas, the United Daughters of the Confederacy, the Woman's Relief Corps, the Art League and the Society for the Federation of Clubs. These women's clubs hoped to raise sufficient funds to purchase the lot from the Perkins Brothers and prevent the demolition of the building.[24]

While the sentiment built throughout 1901, it was not until early 1902, however, that the Perkins brothers completed their plans for the replacement of the building and actually began to move against the historic building. They had (for reasons discussed in the next chapter) selected an architectural firm out of Fort Worth, not D. Rulfs, to prepare the plans for the Stone Fort's replacement. The Perkins brothers advertised for a contractor to take the building down and posted the stones and woodwork for sale.[25] Haltom summarized the dilemma:

> Whatever sentiment may exist, pro or con, the subject is brought down to a square business proposition, and it will take money and plenty of it to change the plans already laid out. Its present owners bought it at a fancy price for a business location for their own use and they are not disposed to sell it at any price. The question of removing the stones and re-erecting them into some sort of monument in memory of the original building and its history, is the only thing to consider.[26]

Carolyn Spears, in her marker application, has written that the Perkins Brothers "eventually donated the whole building to the Daughters of the Confederacy with the understanding that it would be removed and the ground entirely cleared by the fifteenth of March. Within days of this announcement in the local paper, the job of tearing down, moving, and re-erecting the building was taken on by a women's club in Nacogdoches, the Cum Concilio Club. The Club planned immediately to rebuild the structure on the public square.[27]

Before the actual destruction began, opponents of the demolition organized *a commemorative funeral* for the building, a last chance for those who wanted to visit the original structure for the last time to do so. Methodists, Baptists, and Presbyterians had all gotten their start in Nacogdoches in the Old Stone House. Forgetting their earlier denunciations of the building, the

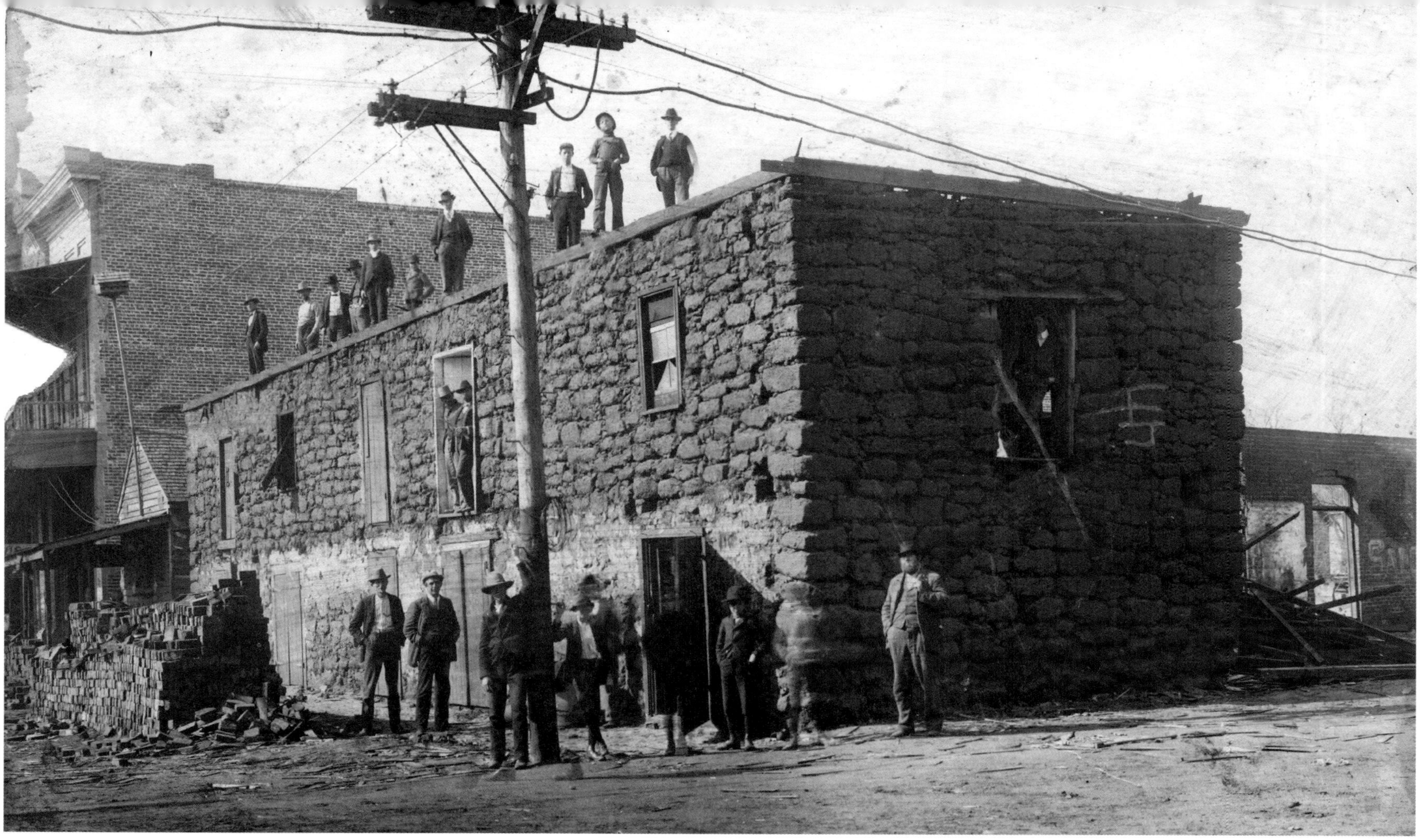

FIGURE 7.5. The Old Stone Fort Being Demolished, 1902.

The workmen and observers, aware of the historic nature of their activity, posed for this photograph. The ladies of the Cum Concilio Club sent this photograph to the Dresden China Factory in Germany to reproduce a copy on china to help in their fund-raising efforts.

FIGURE 7.6. Dresden China Commemorative Plate of the Old Stone Fort.

This china plate, based on the image at the top of the page, even to the inclusion of the 1901 Blount Building and Dial Saloon, is in the collection of the Stone Fort Museum, at Stephen F. Austin State University. The image is used with their permission.

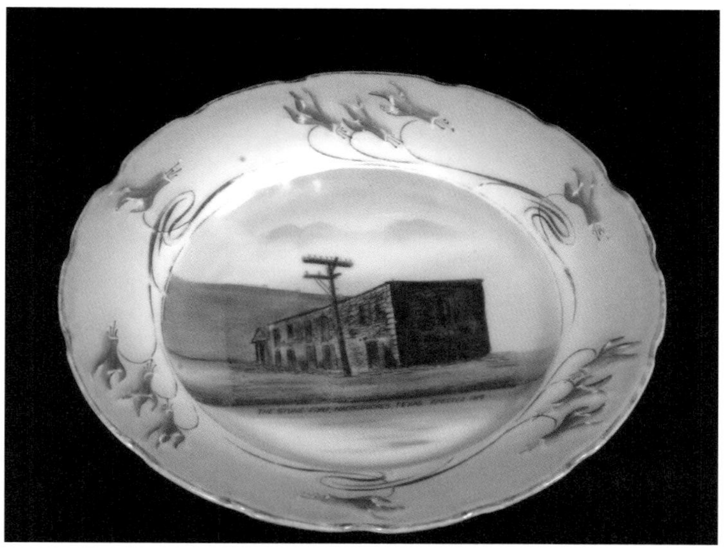

coalition campaigning for prohibition now joined hands with the pastors of these congregations to hold one last religious service in the building, which, according to Mrs. Charles W. Butts, "consisted of Bible reading, prayer and song services, followed by informal talks from various visitors."[28] Later, when the Cum Concilio Club sponsored the idea of selling commemorative china souvenir pieces–cups and saucers, vases, and bon-bon dishes–to raise money for their efforts to build a replica of the historical building, Perkins Brothers quickly sponsored the project by ordering and selling the Dresden china representations. Perkins undertook several initiatives to mollify his feminine opponents. The Cum Concilio Club, to heighten interest in their campaign, countered by inviting William Jennings Bryan to come to Nacogdoches. (John Schmidt, as a prominent Democrat, helped to pull off this event.) Bryan lectured on "The Common Man."

Demolition of the Old Stone House started in January and continued throughout the spring of 1902. Some of the stones, as promised, went to the Cum Concilio Club, which stored them on Washington Square north of the Old University Building. Other stones went elsewhere, contrary to tradition. For instance, many went to construct secure embankments along Virginia Avenue.[29] The stones on Washington Square sat for five years before being assembled into what was called the Memorial Building.[30]

The new Perkins building was ready in September and hailed by *The Daily Sentinel* as "a representative of the new and larger era in which we live." In his editorial, Haltom wrote:

> We live in a prosaic age, in which imagination counts for less than facts, and its is simple truth to say that the Fort was an architectural blot on the horizon, an ugly protuberance thrusting its ugliness continually in the face of the town, a survivor of primitive conditions painfully out of place in modern Nacogdoches, and its most

devoted, and super-sentimental friends, deep down in their heart of hearts, were glad to welcome the enterprise that decreed its doom.[31]

Haltom wanted to move on, as did the Perkins brothers and others, but moving on is not always easy or pleasant. Will Perkins had experienced a bruising fight. He was not able (as he might have wished), to shrug off quite so easily his destruction of the architectural centerpiece of Nacogdoches history. He tried to make amends by insisting that the name of his new bank take the name Stone Fort Bank. He sold porcelain commemoratives in the new Perkins Brothers to aid the ladies of the town in their efforts to erect a replica. But, as his daughter, Virginia Perkins Nelson, related with irony in the 1970s, "My father lived with the label 'the man who tore down the Old Stone Fort, for the rest of his life."[32] Will Perkins very soon (1905) sold part of his drugstore business and began a retreat into a less public enterprise. His new building that replaced the Old Stone Fort burned to the ground in 1906, victim to an arsonist's torch. In January 1907, following the fire, *The Daily Sentinel* announced big news: "W. U. PERKINS WITHDRAWS FROM BUSINESS IN NACOGDOCHES."[33] Perkins did rebuild his building and kept an office upstairs, but he sold his famous emporium, Perkins Brothers, outright. Still very sensitive in the 1930s, Perkins refused to allow a Texas Historical Marker to be placed on the site because it reminded everyone of what he had done.[34]

The destruction of the Stone Fort left its mark throughout Texas, as well as in Nacogdoches. First and foremost, the destruction of the Nacogdoches landmark marked the beginning of the state's dedication to preservation and triggered the movement to save the missions in San Antonio:

> The fate of the Old Stone Fort at Nacogdoches has aroused the United Daughters of the Republic with renewed activity in the effort to preserve the old historic land marks so prominent in Texas history. The demolition of the Old Stone Fort was permitted by sheer procrastination, and this association of Texas' patriotic women are determined that it shall not occur again, and they have already inaugurated a vigorous move for the purchase and preservation of the old Missions near San Antonio. These missions are not threatened as yet by the march of commercialism, and as these noble women have begun an early campaign, we have every assurance that their efforts will be crowned with success.[35]

Haltom had always cited the town's history as an integral part of his promotional advertisements for luring tourists to the old town. Haltom was, even in 1902, courting tourists "in hopes that they would invest, buy land, establish factories, and turn this patch of woods into the paradise its boosters were convinced it soon would be."[36] While the railroad made this feasible for the first time, ironically, Haltom had just stood by and watched as one of the town's leading citizens destroyed the most important historic building in the town and East Texas. When Giles Haltom, Bill's younger brother, put together one of the famous commemorative issues of *The Daily Sentinel* in 1928, he simply skipped over the whole embarrassing episode.[37]

Along with the Red House, the Old Stone House was one of the few buildings that could have *visibly* proved that the town had a distinguished Spanish heritage. With its concrete link to the past destroyed and its visual authenticity compromised, the town would discover that the damage done by this radical act would not go away easily. Nacogdoches has never really recovered. Its citizens had failed to understand the extent to which all of Texas gloried and shared in its past through the presence of the Old Stone Fort. The town immediately attempted to repair the damage, but its first attempts to correct things—the building of the rather pitiful Memorial Building on Washington Square—really only added laughter and ridicule to tragedy. To repair the town's image, Nacogdoches had to *beg* the State in the 1930s to rebuild a better replica as part of the Texas Centennial Celebration. To this day, when tourists ask for tangible proof of the early colonial period, only perceptions and legends of reality can be offered by pointing to the Stone Fort Museum, a replica of the original.[38] Other towns, as stated in the newspapers in 1901, would have paid gold to have the history associated with Nacogdoches, especially with visible proof of the Stone Fort to substantiate this history. Nacogdoches would replay this historical scenario over and over—paying lip service to the town's history while at the same time actively compromising it. Oftentimes, the farcical nature of this becomes quite obvious.

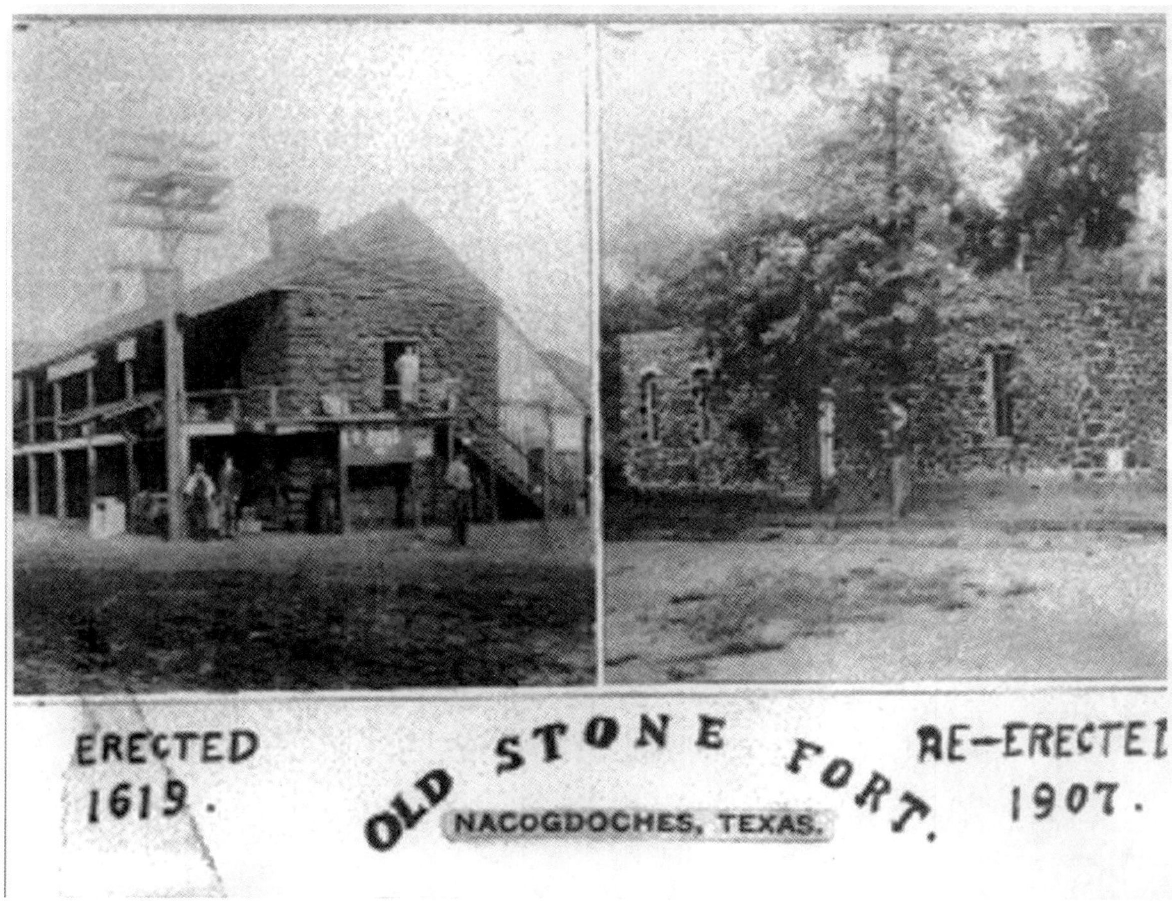

FIGURE 7.7. Nacogdoches Post Card, ca. 1907.
In 1907, to celebrate the construction of the "Memorial Building" to represent the demolished Old Stone Fort, the Cum Concilio Club hosted a dedication ceremony. Afterwards, someone put together the above commemorative postcard marking the occasion and made it available for the public at local stores. The attempt to elicit comparison between the buildings did not inspire confidence in the authenticity of the efforts to create a replica. Photograph compliments of Cecil Sparks

Floods. While the destruction of the Old Stone Fort continued as a "hot issue in early 1902,"[39] the troubles of this year did not end there. In the spring, upset over the Stone Fort, the public refused to approve a bond issue to tear down and replace the county's courthouse. (Ironically, the courthouse was in bad condition and sliding off the hill.) In June, Mother Nature threw in her vote against normalcy in Nacogdoches. Over fourteen inches of rain fell within a twenty-hour period. Water levels reached eighteen inches over previously recorded flood levels. Haltom called it the "worst flood in history."[40] Damage in the county was heavy, with bridges and houses being swept away, especially in Garrison. Downtown Nacogdoches, normally well-drained, had houses and cotton bales in low-lying areas swept downstream.[41] Rescuers had to paddle through downtown in flat-bottom boats to bring residents to safety. "At one point the water at the corner of Fredonia and Hospital streets, in downtown Nacogdoches, reached a depth of three feet."[42] As Gary Borders has recently written, by "late 1902, Nacogdoches was still reeling from the effects of a disastrous flood, a weak economy, and a sinking sense that progress was passing it by." In one of his booster editions, Bill Haltom glorified the prospects of the town: "there is every reason to believe that it will expand into a city of manufacturing industries."[43]

The flood of 1902 once underscored the problems that Nacogdoches was experiencing in a variety of areas. The infrastructure of a frontier town would not support a modern city. The absence of permanent bridges, drainage controls, paved streets with gutters, sidewalks, zoning to prevent building in flood plains, fire prevention, etc., were problems that would not go away. Citizens were unwilling to accept the tax obligations to undertake corrective measures. As a result, some of these problems would not find remedies for three-quarters of a century. The town resisted creating a fire department until 1907, paved roads until the 1920s, zoning laws until the 1970s, and flood zones until the 1980s.

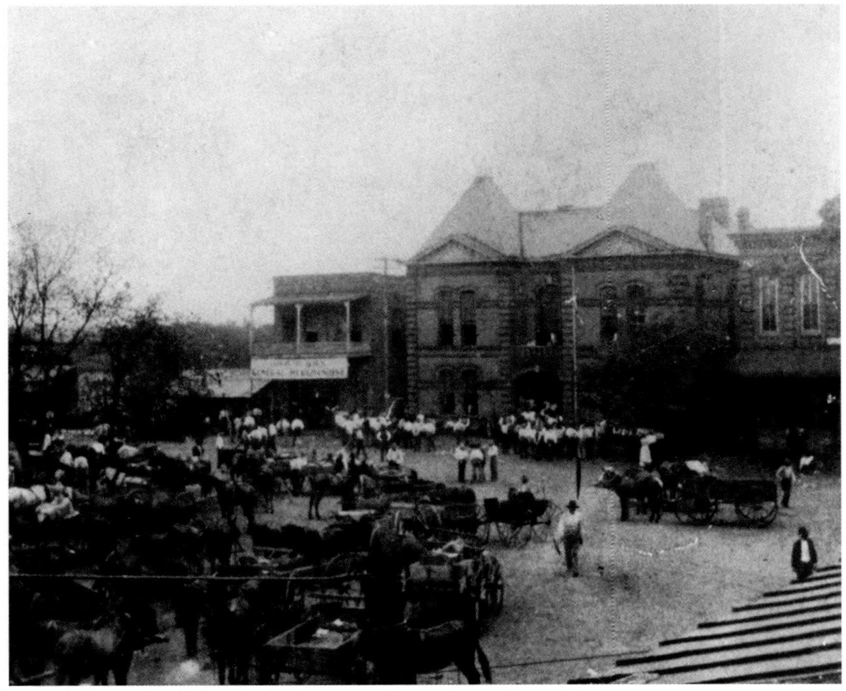

FIGURE 7.8. Awaiting the Verdict., James Buchanan Trial, 1902.
Large crowds gathered outside the 1887 courthouse to await the results of the trial of James Buchanan in October of 1902. Courtesy of ETRC.

FIGURE 7.9. The Verdict Hastily Implemented.
While there are several photographs of this gruesome scene of the hanging of James Buchanan in 1902 looking south, this the only existing photograph taken looking north. The building in the background, from which most other pictures of the hanging were taken, is the newly built E. A. Blount Building (1901). The building only lasted from 1901 to 1906 when it was consumed by fire. Photograph compliments of Gary Borders.

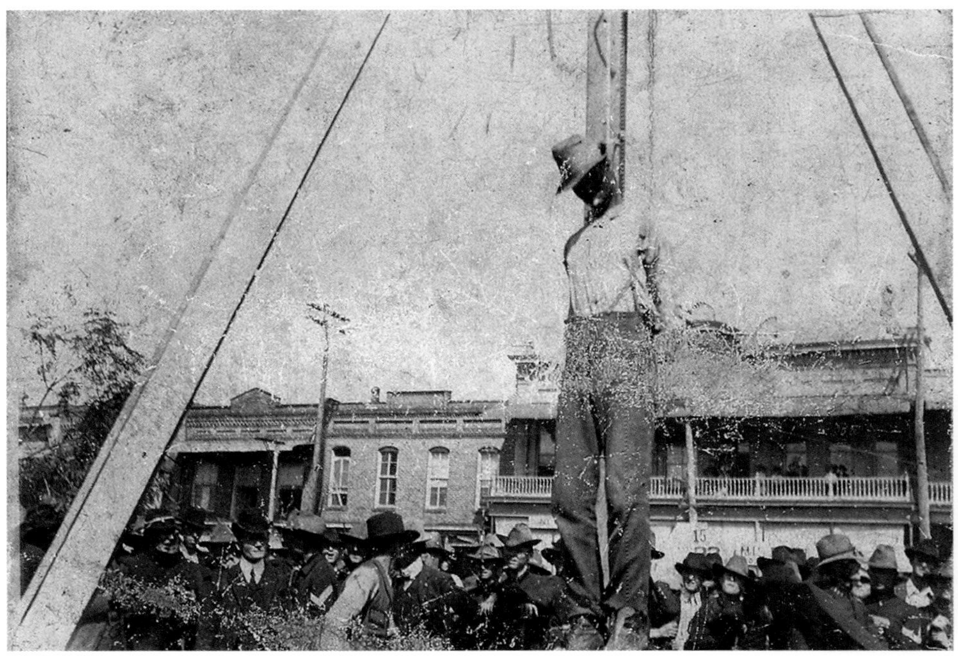

The Role of Race in the Emerging City: A Hanging in Nacogdoches.

Overshadowing the flood, a more serious crisis challenged the reputation of the town in the fall of 1902. Gary Borders, a former editor of *The Daily Sentinel*, dramatically narrates the 1902 crisis in his recent book, *A Hanging in Nacogdoches: Murder, Race, Politics, and Polemics in Texas's Oldest Town, 1870-1916.* It started with the murder of three members of the Hicks family in the community of Blackjack and culminated with the hanging of the murderer in the Public Square of Nacogdoches on October 17, 1902. The suspect, a black man named James Buchanan, was tried without representation, convicted within three hours, and rushed to the gallows on the Public Square three hours later. The state had to send hundreds of state militia troops to maintain order in Nacogdoches and throughout East Texas to prevent mobs from lynching or burning Buchanan at the stake before he could receive even a semblance of justice.

Borders does not paint a rosy picture of Nacogdoches at the turn of the century. The period is full of contradictions and hypocrisies, with religious fervor coexisting with intense racism, and with some leading citizens promoting outrageously speculative schemes and others opposing even the mildest of reforms. This realism needs to be injected here as a counterbalance to the overwhelmingly romantic and pleasant picture of Nacogdoches, which emerges from the pictures of wonderful architecture. Although unflattering, the observations of Borders are accurate, and his summary worth quoting:

> Nacogdoches in 1902 was a sleepy little place inhabited by a goodly number of trigger-happy citizens, who were called "gun toters" by the state's newspaper writers. Local voters proved time and again unwilling to pay for public improvements, apparently satisfied with muddy streets, a porous jail, and raw sewage running down the ditches. They scrapped constantly over politics. Most folks barely scratched out a living on red-dirt land that was nearly played out from the ravages of raising cotton and cows, or else they worked in the forests, cutting down huge pines and hardwoods for lumber. Blacks were treated barely better than chattel by most whites. The town's boosters constantly pushed the latest far-fetched get-rich scheme—whether it was growing tens of thousands of tomatoes, establishing a cigar factory, or attracting Northerners on excursion tours with the lure of cheap land and cheaper labor.... In many ways it was a typical small southern town.[44]

The lynching of black men was all too frequent in the South after the Civil War. The years around the turn of the twentieth century, when the numbers increased, were particularly grim.[45] Nacogdoches, unfortunately, fitted into this grim pattern. R. W. Haltom—the founding editor of *The Daily Sentinel* and the chief booster of the town, the man who consistently defended Rulfs—emerges as a gut fighter in political matters. He cynically manipulated racism when it suited his purposes.[46] Haltom denounced Sheriff Andrew Jackson Spradley when he tried to protect the life and the rights of the suspect. Haltom justified the lynching of Buchanan as an act of quick justice while at the same time he argued against lawlessness in the town. Leading businessmen, such as John Schmidt and Will Perkins, rushed to place their advertisements as near to the most sensational editorials or news items in order to profit from the heightened circulation. When the town came under blistering criticism throughout the state and nation, Haltom responded by rushing out one of his special editions of the *Daily Sentinel* (Fall, 1902), touting the accomplishments of the town.[47] While certainly many residents deplored the violence, the town continued to terrorize black families deep into the spring of 1903, forcing many families to flee the county.

Civic Responsibilities in the Emerging City: The Wettermark Bank Collapse

Citizens, with a sigh of relief, welcomed the end of 1902. Unfortunately, not only did "the violence of the previous decade or so continue unabated,"[48] but 1903 also brought new sorrows. On January 5, 1903, the newspaper announced that the Wettermark Bank, the first bank in Nacogdoches, was bankrupt and that the owner, Colonel Benjamin Wettermark, had fled the county, taking an estimated $500,000 with him! The town hardly had time to absorb this economic blow before the first in a long series of disastrous fires occurred downtown, many as a result of arson. In addition, civility was breaking down: "Just after Valentine's Day, Sheriff Spradley, in front of Dial's Saloon, walloped editor Haltom about the head with a heavy stick."[49]

The collapse of the Wettermark Bank, a fixture since 1883 (the year the railroad arrived), shocked and hurt both the business community in general and individual citizens. Ben Wettermark, forty years old at the time, was a very active civic leader. His father was a respected banker in Henderson. Yes, the town knew he was a wheeler-dealer of sorts, a promoter, and a booster of almost anything new, but these qualities inspired admiration as often as they triggered caution. Wettermark was the serving Mayor of Nacogdoches in 1900. He was a respected member of the Presbyterian Church, the Masons, and the Stone Fort Rifles. Through his bank and personally, he had lent money to almost every entrepreneur in town, men such as John Schmidt, Will Perkins, E. A. Blount, and Ira Sturdevant.[50] He sat on many corporate boards, including the Commercial National Bank and the Nacogdoches (Wholesale) Grocery Company. His wife was a leading light in the new Cum Concilio Club. The Wettermark Bank's collapse came, in Haltom's words, "like a clap of thunder from a clear blue sky."[51]

Wettermark's troubles stemmed from his speculation in cotton futures and later in drilling oil wells in the eastern part of the county, where he was running a Ponzi-like scam.[52] At first, friends like Haltom and June Harris expressed confidence that everyone would receive their money back. When the story broke, Haltom wrote in the *Daily Sentinel*:

> The entire community greatly deplores the embarrassment that has befallen the Wettermark Bank. Their many years of work have given them very great prominence and popularity. Public confidence remains strong, and public sympathy is unbounded, both at home and abroad. Col. B. S. Wettermark's unlimited devotion to the public, especially to this town and county is proverbial. His big-heartedness is beyond question .... His creditors all have faith in his father, too, and so they will stand by these noble men to the end, trusting in their paying dollar for dollar.[53]

The next day Haltom had to temper his own words with a more sober assessment. The bank was a total loss. The losses, variously estimated from a half to three-quarters of a million dollars, were staggering for a small town. Wettermark had absconded with the Christmas sales receipts deposited by local merchants and with investments by his stockholders and business partners. Personally, he left his second wife and their three children stranded without funds. Sheriff Spradley and his brother, Duncan, were on the list of depositors who lost money; everyone knew, therefore, that the law would do its best to track Wettermark down. When a Jacksonville banker absconded with funds in a similar manner at the end of January 1903, Haltom at least introduced a note of levity into the very serious crisis: "The Jacksonville banker is evidently copying after the Nacogdoches pattern. Nacogdoches always leads."[54] No one, however, ever caught Wettermark or brought him to justice. He had left the country.[55] The Commercial Bank and the Stone Fort Bank (the latter opened in the wake of the Wettermark failure), soon restored confidence without too much damage because they were under state and national regulations. Nacogdoches was beginning to learn hard lessons about its free-wheeling past. Regulations could serve everyone's interests. In other areas, too, the town's procrastination and refusal to address needed reforms and obvious solutions began to catch up with it.

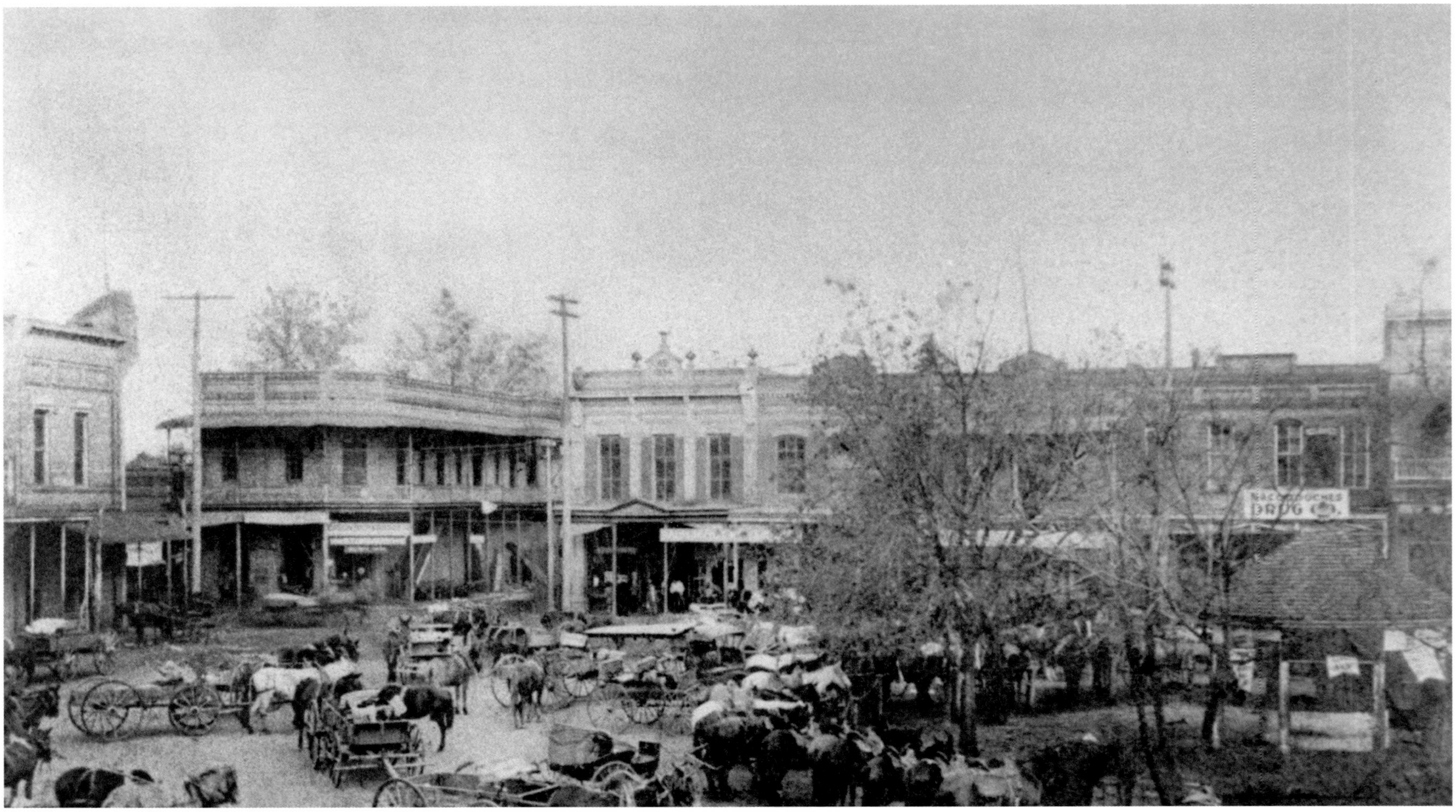

FIGURE 7.10. A Last Look at the "First Brick Block," ca. Fall, 1906.

This may be one of the last pictures taken of the First Block, the west end of the North Square before the great fire of Christmas Eve, 1906. It is also one of the last views of the Old Town Well, which was filled in as a part of the refurbishment of the Square after the great fire. The Wettermark Bank, the first building on the left side of the photograph, and the Cox Building across Main Street survived the fire. Courtesy of ETRC.

Services in the Emerging City: Fires and The Need For a Fire Department

One week after the Wettermark scandal, the January 12, 1903, headline in *The Daily Sentinel* read: "The Fire Fiend Follows on the Heels of the Bank Calamity."[56] Fires were not uncommon in Nacogdoches, dating back to the earliest Spanish settlement. In any town of primarily wooden buildings, fire was a constant hazard. For instance, in the middle decade of the previous century, a large fire destroyed one whole side of the square from corner to corner. However, the 1903 fire, which destroyed the south side of East Main, inaugurated a long series of disastrous conflagrations. While some of the fires between 1903 and 1908 had seemingly innocent origins, the specter of arson was ever present throughout the town, even though the newspaper tried to play this down, for fear of encouraging even more. A building's brick façade was no protection against an arson. Possibly as many as one-third of the buildings Rulfs had built in the downtown area since 1884 fell to fire in the years between 1902 and 1908.

According to the newspaper, the 1903 fire originated in the kitchen of a restaurant and spread too fast for a bucket brigade to handle. "A large crowd stood with gaping mouths gazing upon the lurid spectacle as if in a trance until the fire began to gush out and envelop the wooden shanties adjoining it on the west side. Nothing could be done to save the wooden buildings, and the only thing that could be done was to keep the flames from advancing further."[57] Another fire occurred on June 30 and destroyed another "bit of old Nacogdoches"[58] – the John S. Roberts House (1832) on the southeast corner of the Public Square. Other fires in 1903 claimed the Ogg Livery Stable in July and a major warehouse owned by Phillip Sanders near the Banita Hotel in November. While the city dallied about the creation of a fire department, the suspicious fires continued in 1904-05. Were citizens of various persuasions using direct action for revenge on their enemies?

The granddaddy of all the fires occurred at the end of 1906. Christmas Eve morning, the newspaper reported destruction of the whole north side of the Public Square. The great fire destroyed Rulfs' original "Brick Block" and its additions, the new buildings built by Rulfs in 1901 for E. A. Blount, which housed both the Commercial Bank and Stripling's Drug Store, and, finally, on the east end, the fire destroyed the new Perkins Brothers building (the one that had replaced the Old Stone Fort). *The Daily Sentinel* coverage of the fire stated:

"Business Block in Ashes"

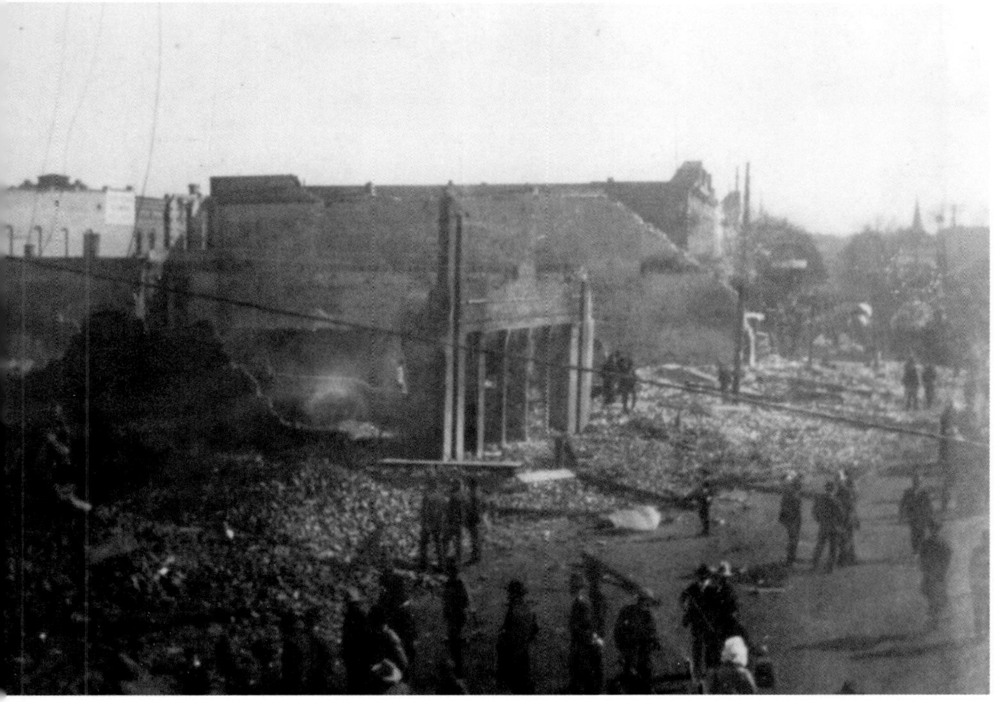

FIGURE 7.11. (Looking East) Ruins of the North Square, Christmas Day, 1906.

The large east wall of the Perkins Building (1902), jutting out into East Main, was the only standing wall on the North Square after the fire. The Mayer & Schmidt Building, the large structure to the east of this wall across Fredonia Street, would in turn succumb to an arsonist in 1908. Courtesy of ETRC.

> BUSINESS BLOCK IN ASHES.
>
> Sunday Morning's Fire Represents about $300,000 Loss
>
> The expected has happened and it happened at an unexpected time, as all things usually do. What was one of the busy blocks of Nacogdoches on last Saturday night when the good people of this town retired for the night and little ones dreaming of the pretty things seen down town, is today a heap of brick and ashes, and which represents a loss of some three hundred thousands of dollars....The only thing that saved the town from total destruction was the fact that the wind was not blowing hard.[59]

The Daily Sentinel, in order not to incite copycats, for years had attributed the fires in Nacogdoches to carelessness, but the numbers were too numerous not to suspect arson. It was not until after the North Square conflagration that the town began to talk seriously about organizing a fire department. Carolyn Ericson, the authority on this subject, writes that by this time, the fires were spreading into the residential areas:

> While a department was being organized, three Nacogdoches homes burned on June 17, 1907. Some area newspapers reported a 'fire-bug' at work in Nacogdoches and urged its citizens to take immediate action. Although *The Daily Sentinel* denied that arson played a part in city fires, they continued to pop up in disturbing numbers. On July 1, 1907, the Burk-Crain Furniture Company on West Main Street was destroyed and the entire city block placed in danger; in August the LaNana Lumber Company plant burned; and on August 16 the Methodist Church, Boger house, and the Dooley residence [on Hospital Street] all were consumed. Several persons were overcome by heat prostration at the church fire.[60]

FIGURE 7.12. Christmas Day, 1906. North Square in Ruins (Looking West).

In the distance, the Wettermark Bank is on the left and the Cox Building on the right of this picture. A partial façade of the original Perkins Drugstore and the 1901 side wall of the Blount Building are still standing in the foreground in front of the Cox Building. The great fire destroyed six buildings by Rulfs in one event. Courtesy of ETRC.

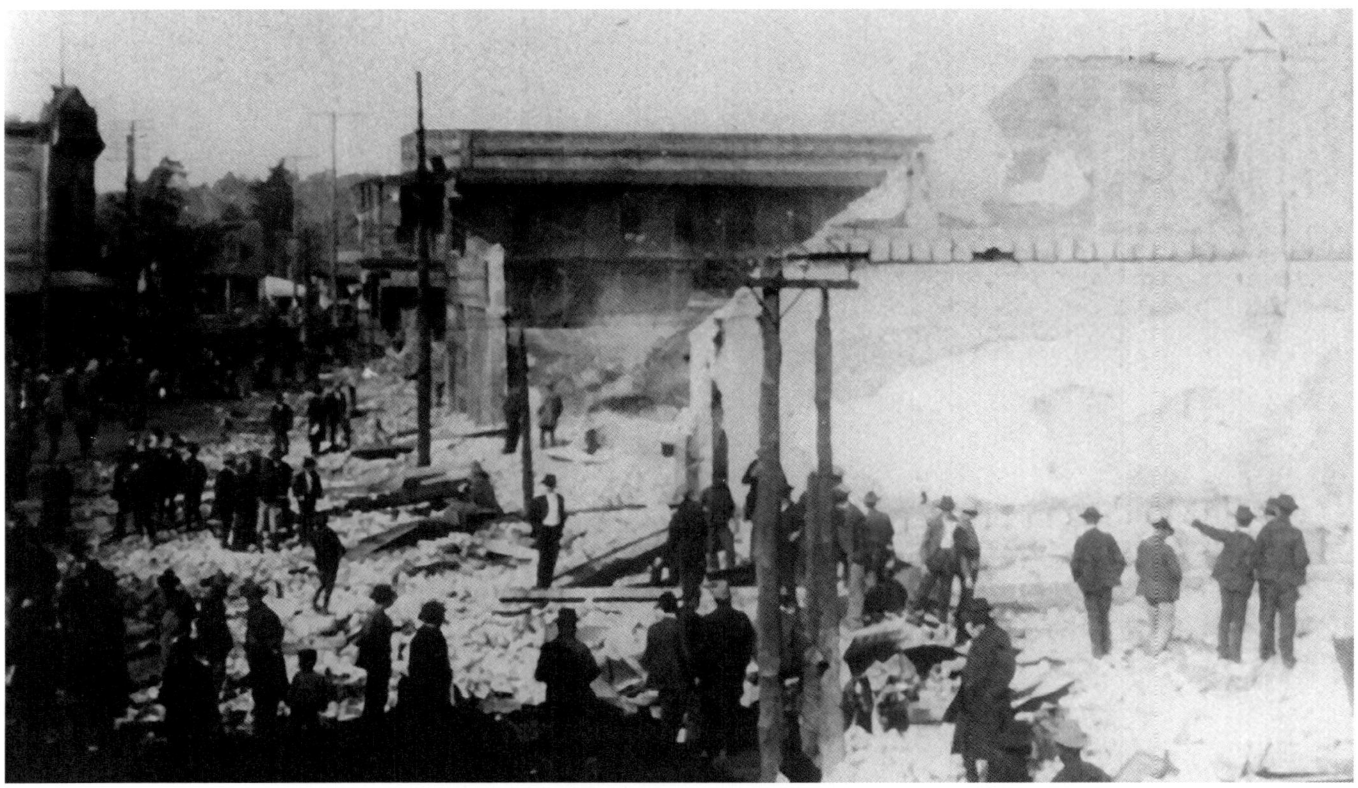

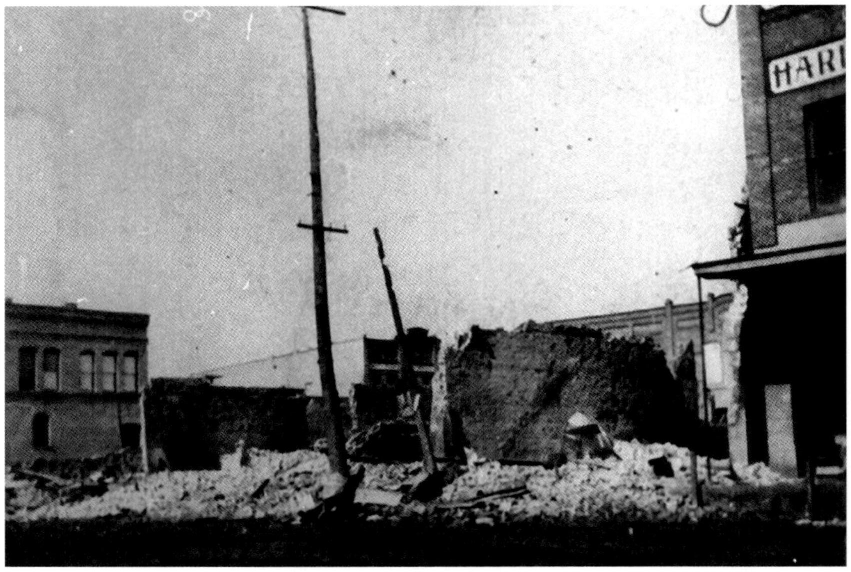

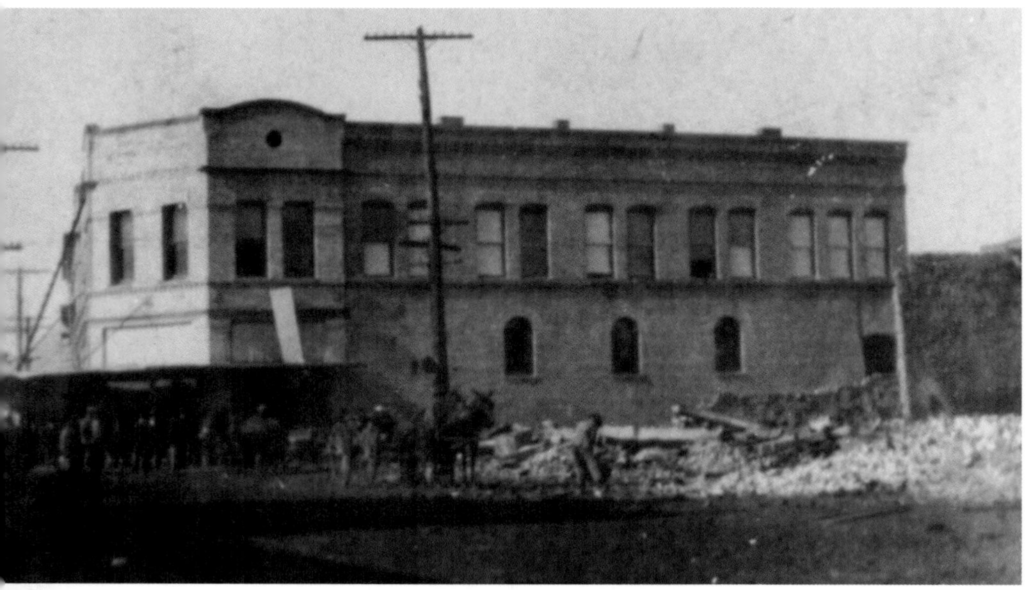

It took one more dramatic fire on January 3, 1908, this time *acknowledged* as arson, to cement the need for action to create a fire department and distribute water hydrants throughout the downtown and main residential areas. The fire, almost as critical as the fire on the north side of the Square, destroyed completely the Mayer & Schmidt and the Davidson Buildings, just east of the Square on the north side of East Main. The fire caused more than $190,000 in damages.[61] The newspaper set forth the major issue: "No water mains had been laid in the business section of the city, and it was impossible to reach the burning buildings with more than one stream of water and that was so weak that it was practically useless."[62]

The need to adopt more urban services came in other areas, too. Disease was another of the crises facing Nacogdoches; plagues do not respect sides in arguments or economic disputes. The town had no sewers, no drainage system, no adequate water supply. Standing water in the unpaved streets provided perfect breeding places for mosquitoes. The town soon discovered, as it tried to recruit a replacement for the Old University, that every prospective institution or committee required good roads, adequate water supplies, drainage, and sewers. When Mayor R. T. Shindler finally announced new ordinances governing sanitation and drainage, there was an outcry against an invasion of personal liberties. Nevertheless, all buildings from that time forward had to be provided with gutters and down spouts; and, in addition, all privies had to be connected to the new sewer lines. Significantly, for this book, a leading advocate of these changes was Diedrich Rulfs, a city alderman at the time.[63]

Across the United States, the years 1907-08 were, in general, very difficult years. The so-called Panic of 1907 revealed many fissures across the nation's financial system. In New York City, the downfall of the Knickerbockers Trust Company brought runs on many banks, recession, and the near collapse of the stock market. Industrial production dropped; the volume of bankruptcies increased, and immigration also dropped.[64]

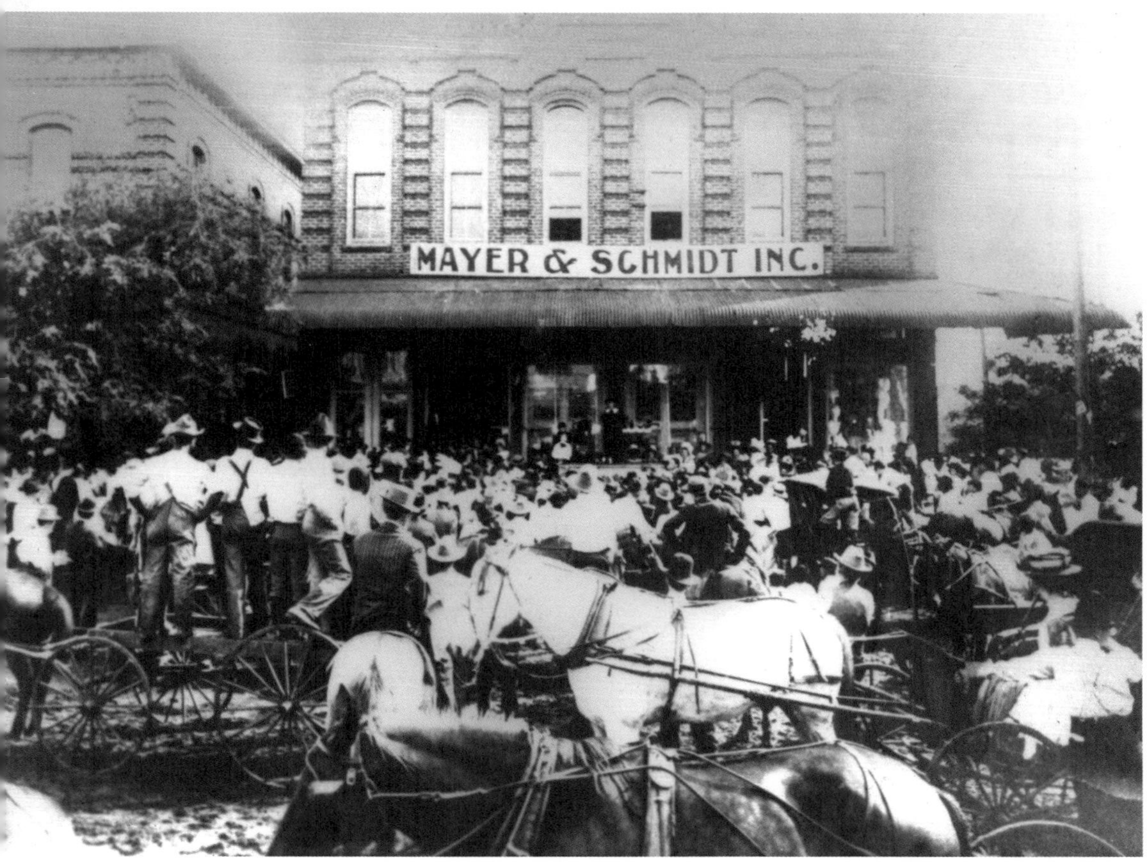

FIGURES 7.13. (Top Left) and 7.14. (Middle). The Ruins of East Main Street.

The 1908 fire destroyed two more of Rulfs' early buildings, the Mayer & Schmidt and Davidson Buildings. In both photographs, the newly rebuilt Perkins Building appears in the background to the left. In the foreground of the small picture to the left, the newly completed Cason-Monk Hardware Store (1906) stood just one wall away from destruction in 1908. Courtesy of ETRC.

FIGURE 7.15. Mayer & Schmidt Company, South Square in the Davidson Buildings, 1907-1908.

After the destruction of their building in the fire of 1908, the resourceful M&S Company reopened their store in the Davidson Building next door to the 1887 Courthouse, on the corner of Pilar and Pecan. The occasion in the picture was a promotional event for Buster Brown Shoes. This building still stands in 2012, and, after many renovations and additions, now houses the Nacogdoches City Offices. Courtesy of ETRC.

A City-Wide Strike

The Role of Labor in the Emerging City: A Strike

In October 12, 1906, the newspaper reported that brickwork on the new Redland Hotel "is being rapidly pushed. It will be ready for occupancy by the first of the year."[65] Ten days later, however, the headline read: "Carpenters on Strike." The Nacogdoches Union of Carpenters and Joiners had called the stoppage, demanding an increase in wages. The newspaper summarized the workmen's case: "The carpenters are demanding $3 per day for their labor stating that the price of living has steadily advanced until they cannot earn enough at the present scale to provide for their families."[66]

The workers, represented by E. D. Moorer and W. S. Chadwick, presented their case in an open letter to the newspaper entitled, "A statement to The People of Nacogdoches." The case rested on the great rise in the "the high-price of groceries, high priced dry goods, and the high price of every other conceivable thing that one has to have to sustain life, and the cheapness of labor." Yet, they had labored under the same wages for the last four years. "Our troubles are these: the carpenters have been working in Nacogdoches for $2.50 per day, and we have asked for $3 per day and have been refused." The letter contained a statement of comparison with other towns:

> We feel we are entitled to $3 per day and are going to get it if we have to leave Nacogdoches to get it. Nacogdoches is about the only town in the state that pays less than $3 and the scale of wages in most towns is $3 to $3.50. We have no ill will towards any of the contractors. If they can't pay it, we lay no blame on them. This is strictly a live and let live proposition for us. We ask the good will of the public, and all who have work to be done, we will make it to your interest if you will please call on some union man.[67]

On October 23, the *Daily Sentinel* reported that "Work has been suspended on all buildings in the city on account of the strike of the local union of carpenters and joiners."[68] Diedrich Rulfs, the architect and the contractor of the Redland, found himself facing bankruptcy. (For the building of the Redland, see Chapter VIII.) Rulfs was very sympathetic to the demands of the carpenters and readily agreed to base future contracts on a new scale, but if he raised the workers's wages under a fixed contract, he personally would court ruin. He had made the contract based on the current wage scale of the union. Rulfs promised to immediately raise the wages if the owners and other contactors agreed.

A compromise, arbitrated by E. C. Branch and H. F. Marr, ended the strike by the 25th of October. "The strike of the carpenters and joiners of this city has been settled to the entire satisfaction of all parties to the difficulty," declared Giles Haltom. The contractors that Rulfs supervised agreed to pay $2.65 on all unfinished work and the union got annual contracts revisions to prevent grievances from building up. Rulfs, always on the side of the carpenters, maintained cordial relations with the workmen and got construction resumed immediately.[69] The business community, however, took notice. When the contracts were let for the rebuilding of the North Square in 1907, everyone heeded the interests of the local contractors and laborers.

At the end of the strike, the *Daily Sentinel* rushed out another Special Edition (discussed in the next chapter) to reassure the town that everything was fine again. The November edition was premature. The worst was yet to come. On Christmas Eve of 1906, the north side of the Square burned to the ground. The fires, which were the work of arsonists, did not stop there. The Mayer & Schmidt Building and the Davidson Building fell to arson a year later.

The Role of Leadership in the Emerging City

Every decade brings forth new leaders and sees the passing of others. In 1907, R. W. (Bill) Haltom, the founding editor of *The Daily Sentinel* and a force in Nacogdoches business and politics for decades, died. In order to run for election as a state representative, he had delegated the editorship of his newspaper to his younger brother, Giles. Bill Haltom, however, regretted this decision and spent his declining years in disappointment, pining for bygone days. Giles Haltom oversaw the *Daily Sentinel* for several more decades, giving the town continuity in its editorial positions. Although Giles and Nacogdoches shared the desires of the progressive era, the town was still mired in its deep frontier and Southern pasts. It became more and more difficult for Giles to sustain the town's optimism and to promote its good reputation throughout the state.[70] The aspirations of Nacogdoches businessmen, which both of the Haltoms voiced, were hard to reconcile with the town's continuing reputation for lawlessness. Even as the Haltoms relentlessly pointed to the town's positive statistics—its increase in population, its ability to attract some industries, its continued ability to exploit agriculture and timber—most realists knew that the salad days of youthful inexperience and easy transformations were over. Even the definitions of manhood and organizations associated with these came under attack from the changing roles for the young men in the community. The prestigious Stone Fort Rifles—an organization, which from 1887 had "provided white males with an organization that satisfied all the needs for community involvement, a community sanctioned outlet for manly activity . . . . a chance to prove one's manhood through the chance of experiencing combat"[71]—fell into decline after 1902. The destruction of its name-sake building provoked discussions that presaged its demise. The Rifles were an anachronism, a remnant more compatible with a mid-Nineteenth Century mindset than the Twentieth Century.

New leadership did emerge from the new banks; but, in some ways, the banks simply divided Nacogdoches into competing camps. Factions defined almost everything. There was cordiality on the surface; but when the economy began to shrink, the competition sometimes turned nasty.

Commercial Bank: Although the leaders who established Commercial Bank were from outside Nacogdoches, they soon sold controlling interest to E. A. Blount and his associates, among whom John Schmidt was the most notable. Blount's team, which included his son, Eugene H. Blount, and Thomas Ellis Baker, continued for many years to provide first-class leadership for Nacogdoches.

Stone Fort: The Stone Fort National Bank's original investors, like those of Commercial Bank, were external to the town; their speculation came as a way to exploit the gap left after the collapse of the Wettermark Bank. When E. A. Blount purchased a sizable block of shares to block outside intervention in the town's affairs, other local investors combined to prevent

Blount from controlling two banks. (E. A. Blount, a major stockholder, however, actually sat on the board of Stone Fort Bank in its early years.) Of the new personalities who emerged, Link Sturdevant, perhaps, was the most successful. While Sturdevant was not a new face in Nacogdoches, having pioneered in the warehousing of cotton and the utility industries, his new position as president of Stone Fort National Bank gave him an important new role. The bank's loan committee included W. U. Perkins, J. J. (Jeff) Hayter, and Charles Hoya. The new bank allowed Will Perkins, still licking his wounds from the Old Stone Fort debacle, to continue to influence events without being on the front line as a merchant serving the public. Hayter, whose wealth was primarily in land, tied the bank to county interests. The new bank survived their initial *faux pas* of selecting the old Wettermark Bank Building, which associated their new venture with a failed one, by accepting Perkins's offer to move into his new building—placing the institution back on the Stone Fort site, next door to Commercial Bank. What irony!

Farmers and Merchants. Dissatisfaction with the two other banks led in 1909 to the formation of a third bank, Farmers and Merchants Bank. This introduced not only more competition into the banking and business world, but it also allowed new leaders to emerge, such as R. D. Whitaker, George C. Ingraham, and the Mast brothers, Hollis and later Blum.[72]

New Commercial Enterprises. The Mast brothers—Hollis, Blum, Henry, and Adlai—also became more directly involved in the leadership of the business class when they purchased Perkins Brothers and opened automobile dealerships. Many leaders advanced from secondary positions into new roles of responsibility. Sam Stripling and his partners, Will Hazelwood and Thomas Ellis Baker, broke away from Perkins Brothers into an independent drugstore business and became respected leaders in the community. John Schmidt's formation of Nacogdoches Wholesale Grocery Company (1904) helped the Hardeman brothers to become more important. With the financial backing and cooperation of John Schmidt, D. K. Cason, R. C. Monk, W. L. Gaston, and J. Edwin Gaston, formed an important new mercantile firm, the Cason-Monk Hardware Company (1906).

Doctors. New doctors leaving medical schools after the turn of the century began to join the older medical doctors to demand new medical facilities. Dr. Joel H. Barham, an older doctor who had come from Rusk County to Nacogdoches in 1883, became president of the County Medical Association in 1905. Barham—active on the local school board, the board of the Baptist Church, and Woodmen of the World, led other new doctors in town to become more civic minded. His son, Dr. George Stephen Barham joined his father in 1908. Dr. Albert A. Nelson, the famous surveyor's grandson, took up his practice in 1898. Dr. Carl Henry Rulfs, the architect's son, joined the ranks of the profession in Nacogdoches in 1906. When Nacogdoches opened its first hospital in 1909, the forerunner of Memorial Hospital, Dr. W. I. M. Smith was the President of the Sanitarium Association, Dr. Francis R. Tucker was the Vice President, Dr. A. A. Nelson was the Treasurer, and Dr. R. P. Lockey was Secretary. Other prominent doctors included Francis "Frank" Cates Ford and Dr. J. E. Mayfield.[73]

Educators. Certain educational leaders, who were to see NISD through the coming years, came to prominence after 1902: Superintendent, R. F. Davis; Principal of the High School, F. P. Marshall; and Headmaster of the Grammar school, J. A. Spear.[74] Davis was to play a key role in the search for a new college for the town.

Women. As across the nation, women were also making their voices heard on public issues. The Cum Concilio Club, begun in 1894, established citywide leadership with their attempt to save the Stone Fort.[75] This was a very unwelcome new force for many men in town. When the women of the Methodist and Baptist Churches took the lead in limiting the sale of alcohol, Nacogdoches went dry in 1905, years before the nation. The regulars at the many saloons around Nacogdoches were hard hit. The "pine top" celebrations hosted by Rulfs at the completion of his building projects became increasingly attractive to thirsty workmen. The drive for women's suffrage, which also allied with the prohibition movement, was to become a major feminine focus in Nacogdoches during the Great War.[76]

In 1907, a young woman with considerable talents, Miss Karle Wilson (later, Baker), decided to make Nacogdoches her permanent home. Her parents, the W. T. Wilsons, had moved from Arkansas several years earlier. Miss Wilson saw what others overlooked. She was to give voice to unexpressed sentiments. In a now-famous letter, which demonstrated the writing skills that were to make her the most celebrated writer in the town's history, the newcomer eloquently expressed, *before anyone else*, the town's yet-elusive search for identity. While the letter is famous and often quoted, the context has escaped modern attention. Her letter appeared on February 18, 1907, at a particularly depressing moment in the crises discussed in this

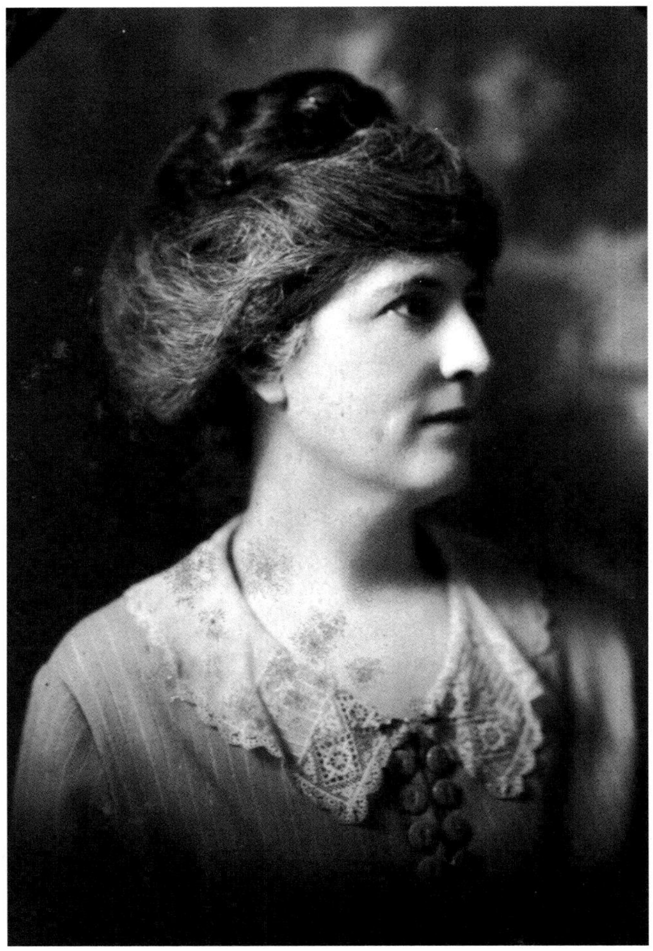

FIGURE 7.16. Karle Wilson Baker, ca. 1926.
In 1924, Mrs. Baker became the first married woman to teach at the new SFA State Teachers College.

chapter. Fires and strikes had just shaken Nacogdoches; the North Square lay in ruins. The leaders of Nacogdoches, finally aware that the town was in trouble, had just met to discuss the economic benefits of enticing the Baptist College in Rusk to move to Nacogdoches. After attending this meeting, Wilson wrote her famous letter about being true to ghosts.

Politely, she scolded the leaders for failing to look beyond the economic benefits. "Perhaps enough has been said, by those competent to speak, about the material advantages Nacogdoches would derive from the location here of the projected college; enough, it would seem, to move her citizens to action if they were to move by such a consideration." She also addressed the persistent local resentment against the right of "outsiders" to speak on town matters. "Sometimes a stranger coming into a place, is more sensitive to the atmosphere of that place than are the residents themselves." She expressed her sensitivity to the history of Nacogdoches with a long passage beginning with this famous sentence. "Nacogdoches has a soul, a spirit, an atmosphere. She is no raw product of today or yesterday. There are ghosts on her streets."[77] On her main topic of education, Miss Wilson wrote:

> One word more. Nobody needs to be told what a college can do for the spirit and atmosphere of a town. The spirit of Nacogdoches today is a gift from the men of the past; the spirit of the future will be the gift of the men of today. There is one form of immortality which nobody disputes: the immortality of influence and good works. And there is one form of ambition to which no man is dead: an ambition for his children. As far back as Cicero's time men were moved by his appeal. "We shall plant trees for others centuries." I heard it said the other day that it is especially hard to move an old town to action. But if any town could be moved by the appeal of the future I would think it would be an old town—a town which owes its superiority, its dignity and traditions, to the fact that long ago somebody planted trees, and built churches, and gave land for schools; a town with a stirring past to live up to, and the presence of dead heroes in its streets. That is the town which should keep the spirit of its forefathers alive; which should cherish its ghosts, and plant trees for other countries.
>
> Karle Wilson.[78]

The publication of this letter, which Wilson's biographer writes "so obviously set Karle Wilson apart from the average inhabitant of the small town,"[79] established a new intellectual foundation for the search for a new college. A few months later, Karle Wilson married the banker Thomas Ellis Baker, and together they helped to lead the college movement.

Where does D. Rulfs fit into these years?

While the following chapters will answer this question in detail, a quick summary will suffice here to place the architect Rulfs in perspective. Rulfs not only designed most of the brick buildings in the period before 1900, but he re-designed and frequently rebuilt many of these same commercial buildings after the sweeping fires of 1902-1908. He was building the Redland Hotel at the time of the city-wide strike. He also interacted with all of the major players in the period in the construction of their residences.

For instance, as a wedding present for his bride in 1907, Tom Baker bought the "Steamboat House" on North Street, which Rulfs had designed for Charles Perkins in 1898. When the Bakers later moved to Washington Square, after the death of Karle's parents, they moved into another Rulfs house, built for the W. T. Wilsons in 1904. Baker worked in buildings by Rulfs before and after the 1906 fire which destroyed the north Square. The Baker story is not unique. Rulfs designed over eight structures for the Blount family. Eugene Blount and Baker in 1919 commissioned him to design another large commercial building, which still stands on the South Square, commonly known as the Mahdeen Building because of its main tenant. The Bakers and the Blounts recommended that the newly named President of Stephen F. Austin State Teachers College in 1922 use Rulfs to redesign his home and a new gymnasium for the school campus. Blount also had Rulfs design a new home for him across from the new college. There are many comparable stories.

Architect Diedrich Rulfs provides a connecting thread to link many of the prominent citizens of the period as he designed the modern architectural legacy of Nacogdoches. All three banks occupied buildings by Rulfs; furthermore, the leaders of these banks lived in Rulfs houses.[80] Of the original members of the Cum Concilio Club, ten lived in houses by Rulfs; without duplicating individuals, ten presidents and an additional ten members over the years lived in houses designed by the north German architect. To this auspicious list, one must add the churches, schools, and hotels he designed for these same people.

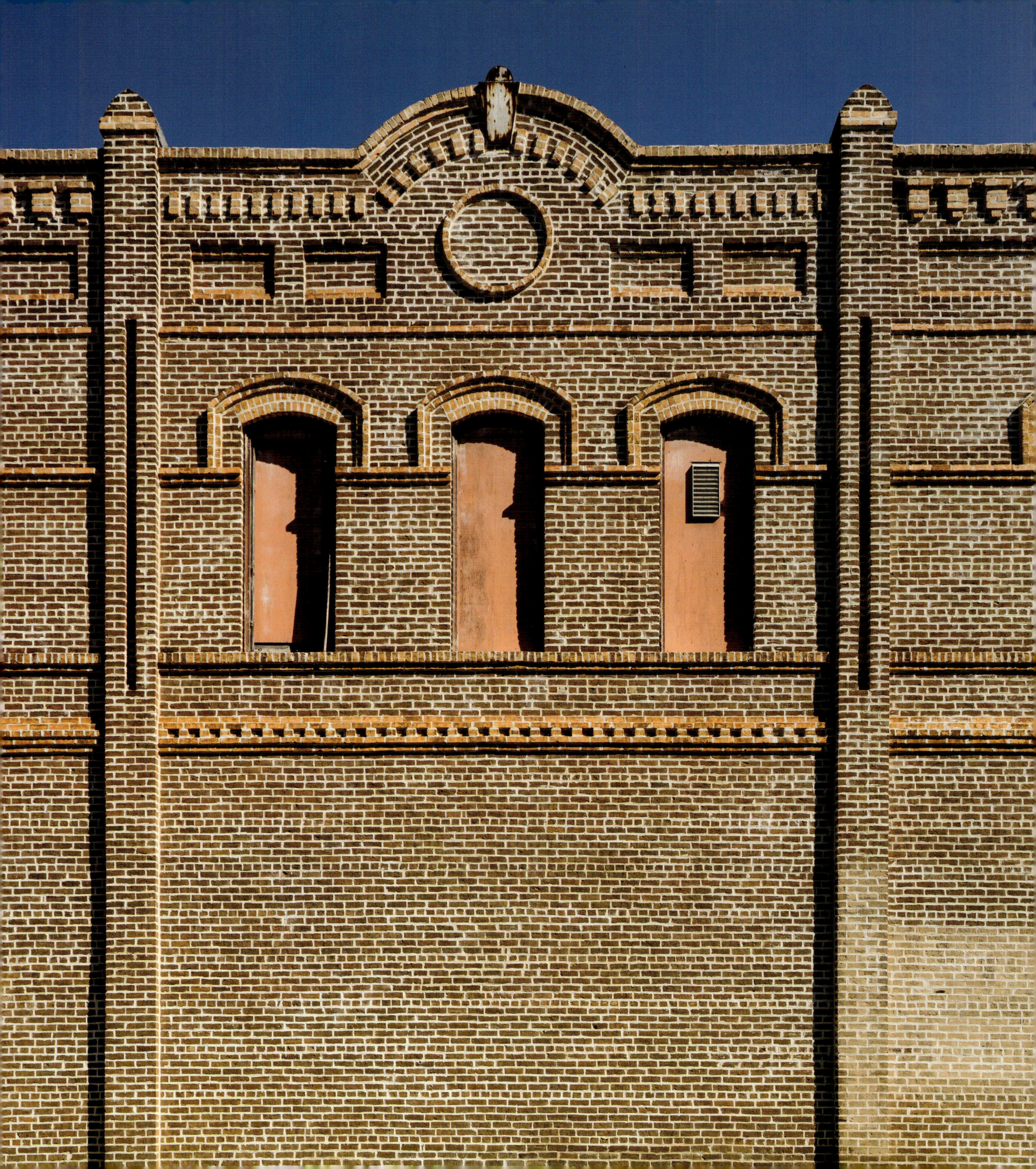

CHAPTER VIII

Commercial Development Continues

Building, Rebuilding, and Expanding, 1900 – 1914

"Nacogdoches, Texas. May 1. Contracts for five brick stores, four one-story buildings and one two-story were let today to Mr. H. L. Austin and Mr. William Rulfs, D. Rulfs architect." *Houston Daily Post,* May 3, 1899.

"The upper story will be built especially for that purpose [a Masonic hall]. The drawing of Mr. Rulfs shows a beautiful design and the building will be an ornament to the business portion of the city." *Daily Sentinel,* March 6, 1900.

The year 1900 marked Diedrich Rulfs' twentieth year in Nacogdoches. In these years, Nacogdoches had moved from a late-frontier, rather unprosperous town of 500 people to become the center of a revived East Texas, with a population of 1,827. Accompanying this awakening, new people, new businesses, new buildings, and new residences seemed to emerge from everywhere. The future looked bright. Unfortunately, as covered in Chapter VII, the new century brought sad as well as joyous moments. Rulfs was by now one of the new pioneers, one of the main leaders in transforming the town. The present chapter traces his attempt to keep his career on an even trajectory in the midst of changing civic leadership and economic upheavals. As before 1900, the details of his contributions will begin with commercial areas, then cover his extensive contributions to church and civic architecture, and finally, move to residential constructions. The years prior to World War I were challenging as well as busy for the master builder. He was to see not only his workers go on strike while staying on friendly terms with the architect, but also increased competition from market forces and outside architects who wanted a share of the Nacogdoches prosperity. He would witness Nacogdoches civic leaders, even when they passed him over for some outside architect, ultimately have to rely heavily on his services.

In an advertisement early in the new century, Diedrich Rulfs observed something about his clients: "Designing and building are items of more than casual interest to the people of Nacogdoches at present." He had just ended one of his most active years, working with committees from the First Baptist Church, downtown businessmen, and owners of the great houses on Irion Hill and Washington Square. The schedule for work in 1900 was already crowded with new commissions. While his ads restated his obvious professional services—architect, contractor, and builder, he added a new tone: his preparedness to provide estimates and to build "houses on any scale."[1] One wonders if this last statement was an appeal for even larger residences; perhaps he feared that the wealthy might seek architectural services from the big cities. Or, did he suspect that his reputation for building large, imposing residences might alienate him from the bread-and-butter houses, which had sustained him in the early period? Because of his early professional experiences in Northern Germany, Rulfs knew what an economic

FIGURE 8.1. (Opposite) Detail, South Elevation, Hoya Building (1900) in 2012.

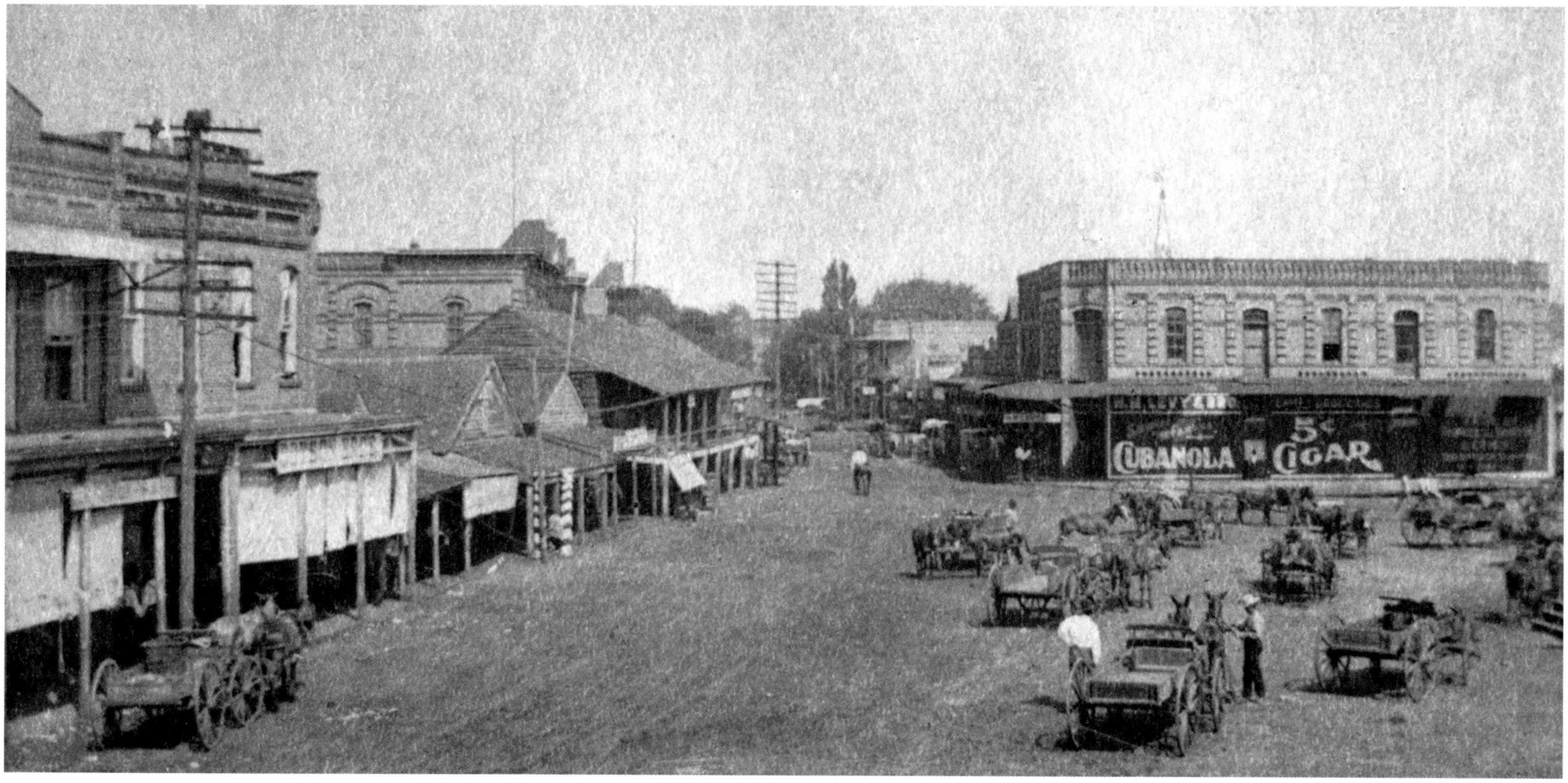

FIGURE 8.2. The North Square and East Main Street, 1900.

Taken from the second floor of the Wettermark Bank (Rulfs, 1896) on the West Square, this photograph reflects accurately how Main Street appeared in 1900. The wagons clearly indicate a time before automobiles, but the pole on the left confirms both telephones and electricity. The view captures the moment before the construction of the E. A. Blount Building in 1901 and the tearing down of the Stone Fort in 1902.

Starting from the left, the buildings of "the First Brick Block" started by Rulfs in the year 1884. The next buildings, the older wooden structures with gables to the street, are pre-1880 and stand between "the First Brick Block" and the Old Stone Fort; the Blount Building of 1901 would replace these. Next, the venerable Old Stone Fort (pre-1800) stands on the corner of Main and Fredonia Streets. It juts into Main Street, obscuring the view of the north side of East Main. Over the roof of the Old Stone Fort, however, one can see the large two-story Mayer & Schmidt Building (Rulfs, 1888-89) on the east side of Fredonia at Main Street. In the distance, down East Main, stands the two-story Huntley Building (Rulfs, 1895), which would burn in 1903.

The two-story building on the East Square, with the large 5¢ cigar sign, is the John Cox Building (Rulfs, 1891). In 1900, the building housed a restaurant on the first floor and the W. T. Wilson Grain Company on the second. The first floor later became Farmers and Merchants Bank in 1909 and Stone Fort Bank in 1919, when the two banks merged. Rulfs remodeled the building in 1919. The Cox Estate sold the property in 1929. In 1992, the building passed to Texas Commerce Bank and in 1993 to Regions Bank. This structure, remodeled often with a succession of façade treatments, retains today its basic shape, height, and chamfered corner. Photograph courtesy of ETRC.

downturn could do to his profession. At that moment, however, he did not need to worry. His commissions in 1900 were more abundant than ever.[2] The editor of the new *Daily Sentinel,* R. W. Haltom, who always had his ear to the ground, predicted: "There will probably be no less than twelve new brick buildings erected in Nacogdoches by next September 1st. The building boom hasn't got fairly started here yet."[3] As the century ended and as the new one began, Rulfs had an enormous backlog of commercial commissions and two churches: for the West Square, the North Square, along Fredonia, Commerce, Church, and East Main streets. Surprisingly, Rulfs even got a request from the town fathers to build a wooden bridge across the Banita Creek near the Depot, which the newspaper dubbed, "splendid."[4] The new century looked rosy.

Four Buildings on Main Street, 1899

The *Houston Daily Post* on May 3, 1899 announced: "Contracts for five brick stores, four one-story buildings and one two-story were let today to Mr. H. L. Austin and Mr. William Rulfs, D. Rulfs architect."[5] As 1900 opened, D. Rulfs had a full agenda of commercial, residential, and church commissions. One of these mentioned serves to set the pattern of the relationship of Rulfs to his brother and to other contractors in the town. The contract reads: "For the erection and completion of four, one-story brick buildings, west of the public square on West Main." At first, this is confusing, but the 100 block of East Main today was West Main in 1899; all designations emanated from the Square. The contract, in the Bennett Blake Papers at the East Texas Research Center, outlines the binding agreement between J. W. Power (two of the buildings), John J. Lilly, and Wm. B. McKnight, and the contractors. Henry L. Austin undertook the brickwork for $3250. William Henry Rulfs contracted for the carpentry work for $3400. All of the work, materials and labor, were to be done "according to and in compliance with the plans and specifications prepared by D. Rulfs Architect which plans and specifications are now in the hands of the parties hereto and hereby made a part of this contract."[6] The architect's fees for drawings and specification, in all examples in the period, were paid up front before the arrangements for construction. While this pattern clearly separated the plans from the construction, others did not always see the transactions as separate. (See Chapter IX.)

The Hoya Buildings (1900)

On March 6, 1900, the *Daily Sentinel* announced that Fritz Hoya had commissioned his friend and neighbor, D. Rulfs, to design brick replacements for the wooden stores at the south end of the West Square. The land, purchased in 1839 by Francis von der Hoya at a forced sale to pay the debts of the former Mexican commandant, was still in the hands of the Hoya descendents until 2012. The deed for the sale can be viewed online at the East Texas Research Center.[7] The Hoyas used the corner for a variety of family enterprises.[8] Fritz Hoya, the older and unmarried brother of Charles Hoya, oversaw the transition from wood to brick acting for the heirs in the building plans of 1900. Before announcing his new building, Hoya obtained a ten-year lease on the second floor from the Nacogdoches Milam

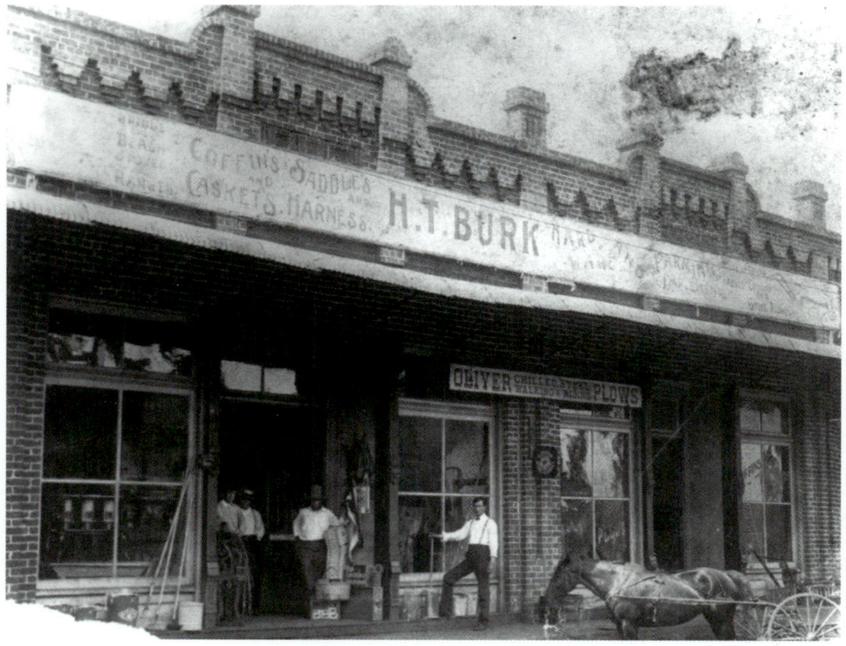

FIGURE 8.3. The H. T. Burk Hardware Business, ca. 1910.
The J. W. Power Building, built in 1899, was leased to the Burk Hardware business after 1908. Courtesy of ETRC.

FIGURES 8.4 Johnson Furniture Company, 2012.

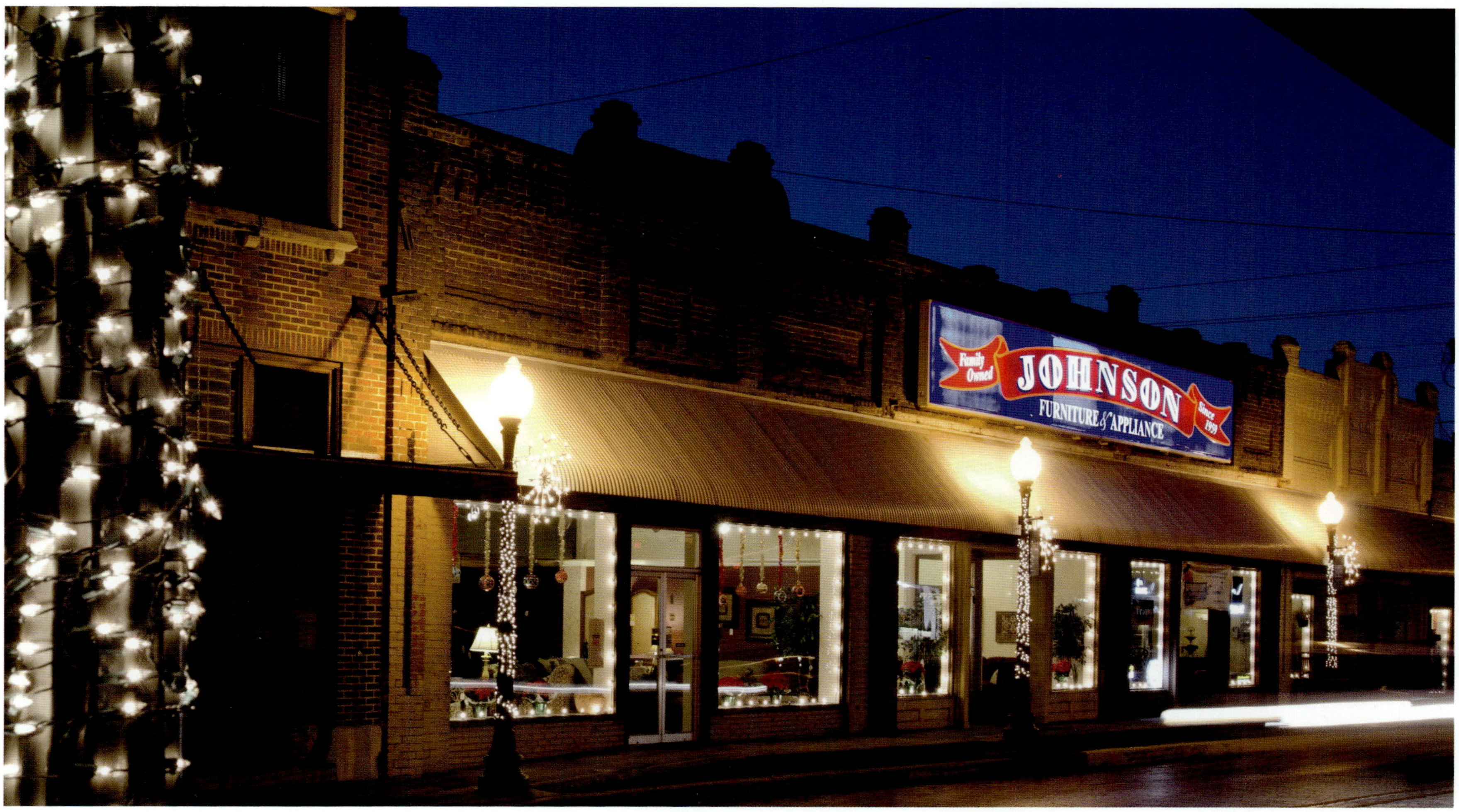

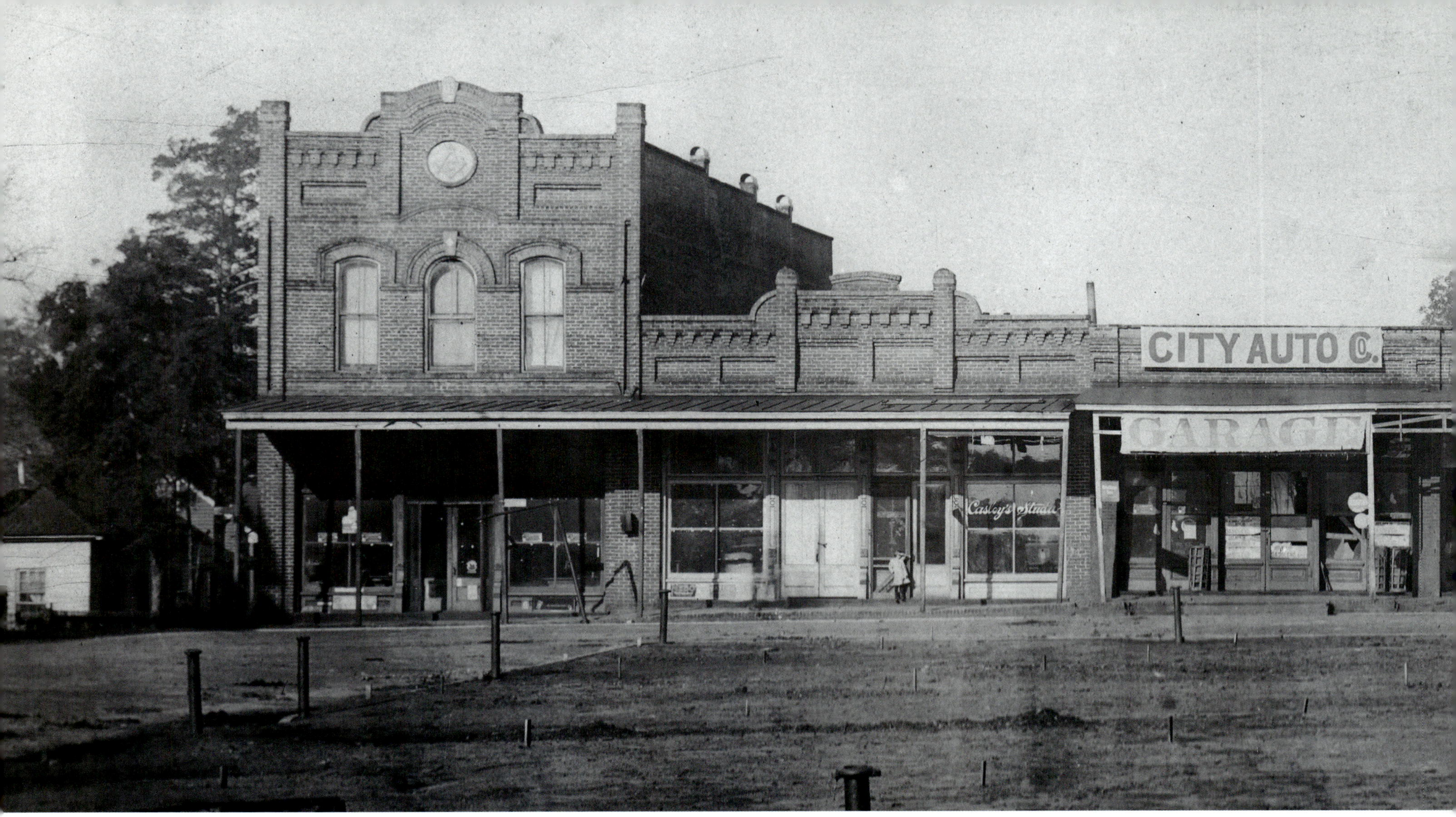

FIGURE 8.5. The West Side of the Square, ca. 1915.

This photograph of the West Square Hoya Buildings dates ca. 1915, when the town was planning to sell the center of the Square for a United States Post Office. On the left side, the Hoya Buildings built in 1900, were the last buildings completed along Pecan Street. The focal point of the upper façade of the two story Hoya Building (left end) was a Masonic Emblem. The Hoyas later replaced the Masonic Emblem with a large clock once the Masons moved out of their second story quarters. Without a picture, the intricate color articulation of the brickwork can only be imagined by looking at the Pilar Street façade (FIGURE 8.1). As one can see, there were no brick streets until after 1917. Courtesy of ETRC.

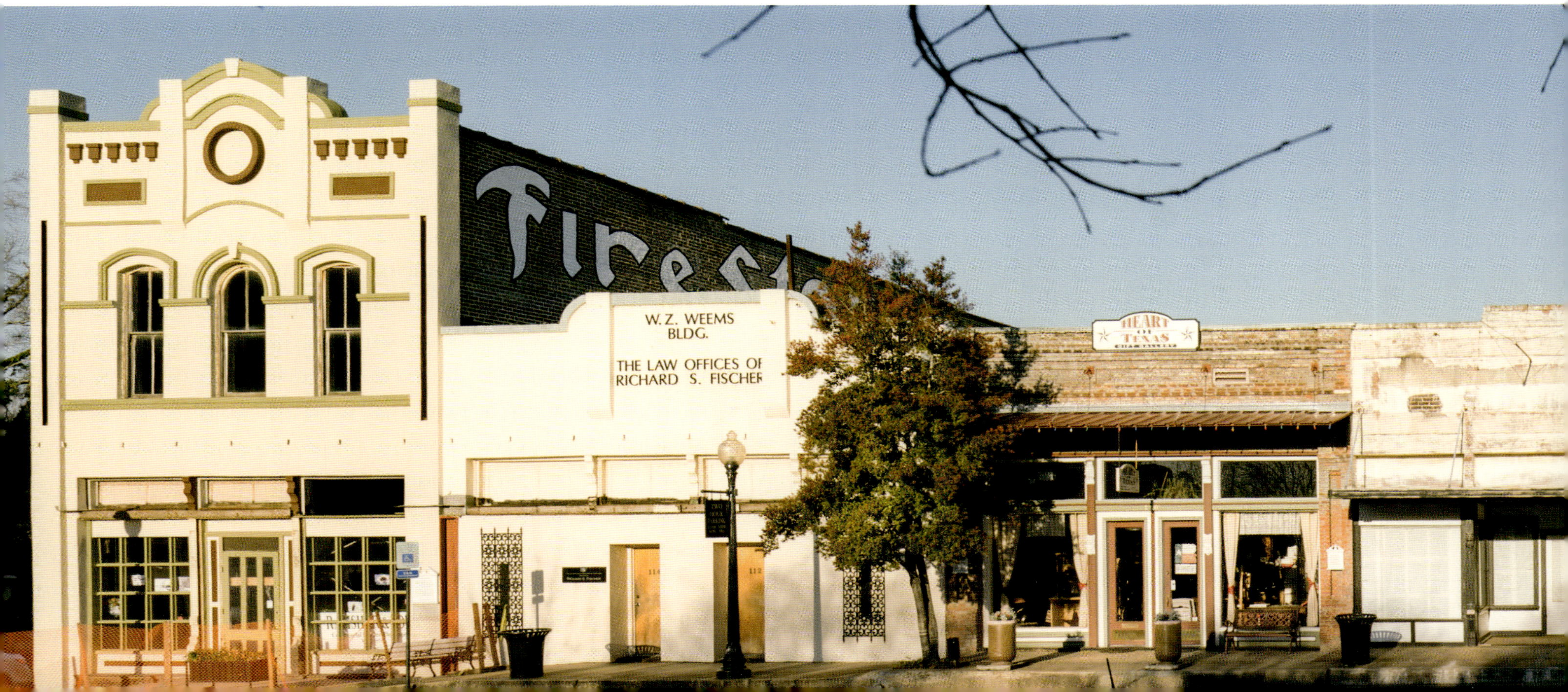

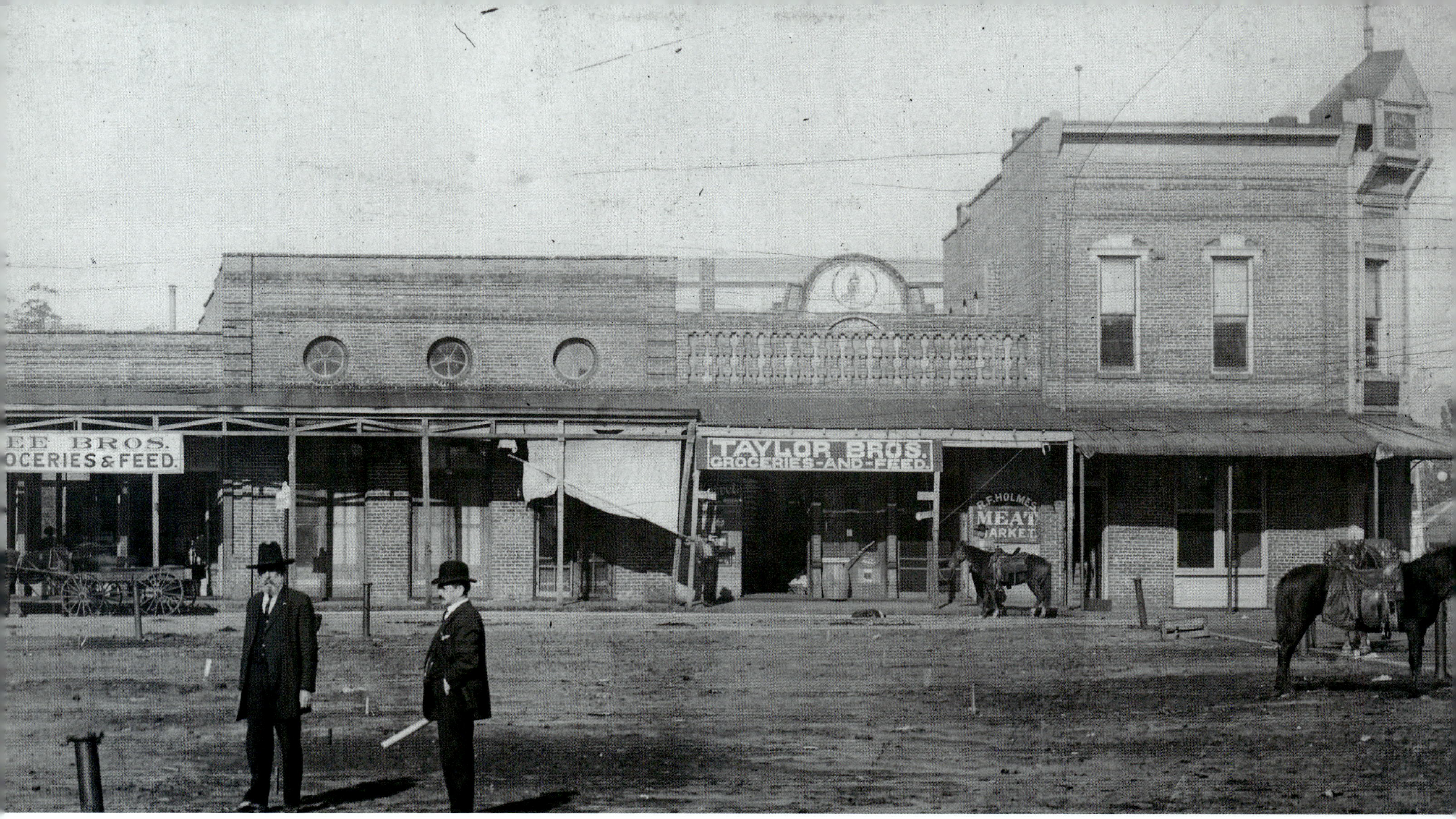

FIGURE 8.6. (Below) The West Square Today, Pecan Street Elevation.

While changes have occurred over the years, the West Square complex constitutes one of the most authentic, extant suite of buildings by Rulfs in the downtown area. The Hoya Building, on the corner of Pecan and Pilar, is undergoing extensive restoration and renovation. The original façade on the Square, destroyed in early renovations, is being recreated in plaster to provide a semblance of its former details.

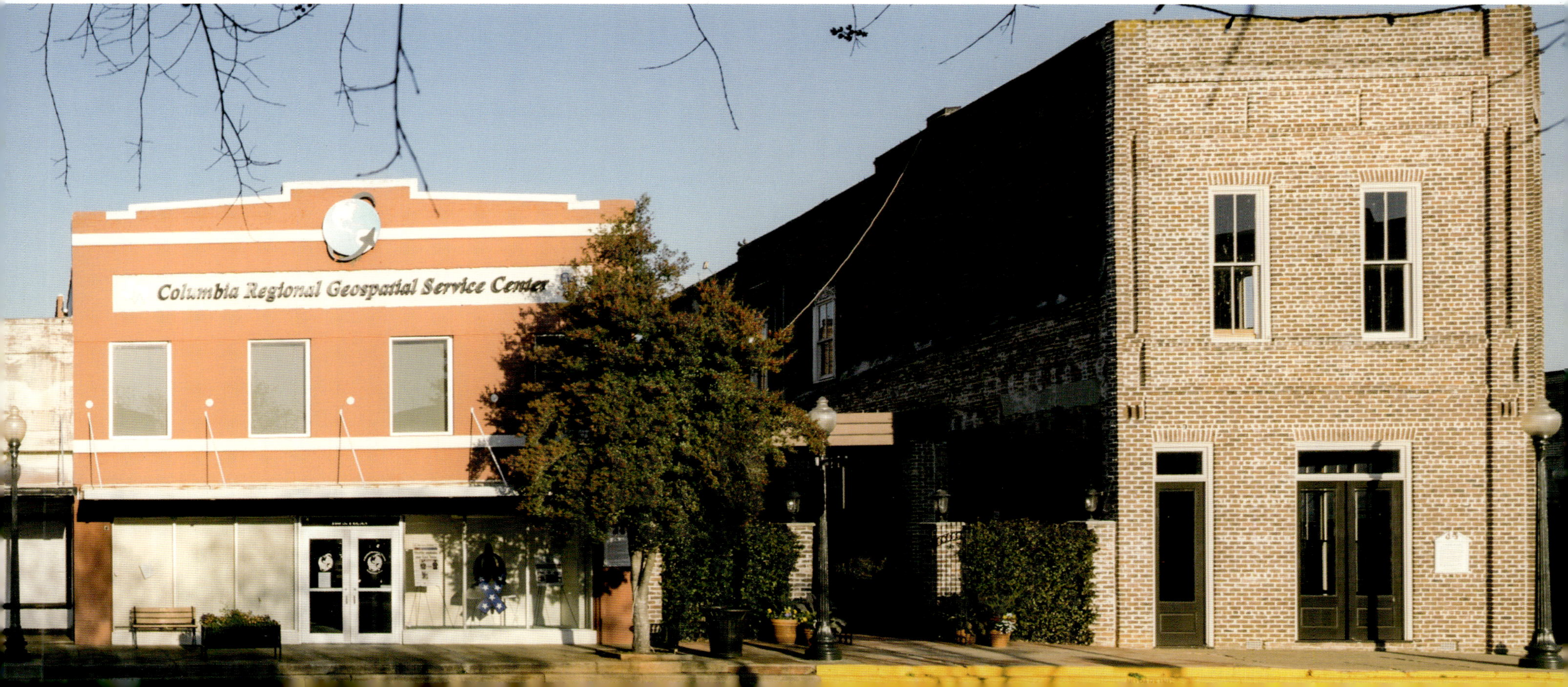

Lodge Number 2 of the Masonic Order. The newspaper hailed the project: "The new brick building will finish the row of brick houses in that part of town and will add much to the dignity and beauty of that locality. It will also be a splendid business location. We hope the day will not be far distant that will witness the removal of all the wooden buildings in town and the erection of commodious bricks in their place. Besides adding to the beauty it also lessens considerably the danger of fire and thereby makes insurance rates less."[9] Later, the newspaper gave a fuller description, confirming the fact that D. Rulfs expressly designed "the upper story to be occupied for a Masonic hall." After viewing the plans, the editor concluded, "The drawing of Mr. Rulfs shows a beautiful design and the building will be an ornament to the business portion of the city."[10] R. B. Shearer, who was working with Rulfs on the Christ Episcopal Church, was the brick contractor.[11]The Masons moved into their new home on November 30, 1900, and they celebrated their first home "especially prepared for them" with a banquet. Years later in 1921, Rulfs drew plans for another Masonic building, but if this building was ever built, the author can find no evidence.[12]

The ground floors of both buildings were very similar, designed for commercial use: each had bay areas separated by cast iron columns (some still visible) and flat wooden awnings to cover the sidewalk. The façades of both buildings, now covered with stucco and heavily altered, once had elaborate brickwork. The one-story northern building had a stepped parapet, with inset brick panels, half-pilasters, and corbelled brick moldings, very much like the parapets used in the block between the Square and North Street discussed earlier. (See Figures 8.3, 8.4) A variety of commercial concerns have occupied these buildings: in 1906, sheet music, pianos, and organs; in 1912, groceries; in 1921, tin; and in 1929, furniture. Montgomery Ward and Jasper Furniture were long-term lessees.[13]

The second story of the Hoya building on the corner of Pilar Street was one of the architect's most elaborate designs, his tribute to the importance of the Masonic Order in Nacogdoches. The focal point of the upper east façade was a Masonic Emblem; the same theme is suggested on the south side of the building. Instead of his traditional Palladian arrangement, Rulfs replaced the elevated central arched window with a triumphal arch surrounding a large Masonic medallion. The parapet and the sides featured elaborate brick cornices, pilasters, inset panels, and a keystone at its pinnacle. Since the façades of both buildings are now covered with stucco and the elaborate brickwork obscured, modern observers must look to the Pilar Street façade to imagine what a striking addition this building must have made on the Square in 1900.[14]

The Cox Building on Pecan Street (The "Tobacco Warehouse"), 1900

The updating of the John H. Cox Building (Rulfs, 1888) at the corner of Main and Pecan Street was part of an elaborate scheme to pacify the ever-expanding Cason, Richardson, & Company.[15] In exchange for a five-year lease, Cox had Rulfs to oversee joining two buildings on Main and building a new one on Pecan, very much like he would join buildings later on East Main. Haltom in the *Daily Sentinel* lays out the whole project.

FIGURE 8.7. (Below) Drawings by D. Rulfs for a Brick Warehouse for Cason, Richardson & Co., 1900.

Although on Cox property, Rulfs drew the elevations below for D. K. Cason as a part of the latter's expanding company on the Northwest corner of the Square and Pecan Street. Later in 1906, when Cason expanded his operations even further, he reconstituted the business and moved to East Main as the Cason, Monk and Company. The elaborate façade above may have existed only between 1900 and 1909; afterwards, as the uses of the building changed, so did the façade. The complete drawings of the building are in the Cason Papers in the ETRC; these photographs predate the transfer of the papers.

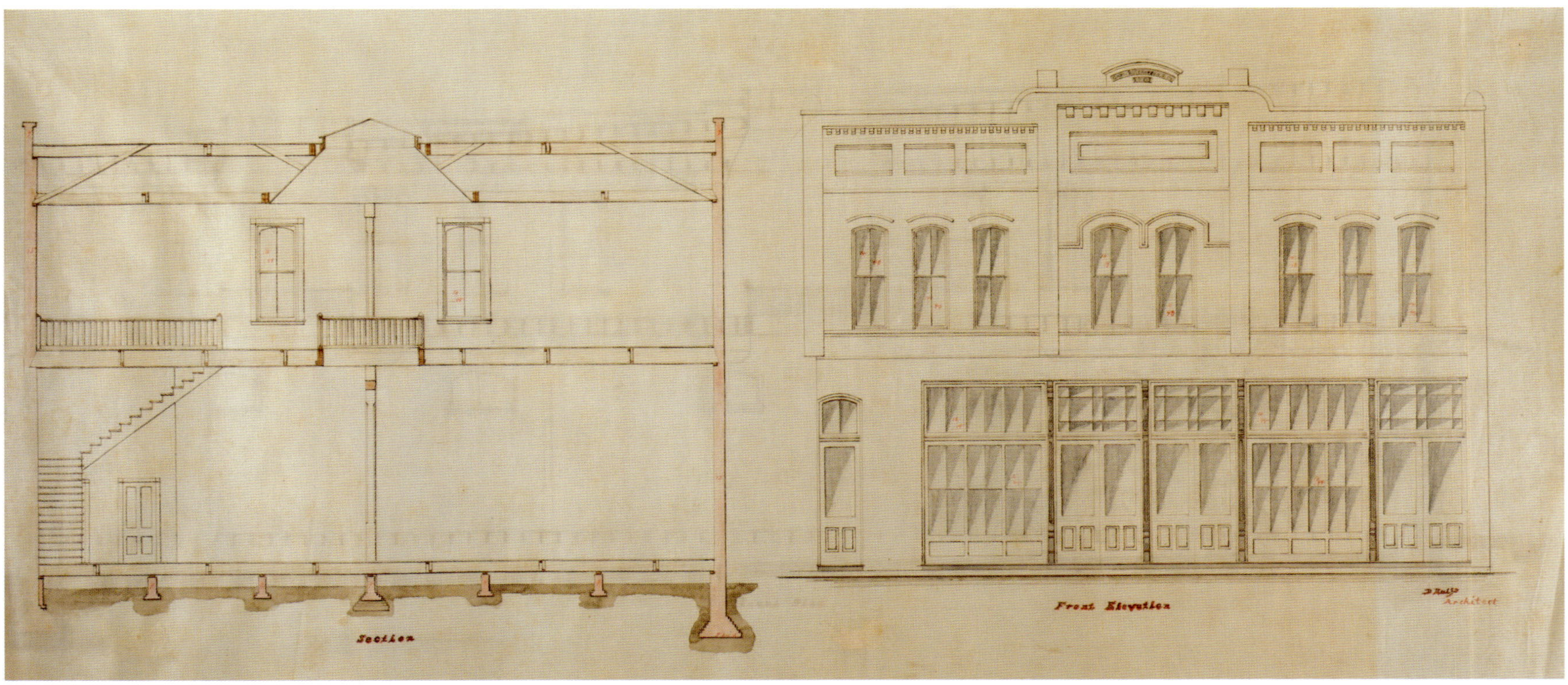

Arch Ways Cut in Cason, Richardson & Co.

> Cason, Richardson & Co. have had two arch ways cut through the partition wall between their two stores and are making several marked changes in the interior of their buildings with the view to greatly enlarging their business and increasing their stock. In addition to the two large stores on Main Street, they will occupy the large new building now approaching completion on Pecan Street. They have ordered new shelving, office furniture, etc., and will have things going in great style within the next 30 days.[16]

The addition of an entirely new structure to the rear of the original Cox Building as early as 1900 was unknown until recently. The author had previously dated the structure, known locally as the Tobacco Warehouse, to 1909 when the Tausig Cigar Company leased the structure.[17]Cason paid to have the building designed and built, not Cox, in exchange for a five-year rent-free lease. Cason and Rulfs reserved the right to supervise and approve all changes, not Cox.[18] Not only are the specifications extant, but also the plans that show front elevations, foundations, second floor details, windows, and cross sections signed by Rulfs. In 1906, at the end of the lease, Cason moved his business to East Main Street and hired Rulfs there, too.

In 1909, Cox remodeled the Pecan Street Warehouse for the Tausig Tobacco Company to serve as a curing, storage, and cigar factory. This business lasted until about 1914. In the remodeling, the facade was changed, the street-level wooden floor specified by Rulfs was removed, and a concrete floor poured at the ground level. The construction contract included provisions for a steam heating system; the building was also equipped with manually operated elevators, one inside and one outside.[19] From 1921, first Tucker-Sitton Hardware and later Branch-Patton Hardware used the building as a multi-purpose warehouse. The building housed buggies, plows, building supplies, lawnmowers, an ambulance, and caskets. The building still has many of the large beams and nice brickwork of the original building. The Cox family heirs sold the building in 1988.[20]

The E. A. Blount Building, North Square (1901)

The important building that Rulfs designed and specified for Edward A. Blount, Sr. in 1901 is one of the most difficult structures to visualize or describe. No drawings have survived; only one grim picture has emerged during research, and the building itself only survived for five years. The origins of the building are deeply involved with a complicated set of local circumstances in the troubled years of 1901-02; the destruction of the building came in the great fire of 1906.

While Rulfs had designed residences for both E. A. and Stephen Blount, neither brother had purchased much downtown property before 1901. Before, they had managed their vast holdings in land and timber around East Texas out of leased offices. Observing that rental property had become a good investment, E. A. Blount bought the prime commercial lots in town when he entered the market: two wood-frame structures between the "First Brick Block" and the Old Stone Fort. He immediately asked Rulfs for plans, and by March they called for bids "for the construction of three brick stores with iron and plate glass fronts."[21] In May, when the *Daily Sentinel* announced that Austin & Herrin had won the contract for the brickwork, the editor noted, "Mr. D. Rulfs is the architect," and the plans "are beauties in design." Upstairs, the plan was to provide for offices. One innovation for the town caught the editor's eye: "A mammoth skylight will be placed in the roof of the building for purposes of light and ventilation."[22]Although not scheduled to be finished until August, Blount at once announced that the major new tenant in his buildings would be a new drug store—Stripling, Haselwood, & Company. Sam Stripling, Will Haselwood, and Tom Baker were to be the principals in the new undertaking.[23]

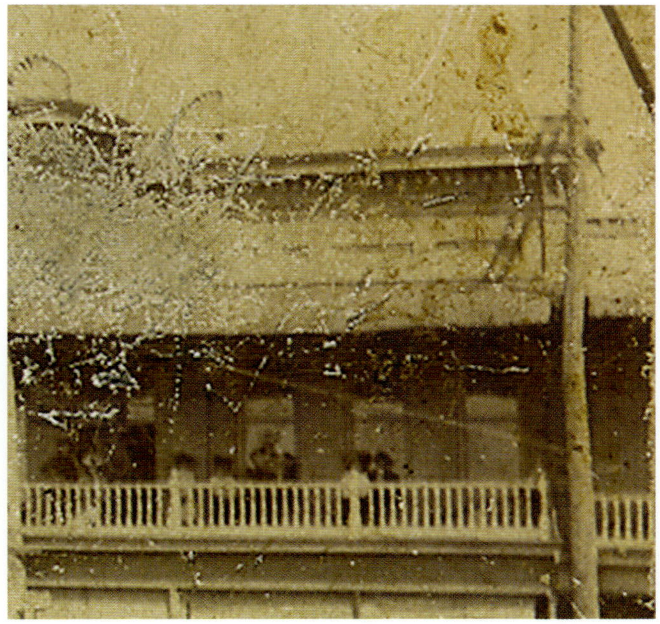

FIGURE 8.8. The Blount Building in 1902.

The only extant picture of the short-lived Blount Building is the one right, which comes from the gruesome hanging of James Buchanan in 1902. For the full picture, see FIGURE 7.8. Photograph compliments of Gary Borders

The announcement of the Blount building brought into the open a private rivalry between Perkins and Blount. With one stroke, Blount had cut Perkins Brothers off from the latter's dream of dominating the whole North Square. To make the situation worse, Blount had given aid and space to a new rival drugstore in the same block. A month later, Perkins showed his willingness to pick up the gauntlet by announcing his purchase of the Old Stone Fort, also on the North Square. There is no proof that Perkins considered asking for a plan from Rulfs, but the architect would have faced a career-limiting dilemma. He had worked closely with both Blount and Perkins, but this dispute was very serious. The decision by Perkins to destroy the Old Stone Fort alienated so many people in the town, especially women, that Rulfs might have found it most difficult to secure commissions for residential construction had the sequence of events played out differently. As stated before, the tearing down of the Old Stone Fort proved so controversial that Perkins himself quit the retail business. Fortunately, well before Perkins purchased the Old Stone Fort, Rulfs had already committed himself not only to Blount's project, but also to a host of new structures in the East Main-Church Street area. He really did not have time for a building for Perkins. As the crisis developed, Perkins decided to go to contacts he had in Fort Worth to escape the local scene. This decision saved Rulfs many headaches. After the fire of 1906, as discussed below, Perkins did turn to Rulfs to work out of a difficult problem on rebuilding the building.

The hatred in town over the destruction of the Old Stone Fort actually offered Blount an additional victory. A single lot owned by Hardy Dial's Saloon stood in between the new Blount Building and the Old Stone Fort property. Furious that Perkins was tearing down the old landmark, Dial sold to Blount and, in the process, got fancy new quarters for his popular watering hole. Rulfs did the plans, and Blount let the bids on May 2, 1902. Since Dial's Saloon was Haltom's favorite pub, the newspaper narrated the whole story.[24] No one remembers these buildings today: both the big Blount Building and Dial's Saloon burned in December of 1906, along with the new Perkins Building.

To offset the impact of the new Perkins store and, at the same time, to take advantage of increased traffic, Blount and Schmidt bought the property to the north along the west side of Fredonia Street, discussed below in a separate section.[25]

New Players and Old Rivals

Prosperity attracts competitors; tough times turn competitors into opponents. After the Civil War, Texas was not favorable to the establishment of banks. "This situation prompted the origin and growth of the institution of private money lenders,"[26] one source writes. Nacogdoches had a long history of private money lending. Bennett Blake and Frost Thorn lent money in Nacogdoches before the coming of the railroad. John P. Davidson was another prominent private lender. After the arrival of the railroads, as other men with money moved to town, the competition among those who lent money (while friendly enough on the surface) became spirited. The Wettermark Bank, a private institution, more or less forced Davidson and others to establish a rival institution in 1890, the First National Bank, but this venture lasted only until 1899.[27] Newcomers to the lending circuit, such as Blount, Perkins, Schmidt, Sturdevant, Hayter, and Hoya, seemed to prefer the private tradition, but after the turn of the century, this became increasingly impractical.

In the fall of 1901, in the midst of the crisis over the fate of the Old Stone Fort, a group of outside investors announced the formation of a new bank in Nacogdoches. In the *Daily Sentinel* of September 24, 1901, the editor announced the name: The Commercial National Bank of Nacogdoches. Haltom assured his readers that T. J. Williams, the principal stockholder, was acceptable: "Mr. Williams, while a stranger to most people of Nacogdoches, is a native Texan."[28] Everyone, however, recognized the well-established attempt of outsiders to fish in troubled waters. The newspaper explained that the new bank had signed a lease for the front corner of the new building Rulfs was building for the Hazle family on East Main.

Perkins was too distracted to respond to the outside challengers and may not have seen a reason to do so, but E. A. Blount immediately began to meet the threat head on; his chief ally in the endeavor was John Schmidt. By January 1902, exactly at the time the demolition crews began tearing down the Old Stone Fort, Blount pulled off a decisive stroke by purchasing controlling shares in the new Commercial Bank. Although Williams stayed on the Commercial Board, Blount and Schmidt ran the new bank. Rulfs quickly refitted the space in the Hazle Building to suit the new owners.[29] The waters in Nacogdoches became even more troubled after the collapse of the Wettermark Bank in January of 1903. A second group of outside investors announced in February that they had received a charter for another bank in town.[30] The group, led by E. S. Woodfin, who never really established any links to Nacogdoches, was looking to be bought out. Blount, who had fended off the earlier outside attempt, quickly bought shares in the new venture. W. U. Perkins and others, however, were not about to see Blount control two banks. Although Blount would be a major investor of the new bank and sit on its board, Perkins and a close group of local investors, which included Jeff Hayter, Charles Hoya, and Link Sturdevant, bought controlling shares in the new entity immediately. Stone Fort National Bank—Perkins suggested the name—trumped Blount by announcing it would open on the Square.[31] Inadvertently, the new coalition outmaneuvered themselves by selecting as their new home the former building, admittedly available, of the discredited Wettermark Bank. Their *faux pas,* from a publicity point of view, gave Blount a chance to relocate Commercial Bank from the Hazle Building to his own new building on the North Square; the Commercial Bank opened on the Square on October 21, 1903.[32] To extricate the Stone Fort Bank from its misstep, Will Perkins offered the bank space in his new building. This, ironically, placed the new Stone Fort Bank on the site of the former Old Stone Fort, *immediately next door to Commercial Bank.*

The Successor to the Old Stone Fort: The Perkins Brothers Building (1902)

Although not a Rulfs design, the Perkins Building that replaced the Old Stone Fort was a major building in downtown Nacogdoches. The demolition of the Old Stone House started in January and continued throughout the early spring of 1902. While Bill Haltom would have covered the new Perkins Brothers Building under any circumstances, the editor of the *Daily Sentinel* had invested heavily in the new venture—not in money, but in credibility—and had, as a result, to give full coverage to the building in order to justify his own position. The *Daily Sentinel* narrated the construction process step by step: on May 9, the brick work was "getting up above the foundation;" on May 16, "a large shipment of St. Louis brick . . . arrived" and "Bedford stone from Indiana;" on July 3, a portion of the building "was injured by a storm" and completion delayed; on August 15, "fast approaching completion;" on August 28, installing "the finest sidewalk made."[33] In a large article on September 1, entitled "Successor to the Old Stone Fort," Haltom began the build-up to the grand opening:

> The building is a representative of the new and larger era in which we live. The Fort was an architectural blot on the horizon, an ugly protuberance thrusting its ugliness continually in the face of the town, a survivor of primitive conditions painfully out of place in modern Nacogdoches, and its most devoted, and super-sentimental friends, deep down in their heart of hearts, were glad to welcome the enterprise that decreed its doom . . . .

Haltom described the structure in glowing terms, touting the imported brick and stone, in short, "a rare and pleasing combination of elegance, simplicity and solidity combined." M. R. Sanguinette from Fort Worth was the architect and I. C. Buchanan, the contractor.[34]

Perkins Brothers moved in late September and put the "finishing touches on the front of the building" on October 5, 1902.[35] The opening was grand. On the other hand, the wounds Perkins incurred during the yearlong period of discussion, demolition, and construction were also grand and did not heal. Perkins had staked his entire company on the new building, his *magnum opus.* Evidently, the fight over the old historical landmark had taken the pleasure out of the retail business for him. As a wealthy man, he certainly did not need to continue. In early 1905, he dissolved his original company, and Charles Perkins sold his interest to M. R. Kleas and Hollis Mast. Haltom called this "the most important business change which has occurred here for many years."[36] As part of the sale, Will Perkins stayed on in the new pharmacy-emporium (Perkins, Kleas, and Mast) for another two years. But, after the great fire in December of 1906, Perkins decided to sever all connections with retail trade in January of 1907. This was front-page news in Nacogdoches. Giles Haltom's coverage in the *Daily Sentinel* was more like an obituary than an item for the business pages. The newspaper headline ran: "W. U. Perkins Withdraws from Business in Nacogdoches."[37] Since Perkins had other options and would still be an important player in Nacogdoches because of the new bank and the Nacogdoches Cotton Oil Mill, he withdrew from the drugstore business completely; he had had enough of dealing directly with the general public. He did, nevertheless, rebuild the Perkins Building in 1907, this time under the supervision of Rulfs who essentially used the older plans.

The Architect's Patron: John Schmidt (1900-1906)

The new century brought many changes in the largest and most important business in Nacogdoches—the Mayer & Schmidt Company. Giles Haltom went so far as to call it "the largest commercial establishment in East Texas." If a history of commercial activity in Nacogdoches were written, Haltom continued, the company's history "would be a history of the commercial development of Nacogdoches for the past twenty-eight years."[38] The firm was important in all types of general merchandising, both wholesale and retail: cotton, dry goods, furnishing, furniture, groceries, and hardware. In addition to Nacogdoches, the company had a very successful branch in Tyler. Because of their great buying and selling, their seasonal visits to markets were no longer practical by the turn of the century. The company needed offices in New York City; as a result, around 1900, Abe Mayer left Nacogdoches "to open up an eastern office and establish a quilt factory."[39] In 1903, the old mercantile firm transformed itself into an official corporation using the same name.[40] John Schmidt was the President, Abe Mayer Vice President, and R. C. Monk was the Secretary and Treasurer. The partners not only incorporated, but they also began a process of spinning off their various divisions and capital assets into separate companies. There were also mergers with other local firms. All of these changes occasioned new buildings and the remodeling of older buildings. Once Abe Mayer left for New York, John Schmidt, who never had many restraints, became even more liberated to make the decisions in Nacogdoches on his own.

Although Rulfs designed buildings for nearly everyone in town, the architect worked so continuously for his patron John Schmidt that it is difficult to know how to analyze their many projects together: by area, type of architecture, or chronological order. Today, one would say that Rulfs worked on retainer for John Schmidt and Abe Mayer throughout most of his career in Nacogdoches. He always gave them first options on his talents and services. Rulfs depended on them,[41] and they on him. Rulfs always made time to fit another one of their schemes into his schedule. In the period from 1900 to 1906, Rulfs undertook many projects for Mayer & Schmidt, but he also designed for associated companies where Schmidt had the dominant influence, and with organizations in which Schmidt played a leading role. Rulfs redesigned the area around the big Mayer & Schmidt store (the area around Fredonia, East Main, Commerce, and Church Streets) and helped Schmidt expand into new enterprises. Some of the buildings from this period still exist, but many have since disappeared.

Cotton Exchange Building (1900-1902)

The National Register labels the Cotton Exchange Building as "one of the premier examples of late 19th-century commercial architecture in Nacogdoches. Although the city at one time boasted many similarly detailed buildings in the downtown, most have been razed or have been so severely altered that their integrity has been compromised."[42]

The building that now occupies the corner of Fredonia and Commerce streets was not the first or the second or the third structure in that location. A wooden "storehouse" on the site dates back to 1854; also, later in the 1870s, R. C. Shindler had a warehouse there.[43] When M&S took the property as part of their expansion of the second brick block in 1888-1889, they remodeled the back building and used it for warehouse space. As their needs changed and expanded, so did their storage buildings. Modifications came in 1891, when the first floor brick building was built, and again in 1896—thus the difficulty in dating the building.[44] The major transformation of the building, which accounts for most of what we see today, came between 1900-1902.

Shortly after 1900, Rulfs undertook for Mayer & Schmidt a major repurposing of the building at the corner of Fredonia and Commerce Street to fit their needs at the time. They wanted to transition the location from warehouse to wholesale commercial uses: their wholesale grocery business, their wholesale hardware business, and their wholesale cotton business. While Rulfs knew the building was still utilitarian and likely to change in the future, he attempted to tie his exterior designs to the interior functions of these three businesses as of 1900. The southwest corner of the building, on Fredonia and Commerce Streets, served as the face of their wholesale grocery operations. There, Rulfs placed a pair of oversized arched openings—a door and a window (which have since been bricked up.) The wholesale hardware operations, to the east on Commerce Street, visually got its own segmentation (a mirror of the central bay on the west. The hardware entrance, offset between pilasters and placed under an arch at the parapet level, had its own distribution of windows and doors. To unify the first floor and provide a strong horizontal element, the architect specified an awning around the entire south and west elevations. He also placed inset panels with corbelled brickwork at the level of the parapets, which created another unifying horizontal element. Rulfs had become fond of this fancy brickwork during his training in Oldenburg. The windows along the upper facade were arched with hoodmolds, despite their various groupings.

Rulfs treated the upper façade of the Cotton Exchange as a unit, a reflection of its single interior business function. He divided the building into three bays or segments. The central bay, over the main door, had pilasters on each side, two arched windows with hoodmolds, and an arch over the center inset panel. (He had used similar arches and hoodmolds on the Hoya Building earlier in the year; the Cotton Exchange, however, was less elaborate.)

Although the exterior brick walls of the Cotton Exchange were load bearing, Rulfs needed to strengthen the support for the large second-story open space. He accomplished the support by inserting huge columns, hewn

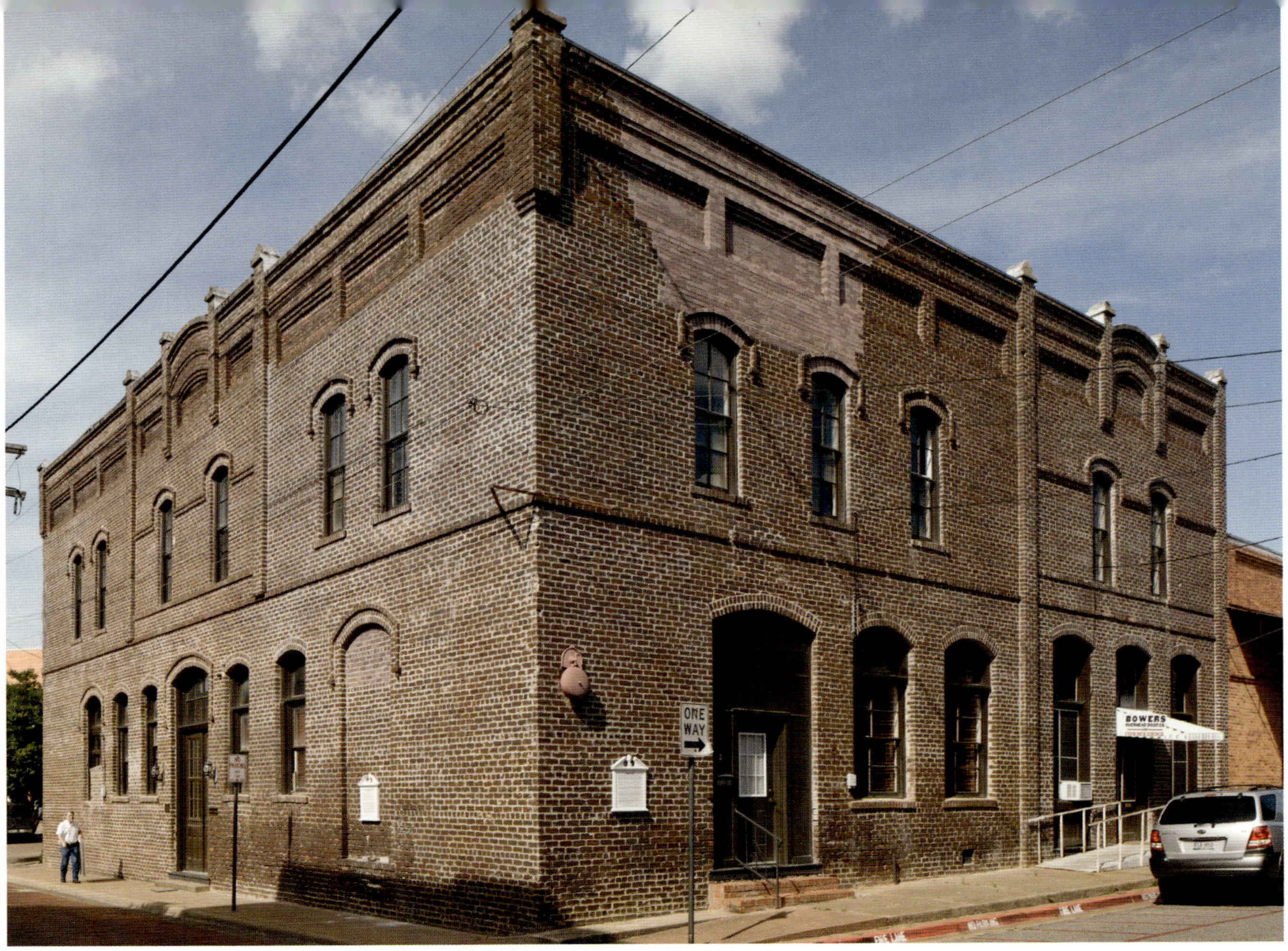

FIGURE 8.9. The Cotton Exchange Building, 2012.
The Mast family now owns the Cotton Exchange Building, and both Travis and John Mast have their offices there.

from singletree trunks, throughout the first floor. Near the exterior loading platforms on the north side of the building, Rulfs installed an open eleva-tor accessible from all the interior partitions. The remodeled buildings had electricity from the beginning. According to the newspaper, Henry Austin supplied the brickwork; Rulfs' brother, William Henry, oversaw much of the carpentry work in the building; and a man named Will Hartgraves was the overall contractor on the hardware division.[45]

However, using the name 'Cotton Exchange Building' has created confusion for the modern observer. The consolidation of the cotton industry was slower and much later than many historians have assessed. By moving their cotton trading operations to Commerce Street, M&S were recognizing the growing importance of this side of their business, but it is unlikely that they used the earlier 1891 building, as one source suggests, as the location for their cotton trading operations.[46] While their brokerage business in cotton started early, the idea of holding auctions away from the actual cotton storage sheds was a new idea. When they first ventured into this model in the mid-1890s, various spaces around town housed the operations, including the upper floor of their establishment on East Main Street. The cotton exchange business was an extension of their quickly expanding wholesale grocery business. Many of the regional grocers had to take cotton as payment for their goods. M&S gave the customers they supplied a way to do the same type of trade for wholesale groceries. The volume of cotton shipped from Nacogdoches increased rapidly, only after the establishment of the Cotton Compress Company in 1897. A rail car would hold about fifty bales of cotton; but if the bales were compressed, it would hold over three times as many. A consortium, of which John Schmidt was a major stockholder and Secretary/Treasurer, owned the Compress.[47] The repurposing and expansion of this building after the turn of the century signals the coming of age of the cotton market. In fact, it is around 1900 that the volume of M & S's trade in cotton became so complicated that it led to a physical separation of the partnership into two branches. Abe Mayer, in order to keep the cotton shipments on track, felt it necessary to move to New York to conduct the complicated operations up there. As their business empire evolved, they would make other adjustments.[48] At every step of the way, Rulfs responded to their spatial needs, expressed to him by John Schmidt, by designing and constructing, or overseeing construction as the case may be, new buildings. (See the Nacogdoches Grocery Company later in this chapter.)

The Blount-Schmidt Buildings on Fredonia Street (1902)

John Schmidt and E. A. Blount, in assessing the future requirements for the town, concluded that the new Perkins corner and the Cotton Exchange would create enormous traffic in the area just north of the Square. Schmidt had just helped Blount acquire controlling shares in the Commercial Bank. They now joined together to control the neighborhood along Fredonia Street, offer new temporary space for traveling salesmen, provide additional warehouse space, and encourage wholesalers in the area. The property they purchased was the old central meat and vegetable market of Nacogdoches, immediately north of the Old Stone Fort. In essence, this limited Perkins to the corner of Main and Fredonia Streets. The entrepreneurs immediately engaged Rulfs to plan a new commercial block along the west side of Fredonia Street. The usual team swung into action: by March of 1902, Rulfs had drawn the plans, his brother William Henry Rulfs did the carpentry work, and Henry Austin did the brickwork. From conception, the structures were speculative and utilitarian; the owners advertised that the interiors could be customized to suit the tenant. Their advertisement in

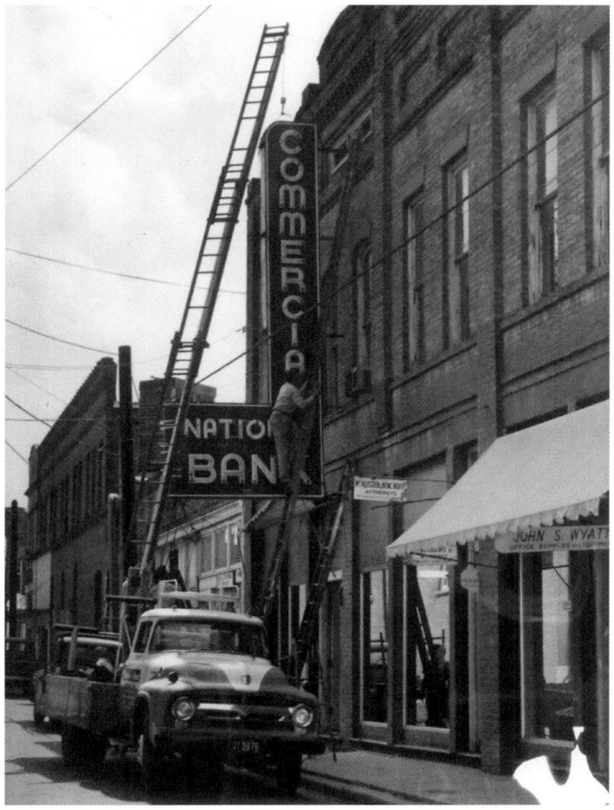

FIGURE 8.10. The Blount-Schmidt Building.
The Blount-Schmidt Building was a general-purpose office structure from the start. In this picture taken in the 1960s, the Commercial National Bank is moving into the building temporarily while their location on the Square was being remodeled. Courtesy of ETRC.

March stated: "We have a nice store room for rent in our new brick on Fredonia street. Also a large hall in the same building, well lighted and ventilated. E.A. Blount and John Schmidt."[49] The Knights of Pythias, to which Rulfs belonged, considered leasing the large second story room, but did not. The buildings, finished in August, appear again in the newspaper in October as they were being partitioned for some tenant. The large hall on the second floor later became the B. P. O. E., Elks Lodge.

Little information survives on these now-gone buildings. They were not, even when new, great pieces of architecture; but they were good examples of the commercial architecture of the period. The ground level storefronts had mixed iron and brick pilasters with glass show windows in between. Rulfs used paired windows with concrete lintels on the second story, inset panels with corbelled brickwork at the parapet level, and small arches over each of the two central bays. The buildings had electricity from the beginning. Because of the Sanborn Maps, we know their footprints and their uses over time. The southernmost building, next door to the Perkins Building, had three one-story "sample rooms" or showrooms, which traveling salesmen leased on a short-term basis. At times, the Banita Hotel leased these rooms as sample rooms for the many salesmen who frequented their establishment. In 1906, furniture, sash doors, and even hay were being sold out of the buildings. By 1912, the tenants were more medium term: the Telephone Office had replaced the sample showrooms; the Post Office leased the middle two-story building; and a printing office had the northern building, with the B. P. O. E. Elks Lodge on the second floor. In 1922, the County leased one of the buildings; but during the Depression, the buildings frequently remained empty, especially the second stories. The Commercial Bank used the properties for temporary offices at various times.

Schmidt Explores the Hotel Business (1902)

As Nacogdoches continued to grow and as the number of people who came to the town for business and shopping increased, the demand for hotel rooms became critical. In response to these demands, in 1901 Rulfs designed, and his brother William Henry built, a ten-room addition to the Banita Hotel.[50] In 1902, John Schmidt decided to build a small hostelry to replace a boarding house that was going out of business at the corner of Main and North Street. This was not intended as a bid for the high-end hotel traffic. Because of its location next to the largest wagon yard in Nacogdoches, they were building additional retail space and, in so doing, trying to solve a need for traveling salesmen. The hotel rooms were on the second floor, leaving space for retail shops, such as a bakery, on the ground floor. The building no longer exists, but it sat diagonally across from the present Courthouse, just north of the old horse trough.[51] Haltom, always fascinated by the German tradition of placing a pine sapling over a finished building, commented:

> The brick work on the new hotel and livery building of Mayer & Schmidt on the old Cruse lot has been completed and the inevitable pine top has made its appearance. The new building shows up immensely and is going to be an ornament to that section of the city. The woodwork is progressing and in a few weeks the building will be ready to turn over to the Messrs. Heath and Ogg. The former has leased the hotel while Mr. Ogg has leased the livery stable.
>
> The building will contain twelve rooms up-stairs and an office, dining room and kitchen down stairs for the hotel, and on the side to be used as a livery stable, there are an office, feed rooms, haylofts, and stalls to accommodate thirty-five horses, besides the open space not cut into stalls. The arrangement for both hotel and livery business is complete and could not be improved upon and is a credit to the architect Mr. D. Rulfs.[52]

As a result of the success of this small hotel, which they christened "The Plaza," John Schmidt purchased the old A. A. Nelson homestead immediately north of the new hotel (at the southeast corner of North and Hospital) and instructed Rulfs to prepare plans for an even larger brick hotel. After hearing of the plans, Haltom observed, "The work of tearing down the old Nelson homestead began this morning. This is one of the old houses of Nacogdoches, and when first built was one of the finest residences in the city. Mr. John Schmidt will erect a handsome modern city hotel on the lot at once, which will both fill a long felt want in our town, and improve the appearance of North Street greatly."[53]

Rulfs proceeded to draw the plans for a large hotel on North Street, but it was never built. Events and other opportunities intervened. The collapse of the Wettermark Bank caught everyone off guard. Schmidt—ever the entrepreneur—then diverted his attention to a more profitable venture than a hotel: the building of the Nacogdoches (Wholesale) Grocery Company. Rulfs devoted his attention to the design and erection of two of the public schools that opened in 1904 (discussed in Chapter IX). The hotel shortage would have to wait to be addressed in 1906 with the construction of the Redland Hotel.

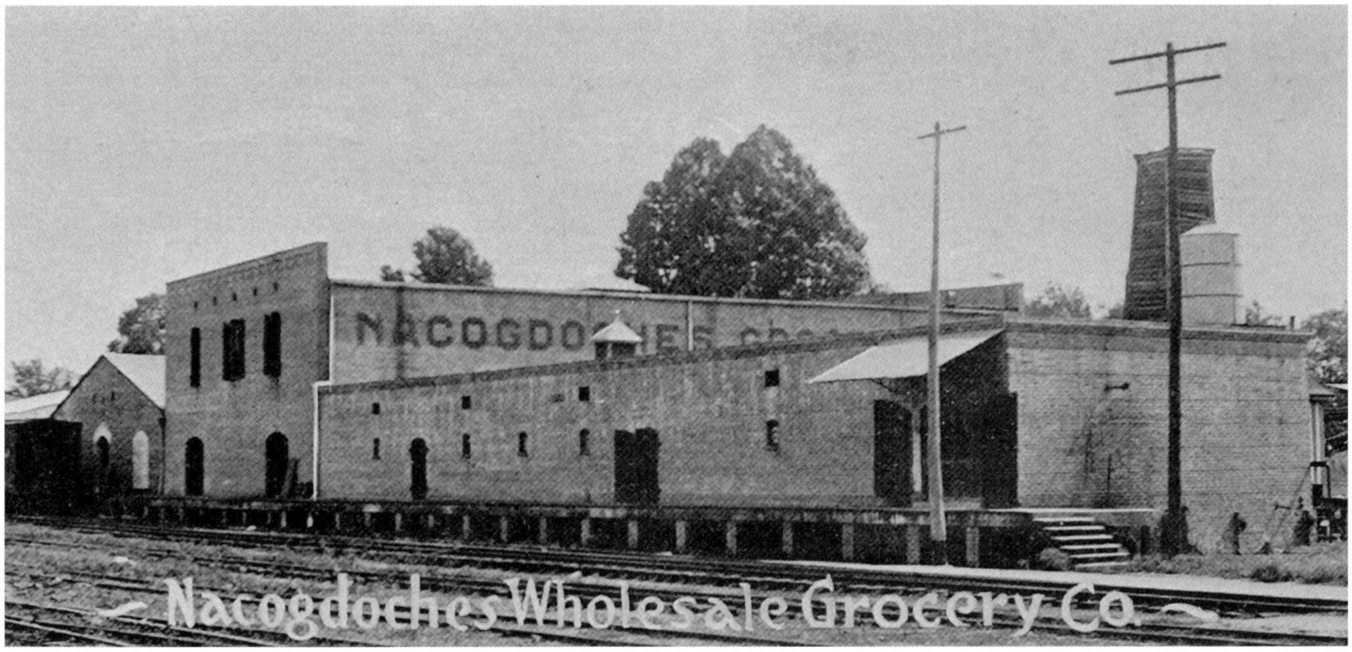

FIGURE 8.11. Nacogdoches Wholesale Grocery Co., 1917.
This extract from the Twenty Three Reasons Why, *the brochure showing scenes of Nacogdoches for the campaign to attract the SFA Normal to the town, shows the loading platforms along the tracks in 1917. Photograph from author's collection.*

Nacogdoches (Wholesale) Grocery Company (1904)

The Mayer & Schmidt Company had originally opened as a grocery business in 1878. By 1900, however, their retail grocery business had become secondary to their wholesale grocery business. While other establishments sold groceries wholesale in the city,[54] M&S was well on its way to being the major supplier to a large percentage of the small grocery businesses in the immediate East Texas Region. Schmidt's first attempt to cope with the growing demand led to the building of the Cotton Exchange Building, but the ground floor space allotted to the grocery business quickly proved inadequate and awkward for receiving and distributing groceries. Schmidt, ever quick to recognize and take advantage of opportunities, took the lead in creating a new company in May of 1902—the Nacogdoches Grocery Company. Schmidt became president of the new company, but he opened the investment to E. A. Blount, B. S. Wettermark, B. F. Hardeman, Oscar Matthews, and S. T. King.[55] Later stockholders and directors included C. W. Butt, Lee Hardeman, and Jacob F. Schmidt (John's nephew).[56] (*All of these men lived in houses designed by D. Rulfs.*) The Grocery Company started with an investment of $125,000, and according to the *Daily Sentinel*, because it inherited the M&S territories and reputation, it had a great foundation from the beginning. After three years in business, Giles Haltom called it a "matchless business."[57] He also wrote: "The Nacogdoches Grocery Company is one of the concerns which has not succeeded so much by force of capital, but by honesty, integrity, and liberal treatment to their patrons, employees and everyone with whom they come in contact."[58]

In 1904, Schmidt requested from Rulfs a set of plans for an expanded warehouse facility for the wholesale grocery operation. The event that occasioned this request was the 1903 purchase by Southern Pacific Railroad of both the H. E. & W. T. and the Texas & New Orleans railroad lines. This opened even more markets to Nacogdoches. The new company could take advantage of the refrigerated cars that were now available on the railroad lines.[59] The commercial building the architect designed still stands at 211 Old Tyler Road, immediately north of the Southern Pacific Passenger Depot (1911). When the new building opened in 1904, the *Daily Sentinel* called it "a splendid two-story building, 60x100 feet" and listed the cost to build as $8000.[60] According to both the Sanborn Map of 1906 and the *Daily Sentinel,* the one-story warehouse to the north (now Auntie Pasta's) was also built at the same time and joined by common interior sliding doors.[61] The two-story structure housed the office and "the higher grade of goods."[62] The company also utilized a large warehouse near the oil mill for overflow staples, making available the combined floor space of 21,000 square feet.

The first picture of the main complex building appeared in the 1906 Special Edition of the *Daily Sentinel.* By 1917, the company added more units to the warehouse along the east side of the railroad tracks, as the picture in the *Twenty-Three Reasons* brochure indicates.

The façades of the building, either on Old Tyler Road or on the railroad track side, were not elaborate, certainly by comparison to the Hazle Building or even the Schmidt-Blount Building, There were no showrooms or retail displays. The facades used standard commercial elements used by the architect during this period: inset panels at the parapet level, wood double-hung arched windows with arched heads, iron shutters, and corbelled brickwork.

The Nacogdoches Grocery Company Building has changed very little over the century of its existence.[63] Later owners have bricked in some of the windows, placed a metal roof and glass enclosure of the old truck dock, and put in some burglar bars. Even today, one can make out the enormous sign painted on the south brick wall in 1904—"NACOGDOCHES GROCERY CO." Inside Clear Springs Cafe, which now occupies the structure, one can still see the old elevator, the large warehouse doors to the railroad tracks, and the adjoining warehouse.

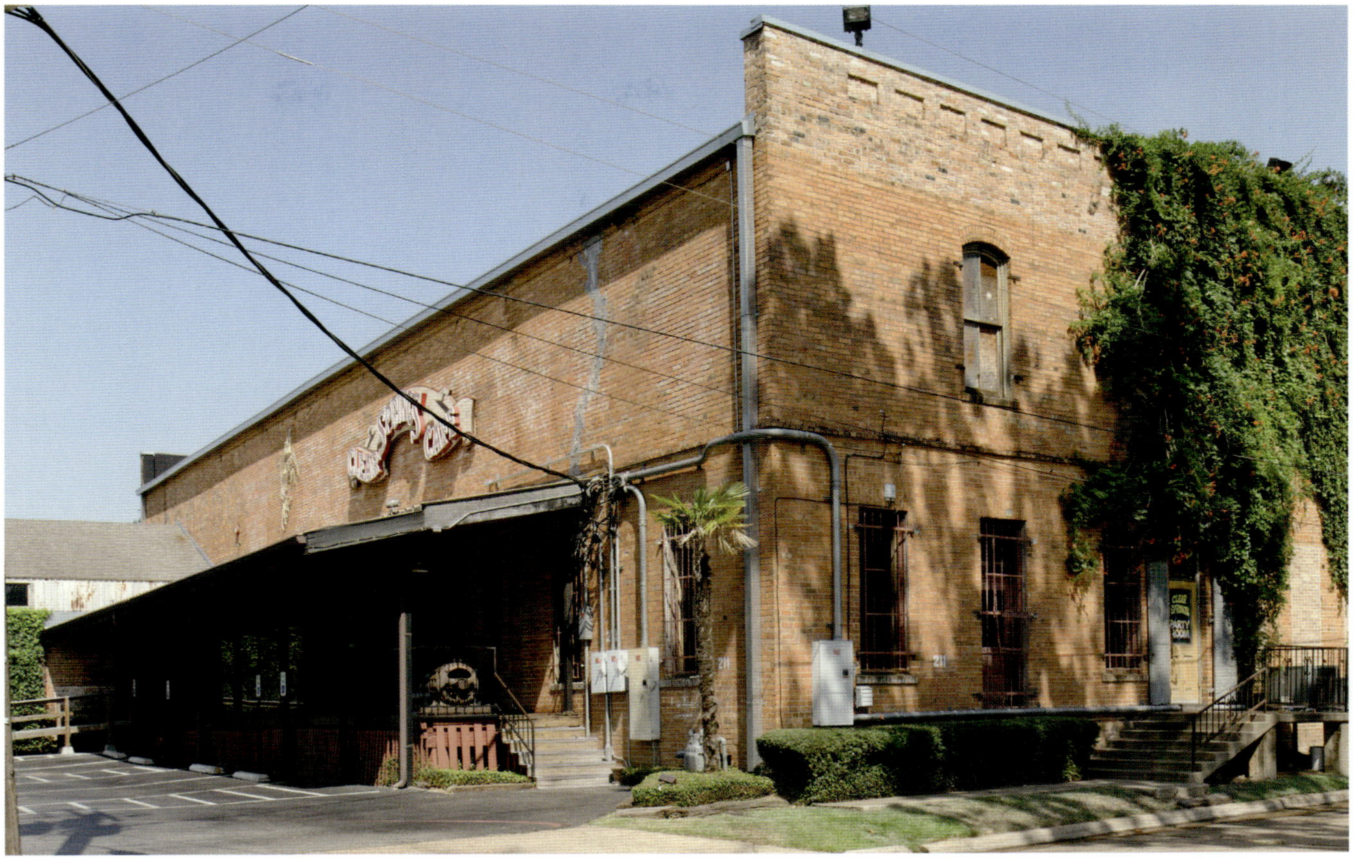

FIGURES 8.12 and 8.13. Nacogdoches Wholesale Grocery Building, 2012.

The Wholesale Grocery Building (1904) today houses the popular eatery Clear Springs Cafe. The first restaurant to use the building, Rossini's Spaghetti Warehouse, featured SFA music students as waiters who sang opera and musical selections while people ate. The interior of the building still shows many of the warehouse features: the large beams, the cold storage units, the large sliding doors to the railroad tracks, and the access doors to the north warehouse.

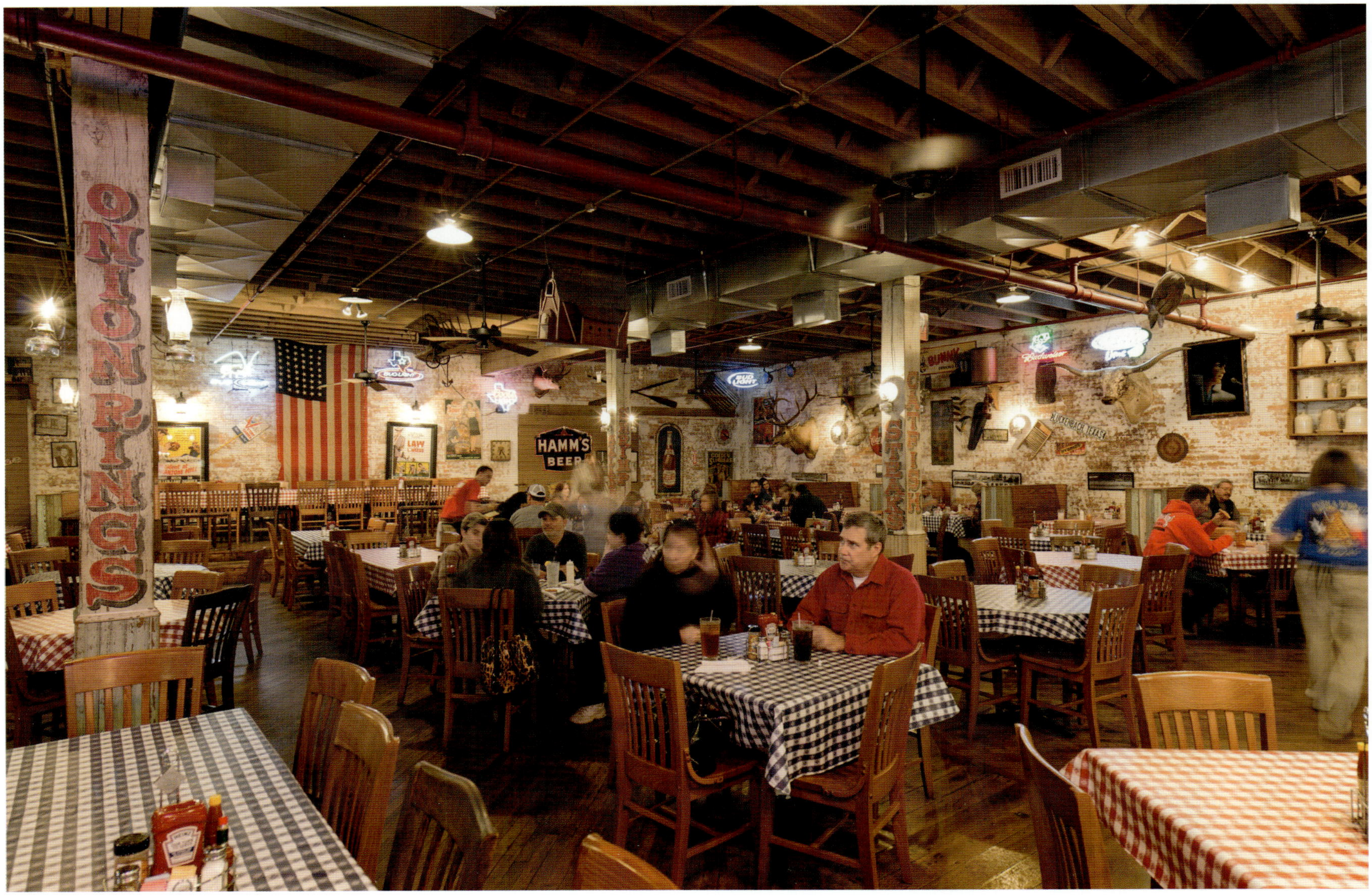

Cason, Monk & Company Buildings (1906)

In introducing the newly incorporated firm of Cason, Monk & Company to the Nacogdoches public in August of 1906, Giles Haltom called it "one of the most important events in the mercantile history of this old and historical city."[64] The new company was a merger between the hardware departments of Mayer & Schmidt (M&S) and the remnants of the Cason, Richardson & Company. (D. K. Cason had bought out his cousin Richardson the year before.)[65] The newspaper stated the mission of the new joint enterprise was "to conduct a wholesale and retail hardware and mill supply house." D. K. Cason became the president and general manager. Although an equal with Cason in terms of stock, John Schmidt did not take the lead in forming this company. Schmidt simply thought the merger made good sense and therefore, took the position of Vice President. Of the other stockholders, Robert Monk and Willie Leroy (Lee) Gaston migrated from the M&S Company, and John Edwin Gaston came from the Cason Hardware Company.

The choice of Rulfs to oversee the spatial needs of their new hardware company was as natural for the major partners as it was for Schmidt: D. K. Cason and R. C. Monk both lived in houses by the architect. Rulfs and Cason had worked together on the commercial warehouse on Pecan Street. Like the partnership itself, the quarters for the new company were in essence a merger–all 40,442 square feet of it. The site chosen as their primary location was in the middle of the north side of East Main, in between the Mayer & Schmidt Building and the Opera House. While Rulfs drew a new facade, the 1906 plan was primarily a remodeling job with some new construction. From the extensive account given in the *Daily Sentinel*, it is obvious that Giles Haltom was fascinated not only by the new company, but also with the whole process of merging the existing buildings in the center of an old block.

Essentially, Rulfs built a new central two-story building between two existing one-story buildings. (Cason-Monk did not own all the real estate, but leased some of the spaces.) Rulfs connected the first floors by cutting large arches between the walls as he had done in the Cox Building on Main and Pecan Streets.[66] He added second stories to the existing buildings. So that the company could sell such goods as "buggies, surreys and undertaker goods [caskets]," the plans called for a large modern elevator in the back of the building to get the goods to the second floor.[67] Across "Progress Avenue," as Commerce Street was called at the time, Rulfs designed, but did not build, three large brick warehouses to accommodate the really heavy items such as boilers, nails, piping, farm implements, and engines.[68]

The facade of the new Cason-Monk Hardware was greatly simplified from his plans for the warehouse in 1900. By raising the height of the new central unit, he created two wings out of the two side buildings. He distinguished the center ever so slightly by placing it between two noticeable pilasters and raised the parapet. While he did use very straight running dentil-brick molding, he reduced the importance of the windows by calling for concrete lintels and included signage from the beginning—gone were the arched windows, the corbelled-insets, and the decorative hood-molds and banding he was using in earlier building. The horizontal nature of the front made the building look larger. The contrast with the Hazle Building, a half-block away at the corner of Church and Main streets, is dramatic. Both the tastes of the clients and the architect's work had evolved between 1901 and 1906.

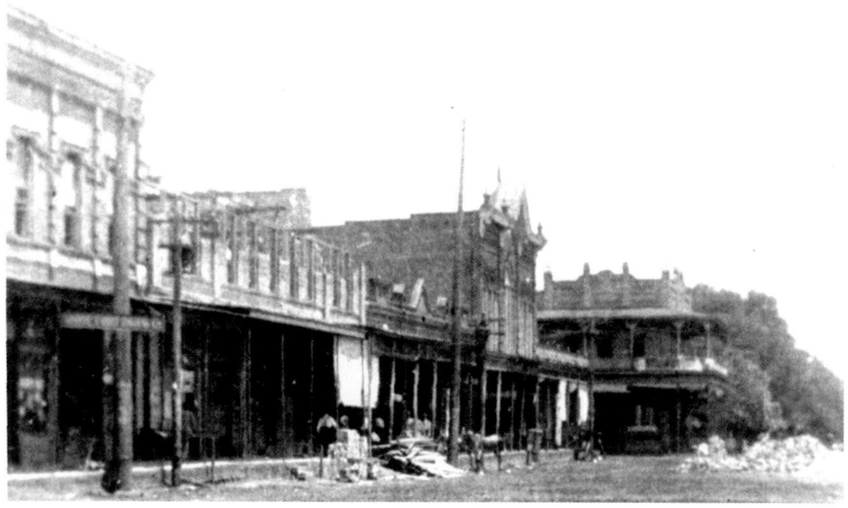

FIGURES 8.14 and 8.15. Construction of the Cason-Monk Building, 1906.

The photograph above shows the main showrooms of Cason-Monk under construction on the north side of East Main. The Opera House is at the end of the block, and the new Hazle Building is at the intersection of Church Street.

The image below, a closer view of the same construction, shows how a new second story was added to the 1889 ground level buildings.

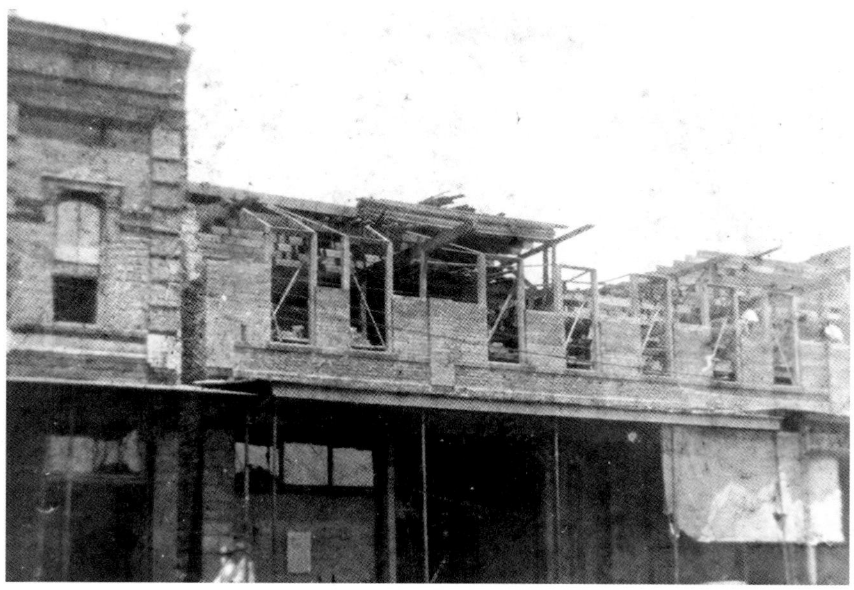

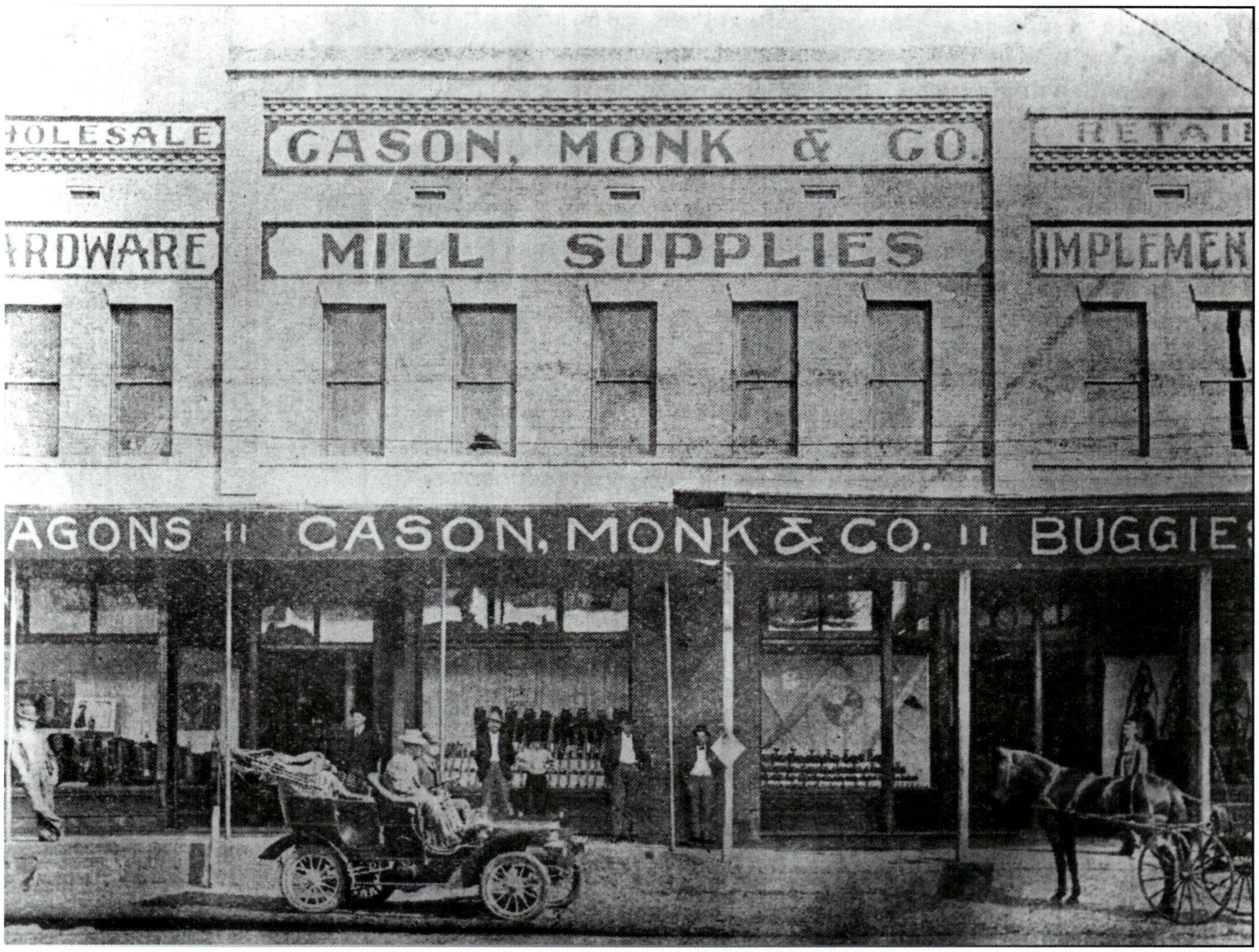

FIGURE 8.16. Cason-Monk Building, East Main Street, 1906.
In his attempt to unify three buildings he had built in 1889, Rulfs in 1906 added second stories and raised the parapet of the center building to give the complex proportion and interest. The signage was there from the beginning. Photograph from the Daily Sentinel, 1906. Courtesy of ETRC.

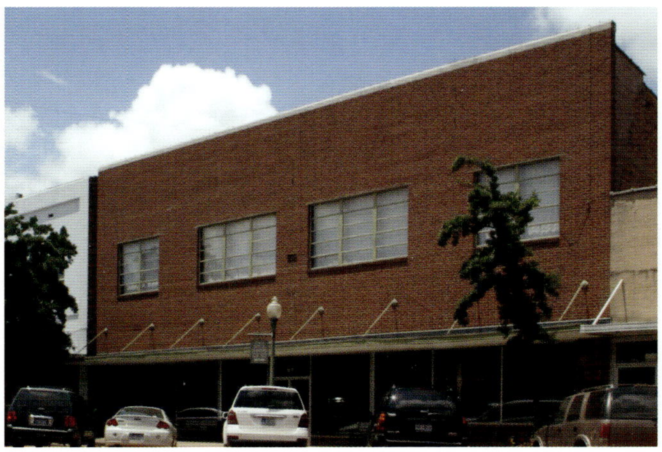

FIGURES 8.17. The Cason-Monk Buildings in 2011.
The front of the Cason-Monk Building (above), remodeled in the 1960s, has no resemblance to the 1906 façade designed by D. Rulfs, but the interior is mostly original.

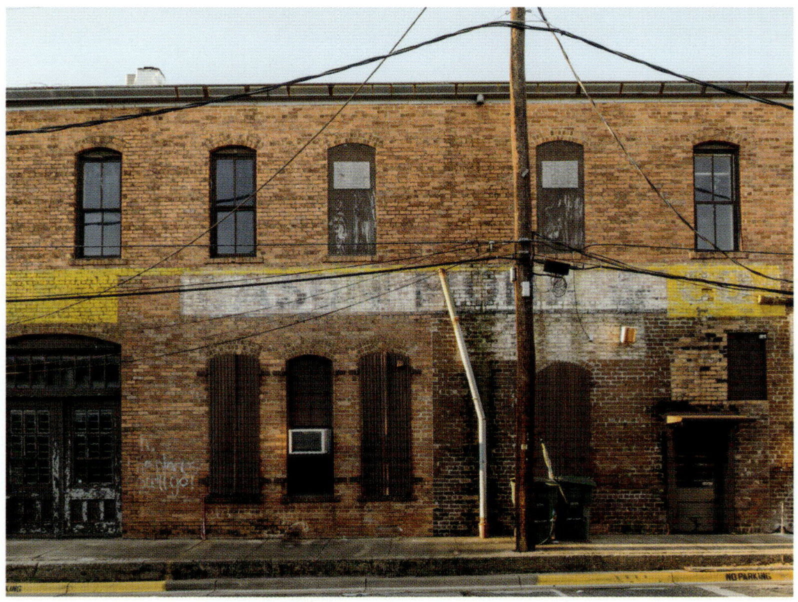

FIGURE 8.18. The Backdoor Façade Tells the Story.
At the service entrance of the Cason-Monk Building, the multiplicity of bricks tells the story of the complex's development. The first stories date to 1889, the second date to 1906. Rulfs specified iron shutters on the backsides of most of his commercial buildings.

"A Building Boom at Church and Main Streets"

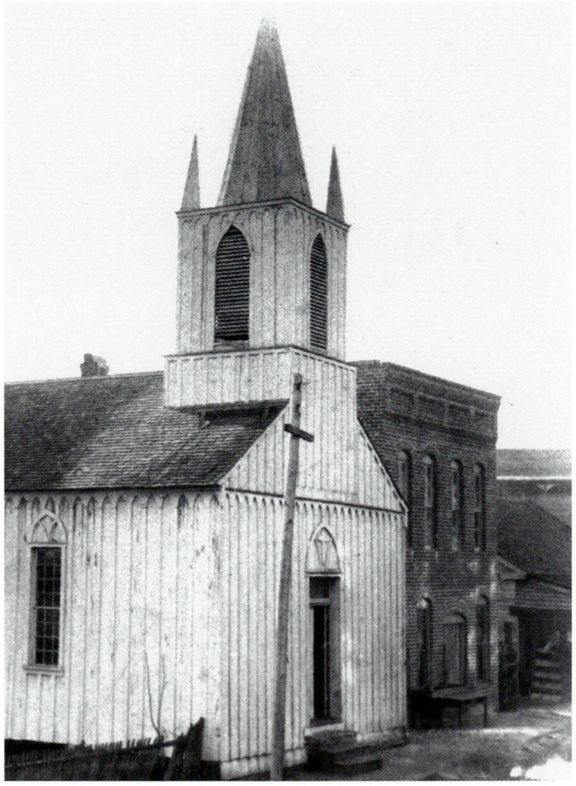

FIGURE 8.19. (Left) Christ Episcopal Church and The Hazle Building in January 1900.

Rulfs finished the Hazle Building, the first home of the Daily Sentinel, before the original Christ Episcopal Church was torn down.

FIGURE 8.20. Lower North Church Street in 2012.

The Bailey Block (where the Christ Church Stood), the Hazle Building (former office for the Daily Sentinel), and the M. G. Hazle Building (first home of Commercial Bank) on the corner of Main Street.

The new daily newspaper, founded in 1899, did not move into this Church Street location until 1900. The newspaper had printing offices on South Church Street, later on the ground level of the Old Opera House, and also in the Bailey Block next door.

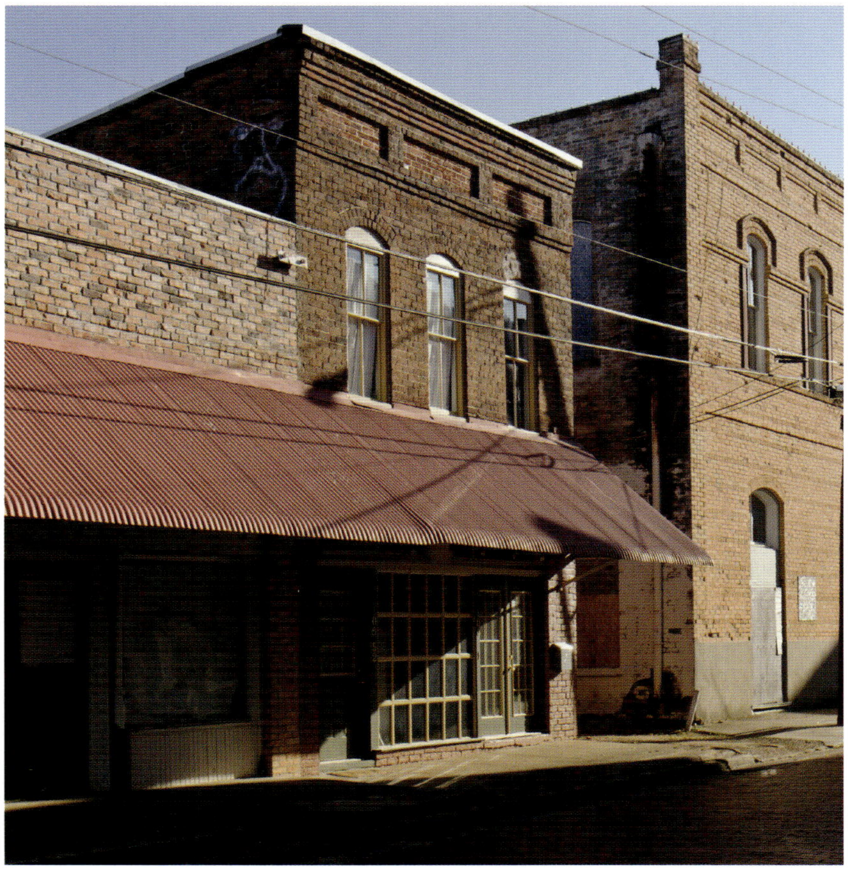

A New Home for the New Daily Sentinel: the Hazle Building on Church Street (1900)

Even before undertaking the work on the West Square for Hoya in 1900, Rulfs had begun planning with John Schmidt to oversee an ambitious addition to the buildings in the area of East Main. R. W. Haltom had just established the *Daily Sentinel* in 1899; Schmidt immediately maneuvered to have the new enterprise within his sphere of influence. John Schmidt believed in advertising and relied heavily on the newspaper as a partner in promoting business deals and keeping the Opera House packed. When the *Sentinel* declared that there was a "building boom" at Church and Main Streets, Haltom was promoting its own new back yard.[69]

Schmidt, who regularly promoted shared interests, convinced the Hazle family that their valuable property at Main and Church was under-developed. Schmidt provided the cash, Hazle the land, and Rulfs the plans. The development called for a large building on the corner, the newspaper building immediately north, and then a series of new one-story retail buildings north along Church Street. The quarters for the newspaper came first. (See Figure 8.19) In honor of moving into the new building, Haltom decided to republish his 1880 *History and Description of Nacogdoches County*.[70] The second phase, the so-called "Bailey Block" of buildings along the east side of Church Street, came next and appeared on the Sanborn Map of October, 1900 with the pre-construction label: "from plans."[71]

The E. C. Branch Warehouse (1900)

While the author located no contract proving this, Rulfs most probably did the warehouse on the northeast corner of Pilar and Church Street, known in modern times as Gallery 107. The owner who built the building was E. C. Branch, a close associate of both Bill Haltom and Rulfs. The building's first use was as a warehouse and printing facility for the *Daily Sentinel* (one block north on Church Street). The elevation on Pilar Street building has architectural features which supports attribution of the structure to Rulfs. The Pilar Street elevation has modified Palladian features and a porthole at the top. Another reason, Rulfs was at the same time constructing a residence for Branch on Virginia Avenue.[72] Branch had purchased his lot from the Harris-Lindsey Real Estate Company, owned by June Harris and Robert Lindsey. Harris and Lindsey were not only partners with Rulfs in development of the Forbes-Irion Hill region, but they were also paired with Rulfs in developing commercial buildings along East Main Street.

The Sanborn Map of 1900 designated the use of this building as a warehouse and printing facility. After the fire of 1903, when the building in front of this property had to be rebuilt, the Branch building was transformed into the "City Hotel," the label it has on the 1906 map.[73] After the opening of the Redland Hotel, however, the City Hotel was no longer viable. In 1909, the idea of Nacogdoches as a center for the tobacco industry took the town by storm. When George T. McNess, "the tobacco man," leased Branch's warehouse-cum-hotel for "his tobacco warehouse and curing plant,"[74] the building was rearranged once again. (Nacogdoches by 1909 had three tobacco warehouses; the Cason Building on Pecan Streets, done by Rulfs in 1900, also became one of the tobacco houses.) Branch sold the Church Street building in 1913. Although modified often over the years, for instance by the addition of stucco, the sturdy building still has architectural interest and a colorful history. In 1967, the structure became the home and working studio, Gallery 107, of Lucille and Reese Kennedy. At present, the building is owned by George and Patricia Lyford.[75]

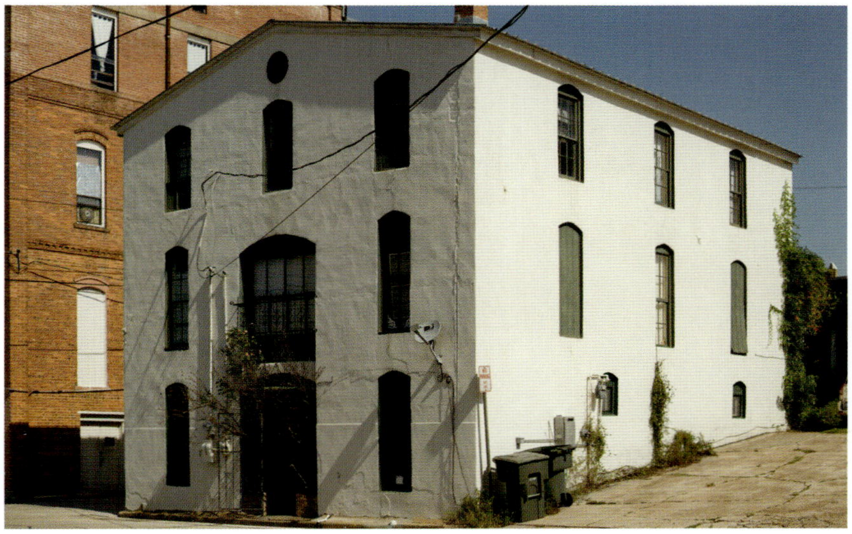

FIGURE 8.21. The E. C. Branch Warehouse.
The warehouse, built at the same time Rulfs was building a home for E. C. Branch, later became The City Hotel, a tobacco warehouse, and for many years Gallery 107.

The M. G. Hazle Building (1901)

The northeast corner of Main and Church Street has an illustrious list of owners. It was part of the land conveyed by the Spanish Government to Ygnacio Y'Barbo in April 16, 1810, and subsequently belonged to the Durst, Roberts, Johnson, Thorn, and Hazle families. In the spring and summer of 1901, Rulfs replaced the Hazle family's grocery and general store with the large two-story M. G. Hazle Building that still stands on the corner.[76] When the main construction was completed on August 2, the architect called the carpenters together to place a "pine top" on the building, as he traditionally did, to celebrate the fact that Hazle had "come across" with his payments for the job. Haltom, who never missed a pine top celebration, commented, "It was a feast and a glow of sparkling wit and other sparkling things to which all us carpenters did ample justice."[77]

The first occupant of the building was to be the Cason, Richardson & Co. Hardware division; they took out a five-year lease after seeing the plans. Almost immediately, however, Cason received a profit by selling the lease to the newly organized Commercial National Bank of Nacogdoches – controlled by a group of outside investors. E. A. Blount and John Schmidt, shocked at this turn of events, immediately began negotiations to purchase control of this new bank. This did not come to fruition until after the opening in the Hazle structure. Later, Blount would move the bank to his building on the north side of the Square in 1903. After he moved the bank, E. A. Blount advertised that if some group so desired, he was willing to put a third story on the Hazle Building "for an elegant third story lodge room."[78] This never materialized because of the depressed economy. Later occupants of the Hazle Building included furniture, general merchandise, a drug store, and McLain's Men's Wear for many years. The Andrews family now owns the building.[79]

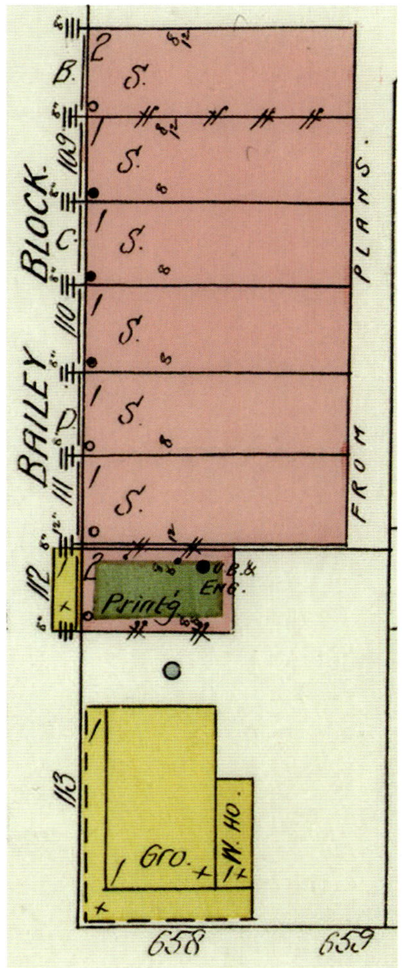

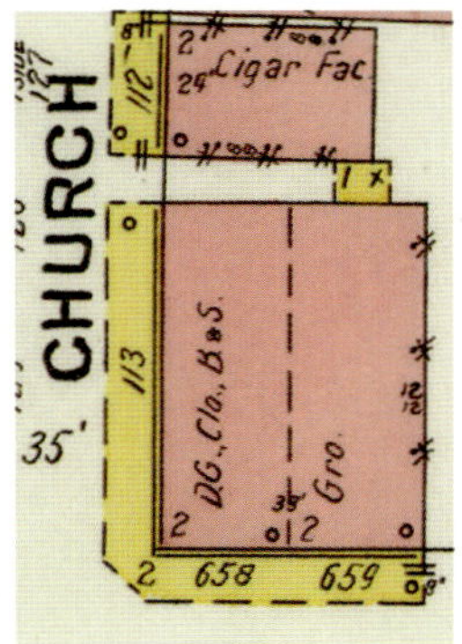

FIGURES 8.22 and 8.23. Details, Sanborn Maps, Church and Main Street Intersection, 1900 and 1906.
On the left, the 1900 Sanborn Map shows the Daily Sentinel Building in place. The buildings of the so-called "Bailey Block," along the east side of Church Street, appear on the October map with the pre-construction label: "from plans." Rulfs worked closely with the mappers, and many of his buildings are on the maps even before construction. At the bottom of the map, at the corner of Main, the old Hazle Grocery building is still shown in 1900.
To the right, this detail from the 1906 Sanborn Map shows the new M. G. Hazle Building (1901) to the south of the newpaper office. Sanborn Maps, UT, Nacogdoches, 1900 and 1906.

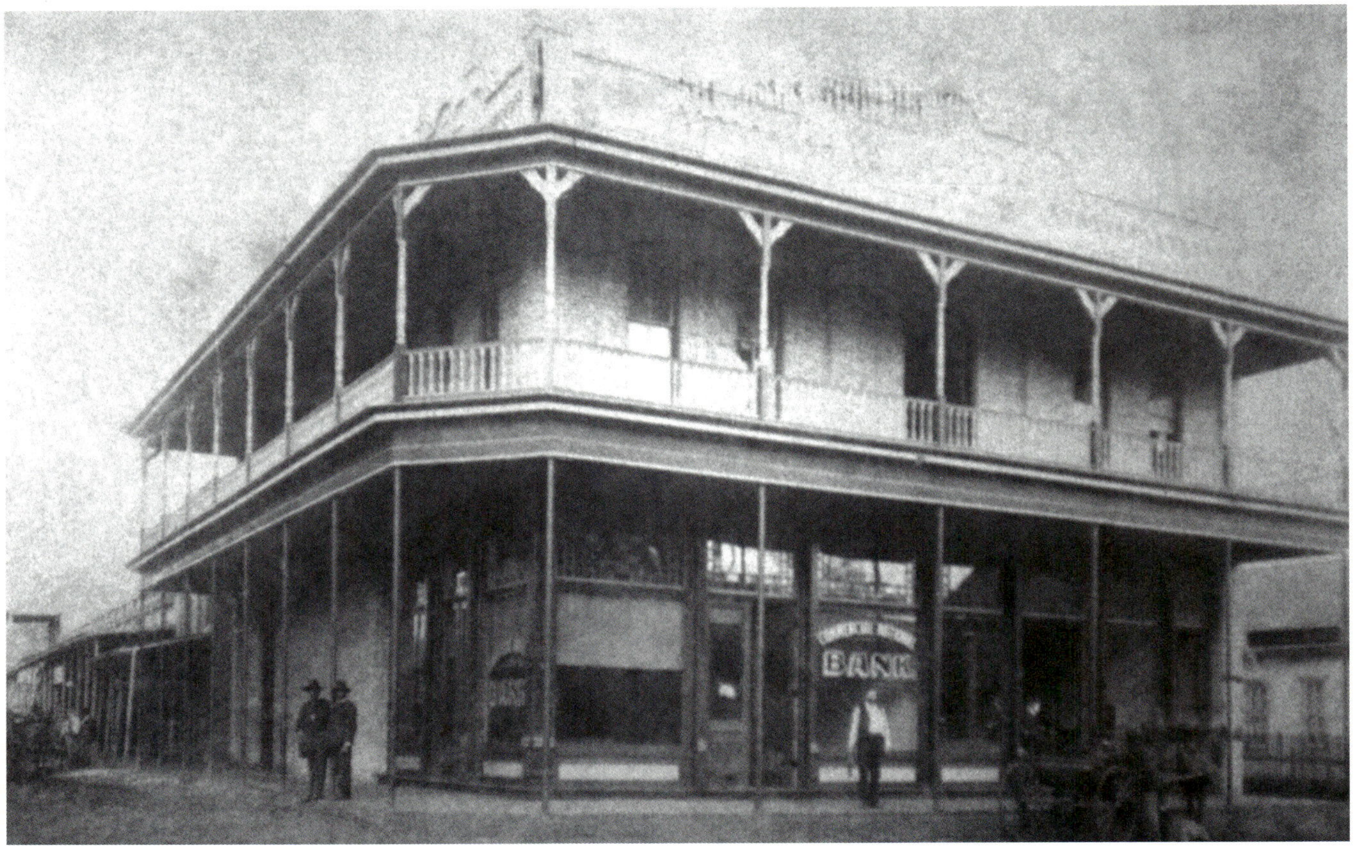

FIGURE 8.24. The M. G. Hazle Building and Commercial National Bank, ca. 1902.

The Hazle Building, as designed and built by Rulfs in 1901, had two-story, wrap-around porches supported by iron posts on the first floor and wooden posts on the second. The first floor commercial areas had a continuous iron threshold, one step high, which ran along Main Street and wrapped around the Church Street corner. Large plate glass windows separated by iron mullions made the first floor businesses look very modern. The brickwork on the upper facade, which was a model of the motifs Rulfs was using around the square and the east side of town at the time, appear clearer in the modern photograph on the next page. The Hazle Building was the original home of Commercial National Bank, until the business moved to the Square in October 1903.

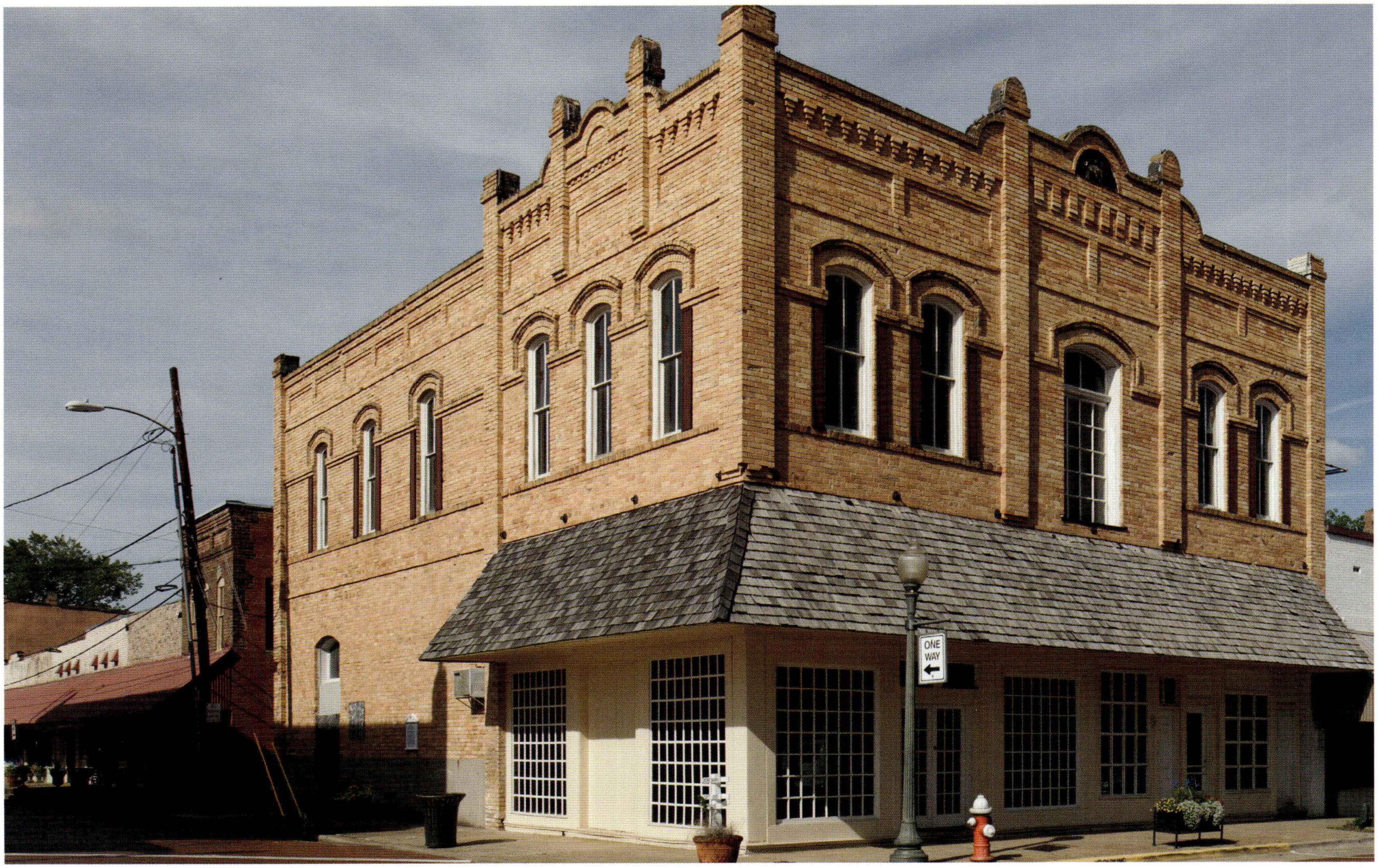

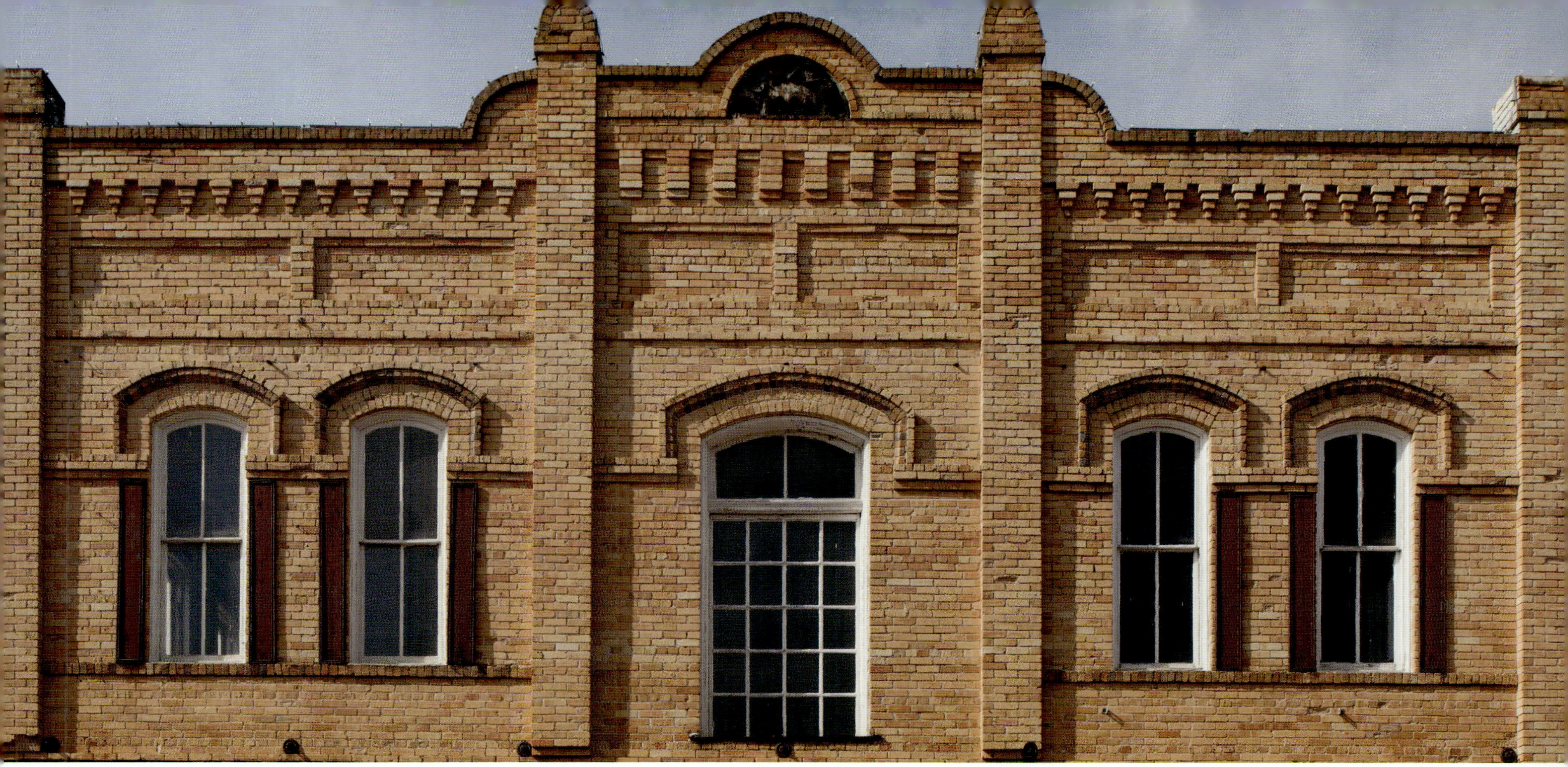

FIGURE 8.25 (Bottom Across) and 8.26 (Above). The M. G. Hazle Building in 2012.
The details of the Hazle Building are more visible today than in 1901 when it was built. The brickwork includes: detailed corbelled brickwork at the cornices, recessed panels, pilasters separating the bays, and continuous bands of brick which formed hood-molds over the arched windows. The use of buff-colored brick is unique and lends a softer quality to the building. The larger arched opening, still in the center of the Main Street façade, was once the door that gave access to the upstairs porch from the hall. While the lower front of the building is now greatly changed, the upper floor, minus the porches, remains very much as Rulfs completed it and one of his best commercial works in Nacogdoches.

The Hazle Building is perhaps the most beautiful commercial building from the period still standing in the downtown area. The use of buff-colored brick is unique and lends a softer quality to the building. One can appreciate the impressive details of the brickwork better today than when the building had the extensive porches attached. The larger arched opening, on the second story in the center of the Main Street façade, was once a door that gave access to the upstairs porch from the hall.

Several other buildings, some of which are still extant, date from the same period as the Hazle structure and were part of the "building boom" in the East Main area. While a large two-story building that Rulfs had constructed for the Hardeman and Huntley families burned to the ground in the great fire of 1903, the buildings at 420 and 422 East Main, however, have survived; both buildings also emerged from the Harris-Lindsey Real Estate Company. These buildings are on the 1906 Sanborn Maps, but no plans for either of these building have survived. On May 6, 1901, the *Daily Sentinel* reported that the two-story building, which later sold to E. D. Williams, was almost finished.[80] In recent years, this building was the home of the David Welch's Wrap-It-Up Company, but the property is now owned by John Sloane. The success of this speculation led quickly to a second building at 420 East Main. This building, for many years the law office of David Adams, now is the home of East Texas Legal Services.[81]

Although the author found no documentation, it is also quite possible that Rulfs built the Roberts Building on the South Square, ca. 1904.

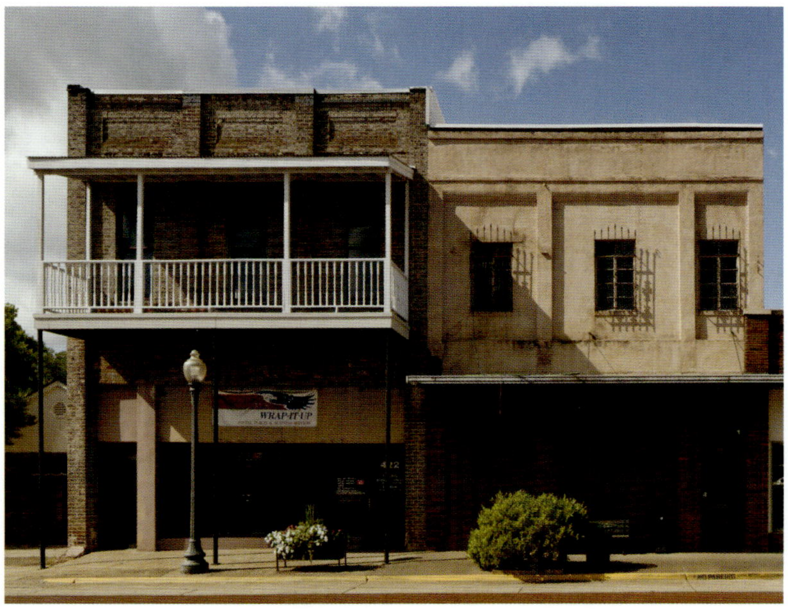

FIGURE 8.27. E. D. Williams Building (1901) on the left.
The two buildings on the south side of East Main near Mound Street were part of a series of buildings built by the Harris-Lindsey Real Estate Partnership in conjunction with Rulfs at the turn of the 20th Century. Several of their buildings perished during the great East End fire of 1903.

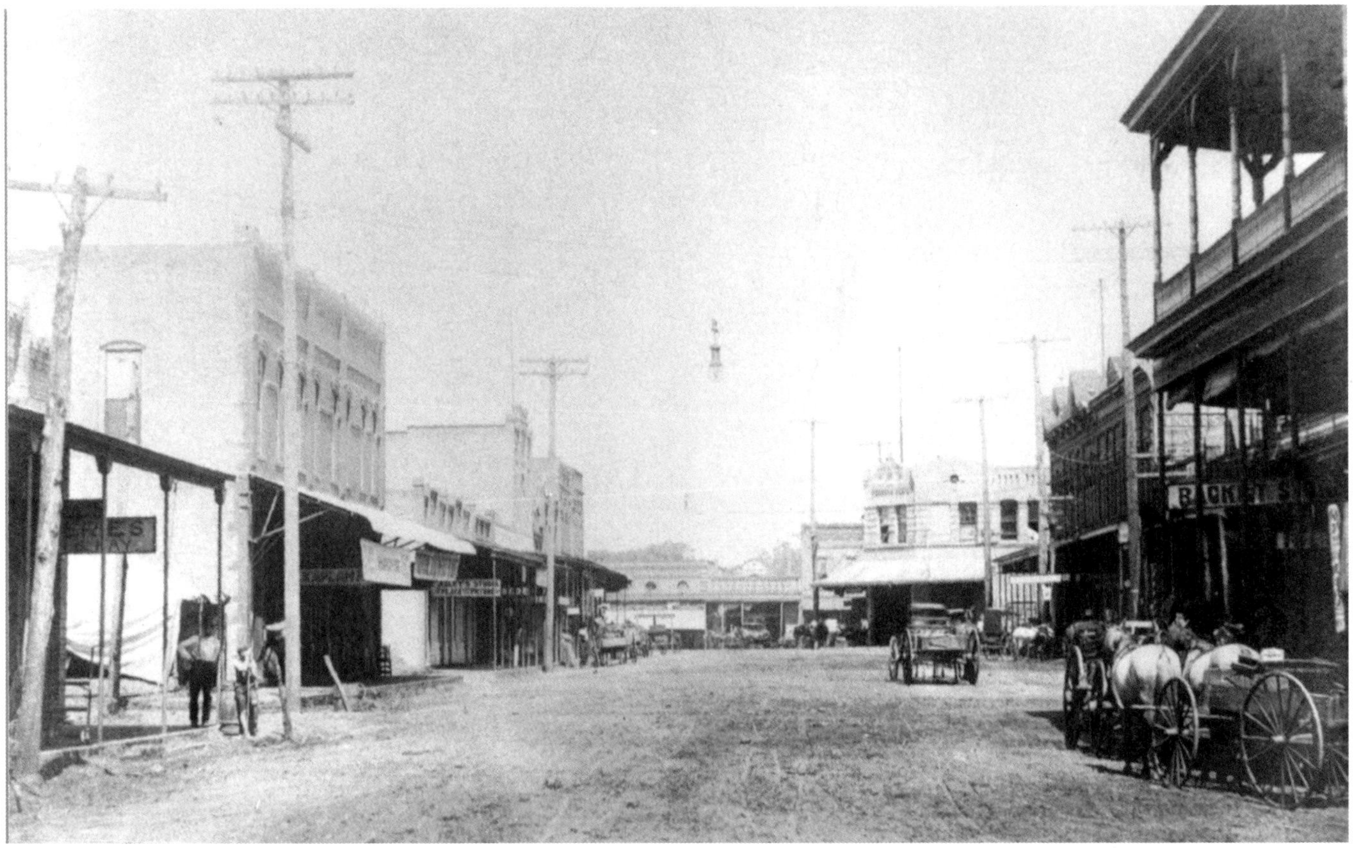

FIGURE 8.28. East Main Street, Looking West toward the Square. (ca. 1905)

From left to right, this photograph shows the Hardeman Building (1904), built in the "Burnt District" destroyed by the 1903 fire; this building was later to become part of the new Redland Hotel complex. Near the Square, the Cox Building; then the west side of the Square and the Wettermark bank. Jutting into Main Street at Fredonia is the Perkins Building which replaced the Old Stone Fort. While the large Mayer & Schmidt Building is somewhat visible, the one-story stands and the Opera House west of Church Street are hidden. The M. G. Hazle Building on the right, which housed the Commercial Bank, has a gallery surrounding the second story. Courtesy of ETRC.

The Hardeman Building (1904)

As discussed in the previous chapter, the great fire of 1903 consumed most of the south side of East Main Street. Not only was the boom over, but also recommitment and rebuilding returned slowly. Over a year-and-a-half later, the *Daily Sentinel* was still complaining about the "unsightly ruins in the burnt district." When B. F. Hardeman committed to a new building in the area, Haltom was gleeful in his encouragement: "Mr. Hardeman's business sagacity and enterprise deserve hearty commendation."[82] Lindsey and Harris also talked about the erection of a brick building in the burnt area, but that did not materialize. In 1905, there were still vacant lots along the Street.

Rulfs had built houses for all the Hardeman brothers.[83] Rulfs almost always showed his plans to Haltom, for he always reaped good publicity for doing this. After seeing the architect's plans for the Hardeman Building, Haltom wrote, "The building is to be thoroughly modern and up-to-date in all respects and will be one of the architectural ornaments of the city when completed." Haltom, anxious to get construction moving again, reported on the progress frequently.[84] Near the completion date, Haltom openly appealed to other entrepreneurs: "The new Hardeman building is just about completed and is a beauty. If a few more of our enterprising citizens would add a brick house or two to this end of the business section of the city, it would greatly help the looks of Main street."[85]

Hardeman's new building, however, was not a financial success. No matter how much Haltom and others promoted the area, office rentals were off throughout Nacogdoches. Even the new Hazle Building had trouble after the Commercial Bank moved. Rulfs, as an architect who had experienced an economic downturn in Oldenburg, knew that architects had to be their most creative in such circumstances. He moved quickly into repurposing the Hardeman Building into a new scheme for East Main.

The Redland Hotel (1906-1907)

In the *Daily Sentinel's* promotions to encourage businessmen to clean up and rebuild after the fire of 1903, one of the rumors circulating was the possibility of building a new hotel, "a three-story hotel building occupying the whole block." Although office demand had fallen, trade in the city was still strong, and there was a need for more hotel rooms. In 1906, the need for a new hotel came up once again. E. A. Blount, knowing that Rulfs had designed a hotel for John Schmidt that was never built, approached the architect for suggestions as to what to do. Always the practical man, Rulfs thought the idea of a totally new hotel was risky, and he discouraged the idea. Instead, Rulfs suggested the idea of wrapping a new hotel around the two-year old Hardeman Building and integrating the two. The new group considering the project – E. A. Blount, B. F. Hardeman, June C. Harris, and Robert Lindsey – liked the suggestions and authorized the architect to proceed.

In July, the *Sentinel* reported that Rulfs had submitted plans to the group, that they had accepted them, and that the owners were ready to move. The specifications called for a structure of "red pressed brick trimmed with stone, and . . . equipped with every modern convenience."[86] Before construction started, they located a company out of Houston who promised to run it when completed.[87] The original name, Hotel Redlands, quickly got changed to the Redland Hotel. The newspaper announced in August, "D. Rulfs, the architect and contractor, secured the contract for the building of the new hotel."[88] The principals signed the contracts on August 2, 1906, with a completion date by December 15, 1906.

The Redland Hotel project showcased the many talents of Rulfs. The idea of wrapping an L-shaped addition around the Hardeman Building, salvaged not only the old building, but it also had the potential of shaving months off the whole project. His incorporation of the older building—by connecting the two by cutting arched doorways to the west, by utilizing the existing street-side space for commercial shops, and by modifying the upstairs office spaces into bedrooms—reserved the new construction for the hotel's entrance, lobby, and dining room. The Rulfs plan reserved the new area behind the Hardeman Building for a large dining room/ball room, kitchen and service areas, and sample rooms popular with traveling merchants. Beneath these additions were the new steam boilers for the central heating. To unify the two structures visually, Rulfs added a long gallery across the entire façade and provided access from the upstairs bedrooms to the gallery's roof. (He had used the same concept on the houses for Drs. Woolam Smith on North Street and Frank Ford on Washington Square.)

In October, about halfway into the project, the Nacogdoches Union of Carpenters and Joiners went on strike. The decline in economic activity had hit the workers even more drastically than the owners of businesses. The workers demanded an increase in wages from $2.50 a day to $3.00. Rulfs, caught between the workers and a fixed contract, faced bankruptcy. In the *Daily Sentinel*, the workers, represented by E. D. Moorer and W. S. Chadwick, published an open letter explaining their case. They cited the high cost of living as the reason for their demands. They explained that they had worked under the same wage scale for four years; and if not satisfied, they threatened to take their services out of town. A compromise, worked out by E. C. Branch and H. F. Marr as arbitrators, ended the strike by October 25. The contractors that Rulfs supervised agreed to pay $2.65 on all unfinished work, and the union got annual contract revisions to prevent grievances from accumulating. Rulfs, always on the side of the carpenters, maintained cordial relations with the workmen and got construction resumed immediately.[89] The problems of modern life were rushing in on Nacogdoches.

While not finished on schedule, the new $30,000 Redland Hotel had a soft opening on March 4, 1907, with a formal opening on March 15.[90] Giles Haltom's hyperbole was not far off: "This is one of the largest and best-equipped hotels in East Texas, and will prove a big drawing card for Nacogdoches."[91] The Redland Hotel was Nacogdoches's first modern hotel. It offered guests private bathrooms, steam heating throughout, and a fine dining experience.[92] The Redland also provided transportation to and from the railroad depot. The formal opening was a gala affair. Huge numbers of people from both Nacogdoches and Lufkin attended. There was a reception in the afternoon and dancing with an orchestra in the evening.[93]

The Redland immediately became the venue of choice in the Piney Woods. At the end of the year 1907, the Cum Concilio Club announced that presidential candidate William Jennings Bryan would stay at the Redland and make a speech from the balcony of the hotel. The *Daily Sentinel* estimated the crowd in front of the balcony on January 3, 1908, at 3000: Bryan, boasted Haltom, "practically announced his candidacy for the Democratic nomination for the presidency."[94] The Redland also provided a boost for the Nacogdoches Opera House. The hotel hosted many theatrical companies and patrons. The Marx Brothers even began their comedy routines in the Opera House while staying at the Redland. When Stephen F. Austin State Teachers College opened in 1923, the town celebrated with receptions at the Redland.

After the original owners sold the hotel in 1909, it briefly took the name "New Murphey Hotel," but later owners returned the name to the Redland. A lumberman named J. H. Buchanan owned the property from 1914 to 1929; he was the one who added, around 1919, the third-story to the hotel structure.[95] It is unknown whether Rulfs had anything to do with this extension. A. T. Mast, Sr. bought the property in 1929; it continued as a hotel until after World War II. In discussing the hotel, his son Adlai Mast, Jr., said in the back of the building behind the Hardeman Building, there was a "a big ballroom, a real pretty ballroom," which also served the hotel as the dining room. "The food was the very best in East Texas. They had quite a menu . . . quite a selection. It was *the* place to eat at the time."[96] In 1935, the Nacogdoches Rotary Club moved from the Liberty Hotel to the Redland.[97]

Over time, the commercial spaces on the street front in the old Hardeman Building accommodated dress shops, the Redland Cafe, a pool hall, the Chamber of Commerce, dry goods sales offices, and various barbershops. On many Sanborn Maps, the spaces were vacant. A. T. Mast sold the old Hardeman portion of the unified complex to the Flany Corporation in 1937; to uncouple the two buildings, the owners needed only to brick the arched passageways between the lobby and the dining rooms. McCrory (Five and Dime) Stores occupied the space for many years thereafter.[98] Although Charles Bright owned the building for some years,

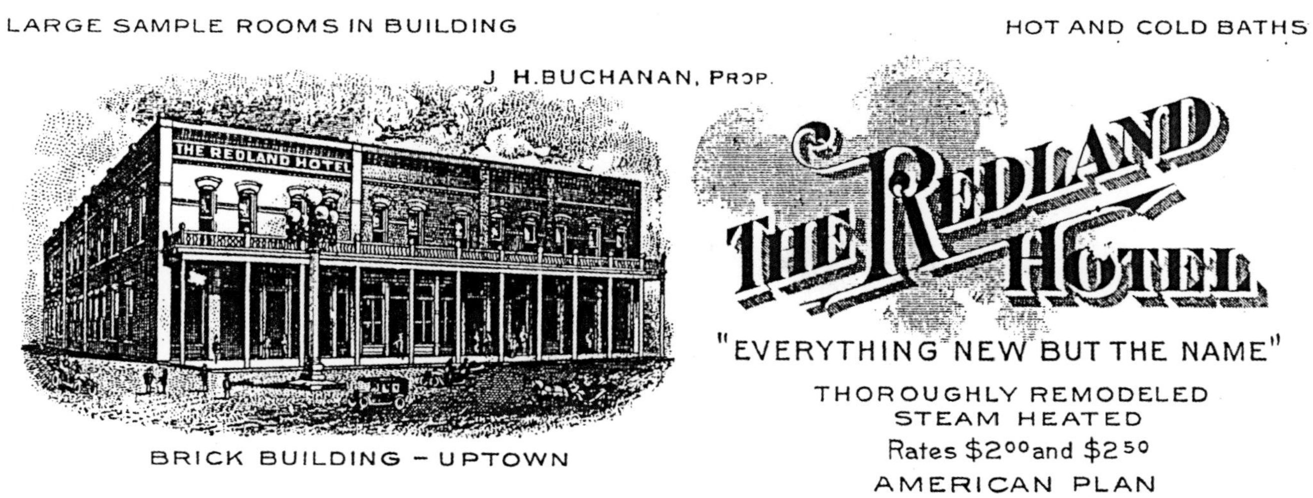

FIGURE 8.29. Letterhead Stationery, Redland Hotel, ca. 1915.
The letterhead displayed right dates from the ownership of J. H. Buchanan, who owned the property from 1914 to 1929. He added the third story seen in the pictures opposite. Letterhead courtesy of Adlai Mast, Jr.

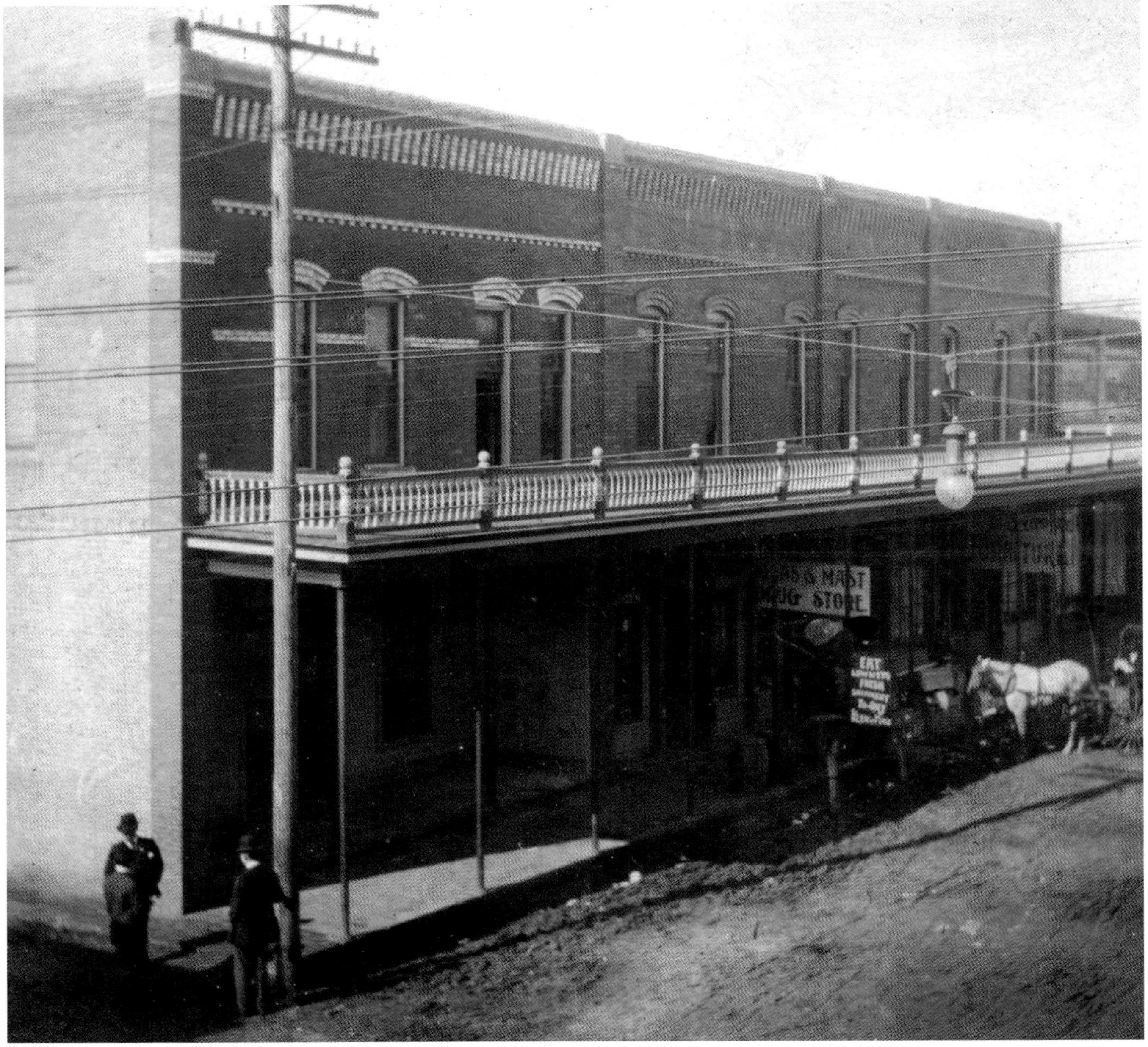

FIGURE 8.30. The New Redland Hotel, 1907.

This photograph shows the new Redland Hotel shortly after its completion in 1907. The first section with the colored brick accents is the new construction and the rest of the building was the 1904 Hardeman Building. The balcony was added to tie the two buildings together; the Hardeman Building originally had a molded tin overhang. Later, a third floor was added to the hotel, as the pictures across show. Photograph courtesy of Linda Greer.

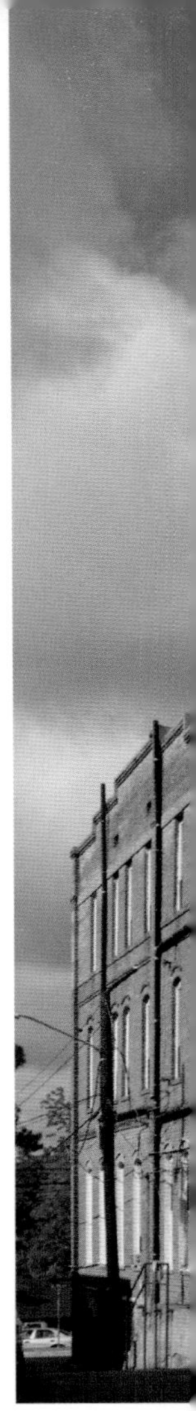

Greer's Fabrics and Design Center (established by Linda and Robert Greer) is the commercial enterprise most associated with the building in recent years. Upstairs in their shop, in the old offices converted to hotel rooms in 1906, the Greers maintain a large collection of photographs of downtown Nacogdoches.

In 1977, the three-story hotel (1906 portion with 1919 additions) sold to GODTEL [God's Open Door To Eternal Life] Ministries, headed by June Gentry. Although the Redland was in a serious state of deterioration at the time, GODTEL has prevented further deterioration to the property in recent decades. The projected move of the Ministries to a new facility makes the fate of the Redland uncertain in coming years.[99]

Another Special Edition of the Daily Sentinel (1906)

The citywide strike in the fall of 1906 and the delay in finishing the Redland had depressed everyone. Giles Haltom, the new owner and publisher of the *Daily Sentinel*, felt the town needed a bit of cheering up. Following a long tradition with the Haltoms, he brought out a special edition to showcase the modernization of Nacogdoches. The edition in early December, designed to boost the town's morale, was premature. His timing was off. The *real* crisis for the year had not yet happened. The special edition appeared just before the great Christmas Eve fire that destroyed the whole north side of the Square.

The 1906 special edition, like the 1897 *Nacogdoches Chronicle*, is important for assessing Rulfs's role in Nacogdoches. Most of the buildings Haltom used to illustrate his feature articles—on churches, schools, homes, and brick businesses of Nacogdoches–featured were works designed by Rulfs.[100] The edition freezes for posterity many commercial buildings and houses that no longer exist, or that exist only in altered forms. The fire of 1906 wiped out six of Rulfs' buildings: the four buildings of the original "Brick Block" from the mid 1880s and the two buildings added for E. A. Blount since 1900. It also destroyed the new Perkins Brothers Building on

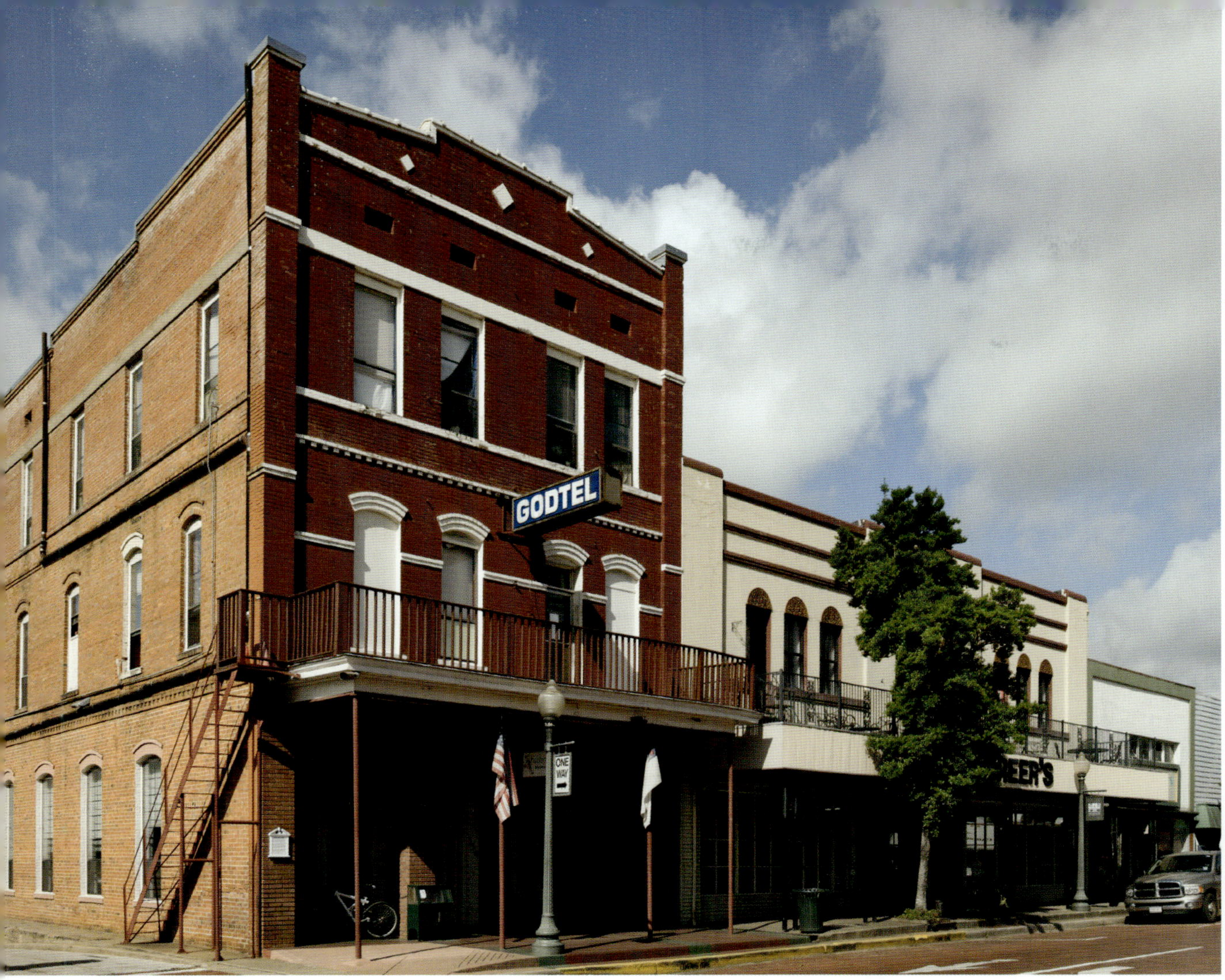

FIGURE 8.31. (Left) The Redland, Home of GODTEL Ministries.

The third story dates to 1919. A. T. Mast, Sr. purchased the hotel in 1929. Mast sold the building in 1977 to Reverend June Gentry as a home for his Godtel Ministries.

FIGURE 8.32. (Right) GODTEL Ministries and Greer's Fabrics.

The Redland Hotel, with its third floor is on the left. In 1937, the old Hardeman Building, joined to the Redland in 1906, became McCrory's Five and Dime and years later Greer's in 1997. The continuous balcony, done in 1906 to join the two buildings, was decoupled into separate units with iron rails.

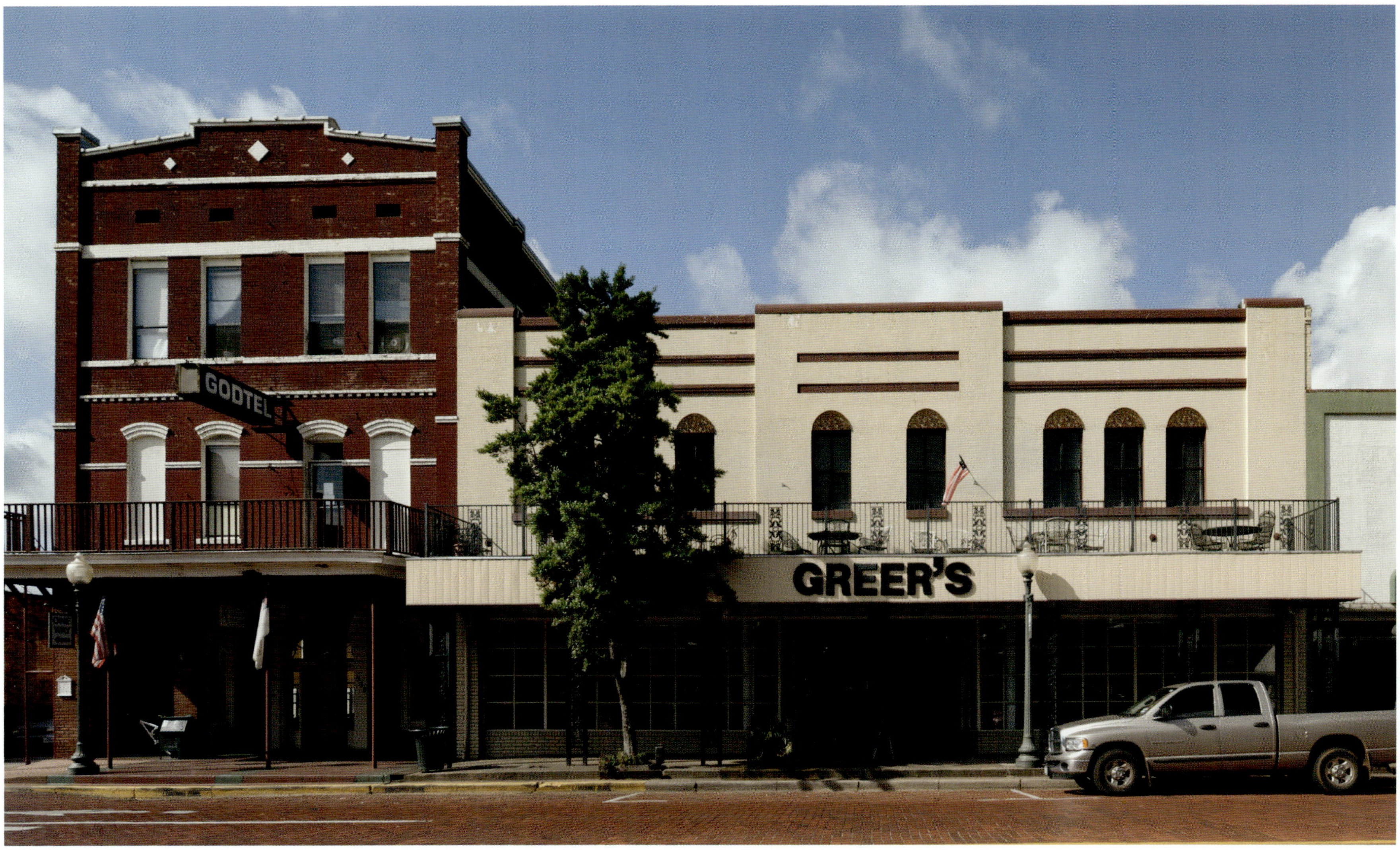

the former site of the Stone Fort. While the fire had the immediate result of solving the unrented office space as every burnt business scrambled to find temporary space, Rulfs knew the community needed more than temporary fixes.[101] He had labored for years with the needs of the emerging city: Nacogdoches had no sewers, no drainage system, no adequate water supply; and, mosquitoes were breeding in the standing water on the unpaved streets. People who desired to settle in the town demanded these things, especially the leaders of prospective colleges who were being solicited. Rulfs happened to be in a position to help move the town forward on these matters. He was serving as one of the Aldermen of Nacogdoches at the time. He teamed up with Mayor R. T. Shindler to pass some new ordinances governing water, sanitation, and drainage. Specifically, Rulfs knew that the new Redland Hotel, which he was building at the time, needed these services.[102] When the city announced their new ordinances, however, there was an outcry against an invasion of personal liberties. Many citizens were not yet convinced that urban existence required more infrastructure and more restrictions on the individual for the common good.

As the town began to pick up the pieces after the great fire, two interesting footnotes to history emerged. One, should the town use eminent domain to straighten Main Street by cutting off a portion of the North Square where the Old Stone Fort jutted out into the middle of the street? The proposal was to use "a line with the Cox building on the west and the outside line of the pavement in front of the Mayer and Schmidt building on the east" to take out the old Spanish configuration. The *Sentinel* showed its surprise that the issue even reached the level of a petition.[103] The subject of beautification of the center of the Square also came up for discussion. E. A. Blount even headed a committee to "fill up the well in the center of the public square," remove the chinaberry trees, build an iron fence around the plot, plant shade trees, and provide seating. "This little park will be provided with seats and can be used by farmers and others as a rest place during the hot summer days."[104] While iron posts were put around the square, in order to keep wagons and cars off it, the park never really materialized. During World War I, the city sold the center of the Square to the Federal Government for a Post Office and other government offices.

The Rebuilding of the North Square (1907)

According to the *Palestine Daily Herald*, December 26, 1906, as the owners watched the smoldering ruins of their buildings, "architects were ordered to prepare plans for new buildings to take the place of those burned."[105] The paper's reference was to E. A. Blount and his immediate instructions to D. Rulfs. Rulfs had the plans for the rebuilding of the E. A. Blount buildings ready by February. In early March, Blount awarded the contract for the buildings to J. M. Innis of Dallas.[106] (Rulfs did not submit a construction bid since he was still working on the Redland for Blount.) After the recent strike, Rulfs encouraged all of the property owners to use as many local firms as possible under the new labor contract. The brickwork for the Blount buildings went to Herrin & Herrin of Nacogdoches; and the sheet iron, tin, and plumbing work went to "Stack & Smith of this city."[107] The editor of the *Sentinel*, always interested in the custom, announced on June 25 that Rulfs had put up a pine top on the Blount buildings and the new home of Commercial National Bank.[108] Although Will Perkins did not require new plans—his building was only four years

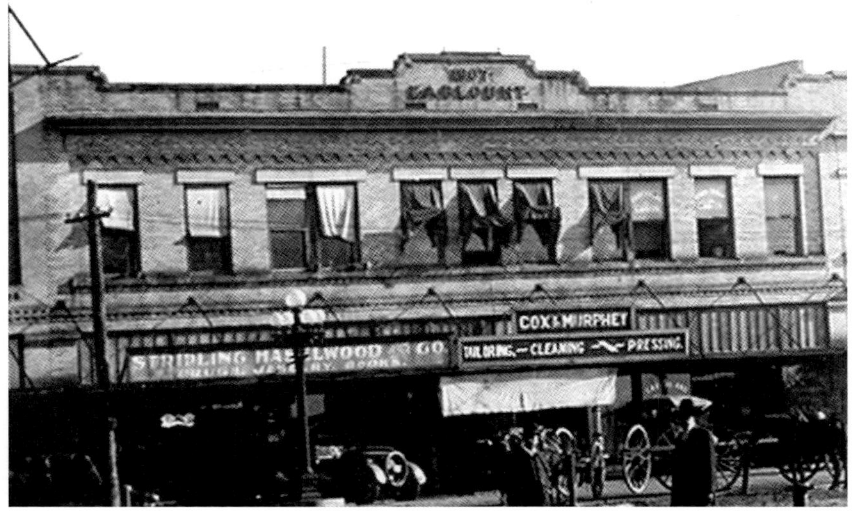

FIGURE 8.33. The E. A. Blount Building, ca. 1915.
The first Blount Building (1901) burned in 1906. The second, shown in this 1915 photograph, dated to 1907 when the North Square was rebuilt.

old at time of the fire—he asked Rulfs to oversee the work of rebuilding his structure. On advice by Rulfs, Perkins asked the Fort Worth firm, who had built the building in 1902, to withdraw and awarded the building contract to a firm out of Lufkin, which had promised to use as many local firms as possible for the subcontracts.[109] By the end of March, Rulfs had the drawings and specifications ready for the west end of the block (Weeks, Hardeman, Sanders, and Reindl Buildings). Although the Sanders decided to build their building using day laborers, the other buildings on the west end were built, as well as designed, by Rulfs.[110] When the workers finished the Perkins Building, Rulfs transferred them to the west end of the block.

The Blount Building (1907)

The Blount Building of 1907 consisted of three different buildings grouped behind one unified façade. Rulfs conceived of the 1907 building in a completely different way than he had when he did the 1901 building. Gone were the inset panels at the parapet, the balcony with balustrades, the corbelled brickwork at the cornice. The continuous parapet was without ornamentation except for the stepped center parapet, where "E. A. Blount 1907" was inscribed. The distinguishing decoration on the upper part of the building, separating the parapet from the roof, was an enormous Ogee molding (concave and convex), which ran the entire width of the structure, so that there was no question who owned the complex.

Between the mold-ing and the windows, the large entablature had some decorative brickwork, more like dentil molding, to create another horizontal, but nothing like the elaborate panels of previous years. He arranged the standard windows (2 over 2) in a 1-1-2-3-2-1-1 pattern. Since the new building had to be tastefully tied into the Perkins Building, which Rulfs was overseeing, the architect copied the idea using a suspended awning over the sidewalk rather than having a porch. Above the awning level, in order to give natural illumination to the interiors, he placed a fixed row of windows. He used this feature across the whole block. Inside the building, the Commercial Bank had the east stand; a barber

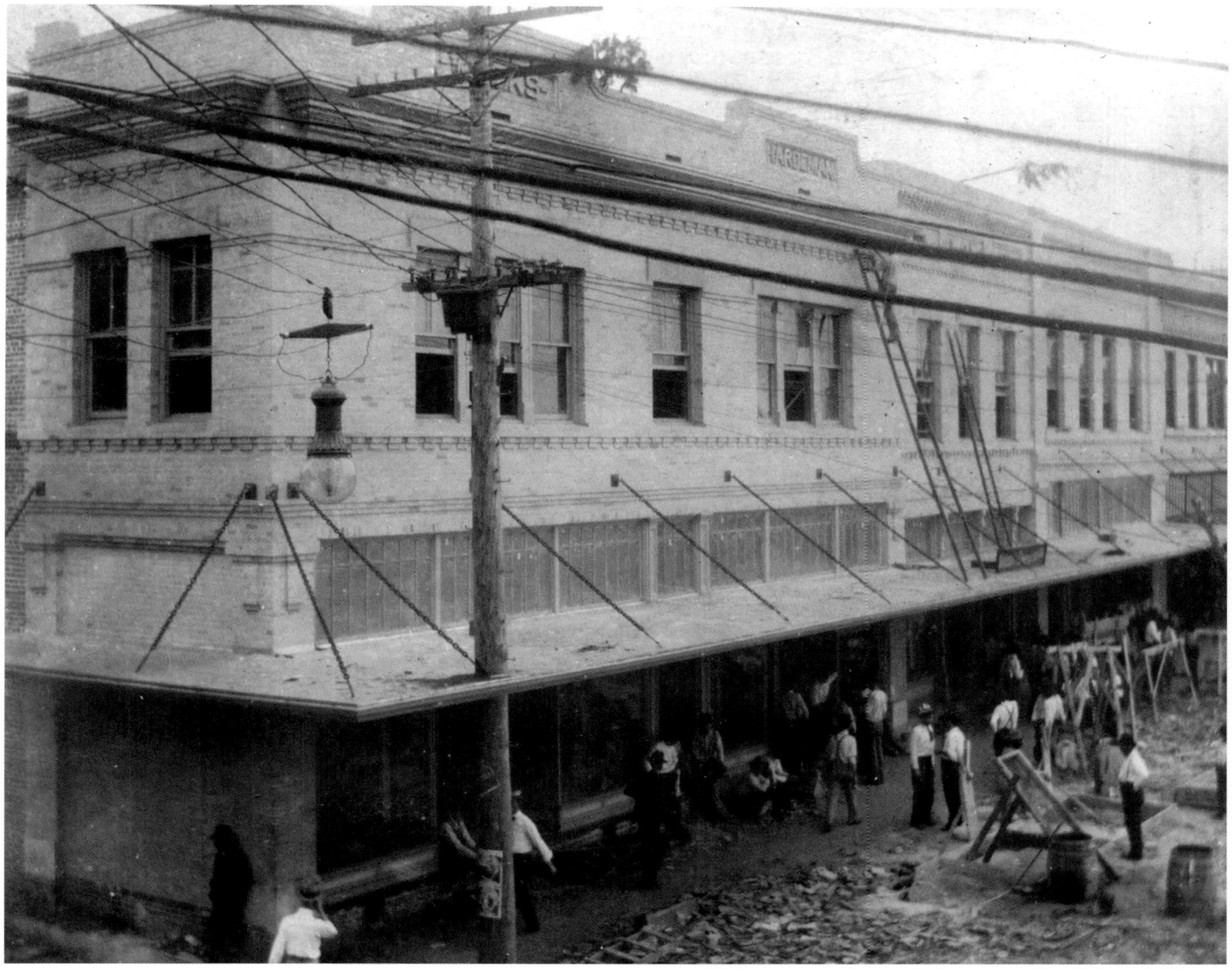

FIGURE 8.34. The West End of the North Square, 1907.

This photograph, showing the west end of the North Square, dates to the completion of the buildings in 1907. The four buildings by Rulfs that still stand on the North Square are shown. All of the buildings had suspended awnings; Rulfs had given up balconies in the downtown area by that time.

shop and tailor shared the next building; and to the west, the Stripling, Haselwood, and Company. The Stripling portion was larger than the others.

The competition of the banks, in building terms, was an interesting phenomenon to watch. When the Commercial Bank moved to the square in 1903, its headquarters were most modest; and even in the 1907 building, their headquarters were only marginally more impressive. The Stone Fort Bank opened in the former Wettermark Building on the West Square, but, recognizing their *faux pas*, quickly moved to space made available to them in the Perkins Building. This put both banks immediately next door to each other on the North Square. The Farmers and Merchants Bank opened across the street in the Cox Building. When Stone Fort Bank merged with Farmers and Merchants in 1919, they used the old Cox Building location and had Rulfs remodel the building. To meet this challenge, the Commercial Bank upgraded by adding a new marble exterior.[111] Today, both the Perkins Building and the Blount Building by Rulfs of 1907 are gone, consumed in the many subsequent remodeling and building expansions of Commercial Bank: 1961, 1980s, and 2000s.[112]

West End of the North Square: Weeks, Hardeman, Sanders, Reindl (1907)

Four buildings designed by Rulfs after the great fire of 1907 still exist on the north Square: Weeks, Hardeman, Sanders, and Reindl. The Rulfs brothers constructed all but the Sanders building, as mentioned. E. A. Blount and the Commercial Bank lent the money to rebuild all of the buildings. The buildings for John Weeks and Tolbert B. Hardeman, on the west end of the block, were a single unit, mirror images of each other. The names of the owners appeared on the parapet of the buildings. John Weeks had purchased the original Perkins Brothers building, on the corner of Main and Pecan, when Perkins Brothers moved to the other end of the block. Although Weeks continued to run a drug store in the building for some years, the building also housed in subsequent years a print shop, meat market, restaurant, dress shop and offices. Various offices with waiting rooms, such as doctors, always occupied the upstairs. After 1915, the building reverted to E. A. Blount and remained in the Blount family until 1965. The J. W. Kennedy family and heirs (J. W., Leroy, and George, later Jean Kennedy and David Stephens), starting in 1915, have conducted a jewelry business in the building until 2013. They purchased the building in the 1975.[113] When Tol Hardeman moved to Oklahoma, he sold his building to Dr. C. C. Pierce, who had an office in the building. Long time District Judge Jack Pierce, a grandson, maintained an office in the building until his death in 2008. Gruebel Enterprises now owns the building.[114]

The North Square has also known fires since 1906. The Sanders Building caught on fire in 1915, but because of the new fire station across the Square, the firemen contained it quickly. In 1984, when the huge fire destroyed much of the middle of the block, the firewall installed between the Sanders and the Reindl building next door saved the Sanders Building, albeit the buildings suffered considerable water damage.[115] The 1984 fire completely gutted the Joe Reindl Building next door.[116]

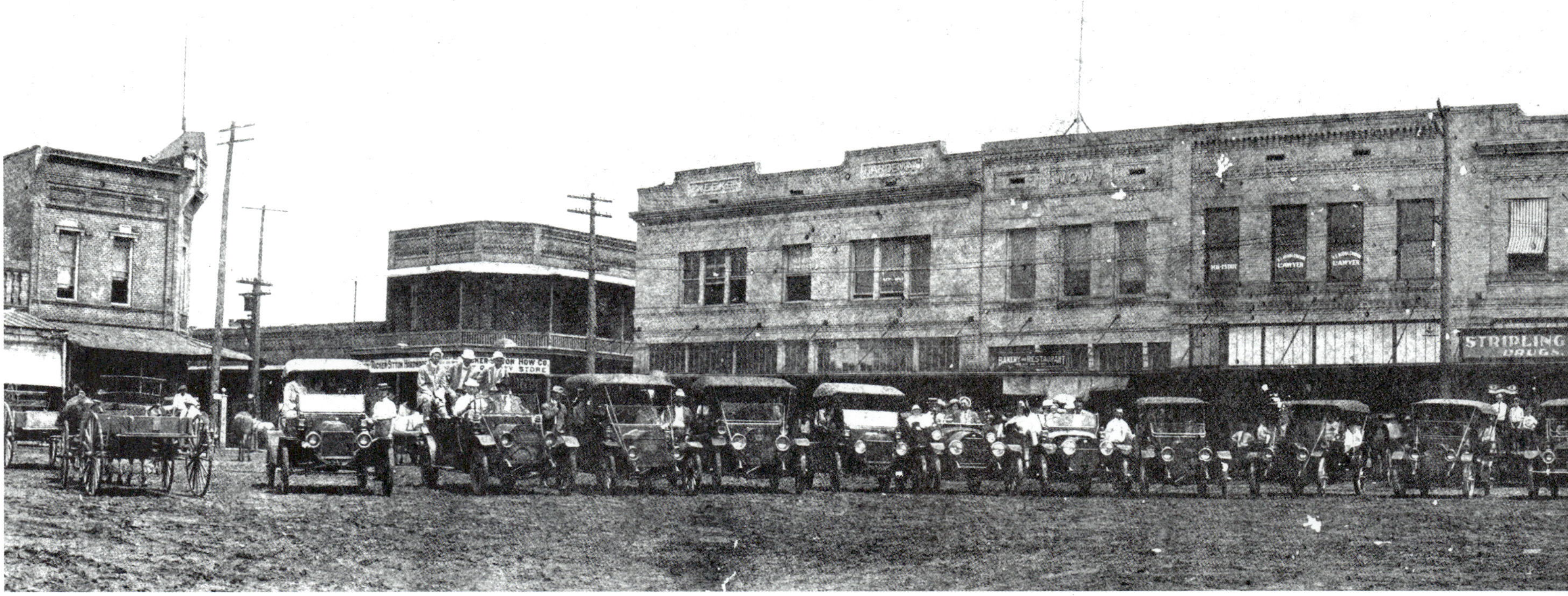

FIGURE 8.35. Panoramic View of the North Square and East Main, ca. 1910.

Despite the poor condition, this panoramic photograph documents the remarkable contributions of Rulfs to the development of the commercial district of Nacogdoches. From the left of the picture (the Wettermark Bank) to the right (the Mayer & Schmidt and Davidson Buildings), there is only one building which Rulfs did not design, the W. U. Perkins Building on the west corner of Fredonia Street. Even so, when Perkins rebuilt in 1907, he asked Rulfs to supervise the reconstruction and make changes as necessary. Photograph was a gift from Gladys Hardeman to the author.

FIGURE 8.36. The West End of the North Square, 2011.

This photograph shows the four buildings by Rulfs that date from 1907, which still stand on the North Square. In reworking the Reindl Building (right side of the image) after the large fire that gutted it in 1984, the owners added the balcony with iron supports; all of the buildings in 1907 had suspended awnings as shown in FIGURE 8.35.

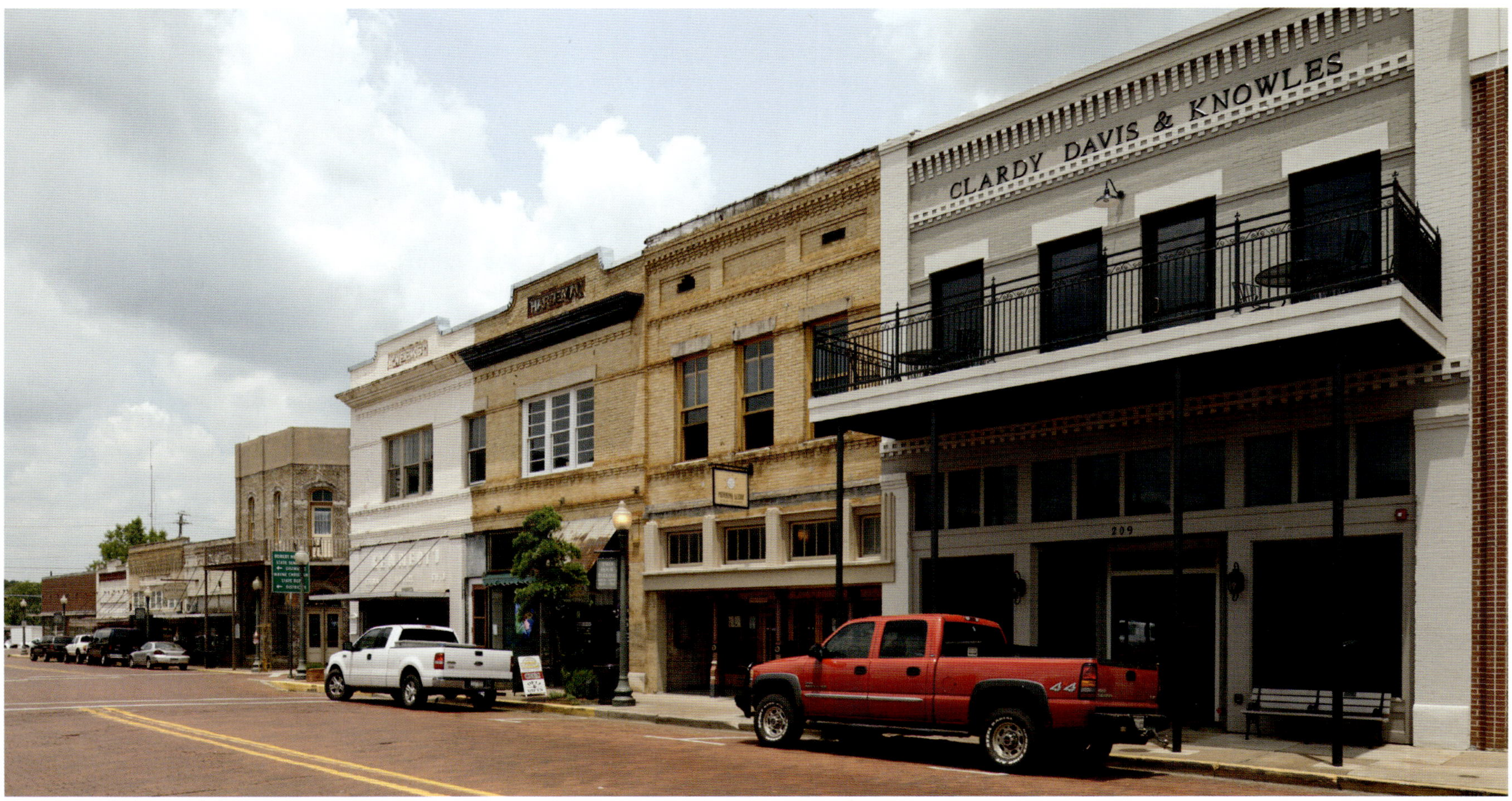

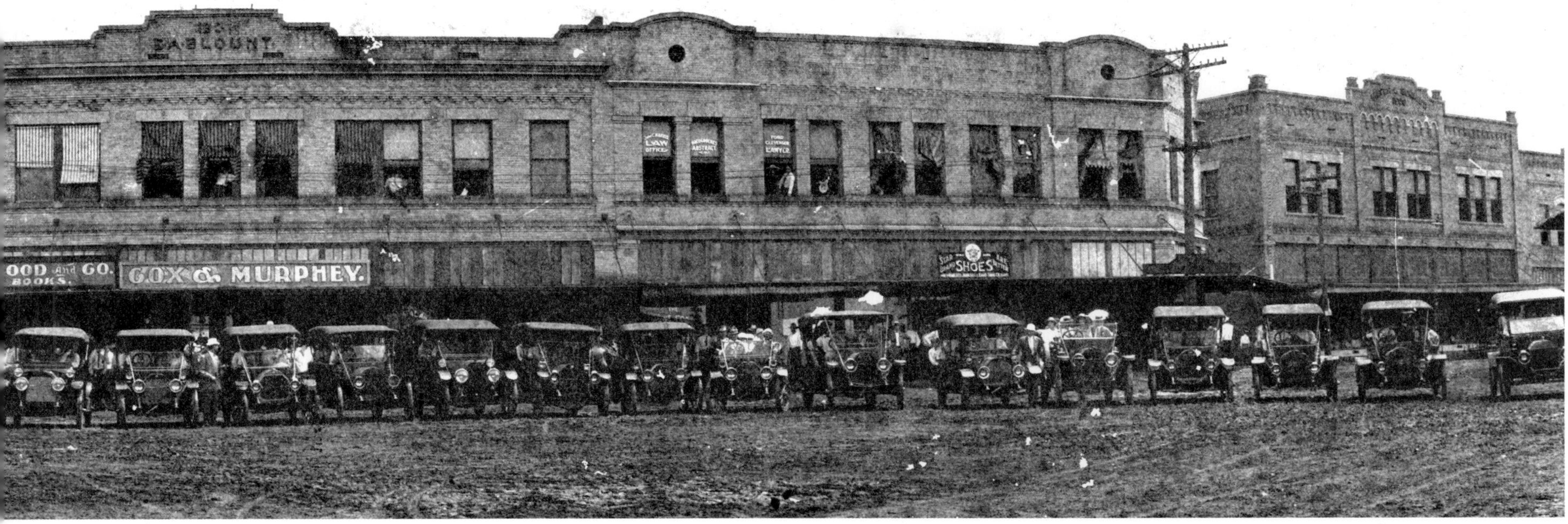

The Mayer & Schmidt Building (1908)

On January 3, 1908, an arsonist set a fire that completely destroyed the Mayer & Schmidt Company's main store at the corner of Fredonia and East Main (Rulfs, 1888-89). "The Total Loss Near Two Hundred Thousand Dollars," according to the *Sentinel's* headline. The fire also took out the Davidson Building (Rulfs, 1889) next door, but spared the new Cason-Monk Building in the middle of the block, barely. While the fire was probably too far advanced when discovered to do anything, the fact that the town had no water mains, fire hydrants, or pumps meant that it was a futile effort by the volunteer firemen. For the first time, Giles Haltom's coverage admitted the presence of arson and, disturbingly, more. Clearly, Haltom was shaken.

> It is universally conceded that the fire was of incendiary origins, and steps have been inaugurated to investigate it. An attempt to set the Davidson building on fire, and in identically the same room where it originated last night, was discovered on last Monday night just in time to prevent a conflagration. Two candles were found burning in a box of excelsior in the middle of the room, and one of the candles had almost burned down to the combustible when detected.
>
> One disgraceful feature in connection with the fire last night was the large amount of goods stolen after they had been carried out of buildings to supposed places of safety. It was astounding to see so much bold pilfering going on and the thieves were white people too.[117]

Arson followed by white people looting? What had happened to the idyllic village, the paradise in the pines? At a rally of town leaders several days later, one could see a new seriousness in the speeches given by E. A. Blount, D. K. Cason, and Charles Perkins. Perkins reported that his fire committee, just since the Mayer & Schmidt fire, "had found 51 defective flues, condemned four stoves, and required fenders to be place in front of all fire places."[118] He also recommended better security for the buildings downtown.

In a press release on January 9, John Schmidt promised to rebuild on an even larger scale—the most modern business house in the city.[119] The easy working relationship between John Schmidt, the patron, and D. Rulfs, the master builder, kicked into high gear. There was no question of putting out bids, waiting for contracts to be signed, or dallying over details. Schmidt just told Rulfs to make it happen, and it did. Within days, Rulfs was hiring hands to clean brick at the burnt block. By the middle of February, the two men previewed their plans for Haltom; and by the middle of April, the masons were laying the foundation.[120] The newspaper eventually confirmed, what everyone at the time already knew, that D. Rulfs was the architect and general contractor. Herrin & Herrin would do the brickwork. Haltom praised the plans as "strictly up to date in every particular" and the building "the most handsome structure in the city, and one that would be a credit to any city in the country."[121]

Rulfs built the new Mayer & Schmidt Building in eight months. At the completion of the structural work on the 13,520 square foot building in August, the principals laid out one of their largest "pine top" celebrations. On top of a 60-foot table of food, supported on sawhorses and nail kegs, Schmidt set a sumptuous spread for local notables. The store opened in October to rave headlines. Features praised were the steam heat, the modern lighting, the private telephone system, the large elevator, and the fact that all of the store fixtures and furnishings were built in East Texas. In waxing about the importance of the Mayer & Schmidt Company to the town, Haltom wrote in 1909, "This is the pioneer dry goods enterprise of Nacogdoches since its inception. No citizens have done more for their home town and neighboring counties than have Messrs. A. Mayer and John Schmidt. The store owned and operated by this pioneer firm is the largest in the city."[122] In 1928, after reflecting over the firm twenty years later, Giles Haltom (the brother) added that the modern history of Nacogdoches was intimately tied up with this company, "so closely woven and interwoven ... that the story of one would be the story of the other."[123] What the Haltoms felt about Schmidt should also extend to the architect D. Rulfs who served the firm in everything they built.

After Mayer died in 1909, the now incorporated M&S firm sold their hardware business to Cason-Monk and continued business in this location until the 1930s. Heavy investments in the cotton market and the Depression had ruined Schmidt's fortune by the time he died in 1934. His son declared bankruptcy and sold his interest in this building to H. R. and A. T. Mast in 1938. The building, remodeled several times since then, still belongs to the Mast family descendents.[124] Important later tenants have included Three Beall Brothers; the City Recreation Department, and at present, the law offices of Adams, Belanger, Atherton, and Lostracco.

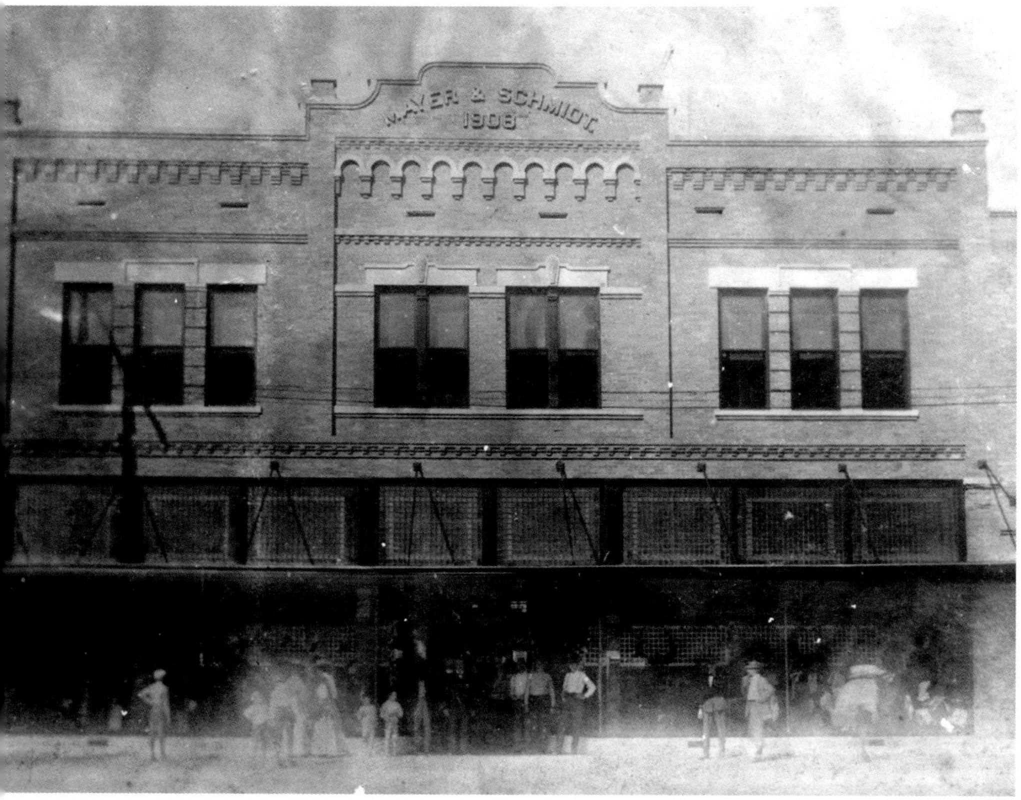

FIGURE 8.37. The Mayer & Schmidt Building, ca. 1910.
The parapet with the company name appears in this photograph. In the photographs of today, the parapet is missing.

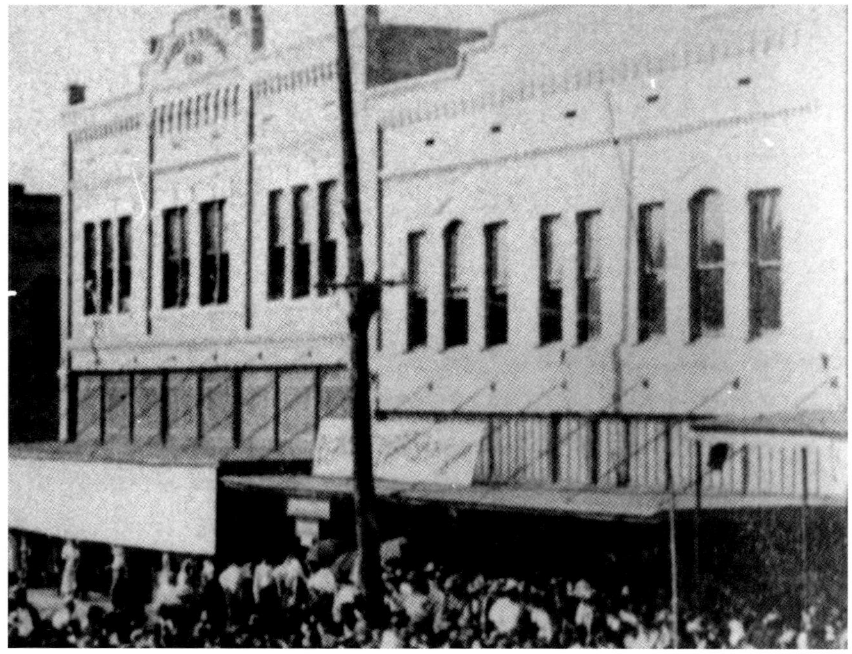

FIGURE 8.36. October 1909: Re-Opening of the Mayer & Schmidt Company.
Both the Mayer & Schmidt and the Davidson Building reopened at the same time. Both buildings had raised parapets with the names of their owners and their dates. This Davidson Building has little ornamentation. The windows, however, have a subtle variation of the Palladian motifs that Rulfs enjoyed using.

The Davidson Building (1908)

Although frequently overlooked, the fire that took out the Mayer & Schmidt Building actually was set and spread from the second floor of the John P. Davidson Building next door to the east. Davidson, primarily an investor, did not run a business or even have offices in the building. The occupant at the time was the Weeks Drug Company. Without a fire department and hoses, there was no way to prevent the fire from spreading to the large M&S establishment, which had adjoined the structure since 1889. Interestingly, the 1906 Cason, Monk & Co. Building's firewall kept the newer building safe. One of the occupants in the Davidson Building was the son of D. Rulfs, Dr. Carl Henry Rulfs. Dr. Rulfs and his mentor, Dr. Frank C. Ford, lost hundreds of dollars of equipment.[125] John P. Davidson, who had his office in another of his buildings, the one which now houses the Nacogdoches City Offices on the south side of the Square, offered this space to the victims of the Main Street fires. The Mayer & Schmidt Company immediately opened there. (See FIGURE 8.37)

Neither Rulfs nor Davidson felt obligated, when rebuilding the Davidson Building, to match the new Mayer & Schmidt Building. The floors, windows, and parapet, therefore, did not present a uniform impression with the neighboring structure. To give the Davidson structure some distinction, Rulfs used a very modern interpretation of his favorite design element, a Palladian window.[126] It is mentioned here because Rulfs would use the motif again for Davidson on the apartments designed later in 1925. The building was the long time home of the J. B. White Company. It is now owned by Reese and Carolyn Andrews and houses the Andrews Law Firm.[127]

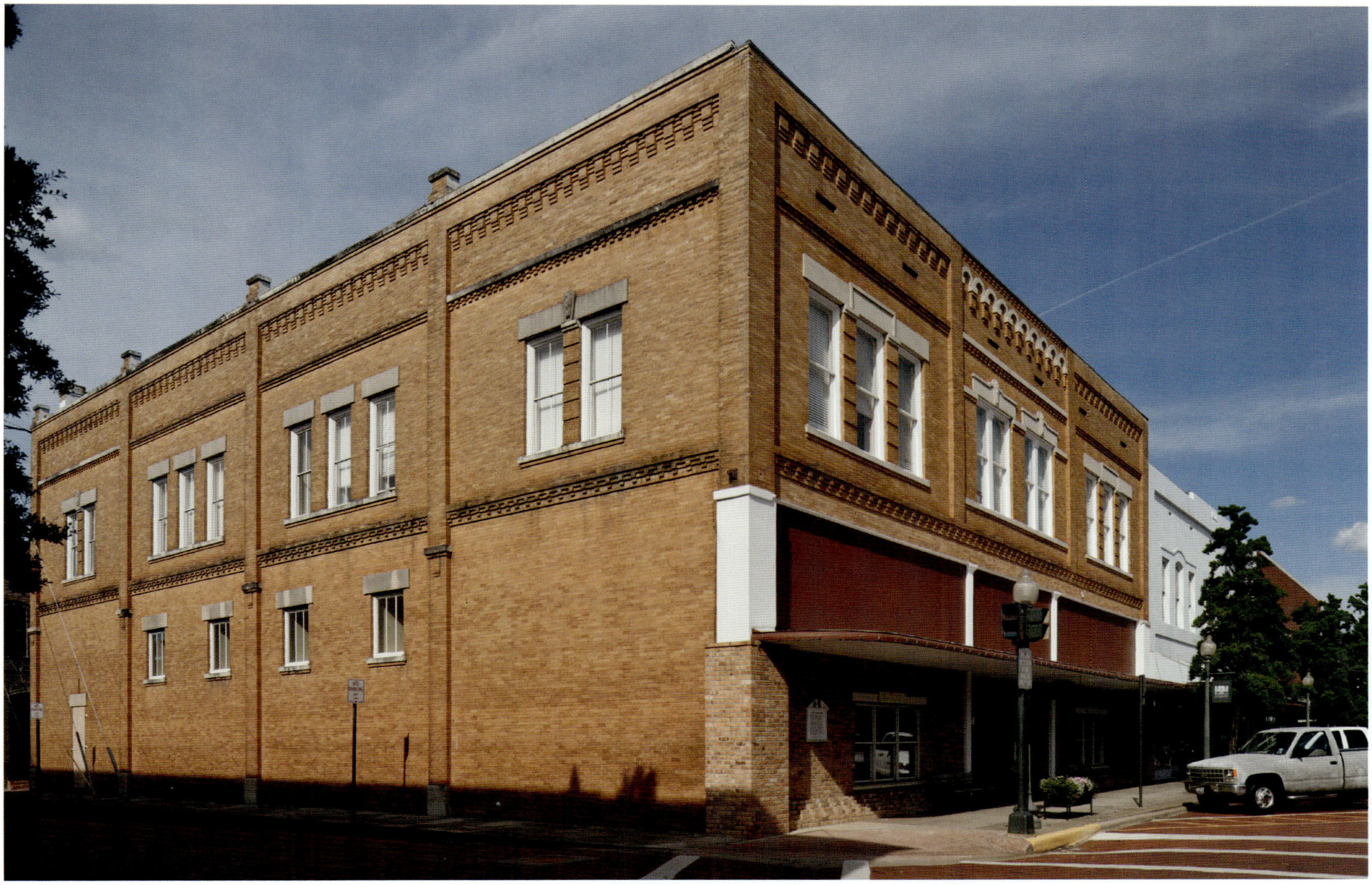

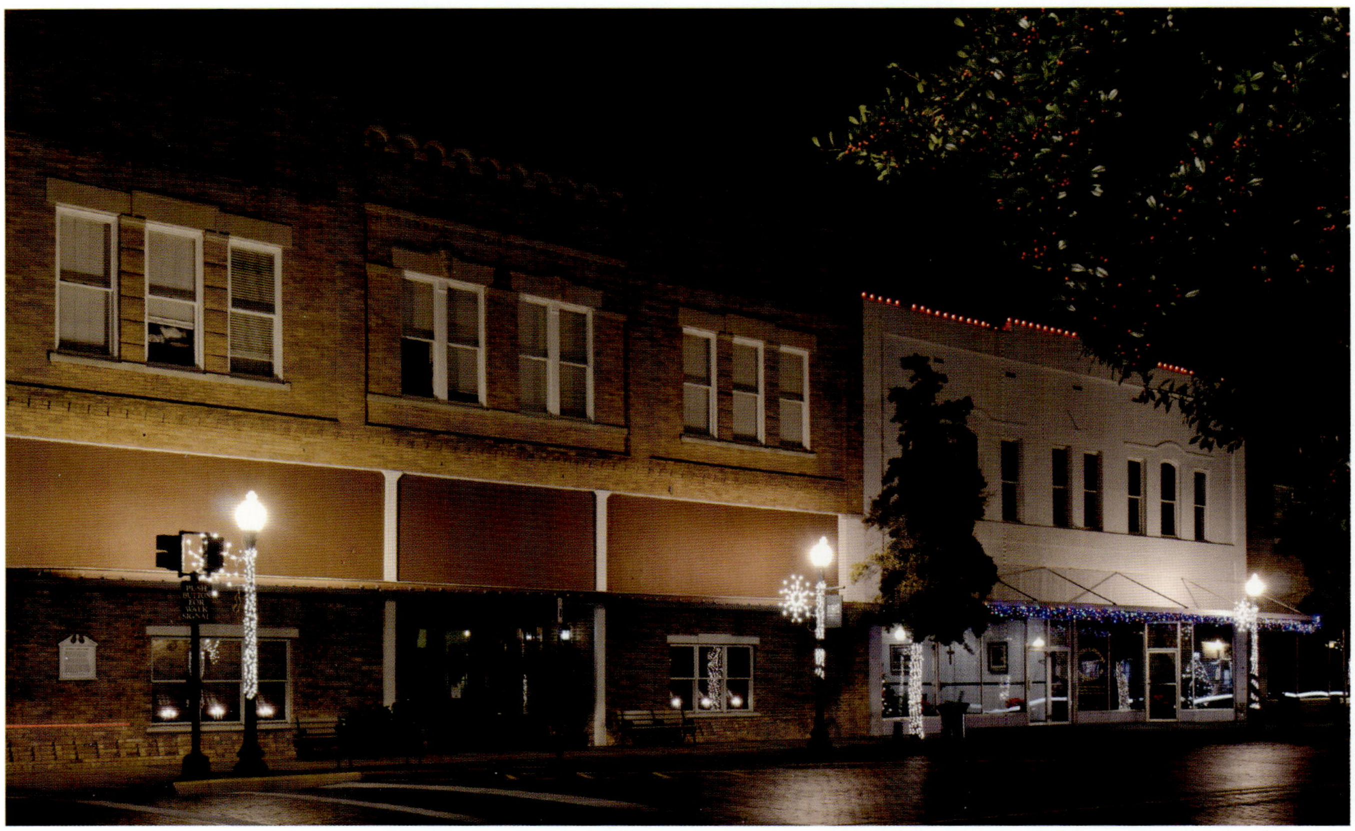

FIGURES 8.38 - 8.39. Day and Night Views of the Mayer & Schmidt and the John P. Davidson Buildings, 2012.

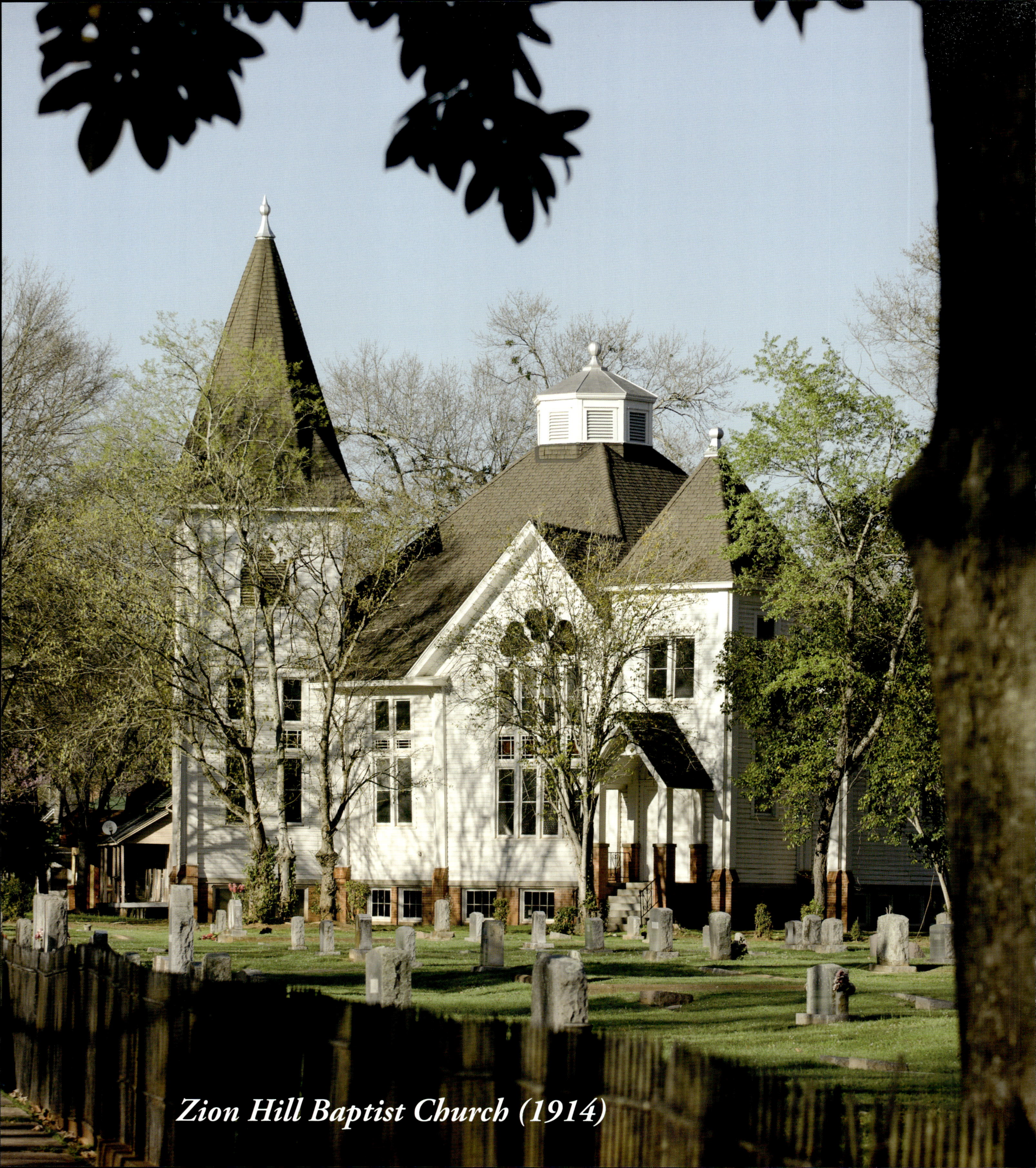

Zion Hill Baptist Church (1914)

CHAPTER IX

Churches and Civic Buildings

A City of Spires 1880-1914

"NEW BUILDINGS FOR NACOGDOCHES. Stores, Residences and a Fine Church Contracted For. . . . The contract for the new Baptist church was let to Mr. D. Rulfs. . . . The building will be of frame work and the plans show an elegant church." *Houston Daily Post*, May 3, 1899.

"The newly completed Cumberland Presbyterian Church building . . .[is] a charming site and a gem of an edifice." *Galveston Daily News*, July 13, 1902.

In 1880, Nacogdoches had many church congregations, but only two of these had their own buildings. The Sacred Heart Catholic Church and Parish, dating back to 1847, was the oldest. It was a small wooden structure on Pecan Street. The Parish originally served the entire East Texas region all the way to the Red River and Dallas.[1] Christ Episcopal Church was the first Protestant congregation to have a building in the town, a small board-and-batten structure (1852) that sat one block north of East Main Street. The access road later became known as Church Street. With no Lutheran congregation in Nacogdoches, many German Lutheran families, including the Rulfs and Schmidt families, attended Christ Episcopal Church. Throughout his career, however, D. Rulfs worked harmoniously with all of the denominations in Nacogdoches: First Methodist (1887, 1892, 1910), First Presbyterian (1889), First Baptist (1899), Christ Episcopal Church (1901), Main Street Presbyterian (1902), a steeple for Sacred Heart Catholic (1906), and Zion Hill Baptist Church (1914). Rulfs used Gothic elements in most of his church buildings in Nacogdoches, albeit the dominance of the Gothic influence varied from building to building: Christ Episcopal Church is totally Gothic; the First Baptist Church had strong Gothic elements; and the First Methodist Church and Zion Hill Baptist Church had selected Gothic accents.

FIGURE 9.1. (Across) The Zion Hill Baptist Church (1914) in 2012.

First Methodist Church (1887)

The first known church building designed by D. Rulfs was for the First (Episcopal) Methodist Church (South). The Methodists were one of the oldest Protestant groups in Texas. Their first attempt to build a permanent house of worship in 1838 failed. "A traveler in Nacogdoches in 1850 noted the absence of any Protestant church building in the town, but declared the Methodists to be the most numerous and active Protestant group in the community."[2] Methodists assembled in homes, a practice employed by all of the Protestant denominations in Nacogdoches at the time, apart from the congregation of Christ Episcopal Church. In 1860, the Methodists purchased their first building, the former Temperance Hall, when the Old Nacogdoches University moved from the Hall into their new building on Washington Square.[3] The Civil War and subsequent economic chaos evidently delayed further action until after the arrival of the railroad. The size of the congregation tells the story: membership fell from 470 white members and 85 colored members in 1857, to 197 in 1879, and to a

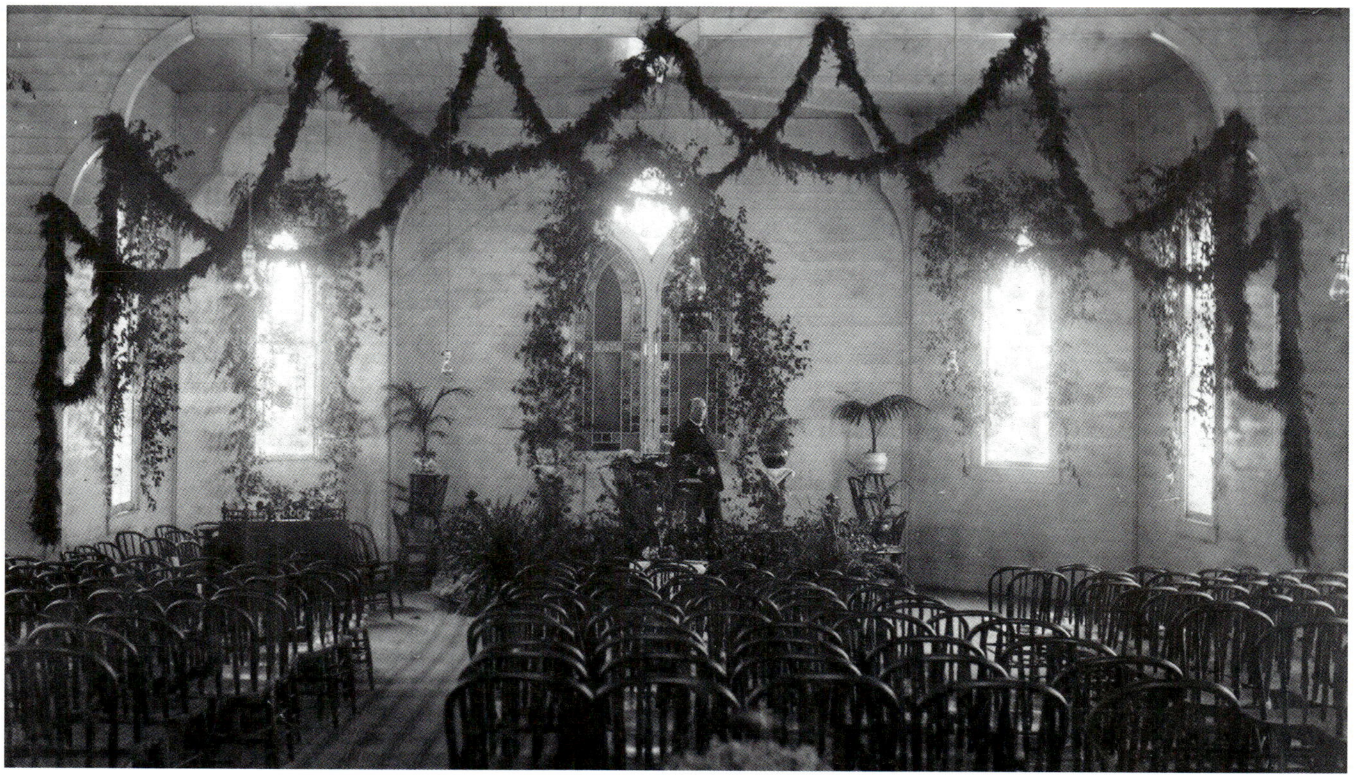

FIGURE 9.2. First Methodist Episcopal Church, ca. 1900
No exterior photographs exist of this early church by Rulfs. On the other hand, this intriguing interior shot, with the extended chancel, does exist. There were no pews, just chairs. This allowed the nave to be completely flexible. In the photograph, the church is decorated for a wedding or perhaps Christmas with garlands of cedar and waxy smilax over the windows. The congregation worshipped in this building from 1887 to 1907 when it burned. Rulfs also designed the building that replaced this one. Photograph Methodist Church Archives.

bottom of 22 in 1883. Resuscitation of the economy and population in the 1880s gave new life to the congregation. By 1885, with a membership of 207, the Methodists tried again. They expanded their property on the corner of Pecan and Hospital by purchasing the adjacent lot, which included the "Old Calaboose" or County Jail. The 1885 Sanborn Map of Nacogdoches shows both the Temperance Hall (as the church) and the jail.[4] When Robert H. Irion offered $500.00 for their two lots and G. D. Boger agreed to buy and move the Hall, however, the congregation sold and purchased new lots on the north side of Hospital Street.[5] Led by the Reverend W. W. Hopper and later the Reverend J. T. Browning, a building committee called for plans, discussed them thoroughly, and in late May 1887, awarded the contract to build the new church to the lowest bidder, "Rulfs and Whitcorn."[6] Whitcorn, on whom no further information was found, was evidently an early contractor in Nacogdoches. Rulfs did not advertise his services as a contractor until a year later.[7]

The building committee endorsed the design submitted by Rulfs, but they were particularly attracted by the option which Rulfs offered to complete the design in two stages. The first stage, completed in 1887, was a simple rectangular building, about the same size as their previous building across the street. The gabled roof measured seventeen feet to the eaves. The main entry porch was to the east front side of the building. The sanctuary had Gothic windows on the east and west sides and larger Gothic windows at both ends of the sanctuary. The new open interior offered much-needed functionality, lacking in the previous structure. While no exterior photograph has survived, the church building resembles the footprint of the church Rulfs built for the First Presbyterian Church several years later. The second stage of the Methodist building, completed sometime around 1894, had an enlarged entrance porch, a forty-five foot steeple and bell tower, and a Gothic chancel that extended the sanctuary to the north by some twenty feet.[8]

For establishing a presence in the community, it was important for the new structure to look like a church. The addition of the Gothic chancel and steeple transformed the original rectangular box into an architecturally interesting structure. By repeating the large brackets (needed when he opened the north wall) as decorative elements between the windows of the bay, Rulfs turned the chancel, an ordinary extension, into a Gothic apse. The placement of five Gothic stained windows in the chancel completed the addition. The simple treatment was effective and charming. The window behind the pulpit, considerably larger than the side windows, consisted of a

FIGURE 9.3. First Methodist Parsonage.
Rulfs designed and built this small parsonage for the Methodists a few years after the completion of the church (ca. 1890). This house sat to the east of the church originally. When, in 1902, Rulfs designed a second and larger parsonage for the church, the original parsonage was moved to Fredonia Street. In the 1970s, Congresswoman Lera Thomas salvaged it for her restoration village at Millard's Crossing. Mrs. Thomas replaced the deteriorated rear portion with a kitchen/dinette area. She used the charming house as a guesthouse for visiting friends and family.

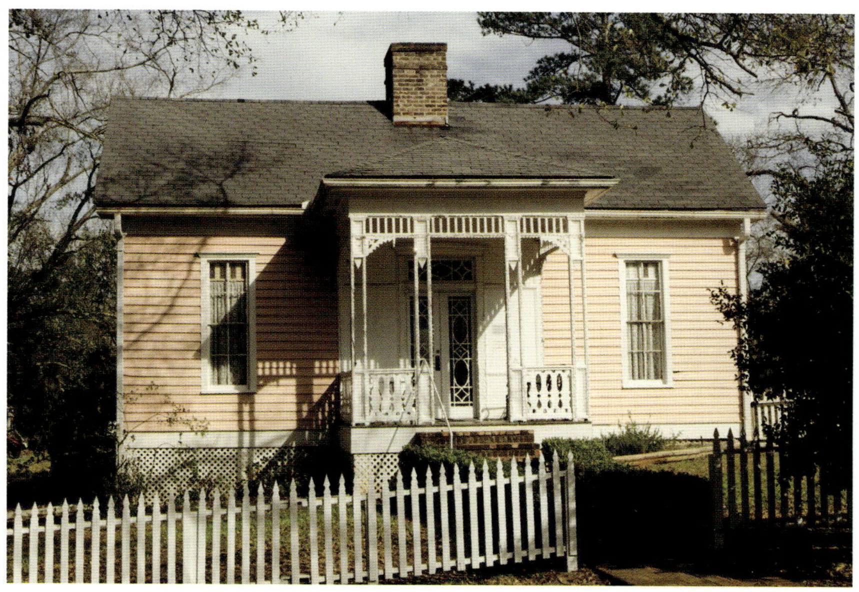

quatrefoil over two lower windows. By furnishing the nave with chairs and not pews, the congregation preserved complete flexibility in the space, very important for a congregation without separate fellowship facilities. Rulfs also designed three of the parsonages for the Methodists. He completed a small parsonage ca. 1890 for the Methodists. This structure, moved in 1902 to Fredonia Street, survives and today is part of Millard's Crossing Historic Village north of Nacogdoches. In 1902, Rulfs designed a second larger parsonage for the church. This house survived the church fire in 1907; the church later utilized this house for Sunday School rooms. When the Haselwood family left their home on Mound Street for use as a parsonage, the congregation inherited another structure by Rulfs, as discussed in Chapter XI.

The First Presbyterian Church (1889)

Presbyterian evangelists came to Nacogdoches very early in the Texas revolutionary years, but with the abandonment of the Old Stone Fort Sunday School in 1849, Nacogdoches' township ceased to have an organized Presbyterian presence although county Presbyterian churches continued.[9] In 1886 Presbyterians re-entered Nacogdoches with the organization of the First Presbyterian Church, United States, known at the time as the "Old School" Presbyterians.[10] Rulfs suggested a program in two stages (as he had for the Methodists), but the congregation showed no interest in the second stage. In 1889, he built a one-story rectangular building with a steep gabled roof at the corner of North Fredonia and East Hospital Streets. It had a small bay window on the east end. Along the north and south walls of the nave (congregational space), Rulfs placed four arched Gothic windows with hoods or caps over the top to deflect the rain. Rulfs later substantially reworked his original ideas for this rejected facade in executing his plans for the new First Baptist Church in 1899; he increased the proportions and made them more refined and elegant. When the Presbyterians decided years later in 1906 to reverse their decision and to replace their modest facade, they approximated what Rulfs had originally suggested: a two-story tower on the south, a one-story tower on the north, and three gabled bays in between the two towers.[11] Rulfs, however, did not build or oversee the 1906 additions, and was, no doubt, somewhat embarrassed that his incomplete first thoughts were being rendered years later without the proper refinements.

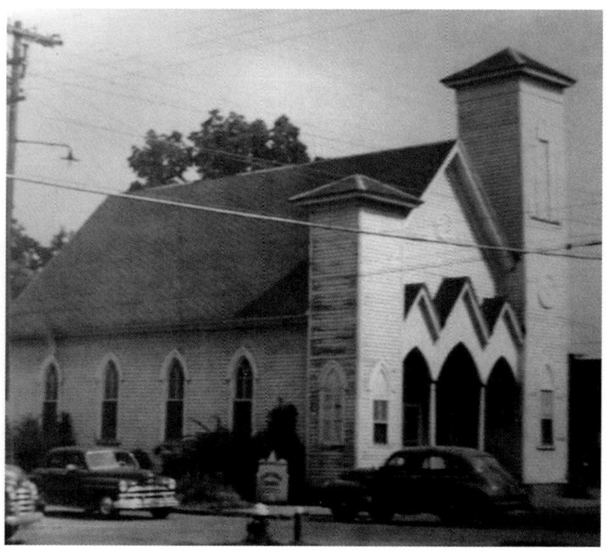

FIGURE 9.4. First Presbyterian Church Building in the 1950s. Courtesy of ETRC.

First Baptist Church (1899-1900)

Like the Methodists, the Baptists were among the earliest Protestants in Nacogdoches County. The Hopewell Baptist Church near Douglass was "the first Baptist church to be organized in Texas," and Elder Daniel Parker even represented Nacogdoches in the Consultation of 1835, where he offered the opening prayer. The Old North Church congregation dates from 1834, its first building to 1852. The congregation of the Zion Hill First Baptist Church dates from 1879.[12]

In 1884, the Baptist General Association of Texas "sent Luther Rice Scruggs to begin Baptist mission work in the small East Texas town of Nacogdoches."[13] The First Baptist Church, the first Southern Baptist group, organized in 1885 and in the next year acquired the property where the church stands today on North Street. They purchased the property from Julia Curl and Anna Marie Shindler, daughters of Charles S. Taylor. According to James G. Partin's *Pictorial History of the First Baptist Church*, the members built their first small wood frame church soon afterwards at a cost of $950.00: "The building featured double front doors and five windows on each side."[14]

Without firm evidence, one can only speculate that D. Rulfs had any role in the design of this first structure for the Baptists. The unfinished nature of the building, as described by one member, suggests that the congregation approached their building needs in stages as did the Methodists. Furthermore, the drawings of the structure indicate that the steeple was a later addition; it stood completely external to the body of the building, not integrated. (As mentioned earlier, one of Rulfs' central architectural goals was to make Nacogdoches into a city of spires.) The design of the steeple strongly resembles one Rulfs later drew for the 1910 Methodist Church. To go beyond speculation, however, is the *fact* that once the congregation had outgrown its first structure, instead of trying to enlarge as the Methodists had done, the Baptist congregation in 1899 turned to Rulfs to design and replace this original building with a larger place of worship. The *Houston Daily Post* noted the importance of the building. "The contract for the new Baptist church was let to Mr. D. Rulf[s], he agreeing to erect same for the sum of $6000. The foundation is being laid on the lot where the old church stood. The building will be of frame work and the plans show an elegant church."[15] One source estimated the cost of the undertaking was $13,000, but this estimate probably also included all the furnishings, too.[16] The Baptists "held their first service in the new building on Sunday, April 1, 1900."[17]

While Rulfs honored the original building in many ways—the same number of windows down the side, the repetition of the two front doors, the emphasis on the steeple—the floor plan for the new sanctuary was more square than rectangular. To keep the shape interesting, Rulfs placed large rectangular bays in the center of the north and the south walls of the sanctuary and placed gabled roofs over these bays. This treatment broke the enormity of the central roof and approximated a transept without creating either a Latin or Greek Cross, which might have affronted Baptist traditions. The building is reminiscent of the open space within the hall-style churches in Germany. Rulfs kept the five-window pattern of the old church, but by pairing the windows on either side of the bay and by enlarging the central Gothic windows in the bays, he increased the interior light and created major focal points at both ends of the semi-circular seating.

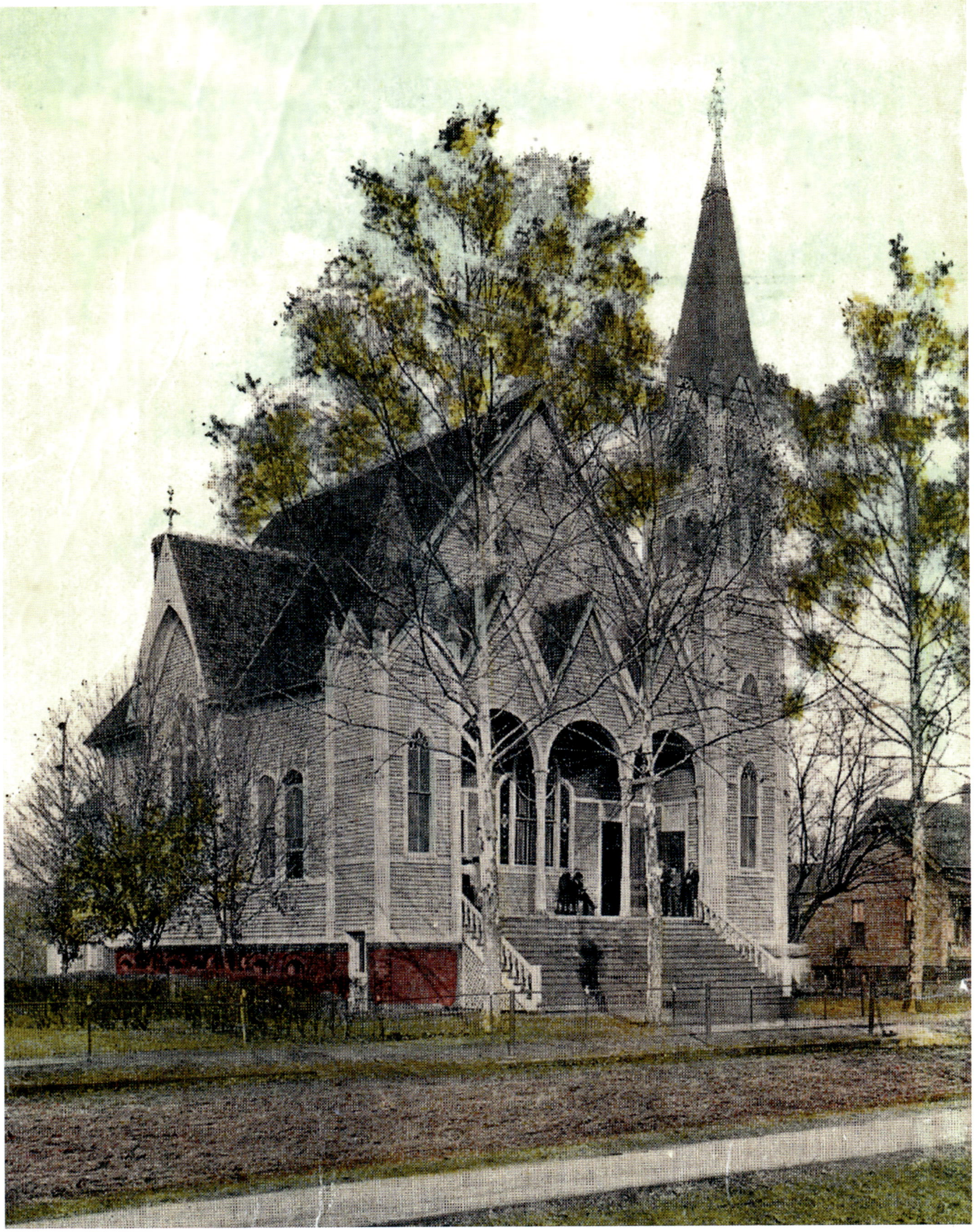

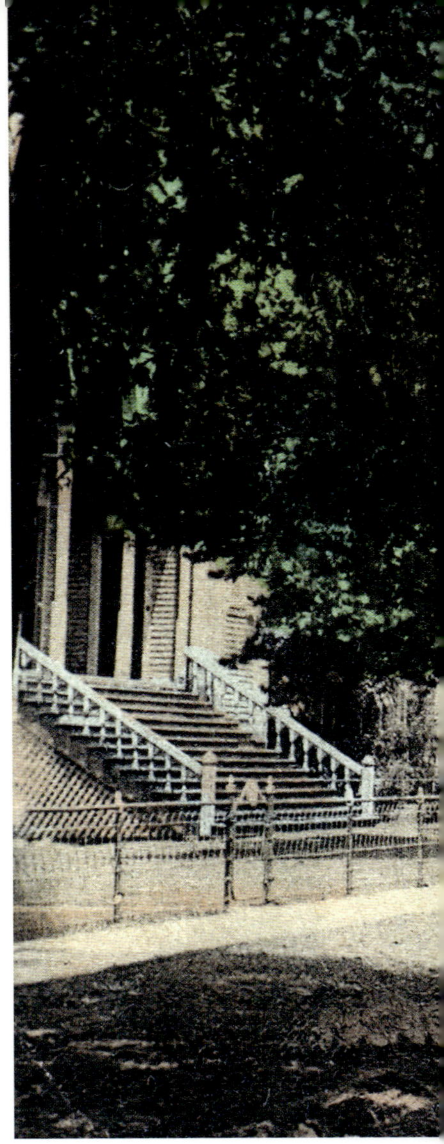

FIGURE 9.5. First Baptist Church

This black and white image, with color added, shows the 1899-1900 building from the southeast. The image gives a good overall idea of the church with its three bays on the façade's porch. The structure was basically a gable front with shorter gables on the side forming a transept. By lifting the main floor, Rulfs made the structure more imposing and also allowed for a basement floor. The towers were asymmetrical. The tower on the north was 80 feet tall. First Baptist Church Archives, courtesy of James G. Partin.

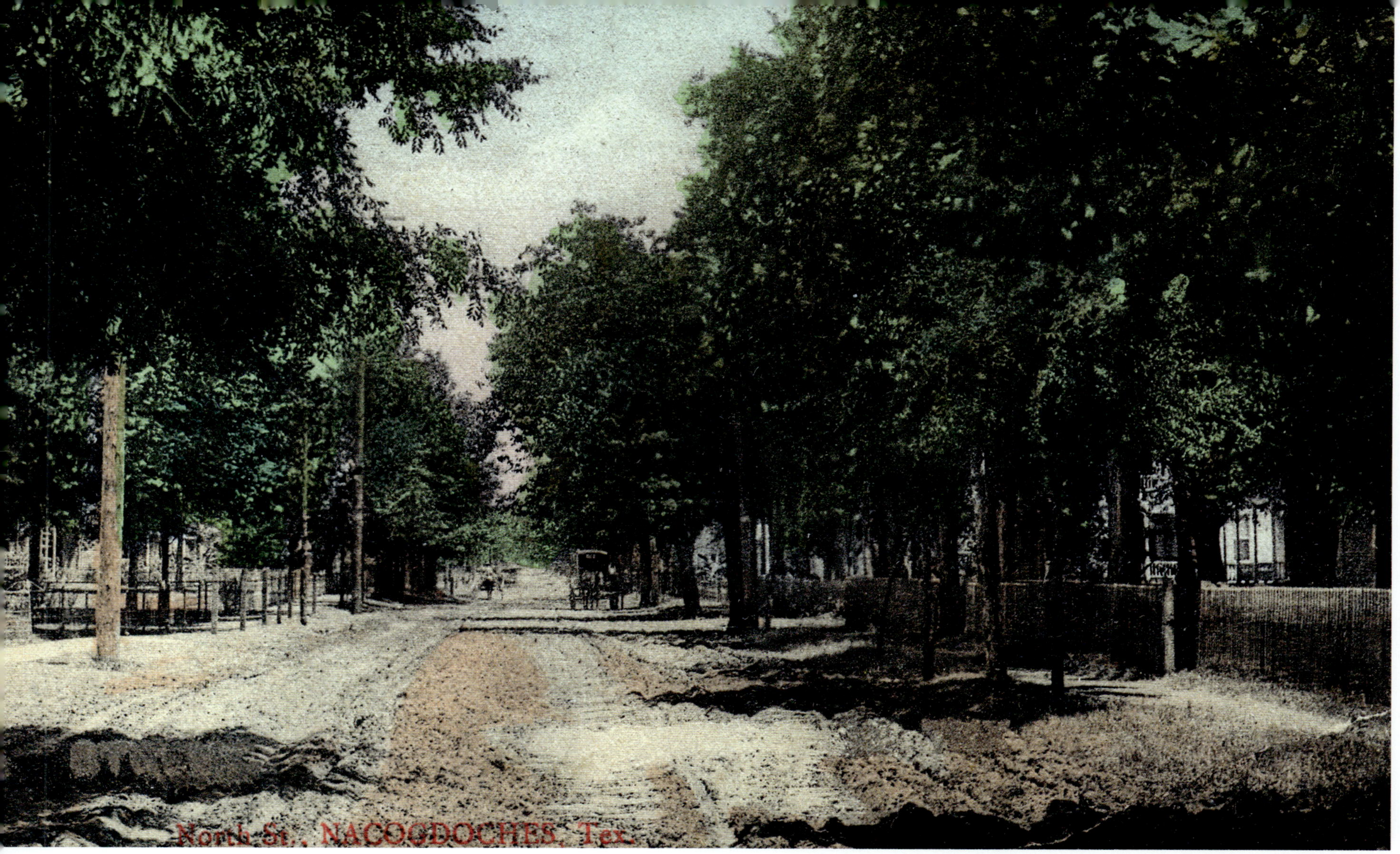

FIGURE 9.6. North Street, ca. 1903.

In this view of North Street, later colorized, the front steps of the new First Baptist Church are visible on the left. The street remained unpaved until Nacogdoches promised to pave it as part of its agreement that secured Stephen F. Austin State Teachers College in 1917. The church building had electricity from the beginning; one can see the poles along the street, but electricity did not extend all the way up North Street at the time. FBC Archives, courtesy of James G. Partin.

Limited by the bounds of the congregation's original property, Rulfs el-evated the main auditorium to provide for a fellowship hall and classrooms beneath. The eaves of the sanctuary itself were thirty feet off the ground, which allowed for windows in the basement floor.[18] The new plan was both efficient and striking. When the congregation replaced the structure, they kept the same relationship of a raised auditorium over their fellowship hall.

Rulfs included clearly defined horizontal elements to give the Baptist building solidity.[19] Overall, however, his emphasis was on the perpendicular. The imposing north tower, by far the tallest steeple in Nacogdoches, stood eighty-feet tall[20] and made a striking impression when one approached Nacogdoches from the north. (See Figure 9.9) The second tower, on the south of the façade, appeared "unfinished," as was often the case in great European cathedrals. It gave the structure historical character or tone. The use of lancet windows and finials at the top of the corner shafts of the towers increased their upward movement. Between the towers on the façade, Rulfs placed an elegant, recessed Gothic portico reminiscent of a loggia, with each bay having its own gabled roof. The central arch on the porch framed a large stained glass window in the form of a triptych, and the other two arches framed the two front doors. Together, the entrance steps, the individual gables over each bay, the gables of the main sanctuary, and the towers gave tremendous verticality to the building. While the number three is prevalent throughout Rulfs' churches because of the Trinity, the numbers four and five and multiples of these were used extensively in this particular building.

The structure had electric lights and wood-burning stoves for heating.[21] Rulfs ingeniously hid the chimneys behind the side gables.[22] The windows on the sidewalls also helped light the auditorium, but the main purpose of stained glass from the Middle Ages onward was to approximate the luminous qualities promised in heaven. The pews, in a semi-circular pattern with two aisles, gentley curved from the northern Gothic window to the southern one. The platform on the west wall followed this same semi-circular pattern. The baptistry, located beneath the platform, required moving the pulpit for access; Rulfs also incorporated this feature in the Zion Hill Baptist Church (1914). At the back of the platform, two double-pocket doors provided a paneled backdrop for the pulpit and Lord's Supper Table. When open, these doors provided access to Sunday School space and additional seating in case of an overflow crowd in the sanctuary.[23] In his later designs for First Methodist and Zion Hill Baptist Churches in 1910 and 1914, respectively, Rulfs designed similar flexibility for the sanctuaries.

In October 1941, when the First Baptists replaced their wood-framed church, they asked architect Hal Tucker, a former apprentice to Rulfs, to undertake the work.[24]

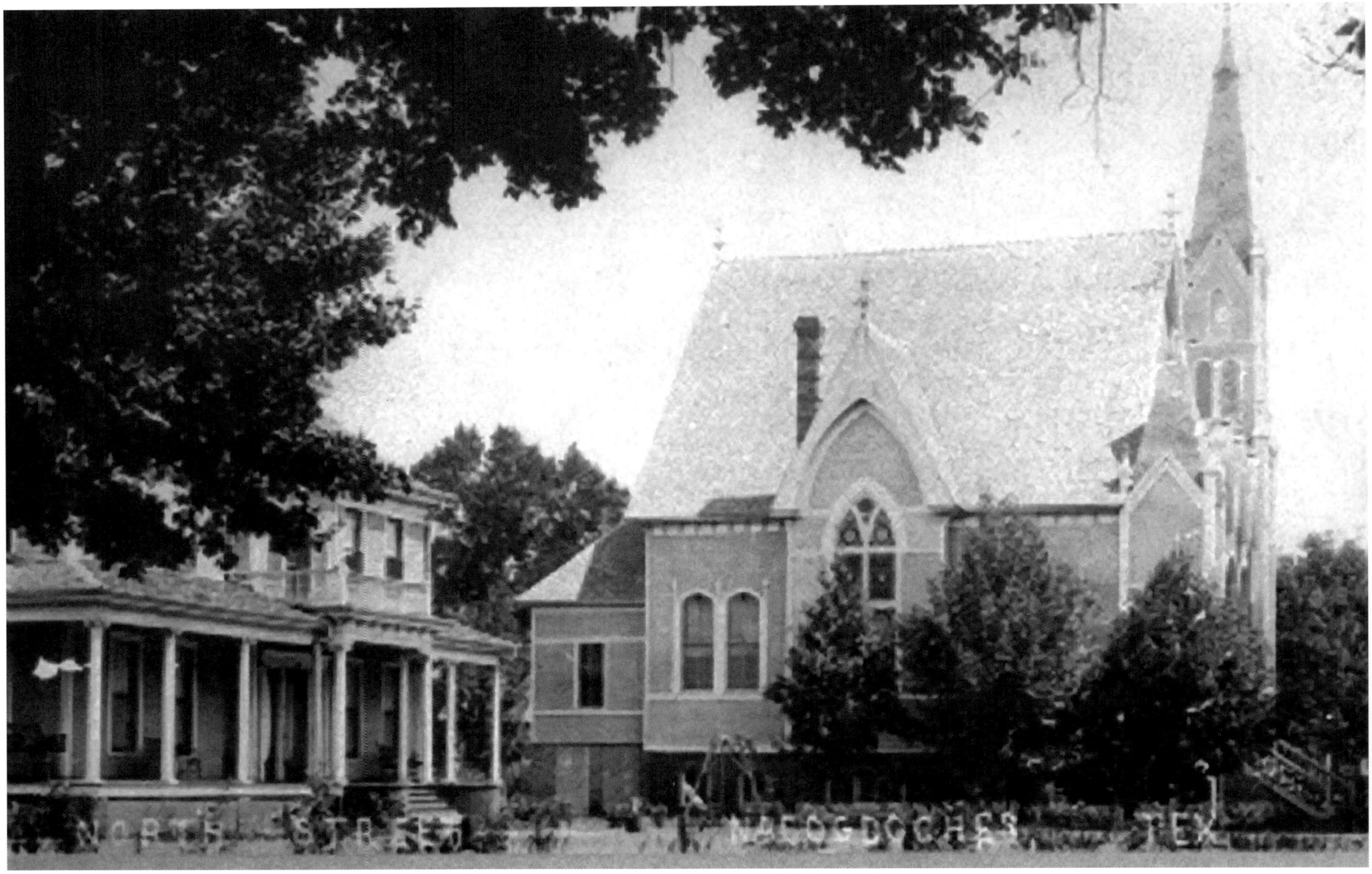

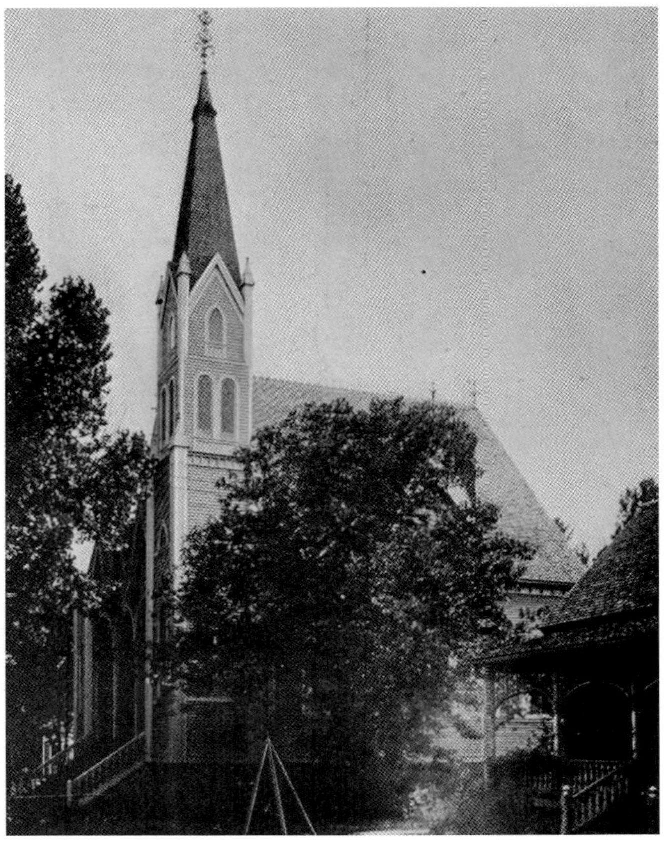

FIGURE 9.7. (Above) South Elevation, Including Matthews House.

This postcard from around 1910 shows the Gothic detailing on the side gable, with its large stained glass windows. These gave the structure a very elegant appearance. The George H. Matthews House (Rulfs, 1905) sat south of the church. It became the Cason-Monk Funeral Home in the 1930s. After purchase in the 1940s, the church utilized the Matthews House for offices, Sunday School rooms, and a center of youth activities. Photograph courtesy of Cecil Sparks

FIGURE 9.8. (Left) North Tower of the First Baptist Church.

The north tower of the First Baptist Church was one of the grandest and most attractive done by Rulfs in Nacogdoches. The Sanborn Map of 1900 states that the tower was 80 feet tall. This photograph appeared first in the booklet, The Twenty Three Reasons Why, which the town assembled to solicit the placement of Stephen F. Austin Normal in Nacogdoches in 1917. The picture also appeared in the volume Nacogdoches County Families, mislabeled as the "Old First Presbyterian Church."

FIGURE 9.9. (Right) Interior of First Baptist Church.

This rare view of the interior of the 1899 First Baptist Church shows the sliding doors, which covered the baptistry. FBC Archives, courtesy of James G. Partin.

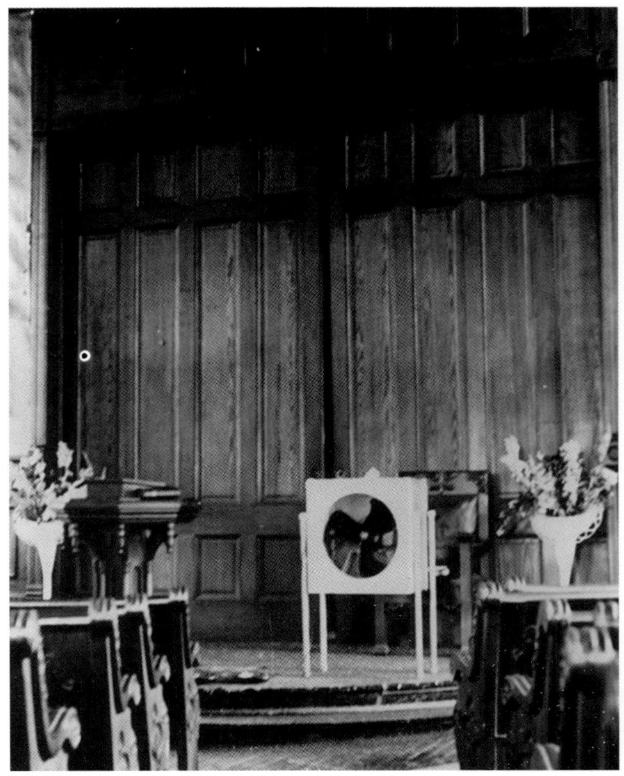

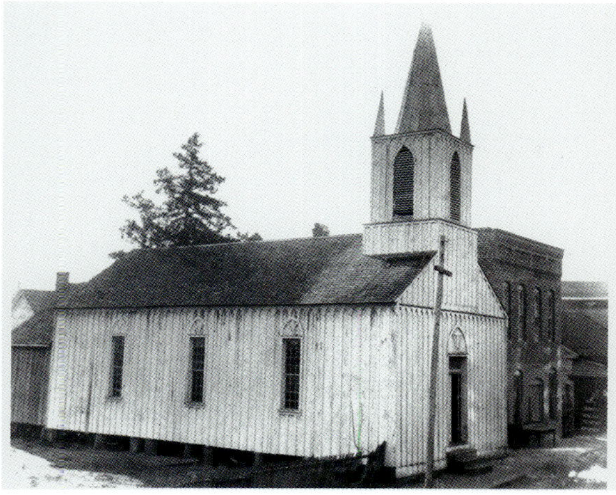

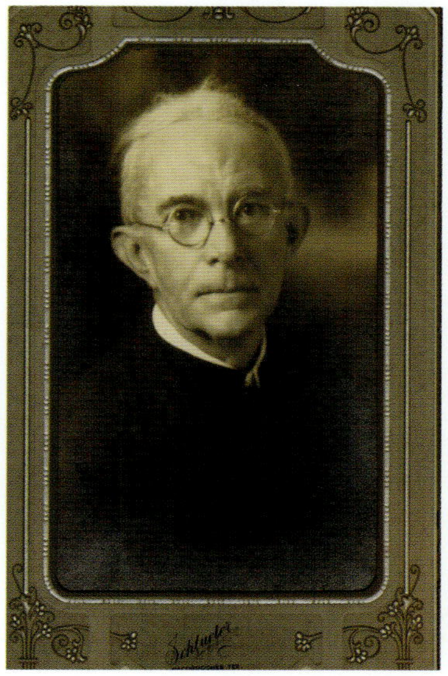

FIGURES 9.10 and 9.11. The Christ Episcopal Church in 1900 and the Rev. George Crocket.
Rulfs finished the Hazle Building for the Daily Sentinel before the Christ Episcopal Church tore down its original 1852 sanctuary. The Rev. George Crocket (above) preached his last sermon in the old building on January 28, 1900. Courtesy of ETRC.

Christ Episcopal Church (1900-1901)

The first Episcopal service in Nacogdoches took place on June 14, 1848, in the wooden courthouse that sat in the middle of the Square at the time. The Reverend Henry Sansom, the rector who conducted this service, was the pastor of the newly created church in neighboring San Augustine. Amos Clark, a lawyer in Nacogdoches, had requested the visitation and later gave $500 to initiate a building campaign. Frost and Susan Thorn donated land; and early members, including the Edwards, Raguet, Arnold, Nelson, Starr, Frost, and Fry families, constructed a small board-and-batten structure for $900.00. This 1852 building, on what became Church Street, was the first Protestant church building in the town of Nacogdoches. The members of Christ Church worshiped in this small building for half a century; Diedrich and Johanna Rulfs worshiped there for their first twenty years in Nacogdoches and saw their children christened and married therein.

The Reverend George Louis Crocket first became the Rector at Christ Church in Nacogdoches in 1888 and served until 1908 in his first appointment.[25] According to the church history, he breathed "new life" into the congregation and ended "a long period of turmoil and uncertainty."[26] Crocket perhaps initiated a drive for a new building program in part as a way to get his parishioners focused. Conveniently, there was a new initiative in town to have churches relocate to the corners around Nacogdoches University. While the educational institution was non-denominational, the presence of churches occupying the four corners, the argument ran, would convince parents that a moral compass for their students was not being ignored. The Cumberland Presbyterians (Main Street) considered building their new church on Washington Square, but in the end declined as did the Baptists. The Baptists argued, with good reason, that their new sanctuary on North Street was within sight of the Old University. Crocket, however, welcomed this initiative as parallel to his own drive to move his congregation to new quarters. In the end, however, it came down to money. When Roland Jones informed the Vestry in late 1899 that the Trustees of the Old University Board were about to close the institution, ironically negating the original purpose for relocating the churches, the congregation responded in order to secure a bargain on prime property.

In a complicated series of meetings, most of which took place at Roland Jones's new house on Church Street (Rulfs, 1896-97) or at the R. C. Shindler & Sons Drug Store on Main Street (Rulfs, 1889), the Vestry decided to act. They authorized E. A. Blount to buy, sell, and trade their properties on Church Street (including the old church building) to M. G. Hazle and W. N. Bailey. They paid the Old University Trustees $500 for the lot on the southwest corner of Washington Square and cleared $1,000 in the whole transaction.[27] Given their later troubles, the bargain was less-than-perfect. Crocket preached the last sermon in the old Christ Church building on January 28, 1900, and the demolition of the old structure began the next day.[28] If the newspaper is to be believed, they acted before they had arranged for an alternative place to meet.[29] As they began to discuss their new building, it became immediately obvious they had a lot that was too small. For the size sanctuary they wanted, they had to build within three feet of the new property line on all sides. Recognizing a problem does not mean dealing with its implications: they had no room for expansion.

The Vestry did not discuss plans for the new building until January 26, 1900, three days before the demolition of their old structure began. Contrary to later accounts, D. Rulfs was not a member of the Vestry; however, his son Carl Henry Rulfs was. Crocket presented the Vestry some ideas he had sketched for a building. The group agreed by unanimous motion "that the plans be put in the hands of D. Rulfs to enlarge and perfect and put in shape to have bids made on same." The designated building committee consisted of Rector Crocket, George H. Matthews, and Roland Jones, the Senior Warden. Jones, evidently at odds with Crocket's suggestion of a Gothic structure, later tried to get the Vestry to emulate a building in his hometown of Shreveport.[30] In the meeting of March 2, however, the Vestry reaffirmed their support for Crocket's ideas as perfected in designs by Rulfs:

> As Mr. D. Rulfs had kindly offered previously to draw up finished designs and working plans, from sketches furnished by Mr. Crocket, [Rulfs] was present with the plans which were accepted after some minor changes in the door and leaving out the belt courses and square trim around windows.
>
> Motion carried that Mr. Rulfs go ahead and finish up the plans in ink as soon as possible, that they may be put on exhibition at Shindler's Drug Store, and that the Vestry now tender their thanks to Mr. Rulfs for his interest in the work he has done in the matter.[31]

The Vestry officially accepted Rulfs' plans on April 5, 1900, subject to Parish acceptance. Nothing, however, ever seemed to be final. On April 23, they were still arguing over whether to go with brick or wood. They had all witnessed, however, the steady progression of the downtown from wood to bricks, and since neither the Baptists nor the Methodists had a brick structure, the opportunity to be the first to have a more permanent structure proved irresistible. The majority concluded that "the increased cost was only a few hundred dollars more for the brick" and that "they should consider the future" because they wanted something to stand for "50 to 60

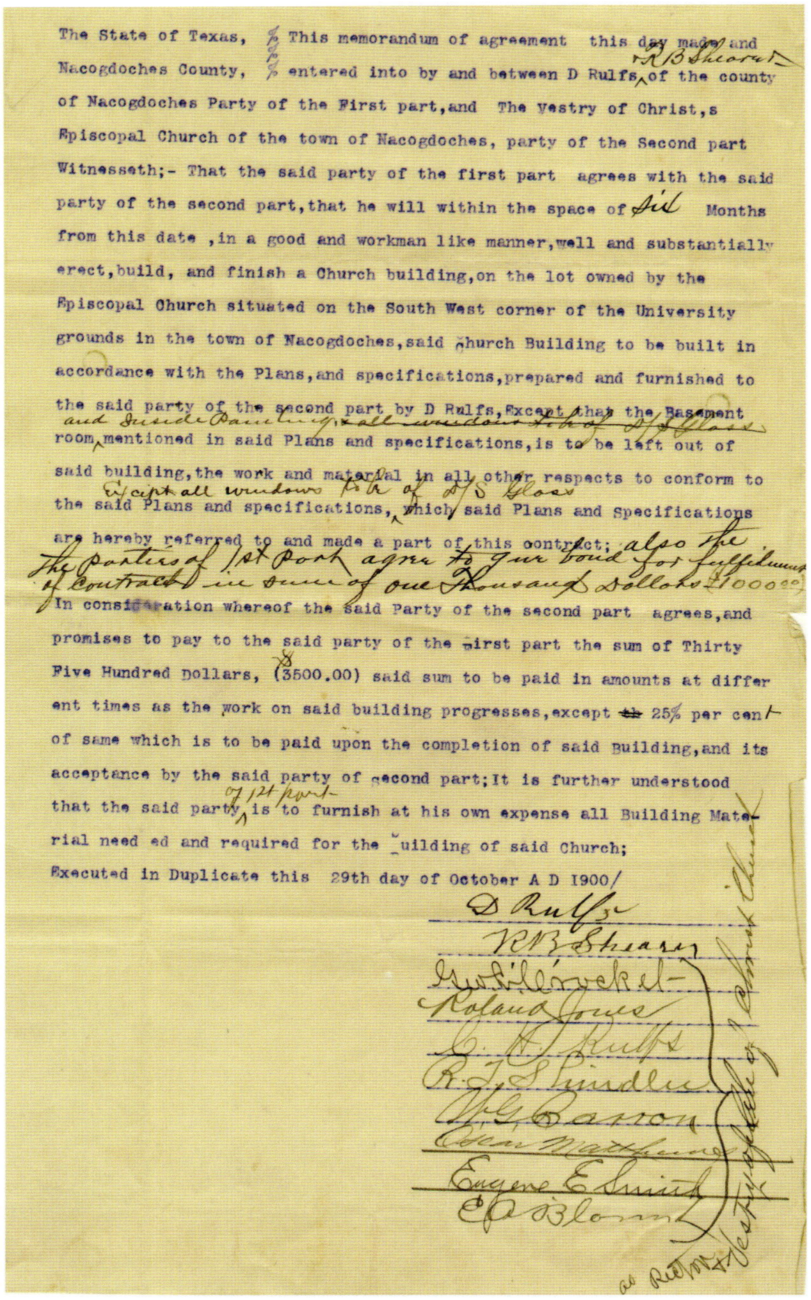

The State of Texas, } This memorandum of agreement this day made and
Nacogdoches County, } entered into by and between D Rulfs, R B Shearer of the county
of Nacogdoches Party of the First part, and The Vestry of Christ,s
Episcopal Church of the town of Nacogdoches, party of the Second part
Witnesseth;- That the said party of the first part agrees with the said
party of the second part, that he will within the space of six Months
from this date, in a good and workman like manner, well and substantially
erect, build, and finish a Church building, on the lot owned by the
Episcopal Church situated on the South West corner of the University
grounds in the town of Nacogdoches, said Church Building to be built in
accordance with the Plans, and specifications, prepared and furnished to
the said party of the second part by D Rulfs, Except that the Basement
room, and inside Painting, all windows ... mentioned in said Plans and specifications, is to be left out of
said building, the work and material in all other respects to conform to
the said Plans and specifications, except all windows ... which said Plans and specifications
are hereby referred to and made a part of this contract; also the
the parties of 1st Part agree to give bond for fulfillment
of contract in sum of one thousand dollars $1000.00
In consideration whereof the said Party of the second part agrees, and
promises to pay to the said party of the first part the sum of Thirty
Five Hundred Dollars, ($3500.00) said sum to be paid in amounts at differ
ent times as the work on said building progresses, except 25% per cent
of same which is to be paid upon the completion of said building, and its
acceptance by the said party of second part; It is further understood
that the said party of 1st part is to furnish at his own expense all Building Mate
rial need ed and required for the building of said Church;
Executed in Duplicate this 29th day of October A D 1900/

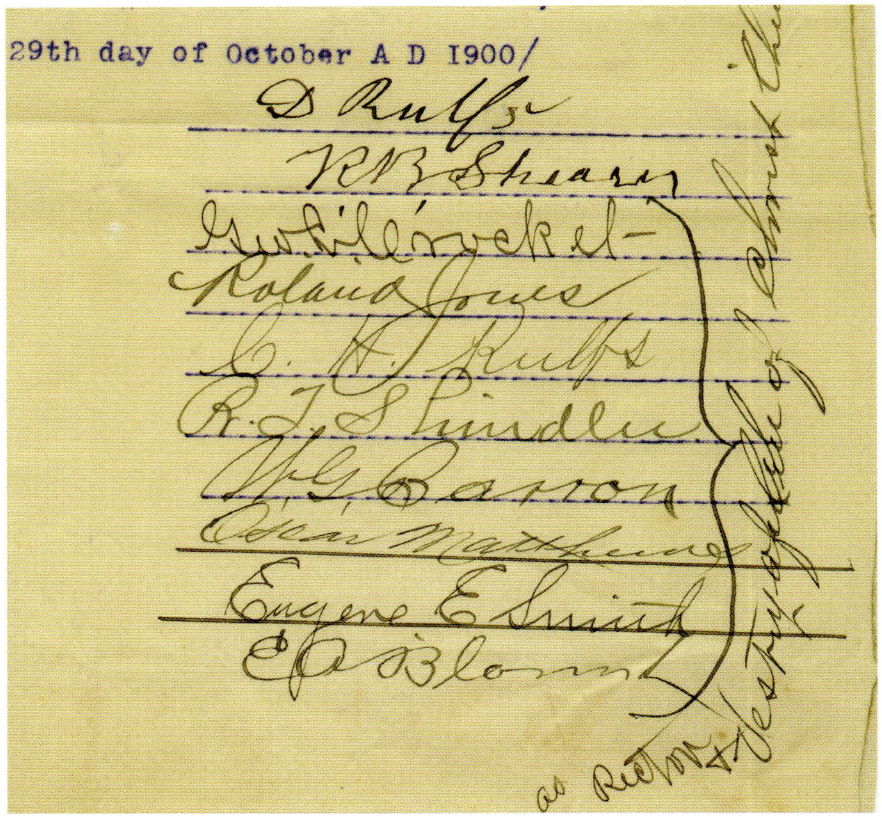

29th day of October A D 1900/

FIGURES 9.12 (Left) and 9.13 (Above). Contract, Christ Episcopal Church; Detail of Signatures. Courtesy of ETRC.

(Left). The full one-page contract for the Christ Church Building, dated October 29, 1900.

(Right). In the detail of the signatures, Rulfs and Shearer signed first, then the Vestry:

D. Rulfs (Architect and Builder)
R. B. Shearer (Brick Contractor)
G. W. (George) Crocket (Reverend, Rector)
Roland Jones (Manager, Nacogdoches Cotton Compress)
C. H. Rulfs (Diedrich's son, Dr. Carl Henry Rulfs)
R. T. Shindler (Druggist, R. C. Shindler & Son)
W. G. Barron (Mechanical Engineer)
Oscar Matthews (Nacogdoches Wholesale Grocery)
E. A. Blount (Banker, Commercial National Bank)

years."[32] Before the Notice to Contractors went out on May 5, they made the idea of adding a basement supplemental.[33] When the Vestry opened the bids on July 3, all of the submissions were higher than expected. After E. A. Blount, the banker, reminded everyone the church had only $3,000 of funding in sight, the Vestry rejected the bids and called for a second round, minus "both tower and basement."

Up to this point, Rulfs had simply drawn the plans; he had submitted no bids. He now personally opened talks with the three brick contractors: Henry Austin of Nacogdoches, R. B. Shearer of Garrison, and Valentine Nerver (Garrison Brick). Shearer proved to be the most accommodating of the three on the brickwork. Rulfs and Shearer put together a compromise bid. On October 29, 1900, Rulfs and Shearer signed a contract with the Vestry. The simple contract, without access to the Vestry minutes, hides a world of angst.

> . . . that he [Rulfs] will within the space of six [entered by hand] Months from this date, in a good and workman like manner, well and substantially erect, build, and finish a Church building, on the lot owned by the Episcopal Church situated on the South West corner of the University grounds in the town of Nacogdoches, said Church Building to be built in accordance with the Plans, and specifications, prepared and furnished to the said part of the second part, by D. Rulfs.[34]

Handwritten modifications to the contract included the elimination of the basement, the cost of interior painting, and decorative stained glass for the windows. Rulfs also agreed to put up a $1,000 bond "for fulfillment of the contract." As specified in the contract, Rulfs had "to furnish at his own expense all building materials needed and required."[35] For this, the church promised to pay the architect the princely sum of

$3,500. (The difference in prices then and now is staggering—what a bargain for the church.) Rulfs donated all of his personal services—plans, specifications, and oversight. The church agreed to disperse some of the funds "as the work on said buildings progresses," but they withheld 25 per cent "to be paid upon the completion of said building, and its acceptance."[36]

Rulfs signed the document first. R. B. Shearer, the brick contractor, signed next. For the church, Reverend Crocket signed first, followed by Roland Jones, C. H. Rulfs, R. T. Shindler, W. G. Barron, Oscar Matthews, Eugene Smith, and E. A. Blount. (See Figure 9.12.)

Oscar Matthews oversaw the collecting of funds, which E. A. Blount received and disbursed; W. G. Barron (an engineer) became the inspector of brickwork; and Roland Jones became the inspector of woodwork. The Vestry "and no other authority" was responsible for all changes. There is no information available on the details which were omitted in the 1900 contract. The basement was not included, but certainly the tower was, as early photographs confirm. Given his obsession with church spires, it is fair to assume that Rulfs himself got the tower reinserted as the negotiations progressed. No doubt Rulfs was able to lower costs by efficient use of his laborers; he had a large number of commissions under construction at the time. Even so, there was no way he could have finished the church within the six months stated in the contract. The congregation knew that the project was especially dear to Rulfs, a labor of love on which he probably lost money. In an interview for the 1973 special anniversary edition on Christ Church, Anna Katherine Holbrook, granddaughter of D. Rulfs and daughter of Carl Henry, said the whole Rulfs family (Diedrich, Carl Henry, Tony, John, and William Henry) helped to produce the Christ Church building—a true family affair.[37] As to the assertion that Rulfs made the beams of the church in his shop, this is quite possible; but before the project was over, he was looking for ways to keep the undertaking from ruining him. The Vestry voted unanimously to accept the building on July 24, 1901, and to return Rulfs's security deposit.[38] On September 9, 1901, the *Daily Sentinel* joyfully announced, "The old Episcopal bell rang Sunday morning announcing services for the first time in their new church."[39]

The story of the completion of Christ Church, however, is sketchy and inconsistent. The day after the Vestry accepted the building, a crisis surfaced (nothing to do with Rulfs). The note on the building, evidently poorly written, required each member of the Vestry to become responsible individually for any liabilities. Since the Vestry Minutes for Christ Church for the period from 1901 to 1938 are missing, there are no records about the consecration of the building. The *Daily Sentinel* is strangely silent on the matter. To fill the the gap in information, several modern accounts, including the 1973 article on the church's one hundred and twenty-fifth anniversary in the *Daily Sentinel,* have Bishop Alexander Gregg, the first Episcopal Bishop of Texas, consecrating the building. However, since Bishop Gregg died in 1893, many years before the building's concept or completion, the building was probably consecrated by Bishop George Herbert Kinsolving, Gregg's assistant and successor.[40] The historical marker uses the date 1902, but there are several mistakes on the marker: D. Rulfs's initials are confused with those of his father, and the architect himself with his son, Dr. Carl Henry Rulfs, as a member of the Vestry.

From the start, the church had trouble with the size and the location of its property on Washington Square. While the congregation utilized the public school's campus for out-of-the-building events, there was no space for parking, and the school children playing sports were a constant danger to the windows of the church. The Parish Hall and the Rectory had to be placed across Fredonia Street. In the mid-1930s, the congregation began thinking seriously about a move. Their dilemma became: how could they take the building with them? Their emotional attachment to the Rulfs building was deep. When Hal Tucker advised Reverend Orin G. Helvey, the Rector in 1933, that the building could be moved, the Rector undertook the challenge. F. I. Tucker persisted in calling this Rector "Goliath"[41]

The original plans by Rulfs have vanished,[42] but according to the tradition, architect Hal Tucker used Rulfs' original plans in 1938 for the reconstruction of the church at the corner of Mound and Starr Streets.[43] Tucker's daughter, Molly Smith, found her father's drawing from the 1930s and has allowed the author to copy it. (See Figure 9.13) There are obvious differences between the replica and the original church. The 1938 plans shifted the tower and entrance to the north side on Starr Street, enlarged the chancel, added a basement, and resurfaced the exterior walls with new brick. The congregation and the contractor, John Hamblin, carefully saved the early stained glass windows and the handmade bricks around them for use in the new building. An elaborate pulpit, given to the church by Mrs. Frank Sharp, incorporated panels of wood carved by Reverend George Crocket. In the early 1990s, the congregation extended the nave to accommodate a new pipe organ and choir loft, and added a new narthex and entrance to the south.

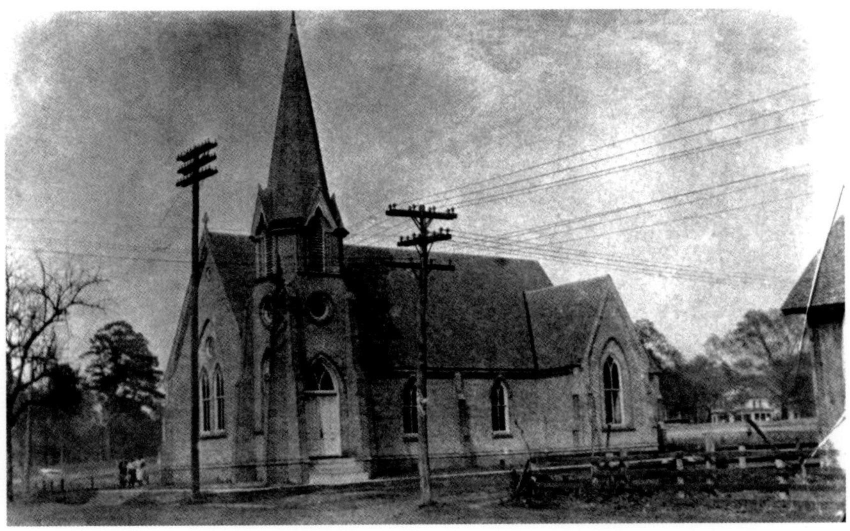

FIGURE 9.14. Christ Episcopal Church, ca. 1903.

This picture of Christ Church on Washington Square, taken shortly after the building's completion, shows the Charles Perkins House in the background and none of the ivy or the cedar trees in the 1935 picture on the next page. The church owned only three feet beyond the walls of the structure. After the building of the public school in 1904, the windows of the building were constantly in danger from the children playing on the field next door. Courtesy of ETRC.

In the promotional booklet (1917) advocating placement of the new East Texas Normal in Nacogdoches, three churches were illustrated on the page entitled "A City of Churches." The Baptist, Methodist, and Episcopal churchs were all by D. Rulfs. (See FIGURE 12.3.)

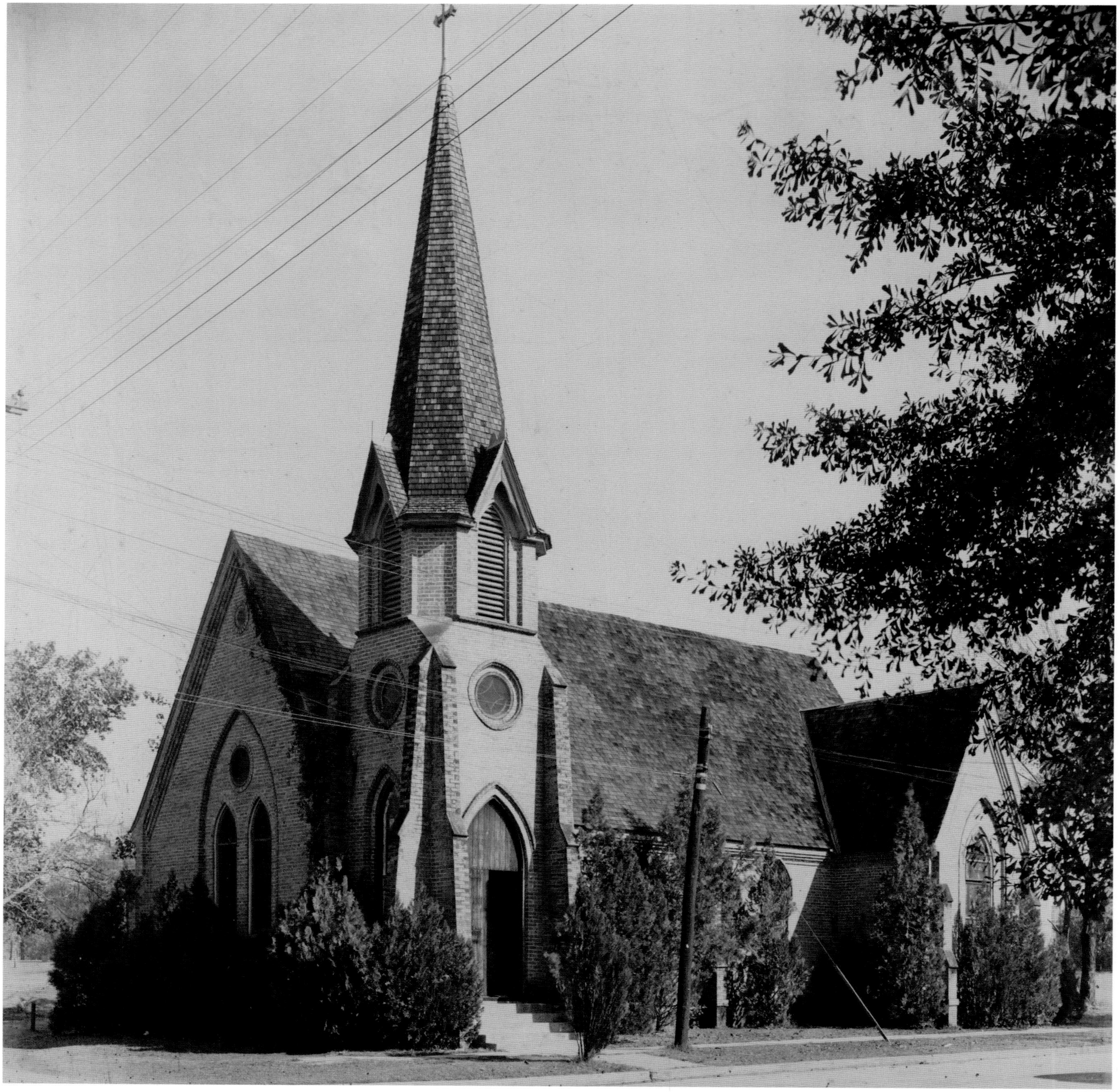

FIGURE 9.15. (Above) Christ Church on Washington Square, ca. 1935.

This photograph of the building, taken shortly before it was moved to Starr and Mound Streets, shows the church surrounded by overgrown cedar trees, high enough to shadow some of the stained glass windows. Courtesy of ETRC.

FIGURE 9.16. (Opposite) The Christ Church Sanctuary, 2012.

"The Reverend Mr. Crocket carved the magnificent altar from native yellow pine along with the Retable on the Chapel altar, the Chapel processional cross, the Psalter Board, and the intricate native red gum pulpit panels representing The Nativity, The Crucifixion, and The Transfiguration." Information supplied by Florence Patton.

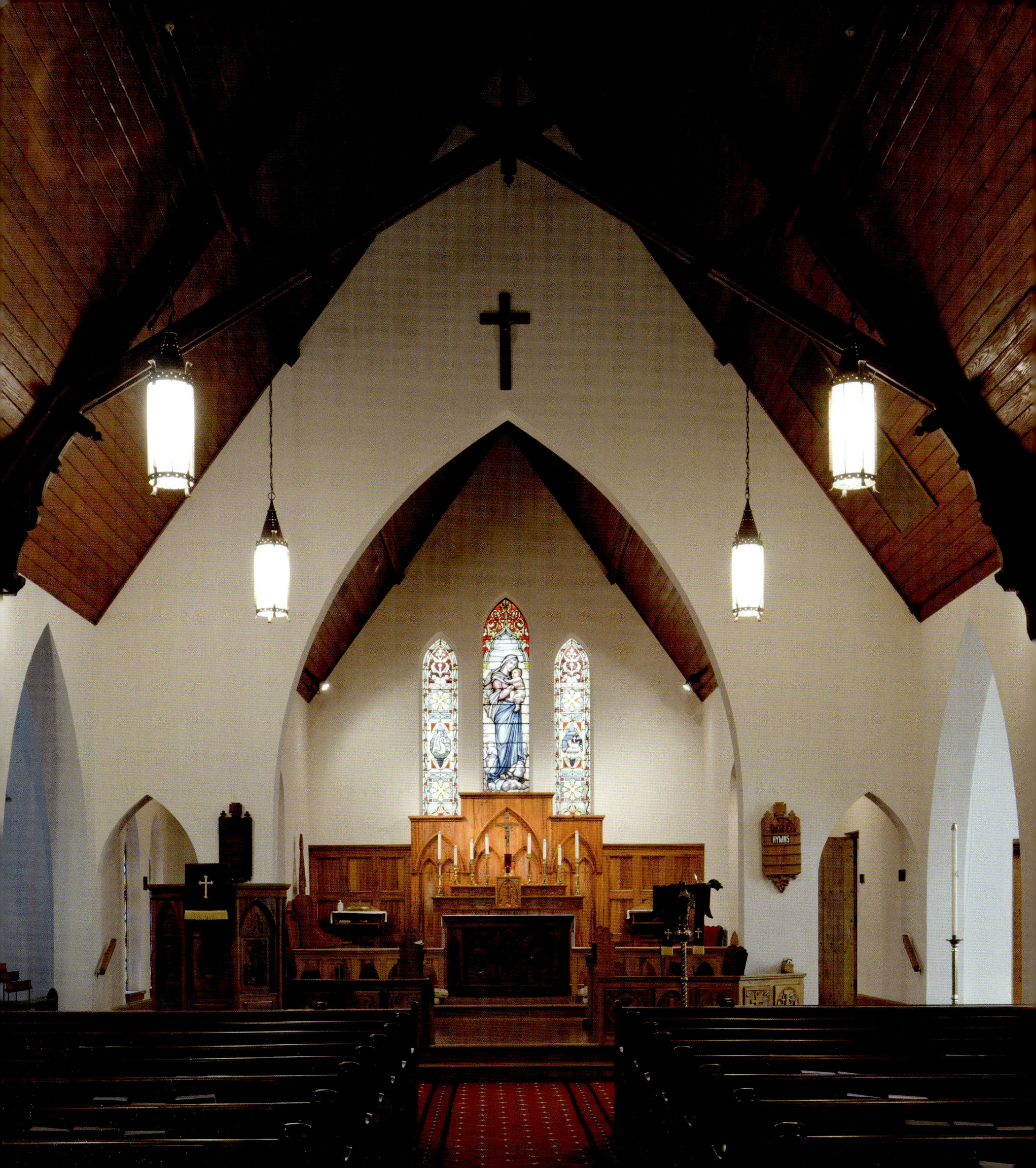
HYMNS

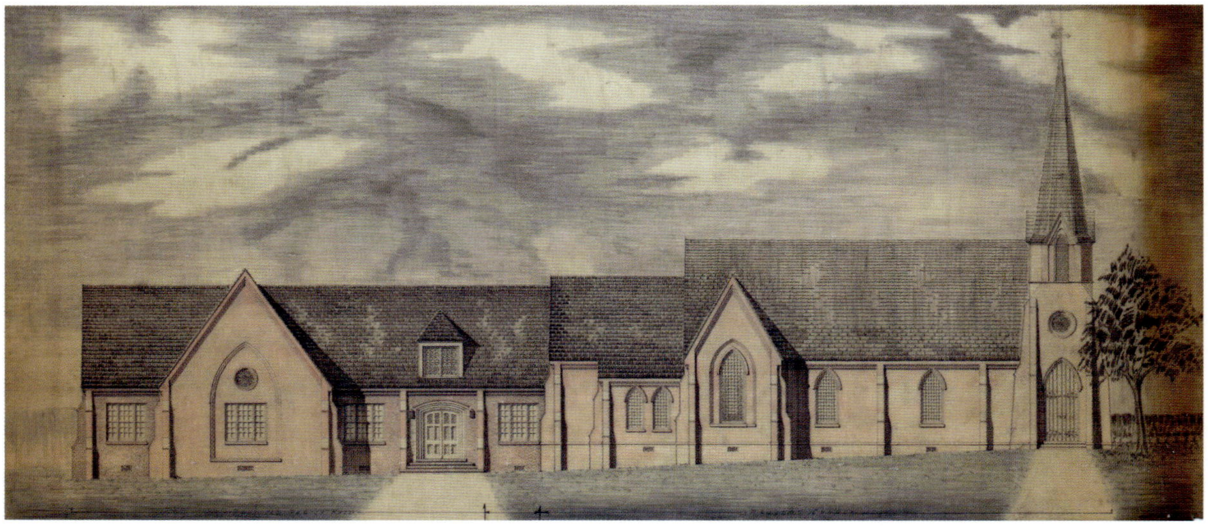

FIGURE 9.17. (Left) Drawing by Architect Hal Tucker, Reconstruction of the Christ Episcopal Church.

This north elevation of the building dates to 1938. Tucker used the original architectural plans by Rulfs in planning the move to Starr Avenue. Access to this drawing graciously provided to the author by the architect's daughter, Molly Smith. The ETRC scanned the image and now has the drawing.

Christ Epicsopal Church

FIGURE 9.18. (Below) North Elevation, Starr Avenue, 2012.

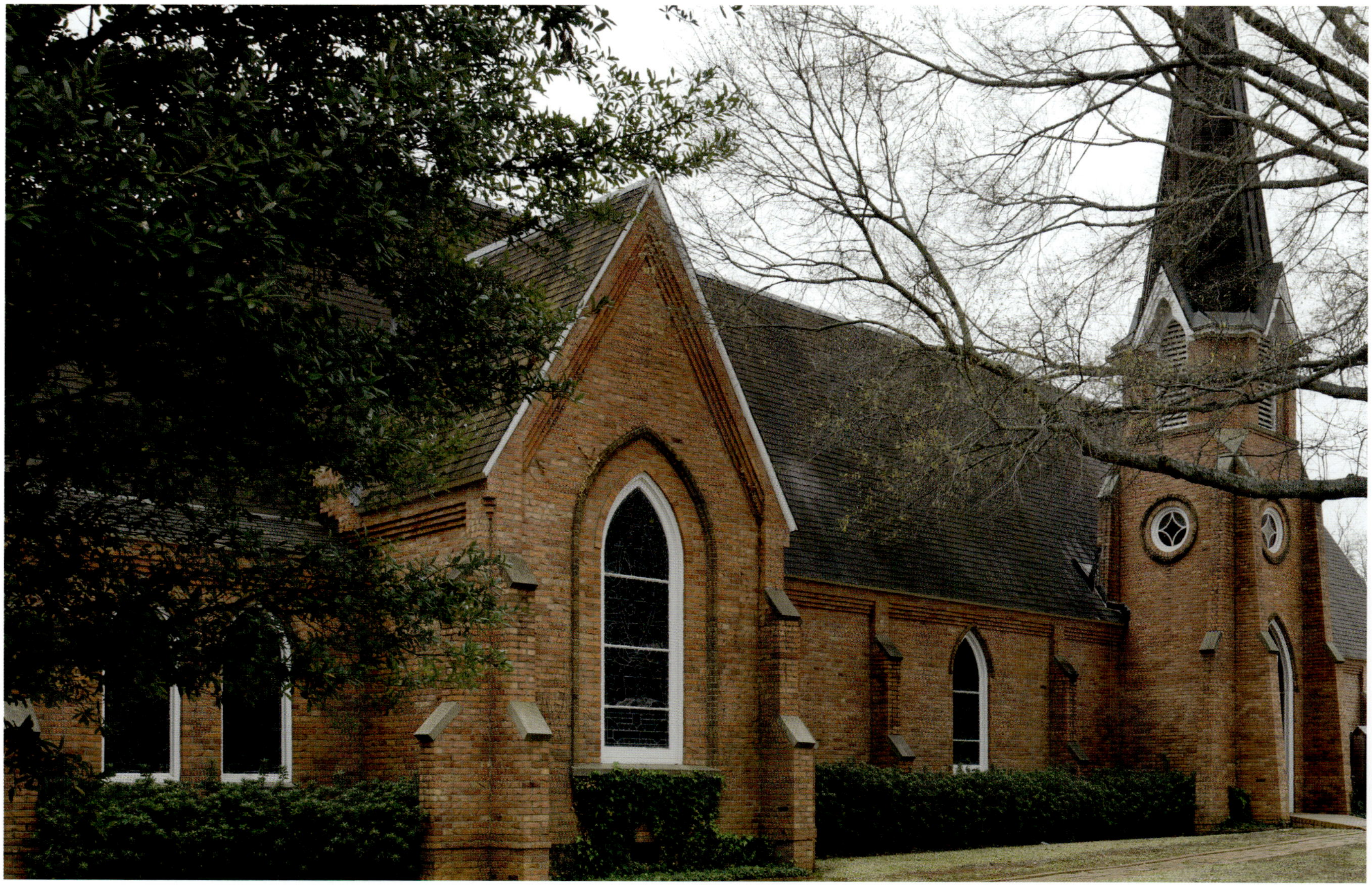

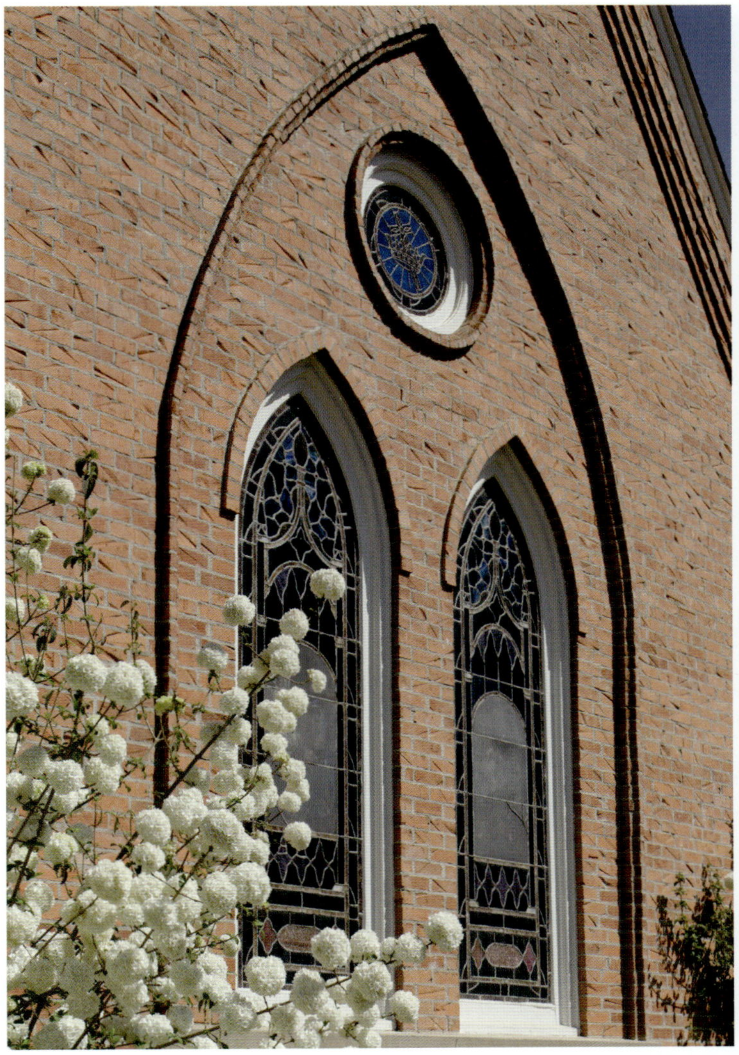

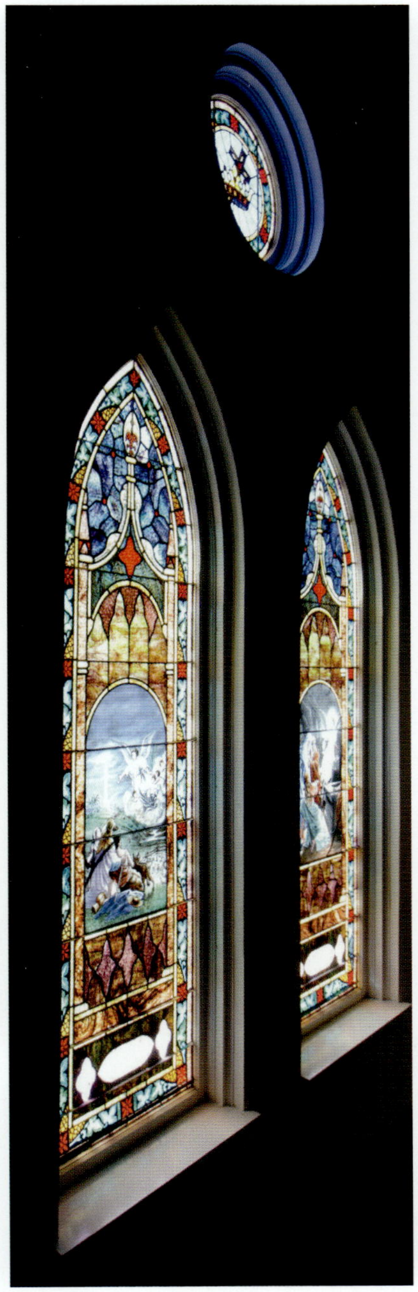

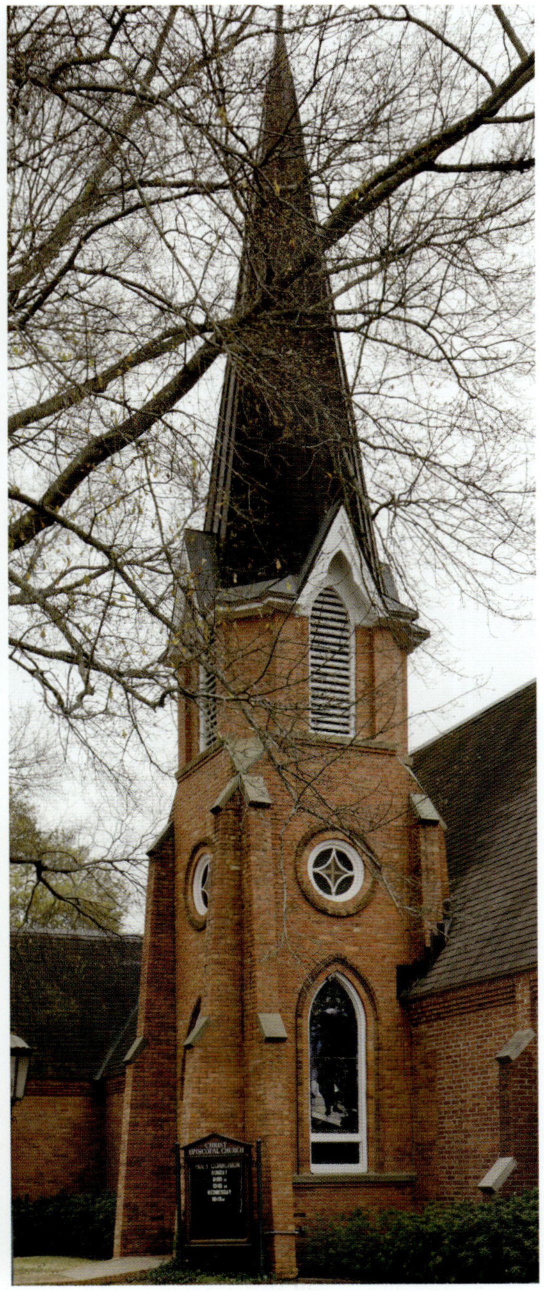

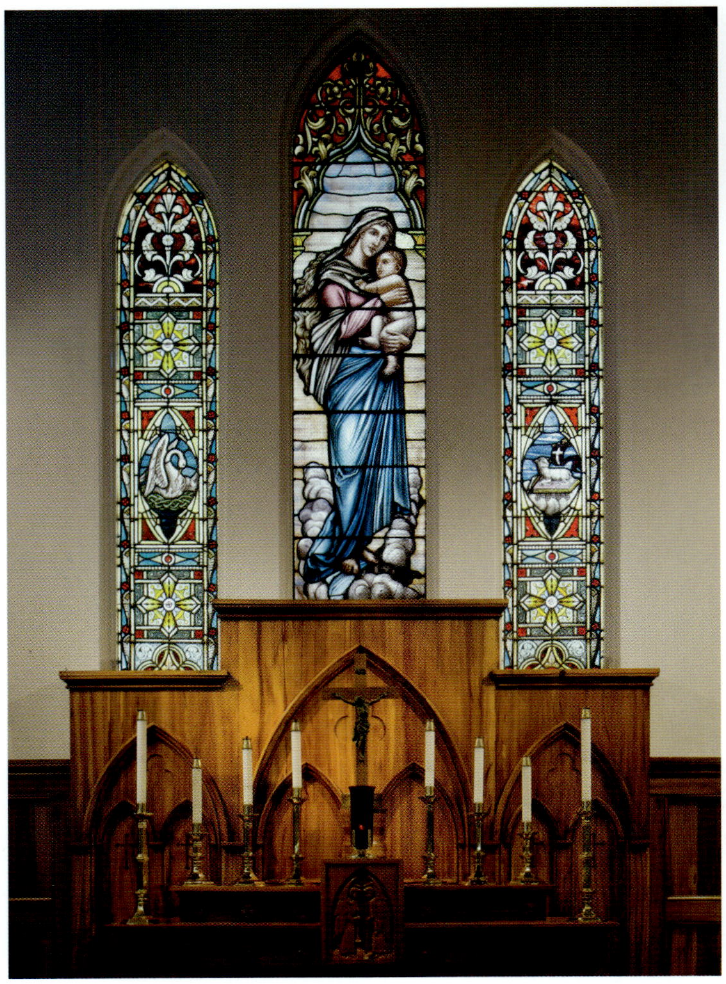

FIGURES 9.19. (Top Left) and 9.20. (Center) The Blount Memorial Windows.
E. A. Blount gave six windows to the church. The ones on the west wall (exterior, left), (interior, center), were in memory of his daughter Laura Blount Chapman, who died after childbirth.

FIGURE 9.21. (Top Right) The Tower, Christ Church.
The tower, influenced by examples in North Germany, originally stood on the south of the building.

FIGURE 9.22. (Left) Madonna and Child Window, Altar.
"Above the altar is a magnificent Madonna and Child flanked by two elaborately beautiful windows--one symbolizing Victory with the enthroned Lamb, and the other symbolizing Sacrifice with a pelican, God's only creature which will pierce its own body to feed its young." Information from Florence Patton.

The Main Street (Cumberland) Presbyterian Church (1901-1902)

The Main Street (Cumberland) Presbyterian Church, a second congregation of Presbyterians and the precursor to today's Westminster Presbyterian Church, organized in Nacogdoches on May 5, 1893. There were twelve founding members, and the founding pastor was Reverend B. A. Hodges. As was common in the day, the members met at first in private homes.[44] At one time, the Main Street Presbyterians considered locating their church on one of the corners of the Old University property on Washington Square; but they decided, after the Trustees announced the closing of the institution, that they preferred being on Main Street. The membership of the church was never large and only stood at fifty-three in 1907, according to the newspaper.[45]

In 1901, during the pastorate of the Reverend A. S. Blackwood, the membership purchased property from Dr. J. E. Mayfield at the southeast corner of Main Street and Mound Street.[46] They asked their neighbor in the next block, D. Rulfs, to design and build a building for them. The building, started after Rulfs completed the Christ Episcopal Church, was complete by July of 1902. The building sat in the middle of a fine lot with existing large trees; the *Galveston Daily News* called it "a charming site and a gem of an edifice."[47] As with the First Baptist Church, designed only a few years earlier, Rulfs used predominantly Gothic Revival architectural influences. Rulfs designed the Presbyterian building to reflect the small size of the congregation. The building was approximately one-half the size of the First Baptist Church: the eaves of this church were only fifteen feet above the foundation piers; its single tower was forty feet tall; and he downsized even the triptych Gothic window on the main façade. Having no lower floor and resting on standard brick piers, the Presbyterian Church needed only modest front steps. The cross-gable roof formed a Greek Cross. Each of the transepts had external doors, which greatly increased the flexibility of the building.

The façade had two entry porches. The main entry, the larger of the two, was beneath the tower—a pattern Rulfs used again in 1910 on the Methodist Church.[48] According to one puzzled interviewee, the congregation tended to enter through the tower entrance and exit through the east door.[49] The steeple on this Presbyterian Church tower is of North German design, inspired by the many churches Rulfs experienced in Oldenburg. The architect placed a similar one later on Zion Hill Baptist Church. (See Figures 9.49, 9.50, and 9.51).[50] The Main Street Presbyterian congregation worshiped in this building until the 1930s, when they moved to North Street.[51]

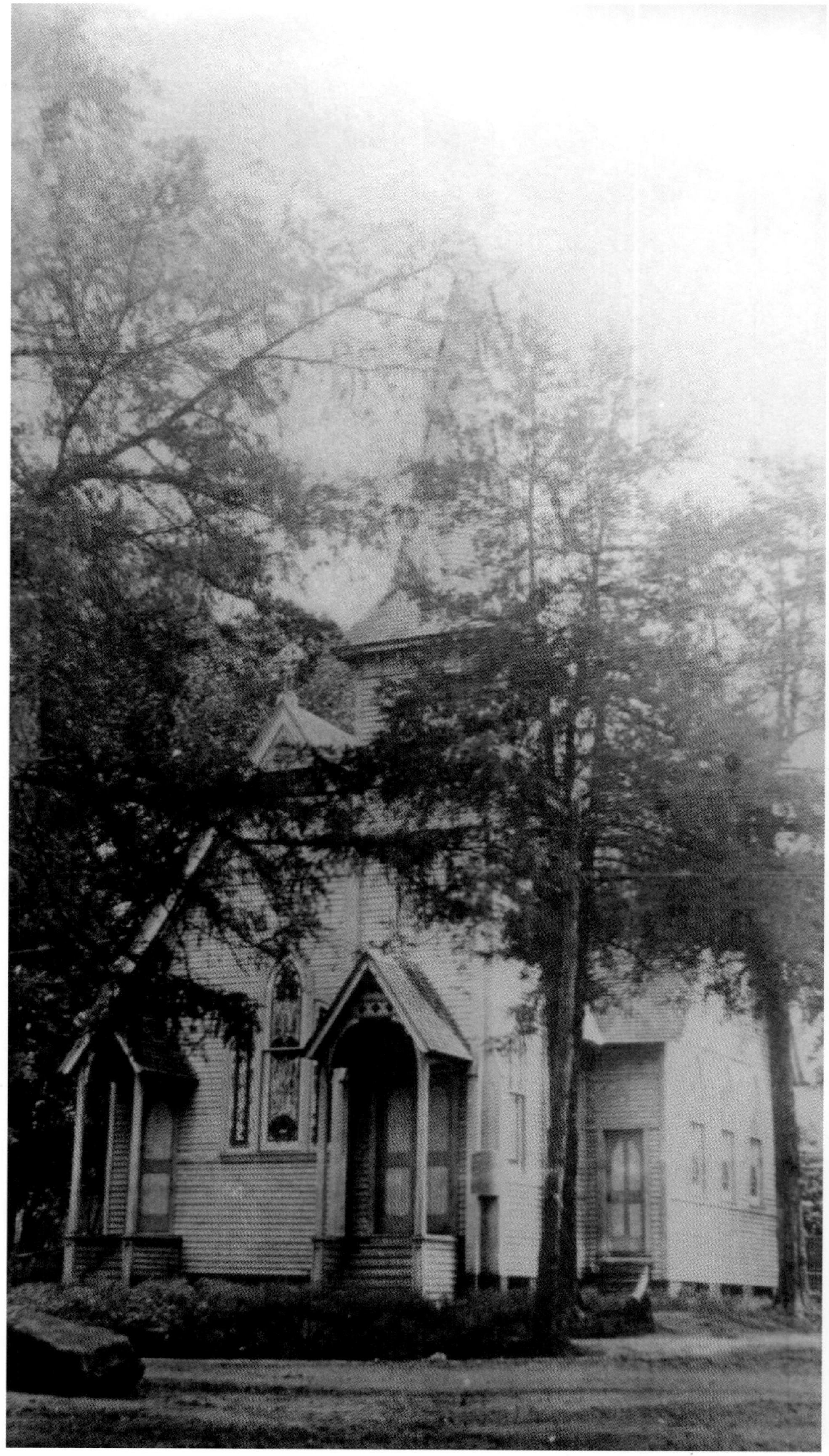

FIGURE 9.23. The Main Street Presbyterian Church.
The gable front façade of the church had two porches, a triptych window, and a tower. The tower, identical to the one Rulfs later used on the Zion Hill Baptist Church, was of North German design. Its four sides tapering into an octagon shape as it rose to the cross at the pentacle. The cross-gables, which extended from the east and west sides of the structure, gave the floor plan the shape of a Greek Cross.
Courtesy of ETRC.

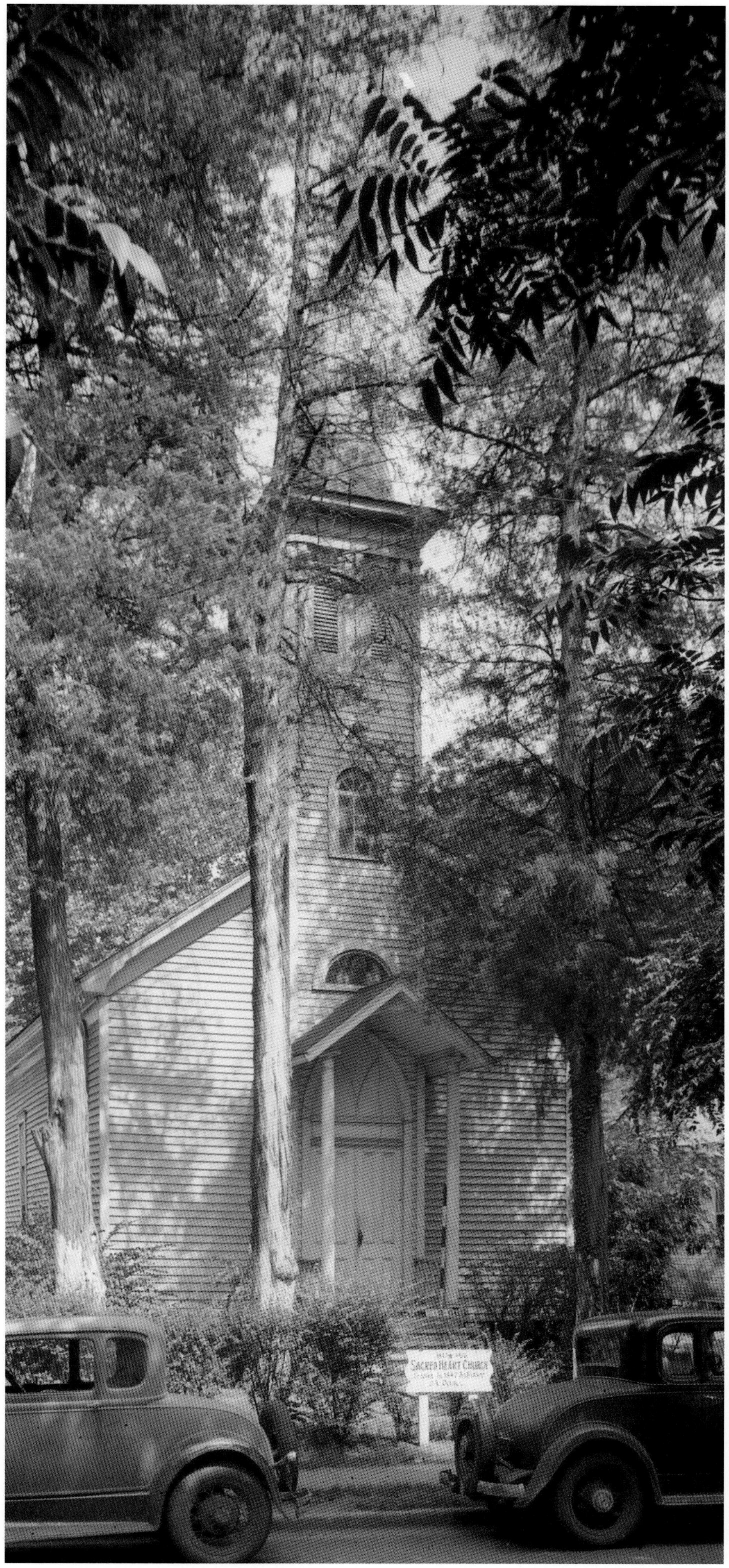

New Tower for Sacred Heart Catholic Church (c1905)

In discussing her uncle's work in Nacogdoches, Mrs. Mary Stewart Duncan related the story of the architect's vision for Nacogdoches as a town of spires.[52] One of the churches she named was the Sacred Heart Catholic Church. Rulfs probably completed the addition of a new steeple for their pioneer structure sometime around 1905, judging from his work schedule. Early Sanborn Insurance Maps, from 1885 to 1900, indicate a small roof-mounted belfry cupola on the mid-nineteenth century building, but the steeple as shown on the 1906 Sanborn Map is two-story.[53] A wonderful, high-resolution photograph, taken in 1933 by the Historic American Buildings Survey (HABS) of President F. D. Roosevelt's New Deal, allows the modern viewer to see the details of the tower up close.[54] The footprint of the church in 1906 indicates new additions to the rear of the sanctuary, too. It is possible that Rulfs oversaw a general remodeling at the same time.

The new entrance porch had slim Tuscan columns and a Gothic arch over the double entry doors. The tower included eclectic architectural elements, a mixture of classical and Gothic elements, at the time in use by Rulfs elsewhere in town. At the base of the tower, immediately above the porch, Rulfs placed a stained glass fanlight window to cast multi-colored light in the entrance foyer. Midway up the tower, there was a small arched window; and at the top, twin louvered panels denoted the bell chamber itself. Unlike the church building, which used older clapboard siding, the tower siding was the newer German or novelty-milled siding which he used on the Fannie Nelson House on East Main. Finally, to complete the 48-foot structure, Rulfs placed an octagon-sided North German steeple. The architect later mixed many of these same elements in the Methodist Church (1910) and Zion Hill Baptist Church (1914) towers. The architect's very slim, elegant tower for the Catholic Church, gave the small pioneer structure a renewed presence in Nacogdoches to rival the structures of larger congregations.

First Methodist Church (1910)

FIGURE 9.24. The Tower and Porch of the Sacred Heart Catholic Church in 1933.

This picture of the Catholic Church, taken by the Historic American Buildings Survey, gives a good view of the tower by Rulfs shortly before the tower was taken down and the building moved. Courtesy of Library of Congress.

"ANOTHER DISASTROUS FIRE," screamed the headline of the *Daily Sentinel* on August 16, 1907. This time, the casualty was Rulfs's wooden sanctuary for the First Methodist Church (1887 sanctuary-1891 tower). The newspaper pinpointed the fire's origin to the kitchen of the G. D. Boger residence next door; it quickly engulfed the church, another residence, and a nearby gunsmith shop. According to the reporter, "The Methodist church was somewhat aged and not in very good repair, hence its value is hard to estimate. It is a total loss and was not insured. Immediately east of the church was the Methodist parsonage, and for a time it seemed that it would be burned, but heroic work saved it."[55] The 1902 parsonage continued in be used as a parsonage and afterwards as Sunday school rooms until the 1950s; in the 1930s the parsonage moved to the Haselwood House on Mound Street. Immediately after the 1907 fire, the congregation began to plan a new sanctuary. This time they wanted a brick structure. The membership of the Church stood at 500. The Reverend J. W. Mills was the minister of the church in Nacogdoches, and, under his leadership, the congregation appointed a building committee under the chairmanship of George F. Ingraham. When the Boger family decided to move, the church purchased their homestead to the west to enlarge their building site. During the three-year planning and building process, the congregation, interestingly, met nearby in other buildings designed and built by Rulfs: in the First Baptist and Cumberland Presbyterian Churches, in the Ingraham Building downtown, and in the Old Opera House.[56] It was not until July 1909 that the congregation assembled for a groundbreaking ceremony. The new building was to cost "$15,000."[57] The church laid its cornerstone on June 30, 1910, and opened in the late fall.[58]

In planning in 1907, the Nacogdoches Methodists decided they needed a unified learning system and a church building to accommodate this. Methodists, historically, were at the forefront of the movement to educate children through the use of Sunday Schools. To integrate the instructional goals and worship, the First Methodist Church in Akron, Ohio, introduced a new style of architecture, which wed the old concept of the one-room schoolhouse to a modern sanctuary for worship. Perhaps little known today, this "Akron Style" surrounded the sanctuary with individual classrooms. Functionally, the style was extremely flexible because, by opening or closing folding or sliding doors, the education space became part of the central worship space. While many denominations adapted the architectural concept, the style was most prominent in New York and the mid-west in the period between 1870 and the First World War.[59]

Oftentimes, the Akron-style buildings in the mid-west were Romanesque Revival, sometimes Byzantine Revival, with heavy stone exteriors, rounded arches, central rotundas or domes, and dark interiors with mosaics.[60] Each of the architects who submitted plans had the Akron guidelines. The church archive fails to document how many plans they considered, but one set of drawing does exist from a Dallas architect. The drawings show a Beaux Arts-inspired design, with a dome, huge columns with composite capitals, and elaborate interior decorations. The committee, evidently, considered the plan pretentious or too ornate or inflexible. While Rulfs enjoyed the local advantage—he had worked with many of the Methodist leaders who, like the committee chairman, George Ingraham, lived in houses designed by him—it was the modest, straightforward, almost severe lines of his interpretation of the Akron principles which appealed to the committee. Rulfs disliked ornate interior ornamentations and avoided these in all his churches in Nacogdoches, apart from the use of stained glass windows.

Rulfs used elements very common in northern Europe at the time. The main façade consisted of a red brick stepped gable, the focal point of which was a large stained-glass window. To symbolize the Trinity, Rulfs utilized the number three throughout the structure. For instance, there were three stepped gables on the building: the largest on the south entrance façade, and smaller ones on the east and west sides. There were three porches: the large congregational entry at the base of the tower on the southeast, with smaller porches positioned at the southwest and northeast corners of the building. There were three small rectangular windows at the apex of the stepped gables, a Palladian arrangement Rulfs used frequently. There were three distinct banks of pews in the interior. There were three divisions of the bell tower. To keep the building visually grounded, Rulfs introduced a number of solid horizontal lines. On the façades he used cut stone banding at the floor and ceiling levels to give one's eye an element to establish relativity. (He had suggested this same treatment in brick for the Christ Episcopal Church, but the Vestry rejected it.) Even the tower had strong horizontal breaks.

The interior seating, arranged in a semi-circle, was not unlike what Rulfs had used for the auditorium of the First Baptist Church. Unlike

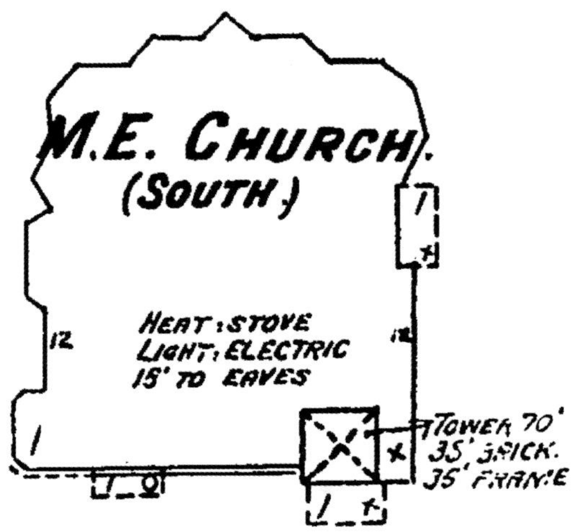

FIGURE 9.25.
(Left) First Episcopal Methodist Church, 1912.
The footprint of the Methodist Church as shown shortly after its completion on the 1912 Sanborn Map.

FIGURE 9.26. (Opposite) The First United Methodist Church (Rulfs, 1909-1910).
As his main design feature, Rulfs used large North German stepped gables on the main façade and smaller ones on the east and west. The focal point of the wall was a large stained glass arched window with a hoodmold of cut stone. At the apex of the gable, the architect placed a grouping of three windows in a Palladian arrangement, a signature he used in many of his buildings in Nacogdoches. He outlined the steps with cut stone and placed another belt course of stone at the floor level of the building. The red brick came from Garrison. The gables, which projected above the roofline, hid the complicated hip-and-gable roof. As he did throughout Nacogdoches, Rulfs placed an impressive tower on the building. It stood seventy feet tall: the first thirty-five feet were brick and the second thirty five, frame. On the frame portion, the tower featured arched windows on two levels. The upper window mirrored the design of the windows on his home church in Stollhamm, Germany, with the added feature of a hoodmold. Photograph, Methodist Church Archives.

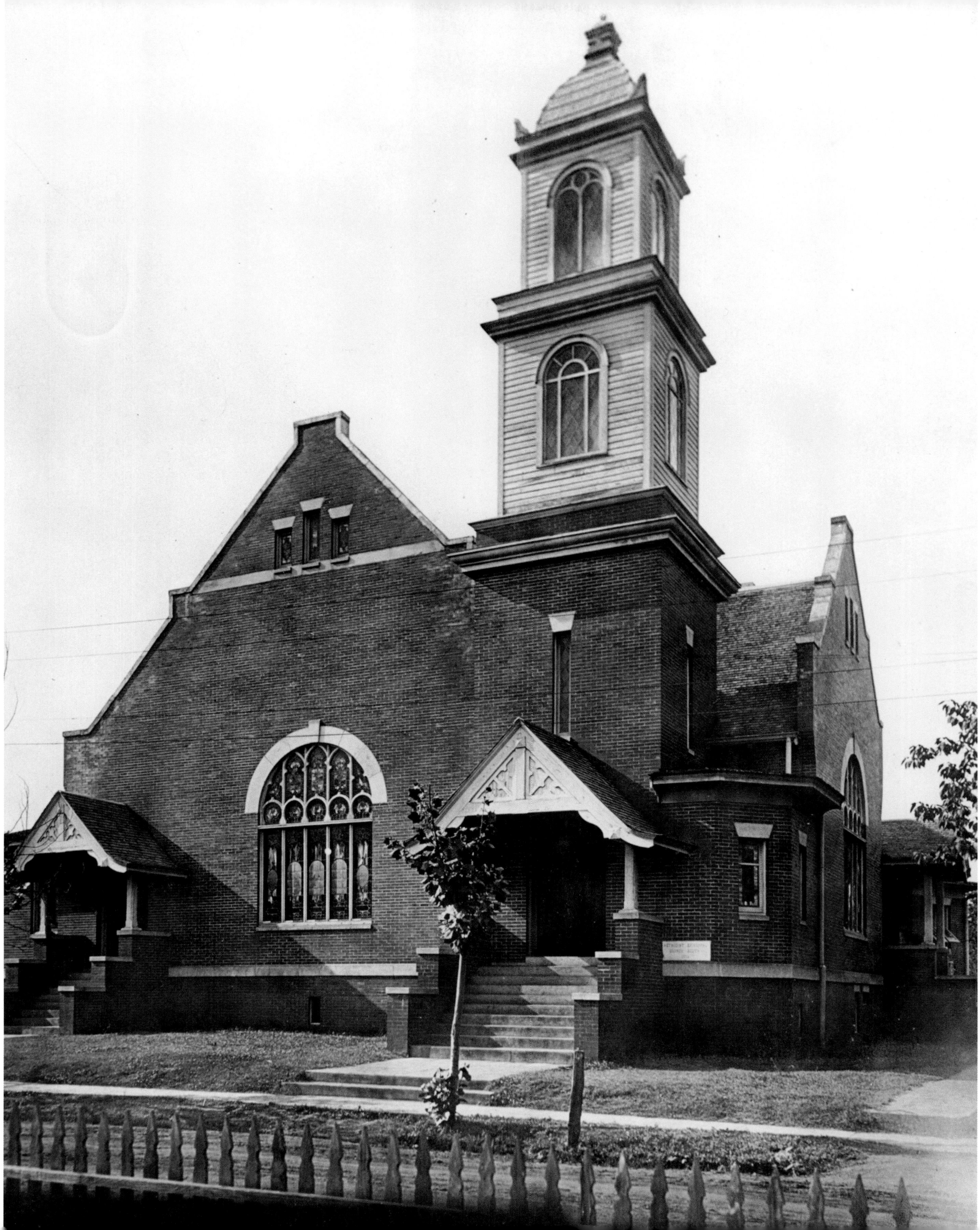

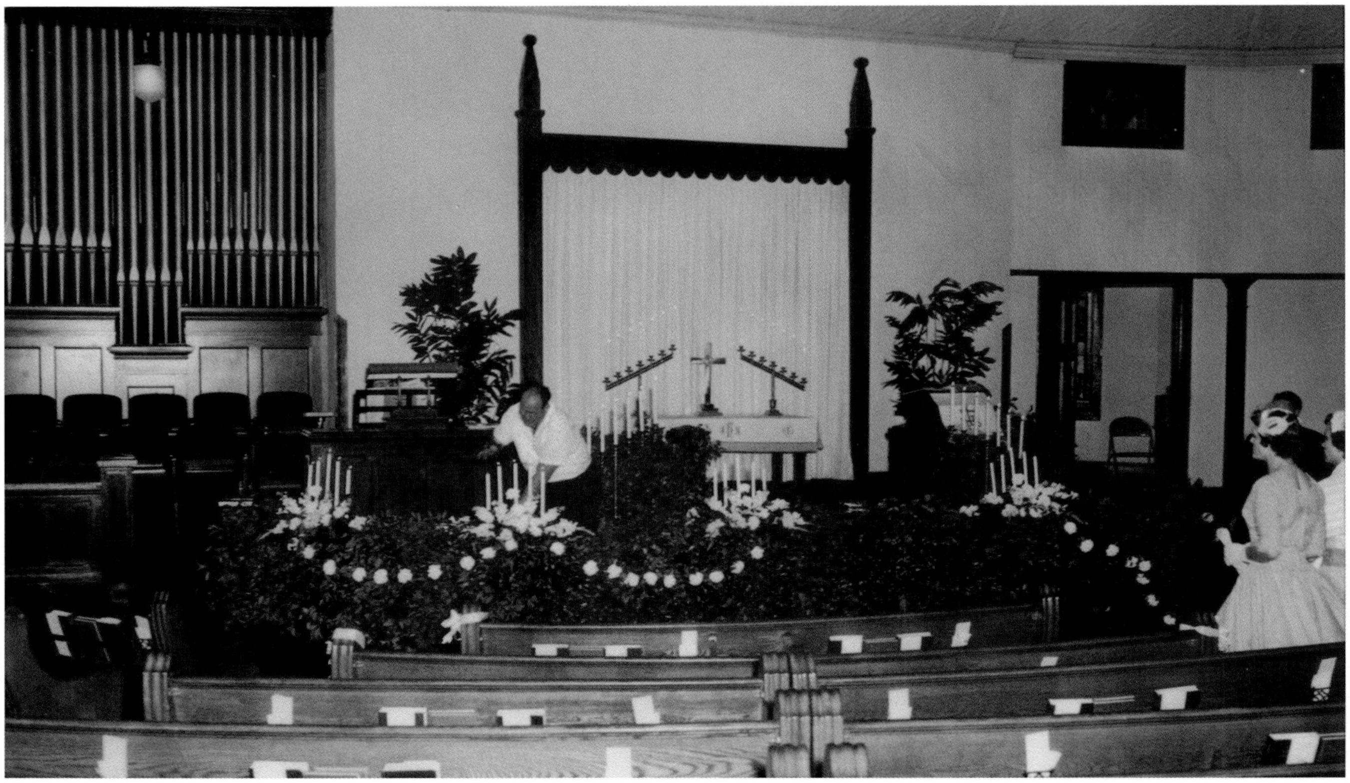

FIGURES 9.27 and 9.28. Interiors, First Methodist Church, 1930s.

(Left) The sanctuary is being prepared for a wedding in the photograph left. At the right of the photograph, one can see one of the north classrooms that opened into the sanctuary. (Below) In normal services, the drape behind the altar was deep red. Photographs from the Methodist Church Archives.

the latter, however, Rulfs graduated the floor of the Methodist sanctuary, thereby giving everyone a good view of the preacher. The classrooms of the building, according to the Akron formula, surrounded the sanctuary on the north side and could be opened into the sanctuary for educational purposes or to increase seating. Rulfs liked the concept so much that he used the "Akron Style" in his design for the African-American congregation at Zion Hill Baptist Church (1914). While the altars in traditional European arrangements were always to the east, in both the Methodist and Zion Hill churches, the altars and the pulpits were on the west walls. In both churches, as in the earlier First Baptist Church, Rulfs made accommodations for a fellowship hall with kitchen beneath the sanctuary. In these churches, the vertical panels of the windows were functional; they pivoted to encourage cross ventilation.[61]

The impressive tower Rulfs placed on the Methodist building stood on the southeast corner of the building. The first thirty-five feet were brick, and the second thirty-five feet were frame.[62] On the frame portion, the tower featured arched windows on two levels. The upper window mirrored the design of the windows on his home church in Stollhamm, Germany, with the added feature of a hood mold.

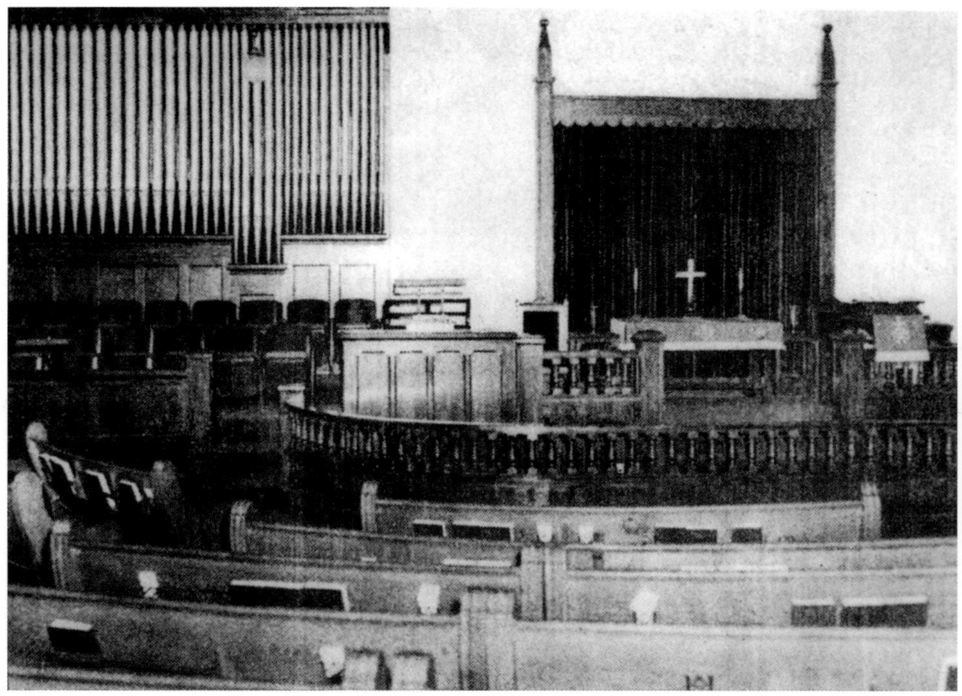

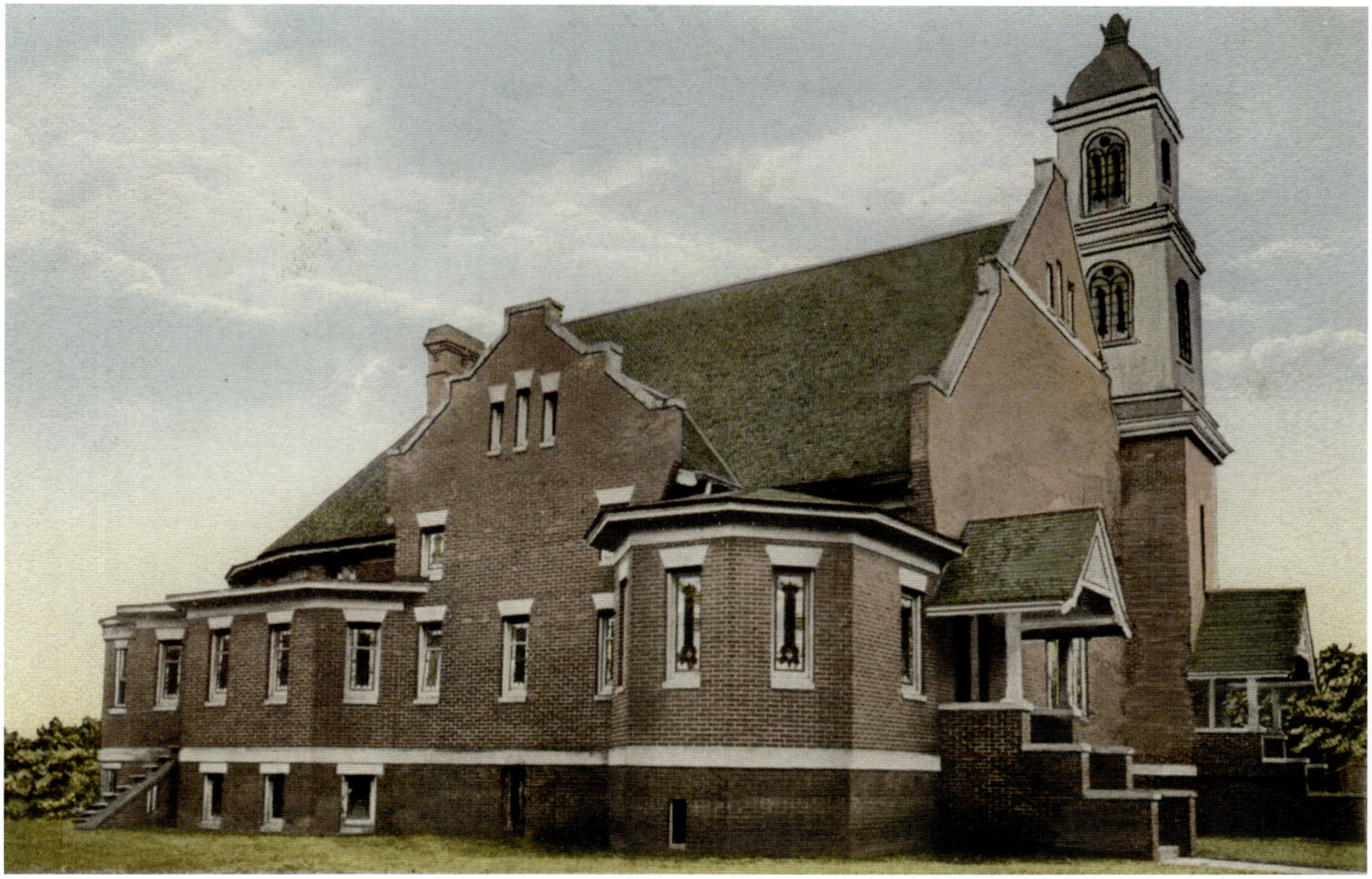

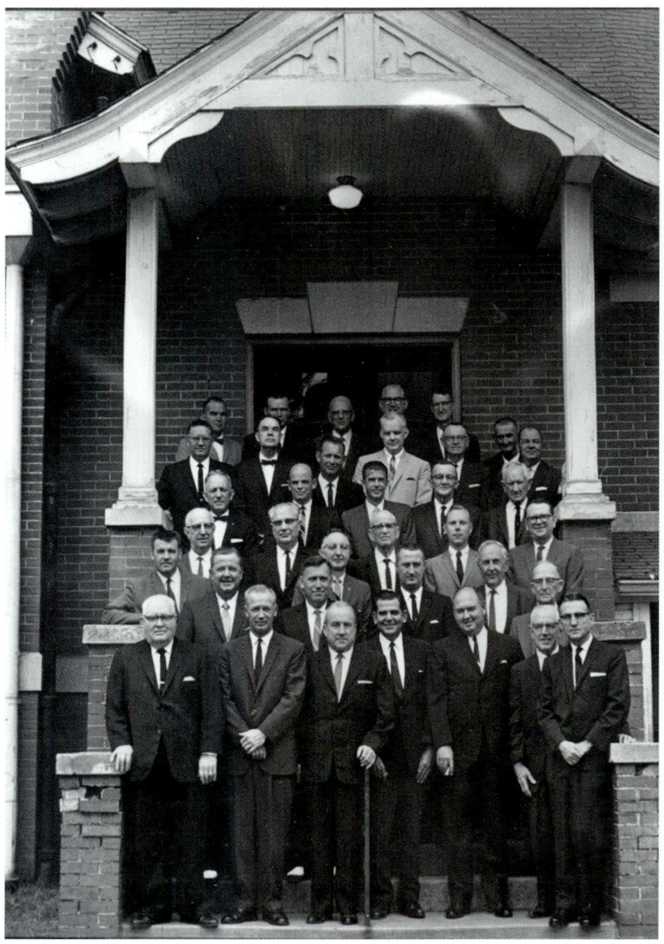

FIGURE 9.29. West Side of the 1910 Methodist Church.

This colorized postcard gives the only view available of the complicated west and north sides of this Akron style building. The classroom, which surrounded the north side of the building, could be opened into the sanctuary. The small porch on the front led directly into the choir room. Image compliments of Cecil Sparks.

FIGURE 9.30. (Left) The Business Men's Bible Class

The Business Men's Bible Class, who met in the basement of the church, are pictured here on the east porch entry to the sanctuary.

FIGURE 9.31. (Below) The 1910 Church Without Its Tower.

During the Depression, when a storm damaged the frame portion of the tower, the church decided not to replace it. Compliments of Cecil Sparks.

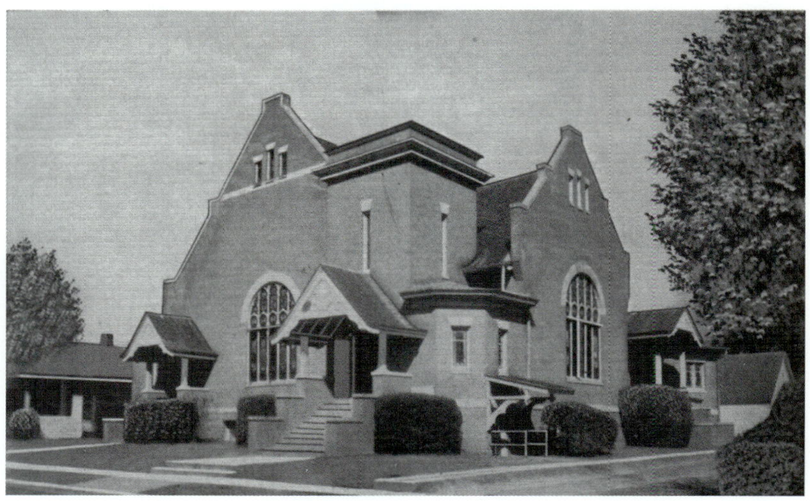

Windows from the 1910 Methodist Church by D. Rulfs

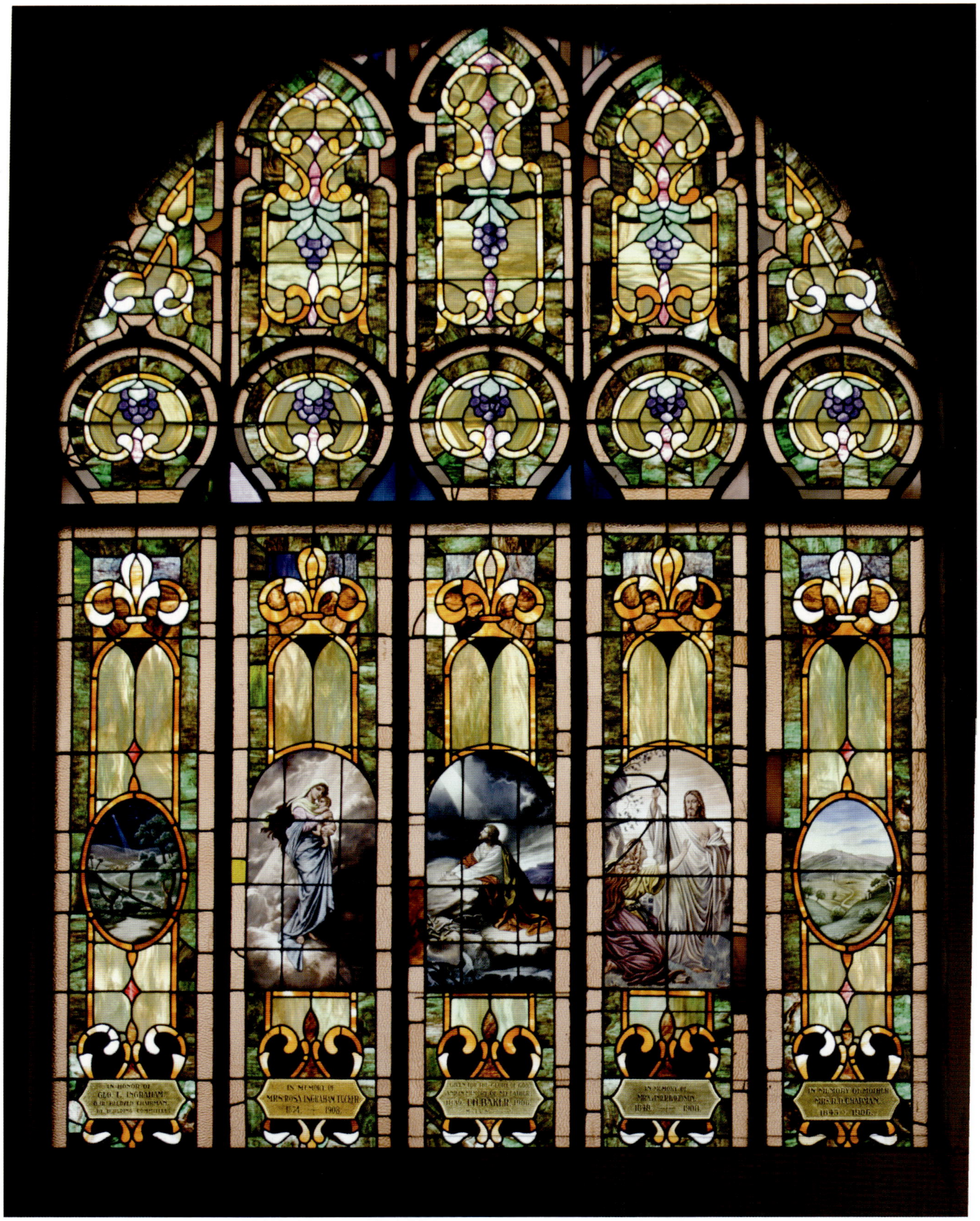

FIGURES 9.32. (Left) South Stained Glass Window, 1910.

The window on the south façade still faces Hospital Street from the tower room off the present sanctuary. From left to right, the panel dedications read: 1) "In Honor of Geo. F. Ingraham, Our Beloved Chairman, by Building Committee;" 2) "In Memory of Mrs. Rosa Ingraham Tucker, 1874-1908 (Ingraham's Daughter);" 3) "Given in Memory of My Father, T. H Baker, 1839-1906, Mrs. I. L. Sturdevant;" 4) "In Memory of Mrs. Jho. P. Davidson, 1848-1908; 5) "In Memory of Mother, Mrs. R. D. Chapman, 1845-1906."

FIGURE 9.33. (Across) Resurrection Window from the First United Methodist Church, 1910.

When the Methodist congregation replaced the 1910 Rulfs church in the late 1960s, they saved the large stained-glass windows which were the focal points of the south and east façades. These windows today are part of the history room in the new tower. The window across graced the east façade. The center panel, given in memory of Mrs. J. T. Hoya, has the dates of her life on either side, (1821-1874); the left side panel was dedicated to Holt Davis (1908-1963); and right to H. Jack Mathews (1897-1950).

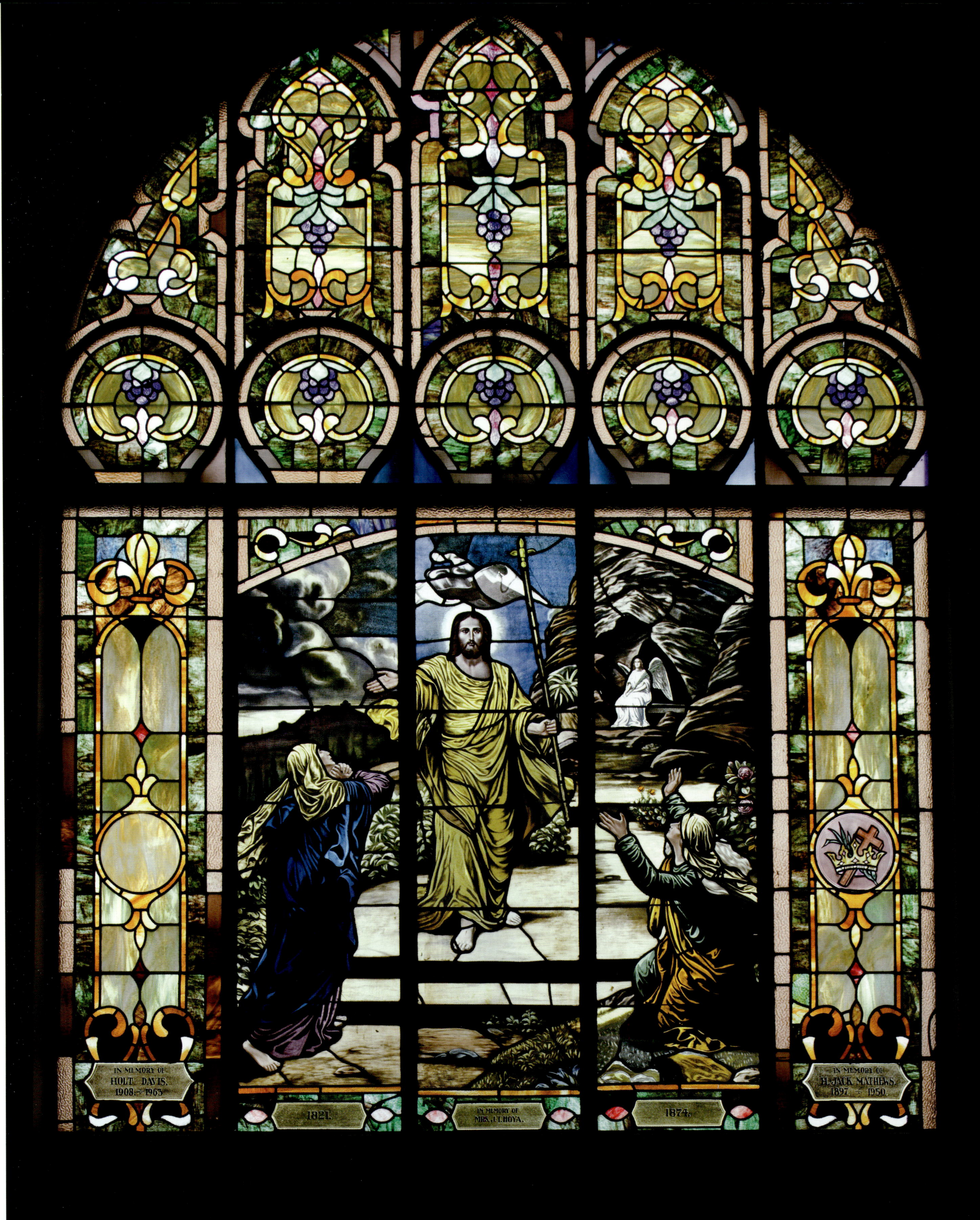

IN MEMORY OF
HOLT DAVIS.
1908 – 1963
1821.
IN MEMORY OF
MRS. J. T. HOYA.
1874.
IN MEMORY OF
H. JACK MATHEWS.
1897 – 1950.

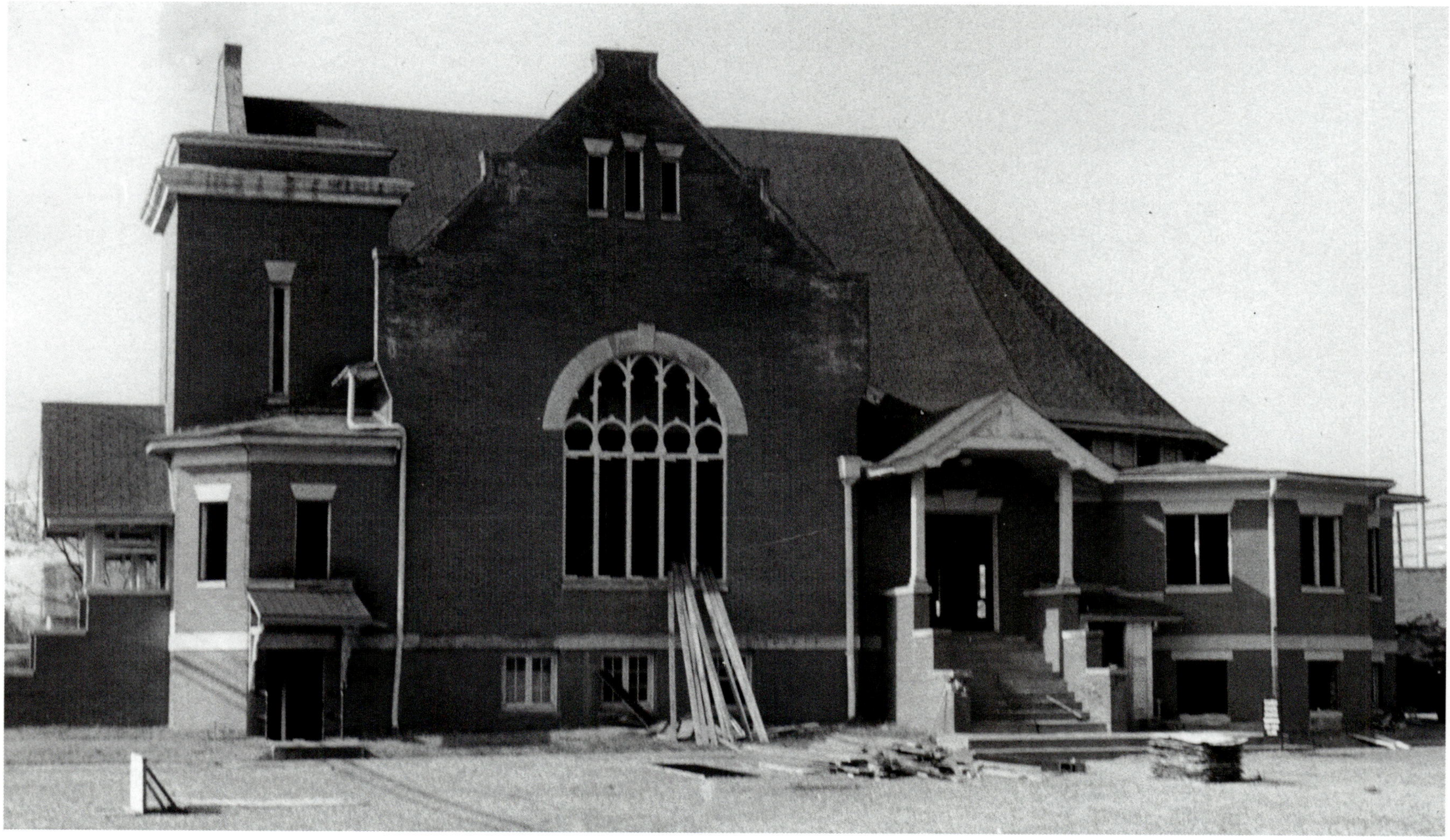

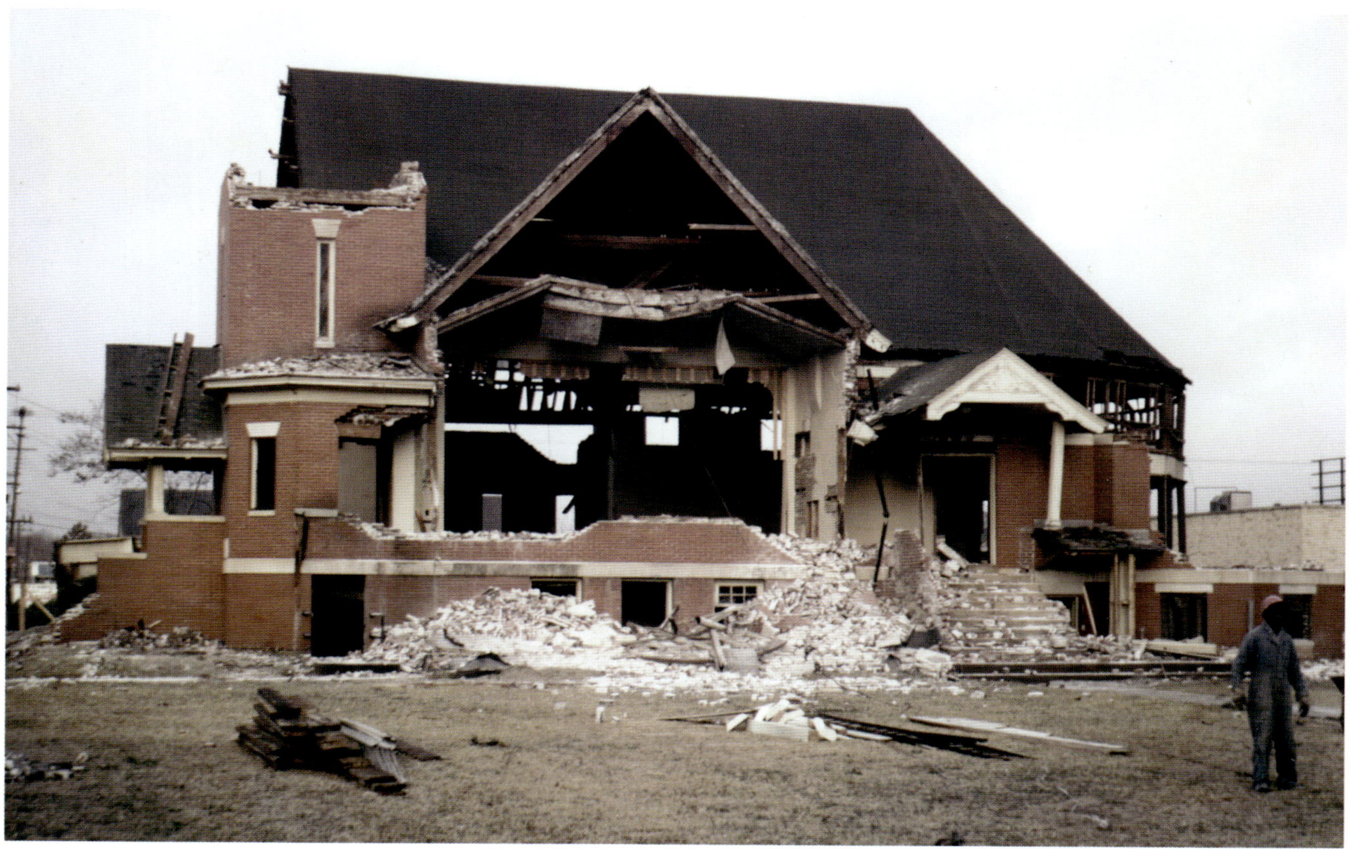

FIGURES 9.34 and 9.35.
The Demolition of the 1910 Methodist Building in 1967.

The early stages above, the later stages below, tell the story of the destruction of the building. As the destruction progressed, the attachment of the congregation to the old building led the building committee to make the decision to salvage enough of the brick to line the interior of the new sanctuary. Photographs courtesy of Campbell Cox, whose son Marcus was the last child to be baptized in the 1910 sanctuary.

The Zion Hill Baptist Church

Zion Hill First Baptist Church (1914)

The only church designed by Rulfs to survive on its original site is the Zion Hill Baptist Church. Built for an African-American congregation, Zion Hill is one of the architect's most interesting works. The Texas Historical Commission has designated an entire National Registry district around the structure.

In its nomination for National Registry status (1992), the Historical Commission wrote: "The Zion Hill Baptist Church, at the intersection of Bois d'Arc and Lanana streets, is the only nonresidential building in the district. It differs in scale and level of craftsmanship and architectural sophistication from the modest residential buildings in the district."[63] The 1976 application for the building's designation as a Recorded Texas Historic Landmark gave a history of the founding of the congregation and the immediate background of the Rulfs building.

> Alwyn Barr has written: 'Black congregations [in Texas] generally remained small with poor buildings and severe financial problems. . . .' This was not true of the Zion Hill Baptists in Nacogdoches. By the 1890s, the Zion Hill congregation needed a larger building. They built their second building, described by one of Rev. Reed's descendants as "a plain, square church," on the original site of the brush arbor meetings, that is on the west side of the 500 block of Logansport Street. While it is true that expansion of the white residential area from Washington Square into Logansport Street brought pressure on the blacks to abandon this second structure, this is only part of the picture. By 1914, the membership of the church had already outgrown its second structure. Furthermore, the importance and the solvency of the Zion Hill congregation was recognized by the white community. Both sides worked out an attractive alternative.[64]

D. K. Cason and Charles Hoya, two of the leading business leaders of Nacogdoches, became interested in the Logansport Road area and began purchasing land along the old roadway. Cason, for instance, bought a lot in 1910 and began planning a new homestead.[65] The presence of the Zion Hill Baptist Church presented a stumbling block. John Schmidt stepped in to suggest a solution. Schmidt, the second largest stockholder and vice president of Cason, Monk & Company, also had an interest in the Zion Hill congregation. Charlie Clay, a leading member of the Zion Hill group, was Schmidt's trusted employee at the Nacogdoches Wholesale Grocery Company. Clay, by all accounts, kept the lucrative grocery business running. Schmidt, therefore, recognized the importance and the solvency of the Zion Hill congregation. Under the very creative compromise for the period, Schmidt agreed to sell and finance the land on which Clay was already living for a new church building. Schmidt offered to underwrite the financial burden of a new sanctuary and, offered the services of his architect, D. Rulfs. Clay became the leading figure on the building committee.

On March 16, 1914, the Trustees of the Church purchased the four acres of land on Lanana Street from Mayer & Schmidt.[66] Schmidt financed the land ($2,500) and the building ($7,223) without a down payment. Rulfs supplied the ideas and plans. His company, under the leadership of William Henry Rulfs, supplied the construction expertise. The building committee, named on the side of the cornerstone, included Charlie Clay, Sr., Rich McBroom, Jeff Powers, R. Horace Scott, and John Townsend. The cornerstone of the Zion Hill First Baptist Church building reads: "Erected in 1914. J. C. Sweeney, Pastor." Although nothing is known about the pas-tor, whose name appears on the cornerstone, one can easily trace the other members of the building committee and the continuing influence of their descendants in the Zion Hill congregation to the present time. Reverend Lawson Reed, without a doubt the driving force in the congregation in 1914, had given up the pastorate but had continued his membership de-spite his work with the Sabine Valley Association of the Missionary Baptist Church. Reed was one of the greatest organizers of his day and has been credited with the founding of 55 Baptist churches in the East Texas area and with the conversion of over 300 candidates.[67] Rulfs also designed the home for Reed's family, where his grandson Clarence (Bo) McMichael lives.

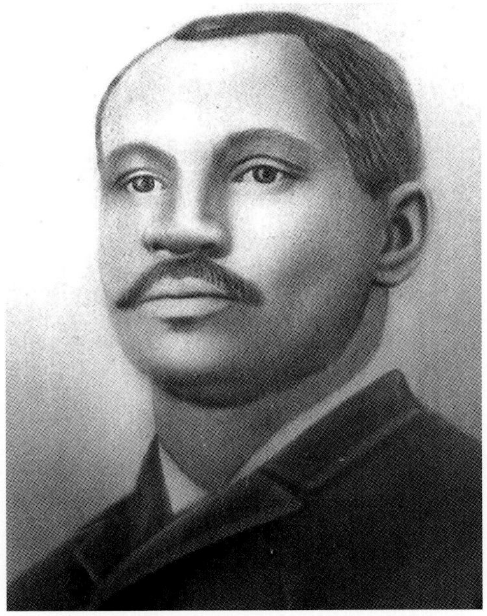

FIGURE 9.36. Reverend Lawson Reed, founder of the Zion Hill Baptist Church. Church Archives.

Recently, questions have arisen concerning the Clay House, which stands on Bois d'Arc Street east of the Zion Hill Church.[68] The question of whether the house was used as a parsonage is interesting and relevant to the sanctuary next door, but, in reality, the house, built sometime after John Schmidt bought the property in 1901, predates the church.[69] In the author's opinion, Rulfs built the Charlie Clay House around 1904-1906. It and the Reed home are the only private structures in the area to possess any architectural finesse.[70] The house's original porch, which has since been removed, faced east and was not oriented toward the later church. The Charlie Clay family was already living there by the time of the 1910 U.S. Census.[71] Schmidt was the patron of both Clay and Rulfs. The latter was not only on retainer to Schmidt for all kinds of architectural services, but he also worked with Clay on a number of projects: the Wholesale Grocery

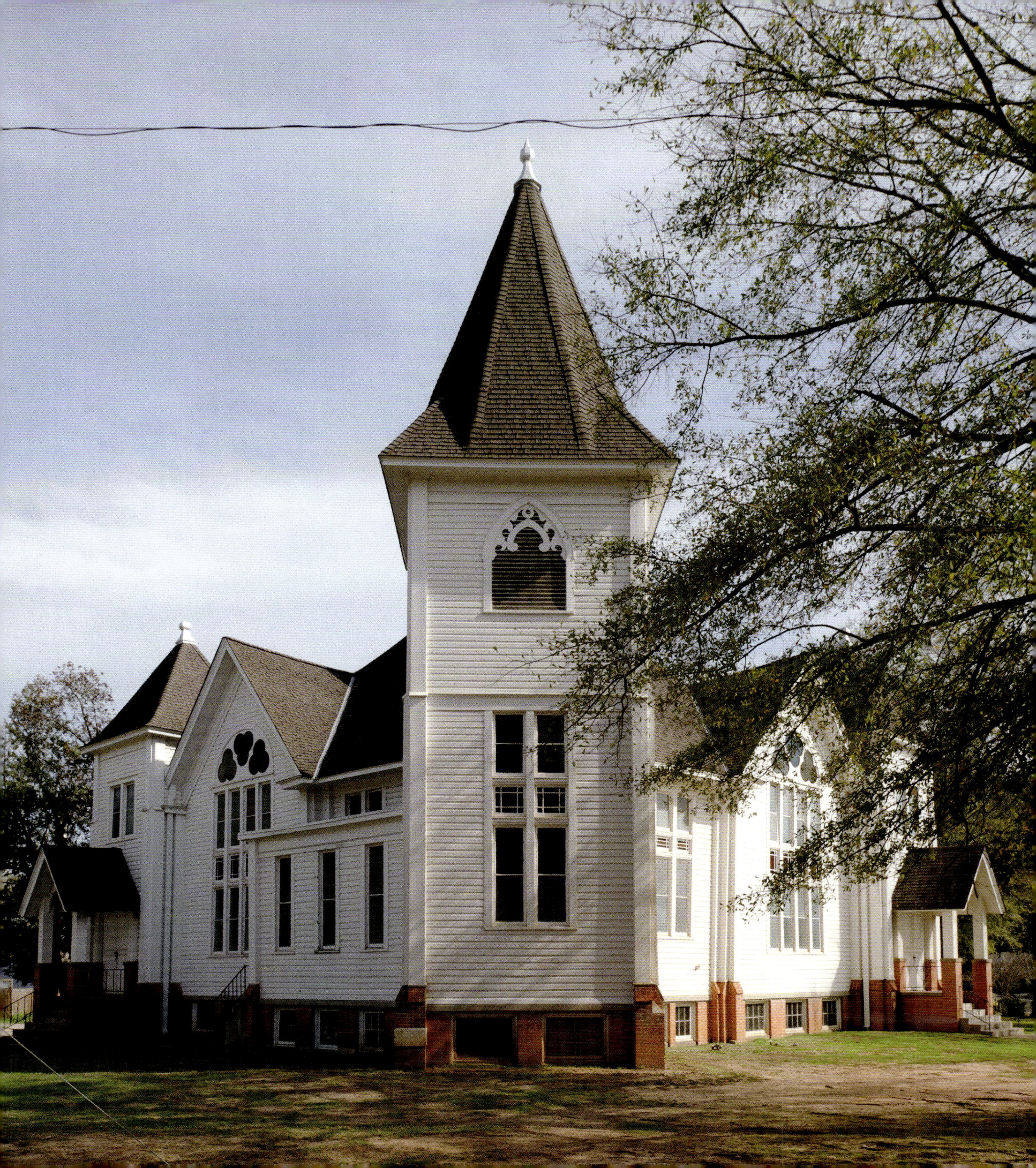

Company, where Clay worked; East End School in 1904, where the Clay children went to school; and, finally, the Zion Hill Church, where the Clays worshipped. Although Rulfs would have undertaken anything asked by Schmidt, Rulfs would not have felt any reservations about aiding in a house for Clay. The architect had many trusted African-American employees of his own; he also worked closely with the African-American community when he designed and built the public school on Shawnee in 1904. Rulfs had drawn many small houses in the 1880s and 1890s, and he would have found the assignment easy to perform. According to Sharon Rulfs Kerr, the architect's great-granddaughter, Rulfs continued to work closely with African-Americans in Nacogdoches for many years. Kerr recounts how her father went with his grandfather to a working meeting where D. Rulfs drew up plans to help the African-American community to rebuild their private houses after one of the periodic floods damaged many homes in the Shawnee Street area. D. Rulfs "drew out a plan for revitalizing the area," and "many of the church deacons and members furnished sweat labor to complete the project."[72] According to Birdie Wade, a long-time leader in the African-American community, Rulfs "did not want credit for his efforts. He was one of the few who was fair to the Black Community and did not take advantage of them as others."[73]

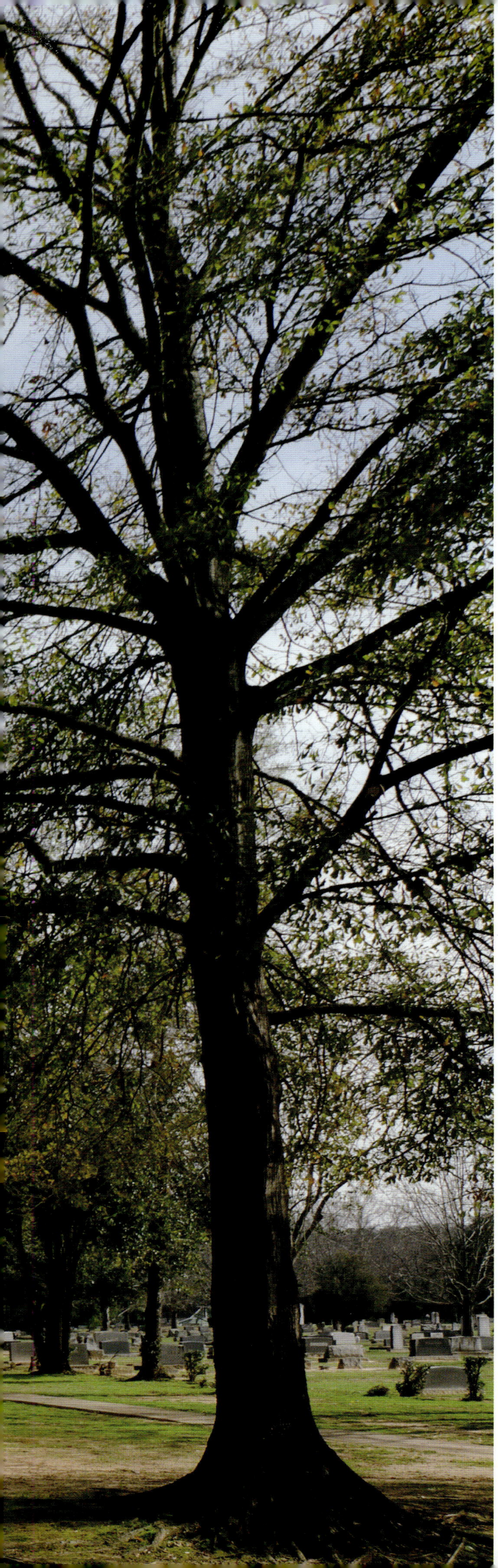

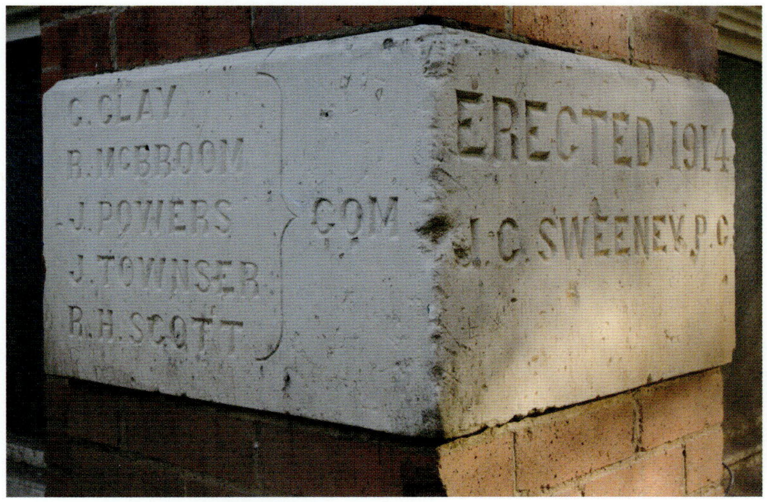

FIGURE 9.37. (Right) The Corner Stone, Zion Hill Church.

The cornerstone of the Zion Hill First Baptist Church building reads: "Erected in 1914. J. C. Sweeney, Pastor." The building committee, named on the side of the cornerstone, included Charlie Clay, Sr., Rich McBroom, Jeff Powers, R. Horace Scott, and John Townser.

FIGURE 9.38. (Left) The Lanana Street Elevation, Zion Hill.

This view, now rarely seen because of the trees, is the view Rulfs would have envisioned when he designed the church. The tower is front and center facing Lanana Street, named Bois d'Arc at the time.

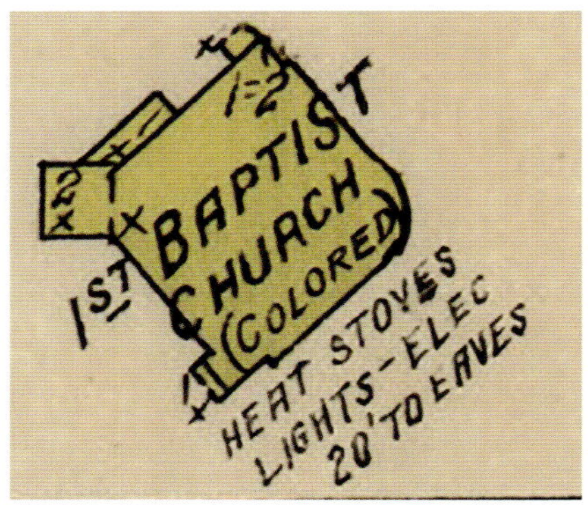

FIGURE 9.39. (Bottom Right) The Sanborn Map of 1922.

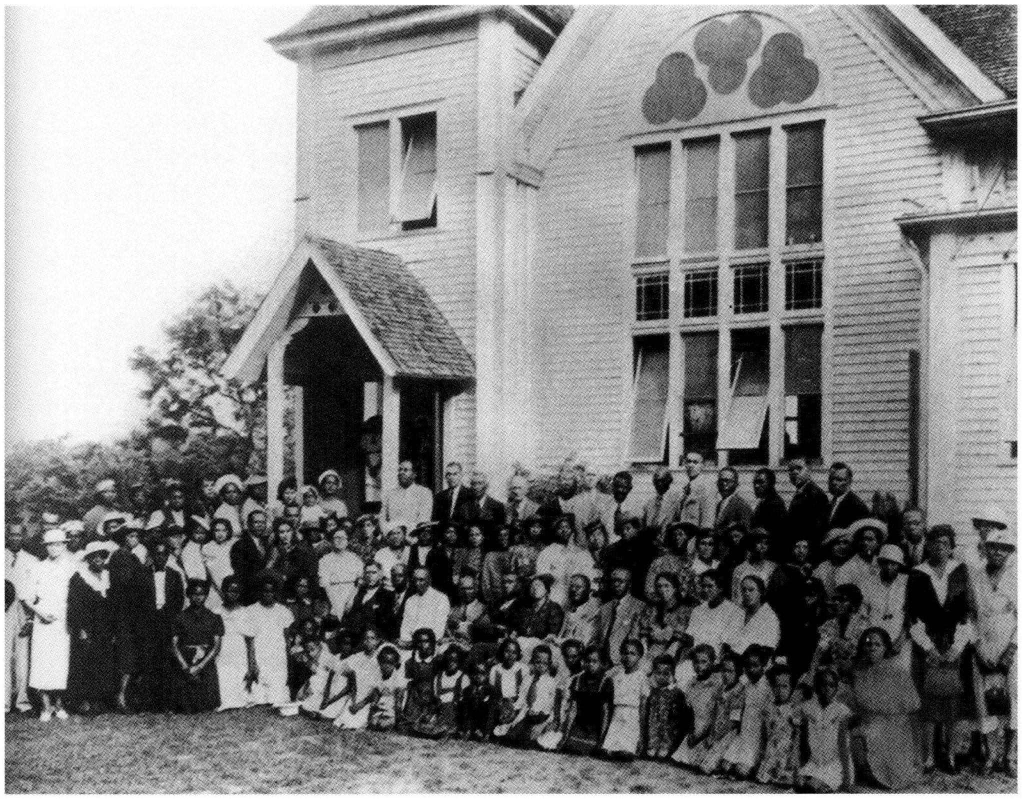

FIGURE 9.40. (Left) Zion Hill Congregation, ca. 1920.
This photograph, compliments of Eddie Orum, is displayed in the church foyer. Church Archives.

FIGURE 9.41. (Across) South Elevation,

Architectural Features of Zion Hill Baptist Church

In discussing the architectural features of Zion Hill Church, the application for Texas Landmark status in 1976 observed:

> The Zion Hill building . . . . is a harmonious blend of Gothic and Victorian elements. The Gothic elements can be seen in the west tower with its pointed belfry vents and shingled spire, the windows on the east side, and the trefoil or "clover" designed lights over the windows on the northwest and southwest fronts. The Victorian elements can be seen in the building's overall opera house shape and occasional lack of symmetry, in the octagonal lantern (dome), which rests on the roof over the sanctuary, and in the irregular placement of passages and shape of the balconies inside.
>
> Rulfs' design is extremely versatile as well as aesthetically pleasing. There are two main entrances under porch-towers at the northwest and southwest corners. Inside are small antechambers with steps ascending to the sanctuary and balconies and descending to the social hall below. Wrapping around the whole east side of the main floor, from the northwest entrance to the southwest entrance, is an enormous vestibule that can be either separated or included in the sanctuary by closing the folding doors. (These doors are original to the building; they were horizontal-panels, hinged together to fold back against the wall.) This built-in system of partitioning allowed for Sunday School space, as did the rooms located over the entrance towers. While the vestibule had a level floor of 1x6 tongue and groove boards, the floor of the semi-circular sanctuary slopes from the level of the vestibule and entrances to a raised chancel or platform on which the pulpit and choir are located. The pews following this semicircular pattern are, therefore, naturally arranged in tiers. The balcony that overhangs the third of the sanctuary area is also tiered. (The original pews in the sanctuary, some of which still are used in the vestibule and in the balcony, were replaced by more comfortable ones in the 1960s.)
>
> Nothing in particular needs to be said about the procurement of materials used in the structure; all of the materials were readily available at any of the major lumber companies in Nacogdoches at that time. The entire structure, except for its brick piers and underpinning, is of wood. The siding on the outside is the older version of "105" horizontal lap siding with the "OG" groove; the inside is almost exclusively beaded board. Rulfs' rather ingenious use of these available materials does deserve mention. For instance, around the west front he used standard 1-over-1 light windows but arranged them in vertical patterns to create a feeling of height. He grouped standard windows on top and four on bottom and separated them by small squares of stained glass and topped the group with a semicircular arch containing three trefoils. These windows did not raise and lower but were made to pivot from the middle to allow for ventilation. Rulfs used combinations of 3 and 8 everywhere on the building; for instance, 3 towers each with 3 openings on the second level; 3 trefoils; an octagonal lantern; an 8 sided roof on the main tower. [74]

The Zion Hill Church has undergone virtually no structural modifications over the years. The congregation, while prominent in the African-American community, had little money to undertake anything more than necessary repairs. When the congregation voted in the early 1970s to replace

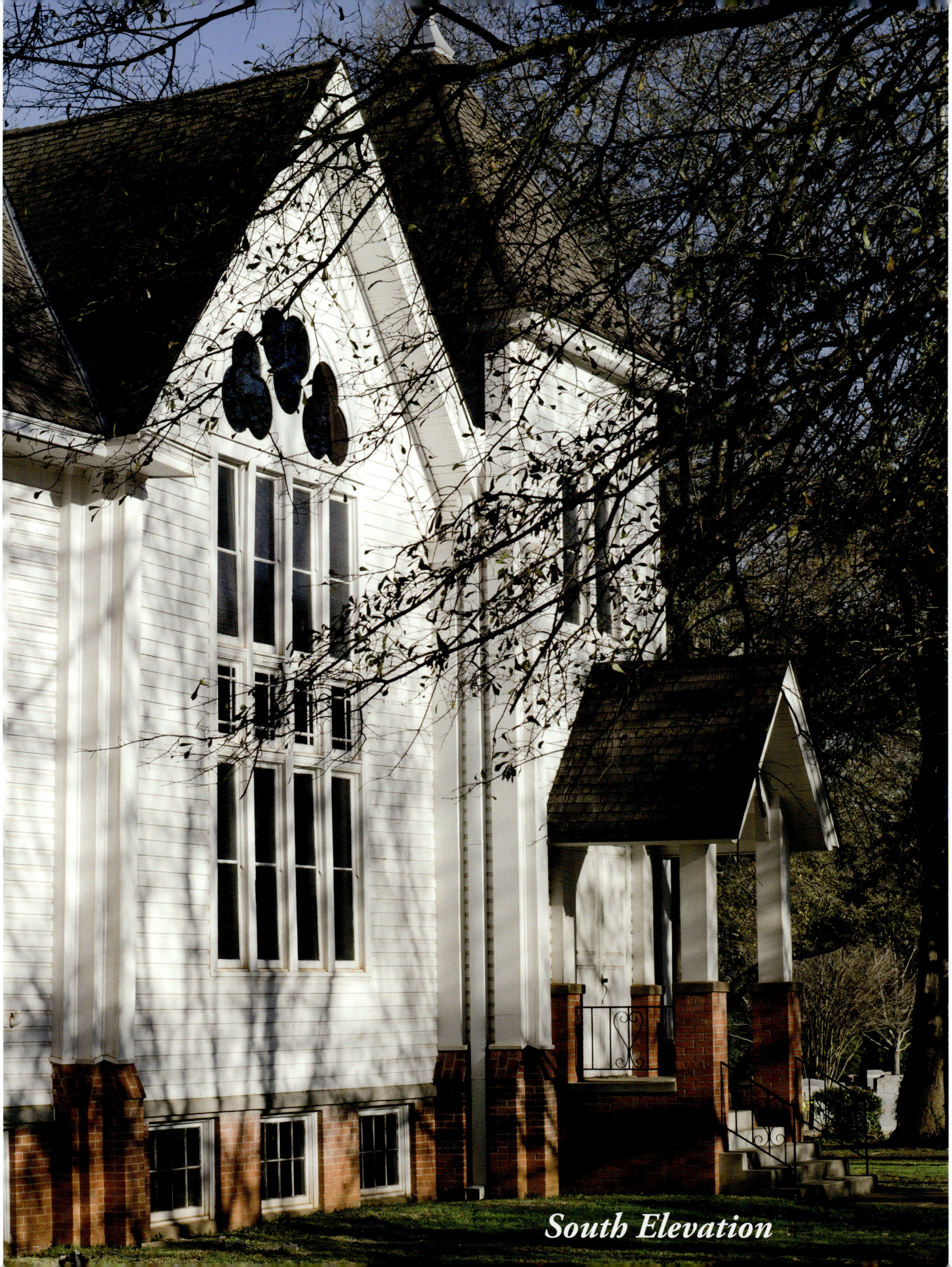

South Elevation

the structure, thinking that the period structure was preventing a more modern outreach, there was immediate reaction from stunned members within the church and many in the community. A coalition of individuals and organizations began to explore ways to preserve the treasure. The Nacogdoches Historical Commission and the Nacogdoches Bicentennial Committee cooperated in securing free paint from the Sherwin-Williams Company for a restoration effort, and the local chapter of the Daughters of the American Revolution volunteered to pay for a Texas Landmark designation. In convincing the congregation, John Anderson and Chuck Phillips joined the author in an appeal. Responding to attempts to honor and preserve the structure, the membership voted to rescind their vote and undertook a stabilization drive of $25,000. They replaced the wood shingle roof, repaired and repainted the interior and exterior, and added central heat and air. Shortly after receiving the Landmark status for the building, the East Texas Historical Association held part of its 1980 fall meeting in the sanctuary. Everyone who attended immediately related to the building as an architectural treasure and a focal point for African-American heritage in Nacogdoches.[75] Eventually, the argument that somehow the out-dated building was preventing the growth of the congregation resurfaced. When an opportunity to purchase a new facility on East Stallings Drive presented itself in 1989, the congregation moved and offered the old building as a home for the Community Action Organization. This arrangement did not last and furthermore, provided no security for the building itself. The building sat vacant for the next fifteen years. Accompanying illustrations show the graphic nature of the deterioration.

In 1998, Lucille Fain, one of the editors of the *Daily Sentinel*, implored this author, as chairman of the Nacogdoches County Historical Commission, to do something for Zion Hill as undertaken in the 1970s. In the article responding to her request, I wrote, "If *location* is so important in business that we repeat it three times, then every time we think of Oak Grove Cemetery, modern promoters of tourism need say Zion Hill Baptist Church three times."[76] By the late 1990s, however, the salvation of the structure took more than words—a larger town and state effort was necessary. While those who have helped are too numerous to list, certain names and organizations need to be mentioned: the Fains at the *Daily Sentinel;* mayors and members of the City Commission; J. C. Hughes, Scott Ingalls, and later Brian Bray from the City's administration. The Texas Historic Preservation Trust Fund and the Texas Historical Commission, under the direction of Dan Utley, Linda Roark, and so many others, offered a $60,000 challenge grant to Nacogdoches. In 1999, the congregation donated the Zion Hill building to the Nacogdoches County Historical Foundation, which raised and invested more than $400,000 for exterior restoration. The officers at the time were Betty Shinn, Mike Bay, Linda Sisk, and Janie Kenner; members of their board included Camille Bolinger, Judy Hale, Arminda Hopkins, Pat Mast, Carolyn Mithchell, Holly Musick, Jean Stephens, Pam Thorstenson, Jackie Warthan, Jerry Baker, Sally Ann Swearingen, Lee Brittain, Gary Lee Ashcraft, and Jan Kingham.[77] Although the efforts to move beyond stabilization will take even more years, now that the Zion Hill Baptist Church belongs to the City of Nacogdoches and is under its direction, a useful future for the buildings can proceed.

This would no doubt please Diedrich Rulfs, who rests within sight of Zion Hill Church in Oak Grove Cemetery.

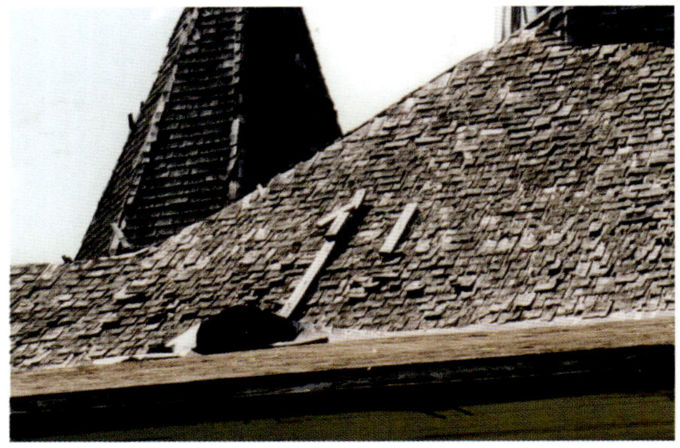

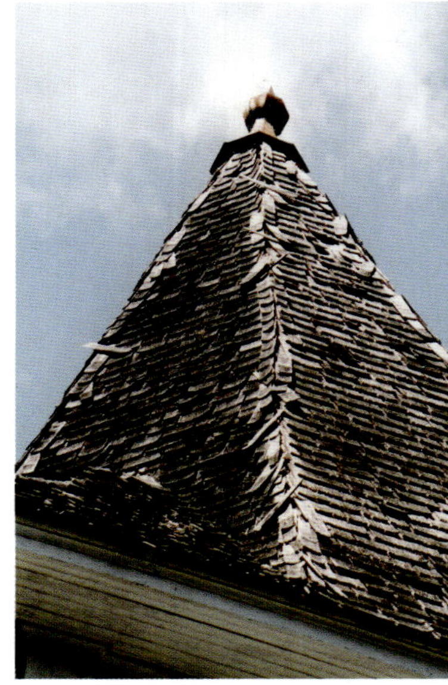

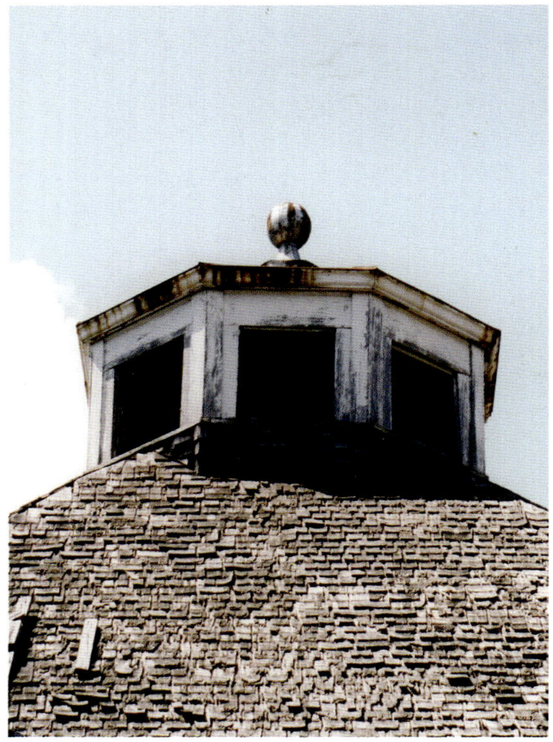

FIGURES 9.42 - 9.45. Zion Hill Deterioration, 1999. Photographs by the author.

FIGURE 9.46 - 9.48. (Across) Zion Hill Stabilized, 2012.

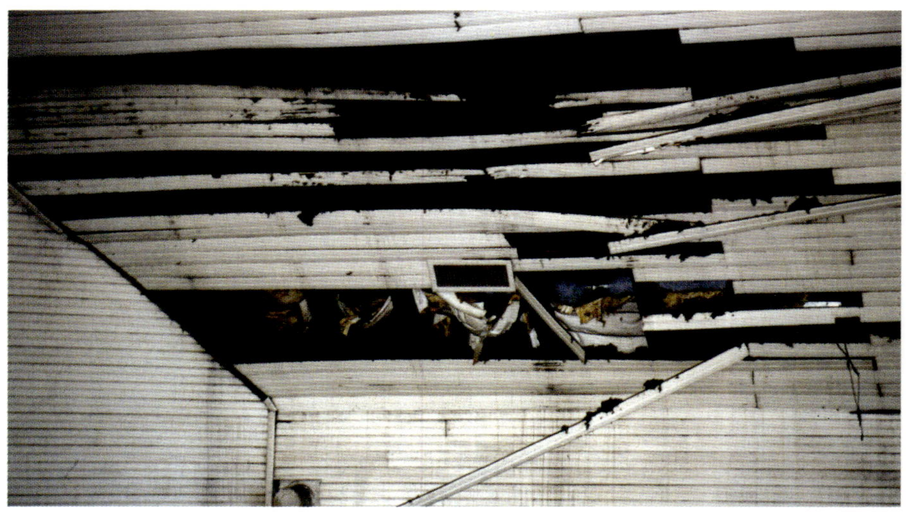

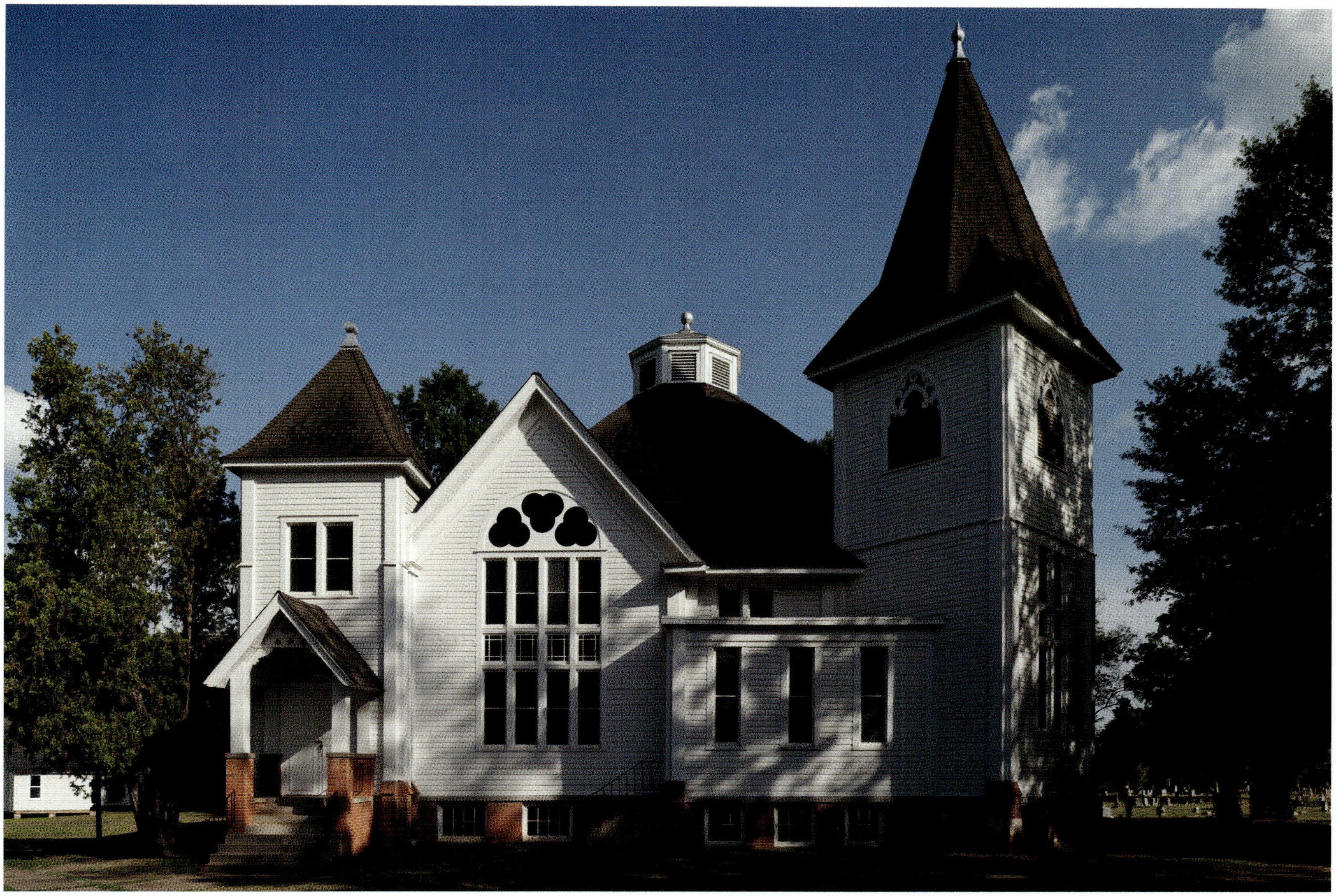

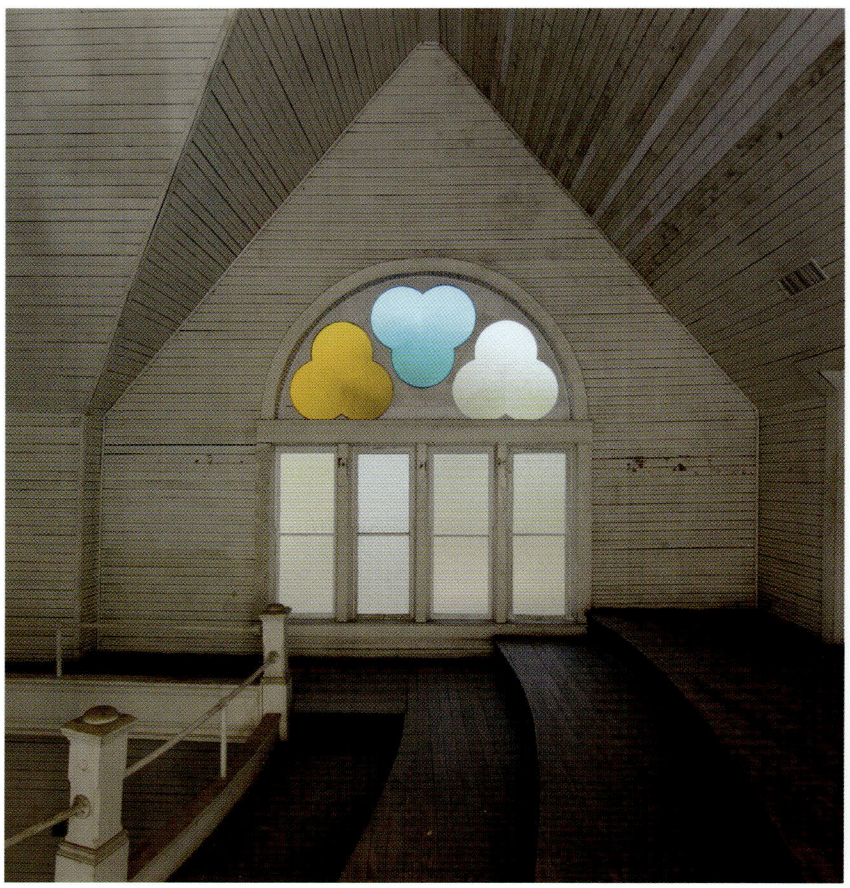

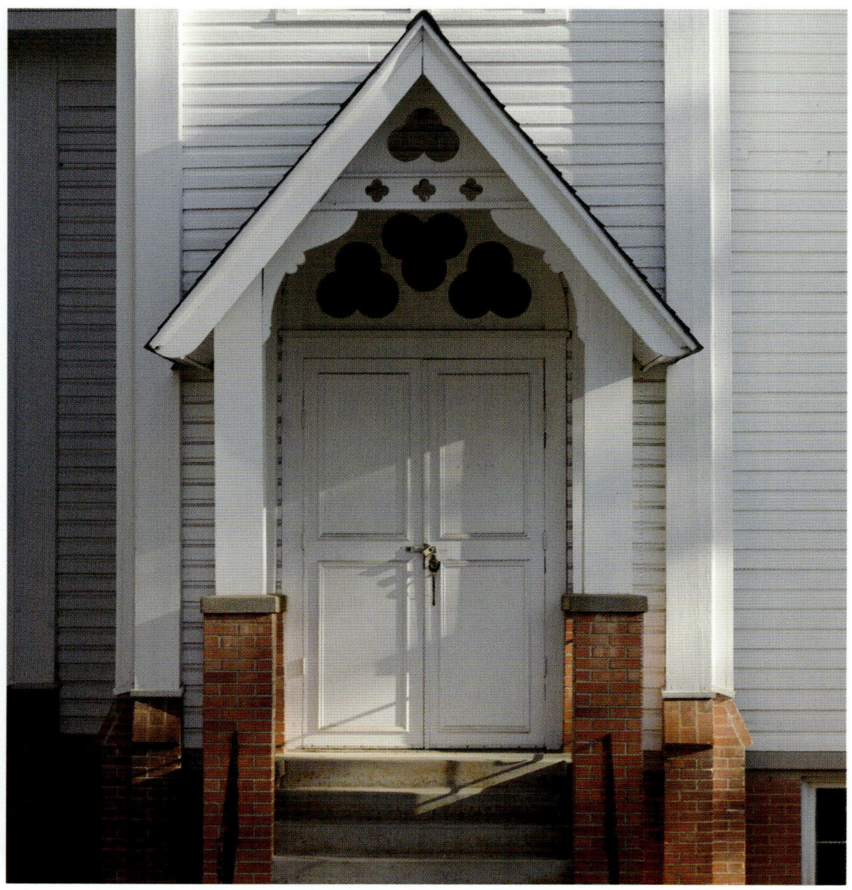

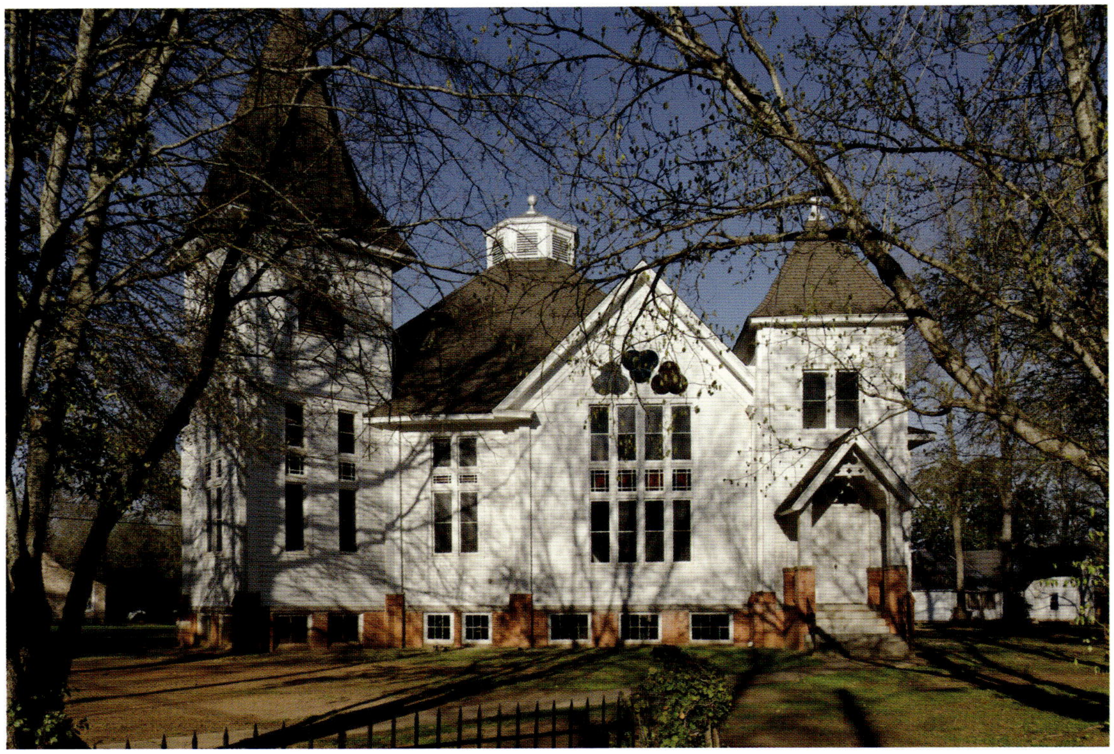

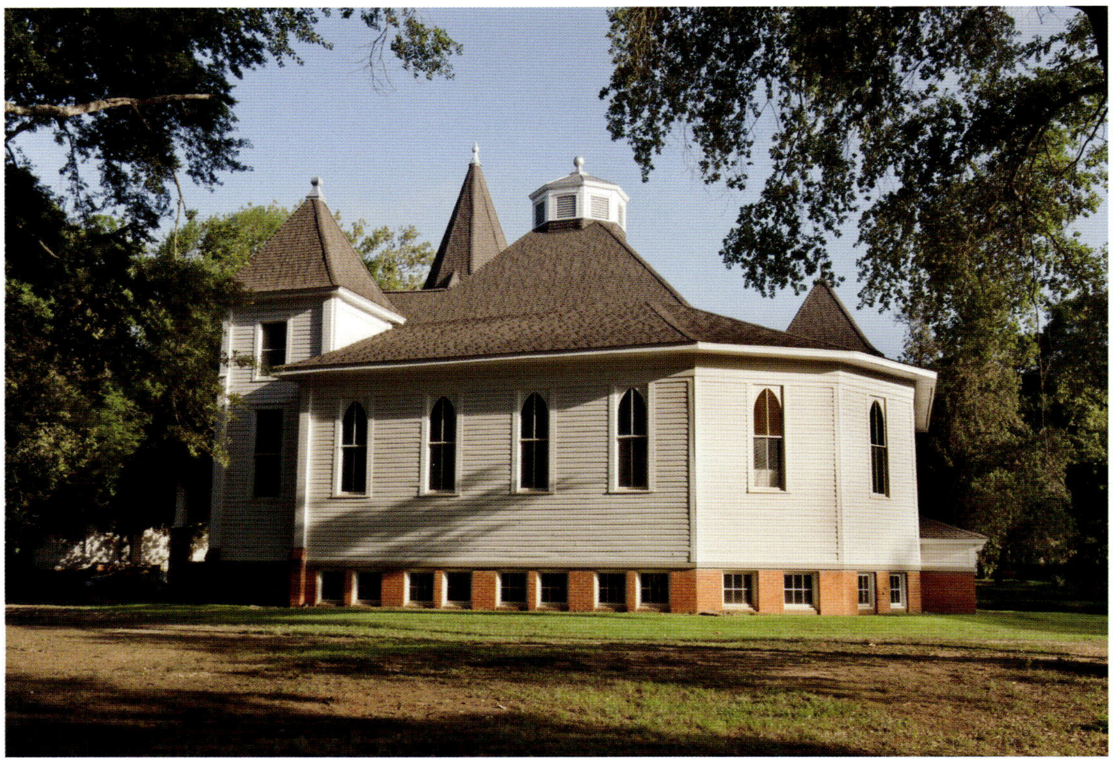

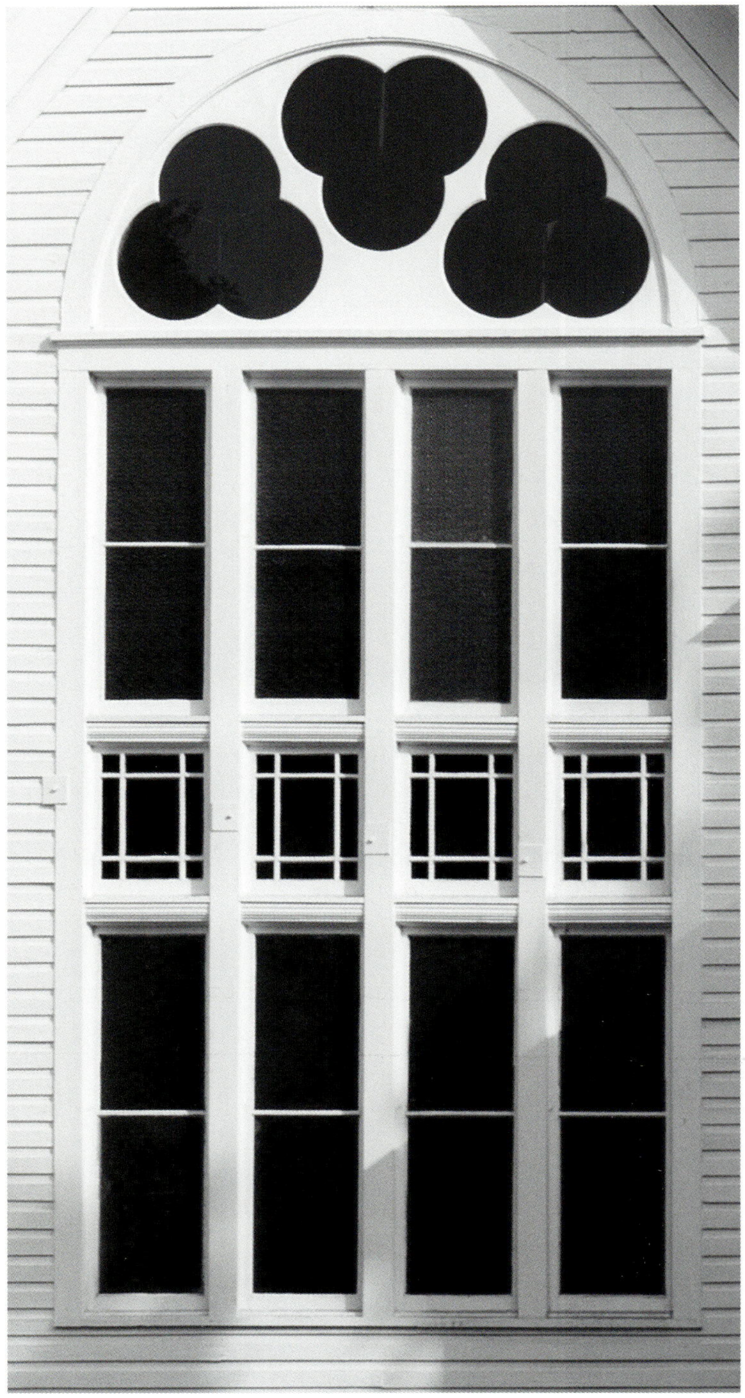

FIGURES 9.49 - 9.51. Photographs of the Restored Exterior of Zion Hill Church.

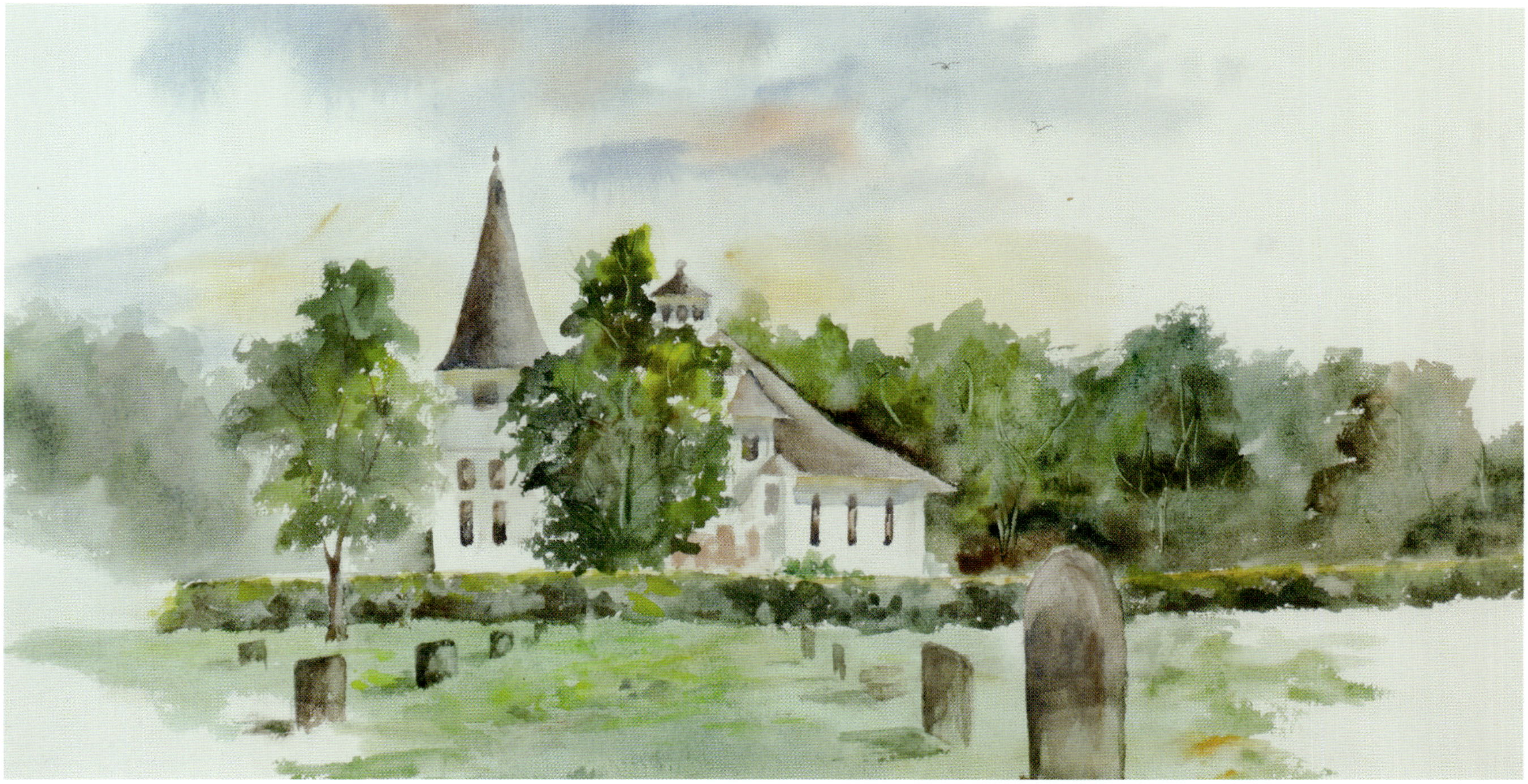

FIGURE 9.52. *Watercolor by Delores Sutton Jenkins, used with her permission.*

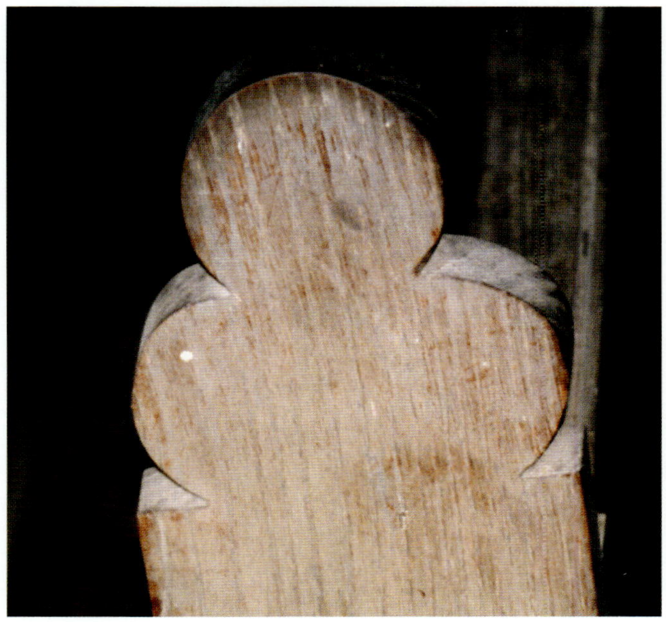

FIGURE 9.53. Pew Made by Rulfs Brothers for the Zion Hill Baptist Church. *D. Rulfs designed the pews for the Zion Hill's sanctuary, employing this trefoil design throughout the church. Transferred to the balcony of the church when the congregation could afford new and more comfortable pews, only one or two of these pews have survived.*

If location is so important in business that we repeat it three times, then every time we think of Oak Grove Cemetery, modern promoters of tourism need say Zion Hill Baptist Church three times. The church stands just north of one of Texas' most historic cemeteries and is an integral and essential part of the cemetery's landscape along Lanana Street. Aesthetically, the Zion Hill and the big oak trees belong there and give Oak Grove its tone; they turn an ordinary cemetery into one of the prettiest tourist sights in this state. The historic people buried in Oak Grove can receive attention in a brochure or colorful lecture; a description of the original land grant from the Government of Spain to Antonio Arriola can be described. Visually, however, with the exception of a few interesting examples of funerary art, the attraction of this location would decrease by one half if Zion Hill falls. With Zion Hill, Oak Grove becomes one of the city's and state's premiere tourist sites; the once isolated church, separated by a large field before World War II, now forms one integral unit with Oak Grove Cemetery.

A Public Plea by Jere Jackson, "Zion Hill: an endangered species," *Daily Sentinel*, 1999.

FIGURE 9.54. (Overleaf) The Interior of Zion Hill, 2012. *Stabilized, but still in need of attention.*

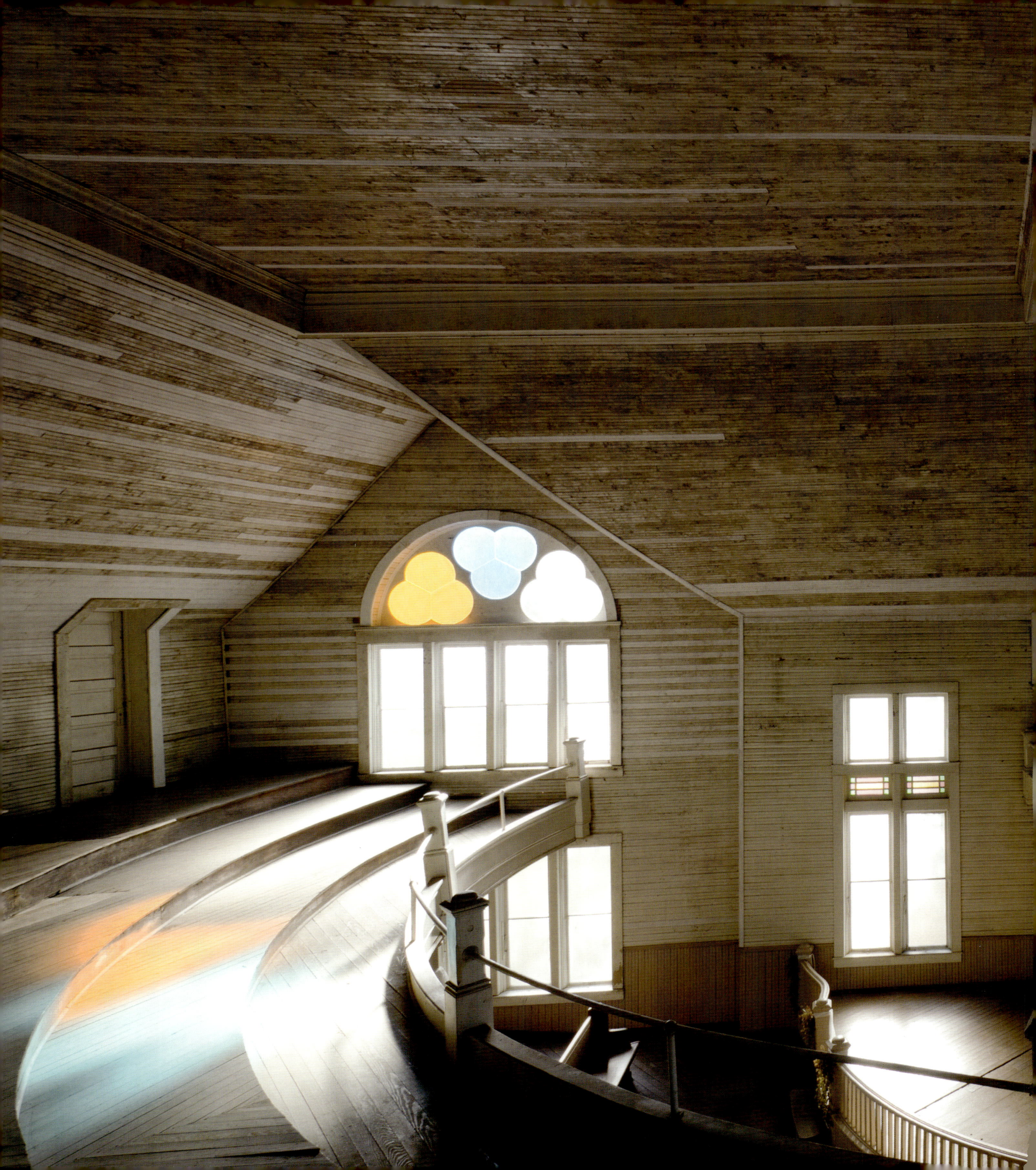

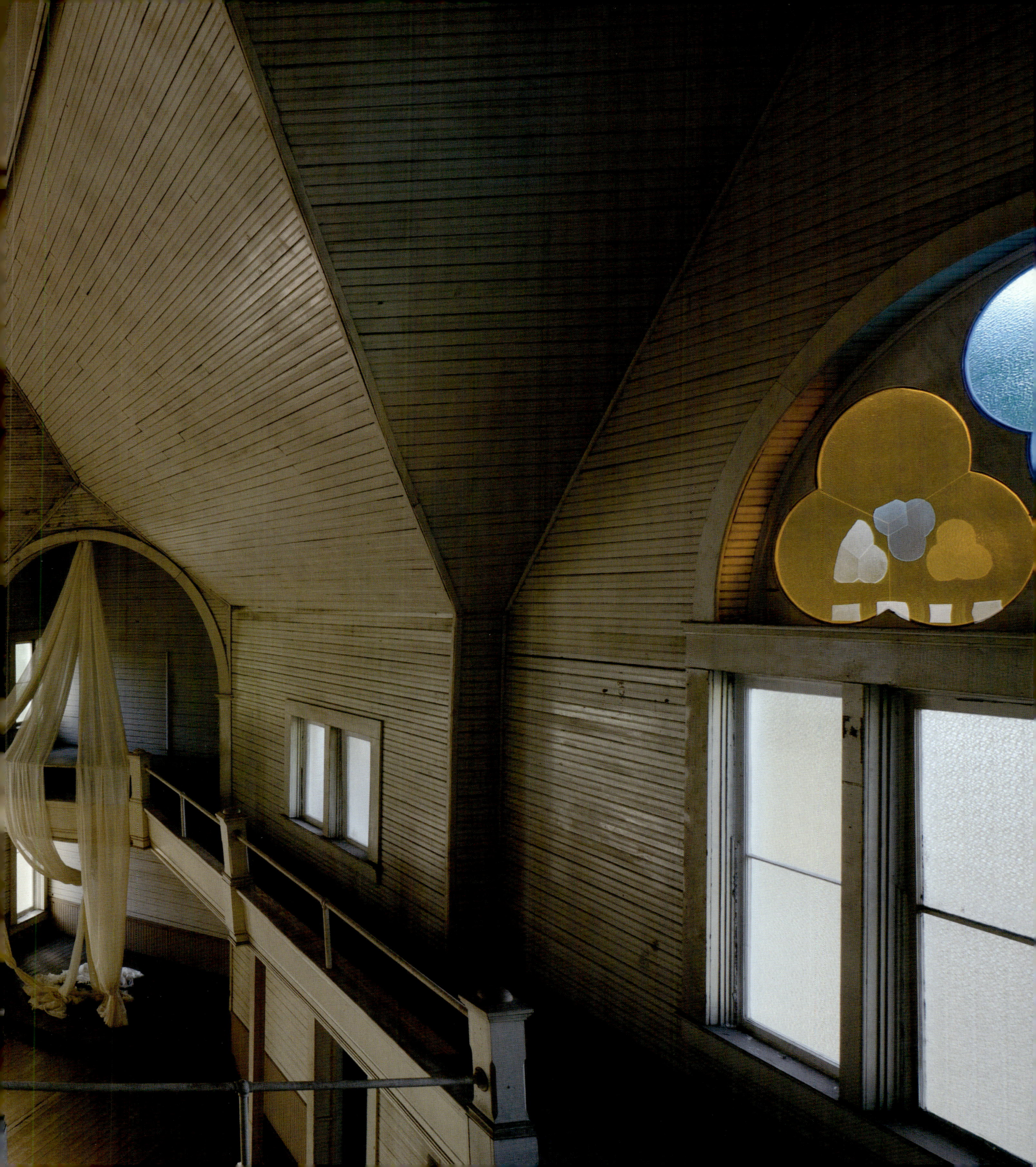

Civic Buildings

The Push for a New Central School

After 1900, cities and towns across Texas had the ability to develop and administer their own schools, "resulting in the formation of independent school districts."[78] Although 1902 was not a good year in Nacogdoches—the year started with the tearing down of the Old Stone Fort and went downhill from there, Nacogdoches did pull together to approve bonds for an Independent School District (NISD). However, former newspaper editor Gary Borders has observed that "most campaigns for civic progress—whether for paved streets, a professional fire department, a waterworks, or a new jail and courthouse—failed miserably."[79] The election to authorize a new bond issue took place in May 1902, granting the district $32,500 with which to work: $25,000 allotment for a new central building on the old college campus, $5000 for a new building on Irion Hill in west Nacogdoches, and $2500 for a schoolhouse for the colored population. The educational leaders who were to see Nacogdoches Independent School District through the coming years were already in place by 1902. The bond election's success guaranteed, or so it seemed, a seamless transition from the old educational system to the new independent school system. Unfortunately, even in the case of the school system, the years 1902 to 1905 were to be anything but smooth. Immediately, there were hurdles for the implementation of the school building program to overcome: land disputes, taxation and jurisdictional disputes, arguments about what to do with the Old University Building, rising costs, and how to allocate the money between the white and colored schools.

Bill Haltom bragged that the new school bill's passage would make "Nacogdoches Second to No City for First-class Schools." Anxious to reassure the town during the midst of the James Buchanan trial and hanging, Haltom intentionally exaggerated: "The schools of Nacogdoches have a fairer promise than at any time since the city grew from an Indian settlement to a white man's habitation." He declared the Old University Building to have "outlived its usefulness," no matter how many memories clustered around it. "It will only be a matter of a few short months when we can point proudly to the new buildings worthy of the new Nacogdoches."[80] Unfortunately, as the wrangling dragged on and birth pangs of the new education system continued, Nacogdoches lost it first real prospects for getting a replacement for the Old University—East Texas Baptist College.

The committee to solve the property issue, headed by John Schmidt, chairman, and aided by Stephen Blount and J. H. Thomas, had to resort to calling in the State Attorney General's office: "In 1904, the grounds and buildings of the University were deeded to the Nacogdoches Independent School District to be used for 'educational purposes only and for white children only'."[81] Since the city limits did not correspond to the NISD district, Nacogdoches had to reincorporate and hold the school bond election again, as well as elections for mayor, marshal, and aldermen.[82]

On January 2, 1904, the town held another school bond election, this time for $36,500 instead of $32,500. Since most people felt the gesture was *pro forma,* the turnout was extremely low–158 for and 16 against.[83] On March 21, 1904, the NISD trustees spent the entire day, which the newspaper called "tedious," poring over architectural plans and specifications. D. Rulfs was one of the seven architects and contractors who submitted designs[84] The committee awarded the central school architectural contract to C. H. Page of Austin;[85] and on May 18, 1904 the construction contract to J. M. Innes of Greenville for his low bid of $20,898.[86] Rulfs received, however, the committee's approval for the two suburban ward schools. In late June, the town hosted a free barbecue for thousands to celebrate the laying of a cornerstone for the central school. All three school buildings opened for classes after the Christmas holidays in January 1905.[87]

None of the committee's deliberations have survived, but no doubt the members found it difficult to answer the question of whether to stay local or to award the contract to an outside architect. There were advantages both ways. Rulfs' drawings have not survived. While Rulfs had many friends on the local committee, the majority obviously preferred the Beaux Arts designs presented by Page. The new school was impressive, and Giles Haltom, at the time of opening, praised it highly: "In her high school building Nacogdoches has the most imposing structure of the kind in East Texas, for its location, nature has provided a most admirable place."[88]

Although Rulfs did not get the contract for the new Central School, he did perform one very useful service to Nacogdoches. The Rulfs plan, which has not survived, tied the new building architecturally to the old building and in location offered a plausible solution to the dilemma of the fate of the Old University Building. The modernists, such as Haltom, wanted the Greek Revival building torn down immediately. Many citizens openly ex-pressed their strong emotional attachment to the building. Rulfs suggested, according to his niece, that if the new building sat directly in front of the old one, the leaders could finesse the emotional issue by postponing the de-cision of *when or if* to demolish the old building.[89] The suggestion by Rulfs was too good to pass up politically, and the architect who won the contract accepted this expediency. The unanimous desire to avoid another state-wide and local crisis so soon on the heels the destruction of the Old Stone Fort, in truth, saved the Old University Building. When the opportunity came later in 1904 to lease the Old University Building to a local business college, the idea seemed like a good business decision, too.[90] Ironically, later school boards were always too desperate for space to consent to the destruc-tion of the well-built building. It was not, however, until after the Second World War that the citizens of Nacogdoches realized what a treasure they had in the Old University structure. While the citizens took down Page's Beaux Arts building in the 1950s, the pre-Civil War building for the Old University still stands and recently celebrated its 150th anniversary.

FIGURE 9.55. The New Central School (1904).

The new Central School, the work of Austin Architect C. H. Page, stood immediately in front of the Old University Building. Courtesy of ETRC.

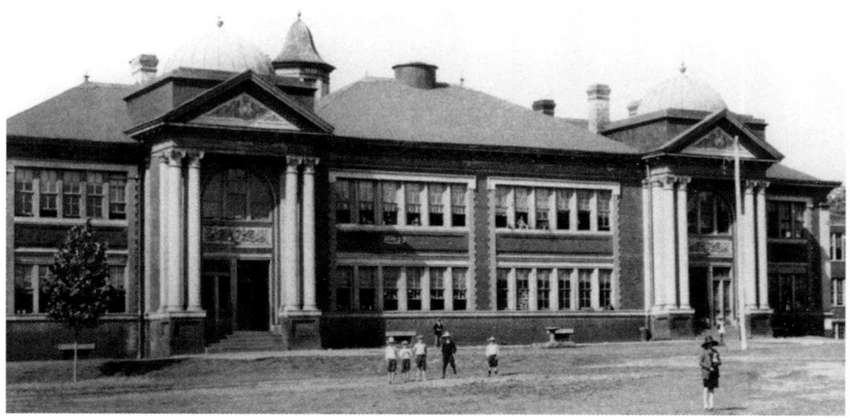

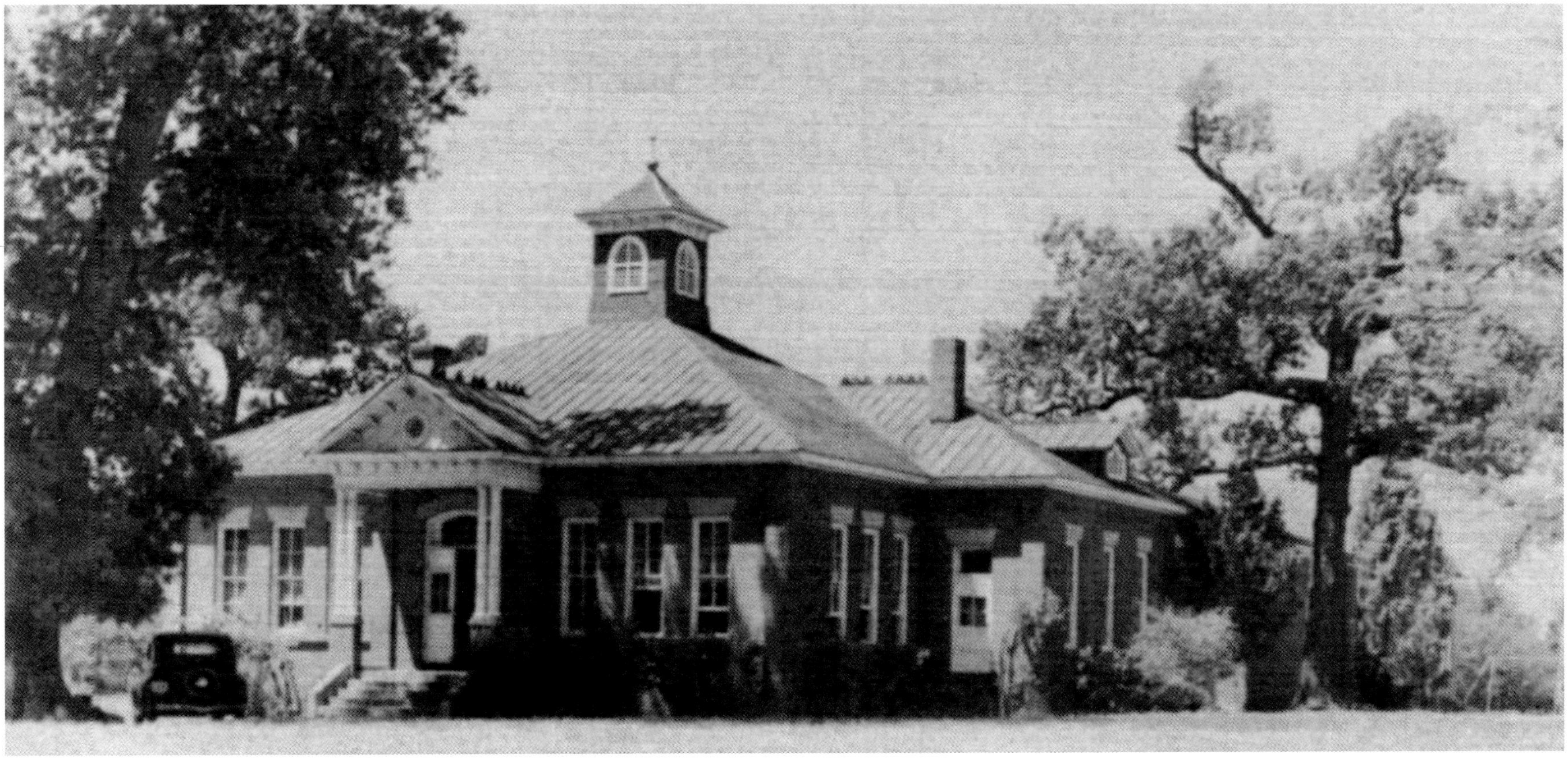

FIGURE 9.56. The West End Public School.
This photograph of the west elementary school dates to the 1930s and comes from a pamphlet published by the Commercial National Bank. Courtesy of Edward B. (Jerry) Baker.

West End Public School (West End Institute, 1904)

Rulfs had a budget of $8,000 with which to build the West End School (later Nettie Marshall Elementary). The design the architect used was an extension of elements he employed in his homes in the Irion Hill area. The Sanborn Map of 1906 shows the building as a T-shaped structure with its main porch on the east and a smaller one on the west. The building had a central hallway and was heated by wood-burning stoves.[91] For the east porch pediment, Rulfs paired slender Tuscan columns on plinth bases on each side. Behind these at the wall, he used pilasters, repeated at the corners of the building, thereby defining the bays for the windows. The three 4/4 windows, with splayed concrete lintels, were within each of the front and side bays. He topped the pentacle of the hip roof with a cupola tower for a school bell. The slight eaves had decorative supports for the overhang. Rulfs placed his signature Palladian windows in the dormers over the north and south wings. The original Rulfs structure survived many renovations and additions, such as when architects Shirley Simon and Hal B. Tucker in 1936 designed an auditorium, two classrooms, and a basement for the structure. Unlike the East End School, which still stands, a fire destroyed this school in 1968, resulting in $100,000 damage.[92] At the time of the fire, it was one of the two oldest buildings in continuous use by the NISD.

The East End School (1904), Later Known as the Old E. J. Campbell Building.

In the early part of the twentieth century, Nacogdoches stacked almost all of its decisions against the Black citizens of the town. (For the climate of racism, see Chapter VII.) The school building discussions were no different. The promise of the 1876 Texas Constitution to be impartial did not rule the day in the Nacogdoches of 1904. The original bond issue and the final one in 1904 allocated twice as much for the white ward school as the one for the colored ward school.[93] The discrimination, however, was in truth much more severe, because the East End School was not just a ward school. The building on Shawnee served all of the Black children, from elementary grades through high school. The official name, used on the Sanborn Maps was the "Nacogdoches High and Grade School (Colored)" on Shawnee Street (later E. J. Campbell).[94] To offer a true comparison, the cost of the Central School ($36,500) would need to be added to the cost of the West End School ($8,000) to offset the facilities for the Blacks: four rooms to serve 125 students in 1904.[95] Edward John Campbell (1877-1937), who was named principal of the East Side School in 1910, became "in effect the superintendent of the black school system."[96] In his twenty-seven years of service, Campbell transformed education for generations of black students in Nacogdoches and surrounding areas. Following his death in 1937, the NISD recognized his service by naming the school for him. Many of his former students have testified to his influence on their lives in recorded oral histories.[97] The old campus on Shawnee Street is now a Community Center under the sponsorship of a strong E. J. Campbell Alumni Association.[98]

Rulfs's East End School at the foot of Orton Hill still stands, the only one of the three 1904 buildings to survive. Architecturally, the East End School appears to be a scaled-down version of the West End School. Its

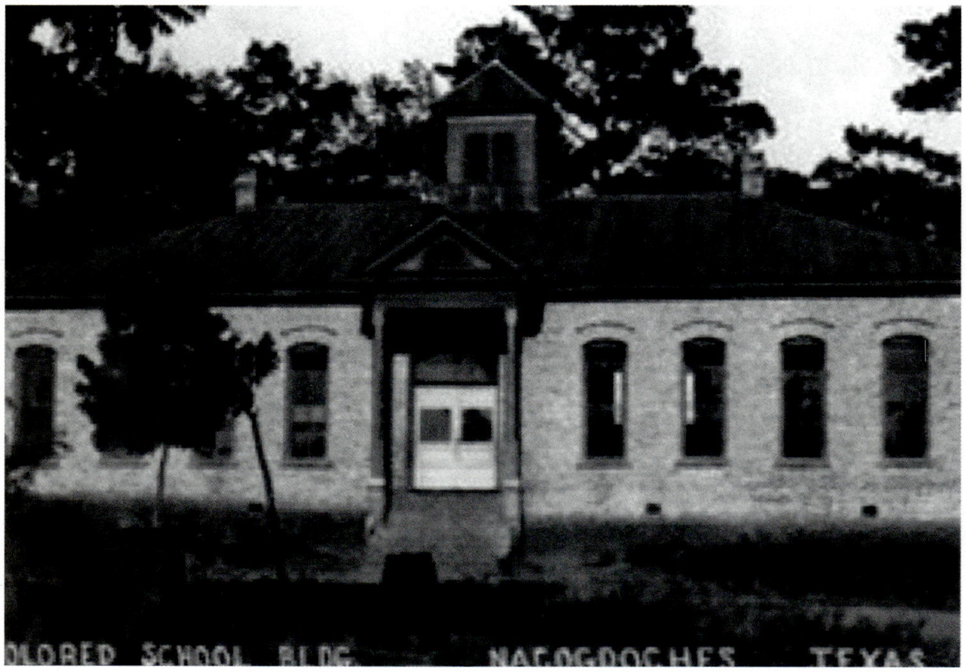

FIGURE 9.57. The East End School.

This is one of the few photographs of the original East End School before the additions of 1917 and later. The front door of the original building later became part of the two-sided entry, between the wings, added by Rulfs in 1917. Photograph courtesy of Anita Farr.

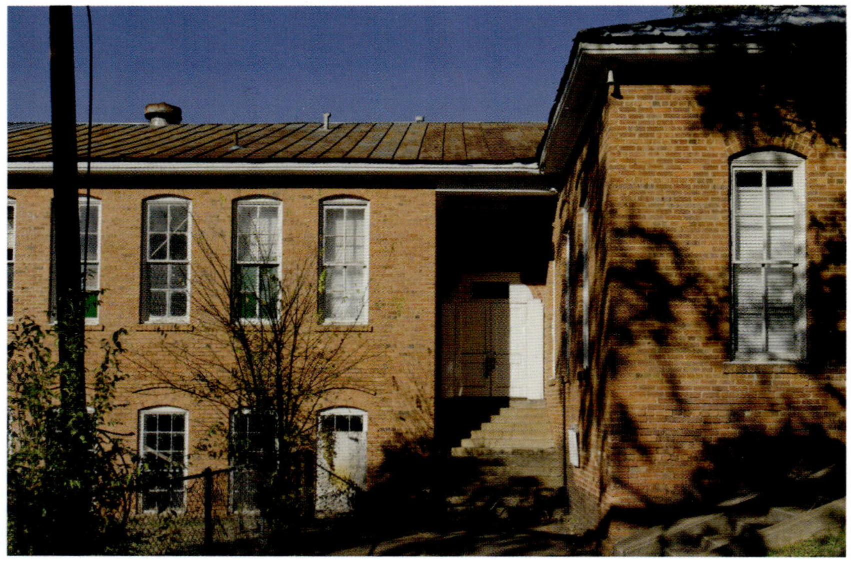

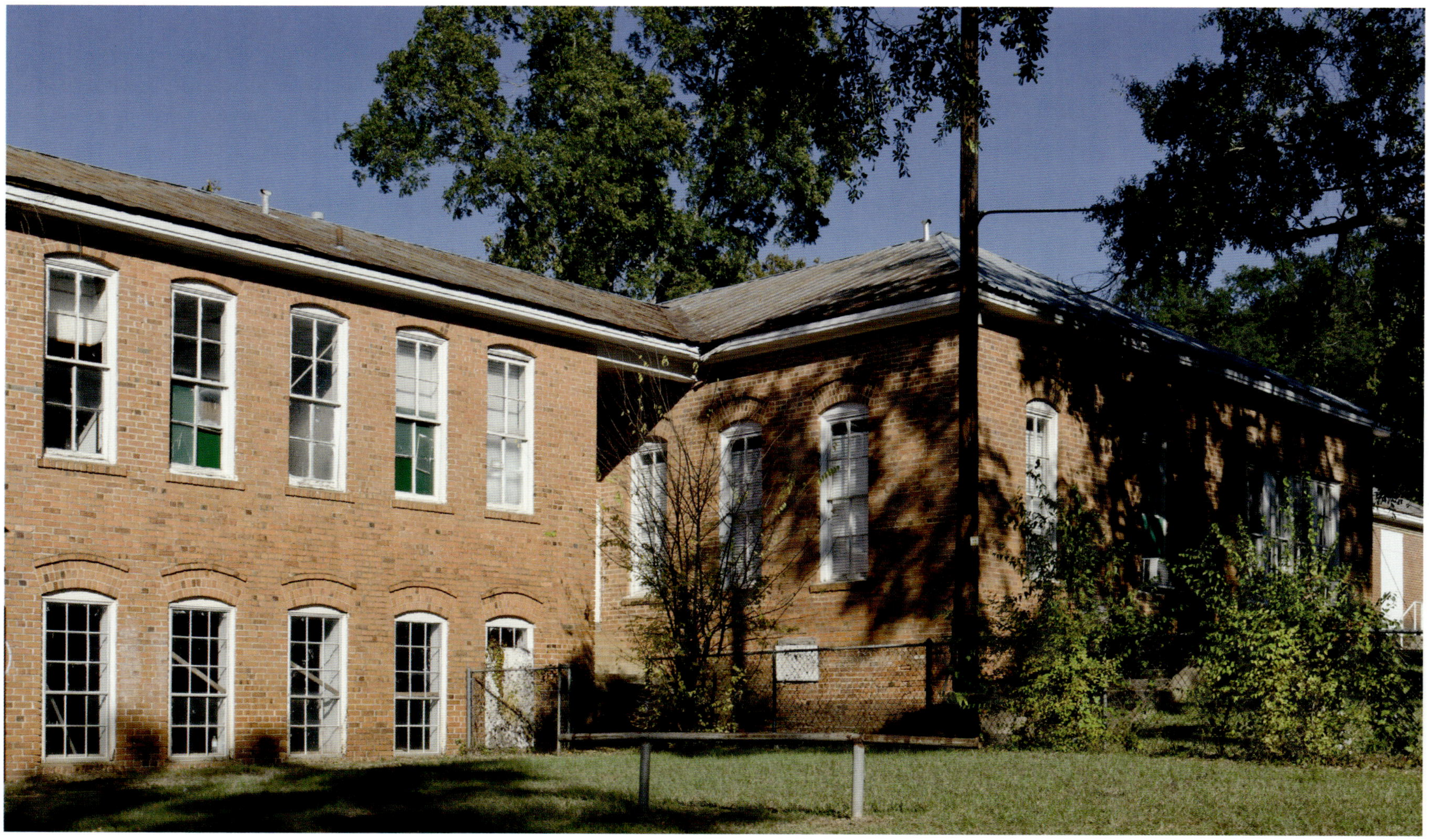

FIGURE 9.58 and 9.59. E. J. Campbell Building After 1917.

When he designed the addition of the East End School, Rulfs appended the new wing to the west, down the hill, which allowed for two stories. He added steps on either side of the original porch to give access to the upper floor and the old building. The original East End School is on the right, the 1917 addition on the left of this photograph. Rulfs had a reputation of working with the Black Community beyond the designs of these two buildings. He aided in the rebuilding of homes along Shawnee after one of the many floods along the Lanana Creek.

pedimented entry porch (now gone) was smaller, with two full-length Tuscan columns and a fanlight window in the tympanum.[99] The building, essentially a square, consisted of four rooms, two on each side of a central hall. Each room had six windows–four windows along the sides and two at each end. Some of the windows were sealed up when additions to the building were made in the 1920s; in addition, some windows themselves were grouped on the north and south walls to increase the amount of available light. The hipped roof had a square bell cupola over the central hall. The budget did not allow Rulfs to include much exterior decoration; there were no pilasters, decorative eaves, or dormers. The windows, however, have very nice curved brick arches. Both the East and West End Schools, and no doubt Rulfs's design for the Central School, had patterns of brick-laying that matched that on the Old University Building: every sixth course was a header, turned inward to strengthen the resulting wall.

Mr. Rulfs was himself one casualty of the building process on the two ward schools. While inspecting the schools before their openings, he stepped "on a nail which penetrated entirely through the foot," according to the *Daily Sentinel.* Rulfs spent the Christmas holidays of 1904 confined to his room.[100]

In 1917, the East End School received an addition, making the school essentially the same size of the original West End School. It is reasonable to assume that Rulfs did this extension: the arched windows (4/4) and the bonding of brickwork match his original design. Later additions done by others did not take the care to follow the original pattern. Because of the sloping terrain of the hill, the extension to the west allowed for a basement of classrooms. A new arched passageway, which replaced the front porch and joined the two wings, has entrance steps on the north and south. The Sanborn Maps are very clear about the dates of the additions to the original building. The 1929 map shows the first expansion (1917) and the 1927 addition of an auditorium and early gym (later used as a cafeteria). The updated map in 1946 offers the best footprint and a complete chronology of the building. The school district attached yet another wing further to the west in 1936, but this later addition introduced a change in architecture—larger windows, larger arches, and different brickwork. To complete the Shawnee Street campus, the NISD constructed a separate building for home economics and agriculture in 1929 and a separate gym/auditorium in 1940 (both now gone).[101] In 1954, a new E. J. Campbell High School opened across Shawnee Street, with a renaming of the old buildings as the Emeline Carpenter Elementary School. When yet a newer elementary school opened in 1964, the Carpenter name was transferred, and the old East End School ceased to be a working part of the NISD. In the summer of 1970, the merged Nacogdoches High School graduated its first integrated class.[102]

The City Hall and Fire Department (1908-1910)

As a member of the City Council, Rulfs had repeatedly pressed for both a fire department and city water lines. The fire at Mayer & Schmidt Department Store (January 1908) was the final catalyst in a series of conflagrations that would force the town to cope with the two critical urban services. In May, Volunteer Fire Chief Sturdevant began negotiations with a committee from the City Council "to investigate the purchase of a horse and the establishment of a permanent fire station in the near future."[103] The City Council and a new Fire Department authorized Cap'n Sturdevant to buy a lot made available by the Hoya family on the south side of the square. In December 1908, D. Rulfs produced plans for a new building to house the fire department on the ground floor and new city offices on the second.[104] Legal questions, concerning the land title and the obligations of citizens to maintain a fire department, delayed the immediate construction of the building. The signage of the new building stated "THE CITY HALL, 1909," but as the minutes by J. R. McKinney noted, the Fire Department was not housed in the building until January 11, 1910."[105] By the time Nacogdoches had its new wagon and one paid fireman, automobiles and trucks had rendered them obsolete. Nevertheless, having a Fire Department, and the underground water and sewer systems that accompanied this, helped to enhance the quality of urban life in Nacogdoches.[106]

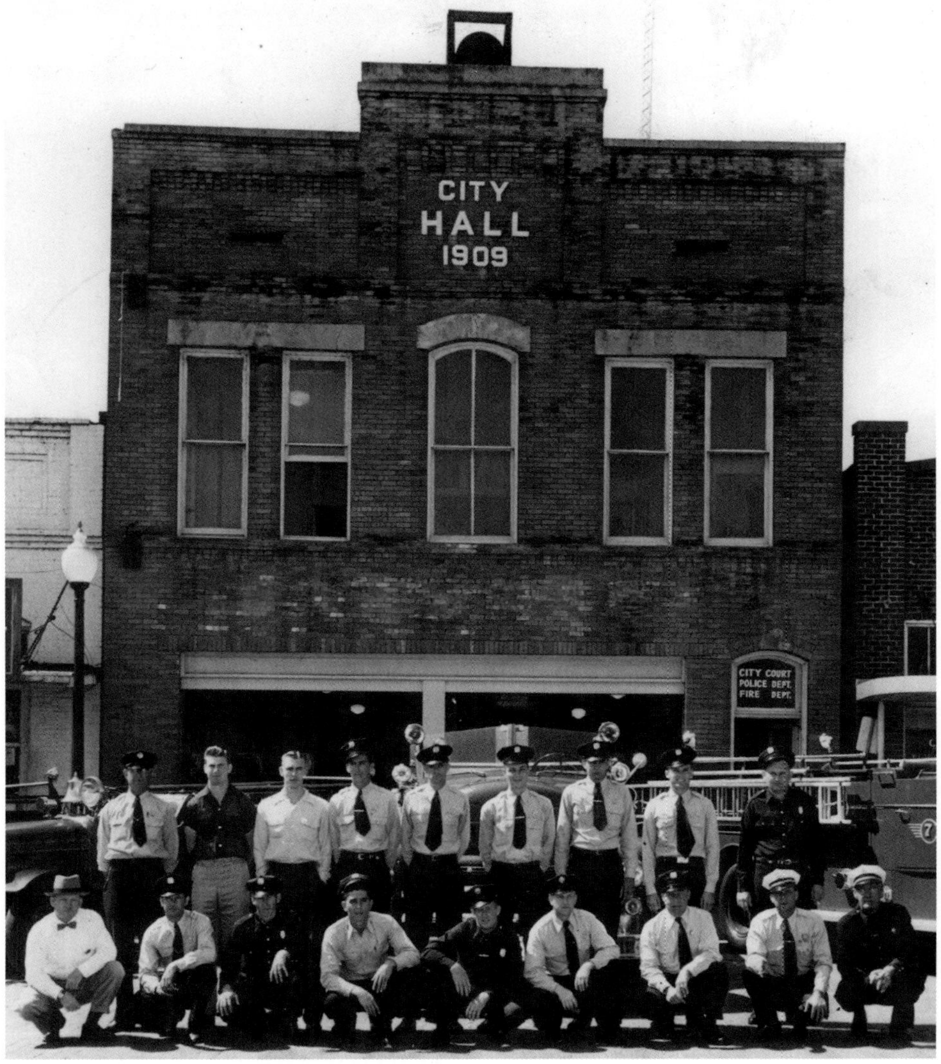

FIGURE 9.60. The City Hall and Fire Department, Photograph from 1940s.
The photograph of the members of the Fire Department shows the building by Rulfs in the background. Rulfs utilized the same subtle modernized form of Palladian motif he had placed on the Davidson building the same year. Photograph compliments of Fire Department Museum.

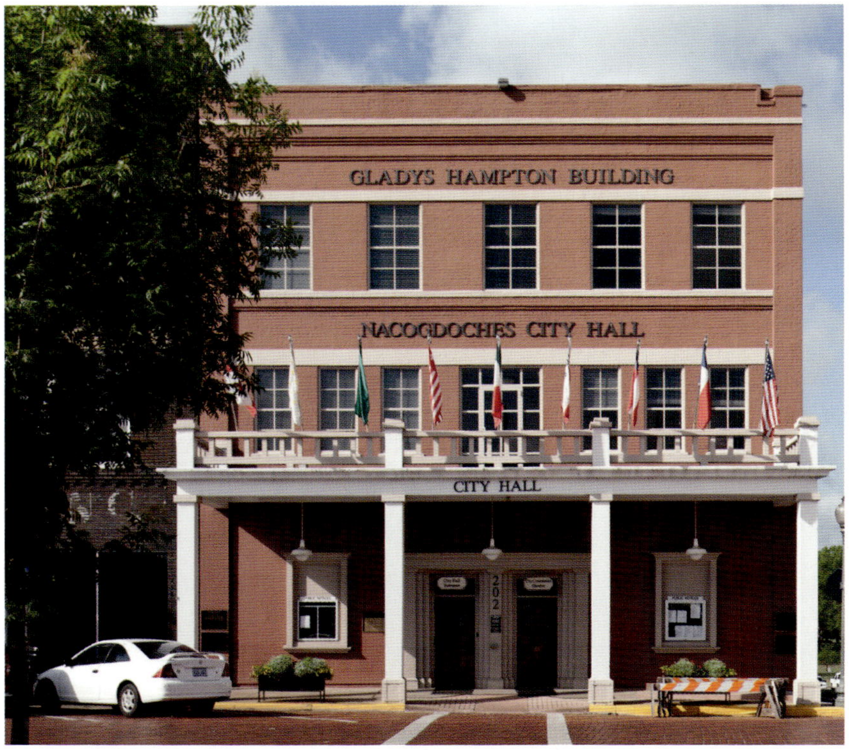

FIGURE 9.61. (Above) The Nacogdoches City Hall in 2012.
Although changed over the years, the City Hall is still in a building by Rulfs - The Davidson Building (1891).

The Nacogdoches Sanitarium (1909) Opens in a Rulfs Building

Dr. Woolam Ira M. Smith (1860-1937), originally from Sabine County, was one of the many doctors who moved to Nacogdoches in the boom of the 1890s. After attending the University of Virginia, he did medical work at Tulane and ultimately graduated from Atlanta Medical College in Atlanta, Georgia; he later did post-graduate work in New Orleans, New York, and Chicago.[107] He started his practice of medicine in 1884 in Chireno, where he continued to maintain an office even in later years, but he practiced all over Nacogdoches County. The lure of the boom in Nacogdoches, however, drew him steadily into the county seat. In 1897, Smith moved his main office and home to Nacogdoches. He leased office space from W. U. Perkins in the Nacogdoches Chronicle Building on Pecan Street. (See Figure 3.20) Smith's homestead was on the west side of North Street, south of Mueller Street, approximately across from where Hughes Street enters North Street.[108] The two-story house Rulfs built for the Smiths in 1898 was large, but undistinguished. The forward front gable room had a rounded bay window, similar to the one used the year before on the Stephen Blount House. The porch, which wrapped from the forward room around the west and south façade of the house, supported a continuous balcony as its roof. Considering the later use of the house, this extensive access to the outdoors was possibly the house's most recognizable feature. Rulfs used this feature several years later on the Dr. Ford House on Washington Square.

In 1909, Smith added a three-room extension to his large fourteen room house and turned the house into the town's first modern hospital. According to the *Galveston Daily News*, which thought the opening important enough to include it in their May 4th edition, the building was "modernly equipped, handsomely furnished, and represents a large expenditure of money." The article ended with the sentence: "The hospital is said to be the only one in East Texas."[109] Smith and his family moved across the street to a house rented from E. A. Blount. In December of that same year, however, this leased house burned to the ground.[110] The Smiths turned a portion of the new hospital back into a family suite for a time. The doctors associated with the sanitarium/hospital, according to a letter from the early 1920s, included: W. I. M. Smith, President; F. R. Tucker, Vice-President; A. A. Nelson, Treasurer; and R. P. Lockey, Secretary. They declared, "The institution is open to all ethical Physicians. Our rates are reasonable, $2.50 to $5.00 per day."[111] The Smith Sanitarium appears on the Sanborn Maps as a hospital from 1912 through 1922; on the 1929 map as a domestic structure, after the opening of Memorial Hospital, its successor; and as a vacant lot on the 1946 map update.[112]

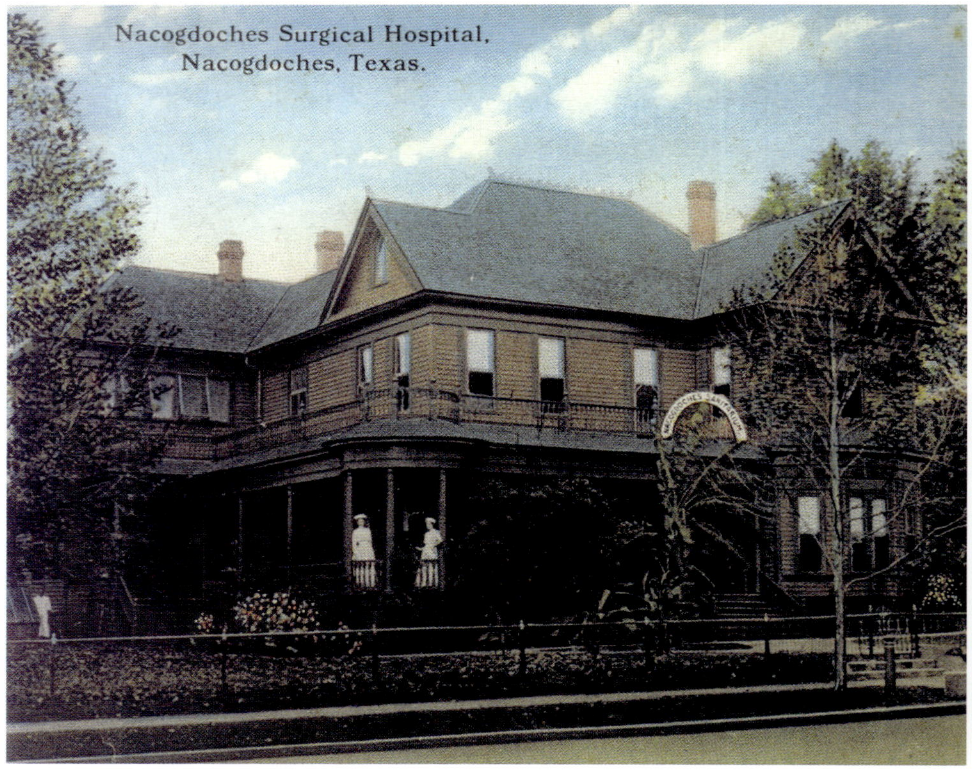

FIGURE 9.62. (Above) The Nacogdoches Surgical Hospital.
This colorized postcard dates from around 1912. Unlike the images of the building on the next page, in this photograph the name "Nacogdoches Surgical Hospital" is used rather than "Nacogdoches Sanitarium." In both photographs, however, two nurses in white uniforms appear. Compliments of Cecil Sparks.

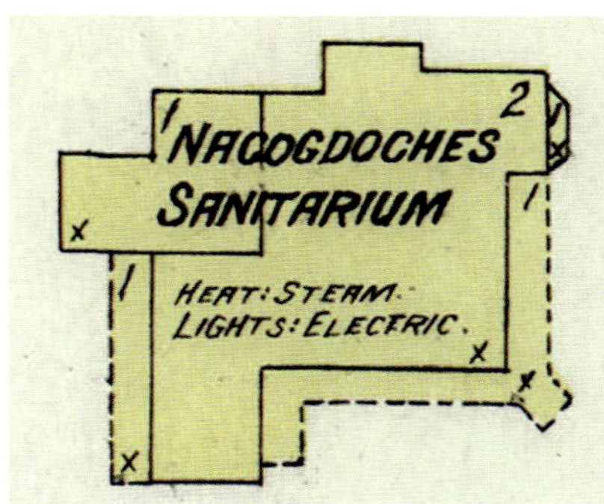

FIGURE 9.63. The 1912 Sanborn Map.
The 1912 Map labels the structure the Sanitarium and states that the building had central steam heat and electricity.

The Movement to Get a New Court House 1902-1912

During these same years, many leaders began to push for a replacement of the County Court House. In 1902, their efforts to secure the bond issue failed. The public was in no mood to accept the argument that a fifteen-year-old building (the 1887 building by Eugene T. Heiner) was worn out.[113] The *Daily Sentinel* launched another effort in 1906 to make the case for a new court house. In 1907, the County Commissioners voted unanimously to give the taxpayers "another opportunity to vote on the question of issuing bonds for a new court house and jail."[114] The skeptics again carried the day, and the bond issue failed. By 1910, the proponents tried again, this time with a better organized campaign. They emphasized how dangerous the old building was, how cheaply it had been built. Giles Haltom in an editorial wrote, "The building is not only indecent, but dangerous."[115] With E. A. Blount and John Schmidt in charge, the campaign included petitions by school children, advertisements, circulars, and public assemblies. The *Daily Sentinel* victoriously announced on May 1, 1911, "BOND ELECTION CARRIES."[116]

In early summer 1911, a controversy erupted over granting the architectural contract for the new building. The headline in the *Daily Sentinel* read, "Architects vs. Construction Company." The newspaper continued:

> The commissioners court yesterday decided to postpone the selection of plans for the new courhouse until the first Monday in July.
>
> The facts in the matter as we have been able to ascertain are about as follows: The court some weeks ago advertised for plans and specifications from architects to be submitted to the court Tuesday of this week. Ten gentlemen, representing themselves as architects, were on hand ready to submit plans and specifications in competi- tion. When the court met and the matter was taken up, eight of the architects represented to the court that two were present who were not architects bona fide, but were connected with construc-tion companies, and refused to enter in comp- etition with them, believing as they did that they would stand no chance. The court, however, refused to eliminate the two companies, of whereupon two of the architects withdrew from the competition, leaving one remaining, and withdrew along with them.
>
> The seven architects lef the city yesterday and say they will not return in July, or in fact have anything further to do with the Nacogdoches courthouse plans so long as they have to enter in competition with agent of construction companies.[117]

Although Rulfs always specified his buildings separate from his construction firm bids, Rulfs withdrew his name from the competition rather than see himself or the town humiliated. On July 12, the Court awarded the architectural contract for a three-story reinforced concrete building to the firm of Lang & Weichel of Dallas; and in September, it assigned the construction contract to W. C. Whitney of Beaumont.[118] Neither the court minutes nor the newspaper gives details, but one can read between the lines. The architects, who were beginning to unionize themselves into professional organizations and tighten their exclusion of any practicing architect that did sever any connections with a construction firm, boycotted Rulfs. The County Commissioners, never keen on going along with the clique in the town, possibly enjoyed seeing Schmidt's architect excluded. As irony would have it, however, because of labor problems and the death of the contractor, the bonding agency and the architect in Dallas had to resort to hiring D. Rulfs to become the supervising architect in order to see the Courthouse to completion. Otto Lang,[119] a fellow German-born architect and the partner in charge of the Courthouse, possibly felt badly about the exclusion of Rulfs; he certainly felt comfortable with Rulfs overseeing the completion of the building. It was D. Rulfs in the end who certified that the Courthouse was "complete and ready for acceptance;" it was his signature that approved the final accounting to both the Lang architectural firm and the Court.[120]

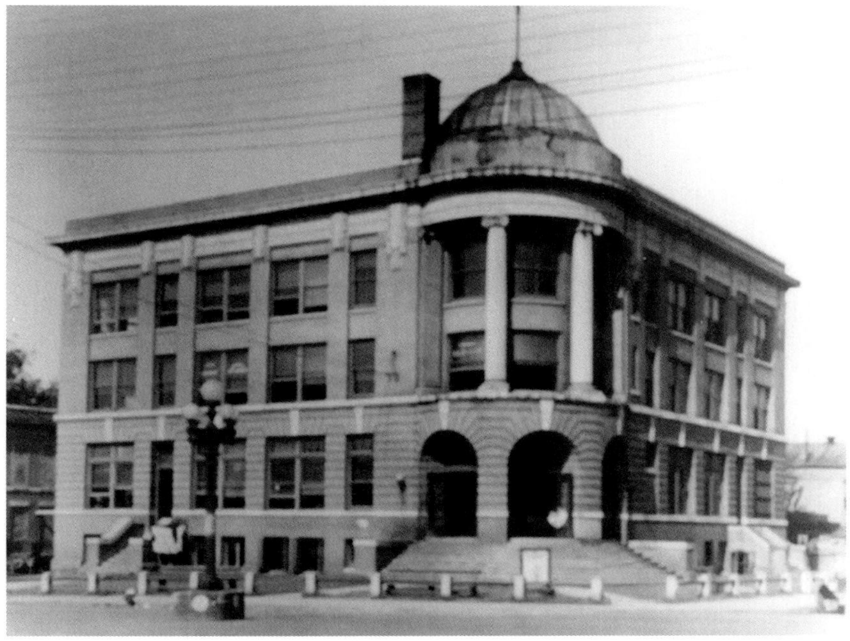

FIGURE 9.64. Nacogdoches Courthouse, 1912.

Although not designed by him, Rulfs was the supervising architect for the new courthouse. Courtesy of ETRC.

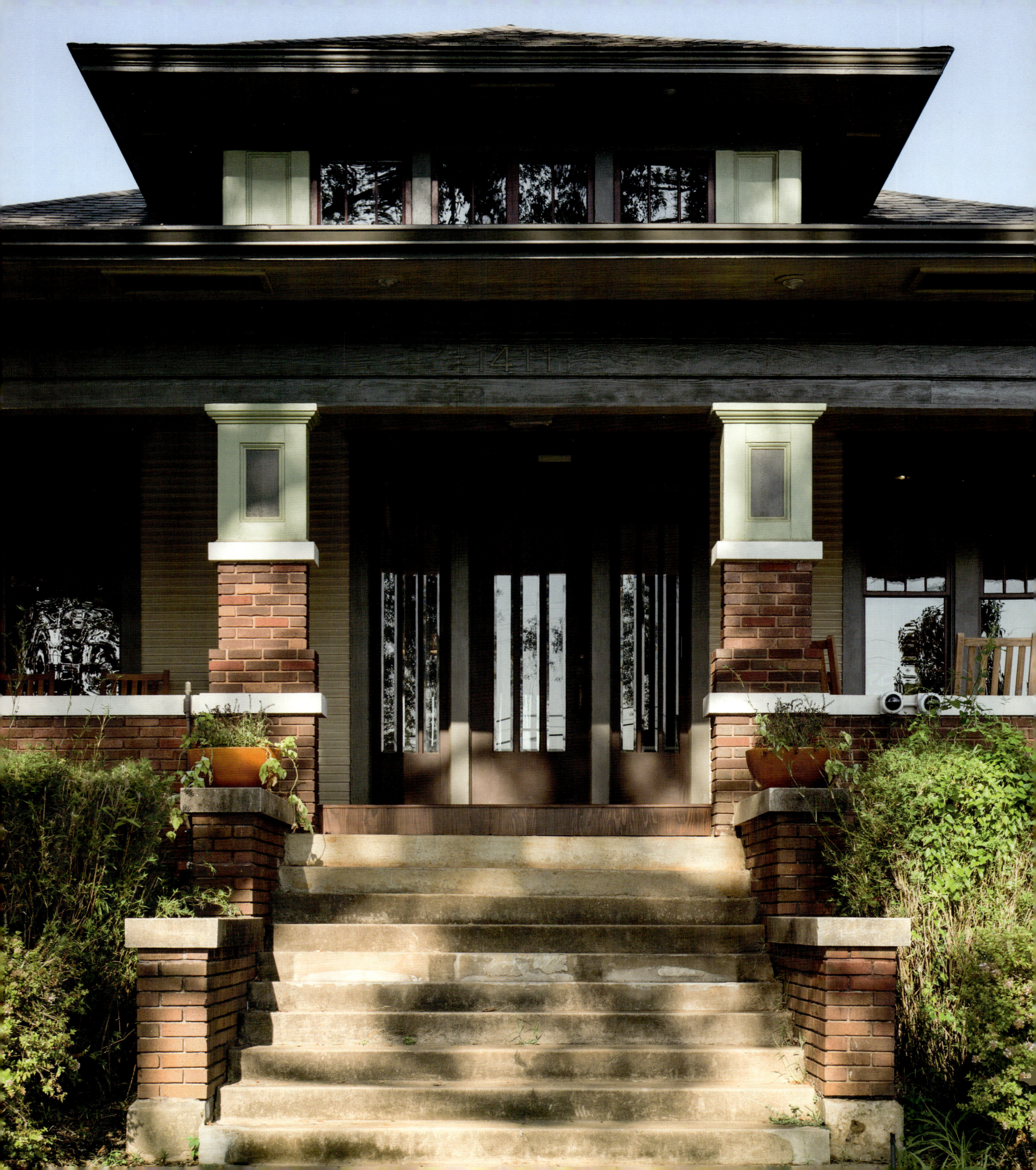
1411

CHAPTER X

Eclectic Domestic Styles

Downtown and North Street, 1900-1916

"Unusual activity in real estate in and around Nacogdoches and the prices keep running up by leaps and bounds." *Daily Sentinel,* June 17, 1901

"Twenty white square pillars, ranged in two step-back tiers on the street façade and half way around the south side gave the residence stateliness without pretension." Memoirs of Bill Wilson, Architect, Grandson of W. U. Perkins, 1999.

In 1906, the *Daily Sentinel* published one of its periodic special editions designed to showcase the progress Nacogdoches was making toward modernization and becoming a city. Wherever Giles Haltom turned to find examples to illustrate his feature articles, most of the photographs were of churches, homes, schools, and brick businesses from the creative genius of D. Rulfs.[1] Whether back in 1897 or later in 1917, to illustrate the town's built environment meant paying tribute to this German immigrant. For the historian, the editions freeze a moment in time that is very helpful. Many commercial buildings and houses pictured in the 1906 Special Edition no longer exist. Some, like the buildings on the North Square, survived for only a month beyond the Special Edition—destroyed in the great fire of December 23, 1906.

The Special Edition featured very few new residences. The years at the beginning of the century had seen a reduction in residential construction. Perhaps the general slowing of the economy in East Texas and the nation can explain this decline. The town slowly realized the need to replace the Old University, but the difficulty in attracting a replacement proved to be a drag on the town's confidence in its future. Nacogdoches was not a large town. The pent-up demand of the previous decade had cooled, the market saturated. This would not change until the next generation of leaders came along. Another important factor, no doubt, was that the demand for residences abated because so much money had to be diverted into rebuilding burned commercial establishments. Rulfs, while not busy designing houses, was extremely busy in these years designing and overseeing the erection of churches, schools, hotels, commercial buildings, and, all too frequently, in replacing structures consumed by fire. He even designed the new fire station. It is, however, a period in which Rulfs undertook as many remodeling jobs as new commissions. His advertisements, as discussed earlier, anticipated these transitions.

Of the residences featured in the Special Edition of the *Sentinel*, very few were of recent construction. Older outstanding examples of work by Rulfs, such as the E. A. Blount and Roland Jones homes, were nearly a decade old. The market for new or remodeled residences recovered only after 1910. By that time, Rulfs had made a substantial paradigm shift as he negotiated the emergence of a new generation, usually reflected in the competition between modernists and the traditionalists.

FIGURE 10.1. (Across) The Mary Buford Hayter House.
Built in 1913, the Hayter House celebrated its 100th anniversary in 2013.

The New Trends

The newest force for change in the upcoming years was the automobile, but that innovation did not change Nacogdoches as quickly as the railroad had. While the concept of what was and was not "in the country" began to become more relative, the race to the suburbs did not occur in Nacogdoches until after Stephen F. Austin State Teachers College (SFA) moved to its new campus in 1924. SFA was to change everything: the median age in the town, the geographic center of both the commercial and residential areas, the use of buildings, the value of land, and city services, such as paved roads, water, and sewage. Before World War I, the determining factors for the development of the town were still geographical and not technological: Irion and Orton Hills and Banita and Lanana Creeks continued to be the same great barriers to the development of suburbs as before; only bridges and paved roads would change this. The plans for and the building of the West End School in 1904 did lure people outside the area between the two creeks, but the new Central School probably brought as many people back into the old central zone as those who left.

In architecture, the lure of modernization became important, but conversely, while people no longer wanted High Victorian elements, such as fretwork or "gingerbread" on their houses, they did not necessarily embrace the straight lines of modernism quickly. A tug-of-war began between those who craved and demanded modern expressions and those who wanted to remain with the more traditional. Diedrich Rulfs had a remarkable ability to anticipate and accommodate these stylistic changes. Always sensitive to national trends and economic conditions, he began to simplify the lines of his houses. Even before the turn of the century, Rulfs realized that the desirability of extensive decorative elements had become passé. He began to steer his clients away from the opulence of the 1890s, for reasons of taste and economic reality. The architect's personal tastes had always been quite eclectic, but, by 1900, he began to specify more classical elements, less ornamentation, and more horizontal lines. Even more remarkably, he did these things in complete harmony with his limited pool of clients and in tune with a faltering economy. He accommodated the new era by remodeling as many houses as he undertook in new construction. He instinctively knew that his clients wanted something different, not necessarily something modern. He updated the houses of the old trendsetters—who became the traditionalists—without shocking their sensibilities or their pocket books.

Like a great composer using the same melody in complicated fugues and variations, architect D. Rulfs utilized his themes and favorite designs repeatedly as he transformed Nacogdoches. He had a unique ability to repeat elements without ever being boring or limiting himself to a single architectural template.

The Mayfield-Reid House (1901)

Not long after the turn of the century, several of Rulfs's clients began to develop the portion of East Main Street between Mound and Lanana Streets—an older section of town, just to the west of his own homestead. One of his early projects was a sanctuary for the recently organized Main Street Presbyterian Church, discussed in Chapter IX. In this block, Rulfs designed homes for Dr. J. E. Mayfield, William A. Nelson and his sister Fannie Nelson, and Miss Mary Hoya. Two of these houses still exist.

The house Rulfs created for Dr. J. E. Mayfield (1843-1924), a long-time resident of Nacogdoches, dates to the spring of 1901. Mayfield had come to Nacogdoches with his family in the 1850s; his father, Walter E. C. Mayfield, served as Sheriff and District Clerk in the County. As a young man, Mayfield had served in the Texas Volunteers and Confederate Army during the Civil War. According to the Census records of 1880, the Mayfields had lived on North Street near the A. A. Nelson family.[2] Although Mayfield had purchased a piece of property on East Main Street from the Henry Raguet family, he did not decide to build on the lot for twenty years. The death of his first wife and his remarriage occasioned the decision to build on East Main as part of an overall shift of both his office and residence to the east side.[3] As part of a report on May 6, 1901 on the "building boom" on the east side of town, discussed in the previous chapter, Bill Haltom at the *Daily Sentinel* included this note: "Dr. Mayfield's new residence is now under headway."[4] Mayfield would live in this house for eight years. In 1909, he relocated to San Antonio, but continued to be very interested in Nacogdoches and wrote a regular column entitled "Nacogdoches Traditions" for the *Daily Sentinel* until his death in 1924.[5]

Mayfield's house, as built in 1901, was a traditional late Victorian cottage. Below the peak of the hipped roof projected gables on the east, north, and west sides, all three with chamfered bays below. There was a balcony above the pediment over the front entrance. On the Main Street façade, a gabled dormer pierced the roof. The porch had Tuscan columns and a tailored balustrade but no fretwork, according to Mary Stewart Duncan (Rulfs's niece), who described the original house to the author.[6] The center windows of the bays were larger than the sides and had fixed upper sashes, not unlike the Tucker-Branch House on Mound Street or the J. J. Baker House on North Street. The paired windows in the dormer, while not used by the architect generally, were very pervasive throughout his native Oldenburg. Postcards from the period and observation today indicate that the use of paired windows in gables is more characteristic in Oldenburg than the three-window configuration normally used by Rulfs in Nacogdoches.[7]

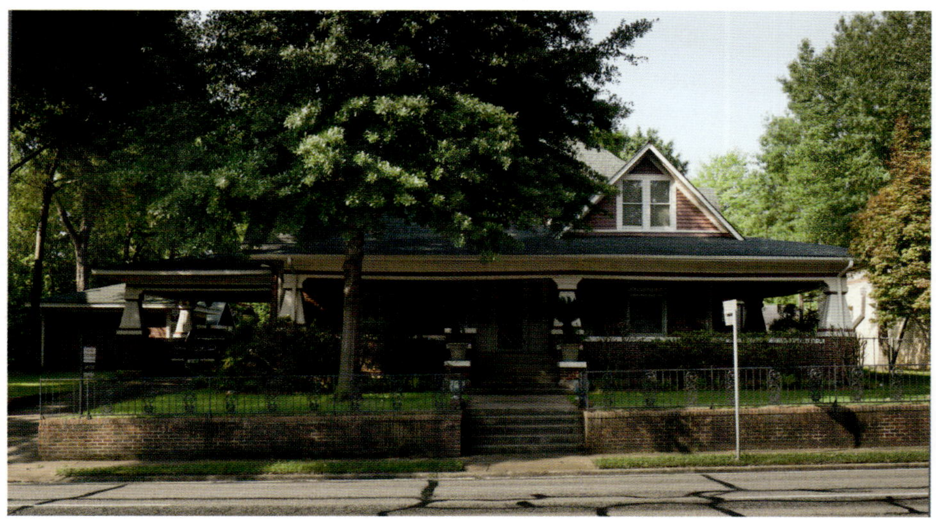

FIGURE 10.2. The Mayfield-Reid House, 2011.

The Mayfield-Reid House today does not look like the house Rulfs built in 1901, but rather has a craftsman look of the 1920s when it was remodeled. These changes came between 1922 and 1929, according to the Sanborn Maps.

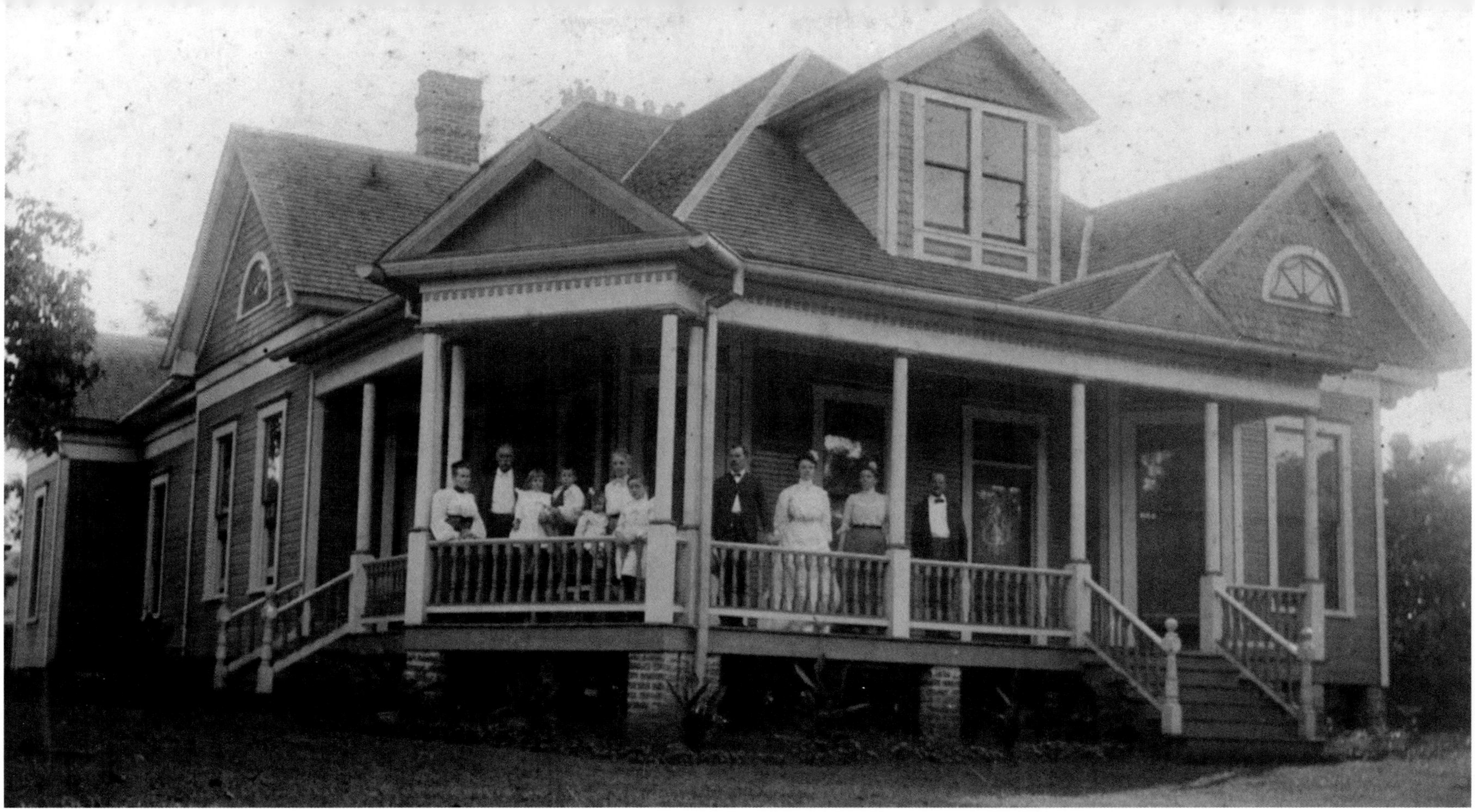

FIGURE 10.3. The Nelson House and Family.

The entire Nelson family assembled on the porch of their new home on East Main. Among those pictured are Fannie Starr Nelson, Gus and Helen Nelson, and Dr. A. A. Nelson. Photograph compliments of Paul Davis, a Nelson descendent.

In 1909, William Green Reid (1874-1943)[8] purchased the house from Mayfield when the latter moved to San Antonio. Sometime in the late 1920s, the house received a rather heavy-handed craftsman's update—not by Rulfs. The removal of the original porch, the use of wooden pyramidal support columns with brick piers and the addition of a carport gave the house a new predominantly horizontal emphasis, popular at the time. Florence Reid, who grew up in the house and inherited it when her father died in 1943, lived there with her husband, C. N. "Choc" Thompson, until their deaths.[9] Paul Davis and Helen Davis Daniel have also talked with the author about the Reid and Nelson houses on East Main.[10]

Fannie Starr Nelson and William A. Nelson House on East Main (1902)

On July 13, 1902, while commenting on the new Main Street Presbyterian Church in the block, the *Galveston Daily News* mentioned another structure designed by D. Rulfs. "On this same block and same side of the street, the fine and spacious new home of Miss Fannie Nelson is nearly complete."[11] The Nelson family was one of the oldest and most prominent in Nacogdoches; their homestead was at the southeast corner of North and Hospital Streets. When Albert A. Nelson (the surveyor) died in 1892,[12] his unmarried daughter, Frances Starr ("Fannie") Nelson (1858-1917), and her younger brother William Augustus (1861-1919) and his wife continued to live in the family home for another decade. Their older brother, however, moved to Mound Street, and in 1902, Fannie and Gus decided to join him. Their long-time friend Dr. J. E. Mayfield made the lot next to his new home available to them. Fannie paid for the lot, and her brother paid for the building of the house.[13] Fannie Nelson only paid $1500 for the lot, but that was enough to turn heads at the time.[14] For the same sum of money, she could have purchased enough acreage along Logansport Road to have constructed a whole subdivision.[15] When the Nelsons sold their old homestead on North Street, Haltom in the *Daily Sentinel* used the incident to champion how history had to give way to progress in the town: "The work of tearing down the old Nelson homestead began this morning. This is one of the old houses of Nacogdoches, and when first built was one of the finest residences in the city. Mr. John Schmidt will erect a handsome modern city hotel on the lot at once; which will both fill a long felt want in our town, and improve the appearance of North Street greatly."[16] (This never happened; see Chapter VIII.)

The Rulfs family lived in the next block to the Nelson lot on East Main; the architect could see the lot from his office. The architect's niece confirmed the attribution of the house to Rulfs, but the design elements he used denote his work without that confirmation.[17] The house, a traditional one-story structure, follows the trends in the architect's work after the turn of the century: few embellishments, classical elements, and plain entablatures with only dentil moldings. The pedimented gable at the northeast corner of the front porch gave the house its most distinctive architectural feature. Rulfs liked this feature and had used it as far back as the Laura Blount Chapman House and as lately as the Tucker-Branch House on Mound Street. The hip-and-valley roof construction was new, but his use of paired windows on the dormer and the use of fanlight windows over bays were used in several houses in these years. As usual, Rulfs combined familiar elements to form a very pleasant and distinctive structure.[18] After the death of Fannie (1917) and Gus (1919), Helen Amelia, Gus' widow, enlarged the house by adding a second story in order to provide rooms for rental income. By 1919-1920, Rulfs had retired from any construction work, due to his advancing age and the death of his brother. Nelson family tradition has Rulfs overseeing this makeover, which is quite possible. The architect possibly drew the exterior and may have suggested the mechanics of the job, but the quality of the workmanship and the detailing on the second floor make it unlikely that he closely specified or supervised the remodeling. At the time of the enlargement, the small pediment over the front door was replaced by a balcony. As can be seen in Figure 10.4, the balcony was open and had no shed roof. "Gingerbread" was never part of this house's development; Rulfs did not use such ornamentation after 1900.[19]

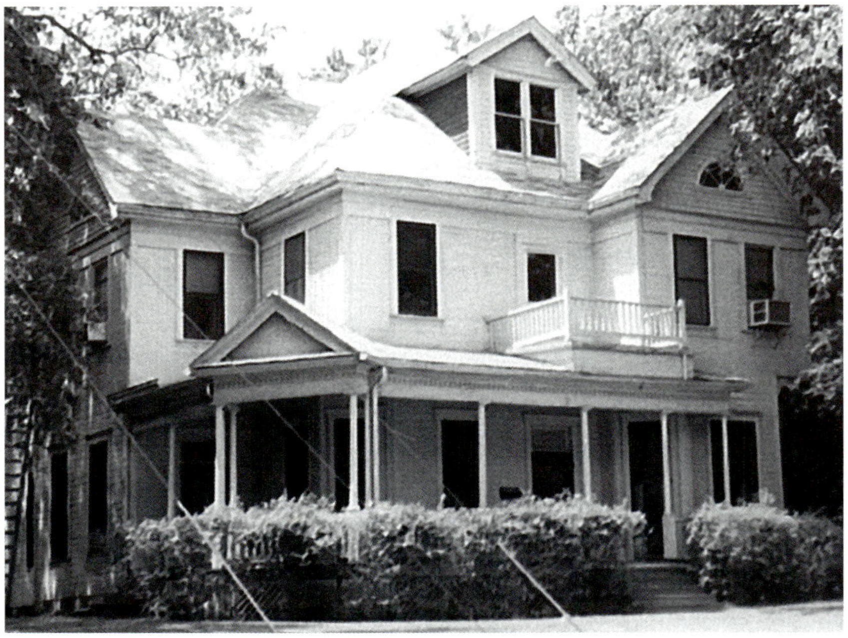

FIGURE 10.4. (Above) The Nelson House, ca. 1976. *Photograph taken by the author.*

FIGURE 10.5. The Nelson House, 2011.

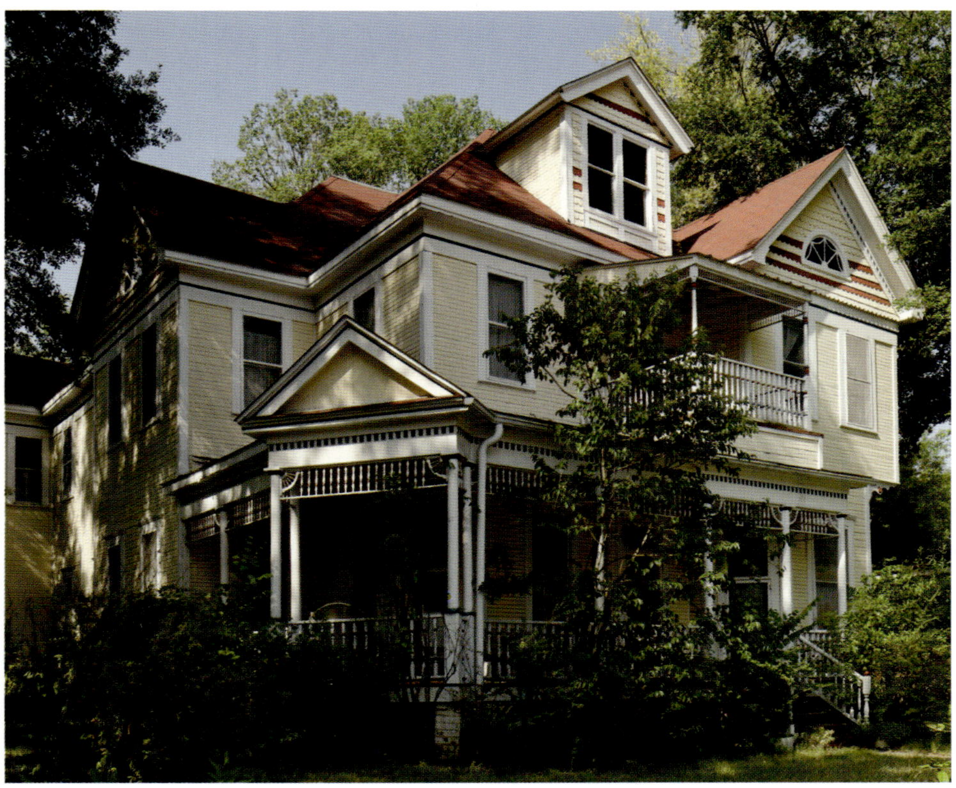

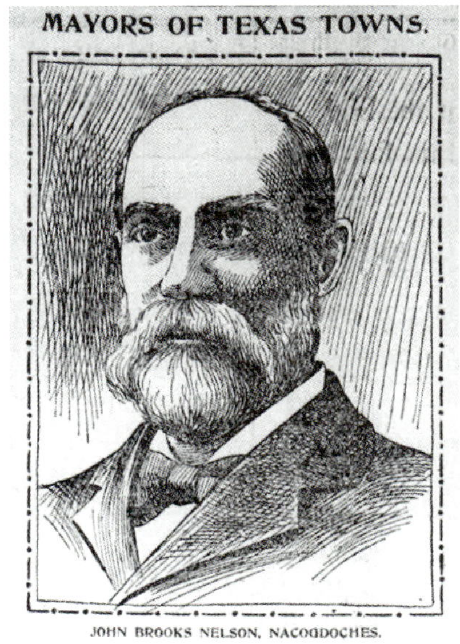

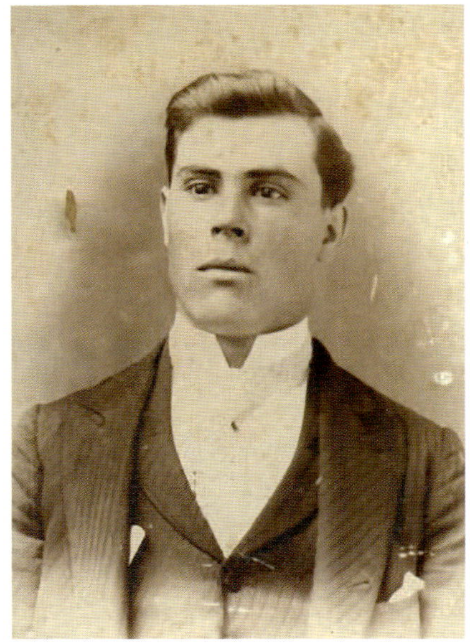

FIGURE 10.6. (Above Left) Mayor John Brooks Nelson, 1900. *Houston Daily Post.*

FIGURE 10.7. (Above Right) Dr. Albert Aldrich Nelson, ca. 1897. *Picture from the Hoya Scrapbook, courtesy of ETRC.*

The Nelson House on Mound Street (1892 and 1905)

John Brooks Nelson (1847-1929), older brother of Fannie and Gus, was the first member of his Nelson family to move to the east side of town. John purchased a lot on Mound Street in 1890 from the Raguet heirs and built a small three-room house there in 1892; he placed the house in his wife's name, the tradition of the time.[20] The house, camouflaged under an extensive makeover, still stands on the east side of North Mound Street, just north of Main Street. In 1898, when his son, Dr. Albert Aldrich Nelson (1875-1934), returned to town after completing his medical training and married Mattie Langston, John gave this small house at 122 North Mound as a wedding present to the couple. Albert Langston Nelson, their first son, was born in this house in 1900.[21]

At first, Dr. A. A. Nelson set up his practice on the second story of the Davidson building in downtown on East Main, but he soon concluded that the second-floor location was too difficult for his older patients to access. This problem, and an attempt to simplify his life, led Nelson in 1905 to ask D. Rulfs to remodel the house on Mound Street to make it his office as well as his home.[22] The remodeled house/office first appeared on the 1906 Sanborn Map.

Much like the Mayfield house, the newly remodeled Nelson house had a hipped roof with a front gable on the right with paired windows, a pediment over the entrance, and dormer, also with paired windows. (See the W. T. Wilson House for another house from this period.) A makeover, however, was much harder than starting from the ground up. Because Rulfs was so proficient in his makeovers, it is hard to distinguish the old parts from the new. According to Langston Nelson, Rulfs turned the front two rooms into a parlor and an entrance hall. He then added the new doctor's office to the south of the entrance, the room projecting slightly from the old rooms and defined by the new front gable. To the east of the original house, he added a complete central, cross-gable wing, running parallel to

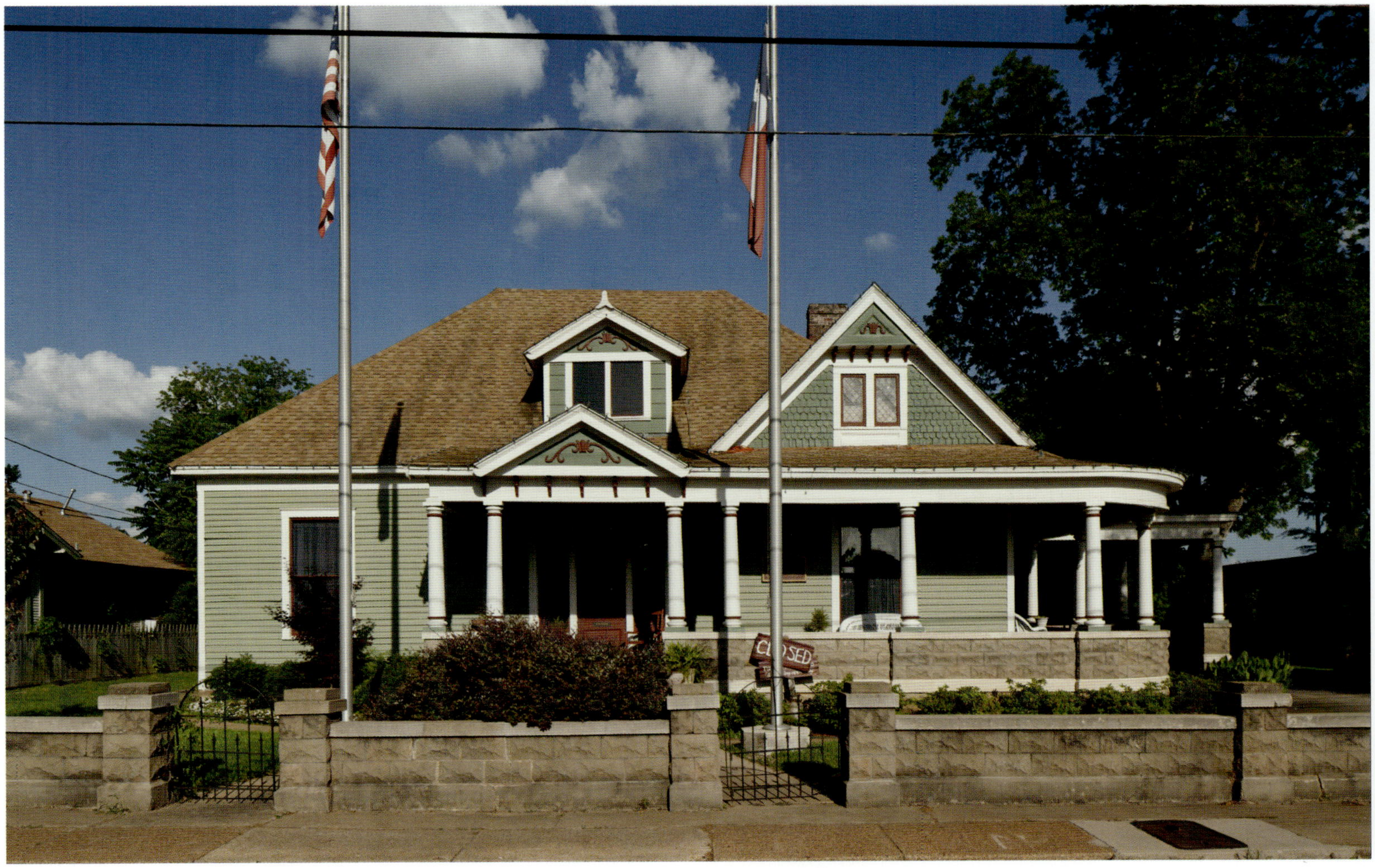

FIGURES 10.8 and 10.9. Dr. A. A. Nelson House, North Mound Street, in 2012.

While built in 1892, the look of the Nelson house dates to 1905 when Nelson had Rulfs remodel the structure. It is hard to distinguish the old parts from the new. The left side of the image right was part of the original house; these rooms became the new parlor and entrance hall. The new front gable to the right was Dr. Nelson's office, with an outside entrance to the south for patients. The rear of the structure was entirely new.

While the pediment and dormer and front gable were standard for Rulfs in the period, the house had unique features. Instead of brick supports, the entire front porch consisted of an entirely new material—molded concrete. The skirt of the porch, the piers for the columns, the solid balustrades, and even the Tuscan columns were simulated stone. Some time between 1912-1922, a carport and a wall at the curb were added.

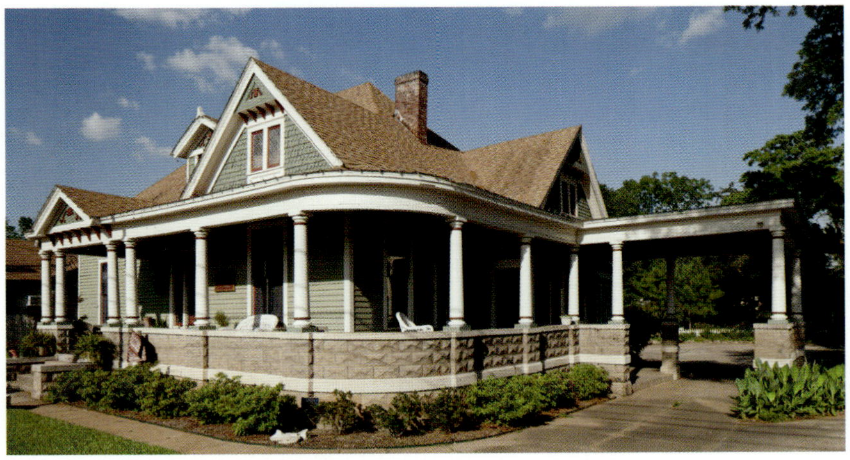

the front of the house: at the north end a new dining room and at the south end a new bedroom. Further to the east, in an L-shaped configuration, Rulfs added a new kitchen and a sleeping porch and sitting room off the bedroom. He completed the living spaces by adding a stairway off the middle hall to an upstairs bedroom. On the exterior, he used a pediment similar to the one on the West End School, paired Tuscan columns on plinth bases. Instead of brick supports, however, the entire front porch, which wrapped around from the entrance to the south side, consisted of an entirely new material—molded concrete. The skirt of the porch, the piers for the columns, the solid balustrades, and even the Tuscan columns themselves were simulated stone. Later, some time between 1912-1922, Rulfs updated the house again, adding a more urban appearance by the addition of a *porte-cochere* (perhaps by then called a "carport") and a wall at the curb of the same simulated stone. (The addition probably took place around 1912-1914 when the architect was adding landscape elements to his designs; for instance, the Hayter, Gray, and B. Mast houses have these.) The architect so expertly blended all of these changes that it is difficult to see the various transformations, except on the Sanborn Maps.[23]

Dr. A. A. Nelson practiced medicine out of this house for several decades. According to his entry in *Nacogdoches County Families*, Nelson "owned and operated the first x-ray machine in Nacogdoches County" and was "instrumental in the establishment of the City Memorial Hospital of Nacogdoches." His son, Albert Langston Nelson, also became a well-respected medical doctor in Nacogdoches with offices across the street on the corner of Hospital and Mound Street in the old June Harris House (Rulfs, 1893).[24]

In recent years, several owners have occupied the Nelson House. In 1973, Langston Nelson sold the property to George and Worth Barham, who opened a popular emporium, "The Importers," with a flower shop operated by John Shaw. In 1981, it became the offices of William A. Stewart and Associates, and, in 2005, the home of Greg Patterson Photography.[25]

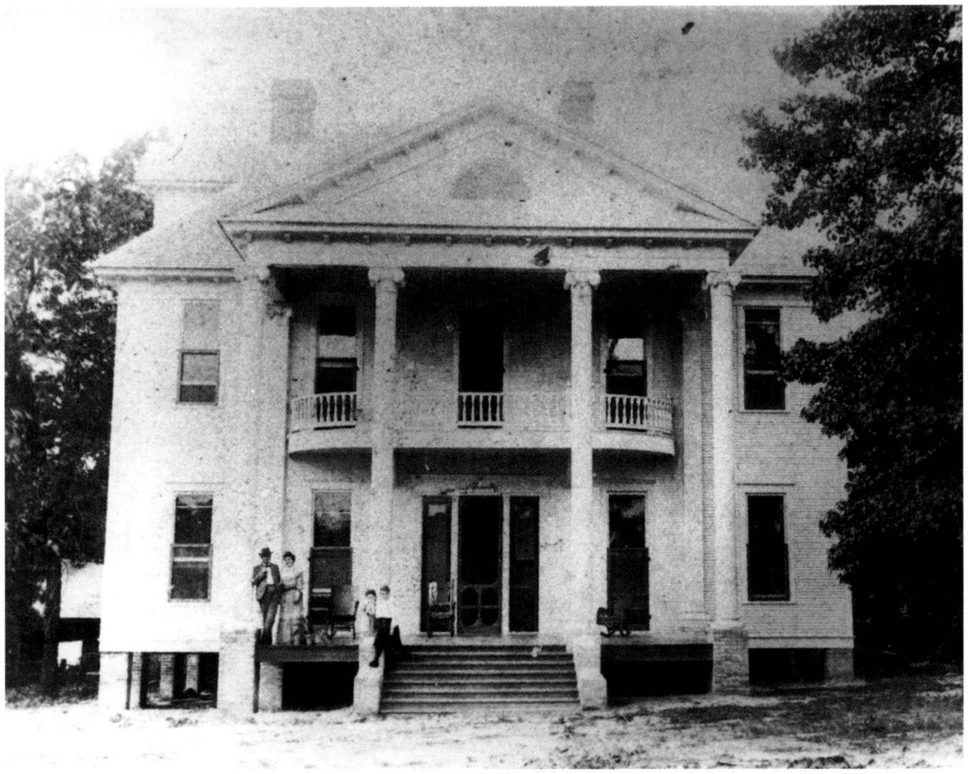

FIGURE 10.10. The Charles W. Butts House.
Built in 1906, the house sat on East Main Street. It burned in 1929. Courtesy of ETRC.

The Charles W. Butts House (1906)

One of the new homes featured in the 1906 Special Edition of the *Daily Sentinel* was the residence Rulfs designed for Charles W. and Cornelia Butts (sometimes spelled as Butte) on East Main Street. It was one of his most unusual houses. It was the only large house built by the architect on the east side of town across Lanana Creek. Perhaps, Rulfs discouraged building across Lanana Creek because of his own unfavorable experience. The house was outside the city limits of Nacogdoches at the time. While Rulfs favored elevated building sites, the property was too far from the crest of the hill to take advantage of the view, like the houses on Forbes and Irion Hills to the west.

Charles Butts, along with his brother James as his partner, ran a wholesale business operation in the 300 block of East Main. The *Sentinel* in 1906 called Butts a popular and progressive businessman, the "cash man" who sold everything at "low and satisfactory prices." In business since 1895, Butts sold "dry goods, groceries, crockery, glassware, hardware, novelties and a general line of racket goods."[26] Their wholesale business burned in the fire of 1903 on the south side of East Main.[27] By 1908, he had rebuilt, invested in several manufacturing and commercial enterprises, and sat on the board of the Nacogdoches Grocery Company by invitation of John Schmidt.[28] Mrs. Cornelia Butts helped to lead the fight against demolishing the Old Stone Fort, and she was the president of the Cum Concilio Club when the Stone Fort Memorial Building was erected in 1907-08.[29]

By 1906, Rulfs was certainly incorporating ever more classical design elements, but this might qualify as his only truly Classical Revival house. While the D. K. Cason House (1914) is also a neo-classical house, the two-story classical columns and pediment front of the Butts House was unique among his houses–an ante-bellum statement. This was the only new house he designed with two-story classical columns. (The architect did use two, full height Ionic columns when he remodeled the Link Sturdevant House in 1910, but not very successfully. See FIGURE 4.40.) The suspended balcony on the Butts home was not unusual; he had used this on the Edwards House in 1888. While neo-classical designs were in vogue across the nation at the time, it is quite probable that the design of the house owed more to Charles Butts than D. Rulfs. Butts had lived his early life in Virginia, where southern colonial architecture maintained its popularity throughout the whole of the nineteenth and twentieth centuries. The Classical Revival style was nostalgic for Butts—a sign of aristocracy. Ironically, there was a prejudice against the two-story southern look in Nacogdoches. Haltom and others associated the style with the 1856 Court House and the Old University, two buildings denounced by the 1890s' "modernists" as being "old style." Rulfs certainly was aware of this sentiment and possibly reluctant to use even an updated, neo-classical version of this style. Excluding the porch, this house looks very similar in window placement, height, and overall plan to the house Rulfs did a few years earlier on South Sanders Street for W. T. Sanders. The slip-head windows, which Rulfs used on the Butts House, were on their way out of style.

The Butts House burned to the ground in 1929. According to the report in the *Daily Sentinel,* the house "was one of the two oldest on Orton Hill and was built in 1906," and it was "outside the city limits and water service in fire fighting was not available."[30]

North Street

Throughout Diedrich Rulfs's lifetime, North Street continued to be the premier residential street in Nacogdoches. Even the opening of Stephen F. Austin State Teachers College (SFA) in 1923 did nothing to diminish the status of North Street. If anything, the arrival of SFA enhanced the street because, in order to secure the college, the town had to pave the street with bricks. Lined with large magnolia trees, North Street maintained its status and attraction for many of the town's most important families. The appeal of North Street survived until the late 1960s when the widening of the artery cut the trees and killed its residential nature. D. Rulfs was long dead by that time.

In 1900, the newest house on North Street was the impressive mansion of the banker Benjamin Wettermark. This house, just north of the future college campus, more or less established the new outer residential limits of the town at the time. Rulfs continued to design and build houses on North Street until his retirement. It would take more than two decades for North Street to fill in the space between downtown and the college. In 1923, when Eugene Blount, one of the leading advocates for SFA, decided to place his new home directly across from the entrance to the new college, it was within the perimeter set by Wettermark in 1900. Ironically, the Wettermark House burned to the ground in 1924, the year SFA moved onto the North Street campus.[31] Had Rulfs lived longer, he would no doubt have designed the new houses for the Bakers and the Sturdevants, who moved to lots across from SFA in the late 1920s. The fascination of Karle Wilson Baker with the houses and families on North Street has greatly aided this study of the legacy of the architect. While the Sanborn Maps can help in the location of a house and suggest its footprint, Mrs. Baker's interest was with the families who occupied the structures.[32]

The John Franklin Summers House (1901)

The Summers family migrated from Alabama to East Texas in 1852 and settled in the northeastern part of Nacogdoches County. Soon after their arrival, Thomas H. and Talitha Summers and two of their sons Jesse Holloway and John Franklin Summers (1850-1921) joined North Union Baptist Church (Old North Church). The younger brothers and sisters of the family were born in Texas.[33] While the older Summers lived and associated with the Appleby communities, Jesse and his younger brother, Frank, gravitated to the city of Nacogdoches, especially after the arrival of the railroad. The property the Summers owned on North Street, at the corner of King, was purchased at a Sheriff's sale in 1896 for the highest bid of $775. Frank bought out his brother Jesse for $500 in 1901. Frank placed his older home up for sale with the Harris-Lindsey Real Estate Dealers and commissioned the construction of a new house at the corner of North Street at King.[34]

D. Rulfs worked with many members of the Summers family, in two different generations.[35] The new house for Frank Summers still exists, albeit greatly altered. It is a standard, late Victorian, two-story house with a hip-and-gable roof, forward facing chamfered bay rooms, and a one-story porch that wrapped around the front and south side of the house. Over the front doorway, the porch had a two-story section, similar to the Tol Hardeman House on Mound Street done two years before.[36] Some of the architectural features of the house still exist: restrained gable ornaments, brackets, and stained glass lights around the front windows, elements Rulfs used in several other houses of the period, on Mound Street and Irion Hill.

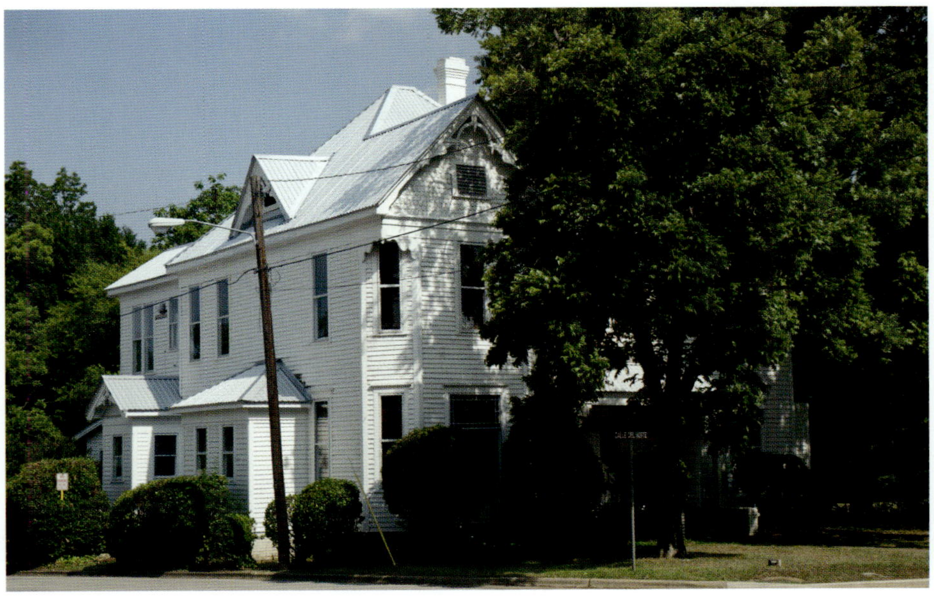

FIGURE 10.11. The John Franklin Summers House, 2011.
The Summers House on North Street, after many modifications and additions over the years, still stands on the North Street lot where it was built in 1901. The two story porch in front is gone as is the decorative window in the front gable, but many late Victorian details remain: the fish scale siding, the gable ornament, and the elaborate chimney.

The Woodall-Tilford House (1902)

In 1902, Rulfs designed and built a new house on North Street for R. O. Woodall (1860-1920) and his family. The house sat at 1717 North Street, now the address of McDonald's Restaurant at the corner of Rusk Street. (The only new house at the time in the area was the Robert Lindsey House (Rulfs, 1898), which still exists on its original site, on the next lot.) There is not much information on Woodall, except that he was listed in the Census as a merchant.[37] For some reason, the Woodalls did not stay in the house very long and sold it in 1904 to James W. Power (1880-1937) for $4,000.[38] Unfortunately, the author could find no pictures of the house. From the footprint on the Sanborn Maps, the house was a one-story structure with a porch across the entire east façade that wrapped around to the south side. The house is noteworthy for two reasons: there is a wonderful description in the *Daily Sentinel* in 1902 about the "pine top" celebration hosted by Mr. Woodall and D. Rulfs; second, immediately after World War I the house became the home of the Tilford family, a very popular Nacogdoches family. Tilden Tilford (1876-1926) is shown on the 1920 Census as living in the house, as was his seventeen year old son, Gillette.[39] Tilden was a writer of some note.[40] After the older Tilfords died, Gillette and his wife, Jewel, continued to live in the house before building a new home east of town.

In the March 4, 1902 edition of the *Daily Sentinel*, R. W. Haltom reported on one of his favorite events in Nacogdoches—a pine top celebration by D. Rulfs.[41]

". . . the 'pine top' annals of Nacogdoches"

Another Banquet Tendered for Carpenters of Nacogdoches

Yesterday afternoon for an hour or more, the back room of Tim Smith's saloon was the scene of one of those pleasant little social affairs peculiar to Nacogdoches, in which a banquet was tendered the workmen who had just completed the frame work of the new residence on North street of R. O. Woodall, and surmounted it with the symbolical pine top, which calls for nothing less than a keg of beer and substantials on the side. Messrs. Gallaway & Wright, the well known lumber firm, who furnished the material for the building, set up the spread for the boys, and Tom Smith put himself on his mettle to make the occasion memorable in the "pine top" annals of Nacogdoches.... Mr. D. Rulfs, the contractor and architect, who has the building in charge, was also on hand to do his part, and in addition to the workmen on the building and the carpenters of the city generally, were lawyers, bankers, merchants, the newspapermen and other invited guests, all hungry, thirsty and sociable, and they made the most of a most delightful occasion. . . . things happen in a quiet, genial, hospitable, and altogether satisfactory sort of fashion.... The feed was of the most appetizing character and abundant in quantity, the beer all that the thirsty could desire, and every guest had all he wanted; formality and ceremony were as conspicuously absent as coarse and boisterous conduct, and when the jolly crowd had had its fill all departed in elegant spirits and wishing all kinds of good fortune to the hospitable promoters of the occasion.

Daily Sentinel, March 4, 1902.

Sam Stripling Houses (1898 and 1905)

Samuel Black Stripling (1872-1957)[42] began his long career as a young boy who kept the mule-powered fan system operating at Perkins Brothers Drugstore. By 1895, he moved into the position of clerk; and, finally, in 1896 he became a registered pharmacist.[43] In 1901, he ventured into his own establishment, a partnership with Will Haselwood, a jeweler and watchmaker at Perkins Brothers, and Tom Baker, an accountant at Mayer & Schmidt.[44] E. A. Blount announced that Stripling's new business was to be the first tenant in the new Blount Building on the North Square. Stripling and the other men were part of a pattern that repeated itself all over Nacogdoches: they began their careers in buildings by Rulfs, opened their first business in commercial buildings by him, later worked in new commercial structures by the architect after the 1906 fire, and went on to live in residences designed by Rulfs.[45]

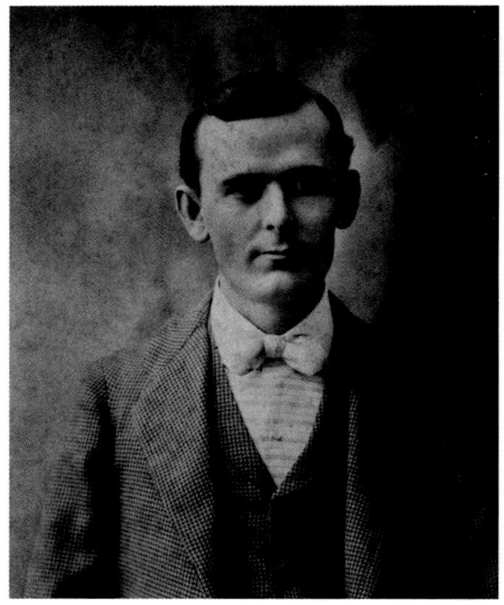

FIGURE 10.12. Sam Black Stripling, 1901.

FIGURE 10.13. (Below) Service Entrance, Stripling Drug Store, E. A. Blount Building, ca. 1905.

Sam Stripling is shown on the wagon loaded with supplies for his drug store, which was in the new E. A. Blount building. This buildings burned in 1906 in a great fire that consumed the whole north side of the Square. Photograph courtesy of Craig Stripling.

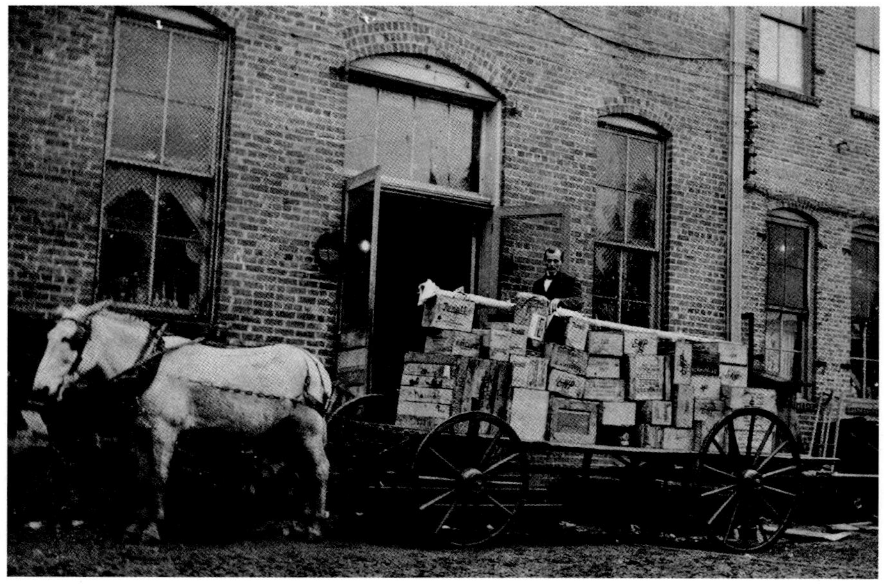

Two years after opening his new business, Stripling married Elizabeth F. Wright in 1903. During the next year, he purchased a new homestead lot on North Street, just above Mims Avenue. After being shown the plans for the house by Rulfs, Giles Haltom reported that Stripling was planning "to build a handsome two-story home on his North Street property."[46] A wonderful commemorative picture of this new home was taken shortly after the Striplings moved into their new house.[47] [For a discussion of this house (now gone), see FIGURE 10.14.]

The Sam Stripling story is instructive in trying to explain and illustrate the intertwined relationships between the German-born architect, D. Rulfs, and the citizens of Nacogdoches. In May of 1905, Rulfs finished Stripling's new home. A year and a half later, on Christmas Eve in 1906, the newspaper announced the destruction of the Stripling business in the great fire that consumed the Blount Building (1901) and the North Square. Stripling, Haselwood & Co. suffered a loss of $30,000 in stock and fixtures. They had only $15,000 in insurance, making their loss one of the highest in the group.[48] Sam and Lizzie Stripling were expecting their first child at the time. Further tragedy struck five months later when their home burned. On May 16, 1907, the headline in the *Daily Sentinel* read: "ANOTHER BIG FIRE. Residences of Mrs. W. P. Mims and Sam Stripling in Ashes." In one hour, the fire completely consumed both structures and damaged other residences nearby. Haltom labeled the Stripling home, "among the nicest residences in the city." The newspaper estimated the family's loss "at about $6000, insured for $5300."[49] After the loss of their charming new home, the Striplings temporarily leased the Laura Blount Chapman House (Rulfs, 1894) at the corner of North Street at Power (today known as the Rudisill House).[50] Their first son, Sam, Jr., was, therefore, born in a Rulfs house.

Next door to the Chapman House stood the William Crouch House (Rulfs, 1898). When Crouch sold his insurance agency in 1906 and moved to San Antonio, he sold the large Queen Anne house to T. J. Williams, the founder of the Commercial Bank.[51] While the Striplings were leasing next door, the young son of Williams died when an old Civil War pistol discharged while he was playing in the attic with friends. The sad tragedy held too many memories for the parents to stay in the house or even in Nacogdoches.[52] Williams abruptly put the Crouch House on the market. The Striplings purchased this Crouch House in 1907 and lived there for the next fifty-three years. All of the Stripling children were born in houses designed by D. Rulfs, and Sam Stripling continued to conduct business for the rest of his life in a commercial building downtown designed by Rulfs—the 1907 E. A. Blount Building.[53]

The Crouch-Stripling House was a restrained Queen Anne style structure without elaborate fretwork or "gingerbread." The architect used slender paired Tuscan columns on raised plinth bases as he had planned for the June Harris House and ultimately used on the Tol Hardeman House. The porch had two wide, slightly projecting pediments: the one over the main entrance to the house had a balcony above, which gave outdoor access via a slip-head window from the upper hall; a second pediment existed over the steps from the south porch. The hip-and-gable roof had two-story bay rooms projecting from the east and south sides. The brackets used at the gable roof level were deliberately tailored. Rulfs augmented the front gable of the Crouch-Stripling House with a Palladian motif. The tower on the house had windows at three levels. Rulfs used a very similar plan for the Robert Lindsey House on Virginia Avenue completed in 1901. The tower on the Lindsey House, however, had windows at only two levels, no pediment on the porch, and a continuous balustrade across the entire front porch roof. (See FIGURE 6.47.)

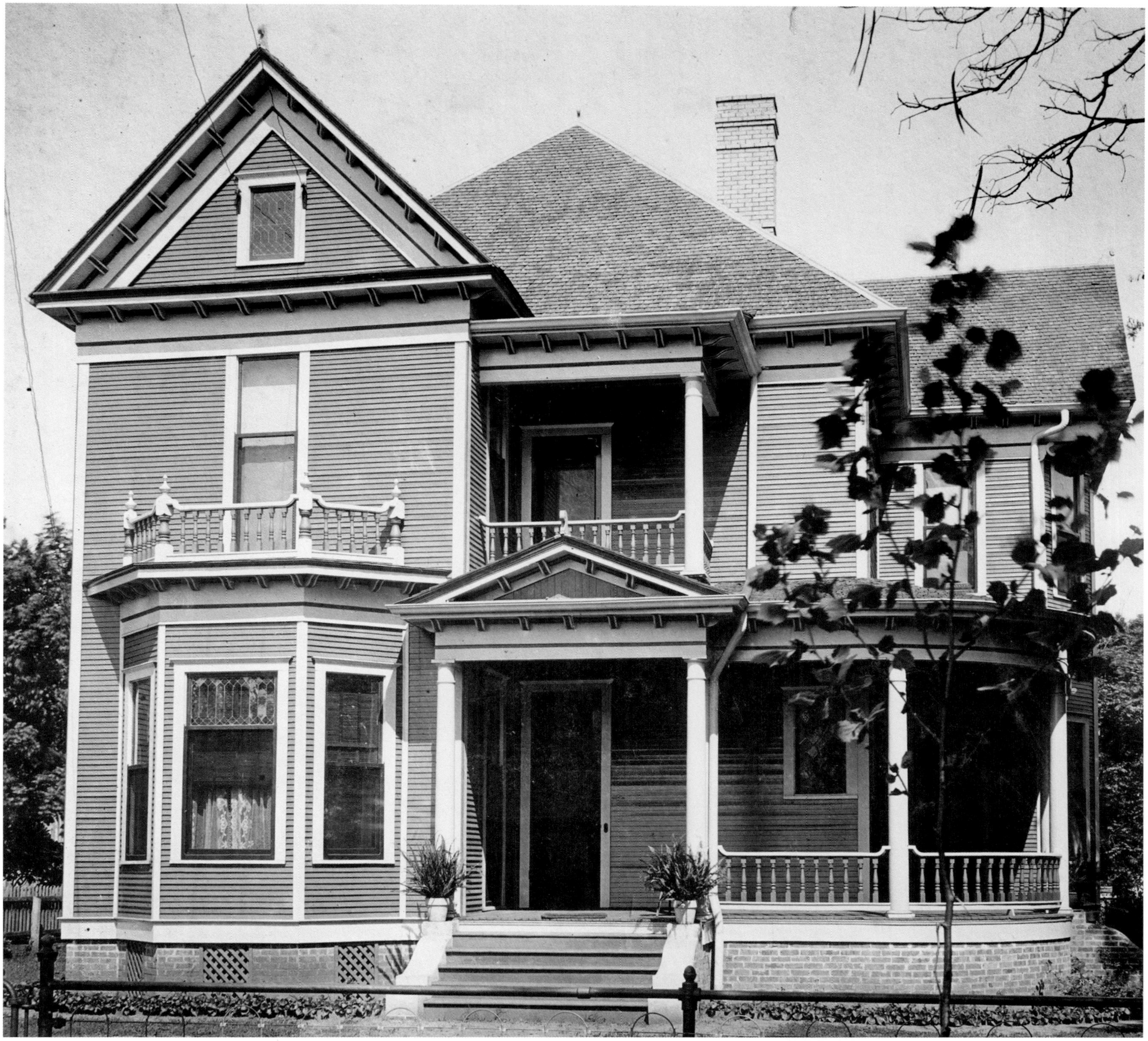

FIGURE 10.14. The Sam and Elizabeth Stripling House, built 1905, burned 1907.

This photograph is more or less the "official" documentation of Sam and Lizzie Stripling's new house. The date May 20, written on the back of the picture, signifies that the house was completed between January and May of 1905. The house, which burned in May of 1907, sat immediately north of the Mimms Hotel (the northeast side of North Street at the corner of Mimms Street, before the building of the Catholic Church there).

The 1905 Stripling House was an elegantly refined, small two-story house. There were similarities in the floor plan of this house and the J. J. Baker House on North Street, which sat two lots to the north. While definitely a late nineteenth century, asymmetrical house, the blending of elements is particularly noteworthy. There is no hint of frou-frou or frills about the house. The standard elements used by the architect include the front-facing gable with the projected bay window, the Juliet balcony above with a slip-head window, the porch that wrapped around to the south, the hip-and-gable roof, the turned balusters on the porch, and the small window on the stairwell landing. The classical elements and refinements on this house, however, place it in a different category of eclectic architecture. The pediment over the front door is one of Rulfs's finest–similar to the Phillip Sanders House on West Main Street. The Tuscan columns, the brackets or modillions that appear beneath the corona, the large entablature, the graceful way the handrails attach to the columns–all lift this Stripling House out of the ordinary. Photograph courtesy of Craig Stripling.

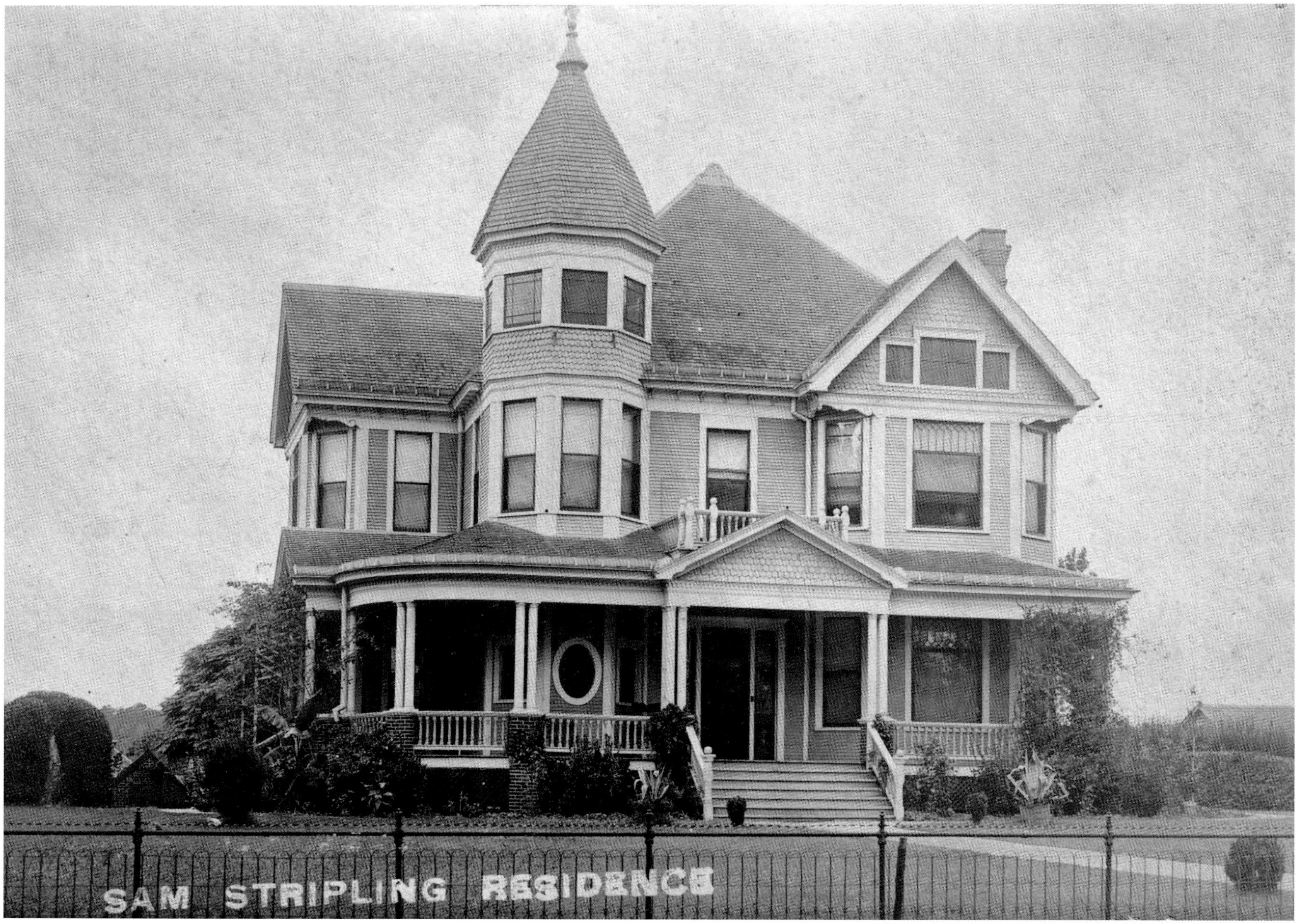

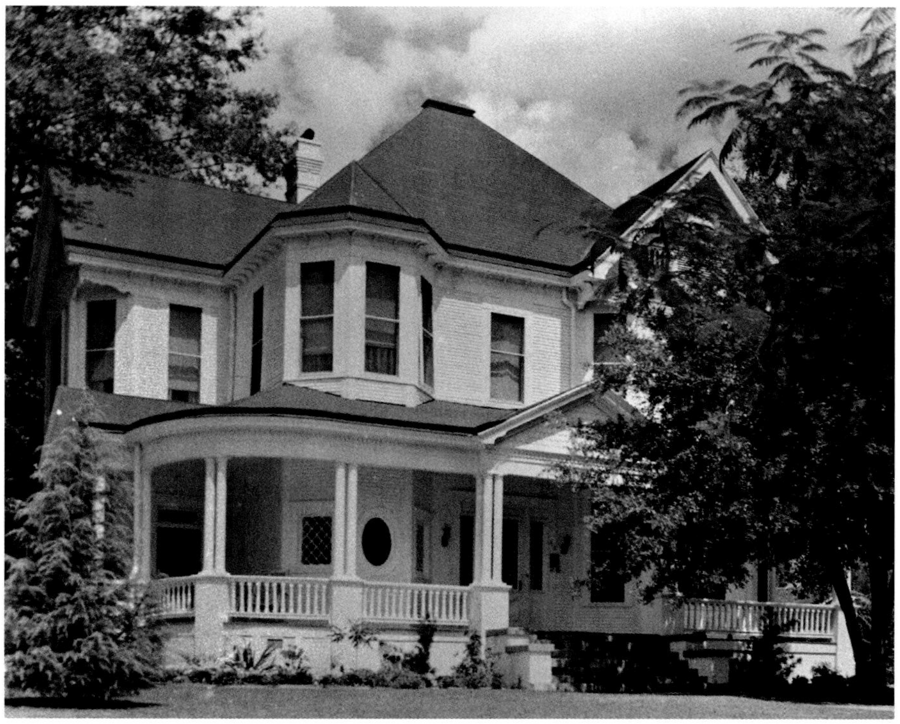

FIGURE 10.15. (Above) Postcard of the Stripling House.

The Crouch House (Rulfs, 1898) became the Sam Stripling House in 1907. The picture above, from a postcard sold at Stripling-Haselwood Drugstore, shows the Stripling home about 1913. Sam, Jr. later commented, "That house was built back when you could get a master carpenter for $1.50 a day." (Daily Sentinel, October 25, 1960.) The projecting gables, on the east front and south elevation, are two story bay rooms with chamfered windows. There is a balcony over the front door pediment and a slip-head window for access from the upper hall. To the south of the front door, at the base of the tower, there was an oval art glass window.

FIGURE 10.16. The Stripling Home, ca. 1950.

In the 1930s, towers were passé; in the Depression they seemed to symbolize earlier extravagances. Stripling, who never cared for the tower anyway, removed the third story when updating the roof. There was no need to remove gingerbread, because the house never had any. The installation of an attic fan at that time led the owner also to remove the central window in the front gable's Palladian motif. At the same time, Stripling had the wooden steps and handrails replaced with brick and concrete. Brick also replaced the lattice between the piers. The house was then painted solid white. Photographs courtesy of Craig Stripling.

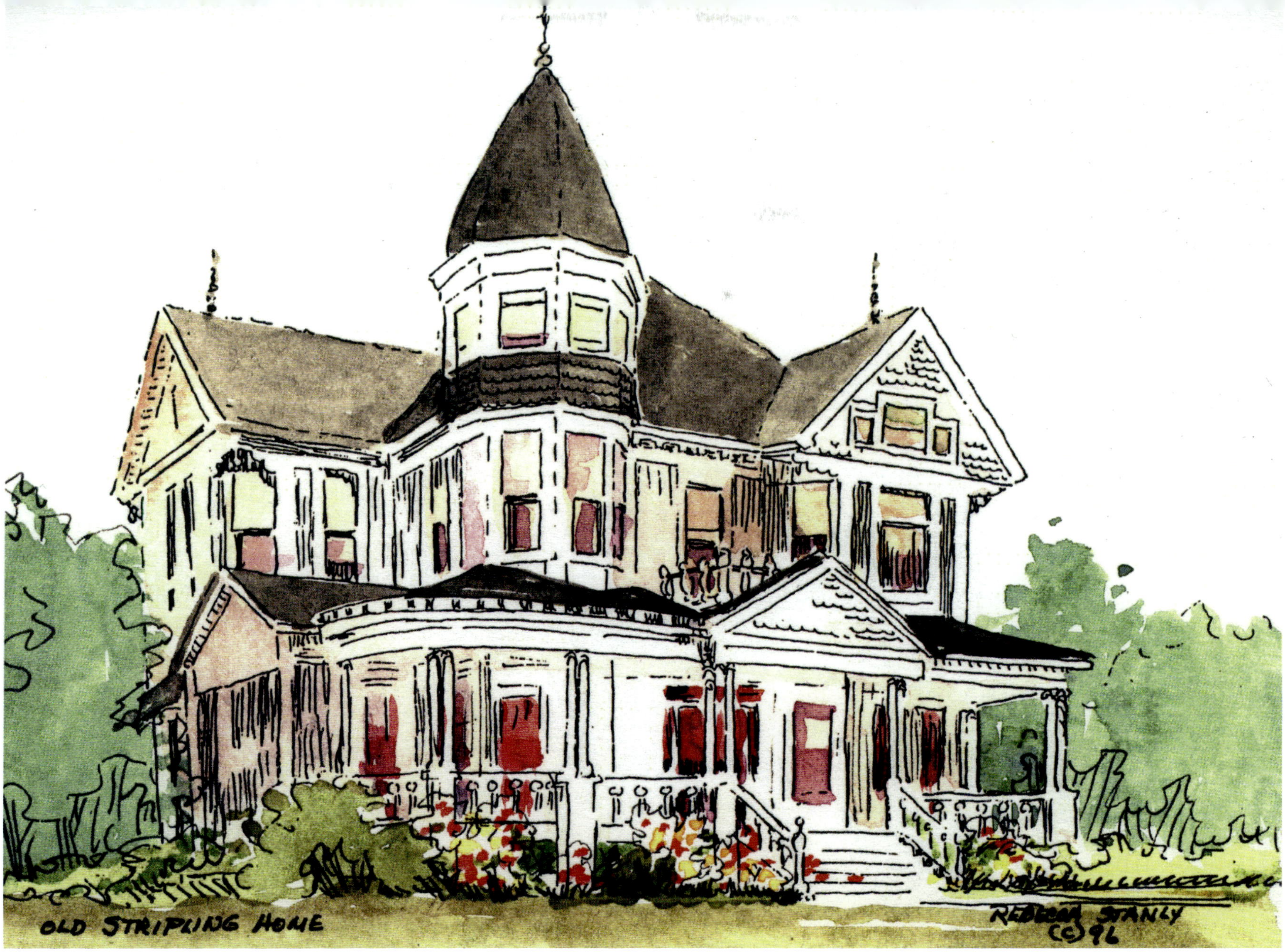

FIGURE 10.17. The Stripling Home by Artist Rebecca Stanly, 1996.

The houses on North Street, around Washington Square, and Irion Hill have from the early years of their existence been objects of art. Postcards, like the one on the previous page, have made their way into many collections. Drawings, like the one above by local artist Rebecca Stanly, have also made their way into many collections. Colored drawing courtesy of Rebecca Stanly.

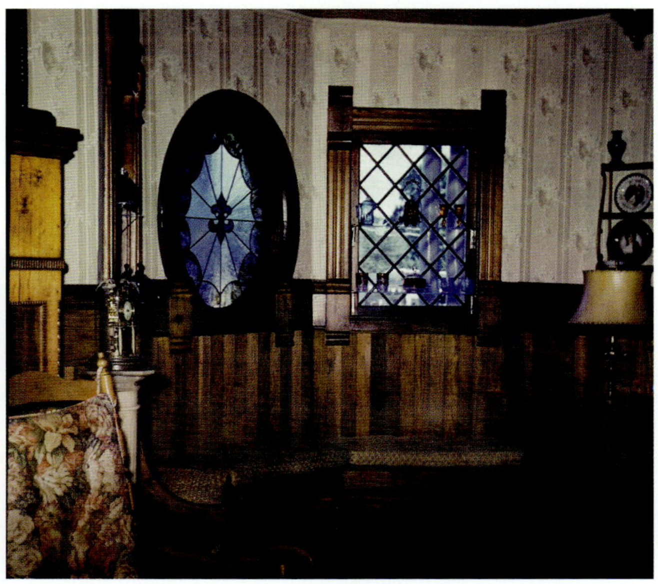

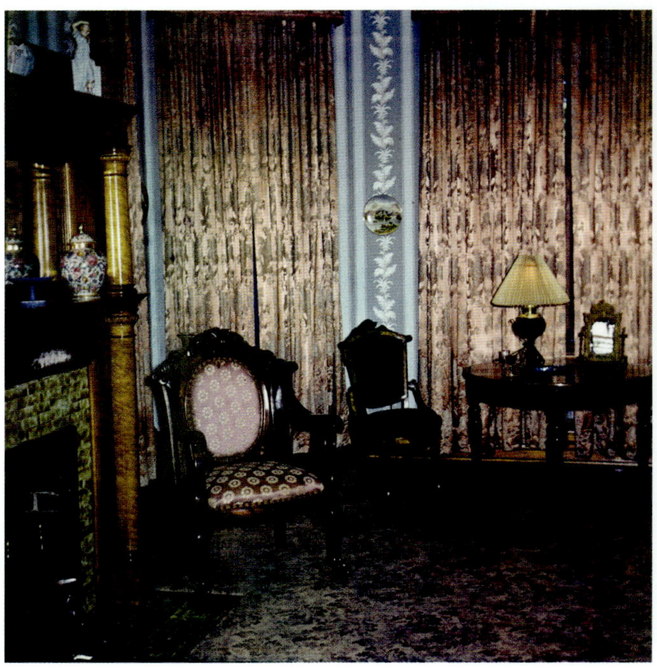

FIGURES 10.18 and 10.19. Interiors, Stripling House, ca. 1956.

The two interior color photographs of the Stripling House date from the mid-1950s, shortly before the demolition of the house in 1960. The photograph left shows the living room and the one above the tower section of the entrance hall. Photographs, taken by Bill Stripling, courtesy of Craig Stripling.

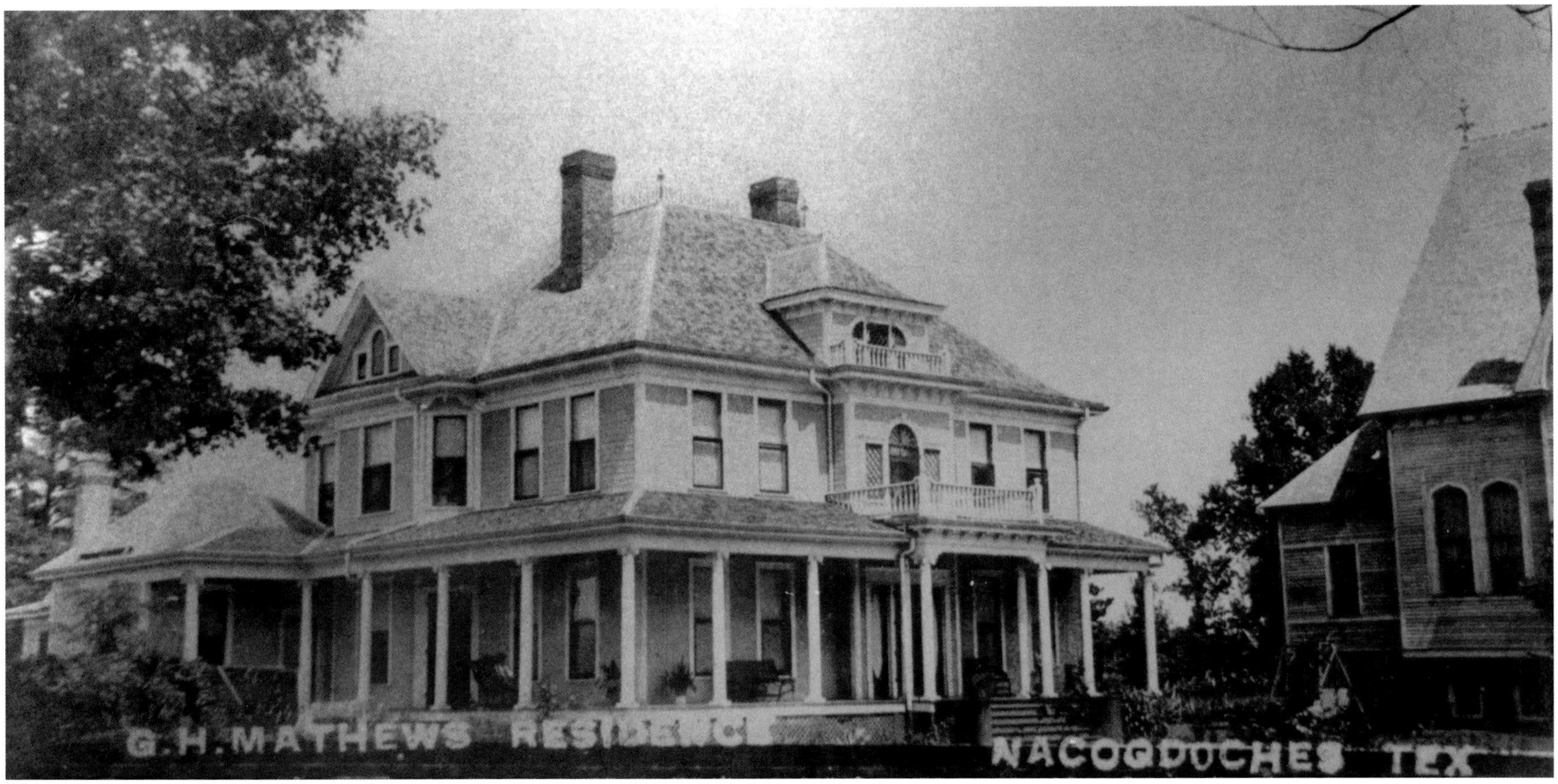

The George H. Matthews House (1905)

George H. Matthews (1858-1938) was a lawyer in Nacogdoches, a Mason, and several times mayor of the town.[54] (His son, Oscar Matthews, worked with Rulfs on building Christ Episcopal Church between 1900-1902.) According to the Census in 1900, George and his family lived on North Street close to the Wettermark House.[55] Around 1905, Matthews had Rulfs design and build for him an imposing house on a lot he had purchased just south of the new First Baptist Church sanctuary on North Street. The completed house is shown on the 1906 Sanborn Map, just north of the George Houston Davison House (now gone, but also built by Rulfs).[56]

The Matthews House strongly resembles the original design of the John Garrison House on Washington Square. (See Chapter V) The three-ranked projection over the main entrance is the most distinguishing characteristic of the house: grouped Ionic columns at the porch level, a Palladian door-window with a balcony and balustrade on the second, and an elaborate dormer on the third floor. The façade was very symmetrical. As part of the hipped roof, the house had cross gables at the rear of the house. As in all of the architect's houses built after 1890, the chimneys are internal.

The Matthews House, purchased by the Cason, Monk & Company in the 1930s, became the home to the company's funeral home division. In 1946, the company conveyed the Matthews House to the First Baptist Church. The church utilized the house for office space and for their Young People's Department. In the building programs in the 1950s, the church moved the Matthews House down the hill, all in one piece, where it continued to serve the congregation.[57] The chapel of the First Baptist Church now occupies the former site of the Matthews House.

FIGURE 10.20. (Above) The George H. Matthews House.
This postcard of the Matthews House dates to ca. 1907. The name is misspelled on the postcard; "Matthews" is missing a "t." Photograph courtesy of Cecil Sparks.

FIGURE 10.21. (Below) The Matthews House, ca. 1950s.
The Matthews home in the 1930s became the Cason-Monk Funeral Home. After World War II, the building passed to the First Baptist Church. Photograph courtesy of James G. Partin.

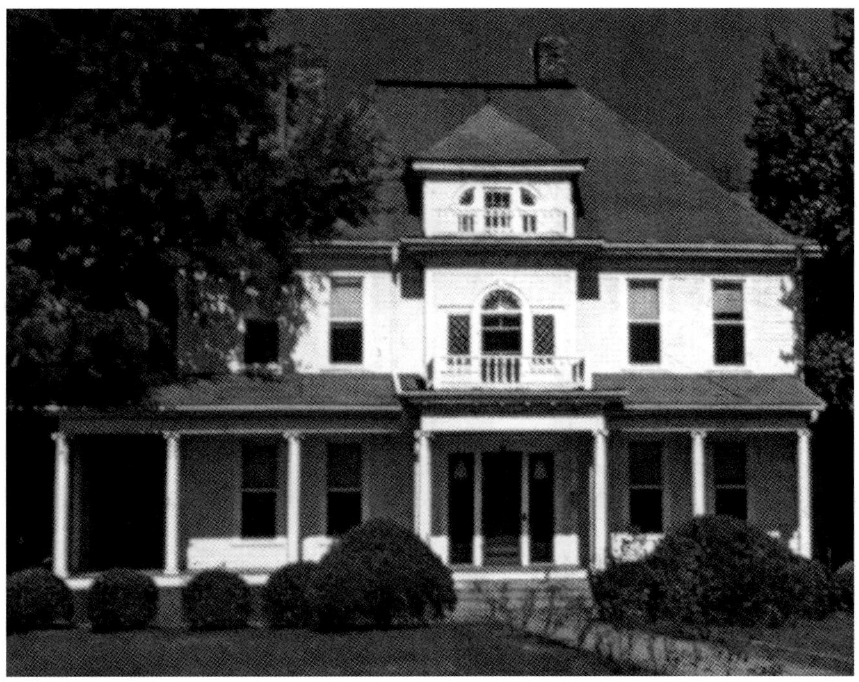

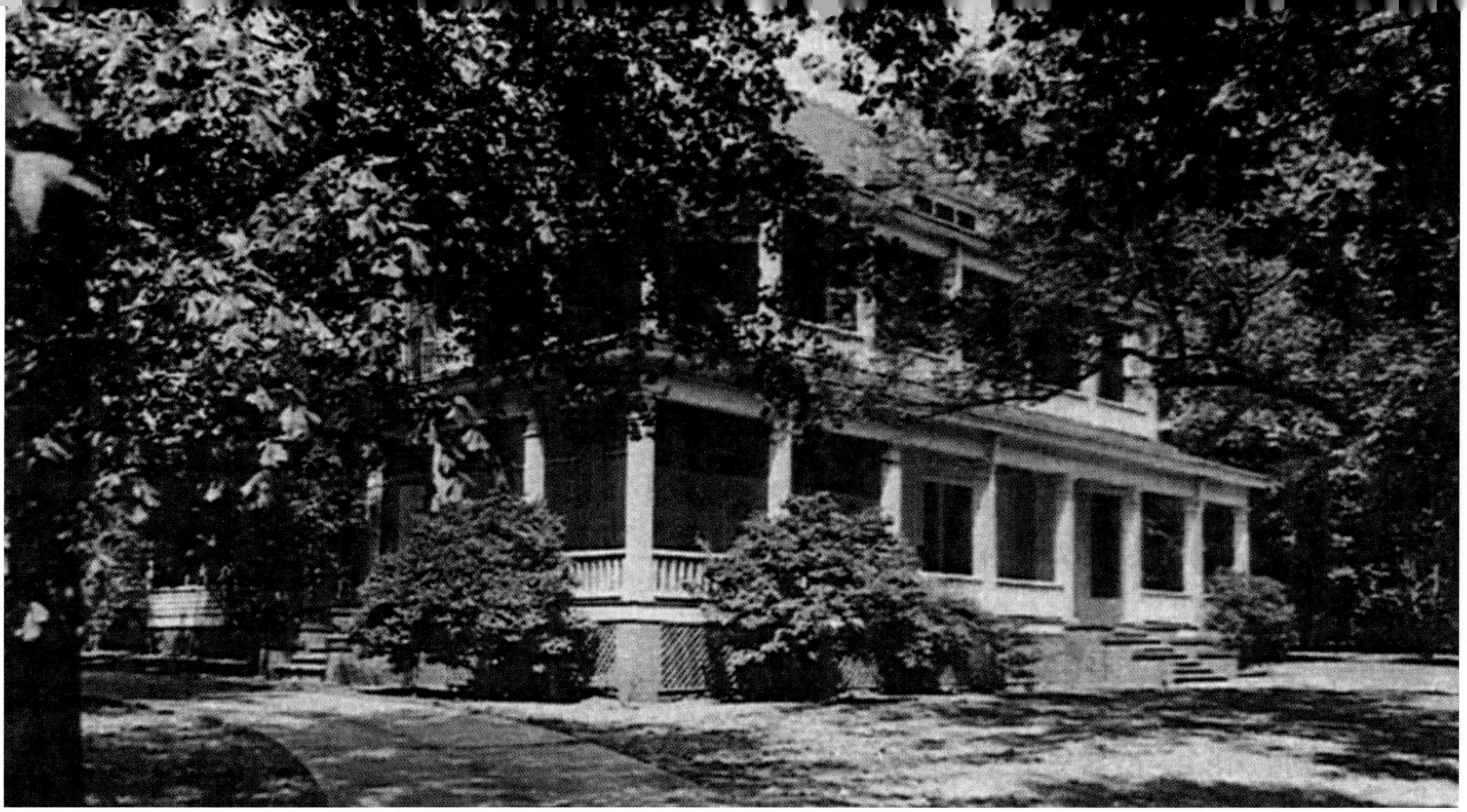

Remodeling the Will Perkins House (1910)

Despite his withdrawal from the retail business in 1907, W. U. Perkins remained active in civic affairs in Nacogdoches; for instance, he was mayor in 1908. The family's domestic arrangements, as early as 1890, had set the pace for construction on North Street. (See Chapter IV.) The newspaper eagerly watched the decision by Perkins to remodel his home in 1910 instead of building a new house. Again, the innovations Rulfs introduced in this makeover set the pace for a whole host of transformations around town: on North Street, Church Street, Mound Street, and Irion Hill. In the Perkins makeover, Rulfs offered an alternative to homeowners who could relate to some of the demands of the modernists: straight lines and a minimum of decorative details. On the other hand, traditionalists like Perkins wanted no part of the national movement towards bungalows. They already had perfectly good structures; furthermore, they still cherished the elegance and gentility of entrance halls, luxurious woodwork, high ceilings, stately roofs, and the utility of back stairs.

In 1910, Rulfs made few internal changes to his 1890 makeover of the house. He updated the kitchen, introduced bathrooms, added closets, and enclosed a porch. Rulfs was introducing these changes all over town in his new designs and renovations; they were made possible by the town's new water and sewer lines. The external changes, however, were dramatic. According to Will's youngest daughter, Virginia Perkins Nelson, the external changes consisted of removing the narrow front gallery, the "gingerbread," and the tower.[58] There are photographs of this remodeled structure. Also, many people remember the Perkins House as remodeled in 1910, because it was not torn down until 1967 to make way for Tipton Ford Motor Company. Bryan and Carolyn Davis have discussed this house in detail with the author.[59]

FIGURE 10.22. The W. U. Perkins House on North Street.
In 1910, Will Perkins had Rulfs update his home on North Street. The clean lines set the pace for various remodelings in town. Photograph courtesy of Dorothy Neblett Perkins.

They agreed with the description offered below by architect Bill Wilson, Will and Annie Perkins' oldest grandson:

> The house was on a lot with perhaps 350 feet of frontage and a back yard which ran a quarter-mile west through orchard, barn yards, pasture, and pine woods down to the Lanana [sic, Banita Creek]. Across the creek and railroad track was a sawmill. In style the house was white clapboard, restrained and almost chaste Victorian. The only purely decorative elements were modest copper ridge acroteria cresting a green-painted cedar shingle roof. Ceiling heights measured thirteen feet on the first floor and eleven on the second. Twenty white square pillars, ranged in two step-back tiers on the street façade and half way around the south side gave the residence stateliness without pretension.[60]

Rulfs replaced the posts on the porches with square boxed columns coupled with square balusters with enlarged handrails. He enlarged the width of the porch and included large screened sections on both levels. The new front steps were concrete. The architect later used all of these same elements when he remodeled the Tom Summers and Sarah Perkins Houses on Church Street, and the R. C. Monk House on Irion Hill. Dr. Joel Barham, a cousin of the Perkins, also had these same decorative elements placed on his house on North Street.[61] The Hollis Mast House on Mound Street (discussed in the next chapter) also shared some of the same proportions and elements.

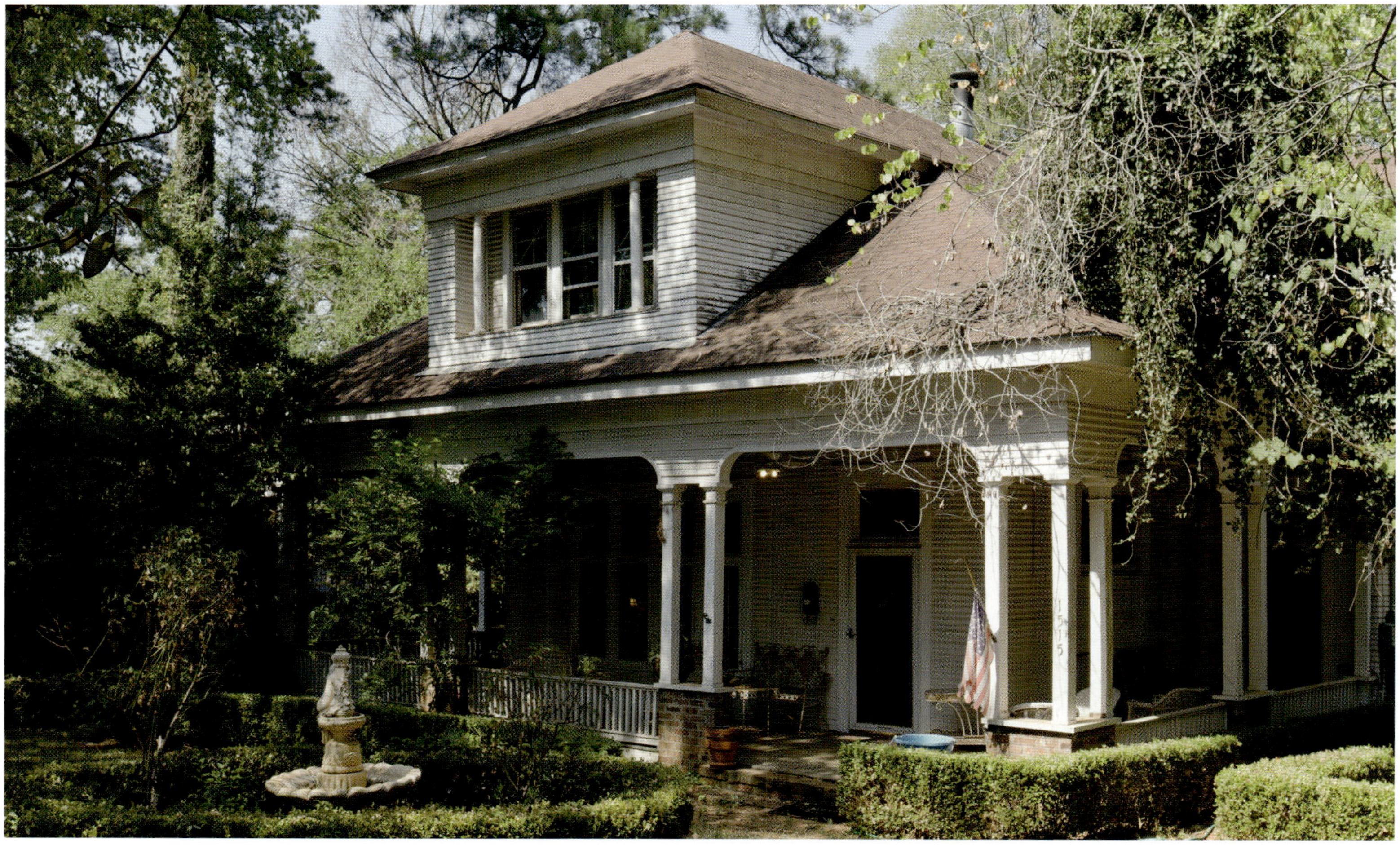

FIGURE 10.23. John Perkins House, 2011.
Now on Pearl Street, the John Perkins House originally sat on North Street north of the Hayter House. Later the corner was the service station of John Wood.

John Perkins House (1910)

John Hardeman Perkins (1877-1937), son of Will Perkins's brother, Richard, grew up and went to school in Rusk County and did not move to Nacogdoches until about 1894. After receiving his pharmacy degree in 1898 from the University of Texas, he joined his uncle as a pharmacist at Perkins Brothers.[62] In1910, John Perkins commissioned Rulfs to design a home for him on the corner of North Street, north of what is now West Starr Street, approximately where Long John Silver's restaurant now stands.[63] The house, still extant but moved down the hill to 1501 Pearl Street in the 1960s, shares common elements with two other houses by Rulfs in the same time frame: the Haselwood House on Mound Street and the Summers House on Church Street.

In his plan for the John Perkins House, the architect began to experiment with ways to utilize the space under large hipped roofs without creating a full second story. From the crest of the roof, he projected large dormer-rooms forward over the front of the house, and on the three other sides of the house. Each dormer-room of the Perkins structure had recessed windows flanked by Doric columns. The unusual front porch of this house wraps around the living room on three sides. The porch supports consist of paired slender, square Doric columns resting on brick piers that rose from the ground to the handrails of the balustrades.[64] The one photograph found of the house on its original location on North Street clearly gives proof why Rulfs preferred to place his creations where one looked up, rather than down, on them from the street.

John Schmidt House, Phase II

John Schmidt had the largest, most opulent Queen Anne style home in Nacogdoches. In 1911, Schmidt decided his house, too, needed some updating. He called on the Rulfs brothers to undertake the design and carpentry work. D. Rulfs specified the replacement of the posts with columns, removed some of the fretwork, removed the large dormer from the roof, enlarged the bathrooms, added closets, and connected the house to the new city water mains and sewerage. The domestic contexts in Nacogdoches were changing as a result of technology in the form of the automobile and urban services such as water and sewerage. Although *anything* Schmidt did was newsworthy, the *Sentinel's* coverage this time focused on the craftsmen imported from Tyler to undertake the interior decorations. Schmidt by this time had a major store in Tyler; his decision to spread his patronage to business associates in Tyler occasioned the following comments.

> H. S. Taylor of the firm of Tayler & Arrat of Tyler, house painters and decorators, arrived in the city yesterday with a force of men and this morning put them to work on the residence of John Schmidt on North Street. Mr. Taylor informs us that he has a contract to overhaul the house from the ground to the roof. The paint on the outside will be burned off and a fresh new coat put on; the inside of the building will be newly varnished and every room will be freshly papered and the roof will also receive a fresh coat of paint. When the work is completed Mr. Schmidt will have one of the neatest, cleanest looking and prettiest residences in the city.[65]

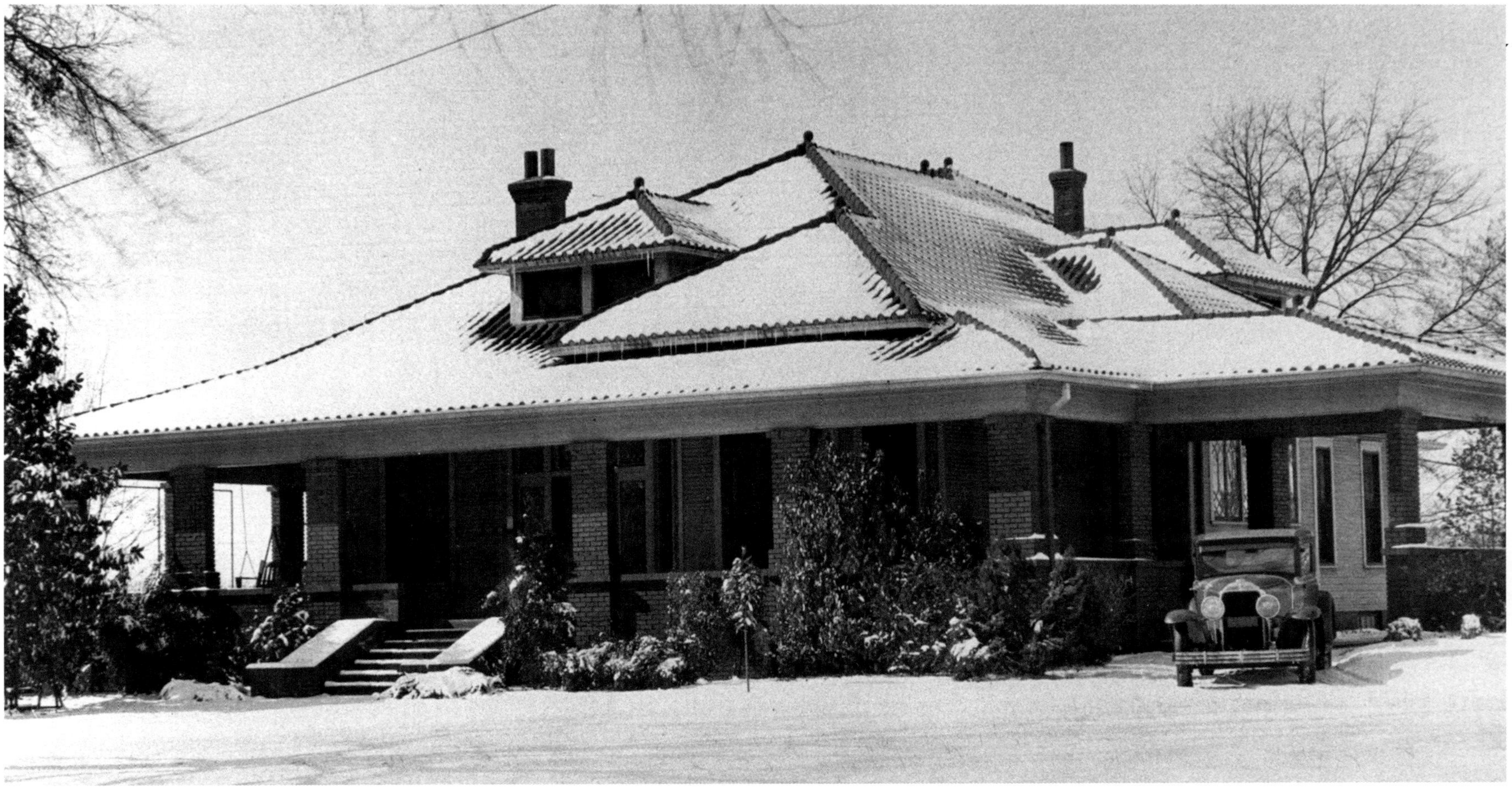

FIGURE 10.24. The Fay and Guy Blount House in 1912.
Dr. & Mrs. James Buckingham extracted the Guy Blount House from the growing commercialization of North Street in 1986. The house now sits off Appleby Sand Road. Photograph courtesy of Judy Buckingham.

The Guy Blount House (1912)

Guy Arthur Blount (1884-1937) was the youngest son of the banker E. A. Blount. He grew up in a Rulfs house on North Street. In 1906, in the wedding of the decade, Guy (22) married Fay Hayter (23). The marriage united two of the most important families in Nacogdoches. The Hayters also lived in a Rulfs house—the house originally built for Ben Wettermark in 1900. The Guy Blounts decided after the birth of their first children, Elizabeth in 1908 and Mamye Ethel in 1911, that they needed more space.[66] Guy's father offered them a lot on North Street, thought to be the site of the Spanish Mission Guadalupe,[67] and, in late 1911, they discussed their interests with D. Rulfs. Guy had become a lumberman and managed the family's extensive land holdings throughout East Texas;[68] Guy wanted a house that would be a showplace for the various woods of the East Texas region. The Blounts also wanted something more modern in style, more suited to a new generation. Contemporary designs across the nation were emphasizing the horizontal lines of the house rather than the vertical. Rulfs incorporated all of these things.

The plans Rulfs submitted to the Blounts were unique for Nacogdoches. It was the first of the architect's prairie style houses. In sharp contrast to the other Blount houses nearby, from the pitch of its roof to its underpinnings, this house represented the modern: it had the town's first low-hipped roof; the first tile roof; one of the first houses (along with the Hollis Mast House) with continuous brick skirt and brick columns and balustrades; one of the first houses with a concrete porch; the first central steam heating; and the town's first carport, rather than a *porte cochere* for carriages.[69] The carport extended the linear look of the house, as did the low profile dormers with their hipped roofs and horizontally grouped windows. While not the first house to build-in internal toilets, it was the first to have a built-in shower. Nor was it the first house to have direct entry into the living room (that is, no entrance hall), but it was among the first beyond the architect's own house.

While the basic floor plan of the house's interior was not that radically different from other houses, the absence of an entrance hall was unusual and forced certain compromises on the house. The two front living spaces, a parlor and a living room, had no hall separating them. The open space was terrific for entertaining, but with no separate entrance hall, the living room by necessity became a hall. This could and did work in the front of the house, but in the back half of the house, where the rooms needed to be separate or private (bedrooms and kitchen), there continued to be a need for a hall. To designate the back half of the house, a permanent, in-wall divider stood between the living room and the back hall. This was fine during the summer when drafts were always welcome, but in winter, this left the front room with a substantial heating problem. The new central heating system was to supposed offset this; but, in reality, the house had to rely on the *portieres* or curtains which separated the front room from the back hall to control drafts.

In this house, as in no other since the Schmidt House, Rulfs had the opportunity to display an extravagance of fancy woods. In the main rooms, the doors were pine on one side and oak on the other. The public rooms had fine inlay borders, each one different. The wood for the inlay in the living room came from the timbers of the Old Stone Fort. Rulfs, quite possibly, would have clad the house in a brick veneer, as he did in the Haselwood

House about the same time, had the owner not been a lumberman. The inclusion of a bay window with chamfered corners in the parlor, a nod to tradition, forced Rulfs to create a break in the roof line to accommodate the floor plan. The architect learned that this anomaly interrupted the linear look and did not repeat it in his subsequent prairie style houses.

Fay Hayter died in 1921. In 1925, Guy married Lois Foster, the first faculty member hired at the new college in 1923. With two children from the first marriage and four from the second, the Blounts enlarged the house in the early 1930s by adding another large bedroom and screened porch off the back of the house.[70] In 1985-86, after the widening of North Street had turned North Street into a commercial thoroughfare and, after the death of Lois Foster Blount, the house received a second life because of the dedicated work of Dr. James and Judy Buckingham. The Buckinghams documented in photographs the entire process of the move. Such a room by room, wall by wall dissection of a Rulfs house exists in no other pictorial record. The house is now home to Michael and Mandy Brewton.

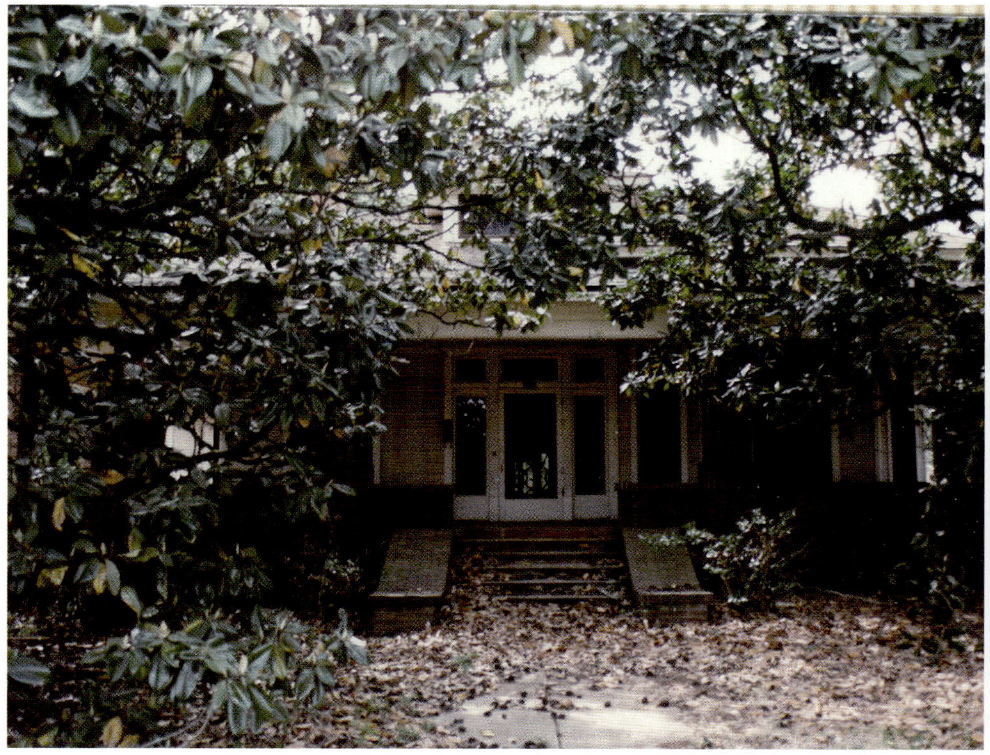

FIGURE 10.25. (Right) Entrance, from North Street
Large magnolia trees completely hid the Guy Blount House in its later years on North Street, making perspective difficult. The unique front steps and the massive front door can be seen in this photograph. Courtesy of Judy Buckingham.

FIGURE 10.26 - 10.27. (Below) The Living Room, Guy Blount House.
In the picture below left, the front living room as it looked in the 1920s. Below, right is the same room in the mid-1980s, shortly before the Buckinghams moved the house. Notice that later owners removed the hood over the mantle and at least started the removal of the paint on the wainscoting. Courtesy of Judy Buckingham.

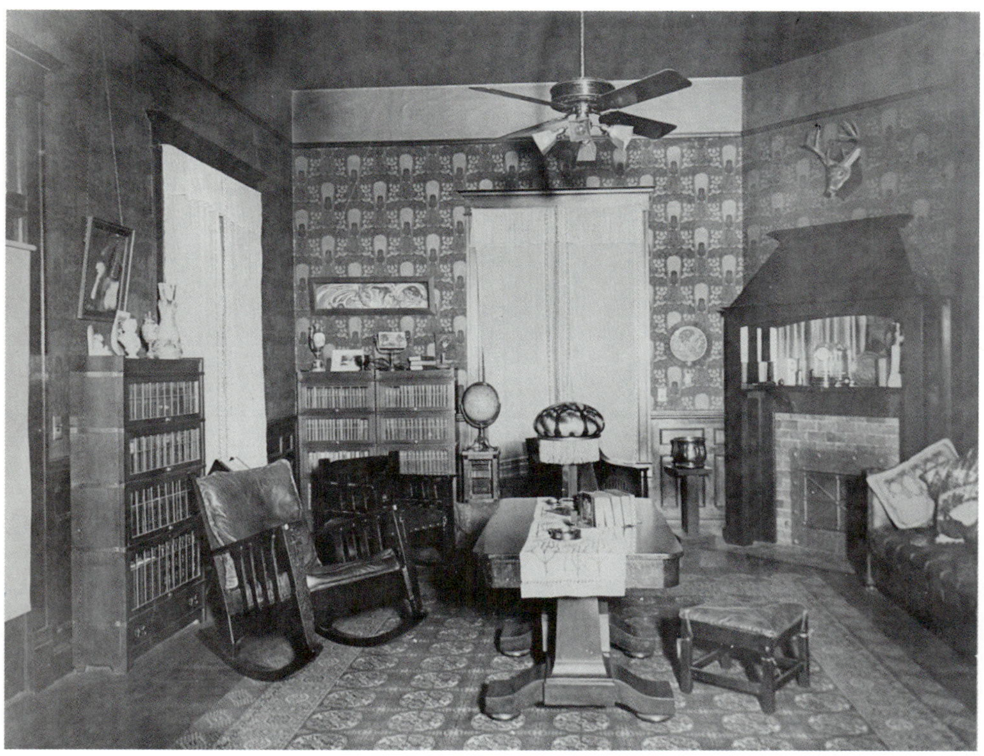

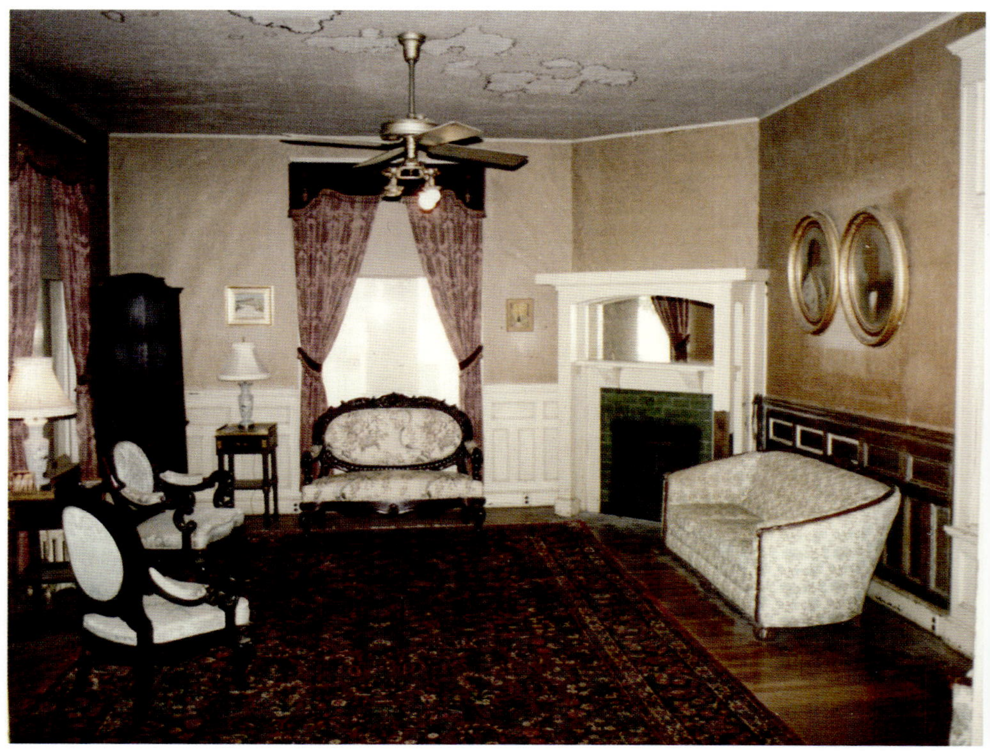

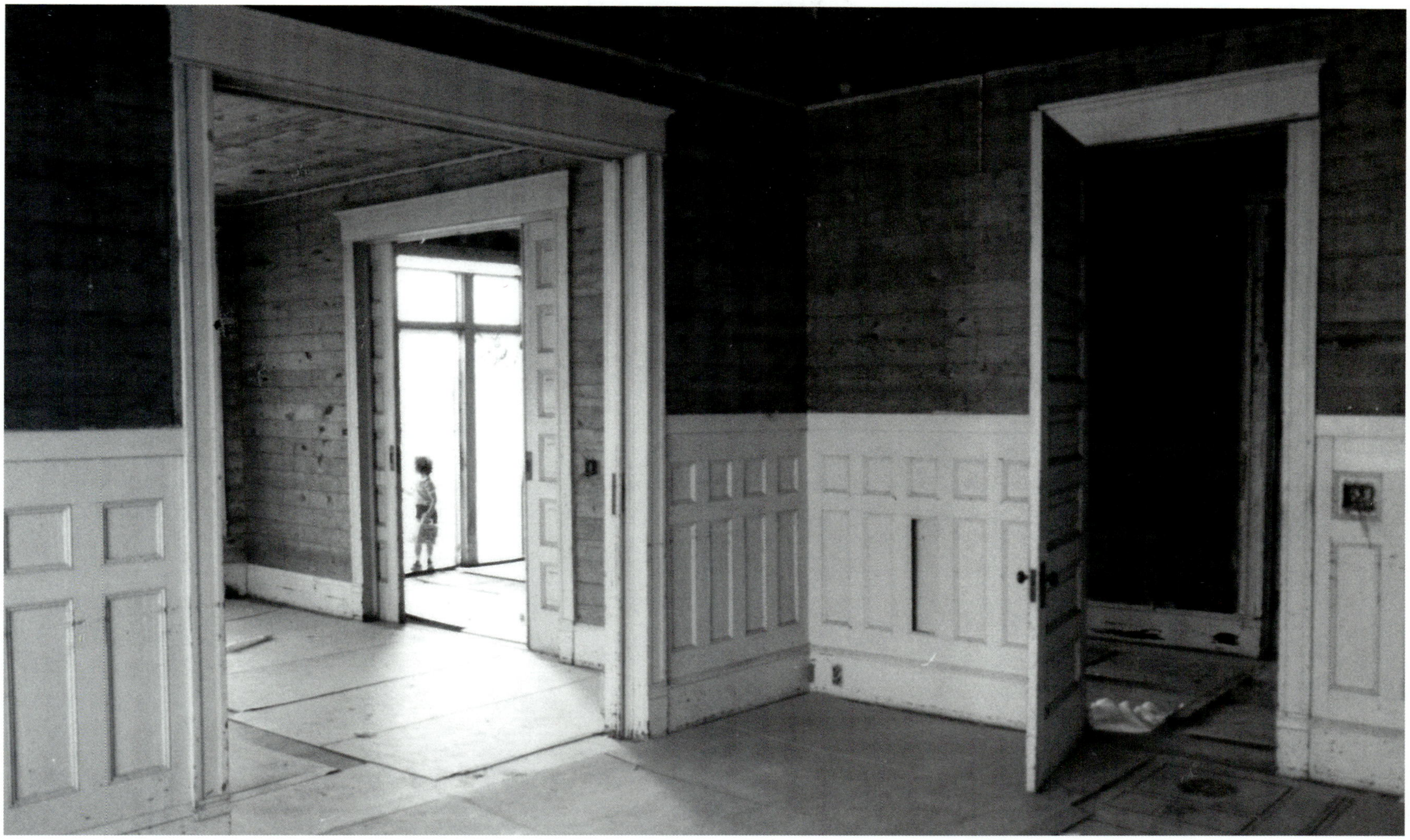

FIGURE 10.28. (Above) Guy Blount House, 1985.

This interior photograph, taken shortly before the house was moved, shows some interesting details looking from the dining room through the parlor to the front door, where young Jordan Buckingham is standing. Plyboard is covering the inlay floors to protect them. Courtesy of Judy Buckingham.

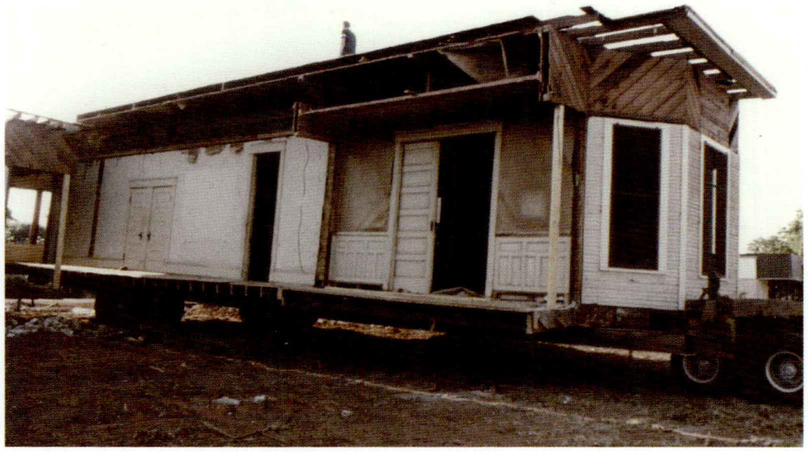

FIGURE 10.29. (Above) Leaving North Street.

The front family room is on the truck, roof removed, but pocket doors in place. Courtesy of Judy Buckingham

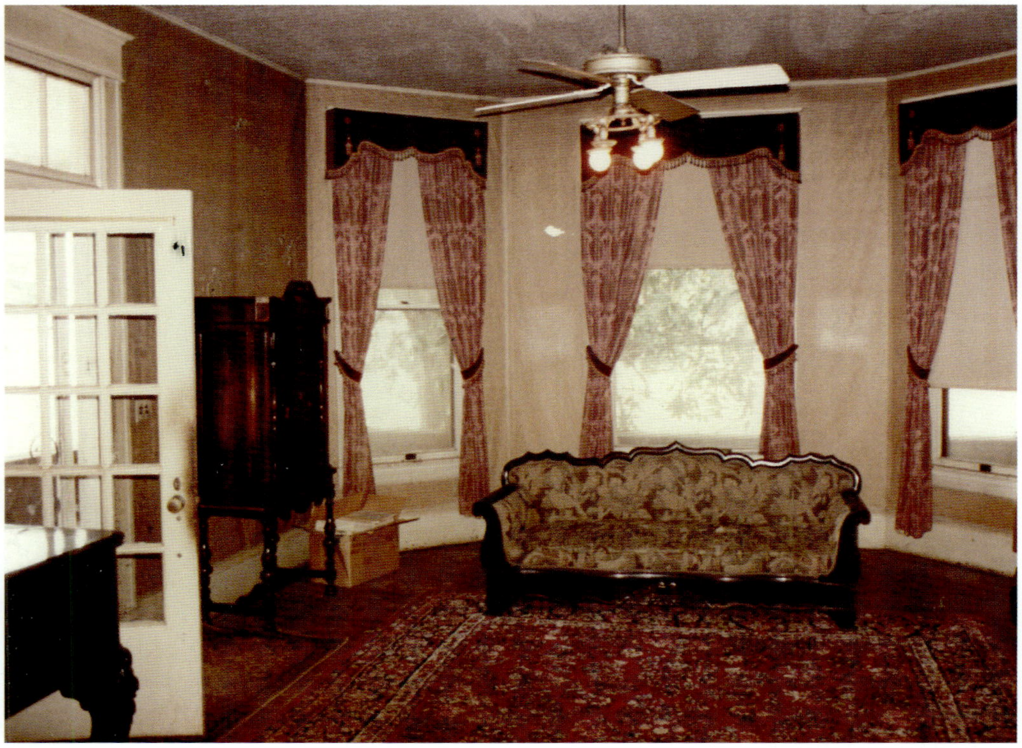

FIGURE 10.30. (Left) Family Room Before the Move, 1985.

This picture shows the doors to the carport area. To conserve space, the house had neither an entrance hall nor a foyer to the carport area. Courtesy of Judy Buckingham.

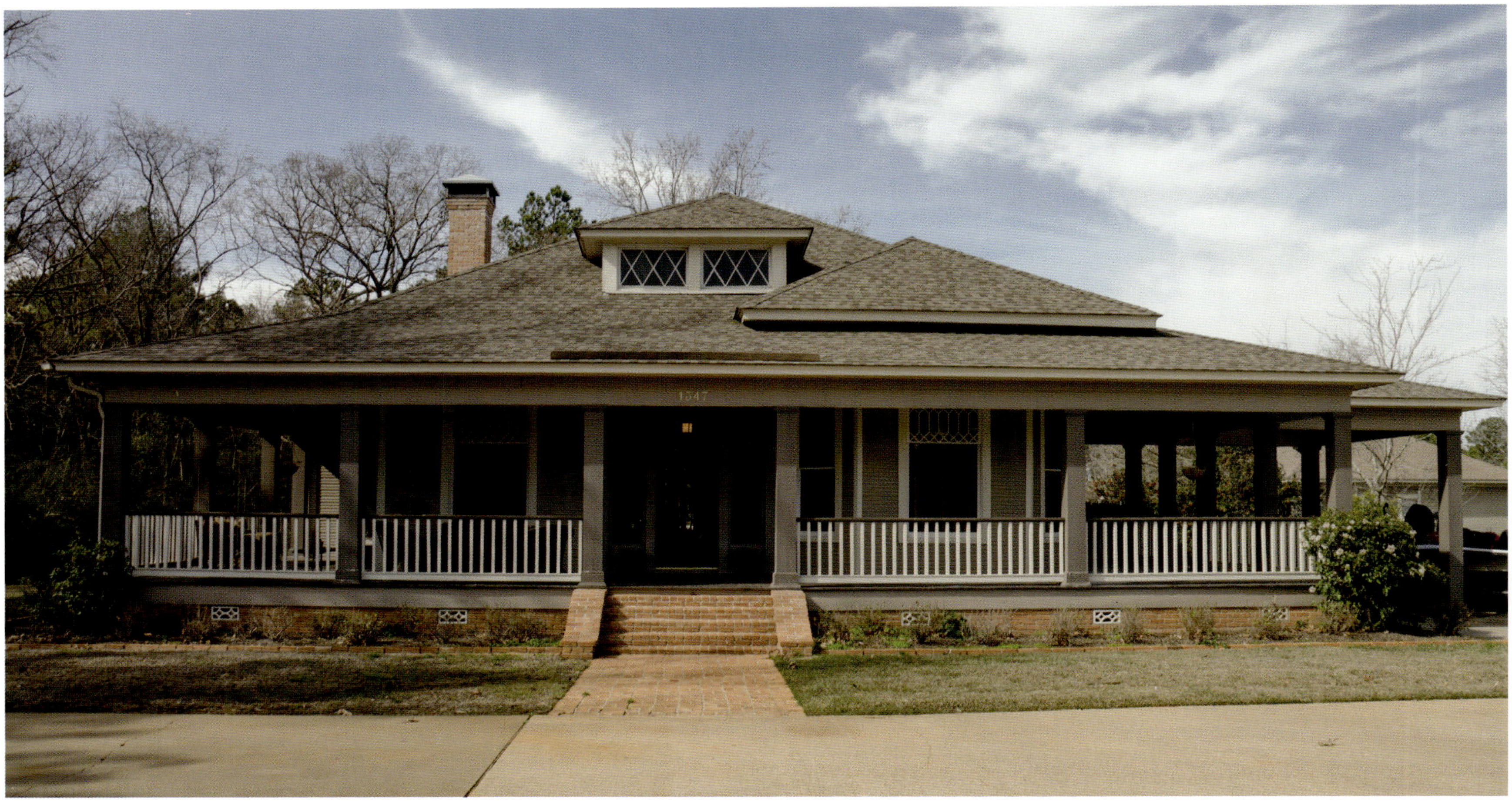

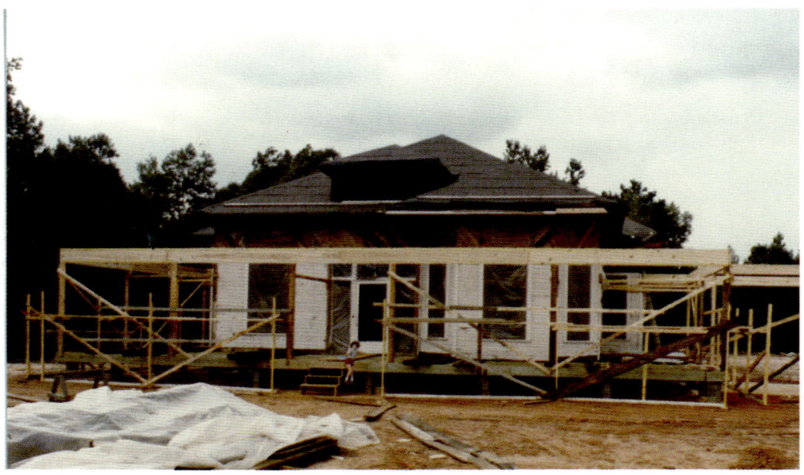

FIGURE 10.31 - 10.32. The Guy Blount House, 1986 and 2012.

Dr. & Mrs. James Buckingham extracted the Guy Blount House from the growing commercialization of North Street in 1986. The house now sits off Appleby Sand Road. (Left) The photograph shows the restoration of the porches surrounding the house. Instead of the brick columns, boxed wood columns used throughout the period were selected for the remodeling. (Above) The house today is owned by Michael and Mandy Brewton.

FIGURE 10.33. (Below) The Family Room, 2000. *Photography by Terry Lewis and used by permission. Courtesy of Judy Buckingham.*

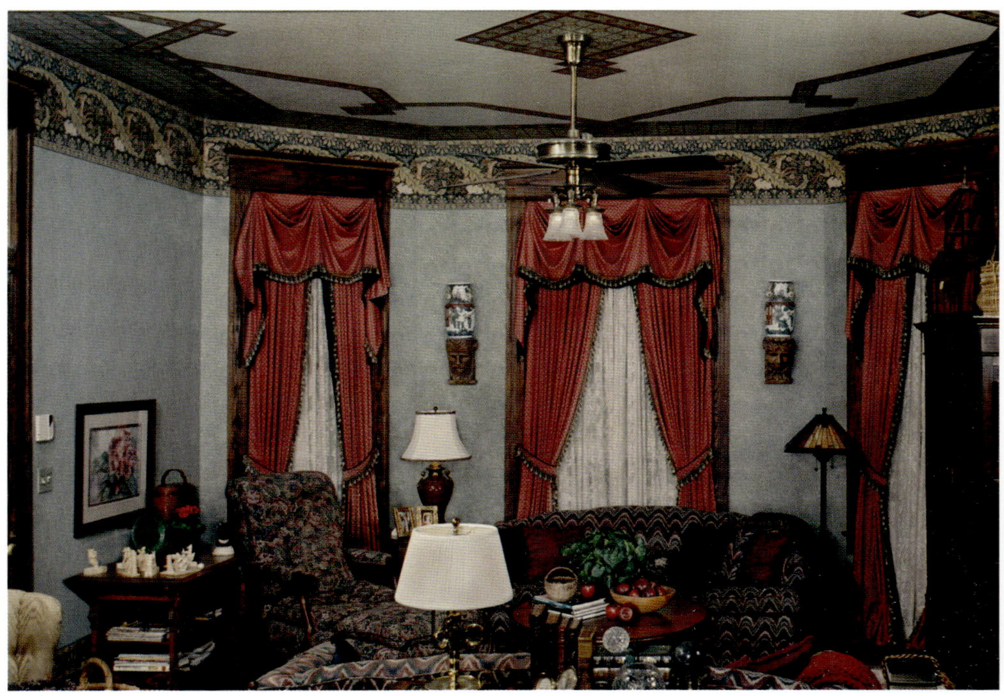

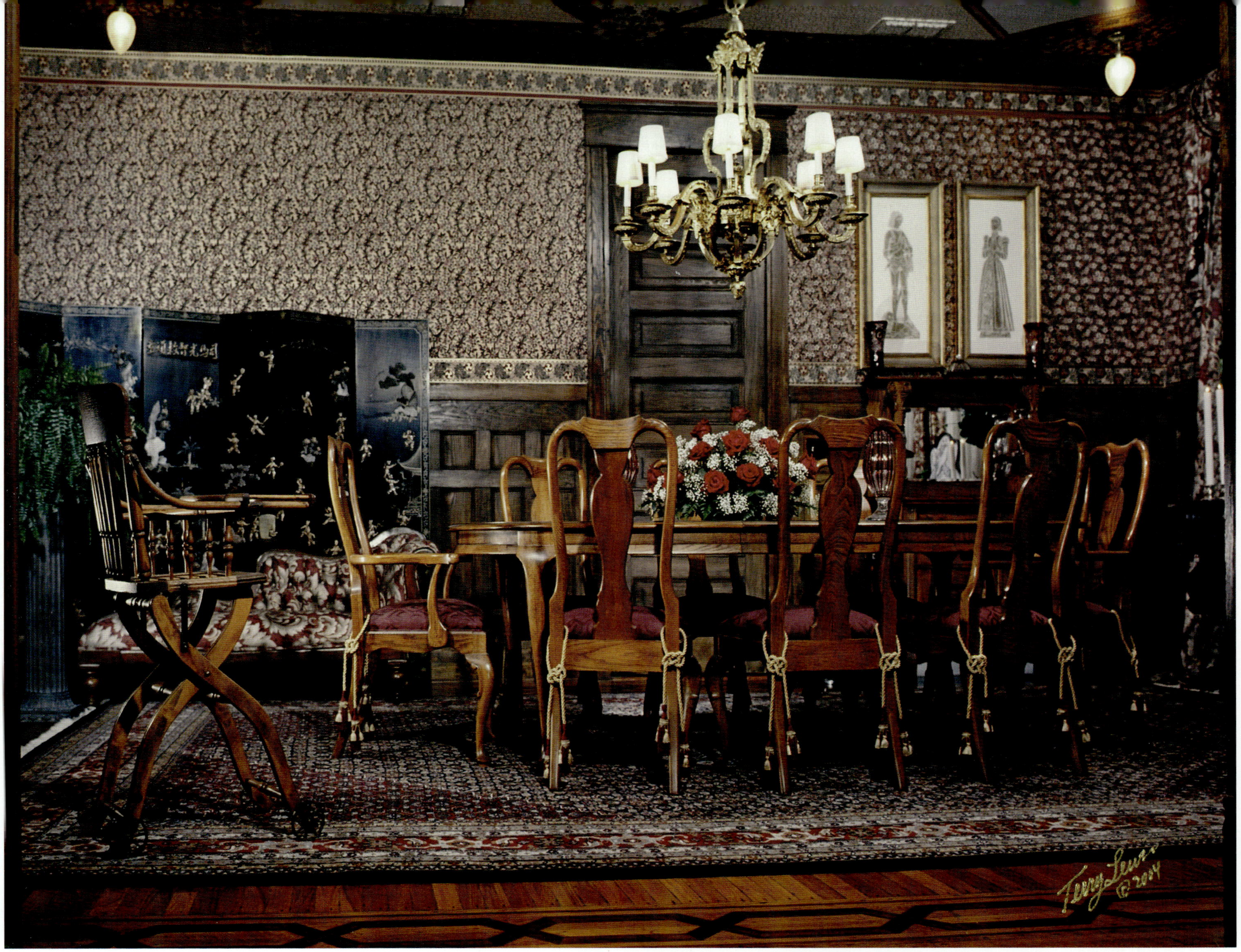

FIGURES 10.34 (Above) and 10.35 (Right). Interiors, The Buckingham Home.

The dining room has lovely paneling, like the front living room. [Compare this photograph just before the move (FIGURE 10.28).] In this photograph, notice the beautiful inlay wood border of the floor; the dark wood came from the Old Stone Fort. Also, notice the nine foot door leading into the butler's pantry. Photography by Terry Lewis and used by permission. Courtesy of Judy Buckingham.

FIGURE 10.35 (Right) The View from the Parlor into the Family Room.

Large pocket doors separated the family room from the parlor and another set opened to the dining room shown above. Tuscan columns and portieres separated the front entry parlor from the back hall.

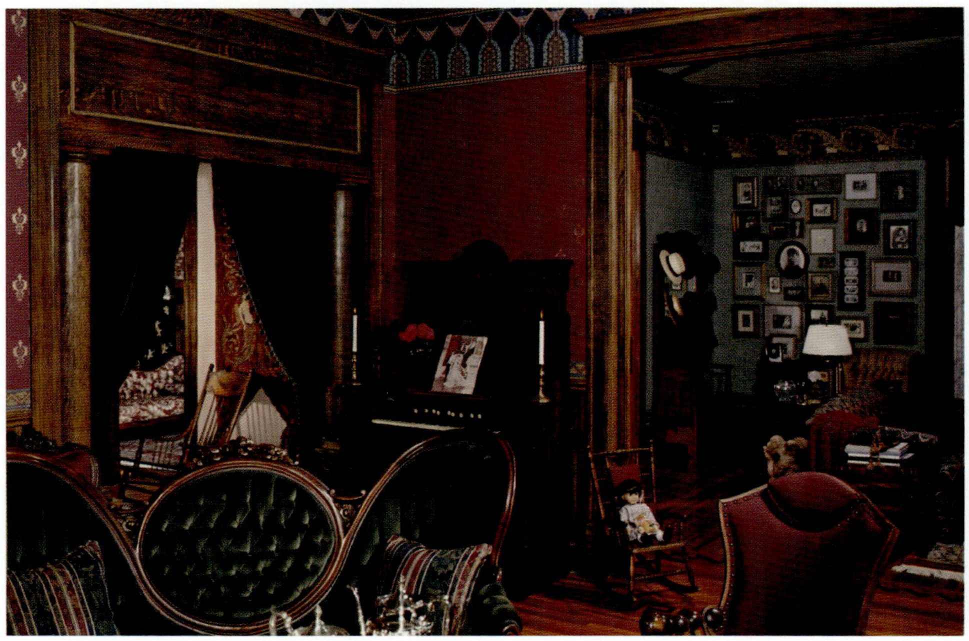

The Hayter House

The Mary Buford Hayter House (1913)

As frequently happened in his career, Rulfs received his next commission as a result of his last one. The connection in this case was more than architectural. Fay Hayter Blount's mother, Mary Buford Hayter (1859-1921) liked her daughter's new house and asked Rulfs to design one for her.

Until her husband Jeff Hayter's death in 1911, Mary Hayter had lived in houses she had no part in planning. Jeff Hayter had purchased the homestead of Dr. W. P. Fears in 1886 for $1900. and lived there until 1904, at which time she moved into the Wettermark House.[71] Hayter had purchased the Wettermark's house "on the courthouse steps," so to speak, after the banker fled town with the deposits in his bank. While the Wettermark residence was one of Rulfs's finest houses, by all reports, Mary Hayter wanted something new and her own. Mary's oldest son, Sam Buford Hayter, whom most people associate with the Hayter House on North Street, was not living in the family home in 1910 and would not marry until 1915. At the time of the 1920 Census, however, she had living in her house two sons (Robert and Sam), Sam's wife and two daughters, Mary's brother, William Hall, and two servants who lived in out-buildings.[72] Only after Mary died in 1921 did the house become the Sam Hayter House.

Jeff Hayter and D. Rulfs were lodge brothers in the Knights of Pythias. When Mary Hayter commissioned Rulfs to do plans for her, she was asking a friend. Mary also knew Rulfs through their mutual membership in several organizations. Had Mary wanted to have Rulfs perform one of his miracle transformations, there was an opportunity. She had enjoyed living closer in to town than the Wettermark property.

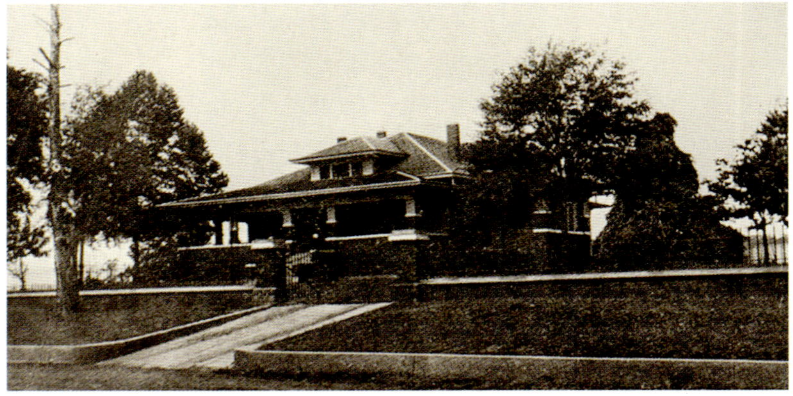

FIGURE 10.36. The Mary Buford Hayter House in 1917.
Mary Buford Hayter wanted a house similar to one Rulfs had built for her daughter, Fay Blount. The house, one of several prairie style houses done by Rulfs in the period from 1910 to 1914, still stands at 1411 North Street. The photograph dates from 1917, as shown in the booklet The Twenty Three Reasons Why, *put together to entice the state to locate the newly authorized "East Texas Normal College" in Nacogdoches. The house was the first house in Nacogdoches to have a landscape plan included with the design.*

FIGURE 10.37. The Samuel B. Hayter Home in the 1950s.
Because of the long residence in the house of Mary's son, Samuel Buford Hayter, most people think that he built it. Sam Hayter and his bride did not move into the house until a few years before Mary died. The photograph dates to the time of Sam's death in the mid 1950s. Photograph courtesy of Francis Abernethy.

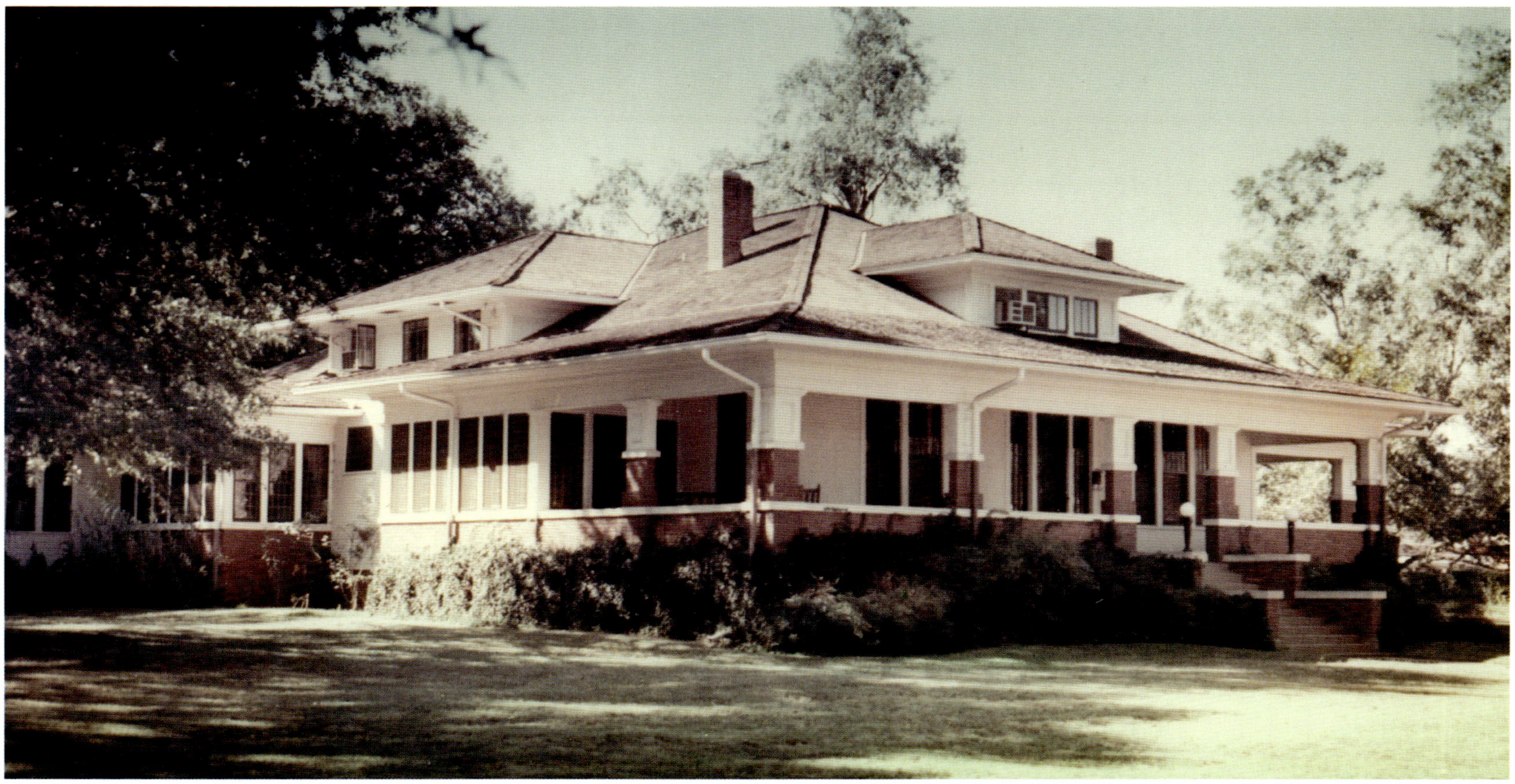

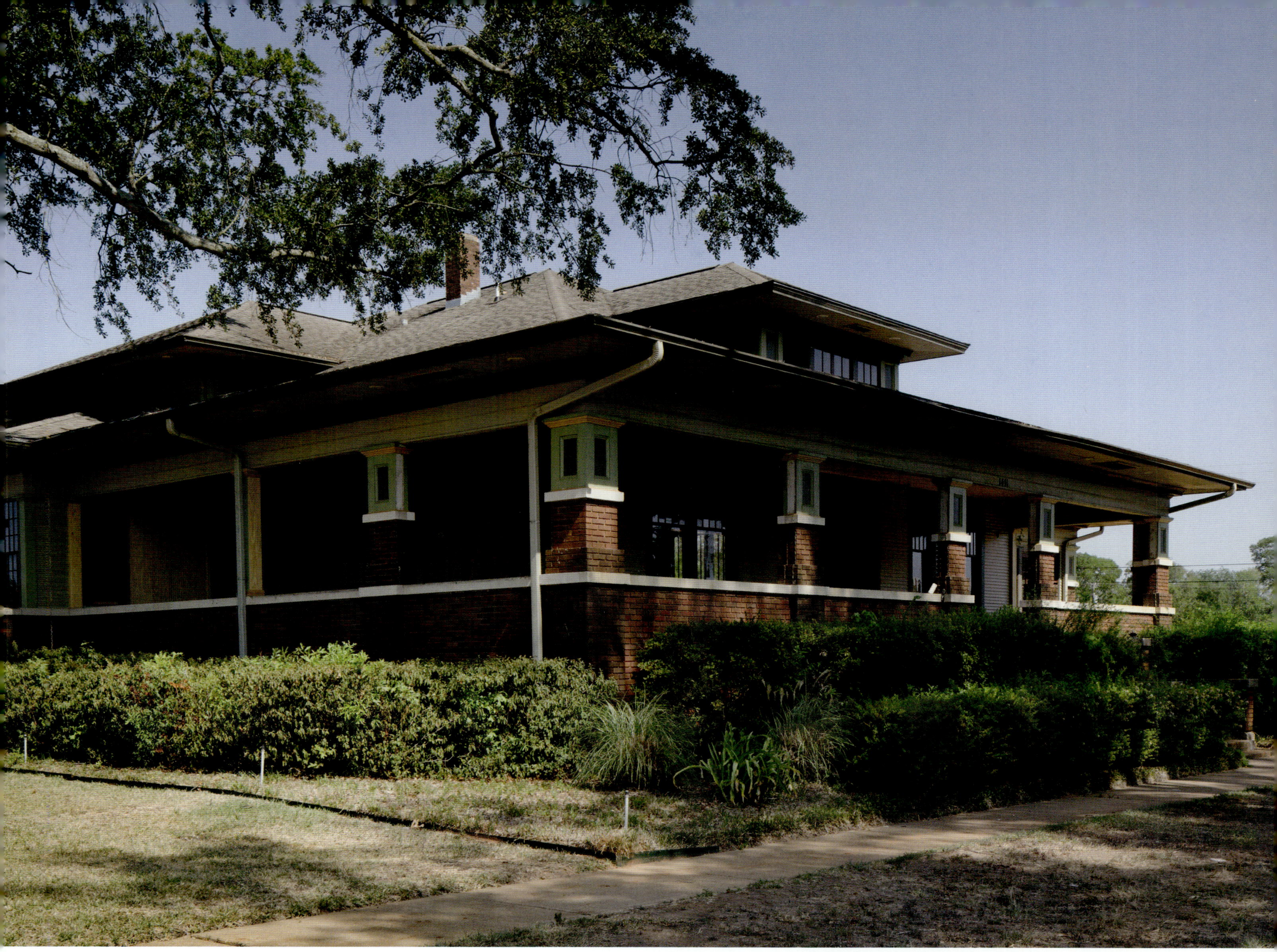

FIGURE 10.38. The Hayter House in 2011.

The Hayter House has served many functions since the family ceased living in the structure. The Legends Corporation, the present owners, have designated the house as the main club and offices for its large apartment complex to the west on the Hayter homestead. The front door has again become the main entrance.

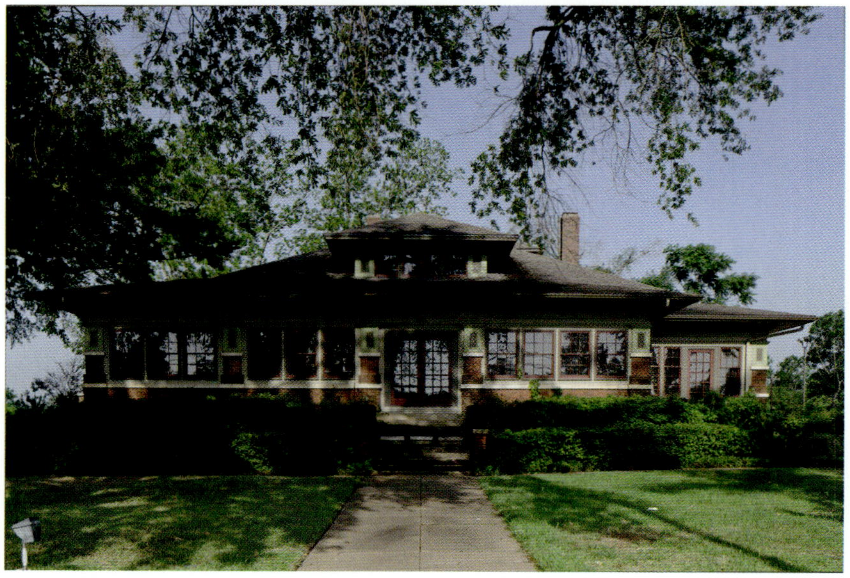

FIGURE 10.39. (Right) The Hayter House in 2008.

When first used as a restaurant in the 1980s, the Hayter Estate enclosed the front porches and carport with windows to give more main floor space and added new second floor space to the rear. In a later more extensive remodeling as a restaurant in the 1990s, the estate shifted the entrance from the carport on the north to a new entry porch on the south.

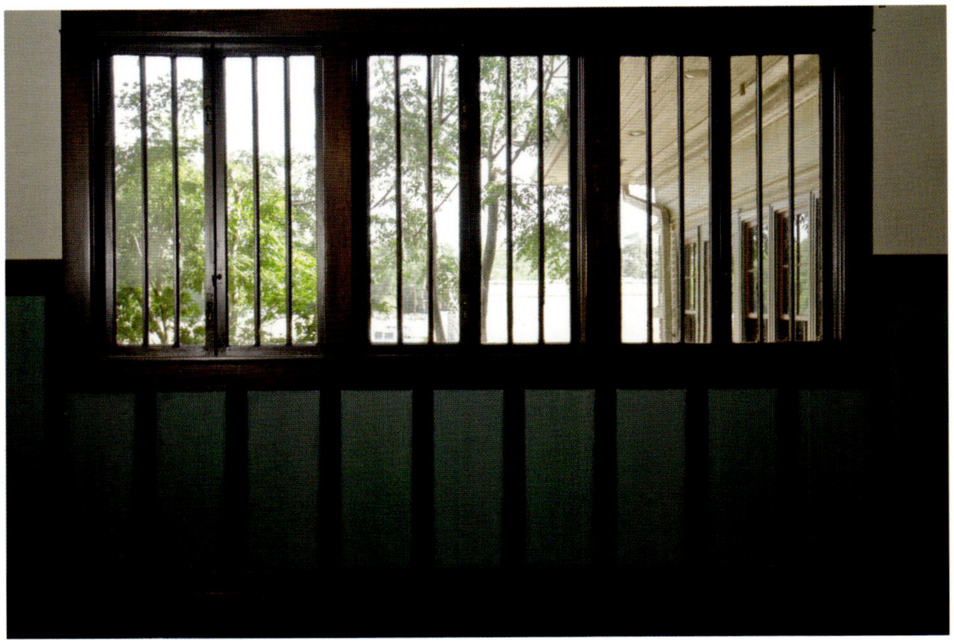

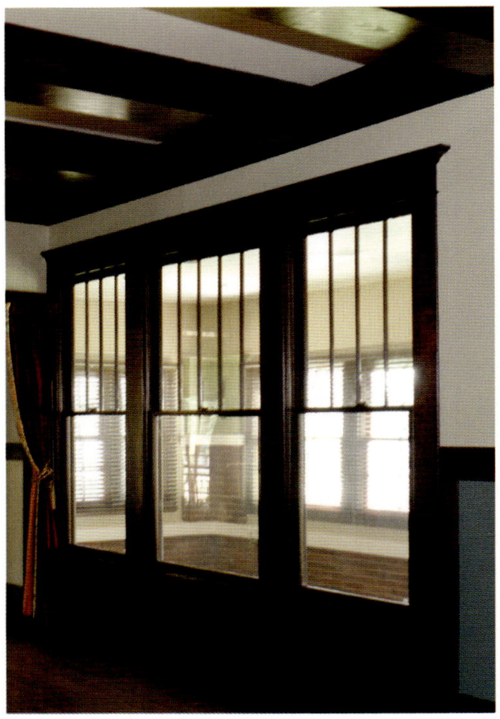

FIGURES 10.40 - 10.41. Windows in the Mary Buford Hayter House.

The Hayter House had modern, custom window treatments – careful studies in contrast between the vertical and horizontal elements. In the dining room, the wooden French sashes, while arranged in a horizontal group, had vertical mullions and muntin. Rulfs grouped even the traditional double-hung sashes into horizontal bands on the front of the house. The front door (See FIGURE 10.1) had the same vertical emphasis.

FIGURE 10.42. (Below) Interior, Front Dormer Room.

The dormer rooms, while low profile on the exterior, were quite spacious on the interior.

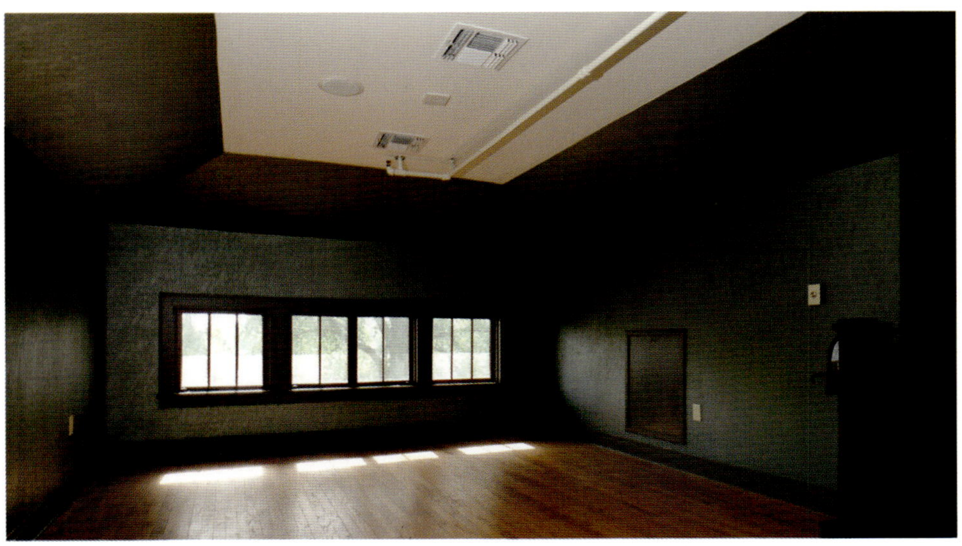

Mary did not want another hand-me-down house, no remodeled house where she had to share titular ownership. She wanted something new, modern, and closer into town—something like her daughter's new house (Fay's house had caused a sensation in Nacogdoches.) She had Rulfs start by tearing down the house of Dr. Fears. The house Rulfs built for Mary Hayter in 1913 still stands on North Street, on its original location. Although modified, extended, and remodeled numerous times, the Hayter House at the corner of North at Starr has survived in part because the next owner, Sam Hayter, included the house in the iron-clad trust that prohibited his heirs from selling the property for at least two generations.[73]

The Hayter House was an updated version of the Guy and Fay Blount House. On Mary Hayter's version, Rulfs did not allow the interior floor plan to compromise the symmetry of the roof. While Rulfs used all the innovations he had used on the daughter's house, he added new elements to make this house even more unique. The wood-paneled columns over the brick piers on the porch lightened the appearance of the supports and thus the porch; the enlarged and centered dormer rooms gave the house added symmetry; and the windows, grouped horizontally in the dining room and vertically across the façade at the entrance, all had vertical mullions which gave the house appealing contrasts to the overall horizontal elements. The house, along with the houses for Charles Hoya's daughters discussed in the next chapter, were the first in Nacogdoches to have an integrated landscape plan included from the beginning. The brick and iron fence in front of the houses increased the horizontal lines. The Hayter House also incorporated a substantial garage as well as a carport from the beginning. The garage, with living quarters for servants above the car stalls, now stands at Millard's Crossing Restoration Village (6020 North Street). A reverse inspiration occurred when this carriage house became the model for the pool house at the moved and restored Fay Hayter Blount house off Appleby Sand Road.

Because of its size, location, and entailment within a family trust, the Hayter House has withstood the destruction of domestic houses, which accompanied the commercialization of the street. It has, however, hosted a series of restaurants in the last thirty-five years. Jim Elder's "La Hacienda" restaurant, a popular Mexican eatery, leased the house for many years; shorter lessees include the "Hayter House" and "Fairchild's" restaurants.[74] Real estate developer Eric Jakimier and the Legends Corporation purchased the property in 2010 from the Sam Hayter Trust and began its incorporation within a huge student apartment complex. Jakimier, in an interview with the author, asked for further information about where the house fit into the architect's career. He said he fell in love with Rulfs' Prairie-style house the first time he saw it.[75] In another interview, the developer said, "This fabulous house will be the centerpiece of our development, and everything will work around it. It's not going to be just the leasing office, but it will also be a lounge area, fitness center, and computer area."[76]

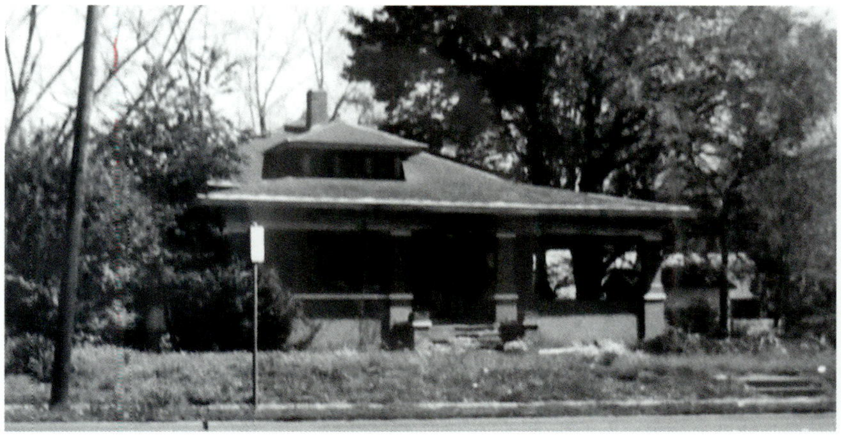

FIGURE 10.43. The Charles Hodges House, 1950s.
While there is no photograph of the original house before Charles Hodges had it remodeled in 1913, the one above shows the house in the 1950s. Rulfs applied horizontal features similar to those on the larger houses for the Blounts and Hayters.

The Charles A. Hodges House (1913)

In October of 1911, the property south of the Frank Summers House, on the corner of Houston and North Street, came into the ownership of Charles A. Hodges (1891-1933).[77] It was part of the James Harper Starr homestead property and once was owned by the Voight family. One of the owners was Major Thomas J. Carraway, who purchased and edited the *Nacogdoches Star-News* after the Haltoms. The property sold for $1250 in both 1887 and 1911.[78] Rulfs remodeled the house for Hodges in 1913. Albeit more modest in scale, the rework of this house followed the same pattern used in other houses designed at the time: low hipped roof, central dormer with banked windows, brick columns and balustrades. While the new front porch wrapped around the south side, there was no carport as was the case in the other houses.[79] The Lee Gaston House on North Street also had a similar porch makeover, but because of the owner's refusal to change the pitch of the roof from high to low, the Gaston makeover was not very successful or convincing.

The Hodges House still survives, although it has been moved twice and undergone considerable modifications.[80] Because of the removal of the brick porch supports in the moves and the substitution of Victorian posts and balustrades in later interpretations, the 1913 appearance no longer exists. The interior of the house, however, still demonstrates the changes Rulfs made to the original structure and tie the house to the changes he made in other houses around the same date, such as the remodeled houses on Church Street. The house is now owned by Vonda and Danny Windham.

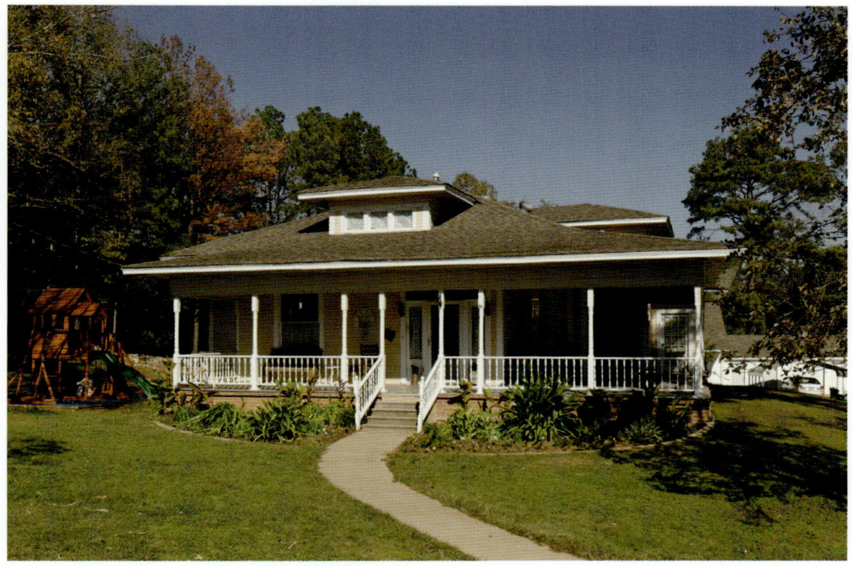

FIGURE 10.44. The Windham Home, 2012.
The Hodges House, moved twice and without its brick columns, now sits off Appleby Sand Road, as shown in the color image above.

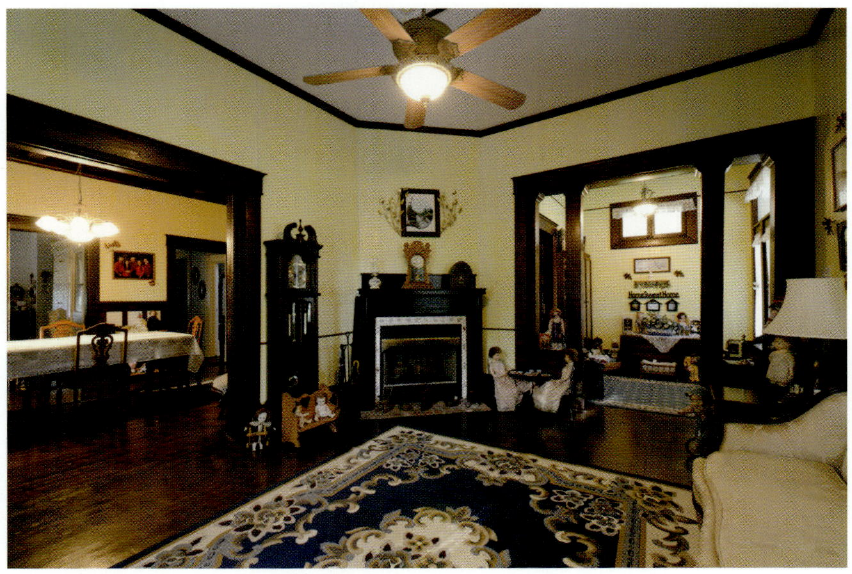

FIGURE 10.45. The Windham Home, 2012.
In reworking the house for Hodges, Rulfs opened the entrance hall to the living room by placing a colonnade between them and pocket doors between the living room and dining room. The house, moved twice and without its brick columns, now sits off Appleby Sand Rood and is the home of Vonda and Danny Windham.

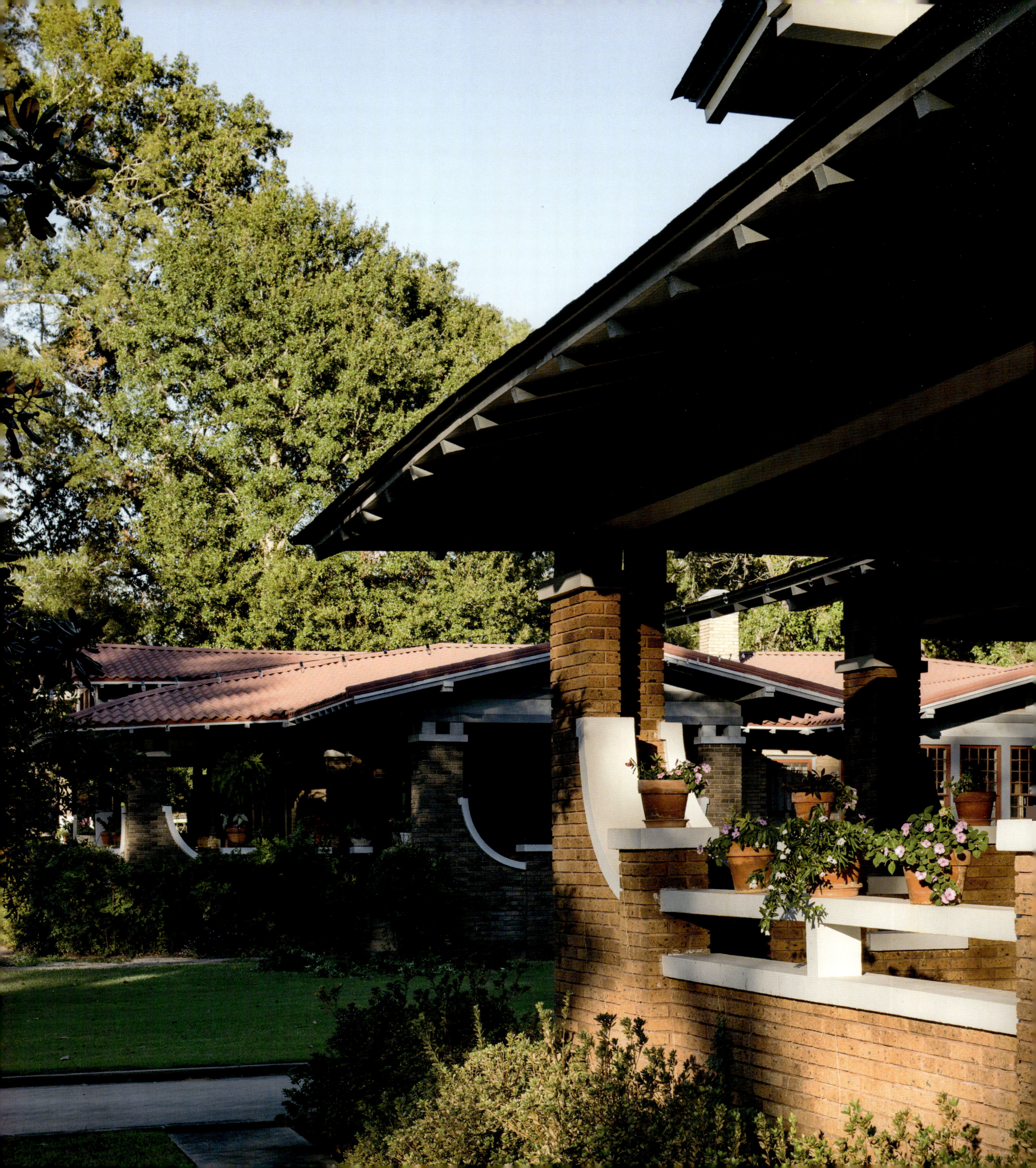

CHAPTER XI

Eclectic and Modern Styles

Washington Square: Phase II (1903-1916)

"My work in Nacogdoches speaks for itself." D. Rulfs, *Nacogdoches Plaindealer,* October 16, 1902.

The building of the new Central School on the campus of the Old University in 1904 injected new viability into the old neighborhood around Washington Square. This chapter will discuss the domestic structures designed by Rulfs in the area between 1901 and 1914. The houses follow the same general trends as discussed on North Street. A new generation of homeowners sought less complicated structures, willingly considered more eclectic styles, and, in some cases, actively requested modern designs. Diedrich Rulfs, as always, knew how to guide his clients into discovering what they wanted and provided designs to match their needs.

"Tanglewood." William T. Wilson House (1903)

While the house built by D. Rulfs at the corner of Mound and Hughes streets on Washington Square disappeared in the late 1920s,[1] its name lives on in Nacogdoches memory because of a little book of essays written about the property–*The Birds of Tanglewood*, by Karle Wilson Baker. Mrs. Baker and her husband, Thomas Ellis Baker, made "Tanglewood" their home from 1916 to 1929.

William T. Wilson (1846-1916), a successful grain dealer in Little Rock until financial difficulties forced him into bankruptcy, stopped off in Nacogdoches in 1898 on his way to San Antonio to join his brothers. Wilson stayed in the new Banita Hotel (Rulfs, 1896) on the trip. "He was so impressed with what he found that he chose Nacogdoches as the place to restart his business and to relocate his family (Kate Floy, Karle, and Ben)."[2] Wilson Grain Company occupied the upper story of the Cox Building (Rulfs, 1891) on the east side of the Square—now Regions Bank. At first, the Wilsons lived in a rented house on the east side of North Mound just north of the present day First Christian Church. They liked the area and purchased two lots across the street on the corner of Mound and Hughes (where the Whited-Barham house now stands).[3] While they did not build immediately, the Wilsons christened the site "Tanglewood." Wilson's daughter, Karle Wilson Baker, later wrote the following to her publisher, Yale University Press:

> Tanglewood takes its name from the riot of sumac and muscadine and Virginia creeper that it was when my father bought it. Before that, there had been a pond in the midst of it, where the boys came to shoot the wild ducks that came down for water and rest on their long flight to the Gulf in November. The new owner did not at once build a house on his property.[4]

The house Rulfs designed and built for Wilson in 1903, after their leased house burned, was a modest 1-½ story structure. The house faced Mound Street with its south side parallel to Hughes Street and Washington

FIGURE 11.1. (Across) The Mast & Gray Houses (1914) in 2012.
Rulfs built houses on Logansport Street for Charles Hoya's two daughters in 1914.

Square. In order to preserve as many trees as possible, the house sat deep in the middle of the property, concealed in the woods, as if it were in the country. The house, similar to others Rulfs was building in the period (such as the Mayfield, Nelson, and Gaston houses), had a hip-and-gable roof, a front-facing gable, and a graceful porch that curved from the front door around the south to the kitchen. The Tuscan half-columns on the porch rested on brick piers, which rose from the ground to the level of the handrails. Over the entrance was the standard pediment. Paint accents enhanced the balusters and molding. In the front gable Rulfs used paired windows; the use of paired windows was very typical of the North German region where Rulfs had grown to manhood. He also used these on the closely related houses of the period–the Mayfield and Nelson houses. On the first floor, the wider windows with patterned mullions were similar to those he had used on the Hal Tucker House nearby on Mound Street. The slightly flared front steps, reminiscent of the Lindsey House (1900), gave the Wilson house another graceful touch.

After the death of her father in 1916, poet Karle Wilson Baker and her husband, Thomas Ellis Baker, moved from the Steamboat House (Rulfs, 1898) on North Street to Tanglewood, where they lived for the next thirteen years.[5] As mentioned earlier, to commemorate the plethora of birds in the area, Baker wrote a charming series of essays, later published as *The Birds of Tanglewood*.[6] She also immortalized the birds in poetry: "Thrushes."[7]

Thrushes

Through Tanglewood the thrushes trip,
As brown as any clod,
But in their spotted throats are hung
The vesper-bells of God.

And I know little secret truths,
And hidden things of good,
Since I have heard the thrushes sing
At dusk, in Tanglewood

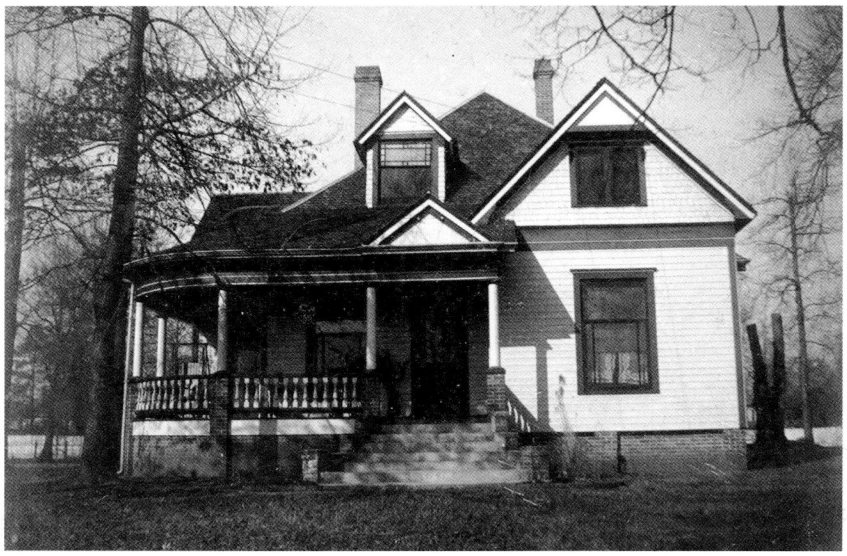

FIGURE 11.2. The W. T. Wilson Home, 1903-04

The picture dates from the period of the construction of the Wilson House, ca. 1903-1904. Except for the turned spindles, the porch is devoid of busy decoration. The house sat on the northeast corner of Washington Square, facing Mound Street at the corner of Hughes Street. Photograph compliments of Edward B. (Jerry) Baker.

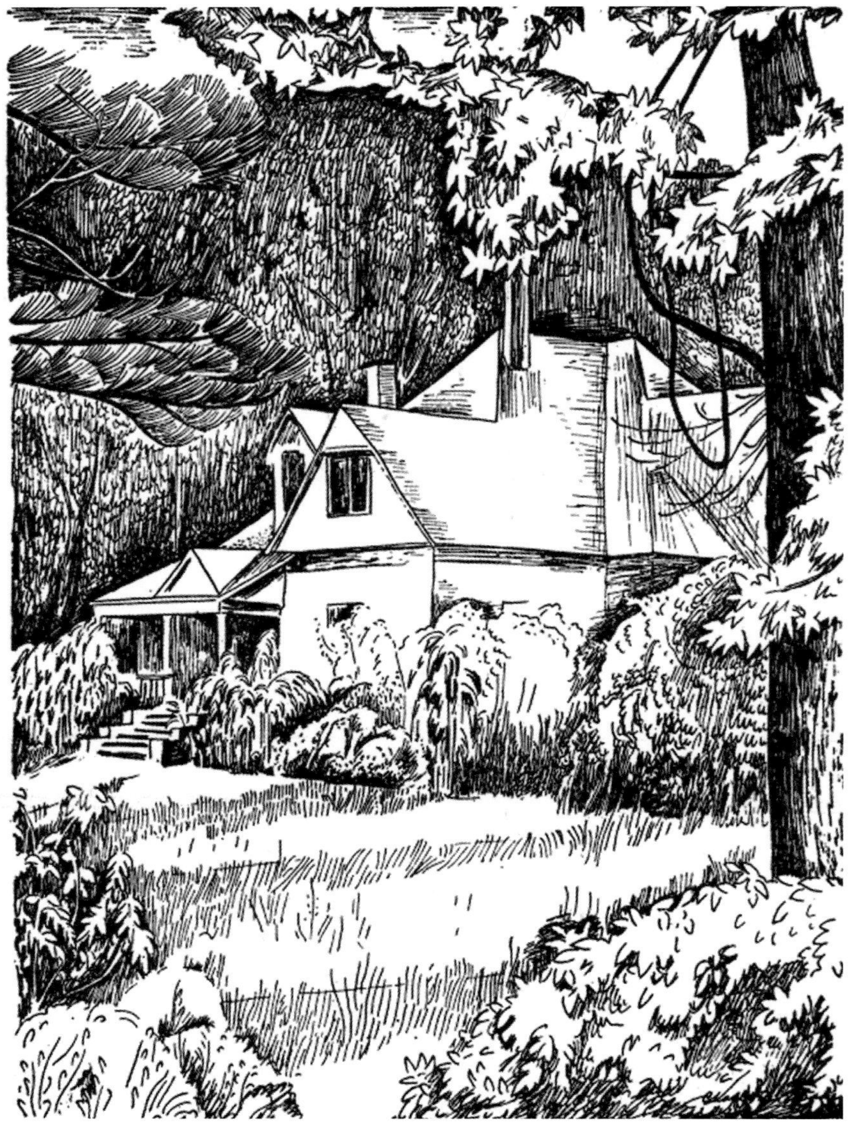

FIGURE 11.3. "Tanglewood," Drawing by Charlotte Baker.

To illustrate her mother's book of essays, entitled The Birds of Tanglewood, Charlotte Baker provided a series of charming drawings. Used by permission of Edward B. (Jerry) Baker.

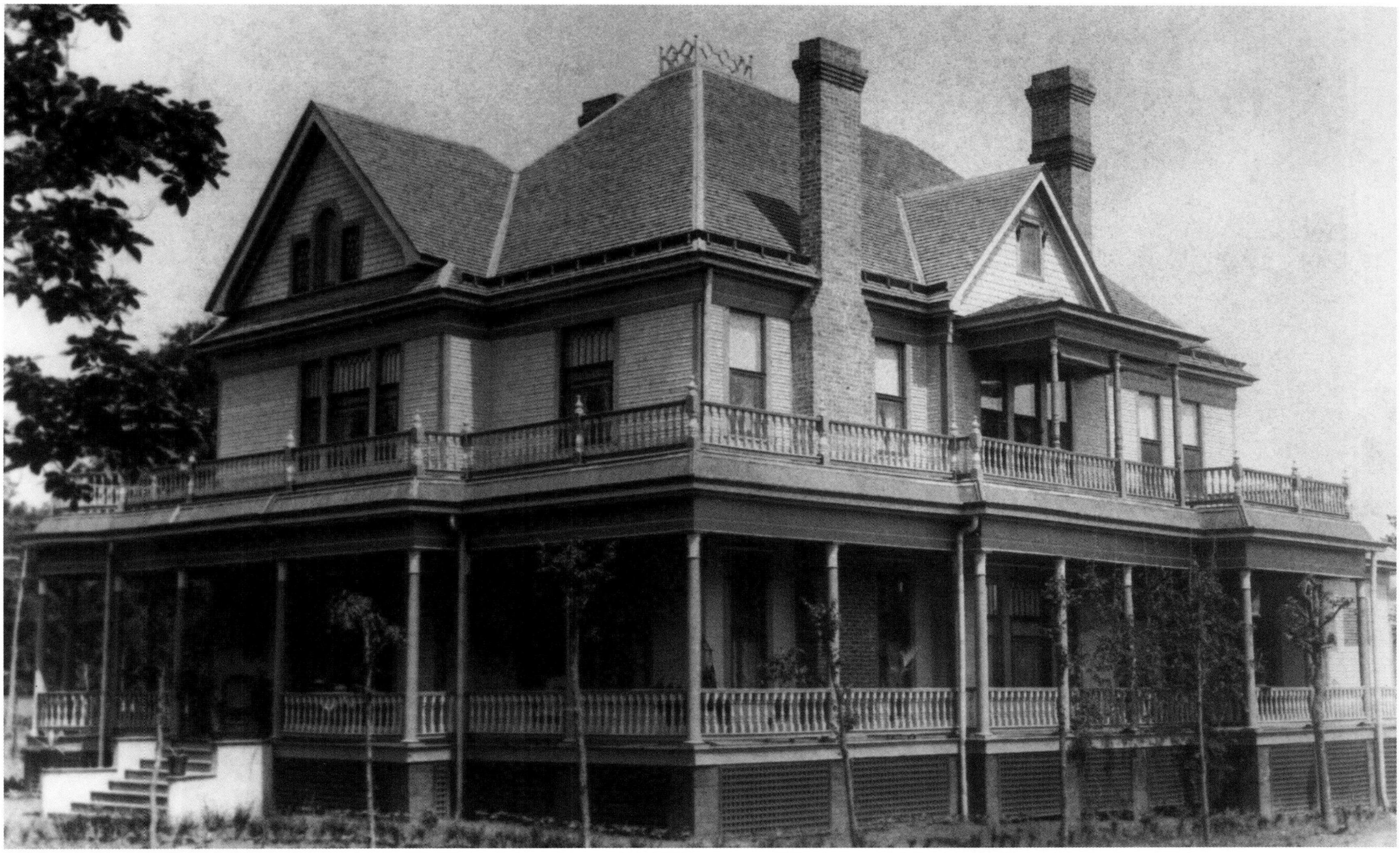

FIGURE 11.4. The Frank Cates Ford House.
Dr. Frank Ford's house sat where the Christian Church is today, on the corner of Mound and Park Street. Courtesy of ETRC.

The Dr. Francis Cates Ford House (1903)

Dr. Francis "Frank" Cates Ford (1849-1925),[8] a medical doctor who had practiced in Nacogdoches since the early 1880s, was a good friend of both Schmidt and Rulfs. Ford served with Schmidt on the Old University Board during the period of transition when they closed the institution and during the building of the new high school building in 1904. Ford was the mentor of Dr. Carl Rulfs, son of D. Rulfs, when the young physician returned to practice in Nacogdoches. When Ford first moved to Nacogdoches, he had received similar assistance from old Dr. George Hyde (1811-1888); in respect of this fact, Jean Hyde, the doctor's widow, lived with the Fords until she died. Dr. Rulfs was sharing offices with Ford in the Davidson Building as late as 1908, when the Mayer & Schmidt fire took out both buildings.[9]

The Fords resided in several locations over the years.They lived on Hospital Street at one time with the Hydes, but in 1900, they were leasing a house on Irion Hill (West Main) near the Vernon Middlebrooks. Ford may have been sampling life on Irion Hill before he decided where to build. In 1903, however, Ford asked Rulfs to design and build a new home on Washington Square. Since Ford's son was beyond school age, the doctor most likely chose the site for convenience and neighbors rather than because of the school. Across from the Wilsons, the lot was on the corner of North Mound and Park Street, where the old sanctuary of the First Christian Church now stands.[10]

The Ford House was one of the new houses in town which Giles Haltom featured in the 1906 Special Edition of the *Daily Sentinel*.[11] Rulfs used an unusually large number of Palladian motifs on the house. On the main facade, facing Mound Street, Rulfs placed the classic Palladian window in the tympanum of the front gable and below that windows and doors in a three-part configuration. He repeated the windows and doors under the south gable. The house had an extensive porch system, the largest ever included on a house by the architect. This must have come as a special request to Rulfs. The full-length porch across the front wrapped around both the north and south sides, all with slender Tuscan columns joined by balustrades using turned spindles. By specifying no roof on the second story porch, the architect created a continuous balcony around the upper bedroom floor without increasing the presence of the house visually, a device Rulfs also used on Dr. Smith's house on North Street.

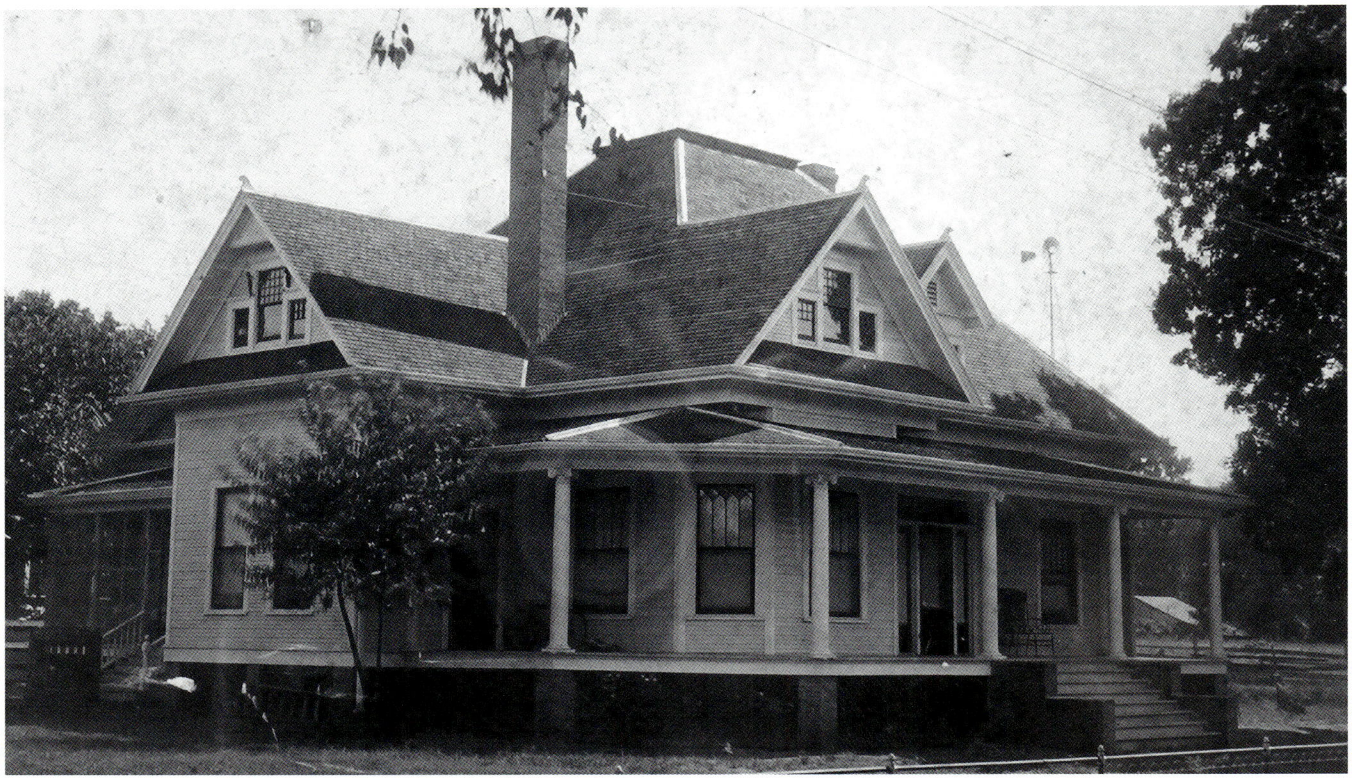

FIGURE 11.5. The Frank Summers House.
The Frank Summers House sat on the northwest corner of Hospital and Mound. Courtesy of ETRC.

The W. F. (Frank) Summers House (1905-06)

Jesse H. Summers (1848-1933), according to Haltom, introduced the wholesale lumber business in Nacogdoches. By 1906, Summers Lumber had become "one of the largest wholesale concerns in the state." Jesse's oldest sons, Frank (W. F.) and Tom (T. H.) were partners with their father in the lumber business. The Summers Lumber (Retail) Company yard sat on the corner of Main and North Street. Haltom lauded the younger Summers highly as being "two of the most competent young lumbermen in the Texas-Louisiana belt."[12] The whole Summers clan–Jesse Summers, his sons and daughter, his brother, and the next generation as well–utilized the service of D. Rulfs.

The 1906 Special Edition of the *Daily Sentinel* also featured the new home of W. F. (Frank) Summers. On the northwest corner of Mound and Hospital Streets, the house featured the first tennis court in Nacogdoches.[13] The house itself was not unusual, a traditional cottage for the period, with an entrance hall between the parlor and living room, and a hip-and-gable roof. In the tympani of the gables, Rulfs configured the Palladian motifs out of square windows. As on other houses in the area, he carried the three-part configuration to the front door, where he used side lights on either side of the door. The house exhibits several transitional features. In contrast to the Ford House, with its anachronistic porches, the Summers residence had a modest porch configuration with unusual variations. The unfluted columns on the porch had no balustrade between them. Of course, the absence of these on the front may just reflect the fact that he house was not high off the ground, but more likely this was a way of making the house look more modern and uncluttered; the back porch was decidedly old fashioned, with posts, balustrades, and handrails down the steps. The chamfered porch roof reflected the oddly shaped living room, odd because it was not a full bay, just two thirds. Perhaps this was a way to limit the size of the overall structure. But a final clue –a definite modern trend– was the front steps: concrete risers with graduated brick sides and no railings. This trend, introduced on the Wilson and Ford houses, would become the order of the day on most of Rulfs' future designs.

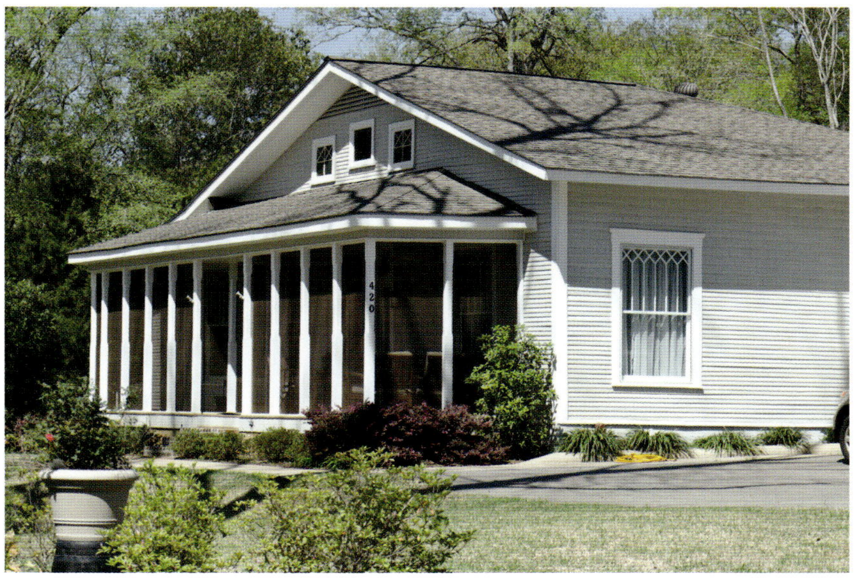

FIGURE 11.6. The Jay Anderson Home, 2012.
The Frank Summers house was moved in the 1980s to Sunset Street, off Virginia Avenue. In the move, the house lost its high hip-and-gable roof structure, but the overall interior configuration and most of the windows survived.

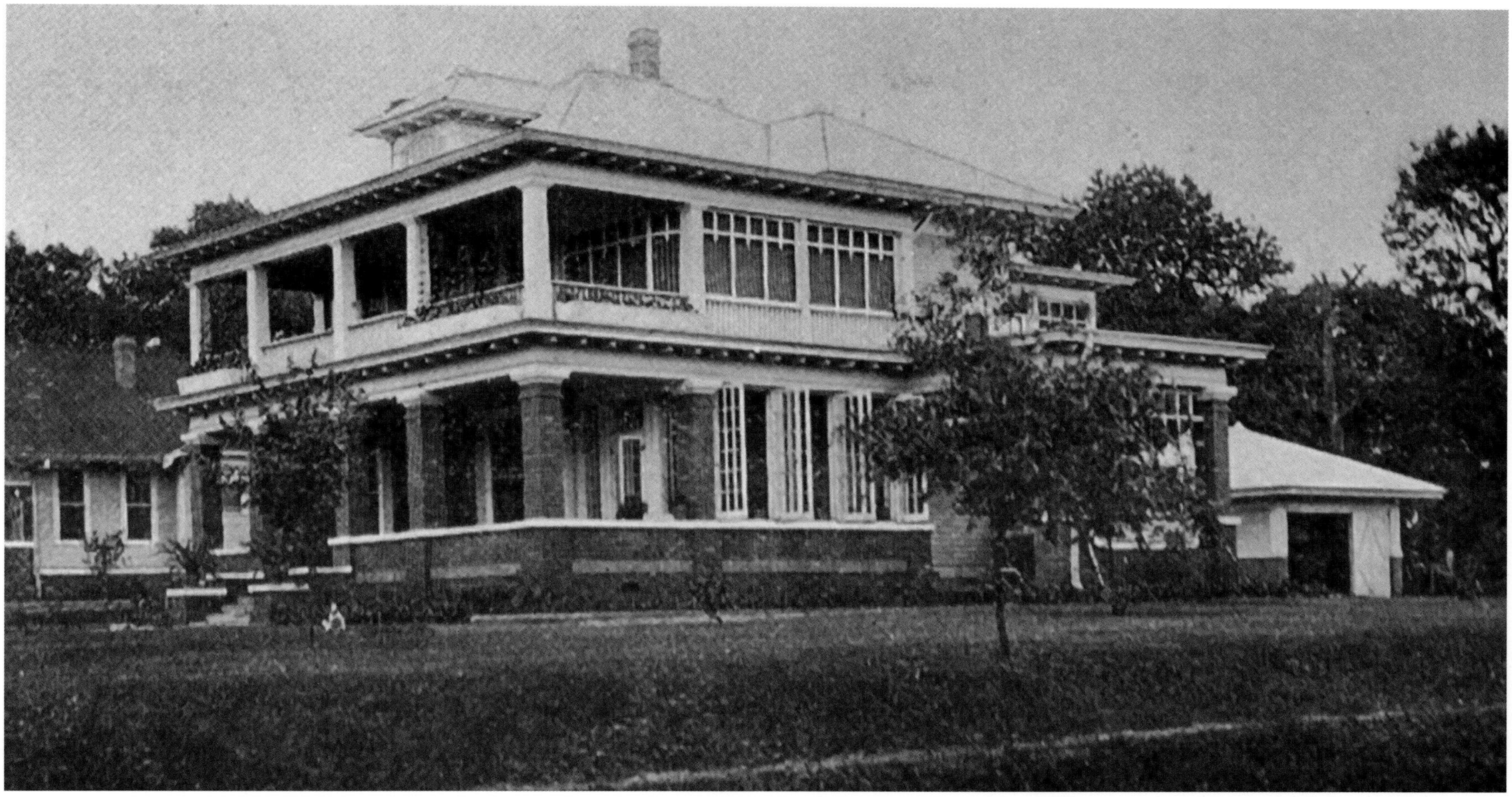

FIGURE 11.7. The Hollis Mast House, 1917
This picture of the house appeared in the booklet entitled The Twenty-Three Reasons Why.

The Hollis Mast House (1910-1911)

When Hollis Mast (1879-1918) married Kate Bridwell in 1901, they lived next door to his parents on North Fredonia Street.[14] Before joining his brother Blum in buying part ownership of the Perkins Brothers Drugstore in 1905, Hollis worked originally for Cason, Richardson and Company. After the great fire in 1906, the brothers Mast bought out Will Perkins completely and renamed the business Mast Brothers. Two years later, Hollis, a bookkeeper by profession, joined the newly created Farmers & Merchants Bank. In 1910, Hollis purchased property on the corner of Mound and Hospital[15] and undertook the building of a new home for Kate and their four children.[16] Kate Mast died in 1913. Hollis married his second wife, Prudie, in 1915, a lady well liked by friends and relatives, according to Hollis' niece, Hollis Mast Barron.[17] Prudie invited Hollis' youngest brother, Adlai, and his bride, Lois, to live in this house until Rulfs could finish overseeing the construction of their new home at the north end of Washington Square (discussed in the next chapter.)[18] Hollis Mast was a very popular man in Nacogdoches and a key supporter of the movement to secure the Stephen F. Austin State Normal for the town. When Hollis died suddenly in 1918, an early victim of the great Influenza Pandemic at the end of World War I, many people considered his death a blow to the town.[19]

The Hollis Mast House was a striking structure, in contrast to the more traditional cottage across the street, built just four years earlier for Frank Summers. The Mast House sat on a large lot, the north half of which Hollis later sold to his brother Henry. The lot was large enough to accommodate a large, one-story house, but the Masts wanted a more traditional two-story structure with the bedrooms upstairs. For Rulfs, the lot was perfect. Not for the first time, the architect took an elevated lot and placed an elevated house on it, thereby enhancing the importance of the structure. The house falls chronologically and architecturally between the W. U. Perkins remodeling and the more modern Guy Blount House.

In remodeling the W. U. Perkins House, Rulfs had used full-width, double porches across the front façade; he enclosed part of the existing wrap-around porches to create screened sitting rooms, both upstairs and down. The Mast residence started from a plan instead of an existing building. Rulfs chose to support the upper gallery on square brick columns on the main level. The upper gallery, with open balustrades with square balusters between square boxed columns, was identical to the porch treatment on the W. U. Perkins House and later the Tom Summers House. In anticipation of what he would use on the Guy Blount residence, Rulfs added weight to the lower level by using square columns on piers which rose to the level of the continuous brick balustrade. Rulfs incorporated, within the volume of the house, a large screened room on the second floor and a large sunroom on the main floor. (Rulfs would use this same concept, in a more modest way, as part of the remodeling of the house for Tom Summers, half a block away.) Rulfs placed pivoting windows in the first floor sunroom, similar to the ones he specified in his plans for the new Methodist Church built

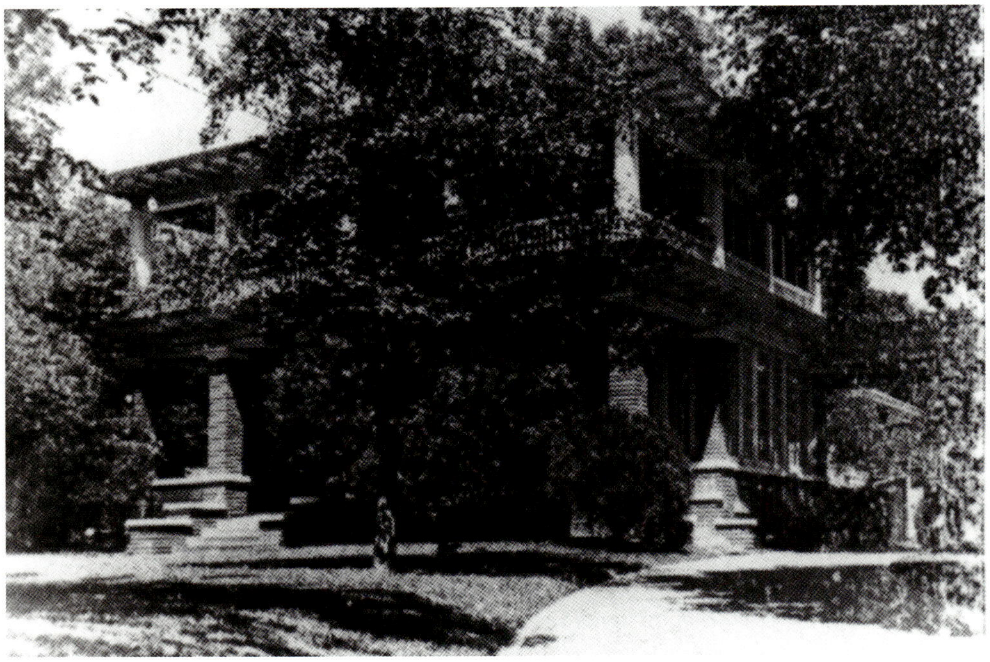

FIGURE 11.8. (Above) The Mast House, ca. 1929.
The driveway and the southern entry steps were added in the 1920s. Courtesy of ETRC.

in the same year. Rulfs specified pressed-metal roofing for the house, as he previously specified on the A. A. Nelson office/residence in the next block down Mound Street.

The façade of the Mast residence had a modernized French-colonial appearance, in contrast to the raised cottage style he had created for June Harris fifteen years earlier. By 1910, Rulfs had more or less abandoned Victorian elements in favor of more modern elements. The small brackets on the offset bay window of the north side are perhaps the one exception. The interior woodwork was tailored and unadorned; the lines of the window mullions were straight. The concrete porch floor was, perhaps, the architect's first.

It is difficult now, after so many modifications, to discern the original internal configuration of the house. As described by niece and namesake, Hollis Mast Barron, the north side had a parlor and dining room (in the square bay) and a large sunroom on the south front.[20] Originally, the house had no access to Hospital Street except to the rear of the structure; the front door and steps were on Mound Street. In the 1920s, when the semi-circular driveway was added, south steps were added to the front porch. The house served as the home of Oakley-Metcalf Funeral Home from 1937-1985. (See Figure 11.8). When it became an office building under the name of Nacogdoches Plaza, the galleries were enclosed, a one-story addition was added on the Mound Street façade, and the orientation was completely refocused to Hospital Street.[21]

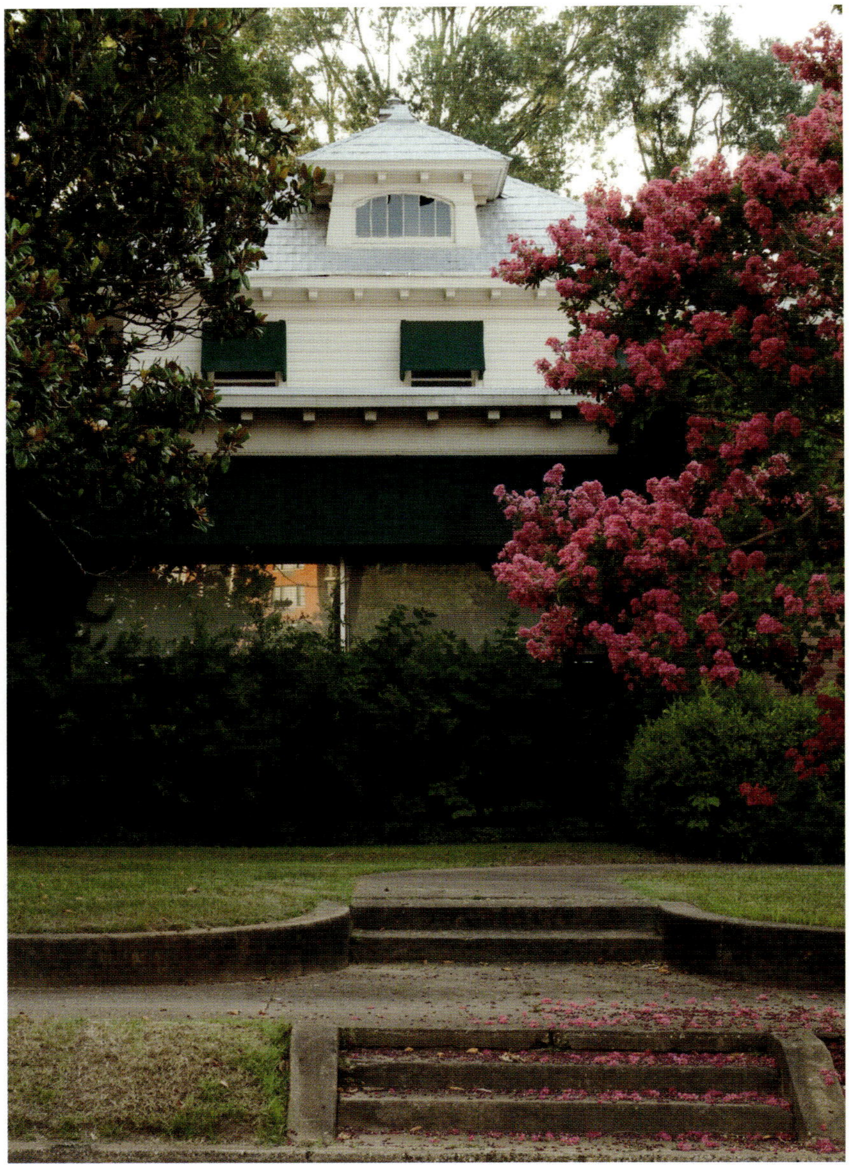

FIGURE 11.9. Nacogdoches Plaza, from Mound Street.
Today, it is difficult to discern the original configuration of the Hollis Mast House. Originally, the entrance and the main façade of the house faced Mound Street, but as the photograph above shows, the façade has undergone extensive changes. When the driveway off Hospital was added in the 1920s, steps were added to the south and the orientation of the house shifted to the new southern steps. The house served as the home of Oakley-Metcalf Funeral Home from 1937-1985, after which it became an office building under the name of Nacogdoches Plaza.

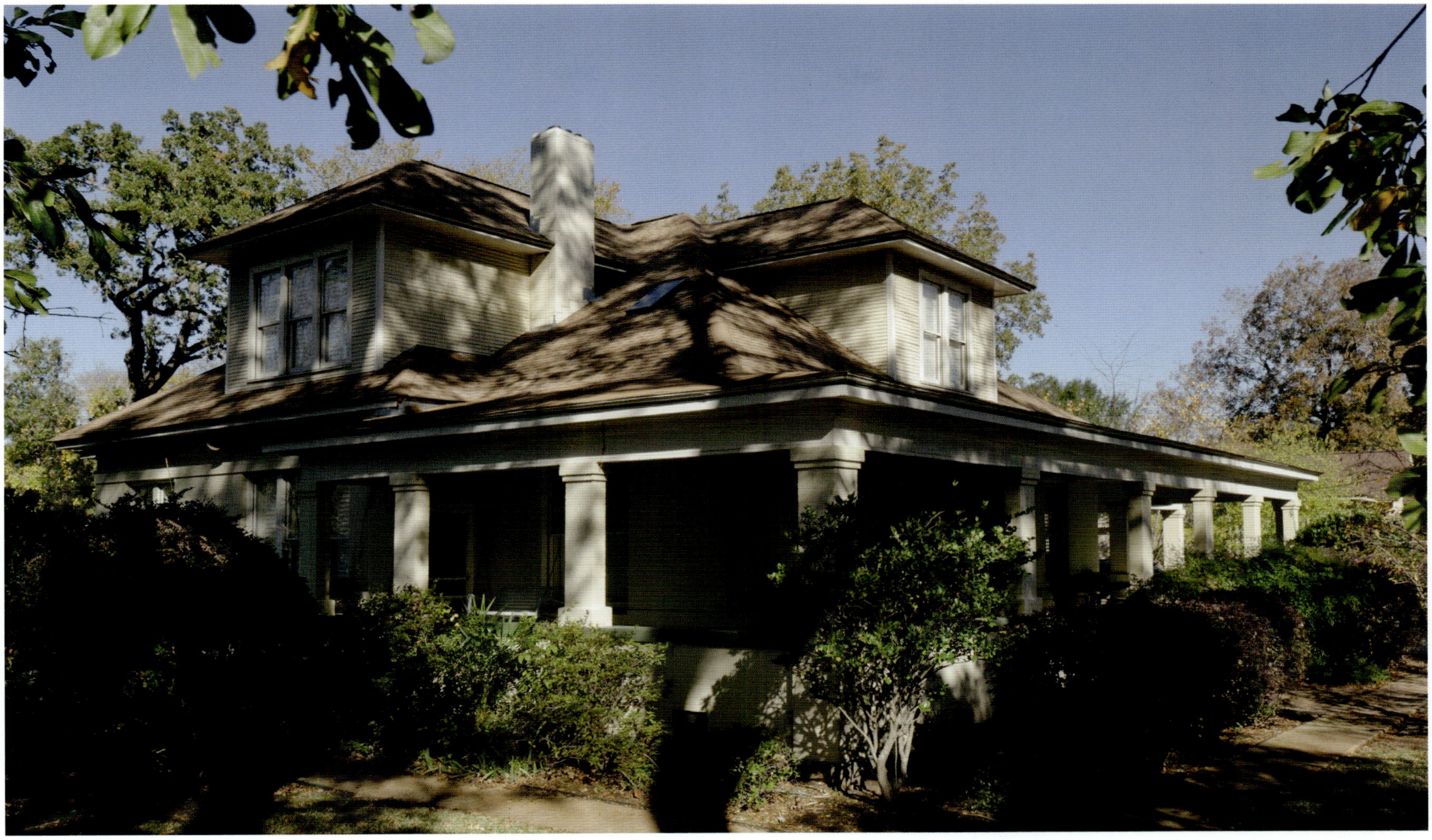

FIGURE 11.10. The Haselwood House in 2012.
The Haselwood House, now the home of Mike and Shannon McClellan, dates back to 1904, but the features seen today date to 1912, when Rulfs reworked the house. The house served as the First Methodist Parsonage for fifty years, from the mid-1930s.

The Robert W. Haselwood House (1912)

Robert William Haselwood (1872-1935) was a jeweler and watchmaker at Perkins Brothers at the turn of the century. In 1901, he left Perkins Brothers to join Sam Stripling and Tom Baker to form a new independent business—Stripling, Haselwood, and Company.[22] Haselwood was also very active in land speculation at the turn of the century, sometimes in partnership with Charles Perkins. After 1920, Haselwood became a fire insurance agent in partnership with John Perkins.

The Haselwoods purchased a house on Mound Street, north of the W. T. Wilson property in 1904; the house dates from the same period as "Tanglewood," the Wilson house next door.[23] Whether Rulfs did the original house is unknown, but he possibly did. The 1910 United States Federal Census shows the Haselwoods living in the original house.[24] Since the Sanborn Maps did not reach the area until 1922, the configuration of the original house is unknown. In 1912, Rulfs, who was designing and building other houses in the neighborhood, was asked to remodel and enlarge the house.

The Haselwood House, as remodeled in 1912, fits into a group of three houses in which the architect was experimenting with the use of room-sized dormers: the John Perkins House on North Street, dates just before this house, and the Tom Summers House dates to 1913.[25] The style of the house is definitely transitional. The brick porch supports, which Rulfs had just begun to use, the brick railings, the straight chimneys, and the extremely plain entablature, give the house some of the features of the newer houses; but the floor plan, materials, and feel of the house are traditional, reflecting both its pre-existing configuration and Haselwood personality. The coffered ceiling in the dining room and the paneling were definite updates to the existing house. It was unusual for Rulfs to employ brick to veneer the first story, but Mrs. Haselwood wanted the remodeled house to have a more substantive appearance than the original house or its neighbors.

The Haselwoods, devoted members of the First United Methodist Church, willed use of the house to the church as a residence for their ministers. In 1936, after the death of the Haselwoods (Billie in 1935 and Nettie in 1936), the house became the Methodist Parsonage and remained so for over forty years.[26] In the 1980s, when the congregation built a new parsonage, the Haselwood heirs sold the 1912 house to the Delta Sigma Phi fraternity, who occupied it for a decade before a zoning dispute encouraged fraternities to locate outside residential areas. Mike and Shannon McClellan have owned the house since 2001.

The Lee Hardeman House – Phase II (1912)

Many of the early details of the houses on Church Street were introduced in Chapter V. The first level of the Lee Hardeman House dates to 1892, shortly after Lee and his wife, Ida, first moved to Nacogdoches from Melrose. In interviews with Miss Gladys Hardeman, she said her father asked his friend D. Rulfs to enlarge the house in 1912. The Hardemans were thrifty, hard working, unpretentious, and uncreative; they, furthermore, were proud of all these attributes. Since the house was first built, the family had increased by two children—Gladys (1893) and her younger brother, Curtis (1904)—but certainly not enough to fully double the house as they did in 1912. Lee's brother Tol decided to move to Oklahoma around 1910. Since the overall Hardeman family was large—many aunts, uncles, and cousins, Lee Hardeman and Ida knew that accommodating the extended family when they visited would fall to them. (B. F. Hardeman, the other brother in town, had remarried, and his new wife had her own large family who visited frequently.) The new upstairs of the remodeled house had four bedrooms and a bath on the hall, a major consideration in all the remodeling commissions around this time. The new flooring throughout the house was beautiful edge-grained pine. The door facings and moldings were pine, too, but stained a rich mahogany.

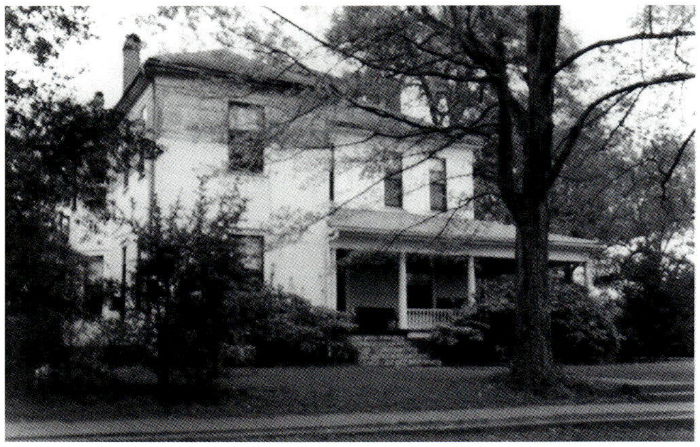

In reworking his original plan, Rulfs turned the north bedrooms of the one-story house into a new living room and dining room, separated by large double pocket doors. By the addition of double pocket doors to the old parlor and moving the fireplace from the southern wall to the southeast corner, Rulfs opened the parlor to the entrance hall. The effect was dramatic, as if the fireplace were actually in the entrance space. The formal staircase narrowed the old entrance hall, but the new open parlor more than compensated for this change. There was a short back stairs at the main landing, which offered flexibility to the house. By the addition of a two-story chamfered bay on the north side, Rulfs expanded the middle of the house. In an extended service area across the back of the house, he provided needed storage space for the kitchen, a back porch, and a new bathroom for the new master bedroom (the old family room).

To tie the interior changes together, Rulfs widened the original short porch along the front façade and wrapped it around the south side to the master bedroom. While he replaced the previous posts with floor-length Tuscan columns, he kept the balustrades and turned spindles. He moved the narrow 1/1 windows upstairs and replaced them with wider 1/1 windows in prominent places along the front elevation. The original roof gave way to a hip-and-valley roof with a new dormer on the front. The dormer window, with its diamond and prism-shaped mullions, was the only decorative touch on the whole update; the Hardemans never liked frills. To tie the exterior together, he re-sided the exterior with #117 finger joint siding and established a wide horizontal entablature at the level of the eaves. He then specified grey paint for the house, with a lighter grey trim.[27] Rulfs, as frugal as the Hardemans, re-used as much of the older siding as he could on the back of the house and the garage, away from public view. The curbing and the steps at the street in front of the house were added the next year as the Summers were remodeling the Bagley House next door.[28]

FIGURE 11.11. (Left) The Lee Hardeman House in 1970.
FIGURE 11.12. (Below) The Lee Hardeman House in 2011.

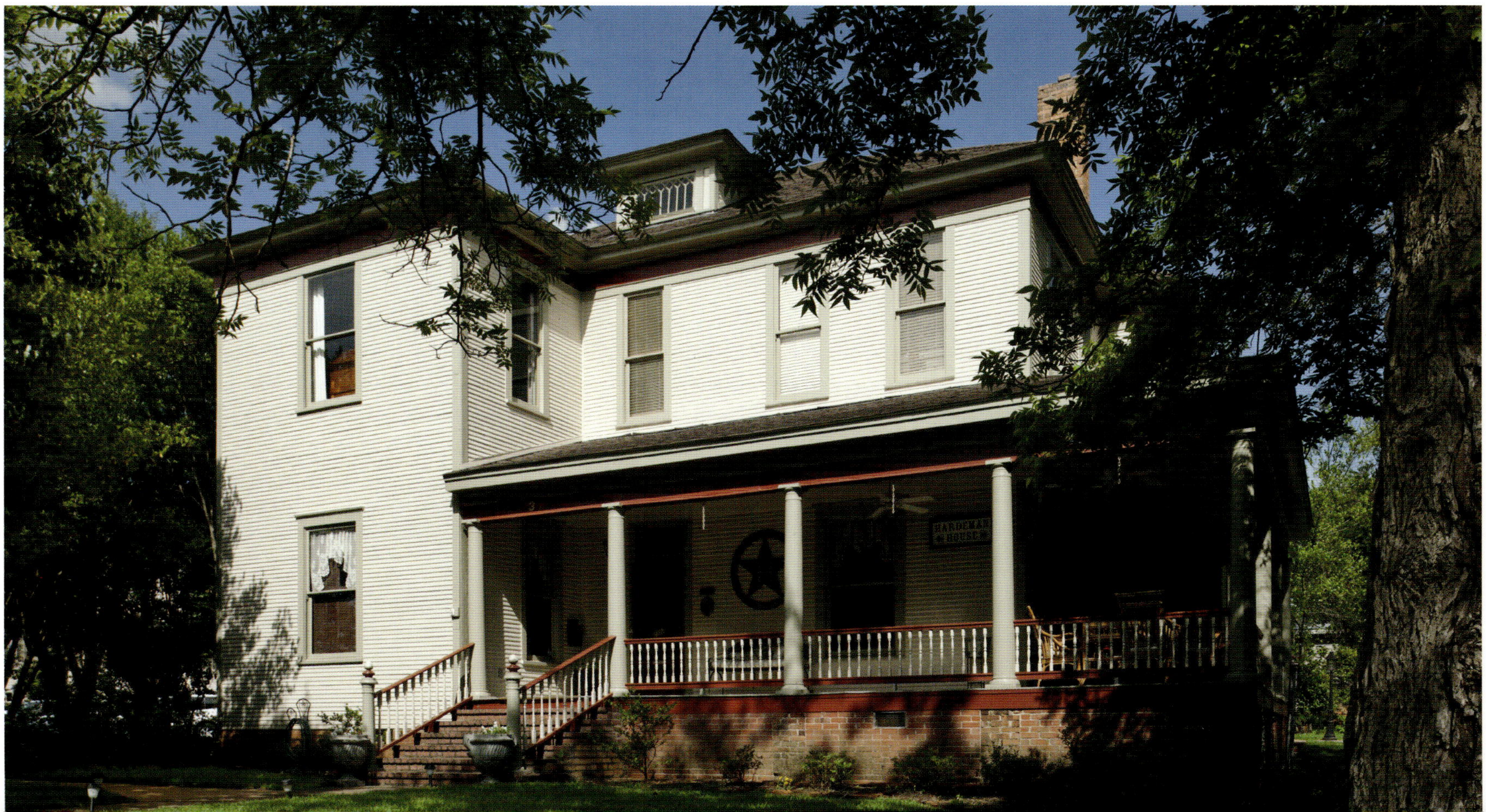

Gladys Hardeman related to the author a funny exchange between her father and Rulfs. She remembered, at the time they were undertaking the remodeling of her home, Rulfs asking her father whether the family intended to keep the space for the milk cow in the backyard? Her father responded, somewhat puzzled, "Certainly, where else would we get milk?" So Rulfs, when providing a storage facility and a house for their new automobile, provided a home for the cow in the rear of the outbuilding. Although modified, this garage with its cowshed still stands in the yard.[29]

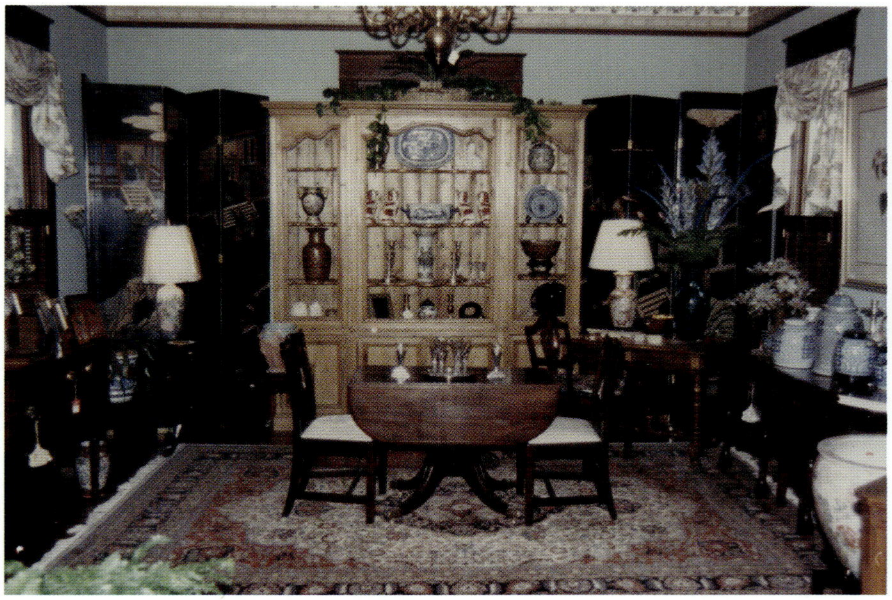

FIGURE 11.13. (Above) The Hardeman House Antique Shop, 1986.
Jere and Sarah Jackson owned the Lee Hardeman House from 1972 to 1991. In the decade of the 1980s, Sarah Jackson owned and operated a fine antique and gift establishment known as Hardeman House.

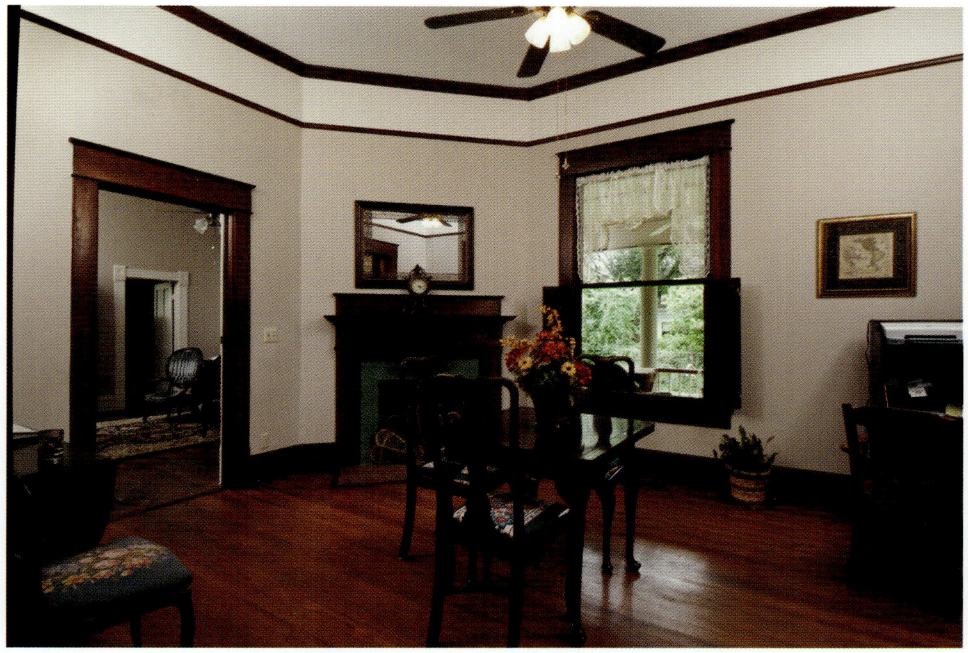

FIGURE. 11.15. (Above) Front Parlor of the Lee Hardeman House, 2011.
The front parlor has double pocket doors opening onto the entrance hall. This arrangement made the fireplace in the room a part of the ambience of the entrance hall.

FIGURE 11.14. (Below) The Living Room of the Lee Hardeman House, 2011.
The open pocket doors show the dining room. Across the enrance hall, the fireplace in the parlor is visible. The mahogany-stained pine woodwork and floors of the Hardeman House are particularly nice, yet simple.

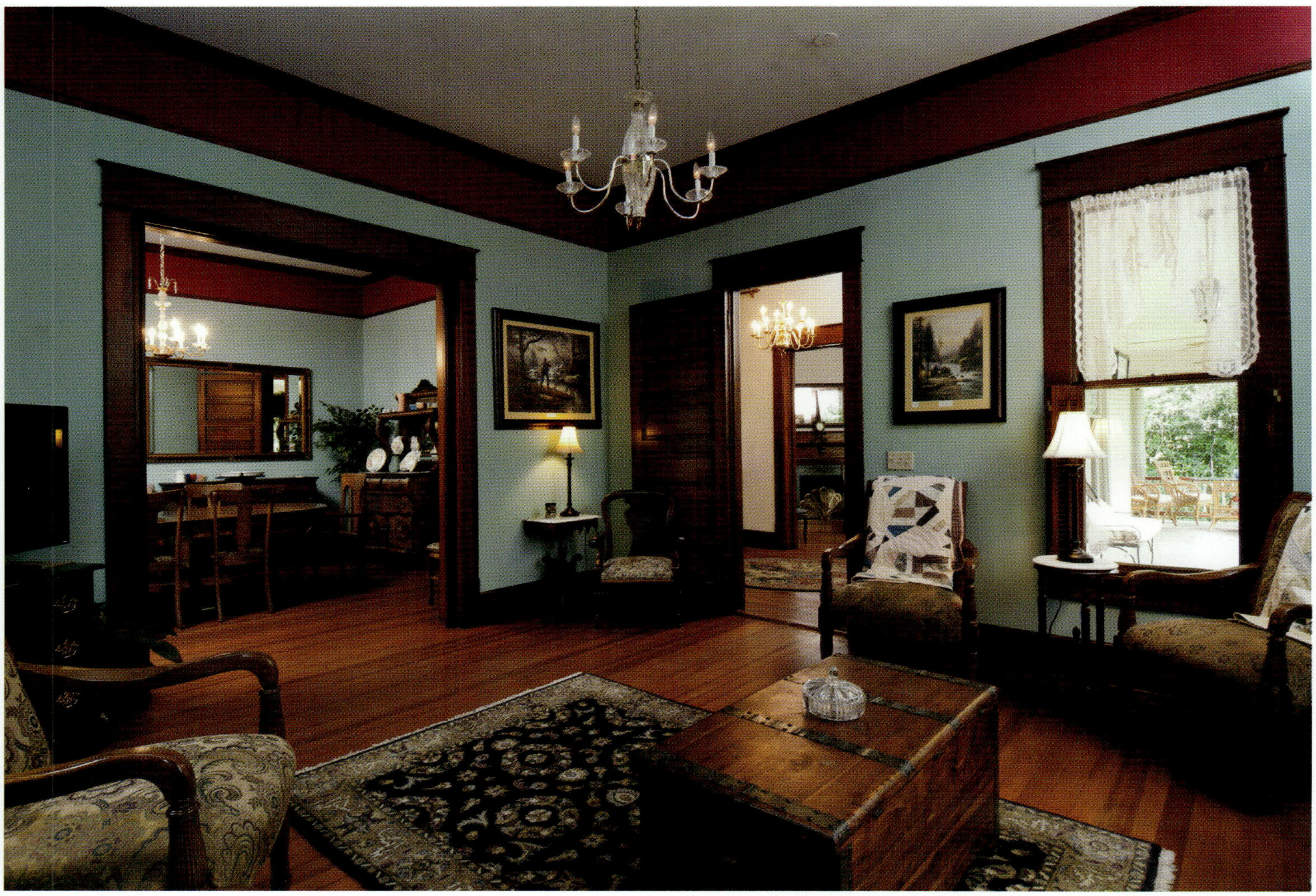

(Overleaf, Pages 296-297)
FIGURE 11.16. The Hardeman and Summers Houses viewed from the Sarah Richardson House, 2012.
The neighborhood that existed along Church Street from the 1890s still exists, in part. Except for the loss of the Cason House, which was torn down in the 1950s, three original houses in the 300 block carved out of the Old University property still retain the charm they exhibited in the period of the First World War.

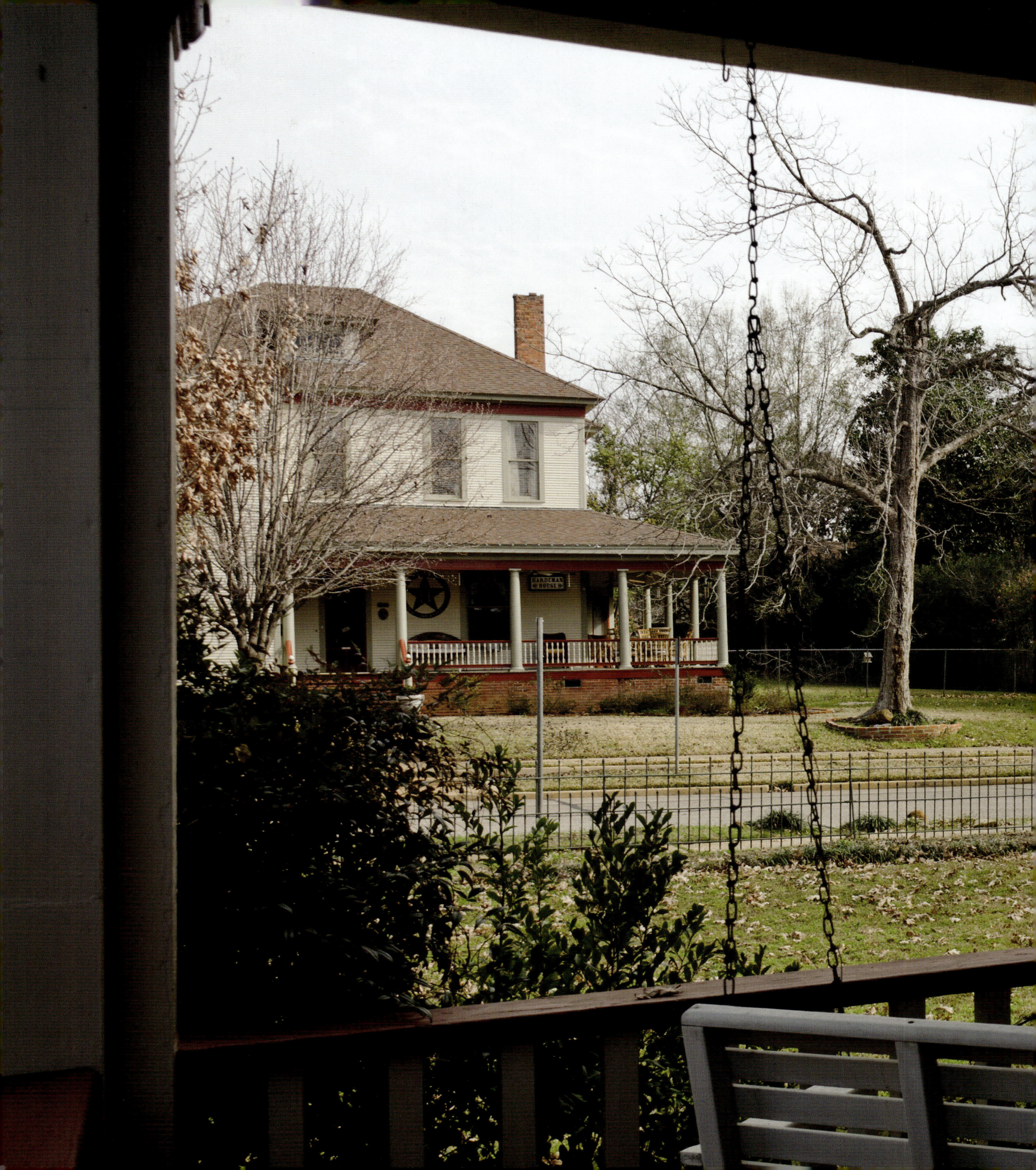

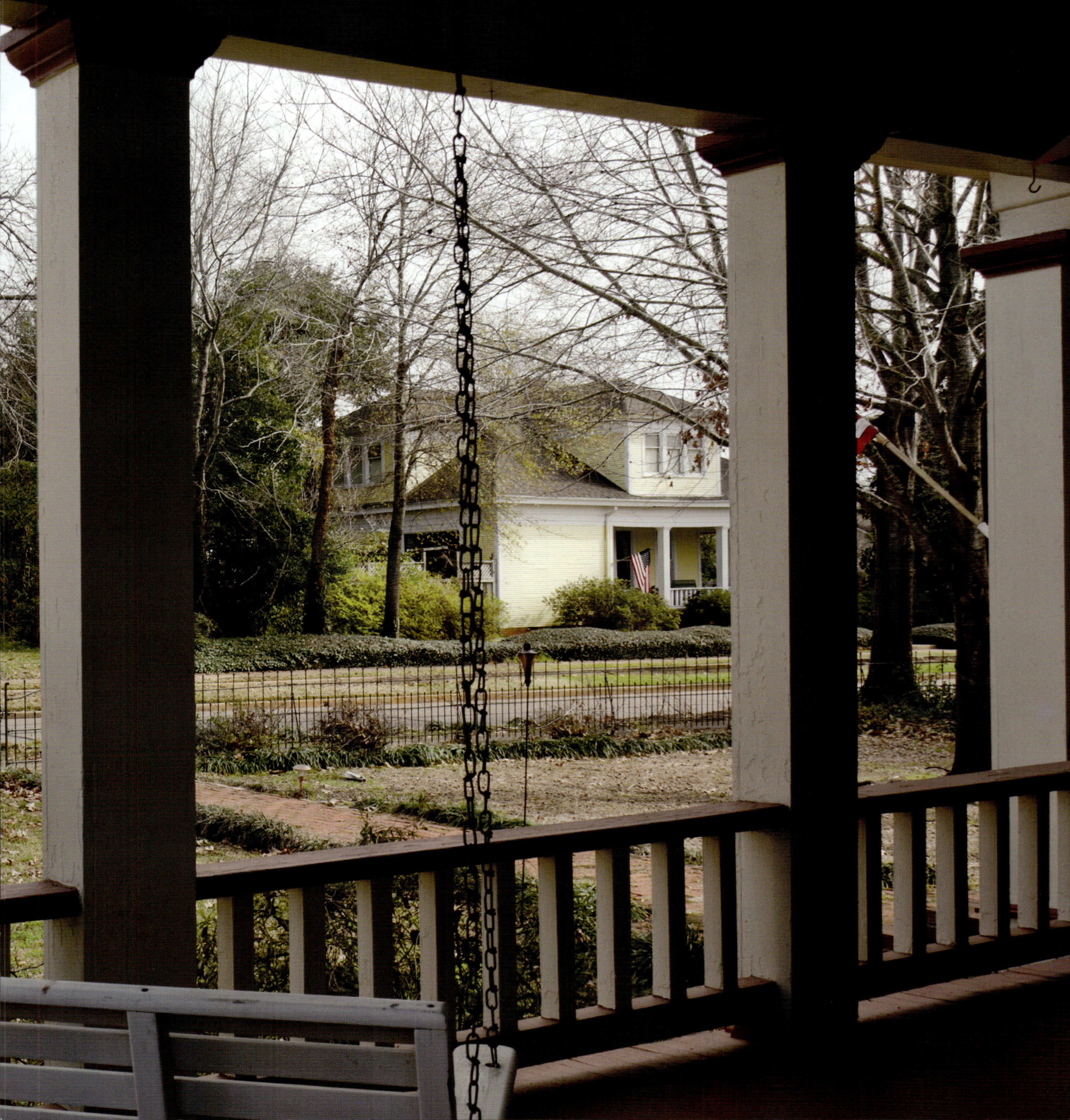

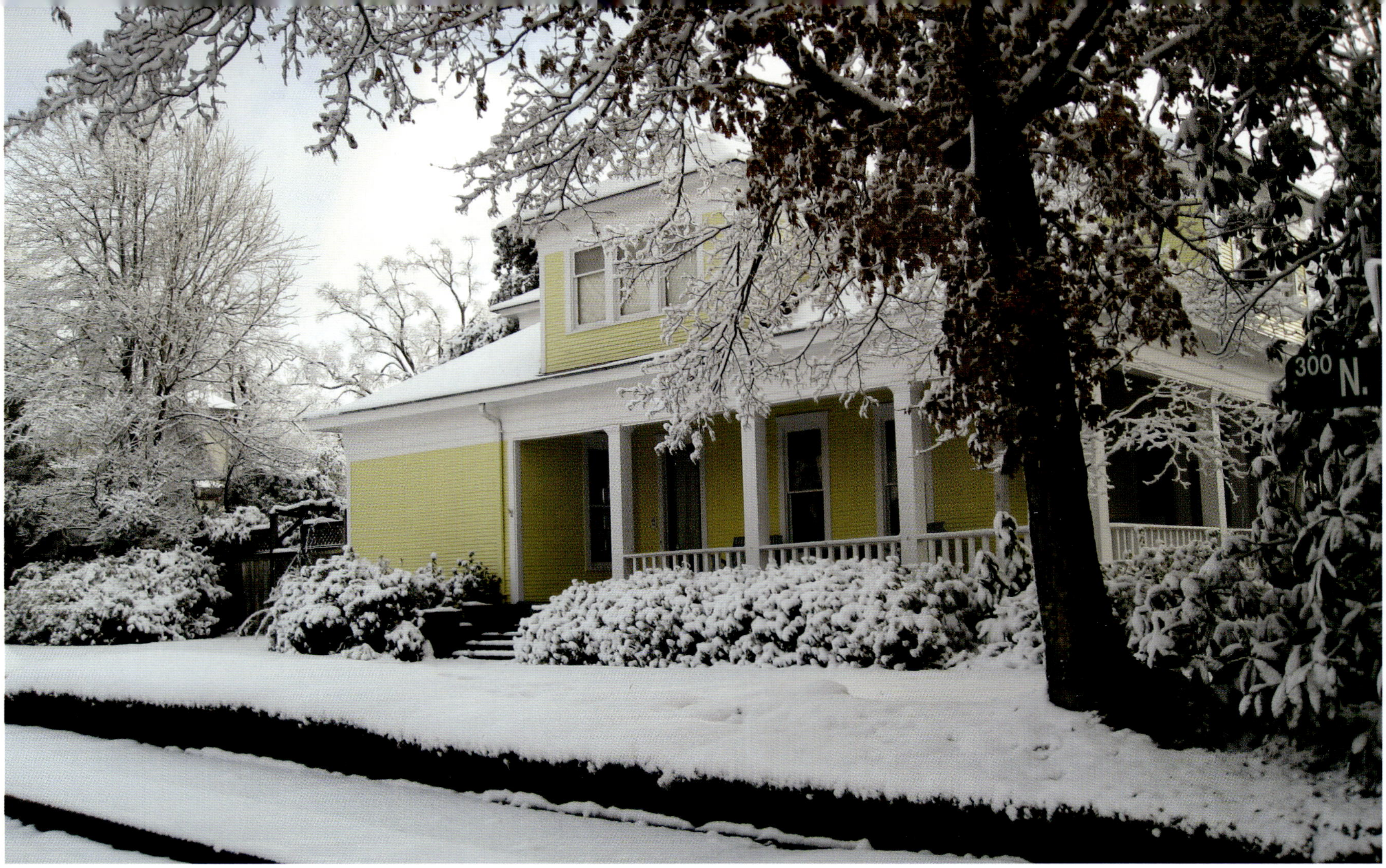

FIGURE 11.17. The Tom and Mary Summers House, now the Jere and Sarah Jackson Home, Winter 2010. Photography by the author.

The Tom Summers House (1913)

In 1913, Tom and Mary Perkins Summers purchased the Sarah Bagley house at 304 North Church Street, next door to the Lee Hardeman House. (The Bagley House dated from the opening of the Washington Square area. (See Chapter V.) The remodeling of the house resulted from the opening of the new Central School in 1904.

When Thomas Holloway Summers, Jr. and his wife, Mary Perkins, first married in 1902, they lived in a new suburban addition put together and promoted by June Harris and Robert Lindsey. The area, nicknamed "Honeymoon Acres," was along Starr Avenue at the end of North Mound Street. While living there, they had their two daughters, Lucille (1903) and Mary South (1908).[30] As the girls reached school age, their parents became interested in the Washington Square area. The Summers "wanted to move back into town from the country to be near the school," according to their granddaughter Florence Patton.[31] In 1913, they purchased the Sarah Bagley house at 304 North Church Street, in part, because Tom's parents (Jesse H. and Emma Summers) lived two blocks away and his brother Frank had a few years earlier built a new house on Hospital at Mound Street, just half a block away. Their sister Emma Mast would soon build close by on Mound Street, creating an enclave of relatives. Tom also wanted to be closer to his job at the Summers Lumber Company on West Main. The area was undergoing a definite renaissance with the building of the Hollis Mast home and the enlargement of the Hardeman home next door.[32]

Rulfs' specifications for remodeling the Bagley house still exist and are in the possession of the author. Unfortunately, no drawings have survived. The additions to the Bagley structure resembled the solutions applied to the Hardeman House next door. Rulfs replaced the wall between the two north bedrooms with a columned divider to create a new living room/dining room combination. He moved the fireplace in the south parlor and shared it with a new bedroom and sleeping porch to the east. Across the back of house, in a new utilitarian addition, he provided for a new breakfast room, a service porch, storage, and a new bathroom for the bedroom addition. Upstairs, he provided for three bedrooms and a sleeping porch by projecting four dormer-rooms from the center of the new massive hipped roof. (He had previously used the dormer-rooms on John Perkins and Haselwood Houses.) On the exterior, he extended the short front porch around the south side of the house and created a screened porch at the side of the new bedroom.

As a lumberman, Summers never considered sheathing the house in bricks. The floors were of heart, edge grain pine; the exterior completely resurfaced in #117 finger joint siding; and the custom furniture for the porch and yard was out of cypress. Supporting the roof over the porch were large boxed columns, identical to the ones on the Will Perkins House in 1910. The Summers did not demand fancy uses of the wood, such as in the Guy Blount or Schmidt homes, but the quality and the quantity of the lumber used were impressive. Throughout the house, Rulfs created wonderfully classic post-and-lintel door facings with a minimum of wood and carefully selected moldings. Following the lines of the older house, the arrangement was traditional, the look restrained with classical elements, the size manageable, and the double wood walls economical for heating and cooling.

The architect specified several innovative uses of windows. A wall of windows—two sets of massive 15/15 double hung sashes, separated by a pair of by-folding glass French doors ten feet tall—partitioned the new downstairs bedroom from the screened sleeping porch. (The research for the windows in the First Methodist Church led Rulfs to use the unusual windows in the Hollis Mast House and this house.) Each of the three dormer-bedrooms had a grouping of three, single-hung windows with fixed, ripple-glass transoms. The head of the lower windows slipped or disappear into the walls above as the window was raised. The front door, nine feet tall, has one large pane of beveled glass, six feet tall. The double-hung windows in the front rooms are seven feet tall. Obviously, the accommodation of light in the house was important for the Summers. When Mary South Summers died in 1969, the house sold to Jere and Sarah Jackson who completely refurbished the house in 1970 and who continue to live there.

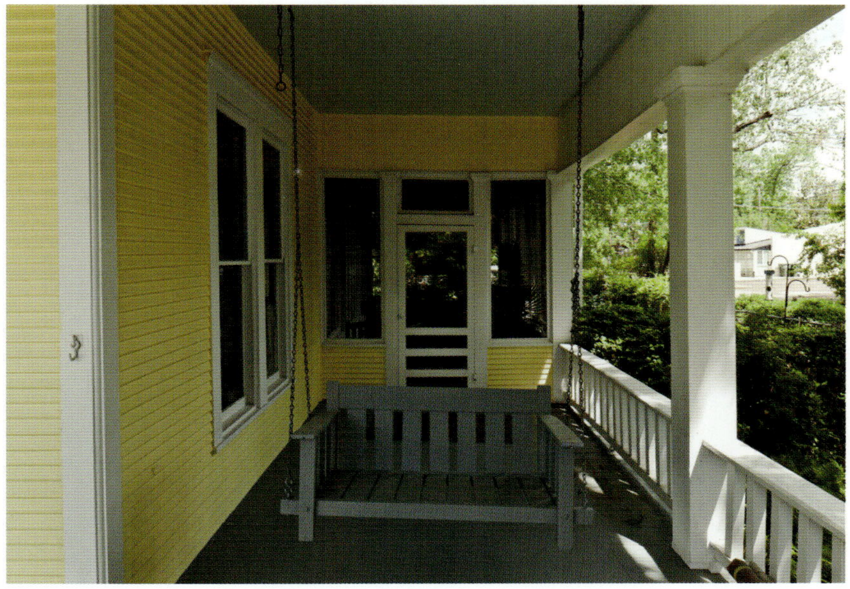

FIGURE 11.19. (Above) Summers House South Porch.
The front porch of the Summers House, incorporated under the main hipped roof of the house, wrapped from the living room aound the old parlor to the new screened sleeping porch on the southeast of the house. D. Rulfs designed and made the cypress furniture shown in photographs above for the house.

FIGURE 11.18. (Below) Living-Dining Room, Jackson Home.
In 1913, Rulfs created a new living-dining room by combining two bedrooms and replacing the wall between them with a colonnade. A library is across the entrance today in the old parlor.

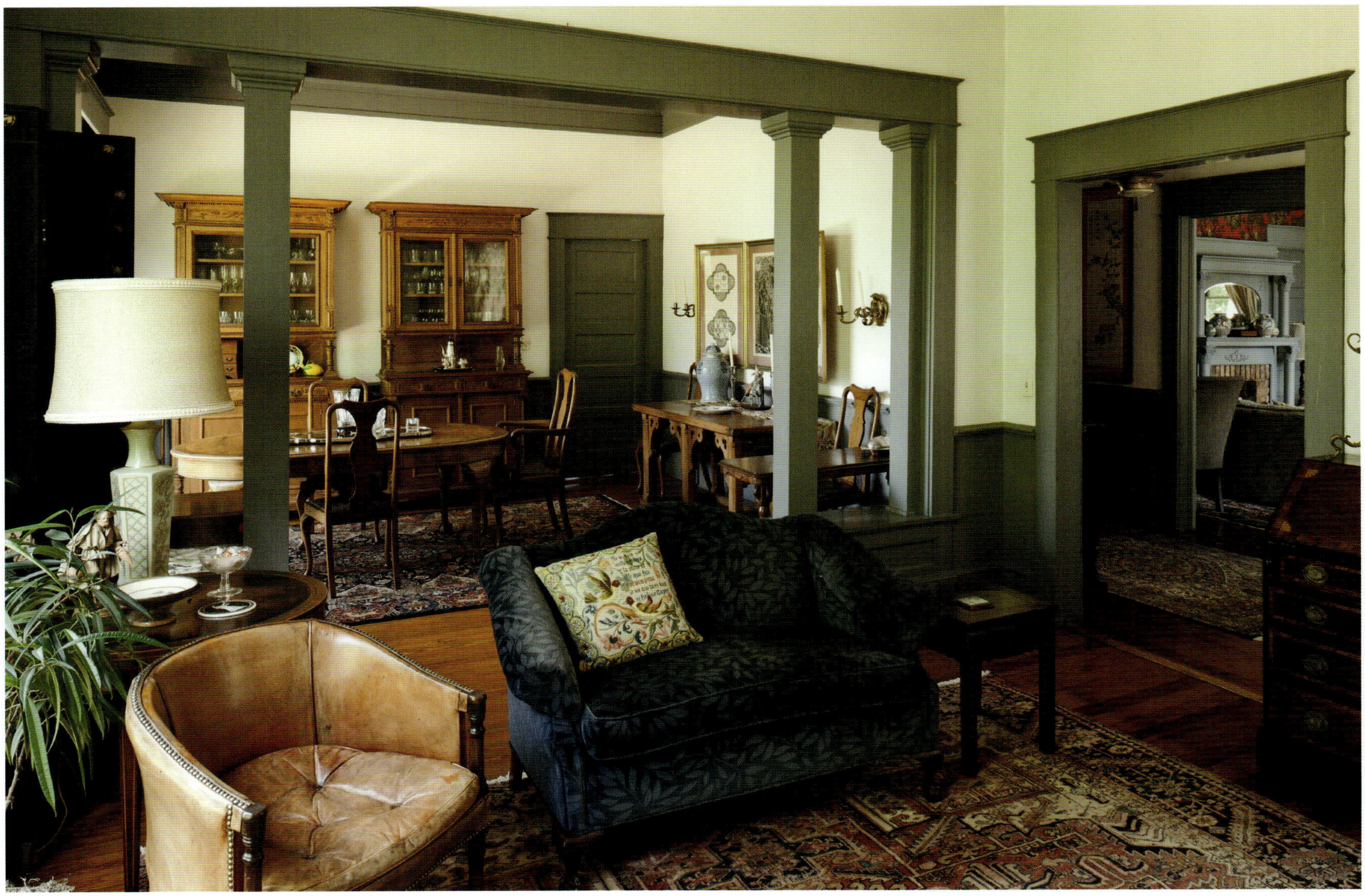

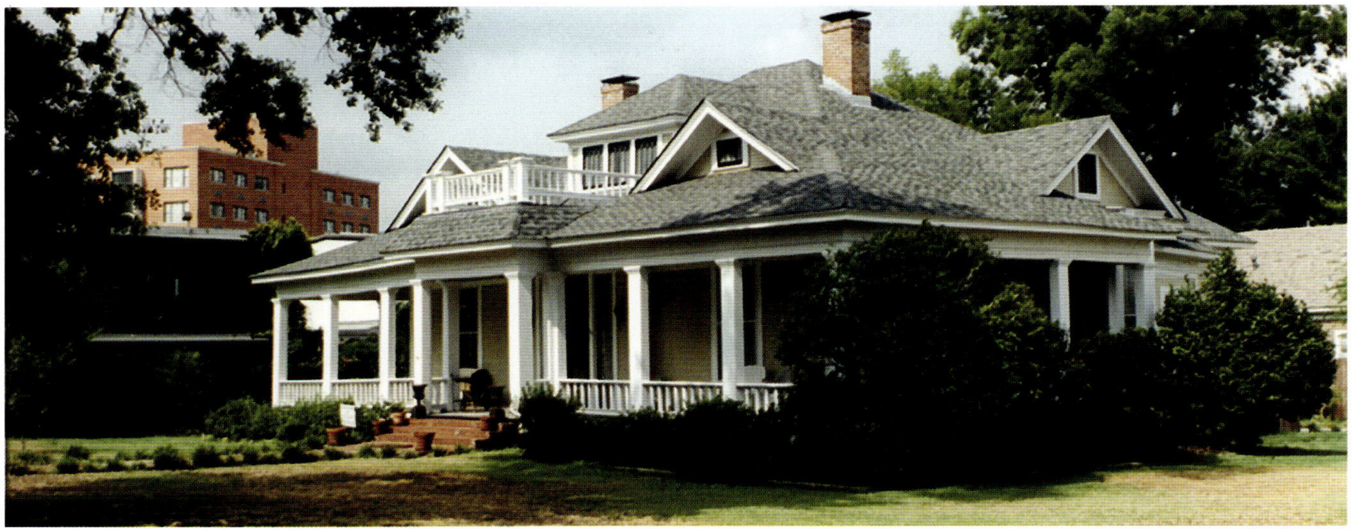

FIGURE 11.20. The Sanders Home, 1970s.
The Richardson House passed to the Haralson family in 1944. This picture, taken in the 1970s, shows the house as lived in by Gene and Mary Haralson Sanders.

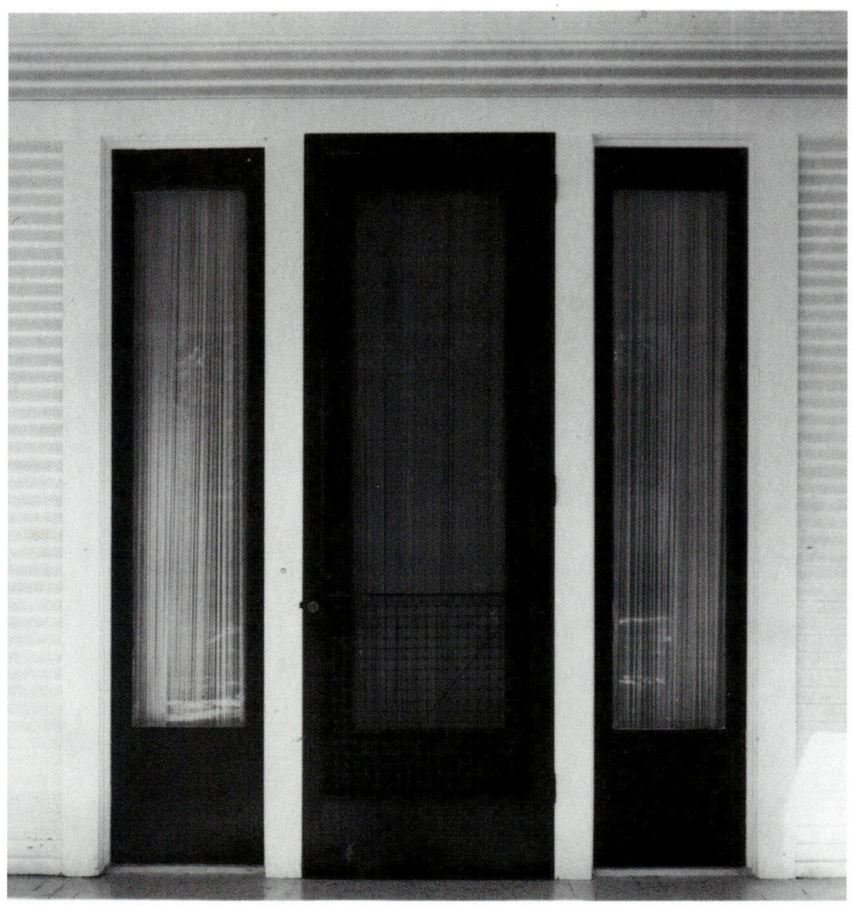

FIGURE 11.21. The Front Door of the Remodeled Sarah Richardson House. Photograph by Bill Murchison, 1986.

The Richardson-Haralson-Sanders House – Phase II (1915)

Rulfs revisited another of his early houses on Church Street in 1915. Alice Perkins Richardson's house, which he had designed in 1897, caught on fire; but the fire department limited the damage to the upper part of the one-and-a-half story structure. Gladys Hardeman, the neighbor across the street since 1893, accompanied the author and Eugene Sanders in the 1970s on an inspection tour of the attic of this house. The burned ceiling joists were clearly visible at that time; later renovations sealed off this remaining damage. [33] The Richardsons immediately engaged Rulfs to work his remodeling magic. Unlike the houses across the street, the task here was to downsize the house to become a single story. Whereas the old house was asymmetrical, built to take advantage of the corner position, the new classically influenced façade focused completely on Church Street. The new façade was symmetrical and featured a hipped-roof dormer with a bank of windows between two front facing gables.

The simplified design followed the pattern begun with the Will Perkins House on North Street in 1910. The floor plan was only slightly altered: the old parlor became one of two south bedrooms; the front entrance hall became part of the living room; the middle hall became the new central dining room; and the old dining room became the new master suite with the addition of a bathroom.[34]

In the 1920s, the Richardson House, like many houses in the Washington Square area, offered housing for new faculty members who opened Stephen F. Austin State Teachers College on the Old University Campus. Lois Foster (first faculty member hired at SFA), Ida Pritchett (head of the Music Department), and Ruth Mays (first Dean of Women), were residents in the house at 315 North Church. The first college song, "The Pine Tree Hymn" by Karle Wilson Baker, was first performed in this house at a *soiree* hosted by these faculty members in 1924, with President Birdwell in attendance.[35]

The William Haralson family purchased the house in 1944 from the Richardson heirs.[36] After her mother's death, Mary Haralson Sanders and her husband, James Eugene Sanders, took over management of the house. Neither the Haralsons nor the Sanders made substantive changes to the house beyond restoring the rotted balustrade over the front entry. Gene's sister, Mary Lee Sanders, lived in the house until her death in 1991; and Jimmy Sanders used the house as a weekend retreat from Houston for a number of years before selling the property to Jill (Muckleroy) and J. R. Ornelas in 1996, who once again stabilized the house. J. R. closed in the attic as a music room for himself. The legal firm of Karczewski and Bradshaw now own the house.[37]

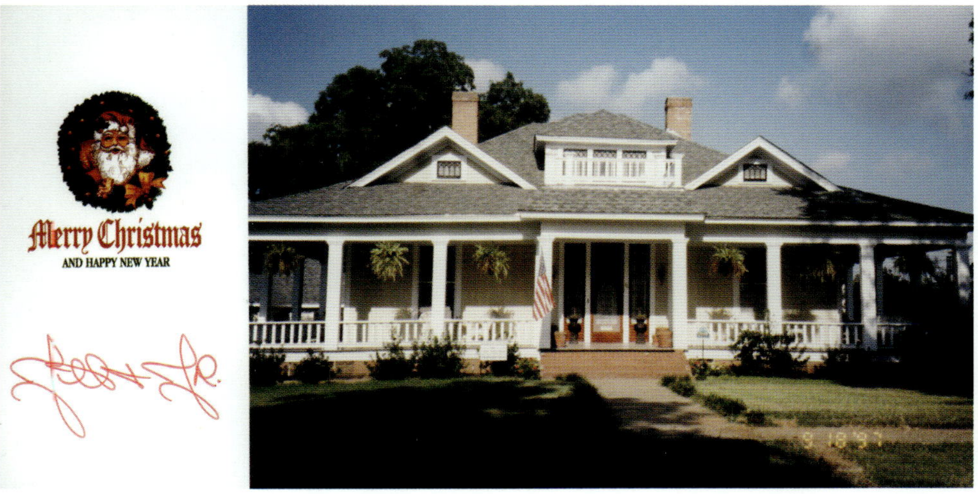

FIGURE 11.22. Christmas Post Card, 1997.

The Sarah Richardson House became the home of Jill and J. R. Ornelas in 1997. To celebrate their complete refurbishment of the house, they sent the above Christmas card and commemorated their achievement.

FIGURE 11.23. (Right) SFA's First College Song Presented in this House.

SFA opened its doors across from this house on the Washington Square Campus of the Old University in 1923. The Pine Tree Hymn, a poem by Karle Wilson Baker, was set to music by Ida Pritchett who lived in this house at the time. Baker herself lived on the north side of Washington Square. President Birdwell was present at the event.

FIGURE 11.24. (Below) Front Porch of Richardson House.

The front porch of this house was a favorite gathering place for early faculty members at SFASTC during the college's yearlong tenure across the street, September 1923 to May 1924.

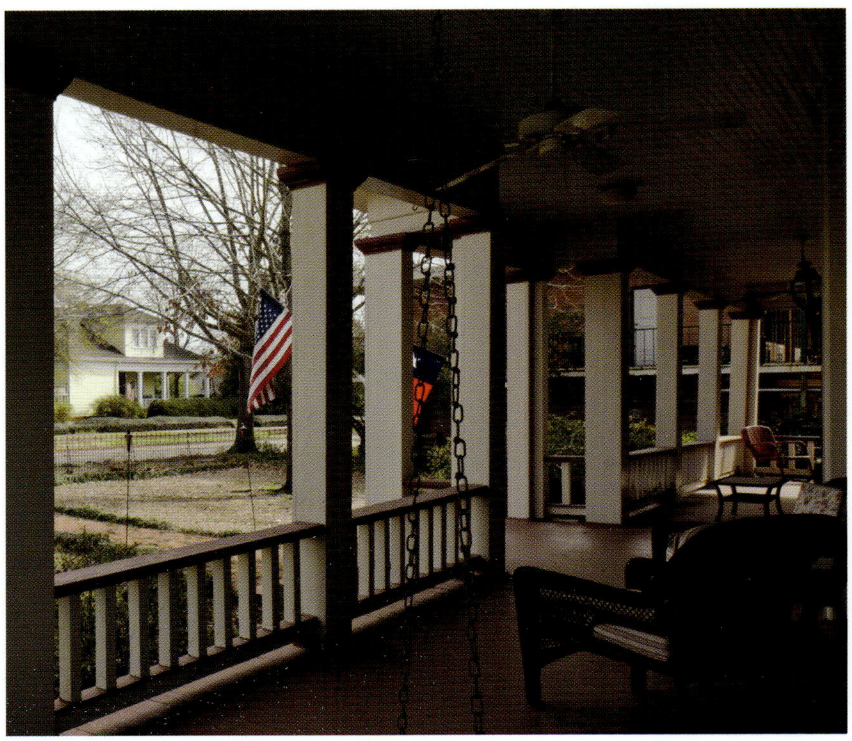

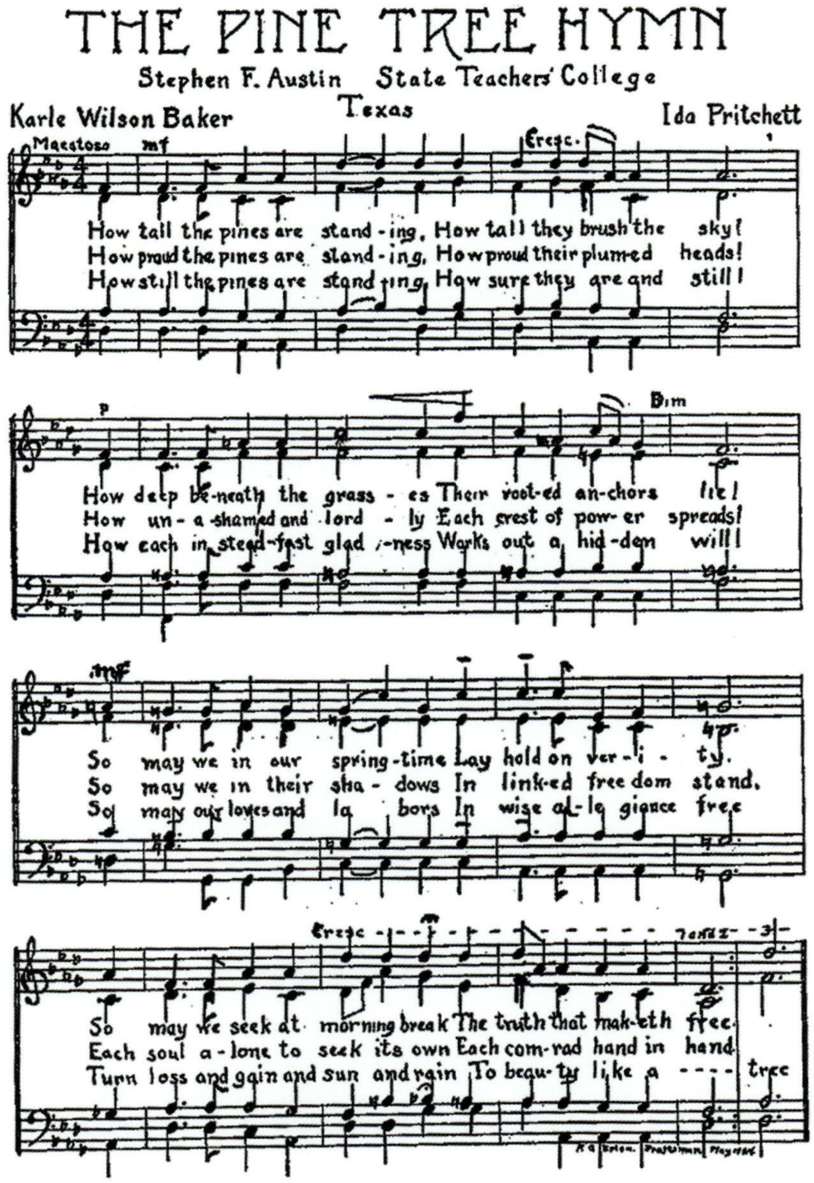

FIGURE 11.25. (Overleaf) The D. K. Cason House (1914).

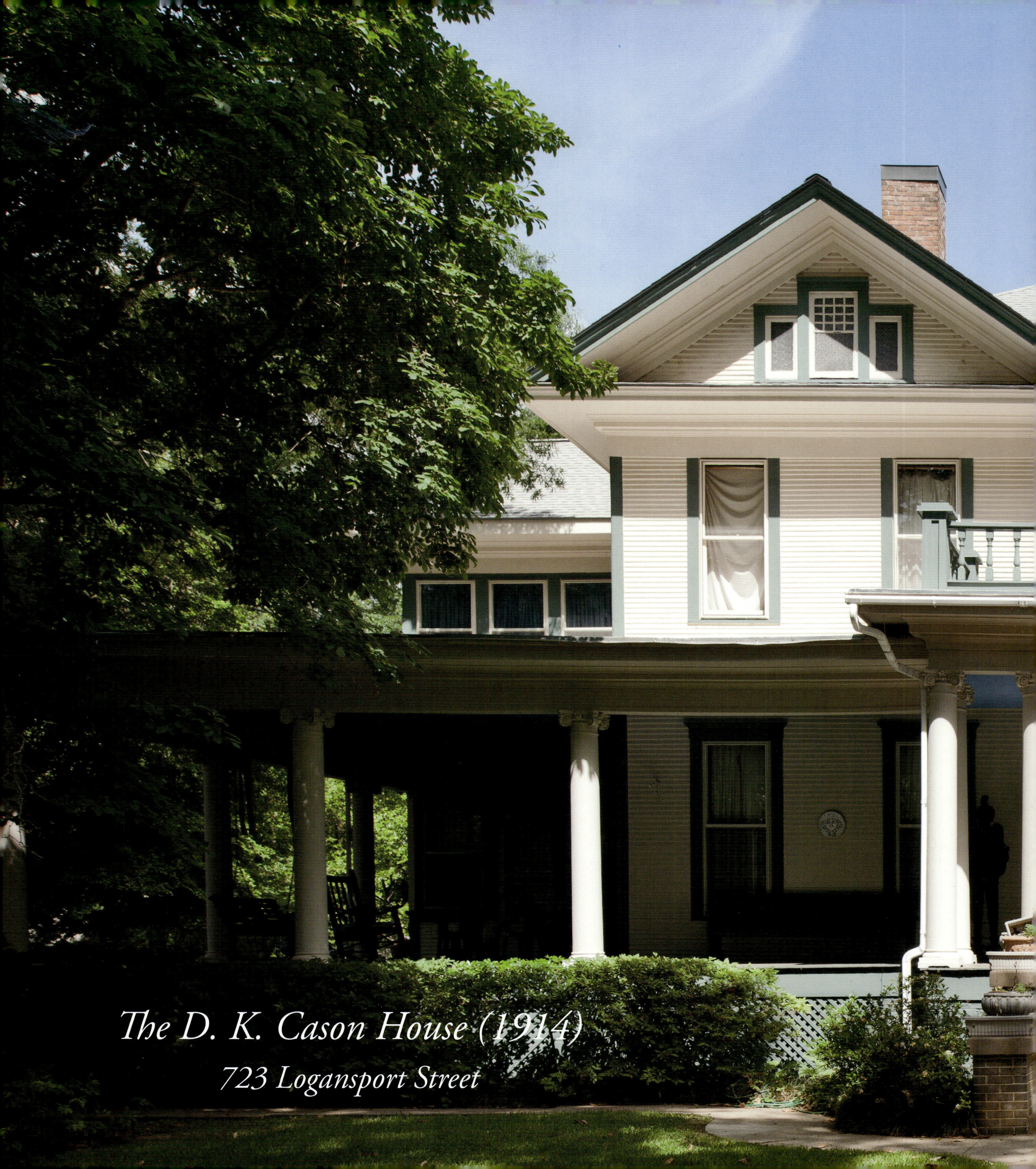

The D. K. Cason House (1914)

723 Logansport Street

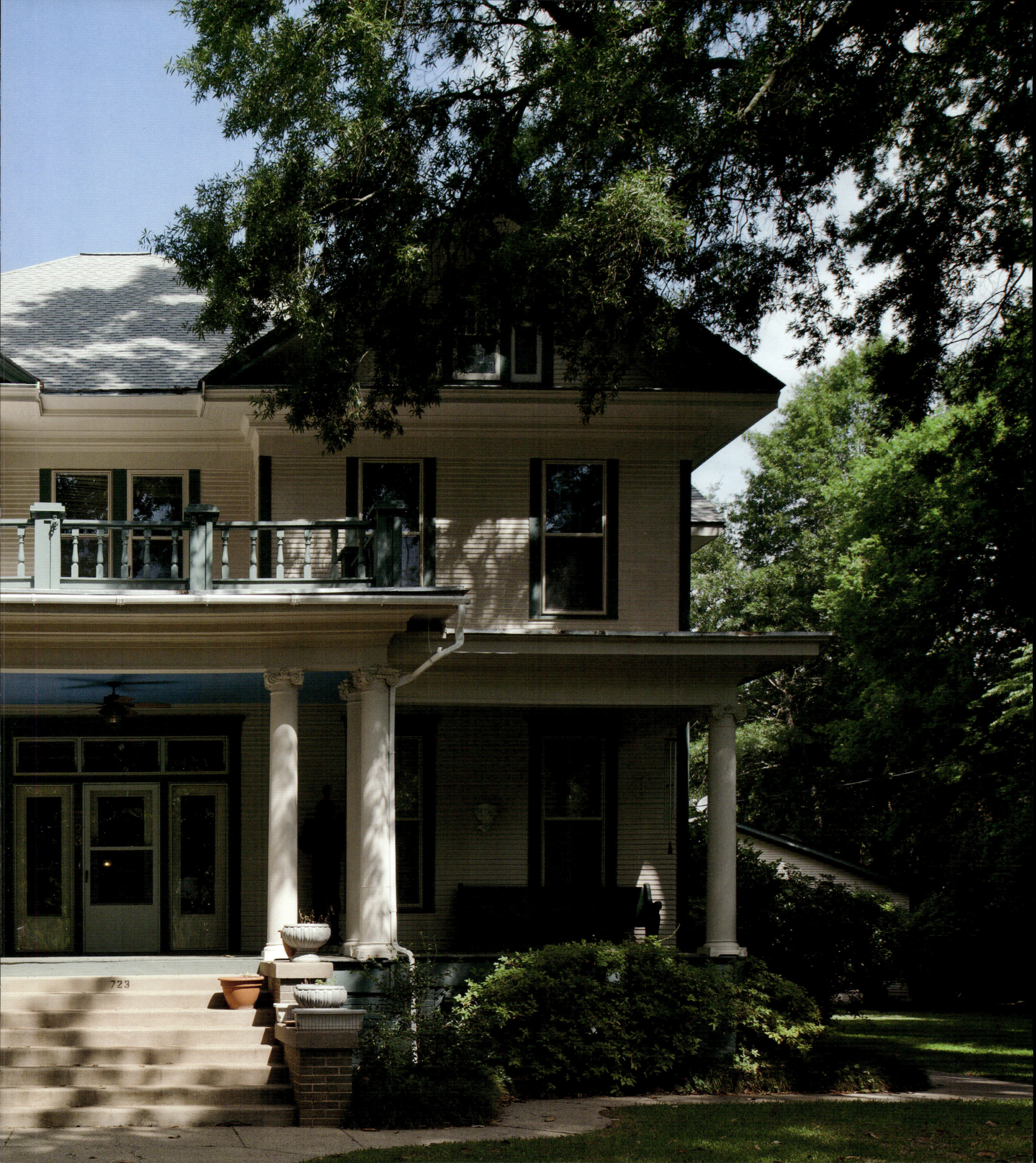
723

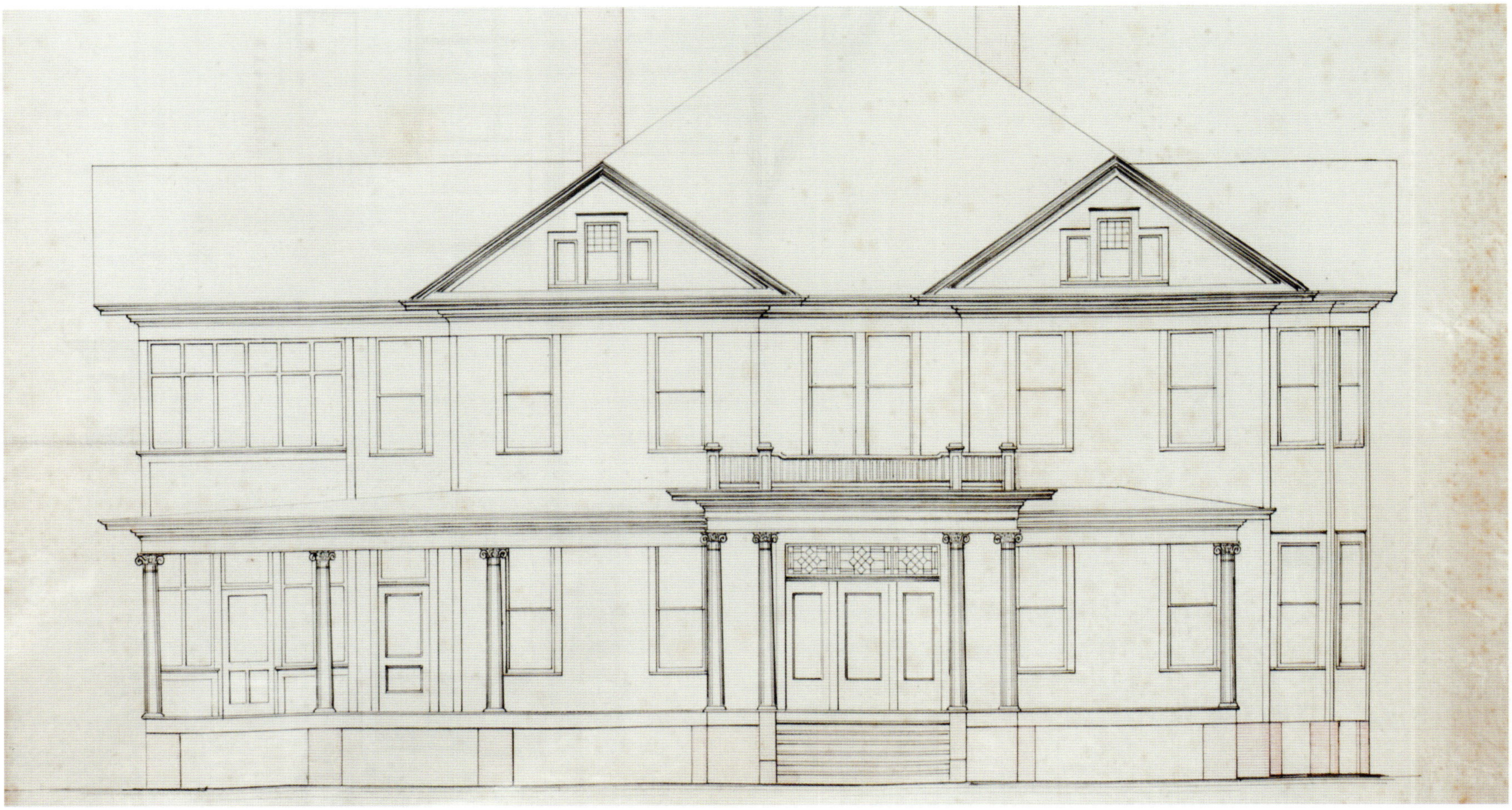

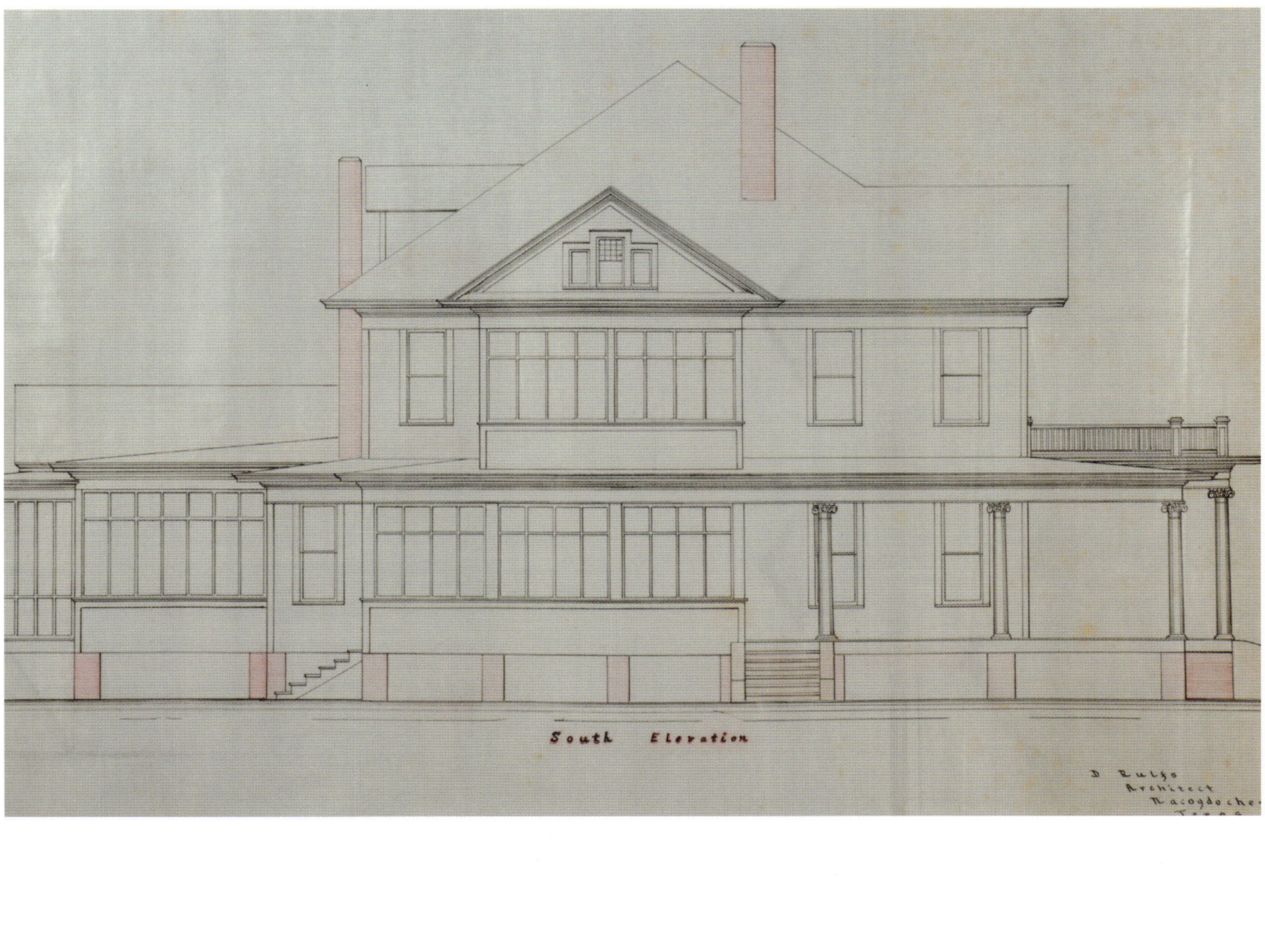

FIGURES 11.26 and 11.27. Architectural Drawings by D. Rulfs for the D. K. Cason House, 1914.

The front elevation (above) and the south elevation (below). The plans, given to the author by the Cason Estate, are now in the ETRC.

The D. K. Cason House (1914)

The Logansport Road area to the northeast of Washington Square seems now a natural extension of the old square, but, in 1910, the area was still farmland, in the country as thought at the time.[38] The building of the F. C. Ford House at Mound and Park Streets seems to have triggered renewed interest in the area. D. K. Cason first purchased land along Park Street, but then shifted his thought to developing a new subdivision along the old Logansport Road. (The story of D. K. Cason and Charles Hoya's interest in the area appeared in Chapter IX as part of the discussion of the building for Zion Hill Baptist Church.)

Dick Cason[39] was a long-time friend and patron of D. Rulfs. The architect had designed Cason's first home on Church Street, built a variety of commercial buildings for Cason, and collaborated with Cason on the Methodist Church. With his children grown and his great business venture launched (Cason, Monk & Company), Cason yearned for a grand, spacious house commensurate with his status in town, the reward his peers had granted for themselves years before. While he and Rulfs had discussed this for years, the house had to wait until the move of the Zion Hill Church became a reality.

The Cason House was a grand residence, the largest house built in Nacogdoches since those of the 1890s for W. U. Perkins, John Schmidt, the Blount brothers, June Harris, and Roland Jones. There was nothing terribly new about the house, but it seemed to be exactly what the traditionalist owner wanted. It most definitely was a response by the old guard to the modern residences on North Street. In using the term "grand," the author limits the use of this adjective to the Nacogdoches context. The largest house in Nacogdoches would compare only to houses of middle standing in cities such as Dallas and Houston at the time. But, for instance, the Cason House, would compare comfortably to many houses along the Swiss Avenue Historical District built around the same time in Dallas, with perhaps one exception: wood, not brick, still dominated the Piney Woods building scene. In fact, when the house was being reworked in the 1970s, restoration architect Rayford Stripling mistakenly attributed the house to a prominent Dallas architect, Robert Witchell, and dated it to 1912.[40] The firm of Lang & Witchell did design the Nacogdoches Court House of the period 1910-1912. Interestingly, Stripling, who lived and worked in the San Augustine area, did not know that a local Nacogdoches architect of Rulfs's stature had ever practiced in the Nacogdoches area or could have designed the residence for Cason. The recently discovered specifications and drawings of the house by Rulfs, included in these pages, should dispel any lingering doubts of the abilities and resourcefulness of the resident architect who designed modern Nacogdoches.

The Rulfs plans called for a house gracious in proportions, restrained in ornamentation, and conservative in organization.[41] Rulfs must have enjoyed the opportunity to confirm in this house the themes of his career. The house had, for instance, a profusion of Palladian motifs. The predominant features of the house included spacious wood porches, an array of classical (unfluted) Ionic columns, two-story front gables, two-story, chamfered bay rooms. The interior organization was traditional: a parlor and living room on either side of a spacious entrance, which had a grand staircase at the rear. The setting for house had enough acreage to make the built-in sunrooms, with their walls of windows, worthwhile. Overall, the house was a fitting setting for the grandee that D. K. Cason was by that time. Unlike the older mansions, this house from the beginning included all the modern conveniences: indoor plumbing, central heating, and closets throughout. Until the invention of air conditioning, the high ceilings of the Cason residence had a distinct advantage over some of the newer houses. Despite all of its lovely features, the house was an anachronism, a symbol of a bygone era.[42]

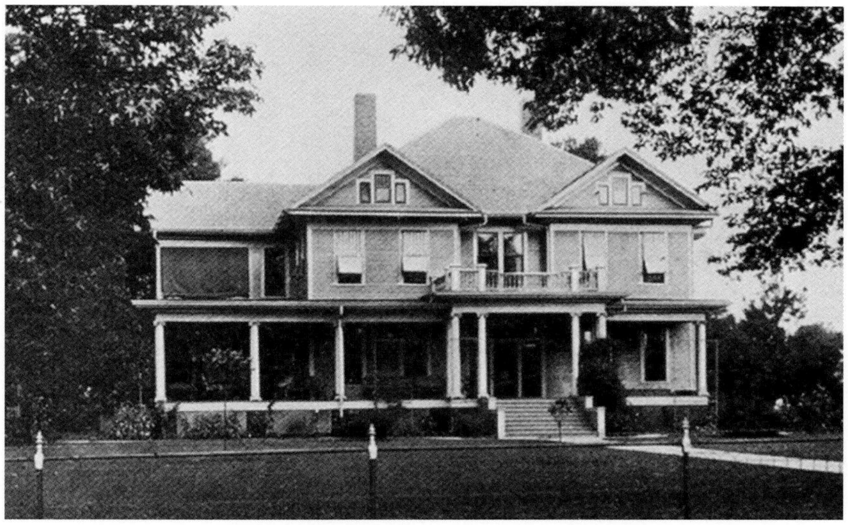

Figure 11.28. The Cason House, 1917.
This picture, from the booklet entitled The Twenty Three Reasons Why, *was part of the solicitation campaign to secure the SFA Normal School for Nacogdoches. The scan is from the author's copy.*

Not long after World War I, the Casons sold their new home and moved into more manageable quarters. Their children did not want the house. The John Edward Stone family owned the Cason House until the early 1970s.

In 1976, John and Linda McKinney purchased the house. "The house needed a family; we needed a house," John told the *Daily Sentinel* reporter. Under the supervision of restoration architect Rayford Stripling from San Augustine, the McKinneys undertook to update the structure. Stripling called the the structure "Classic Revival," free of the gingerbread embellishments of earlier houses. By including the large sun porches into their new bedroom suite, the original spaces now have new uses. The outdated kitchen received the most complete transformation. The parlor became a new library. The edge-grained pine floors, sanded and refinished, became the backdrop of lovely oriental rugs.[43] Dr. Matthew Lowe purchased the house in 1983.

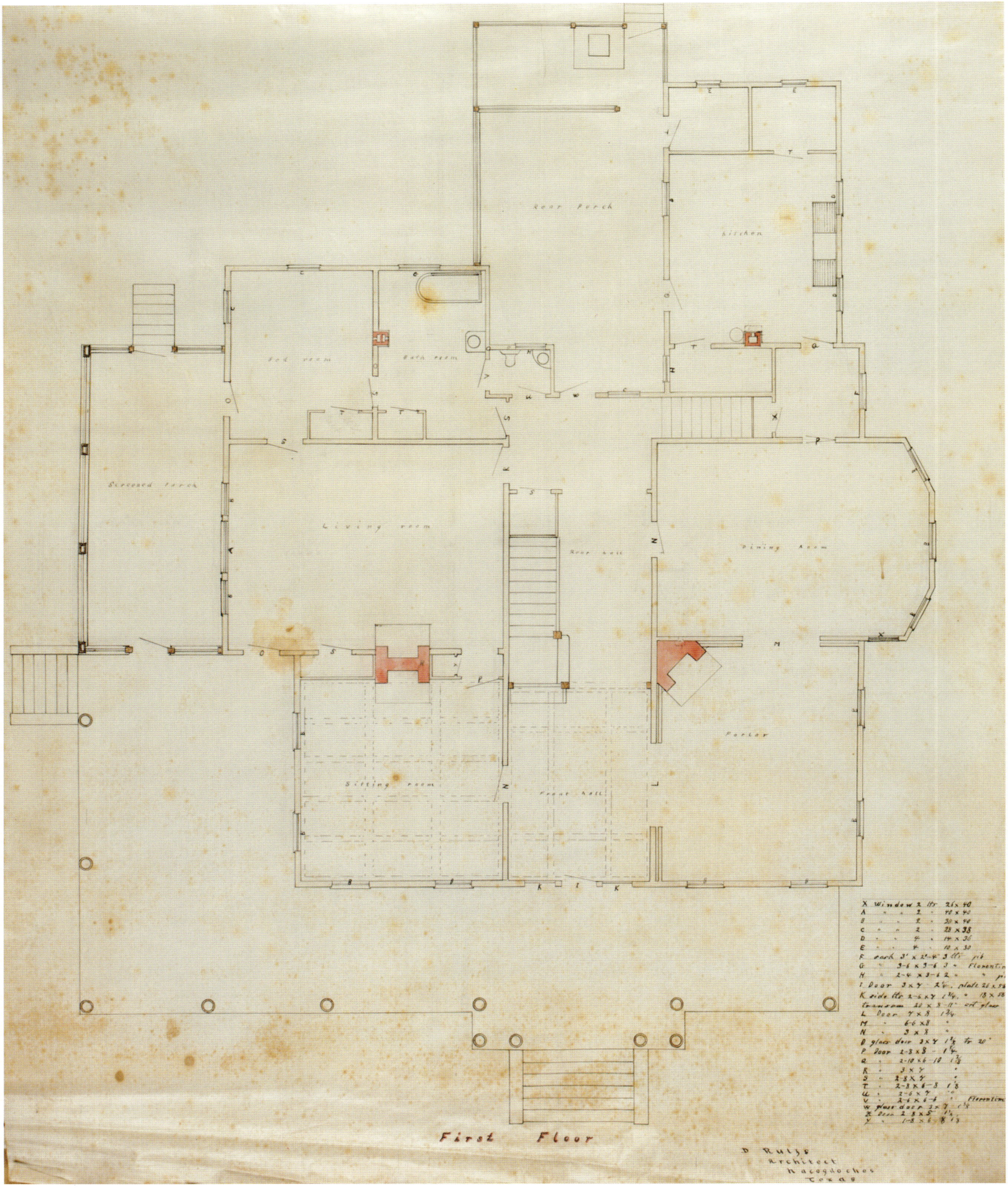
Rear Porch
Kitchen
Bed room
Bath room
Screened porch
Living room
Rear hall
Dining room
Parlor
Sitting room
Front hall
X Window 2 lts 26 x 40
A " " 2 " 40 x 40
B " " 2 " 30 x 40
C " " 2 " 28 x 38
D " " 4 " 14 x 36
E " " 4 " 12 x 30
L Door 7 x 8 1 3/4
M " 6-6 x 8 "
N " 3 x 8 "
P Door 2-8 x 8 - 1 3/4
R " 3 x 7 "
S " 2-8 x 7 "
T " 2-8 x 6-8 1 3/8
First Floor
D Ruizs
Architect
Nacogdoches
Texas

Plans for the D. K. Cason Home, 1914

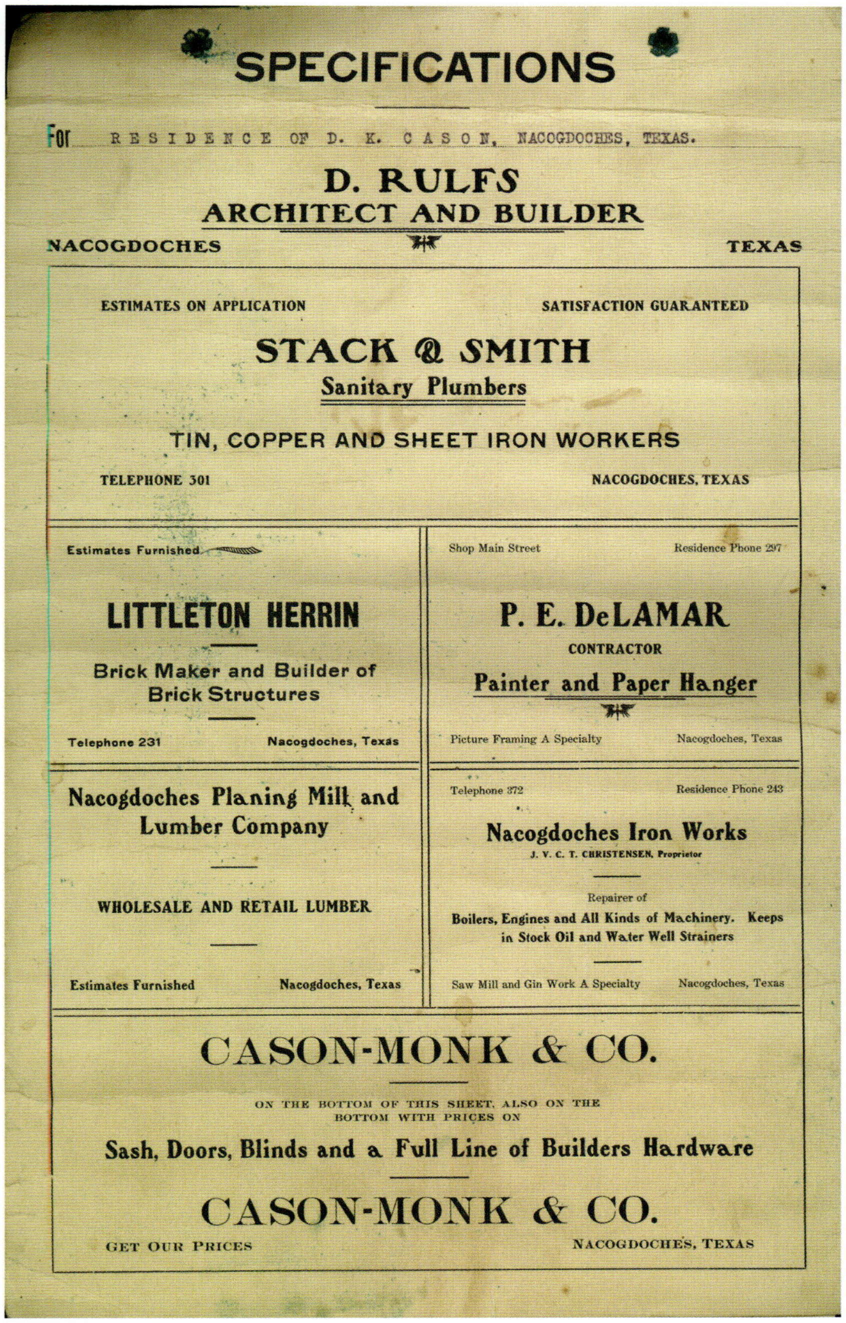

SPECIFICATIONS

For RESIDENCE OF D. K. CASON, NACOGDOCHES, TEXAS.

D. RULFS
ARCHITECT AND BUILDER
NACOGDOCHES TEXAS

ESTIMATES ON APPLICATION SATISFACTION GUARANTEED
STACK & SMITH
Sanitary Plumbers
TIN, COPPER AND SHEET IRON WORKERS
TELEPHONE 301 NACOGDOCHES, TEXAS

Estimates Furnished
LITTLETON HERRIN
Brick Maker and Builder of Brick Structures
Telephone 231 Nacogdoches, Texas

Shop Main Street Residence Phone 297
P. E. DeLAMAR
CONTRACTOR
Painter and Paper Hanger
Picture Framing A Specialty Nacogdoches, Texas

Nacogdoches Planing Mill and Lumber Company
WHOLESALE AND RETAIL LUMBER
Estimates Furnished Nacogdoches, Texas

Telephone 372 Residence Phone 243
Nacogdoches Iron Works
J. V. C. T. CHRISTENSEN, Proprietor
Repairer of
Boilers, Engines and All Kinds of Machinery. Keeps in Stock Oil and Water Well Strainers
Saw Mill and Gin Work A Specialty Nacogdoches, Texas

CASON-MONK & CO.
ON THE BOTTOM OF THIS SHEET, ALSO ON THE BOTTOM WITH PRICES ON
Sash, Doors, Blinds and a Full Line of Builders Hardware
CASON-MONK & CO.
GET OUR PRICES NACOGDOCHES, TEXAS

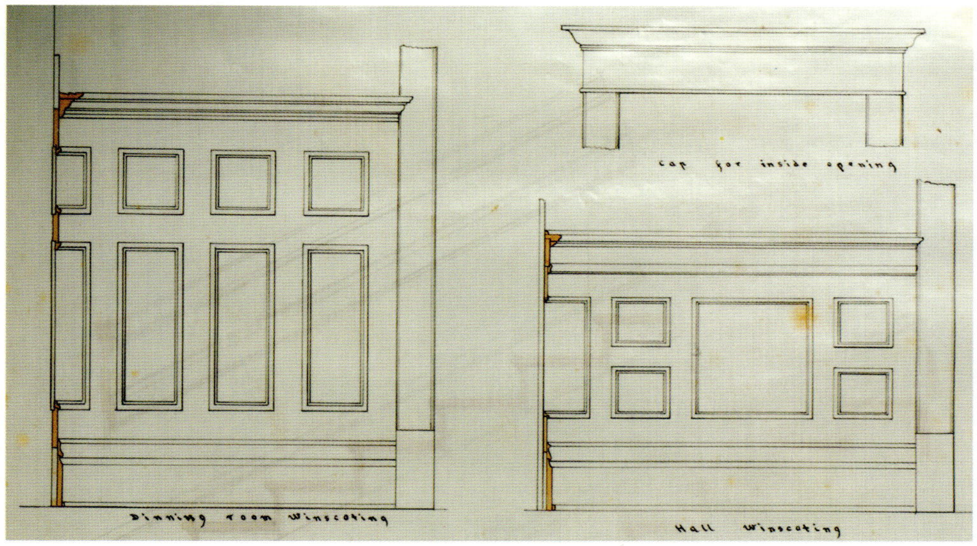

FIGURE 11.30. Original Drawing, Detail of Wainscoting for the Dining Room and Entrance Hall, 1914.
The plans, given to the author by the Cason Estate, are now in the ETRC.

FIGURES 11.31 and 11.32. Architectural Plans, D. K. Cason House, 1914.
(Left) The Cover of the Specifications;
(Below) Blueprint of the Front Elevation. The plans, given to the author by the Cason Estate, are now in the ETRC.

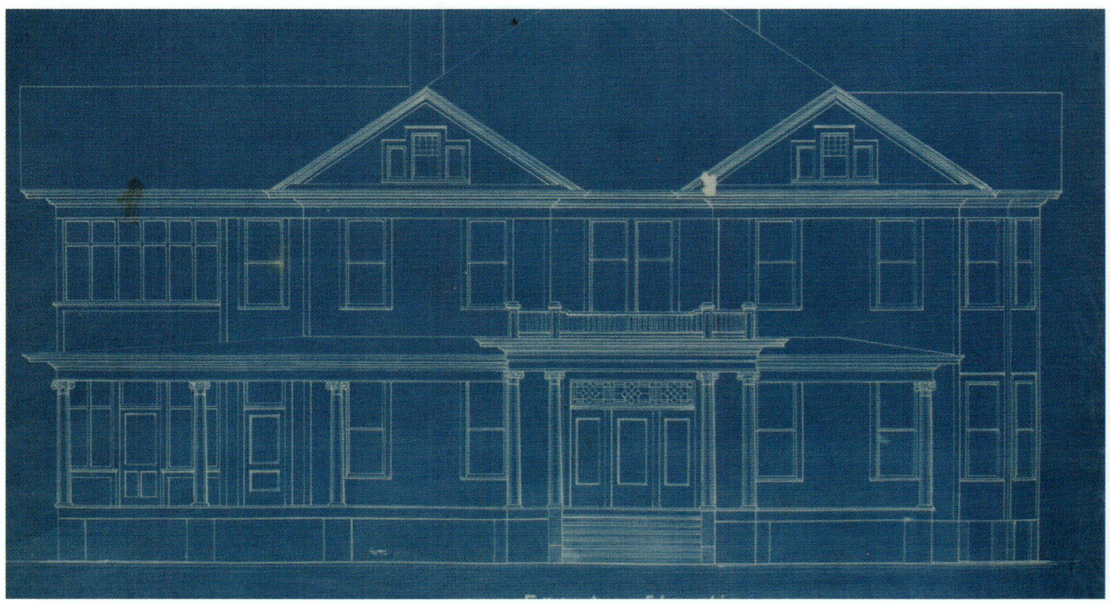

FIGURE 11.29. (Across) Original Drawing by D. Rulfs, 1914.
This drawing of the first floor of the Cason House is one of a complete set, signed by the architect. There are also blueprints for all the drawings. The plans, given to the author by the Cason Estate, are now in the ETRC.

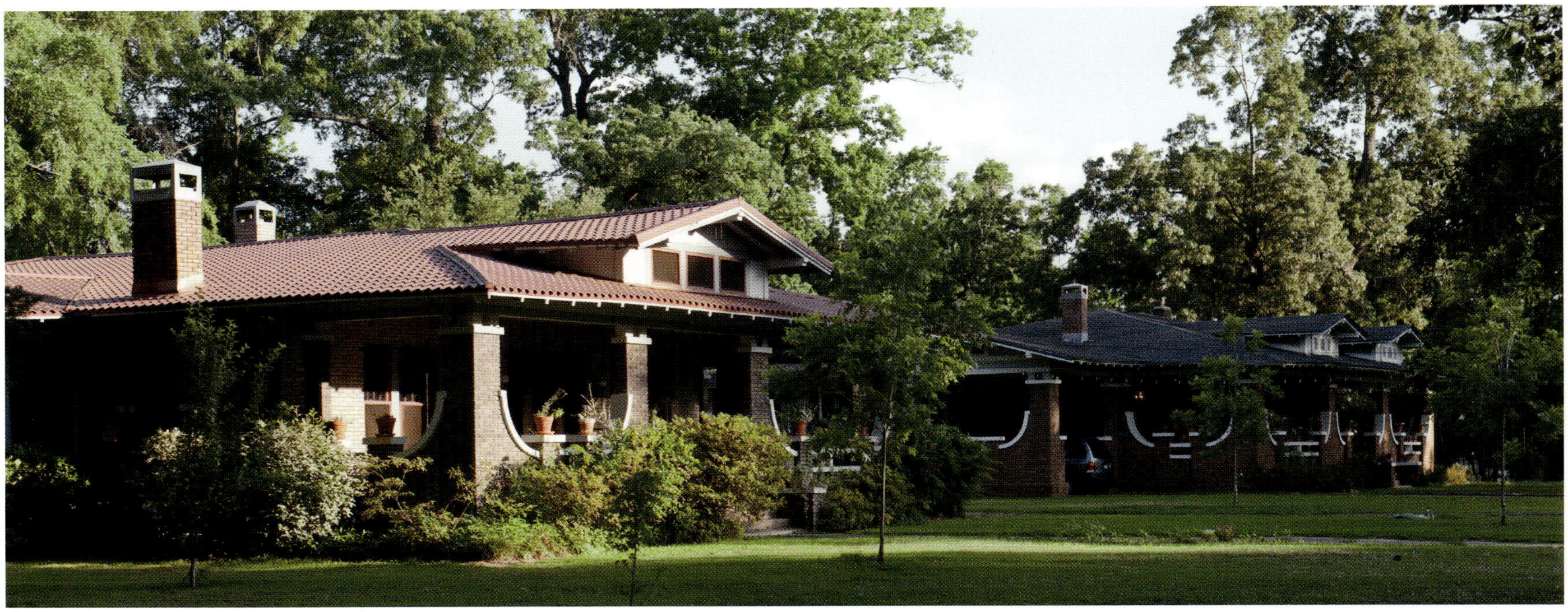

FIGURE 11.33. The Gray and Mast Houses on Logansport Street.

The Jennie and Blum Mast House (1914)
The Clara and Roy Gray House (1914)

On Logansport Street, the clash of traditional vs. modern trends in Nacogdoches came to a dramatic confrontation. Interestingly, when Nacogdoches compiled promotional literature in 1917 to highlight the best features of the municipality, both sides of Logansport Street became leading examples of the best Nacogdoches had to offer.

Across the street from Cason's neo-classical mansion, Charles Hoya commissioned Rulfs to design and build two new homes for his recently married daughters. In 1911, Hoya's eldest daughter, Jennie, had married Leon Blum Mast (1882-1958).[44] Mast originally joined his brother, Hollis, in purchasing the Perkins Drugstore in 1907; but, by 1909, he embarked on his career as a banker, first with the new Farmers and Merchants Bank and later with the Stone Fort Bank after the two banks merged in 1919. In 1914, Charles's younger daughter, Clara, married J. Roy Gray (1888-1966),[45] who joined the Hoya family's land abstract business. Diedrich Rulfs, with an office and homestead across the street from their childhood home, knew Hoya's daughters well, from their earliest childhoods. He had built their family home and remodeled it to facilitate their coming of age.

Clara and Jennie wanted something modern, something akin to what the architect had done for the younger Blounts on North Street. (The impetus for change in Nacogdoches appears more generational, from individuals who wanted to separate themselves from their progenitors.) The houses Rulfs designed for the Hoya daughters seem to reflect, in a general way, the Arts & Crafts Movement. In part, the Arts and Crafts Movement in the United States originated from complaints about assembly line houses with inferior woodwork and mass-produced parts. No one, however, could accuse Rulfs of producing houses that looked prefabricated or overly repetitious or lacking in craftsmanship. Whether Rulfs really preferred the modern trends is debatable, but he either had to demonstrate flexibility or to see his patrons go out of town. In this book, the author has chosen to illustrate the continuity of the architect's work–how his thoughts and designs progressed from one house to another–rather than try to stuff his structures into predefined categories. His tastes were eclectic and his career more interesting because of this.

Locally, people call the Mast and Gray homes "The Twin Houses on Logansport." The nickname demonstrates the extent to which Rulfs succeeded in his objective to create two unique houses with a unified theme for the sisters. Rulfs knew the young women and their husbands too well to put them in identical houses. Clara Gray's house is as straightforward as she was; Jennie Mast's has many frilly elements in line with her nature. The houses are not the same size, nor do they have identical interiors. The house for the Grays is smaller than that for the Masts.[46] They, nevertheless, share many design elements: elongated profiles, low-pitched hipped roofs, overhanging eaves, horizontal massing, distinctive porch supports, open floor plans, and, a shared driveway between the houses. By placing architectural fencing at the street level, Rulfs provided the ultimate unifying element for the "twins" and reinforced their predominantly horizontal impression. While these houses share characteristics of the Craftsman and Bungalow Movements, Rulfs never truly warmed to the Bungalow Style. The houses for the Hoya daughters were part of his experimental nature and part of his career's progression; he borrowed and modified elements as he needed them to satisfy his clients' wishes.[47]

The Gray House is today the home of Tom and Kathleen Belanger since 1992. The Mast House now is the home of Richard and Maria Fischer since 1994.

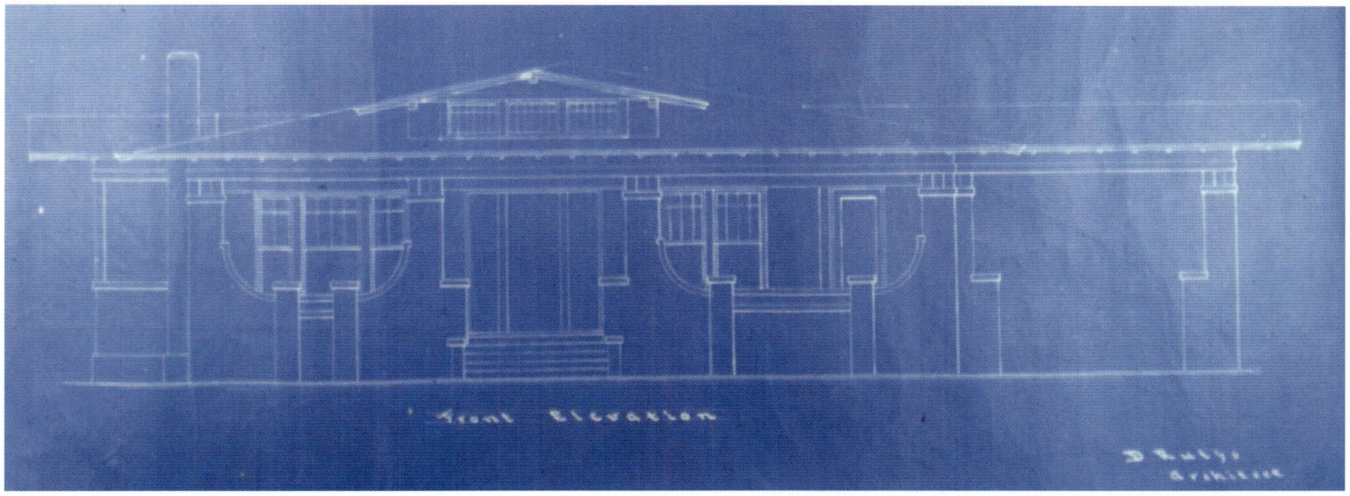

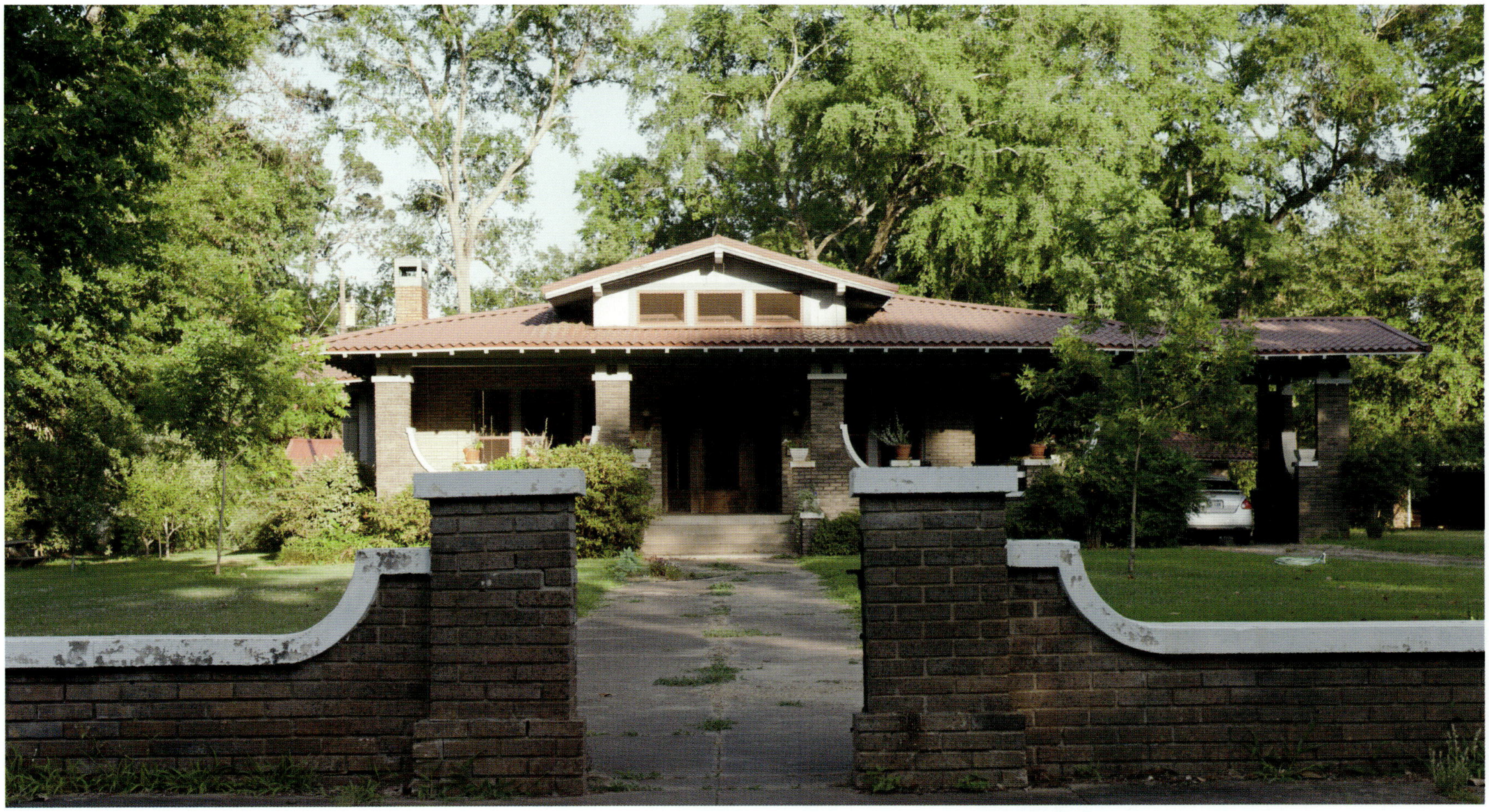

FIGURE 11.34. (Top) The Blueprint of the Clara and Roy Gray House (1914).
Mrs. Clara Gray gave the author permission to take this photograph of her blueprint in the early 1970s.

FIGURE 11.35. (Above) The Architectural Fence and Gate of the Gray House.
Rulfs echoed the Gray and Mast residences in the architectural fencing at the street. The fencing increases the horizontal nature of the houses and helps to give the impression the houses were "twins."

The architect liked to designate the entrance of his houses with varying types of pediments. The effect of the dormer and the front columns of the porch of the Gray House do this in a new way. Because of the larger size of the Mast House next door, this device did not work there.

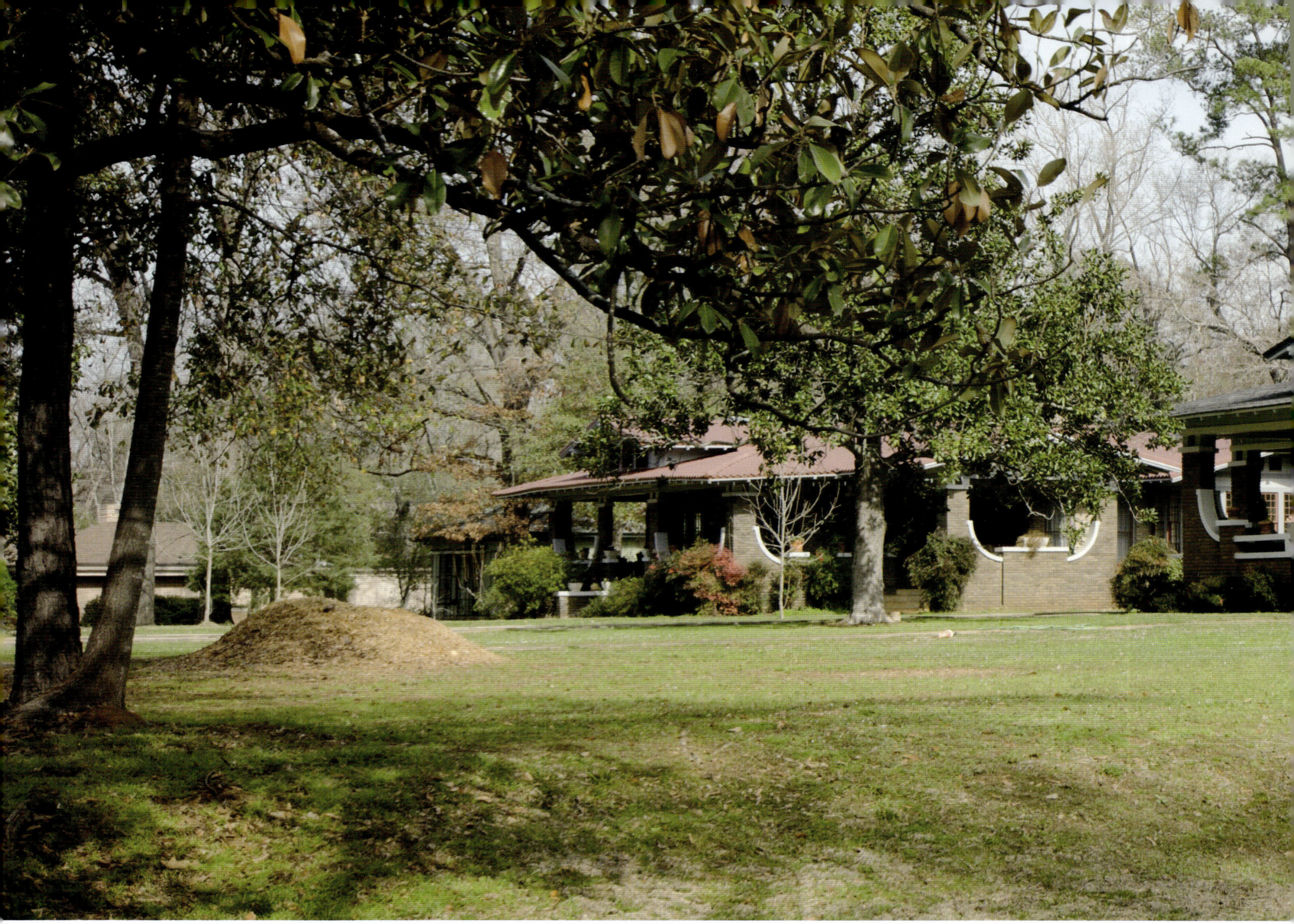

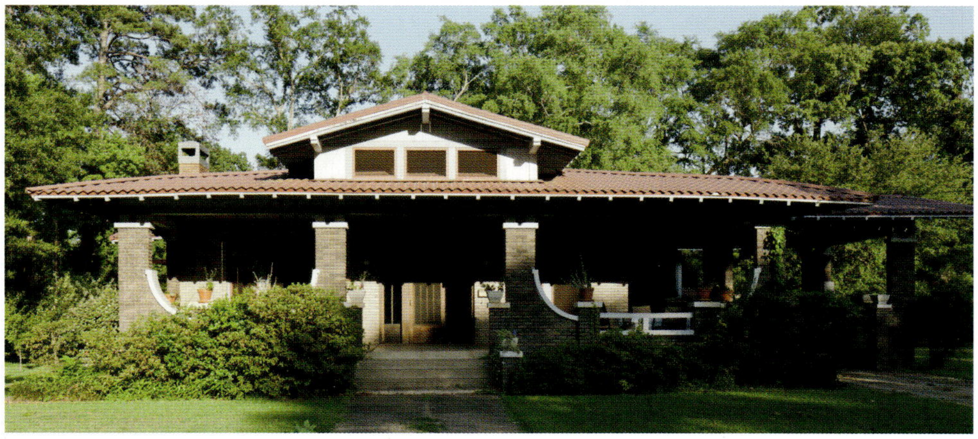

The Clara and Roy Gray House (1914)

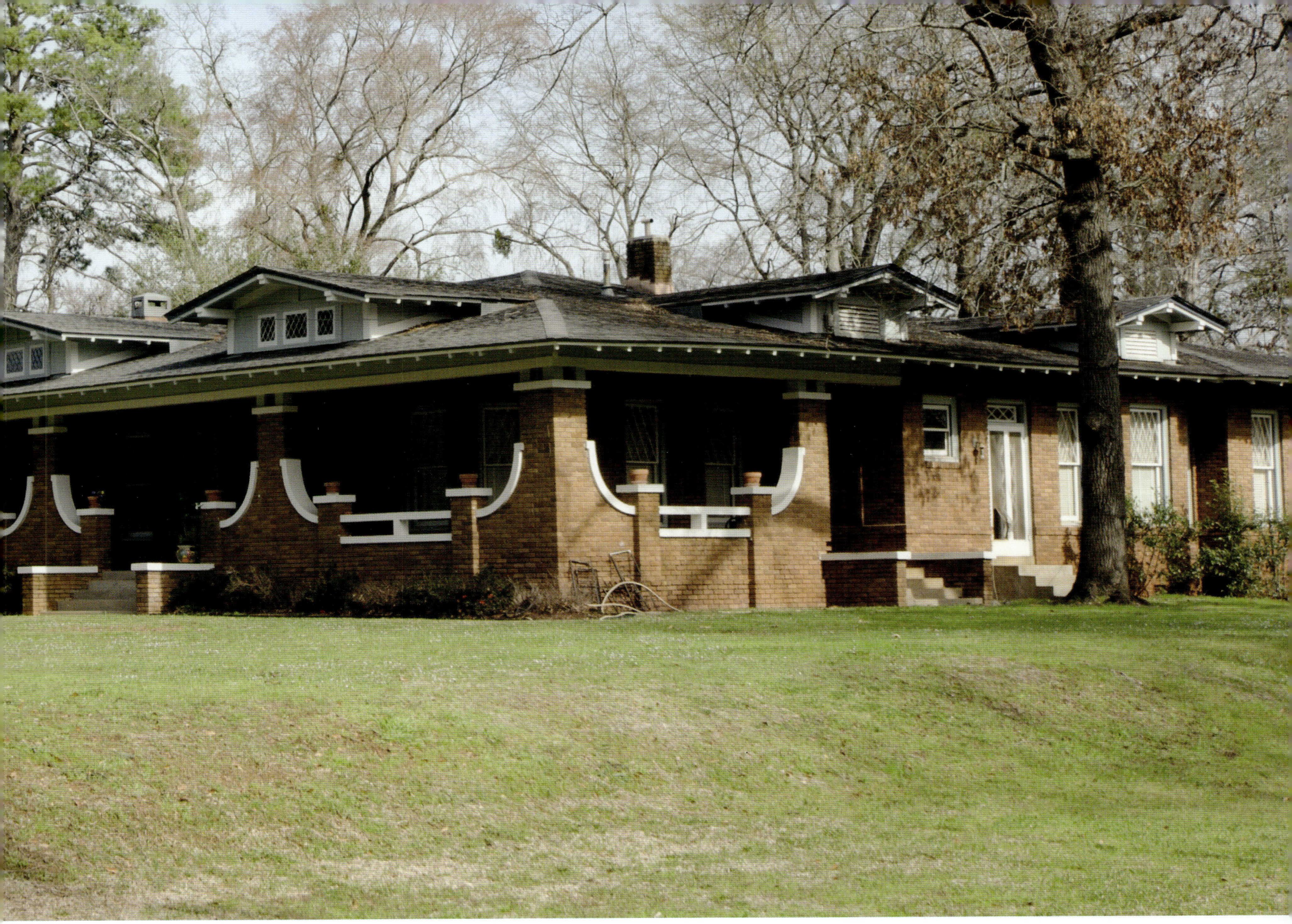

FIGURES 11.36, 11.37, and 11.38. The Differences Between the "Twin Houses."

Although unified by common architectural elements, fence and driveway, the Gray and Mast residences on Logansport Street are not identical. The Gray House is much smaller than the Mast House. The Gray House has only one dormer, the Mast House two. The Gray House has straight walls on the front, while the Mast House has two bay windows. The windows on the Gray House have few decorations, while the windows on the Mast House are adorned with diamond-shaped muntins separating the small panes within the sashes. The porches are different, too. The Gray porch does not wrap around both sides of the structure as does the porch on the Mast House. Both houses were brick veneered, had carports, as well as garages, and had tile roofs. The front doors, although similar, are not the same.

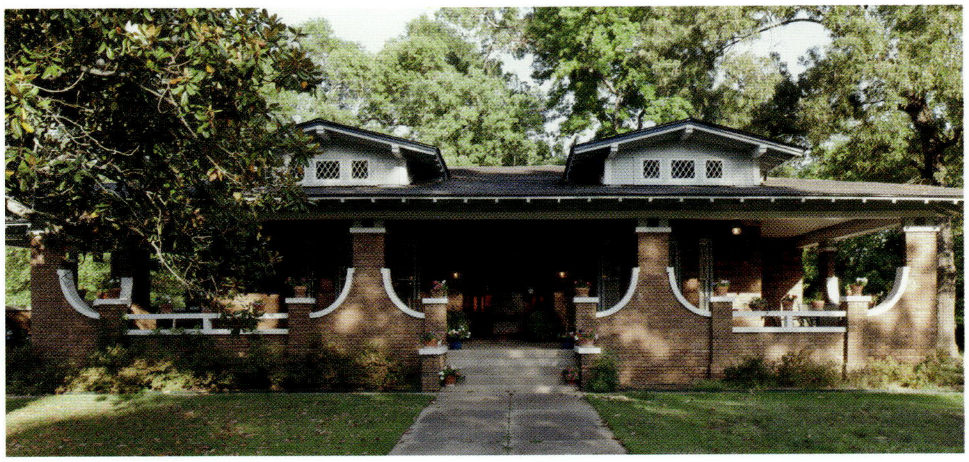

The Jennie and Blum Mast House (1914)

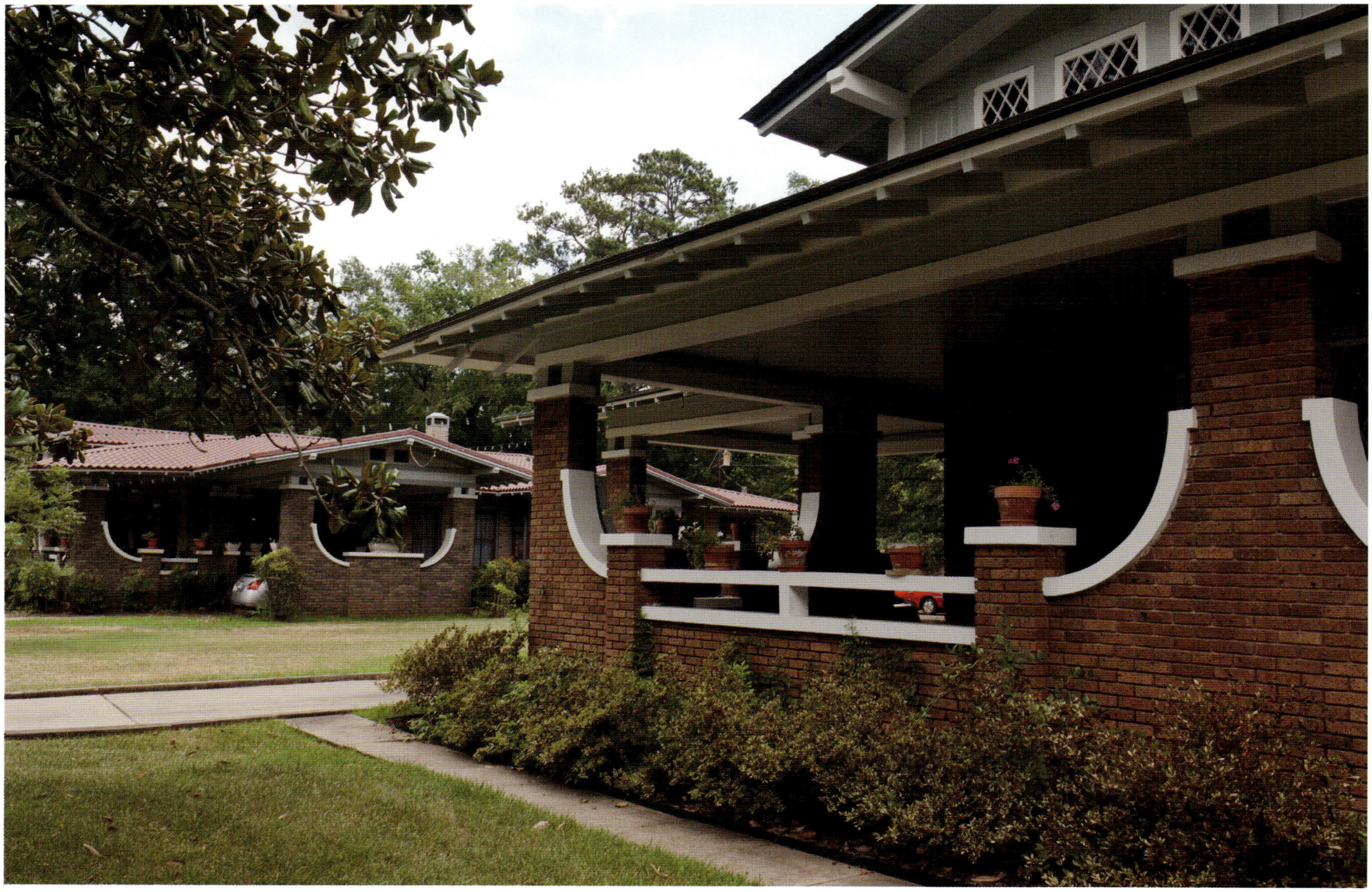

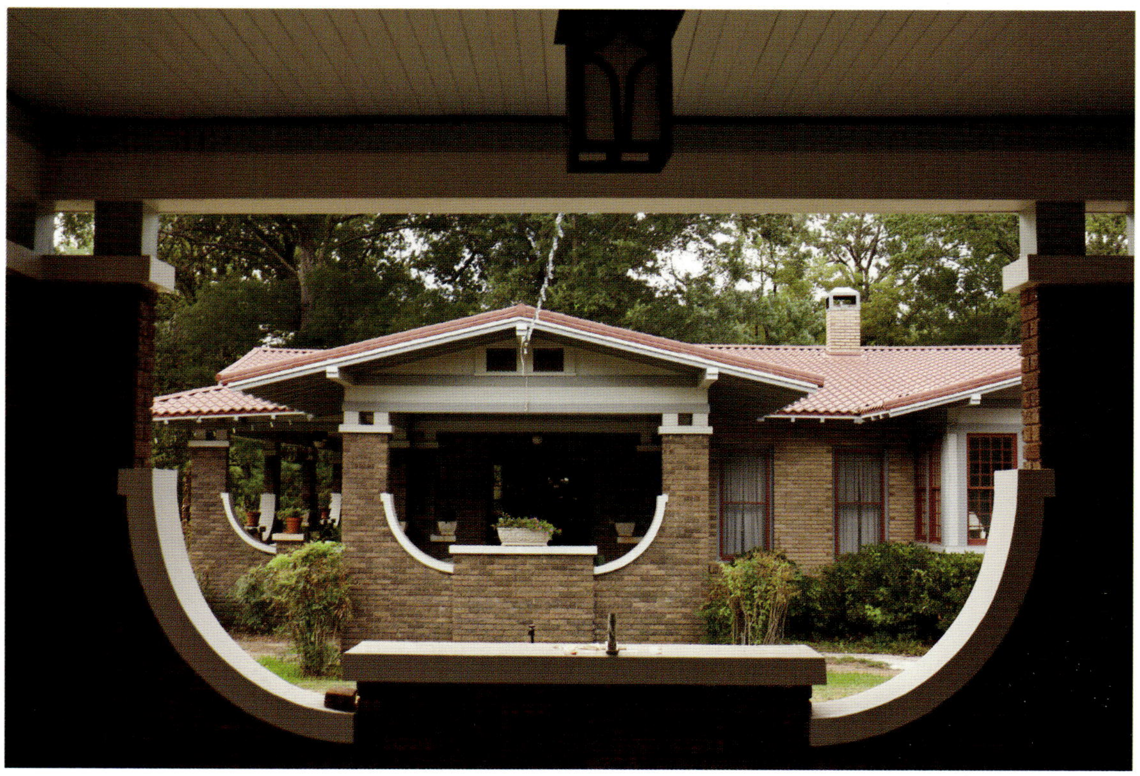

FIGURE 11.39. Detail of the Mast Front Porch.

FIGURE 11.40. The Gray Carport From the Mast Carport.

Emma (Summers) and Henry R. Mast House (1916)

In 1913, Henry Ruben Mast, in anticipation of his forthcoming marriage to Emma Summers, purchased the north portion of the Hollis Mast lot on Mound Street;[48] this purchase would place the couple across the street from her brothers, Frank and Tom Summers, a block and a half away from their parents. Henry Mast, an automobile dealer, traveled frequently on business to other towns. Whether he was struck by a house on one of his trips or was just keen to assert his individuality, Mast decided not to use D. Rulfs as his architect. In 1916, when he decided to build, Mast purchased plans from Edward A. George, an architect in Shreveport, Louisiana. The plans have the label "PLAN NO. 255," which makes one assume the plans were from a collection of pre-drawn templates.[49] The problem, faced by others in town who might have been tempted to seek something by an outside architect, were: who would oversee the construction to their satisfaction; who would correct problems as they arose? Mast eventually turned to Henry Rulfs to construct his new house. While Henry Rulfs actually built the house, according to testimony from Hollis Jean Mast Barron, Henry and Emma's youngest daughter, D. Rulfs agreed generally to oversee the endeavor.[50]

This very unusual undertaking for D. Rulfs invites some speculation. Since the building of the houses on Logansport, the market for houses had collapsed. The war with Germany in Europe brought uncertainty for the country in general. In Nacogdoches, specifically, building activity was depressed. Rulfs welcomed the work for Henry and their carpenters. Also possible, Rulfs helped Mast because he had a tradition of helping other members of both the Summers and Mast families. Albeit the architect did build a double-gable-front house using Craftsman Style elements (the Cason-Baxley House discussed in Chapter XII), the Henry Mast house, a true bungalow, set no pattern for the career of D. Rulfs.

According to Hollis Jean Barron, the house changed very little over the years.[51] The Masts lived in the house until 1941. Later, owners of the house at 216 Mound Street, include the First Methodist Church, Bessie Grant, Tom and Sylvia McGrath (from 1977-2008), and since then Jerry and Patricia Wood.[52] The Woods completely refurbished the interior, restoring the woodwork to its orignal luster.

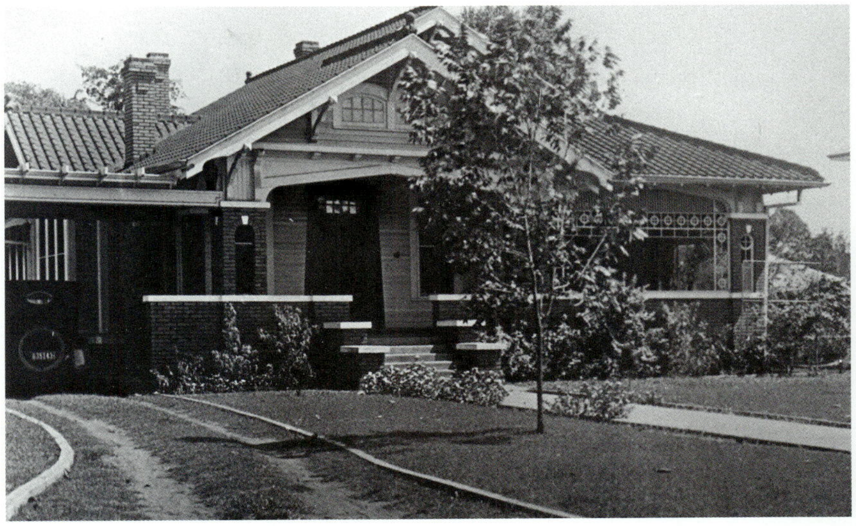

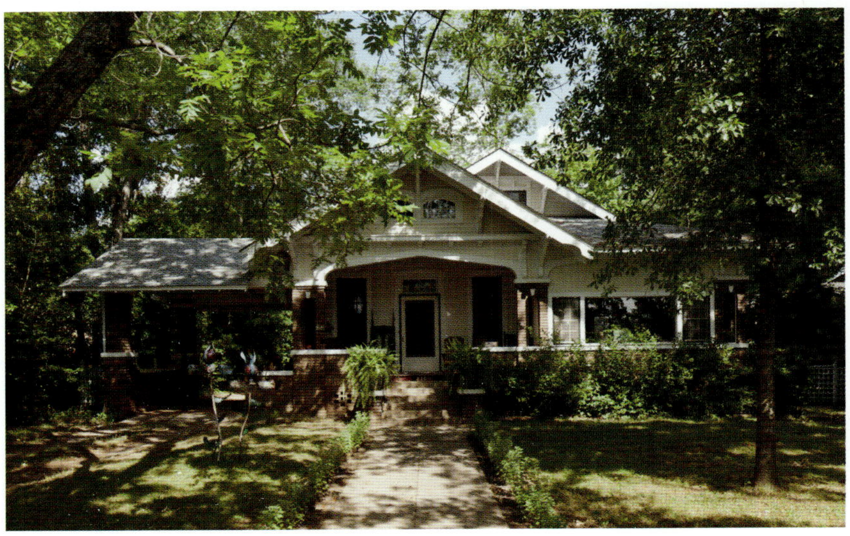

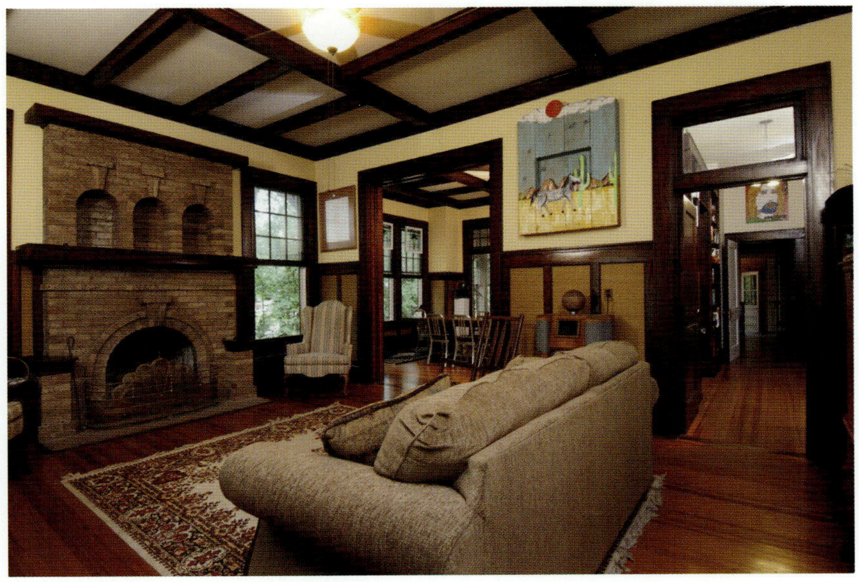

FIGURES 11.41 (Left, Top) - 11.42 (Left, Bottom). The Henry Mast House.
The top photograph is the Mast House around 1925; below in 2011. The right side of the front porch, screened originally, had windows added in the 1930s.
The period photograph is courtesy of ETRC.

FIGURE 11.43. (Above) The Wood Home.
Jerry and Patricia Wood purchased the Mast House from the estate of Tom and Sylvia McGrath in 2008. The picture above shows the interior as refurbished by the Woods: the view is of the living room, looking into the dining room and the middle hall.

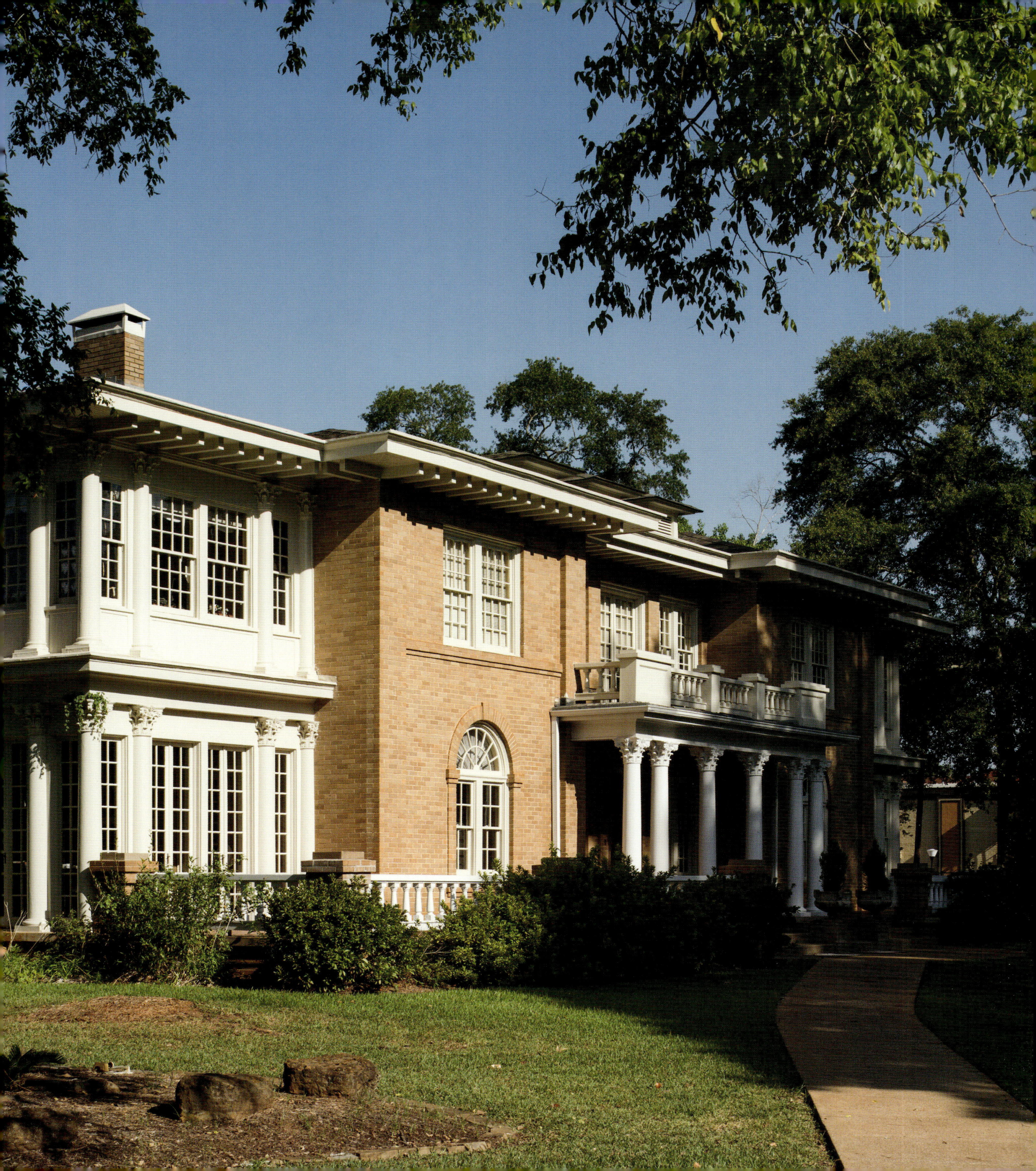

CHAPTER XII

A New Era Begins

The Final Years of the Architect's Career, 1917-1925

"With the capture of the location of Stephen F. Austin Normal, a new era has been born in the industrial, commercial, and social life of Nacogdoches." Editorial, *Daily Sentinel,* July 16, 1917.

[The Blount-Baker Building] *"represents an outstanding example of Rulfs' architectural skill. . . . The composition of this building is simple and straightforward, contributing to its sense of mass and repose."* National Registry Document (2007).

In the years following closure of the Old University in 1900, the initial reaction was to seed a replacement for the lost economic stimulus. In 1907, a new resident reminded everyone that there was more to having a college than economic benefit and enjoined them to remember: "The spirit of Nacogdoches today is a gift from the men of the past; the spirit of the future will be the gift of the men of today."[1] As time passed and several attempts to secure a new college had failed, the eloquent way Karle Wilson Baker expressed her sentiments began to penetrate the town's self-image. By 1914, the search for a college had become almost an obsession. Any discussion, therefore, must include and, in part, revolve around the quest to secure a new college. A determination to tie its fortunes to education has had consequences of historic proportions for the social, cultural, economic, and geographic development of the town into a city. 1917 was not only the most important year in twentieth century world history,[2] but it was also the most important year in the modern history of Nacogdoches. In 1917, the town united in a quest for the state's newly projected Stephen F. Austin Normal, or as some called it, "the East Texas Normal." The year was also an important year in any assessment of the legacy Diedrich Rulfs was amassing in the town. As in other years of review, 1897 and 1906, when the town wanted to tell its story in something beyond statistics and words, the only way to visually represent the town was to feature the architectural designs of D. Rulfs. Rulfs had given concrete, spatial forms to the aspirations of the town's prominent citizens. Before the end of his career, the pioneer town had emerged into a modern city.

FIGURE 12.1. (Across) The Eugene H. Blount House.
Built in 1923, the Blount House was the last major architectural residence undertaken by D. Rulfs.

The World War produced lean years for Nacogdoches. The war dampened interest in large commercial or even residential construction. The future of Nacogdoches appeared bleak. In a desperate attempt to boost the economy in 1915, the citizens voted to sell its open Square, a unique feature of the Old Spanish town, to the Federal Government as the home for a new Post Office. The decision was not an easy one; in previous decades the townspeople had resisted any such move. The architects for the Federal Building were James Wetmore and Wayne Pope. Their modified colonial-federal design cost $50,000 to build in 1917-1918. Ultimately, when the Post Office decided in 1973 to build another facility, the Government gave the building to the City of Nacogdoches for "educational use." At first, it served as a public library and currently serves as the Nacogdoches Convention and Visitors Bureau.

The Quest for the Stephen F. Austin Normal

The search by Nacogdoches for answers to educational dilemmas was part of a wider movement evident in both Texas and the rest of the nation. As early as 1879, the State had established Sam Houston Normal Institute in Huntsville, which offered a curriculum to prepare teachers.[3] By 1915, Texas leaders recognized the need for more colleges to educate teachers if they were to expand the primary and secondary systems. This was especially true for rural school districts of Deep East Texas, a key rural area targeted in the legislation and referred to as "east of the 96th meridian." Nacogdoches elected John Schmidt to head the local effort to secure the "East Texas Normal."[4] Schmidt immediately sent a delegation to Austin for particulars and called a mass meeting in town for March 22, 1915.[5] The *Daily Sentinel* reported: "There were 63 leading business men of the town present, and each and every one voted himself on a committee to promote the work .... Nacogdoches is out after that plum, and you need not doubt that she will get it."[6] From this meeting, the arguments Nacogdoches would use in presenting its case emerged.[7] While the Thirty-Fourth Texas Legislature named the College after the Father of Texas and attempted to fund the college, the session botched the legal work, and the Texas Supreme Court immediately declared the legislation unconstitutional for technical reasons. The amended bill died a second death as the legislative session closed without completing action.[8] Bureaucratic bumbling dashed the great hopes that Nacogdoches had generated.

In the next legislative session in 1917, Nacogdoches took the lead in reintroducing the legislation. Giles Haltom, in announcing another mass meeting, put pressure on the town: "As the *Sentinel* sees it, this will be the most important mass meeting ever held in Nacogdoches for the reason that it has the most important purpose in view, and every citizen with a spark of loyalty and patriotism will be present."[9] After the meeting, Haltom triumphantly praised the enthusiastic mood of those who attended: "Nacogdoches is going after it!" This meeting dispelled any doubts: "The great crowd . . . with one accord agree to any and every measure, no matter what sacrifice might result, to go after the institution."[10]

Although the cities of Austin and Dallas tried to delay the bill, House Bill 72 passed both houses on April 4, 1917. East Texas would get its normal college, but the legislation still used the vague phrase "east of the 96th meridian," which meant that the location of SFA was *still to be determined.* Just two days later, Fate intervened. The headline in the *Daily Sentinel* read: "WAR IS DECLARED BY CONGRESS."[11] The SFA charter legislation eventually survived the tortuous Texas political scene that year, which included the impeachment of Governor James E. Ferguson and the entrance of the United States into war against Germany, but the war forced the Legislature to strip the bill of its appropriations component. In April of 1917, unfortunately, Nacogdoches, unaware of what its future would hold, geared up to present its case to the state. Everyone in Nacogdoches understood that many other towns in East Texas were also preparing applications: Tenaha, Carthage, Jasper, Hemphill, Henderson, Beaumont, Tyler, and Longview.

The Nacogdoches Case

The citizens of Nacogdoches assembled their case in a now-famous booklet entitled *The Twenty-Three Reasons Why.* The publication, a snapshot of an East Texas town in both pictures and words, was exceptionally rare for a town the size of Nacogdoches. The authorship of the booklet was collective, anonymous except for the designation, "Brief Presented by The Citizens of Nacogdoches Through Their Committee." The famous list of reasons why Nacogdoches should be chosen, often reprinted,[12] repeated the word NACOGDOCHES twenty-three times as it summarized the town's case. This booklet and the story of the quest for the East Texas Normal by Nacogdoches can be accessed via the Internet.[13]

Like all promotional publications, the *Twenty-Three Reasons Why* was a flattering view of the town. A close analysis of the booklet reveals some charming promotional fabrications, such as, "[in the summer] the temperature never mounts to unpleasant heights for many days at a time" or "the jail is the only vacant house in the city." The booklet extols the town's interest in history, but omits the painful episode of the Old Stone Fort demolition. It overlooks or finesses all the hostility that had accompanied every step toward providing modern city services.

The local committee's attention to detail (such as covering all the potholes in the roads with automobiles when the Location Committee visited) resulted in the selection of Nacogdoches in July 1917 as the site for the new college. When news arrived from Austin, there was dancing in the streets—"the fire whistle blew, bells rang out with lively peels, . . . the band played." Haltom's editorial, "OUR NEW ERA," proclaimed: "With the capture of the location of Stephen F. Austin Normal, a new era has been born in the industrial, commercial, and social life of Nacogdoches." Mayor Matthews consigned the divisions of the past to history: "This happy result demonstrates beyond question the power of a united people, and should inspire us all to stay together, work together, and pull together."[14] Even the neighboring towns in East Texas, although passed over, seemed willing to share Nacogdoches's good fortune, as this quote from the *Silsbee Signal* illustrates:

> While there were many towns and cities asking for the school, one thing can be said: no other town would appreciate it more than Nacogdoches. . . . The historic interests of the city are unsurpassed in the state; the town is truly a town of homes—beautiful homes . . . . But the fact that every man, woman, and child in Nacogdoches county wanted the normal, talked the normal, wrote the normal, . . . had more to do with the selecting than her beauty or historic lore.[15]

The quest for SFA changed Nacogdoches. Unity came because Nacogdoches wanted SFA more than other towns and sold itself more effectively. This unity of spirit, however, would be tested in the coming years. The costly promises were made to the state: to change its infrastructure by

FIGURES 12.2, 12.3, 12.4 and 12.5. (Across) Promoting Nacogdoches.
Pages from the booklet The Twenty Three Reasons Why The Stephen F. Austin State Normal Ought To Be Located at Nacogdoches, 1917. *From author's copy.*
(Top Left) The Cover of the Booklet, Detail.
(Bottom Left) "Nacogdoches – A City of Churches."
(Top Right) "The Business Side of Nacogdoches."
(Bottom Right) "City Schools." Detail.

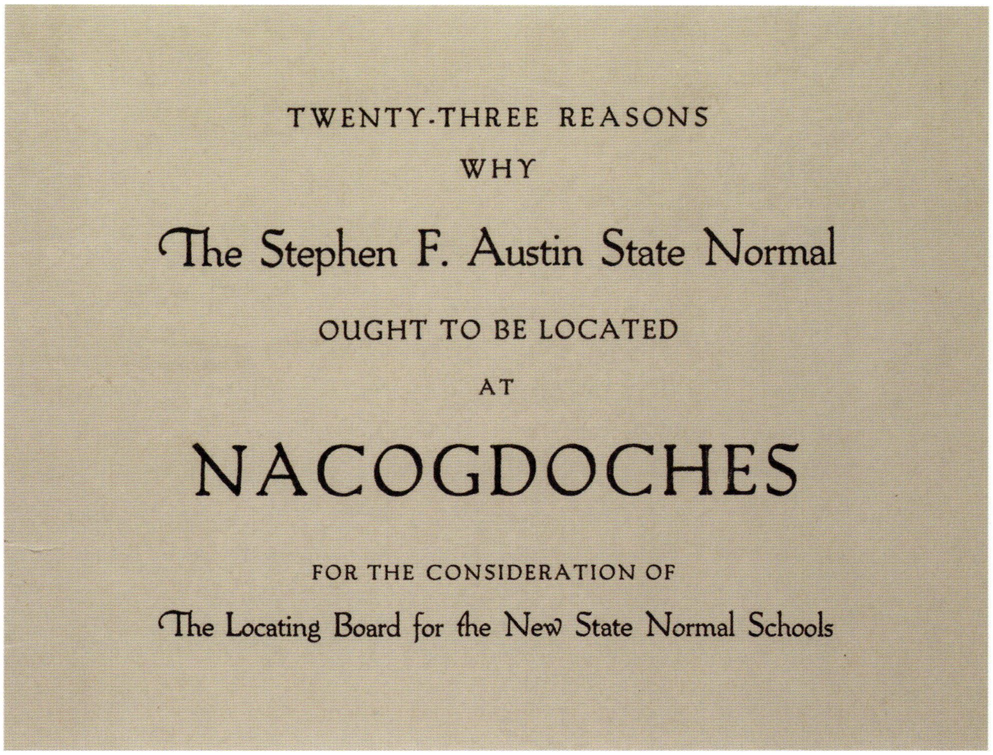

TWENTY-THREE REASONS
WHY
The Stephen F. Austin State Normal
OUGHT TO BE LOCATED
AT
NACOGDOCHES
FOR THE CONSIDERATION OF
The Locating Board for the New State Normal Schools

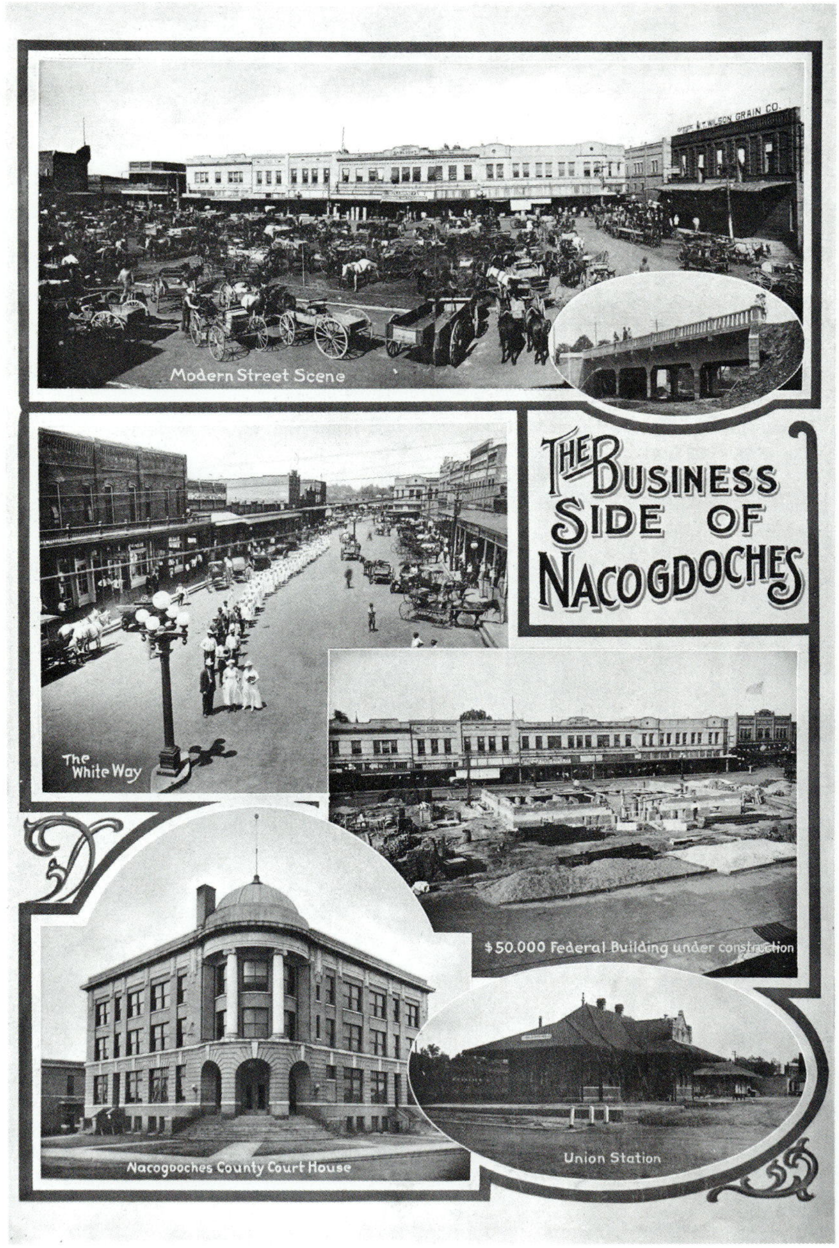

Nacogdoches—A City of Churches

The community life of Nacogdoches is wholesome and highly moral. It may be called a city of churches with perfect correctness. There are nine churches for white people, including thriving congregations representative of the Baptist, Methodist, Episcopal, Christian, Presbyterian and Catholic faiths.

The Sunday Schools have very large attendance records and the people are known as a church-going community.

On the other hand, Nacogdoches has rid herself of the great allies of immorality, including the immoral resort. Pool halls followed other undesirable institutions in their exit from the city. Nacogdoches, once known as the rendezvous of every type of frontier desperado and bad man, is now a model of civic righteousness, a clean and wholesome community in which young students may find a desirable homelike atmosphere, free from contaminations and interruptions. Here the young man or woman seeking educational advancement and mental growth will be surrounded and safeguarded by every natural advantage and protection, so that studying will be easier and the culture of heart and mind will be promoted in the highest degree.

The jail is the only vacant house in the city. With 32,000 people in the county, and a jail that often stands for long periods absolutely untenanted save for the pine-laden breezes from the hills, Nacogdoches can claim a moral tone that is rare indeed.

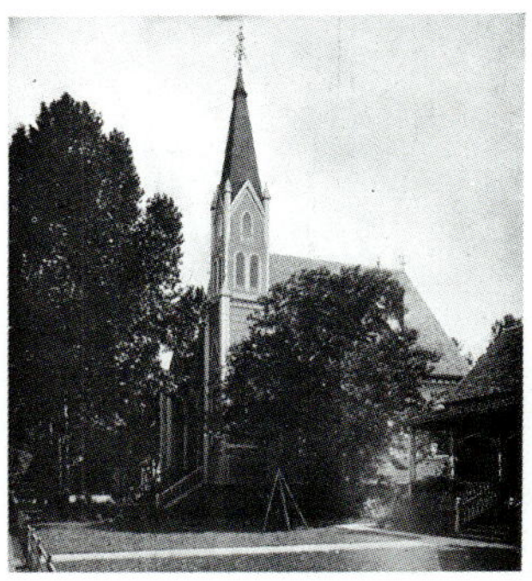

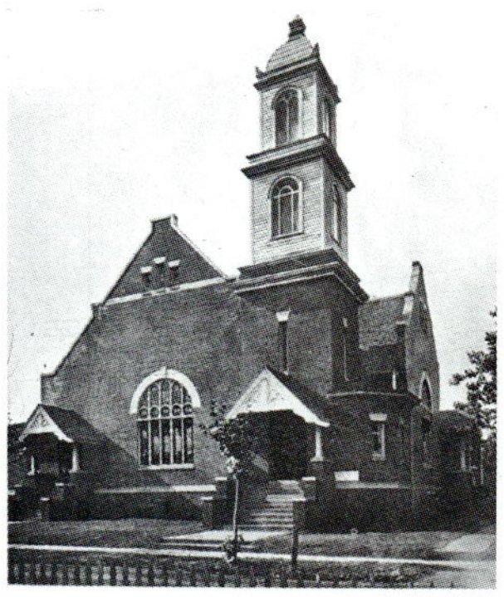

There is nothing stronger to drink than drug store refreshments to be had in the city. There are no "dives" or illegal "joints" for the selling of liquors.

It is not likely that there is any city in Texas of its size that maintains a more wholesome moral atmosphere for its own people or for those who sojourn within its gates than does Nacogdoches.

From the moral and cultural standpoint Nacogdoches is the ideal spot for the Stephen F. Austin State Normal.

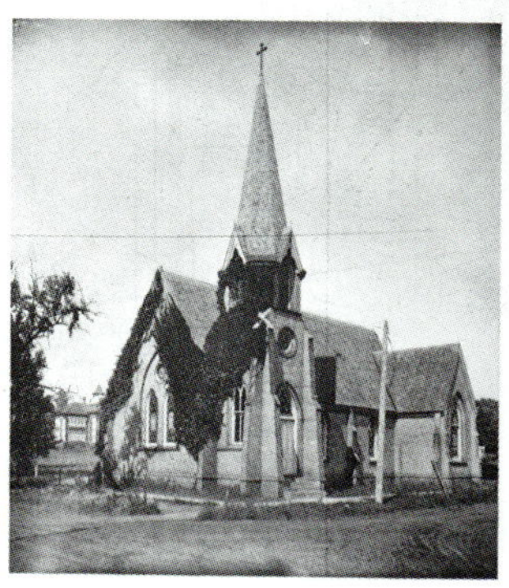

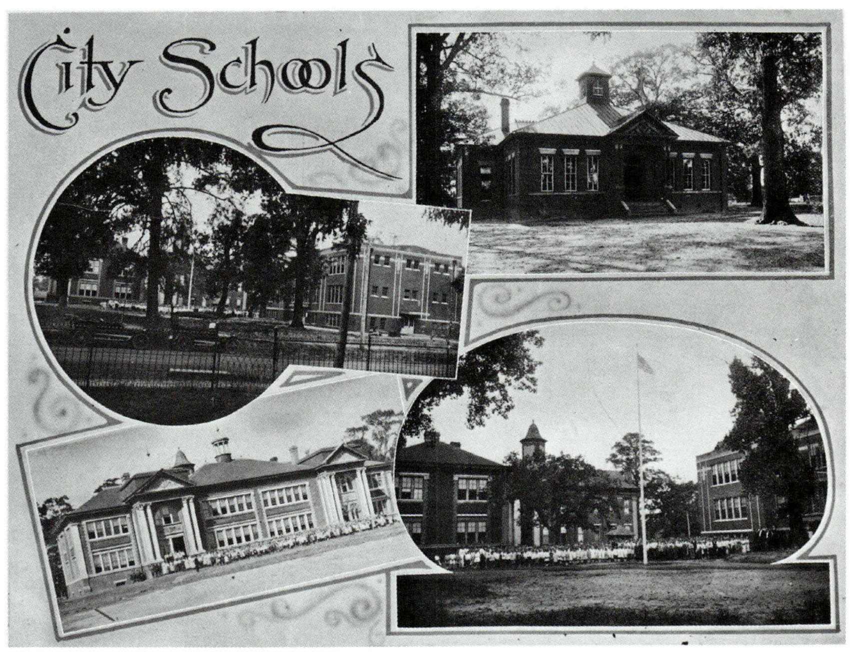

paving roads and providing city services, as well as recruiting and housing 250 students. The crusaders were unaware of the emotional ups and downs, financial strains, and false starts that were to accompany the rest of the saga. Tragically, the triumphant moments of July quickly faded. The year 1917 ended in a flurry of statewide politics, with the legislature snatching away the appropriations (ostensibly because of the war with Germany, but in actual fact as part of the impeachment of Governor James E. Ferguson). Ultimately, Senator Eugene Blount worked out a compromise whereby Nacogdoches salvaged the charter and its designation as the site for the new teachers college despite the postponement of the funding. Haltom's editorial in the *Daily Sentinel* called the loss of the funding a "great injustice."[16]

Sobering and costly years lay ahead for the town. The labor and local expense required to secure the opening of SFA taught Nacogdoches new lessons and surprised everyone. The town itself had to compensate for the delays caused by bad weather, underestimated costs, and a bankrupt contractor. These expenses were in addition to their pledge to recruit and provide housing for new students. Ultimately, the town had to provide temporary classrooms for the homeless college. These setbacks, which easily could have divided the town again, produced more civic unity. The townspeople, learning to think beyond their petty differences, found the new leaders of the "gown" to be very compatible and helpful. Alton Birdwell, the new college president, became one of the most popular additions to Nacogdoches in decades. Since Nacogdoches had to work to secure the college, there really was a feeling in the town that it was "our college." The bond struck during these early years lasted for decades. Nacogdoches was maturing, leaving its frontier past behind. The town was becoming a city, and its primary business was education.

The presence of SFA also changed Nacogdoches geographically. Since the university had to open on Washington Square, that area felt the impact first, as demand for housing downtown soared. The oversized homes around Washington Square, built several decades earlier in a more prosperous era, became boarding houses in 1923 for both students and faculty. When the official SFA campus on North Street opened in May 1924, Nacogdoches also began to drift northward. The space between the town center and the campus filled in first, followed by new residential and service areas north and west of the campus. The Sanborn Maps of 1929 showed Nacogdoches as a city for the first time. Expansion of residential areas to the northeast of the campus across the Lanana Creek would have to await the building of bridges in the mid-1970s.[17]

FIGURE 12.6. Paving of the Square, ca. 1918.

Starting in 1900, from the Square outward, Nacogdoches used wood blocks of bois d'arc to pave Main Street. When it rained, however, the blocks would swell and pop out of the ground in places. As part of the contract the town made with the state to secure the placement of SFASTC in 1917, Nacogdoches promised to begin paving three-and-a-half miles of streets with red brick laid on a concrete base. This began in 1918 and continued until the brick streets reached the new college campus in 1924. Thereafter, they used concrete alone without the bricks. Courtesy of ETRC.

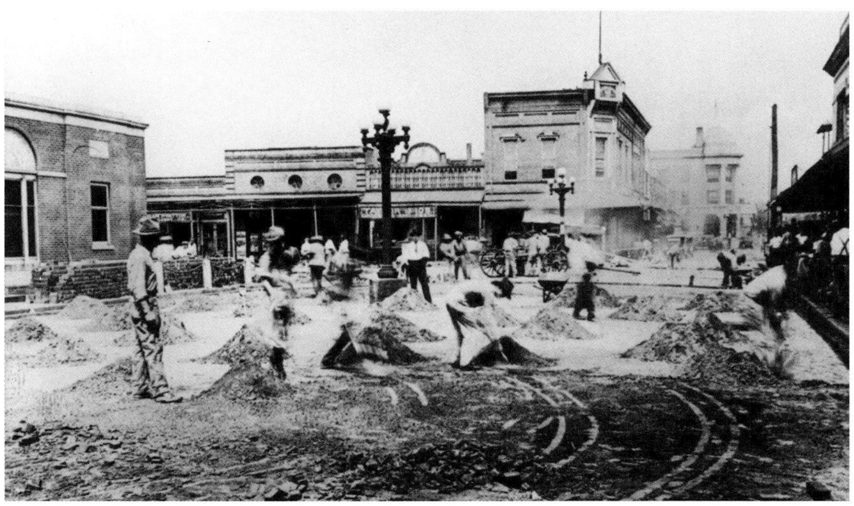

The Twenty Three Reasons Why: A Summary of the Career of D. Rulfs to 1917

For the present book, the *Twenty-Three Reasons Why* offers the modern historian a rare gallery of the legacy of Diedrich Rulfs as of 1917. Visually, the architecture of Rulfs provided the glue for the Nacogdoches case and dominated the illustrations. While the booklet itself was anonymous by design, the newspaper credited the civic leaders who led the effort.[18] Of the leaders on the various "Citizens Committees" who put the booklet together, eighty percent of the active members owned or worked in buildings designed by Rulfs. John Schmidt, Rulfs's most consistent patron, was the chairman of the first committee; and Senator Eugene H. Blount chaired the second; both lived and worked in structures designed by the architect. (Rulfs had by that time built over eight buildings for Schmidt and just as many for the Blounts.) Other leaders in the SFA movement, such as W. U. Perkins, Judge Stephen W. Blount, Judge V. E. Middlebrook, June Harris, W. T. Wilson, Link Sturdevant, T. B. Hardeman, Mayor George Matthews, Sam Stripling, Charles Hoya, and D. K. Cason, to mention only a few, were patrons of the architect and worked closely with him on their homes, churches, and commercial buildings.

Section after section of the *Twenty Three Reasons* illustrated how much the Nacogdoches case owed to the creative genius of Diedrich Rulfs. For instance, in the section entitled "NACOGDOCHES, A CITY OF HOMES," every picture on the page depicts a house designed by Rulfs: the J. Roy Gray and Blum Mast Houses (1914) on Logansport, the Guy Blount House (1912) on North Street, the Robert Lindsey House (1900) on Virginia Avenue, the D. K. Cason House (1914) on Logansport, the Mary Buford Hayter House (1913) on North Street, and the Hollis Mast House (1911) on Mound. In the section entitled "NACOGDOCHES, A CITY OF CHURCHES," *all* of the houses of worship shown—the First Baptist (1899), the Christ Episcopal (1902), and the United Methodist (1910)—were designed and built by Rulfs. In the section entitled "THE BUSINESS SIDE OF NACOGDOCHES," most of the downtown buildings were designed by Rulfs, and many were redesigned by the architect after fires. (Of the design exceptions—the Perkins Building (1907), the Railway Station (1911), and the Court House (1912)—only the Railway Station did not necessitate his supervision.) When the State Location Committee visited the town in July 1917, the members had breakfast in the Banita Hotel, toured both North Street and Washington Square, and ended their visit with entertainment in the Redland Hotel. The showcase that impressed them was the handiwork of this talented North German architect.

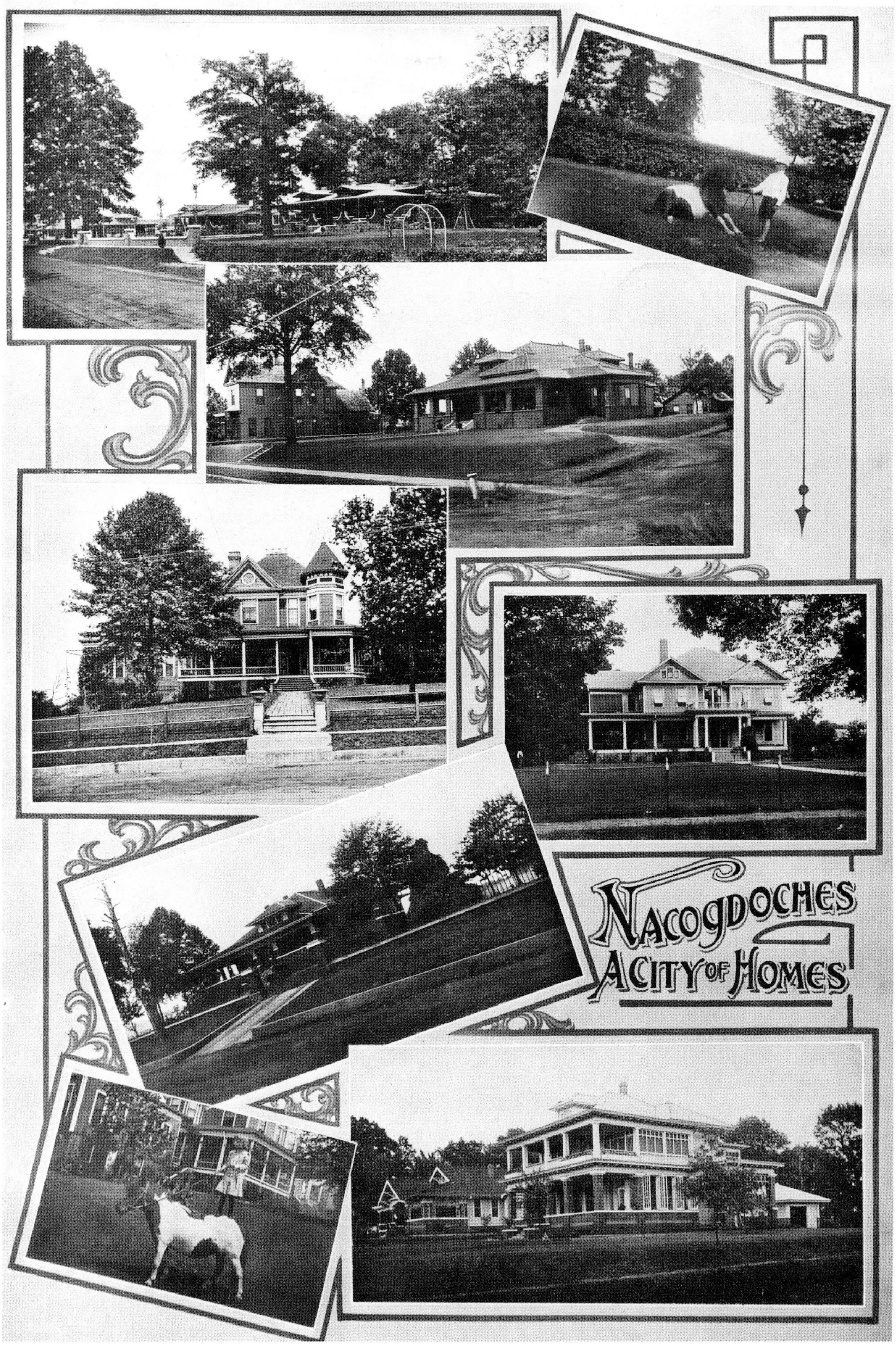

FIGURE 12.7. "Nacogdoches–A City of Homes."

Rulfs designed all of the houses chosen to illustrate the promotional booklet, The Twenty Three Reasons Why. (Top to Bottom) the Gray and Mast homes on Logansport; the Guy Blount home on North Street; the Robert Lindsey home on Virginia Avenue; the D. K. Cason home on Logansport; the Mary Hayter home on North Street; and the Hollis Mast home on Mound. Interesting to note, all these structures still sit on their original sites, with the exception of the Guy Blount House, which has been moved to a different location.

A Period of Family Transition

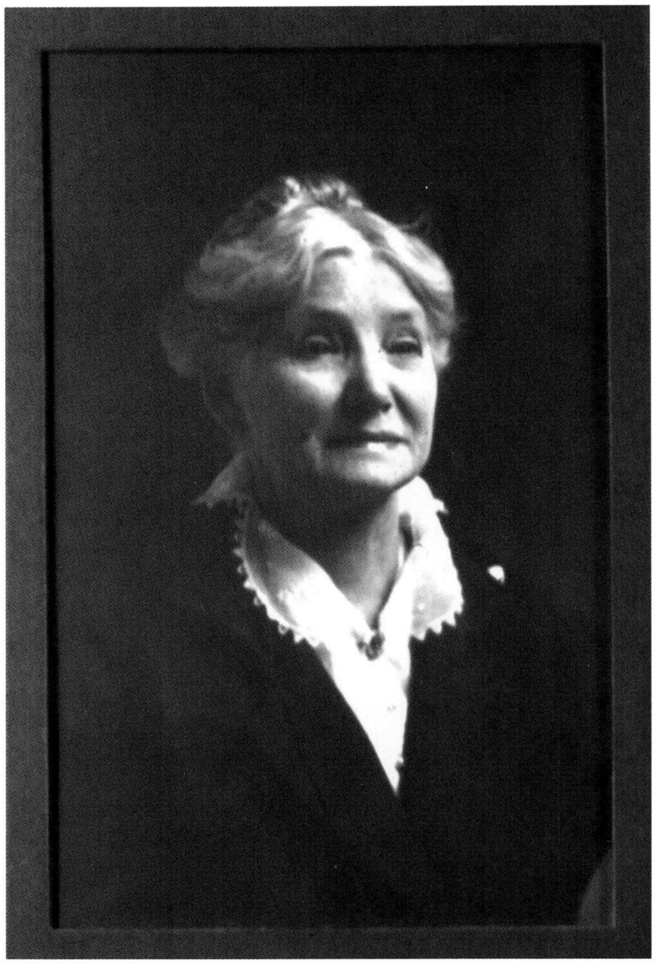

FIGURE 12.8. Johanne Emilie Helene Wilhelmine Böschen Rulfs, September 26, 1849 - April 22, 1918.
Compliments of Anna Kathryn Holbrook.

The Death of Mrs. Johanne Rulfs

While the United States was at war with Germany, there is no evidence that the Rulfs family or any of the other German-immigrant families fell victim to any overt discrimination, although subtle prejudices are difficult to discern. Two factors most likely prevented problems. First, most German immigrants to Nacogdoches came in pre-1900 waves and were fully integrated into the town. Carl Henry Rulfs, Diedrich's son, for instance, was on the Vestry of Christ Episcopal Church and the last captain of the locally famous Stone Fort Rifles. Second, the German community's decision decades earlier to speak only English in public and to fully integrate into the society and religious communities of the town placed them in different categories. Nationally, however, these were tough times for Americans of German heritage, especially after the United States entered the war in 1917.

Diedrich Rulfs celebrated his seventieth birthday on March 6, 1918. He and his family could look back on a very happy and productive life in Nacogdoches. Tempering the celebration, however, was the fact that Johanne Rulfs had not been in good health for over a year. Less than two months after Diedrich's birthday, Johanne, his wife of forty-five years, died at the age of sixty-nine. Johanne had delivered four children in Germany (one stillborn) before making the trek to the United States and bore two more in Texas. The Rulfs family was unusually close. Both Johanne and Diedrich placed their familial duties before career considerations. In addition to her devoted support for her husband and family, Johanne was active in civic, social, and religious activities, working diligently in her way to contribute to Nacogdoches life. The newspaper occasionally gave glimpses of her activities, as she participated in club and church activities or when she accompanied her husband on business trips to Houston or Galveston. The social columns in the Galveston newspaper even mentioned when the couple were in town to visit their children. At the time of her death, all of her children, except John, who lived in California, were at their mother's bedside. The Knights of Pythias passed a resolution honoring both Johanne and Diedrich. Of Johanne, the resolution read,

> Be it resolved, that in the death of Sister Rulfs, Nacogdoches has lost a good and true woman, loved most by those who knew her best; her children have been deprived of a loving, painstaking mother, who always looked forward and bent every effort for the good of those whom God had seen fit to give unto her; and her husband, our Brother Knight, is made to mourn as Solomon would put it; 'For the Dove of his heart, the light of his home, the sweet spirit of his life.'[19]

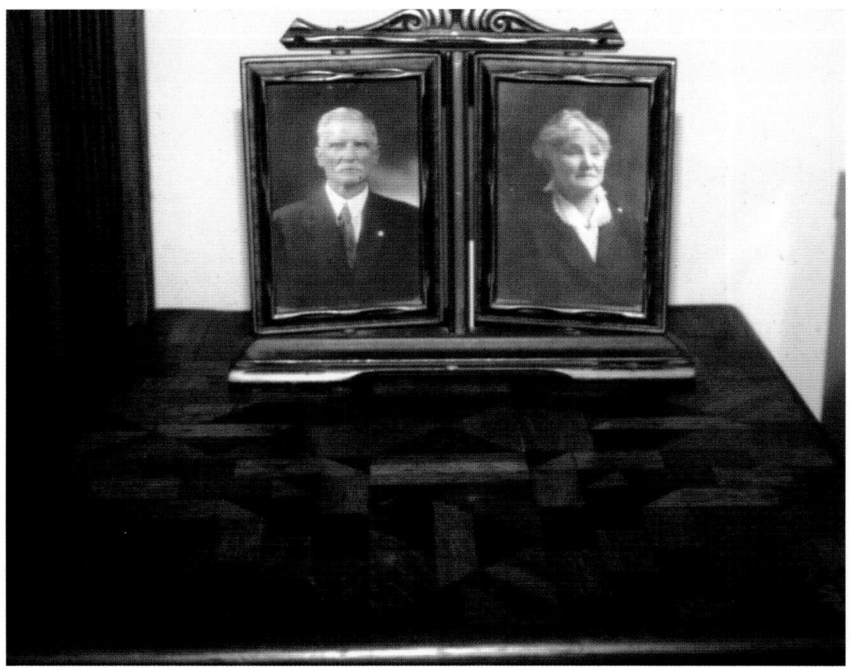

FIGURE 12.11. Inlay Table Made by D. Rulfs.
The portraits of Diedrich and Johanne Rulfs rest on a table made by the architect-carpenter-woodworker himself. Photograph by the author in the home of granddaughter Anna Kathryn Holbrook in 1972.

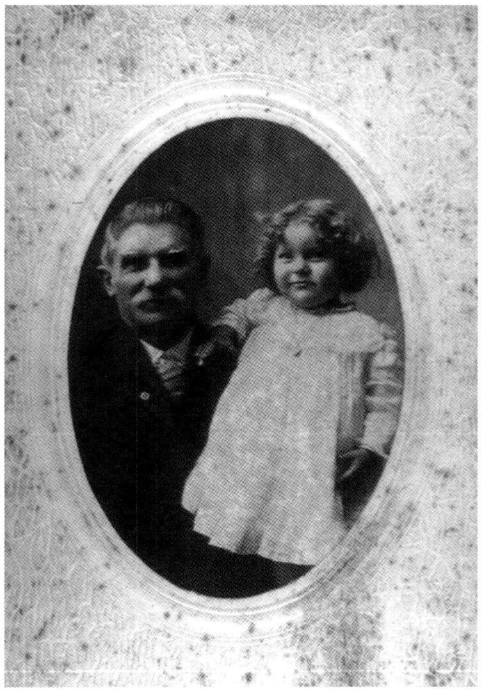

FIGURE 12.9. (Right) Rulfs with his Granddaughter Helene.
Helene was the daughter of Rulfs's son Anton. Compliments of Anna Kathryn Holbrook.

FIGURE 12.10. (Below) Rulfs with Grandson, Lawrence.
Lawrence was the son of Carl Henry and Anna Taylor Rulfs, brother to Anna Kathryn (Holbrook). Compliments of Anna Kathryn Holbrook.

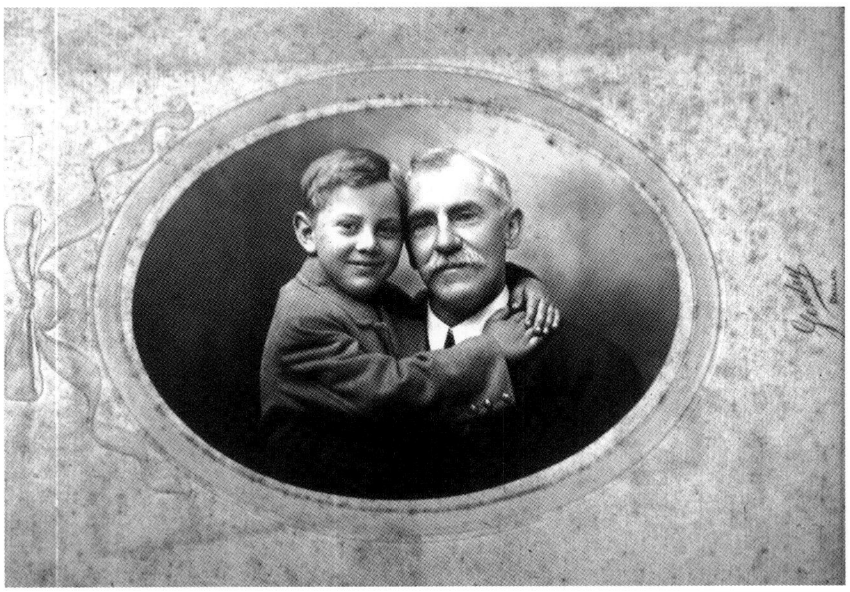

The Death of William Henry Rulfs

Johanne's death was not the only cruel blow in the architect's personal life at this time. On December 11, 1919, William Henry died; he is buried in Oak Grove Cemetery. William Henry was not only Diedrich's brother, but he was also the architect's business partner, his right arm in the construction side of Diedrich's commissions.[20] Their partnership had endured for over 35 years, from 1884 when William Henry followed his older brother to East Texas. Having similar training by their father, who was a Master Builder, their professional relationship was extremely close and intuitive. Will (as locals called him) instinctively seemed to know what Diedrich needed in a project before the architect specified it. He understood Diedrich's meaning even when it was not clearly stated. He shared his older brother's passion for quality, his disdain for slipshod work, his understanding of the basic principles of construction, and his close personal relations with their fellow carpenters. Without Will's assistance, Diedrich would have had a very different career.

Information on Will Rulfs is even more elusive than on D. Rulfs. Finding records, pictures, and documents on William Henry is almost impossible because their family home, on South Fredonia Street, burned to the ground the year before the man's death. According to his grandson, John D. Rulfs, Jr.,[21] the fire was a psychological blow as well as a material one; a lifetime of memories, records, and accomplishments gone in one event. For traces of Will, we are dependent on public records, such as census records and deed records, where Will signed mechanics liens.[22] Although both of the brothers were very reserved and quiet, Diedrich, as the public face of the partnership, had to overcome his reticence in order to plan, negotiate, and oversee various obligations they undertook. D. Rulfs had to promote his career to the patrons and to the newspapers. Will, on the other hand, lived and worked among carpenters.

The basic information on William Henry for this book comes from his daughter, Wilhelmina Rulfs Thompson. The author has Gladys Hardeman to thank for introducing the author to this friendship and interview. Mrs. Thompson, herself very shy and reserved, opened her memories to the author because of her pride in her father's work and her desire to explain his role in the famous partnership of the two brothers. In particular, Mrs. Thompson testified to her father's personal pride in executing the fretwork for the Roland Jones and Stephen Blount Houses. This leads to the conclusion that some of Diedrich's best designs would not have come to fruition without the efforts of his brother. Wilhelmina wanted the story known that "a Rulfs house" meant more than a design by the architect D. Rulfs. The family building trade depended heavily on Will; he signed many of the building mechanic liens. Patrons usually paid the architect's fees in cash, up front before the letting of contracts. Wherever there was a "pine top" party, the brothers would share the accolades. While the two brothers formed a dynamic team, there was no question who was the leader. D. Rulfs designed numerous structures that his brother did not build; and, no doubt, Will, in turn, undertook construction projects on his own. These buildings, however, are more difficult to discern than those by the architect. As an architect, D. Rulfs *signed* a building in unmistakable, stylistic ways that his brother the carpenter/contractor could not.

After his brother's death, Diedrich Rulfs continued to draft, design, specify, and generally oversee building projects until 1925. He did not, however, undertake to contract major projects after Will's death. What people wanted, however, was the architect's meticulous oversight. This continued as before. The years after the First World War were some of his most innovative and impressive. Because of advancing age, however, he rejected more requests than he accepted. In 1923, for instance, when his old friend and patron Dick Cason asked him to undertake the remodeling of the Old Opera House, which Cason had purchased from John Schmidt, Rulfs declined and suggested his young protégé Hal Tucker for the job.

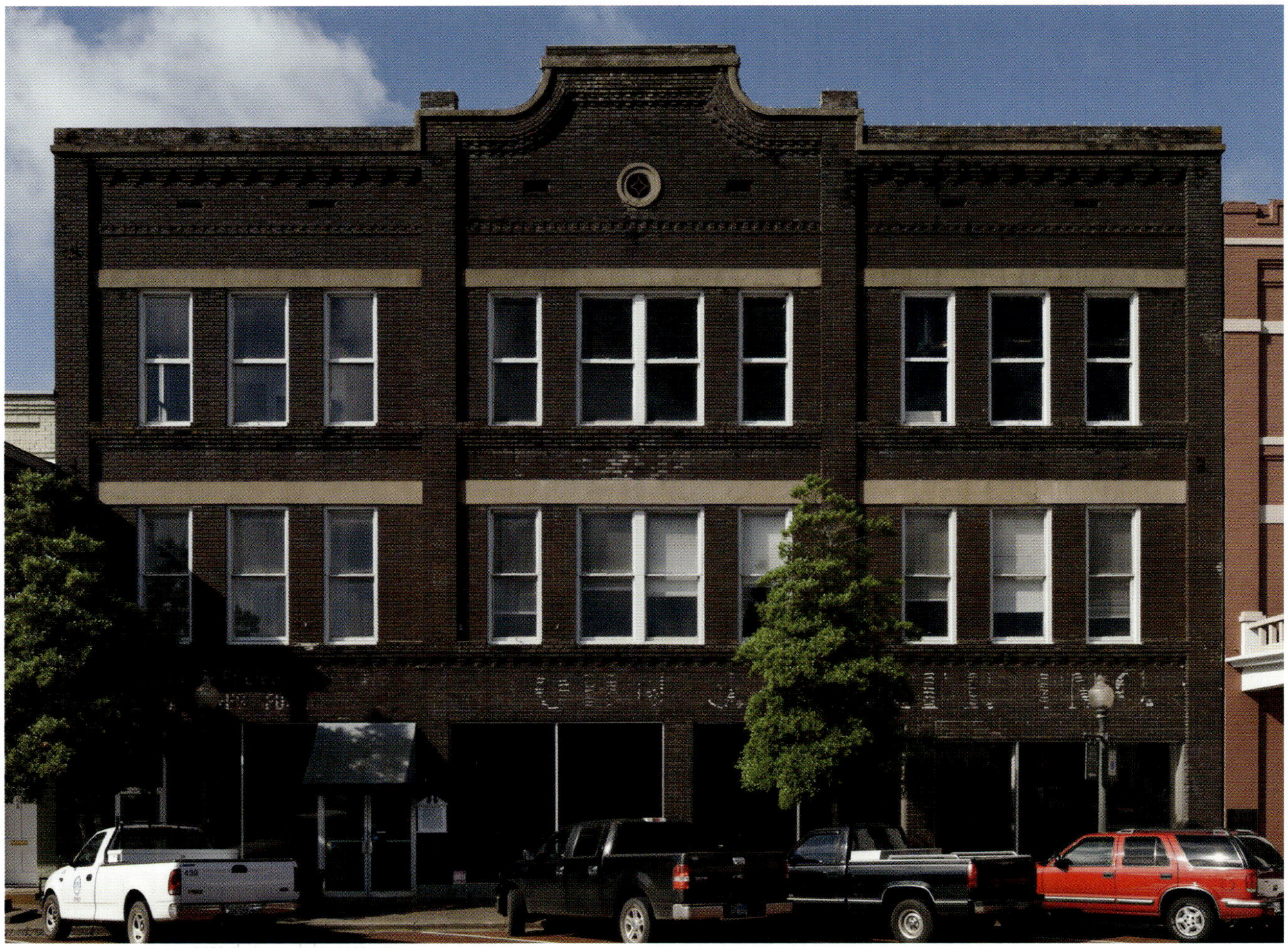

FIGURE 12.12. The Home of Mahdeen Hair Tonic.

The main tenant in the Blount-Baker Building was Frank Aikman's Mahdeen Hair Tonic Company from 1918-1965. The third floor windows had MAHDEEN spelled out in big gold letters. The lower floors facing the Square housed for many years the showrooms for Ben T. Wilson's Ford and later Chevrolet dealerships. Later, John S. Wyatt Office Supply occupied these same floors.

The E. H. Blount-Thomas E. Baker Building for the Mahdeen Company (1918-1919)

When the Nacogdoches Courthouse moved from the square to Main and North street, Eugene H. Blount and Thomas Ellis Baker purchased the old site in 1913.[23] It was not until after the commitment of the federal government to place the post office in the center of the square that the new owners enlarged their holdings to include enough land to accommodate a large modern commercial building. The war and the absence of a suitable major tenant, however, delayed their development. Plans did not proceed until 1918.

Frank Speir Aikman, a native of Brooklyn, New York, was another quiet outsider who played an important role in Nacogdoches. Aikman first visited Nacogdoches in his occupation as a traveling salesman of drug and barber shop supplies. He always lodged at the Banita Hotel. He was continuously looking for a suitable business in which to invest so that he could stay in Nacogdoches. According to one source, "J. R. McKinney, the proprietor of the hotel, told Aikman about an investment opportunity."[24] A local barber, Conrad Needham, had invented a formula for a new hair tonic for men in 1907 and needed a partner to underwrite the manufacture and marketing of the product. Aikman purchased a share in the formula in 1912 and joined Needham to form the Mahdeen Company to manufacture the tonic. (Mahdeen is Needham spelled backward.) The company became very successful—so successful that in a few years the tonic "...was being sold in most of the best barber shops and drug stores in the United States."[25] Men from Nacogdoches even saw the product in France in World War I.[26] At the end of the war, just before his death, Needham sold the formula and controlling interest in the company to Aikman. Aikman could finally expand the company's production, and he asked Jack McKinney to join him. The expansion made Aikman a very wealthy man. He became a director at Commercial Bank and became a generous philanthropist in Nacogdoches, underwriting many projects. In 1924, Aikman became the new state college's first benefactor by donating money for its first gymnasium, "one of the very few such generous residents in our small town," according to an early Nacogdoches graduate of the college.[27] Aikman died in 1939, but his company continued until 1965 under the ownership of W. A. Mize and others.[28]

In late 1918, Baker and Blount contacted D. Rulfs to design a new building for the south side of the Square to accommodate Aikman's expanding company. The hair tonic business was to occupy the third story and the basement of this rectangular brick structure. To this day, the cypress wood casks and metal vats for preparing the company formula can be seen in the building. MAHDEEN was spelled out in big letters on the third floor windows facing the square. The large freight elevator, used by the Mahdeen Company, is still in the building, albeit no longer in use. Ben T. Wilson, Tom Baker's brother-in-law, leased the ground floor as an automobile showroom; for this reason, large display windows were part of the original plan by Rulfs. Fords and later Chevrolets were eventually sold from the main level. In the 1930s, another building in the rear expanded the automotive services to include paint and body work. The structure has housed many businesses over the years. In 1971, the John S. Wyatt Company purchased the building to accommodate their office supply and furniture sales rooms and printing facilities. Cherry Baker now owns the building.[29]

The National Register Nomination for the Blount-Baker building is worth quoting:

"An outstanding example of Rulfs' architectural skill."

National Register Nomination, 2007. [30]

> 'This three-story building is constructed of brown brick, made locally on the banks of Banita Creek. The symmetrical façade is divided into three bays; the central bay is slightly wider than the outer two, and features a stepped parapet. The vertical bays are delineated by pilasters, which extend from the second floor upward to the parapet. This building is given horizontal accent by a band of buff-colored stone (or concrete) that externally demarcates the interior floor division. These bands are broken at each pilaster, but otherwise run the length of the bay. Decorative details are limited to triangulated, corbelled brickwork beneath the banks of windows, the same brickwork at the parapet, and a single decorative medallion adorning the cornice. . . . The composition of this building is simple and straightforward, contributing to its sense of mass and repose."

The Redesign of the Cox Building for the Stone Fort Bank (1919)

As the Blount-Baker building was being built for Aikman's company, a second design opportunity presented itself. As far back as 1908, the Farmers and Merchants Bank had secured a lease on the Cox Building (Rulfs, 1891) that dominated the east side of the Square.[31] In 1919, when the bank merged with the Stone Fort National Bank, the two banks deemed the location of the Cox Building was too good to sacrifice. Therefore, they leased the building for another ten years. To launch the combined bank, the directors asked Rulfs to give the Cox Building a face-lift. (The majority of the directors of both banks lived in houses designed by Rulfs.) While the remarkable 1919 façade no longer exists, a description using period photographs will serve to illustrate the architect's thinking at this time.

The Square in Nacogdoches rests on a plateau. Unlike the new Blount-Baker building, where the architect could compensate for the slope to Banita Creek behind the façade, the slope from north to south on the Cox lot had to be addressed in the building's main façade that faced the Square. In 1891, Rulfs solved the elevation problem by using a chamfered corner, a presence on both Main Street and the Square, and overcame the slope by establishing a strong horizontal line for eye at the level of the parapet. In 1919, he reaffirmed these solutions. He kept the chamfered entrance and, without calling attention to it, camouflaged the slope of the lot by adjusting the length of the Tuscan pilasters which surrounded the entire structure. At the roof line, the majestic brick pilasters supported a very broad classic entablature. The removal of the intricate brickwork of the 1890s and its

FIGURE 12.13. (Below) Cox Building Received a New Façade in 1919.

This photograph, ca. 1936, shows the facade that Rulfs designed in 1919 for his earlier 1891 building for Cox. Photograph from A. P. McDonald's book on the Stone Fort National Bank.

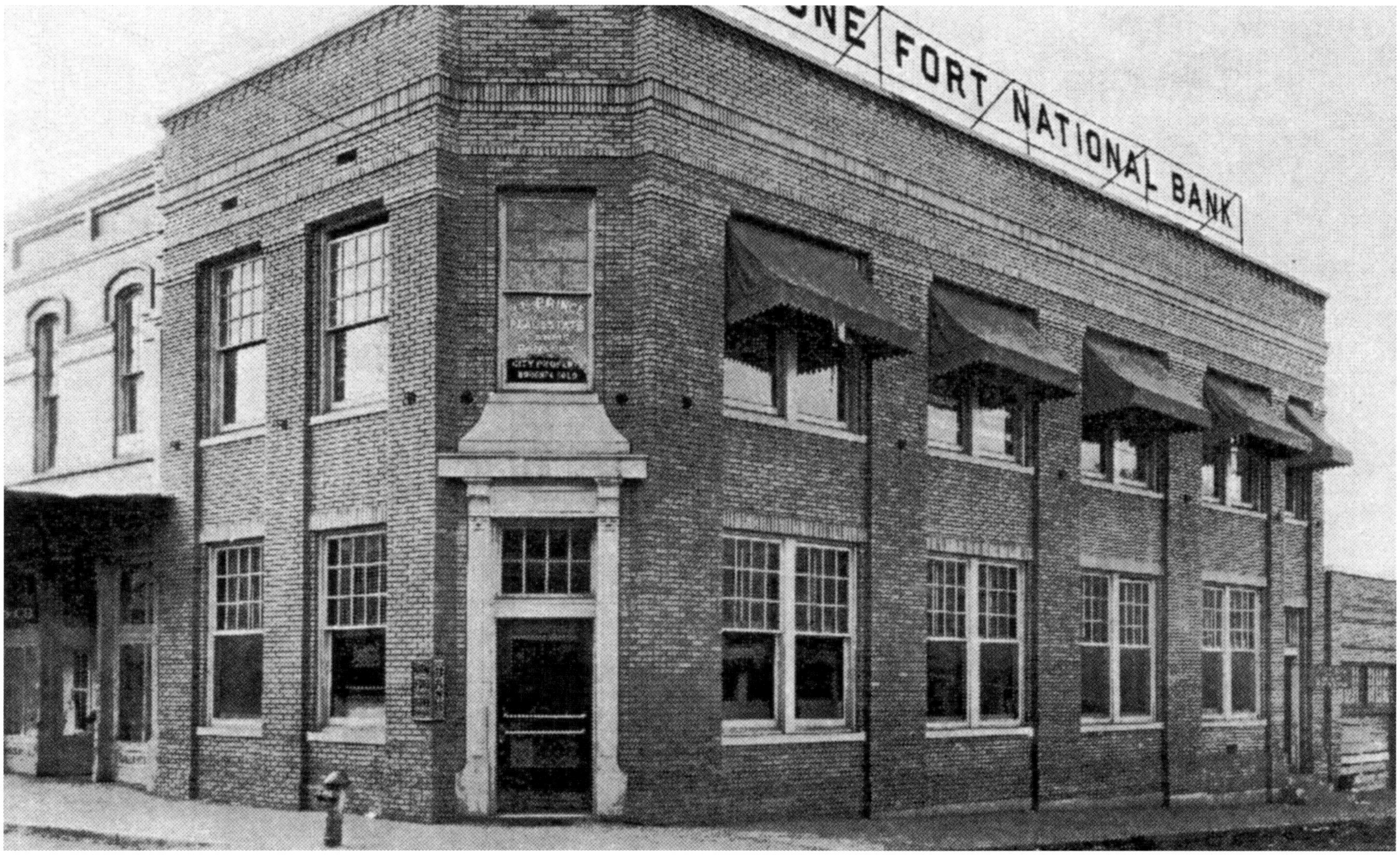

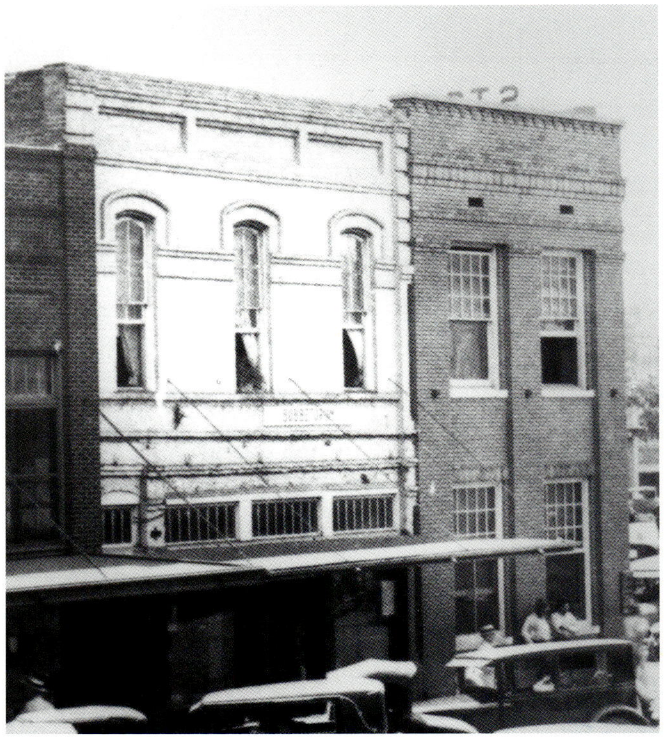

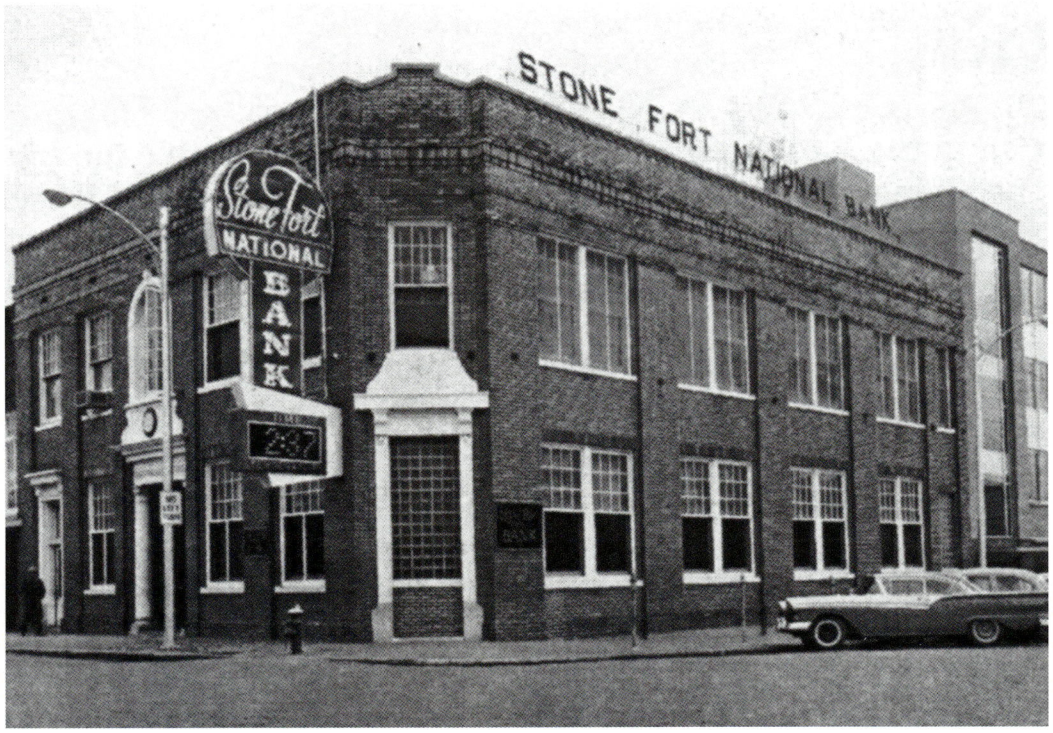

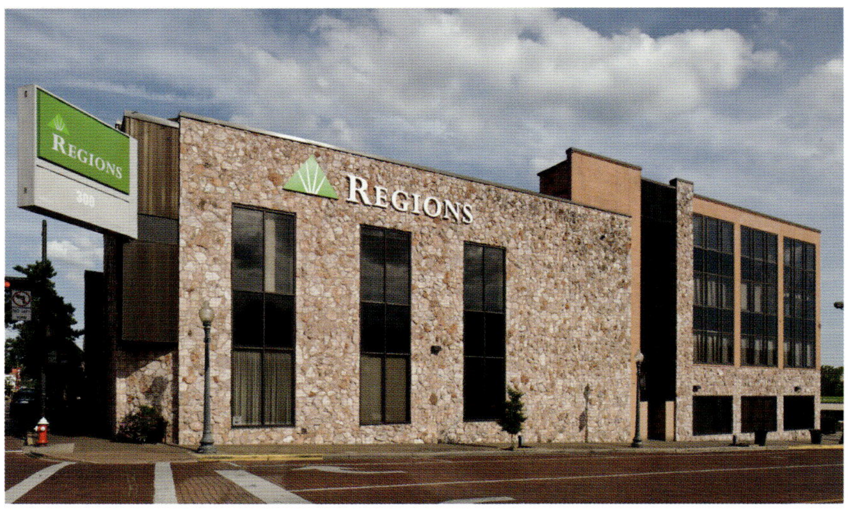

FIGURES 12.14 - 12.16. The Evolution of the Stone Fort Bank Building

(Above Left) The 1919 façade by Rulfs seen from Main Street in the 1930s. The build-ing to the east, which also dates from 1891, can be seen in this picture before the bank unified the façades in 1955. Courtesy of ETRC.

(Above Right) In 1955, the bank extended the features of the Rulfs facade to the building east of the Cox Building. The modern tower office building seen in the picture at bottom right dates to this remodeling. Photograph, Robinson's Studio as used in Archie McDonald's Stone Fort National Bank.

(Left) The Stone Fort Bank replaced the façade by Rulfs in 1966 with stone. This stone façade remains, albeit the building is now owned by Regions Bank. The vertical windows treatments of today cover the bays originally defined by Rulfs in 1919. Despite all these changes and encasements, however, Rulfs's 1891 building with its chamfered corner still survives.

replacement with a Greek-inspired motifs followed a pattern long since established by the architect's work in his residences for several of the bank's leaders (Will Perkins and Hollis Mast). The effect was one of solidity and efficiency. Within the bays created by the pilasters, Rulfs paired windows with twelve lights in the upper sash and one large pane in the lower sash, a popular treatment because it offered both decoration without obscured vision. Rulfs had used a similar treatment on many houses, sometimes in stained glass or diamond mullions, as in the Blum Mast House. (Blum Mast was a major principal in the combined banks).

In 1929, the Stone Fort Bank decided to purchase the Cox Building and the one adjacent to it along Main Street.[32] In 1955, when the directors felt the need to remodel again, the bank reaffirmed its Main Street address by moving the main entrance from the chamfered corner to a portal further along Main Street. At that time, they extended the temple façade created by Rulfs to the east and added a few classical elements of their own. When the urge to refurbish again struck in 1966, the bank replaced the 1919 temple façade completely with stones to simulate their name on their building's exterior.[33]

The Woodmen of the World Building (1922)

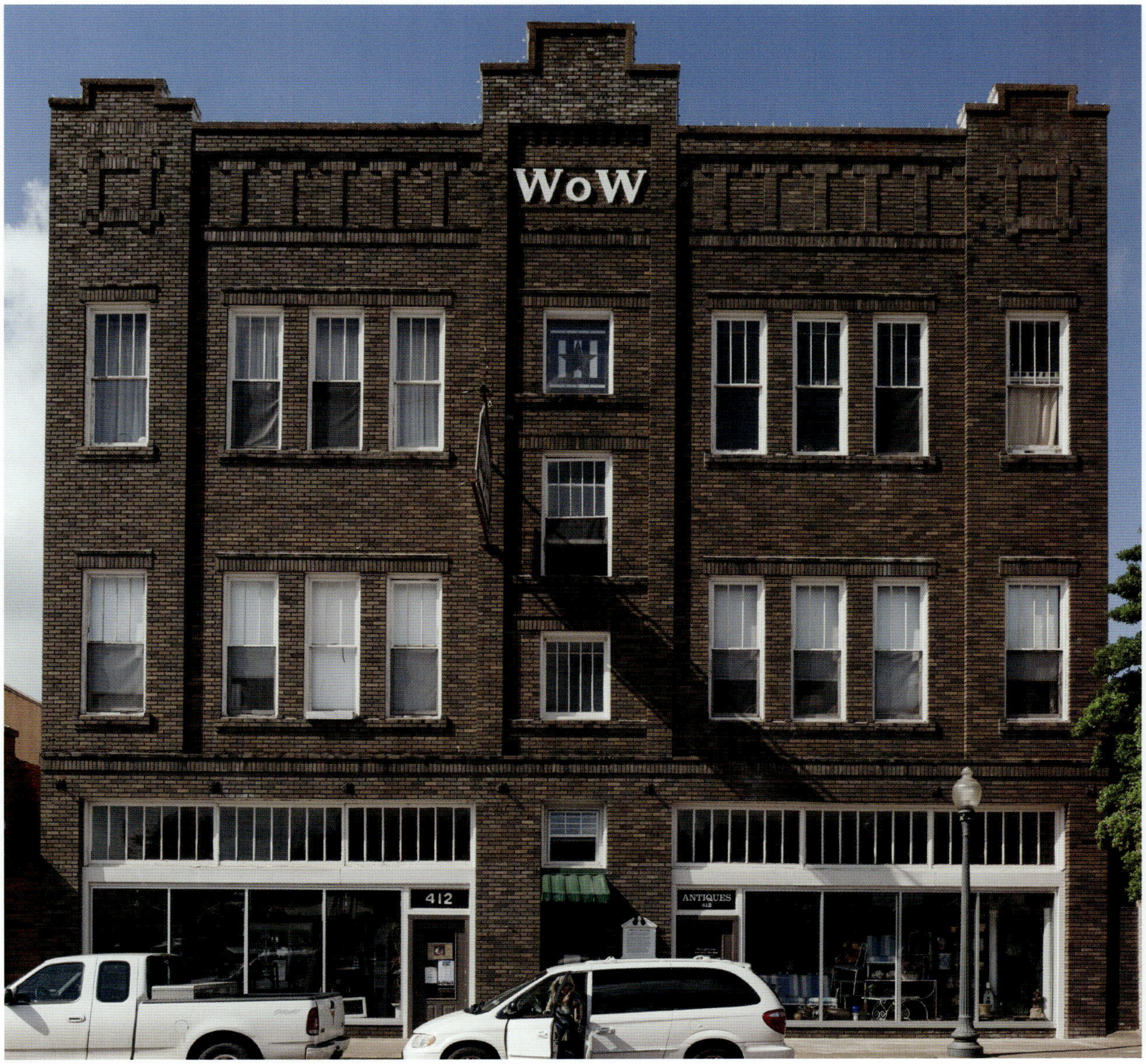

FIGURE 12.17. Woodmen of the World Building in 2011.

Block 16 in the downtown area, on the south side of Main between Church and Mound Streets, was part of the Y'Barbo family grant before it was sold in 1838 to Frost Thorn, an early Texas *impresario* and one of the first millionaires in the state. Thorn made the block his homestead and built a large house there. After Frost's death, his wife Susan transferred the original homestead, shown on Nacogdoches Plat #1 (see FIGURE I.14)], to her niece, Susan Durst, who turned the house into the Hart Hotel. During the boom years between 1880 and 1900, the Hart Hotel played an active role in servicing the trade in and out of the east side of Nacogdoches. By the turn of the century, however, the building was dilapidated; when it caught on fire in 1900, the damage was too extensive to consider repair. The owner demolished its remains and turned the site into a wagon yard with a camp house for freight men. Over a decade later, it became an auto repair warehouse for a time. In 1919, B. H. Wells, Tom H. Summers, and Joe A. Spears, managers for Liberty Elm Camp No. 210 of the Woodmen of the World Fraternal Association, bought this site.[34] The Woodmen, a nonprofit society owned and governed by its members for the benefit of their families and community, was a very popular organization in Texas from the turn of the century.

In 1921, in order to provide a meeting place and rental space for income, the Nacogdoches chapter decided to build a three-story building. They asked D. Rulfs, a member of the group, to provide a design and specifications. Although Rulfs at first declined, the challenge of working with the group and overseeing their project proved irresistible. The Woodmen published his design requirments in a 1922 public notice in the *Deed Records*: "Specifications . . . according to the plans prepared by D. Rulfs, Architect."[35] In the specifications, the owners and Rulfs reserved the right to supervise and make any changes necessary during the construction period. The document discussed in detail everything from the concrete work and brick work ("all brick work to have headers every sixth course"), to the custom show windows. Although the drawings are missing, the written details mention floor plans, elevations, cross sections, details of stairs, plumbing, electricity, examples of the custom windows, layouts of the beams, casing for openings and doors, layers for the flat roof, and more. The Woodmen awarded the brick, cement, and plasterwork contract for $15,656.00 to Moore Construction Company; the woodwork contract for $10,000.00 went to R. W. Parrish.[36]

The Woodmen Building, which stands at 412 East Main, is a three-story rectangular commercial structure with a flat roof. The strong verticality of the building is offset by a first floor, the design of which is different from the upper floors. Two horizontal elements, a stringcourse of bricks and a continuous ribbon of fixed-pane windows with vertical mullions, separate the main floor from the two upper floors. While the unusually high parapet has vertical decorations in its decorative brickwork, in general it provides an overall impression of horizontality. The brickwork of the façade, which according to the specification was to have "black mortar with 3/8" open joints," was different than the brick used on the side of the building.[37]

Over the years, the Woodmen sponsored popular public dances in the upstairs of the building. Many different businesses have occupied this building since 1922. K. P. Branch and Orland Patton opened their first partnership in this space, originally selling groceries as well as hardware. Gilbert's Furniture and Appliance Co., Massey Business College, G. I. Surplus, and Ken Wood's Antique Market have occupied various parts of the building. In 2002, Gary Ashcraft and Bill Taylor acquired and renovated the building.[38]

The Aikman Gymnasium on the SFA Campus (1924)

Stephen F. Austin State Teachers College received its first philanthropic gift before it even moved to its main campus in 1924. Seeing that the college had no auditorium or indoor sports facility, Frank Aikman shared his wealth with the new college by giving a sum of money to build a gymnasium, which could also serve the college as an auditorium and theater. Aikman had witnessed the trauma the town had undergone between 1914 and 1923 to get the College; he wanted the college to have a fighting chance to survive.[39] While no document has surfaced confirming that D. Rulfs planned the gym, without undue speculation the author feels confident in asserting that Rulfs designed the building. First, it was not the type of building that local carpenters would have undertaken or felt comfortable to specify without an architect. While the State Board of Regents did give their permission to proceed, they offered no funds or assistance or a suggestion of an architect as they invariably did for other buildings on campus; there was no bidding. Second, the Nacogdoches team overseeing the struggle to get the school open would have wanted to proceed as economically as possible; this meant they most likely used a local architect, of which D. Rulfs was the only one. Furthermore, the oversight committee consisted of President Birdwell, Senator Eugene Blount, Thomas Baker, and other men who worked closely with Rulfs on their homes and businesses. Rulfs had recently designed the Blount-Baker Building for Aikman's hair tonic business, had even more recently remodeled the Hall House for Birdwell's use, and he was, at the same time, completing Blount's majestic new home across the street from the college. Rulfs quite possibly did the plans *pro bono* as his contribution to the community effort. Third, the structure is completely utilitarian. There was only one noteworthy decorative detail on the entire building–the entrance porch on the south. At this main entrance to the building, next to the ticket kiosk, the supports for the roof were identical to those used by Rulfs on the front of the Frank Sharp House the year before.

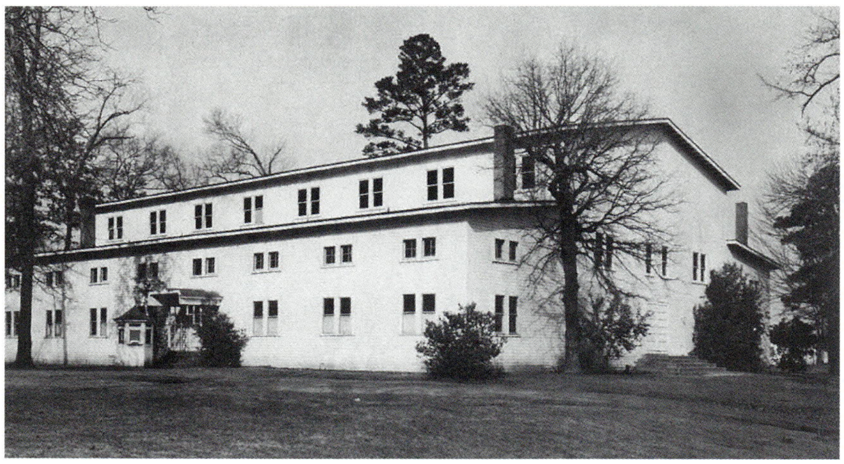

FIGURE 12.18. Aikman Gymnasium (1924-1975).
Photograph from the 1938 Stone Fort Yearbook.

Aikman Gym was a multipurpose building, constructed from readily available materials. While plain, its design was thoughtful and proved to be highly successful. No building on the SFA campus ever received more severe and constant use. The Gym was the center of student activities on campus for almost fifty years, from 1924 to 1975, when it was demolished. It served as a basketball court, theater, auditorium, lecture hall, and dance hall. Famous people like Robert Frost, the poet, and Carl Sandburg, the biographer of Abraham Lincoln, spoke in the Aikman Gym.

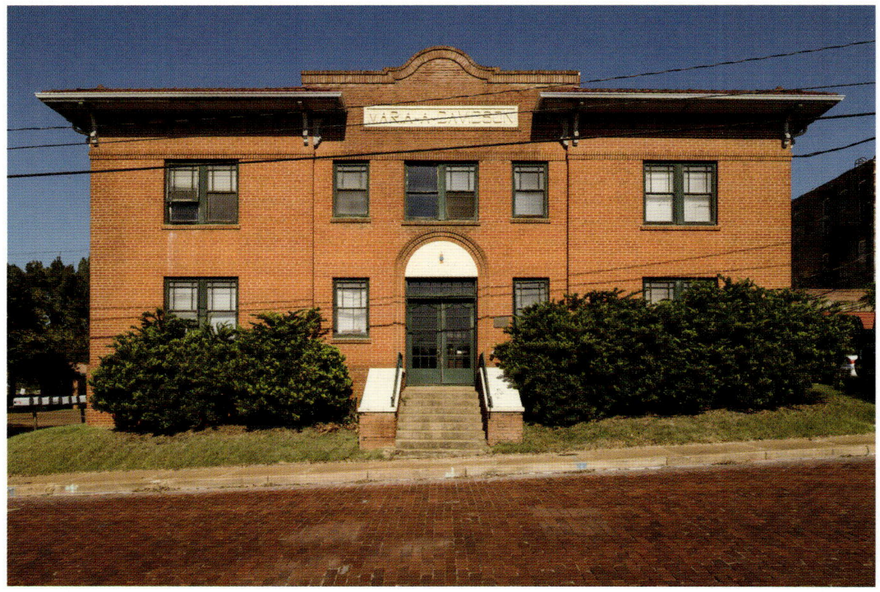

FIGURE 12.19. Marie Davidson Apartments in 2012.

The Marie Davidson Apartments (Designed 1925; Constructed 1927-28)

D. Rulfs designed seven buildings for Nacogdoches businessman and financier John P. Davidson.[40] After the death of his wife, Maria, in 1908, the widower Davidson modified the Davidson Building on the south Square from commercial use into a residential structure, as he had done for the Hardeman Building. The Davidson structure later became the Inn Hotel, then the Liberty Hotel, and finally City Hall.[41] According to the 1910 Census, Davidson rented an apartment to his wife's niece, a school teacher.

Seeing the growing need for rental housing in the central area, Davidson began to contemplate an apartment complex. The tipping point in his calculations probably was the rush of requests for housing downtown due to the opening of SFASTC in 1923-24. Davidson had owned property on the west side of Block 23, on South Fredonia Street, as early as 1904 and had added to this in 1916 and 1917. Davidson's talks with Rulfs began in late 1924 or early 1925, but the plans as developed by the two men necessitated more land than Davidson owned. Execution of the designs by Rulfs for the Maria Davidson Apartments, therefore, had to await the acquisition of additional property and were not completed until late 1927 or 1928. The construction of the apartments, therefore, did not commence until after the death of D. Rulfs.[42] The building was his last commercial design. The building is now listed in the National Register of Historic Places (1992), the official list of the Nation's treasures worthy of preservation.[43]

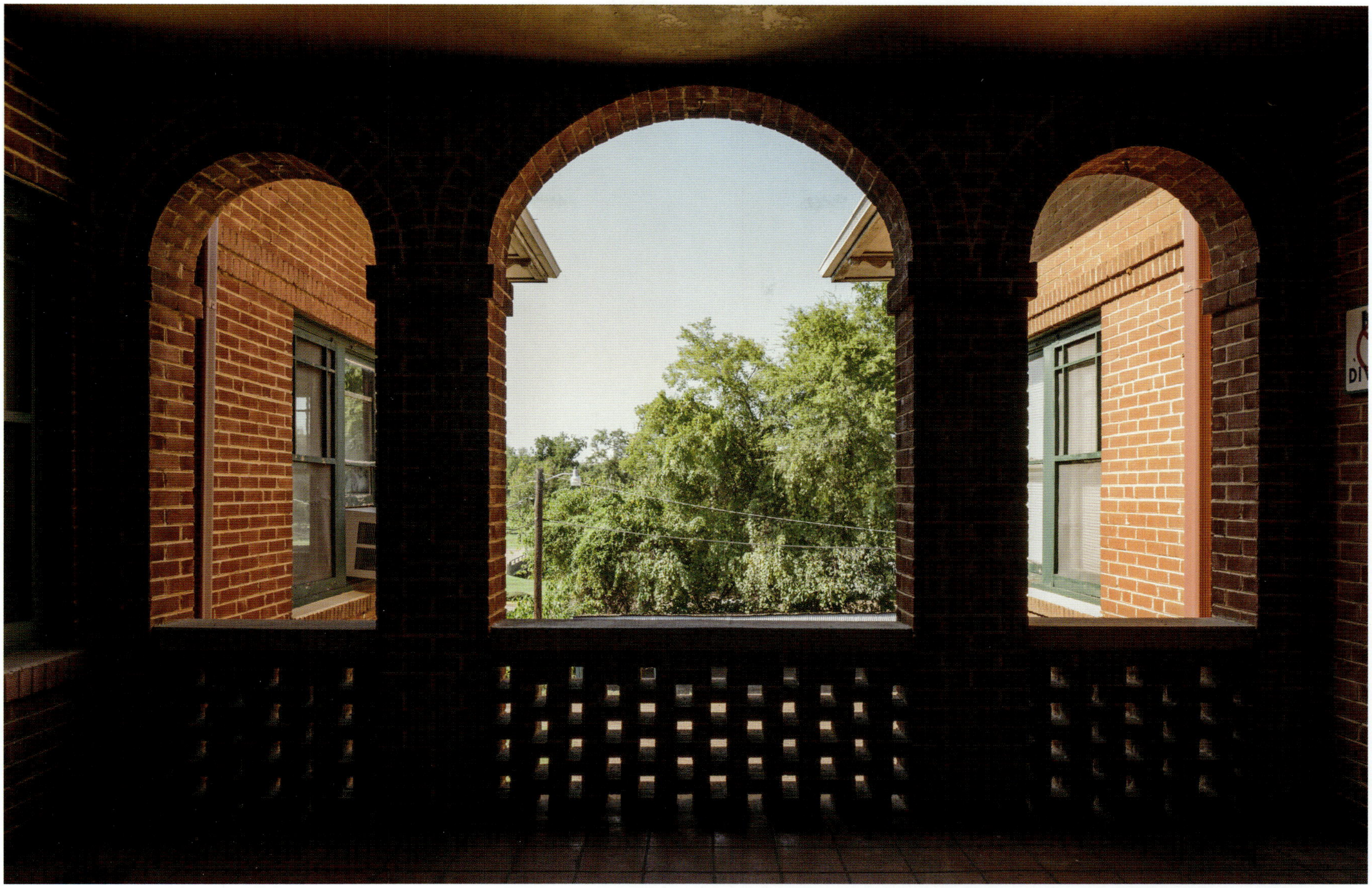

FIGURE 12.20. Arches, Upper Courtyard, Marie Davidson Apartments, 2012.

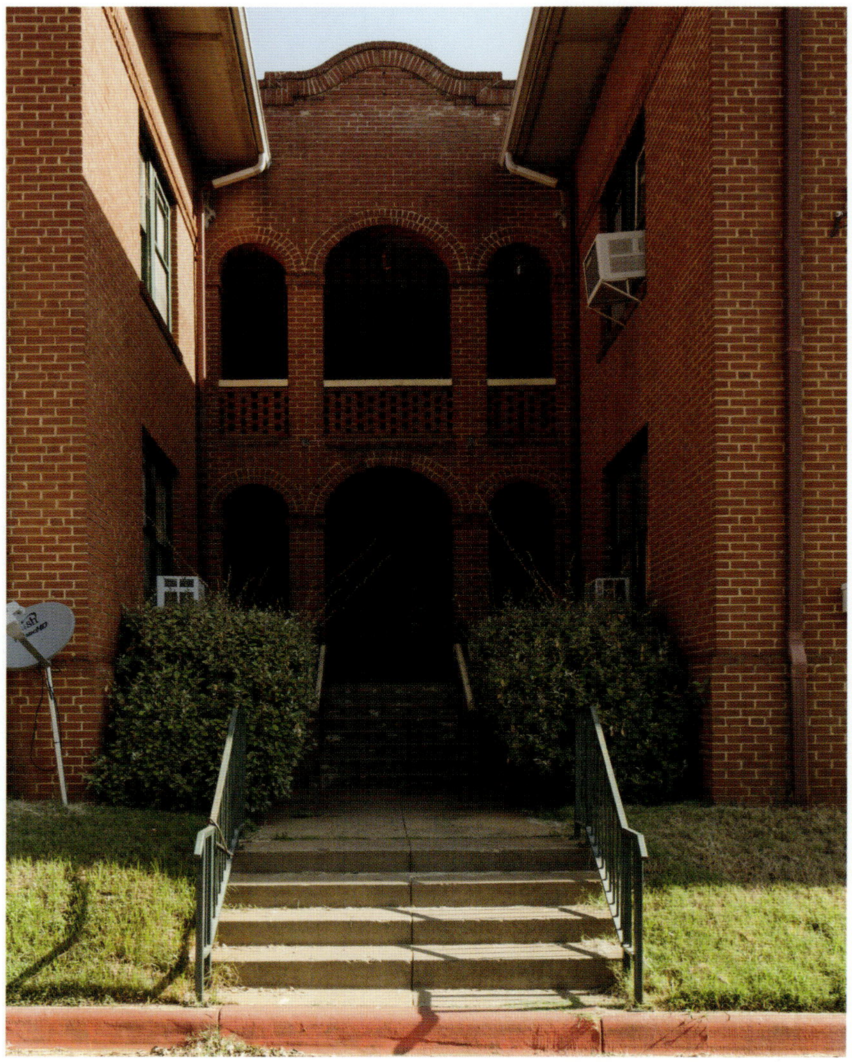

FIGURE 12.21. South Entry Courtyard, Marie Davidson Apartments, 2012.

The nomination for National Register status designates the building "the only historical apartment building in Nacogdoches originally constructed for the purpose that it retains today." The application labels the architecture as "an intact example of a simplified Mission or Spanish Colonial Revival architectural style, which despite the Spanish heritage of Nacogdoches, is rarely seen in the extant building stock."[44] While most of the individual descriptions in this application are accurate, the overall impact of the interpretation is misleading. By treating the structure as simply another example of the architect's eclecticism, the nomination's conclusions are misleading. Only by placing the structure in the context of his earlier designs and then current preoccupations can the building really be seen to bear the Rulfs signature.

First, Davidson was an old man, familiar in every way with the prejudices of the business classes in Nacogdoches. The patrons Rulfs served had a well-voiced aversion to anything influenced by the Spanish-Mexican Colonial period. For this reason, Rulfs never emphasized any Spanish or Mission colonial influences in any of his architectural designs, whereas he began his career in Nacogdoches with Italianate creations. Second, the community in Nacogdoches was accustomed (unlike *our* frame of reference) to viewing raised parapets by Rulfs all over town: the Perkins Building (1884), the Davidson Building on East Main (1889), the Opera House (1889), the Davidson Buildings on the South Square (1891), and the Wettermark Bank (1896). Modified parapets with arched central design graced the Cotton Exchange, the Cox Building (1901), and the Blount-Schmidt Building (1904). Most of these buildings are gone or modified. Third, Rulfs did not have to look outside his own design portfolio for inspiration for these apartments. The east façade of the apartments is a simplification of the south facade of the Hoya Building of 1900–a design Davidson himself observed every day from his bedroom window. The Hoya façade even has three bays and an arched protrusion (the Alamo element) to break the parapet and define the design below. To vary the older design, Rulfs recessed the central bay, as he had done on the Eugene Blount home, utilized the tile on the pent roof as a substitute for the intricate brickwork, which was by then passé, and finally simplified the lines of the building, as he had done all over Nacogdoches since 1910. Fourth, Rulfs was ill at the time and certainly knew this was likely to be his last commercial building. Rulfs returned to the Palladian motifs that had obsessed him for his whole career–his signature, so to speak, and to the Renaissance and Baroque parapets and brackets that were ubiquitous around Oldenburg in his youth. Rulfs had used modern interpretations of the Palladian window for Davidson on his home and on the redesign of the Davidson Building on East Main after the 1908 fire. Five, many of the other elements come from his recent works: the pent roof from the Sharp House, the wide soffits from most of his modern houses, and window selections like many of his recent commercial buildings. Even the large decorative brackets under the eaves, used in most Italianate designs, reflect his design work from the 1890s onwards. The brackets on the apartments are as much practical supports for the pent roof as major stylistic statements of colonial architecture.

While the Palladian influences on the main Fredonia entrance are subtle, the three-arched configurations on the south, recessed in the courtyard entrance, are very strong and very clear. The two-story galleries, which connect the two blocks of the apartments, are definitely neo-Romanesque or Constantinian configurations. His use of this configuration, as opposed to other versions involving rectangles, was very nostalgic for the architect–an emulation of his home church in Stollhamm, Germany. This is the only structure in which he used both types of Palladian windows. While the National Register description sees the brick wall behind the galleries as a wall whose roofline was "broken by a protruding Alamo parapet," it is not, in the author's opinion, necessarily obvious that this was Rulfs's intention.

Post-War Residential Design

The Lois and Adlai Travis Mast, Sr. House (1921)

One of the few residences Rulfs designed after World War I in Nacogdoches was for Adlai Travis Mast, Sr. (1892-1985). Mast, from a pioneering Texas family, was born and lived his early life in Melrose. By the time of the 1910 Census, he was living with his parents on Fredonia Street, across Washington Square from where he would later build his home. When he returned from World War I, Mast (28) married Lois Wilson (27) of Sugar Land. While their new house was being built, the couple lived with their sister-in-law, Prudie Mast, in the Hollis Mast House (Rulfs 1910) at the corner of Mound and Hospital Streets.[45]

The A. T. Mast House was innovative, much like the Guy Blount House a decade earlier, and set new standards for many post-war dwellings. It was the first house in the town to be built on a slab; the first by Rulfs to be completely brick veneered; one of the first houses to feature the lower ceilings which made houses in the interwar period easier to heat; the first of the houses by Rulfs to have no covered porch; the first house to feature a series of arched windows as the central feature of the house; one of the first houses (in decades) to have an external chimney; and, importantly, the first house to have an elaborate brick drive to accommodate the prominent carport on the front approach to the house.

Rulfs had designed many earlier houses with carports, for example the houses for Guy Blount, Mary Hayter, and the Hoya sisters; but, all of these had dirt floors.[46] The A. T. Mast House was the first in town to integrate the driveway into the house; even the houses for Frank Sharp and Eugene Blount, which had brick driveways, did not integrate them as fully. Although Mast was trained as a pharmacist and worked with his brothers in the drug stores around the Square, his later business interests overtook his early profession. He and his brother, Henry, were among the pioneers of the automobile business in town. No doubt his business interests led him to feature the new mode of transportation so prominently in his home. According to an interview with his son, Adlai, Jr., the senior Adlai carefully supervised the intricate work that was necessary to piece the drive together.[47] Fortunately, the city recognized the unique integration of this drive with the house when they preserved the legacy while installing sidewalks along Park Street.[48] In the 1980s, after his father died, Adlai, Jr. supervised the addition of a bedroom wing off the southeast corner of the house and a glassed-in breakfast room near the carport. The senior A. T. Mast willed the house to his grandson, Dr. A. T. Mast, III, who has, in turn, reared another generation of Masts in the house.

When the Mast home was included in the tour of homes in 1962, the architect's name was not featured. This was not unusual. Most of the other houses on the tour during that decade were by D. Rulfs, and none of the supporting literature mentions the Rulfs name. The brochure of the Colonial Dames for the Mast House featured only the rosewood dining furniture, the Venetian glass, the John Belter chairs, and the yellow onyx fireplace mantle.[49] The members of the tour committee at the time, no doubt, knew Rulfs had designed the house. *Everyone* knew that fact, as both Miss Gladys Hardeman and Adlai Mast, Jr. admitted a decade later to the author.[50] Subsequent generations of the public forgot these things.

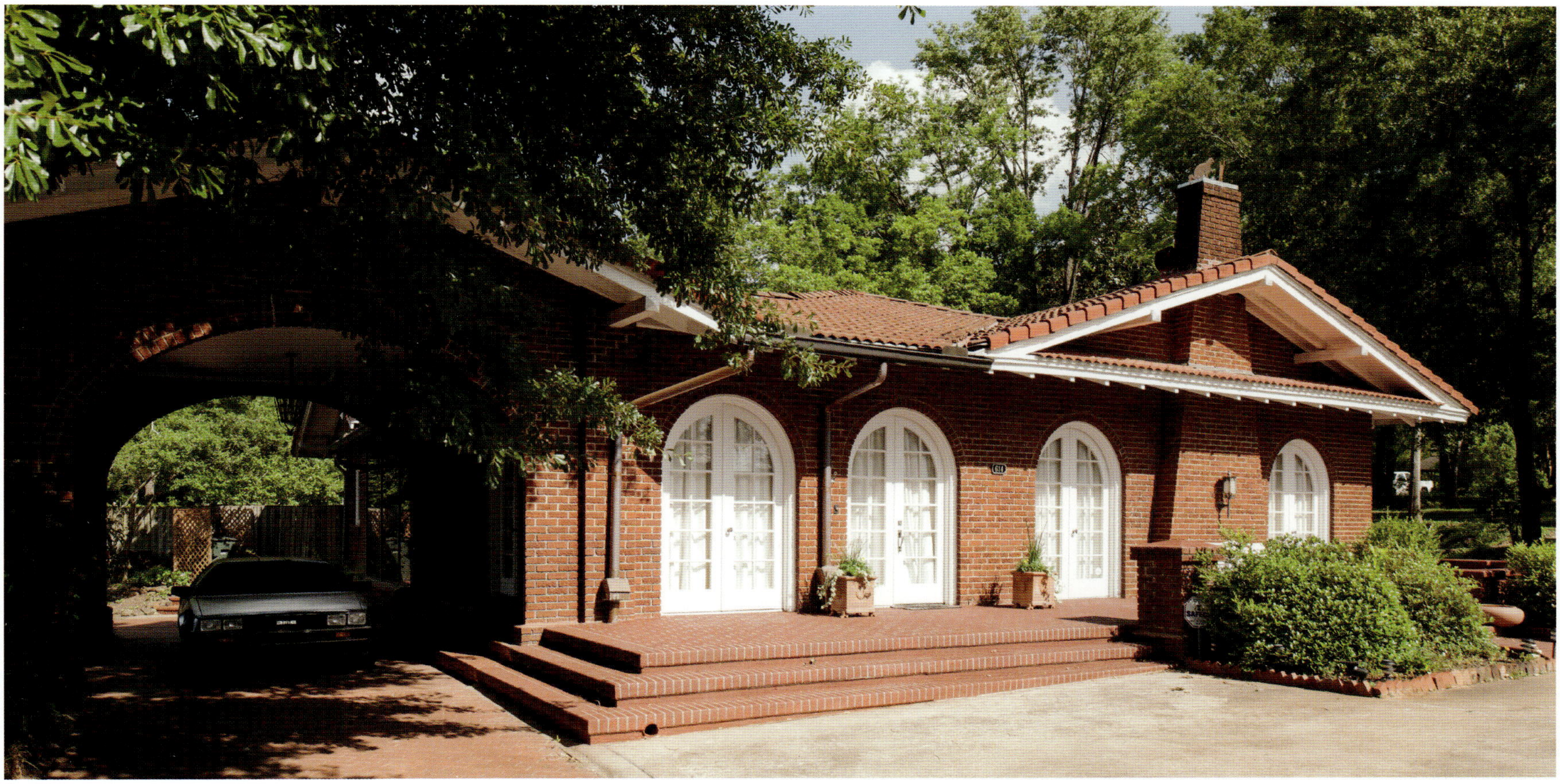

FIGURE 12.22 - 12.24. The Adlai T. Mast, Sr. House, now the home of Lupe and Dr. A. Travis Mast, III.

The Mast house dates to 1921. It was the first house in Nacogdoches to be constructed on a slab. The lot had a natural elevation above the street level; this made the use of a slab more acceptable to Rulfs. It was also the first house done by Rulfs which integrated the carport into the design of the house. The arched windows wrapped around the house on the south side, giving the house a unique appearance. The intricate brickwork on the driveway (below) is another special feature of the house. The concrete circular drive in front of the house was added later.

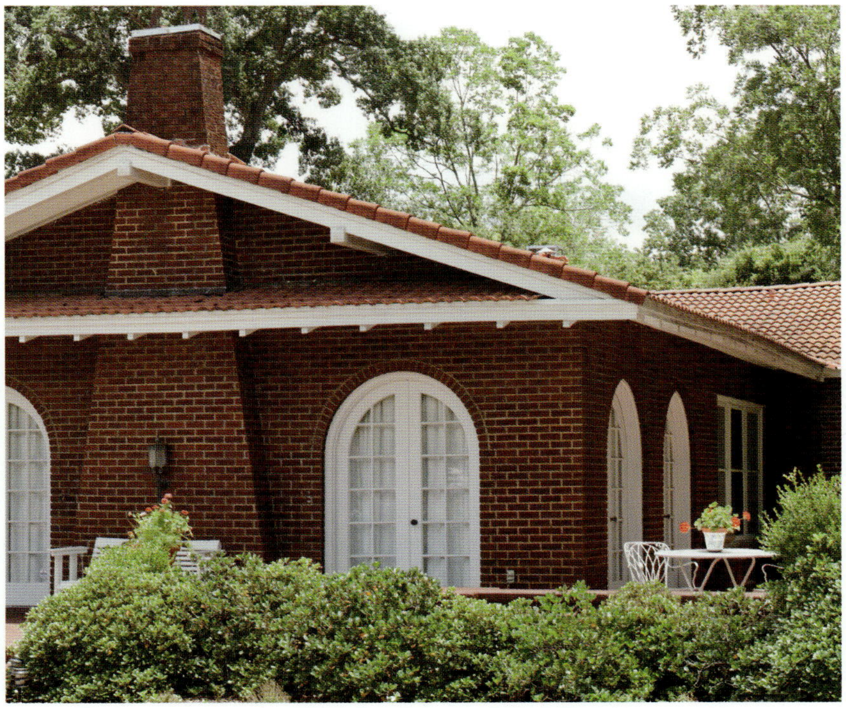

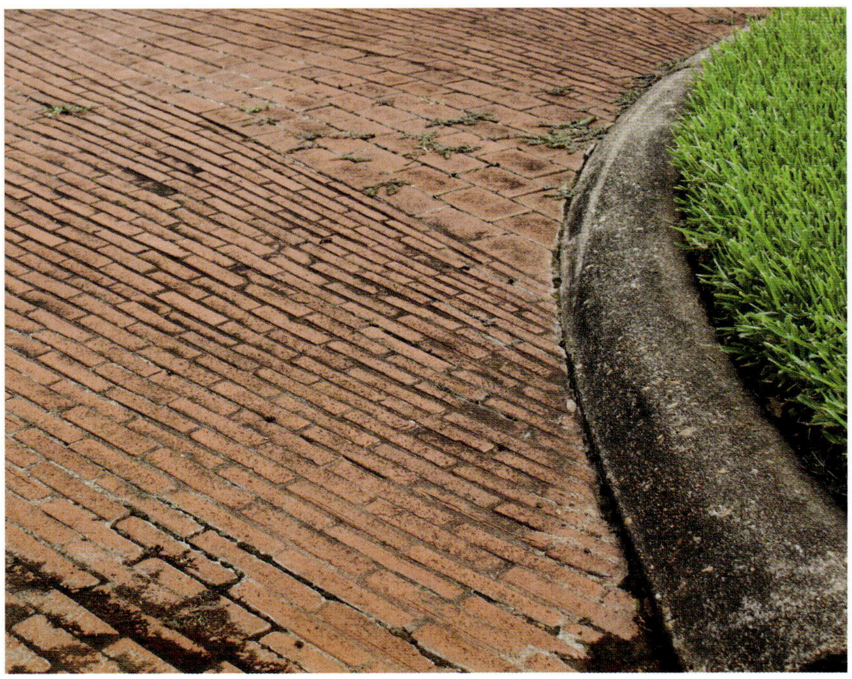

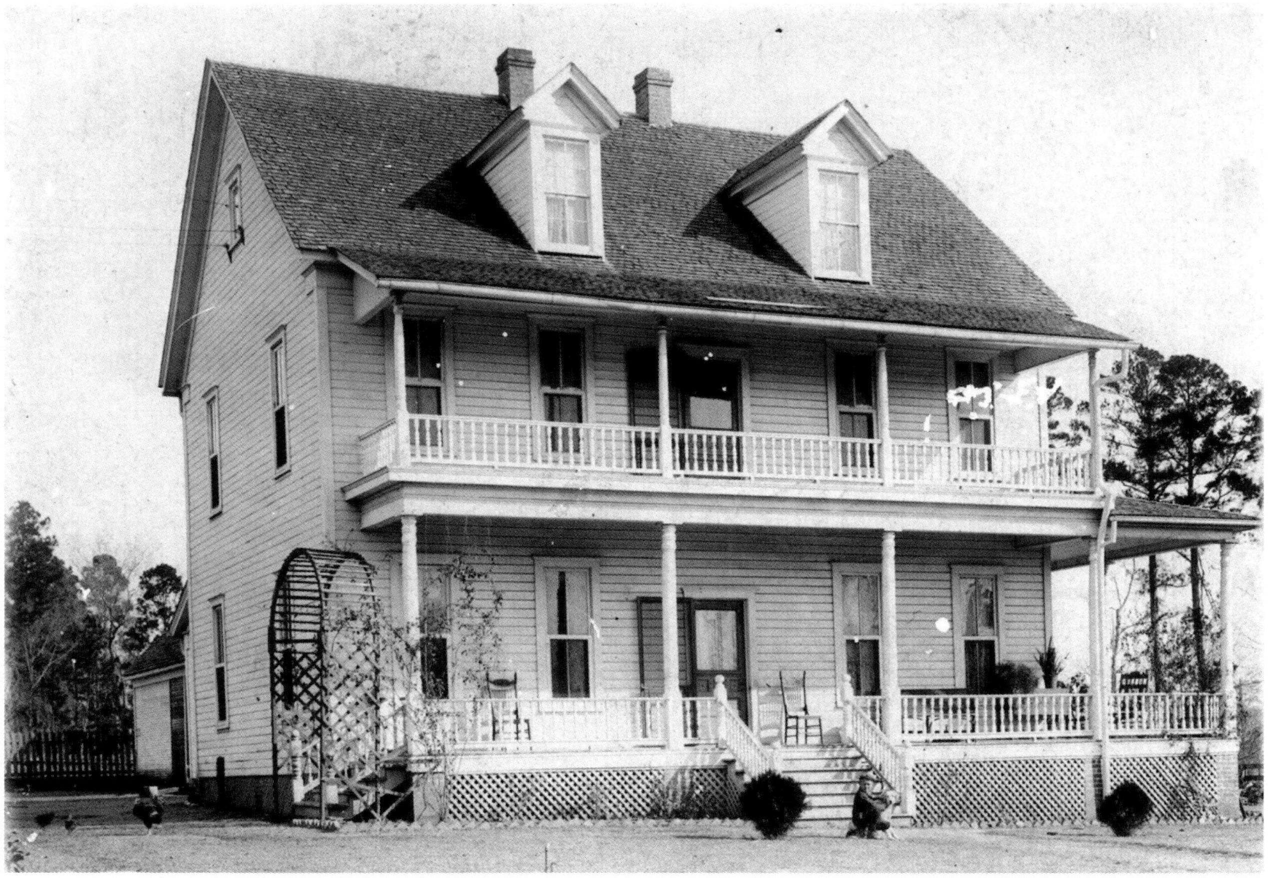

FIGURE 12.25. The R. A. Hall House in 1920.

The R. A. Hall homestead, one of the original tracts purchased for the campus of Stephen F. Austin State Teachers College, included a nice frame house, shown above. The building, remodeled by D. Rulfs in 1922, became the first President's house. The architect retained the wrap-around south porch as a small eastern screened porch in 1922. Photograph provided by SFA Regent and State Senator Roy Blake, grandson of R. A. Hall.

The Hall-Birdwell House (1922)

When the Nacogdoches Citizens Committee's subcommittee on land acquisition, led by Eugene H. Blount, assembled the tracts of land in 1917 that would make up the future campus for the SFA Normal, they included as one of the parcels the homestead of Richard Alexander Hall (1862-1931).[51] With the property came a nice frame house built around 1901.[52] As fate would have it, this nineteenth-century house was to become the first home of the College's new President, Alton W. Birdwell.

Birdwell and his wife, Maud, lived off campus when they first moved to Nacogdoches in early 1922. Birdwell immediately asked the State Regents if the Hall house could be remodeled to serve as his home. The Regents authorized him to proceed with the remodeling of the frame house, but the Texas Governor vetoed the appropriation. When the contractor of the Austin Building defaulted, all the parties in Austin recognized the need to have Birdwell on site to oversee the completion of the campus. The plan to remodel the Hall home proceeded. While any number of those advising Birdwell could have informed the newcomer that Rulfs would be the man to redesign the house, most probably Eugene Blount, the State Legislator at the time and the man in charge of the property, did the honors. Karle Wilson and Thomas Baker, close friends of the Birdwells, were also capable of recommending the architect; they lived at Tanglewood at the time.

Rulfs completely modernized the exterior of the Hall House with a minimum of effort by removing the porches and dormers and adding ribbon windows. The sashes reflected the same concept he had used on the windows of the remodeled Stone Fort Bank: multiple lights on the upper sash and a large single pane on the lower sash. He then repeated the same appearance in the square latticework on the east screened porch. For the entrance, he used a simple entablature supported by Tuscan columns. A new decorative window replaced the upper porch door and gave illumination to the upper hall and stairwell. The design possibly came from the guardhouse in the Ducal Palace in Oldenburg.[53] Rulfs repeated this same window design on the front of the Eugene Blount House the next year.

The cosmetic changes given to the Hall-Birdwell House were meant as a temporary solution. Rulfs did not thoroughly reconfigure the 1901 house. President Birdwell later called the house "indifferent but comfortable." This most modest of presidential homes received only slight modifications between 1922 and 1957: the enclosure of the east screened porch with windows to form a small morning room and addition of a carport to the west. The College moved the Hall-Birdwell House eastward where it served as the home-demonstration house for the SFA Home Economics Department. When it later faced demolition, Professor Andrew Eugene Huffty moved the house to South Shawnee Street (2052 Rayburn Drive), where it took on new life as a bed-and-breakfast inn for some years. Dr. Jeffrey Roth, a professor at SFA, currently, makes the house his home.

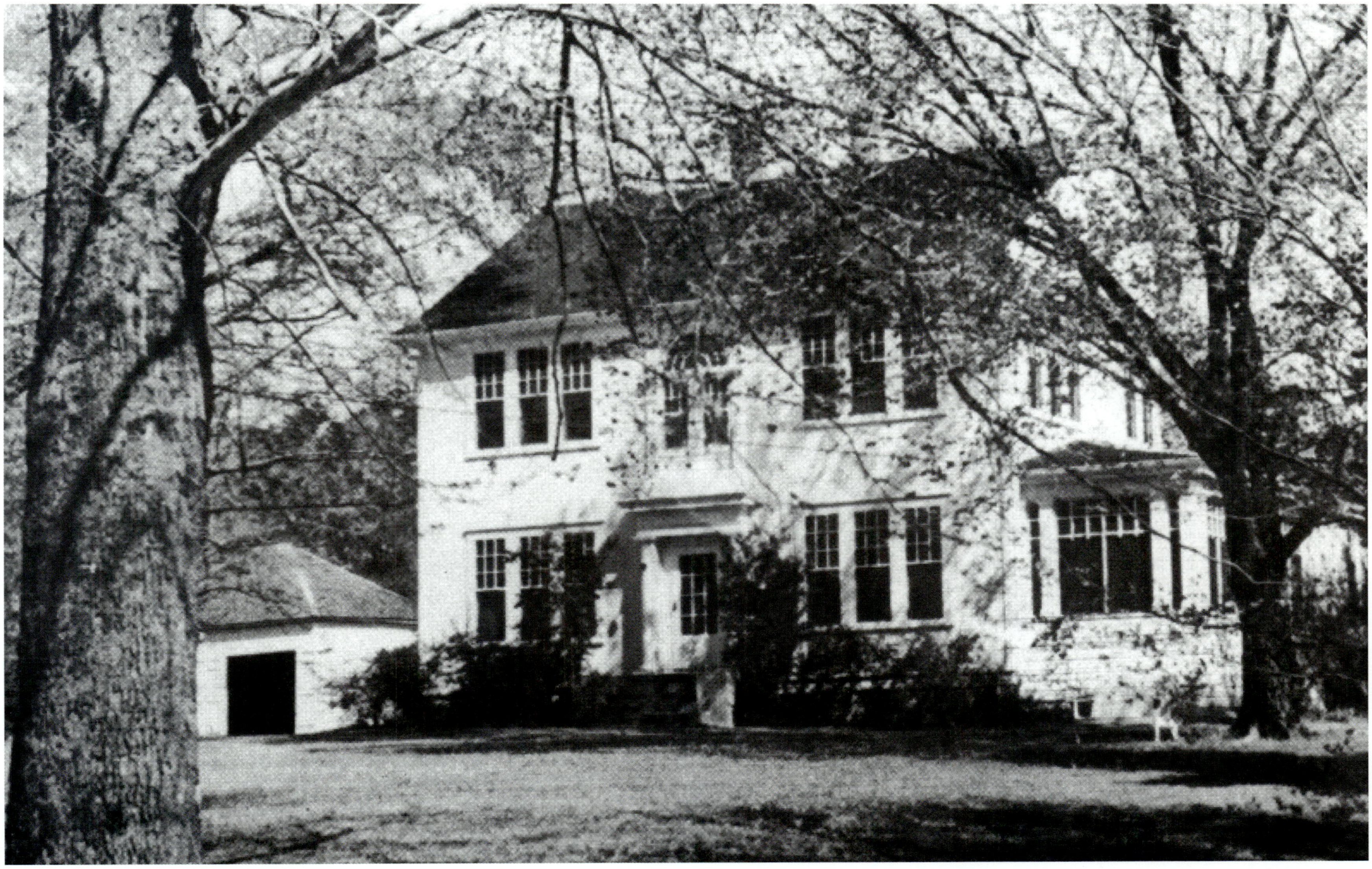

FIGURE 12.26. The Alton Birdwell House, 1922.

This 1901 house, as remodeled by Rulfs in 1922, served as the presidential residence at SFA from 1922 to 1956.

FIGURE 12.27. (Right) The Jeff Roth Home.

The Birdwell House has remained in the SFA family, so to speak. Gene Huffty moved the house, and another professor now lives in the house and is in the process of restoring the structure. Photograph compliments of Jeff Roth.

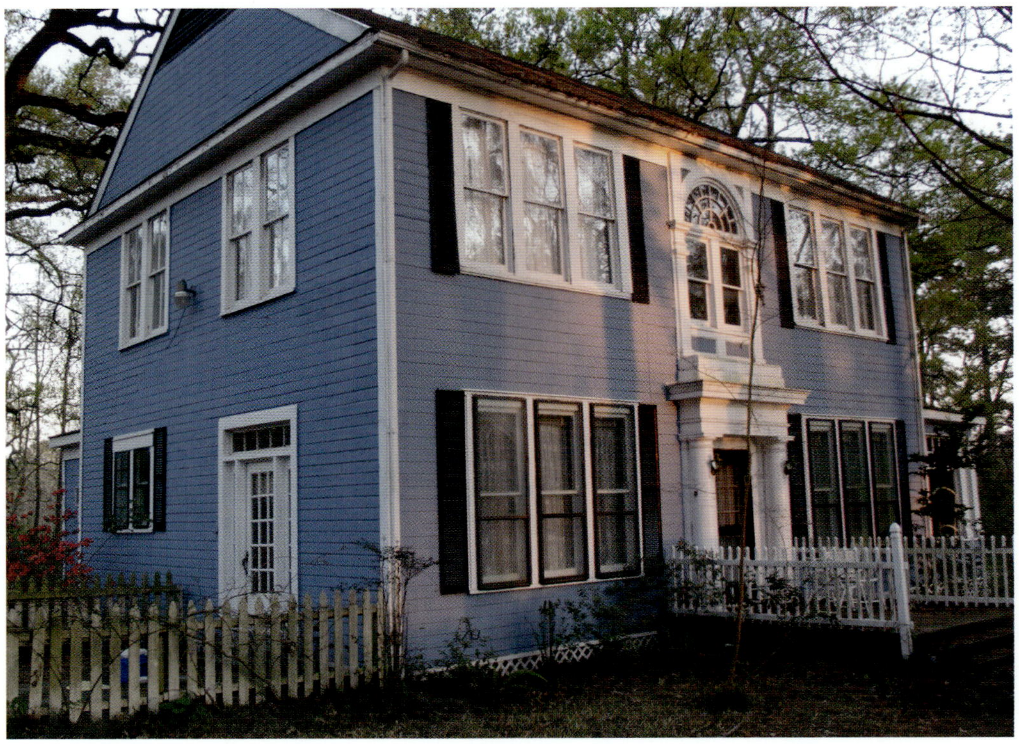

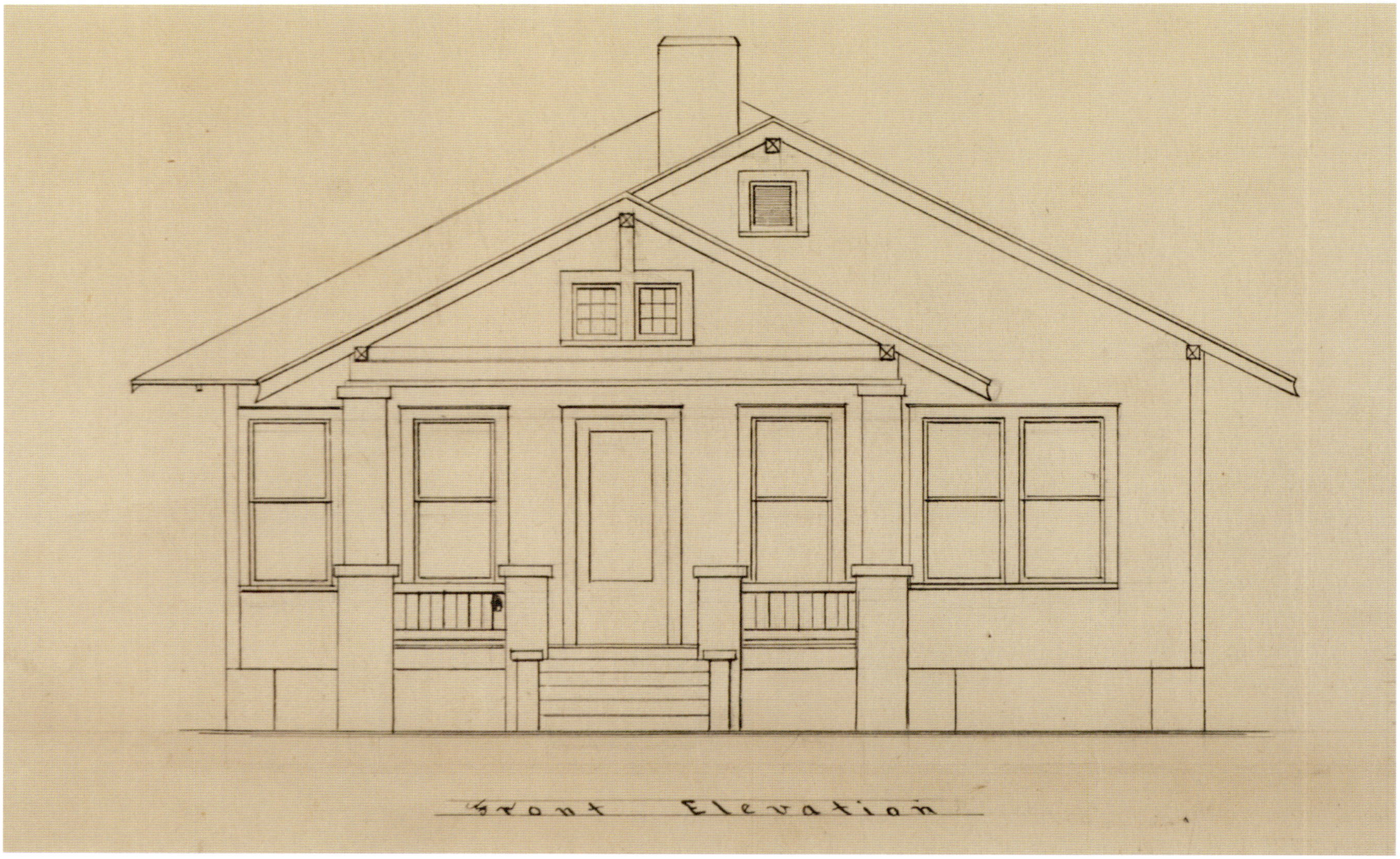

The Cason-Baxley House (ca 1921-1923)

One complete set of original drawings signed by Rulfs and preserved in the Cason Estate Papers is entitled, "Building Plan of a One Story Residence Erected by Robert Cason. D. Rulfs Architect."[54] The plans have no date, but the house as built at 623 Logansport Street has no association with Robert Cason, but with his older sister, Willie Maud. Since neither Willie Maud nor Robert lived at this location in the 1920 census, the house probably dates to late 1920 or 1921. The 1920 census shows Willie Maud and her husband, Austen Baxley,[55] on North Street, and Robert, unmarried, at home with his parents. The 1930 census, however, shows the Baxleys and their two daughters on Logansport, but Robert and his wife, Nell, were still not listed on the street.[56]

Piecing together the various official records, what probably happened was that after Robert and Nell married in 1921, D. (Dick) K. Cason transferred property on either side of his home to both Willie Maud Cason Baxley and Robert in the 1923-1924 period for the building of homes.[57] The talks with Rulfs could have started earlier, preparing a bachelor house for Robert, but most likely came in anticipation of a honeymoon house for Robert and Nell in 1921. After commissioning the plans, Dick probably decided to use the plans for the Baxleys instead; the Casons wanted their two granddaughters nearby. D. K. Cason built the house, most likely, between 1921 and 1922, when he transferred the land to Willie Maud.[58] While the 1922 Sanborn Map shows the area, the Baxley House does not appear until the 1929 Map.[59]

Although the house as constructed is the mirror image of the drawings, the detailed plans obviously match the house designed by Rulfs. The extant plans for this double gable-front, Craftsman house consist of the following: floor and foundation drawings; front, north, and south elevations, rear and sectional elevations, as well as details for balustrades, rafter bases, and wiring. While no detailed specifications have survived, the various Nacogdoches surveys have supplied the basics: a one-story house clad in bull-nosed siding, with a hip-and-gable roof with "deep overhang, extended rafter and beam ends."[60] The front porch has square brick supports. The original structure had only one fireplace, in the front room, with one interior brick chimney and a flue for the kitchen. The additional chimney on the north, the carport-garage, the room at the back, and the south porch, all part of the house today, were not on the original plans.

Dr. George R. Hugman, Jr. and his family have owned and lived in the house since 1986.[61]

FIGURE 12.28. (Across) The Front Elevation, Plans by D. Rulfs for the Cason-Baxley House (ca. 1921-1923)

As one can see, the house as drawn is reverse from the house as built; the pair of windows is on the right in the drawing and on the left of the porch on the existing house. This is not unusual as the plans were adjusted to fit the lot better. D. K. Cason Papers, ETRC.

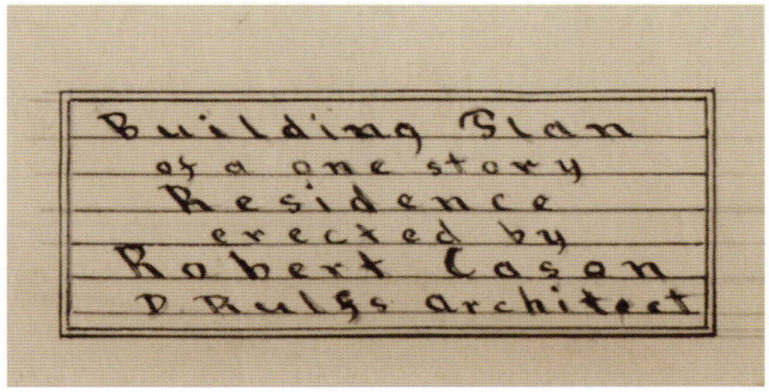

Building Plan
of a one story
Residence
erected by
Robert Cason
D. Rulfs Architect

FIGURE 12.30. The Architect's Caption on the Plans Drawn for Robert Cason, ca. 1921-1923.

FIGURE 12.29. (Below) The Hugman Home, 2012.

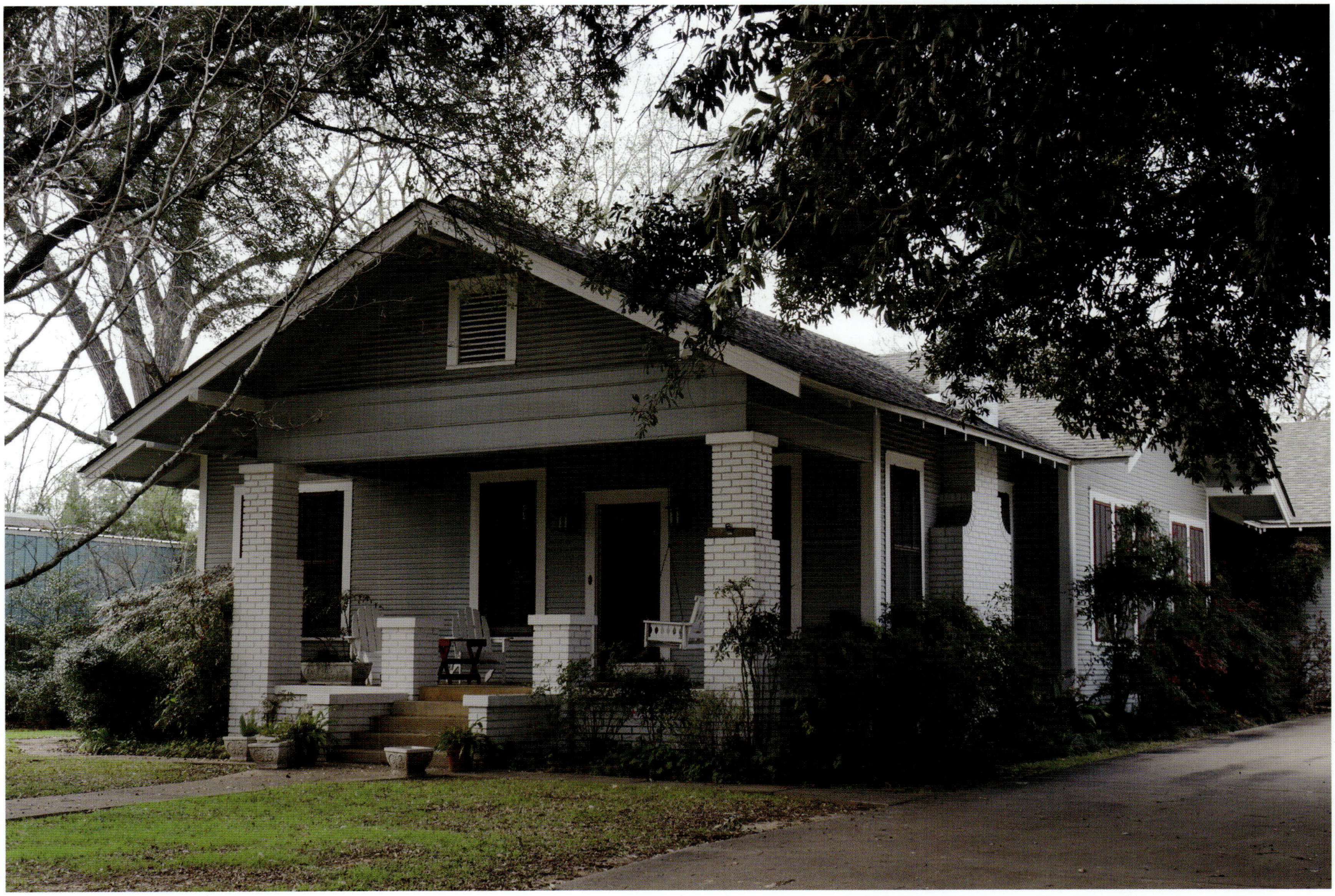

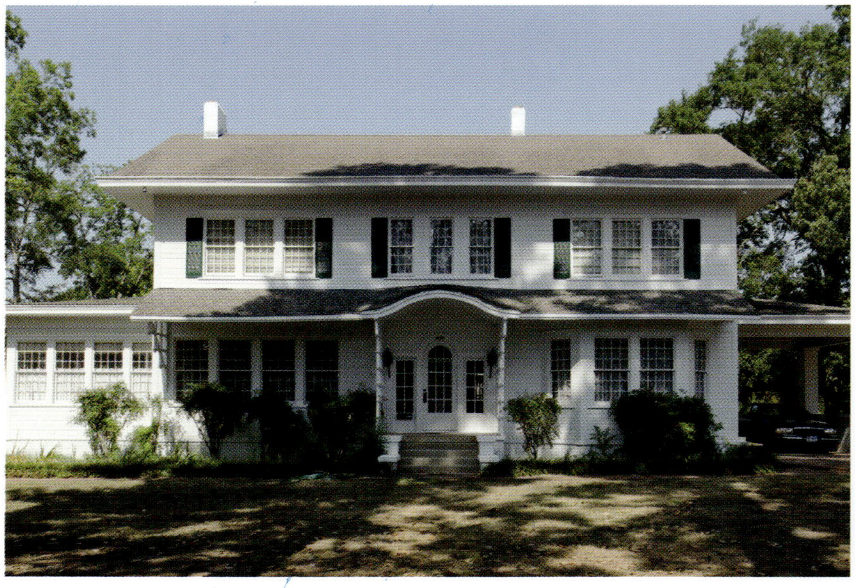

FIGURE 12.31. The Sharp House on Mound Street, 2011.

The Frank and Mamie Sharp House (1923)

A half block from the Hall-Birdwell House at the north end of Mound Street was the homestead of Anna Mary and Benjamin Franklin Sharp. Frank Sharp (1877-1930)[62] first worked as a clerk and secretary to E. A. Blount at the Commercial Bank, and later continued as an officer in the bank under the leadership of his brother-in-law Eugene H. Blount. When Frank married Mamie Shindler in 1902, he inherited a strong family loyalty to D. Rulfs. The architect, a close friend of the R. C. Shindler family, built many houses for them. No picture of the first house Rulfs did for the Sharps (ca. 1909) has surfaced; the Sanborn Maps did not include the area until 1929. Both the 1910 and 1920 Censuses, however, show the Sharps living on this corner.[63] The emphasis must focus, therefore, on the house Rulfs remodeled for the family in 1923, the one that currently stands on the same property at 1417 North Mound.[64]

The 1920 Census indicates that Mamie's brother, Herbert Shindler, was living with the Sharps; they also had a new baby, Lucette, born in January of that year, and a servant living there, too.[65] Their living accommodations needed updating and reordering. No doubt the Sharps were impressed by the remodeling Rulfs had done across the street for the Birdwells. More likely, however, the Sharps were influenced by the grand opus that the architect was planning for Mamie's sister, Rosine, and Eugene Blount on North Street. Whatever the reason, Rulfs suggested that the older Sharp house be split into two parts and pulled closer to Mound Street.

The remodeled Sharp House, later known to many as the Dr. Stephen B. Tucker House, has many of the same features Rulfs used on the Birdwell House: the ribbon windows, the pent-roof insets on the gables, and a sun room. The Sharp House, however, was much larger than the Hall-Birdwell structure. The defining feature of the remodeling was the addition of the new pent roof, injected between the two floors on the main façade, and the inclusion of a Palladian-inspired entrance. The large overhang introduced

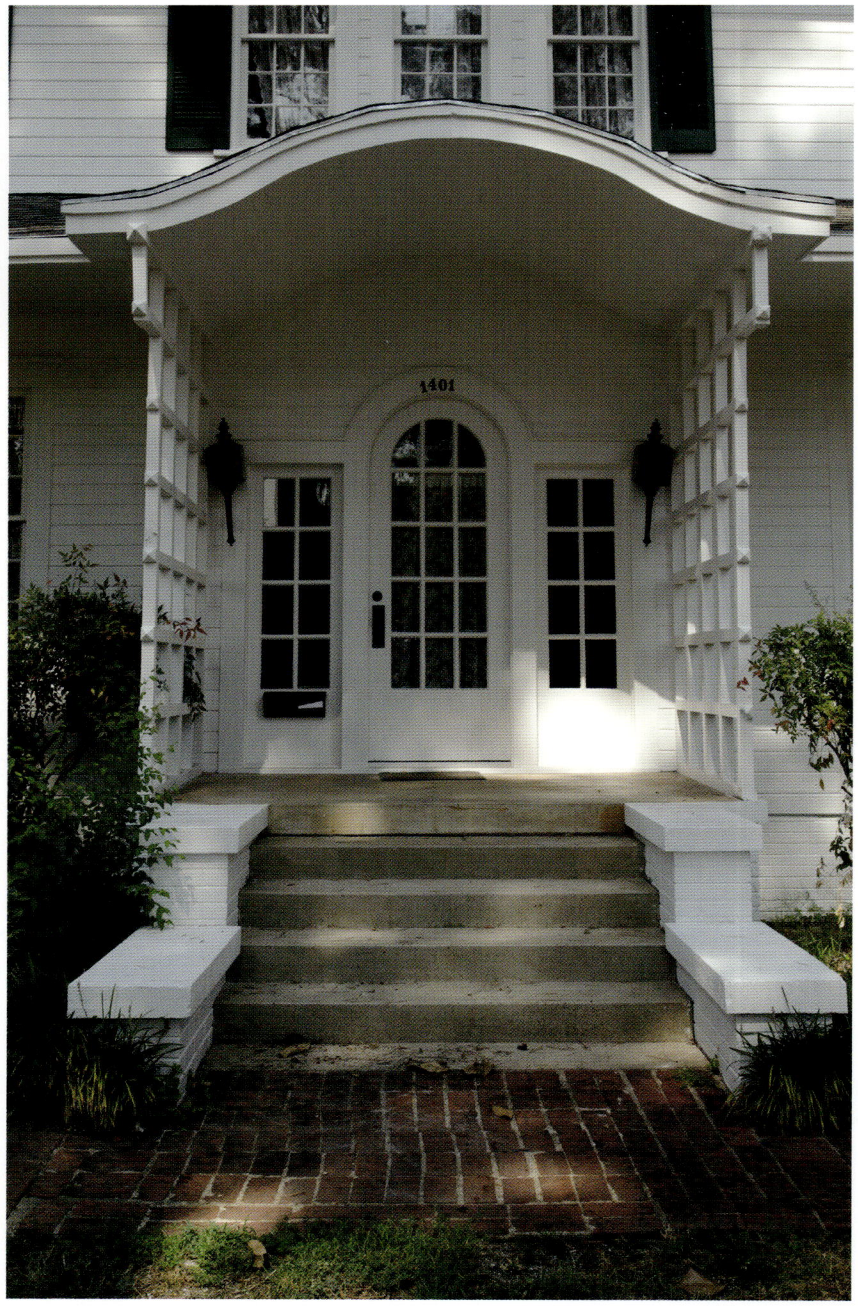

FIGURE 12.32. The Palladian Front Door.

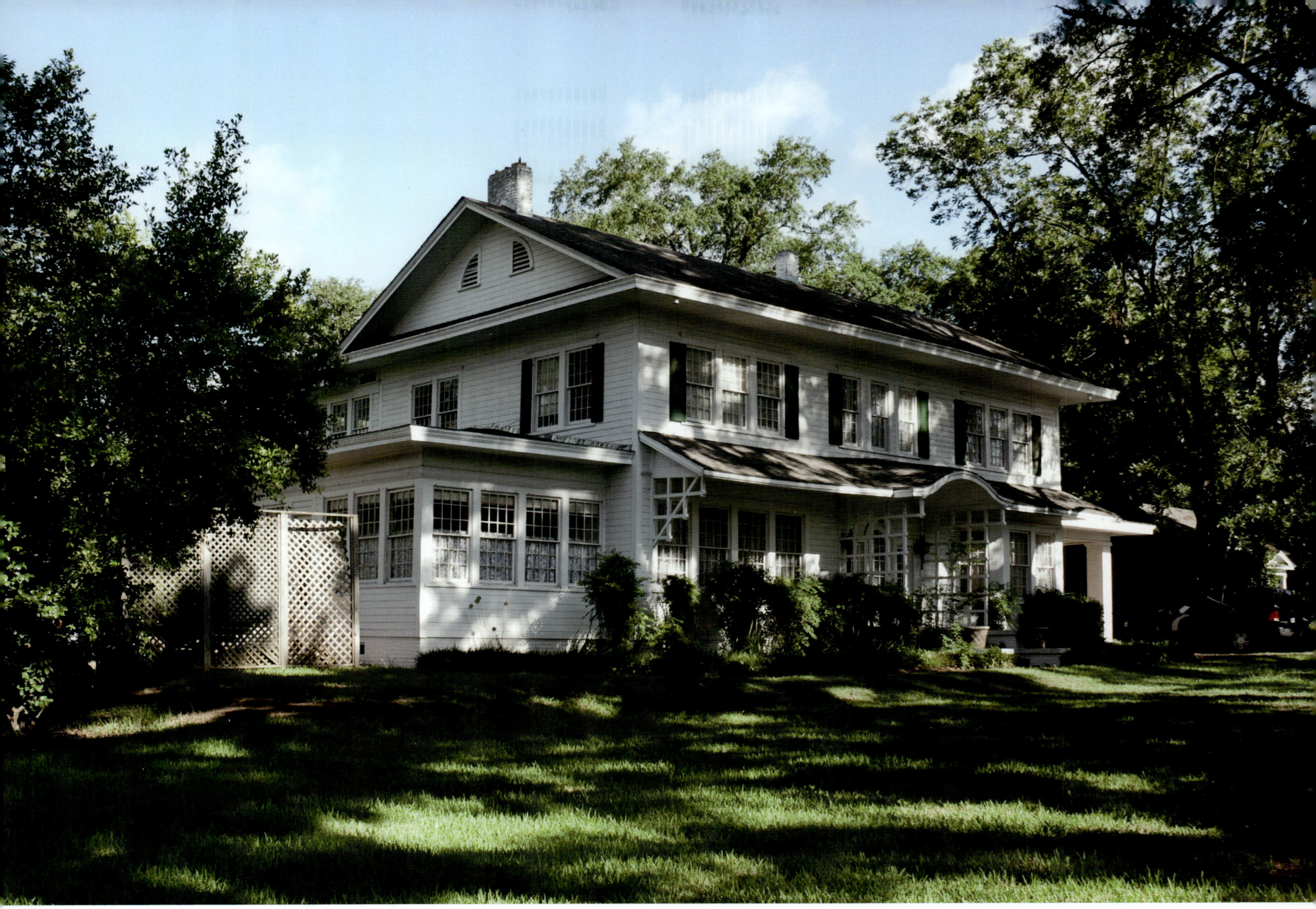

FIGURE 12.33. The Sharp-Tucker-Hutchison House on Mound Street.

on the main roof and the pent roof offered more protection for the windows and siding below. Rulfs placed a carport on the north side. When he moved the house forward, the architect transformed the L-shaped extension of the original house into a separate cottage for Mrs. Sharp's brother. By placing the cottage up front rather than further back on the lot, Rulfs offered an attractive alternative that was to work in subsequent family transitions. As the Hall-Birdwell and the Sharp Houses demonstrate, Rulfs maintained his genius for creative remodeling to the very end of his career.

Dr. Stephen B. Tucker (1897-1977) came into the Sharp family in 1928 when he married Rosine Sharp. He had just returned to Nacogdoches to start his practice. In 1925, he and his father, along with his brother, Henry, and his cousin Fred T. Tucker, established the Tucker Clinic.[66] Stephen and Rosine at first lived on Walker Avenue,[67] but sometime after the death of Frank Sharp in 1930, the couple and their three children moved into the big house on Mound Street with Mamie Sharp. Two years after Rosine died, Dr. Stephen married her younger sister Lucille; Lucille had one child by her first marriage to Fred T. Tucker, Stephen's cousin. According to a relative, at the time Lucille and her young son, Fred, moved into the Sharp House, grandmother Mamie and her youngest daughter, Lucette, who had never married, moved to the side-front cottage.[68] In 1943, Mamie Sharp sold the homestead to Lucille and Stephen Tucker, who lived there until their deaths.[69] After a brief ownership by the Mast family, the Sharp House returned to the original family. In 2004, The Honorable Kay Bailey Hutchison, United States senator from Texas, purchased her mother's childhood home and is the current owner.[70] The senator is the granddaughter of Frank and Mamie Sharp and the daughter of Ella Kathryn Sharp (1912-1998).[71]

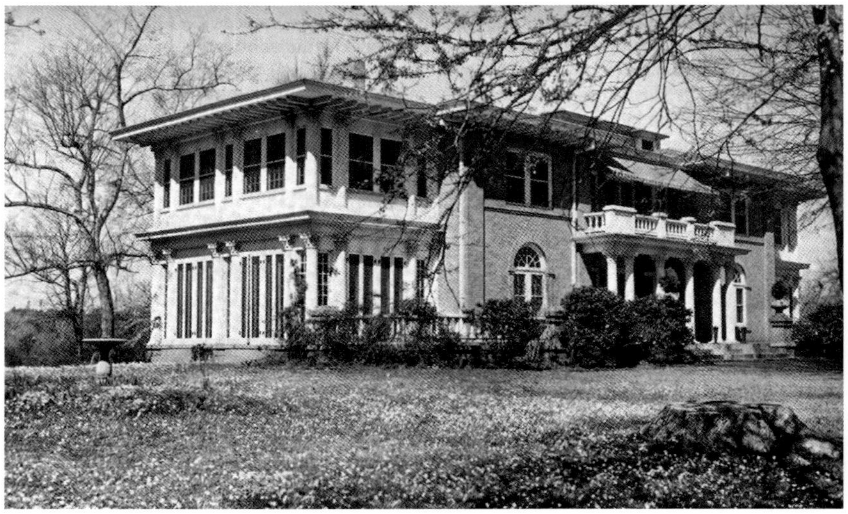

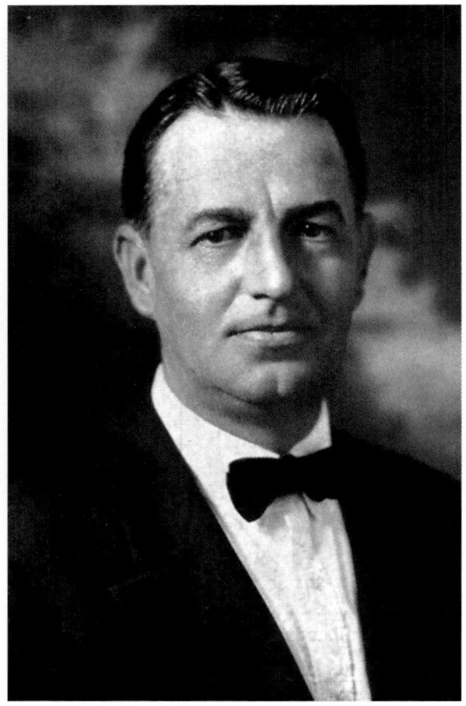

FIGURE 12.34. (Far Left) The E. H. Blount House, ca. 1925.
Photograph compliments of Edward (Jerry) Baker.

FIGURE 12.35. (Left) Texas Senator Eugene Harmon Blount.
In 1923, when this picture was taken, Blount was the President of Commercial National Bank. Blount played an important role in securing Stephen F. Austin State Teachers College for Nacogdoches. Photograph compliments of Edward B. (Jerry) Baker.

The Rosine and Eugene H. Blount House (1923)

The Eugene H. Blount House at 1801 North Street is one of the finest houses ever built in Nacogdoches. It was the last major house designed by Diedrich Rulfs. Both Blount and Rulfs were cognizant of the potential historical importance of this new house. Eugene Blount—a state senator, president of Commercial Bank, and a major force in securing the placement of the college in Nacogdoches—induced Rulfs out of semi-retirement to design the new landmark. Although Rulfs had worked with the Blount family on many projects, Rulfs knew that Senator Blount was offering him one last chance to set his mark in the town. The site was important: the homestead of one of the town's most illustrious citizens, Thomas J. Rusk. Two of Blount's ancestors had signed the Texas Declaration of Independence at the same time as Rusk. More importantly for the future, the site was directly across North Street from the entrance to the new Stephen F. Austin State Teachers College campus–the new centerpiece of modern Nacogdoches. Blount hoped that the house would attract other great houses to the area, but in the long run this did not happen. Blount himself died only four years after the house's construction. While the house did reign for some years as a symbol of the town's prosperity after 1917 and encouraged the Sturdevants and the Bakers to build nearby in the late 1920s, the Depression and the dynamics created by SFA's growth into a university in the 1960s, isolated the Blount House and destroyed the grandeur of the street on which it stood.

The background of the Eugene Blount House reads like a partial review of the career of D. Rulfs. Both Rosine and Eugene were heirs to families who had trusted Rulfs with their architectural needs for decades going back to the 1880s. Rosine's father and Eugene's father had each used Rulfs to design their homes and commercial establishments.[72]

Carolyn Ericson, writing in *Nacogdoches County Families,* gives the basic details of Eugene Blount's life and career. Born in San Augustine and educated through primary school there, Blount received his secondary education in Nacogdoches and his undergraduate work at Sewanee, University of the South. Following his graduation, Blount "traveled abroad extensively before returning to Texas to join the staff of the Commercial National Bank when he was twenty-three years of age." He became President of Commercial Bank when his father died in 1914. He served in the 37th and 38th Texas Legislatures.[73] In a very insightful portrait of Eugene Blount, Martha Turner has written: "Sometimes Nature in a rare mood invests a single person with her richest gifts–distinguished heritage, exemplary leadership, brilliant intellect, unmatched eloquence. Eugene H. Blount–financier, statesman, philanthropist, and orator–was such a person. He was also a singularly handsome man who comported himself with an imperial air that set him apart from his contemporaries without being in the least offensive."[74]

In writing about hte Blount House, the National Registry nomination states:

> The setting helps evoke a sense of grandeur to the building. The principal facade, which faces east, consists of a 5-part plan dominated by a recessed central section or bay where a one-story porch with balcony is located. Corinthian columns support the porch. The projecting sections on the front (which frame the recessed bay) are of brick and have round arched first-floor windows. The windows on the second floor are paired and have 12/12 lights. The outer sections are of frame construction and have vertical wood siding. Pilasters with Corinthian capitals provide visual interest. The symmetry and architectural details suggest a Colonial Revival (Georgian Revival) style while the horizontal thrust of the building indicates a Prairie School influence.[75]

In the author's opinion, the classification of the house in the last sentence is misleading. The Blount House is of Mediterranean or Italian Renaissance Revival architecture, right down to the compulsory terrace overlooking, in this case, the entrance to Stephen F. Austin State Teachers College instead of a sea, lake, or terraced vista. The style of the house reflects Blount's affinity for things formal and his extensive visit to the northern Alpine lakes in Italy and along the Riviera. Rulfs also had a weakness for elements of Italian Renaissance architecture as evidenced by his extensive use of Palladian motifs all over Nacogdoches. While Rulfs was enamored with the low horizontal emphasis of the Prairie School, as witnessed by his designs since 1910,

The Rosine and Eugene H. Blount House (1923)

his Prairie style houses eschewed the use of so many neo-classical elements. The two prominent arched windows, centered on the slightly projected walls flanking the main entrance, are identical to the upper single window treatment used by Rulfs on the Hall-Birdwell makeover the year before. Rulfs saw these windows used frequently in Oldenburg where he studied.[76] The side porch extensions, although multiplied and placed on both levels at the ends of the house, are evolutions from the houses at the end of Mound and Starr Streets. The placement of the house, at the crest of the property, was a tradition employed by Rulfs from the beginning of his career.

The design element which sets this house apart, perhaps even from the architect's own works, is the formal symmetry of this house. While works of the Prairie School or the Arts & Crafts Movement are rarely formal, the works of the Italian Renaissance Revival or Mediterranean houses almost always are. Rulfs normally avoided Corinthian columns, the most elaborate of the ancient orders and the most prohibitive in terms of cost. For this patron, however, money was no object. Since Rulfs limited ornamentation on the exterior of his later houses, Blount's desire to use Corinthian columns probably posed a problem for the architect. He limited the formality of the columns by specifying unfluted shafts. The ornamentation was confined to a profusion of the columns, to large balusters on the terrace and upper balcony, and simple horizontal modillions under the wide roof soffits. The only fully-rounded Corinthian columns stand on the loggia-like front porch. The columns around the various sun-porches or solaria give the impression of being whole, with doors and windows inserted in between; but, in fact, they are paired-pilasters, one on the interior and one on the exterior–a very expensive installation.

The position of the house and its unique architectural features, certainly for provincial Nacogdoches, made the Blount House more imposing than its actual size in square feet might suggest. The houses of the 1890s were much larger. Although nice houses needed a carport, preservation of exterior symmetry dictated the placement of the carport to rear of the house. Blount wanted no modern intrusion like the automobile to spoil his classically balanced façade. No concrete walkway, as was added later, spoiled the esplanade of grass and pine trees leading to the east and its view of the new college entrance. To accommodate cars, Blount had Rulfs design a long and graceful brick driveway that entered off North Street, some distance from the house, then unobtrusively formed a brick terrace behind the house, as it connected with the carport-pavilion behind the center of the house, before exiting on to Rusk Street.

The symmetry of the interior is no less remarkable than the exterior. From the 1920s to today, the grand central staircase in the entry instantly became a favorite venue for bridal pictures in Nacogdoches. Because the house was centrally heated from the basement, fireplaces existed only for esthetic reasons. Eugene's daughter, Jean Baker, said they rarely used them. In an amusing twist, she remembered using the one in the south sunroom for roasting marshmallows.[77] The south solarium itself was frequently the venue for refreshments served at the many parties in the formal garden outside. Hostesses, at such times, opened all the fully-functional French doors, each of which had its own set of concrete steps on the exterior.

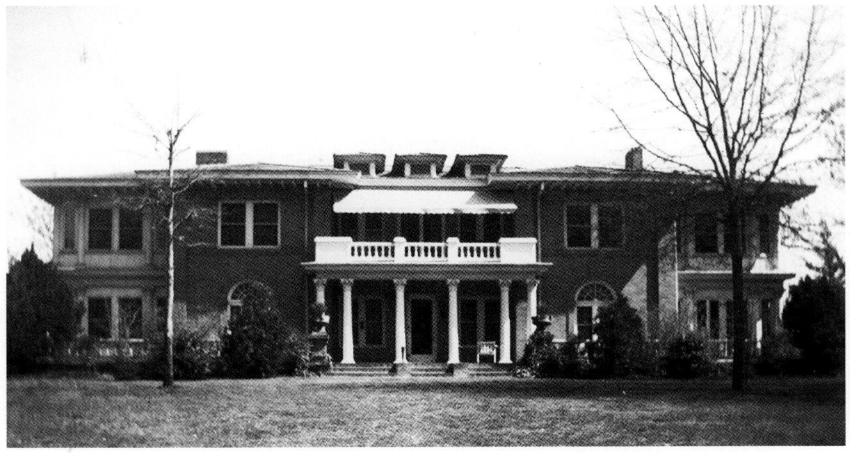

FIGURE 12.36. Front Elevation, 1930s.
Photograph complements of Edward B. (Jerry) Baker.

Eugene Blount, well aware of the importance of the houses in Houston around Rice Institute and in Dallas close to Southern Methodist University, planned to duplicate this ambience around the new Teachers College, but he did not live to see this. (In fact, it never happened.) Blount's choice of North Street led directly to the building of residences by Thomas E. Baker and Ira Link Sturdevant to the south, but the 1920s signaled the high point of the residential construction on North Street. Blount's personal career reached a peak in 1925-1926. As the very successful chairman of the appropriations committee in the Thirty-Ninth Legislature, he shattered a sixty-year-old precedent when he succeeded in getting his appropriations bills through the regular session of the Legislature. Blount's death in 1927 ended an exceptional career.[78] At the time, he was the most prominent banker in East Texas, president of the Commercial National Bank, the Commercial State Bank of San Augustine, and the Chireno State Bank. He was also a considerable philanthropist. A popular man throughout the state and a noted speaker, he had addressed an audience of 50,000 at the annual celebration of the San Jacinto battleground monument. It was entitled "San Jacinto's Place in History," and it was reprinted in school textbooks for years as a classic review of the importance of the famous battle.[79]

This Blount House continued in the family until Rosine died in 1959. For some years, in the 1970s, the house served as the home of Christ the Redeemer Lutheran Church. In 1980, the Nacogdoches County Historical Trust purchased the property and leased the building to the Nacogdoches Chamber of Commerce (1980-1997). Since 1998, the law firm of Fairchild, Price, Haley, & Thomas has owned the property and utilized the house for its legal offices.[80]

FIGURE 12.37. (Overleaf) Front Elevation, Eugene H. Blount House, 2012.

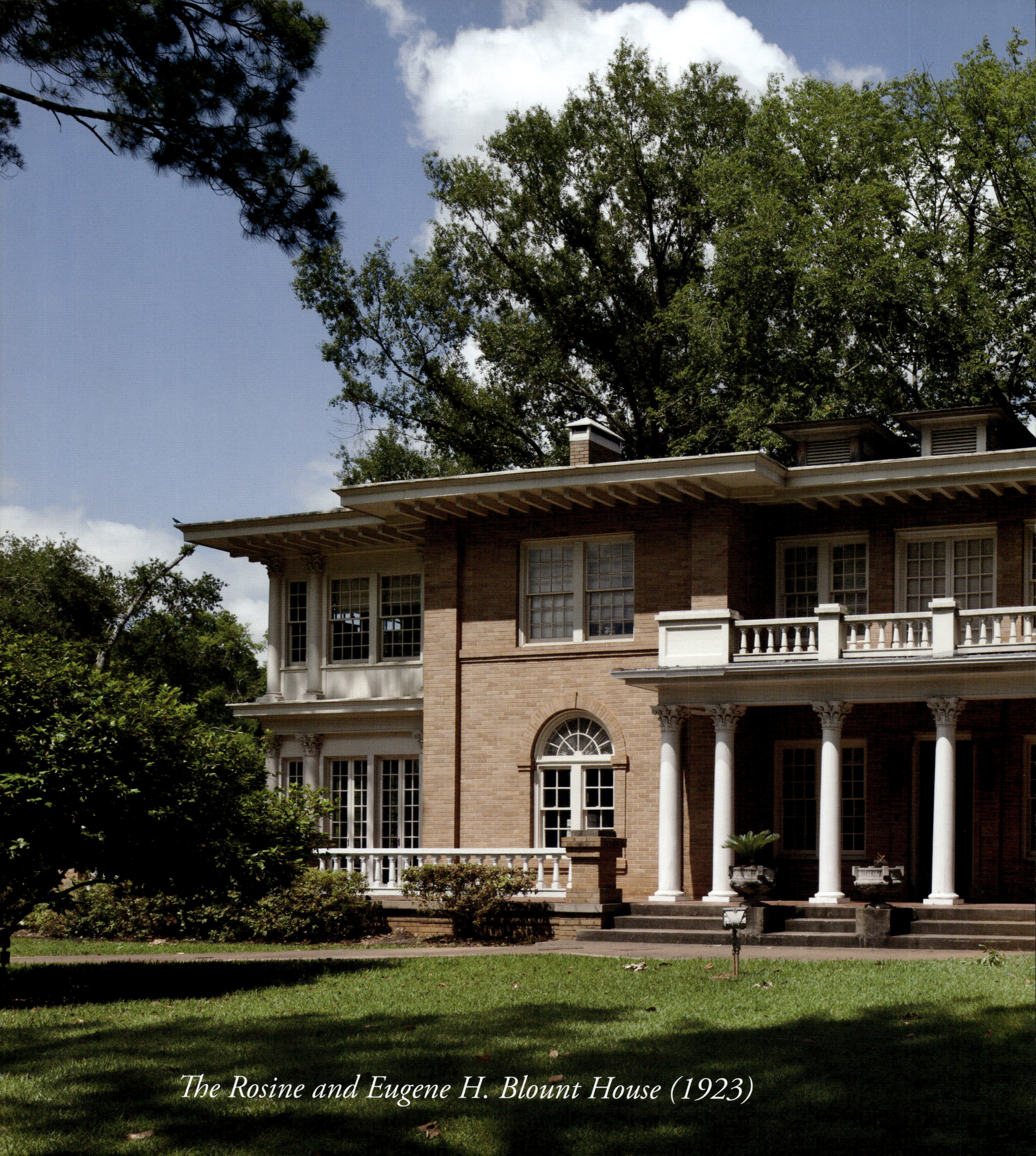

The Rosine and Eugene H. Blount House (1923)

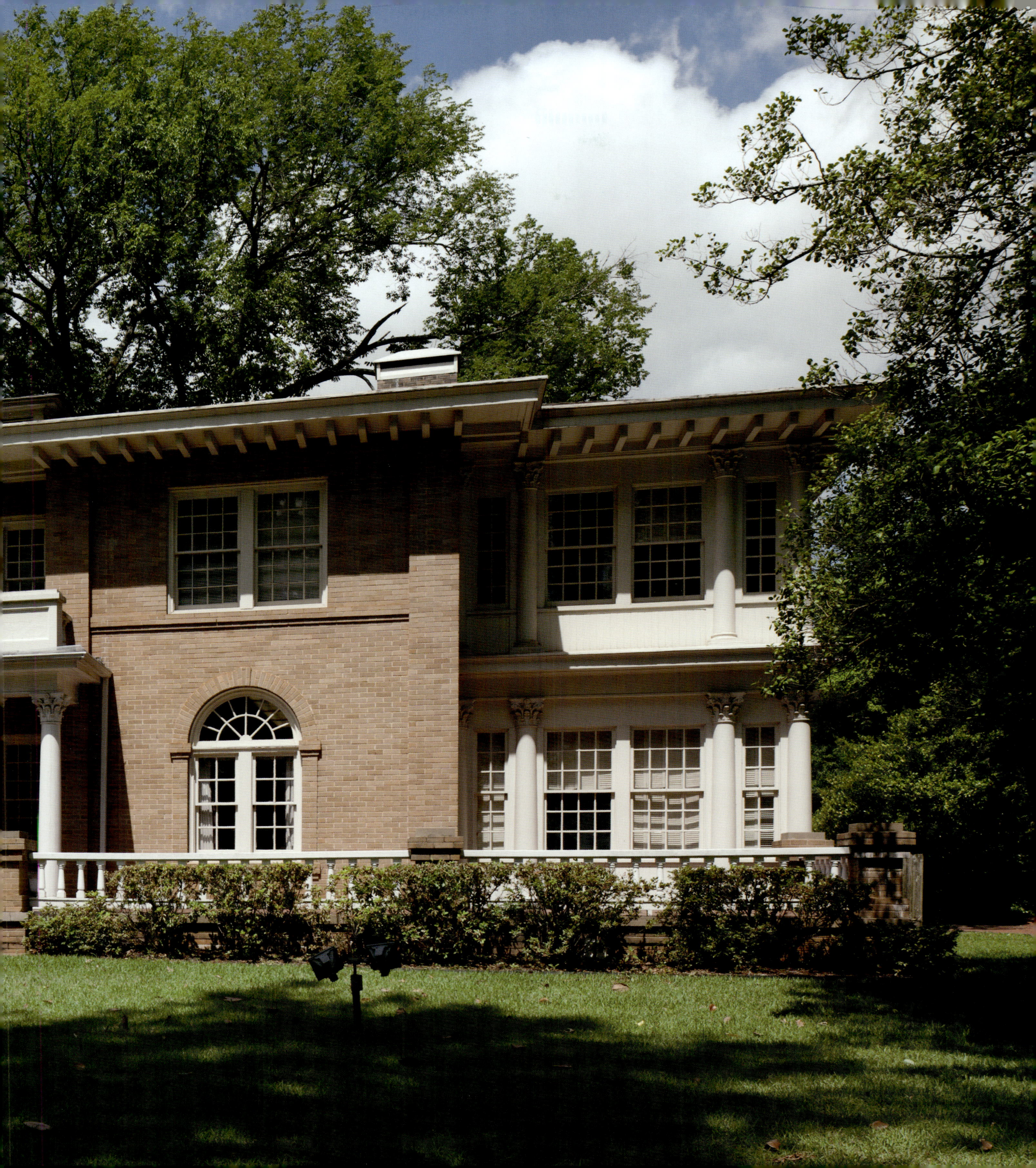

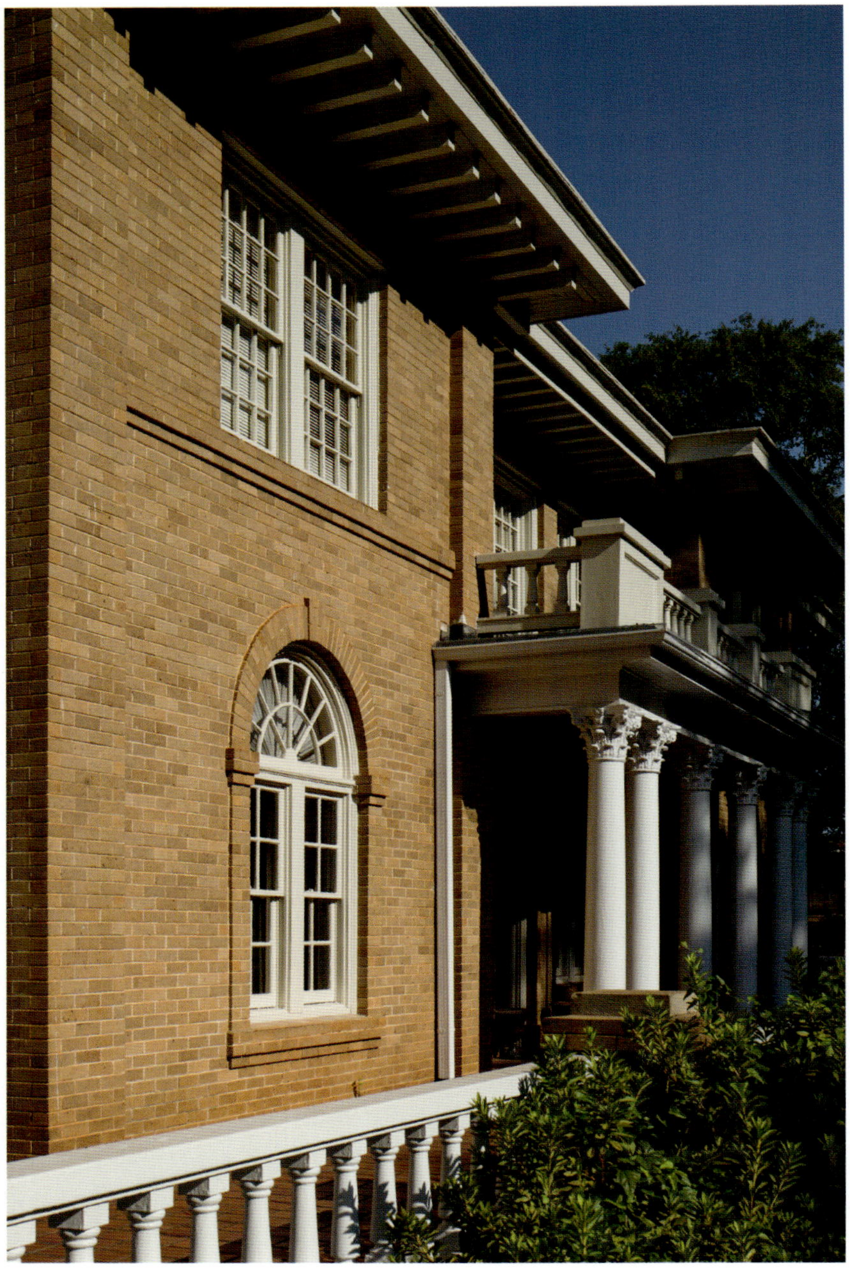

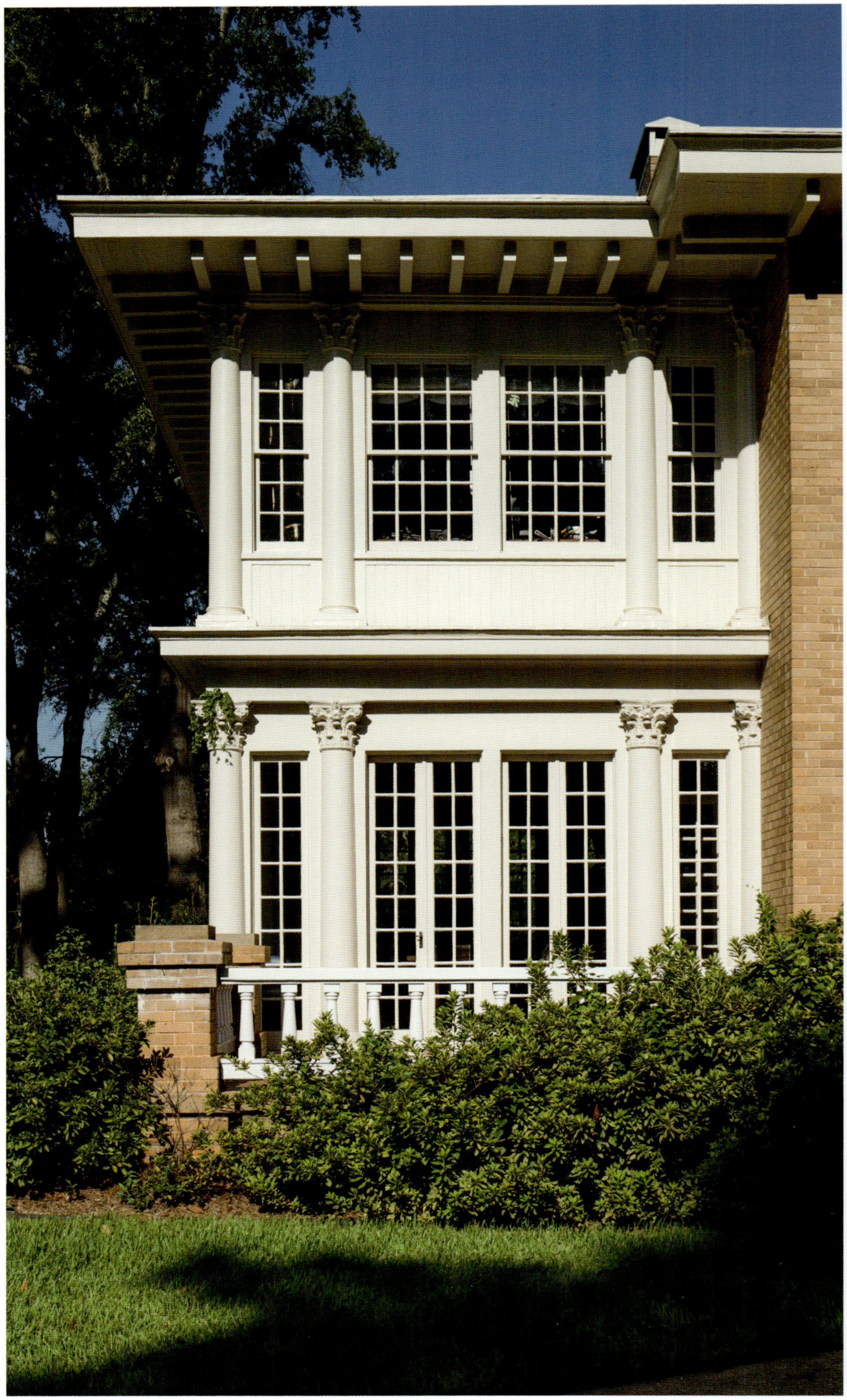

FIGURE 12.38. Details, Front Façade and Terrace overlooking SFA.

FIGURE 12.39 Double Porches.

Blount wanted a very formal and symmetrical façade. Rulfs placed double solariia on both ends of the house. These solariums with their Corinthian pilasters were truly elegant. Three of these rooms were glass-enclosed with windows. The dictates of the exterior necessitated the oddity of a window in a closet on the north side of the house.

Only the southern solarium had doors to make it a true porch. It had a series of French doors around the room on three sides, each set with its own steps to the garden or the front terrace. The southern solarium also had a fireplace, which foreshadows the external fireplaces popular at the present time.

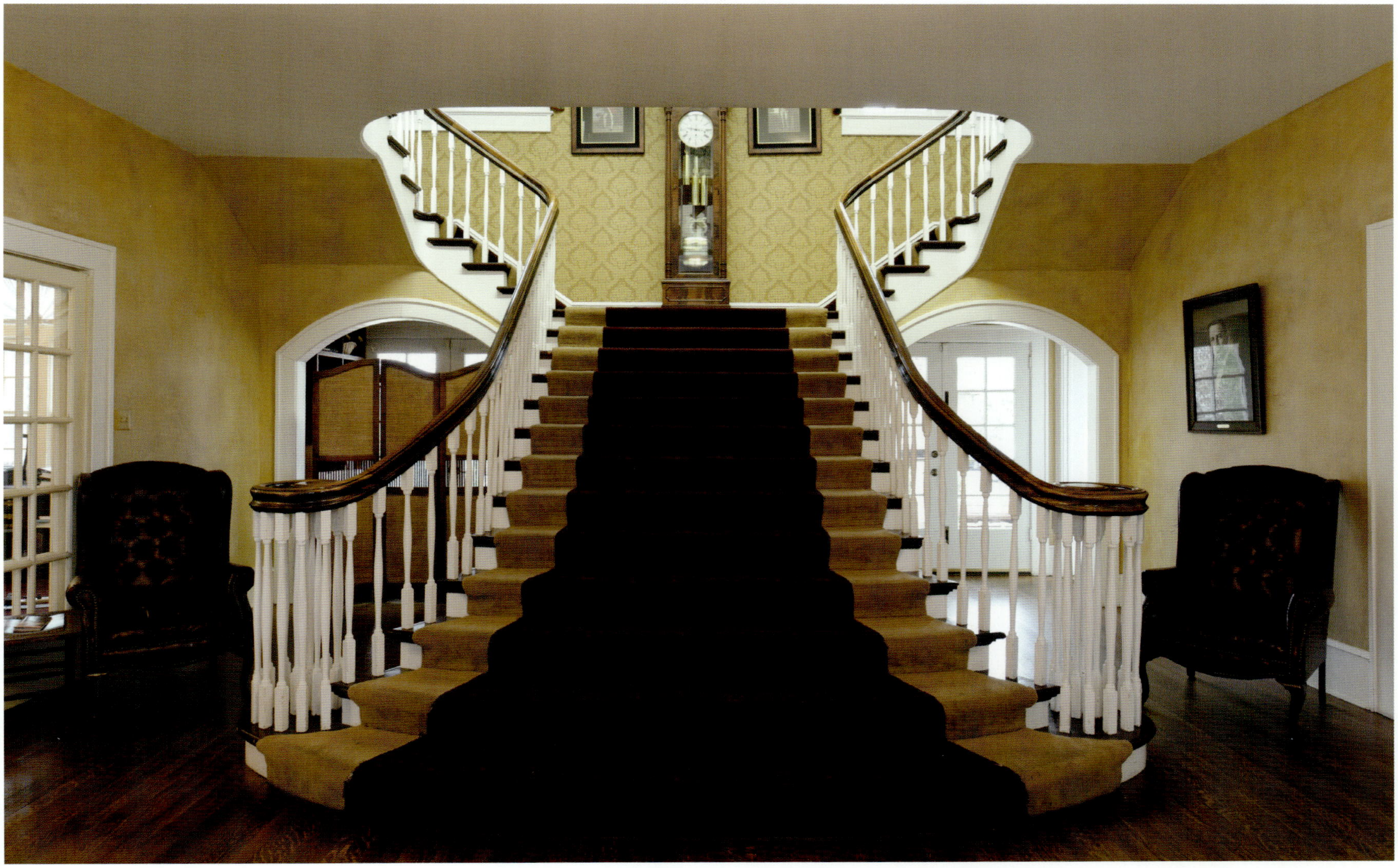

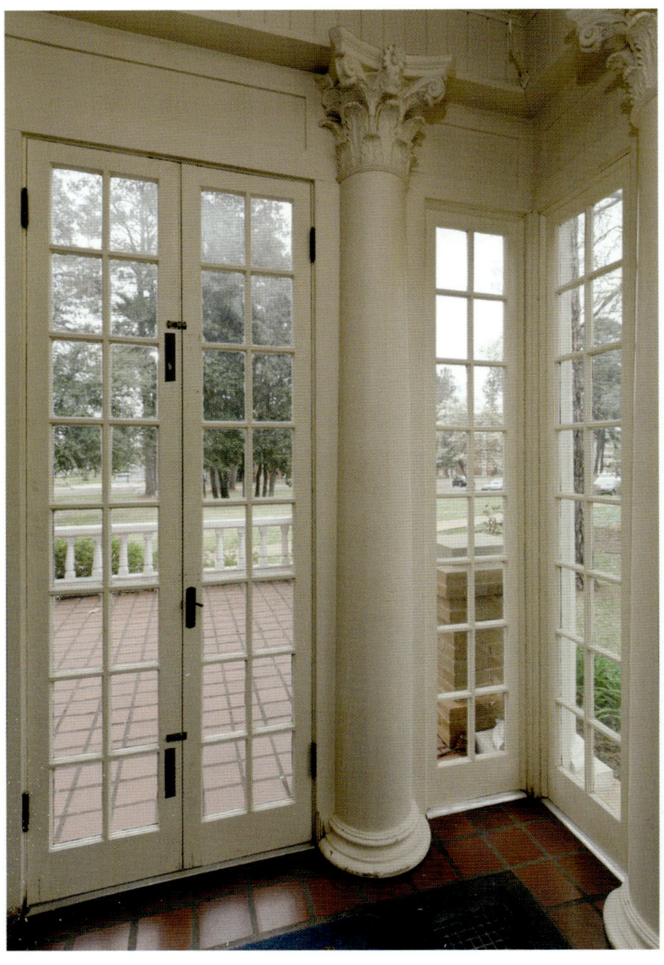

FIGURE 12.40. The Grand Staircase.

The entrance hall consumes the whole center of the house, with access from the front and the rear of the house.

FIGURE 12.41-12.42. (Left and Below) The Southern Solarium.

The southern enclosed porch was one of the most important rooms in the house. Most of the windows were working doors, which opened onto the front terrace and to the formal garden to the south.

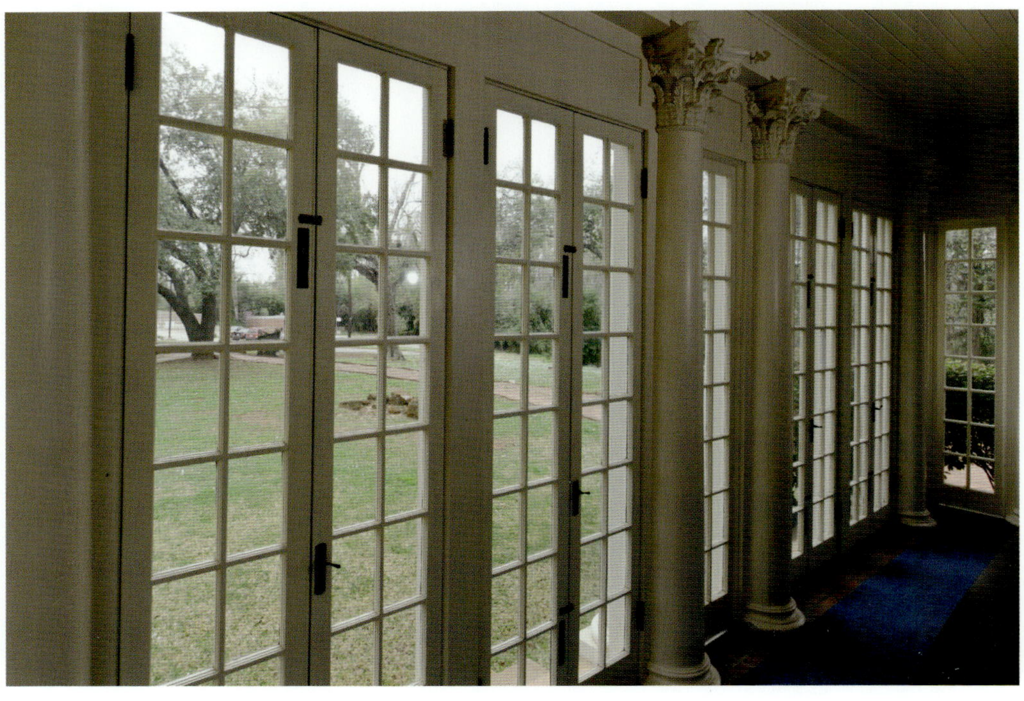

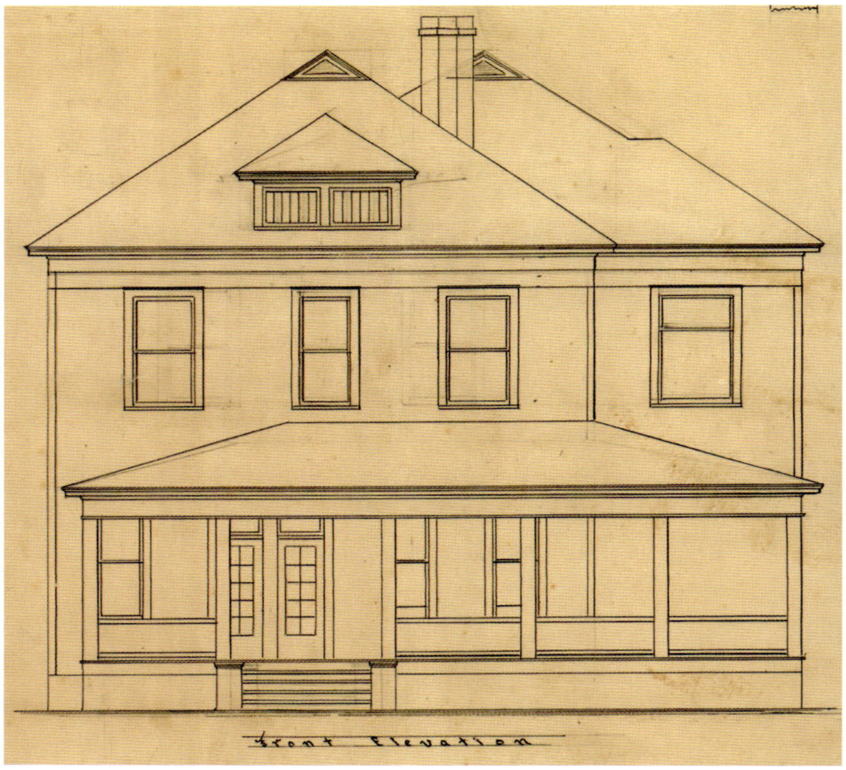

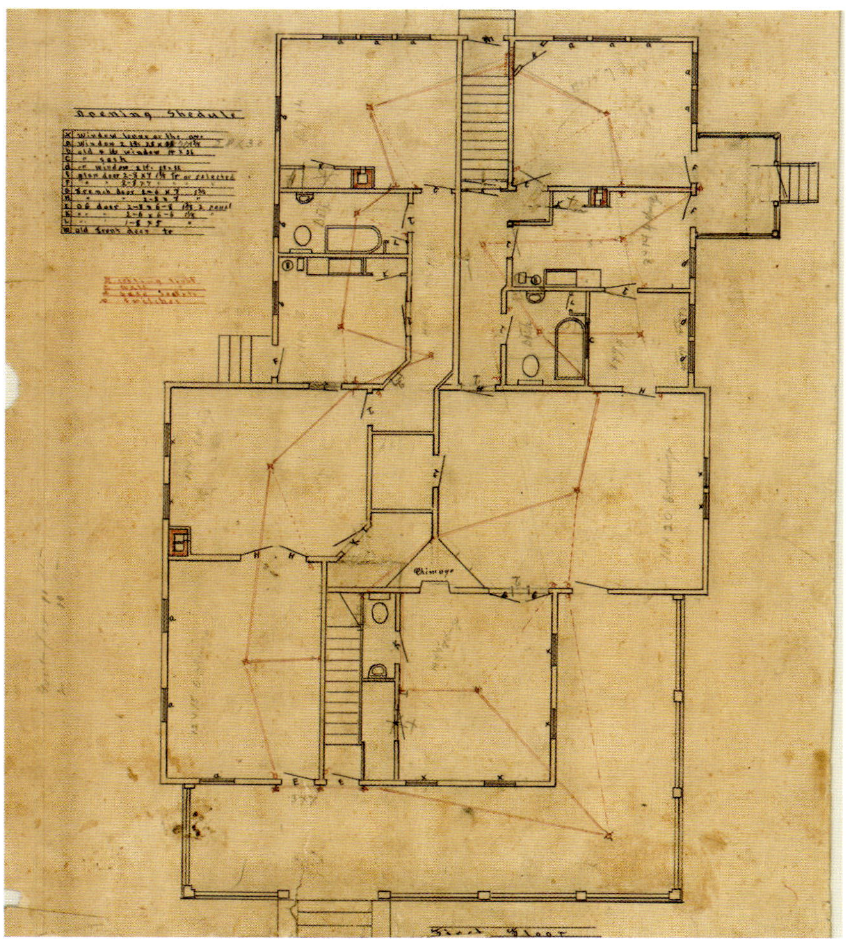

FIGURES 12.43. and 12.44 Drawings by D. Rulfs for the W. F. Price House on Mound Street, 1925.

(Above) Front elevation. (Below) The Plan for the First Floor.

Missouri Price saved the complete plans by Rulfs in her papers, which are now in the East Texas Research Center at the Steen Library on the Stephen F. Austin State University campus. Courtesy of the ETRC.

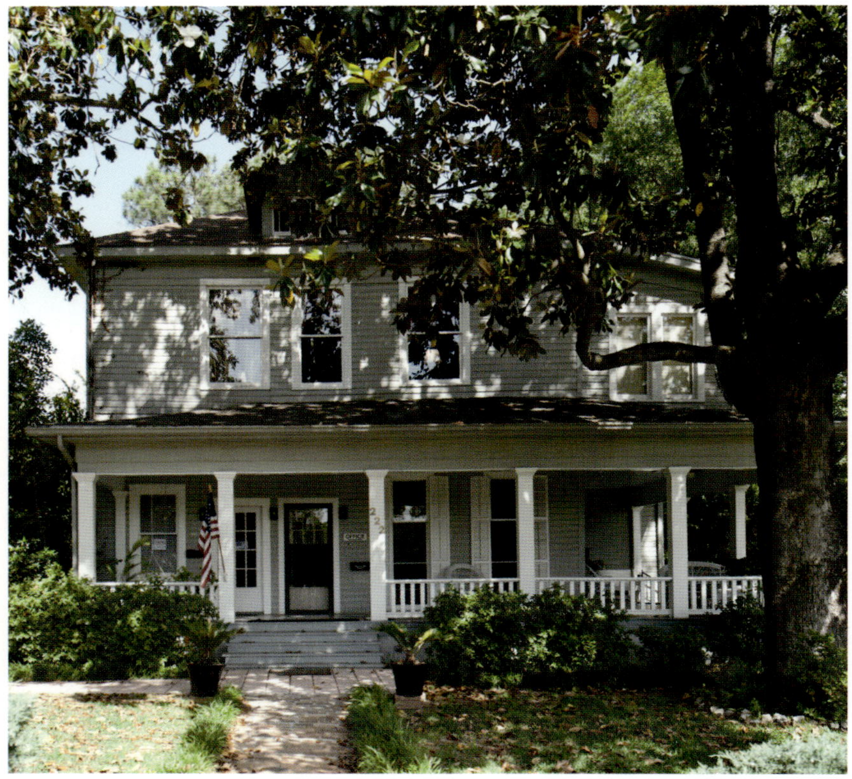

FIGURE 12.45. Front Elevation of the Price House, 2012.

The W. F. and Missouri Price House, Phase II (1925)

The house at 222 North Mound Street, designed and built by D. Rulfs for John Schmidt's nephew, appeared in Chapter V of this book. From 1896 onward, the house belonged to W. F. and Missouri Price.[81] The house maintained its consistent footprint on the Sanborn Maps between 1906 and 1922.[82] On January 17, 1925, a *Daily Sentinel* headline announced, "Price Home Destroyed." Although not as drastic as the headline suggested, the house was severely damaged by fire. The building was saved by the new and powerful pump acquired by the Fire Department. According to the newspaper, "Most of the roof was burned off and a part of the inside walls damaged, the whole house being pretty badly wrecked. Mr. Price carried insurance of $1000 on the building, a ten-room, two story structure and $1000 on the furnishings. These sums will not nearly cover the damages to the properties they were designed to protect, it was stated." Citing that he had "one of the most desirable locations in the city and no other place would feel like 'home,'" Price pledged that he would reconstruct the house immediately, with the hope of having it completed "within six weeks to two months."[83]

Although D. Rulfs was, for all practical purposes, retired, Price wanted the original architect to restore the house. Whether from a deep sense of responsibility to sustain and remodel his earlier works or because Price was a fellow fraternal brother in the Knights of Pythias, the aging Rulfs immediately took up the challenge. It was to be his last domestic design, fittingly a redesign of one of his earlier houses.[84]

Rulfs retained as many features of the original structure a possible. The mixture of sidings tells part of the story. He simplified the design of

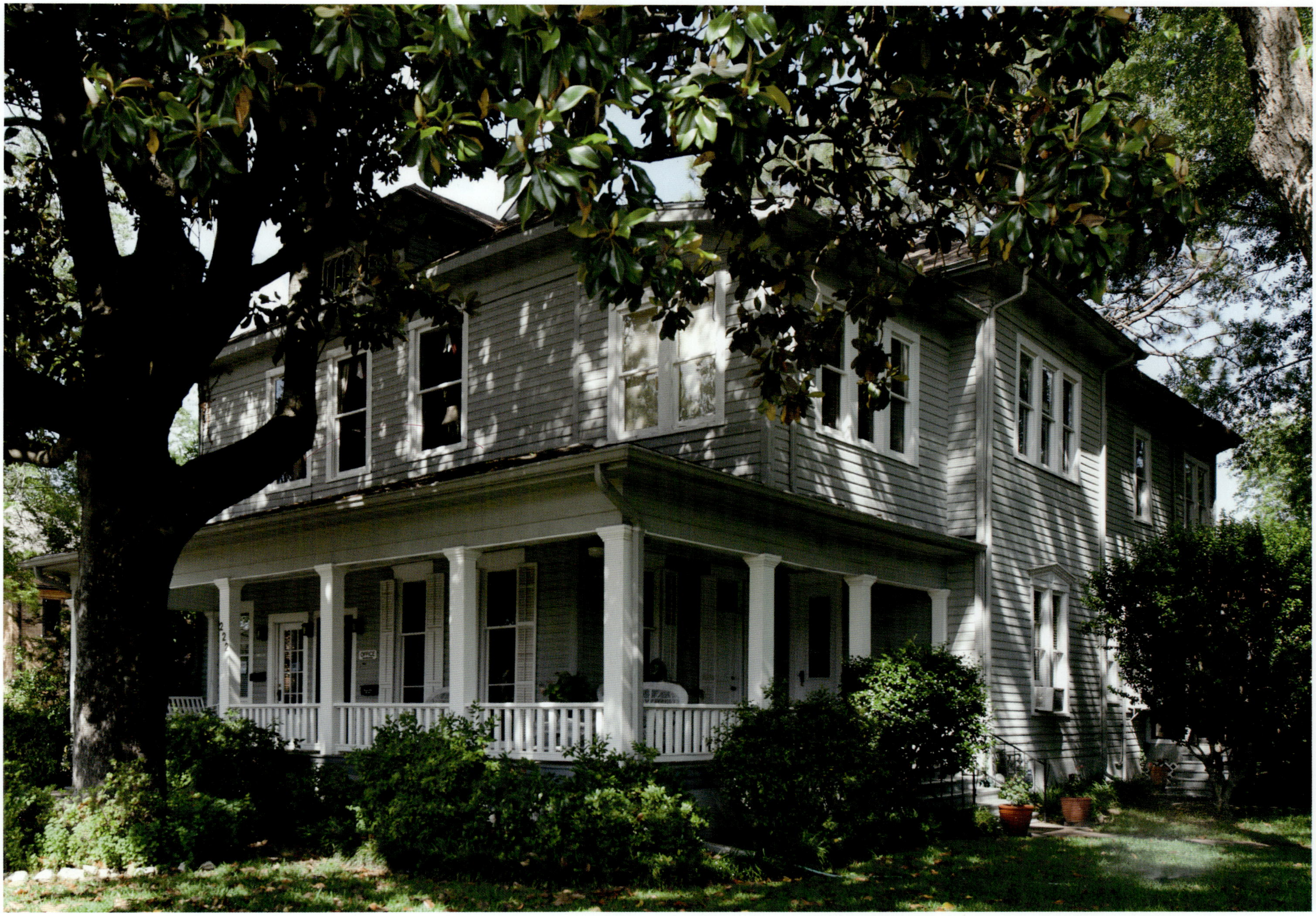

FIGURE 12.46. The Home of Milton Pitts, 2012.

The room over the south portion of the front porch was added later. Rulfs used the same columns and balustrades on the remodeled house as used on the Summers and Richardson Houses nearby.

the front porch (straight boxed columns with square balusters and simple handrails) similar to the other houses in the area, such as the Summers and Richardson Houses. He reconfigured the upper story which was the most damaged by extending the second floor bay to square the south wing, and added a second story on the L-shaped rear section of the house. Because the Prices by that time rented out many of the rooms and the upper floor of the building, Rulfs made an unusual accommodation by placing two doors together at the front entry. The drawings by Rulfs, featured on these pages, can be seen in the East Texas Research Center at the SFA Steen Library.[85]

The Price House is now owned by Milton Pitts, who enjoys the central location, which so pleased Mr. Price in 1925. The upstairs is still leased as rental property as it was when Rulfs remodeled the house in 1925.[86]

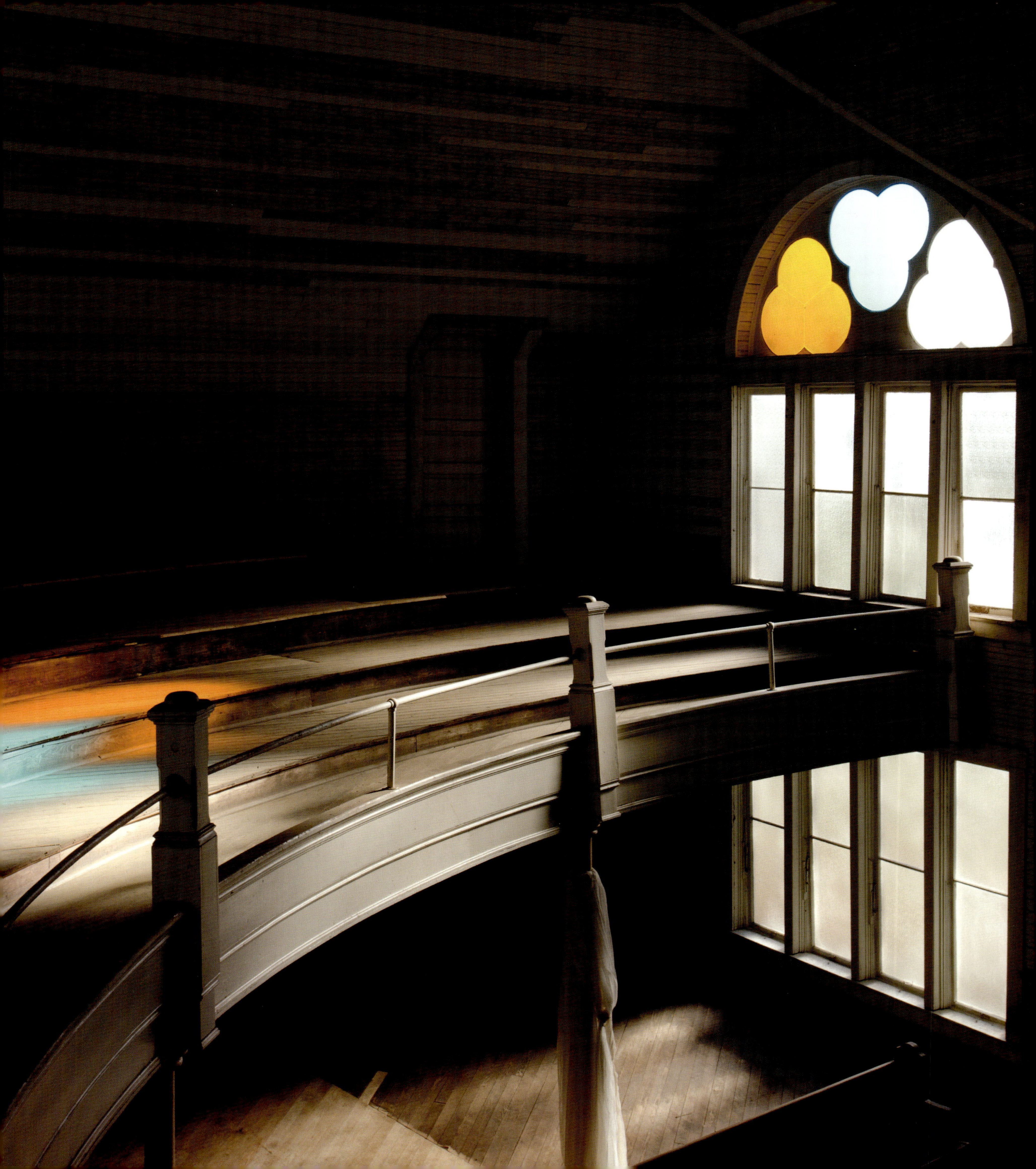

REFLECTIONS

The Rulfs Legacy

D. A. W. Rulfs Dies in 1926

"Nacogdoches holds the memory of a pioneer citizen in high honor, one who always worked for the best, for the town and stood for the right. One of the largest concourses of recent years was gathered at the grave, and the floral offerings from many cities were magnificent." Obituary, *San Augustine Tribune*, February 25, 1926.

"The present is the flowering of the plantings of the past....Our studies of the past, therefore, with its great leaders, its conflicting ideals, its organizing ideas, have resulted in pride of achievement, and let us hope, in new and clearer visions and purposes." *A. W. Birdwell, President of SFASTC – 1936.*

The Death of Diedrich Anton Wilhelm Rulfs

By the end of 1925, Diedrich Rulfs was in poor health. To secure needed assistance, the architect moved to the home of his daughter Mary Rulfs Neyland, in Shreveport, Louisiana.[1] A few months later, at eleven o'clock A.M. on February 15, 1926, Rulfs died, just short of his seventy-eighth birthday.[2] The front page of the *Daily Sentinel* reported, "FUNERAL FOR D. RULFS WILL BE HELD HERE ON TUESDAY." The newspaper article said his remains would arrive by train, and the funeral would be conducted from his home on East Main Street. "Mr. Rulfs was well known in this city, having lived here for a number of years, and being associated in the business circles of the city, had made hundreds of friends. He was known for his honest dealings in whatever he undertook, and in his going, Nacogdoches lost a good man, a progressive citizen, and his loved ones lost a kind, tender and affectionate father and friend."[3] In the same edition, a notice immediately went out to the Knights of Pythias for all members of the Lanana Lodge No. 106 to meet "to form for the funeral of Bro. D. Rulfs."[4]

FIGURE 13.1. (Opposite) Interior of Zion Hill Church.

The Reverend George L. Crocket performed the service, and the Pythians took care of the graveside service. The editor of the *Daily Sentinel* paid tribute to D. Rulfs, as did the *San Augustine Tribune*: "A good man, and a good citizen has passed to his reward after a long and useful life. Children and grandchildren revere his name and carry on his work in the world. And Nacogdoches holds the memory of a pioneer citizen in high honor, one who always worked for the best, for the town and stood for the right." The newspaper added: "One of the largest concourses of recent years was gathered at the grave, and the floral offerings from many cities were magnificent."[5]

The contemporaries, who followed Rulfs' casket that day as he was carried from his home to nearby Oak Grove Cemetery, knew what subsequent generations would forget: D. Rulfs designed modern Nacogdoches. The architect rests *sine die* in the historic cemetery, his grave within sight of a *magnum opus,* Zion Hill Baptist Church. Rulfs rests alongside a host of other members of his family and their relatives.[6] Nearby lie the many patrons who respected him as an individual, who commissioned his architectural works, and who collaborated with Rulfs to transform Nacogdoches into a city.

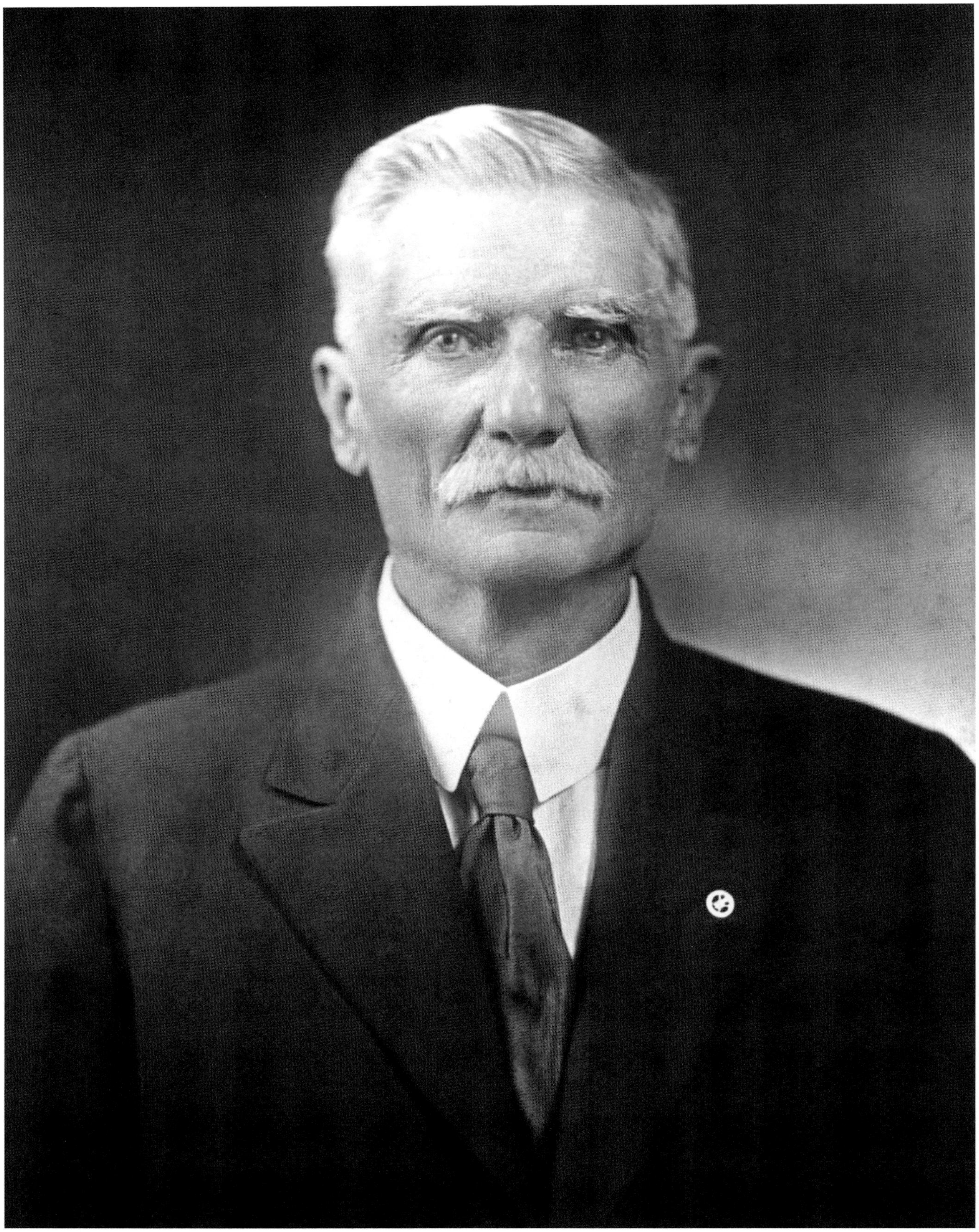

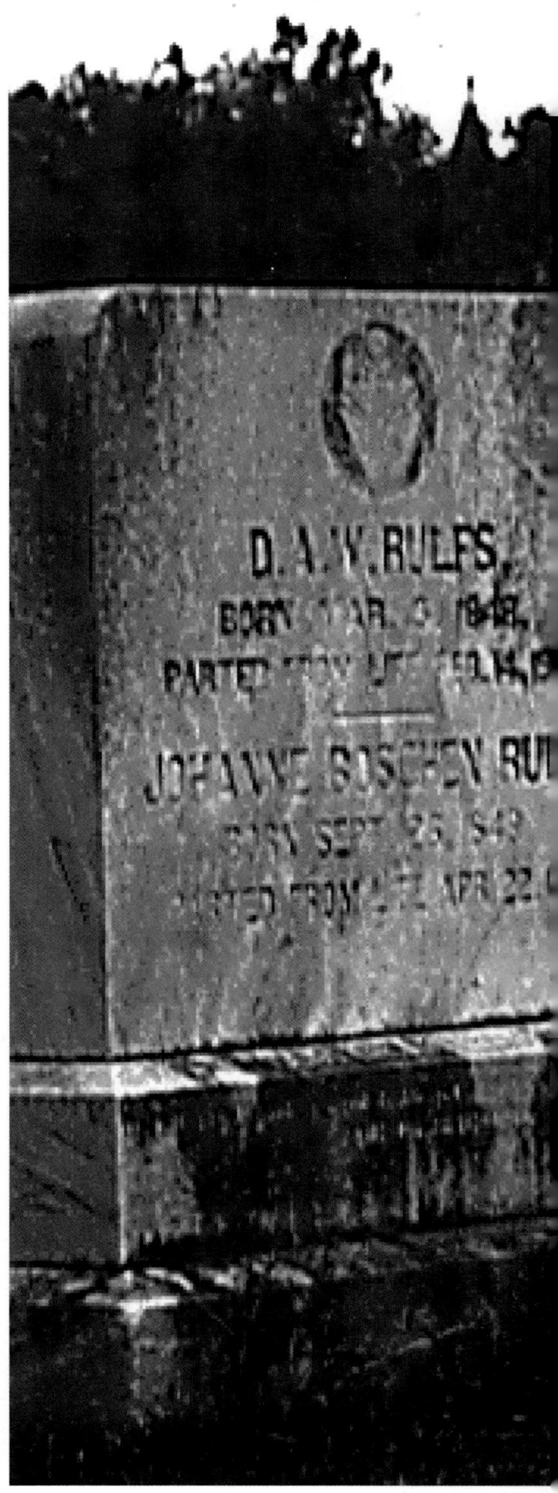

FIGURE 13.2. D. Rulfs, 1918.
Photograph compliments of Anna Kathryn Holbrook.

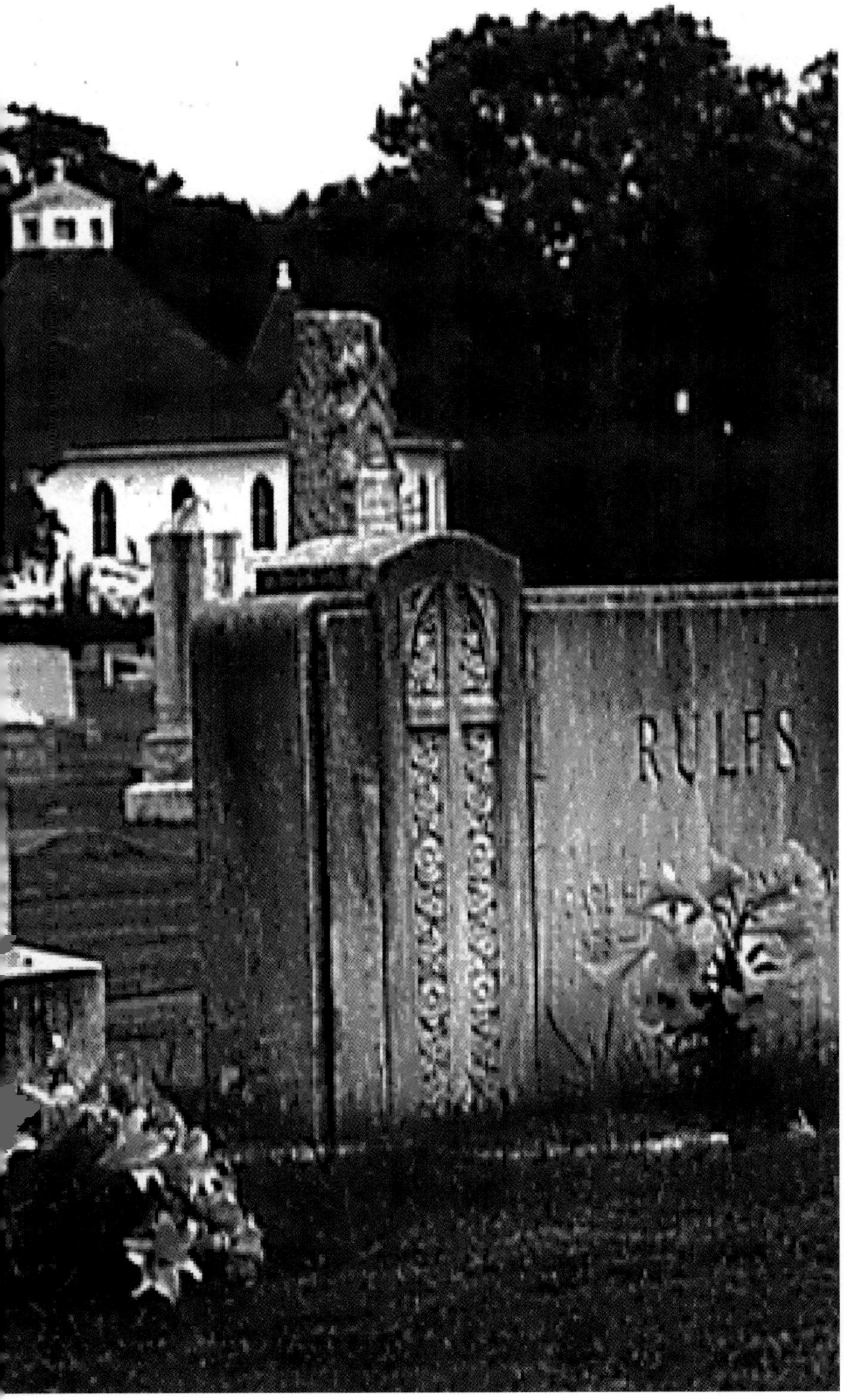

FIGURE 13.3. Grave of D. A. W. Rulfs, and Johanne Böschen Rulfs, Oak Grove Cemetery, and Zion HIll Church.

The headstone of Diedrich Rulfs only has his initials due to the many misspellings through the years. He rests next to his wife and his son Dr. Carl Henry Rulfs. There are more than twenty of his relatives buried nearby. Zion Hill Church, a masterpiece, is in the background. Photograph by the author in the 1970s.

Reflections on Rulfs as an Architect

This book originated from an attempt to correct the lapse in collective memory about the architect who designed modern Nacogdoches, Diedrich Anton Wilhelm Rulfs. As the research progressed, the author slowly came to recognize the book could not be definitive. It simply represents a mere survey. First, Nacogdoches is the only town covered; his work outside Nacogdoches will have to wait for an addendum. Second, comprehension even in Nacogdoches eluded the author; records have vanished, transformations and moves have made buildings unrecognizable, people who could tell the stories have died, and private individuals who may have more information have remained unknown. Third, the paucity of documentation from the architect himself is a primary limiting factor on interpreting the Rulfs legacy. There are no memoirs, no great archive of drawings or sketches, no inventory of letters, no library of resources he might have used. Fortunately, newspapers and public records have provided coverage for many of the gaps, and oral interviews have proved invaluable to help connect the disparate information. Unfortunately, many of the original interviewees were not recorded on tape; without tapes, nuances may have disappeared. The author has, however, supplemented these interviews with re-documentation through other credible sources, such as census, tax records, private archival materials, and recent interviews. The productivity of D. Rulfs and his brother continues to amaze. Some houses, known to be by the Rulfs brothers, are missing in the book because the author could not determine what the newspaper meant when it would comment, 'Rulfs is building another new house on Main Street.' Without pictures, with incomplete coverage by the Sanborn Maps, and confusing deed records, there are few ways to confirm such vague leads.[7]

A note of definition. 'Architecture' and 'architect' are elusive concepts. Vitruvius, the Roman architect and engineer, was the first to define and write on the subject. Reflecting the Roman master, the *Encyclopedia Britannica* defines architecture as "the art and technique of designing and building, as distinguished from the skills associated with construction"; it is "both utilitarian and esthetic"; architecture must be adaptable "to particular human activities"; offer "stability and permanence of the work's construction;" and communicate "experience and ideas through its form."[8]

Diedrich Rulfs, the master architect of modern Nacogdoches, most certainly followed the Vitruvius model by producing buildings that were durable, functional, and beautiful. His training in Germany prepared him to integrate the art of designing with the skills associated with assemblage of these plans. An architect with rigid preconceptions could not, quite possibly, have survived in the late frontier backwater that Nacogdoches represented in 1880. There were, however, men such as John Schmidt, E. A. Blount, W. U. Perkins, and Dick Cason–sophisticated patrons all–who could use the talents and services of Rulfs. They set before Rulfs their goals and their means, and the master builder returned plans and specifications to achieve these goals. The mutually beneficial relationship that developed between this North German architect and Nacogdoches community lasted forty-six years. In every decade after his arrival, Rulfs led the town into new modes of expression that brought the town in line with national trends. As a result, his designs have endured the test of time because his buildings were useful to generations beyond the owners who commissioned them. His creations were esthetically pleasing, prized for more than their utilitarian functions. His contemporaries saluted him for this, and present-day judgments confirm this. The legacy he bequeathed to Nacogdoches and Texas testifies to his abilities as an architect, a builder, a supervisor of construction, a creative advocate for adaptive use, and, oftentimes, as a diplomat between warring factions.

Reflections on His Methods

Numerous drawings survive to illustrate how Rulfs communicated his ideas: elevations, floor plans, sections, measurements, scales, annotations, cross-referencing, and details (such as wainscoting and stairways.) Although numerous references to drawings and specifications appear earlier, the first elevation to survive dates to 1895–a pencil drawing with ink and coloration added of the June Harris House on Virginia Avenue. The Harris elevation provides ample testimony to the quality of Rulfs' abilities as a draftsman. The first surviving specifications are for the Roland Jones House on Church Street (1896). When the volume and complexity of his buildings increased, and other contractors besides his brother were involved in construction, detailed specifications became more commonplace. The most thorough sets of drawings and specifications extant exist in the D. K. Cason Papers, now housed in the East Texas Research Center in the Steen Library at SFASU.[9] One set of specifications, for the Woodmen of the World Building (1922), was found in the Nacogdoches *Deed Records*. His last drawings and specifications date to 1925 for the Price House. Many drawings that have not survived, however, are referenced in letters, newspapers, and testimonials. Rulfs was not only a competent draftsman, but he was also a good salesman. He frequently showed his drawings to the newspaper editor, who provided comments and thus advertisements for the architect. The drawings for Christ Episcopal Church received public display, as well as extensive documentation in the church minutes. Rulfs frequently showed his plans to the mappers of the Sanborn Fire Maps Company, who relied heavily on his work. The Sanborn Maps, used extensively in this book, have provided 'footprints' to Rulfs's structures in both the downtown and later in the residential areas. The maps are particularly good at determining the original configuration of porches and allowing the historian to speculate intelligently about the arrangement of some interior spaces when no pictures exist.

Occasionally, D. Rulfs helped a patron (such as John Schmidt) select a building lot for a project, but usually he had to work within predetermined parameters. His patrons appreciated how adeptly Rulfs could maximize the options of a piece of property. Rulfs always wanted the public to look up, literally, on his houses rather than down on them. Even when the lot was not elevated, he chose to elevate his houses on high piers and emphasized the height of a house as a way of increasing its importance. He positioned his houses on the crests of hills. He especially related to the houses on the hills west of downtown. He always preferred the one-and-a-half story houses to the single story; he preferred the two-and-a half to the two-story. Likewise, he wanted his patrons to enjoy great views from their houses. This predilection came from his upbringing in a flat region of Oldenburg. After he arrived, Rulfs learned how volatile weather conditions in Texas could turn innocent-looking creeks into raging torrents. From his early years in Nacogdoches, Rulfs refused to build houses in low lying areas. His buildings always provided for the effects of the sun, wind, and rainfall.

The citizens of Nacogdoches valued the architect's mastery in the allocation of space, attention to details, and quality. He was particularly conscientious about access and egress, the placement of porches, the utility of loading areas on commercial buildings, and orientation to assure the best visual perspectives. Beyond initial conceptions, Rulfs followed his plans to fruition by close supervision during construction, even to the point of visiting his projects on a daily basis–whether or not he or his brother were the contractors. He maintained cordial relationships with his contractors, subcontractors, craftsmen, and workers who contributed to his projects. He frequently elaborated a concept by drawing on a piece of lumber. Although he rarely involved himself in landscape architecture, there are occasions when he also designed an architectural detail for the landscape, for instance the street-side walls for the Hayter House (1913) and the Gray and Mast Houses (1914). Rulfs relentlessly advocated for improvements in the town's infrastructure and building codes: fire protection, easements, paved streets, and city services, such as water mains, sewage, and drainage.

Reflections on What Influenced Rulfs

By way of summary, D. Rulfs exhibited influences from his homeland of Oldenburg, from his training in classical masters (whether Gothic, Italian, French, or Victorian), from current trends (Queen Anne, Stick, Eastlake, Arts & Craft, Prairie, or Bungalow), and from personal observations, including his frequent trips to Houston and Galveston. He undoubtedly received inspiration from various publications at the time, but this is difficult to trace without a detailed personal library. Modern surveys of extant architecture in Nacogdoches cannot adequately cover these influences because so many of the examples have not survived. For instance, his extensive use of Italianate influences has received very little attention, namely because his original buildings have not survived: the first Perkins Drug Store, the first Mayer & Schmidt Building, the initial façade of the Opera House, and his own home. Having said this, the influence of the major Italian Renaissance master Andrea Palladio (1508-1580) was widespread throughout Rulfs's career. Although Rulfs in later years moved away from Italianate influences, he used Palladian influences to the end of his career and his last great work was an impressive Mediterranean villa for Eugene Blount in 1923.

Palladio's *Four Books of Architecture* were the most influential textbooks on architecture in modern times. Europeans greatly admired Palladio at the time Rulfs undertook his apprentice work. Architectural historians call the revival movement Palladianism to distinguish it from the Italianate Renaissance Style, which was more romantic and expressive. While impossible to say the extent of Rulfs's knowledge of the theories of Palladio, condensed versions of the Italian master's ideas were ubiquitous at the time.[10] What is obvious, however, is that Rulfs applied many of the Renaissance master's design principles as he worked to transform Nacogdoches. Rulfs liberally placed Palladian windows and motifs and elements of the Roman Tuscan Order throughout Nacogdoches–his homage to the genius of the great Renaissance Italian. Beyond that, however, the frontier town of Nacogdoches was no place for Palladian or Italianate villas. Rulfs slavishly emulated no fixed set of architectural examples; but then, neither did Palladio. Rulfs created his own architectural formulae by applying his considerable talent and background to the circumstances and materials he had available. To augment his talent, his cheerful disposition and refusal to let challenges darken his vision allowed Rulfs to serve a complex set of patrons for forty-six years and to bequeath to Nacogdoches a remarkable legacy. The new moneyed class, for the most part, preferred "new architecture" to traditional architecture. As each period defined "new" in different ways, Rulfs adapted, whether it was by using Queen Anne details as modern, or, in their turn, Arts & Craft, Prairie, and Bungalow, and eventually even Neo-Classical styles. The patrons of Rulfs intensely disliked the Greek Revival styles; they considered the Old South's plantation architecture as outdated. Rulfs understood the aspirations of his clients and led them at every stage in his career to achieve their goals. His success stemmed from his impeccable taste in applying current trends to specific needs and by underpinning these with the importance of quality.

Rulfs overwhelmingly preferred the Roman Tuscan Order, as refined by Palladio, to the traditional Greek orders–Doric, Ionic, or Corinthian. He used Tuscan elements even on houses where the patron would have disliked classical elements. Purists sometimes refer to the less ornamental Tuscan Order as "carpenter's Doric." Perhaps Rulfs preferred the order for this reason, because he *could* construct the elements of the order out of locally available materials. The cost-conscious Rulfs could get Tuscan columns replicated locally, allowing him not only to keep costs in line, but also to include other businesses in his plans. The endless variations of heights possible with Tuscan columns allowed Rulfs great flexibility.[11] There were, however, philosophical reasons (appreciated by Palladio and Palladianists) why Rulfs employed so many elements of the Tuscan Order.[12] As he moved from traditional to transitional to modern styles, the plain entablatures and uncomplicated decorative elements of the Tuscan Order seemed to promote his constant desire to reconcile form with function.

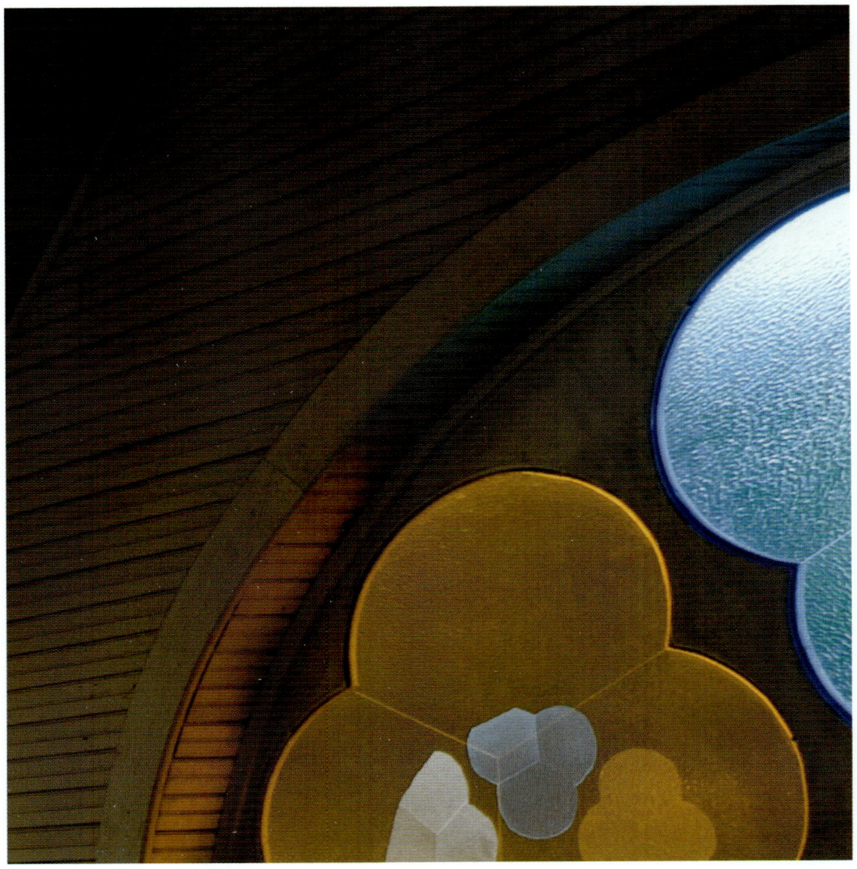

FIGURE13.4. Window Detail, Zion Hill Church.

The Architect's Use of Numerology

While D. Rulfs never rigidly adhered to a set of mathematical formulae, he knew from his training among master builders, such as his father, that one way to assure well-proportioned buildings was to follow a system of numbers. Since ancient times, architects had used "the golden mean" ratio of *Pi* (π)[13] to calculate the mathematical proportions of their buildings. Rulfs employed numerology not only to assure good proportions, but also to execute a theme. Rulfs liked any motif containing a tripartite arrangement. From his training, Rulfs knew that even the untrained eye, without really knowing why, could recognize when things were mathematically incorrect. The correct structural proportions were more pleasing to the eye. He coupled his clear sense of proportions to an equally clear preference for variety. That certainly is one of the reasons architecture by Rulfs is still appreciated.

One group in Nacogdoches, known for its adherence to ancient ratios, symbols, and examples, was the Masons. Rulfs built meeting halls for the group. Many of his patrons, including his patron-in-chief John Schmidt, were Masons: Thomas E. Baker, E. A. Blount, Sr., Eugene H. Blount, Guy A. Blount, H.H. Cooper, Dr. Frank Cates Ford, June C. Harris, Lee Gaston, George Francis Ingraham, Roland Jones, Hollis T. Mast, Leon Blum Mast, George H. Matthews, Robert C. Monk, Dr. Albert Aldrich Nelson, William B. Pearson, Henry Schmidt, J. F. Summers, W. F. Summers, Benjamin Wettermark, and, possibly, others.[14]

In his churches, Rulfs adopted numerology from the Bible, especially the symbolism of the Trinity. This allowed him to employ the ancient ratios of *Pi* by giving them Christian meanings, as did the builders of cathedrals in the middle ages. The First Baptist Church, Christ Episcopal Church, the Main Street Presbyterian Church, Zion Hill Baptist Church, and the First Methodist Church were all imbued with recognized and unrecognized numerology, *all in plain sight*. For instance, the numbers of Zion Hill Church were eight and three, or multiples and divisions thereof. Rulfs implemented his number systems, however, in a non-rigid manner. He skillfully combined local materials, existing craftsmanship, and patron expectations to create unique designs with a mix of classicism, geometry, and practicality.

Reflections on His Career

This book, in general, divides his career into nineteenth (late Victorian) and twentieth century (post-Victorian) segments.[15] The demarcation point came during the years of crises, described in Chapter Seven, around 1906, if a date needs to be interjected. The best term to describe the architectural style of Rulfs is "eclectic." He moved effortlessly from locally important norms to Queen Anne styles, then followed these with easy transitions into various modern styles. The pinnacle of his eclecticism came in 1914 along Logansport Street and with the building of Zion Hill Church. The conservatism and limited wealth of Nacogdoches, however, restrained how much "style" he could introduce into his commercial, civic, or residential structures. He began and ended his career using high Italianate style, but this did not seem to captivate Nacogdoches. The town was more comfortable with somewhat anachronistic styles. Despite this, Rulfs was successful in introducing stylistic changes that kept his patrons equal or ahead of the towns around them. In both halves of his career, he did commercial, domestic, and civic buildings. Recruited as a commercial architect, the range of his commercial buildings is, indeed, impressive: stores, banks, exchanges, warehouses, exhibition space, office buildings, production, distribution centers, apartment houses, hotels, and an opera house. In the civic realm, Rulfs proved equally prolific: churches, schools, and municipal buildings. He built at least one wooden bridge across the Banita Creek. In order to survive, however, he turned to domestic architecture; and it is for this genre that he is primarily known today. The catalogue of his *extant* residential homes numbers over one hundred. In all undertakings, however, Rulfs proved himself remarkably in tune with the resources of his patrons. When resources contracted, he expended his talents by extending the life of his original designs.

While architects work primarily for moneyed patrons, Rulfs was not an elitist. According to the testimony of many, Rulfs worked extensively with people who could not afford polished drawings and specifications; he gave generously of his talents. His association with and respect for the craftsmen with whom he worked was quite obvious. Even in the midst of Nacogdoches' first major labor dispute, Rulfs was not the target of the action and maintained the respect of his workmen. Interestingly, Rulfs easily bridged generational gaps and worked amicably with young patrons.

For patrons who allowed him flexibility, Rulfs quickly proved how good design and quality construction could underpin their ambitions. He assisted men like Schmidt, Perkins, Blount, Cason, Davidson, Sturdevant, and others, to augment their fortunes in commercial buildings. Afterwards, Rulfs aided these same businessmen to redefine their domestic contexts to provide not only creature comforts, but also refined social status. While offering the proviso that the most lavish structures in Nacogdoches were modest by metropolitan examples, Rulfs designed and, more often than not, built homes equal to many currently fashionable in cities across the nation. As the locations of these homes expanded, Rulfs became a strong advocate for better utilities, services, and infrastructure.

Reflections on the Preservation of the Rulfs Legacy

Nacogdoches, because of its age, faces a particular dilemma that younger cities with less history never confront. How does one define history in Nacogdoches? In researching Nacogdoches around 1900, it became quickly evident that anything with less than a century-and-a-half of age was considered modern and, therefore, not historical. The modern development of the town since 1880 was a no-man's-land, an unclaimed and ambiguous area of value to the history of the ancient town.

The relationships of the past to the present and the present to the future are always problematic, in any age. The modern city of Nacogdoches has found it difficult to come to a comfortable relationship with its past. In 1901-1902, it was the tearing down of the Old Stone Fort that provoked the first major confrontation. At moments of prosperity, when leaders focus on the future, the past oftentimes appears as an obstacle to be overcome. In less prosperous moments, the past becomes an asset which might be exploited to produce benefits for the town. Notably, this was the case when the town marshaled its historical record to solicit the placement of a new college here. In the 1960s, however, when Nacogdoches was again prosperous, it went through another identity crisis, and, ironically, cloaked its discomfort with its past with a new slogan, "The Oldest Town in Texas." The slogan covered the reality that the city of Nacogdoches was systematically aiding state highway developers to destroy one of its most beautiful historical assets–North Street. Only afterwards, within a few years, did they see the possibility of routing highway traffic through the pasturelands of the Lanana Creek bottom by creating University Drive. The architect Diedrich Rulfs was long dead by then, but the fate of many of his architectural creations carries the story of this book deep into this period. Except for a discussion of the buildings lost during this later period, the history of Nacogdoches after the coming of SFA must wait for a sequel book.

FIGURES 13.5-13.7 Document Preservation.

Preservation is not just for buildings. The collection and preservation of documents such as drawings and blueprints are important for historic interest, but also important for restoration efforts. This book research discovered the architectural drawings and blueprints of the D. K. Cason House. No doubt there are other treasures out there.

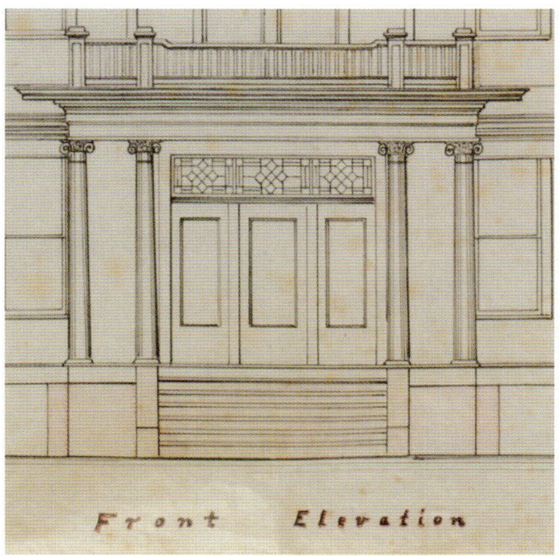

The drawing of the June Harris House (Right), dating from 1895, helped with the restoration of the house by Dr. & Mrs. Richard Baker (Far Right).

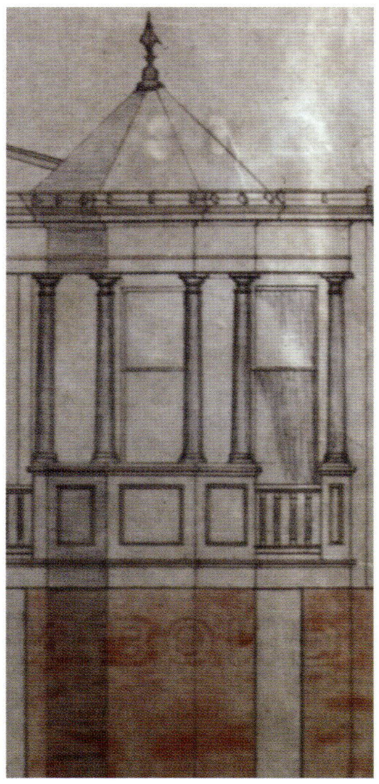

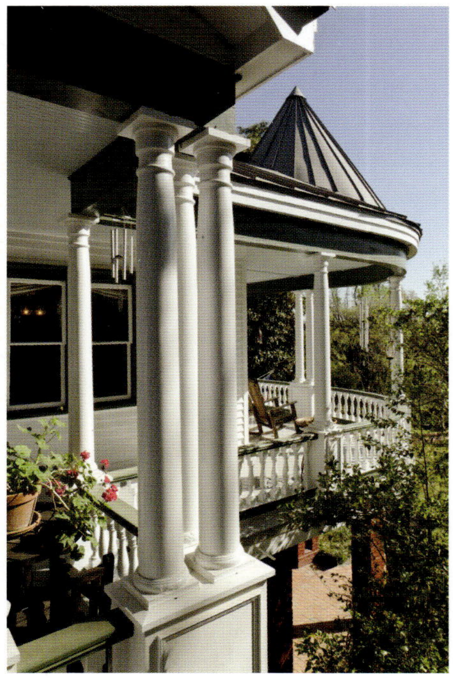

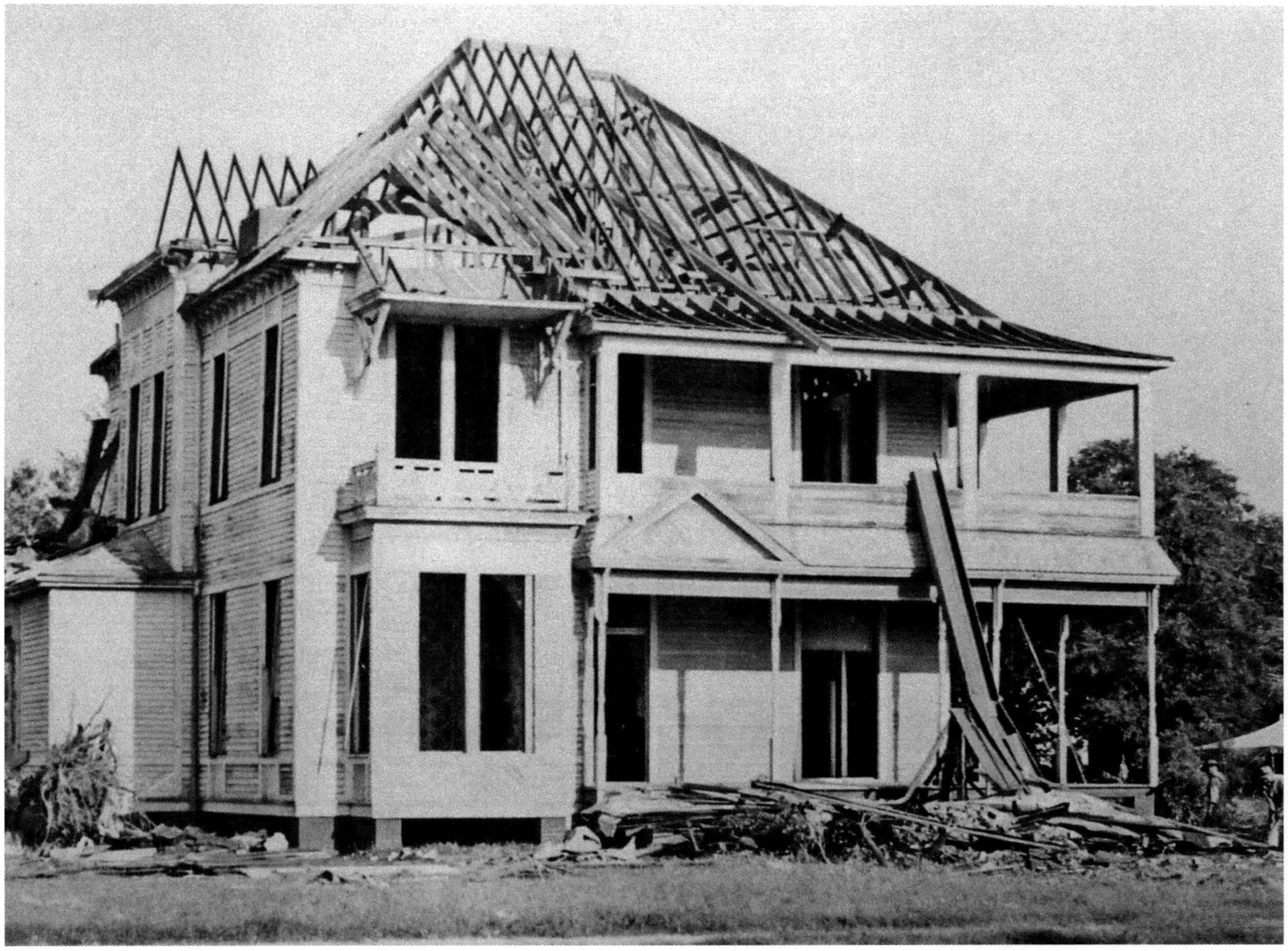

FIGURE 13.8. Demolition of the John Schmidt House in 1962.

The John Schmidt House was, arguably, the finest house Rulfs ever built. The newspaper commented whenever the house got new paint and wallpaper. The house went through several face-liftings. This picture indicates that the front dormer in the roof had been removed during one of the reroofing jobs. At some point, the turned posts of the original house became boxed columns and the decorative balustrades removed. The old posts are visible on the first floor and the boxed ones can still be seen on the second floor porch, This was done after Rulfs set the whole modernization craze in motion after reworking the Perkins House in 1910. It was only fitting that the newspaper discussed its demolition, too.

Courtesy of ETRC.

Until the 1970s, the town "protected" the extant Rulfs buildings because they existed in the parts of town that were so anachronistic that their anonymity protected them. Nacogdoches was so far out of place in time that it actually seemed "in" with the national attempts to preserve structures. With the institution of zoning laws, surveys of historic properties, and the creation of National Register Districts, the organized efforts have now caught up as well, at least on paper. This probably went as well as it did because these were non-commercial parts of town–Washington Square and Irion and Forbes Hills. Historical zoning, bitterly opposed at first, has gradually gained currency in the city, but its modest gains have recently been challenged.[16] Leading city leaders still cannot decide what the role of history is in the city. London and Paris officials know that most of their tourist dollars come from the visitors seeing what they expect to see. Nacogdoches City Commissioners, who would not dare to exempt property owners from plumbing and fire codes, find it more difficult to uphold preservation laws, which guarantee city interests, too. In a city that values its history, some definition of "progress" should include protecting the best of the past as we move into the future. While Nacogdoches still has enough treasures that it does not have to create Disney-like fantasy lands, the city faces some hard choices: can replicas really replace our trashed visual history? Are we so proud of being historic in the period of the Texas Revolution, that we overlook or are cavalier about the monuments still extant from the turn of the twentieth century?

There were two parts to the main sentence Karle Wilson Baker wrote in 1907, echoed later by President Birdwell of the new college: "The spirit of Nacogdoches today is a gift from the men of the past; the spirit of the future will be the gift of the men of today." She also observed that Nacogdoches was more enamored with being historic than knowing about her history. This book is an attempt to broaden the definition of history in Nacogdoches to include the modern period after 1880. Had a detailed account of the career and creations of D. Rulfs been published earlier, is it possible that North Street would not have fallen into the wasteland of commercialism that now occupies it? Since history is a living context, every day we make decisions which will either enhance or degrade the history for future generations. There must be some middle ground between the reactionaries who want to return to the past, even if they cannot decide which modern convenience to abandon, and the hypocrisy of the modernists who sanction the destruction of everything old, yet want to exploit being "historic" and advocate historical theme parks. Nacogdoches should avoid concocting untruths or creating a false sense of historical development on existing treasures. Above all, the town needs to avoid the sophistry of constantly lamenting lost treasures while ignoring steps to protect those that are still around: preservation yesterday and preservation tomorrow, but never preservation today.

To increase awareness, those who created surveys have inventoried things worth preserving. This work continues that purpose, but it adds a survey of the visual treasures, gone and extant, bequeathed to the town between 1880-1926 by the North German architect, D. Rulfs. For the tourist who visits modern Nacogdoches, a paraphrase of the inscription written on Sir Christopher Wren's tomb in Saint Paul's Cathedral in London should accompany every brochure on Nacogdoches, 'If you seek a monument to D. Rulfs, look around you.'

Reflections on Patterns in His Designs

In reflecting on patterns established during his career, a somewhat different approach seems warranted. By using more profuse illustrations, captions, and explanatory essays, the next section will explore the architect's preferences in the following categories:

- Commercial Façades in the Downtown
- Italian Renaissance Influences
- Palladian Influences
- Tuscan Order, Pediments, Front Facing Gables
- Windows
- Exotic Influences and Towers
- Roofs, Chimneys, and Dormers
- Porches
- Staircases, Mantels, and Woodwork
- Art Glass and Gothic Elements

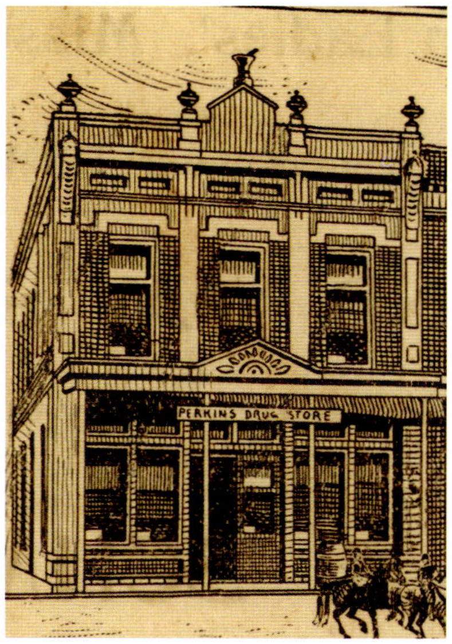

FIGURE 13.09. (Left) The Architect's First Commercial Building: Perkins Brothers Drug Store in 1884.

FIGURE 13.10. (Below) The Architect's Last Commercial Building on the Square: Blount-Baker Building in 1919.

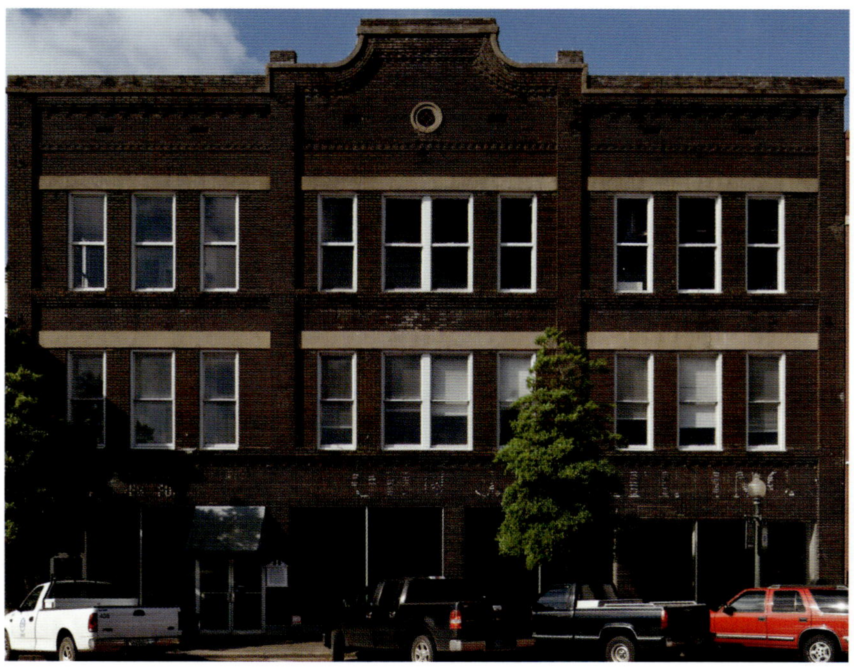

Commercial Façades

The only known set of drawings by Rulfs for a commercial building is the collection for the Cason, Richardson and Company warehouse on Pecan Street. After many changes, this building no longer looks like the drawing, but the drawing itself gives clues to the way the architect standardized the façades of his other commercial buildings by using parapets, the placement of windows, the use of running bands, second story pilasters, showcase windows, and brick patterns.

All commercial designs by Rulfs have certain things in common. The roofs, which actually sloped to the rear of the buildings, were encased or hidden behind parapets. The parapets gave fire protection and lent classical proportions to the appearance of the building. The parapets of his buildings were distinguished by a variety of decorative brickwork in the form of panels, corbels, bands, coffers, turrets, and coping. The front façades were almost universally divided into three segments, sometimes as simple as three windows, but usually divided into bays by pilasters above the ground floor level. The central bay had its parapet raised above the standard parapets in order to allow for individualization: to designate owners, dates of construction, or functions such as entrances. The flexible bays and parapets allowed Rulfs a formula by which to execute plans quickly, yet adjust the size to fit the property. (The series of buildings along the south side of East Main, between North Street and the Square, is the best example of the variations.) In the nineteenth century, his buildings were likely to have porches and balconies, but not always. It depended on the owner, evidently. The 1891 Cox Building (now Regions Bank) and the 1891 Davidson Building (now City Hall) did not. The Opera House, designed about the same time, had a porch on the first floor, which served as a balcony above for the theater goers to stroll during intermissions. More common, however, the two-story buildings had porches on both levels. The Blount Building on the north Square was the last Rulfs did like this. After 1903, when suspended covers for the entrances became popular, the upstairs porches vanished.

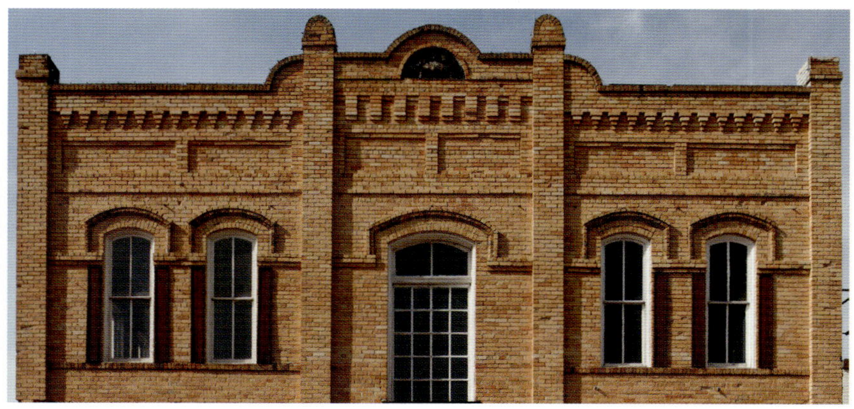

FIGURE 13.11. (Above) M. G. Hazle Building (1901).
FIGURE 13.12. (Bottom) Mayer & Schmidt Building (1908).

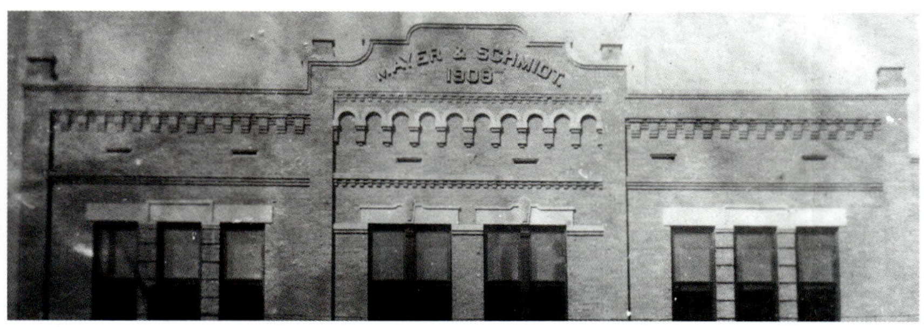

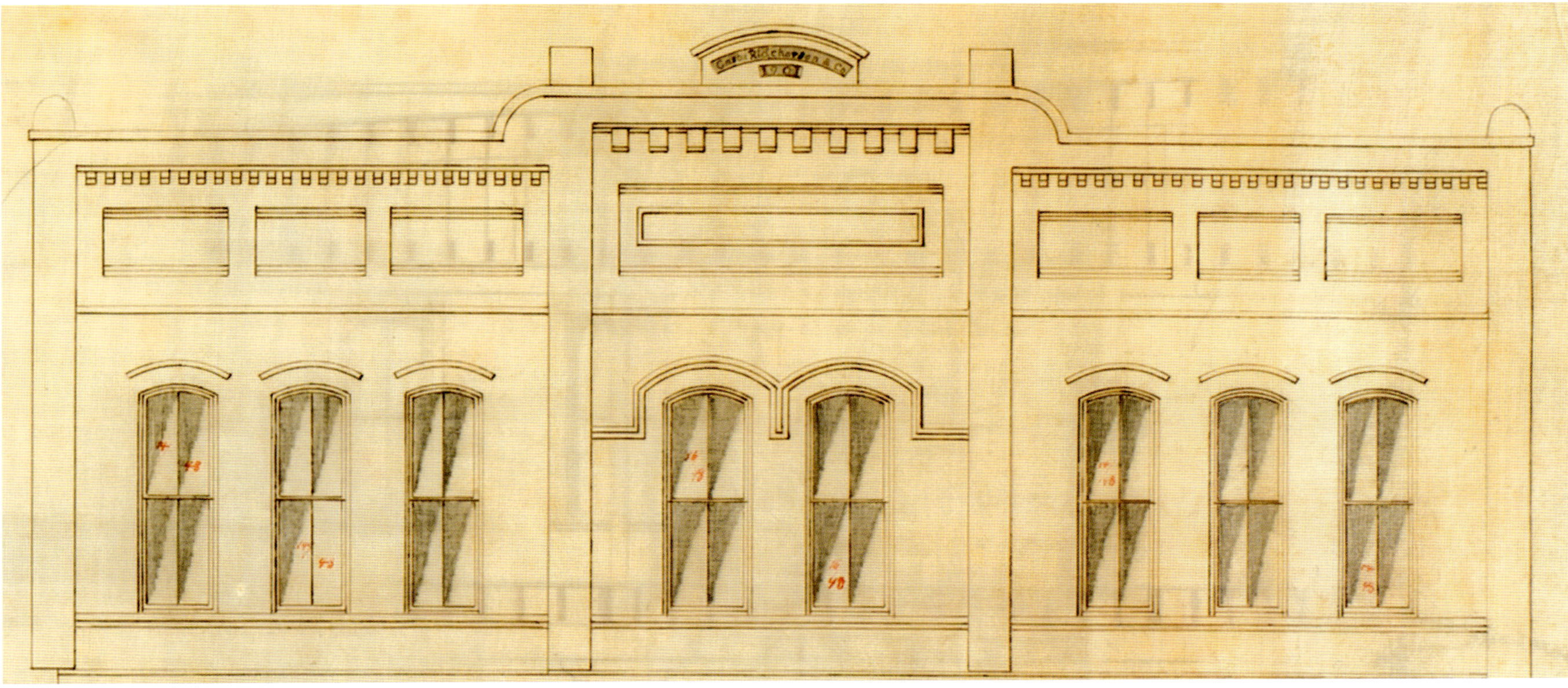

FIGURE 13.13. (Above) Front Elevation by D. Rulfs, 1900.
These elevations for the Cason, Richardson & Co. are the only original drawings of a commercial building by D. Rulfs. The upper façade, divided into three bays, separated by pilasters, is typical of the formula employed by Rulfs on other buildings.

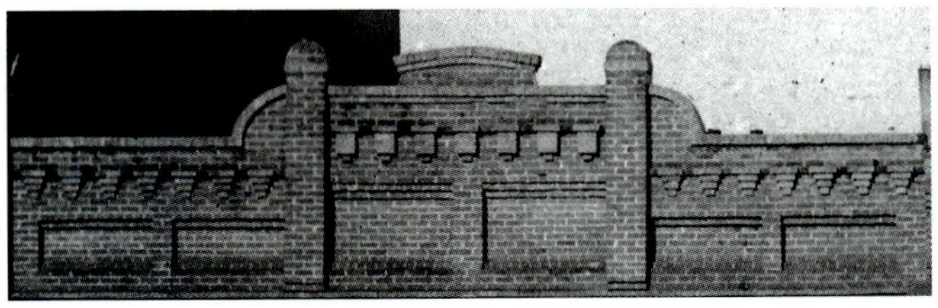

FIGURE 13.14. (Above) North Hoya Building (1900).

FIGURES 13.15. and Figure 13.16. (Below) Parapets (1899).
These parapets on the Johnson Furniture buildings date to 1899; photograph is 2011.

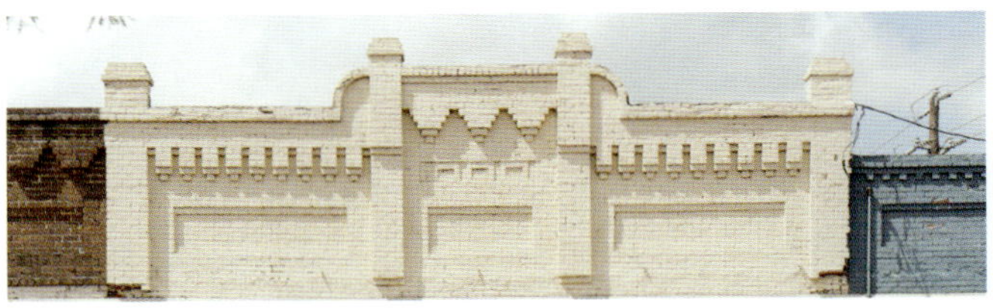

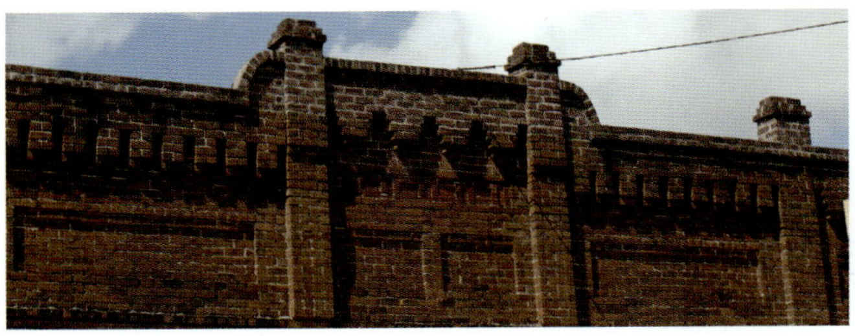

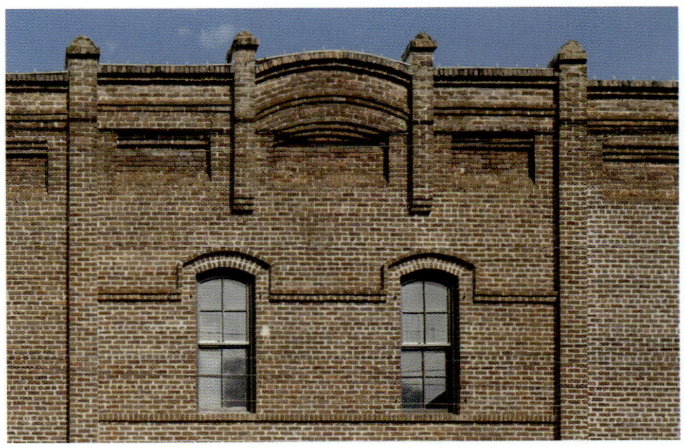

FIGURE 13.17. (Above) Cotton Exchange Building (1902).
FIGURE 13.18. (Below) Hoya Building (1900).

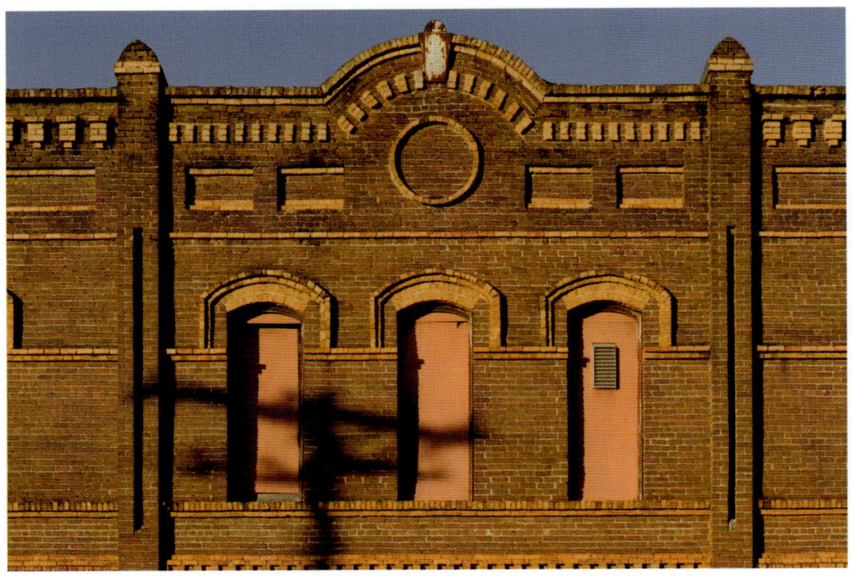

Italian Renaissance Influences

Modern surveys of existing buildings cannot adequately comment on the extent to which Rulfs incorporated influences from the Italian Renaissance. The more one incorporates demolished structures into the body of the architect's work, the more influential the northern Italian influences become. Many of the early commercial buildings by Rulfs used Italianate influences: the Perkins Drug Store, the Mayer & Schmidt Building, the Opera House, and his own home, for instance. However, none of these buildings has survived. Few of his later buildings were overtly Italian, except perhaps the Mediterranean features of the Eugene Blount House in 1923; but the influence of Andrea Palladio and the Palladianism of the nineteenth century was widespread throughout his career. While Rulfs regularly employed various iterations of the Queen Anne Style and occasionally used elements of neo-classical architecture; he specifically avoided the grandiose French Beaux Arts Style that emerged by combining various Italianate design elements. He also declined to use any Neo-Tudor and Neo-Spanish or Mission Revival Styles.

Palladian Influences

While the architectural components employed by Rulfs evolved and changed to suit the requirements of each individual client and the times, a consistent theme was his use of Palladian motifs. These became his signature in Nacogdoches. That D. Rulfs greatly admired Andrea Palladio (1508-1580) is not in question, but it is unclear how carefully Rulfs studied Palladio. He may have simply been imitating mid-19th century Palladianism or various examples from architectural books in publication across the nation at the time. In Northern Germany, on the other hand, Rulfs had experienced the favorable reactions from patrons as touches of Palladianism found their way into contemporary designs there. In Nacogdoches, Rulfs worked at a time when the patrons he served were becoming increasingly at ease with public displays of personal wealth as those in Germany had in the 1870s. Nacogdoches, however, was never ready to copy the villas in the Veneto. Rulfs balanced his admiration for the classical themes of the great Italian's work with an almost casual ability to reinterpret them when it suited his own needs. Rulfs bent the rules of Palladianism to give his patrons touches of classical influence, sometimes placing these in wildly diverse settings from Gothic to modern.

The definitions of what constitutes a Palladian window vary, even whether it should be attributed to Andrea Palladio or to the Italian architect Sebastiano Serlio. A basic configuration—called variously a Palladian window, a Serlian window, and sometimes a Venetian window—was a three-part window where the center window is arched and wider than the two straight-topped side windows. In his essential numbering system, Rulfs liked any motif containing three parts: Palladian windows, Palladian doors, Palladian motifs, three-part windows, three-part doors, treble sashes, treble bays in façades, *et cetera*. Rulfs placed these motifs everywhere in Nacogdoches. He coupled these with generous additions of Tuscan columns and entablatures – on his porches, pediments, gables, brick commercial façades, and interior divisions between rooms. His later move to boxed columns was a further step in the simplification of the Tuscan Order.

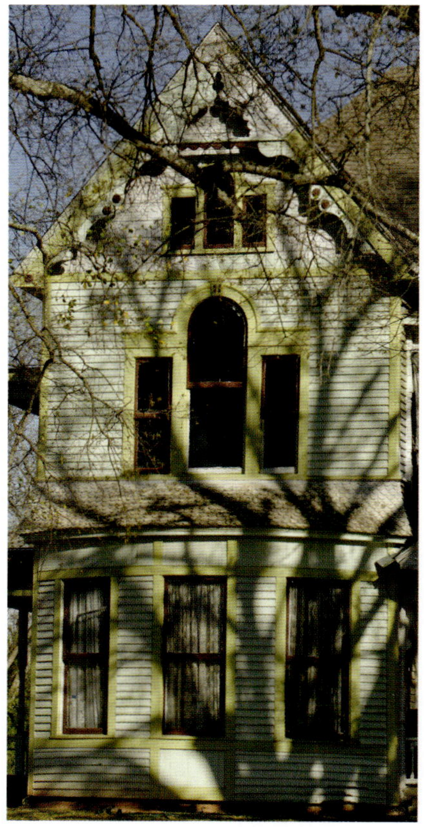

FIGURES 13.19 and 13.20. Two Blount Family Houses.

These two examples of houses done for the Blount family, the Stephen W. Blount House (1897) and the Eugene Blount House (1923), have a profusion of classical and Palladian motifs.

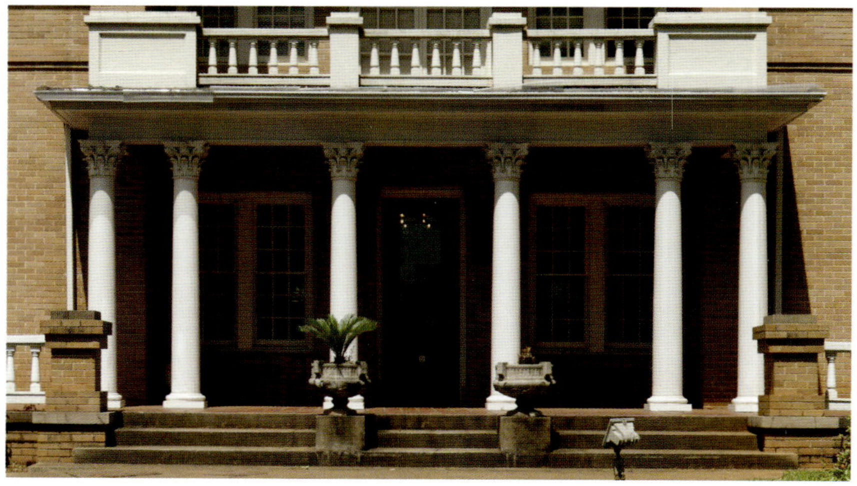

FIGURE 13.21. (Below) The Davidson Building on East Main. (1908)

Occasionally, Rulfs used Palladian motifs on commercial buildings.

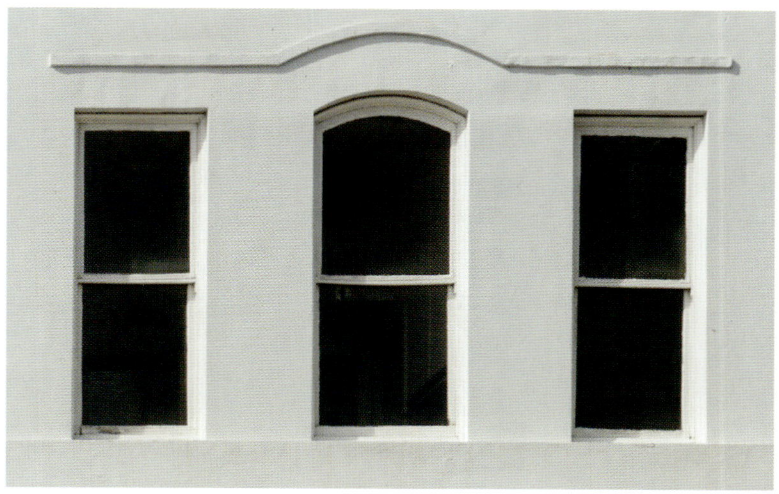

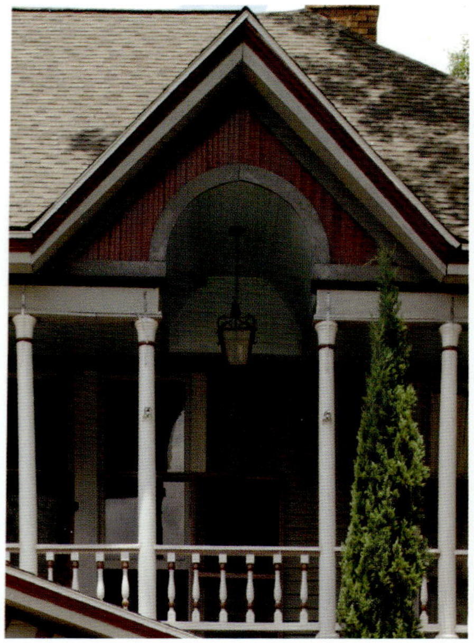

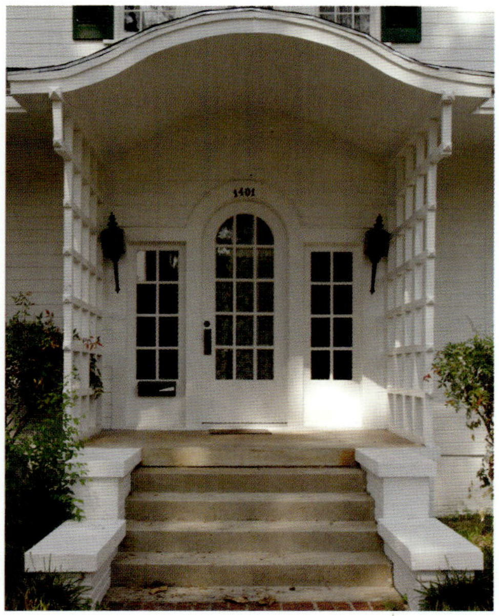

The Constantine Arch

The configuration of windows in the parish church in Stollhamm, Germany, contained three arched windows. Rulfs was very fond of this tripartite variation and used it instead of the traditional Palladian configurations in many places in Nacogdoches.

This configuration followed the ancient Roman Arch of Constantine (the first Christian Emperor) rather than the Arch of Titus in Rome, which inspired the traditional Palladian configurations. The naves and side aisles of Romanesque churches form the same configuration.

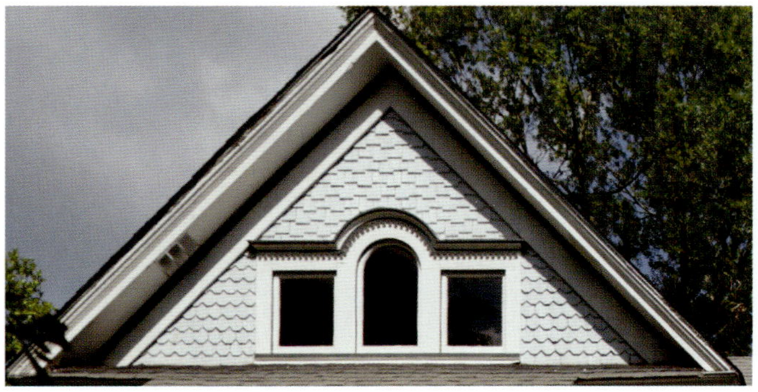

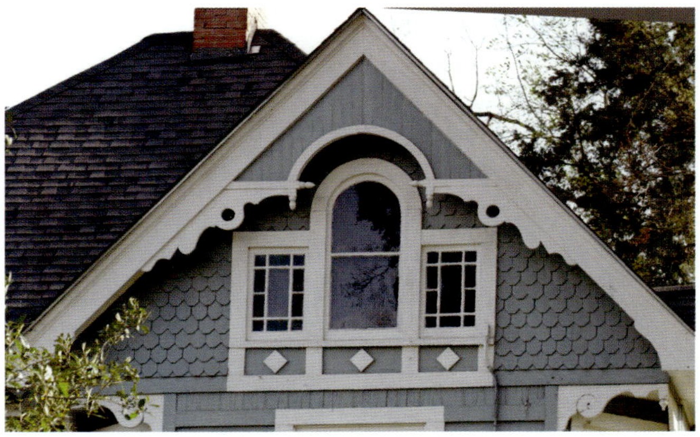

FIGURES 13.22-13.26. Illustrations of Palladian Motifs.
(Top Left) The Upper Porch of the Pearson-Spradley House;
(Top Right) Front Door, Frank Sharp House;
(Middle) The Tol Hardeman House on Mound Street;
(Above) The Middlebrook House on West Main;
(Below) The Phillip Sanders House on South Sanders Street.

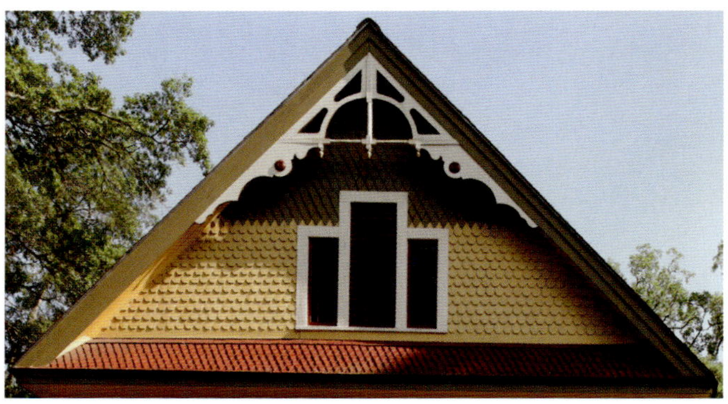

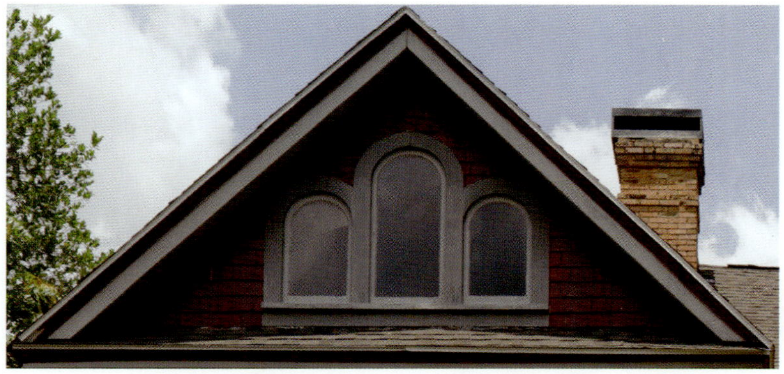

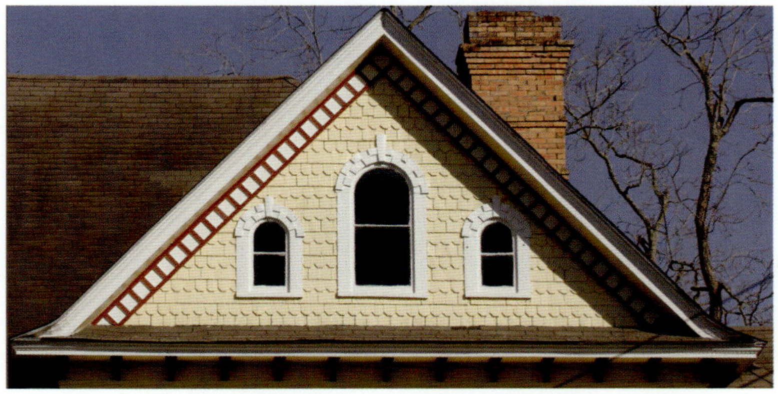

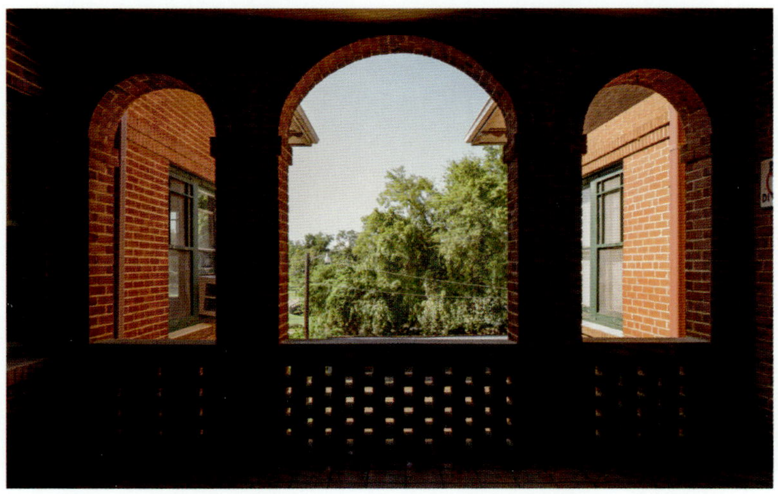

FIGURES 13.27-13.29. (Above) Examples of the Constantine Arch in Nacogdoches.
(Top) Pearson-Spradley House.
(Middle) Charles Perkins House.
(Bottom) Davidson Apartments on South Fredonia.

The Use of the Tuscan Order

Examples of Tuscan columns abound across Nacogdoches. Rulfs could get the plain wooden columns milled in Nacogdoches. Rulfs liked the columns because they allowed him to keep costs down, could be ordered in various lengths, and helped him include other local businessmen in his contracts. Sometimes, Rulfs used Tuscan plain shafts with Ionic capitals, which he ordered by catalogue at local lumber yards. Rulfs even ordered the Tuscan columns in prefabricated concrete. Once the boxed version became popular, the pilasters and columns could even be made on site by his carpenters; he used them in interiors, too. As he moved from traditional to transitional to modern styles, the plain entablatures and uncomplicated decorative elements of the Tuscan Order seemed to promote his constant desire to simplify his designs.

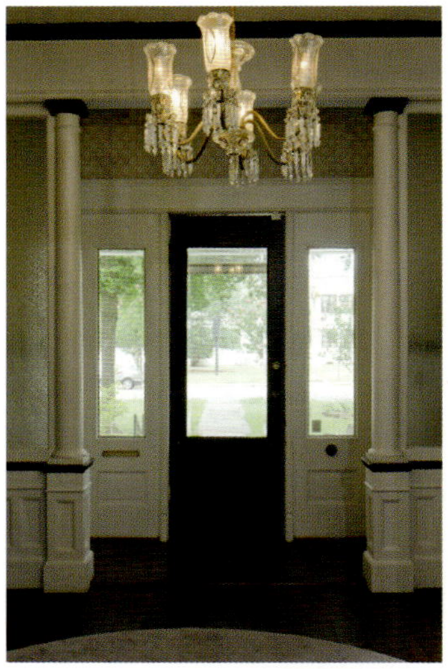

FIGURES 13.30 to 13.34. Tuscan Columns:
(Left) Garrison House on Mound St.;
(Left Middle) Harris House on Virginia Ave.;
(Left Bottom) A. A. Nelson House on Mound St.;
(Below) Chs. Perkins House on Mound St.;
(Bottom) Hardeman House on Mound St.

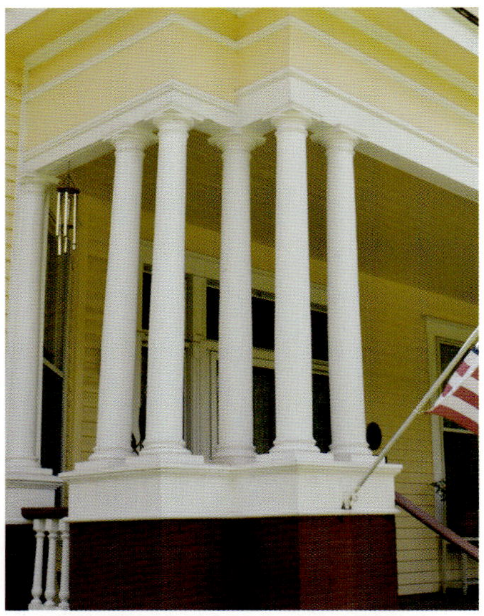

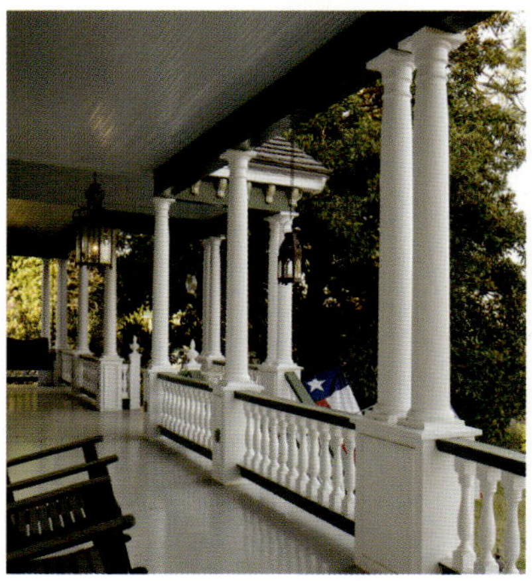

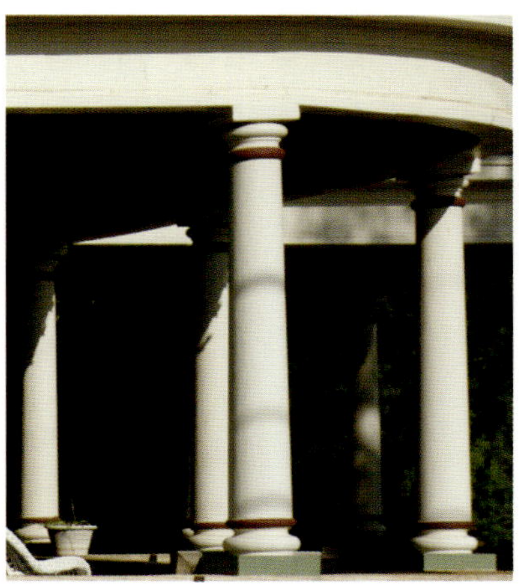

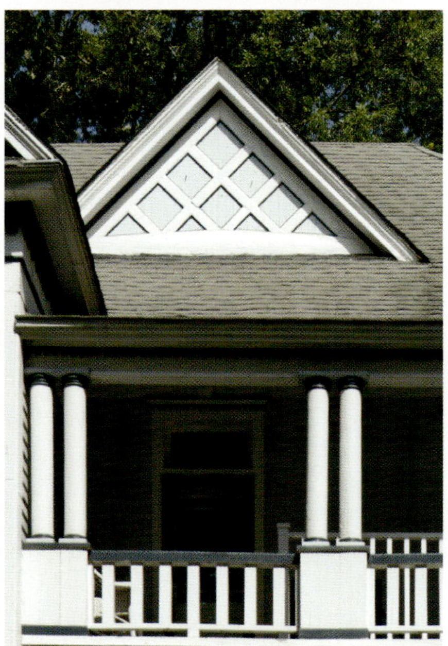

Pediments

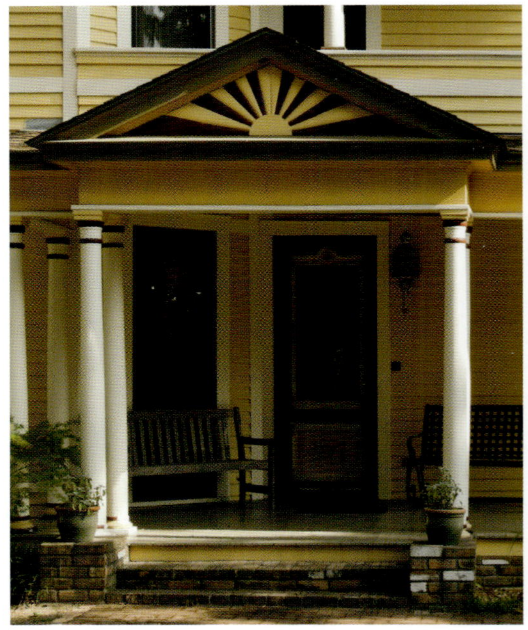

Rulfs used pediments everywhere, from his earliest commercial buildings to his school buildings and residences, even the modern ones. Most of his pediments were classical, consisting of a triangular section above a horizontal entablature supported by columns. The styles varied, as in the Gothic porch pediments on the Shindler House and the Craftsman pediment on the Gray House. The pediments could be free-standing or incorporated within parts of the porch. Some were even multi-stories high. In most cases, the functional use of a pediment, to designate an entrance, seemed supremely practical to him. Where expense limited a free-standing pediment, he simply truncated the concept by placing a triangle in the roofline of a porch. He did, on occasion, use a pediment as a decorative element, for example at the corner of the porch on the Laura Chapman Blount House or the Nelson House on Main Street. In the early years, he used a carpenter's solution to give ordinary windows a pediment-like appearance, allowing the fascia boards to serve as the columns. While his tympana or triangular areas within the pediment were often decorated, these decorations were extremely modest and made within his own shop. The sun-burst tympanum on the Phillip Sanders House is especially nice.

FIGURES 13.35-13.37. Illustrations of Pediments:
(Above) Sanders House on Sanders Street, Irion Hill;
(Right) Sam Stripling House of 1905;
(Below) Gray House on Logansport .

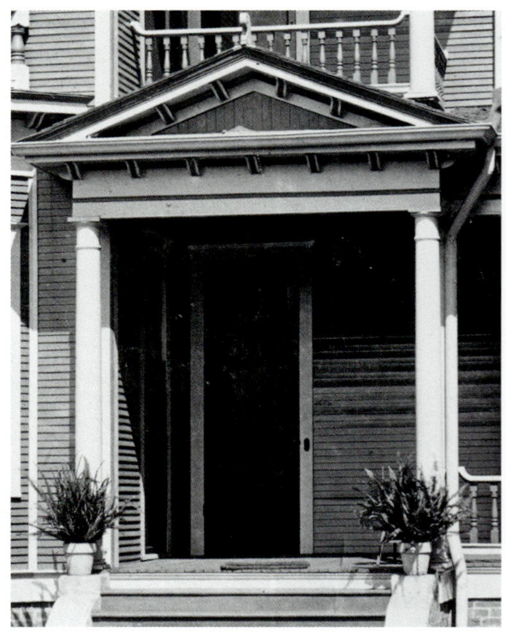

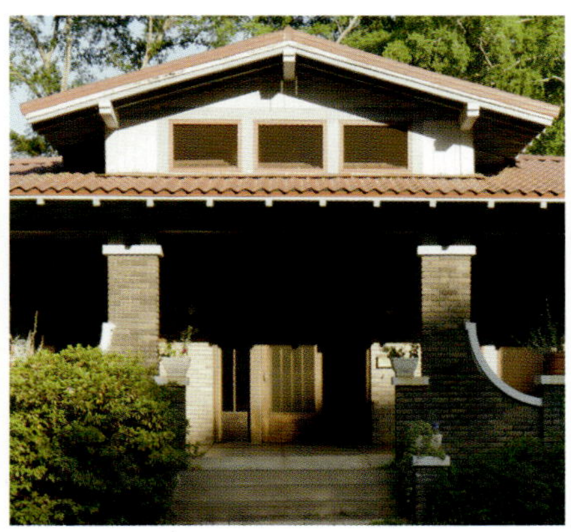

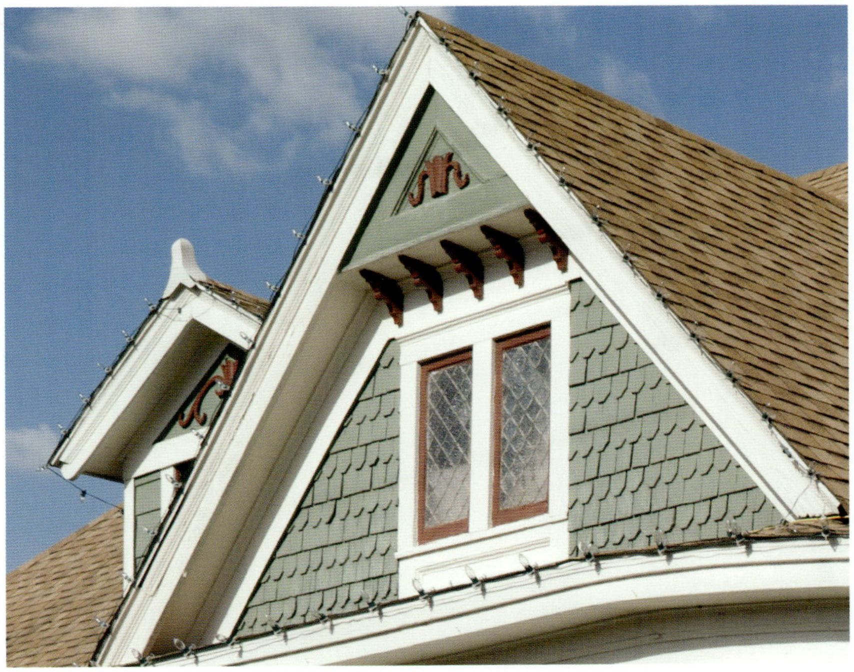

Front-Facing Gables

One of the most characteristic features of a Queen Anne Style house was the front-facing gable. Rulfs used these to make major decorative statements on most of his asymmetrical façades. He even designed double-front-facing gables on several houses (Tucker, Richardson, Cason houses). His gables were almost always load-bearing wall structures. Oftentimes, the gable stood forward to the main body of the house, some designed so far out of the main plane of the house as to be whole rooms. In the earlier house, the gable frequently included chamfered bays with brackets to support the triangular portion. Most of his gables were part of a hip-and-gable roof configuration. The tympana usually had windows and different siding from the house, oftentimes with Palladian windows. Sometimes, the front-gable had bay windows with balconies and shed roofs in addition. He designed a large front-facing gable in line with the main facade of the Charles Perkins House—a purely decorative element. The Cooper House on Irion Hill has a similiar treatment. A charming example of a small house with forward gable is the remodeled A. A. Nelson House; the Tucker-Branch is the best of the two-forward gable houses; and the Edwards, Schmidt, and Tol Hardeman Houses are grand examples of the two-story variety.

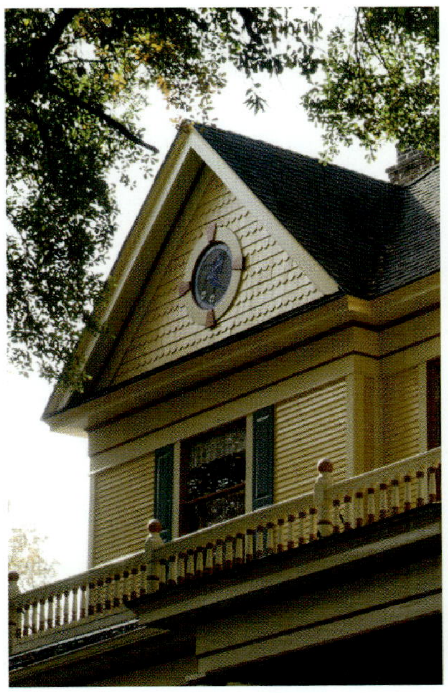

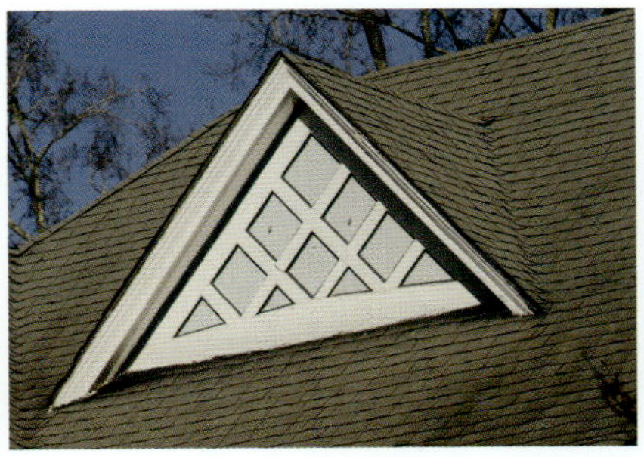

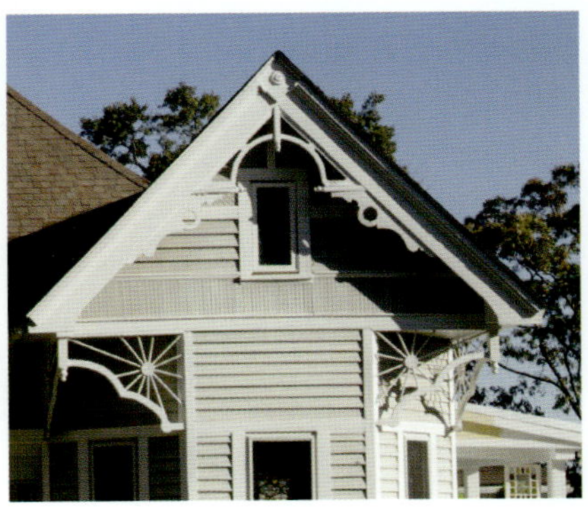

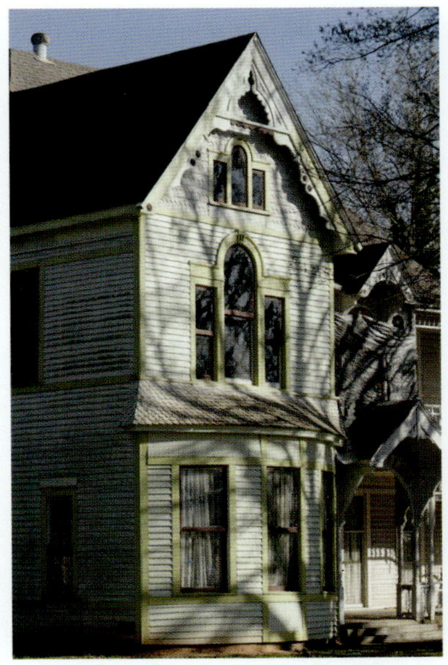

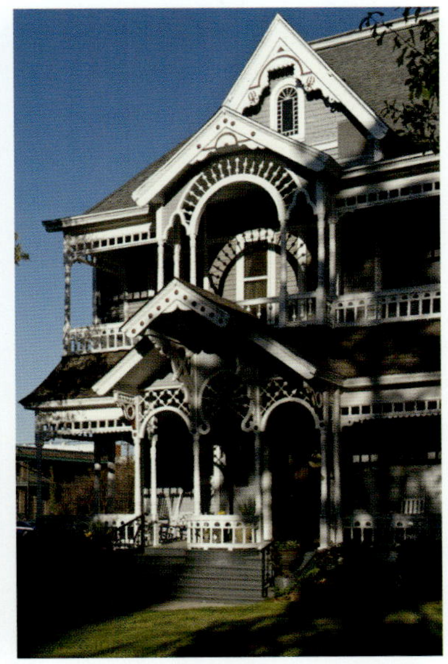

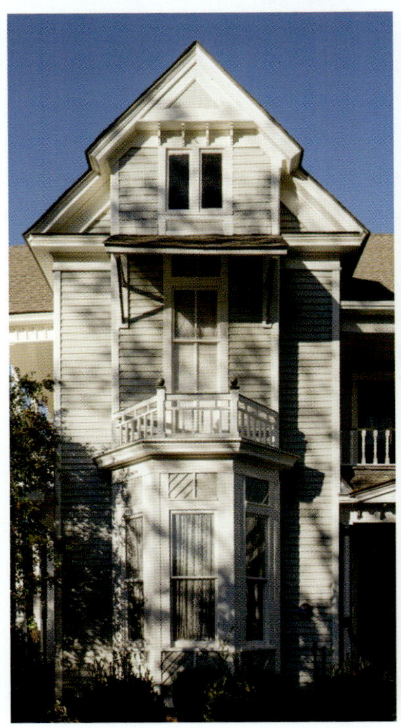

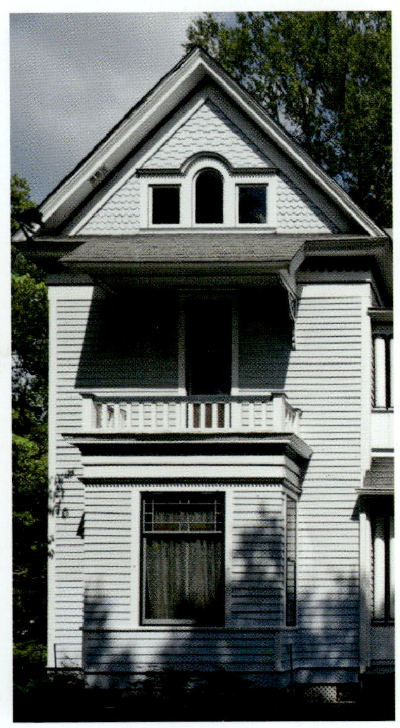

FIGURES 13.38-13.41. (Above) Four Illustrations of Front Facing Gables *(Top) Nelson House on Mound Street; (Above Left) Lindsey House on Virginia Avenue; (Above Right) Roof Gable, Tol Hardeman House on Mound; (Above) Monk House, originally on Virginia Avenue.*

FIGURES 13.42-13.45. (Right) Four Illustrations of Tiered Gable Fronts *(Top Row) S. W. Blount House on Mound Street; Jones House on Church Street; (Lower Row) Edward House on Lanana; Tol Hardeman House on Mound Street.*

Windows

While Rulfs used all types and styles of windows, the most consistently popular was the double-hung sash window. The importance of the circulation of air was no doubt the reason. As Gladys Hardeman explained, every day they would open both sashes, allowing the cool air to flow in the bottom and warm air to escape out the top; by noon, they would close both, and the house with all the wood insulation would stay pleasant the rest of the day. Later, attic fans changed that.

The number of lights or panes varied. His early houses in the 1880s had two over two lights; later, one over one was usual. The sashes became wider after 1900, and some almost presage the picture windows of a much later time. In 1913, Rulfs used his largest application of double-hung sashes–two sets of massive 15/15 double-hung sashes, separated by a pair of by-folding glass French doors ten feet tall–to create a glass wall to separate a sitting room from a screened sleeping porch. This was most unusual, and because the sashes were too heavy to raise easily, it was never repeated. More popular, Rulfs turned to single-hung windows with fixed upper sashes. They were cheaper to construct and offered more decorative alternatives. The fixed upper sashes oftentimes had art glass linings, or opaque lights, or multi-paned upper sashes.

Rulfs genuinely liked slip-head windows, the ones where the lower sash disappeared into the wall above when raised. The large ones, with one-over-one fixed panes, served as doors on the porches of many of his houses. The smaller ones, such as those used in dormer rooms, he used for ventilation where the fixed upper sash would not normally allow for a fully open window.

The arrangement of windows also followed a pattern. In the period from 1890 to 1914, most houses, even many of the Prairie Style ones, had bay windows. Whether from habit or added space and light, patrons demanded bays. Quite possibly, chamfered bay configurations continued to be popular because the viewer could look around the corner, so to speak. Rulfs used small bay window extensions on both the Edwards House and the Shindler House in the 1880s; two-story chamfered bay rooms were used from the W. U. Perkins House in 1890 through 1914. The three-sided sitting or sunroom, however, replaced the chamfered arrangements after 1914.

Rulfs used both hopper and casement windows. In the basements of the First Baptist, Zion Hill Baptist, and First Methodist churches, he used top-hinged hopper windows, which offered the maximum ventilation. He used center-pivoted windows in all of these churches in the main chambers, as he had in his first house in Stollhamm. Rulfs used casement windows in many residences, sometimes in single and sometimes in group or ribbon arrangements. Rulfs designed and had milled in town special windows for the Mary Hayter House; double-hung sash windows, single-hung sash windows with fixed upper sashes, and even casement windows, all with vertical mullions.

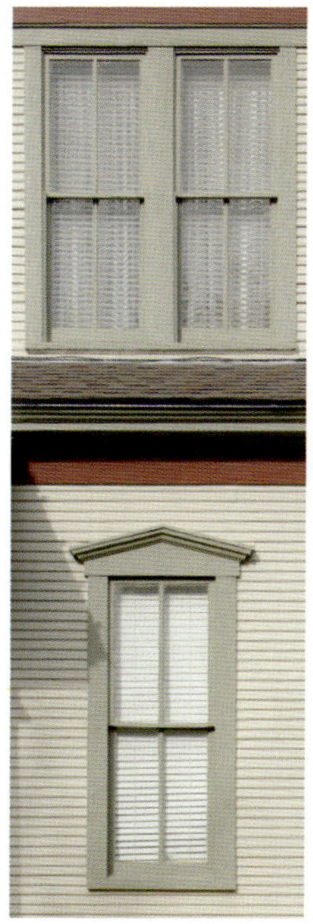

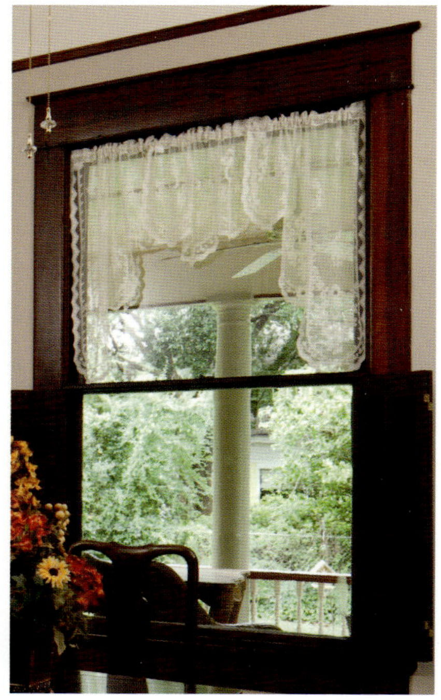

FIGURES 13.46 and 13.47 (Above) The Windows on the Lee Hardeman House.
(Above Left) The smaller windows fron the 1892 front were moved upstairs and paired together; the lower window remained the same.
(Above Left) The new 1912 front windows were wider.

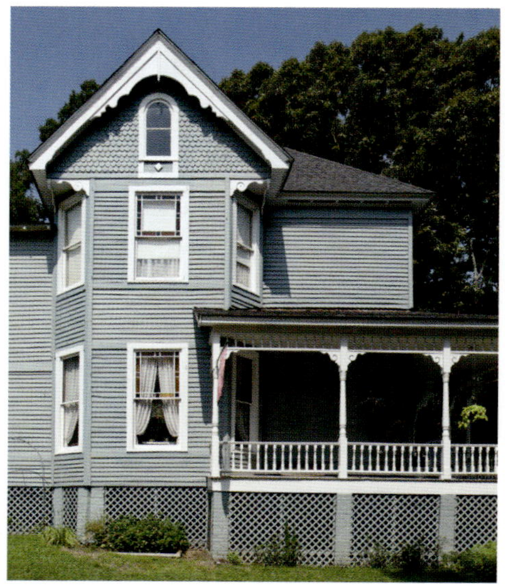

FIGURE 13.48 (Above) The Middlebrook House East Bay.
The Middlebrook House has three, two-story bay window arrangements.

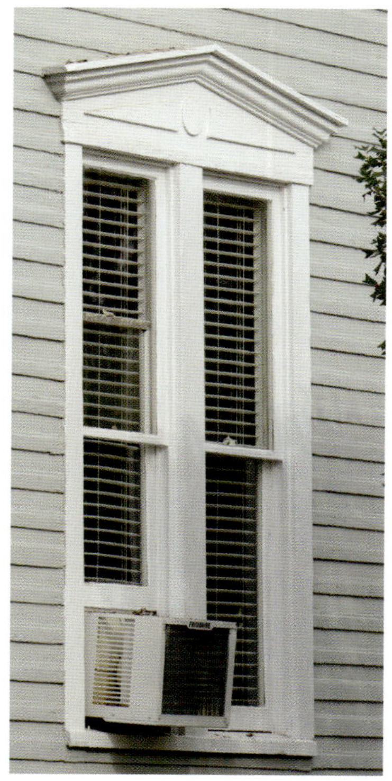

FIGURE 13.49. (Right) Price House.

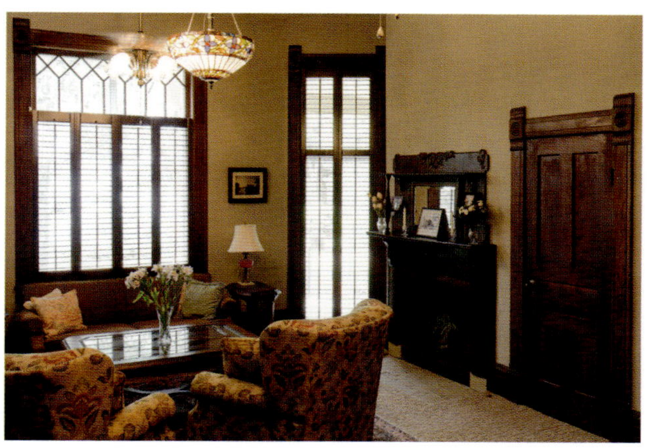

FIGURE 13.50. (Left) Tucker-Branch House.
The Tucker-Branch House had wide windows with a fixed upper sash. To the left, a slip-head window now replaced with a door.

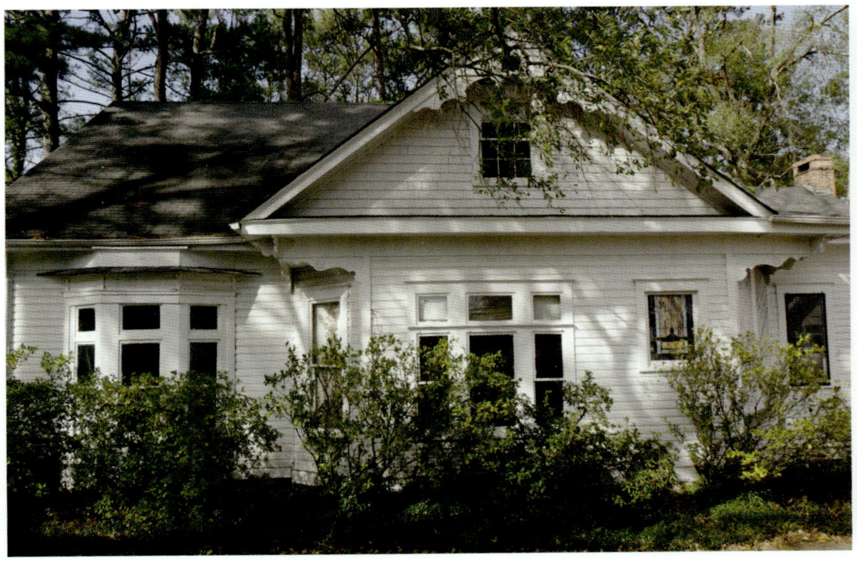

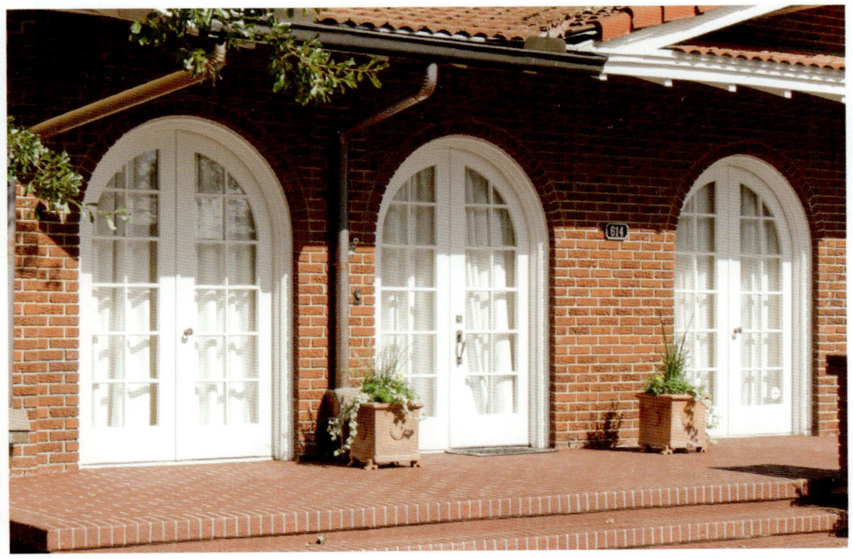

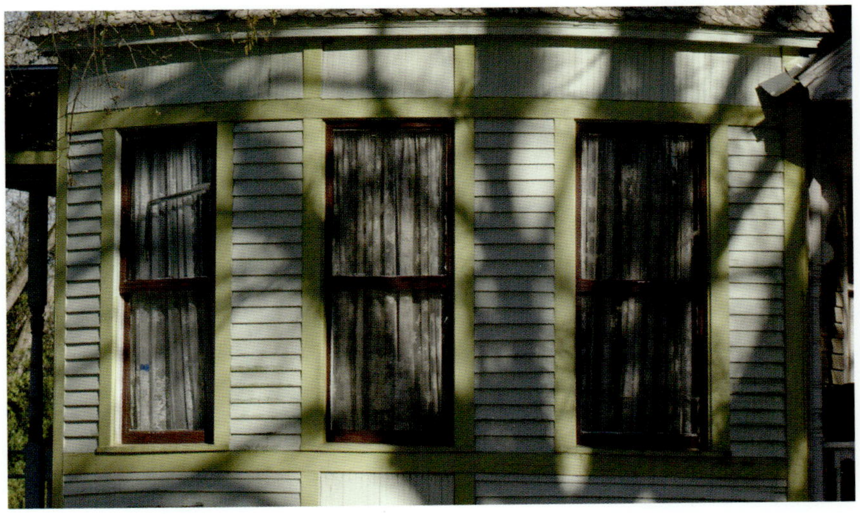

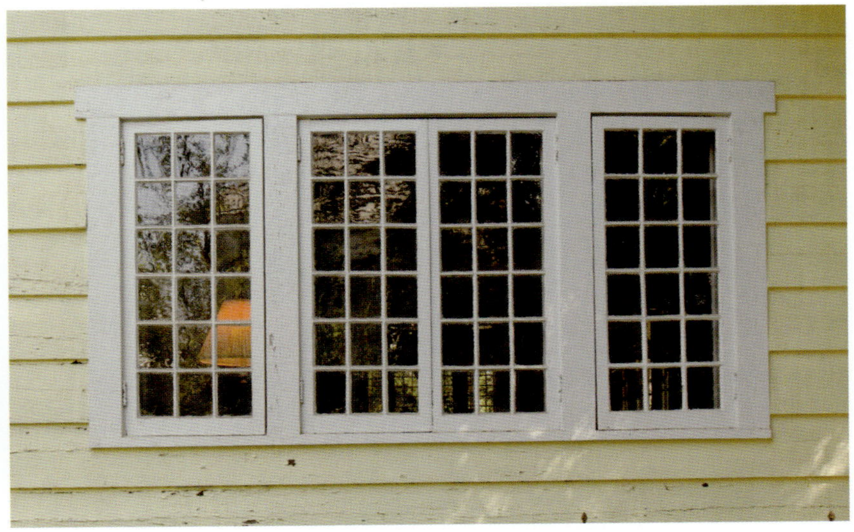

FIGURES 13.51-13.52. Window Groups.

(Top Left) Gaston House at Millard's Crossing: two treatments using three windows, the one on the left in a bay configuration and the one on the right, three light and flat use of the same grouping;

(Above Lower) S. W. Blount House on Mound Street: a massive bow window grouping as the base supporting two Palladian window treatments.

FIGURES 13.53-13.54. Window Groups.

(Top Right) The A. T. Mast, Senior, House on Mound Street;

(Above Right) Ezell-Davison Cottage on Virginia Avenue;

(Below) Hayter House on North Street.

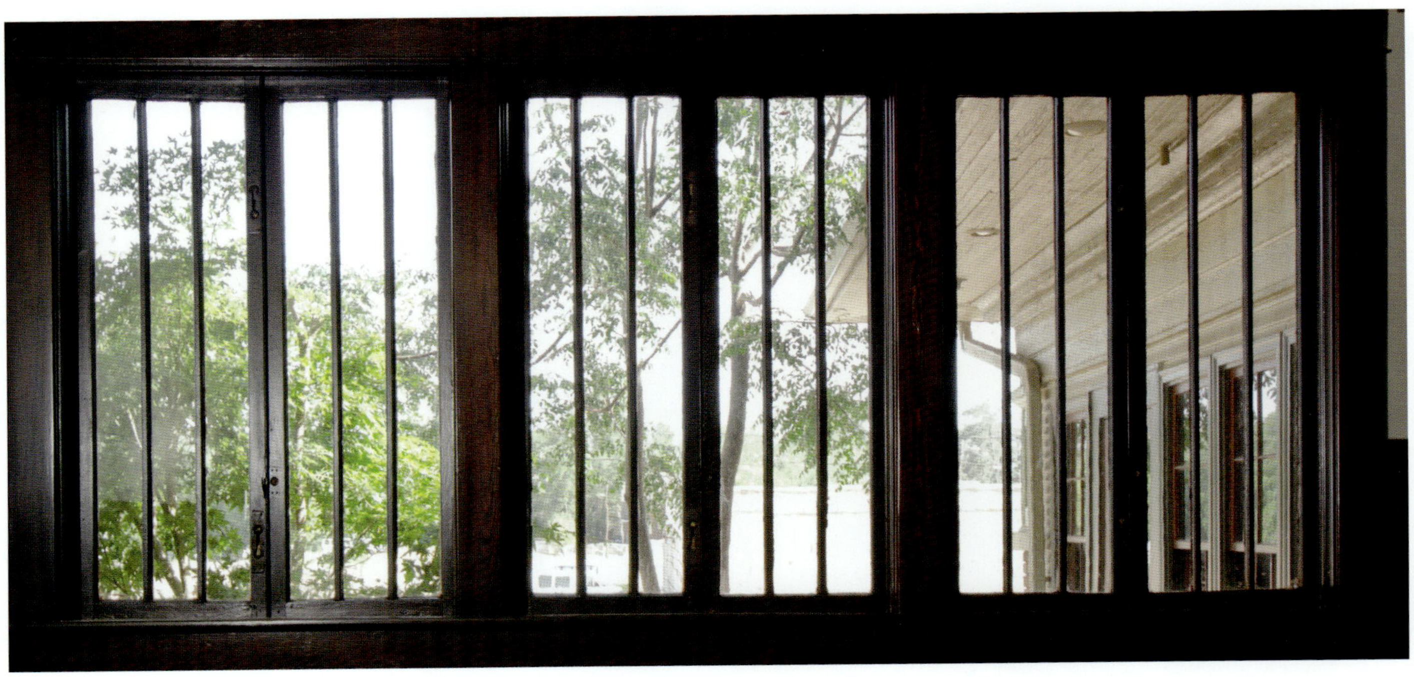

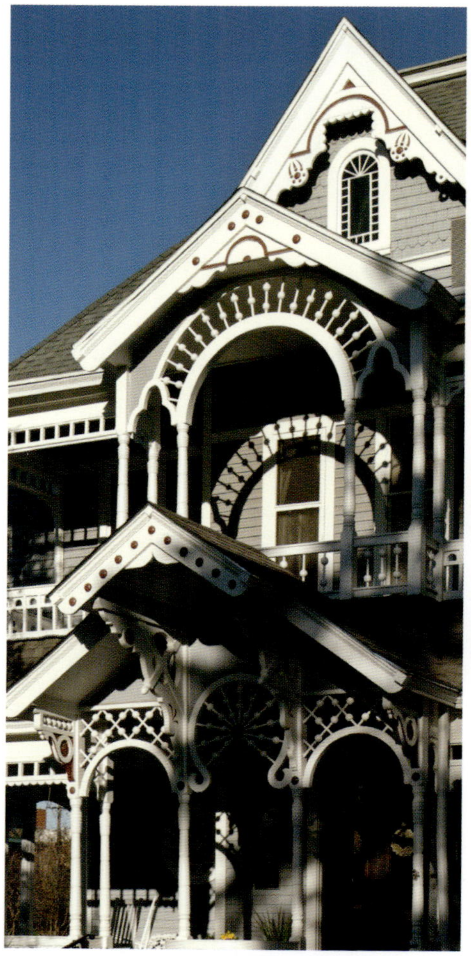

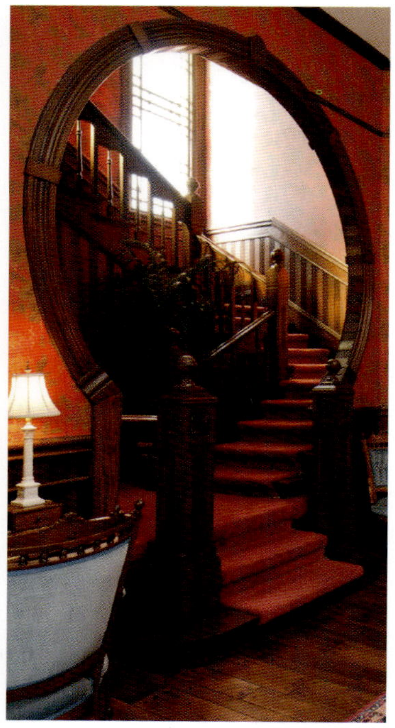

Exotic Influences and Towers

Many of the features Rulfs included in his architecture were standard Queen Anne Features: asymmetrical façades, front-facing gables, wrap-around and second-story porches, bay windows, and pediments. He borrowed, adapted, and invented designs, like most architects. Always, the trick was to balance the demands of functionality, taste, and materials. At one point in his career, however, he became enamored with the romantic and exotic styles sometimes called Moorish Revival or Neo-Moorish. He used elements of Moorish design on the Shindler House, but it was on the Roland Jones House and the Link Sturdevant House that he incorporated the most extensive ornamentation drawn from the exotic styles.

Rulfs used towers on all of his churches, desiring to make Nacogdoches a city of spires. North German towns, especially Oldenburg Stadt, were dominated by church spires. In the period from 1890 to 1901, he also placed towers on his residential designs. The idea of a tower on the corner of buildings was standard fare in Germany and Europe in general since the period of the Baroque. The Ducal Palace in Oldenburg had a prominent corner tower. The W. U. Perkins House (1890) was the first house in Nacogdoches to have a tower; the Jones House had the grandest of his towers.

FIGURES 13.55-13.57. Exotic Influences on the Jones House. *(Left) Jones House Front Porch; (Above) Stairwell (Below Left) the Jones House Tower..*

FIGURE 13.58. (Below) The Link Sturdevant House.

FIGURES 13.59-13.60. (Right) *Towers on the Crouch-Stripling House and the Lindsey House.*

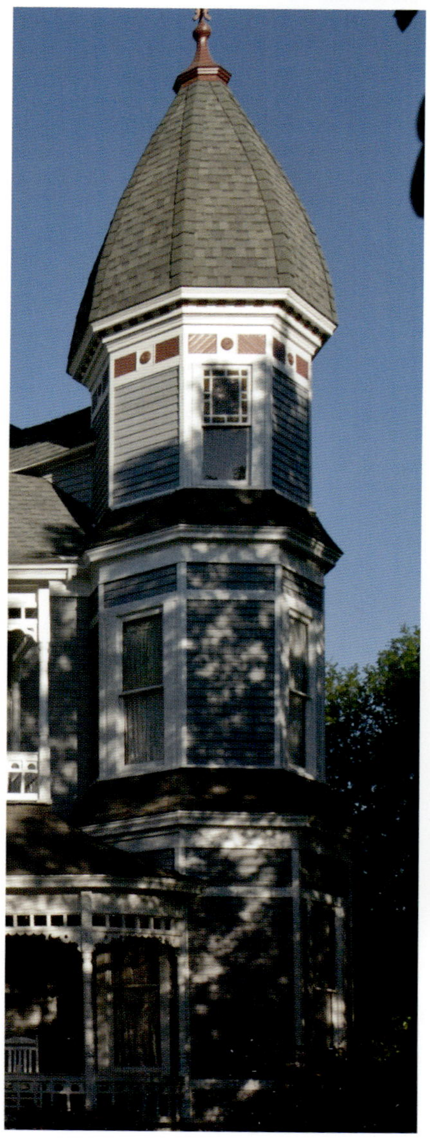

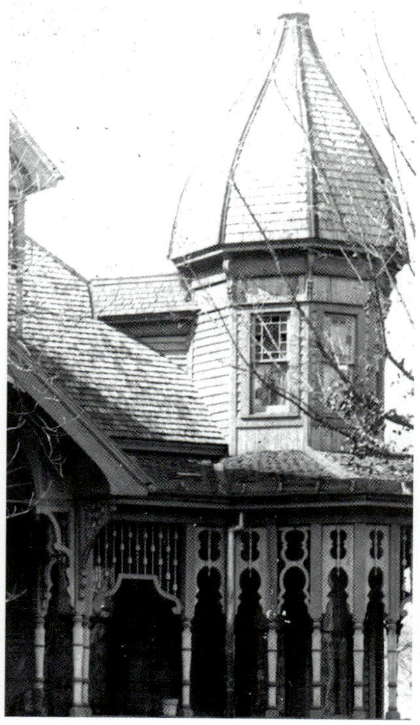

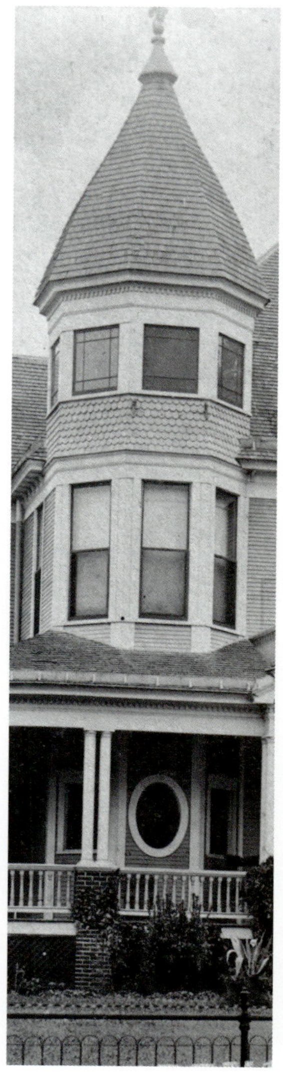

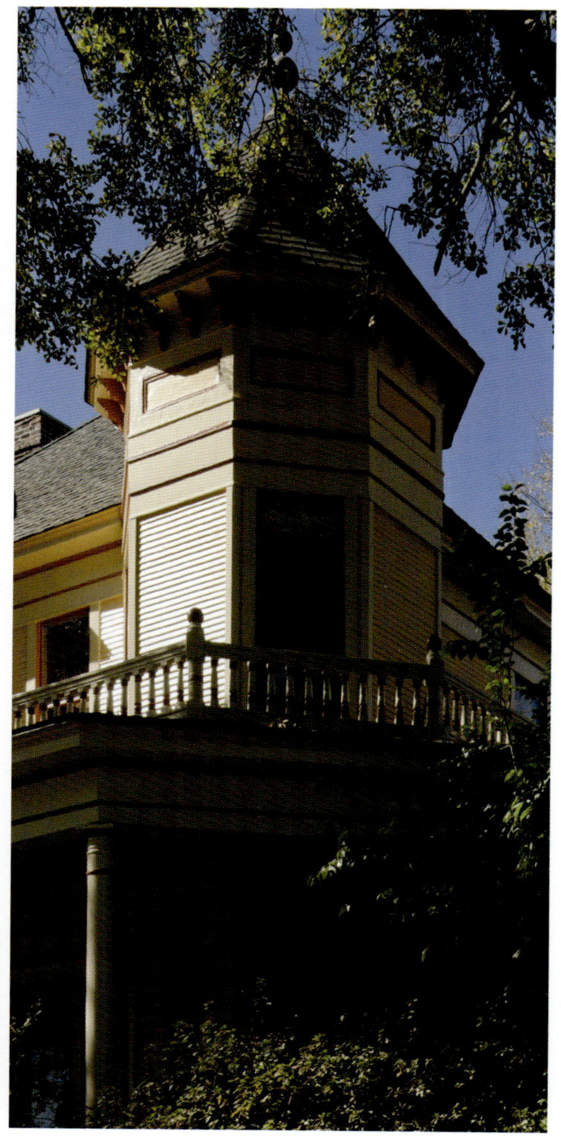

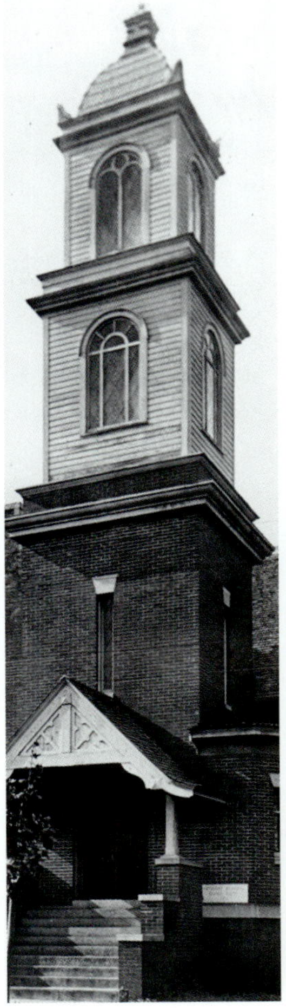

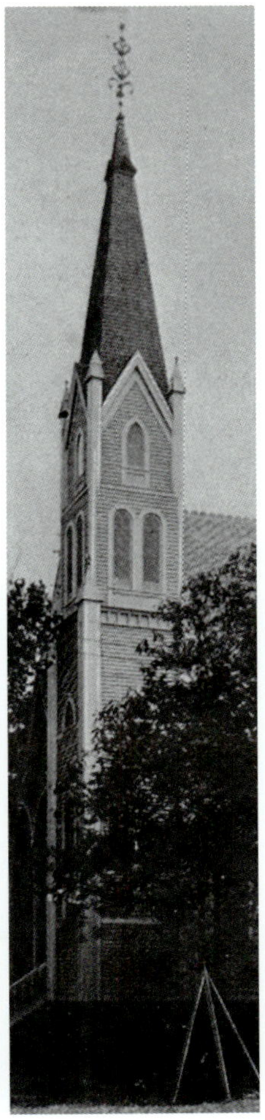

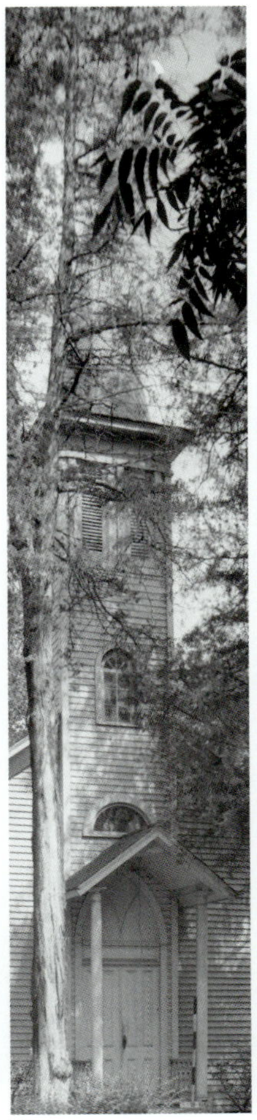

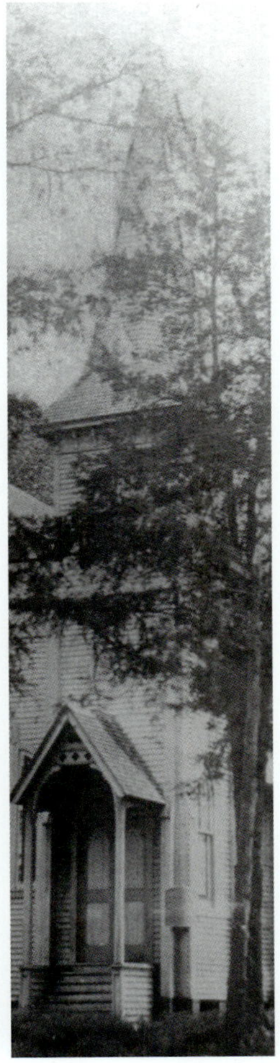

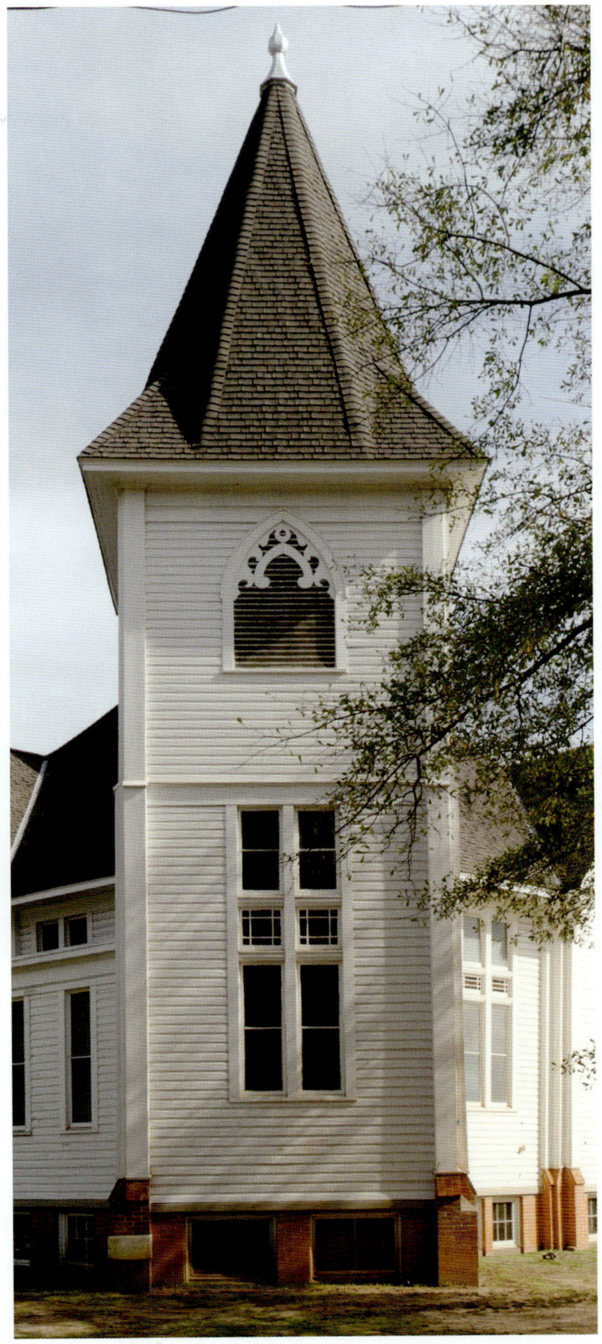

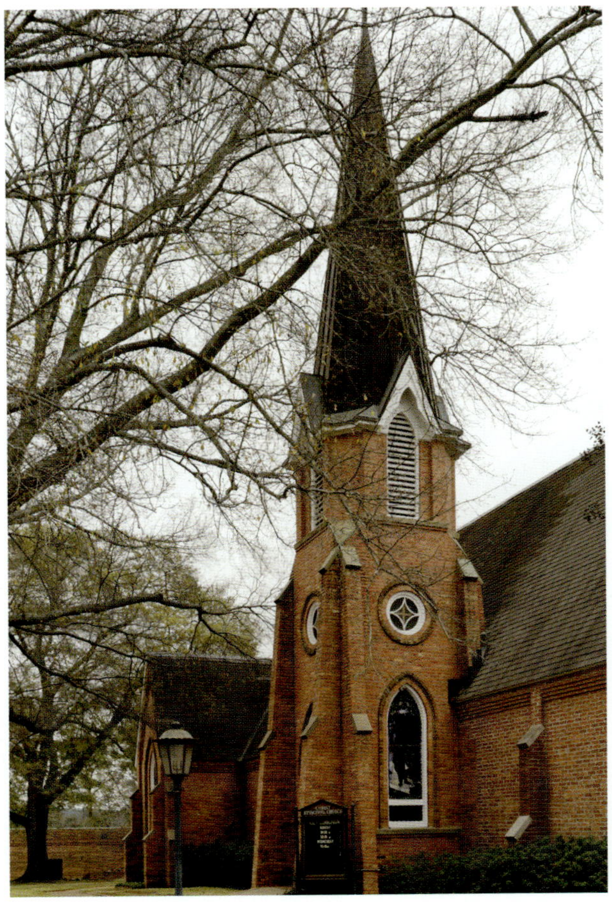

Church Spires

FIGURES 13.61-13.64. Church Towers by Rulfs.

(Above, L to R) First Methodist in 1910; First Baptist in 1899; Catholic in 1905; Main Street Presbyterian in 1902.

FIGURE 13.65

(Left) Christ Episcopal Church Tower in 2012.

FIGURES 13.66-13.67. Zion Hill Baptist Church.

(Top Right) Zion Hill Baptist Church Tower (1914) in 2012.

(Bottom Right) Zion Hill Baptist Church Tower as seen from Space Satellite in 2012.

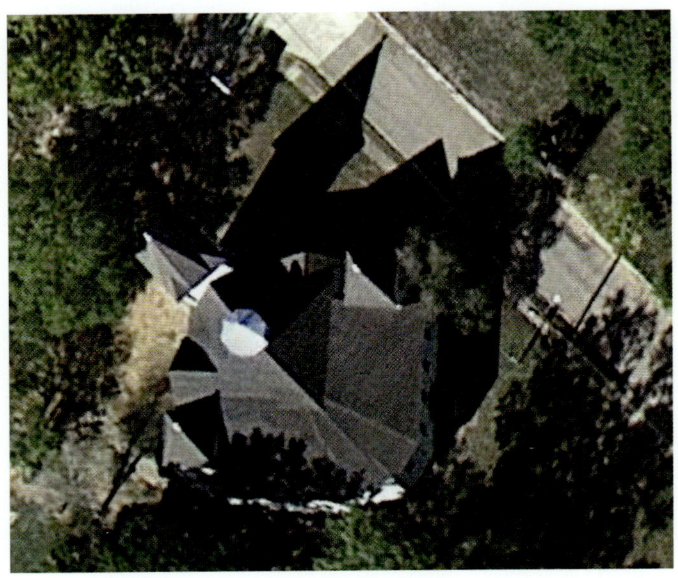

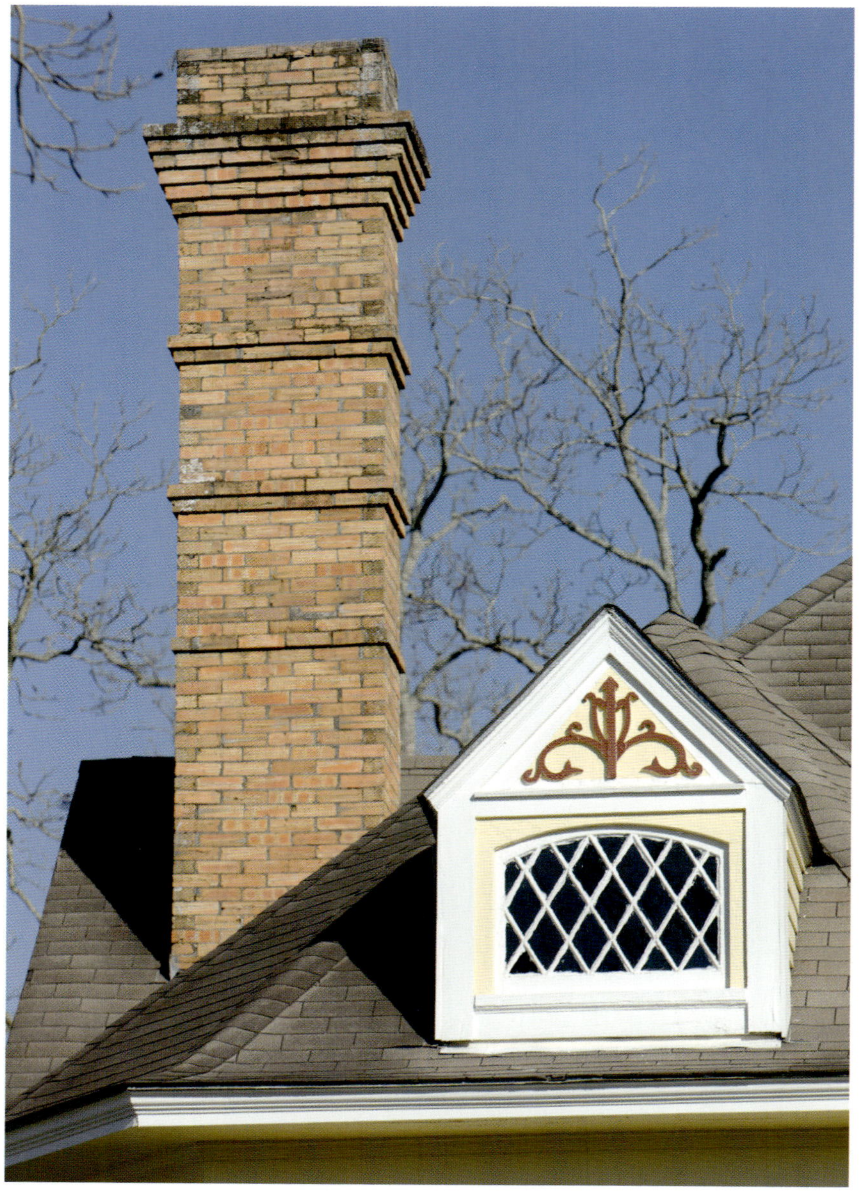

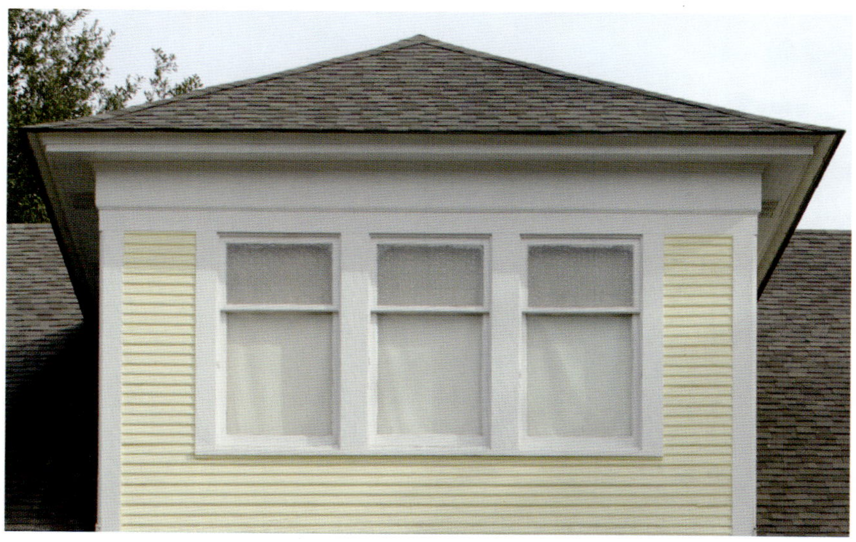

FIGURE 13.68. (Top) Charles Perkins House (1900).
FIGURE 13.69. (Above) Summers House (1913) has four room-size dormers.
FIGURE 13.70 (Right) Cooper House (1898).

Roofs, Chimneys, and Dormers

Rulfs favored complex roof constructions. He used the standard gable roof construction in his early houses, for instance on the Charles Hoya House (1888) and the R. C. Shindler House; but from the moment he was given the opportunity by his patrons, as he was on the Bullen Hotel and the Edwards House, he combined his use of gable roof construction within the framework of an overall hipped roof. Vernacular planners found these Queen Anne roofs difficult. In the 1890s, the disadvantages of the hipped roof—less space in the attic for access and maintenance—did not cause problems because of the high pitches of the roofs. Some pyramidal roofs had to be clipped at the top because of their soaring heights. Increasingly, after 1906, he used more and more hipped roofs, with increasingly lower pitch. The dormer rooms under these low-pitched roofs had portions of their walls chamfered in order to achieve acceptable headroom space. This pattern of development followed trends across the nation.

The architect placed dormers on his houses for a variety of reasons, both practical and decorative. Similar to his use of skylights in his commercial buildings on Main Street, the dormer helped to create usable space and make repairs easier in an attic. Since most attics originally were not floored, however, the dormers served Rulfs as a way of making the house look more impressive. Rulfs also made use of windows in the tympanum of front-facing gables for the same purposes. The device worked. Even today, when any careful analysis of a house would clearly indicate that there are only two stories, the presence of a dormer in the roof or gable front leads the viewer or the architectural surveyor to declare the house to be a half-story larger than it really was. The Sanborn Map surveyors frequently could not make up their minds. Frequently, Rulfs further enhanced the decorative purposes by using special shapes, mullions, lights, materials, or art glass. After electricity, many of the dormers were fitted with fans or louvers to facilitate ventilation. The architect experimented with room-size dormers in the period after 1910, in such houses as the John Perkins, Haselwood, and Tom Summers houses.

While some of his chimneys in the early days were external, almost always Rulfs designed internal chimneys. The Lee Hardeman and the Sarah Bagley houses had their external chimney removed when the houses were reworked. Almost always, the chimneys had multiple flues and served several fireplaces. Rulfs particularly like corner fireplaces. Only the A. T. Mast House, of the architect's later works, has an external chimney. The chimney's brickwork depended on how much the client wanted to spend. The Blount, Charles Perkins, and Schmidt houses had particularly decorative chimneys.

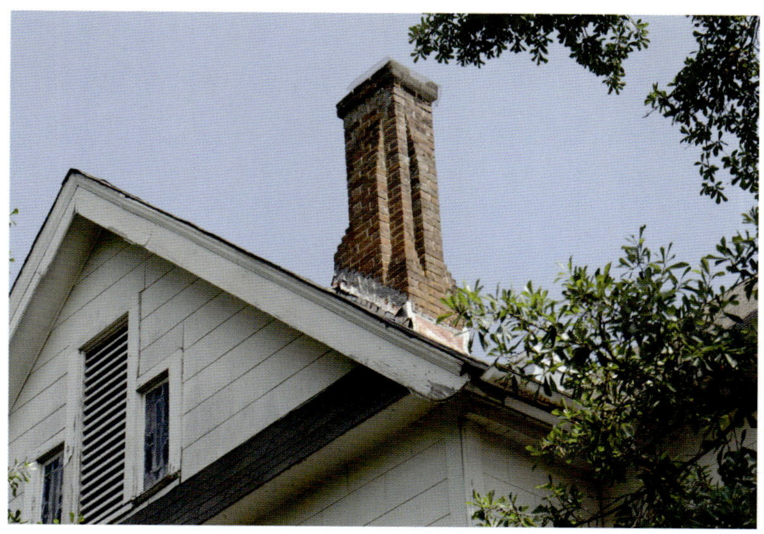

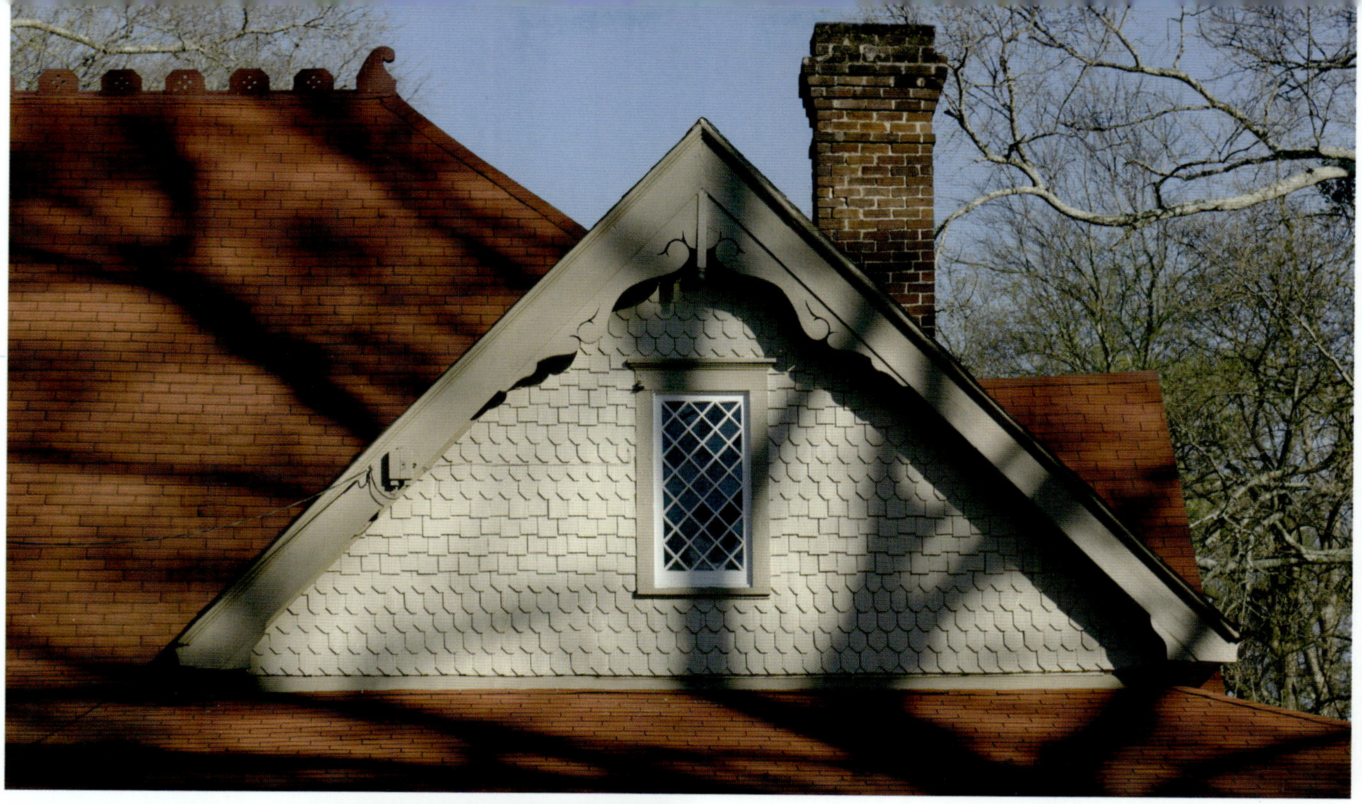

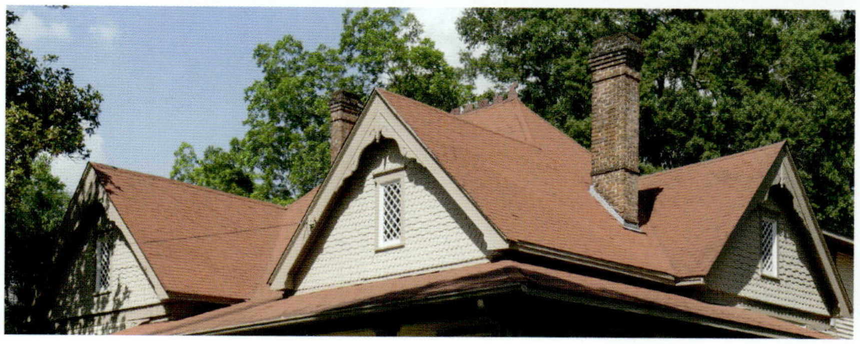

FIGURE 13.71. (Above) Tucker-Branch House (1899)
FIGURE 13.72. (Left) Tucker-Branch House - Roofline.

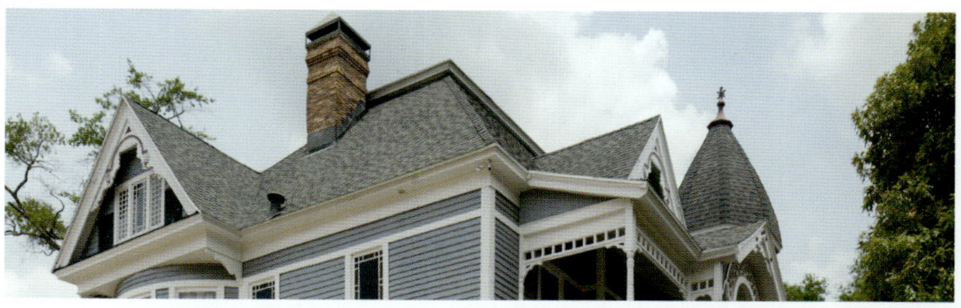

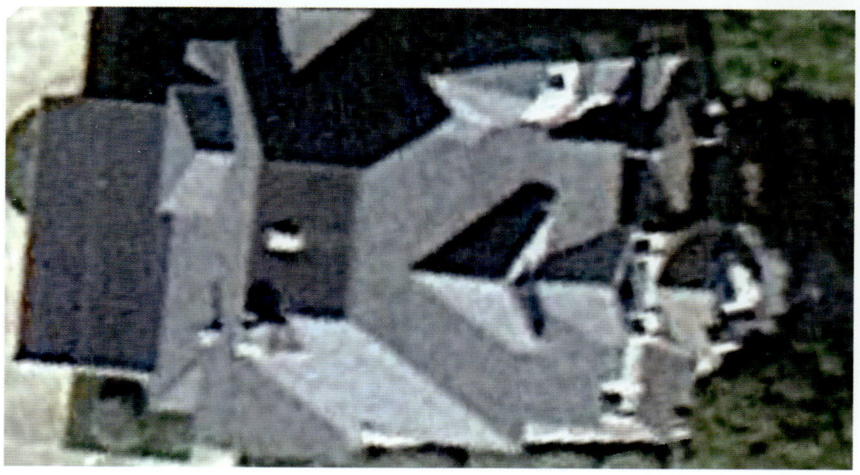

FIGURES 13.73-13.74. (Above) Two views of the complicated roof on the Jones House (1896-97): the south elevation and a view from Space. *From Google Earth.*

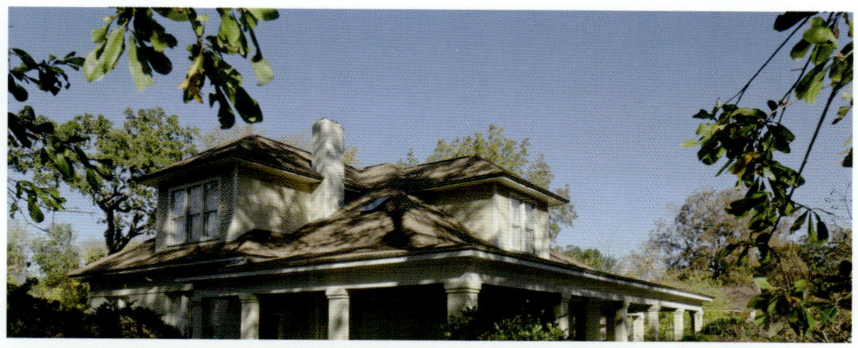

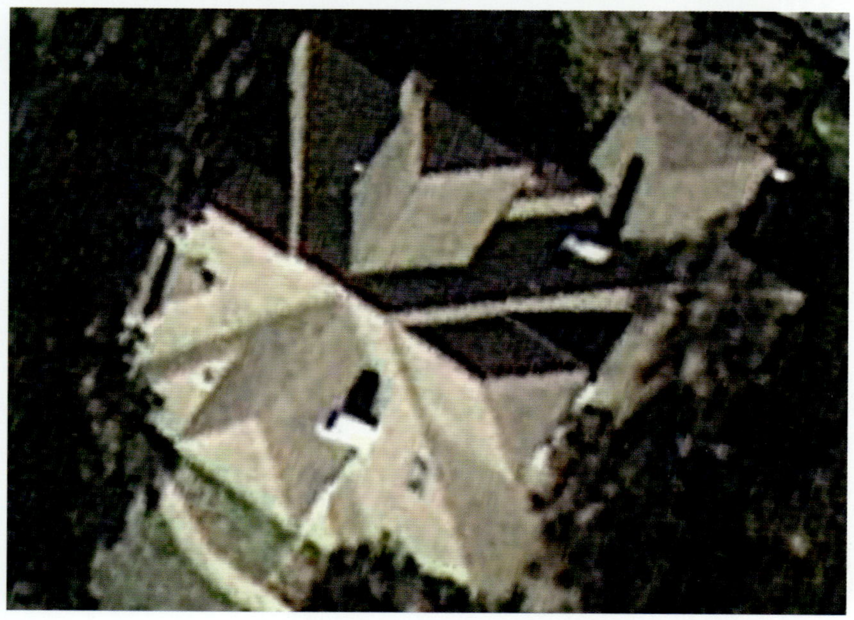

FIGURES 13.75 and 13.76. (Above) Two views of the Haselwood House (1912); the south elevation and from Space. *From Google Earth.*

Porches

Since porches were quintessential in East Texas, a special comment on the architect's treatment of porches is in order. Porches to give shelter at a doorway were common in Oldenburg, but porches as galleries for outdoor living were not. Rulfs had to rethink the uses of porches after he arrived in Nacogdoches. Certainly, porches helped the architect define his houses. While the styles of his porches evolved, Rulfs was as much enamored with porches as utilitarian objects as with their framework for decorative statements. After living in East Texas, Rulfs recognized that porches extended the living spaces: to escape the heat; to accommodate overflow guests with a variety of seating and table arrangements; as a place to dry clothes, play, stack wood, etc. Metal screening extended the possibilities.

Before 1897, posts dominated the support system of his porch roofs. Many porch elements could be and were ordered from the extensive millwork catalogues of the period. But, on many of the large houses of the 1890s, the Rulfs brothers created many of the elements in their own shop. By the turn of the century, complex millwork was gradually replaced with classical elements, followed by boxed columns, and, eventually, brick columns. Since porches were such an important part of defining the overall historical character of the architect's building, the attempts by later owners to add porch structures to create a false sense of historical development have rarely been successful. These alterations usually just diminish the historic nature and give a house a Disney-like quality.

Access to the porch space was always a concern. In addition to the standard entrances (front and side), Rulfs frequently augmented access by using slip-head windows in individual rooms along the porch. Several houses with these auxiliary entrances still exist today: the Chapman, Pearson-Spradley, and Charles Perkins houses. Sometimes, in later remodelings, these slip-head windows have been replaced by doors with transoms, as in the Tucker House. Because of the changeable weather conditions, the porch wrapped around two sides. Some houses, such as the Ford House had porches on all sides. Usually, Rulfs avoided north porches unless the town lot made this a necessity. West-facing porches were usually accompanied by a southern exposure, as they wrapped around the house. He designed many of his porches within the cover of the principal roof. In later years, he placed most screened porches on the south side, as in the Perkins, Summers, Price, Hollis Mast, and Lindsey houses. The houses on the western hills above town had porches designed to take advantage of the views.

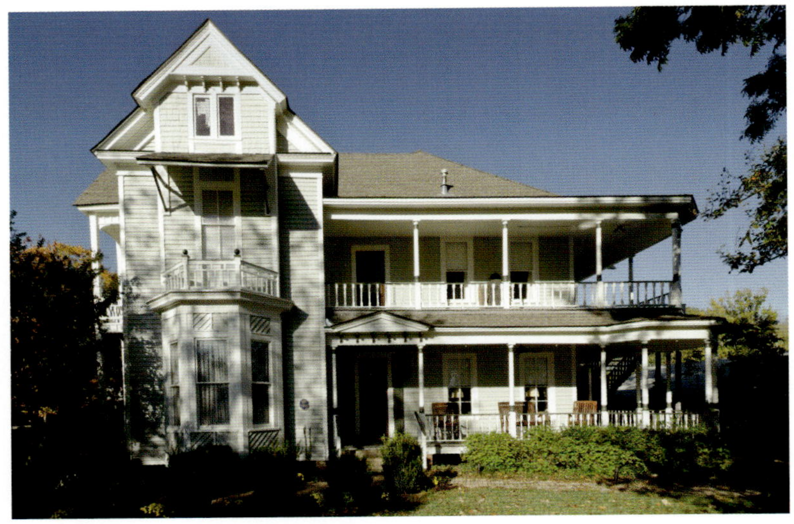

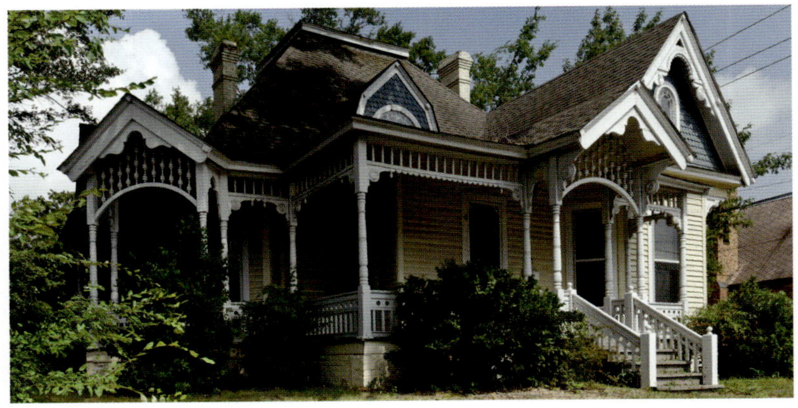

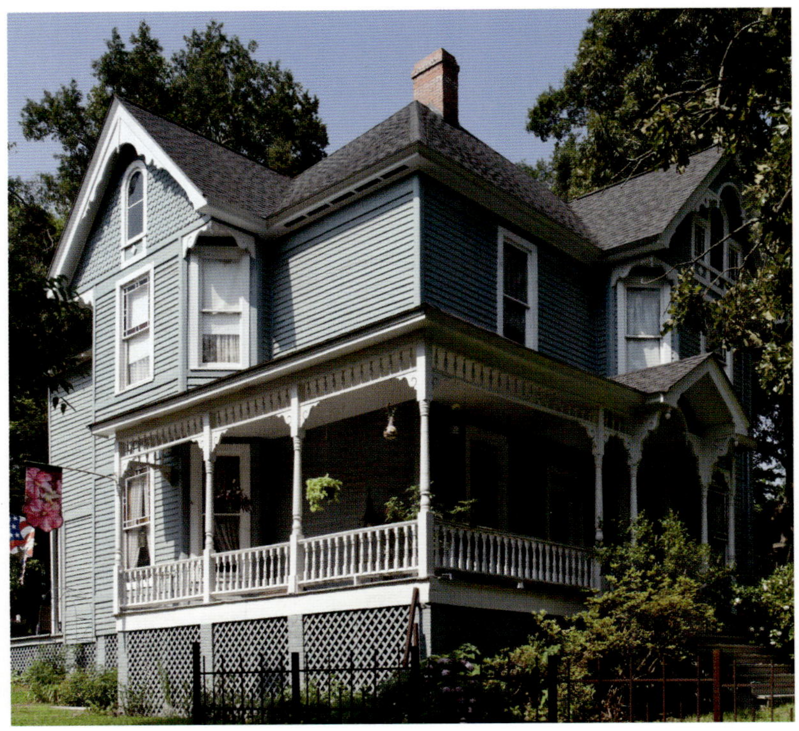

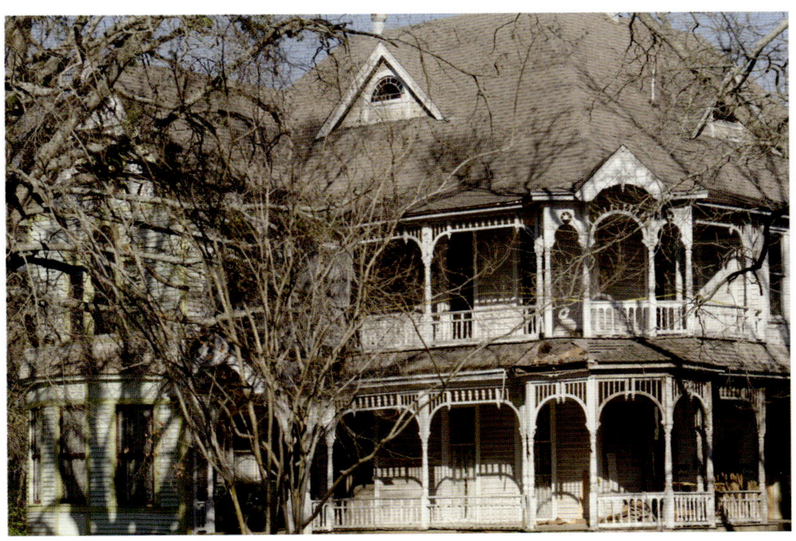

FIGURES 13.77 - 13.80. Porch Illustrations from the 1890s.
(Top) Edwards House (1888);
(Middle) Laura Blount Chapman House (1894);
(Above) Middlebrook House (1898);
(Left) Stephen Blount House (1897).

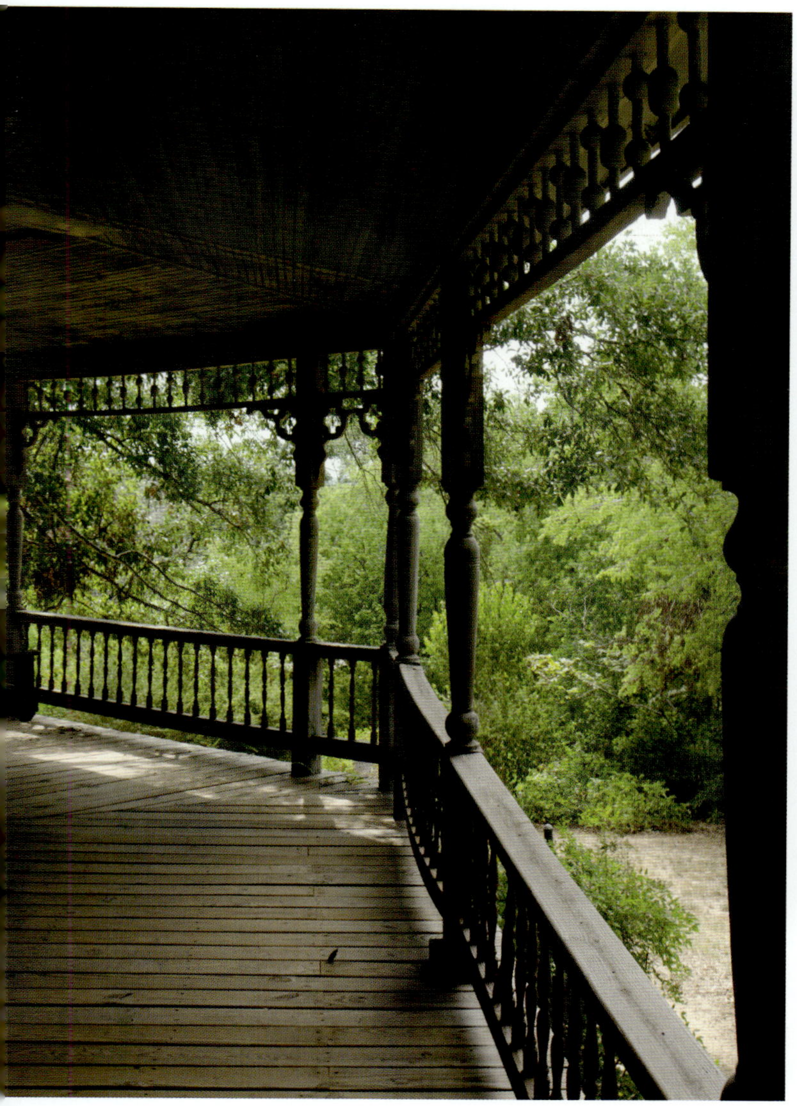

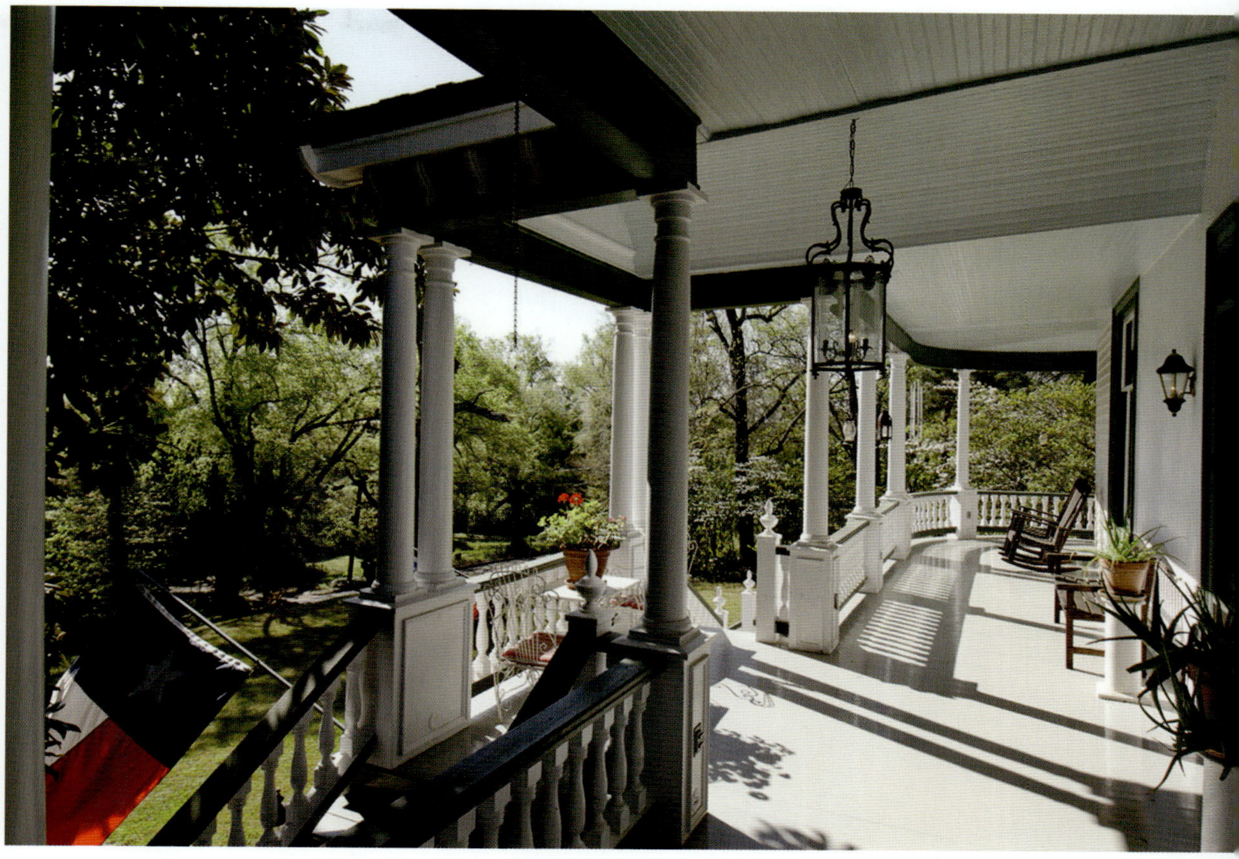

FIGURES 13.81 - 13.83 Porches from the 1890s.
(Left) Cooper House (1898) on Irion Hill;
(Above) Harris House (1895) on Virginia Avenue;
(Below) Robert Lindsey (1900) on Virginia Avenue.

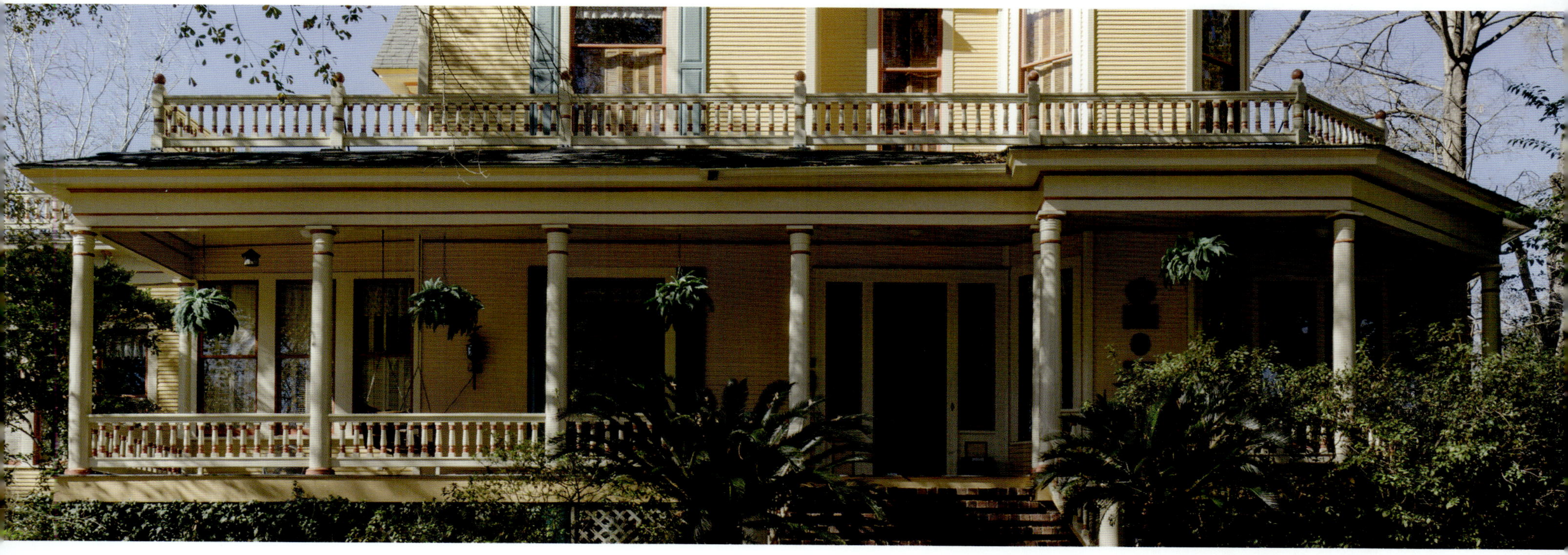

Twentieth Century Porches

While porches like the one on the Lindsey House continued to be popular in the twentieth century, the maintenance of these porches grew more and more burdensome. Some owners enclosed part of them. By the time of the First World War, modifications began to creep into the houses built by Rulfs. Some houses like the Cason House had both open and enclosed porches; others had brick columns and even concrete floors; and, the houses after the war had terraces and enclosed sunrooms.

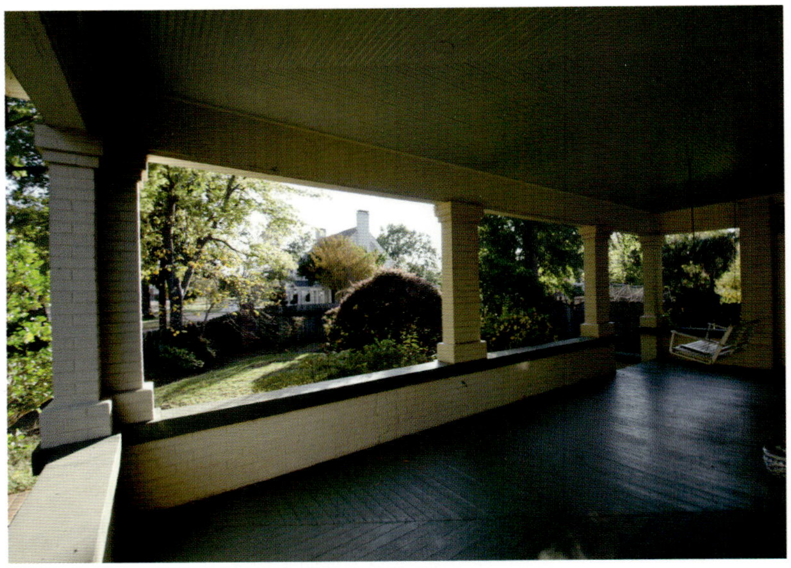

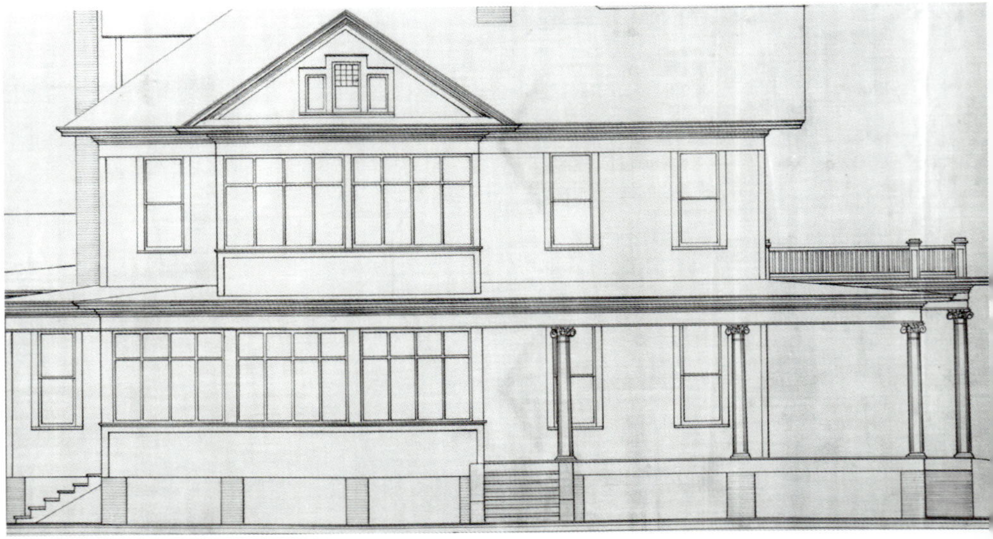

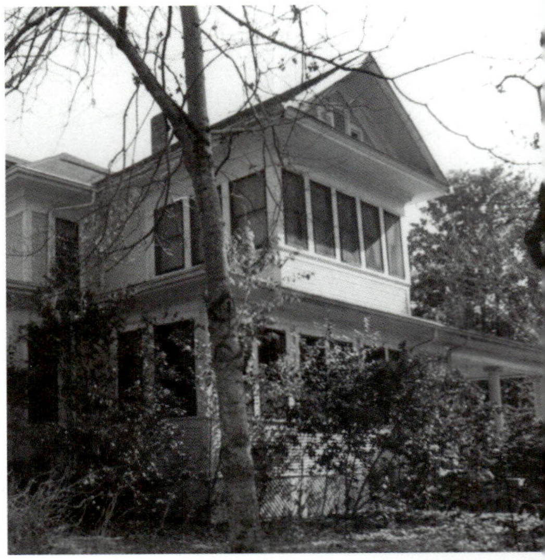

FIGURES 13.86 and 13.87. (Above and Right) The D. K. Cason House.

The D. K. Cason House, designed and built in 1914, had one of the most extensive porch systems that Rulfs ever designed. Unlike other houses with surrounding porches, for instance the ones for Harris (1895) and Ford (1903), Rulfs placed both open and enclosed porches, with windows and screens on the Cason house.

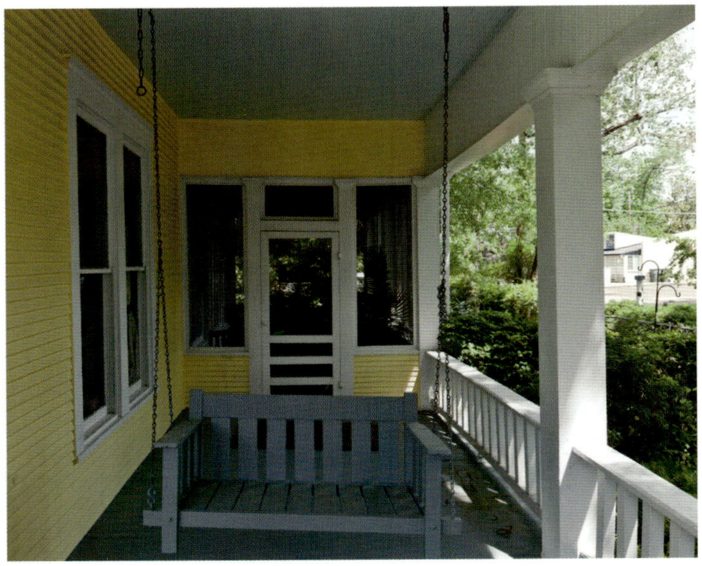

FIGURES 13.84-13.85. (Top Left & Left) Remodeled Houses.

The front porch of the Haselwood House (1912) had brick columns, but wooden floors. The porch on the Summers House was all wood (he owned a lumber yard!), but it included a screened porch.

FIGURE 13.86. (Below Left) The Blum Mast House (1914).

The "Twin" houses for the Hoya sisters had brick columns and concrete porches.

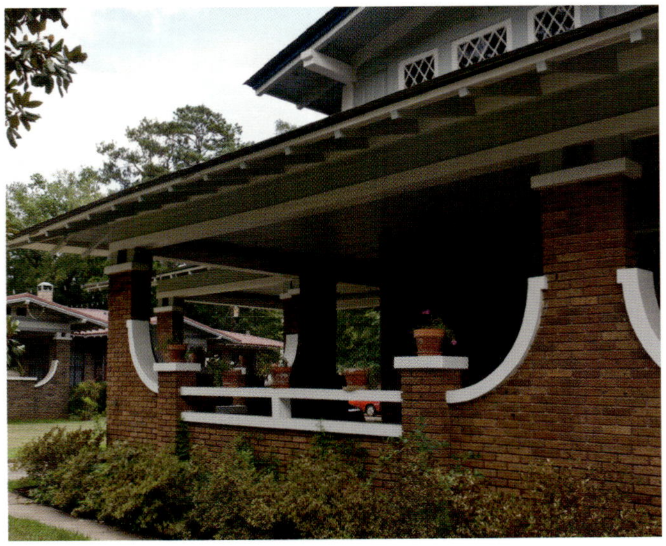

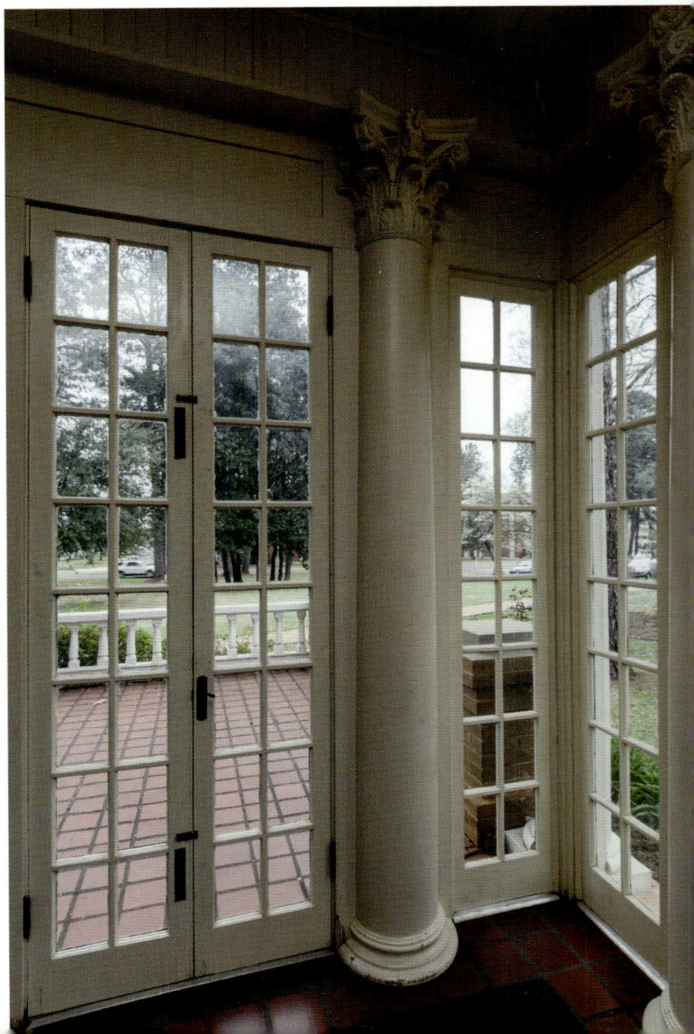

FIGURE 13.88. (Right) The Eugene Blount Solarium.

The porch on the south side of the Blount House was elegantly enclosed with Corinthian columns and French doors; the porch joined a tiled terrace that ran across the entire front of the house. This terrace joined the small porch at the main entrance to the house. The entrance columns supported a balcony accessed from the second story.

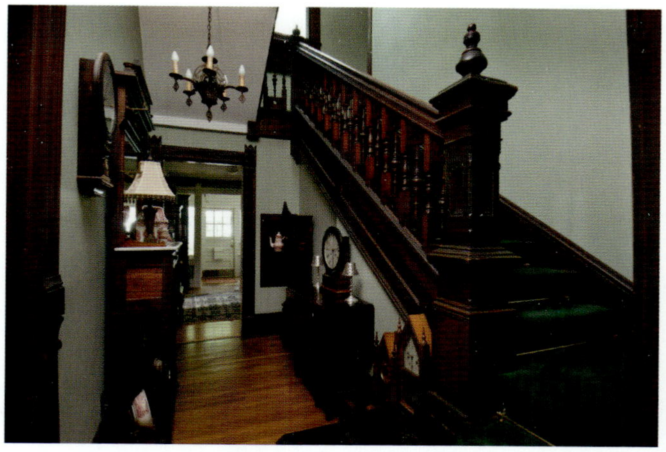

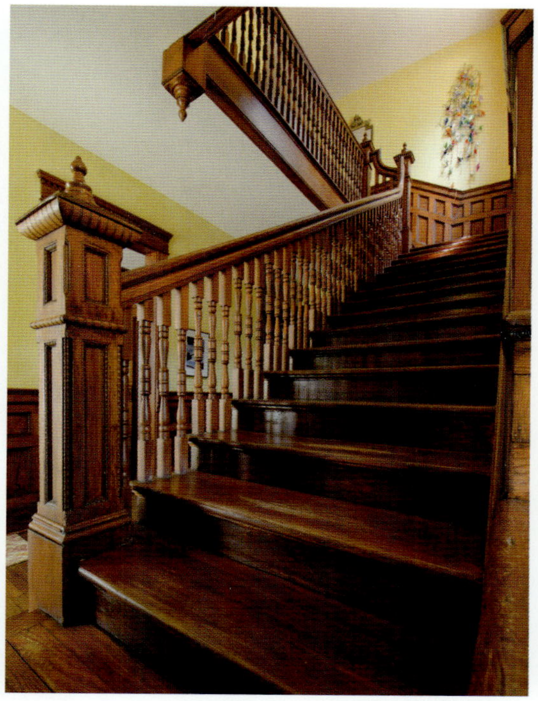

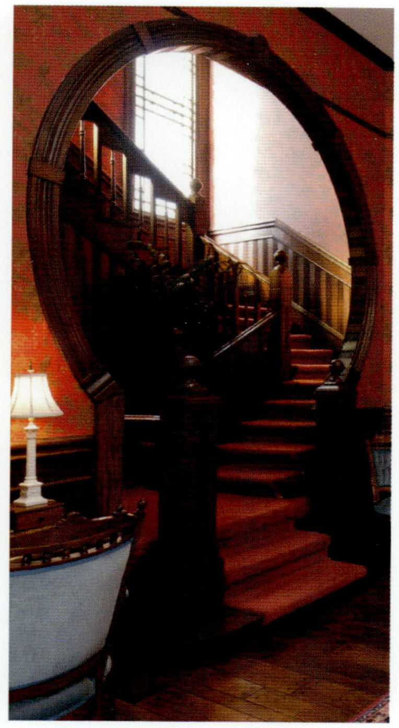

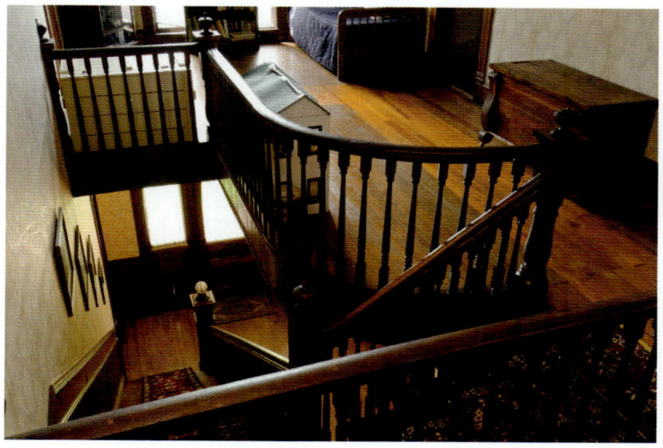

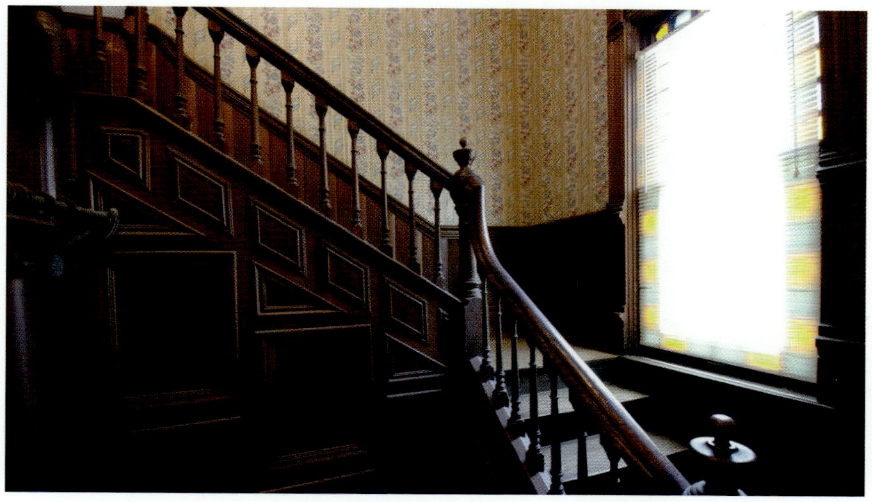

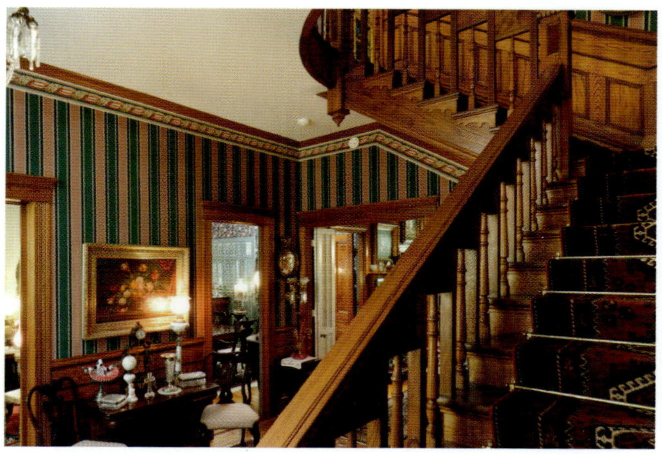

Stairways

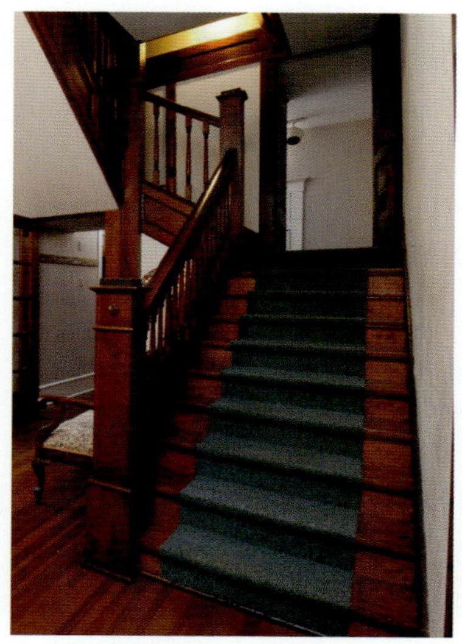

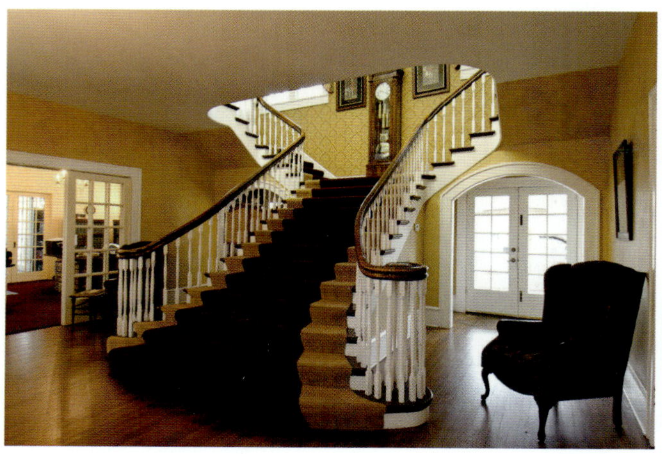

FIGURES 13.89-13.96. Stairway Illustrations.

In clockwise order: (Top Left):
Tol Hardeman House on Mound;
Phillip Sanders House on Sanders Street;
Jones House on Church Street;
Cooper House on Cooper Street;
Lee Hardeman House on Church;
Eugene Blount House on North St.;
Lindsey House on Virginia Avenue;
Charles Perkins House on Mound.

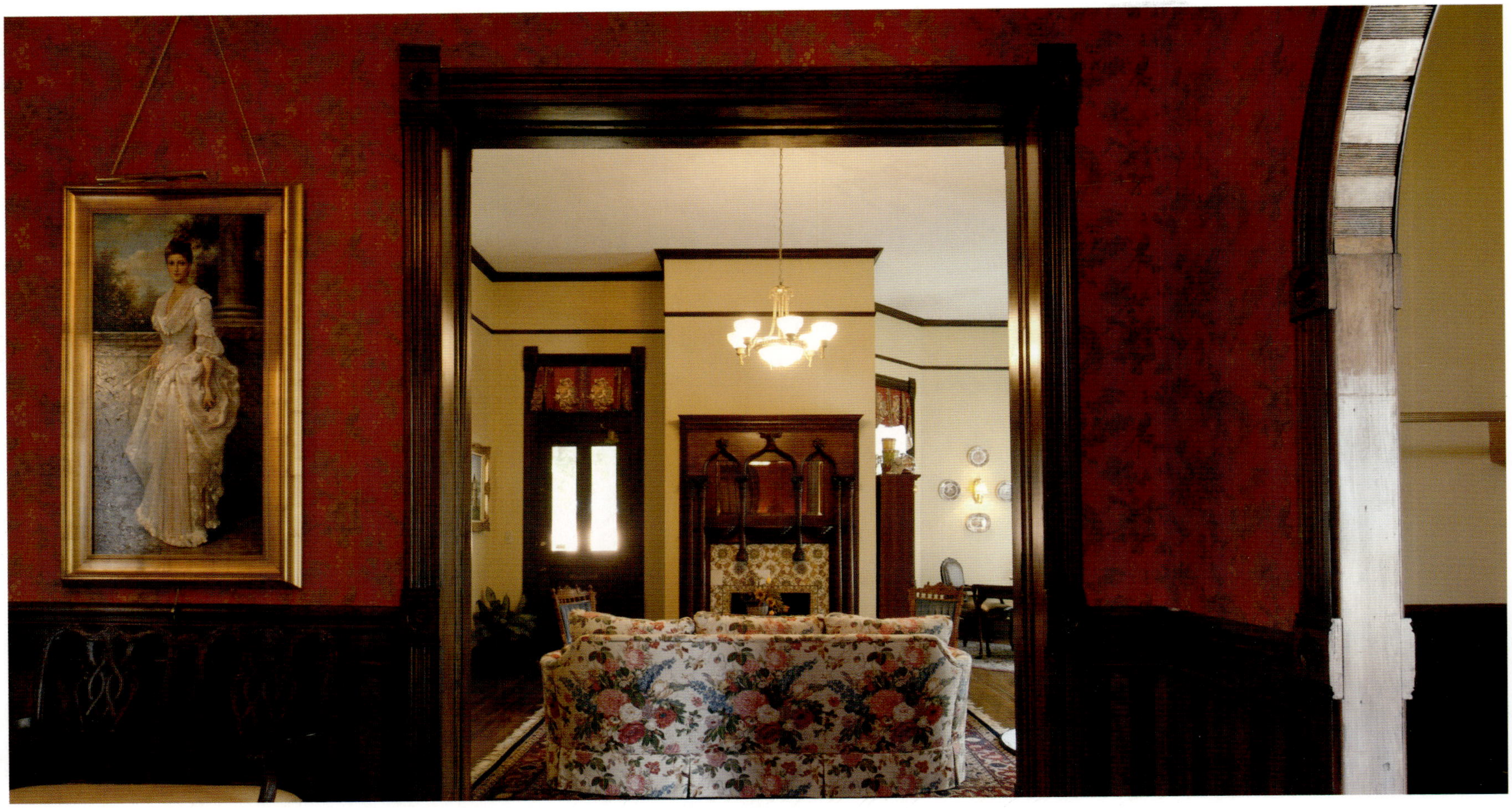

FIGURES 13.97. - 13.101. Woodwork in the Roland Jones House.
(Above) Entrance to Parlor with doors open; imported mantel from St. Louis;
(Below L to R) Wainscoting on the stairwell, Built-in China Cabinet in the Dining Room;
Wainscoting in the Dining Room; Double Pocket Doors, Between the Entrance and Parlor.

Woodwork

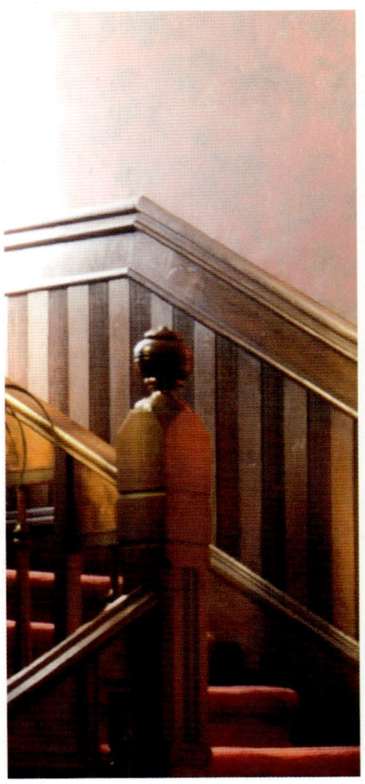

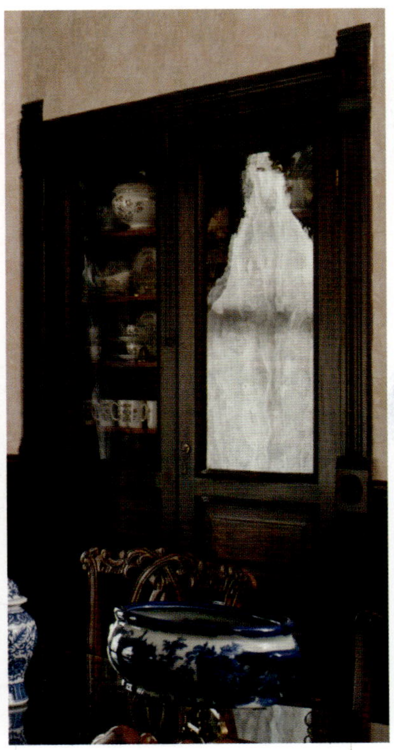

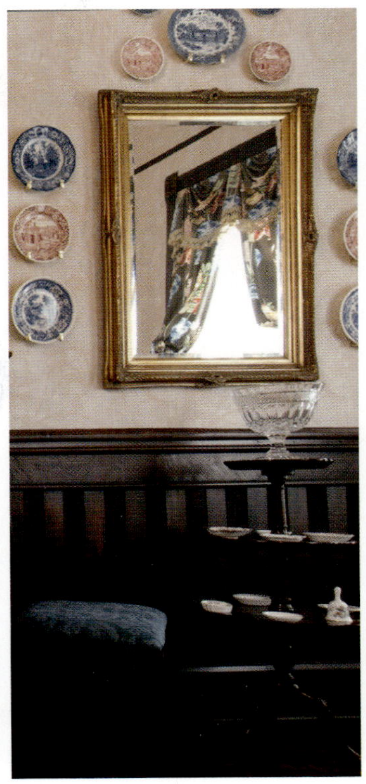

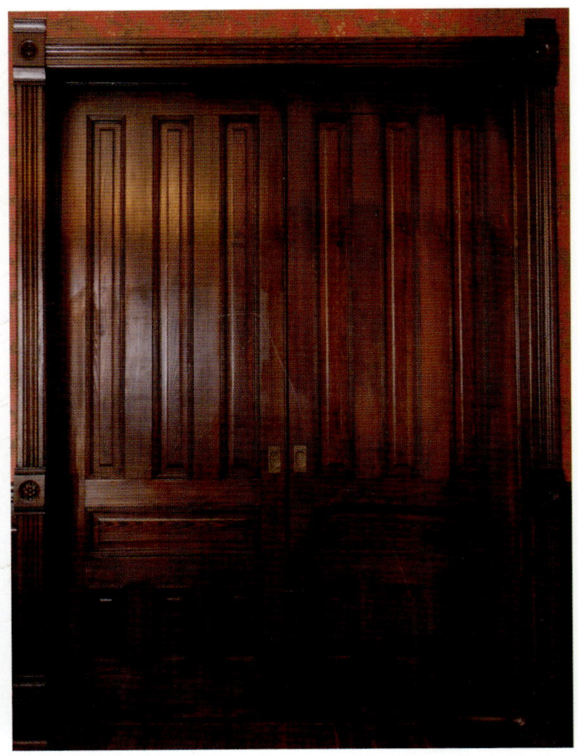

Mantels and Woodwork

For philosophical as well as economic reasons, Rulfs preferred wood to bricks. The plentiful and inexpensive supply of wood in East Texas excited the North German. In his homeland, with few great forests, wood was more expensive than bricks; it was prized for its uniqueness and decorative value. Rulfs, as a carpenter, loved to work with wood and did so to make intricate designs for furniture and houses. While the exterior of his commercial buildings from the beginning were brick and mortar, many of them had extensive wood in their interiors; economic reasons necessitated this. Most commercial building originally had pier-and-beam construction with wooden floors. As the fire hazards increased, Rulfs limited the use of wood. Of course, this increased the expense of doing business in the commercial district, but it was a practical necessity. The commercial buildings in the period after 1906 had almost no wood; the Mayer & Schmidt Building in 1908 was the most fireproof building in Nacogdoches.

In his domestic designs, Rulfs relegated bricks to the areas of necessity: foundations and chimneys. As general esthetic values changed and maintenance became an overriding concern, Rulfs gradually introduced more bricks into his domestic architecture: columns, continuous brick skirting, and brick veneering around 1910-1914.

His love for wood, however, did not prevent him from experimenting in the use of other building materials: permanent roofs (metal and tile), molded concrete blocks, and concrete for slabs, porches, posts, and lintels. He also introduced other innovations quickly, such as metal framing, screening for windows, and central heating.

When patrons allowed, Rulfs reveled in selecting and using a variety of woods for his residences. He and his brother did their most impressive woodwork for the homes of the Perkins brothers, Schmidt, Jones, the various Blounts, Hayter, Pearson, Sanders, and Cason homes. He designed intricate patterns of solid wood paneling for walls, stairs, dining rooms, ceilings, and wainscoting. His wainscoting in the period from 1895-1900, in the Jones, S. W. Blount, Pearson, and Charles Perkins houses, which consists of alternating plain and ribbed boards, is particularly noteworthy. His use of egg-and-dart molding is unique in the Lindsey House. His incorporation of period wood from the Old Stone Fort into the inlay decorations of the Guy Blount House is also worth mentioning.

Following the trend across the nation, Rulfs ordered most of the wooden mantels in these houses from readily available catalogs. The mantels in the Schmidt House came from Europe. The mantels in the Jones house came from St. Louis. Others came from less auspicious venues. A nice mantel cost only a few dollars. The Rulfs brothers did make mantels, however. The one in the front parlor of the Lee Hardeman House is fine; the one on the back side of the same chimney, made using layered molding, is also attractive.

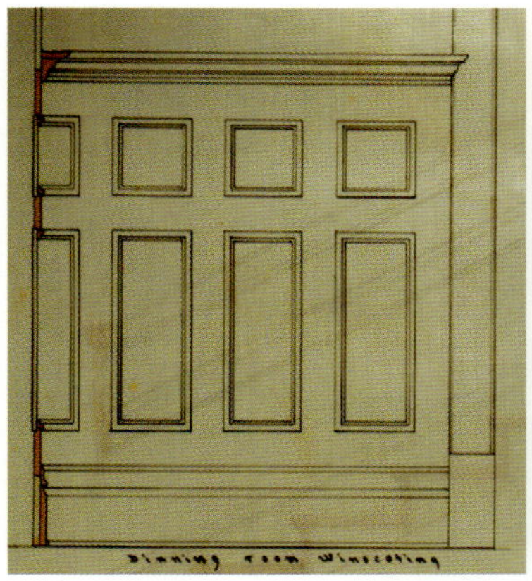
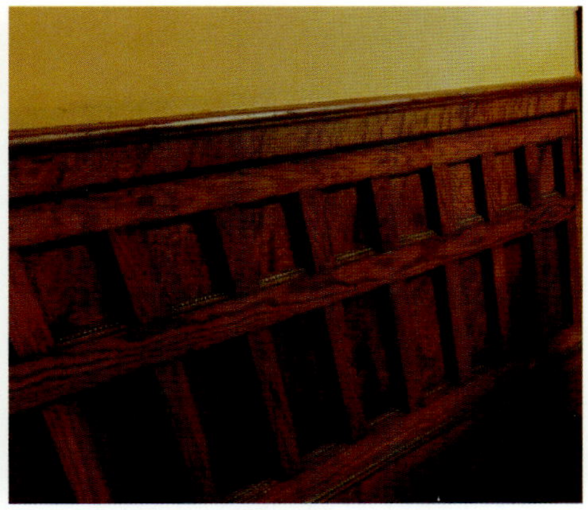

FIGURES 13.105-13.106. (Above) Patterns of Paneling.
Drawing, Cason House and Sanders House Stairwell.

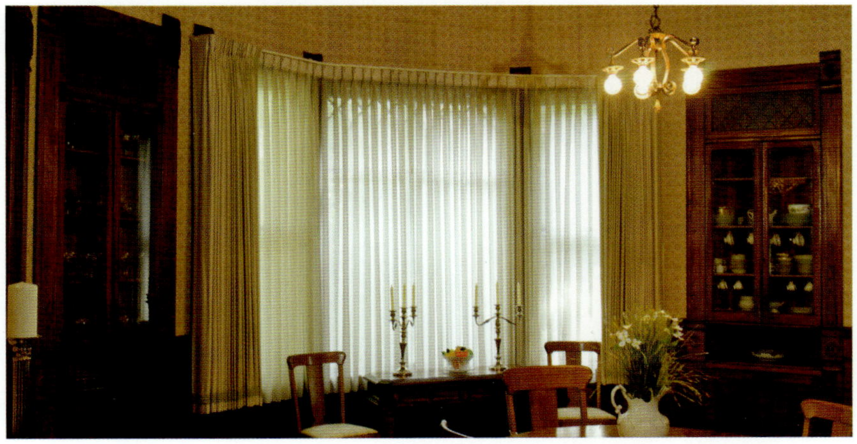

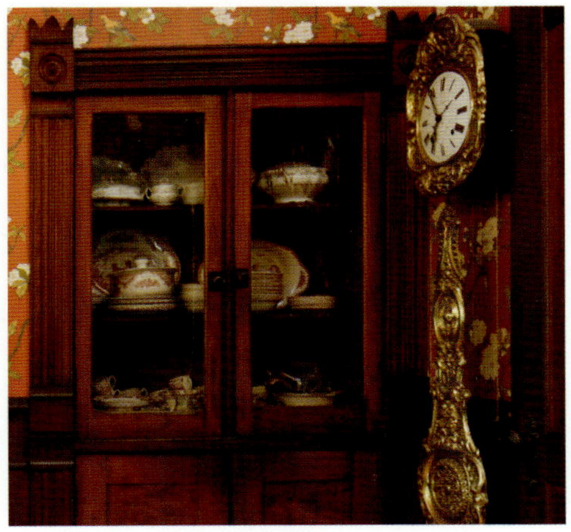

FIGURES 13.107 - 13.108. Built-in Cabinets.
(Above) Twin Corner Cabinets, Tucker-Branch House;
(Right) Tol Hardeman House.

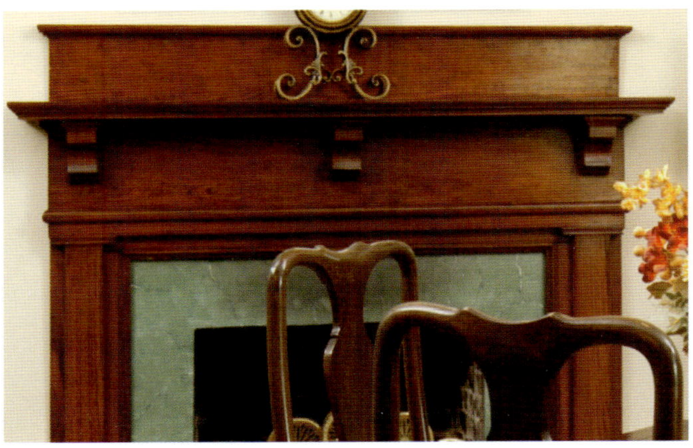

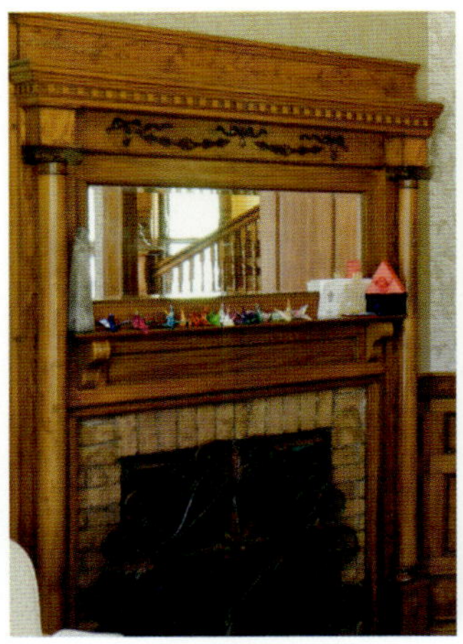
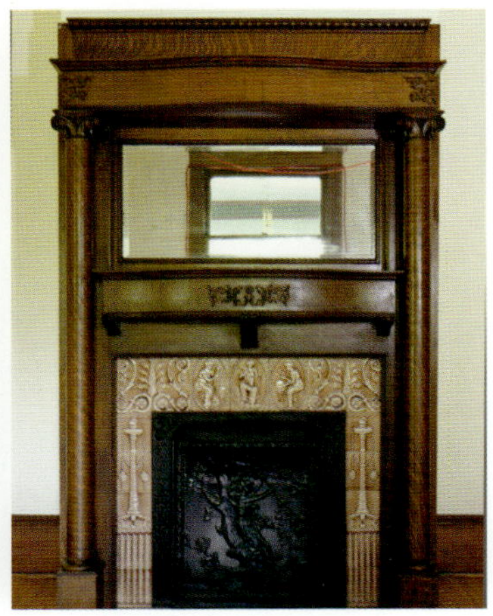

FIGURES 13.102-13.104
Mantels.
(Left) Lee Hardeman House;
(Right) Phillip Sanders House;
(Far Right) E. C. Branch House.

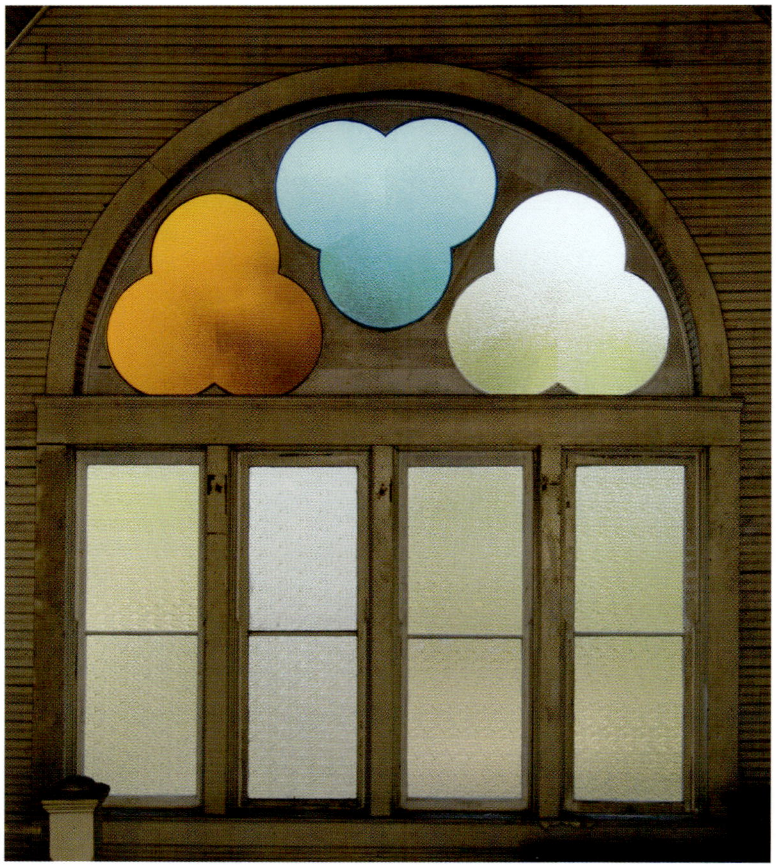

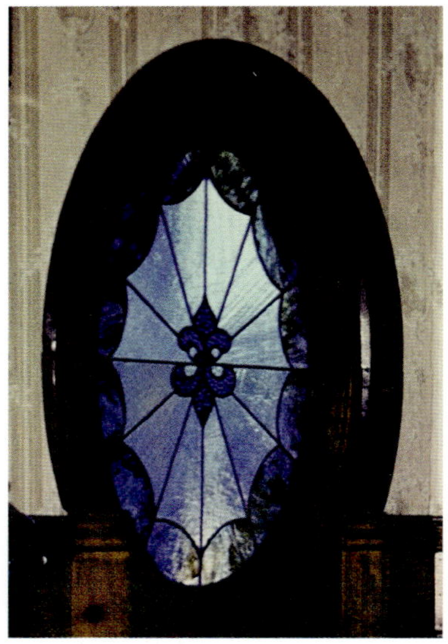

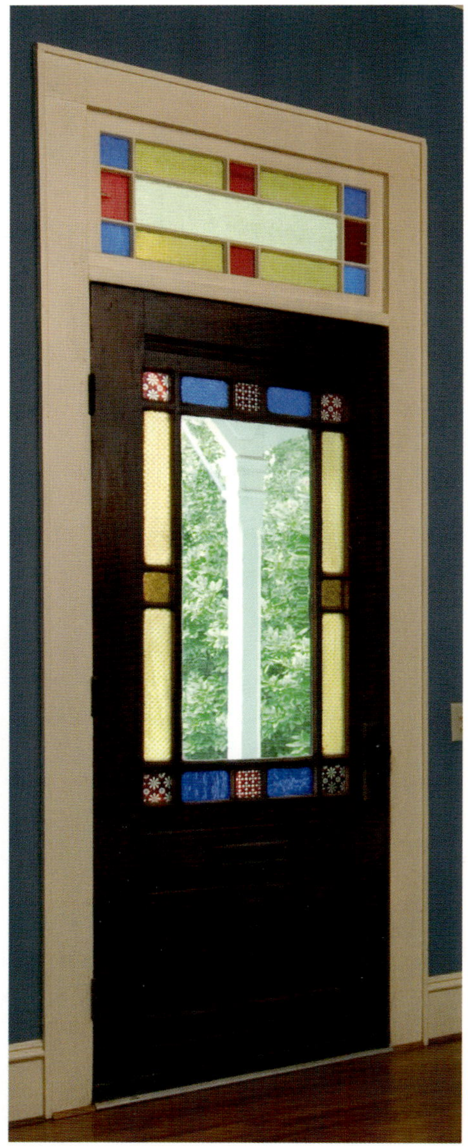

Art Glass

Rulfs incorporated stained glass into most of his churches. When the church could not afford stained glass windows, Rulfs used colored glass to create wonderful illumination of the interiors. In their homes, however, the clientele Rulfs served in Nacogdoches were not inclined to display true stained glass windows or "art glass." The architect did specify a variety of colored glass and leaded glass windows in his domestic structures to add special effects or distinctiveness. Sometimes, he specified it for lining larger windows, sometimes for creating special lighting for an entrance hall (the Crouch-Stripling House), or sometimes he used its opaqueness to give privacy, as in the great staircase of the Roland Jones House. In several instances, he used colored glass in the front gables of houses (Laura Blount Chapman, Sanders, and Middlebrook Houses). In restoring his home, Charles Bright replaced the ventilation louvers added in the 1930s with new stained glass.

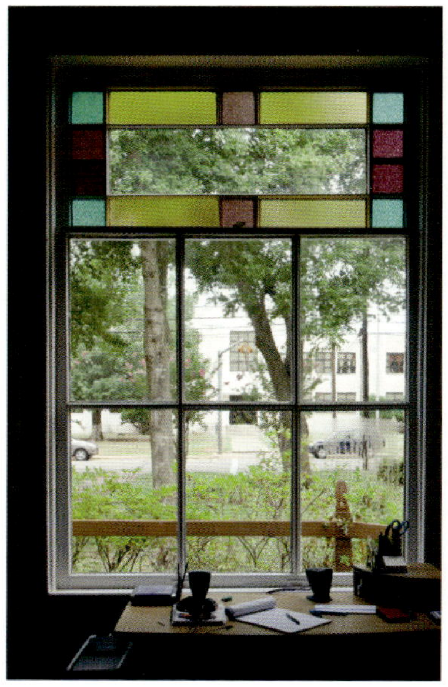

FIGURES 13.109-13.114. Art Glass Examples
(Top Left) Zion Hill Church;
(Top Middle) Stripling House;
(Top Right) Steamboat House Door;
(Middle) Garrison House Window;.
(Right) Sanders House Sidelights from Tympanum;
(Bottom) Charles Perkins House Transoms.

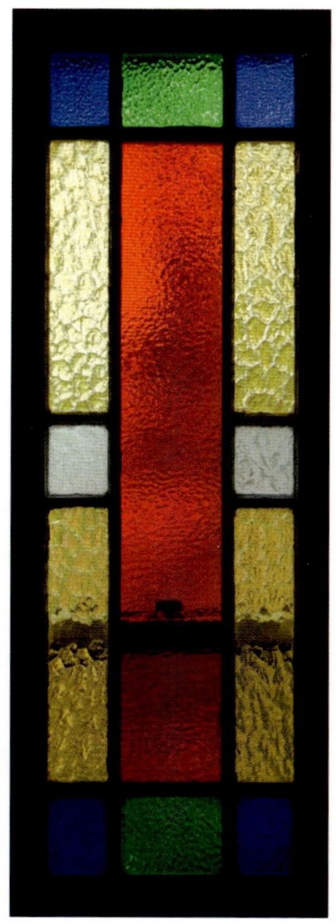

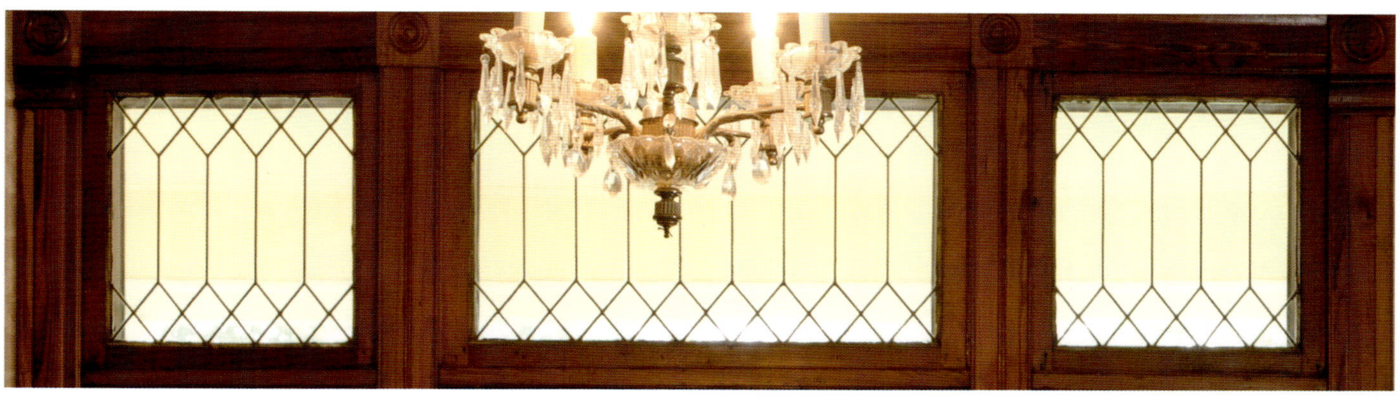

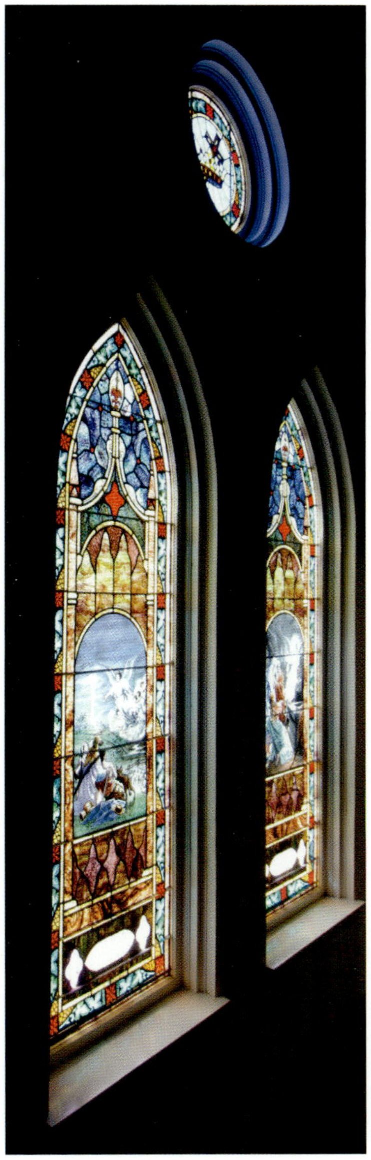

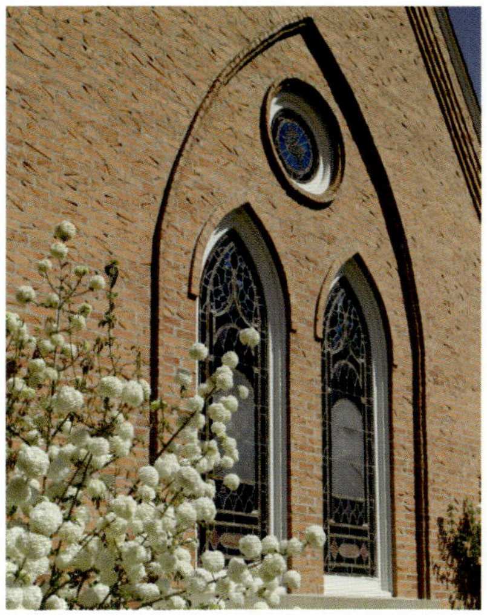

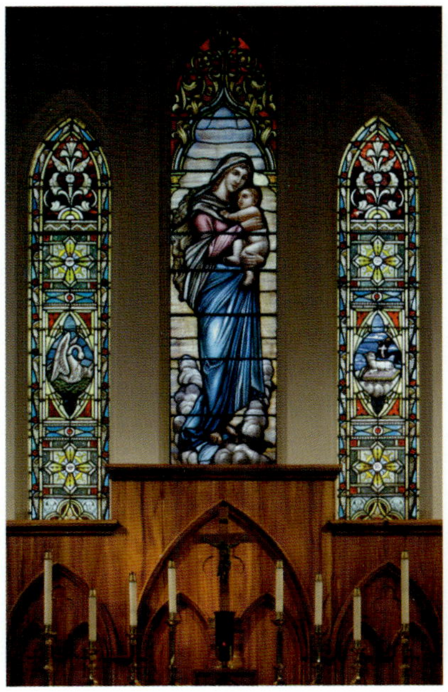

FIGURE 13.115-13.117. Gothic Influences:
(Above) Christ Episcopal Church; Blount Windows on the West Wall; these same windows on the exterior; West Façade; Madonna and Child Windows above the Altar. The Blount windows were by Tiffany and Company.

Gothic Influences

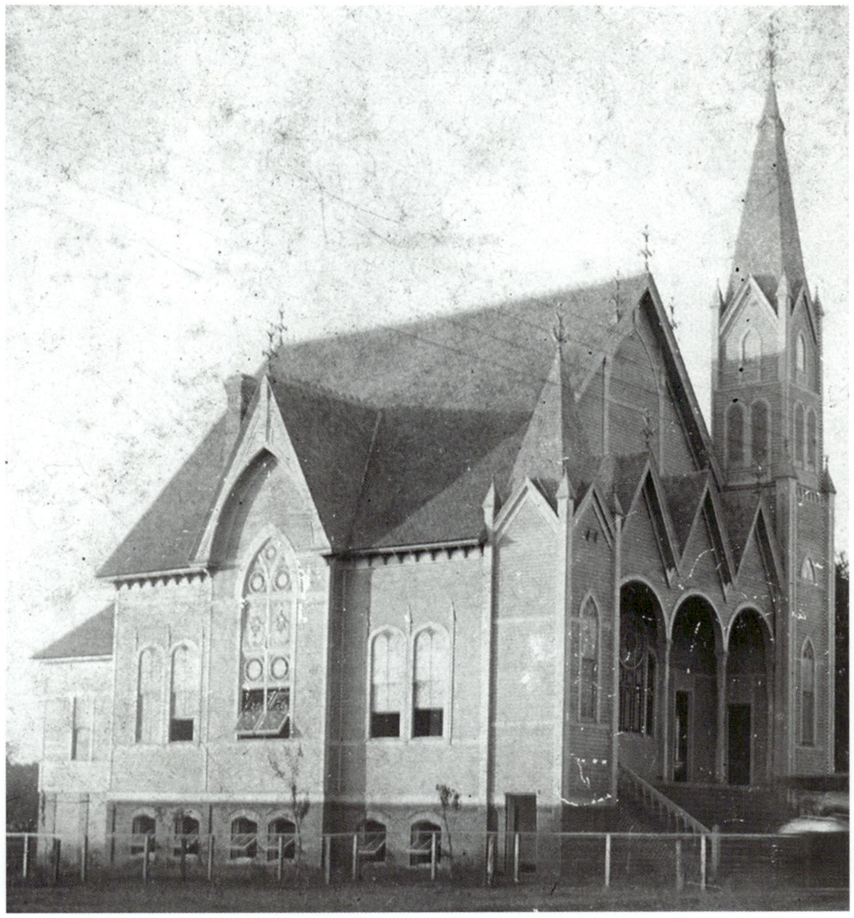

FIGURE 13.118. Gothic Influences: Towers, Bays, Windows.
Southeast Elevation, First Baptist Church (1899-1900).

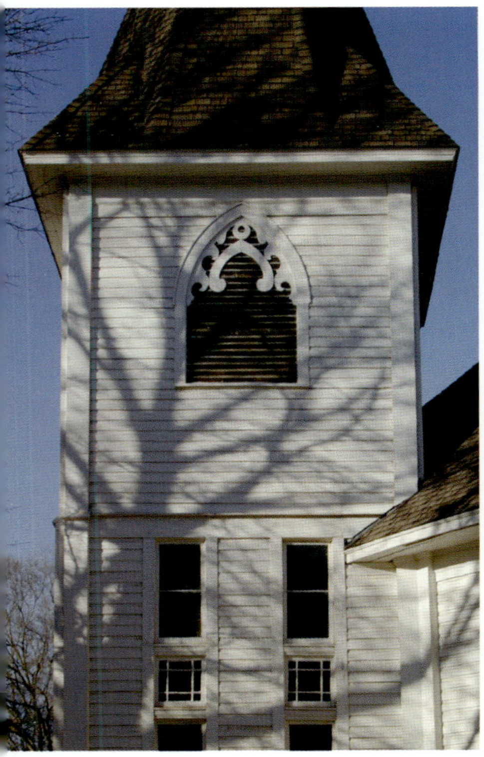

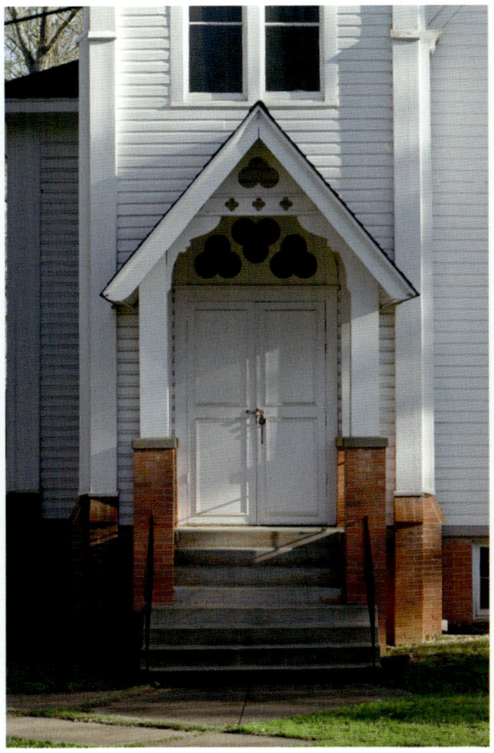

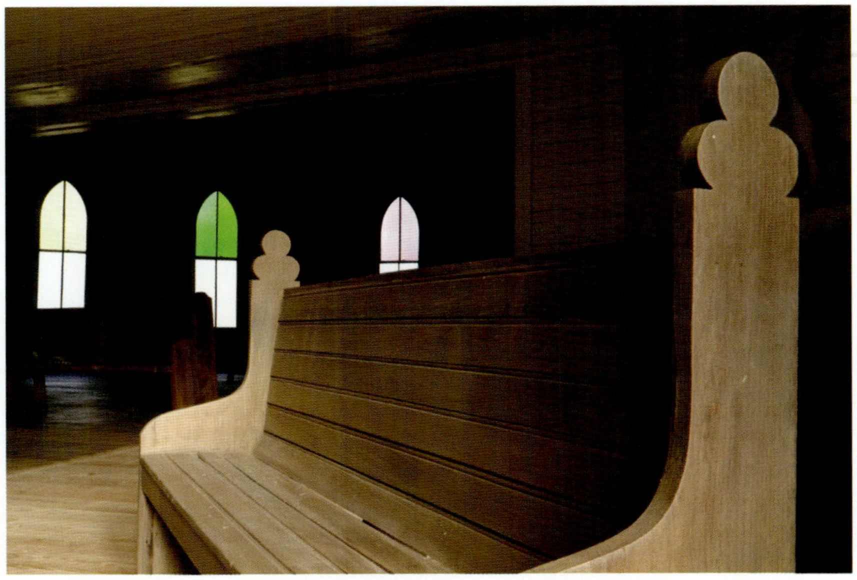

FIGURES 13.119-13.121 Gothic Influences on Zion Hill Baptist Church:
(L to R) West Tower; North Porch; Interior (with detail of Pew made by Rulfs).

SPECIFICATIONS

For RESIDENCE OF D. K. CASON, NACOGDOCHES, TEXAS.

D. RULFS
ARCHITECT AND BUILDER

NACOGDOCHES TEXAS

CASON-MONK & CO.

ENDNOTES

Preface

1. Jere Langdon Jackson, "The Roland Jones House: A Texas State Historical Landmark," Dedication Program with History, December 29, 1973, Nacogdoches County Historical Survey Committee. The program had a history of the structure written by the author.

2. It was with great pleasure, as I began my research on the architect, that I shared with Anna Kathryn Holbrook the quotation about her grandfather by Richard Haltom in the *Nacogdoches Chronicle* in 1897. She published the quote in the biographical information on D. Rulfs in the edited volume by Carolyn Ericson, *Nacogdoches County Families* (Dallas, Texas: Curtis Media Corp., 1985), 580-581 [hereafter Ericson, *Nacogdoches County Families*].

3. "Historic and Architectural Resources Of Nacogdoches: Community Planning And Development In Nacogdoches: 1830-1940," US Department of Interior, National Park Service, National Register of Historic Places, Multiple Property Documentation, (December, 1991): 51, http://pdfhost.focus.nps.gov/docs/NRHP/Text/64500647.pdf.

4. Jere Langdon Jackson, "Nacogdoches' Visible Past: A Review of Our Architectural History," a chapter in Edward B. Baker, editor, *The Bicentennial Commemorative History of Nacogdoches* (Nacogdoches, Texas: Nacogdoches Jaycees, 1976), 199-211[hereafter Jackson, "Nacogdoches' Visible Past," *Bicentennial History of Nacogdoches.*]

5. While both of these markers were submitted by Chuck Phillips as Chair of the Nacogdoches Survey Committee to the Texas Historical Commission, I was on the local commission at the time and did not catch the mistake. See, "A Spelling Problem," in Chapter II.

6. The recent public row over the fate of the Stephen Blount House on Mound Street is a good example of how tenuous, misunderstood, and political the ideas and statutes of historical preservation are in Nacogdoches. For references on this subject, see Chapter V.

7. I was reading Churchill's volumes on World War II for a graduate seminar at the University of North Carolina under a mentor, Dr. James L. Godfrey. Godfrey directed me to the quote and predicted that it would be of comfort to me in the future. He was correct. For many years, as my wife and I would visit Chartwell, one of our favorite places, we would see this quote on his desk. Often quoted, few people cite the correct sources. Winston Churchill made this statement at Britain's National Book Exhibition in 1949 while discussing his memoirs. Until recently, I did not realize how popular this quotation was in motivational writing circles. Here are a few examples after doing an Internet search: "The Nobel Prize in Literature 1953," Nobelprize.org, http://nobelprize.org/nobel_prizes/literature/laureates/1953/; "Inspirational Quotes For Writers," Hubpages, http://hubpages.com/hub/Inspirational-Quotes-For-Writers; "Churchill Quotes and Saying," Search Quotes, http://www.searchquotes.com/quotes/author/Winston_Churchill/; "Winston Churchill Quotes," http://homepage.eircom.net/~odyssey/Quotes/History/Churchill.html.

FIGURE 14.01 (Overleaf) Specifications for the D. K. Cason House, 1914. Compliments of East Texas Research Center.

Introduction

1. Richard W. Haltom, "D. Rulfs, Architect, Contractor, and Builder," *Nacogdoches Chronicle*, September 30, 1897.

2. Sarah Jackson, *Texas Woman of Letters: Karle Wilson Baker* (College Station: Texas A&M Press, 2005), 12-13 [hereafter Sarah Jackso*n, Baker.*]

3. Richard W. Haltom, *A History and Description of Nacogdoches County Texas* (Nacogdoches, Texas, 1880), 45 [hereafter Haltom, *Nacogdoches.*] Haltom was the proprietor of the *Nacogdoches News*; in 1899, he reprinted this book as he launched his new venture, the *Daily Sentinel*. The book was republished in 1976 by the East Texas Historical Association (Austin: Jenkins Press, 1976).

4. This name continued throughout the Spanish period. See Robert Bruce Blake, "Nuestra Senora del Pilar de Nacogdoches," *Handbook of Texas Online* (http://www.tshaonline.org/handbook/online/articles/uen04).

5. Alonso De León and a Canadian-born French explorer named Louis Juchereau de St. Denis each mapped out part of the El Camino Real. *See:* "OLD SAN ANTONIO ROAD," *Handbook of Texas Online* (http://www.tshaonline.org/handbook/online/articles/exo04), accessed March 03, 2012. Donald E. Chipman, "DE LEON, ALONSO," *Handbook of Texas Online* (http://www.tshaonline.org/handbook/online/articles/fde06), accessed March 03, 2012. Donald E. Chipman and Patricia R. Lemée, "ST. DENIS, LOUIS JUCHEREAU DE," *Handbook of Texas Online* (http://www.tshaonline.org/handbook/online/articles/fst01), accessed March 03, 2012.

6. Jackson, "The Nine Flags of Nacogdoches," Application for a Texas Historical Marker #14312, Texas Historical Commission, Vertical Files (2008), Austin, Texas.

7. Jackson, "The Battle of Nacogdoches (August 2, 1832)," Application for a Texas Historical Marker #9252, Texas Historical Commission, Vertical Files (1980), Austin, Texas. Most of the texts of the historical markers in Nacogdoches County can be found at the Texas Historical Commission's Texas Historical Sites Atlas, online at http://atlas.thc.state.tx.us/.

8. Jackson, "Sam Houston's First Home in Texas," Application for a Texas Historical Marker, Texas Historical Commission, Vertical Files (2009), Austin, Texas.

9. Jackson, "Site of Bivouac and Banquet for The New Orleans Greys," Application for a Texas Historical Marker #9253, Texas Historical Commission, Vertical Files (1977).

10. "Houston vs. Starr," tried in May, 1849, *Nacogdoches County District Court Records*, District Clerk's Office, file 2188, Transcript in R. B. Blake Papers, East Texas Research Center, Stephen F. Austin State University. This affidavit was part of a legal controversy in the 1840s involving part of a grant to Sam Houston, a one acre tract from the James H. Starr Survey. When the City of Nacogdoches transferred property to the newly chartered Stephen F. Austin State Normal College in 1917, this one acre tract of land had to be held in trust by George F. Ingraham until the title was cleared. Eventually the State Attorney General's investigation of the deeds discovered a document, signed by Houston in the presence of Thomas J. Rusk in 1855, which sold the land to Starr for $1,200.00. The affidavit and other documents are in the Abstract of Title for SFASTC.

11. Jackson, Jere, "Old Nacogdoches University Building," Application for a Texas Historical Marker #16000, Texas Historical Commission, Vertical Files (2008), Austin, Texas.

Chapter I: Nacogdoches in 1880

1.Karle Wilson, Letter to the Editor, *Daily Sentinel*, February 18, 1907. At the time she wrote this letter, Miss Karle Wilson had not yet married Thomas Ellis Baker which she did in August of 1907. A copy of the letter exists in the Karle Wilson Baker Papers, ETRC, Stephen F. Austin State University; it is also published in a volume edited by her grandson, Edward Blount (Jerry) Baker, *Bicentennial History of Nacogdoches,* iii-iv. See also, Sarah Jackson, *Baker* , 12-13.

2. Hasia Diner, "Immigration and U.S. History," http://www.america.gov/st/peopleplace-english/2008/February/ 20080307112004ebyessedo0.1716272.html.

3. Carolyn Reeves Ericson, "German Immigrants to Nacogdoches," *Yesterdays*, Nacogdoches Genealogical Society, Issue XXIV-2, September, 2004, 39-43.

4. Carolyn Reeves Ericson, *Nacogdoches—Gateway to Texas: A Biographical Directory, 1881-1920*, Vol. III [CD, Computer File: LC 20100113] (Nacogdoches: Ericson Books, 2002), 559 and 807 [hereafter Ericson, *Gateway* III].

5. Ericson, *Gateway* III, 356-57.

6. Special Edition, *Nacogdoches Chronicle*, September 30, 1897; Special Edition, *Daily Sentinel*, November, 1906; *Daily Sentinel*, January 1, 1909; "Nacogdoches Forty One Years Ago," speech from 1926, reprinted in December 8, 1928.

7. "Mayer & Schmidt," *Daily Sentinel*, December 30, 1928. A copy is in the Lois Foster Blount Papers, CA. 1750-1980, (A-107), East Texas Research Center [hereafter ETRC], Ralph Steen Library, Stephen F. Austin State University, Nacogdoches, Texas, http://libweb.sfasu.edu/proser/etrc/collections/manuscript/personal/index.html#b, accessed July 10, 2011.

8. *Daily Sentinel*, December 8, 1928.

9. Ericson, *Gateway* III, 792. The School of Business at SFASU is named after this Rusche family. See, Rusche Family Papers (A-131), 1848-1895, ETRC. See also, Marian M. Goodrum, "Rusche, Francis and Mariana Meier," Ericson, *Nacogdoches County Families*, F912, 584.

10. Carolyn Reeves Ericson, "German Immigrants to Nacogdoches," *Yesterdays*, Nacogdoches Genealogical Society, Issue XXIV-2, September, 2004, 39-43.

11. Dorothy Neblett Perkins, *Descendants of Samuel, James, and Martha Perkins* (California: Neblett Press, 1999), 259-297 [hereafter Perkins, *Perkins*]. Ericson, *Gateway* III, 700.

12. *Daily Sentinel*, December 8, 1929. See also, Perkins, *Perkins*, 242-260. W. U. (Will) Perkins, of English heritage, arrived in Nacogdoches according to family tradition on horseback in 1879 from Laneville (near Henderson) in Rusk County. Perkins, who came to the town to establish a drug store, at first had his brother-in-law as this partner, George P. Garrison, but within a year, the firm become Perkins Brothers when Will's brother, Sam, joined him.

13. *Daily Sentinel*, December 8, 1928. "The society was of a high-toned character for at that time the Griffiths, Hollis, Engledows, Sparks, Hustons, Mullers, Voigts, Gilberts, Hydes, Rusches, Hillenkamps, Hariss, Lees, Iresons, Wells, Haltoms, Ingrahams, Crains, Nelsons, Taylors, Edwards, Irions, Shindlers, Hoyas, Davidsons, Ortons, Mayfields, Rusk, and other distinguished families lived here."

14. *Daily Sentinel*, December 8, 1928.

15. Ericson, *Gateway* III, 953.

16. In later accounts, there was confusion as to which building they rented at first: "They rented part of the lower story of the building on the west side of the public square known as the old court house building, which was owned by Asa Moore." *Daily Sentinel*, December 8, 1928. "They established themselves in the building which they had rented from Capt. Fred Voigt." These buildings were side by side, so it really does not matter. The first two loads of goods were hauled on wagons from Henderson by A. H. Crain and Pilly Huey, the last named being the well-known colored man who for many years operated a wagon from Nacogdoches to Henderson, spending most of his time on the road. Other men who did a great deal of hauling in those days were Muck Burrows, Sam Smith and Josh Millard." *Daily Sentinel*, December 8, 1928.

17. Ancestry.com: *1880 United States Census* [database on-line] *Nacogdoches, Texas*; Roll: *1320*; Family History Film: *1255320*; Page: *166C*; Enumeration District: *47*.

18. William Shakespeare, *Julius Caesar*, Act IV, Scene 3.

19. The German elements in Nacogdoches start in the early immigrants. Adolphus Sterne came from Germany, as did Joseph Theodore von Hoya, Sr. See, Ericson, "German Immigrants the Nacogdoches," *Yesterdays*, 39-43.

20. The history of newspapers, even limiting the story to the years 1880 to 1926, is complicated. The Ortons and Haltoms owned several papers in the period: *Chronicle; Nacogdoches News*; *Nacogdoches Star; Nacogdoches Star-News;* a revived *Nacogdoches Chronicle*; and, finally, *Daily Sentinel* in 1899. See, Joe Ericson, "History of Nacogdoches Newspapers," *Bicentennial History of Nacogdoches*, 195-198.

21. D. W. C. Barker, *A Texas Scrap-Book: Made Up of the History, Biography, and Miscellany of Texas and Its People* (New York: A. S. Barnes & Company, 1875). *Bryant's Texas Almanac and Railway Guide: All About Texas, As It Was, As It Is!, and As It Will Be!* (Dallas: W. N. Bryant, Editor and Publisher, 1879).

22. Haltom, *Nacogdoches,* 14.

23. Haltom published his book in April of 1880; Rulfs did not leave Bremerhaven until July of 1880, but it is unlikely a copy of the book made its way to him in those months.

24. Ericson, *Gateway* III, 882:

25. For instance: James Reese, "Economic Growth of Nacogdoches," in *Nacogdoches: Wilderness Outpost To Modern City, 1779-1979,* ed. by Archie P. McDonald (Burnet, Texas: Eakin Press, 1980), 78-90. James G. Partin, Carolyn Reeves Ericson, Joe E. Ericson, Archie P. McDonald, *Nacogdoches: The History of Texas Oldest City* (Lufkin, Texas: Best of East Texas Publishers, 1995 [hereafter Partin, *et al, Nacogdoches]*. Robert S. Maxwell, "Nacogdoches and the Railroads," in Baker, *Bicentennial History,* 132-141. For his book, see Robert Maxwell, *Whistle In the Piney Woods: Paul Bremond and the Houston, East and West Texas Railway* (Houston: Texas Gulf Coast Historical Association, 1963); Reprinted by the East Texas Historical Association in 1998, with an introduction by Archie P. McDonald [hereafter Maxwell, *Whistle*].

26. The re-publication of Haltom's *History* came when the *Daily Sentinel* opened its new offices in the Hazle Building. *Daily Sentinel,* July, 10, 1901. Haltom used parts in his various contributions to Almanacs, even as late as 1904. [See *Burke's Texas Almanac and Immigrant's Handbook for 1883* (Houston, Texas: J. Burke, 1883).

27. Sarah Jackson, *Baker*, 85. See Haltom, *Nacogdoches*, 57.

28. Partin, *et al*, *Nacogdoches*, 95. James Gallaway Partin, "A History of Nacogdoches and Nacogdoches County, Texas to 1877," MA Thesis, at University of Texas, Austin, 1968. In both works, Partin uses Haltom extensively.

29. Haltom, *Nacogdoches*, 60-61.

30. Haltom, *Nacogdoches*, 46.

31. Haltom, *Nacogdoches*, 57-58.

32. Haltom, *Nacogdoches*, 14 (1834) and 58 (1880). National Register of Historic Places, "Historic and Architectural Resources of Nacogdoches, Texas;" "Community Planning and Development in Nacogdoches: 1830-1940," [Online Resource] http://pdfhost.focus.nps.gov/docs/NRHP/Text/64500647.pdf. This National Register Document can be found now at the Nacogdoches Historic Sites Survey Online, http://www.sfasu.edu/heritagecenter/622.asp, accessed August, 11, 2012. This document cites the population as 300, but this probably not correct. The document is quoting Haltom in 1880, but attributing it to Nugent Brown. Brown's work was published in 1927, not in 1880 as stated. [Nugent Brown, *The Book of Nacogdoches County, July 1, 1927.* Nacogdoches, Texas: Nugent Brown Publisher, 1927.]

33. Haltom, *Nacogdoches*, 56-57.

34. D. B. Alexander, "Influences in Texas Architecture," in *Historic Preservation in Texas: The Comprehensive Statewide Historic Preservation Plan for Texas*, Vol. I (Austin: Texas Historical Commission, 1973), 50-53. *See also*, D. B. Alexander, *Texas Homes of the Nineteenth Century* (Austin: University of Texas Press, 1966), 3-8. The Texas Historical Commission's surveys of Nacogdoches are now available on the Internet; see citation in Endnote 32 above.

35. Not only were the Spanish mission buildings gone by 1880, but their locations were also forgotten. When the Catholic Church reentered the city in 1847, it ignored the location of the former church and cemetery. For cultural reasons, the new congregation overtly disassociated the congregation from the Spanish traditions. The new priests were French, the style of the new church was generic, pioneer or vernacular in its architecture. Joe Devine, "Original Site of Sacred Heart Catholic Church, 1847-1936, Nacogdoches, Texas," Application for a Texas Historical Marker #09NA06, Texas Historical Commission, Vertical Files (2009), Austin, Texas.

36. "Historic and Architectural Resources of Nacogdoches: Community Planning and Development in Nacogdoches: 1830-1940," historic context submitted for the National Register of Historic Places, 1989. Accessed through the *Texas Historic Sites Atlas* on the Texas Historical Commission website (http://atlas.thc.state.tx.us/index.asp), [hereafter cited as "Historic and Architectural Resources of Nacogdoches"]. From THC architectural survey: "He [Y'Barbo] laid out the plaza with respect to the Indians well-traveled trails within the area (Nuttal 1921:750; Stanislawski 1947:95). Consequently the plaza's corners faced northwest, northeast, southwest and southeast."

37. Jackson, "Nacogdoches' Visible Past," *Bicentennial History of Nacogdoches*, 199-236.

38. The Adolphus Sterne House, the Millard-Lee House (which originally sat on the southeast corner of the city square and is now at Millard's Crossing). There are, in fact, many examples of East Texas houses still in use in the county: to mention only two, the John Sparks House and Tolbert Barret House, both restored by Captain and Mrs. Charles Phillips. The typical East Texas house, with its porch across the front and its symmetrical floor plan could be easily adapted to fit Greek Revival influences. Carpenters on the spot could easily satisfy the desire for classical elements in architecture by substituting columns for simple posts, adding moldings inside and out and wider baseboards. The Burrows house at Millard's Crossing is an interesting example.

39. Haltom, *Nacogdoches, 60-61.*

40. Sanborn Fire Insurance Maps – *Texas*, University of Texas, Perry-Castañeda Library Map Collection [Online collection], *Nacogdoches*, available at http://www.lib.utexas.edu/maps/sanborn/n.html [hereafter Sanborn Maps, UT, *Nacogdoches*, (date)].

41. *Daily Sentinel*, December 22, 2009. Jere Langdon Jackson, "Old Nacogdoches University Building," Application for a Texas Historical Marker #16000, Texas Historical Commission, Vertical Files (2008), Austin, Texas.

42. Alexander does not attribute any of these new elements to Diedrich Rulfs. For trends in other parts of Texas, see Alexander, *Texas Homes of the Nineteenth Century*, 167-169. Also, Ernest Allen Connally, "Texas Architecture," *Historical Preservation*, Vol. 16, No. 6 (Nov.-Dec. 1964), 220-228. See the Greek elements added to what were essentially pioneer structures as represented by the Millard House at Millard's Crossing. The most complete coverage of Nacogdoches architectural resources can be found at the Texas Historical Commission's site: "Historic and Architectural Resources of Nacogdoches," *Texas Historic Sites Atlas,* Texas Historical Commission [Online Database] http://atlas.thc.state.tx.us/index.asp [hereafter *Texas Historic Sites Atlas*].

43. Old Dorsey House (122 South Sanders); House at 113 S. Lanana; Swift House (703 E. Main); First Methodist Parsonage (Millard's Crossing), Buchanan-Gray-King House (600 S. Church), Bell House (536 East Pillar); George Muckleroy house (216 N. Church.)

44. While perhaps the norm in Nacogdoches before 1880, the practice of mixing residential and business quarters returned to Nacogdoches in the 1980s. The Mast family renovated the Mayer & Schmidt Building (1908 Rulfs) into apartments, the Hayter Office building also includes an apartment. In Paris, France, most urban properties from the 16th century forward mixed commercial establishments on the ground floor with residential quarters on the upper floors. (Place de Vosges and Palais Royal both consisted of structures and uses of this type.) These mixed use structures dominated life during the French Revolution and are highly desirable even today.

Chapter II: Rulfs in Germany

1. Stollhamm Church Records, Book 1832-1861, 503. Since the author first used them, these records have moved from their original location in the church rectory in Stollhamm to the State Archives in Oldenburg. Of course, it is possible that the cleric who entered Rulfs name into the Stollham registry made a mistake and added the second "e" in the name, but this is doubtful given the fact that his maternal grandfather had the same spelling.

2. Ancestry.com. *New Orleans Passenger Lists, 1820-1945* [database on-line]. Provo, UT, USA: The Generations Network, Inc., 2006. Original data: New Orleans, Louisiana. Passenger Lists of Vessels Arriving at New Orleans, Louisiana, 1820-1902. Micro-publication M259. RG036. Rolls # 1-93. National Archives, Washington, D.C.

3.. Ancestry.com. *1910 United States Federal Census* [database on-line]. Provo, UT, USA: Operations Inc, 2006. Census Place: *Justice Precinct 1, Nacogdoches, Texas*; Roll: *T624_1581*; Page: *16A*; Enumeration District: *0096*; Image: *204*; FHL Number: *1375594*.

1920 United States Census [database on-line]. Provo, UT, USA: Ancestry.com Operations Inc, 2010. Place: *Nacogdoches, Nacogdoches, Texas*; Roll: *T625_1835*; Page: *12A*; Enumeration District: *122*; Image: *691*.

4. See the articles written by Rulfs' granddaughter Anna Katherine Holbrook in Ericson, *Nacogdoches County Families* F908-909: 580-581. The family's spelling is based on the marriage records supplied by St. Marien Kirke in Atens, Germany.

5. Jackson, "Nacogdoches' Visible Past," *Bicentennial History,* 206.

6. Mary Stewart Duncan, interviews with the author, 1972-1974. D. Rulfs to his son Tony, Nacogdoches, September 14, 1921 (letter, in the possession of Mary Stewart Duncan, shown to the author in June of 1972). Mrs. Duncan also had a copy of the District Court Certificate Naturalization , dated March, 1887, and signed by Judge George H. Matthews, and witnessed by William Hillenkamp. For his petitions for citizenship and grant, see *Index to Naturalization Records: 1851 – 1915*: RULFS (RULF), D. A. W. (DANIEL) GERMANY, 1848. Nov. 8, 1886 - Pet. for Nat. - Dist. Ct. - Dist. Ct. Filed Box R-103; Nov. 8, 1886 - Pet. for Nat. - Dist. Ct. - Dist. Ct. Civ. Dkt., Vol. L, p. 151, p. 220; Nov. 8, 1886 - Petition for Naturalization, Dist. Ct. - Dist. Ct. Civ. Dkt., Vol. 1, 167 ; Apr. 15, 1887 - Grant of Cit. - Dist. Ct. - Dist. Ct. Min., Vol. M, 261-262, Case # 5662; ETRC, Steen Library, Stephen F. Austin State University. These papers are also referenced online: Rootweb, Naturalization Records of Nacogdoches County, Texas, http://www.rootsweb.ancestry.com/~txnacogd/naturalization.htm.

7. D. Rulfs to his son Tony, Nacogdoches, September 14, 1921.

8. See the spellings of the great-grandchildren written by granddaughter Anna Kathryn Rulfs Holbrook, in Ericson*, Nacogdoches County Families*, F908-909, 580-81. When Rulfs' grandson was born in 1913, "Dietrich" was used. To add to the confusion, the same first names are used over and over in the family. When they died before leaving which of their first names to use, it is very confusing to know. This added to the official spellings problems.

9. Gerhard and Helene were engaged on March 18, 1847, their banns were published on March 21 and 27, and they were married on April 21st of 1847. "Verzeichniss, der im Jahre 1847 im Kirchspiel Stollhamm Verlobten, Proclamirten und Copulirten. No. 2 Verlobt: März 18, Proclamirt März 21 und 27. Copulirt: April 21." Stollhamm Church Records, Book 1832-1861. Anna Kathryn Rulfs Holbrook had transcripts of these records which she shared with the author in 1974.

10. Hans-Rudolf Mengers, "Genealogy of Gerhard Wilhelm Rulfs, Meister in Stollhammerwisch," correspondences with the author, June 21, 2010 [hereafter Mengers, "Genealogy"]. Gerhard Wilhelm Rulfs, Diedrich's father, was the son of Wilhelm Rulfs (1791-1839) and Anna Katharine (née Dieckmann) Rulfs (1796-1848). The grandfather was born in Stollhamm and died in Iffens (a nearby town); the grandmother died in Stollhamm in 1848, the year Diedrich was born. Gerhard Wilhelm was a hireling at one point and a barrel binder in Iffens northwest of Stollhamm.

11. Mengers, "Genealogy." Other siblings listed in the genealogy sent from Germany by Herr Hans-Rudolf Mengers: 8 children, some stillborn and died near house in Stollhammerwisch. 1) Anna Helene Rulfs (1857-1865), 2) Heinrich Wilhelm Rulfs (1860- to USA in 5July1884), 3) Sophie Rebecka Rulfs (1862 went to USA in March of 1962 and married Johann Diedrich Gerhard Wilken in 1859; 4) Anton Gerhard Rulfs (1863-1867) died in the canal; 5) Johann Elise Gerhardine Rulfs (1865-?) 6) Anna Helene Katharine Rulfs (1865-?); 7) Heinrich Gerhard Wilhelm Rulfs (1870-1877); 8) Anna Helene Wilhelmine Rulfs, (1874-?).

12. Ericson, *Gateway* III, 791. In the German genealogies, Diedrich's brother is listed as Heinrich Wilhelm; in the United States records, the first names are reversed to William Henry.

13. Mengers, "Genealogy." The term *zimmermann*, while roughly translated as "carpenter" in English, signified in Germany a craftsman, not a day-laborer; we might use the term "builder." Diedrich's brother, William Henry, was the *zimmerman* in the Nacogdoches firm.

14. Photographs of the Rulfs house in Stollhammerwisch were sent to the author by Hans-Rudolf Mengers, correspondence with the author, August 4, 2010. The author owes a debt to Mr. Mengers for sending many period postcard photographs of the Stollhamm area at the time D. Rulfs would have lived there.

15. Pfarrer J. Tönjes (the Lutheran pastor at St. Nicklas Church in Stollhamm), conversation with the author, June 4, 2010.

16. Churches where Rulfs witnessed active rebuilding initiatives include: Stollhamm, Blexen, Burhave, Eckwarden, and Oldenburg (Stadt).

17. "List of Rulers of Oldenburg," *Wikipedia*, http://en.wikipedia.org/w/indexphp?title=List_of_rulers_of_Oldenburg&oldid=377486607.

18. The languages of the great Marsh Lands were dialects of German, or "Low German" (*Plattdeutsch*), the "low" referring to flat plains and coastal areas, as opposed to the German in the "high" mountain areas. At the time of his birth, Germany did not exist. The Rulfs were Lower Saxons, subjects of the Grand Duke of Oldenburg. The ruling Grand Duke at the time was Peter II (Reign, 1853-1900). The principal cities of Lower Saxony included Hanover, Braunschweig, Bremen, Lüneburg, Osnabrück, Oldenburg, and Göttingen.

19. "Oldenburg," *The Encyclopaedia Britannica: A Dictionary of the Arts, Sciences, and General Literature,* Vol. XVII (Chicago: Peale Company, 1891), 756-759; [Online at Google Books], accessed July 20, 2011.

20. When Oldenburg sold the port to Prussia, the citizens must have raised their eyebrows when the Prussian King Wilhelm in 1869 named the new port on the North Sea after himself. The Prussians had leased the port from the Duchy of Oldenburg from 1853, according to the Jade Treaty, with about 3.13 km of territory. In 1869, King William I of Prussia established a town as an enclave, but the inland areas remained a part of Oldenburg. "Wilhelmshaven," Wikipedia, The Free Encyclopedia, http://en.wikipedia.org/w/index.php?title=Wilhelmshaven&oldid=376732892.

21. "The Cultural Entities of Niedersachsen: Butjadingen" http://www.lancewadplan.org/Cultural%20atlas/LS/Butjadingen/butjadingen.htm. The towns of the peninsula are well represented on the Internet: http://www.touristik-butjadingen.de/burhave.html; http://www.touristik-butjadingen.de/information-langwarden/52-langwarden.html; http://www.touristik-butjadingen.de/eckwarden.html.

22. "Grand Duchy of Oldenburg," 11th edition of *Encyclopaedia Britannica*, [Online Resource; Google Books], http://1911encyclopedia.org/Oldenburg,_Germany_(Grand-Duchy. They also marketed cork. When Rulfs first came to Texas, he tried to recreate what he was familiar with. He rented a house in the country and rode to town every day. He also remained interested in horses and fishing his entire life.

23. The cloth is named after Osnabrück, south of Oldenburg; it is made from flax, tow, or jute yarns. Both Bremen and Osnabrück were part of the Hanseatic League in the Middle Ages. "Oldenburg," *The Encyclopaedia Britannica: A Dictionary of the Arts, Sciences, and General Literature,* Vol. XVII (Chicago: Peale Company, 1891), 756-759; [Online at Google Books].

24. "Grand Duchy of Oldenburg, 11th edition of *Encyclopaedia Britannica,*[Online Resource; Google Books], http://1911encyclopedia.org/Oldenburg,_Germany_(Grand-Duchy. They also marketed cork.

25. "The Cultural Entities of Niedersachsen: Butjadingen" http://www.lancewadplan.org/Cultural%20atlas/LS/Butjadingen/butjadingen.htm. A road map of around 1893 depicts roads in Butjadingen and Nordenham, these are still important (the L 858, L 860, B 212).

26. "Stadtgeschichte (History)", http://www.nordenham.de/en/tourismus-und-freizeit/stadtgeschichte.html. For an summary in English, see "Nordenham," *Wikipedia,* http://en.wikipedia.org/w/index.php?title=Nordenham&oldid=436533948.

27. Mary Stewart Duncan (niece of D. Rulfs), interviews with the author, March, 1974.

28. There are various spellings of her names to note. On her birth certificate, Johanne's name is spelled with an "e" at the end, while her mother's is spelled without the final "e". Of course, it could be a typographical error, but Anna Kathryn Rulfs Holbrook in Ericson, *Nacogdoches County Families*, F908-909, 580-81, spells the name with a final "a," not an "e," trying to approximate the sound of the name in English. On her tomb in Oak Grove Cemetery, her name is detailed: "Johanne Böschen Rulfs."

29. "Certifiate of Residence, Article 29 of the Community Regulations ... Community of Atens, 9 Mai 1866," Photocopy of German Document, shown to the author by Anna Katherine Rulfs Holbrook, June 1974. Johanne Böschen may not have lived continuously in Atens before 1866. In response to a law passed in 1855, which required recertification if someone moved from one community to another in the Grand Duchy, Johanne registered as a part of the community of Atens as of May 9, 1866. The records show that at age 17, Johanne had to re-certify her residency in Atens. There were some prominent Böschens in Stollhamm in the 1840s, and the last name was widespread in this area of the Duchy. There are still Böschens being buried in the cemetery in Atens today confirmed in the author's photographs of the cemetery in Atens-Nordenham.

30. Records from the St. Marien Kirke in Atens, Germany, shown to the author in an interview with Anna Kathryn Holbrook (granddaughter of D. Rulfs), June, 1972.

31. Hans-Rudolf Mengers, correspondence with the author, June 21, 2010.

32. Mary Stewart Duncan (niece of D. Rulfs) and Anna Kathryn Holbrook, interviews with the author, June, 1972 and March, 1974.

33. "Oldenburg," *Wikipedia, The Free Encyclopedia,* http://en.wikipedia.org/w/index.php?title=Oldenburg&oldid=367712025. "Peter II, Grand Duke of Oldenburg," *Wikipedia, The Free Encyclopedia,* http://en.wikipedia.org/w/index.php?title=Peter_II,_Grand_Duke_of_Oldenburg&oldid=360604368.

34. "Grand Duchy of Oldenburg State Railways," *Wikipedia*, The Free Encyclopedia, http://en.wikipedia.org/w/index.php?title=Grand_Duchy_of_Oldenburg_State_Railways&oldid=459820986. "Finally in 1864 a treaty was agreed between Prussia and Oldenburg over the construction of a railway line from Bremen to Oldenburg. At the same time Prussia committed itself to building a railway line from Heppens – later Wilhelmshaven – to Oldenburg (the Wilhelmshaven–Oldenburg line). The Grand Ducal Railway Commission, set up in 1864, was transferred on 1 April 1867, to the Grand Ducal Railway Division of Oldenburg."

35. Herman Cording, *Als Oldenburg Noch Residenzstadt War: Stadtenwicklung and Stadtleben von der Grafenzeit bis zum Ende de grossherzoglichen Residenz im Jahre 1918* (Oldenburg: Ostendorp Verlag, 1985), 59-73. See also, Erwin Nasse "The Economic Movement in Germany," *The Quarterly Journal of Economics,* Vol. 1, No. 4 (Jul., 1887), 498-506, published by MIT Press Stable URL: http://www.jstor.org/stable/1879345.

36. Paul Zucker, "Architectural Education in Nineteenth Century Germany," *The Journal of the American Society of Architectural Historians*, Vol. 2, No. 3 (Jul., 1942), 6-13, published by Society of Architectural Historians Stable URL: http://www.jstor.org/stable/901158, accessed, October 5, 2010. Dr. Paul Zucker was, from 1938 onward, Professor of History of Architecture and Art at Cooper Union, New York City, formerly having taught in Berlin.

37. Susan Jean Dickey, "F. E. and Oscar Ruffini: Texas Architects, 1877-1917," (PhD Dissertation, Texas Tech University, 1993). See also, Richard Michael Levy, "The Professionalization of American Architects and Engenieers, 1865-1917" (Phd Dissertation, Berkeley, 1980).

38. Zucker, "Architectural Education in Nineteenth Century Germany," 6-13.

39. There is a wonderful array of historical photographs on the history of Oldenburg at the following site on the Internet: "Historische Fotos zur Geschicte Oldenburgs," http://www.alt-oldenburg.de/index.html.

40. Notes supplied by the State Archivist in Oldenburg during my trip in 1978. Also see D. G. Williamson, Chapter 9, "The Financial Crisis of 1873 and the Great Depression," *Bismarck and Germany, 1862-1890,* 2nd Edition (New York: Longman, 1998); also, Gordon Martel, *Modern Germany Reconsidered, 1870-1945* (London: Routledge, 1992), 286.

41. Mary Stewart Duncan and Anna Katherine Holbrook, interviews with the author, 1972-1976.

42. Wolfgang Runge, *Die St.-Nikolai-Kirche in Stollhamm*, (Oldenburg,: Isensee, 1981), 2. The pamphlet attributes the work on the building to Baumeister Wrede, who also did the work in Burhave.

43. The author took photographs of the history of Burhaven and Blexen posted outside these two churches.

44. Ericson, *Gateway* III, 882:

45. Mary Stewart Duncan, interview with the author, March 1974.

46. *The Rulfs Name in History* (Provo, Utah: Generations Network, 2007), 16.

47. *Ibid*, 8-9.

48. Anna Kathryn Holbrook published this in Ericson, *Nacogdoches County Families*, 580-81.

49. Ancestry.com: *New Orleans Passenger Lists, 1820-1945*, [database online], Microfilm publication M259, Record Group 36, Record for "Anton Boschen," the ship *Hannover*, arriving from Bremen, October 1879. In the transcribed records, Anton is listed as a female, 24 years of age, but in the image of the original record, Anton is listed as a male, 21 years of age, from Oldenburg, and labeled a farmer.)

50. Mary Stewart Duncan, whose memory was very clear, was certain that her grandmother and the Rulfs family arrived in 1880. She transmitted this memory to both Anna Kathryn Hollbrook, a younger great, granddaughter, and the author in the 1970s. [For reference, see Anna Kathryn Holbrook, in Ericson, *Nacogdoches County Families,* F909, 580-581.] In her conversation with the author, Mrs. Duncan said nothing about Anton; Holbrook's account places Anton in the group.

51. Ancestry.com: *New Orleans Passenger Lists, 1820-1945* [database on-line]; Original data: New Orleans, Louisiana. *Passenger Lists of Vessels Arriving at New Orleans, Louisiana, 1820-1902.* Micropublication M259. RG036. Rolls # 1-93. National Archives, Washington, D.C. The *New Orleans Passenger Lists* obviously have the children's names confused. They refer to "Willy" as one month old, when it was Anton who was one; Gerhard William (Willy) was five at the time. They refer to "Anton" as the two year-old, when it was Carl Henry who was two. [The author has a photocopy of the birth certificate of "Edward Diedrich Anton" Rulfs, dated July 20, supplied by the Church in Blexen, Oldenburg, Germany.] Carolyn Ericson (*Gateway* III, 791) has the living children correct; she omits the short-lived Emilie Helene, born in Germany in 1877.

52. Concerning the date of arrival, modern accounts range all over the place, having Rulfs arriving anywhere from the mid-1870s to the 1890s. ["1990 NRHP Multiple Property Documentation Form: Historic and Architectural Resources of Nacogdoches, Texas," (link to http://pdfhost.focus.nps.gov/docs/NRHP/Text/64500647.pdf), Nacogdoches Sites Survey Online, accessed December 3,

2011.] In the text submitted on the registration forms for the nomination of the downtown area to be included in the National Registry, the document has Rulfs arriving "in 1879 or 1880" in one place and then in another, hopefully a typographical error, includes this phrase: "Dietrich Rulfs, who arrived in Nacogdoches in 1889." ["1990 NRHP Multiple Property Documentation Form: Historic and Architectural Resources of Nacogdoches, Texas," (link to http://pdfhost.focus.nps.gov/docs/NRHP/Text/64500647.pdf), Nacogdoches Sites Survey Online.] Another source has Rulfs arriving in the 1890s. [Partin, *et al, Nacogdoches*, 136.]

Chapter III: Commercial Development before 1900

1. *Galveston Daily News*, September 2, 1890.

2. "D. RULFS. Architect, Contractor, and Builder," *Nacogdoches Chronicle*, September 30, 1897.

3. Richard V. Francaviglia, *Main Street Revisited: Time, Space, and Image Building in Small-Town America* (Iowa City: University of Iowa Press, 1996), 7-11.

4. In colonial times Nacogdoches was an east-west town. East Main Street up to and including the Square was the major commercial area. On the west, travelers arrived and exited the Square primarily on Pilar, not Main Street. Pilar had the best ford across the Banita, later got the first bridges, and was a gentler grade than Main Street. The north-south corridors, North Street and South Fredonia, were relatively unimportant until after the Civil War. There was no South Street for a long time because there was no ford or bridge until the twentieth century. Travelers from the north doglegged into the Square at the small or Church Plaza and exited the Square on South Fredonia Street. (Fredonia Street north of the square was and is purely local.) All one has to do to understand the above, is to review attempts over recent decades to relocate Highway 21 and 59 in Nacogdoches before the building of the loops.

5. The 100 block of East Main today, the part between the Square and North Street, would have carried the name West Main in the 19th century. The numbering of the Block 13 in the *Nacogdoches County Deed Records* is difficult to follow. Not only are the lot numbers confusing, the property titles in this oldest part of the town are confusing. Since few lots are symmetrical, title companies and lawyers, as they advise their clients, have complete job security in the old one-mile square town of Nacogdoches.

6. These included the homes of John S. Roberts, Charles S. Taylor, Adolphus Sterne, Sam Houston, Thomas J. Rusk, Henry Raguet, A. A. Nelson, and Haden Edwards.

7. Sam Houston selected the corner of Pilar and the Square for the site of his first house in Texas. Jere Jackson, "Sam Houston and Nacogdoches," Application for a Texas Historical Marker #09NA03 , Texas Historical Commission, Vertical Files (2009), Austin, Texas. For the marker text, see Texas Historical Commission Atlas.

8. Robert S. Maxwell, "Nacogdoches and the Railroads," *Bicentennial Commemorative History of Nacogdoches,* 132-141.

9. Maxwell, *Whistle*, 25-26.

10. Partin, *et al, Nacogdoches.*

11. D. Rulfs to his son Tony, Nacogdoches, September 14, 1921. Mary Stewart Duncan, Rulfs' niece, gave a copy of this letter to the author in June of 1972.

12. Perkins, *Perkins*, 242 and 260. For quick genealogical information on Perkins, see Ericson, *Gateway* III , 700.

13. George P. Garrison, Will's first partner for two years, was married to Annie Perkins. He left the drugstore business in 1882 and became a noted professor in the Department of English at the University of Texas in Austin. Garrison's place in the business was taken by Will's brother, Dr. Sam J. Perkins, until his untimely death a year later, but the name "Perkins Brothers" came from this short association. After 1900, Will's younger brother, Charles, joined the firm, and after that, his nephew John. See Perkins, *Perkins,* 242 and 260. See also, Giles Haltom's tribute to Perkins, "W. U. Perkins," *Daily Sentinel*, December 8, 1928.

14. The Haltoms came back into Nacogdoches in 1890 with the *Chronicle*. See Melinda Ann Crain Ivy, "History of Nacogdoches Newspapers," *Bicentennial History of Nacogdoches*, 197.

15. The detailed Plat Map found in the *Nacogdoches County Deed Records* clearly shows the transactions in the block as of the 1886 date, including the backlots. [G. D. Boger *et ux* to Perkins Bros, *Nacogdoches County Deed Records,* September 3, 1886, X: 380-381 (hereafter cited as *Deed Records*)]. The entrepreneurs purchased portions of lot 14 (formerly lot 8) and traded footages among themselves to make everything work out. Sometimes the trades were as low as a few inches and as much as 15 feet. After the great fire of 1906, there was an attempt to correct the orientation of the North Square, to correct the protrusion into East Main caused by the Old Stone Fort, but this came to nothing. (*Daily Sentinel*, January 19, 1907.)

16. Thomas W. Ellison (CEO and Chairman of the Board of Commercial Bank of Texas), conversation with the author, November 30, 2010.

17. *Nacogdoches News*, October 23, 1884.

18. Block 8, Lot 9, and Lot 3: *Deed Records*: R. C. Shindler to Julius Kauffman and Julius 5/29/1882; R. C. Shindler et ux to Julius Kauffman and Julius Runge, January 1, 1887; Kauffman and Runge to Clara Kauffman, July 12, 1887; Clara Kauffman to Mayer & Schmidt, January 2, 1888.

19. Rulfs suggested the same approach to the First Methodist and the First Presbyterian Churches, as discussed in Chapter IX.

20. Sanborn Fire Insurance Maps – Texas, University of Texas, Perry-Castañeda Library Map Collection [Online collection], Nacogdoches (1885), available at http://www.lib.utexas.edu/maps/sanborn/n.html [hereafter Sanborn Maps, UT, *Nacogdoches* (date)].

21. Ericson, *Gateway* III, 616-621. Asa Moore (1815-1890) was the one who opposed the concept of connected brick buildings. When he died in 1890, his sons, Sterling Price Moore (1862-1938) and Richard Asa Moore (1864-1912), undertook to develop the property. See Jere Jackson, "JENKINS SEED STORE (108 South Pecan)," Markers Written for the Nacogdoches Heritage Club and the Texas Historical Commission, Texas Historical Commission Grant, 2003 [hereafter Heritage Club Marker Project].

22. Mrs. E. M. Longhery *A Pen Picture of the City of Nacogdoches and Nacogdoches County: Their Present and Future* (Nacogdoches: Spradley and Hutt, Printers, 1895), 33.

23. Haltom, *Nacogdoches,* 61. See Partin, *et al, Nacogdoches,* 95.

24. *Minutes Commissioners Court Nacogdoches County*, December 13, 1886, Book F, 223.

25. Handbook Texas Online (HTO), s, v, "Heiner, Eugene T.," http://tshaonline.org/handbook/articles/HH/fhe.html.

26. *Minutes Commissioners Court Nacogdoches County*, Book F, 270-271. The 1856 building cost $12,000 and the new 1887 one cost $11,995.00, five dollars less. On March 12, 1887, the Court formally declared that the old Court House building was "in an unsafe and dangerous condition." *Nacogdoches News*, March 12, 1887.

27. Partin, *et al, Nacogdoches*, 94-95.

28. The Court wanted to help Asa Moore in his resistance to plans by John Schmidt to build a brick block in the middle of the west square. They rented Moore's building next to the new M&S brick building.

29. There are several possible explanations for this. The newspapers that discussed the building may not have survived. The same is true for regional newspapers, such as the papers in Jacksonville, Palestine, Galveston , and Houston. A regional newspaper made a mention of a workman being injured or killed in the process of building the building. The article appeared in the *Fort Worth Gazette,* April 14, 1887. Mark Cowen (Texas Historical Commission), e-mail correspondence with the author, June 17, 2010.

30. David C. Bucek, "The Architecture of Eugene T. Heiner (1852-1901)," unpublished study, cited on the *Texas Historic Sites Atlas,* keyword search, "Nacogdoches: Courthouse." Correspondence with David Bucek produced no further information on Nacogdoches. David Bucek, e-mail correspondence with the author, June 17 and 22, 2010. For more information on Heiner, see: Stephen Fox, "HEINER, EUGENE T.," *Handbook of Texas Online* [Published by the Texas State Historical Association] http://www.tshaonline.org/handbook/online/articles/fhe48. Johnny Stucco, "The Courthouses of Eugene Heiner (1852-1901)," http://www.texasescapes.com/TexasCourthouses/Courthouses-of-Eugene-T-Heiner.htm.

31. For instance, he used the chamfered doors on the Charles Hoya (built 1888, remodeled in 1900), the Jesse Summers House, (c1894), and the architect's own home.

32. "Arch Ways Cut in Cason, Richardson & Co.", *Daily Sentinel,* July 29, 1900.

33. Sanborn Maps, UT, *Nacogdoches,* (1900).

34. In 1988 the Meisenheimer family, direct descendants of the Cox family, sold the building to Dr. Robert Gruebel and his wife, Diane Ford, who began the process of renovation and restoration. NCAD, Property 22930, http://www.nacocad.org/ accessed February 13, 2011. Victor & Victor Survey, Site No. 148. In 2003, the author researched and wrote a marker for the building for the Heritage Club and the Texas Historical Commission: Jere Jackson, "The John H. Cox Building," Heritage Club Marker Project, 2003.

35. ETRC, "Nacogdoches, Texas; Main Street, Public Plaza, c. 1882, P70A_8(1)," ETRC, http://digital.sfasu.edu/cdm4/item_viewer.php?CISOROOT=/EastTexRC&CISOPTR=30. For some uses of this photograph, see Archie P. McDonald, *Nacogdoches, Texas: A Pictorial History,* (Virginia Beach, VA: Donning Press, 1996), 39. Christopher Talbot, *Nacogdoches: Then and Now* (Nacogdoches: Stephen F. Austin University Press, 2010), 62. For a discussion based on the photograph, see Jubilee Pamphlets, "1882 . . . Nacogdoches, Texas," Printed by Old Town Printing, provided to the author by Mr. Charles Bright. [The historical notes for this pamphlet were provided by Dianna Scott and Dorothy Nelson (Sterne-Hoya Museum), Linda Nicklas (Ralph Steen Library), Charles Bright, and Ruth Pochmann.]

36. Ericson, *Gateway* III, 559. Ericson, *Nacogdoches County Families,* 587-588.

37. Longhery, *Nacogdoches,* 33. The Mayer & Schmidt Company sponsored this publication.

38. *Nacogdoches Star* , March 9, 1888.

39. "Mayer and Schmidt," *Daily Sentinel,* December 30, 1928.

40. Jere Jackson, "Commerce Street," Heritage Club Marker Project, 2003.

41. For published material on the Opera House, see Lawrence Zillmer, "Theater in Nacogdoches," *Bicentennial History of Nacogdoches,* 107-110; Ericson, *Nacogdoches County Families,* 81-82; Victor & Victor, Site No. 166; Nacogdoches Sites Survey Online, 329 East Main, http://www.sfasu.edu/heritagecenter/1212.asp, accessed August 15, 2011; Jere Jackson, "Old Nacogdoches Opera House," [Marker on the Building], Heritage Club Marker Project, 2003. Tom McKinney, while serving as an assistant to the author in the Center for East Texas Studies, wrote a fine paper on the "The Nacogdoches Opera House" (1999), which was the basis of the promotional material used when the art gallery opened.

42. John Cason, grandson of D. K. Cason, once showed the author a photograph given to him by Groucho Marx , on which Marx wrote that this story was correct. The whereabouts of this photograph is now unknown. Perhaps when the Cason Papers are catalogued in the ETRC, it will be found.

43. Jere Jackson, "The West Side of the Square," Heritage Club Marker Project, 2003. Ann Phillips (granddaughter to S. P. Moore), interview with the author, June, 2010. For information on Sterling Price Moore (1862-1938) and Richard Asa Moore (1864-1912), see Ericson, *Gateway,* III, 620-621. The brothers continued to own the middle building, between M&S and the First National Bank, until deep in the twentieth century. Victor & Victor, Site 206. For the *Deed Records,* see S. P. and Richard Moore to First National Bank, September 18, 1890. NCAD, Property Nos: 22963 & 22964, http://www.nacocad.org.

44. For a picture of the iron plate on the steps of the Moore's building, see Nacogdoches Sites Survey Online, 108 South Pecan, http://www.sfasu.edu/heritagecenter/1176.asp.

45. Joe Ericson, "Nacogdoches Banks and Bankers," *Bicentennial History of Nacogdoches,* 192. The closure of the First National Bank paved the way for the creation of the Commercial National Bank (1901); the collapse of the Wettermark Bank in 1903 paved the way for the creation of the Stone Fort National Bank (1903).

46. Jere Jackson, "Jenkins Seed Store," Heritage Club Marker Project, 2003.

47. Jackson, "Sam Houston's First Home in Texas," Application for a Texas Historical Marker, Texas Historical Commission, Vertical Files (2009), Austin, Texas.

48. Sanborn Maps, UT, *Nacogdoches,* (1896).

49. Sanborn Maps, UT, *Nacogdoches,* (1929). "Nacogdoches Downtown Buildings," Notes by Charles Bright, 2003, made available to the author, Fall, 2010. Mr. Bright only remembered the property as the Liberty Hotel and Coffee Shop, first operated by Mr. J. N. Berry, and then by the Hathcocks. "It was a very good hotel and banquet hall." Bright said that Doug and Joyce Swearingen operated a Credit Bureau several years in the west side. The City purchased the property in stages, starting in the 1960s. They moved their office into the building in 1986. See also, Jere Jackson, "Walking Tour of the Square: Old Liberty Hotel," 2003.

50. *Daily Sentinel,* September 26, 1947.

51. For a survey of the property from 1960 to the present, see NCAD, Property 23059, http://www.nacocad.org, accessed September 6, 2011. See also, Victor & Victor, Site No. 217; and Nacogdoches Sites Survey Online, 202 East Pilar, http://www.sfasu.edu/heritagecenter/1156.asp.

52. Archie P. McDonald, *Sentinel of Service: Stone Fort National Bank* (Nacogdoches: Privately Printed by Regions Bank, 2003).

53. Colonel R. D. Orton (1841-1885) was the brother to Mary Louise Adeline Orton. Mary Louise Adeline Orton married James Harvey Haltom; she was the mother of both R. W. and Giles Haltom. Ericson, *Gateway,* III, 664-665. Bryan Davis, Jr., "The Orton Family," Ericson, *Nacogdoches County Families,* F756, 499-500.

54. *Bicentennial History of Nacogdoches,* 196.

55. The first home of the Wettermark Bank was on the corner of Main and North Street. The Wettermarks purchased an existing wooden structure from Bennet Blake, Sr. for the sum of $1000. In 1896 the bank moved to the other end

of Block 13; at that time the lots were renumbered starting from North Street instead of the Square. In 1905, the original location burned and Rulfs designed the replacement, which still stands. See Chapter VIII.

56. Sanborn Maps, UT, *Nacogdoches,* (1896).

57. Jere Jackson, "Old Wettermark Bank Building," Heritage Club Marker Project, 2003:

58. Additional information on this building can be found at Nacogdoches Sites Survey Online, 124 East Main, http://www.sfasu.edu/heritagecenter/2100.asp.

59. The *1880 Census* has N. G. Wade, his wife, Mary Ann, in the Liberty Community. Ancestry.com *1880 United States Census* [Datebase Online] *Liberty, Nacogdoches, Texas;* Roll: 1321; Family History Film: 1255321; page: 275D; Enumeration District: 53. Wade's parents were living with him in 1880 as well as four of his children. At the time the hotel was built in 1896, Wade was 53 years of age; he died two years later.

60. *Nacogdoches Chronicle*, September 30, 1897.

61. *Daily Sentinel*, 1906 Special Edition, "The Banita Hotel."

62. *Daily Sentinel*, May 23, 1901.

63. Pamela Aronson Kulhavy, December, 1980, "A Survey of Nacogdoches Hotels, 1830-1910," an unpublished paper from the author's local history seminar, Vertical Files, ETRC, 28; Kulhavy is quoting from an interview she did with Richard Wade McKinney, the grandson of Mr. Wade, and son of John Richard. Kulhavy is correct is citing that there were originally only 32 rooms; see *Daily Sentinel*, May 23, 1901.

64. There are four J. R. McKinneys: John Richard McKinney (1876-1951); Jack Rains McKinney (1911- 1997); John Richard McKinney II (1937 - 1982); and John Richard McKinney III (1966 -).

65. "1896 . . . Nacogdoches, Texas," Jubilee Pamphlets (Printed by Old Town Printing, nd [1990s], provided to the author by Mr. Charles Bright. [The Historical Notes provided by Sally Batchelor (ETRC), *Daily Sentinel,* Ericson, *Nacogdoches County Families*, Mr. & Mrs. Jack R. McKinney, Campbell Cox, Mrs. Delbert (Pyrtle) Teutsch.] This pamphlet or brochure can now be read online: http://www.sfasu.edu/heritagecenter/images/FrontScan_copy.pdf. Interesting, but this pamphlet, produced in the 1990s did not credit Rulfs with designing the Banita; nor did it credit him with the enlargement of the hotel after the turn of the century.

66. D. Rulfs, "Specifications of change of part of said Banita Hotel into a Department Building for Zeno Cox, Jr., according to plans prepared by D. Rulfs, Architect, Nacogdoches, Texas." (1920). Campbell Cox, a relative, generously shared these specifications with the author.

67. There are photographs of the East Banita Apartments, as the Ford Studios, at the following website: Nacogdoches Sites Survey Online, 201 West Pillar, http://www.sfasu.edu/heritagecenter/1293.asp, accessed September 7, 2011.

68. Geo. F. Ingraham to G. N. Bright, February 13, 1917, *Deed Records,* 90: 80. The Jubilee Pamphlet entitled "1933 ... Nacogdoches Texas," (Printed by Old Town Printing, nd [1990s], discusses the Bright Grocery Store. The date cited for the Ingraham Building in the pamphlet, 1865, is clearly a mistake.

69. NCAD, Property No: 23064, http://www.nacocad.org. The property now belongs to the Charles Bright Trust.

70. The author was chairman of the NCHC at the time (1998). Tom McKinney, my assistant at SFASU, did the research and the writing of the marker. [Tom McKinney, "The George F. Ingraham Building," Application to the Texas Historical Commission for Recorded Texas Historic Landmark, 1998, Marker No. 12099.] For the text of the marker, see Texas Historic Sites Atlas, Nacogdoches, Ingraham Building, http://atlas.thc.state.tx.us.

71. *City of Nacogdoches, Nacogdoches County* (Nacogdoches: Spradley & Hutt, Printers, 1895.)

72 The *Houston Daily Post,* on Sunday, December 13, 1896, 38. The majority of the article recounts the colorful history of the frontier town.

73. *Houston Daily Post*, Thursday, December 17, 1896, letter written on December 14, 1896. The author cannot decipher who "R. D. C." is.

74. *Houston Daily Post*, Thursday, December 17, 1896, letter dated December 14, 1896. The two banks he referred to were the Wettermark and First National Banks.

75. This was the first of many special editions which the Haltom brothers published during their lifetime, usually in response to a challenge to the town. Other special editions referred to in this work came in 1900, 1902, and 1906.

76. *Nacogdoches Chronicle*, September 30, 1897, East Texas Research Center, Steen Library, Stephen F. Austin State University, Nacogdoches, Texas.

77. *Houston Daily Post*, May 3, 1899.

Chapter IV: Houses, Downtown and North Street

1. The author helped to initiate and conduct the first inventory in Nacogdoches in 1974-1975. The first survey was a combined effort between the Nacogdoches County Survey Committee (later Nacogdoches County Historical Commission) and the Texas Historical Commission. Subsequent surveys, for example the Victor and Victor Survey, were under-taken later under the auspices of the Nacogdoches Historic Landmark Committee. The Victor and Victor Survey (1986) expanded the original survey to the whole core of the town, incorporating the 1975 study. These, and the continuing studies done under the supervision of state and local Historic Sites Department and Landmark Committees, have had a material impact on the preservation of Rulfs' houses over the years. The town has not lost many of his buildings since 1975.

2. For a summary of the National Register Districts, see the "City of Nacogdoches Historic Sites Survey," Nacogdoches Historic Sites Department, [Online Resource] hosted by the Regional Heritage Center, Stephen F. Austin State University, http://www.sfasu.edu/heritagecenter/622.asp [hereafter Nacogdoches Sites Survey Online]. The Victor & Victor Survey, the applications for the National Register of Historic Places, and updates to the survey efforts are all available at this site. This online resource, while a work-in-progress, is easy to use. See also, the Historic Sites Department: http://www.ci.nacogdoches.tx.us/departments/historicsites.php. Increasing daily are the online resources at the East Texas Research Center, Steen Library, Stephen F. Austin State University: http://library.sfasu.edu/etrc/ [hereafter, ETRC].

3. All NR District maps can be found from this site: http://www.sfasu.edu/heritagecenter/622.asp. Washington Square: http://www.sfasu.edu/heritagecenter/images/WASHINGTON.tif; Zion Hill District: http://www.sfasu.edu/heritagecenter/images/WASHINGTON.tif; Virginia Ave: http://www.sfasu.edu/heritagecenter/images/VIRGINIA_AVE.tif; Sterne-Hoya: http://www.sfasu.edu/heritagecenter/images/STERNE_HOYA.tif.

4. Jere Jackson, "Nacogdoches' Visible Past," *Bicentennial History of Nacogdoches*, 206. The Victor & Victor Survey and subsequent surveys, including the National Register Applications have repeated my mistakes. See "Historic and Architectural Resources of Nacogdoches: Community Planning and Development in Nacogdoches, 1830-1940, Texas Historical Commission, *Texas Historic Sites Atlas*, http://atlas.thc.state.tx.us/. In this document, the *general* research is not as strong as the *specific* site entries. This document is now available at the Nacogdoches Sites Survey Online, http://www.sfasu.edu/heritagecenter/622.asp.

5. *Nacogdoches Star-News,* May 31, 1889. Nacogdoches County to Tom R. Jennings, September 22, 1883, *Deed Records*, W:321, Old Town.

6. Carolyn Reeves Ericson, *Fires and Firemen of Nacogdoches*, Texas (Nacogdoches: Pineywood Printing, 1976), 1-17 [hereafter Ericson, *Fires and Firemen.*]

7. For several of these houses, see discussions of the Lee Hardeman, Tom Summers, and Sarah Richardson houses in Chapter XI.

8. The D. K. Cason Papers and the Missoura (Garrett) Price Papers are available for public use in the ETRC.

9. "D. Rulfs. Architect, Carpenter, and Contractor of Buildings. Nacogdoches, Texas," *Nacogdoches Chronicle,* March 9, 1888.

10. Susan Jean Dickey, "F. E. and Oscar Ruffini: Texas Architects," PhD Dissertation (Lubbock, Texas: Texas Tech University, 1993), 17-42. See, Johnson Mahony, Cathey Searls, *Eugene Thomas Heiner: 19th Century Texas Architect* (Charleston, S.C.: C. S. Johnson Mahony, 2001).

11. Along with the application for Recorded Texas Landmark status, a copy of the specifications for the Roland Jones House was submitted dating to 1895-96; this is the only extant copy found. The original elevation of the June Harris House dates to 1895; it is still in the hands of the descendents of the family.

12. See the 1899 contract between William Henry Rulfs and others, Bennett Blake Papers, Box 9, Folder 24, ETRC.

13. See the Redland Hotel dispute in Chapters VII and VIII.

14. *Nacogdoches Star*, March. 9, 1888. This ad ran often: see *Nacogdoches Star*, December 24, 1888; January 11, 1889; May 31, 1889; December 5, 1890; July 22, 1892; ETRC.

15. *Nacogdoches Chronicle*, June 15, 1892.

16. See: *Daily Sentinel*, February 22, 1900; May 15, 1902.

17. *Nacogdoches Plaindealer*, October 16, 1902.

18. Mary Stewart Duncan (maternal niece of D. Rulfs), interview with the author, March, 1974. Rulfs' granddaughter, Anna Kathryn Holbrook relied upon and repeated the words of her cousin Mary Stewart Duncan when she wrote the selection on D. Rulfs for the volume edited by Carolyn Ericson; *Nacogdoches County Families*, 581. Mary Stewart Duncan (1883-1986) was the daughter of Rulfs' brother-in-law William Henry Stewart [born Wilhelm Heinrich Boschen] and Nellie Delilah Miller who married in 1881. See Ericson, *Gateway* III, 882.

19. Bryan Holt Davis (descendant of the Orton Family) interview with the author, August 4, 2010. Grandmother Orton continued to live in the House on the hill during this period, according to Bryan.

20. Mary Stewart Duncan, interviews with the author, March, 1974.

21. Diedrich and Johannah Rulfs had five children other than the infant buried in Germany. According to Anna Kathryn Holbrook, in Ericson, *Nacogdoches County Families*, 581: Gerhard William (1875-1943) m. Sadie Miller, had G. W. Jr., David, Mable; Carl Henry (1878-1955) m. Anna Taylor, had Carl Henry, Lawrence Dietrich, Dietrich A. G. W. E., Anna Kathryn (Katherine) m. Richard Holbrook, Milam Irion; Edward Anton (1880-1948) m. Lily Dell Jones, had Helen; Mary (1882-1953) m. J. C. Neyland, had J. C. Jr. and Dietrich; John (1885-1955) m. three times, no children. See also, Ericson, *Gateway* III, 791.

22. See Holbrook, in Ericson, *Nacogdoches County Families*, 581. The deeds transferring property from Friedrich von de Hoya to Francis and Joseph von der Hoya can be viewed in the East Texas Research Center, Stephen F. Austin State University. Folder 8: Deed from Freidrich von der Hoya Grand Duchy of Oldenburg, Germany and Francis von der Hoya, Nacogdoches, to Joseph von der Hoya, Nacogdoches, for 200 acres on the Lanana Creek, August 24, 1859. Folder 9: Letter in German script, from Friedrich von der Hoya, Germany to his brother, Joseph von der Hoya, Nacogdoches, October 1, 1881.

23. Mary Stewart Duncan, interviews with the author, March, 1974.

24. Z. T. Mast *et ux* to D. Rulfs, September 11, 1888, Block 18 "City," *Deed Records*, Z:60. The deed states that Mast had only recently purchased the lot from T. J. and W. H. Swift in 1884. For Zachary Taylor Mast, see Ericson, *Gateway* III, 552.

25. Ancestry.com, 1880 *US Census* [database on-line] *1880, Melrose, Nacogdoches, Texas;* Roll: 1321; Family History Film: 1255321; Page: 212B; Enumeration District: 49. Also, *1900 US Census*; *Melrose, Nacogdoches, Texas*; Roll: T623_1661; Page: 19A; Enumeration District: 43.

26. Mary Stewart Duncan, interviews with the author, March 1974. For an example of the occasional listing of these houses for rent, see *Daily Sentinel*, November 27, 1900: "For Rent. 5 room house, Main Street, Apply to D. Rulfs."

27. Mary Stewart Duncan, interview with the author, March, 1974.

28. Rulfs used similar corner projections on the Laura Blount Chapman House on North Street, the F. H. Tucker House on Mound, and the Nelson-Davis House on Main Street.

29. *Nacogdoches Chronicle*, June 15, 1892.

30. Thomas Tracy, conversations with the author, October, 2010. See also, *Daily Sentinel*, October 1, 2010. Correspondence supportive of this article took place between Will Goodwin (*Daily Sentinel*, September, 2010. The Rulfs Office was on tour in December of 2010; see *Daily Sentinel*, November 25, 2010. See, Nacogdoches Sites Survey Online, http://www.sfasu.edu/heritagecenter/1311.asp.

31. The Eugene Blount House, done in 1923 when Rulfs was 75, is a prime example of this. See Chapter XII.

32. Ericson, *Gateway* III, 791. "William H. Rulfs," Ancestry.com. *Texas Death Index, 1903-2000* [database on-line], Texas Department of Health, Certificate 36316.

33. Ericson, *Gateway* III, 879.

34. The addition to the Hoya House appears on the 1906 Sanborn map. Sanborn Maps, UT, *Nacogdoches*, (1906).

35. Francis E. Abernethy, correspondence with the author, September 31, 2010. Ab said that Mrs. J. Roy Gray (Clara Hoya) always complained that her husband hired a distant relative who produced an addition of inferior quality.

36. *Nacogdoches Plaindealer*, October 16, 1902. "D. Rulfs, Architect Contractor and Builder. Plans and estimates furnished on buildings of all kinds and sizes. I can both design and build your house, saving you time and annoyance. If you contemplate building, call on or correspond with me. My work in Nacogdoches speaks for itself."

37. Mistakenly, several sources have dated the Baxter Hotel to this early period, the 1890s. The Baxter Hotel, however, does not appear on the Sanborn Maps until 1912 period, although its empty lots appear on early maps. The old Hart Hotel still stood on the south side of East Main near the Opera House, and the Hyde House existed until the Matthews tore it down to built the Bullen. *Nacogdoches Star*, May 11, 1888, lamenting the destruction of the Hyde House: "This lovely, attractive place has been so long a feature of beauty in our town, that it looks almost like an act of vandalism to disturb any portion of the premise."

38. Esme Bullen's husband was a descendant of the Boleyn family in England. The family spelling changed in America. Ericson, *Gateway* III, 556.

39. *Nacogdoches Star*, May 11, 1888.

40. Giles Haltom, in the *Daily Sentinel,* December 30, 1928, stated: "The writer of this tribute well remembers the occasion when United States Senator Roger Q. Mills, delivered an address at Nacogdoches and Henry Brewer marshaled about 100 citizens of Linn Flat and rode to town, two by two, Brew and Dunk Caver leading the procession and carrying a banner on which was inscribed: 'For Roger Q, Mills and Democracy.' A great reception was held at the Bullen Hotel in honor of Col. Mills and the Linn Flat calvacade rode up to the front of the hotel, formed in line and gave several rousing cheers in honor of the speaker of the day who responded briefly and thanked the Linn Flat men for their patriotism and zeal in the name of democracy."

41. Archie P. McDonald, ed., *Hurrah for Texas! The Diary of Adolphus Sterne, 1838-1851* (Waco, Tex.: Texian Press, 1969), 198-199.

42. *Daily Sentinel,* June 12, 1988. The background of the Edwards family is discussed in an article of research on this house conduced in one of my seminar students, Jonathan Jeffry.

43. Victory & Victor Survey, Site No. 957. The three volumes of this survey are now online: Nacogdoches Sites Survey Online, http://www.sfasu.edu/heritage-center/2079.asp.

44. J. D. Martin and Sarah Martin conveyed to J. H. Summers and Emma Summers for $250, April 16, 1887, *Deed Records,* Y: 17. The author has had multiple conversations and e-mail messages from Henry and Tom Middlebrook (great grandsons of Jesse and Emma Summers), June 2011.

45. Affidavit W. D. Burrows and A. G. Gatlin, re: J. H. Summers, deceased, May 22, 1946, *Deed Records*, 172: 356. See also, Ericson, *Gateway* III, 899-900. The children of Jesse and Emma Summers were: Minnie, b. 27 Apr 1874; William Franklin "Frank," b. 1 Dec 1875; Thomas Holloway, b. 18 Jan 1880; Joseph Elbert, b. 11 Feb 1882; Jesse Hubbard, b. 28 Sept 1883; Pearl, b. 17 Aug 1885; Sallie Talitha, b. 19 July 1888; Emma Richardson, b. 9 June 1890; Margaret "Maggie," b. 11 Aug 1892; James Robert, b. 13 Mar 1894.

46. Sanborn Maps, UT, *Nacogdoches*, (1891).

47. Affidavit by W. D. Burrows et al. May 22, 1946, *Deed Records*, 172: 356.

48. "Historic and Architectural Resources of Nacogdoches," (1990) http://www.sfasu.edu/heritagecenter/622.asp.

49. The East Texas Research Center at SFASU has an inventory of the photographs returned to SFA by Evans; they are now online at http://digital.sfasu.edu/cdm/search/searchterm/Elliot/order/.

50. Elliot Evans, "The East Texas House," *Journal of the Society of Architectural Historians*, Vol. XI, (1952) No.4 , 1-2.

51. There are several Rulfs houses in the Evans Collection.

52. Ericson, *Nacogdoches County Families*, F910, 581.

53. *Nacogdoches Star*, March 9, 1888.

54. *Ibid.*

55. *Daily Sentinel,* January 31, 1900. *Nacogdoches Star*, March 9, 1888.

56. *Daily Sentinel*, June 7, 1955, "LANDMARK COMES DOWN." The newspaper incorrectly estimated the date of the house as 1870. The house was in good condition; it could have been moved and saved.

57. *Daily Sentinel,* January 31, 1900.

58. *Daily Sentinel*, January 16, 1900. For other articles on the pine top celebrations, see: *Daily Sentinel*, August 2, 1901; January 18, 1902; March 4, 1904.

59. Ann Phillips, interview with the author, September 18, 2010.

60. Mrs. Richard B. Hardeman, "Hardeman Family," in Ericson, *Nacogdoches County Families*, F436, 340-341.

61. Gladys Hardeman, interview with the author, 1975. See also, *Nacogdoches Star*, May 11, 1888. "The Schmidt building on Main Street in the Perkins brick block, has passed into the hands of B. F. and T. B. Hardeman."

62. The collaborations began when B. F. Hardeman built his residence on North Street, followed by Lee Hardeman House on North Church Street, and then the Tolbert Hardeman House on Mound. They moved their offices into Rulfs' First Brick Block, continued in 1904 with the building of the Hardeman Building on East Main (twice!) and then remodel their building by incorporating it within the Redland Hotel.

63. Gladys Hardeman, interview with the author, 1975.

64. The photograph of the First Baptist Church tower placed in the 1917 booklet, *The Twenty Three Reasons Why*, partially shows the B. F. Hardeman House. A special thanks to Jimmy Partin for providing one of the pictures of the house, which sat north of the First Baptist Church and was used by the church for Sunday School space.

65. State of Texas, Highway Department, *Plans of Proposed State Highway Improvement, U. S. Highway 59, From the South City Limit Line of Nacogdoches to the North City Limit Line,* Federal Aid Project, F201 (10), September 24, 1948.

66. Bryan Holt Davis (descendent of John Greer Orton), interview with the author, January 29, 2012. See also, Ericson, *Nacogdoches County Families*, 422-423; Ericson, *Gateway III*, 529.

67. Lucas to Wade, December 1, 1903, *Deed Records*, 45:501. The property sold for $2350 in 1903 and for $1800 in 1910 when John F. Floyd purchased it from Wade. For some of the modern transactions, see NCAD, Property ID 22653, http://www.nacocad.org/.

68. Among the families who made their homes on North Street were: Perkins, Schmidts, Blounts, Sturdevants, Shindlers, Barhams, Rhines, Gastons, Hardeman, Summers, Matthews, Davidsons, Taylors, Tom Bakers, J. J. Baker, Mize, Hayters, Banks, Adams, Ingrahams, Campbells, Weeks, Irions, Gintzes, Thomases, Wettermarks, and others.

69. *Daily Sentinel,* December 8, 1928. This article also appeared, in an earlier version, in 1906.

70. *Ibid.*

71. Louise, born in this house in 1890, died in 1993. Another daughter, Virginia Perkins Nelson (1902-1986), confirmed this statement in an interview in the newspaper on the occasion of a tour of her home. See *Daily Sentinel*, April 9, 1963. Mrs. Nelson was born in the house in 1902.

72. Virginia Perkins Nelson as reported in the *Daily Sentinel*, April 9, 1963.

73. Other houses with entrance fireplaces and similar treatments include the houses for John Schmidt, Stephen Blount, Roland Jones, William Pearson, and Benjamin Wettermark. The front doors of the Prairie Style houses, while having no entrance hall, opened directly into rooms with fire places; examples include the houses for Guy Blount, Mary Hayter, Clara Hoya Gray, and Jennie Hoya Mast.

74. Carolyn and Bryan Davis, interview with the author, April 14, 2011. Memoirs of Bill Wilson (grandson), December 16, 1992, as reported in Perkins, *Perkins,* 263-264. When Bill Wilson designed a new home for Virginia and Langston Nelson in the late 1960s, he replicated the dimensions of the large drawing room from the Perkins House for their new residence on Parker Road.

75. *Nacogdoches Star*, May 22, 1891.

76. The parents of Will Perkins moved to North Street in 1893, a few miles north of Will. Perkins, *Perkins Family, 265.*

77. *Ibid*, 246.

78. *Nacogdoches Star*, July 22, 1892.

79. Frank Johnson, *A History of Texas and Texans*, Volume 4, Ed. by Eugene Barker (New York and Chicago, American Historical Society, 1916), 197-198. To list a few: the founder of Mayer-Schmidt Co. of Nacogdoches & Tyler; a founding director of Commercial National Bank; a founding director of the Nacogdoches Oil Mill Company and Compress; Vice-President and founding director of the Cason, Monk & Co.; founder and president of the Nacogdoches Grocery Company; founding director of the Nacogdoches Tobacco Co.; director & stockholder of Crain Furniture Co.; major stockholder in the firm of Titche-Goettingers of Dallas, and one of the owners of the Titche-Goettinger Building downtown Dallas; director of Schwartz-Landauer of Dallas; director of the Guarantee and Trust Company in Dallas, Southwestern Life Insurance Co of Dallas, the Fort Worth Elevators Company; director of the Lufkin National Bank, of Lufkin, Texas; director of the Paunee Land and Lumber company, Paunee, Louisiana; Wadel-Dickey Hardware Company, of Tyler, Texas.

See also, Nugent E. Brown, *The Book of Nacogdoches County* (Nacogdoches, Tex: Nugent Brown Publisher, 1927). This book, compiled by an advertising and publicity specialist, had John Schmidt's picture across from the title page with the caption: "John Schmidt, Best known business man and cotton buyer in East Texas. His firm now in 50th year." Brown's volume is in the East Texas Research Center, SFASU.

80. For essential biographical information, see Ericson, *Gateway* III, 807; Carolyn Ericson, "John Schmidt," *Nacogdoches County Families*, F919, 587-588. John Schmidt's nephews were Jacob F. Schmidt and Henry Phillip Schmidt (father to Henry and John Lewis Schmidt).

81. For major reviews of the Mayer & Schmidt business, see the *Nacogdoches Chronicle*, September 30, 1897; *Daily Sentinel*, Special Edition, November 1906; *Daily Sentinel*, December 8, 1928.

82. Obituary for John Schmidt, *Daily Sentinel,* July 24, 1934.

83. *Daily Sentinel,* February 19, 1962.

84. "Edward Augustus Blount, Sr.," and "Stephen William Blount, Jr.," Ericson, *Gateway* III, 83-84; "The Blount Family," Ericson, *Nacogdoches County Families*, F98, 170-180.

85. Regarding E. A. Blount's affluence, a 1950 *Dallas Morning News* article about an S. Seymore Thomas portrait of Col. Stephen W. Blount (E. A.'s father, and Thomas' grandfather) describes Col. Blount as "a large landowner and prominent merchant at San Augustine until his death on Feb. 7, 1890." Col. Blount appears to have received 1/3 league of land when he arrived in Texas in 1835 (Headright Certificate 49, San Augustine County Board of Land Commissioners). He helped his 4 sons start their fortunes and was, apparently, generous with his 4 daughters. Edward (Jerry) Blount, interview with the author, August, 2010. Haltom also confirmed the main source of Blount wealth; *Daily Sentinel*, Special Edition, November, 1906.

86. Joe Ericson, "Nacogdoches Banks and Bankers" *Bicentennial History of Nacogdoches*, 192-193.

87. On North Street alone, Rulfs built: the E. A. Blount House (1894-95), the Laura Blount Chapman House (1894-95), the first Eugene H. Blount House (c1903), the Guy Blount House (1910), and finally, a second Eugene H. Blount House (1923). Rulfs also built for E. A.'s younger brother the Stephen W. Blount, Jr. House (1897) on Mound Street, discussed later. The commercial buildings are discussed in Chapter VIII and XII.

88. Mary Stewart Duncan, interview with the author, June, 1972.

89. "Roaring Fire Destroys 'Old Blount Home' Here; Ancient Landmark Burns to the Ground: Much Valuable Furniture Is Lost," *Daily Sentinel,* January 31, 1945; also reported in Ericson, *Fires and Firemen,* 140-141.

90. *Galveston Daily News*, May 14, 1905.

91. Margaret Culbertson, *Texas Houses Built by the Book* (College Station, Texas: Texas A&M Press, 1999), 35. Culbertson is relying on material by Martha Ann Turner, *Old Nacogdoches in the Jazz Age* (Austin, Texas: Madrona Press, 1976). Turner has, by her own admission, written a highly impressionistic book which relies more on "mood and theme" than deep research. There are no good pictures of the Blount House. Culbertson is writing about the J. E. Downes House in Crockett, which was copied out of the Barber catalogue, in 1891.

92. Margaret Culbertson used the George F. Barber, *Victorian Cottage Architecture: An American Catalog of Designs, 1891* (New York: Dover Publications, Inc., 1982), 112-113; originally published by George Barber, *The Cottage Souvenir no. 2* (Knoxville, Tenn: S. B. Newman & Co, 1891).

93. The author consulted many pattern books in the preparation of this book. They are all listed in the bibliographic referenced, albeit in many cases only the modern selection-books (summations) were easily available. Besides Culbertson's *Texas Houses Built by the Book*, Daniel Reiff's *Houses from Books: Treatises, Pattern Books, and Catalogues in American Architecture, 1738-1950: A History and Guide* (University Park, Pa.: Pennsylvania State University Press, 2000), was helpful in a general way. Period books include: Barber, Bicknell, Comstock, Palliser, and Shoppell.

94. There are successful similarities, such as Crouch-Stripling House and the Robert Lindsey House; then there are the unsuccessful attempts to adapt the Charles Perkins (Steamboat) House. The Perkins plan may have been reused by Perkins himself, not Rulfs, but its replication as a one-story house (at least three times) proved less than perfect. Only one of these, on South Fredonia Street still survives; the others, on North Street and Church Street, have disappeared.

95. E. A.'s daughter, Laura Adelaide Blount (probably named after her mother's sister, Laura Adelaide Sims), was 19 at the time of her marriage to William McNeil Chapman on October 19, 1894. Laura died five days after the birth of her daughter, Laura Blount Chapman, in July of 1896. The child then lived in the household of her grandfather. [Edward (Jerry) Baker, interview with the author, August 2010.] For information on W. M. Chapman, see Ericson, *Gateway* III, 162.

96. For instance, his own home on Main Street, the Tucker-Branch House and S. W. Blount houses on Mound Street, and the Nelson-Davis House on East Main.

97. Clifford, Jean, and Johnny Rudisill, discussions with the author, May, 1998.

98. The windows appeared on the Nelson House on Mound, the Edwards House on Main, the Charles Perkins House on Mound, the Butts House on Main, the Pearson-Spradley House, and several others.

99. Ericson, *Gateway* III, 161-162.

100. Rudisill Foundation, http://www.rudisillfoundation.org/. The site has interior views of the Chapman-Rudisill House as well as some history of the structure.

101. Marc B. Smith, "Judge George Frances Ingraham," Ericson, *Gateway* III, 371-372. Also, Ericson, *Gateway* III, 433.

102. Some of Ingraham's papers are located in the documents of his grandson, F. I. Tucker, A/249, ETRC.

103. *Ibid.* For the 1929 Sanborn Map, see http://sanborn.umi.com/tx/8670/dateid-000009.htm?CCSI=894n. The maps at the University of Houston do not include 1929 or 1929-1946 for Nacogdoches.

104. Ericson, *Gateway* III, 433.

105. Tom R. Jennings to John J. Baker, *Deed Records*, Book 35, 1-2. The transfer to the descendents, the Weavers, after the Bakers died; December 16, 1961, Deed Records, 300: 177.

106. Elizabeth Deanne Malpass, conversation with the author, February, 2011.

107. Mary Stewart Duncan, conversation with the author, March, 1974.

108. NCAD, newspaper in 1988 when it was moved: *Daily Sentinel*, July 17, 1988.

109 Perkins, *Perkins*, 190-191. The deed records contain many transactions by Charles, W. U., and Perkins Brothers in the 1880-1900s throughout Nacogdoches. See also, Ericson, *Nacogdoches County Families*, F801, 524-525; *Gateway* III, 698.

110. *Daily Sentinel*, March 14, 1900.

111. Professor Elliot Evans in his 1948 survey took two views of the Kate Powers Samuels House, which sat on the corner of North Street and King Street. These photographs, while not correctly identified, are available on the website of the East Texas Research Center: Elliot Evans Collection, East Texas House P95T_13 and P95T_18, http://libweb.sfasu.edu/etrc/ accessed July 17, 2012.

112. Sarah Jackson, *Baker*, 17 and 211 *note* 49. For an annotation of the poem "Altair" by Sarah Jackson, see the forthcoming republication of Karle Wilson Baker's *Dreamers on Horseback* (Nacogdoches, Texas: Stephen F. Austin State University Press, 2012), 199. Mrs. Baker, who did a holograph map of North Street in the late 1920s, still labeled the house as belonging to "the Bakers." Baker-Montgomery Estate Papers; Edward (Jerry) Baker, correspondence with the author, correspondence with the author, October 3, 2010.

113. *Daily Sentinel*, July 17, 1988. See also, Nacogdoches Sites Survey Online, "808 Texas Street," http://www.sfasu.edu/heritagecenter/2430.asp. The 2011 summer updates to this site provided new photographs and the story of the 1988 move, a distinct improvement over the Victor and Victor Survey (1986: Site 344) earlier used. The "vintage photograph" which is cited, however, belongs to the Elliot Evan study in 1948 when the house faced Baxter Duncan Street. The photograph Figure 4.24 in this work from the Baker-Montgomery Archive correctly shows the house on North Street. The date of the move to Baxter Duncan Street is uncertain. It sat on North Street in the 1929 Sanborn Map, but on Baxter Duncan Street in 1946. [Sanborn Digital Maps, 1929 and 1929-1946, http://sanborn.umi.com/tx/8670/dateid-000010.htm?CCSI=894n.

114. Kathryn Hooper Davis and Carolyn Ericson, *1900 Census Nacogdoches County, Texas* (Ericson Books: Nacogdoches, Texas, 1989), 15. See also, Ericson, *Gateway* III, 514.

115. *Deed Records*, 37: 429. Lindsey paid $500 for the lot, then sold the house and lot for $3000 in 1900. At the time of the original survey by the Texas Historical Commission in 1975, the house's date was estimated at 1902, based on interviews with the owner at the time, Charlotte Baker Montgomery. The deed records, however, are clear on the date 1898, and the resale in 1900.

116. Edward (Jerry) Baker, correspondence with the author, Oct. 2, 2010. Baker shared with the author a number of pictures from the 1950s when his aunt, Charlotte Baker Montgomery, purchased the house.

117. On May 11, 1900, the Lindseys sold the property and the improvements to J. J. Lilly and his wife for the sum of $3000, consisting of cash and two promissary notes of $1,100 each at 10% interest. The Lilly family lived in the house until 1907 when they probably moved to Tyler; the notes designate a Tyler address for payments. The July 12, 1907 deed record states that they sold the house for approximately what they had paid for it: $800 and two promissary notes of $1,100 each at a rate of 10% interest, (Lilly to Miller, *Deed Records*, 66: 596-598). Giles Haltom bought the house in 1913 and sold it in 1919 to Gintz, who lived there until the 1950s.

118. Ericson, *Nacogdoches County Families*, 112-113. For biographical information, see Ericson, *Gateway* III, 859.

119. *Deed Records,* October 5, 1897, 34: 528 and 560; see also, November 28, 1898, 38: 79.

120. Rulfs used the continuous balcony over a flat-roofed porch again on the Dr. Frank Ford House on Mound Street; see Chapter XI.

121. "Commercial National Bank" from the Nacogdoches *Daily Sentinel*, 1906 Special Edition.

122. *Daily Sentinel*, Sept 16, 1944.

123. *Daily Sentinel*, November 30, 1938. Special Edition.

124. *Nacogdoches Chronicle*, September 30, 1897.

125. The Nacogdoches Compress, organized in June of 1897, had the following list of stockholders and officers: E. X. Andem (Pres.), E. A. Blount (1st V. P.) George H. Davidson (2nd V. P.), Benjamin Wettermark (Secretary-Treasurer), I. L. Sturdevant (General Manager), and John Schmidt, Dotson Bros., W. U. Perkins, F. H. Tucker, R. D. Whitaker, W. D. Rattcliff, and H. E. Dyson. See *Nacogdoches Chronicle*, September 30, 1897.

126. Ericson, *Gateway* III, 97.

127. *Daily Sentinel*, Nov. 30, 1938. Says the founders of SFNB were Chs. Hoya, J. J. Hayter, D. K. Cason, W. U. Perkins, and Sturdevant.

128. Sturdevant helped organize the first volunteer fire dept and became First Fire Chief [*Daily Sentinel,* November 30, 1938; "Happy Birthday," Aug 15, 1946; and September 16, 1944.] For Sturdevant's career see: "Citizens of Nacogdoches Honor Captain I. L. Sturdevant, Who Has Contributed Much to City's Growth," Special Edition, *Daily Sentinel*, November 30, 1938; "Capt. Sturdevant Is Honored for Long and Distinguished Service," *Daily Sentinel*, May 21, 1942; "Capt. Sturdevant Sets Pace for Progressive Nacogdoches," *Redland Herald*, September 21, 1944; "Golden Wedding Anniversary," *Daily Sentinel*, February 18, 1948.

129. Carol Willis (granddaughter of the Sturdevants), interview with the author, March 15, 2011. Carol's mother, Carolyn Miller, grew up in this house; she later became the organist at the First United Methodist Church.

130. *Daily Sentinel*, March 8, 1900. Wettermark sold his old home on North Street to Polk Roberts.

131. Jere Jackson, "The Impact of SFA on Nacogdoches," *Daily Sentinel*, Special 100th Anniversary Edition, 1999. The Wettermark House burned in April of 1924; Ericson, *Fires and Firemen*, 89-90. J. J. Hayter added the porte-cochère on the south side of the Wettermark House after 1903; it was one of the first in Nacogdoches.

132. *Daily Sentinel*, June 11, 1900.

Chapter V: Washington Square

1. "Washington Square Historic District," National Register of Historic Places, 1989, *Texas Historic Sites Atlas* on the Texas Historical Commission website (http://atlas.thc.state.tx.us/index.asp). The document "Historic and Architectural Resources of Nacogdoches: Community Planning and Development in Nacogdoches: 1830-1940," can be found in many places. The most convenient is from the Nacogdoches Sites Survey Online, http://www.sfasu.edu/heritagecenter/622.asp, where it is part of the multiple property applications to the National Register.

2. Today, the only pre-1880 house still left on Hospital Street is the Greek Revival domicile built by Joseph Durst, on the southeast corner of Church and Hospital. It was at one time used as the Rectory of Christ Episcopal Church. It still retains much of its integrity although modified in later years to serve as a residence, a medical office, a gift shop, a restaurant, and now an interior design studio. It is one of the oldest houses in downtown Nacogdoches.

3. The 1891, 1896, and, for the most part, 1900 Sanborn Maps ignore the Washington Square area. Only after the completion of the new Central School in 1904 do the maps extend into the area. The 1906 map shows Washington Square, at least up to the new school, and includes the houses in the 300 block of Church Street (Bagley, Hardeman, Cason, Richardson). The 1906 and 1912 maps show the area accurately, but the later maps (1921-1922) ignore all of the changes in the houses done in the 1910s. Color maps of Nacogdoches, up through 1922, are available online: Sanborn Maps, UT, *Nacogdoches*, (1885-1922) available at http://www.lib.utexas.edu/maps/sanborn/n.html. The only map to documents these houses accurately is the 1929 map, available throught the ETRC: Digital Sanborn Maps, 1867-1970, Texas: *Nacogdoches*, 1929 and 1929-46 [Online Resources], http://libweb.sfasu.edu/proser/etrc/collections/maps/index.html.

4. Jere Jackson, "Church Street," Heritage Club Marker Project, 2003. Church Street, one of the first streets named in Nacogdoches, derived its name from Christ Episcopal Church, which sat just north of Main. From the late 1850s, after the construction of the Old University Building, the street leading north into Washington Square bore the name "College Boulevard," a sixty foot wide street. When the street became residential after 1889, the city decided to eliminate the name College Boulevard and to extend the name "Church Street" northward into Washington Square. When the Jacksons purchased the property at 304 North Church in 1970, lawyer and local historian F. I. Tucker, after looking over the deed abstract he had ordered from the title company, exclaimed, "The Summers never really owned their front porch; the city did!" He immediately filed a quit-claim for the city to remedy this.

5. Carolyn Reeves Ericson, *Sesquicentennial History Of First United Methodist Church Nacogdoches, Texas 1837-1987* (Nacogdoches, Texas: 1987), 16 [hereafter Ericson, *First Methodist Church*]. See also, Carolyn Reeves Gateway III, 28 and 874. Mrs. P. B. Stanley and her sister-in-law, Sarah Bagley, joined the First Methodist Church by certificate in 1889.

6. Victor & Victor Survey, Site No. 445. The Victor & Victor Survey only references the 1890 house as a part of the 1913 remodeled in structure. For more on the structure today, see Chapter X.

7. D. Rulfs, "Specifications for a Residence for Tom and Mary Summers, 1913" in the author's possession since the purchase of the house in 1970.

8. See a discussion of the Hardeman family, see Chapter IV. Also: Ericson, *Nacogdoches County Families,* 340. Gladys Hardeman, "The History of Melrose," Gladys Hardeman Collection A-69, East Texas Research Center, Ralph Steen Library, Stephen F. Austin State University.

9. Gladys Hardeman (daughter of Lee and Ida Hardeman), interview with author, 1974. See also, "Robert Lee Hardeman," Ericson, *Gateway* III, 368. Victor & Victor Survey, Site No. 448. "Miss Gladys Hardeman," (Obituary) *Daily Sentinel*, August 11, 1980.

10. "Ida M. Langley Hardeman," Ericson, *Gateway* III, 368. "Pioneer Resident Is Dead; Mrs. [Ida Langley] Hardeman Passes After Illness," *Daily Sentinel*, March 15, 1946.

11. When Sarah and Jere Jackson bought the Lee Hardeman House in 1972, Carl (Buddy) Monk, Jr., who owned the Wholesale Florist Company behind this house on Mound Street, said in an irritated tone, "I have been waiting decades to purchase that house." The response: "Ah, but I bought the house with Gladys having a lifetime estate in living in the house." He acknowledged the advantage as justified.

12. Ericson, *Gateway* III, 149; Ericson, *Nacogdoches County Families,* F162, 203-204. For more on Cason, see Chapter X, and his obituary *Daily Sentinel*, December 3, 1932. On his company, see the review in the *Daily Sentinel*, September 12, 1935. For information on his family at the Church Street address, see, Ancestry.com: *1900 United States Federal Census* [database on-line]. Place: *Nacogdoches, Nacogdoches, Texas*; Roll: T623_1661; Page: 9A; Enumeration District: 41. Also, Ancestry.com, *1910 United States Federal Census* [database on-line]. Place: Justice Precinct 1, Nacogdoches, Texas; Roll: T624_1581; Page: 6A; Enumeration District: 0096; Image: 184; FHL Number: 1375594 [hereafter cited as Ancentry.com, (Date) *US Census*.]

13. Sanborn Maps, UT, *Nacogdoches*, (1906).

14. Gladys Hardeman, conversations with the author, 1972. Sanborn Maps, UT, *Nacogdoches*, (1906 and 1912).

15. F. I. Tucker, discussions with the author, May, 1970. The Cason Estate gave their entire archive of documents to the author in the 1990. The papers now reside in the East Texas Research Center, Steen Library, Stephen F. Austin State University.

16. Victor & Victor Survey, Site No. 447. See, Chapter X for a discussion of these houses.

17. For a thorough coverage of a complicated family genealogy, see Perkins, *Perkins*, 158 [Charlie Richardson]; 190-191 [Charles Perkins], 259ff [W. U Perkins]. For quick biographical information, see: Ericson, *Gateway* III, 698-700.

18. National Register of Historic Places, Nacogdoches, Site No. 447. Both the National Register Survey and the Victor & Victor Survey (on which it is based) for this house are available online: "Washington Square National Register District," 315 Church Street, Stephen F. Austin State University, Regional Heritage Center, [Online Resource] at http://www.sfasu.edu/heritagecenter/622.asp [hereafter cited as Nacogdoches Historic Sites Online]. For more up to date information, see Perkins, *Perkins*, 190-191. (Will Perkins lived continuously on North Street from 1890 onward, and Charles, while dabbling in real estate development at the time, maintained his home in Melrose until 1900 and, according to U. S. Census records and family records, did not commit himself fully to being a druggist in Nacogdoches until later in 1900.)

19. Also, see Chapter IV for the W. U. Perkins House and the Steamboat House on North Street; Chapter V for the Charles Perkins House on Washington Square; and Chapter X for the W. U. Perkins House phase two and the John Perkins House.

20. Gladys Hardeman, discussions with the author, 1972.

21. For title information, see Endnote 23 below.

22. Hall and Schmidt had worked together on the transfer of lands on North Street as early as 1888. *Deed Records*, 532:250. The Hall homestead became the tract where the President of SFASU now lives.

23. *Nacogdoches County Record of Wills*, Elizabeth (Edwards) Mayo, August 14, 1849, A: 238. For transfers between 1883, when Elizabeth Mayo sold it to Schmidt, see: *Deed Records*, May 19, 1883, W: 258-259; December 16, 1889, Vol. 27: 82; January 5, 1890, 27: 83; January 5, 1891, 28: 84. W. T. Price purchased the land in April 18, 1896, 33: 320, and passed part of it on to Stephen Blount (November 28, 1898, 37: 336-338).

24. *Deed Records*, W. T. Price purchased the land in April 18, 1896, 33: 320.

25. Gladys Hardeman, conversations with the author, 1972-1976.

26. *Daily Sentinel*, January 17, 1925.

27. Dr. Langston Nelson and Mrs. Virginia Perkins Nelson, *aide-mémoire* of multiple conversations with the author, between 1972 and 1976. While not on the 1885 Sanborn map, the house does appear on the 1891 map as a modest house. Between 1891 and the 1896 map, the house was considerably enlarged by Rulfs; as such, it appears on the 1896 map and remains the same until 1922. On the 1922 map, it appears changed and modified like the houses on Church Street. Sanborn Maps, UT, *Nacogdoches*, 1885-1922. For additional information on Dr. Nelson, see Perkins, *Perkins*, 392 ff.

28. *Texas Historic Sites Atlas*, Nacogdoches: National Register Properties, "Jones, Roland, House." The National Register Nomination Application for the Roland Jones House is now online. See Nacogdoches Historic Sites Survey [Online Resource], http://www.sfasu.edu/heritagecenter/documents/NR_Individual_-_Jones_Roland_House.pdf.

29. Frank White Johnson, *A History of Texas and Texans*, Vol. 4, Edited and Updated by Eugene C. Barker, (Chicago and New York; American Historical Society, 1914), 1617-1618.

30. For information on the Cotton Compress, see *Daily Sentinel*, November Special Edition, 1906. For a review of the history of the company, written after Roland Jones' death, see *Daily Sentinel*, May 11, 1934.

31. Genevieve Patterson (formerly Genevieve Bullen-Jones), interview with the author, January 1972. May Irvin Jones and Ashford Jones (son of Roland Jones), interviews with the author, January 1972 and February 1973.

32. One reason the principals placed the house where they did was the location of the outhouses of the Bullen Hotel. These facilities were still operational, and since the new Jones House was not built with indoor plumbing, they needed to use them. The bathrooms were added after the city finally installed a water and sewage system after the breakdown of services in 1906-07.

33. "Notes on the Roland Jones Family to accompany applications for building marker," compiled from an interview between Genevieve Patterson and Charles Phillips, May 9, 1973; copy in the Texas Historical Commission Archives (Austin), Ref. No. 3822-A. In another interview with Mrs. Patterson, reported in the *Daily Sentinel,* June 17, 1973, the reporter Barbara Bond reverses the attribute by saying Mr. Jones wanted the Queen Anne-Victorian house, and not Mrs. Jones. [Actually, Mrs. Leila Hill Matthews, Esme's mother, is possibly the one who wanted the Greek Revival home; her uncle US Senator Ben Hill of Georgia lived in a famous example. See, University of Georgia's President's House, http://iep.cviog.uga.edu/athens/historicimg/ugapres.htm.]

34. In the *Daily Sentinel*, June 17, 1973, an article by Barbara Bond reverses the version of who wanted the colonial and who wanted the "modern" Victorian house. Bond wrote that Genevieve Patterson had told her that it was Mr. Jones who wanted the Queen Anne-Victorian house, not Mrs. Jones. The Jones House, however, was not Bond's main focus; the interview appeared as a part of the Christ Church anniversary celebration.

35. Charles Phillips, "The Roland Jones House: A Texas State Historical Landmark," Dedication Program with History, December 29, 1973, Nacogdoches County Historical Survey Committee. Dr. Jere L. Jackson delivered the dedication address on this occasion, as reported in the *Daily Sentinel*, December 27, 1972. Note: As always in research, new documents bring clarifications. When we printed this program, we made the mistake of saying that the architect was "Dietrich Anton Gerard Rulfs," who "lived principally in Louisiana, but had familial connections with Nacogdoches." The initial research for the Jones marker was done by Chuck and Ann Phillips. Mrs. Ralph Ellis Gun of Houston (granddaughter of Roland Jones) made some additions, and Deolece Parmelee, Director of Research with the Texas Historical Commission (Austin), collated the research.

The author corrected some of these mistakes by 1976 but made some new ones. [Jackson, "Nacogdoches' Visible Past," *Bicentennial History of Nacodoches*, 199-236.] For instance, the assertion that the Jones House was his second big commission. This was a naive mistake, made out of incomplete research on the mysterious career of Rulfs. Between 1926 when he died and 1970, Rulfs is the best kept secret in Nacogdoches.

36. May Irvin Kennedy Jones (wife of Ashford Jones, and daughter-in-law to Esme Bullen Jones), interview with the author, March, 1974. In preparation for delivering the speech at the dedication of the Texas Historic Landmark application, the author also did interviews with the following people: Genevieve Patterson (formerly Genevieve Bullen-Jones), January 1972; F. I. Tucker, September 1972; May Irvin and Ashford Jones, January 1972 and February 1973.

37. Texas Historical Commission, *Texas Historic Sites Atlas:* "Nacogdoches, National Register Properties," "Jones, Roland, House." The entire National Register Nomination Application for the Roland Jones House is now online. See, Nacogdoches Sites Survey Online. The Jones House received a local landmark plaque in October of 2010. (*Daily Sentinel*, October 3, 2010.)

38. Notes written by the staff and Dolece Parmelee on application #3822-A, October 17, 1972, Texas Historical Commission Archive.

39. "Specifications for Residence of Roland Jones, Nacogdoches, Texas, 1896-7," Texas Historical Commission Archives, File No. 3822-A, Austin, Texas. The specifications end with the Latin phrase, *Hic Jacet &*, which means "as is the custom" or "as seen locally, et cetera." A special thanks to Amanda Dyer at the Texas Historical Commission for sharing these specifications with the author (June 16, 2010).

40. "Progress Threatening Relic of Gay Nineties," *Dallas Morning News*, November 6, 1953.

41. October 2, 1972, *Deed Records*, 378:71.

42. In 1972, Dr. and Mrs. John Thomas purchased the Jones house and completely reworked it. Many internal partitions added through the years were removed, but the doctor also made changes, the most unfortunate of which was his introduction of new flooring throughout the main downstairs rooms. The author personally was able to talk him out of removing the massive pocket doors between the living room and the parlor and dining room. Instead, he built within the large living room, leaving the doors), a whole new suite of offices for his practice: an office in the north bay, a hall, and two examining rooms. He did replace the north window of the parlor with a door and a semi-circular roof on the exterior, but these were minimal intrusions on the exceptional exterior.

43. Adlai Mast, Jr., conversations and interviews with the author, 1985-1890. At the time we were working together to renovate the Fredonia Hotel by adding a Convention Center, the author visited with Mr. Mast many times about the land and houses around the hotel. We discussed all of the houses on Church Street as being adjunct properties to the Fredonia. The Jones House was the first.

44. Adlai Mast, Jr. wrote histories for many members of his family. See, "Adlai Travis, Jr.," Ericson, *Nacogdoches County Families*, 439-443. For information on the property, see "Roland Jones House, LT 8 BK 8 AND PT LT 7-B, Property No. 22902, NCAD, [Online Database], http://www.nacocad.org/.

45. The text of the Official Texas Historical Marker on Rulfs can be found at *Texas Historic Sites Atlas*, [http://atlas.thc.state.tx.us/shell-site.htm], Nacogdoches: "Rulfs," Site No. 14540. At the time of this printing, a statue of D. Rulfs, sponsored by the Masts and Historic Nacogdoches, Inc., is in the process of being commissioned for the property.

46. The many comments on this house are sometimes hard to follow. For its general context, see: *Texas Historic Sites Atlas*, : Site Name Search: County: Nacogdoches: "Washington Square Historic District"], Address 310 N Mound (NR 1991) Date: 1897 Site No. 1008. For more specific references to the Stephen Blount House itself, see Nacogdoches Historic Sites Online for both the Victor & Victor Survey comments (1986) and National Register comments (1990): "Washington Square: 310 Mound Street," http://www.sfasu.edu/heritagecenter/868.asp, accessed August 8, 2011. An important National Register document entitled "Historic and Architectural Resources of Nacogdoches, Texas; Community Planning and Development in Nacogdoches: 1830-1940," can be accessed: [Online Resource] http://pdfhost.focus.nps.gov/docs/NRHP/Text/64500647.pdf. A careful study of this house, undertaken by one of the author's students, Jonathan Jeffrey, appeared in Lucille Fain's Heritage Column: "The Stephen W. Blount House," *Daily Sentinel*, July 3, 1888.

47. Ericson, *Gateway* III, 84.

48. For the best information on the older Stephen W. Blount, the patriarch of the family, see Frank White Johnson, *A History of Texas and Texans*, Vol. 5, Edited and Updated by Eugene C. Barker, (Chicago and New York; American Historical Society, 1916), 2161-2162. A short biography of the older Stephen Blount, see "Blount Family Papers," ETRC, http://libweb.sfasu.edu/proser/etrc/collections/manuscript/personal/blount/index.html. The information on this site, however, does not include papers by Stephen W. Blount, Sr. or Jr.

49. S. Seymore Thomas, in the *Dallas Morning News*, 1950, wrote of Col. Stephen W. Blount (Stephen Father), "Col. Blount was a large landowner and a prominent merchant at San Augustine until his death on February 7, 1890." Jerry Baker (descendent) provided this news clipping to the author, July 2010. See also, Haltom on the Blount family, Special Edition, *Daily Sentinel*, November 1906. See also, L. W. Kemp, "BLOUNT, STEPHEN WILLIAM," *Handbook of Texas Online* (http://www.tshaonline.org/handbook/online/articles/fbl31).

50. Jonathan Jeffrey, "The Stephen William Blount House," a study which originated in a local history seminars, was later published in the *Daily Sentinel*, July 3, 1988. The information made its way into the Victor & Victor Survey, the National Register application, and other publications. See, Lucille Fain, "Blount home is recommended as historical place," *Daily Sentinel*, December 9, 1990.

51. Pam Thorstensen (owner of the S. W. Blount House from 1988-2001) to the Members of the City Commission, February 1, 2011), e-mail copy sent to the author, February 1, 2011. Some of her information came from Samuel Houston Dixon's *Encyclopedia of Texas History and Biography* (Houston: Texas Historical Publishing Co., 1924), 192-193.

52. Ericson, *Gateway* III, 895.

53. W. F. Price to S. W. Blount, Instrument date November 28, 1898, File Date, April 5, 1899, *Deed Records*, 37: 336-338.

54. April 1, 1943, *Deed Records*, 163: 31; November 28, 1945. Oakley Metcalf Funeral Directors bought out Cason-Monk later. For a list of owners from 1945 onward, see *NCAD*, "Stephen and Mary Blount House," 310 Mound Street, Property ID: 22788, http://www.nacocad.org/(3z25sfian2cbk2zm-cvilz145)/rprevowner.aspx.

55. Wilhelmina Rulfs Thompson (daughter of William Henry Rulfs, niece of D. Rulfs), interview with the author, February, 1973. Mrs. Thompson was a close personal friend of Gladys Hardeman and Mamie Middlebrook, neighbors of the author on Church Street. We visited with each other on several occasions.

56. "National Register Properties: Nacogdoches County: Blount, Stephen William and Mary Price, House," *Texas Historic Sites Atlas,* http//atlas.thc.state.tx.us.

57. Mary Stewart Duncan, interview with the author, June, 1973. (Ericson lists 12 children born to the couple, not all of whom survived. Ericson, *Gateway* III, 84.) One of author's more thorough papers, "D. Rulfs: Master Architect of Nacogdoches," was delivered as the Opening Speech to the East Texas Historical Association in the Fall Meeting, Nacogdoches, 1980. This speech concentrated on the Zion Hill Baptist Church building itself, but also houses very close to the church. From the back of the Blount House, one can see Zion Hill, for the property ran all the way to Lanana Street at one time.

58. While metallic screening used in screen doors and windows was patented, as far back is 1884, it did not reach Nacogdoches until the mid-1890s. According to Giles Haltom, "The firm of Perkins Bothers were pioneers in two great conveniences—the revolving fans that kept the drug store cool and pleasant and wire screen doors. Both these necessities of modern civilization were introduced here by the enterprising drug firm." See, "W. U. Perkins," *Daily Sentinel*, December 8, 1928. [John Golding of Chicago, Illinois invented metallic screening material (US Patent, #297,382 on April 22, 1884; http://inventors.about.com/library/inventors/blhome.htm.]

59. The funeral home in the 1940s did enlarge the arch leading to the back hall in order to accommodate coffins.

60. Pam Thorstenson, correspondence & interview with author, June 2012.

61. For property records indicating owners back to 1945, see: *NCAD*, Property ID 22788, http://www.nacocad.org/. Robert Gruebel and Jo Ellen Carlson Gruebel are the current owners.

62. Mark Wolf (THC) to (Mayor) Roger Van Horn, January 27, 2011, entered into the City Commission Minutes, February 1, 2011. [A copy of this letter came to the author.] The letter concluded:

> Based on our interpretation of the Standards it is our informal determination that the proposed project does not meet the Standards, and that the location of the new addition is inappropriate. When exterior additions to a historic building are necessary, they should be located preferably at the rear or on an inconspicuous side of the building rather than on the front façade, and should be limited in size and scale in relationship to the existing historic building. Porches and entrances are often the focus of historic buildings, particularly on primary elevations, and especially in a highly-decorative Queen Anne building such as this. These elements are extremely important in defining the overall character of a building. Adding a new porch on the front of this particular building would alter exterior features and spaces that characterize this Queen Anne property, such as the asymmetry and distinctive front porch, which are character defining features of Queen Anne architecture. Moreover, construction of a new porch in the style of the historic would create a false sense of historic development by attempting to mimic architecture of the historic home. Duplicating the exact form, style, and detailing of the historic building in the new addition so that the new work appears to be part of the historic building is not recommended.

63. The entire controversy can be followed in the newspaper between November 2010 to February 2011: *Daily Sentinel,* January 8, 12, 16, 23, 27, 31, February 1, 2, 2011. The newspaper reports do not, however, capture the subtleties of the arguments. For those, the minutes and the tapes of the City and Landmark Commission sessions are necessary and are available for these same time frames. In the midst of the heated exchanges over the proposed changes, the author wrote a letter of support for the Landmark Committee's refusal to grant the variances. The concluding sentences stated a warning: "As for the Blount House, any picture 'then and now' will tell the story. A simple statement of facts will explain the harm: 'Against the evidence, the ordinances, the advice of experts, appeals, and alternatives offered by the Landmark Committee, the owners altered the 115 year old façade of this building in 2011.' "

Jere Jackson, "A Case for the Landmark Committee," *Daily Sentinel*, January 27, 2011:

A Case for the Landmark Committee

There is something sad about having to fight, even in private not to mention in public, about historic preservation in Nacogdoches. The town does not need a black eye on this subject. Too many have fought to raise historic awareness now to be jousting with obvious supporters of things historic over the question of the front façade of the Stephen Blount House.

I am appreciative of the work the Gruebels have done in downtown Nacogdoches. What is puzzling is, how could they have fought so hard to preserve a generic warehouse in the downtown and are now so cavalier in protecting the front façade of one Nacogdoches' finest historic buildings. The Stephen Blount House is one of Diedrich Rulfs' masterpieces; it helps to place Nacogdoches on state and national maps for tourists. It is no nameless structure. Its classification is such because of who commissioned it, who designed it, and where it stands. Placing the highest importance on it, the architects at the National Register office call part of "the most intact grouping of late 19th and early 20th century residential architecture" in Nacogdoches.

Were the landowners unaware of the restrictions on the building when they purchased it? Since the sides and the back of the Blount House had already been altered in the past, the Landmark Committee's decisions agreed with 90% of the requests by the landowners. A 90% win is: more than accommodating and more than offering a compromise. The Landmark Committee is defending the public's only real interest in a historic private structure. The Committee has been most differential. All the Landmark Committee asks of the homeowner is: PRESERVE THE PUBLIC'S INTEREST; PRESERVE THE FRONT Façade. Other major cities in the world put façades in a different category to interiors. What the landowners have done to the interior is not in dispute; it will never be on public view unless the homeowners desire to make it public.

The Landmark Committee, a group of ordinary citizens not preservation zealots, is doing the job they were appointed to do: watching out for the historic buildings of Nacogdoches. By not following the ordinance rules, the Gruebels are asking their friends to make a call based on friendship. If they were asking a variance for substandard wiring or to place a mobile home in a neighborhood such as Knollwood, what would be the city's response? Would someone not ask: why are the plaintiffs asking us to decide between friendship with them and protecting our property interests? Laws and regulations are here to protect common interests.

Since the city passed the historic overlay ordinances, I personally thought we had elevated the history of the town and the need to protect our visual heritage for the tourist/visitor, at least, to the level of a mobile home ordinance. How do we answer the tourist's question: what does Nacogdoches have to show for its claims to being interested in its heritage? A replica of the Old Stone Fort, pictures of what North Street use to be ...

Much of the Blount House's original integrity was lost maybe years ago. Only the entrance hall and the front façade have a claim to authenticity. Unfortunately, the public will not focus on what is being sacrificed until the alterations actually begin. The 3-D effect will be shocking. I call on the Gruebels to rethink their request to the City Commission. If they win their exemption, it will cost them and the city's credibility dearly. No new buyer will have confidence of any historic zoning protection. As for the Blount House, any picture "then and now" will tell the story. A simple statement of facts will explain the harm: 'Against the evidence, the ordinances, the advice of experts, appeals, and alternatives offered by the Landmark Committee, the owners altered the 115 year old façade of this building in 2011.'

Nacogdoches as a center for historic tourism will also lose.

Jere Jackson
Professor of History
Member of the Nacogdoches County Historical Commission
Author of forthcoming book, *Diedrich Rulfs: Designing Modern Nacogdoches*
Resident of Washington Square at 304 North Church Street

64. Ericson, *Nacogdoches County Families*, F436, 340; Ericson, *Gateway* III, 369. See also, Francis W. Wilson, *The Hardeman Impact on Early East Texas*, March 1986. Nicholas P. Hardeman, *Wilderness Calling: The Hardeman Family in the American Westward Movement, 1750–1900* (Knoxville: University of Tennessee Press, 1977). Gladys Hardeman, Gladys, "The History of Melrose," Gladys Hardeman Collection A-69, East Texas Research Center, Ralph Steen Library, Stephen F. Austin State University. It might be of interest to some that the precinct now known as Chireno was originally called Hardemans.

65. Gladys Hardeman, "Historic T. B. Hardeman Home To Be Open For Tour May 3," *Daily Sentinel*, April 22, 1963.

66. Gladys Hardeman lists the subsequent owners as: "After the Hardemans moved to Oklahoma City in 1912, the residence became the home of Judge Beeman Strong's family for the next three years, after which he moved elsewhere to follow his profession. In 1915, Mr. and Mrs. Lamar Acker bought the place, did some redecorating and changed the living room to the south side. The period 1931-1961 was one of much gracious living and charming entertaining under the ownership of Mrs. Mary Moon and her daughter, Miss Sarah Jane Moon." *Daily Sentinel,* April 22, 1963. The Julia and Martin Taylor family owned the house from 1961-1974, the William J. Brophy family from 1974-1995, and the present owners are Mary Elizabeth and Chappell Jordan, Jr. since 1995.

67. Colonial Dames XVII Century, James Haggard Chapter Records, Nacogdoches, ETRC.

68. Gladys Hardeman, interview with the author, 1974.

69. *Ibid.* The gas pipelines came into Nacogdoches in 1927-1928. For a pictures showing this, see Archie P. McDonald, *Nacogdoches: A Pictorial History*, 88.

70. NCAD, Property ID 22785, http://www.nacocad.org/.

71. Victor & Victor Survey, Site No. 1011: Nacogdoches Site Online, http://www.sfasu.edu/heritagecenter/881.asp.

72. Ancestry.com. *1900 United States Federal Census* [database on-line]; *Nacogdoches, Texas*; Roll: T623_1661; Page: 9B; Enumeration District: 41.

73. Sanborn Maps, UT, *Nacogdoches*, (1900). Two other buildings indicated in this way were the Wettermark Bank in 1896 and the Cox Building (later Stone Fort Bank).

74. Jere Jackson, "SFA Opens on Washington Square," *Daily Sentinel*, August 30, 1998. This essay is online: *The SFA Story,* http://cets.sfasu.edu/story/founders/Aug30/1923_Intro.html. Craig Stripling, interview with the author, April, 2011.

75. For instance, the Shindler, the Charles Perkins, and Matthews Houses on North Street, and the Austin House on Virginia.

76. Gladys Hardeman, interview with the author, 1974. For modern property owners, see NCAD, Property ID 22782, http://www.nacocad.org/.

77. January 21, 1899, Geo. F. Ingraham to F. H. Tucker, Deed Records, 36: 459-460.

78. Joe Ericson says Hal Tucker became the Cashier when Blount took over Commercial bank in 1903 after the first transition. Ericson, *Bicentennial History of Nacogdoches*, 193.

79. George S. and Lollie Dee King to K. Pl. Branch, April 2, 1913, *Deed Records*, 79: 380.

80. Ancestry.com. *1920 United States Census* [Datebase Online] *Nacogoches, Texas* Roll: T625_1835; Page: 3B; Enumeration District: 124; Image: 720. Also mentioned in Ericson, *Gateway* III, 98.

81. Mary Ellis Elliott, conversation with the author, 1974. My questions to Mary Ellis did not included family genealogy beyond what was needed to document the owners. Myrtis Bryan Woodward's son, Mack, has recently written: "Mother & Mary Ellis were not orphaned in 1924. Our grandmother Mary Ellis Smith Bryan (1896-1924) died, and she wanted her aunt Flossie Branch to rear her girls. Our grandfather William Jennings Bryan (1898-1973) moved to Cleveland, TX, where he was eventually mayor & owner of a Dodge-Plymouth dealership." Mack Woodward to author, August 29, 2011. See also, NCAD, Property ID 22779, http://www.nacocad.org/.

82. It must have looked similar to the original Nelson-Davis House built on Main Street built several years later. Other houses on which Rulfs used this same feature, albeit more ornate, were the Laura Blount House (North Street), his own residence (Main Street), and, in the most dramatic example, the upper corner porch of the Stephen W. Blount House (Mound Street). The footprint of the porch gable can be seen in the Sanborn Maps of 1900 and 1906 and 1912, but not on the 1929 map.

83. Sanborn Map, ETRC, Digital Sanborn Maps, 1867-1970, *Texas: Nacogdoches*, 1929 and 1929-46 [Online Resources], http://libweb.sfasu.edu/proser/etrc/collections/maps/index.html.

84. Mary Ellis Elliott, conversation with the author, 1974. Victor & Victor Survey, Site No. 1012.

85. Perkins, *Perkins*, 190-191. Dorothy Perkins, author of the Perkins family

history, writes: "George Wilson [a great nephew] says that Charles was a medical doctor and went to medical school in Louisville, Kentucky. He never practiced medicine and Louisville College of Medicine has no record of his having attended school there. I also checked Washington University College of Medicine for records in St. Louise, but they find no record of him. If he was a doctor, he must have apprenticed with a local doctor."

86. *Daily Sentinel*, March 14, 1900.

87. Sanborn Maps, UT, *Nacogdoches*, (1900). Victor & Victor Survey, Site No. 1014.

88. Charles Perkins did not stay in the pharmacy profession for very long. As far back as 1905 when Perkins Brothers Pharmacy had sold to M. R. Kleas and Hollis Mast, Charles Perkins told Giles Haltom he had "not yet decided upon his plans for the future." *Daily Sentinel*, February 11, 1905. In 1920, Charles listed no occupation in the 1920 Census. Charles died on March 7, 1926. Maude died a month later in April 1926. Both are buried at Oak Grove Cemetery in Nacogdoches.

89. Henry and Tom Middlebrook, conversations with the author, June and July, 2011.

90. The Reavley's son, Thomas Morrow Reavley, became a distinguished Texas and Federal Judge. See, "Thomas Morrow Reavley," Wikipedia, http//en.wikipedia.org/w/index.php?title=Thomas_Morrow_Reavley&oldid=436434667.

91. Robert and Ruth Carroll, conversations with author, April and July 2011.

Chapter VI: Irion Hill

1. Old Dorsey Homestead (122 South Sanders) and the Anna Raguet House that Judy Hale owned. *See*, Sally S. Victor, et al, Nacogdoches Historic Site Survey and Preservation Feasibility Study, 1986 (Austin, Tex.: Victor and Victor Consultants, Inc., 1986), Site No. 1275 [hereafter Victor & Victor Survey]. Some of these resources are now available online: "City of Nacogdoches Historic Sites Survey," at http://www.sfasu.edu/heritagecenter/622.asp [hereafter Nacogdoches Sites Survey Online].

2. "Washington Square Historic District," historic context submitted for the National Register of Historic Places, 1989. Accessed through the *Texas Historic Sites Atlas* on the Texas Historical Commission website (http://atlas.thc.state.tx.us/index.asp). See the Assessment document for the city: From the THC Atlas Site: HISTORIC AND ARCHITECTURAL RESOURCES OF NACOGDOCHES COMMUNITY PLANNING AND DEVELOPMENT IN NACOGDOCHES: 1830-1940 as cited below: "Historic and Architectural Resources of Nacogdoches: Community Planning and Development in Nacogdoches: 1830-1940," historic context submitted for the National Register of Historic Places, 1989. Accessed through the *Texas Historic Sites Atlas* on the Texas Historical Commission; http://atlas.thc.state.tx.us/index.asp [hereafter Architectural Resources of Nacogdoches]. This document has recently appeared on the Nacogdoches Sites Survey Online, http://www.sfasu.edu/heritagecenter/622.asp.

3. Carolyn Reeves *Gateway* III, 377.

4. In writing the article of 1976, the author made mistakes because of insufficient research, especially in sequencing the houses of the architect; many of his houses on North Street, and elsewhere, were already gone by the time the article appeared. *See*, Jackson, "Nacogdoches' Visible Past," *Bicentennial History of Nacogdoches*, 199-236. Since Schmidt brought Rulfs to Texas, the author called Schmidt's great house on North Street the first house done by the architect, the Jones House his second, and the Harris House his "third commission in the city." Regrettably, others have repeated these simplifications, for instance the Victor and Victor Survey (Site No. 1451) in 1986 and the National Register Application in 1989. These surveys have also made their own mistakes, without my help, on the Harris family genealogy. For the Harris and Davison genealogy, see: Ericson, *Gateway III*, 377. Enid Davison, "Harris, Junius Clark," Article F439, in Ericson, *Nacogdoches County Families*, 341-42. Star of the Republic Museum, "Family of Junius Clark Harris and Margaret Lorena Seale," available at http://www.starmuseum.org/Signers%20Web%20Page/Clark/rr01/rr01_008.htm#P242.

5. Thomas Ellis Baker read the law with him as did others. "Now at His New Desk," *Daily Sentinel*, March 15, 1910. See also, James Clark Fifield, "Harris and Harris," in *The American Bar; Contemporary Lawyers Of The United States and Canada* (Minneapolis, Minnesota: The James C. Fifield Company, 1918), 656.

6. See Chapter V.

7. Enid Davison, interview with author, February, 1976. Enid Davison had given the same information to the *Daily Sentinel*, April 30, 1963, and again in Ericson, *Nacogdoches County Families*, 341-42.

8. The formal division of the acreage into a subdivision did not come until 1919, according to *Nacogdoches County Plat Records*. When housing construction took place in the addition during the 1930s and 1940s, the area was comprised of modest residences.

9. "Historic Home Overlooking City To Be Open For Tour," *Daily Sentinel*, April 30, 1963.

10. *Ibid*. See also, Martha Ann Turner, *Old Nacogdoches in the Jazz Age*, 134-35.

11. Tom Davison, interview with the author, February, 1976. Mr. Davison, at the time of this interview, showed the author the drawing of this house for the first time. The drawing is signed by Rulfs and dated 1895.

12. *Ibid. See also*, "June C. and Maggie Harris to H. L. Austin," August 24, 1898, *Deed Records*, 36:, 322-323.

13. Richard Baker, interview with the author, February, 2011.

14. Tom Davison, interview with the author, February, 1976.

15. Charles Bright, Richard and Cherry Baker, interviews and conversations with the author, Spring, 2011. For official records, see: NCAD, Property ID 23234, Lot 18, Block 35.

16. Ericson, *Gateway* III, 610. Monk served as a member of the school board (NISD), City Council (15 Years), as Secretary-Treasury for the city when streets were paved; *see* Ericson, "Robert Columbus Monk," F701, *Nacogdoches County Families*, 470. For his obituary, see *Daily Sentinel*, August 10, 1933; August 11, 1933. Affidavit to Public Concerning R. C. Monk and Mamie Monk Estates and Their Successors, M. M. Stripling, Bryan Holt Davis, and J. T. Lucas, 15 September 1989, *Deed Records*, 738: 647. See also, *Texas Death Index*, Certificate, 38331. Ancestry.com. *Texas Death Index, 1903-2000* [database on-line]; Austin, TX, USA: Texas Department of Health, State Vital Statistics Unit. For the wonderful photograph of the young Henry B. Monk and Audley Harris in the Sterne-Hoya Museum and House Scrapbooks, ETRC.

17. While the Monks may have owned other land on Irion Hill, R. C. Monk did not build on family land as some of the architectural surveys claim. F. M. Bowman had purchased five acres from June Harris in 1896 and then sold the lot to Monk in 1897. Monk paid $400.00 to Bowman. See: "June C. and Maggie Harris to F. M. Bowman," March 9, 1896; "F. M. and Lizzie Bowman to R. C. Monk," March 13, 1897, *Deed Records*, 34: 217. See Victory & Victor, Site No. 1488.

18. See section on Cason-Monk Hardware in Chapter 8. See *Daily Sentinel*, August 18, 1906; August 27, 1906. He also invested with Schmidt and others to found the Nacogdoches Oil Company, which Will Perkins came to head.

19. *Daily Sentinel*, June 20, 1976.

20. For 1898, see records: *Assessor Abstracts*, 1800-1899, 2: 289; see also,

Nacogdoches Tax Records 1907, 2: 288, ETRC, Steen Library, SFASU. For more information on the lots and house, see "Robert C. Monk to E. W. Monk, Henry B. Monk, and Ida Monk Williams," *Deed Records*, 377: 491; Affidavit, 738: 647.

21. *Daily Sentinel*, December 30, 1928. Mentioned in the review of Mayer & Schmidt.

22. See *NCAD*, Property ID, 10061, [May 25, 1998, 1221: 206; and April 19, 2002, 1724: 8.] http://www.nacocad.org/(i53lzv3adwasje453jeqzb55)/rgeneral.aspx?ID=10061&seq=1.

23. *Daily Sentinel*, June 11, 1900. "Contractor H. L. Austin has begun the brick work on the new Mayer & Schmidt building on Fredonia street." For contract information, see Bennett Blake Papers, Box 9, Folder 24, ETRC, SFASU; "New Buildings for Nacogdoches," *Houston Daily Post*, May 3, 1899. For biographical information on Henry Austin, see Ericson, *Gateway* III, 26.

24. *Houston Daily Post*, May 3, 1899.

25. Victor & Victor Survey, Site No. 1448. See Nacogdoches Sites Survey Online, http://www.sfasu.edu/heritagecenter/1326.asp. John Anderson, in telephone conversations with the author, April 17, 2011, confirmed that from his research, the house does not date to the 1880s.

26. "June C. and Maggie Harris to H. L. Austin," August 24, 1898, *Deed Records*, 36: 322-323. *See also*, "H. L. Harris to T. F. Bridwell" ($1500.00) April 11, 1900, *Deed Records,* 40: 138. The census has the Austins living on North Street near Hardeman Perkins. See Ancestry.com, *1900 United States Federal Census* [database on-line]; *Nacogdoches, Texas*; *Justice Precinct 1,* Roll: *T623_1661*; Page: *9A*; Enumeration District: *39.*

27. Victor & Victor Survey, Site No. 1448.

28. John Anderson, interview with the author, April 17, 2011. Ann and David Norton, conversations and correspondence with the author, February, 2011. For the recent official records, see NCAD, Property ID 23232, http://www.nacocad.org/(xbutnx55ro14vma4wwfs1crp)/rgeneral.aspx?ID=23232&seq=1.

29. Tom McKinney, conversations with the author, October, 2011. McKinney is undertaking a thorough study of the Stone Fort Rifles.

30. October 10, 1896, *Deed Records*, 34: 29. See October 21, 1896, 34: 29.

31. Vergie Sanders Scrapbook, ETRC, article from the *Daily Sentinel*, A/94, Box 4, Folder 2.

32. Charles Deaton, "Post Offices and Postmasters of Nacogdoches County," in *Bicentennial History*, 164; for the list of Nacogoches Postmasters, see 173-174.

33. October 10, 1896, *Deed Records*, 34: 29 ; and October 21, 1896, 34: 29. See also, *Deed Records*, Deed of Trust, 2: 214.

34. Documents and photographs provided to the author by Mr. Cole Sessom, July 10, 2011. One of the original documents in Mr. Sessom's possession is the marriage certificate of the Coopers, December, 1897.

35. Documents and photographs provided to the author by Mr. Cole Sessom, July 10, 2011. According to a handwritten message by Mrs. Mary Dorsey Bates (the second owner on the house) in 1976, the house dates to 1898. She said the Coopers and Mary Hofmann, Mrs. Cooper's sister, "lived at the Banita Hotel while house being built." Construction probably began in 1897 when Cooper borrowed the money, however, and was finished in 1898. The US Census records offer some confusion to the dates referenced above. At the time of the 1900 Census, the Coopers and Miss Hofmann were again at the Banita Hotel for some reason. This may have had something to do with Cooper's active service in the Texas Militia and the Spanish-American War. [Ancestry.com. *1900 United States Federal Census* (database on-line). Provo, UT, USAUS; Place: *Nacogdoches, Nacogdoches, Texas*; Roll: T623_1661; Page: 21A; Enumeration District: 41.] The house was valued for $2250; ETRC, *Nacogdoches County Texas Tax Roll*, 1907-1908, Vol. 288.

36. *See*, Cooper Estate (Mary Hofmann, executrix) to Mary D. Bates, wife of W. B. Bates of Houston, *Deed Records*, 165: 27-28. Mary D. Bates Trust to Eugene Cole and Sidney S. Sessom, *Deed Records*, 957: 110-111.

37. See Victor &Victor Survey, Site No. 488 for further descriptions. The Victor and Victor Survey, based on information from Mary Bates, said Cooper not only built the house, but he was also the architect. This euphemistic statement is inaccurate. Certainly, Capt. Cooper was the "builder" of the house, in the sense that he commissioned and paid for the house and probably supervised its construction, but the house obviously had an architect—not just a postmaster who was a Mason!

38. Cole Sessom, interview with the author, July 10, 2010.

39. Mary Steward Duncan, interviews with the author, March, 1974. While Duncan confirmed the attribution of this house to the architect, the architectural evidence itself confirms the attribution to Rulfs. The fact that Rulfs used almost a mirror image of this house's gable front to design the Phillip Sanders House across West Main Street is also proof of the attribution to the architect. Chronologically it fits into his other works that year; the use of the Palladin window as the main feature of the forward gable; the exploitation of the vistas; the use the water collection system (like the Schmidt House), the pattern of the roof and the stacked chamfered bay rooms; the windows outlined in colored glass (used across the street in the Middlebrook House). Only the cellar, which obviously Cooper suggested, is unique.

40. Ericson, *Gateway III*, 596-597. Farmer, Lorena M. et al, "Affidavit of Heirship," 22 September 1969, *Deeds Records*, 357: 438.

41. August 21, 1897, *Deed Records*, 37: 55-57. Purchased from George F. Ingraham, W. G. Ratcliff, and W. U. Perkins (See also *Deed Records*, 34: 59-60.) Victor & Victor, Site No. 941.

42. The lot Middlebrook purchased was owned by people who thought they also would move up to Irion Hill: George Ingraham, W. G. Ratcliff. (See *Deed Records*, 34: 59-60.)

43. Ancestry.com. *Texas Death Index, 1903-2000* [database on-line]. Provo, UT, USA: The Generations Network, Inc., 2006. Original data: Texas Department of Health. *Texas Death Indexes, 1903-2000.* Austin, TX, USA: Texas Department of Health, State Vital Statistics Unit. See also, Ancestry.com; *1900 United States Federal Census,* [database on-line]; *Nacogdoches, Texas*; Roll: T623_1661; Page: 19A; Enumeration District: 41.

44. Mamie Middlebrook, interview with the author, March, 1976. Miss Mamie's birth date was January 19, 1899. See Ericson, *Gateway* III, 597. Ericson lists the following Middlebrook children were: "Anna Lorena, b. ca Sept 1888; Affie Augusta, b. 25 Aug 1890; Vera Olivia, b. 25 Feb 1893; infant daughter, b. 25 Feb 1893; [twins] Fannie P., b. 7 June 1896; Mamie, b. 19 Jan 1899; Ruth E., b. ca 1902; Vernon E., b. ca 1906; Edward Walker, b. 9 Mar 1907."

45. August 14, 1969, *Deed Records*, Vol. 357, 438.

46. Suzie and Dick Lower purchased it in 1969 (see *Deed Records*, 357: 438); the Lowers sold to Fred G. and Kay A. Hooper in 1983 (*Deed Records*, 487: 732.)

47. Suzie Lower, telephone conversation with the author, July 9, 2011. For other descriptive coverage of this house, see the Victor & Victor Site No. 941, where they simply estimate the age of the house to be between 1898-1905.

48. Ericson, *Gateway* III, 802-803.

49. The Sanders had horrible luck with both of these buildings. An arsonist set fire to the warehouse in 1903. Their building on the North Square burned in the great fire of 1906. Although they rebuilt in 1907, fire gutted the rebuilt office building in 1915. Ericson, *Fires and Firemen*, 45-46; 51-52; 76.

50. Will Sanders bought land on Irion Hill in 1887 and was on the tax roll in 1890; Phillip bought in 1891 and was on the tax rolls for 1900. *See also*, Ericson, *Gateway* III, 802-803.

51. See *Deed Records*, Jan. 26, 1887, I: 555; March 17, 1888, Y: 519; A. V.

Sanders Subdivision, 184: 343. Victor & Victor Survey, Site No. 1279. Next door to the Will Sander's homestead was the old John B. Dorsey homestead. (Mary Dorsey Bates who later purchased the Cooper House grew up on this property.) Phillip had more extensive property (fifty-two acres in all); on the corner on Sanders and West Main Street, but his land, much of which was not suitable for building and having limited access and limited views, never sold as a subdivision.

52. *Deed Records*, 93: 99. Sanborn Maps, UT, *Nacogdoches,* (1922).

53 Ancestry.com. *1900 United States Census,* [database on-line]; *Justice Precinct 1, Nacogdoches, Texas*; Roll: *T623_1661*; Page: *16A*; Enumeration District: *40*. Amanda Sanders died on July 4, 1939. See Ancestry.com. *Texas Death Index, 1903-2000* [database on-line]; Texas Department of Health. *Texas Death Indexes, 1903-2000*. Austin, TX, USA: Texas Department of Health.

54. "Miss (Virgie) Sanders Dies Friday," *Daily Sentinel*, October 1, 1960. Some of her papers are in the ETRC: "Annie Virginia Sanders," Biological Sketch and Papers, East Texas Research Collection, Steen Library, SFASU, http://libweb.sfasu.edu/proser/etrc/collections/manuscript/personal/sandersannie/index.html.

55. *Deed Records*, 343: 184.

56. Audrey Quick, interview with the author, April 15, 2011. Jimmy Eugene Sanders (1907-1977), interview with the author, 1974. For more information on the Sanders family, see Ericson, *Gateway* III, 799-803. See also, "Garland Roark," Wikipedia, *The Free Encyclopedia*, http://en.wikipedia.org/w/index.php?title=Garland_Roark&oldid=404191810.

57. April 11, 1967, *Deed Records*, 343: 291. Victor & Victor Survey, Site No. 1279.

58. For reference, see the Butt House, the Phillip Sanders House, and even the Jones House.

59. Ericson, *Gateway* III, 514. See Ancestry.com: *1900 United States Census* [database on-line]; *Nacogdoches, Texas*; Roll: T623_1661; Page: 9A; Enumeration District: 39. *1910 United States Census* [database on-line]; *Nacogdoches, Texas*; Roll: T624_1581; Page: 14B; Enumeration District: 0095; Image: 173; FHL Number: 1375594. 1920 *United States Census* [database on-line]; *Nacogdoches, Texas*; Roll: T625_1835; Page: 2B; Enumeration District: 122; Image: 672.

60. *Daily Sentinel*, September 11, 1901. "Lindsey & Harris have moved to the Northeast corner of the Hazle building up stairs where they have a swell real estate and insurance office." Shortly thereafter, they were advertizing properties on Irion Hill; *Daily Sentinel*, September 19, 1901.

61. Victor & Victor Survey, Site No. 1455. See Nacogdoches Sites Survey Online, http://www.sfasu.edu/heritagecenter/1335.asp.

62. Charles Bright (current owner of the Lindsey House), interviews with the author, July-December, 2010.

63. Bryan Davis, interview with the author, April 15, 2011.

64. "Lindsey, Emily Virginia Willis Papers**,** 1887-1958," (A-18), ETRC, http://libweb.sfasu.edu/proser/etrc/collections/manuscript/personal/lindseyemily/index.html. The collection has many of Emily's hand drawn programs and invitations.

65. Charles Bright, interview with the author, October, 2010. According to Bright, Penelope Hayter Anderson, never really liked the Lindsey house. When the author interviewed them in the early 1970s, they seemed quite happy in the house. Penelope and Guy Anderson, interview with the author, July, 1974. It is quite probable that, as they got older, their needs changed.

66. Rayford Stripling turned the music room into three bedrooms with baths. The diagonal flooring, which formed a diamond shape, can still be seen running under the partitions in the south wing. Charles Bright has Stripling's drawing for the renovation of the house. Charles Bright, interviews with the author, October, 2010.

67. Florence Patton, interview with the author, February 17, 2011. William S. Patton was a junior lawyer in the Branch legal firm. Having no children, the Branches took both William and his young son Orland under their wings after the death of the child's mother, Georgia. In the 1910 census, Orland was living with the Branches. Orland was later adopted after William's death in 1915. Later, E. C. Branch furnished the money for his younger brother, K. P., and Orland Patton to create Branch-Patton Hardware which opened in the Woodmen of the World Building, then latter on the Square in the Cox Building on Pecan and Main Streets.

68. Interview with Florence Patton on Feb 17, 2011. Fran and Ed Moore (later owners of the 216 Church Street house), interview with the author, July 1974.

69. Ancestry.com. *1900 United States Census* [database on-line]; *Nacogdoches, Texas*; Roll: *T623_1661*; Page: *7A*; Enumeration District: 41.

70. Ancestry.com. *1910 United States Census* [database on-line]; *Nacogdoches, Texas*; Roll: T624_1581; Page: 10B; Enumeration District: 0095; Image: 165; FHL Number: 1375594. E. C. Branch to Marcus C. and May Smith, May 23, 1912, *Deed Records*, 76: 381. Marcus C. and May Smith to John Richard and Laura McKinney, June 20, 1918, *Deed Records*, 93: 555.

71. "1896 . . . Nacogdoches, Texas," Pamphlet Series Printed by Gary and LaDona Garber, (Nacogdoches, Texas: Old Town Printing, nd [c1990]). [The historical notes for this pamphlet came from Sally Batchelor (ETRC), *The Daily Sentinel*, Ericson, *Nacogdoches County Families*, Mr. & Mrs. Jack Raines McKinney, Campbell Cox, and Mrs. Delbert (Pyrtle) Teutsch.]

72. "McKinney and Wade Family Reunion Old Home Place on Virginia Avenue, Christmas 1932," photograph provided to the author by Libby Bussa Waverly, granddaughter of Jack Rains McKinney, August, 2011. Thanks to Dr. Tom McKinney, SFASU, for helping to clarify the following notes by his grandparents, Claudine and Jack McKinney:

Left to Right – Top down: Luther Irvin Wade (b.1872); Carrie Powers (Mother's Cook); Willie Andrew Wade (1887-1936); [J.?] Kennedy (b.1886); John Richard McKinney (1876-1951); "Aunt" Ella Burke; Edgar Warrington Wade (1876-1952); Frank S. Aikman (1862-1939); Zeno Cox (1879-1944); Lloyd Doolittle (1887-1953); Coke Murphey; Irwin Wade; Fannie Luella Wade Cox (1884-1971); Mary Glenn McKinney (1928-1987); Laura Vernettia Wade McKinney (1879-1976); Lucy Robinson Wade; Dora McConnico Wade; Rose Jordan Wade; Edgar Prentice McKinney (1908-1959); Jack Rains McKinney (b. 1911); Mattie Baxter Wade McKinney (1893-1943); Ella Mae Wade Doolittle (1890-1976); Aunt Texana Baxter Whitaker (1/14/1852-4/9/1952); Joseph William McKinney (1916-1957); Mary Glenn Vick McKinney (b. 1901); Richard Wade McKinney (b.1900); Dr. Mary Ann McKinney (b. 1904); Kenneth Wade Kennedy (b.1918); Dorothey Wade; Lloyd Doolittle (1887-1953); Elizabeth Wade.

73. Laura Wade McKinney (sole heir and as executrix of John Richard McKinney, deceased) to B. H. and Mattie J. Moore, March 3, 1959, *Deed Records*, 281: 304; for tract two, see Genevieve Patterson et al to B. H. and Mattie J. Moore, November 25, 1957, *Deed Records,* 271: 439.

74. See NCAD, Property ID 23237, (Deed Records, 2463: 208. Linda Lindsey (owner of the house in 2011), discussions with the author, July15, 2011.

75. Diane House (granddaughter of Duncan Spradley), interview with the author, July 13, 2011.

76. Charles Deaton, "Post Offices and Postmasters of Nacogdoches County," in *Bicentennial History*, 173-174.

77. He became a Master Mason in Milam Lodge No. 2 in June of 1896, and he served as Worshipful Master of the lodge in 1901. He held many offices at the local and state level. He held certificates to teach in the Grand Lodge of Texas, and was named Grand Secretary Emeritus for life. Research information requested

from the Masonic Grand Lodge of Texas Archival Membership Index Files by Mary and Robert Whitten (owners of the house), shared with the author, July 2011.

78. *Deed Record*, 43: Ol 23-A.

79. Lindsey is on the deed, January 1, 1900, Property ID 23678, *Deed Records,* I: 1; see also, September 11, 1915, Spradley Sisters, 84: 213; 1505: 317.

80. Ericson, *Gateway* III, 696.

81. Dianne House, correspondence with the author, July 15, 2011.

82. Invitation and newspaper clippings from the "Twenty-Fifth Anniversary" from the *Daily Sentinel*, 1908. Documents passed from the Pearson's great granddaughter to the Robert and Mary Whitten, the present owners of the house, who shared them with the author, July 2011.

83. The early outbuildings on the property included a barn, chicken houses, and a "flower house." Later, a double car garage replaced the barn. Dianne House, conversations with the author, June-July, 2011. Victor & Victor Survey, Site No. 946.

84. Dianne House, conversations with the author, June-July, 2011. Dianne House was one of the proofreaders of this manuscript. She talked regularly with the author about the Pearson-Spradly House. As the granddaughter of the man who purchased the house in 1915, she grew up visiting the house on a regular basis. She inherited the property. Dianne wrote comments of interest on several houses in the manuscript.

85. Dianne House, in correspondence with the author, July 15, 2011.

86. See Jan. 26, 1887, *Deed Records*, I: 555; March 17, 1888, Y: 519; A. V. Sanders Subdivision, 184: 343. See Endnote 55 under the W. T. Sanders House.

87. Mary Stewart Duncan, interviews with the author, June, 1974. Gene Sanders, conversations with the author, 1974. [The Sanders family, like many others, used certain names over and over. "Eugene" and "Phillip" were two of the most popular names in the family. W. T. had a son named Eugene.] Gene's sister, Miss Mary Lee Sanders, also lived across the street from the author for many years.

Barbara Stump (current owner of the Phillip Sanders house), private collection shared with the author, July 2011. The correspondence between Barbara Stump and Loy Scoggins, October 10, 2003, reporting a conversation with Dave Patterson (owner of the house in the 1970s), is particular interesting. ""Dave Patterson who was the owner then, told me of the history of how the place was built, by whom (carpenter), and I think he said Diedrich Rulfs was the designer. During that time Rulfs supervised all construction. Not many of the carpenters today could carry the curved walls up to the floor above. Wall in the Hall was curved into all of the living quarter area as I remember."

88. *Nacogdoches Central Appraisal District*, Property ID 26383, 1801: 84. October 16, 2002.

89. June C. Harris to Robert Lindsey, April 9, 1904, *Deed Records*, 45: 624.

90. Ericson, *Gateway* III, 375. Ancestry.com, *1920 United States Census* [database on-line]; *Nacogdoches, Texas*; Roll: *T625_1835*; Page: *2B*; Enumeration District: *122*; Image: 672.

91. Robert Lindsey to W. H. Harrington, October, 1908, *Deed Records,* 61: 580; Harrington *et al* to O. F. Baxter, *Deed Records,* 163: 288-289. The house was sold within the Baxter family to Bert and Mary Jo Baxter when O. F. Baxter died; *Deed Records, (*1950*)* 358: 150. The Baxters were living no where close to this site in 1910: Ancestry.com, *1910 United States Census* [database on-line]. *Justice Precinct 1, Nacogdoches, Texas*; Roll: *T624_1581*; Page: *4A*; Enumeration District: *0095*; Image: *152*; FHL Number: *1375594*.

92. Sanborn Maps, UT, *Nacogdoches,* (1922).

Chapter VII: Crises

1. Maxwell, *Whistle*, 46.

2. Robert Browning, *Pippa Passes*, Part i.

3. Partin, et al, *Nacogdoches,* 113. The source for this quote is Rupert N. Richardson, *Texas Lone Star State* (New York, 1943), 364.

4. Gary Borders makes only passing mention of this in his book, *A Hanging in Nacogdoches*. In Partin, *et al*, *Nacogdoches*, the subject is relagated to the World War I period.

5. Lois Foster Blount, "Some Leaves from the 'Treasurer's Register of Property and Claims Belonging to the Trustees of the Nacogdoches University and of Debts Due by the Trustees," Bulletin of the Stephen F. Austin State Teachers College, Historical Number (East Texas Historical Association Meeting, 1928-1931: Bulletin 38, January, 1932), 47. Note: there is conflict in the way dates are cited. The Texas Handbook Online dates the loss of the charter to 1895, which is incorrect. [An unpublished, slightly different version of this paper is located in the Lois Foster Blount Papers, ETRC, UA, A-147, Box 31, Folder 3: "Some Notes on Nacogdoches University, 1845-1900" by Lois Foster Blount.]

6. *Ibid.*

7. The chance of luring East Texas Baptist College from Rusk (at the time) was the big issue in December of 1904. (See *Daily Sentinel*, December 14 and 28, 1904.) See "Tyler Gets College," *Daily Sentinel*, June 10, 1907.

8. Sarah Jackso*n, Baker*, 7.

9. Charles Sterne, "Letter to Editor," *Nacogdoches News*, October 16, 1884.

10. *Houston Daily Post*, Sunday, December 13, 1896, republished from the *New York Sun*, "IN OLD NACOGDOCHES TOWN. A Little Place That Has a Stirring History. WAS THE FIRST CAPITAL OF TEXAS. It Is Supposed to Have Been Founded by La Salle, the Explorer –The Scene of Many Battles."

11. *Houston Daily Post*, Thursday, December 17, 1896. The date of the letter was December 14, 1896.

12. *Daily Sentinel,* June 5 1901.

13. The deed records are in the ETRC; the selling price was $18,000, a princely sum.

14. Carolyn Spears, "The Old Stone Fort and The Stone Fort Museum," Application for Recorded Texas Historic Landmark Marker (Renewal), Texas Historical Commission, January, 2008 (hereafter cited as Spears, "Old Stone Fort."

15. Borders, *Hanging*, 39-40.

16. *Timpson Herald*, June 15, 1901.

17. "Daughters of the Republic to Save Stone Fort," *Daily Sentinel*, June 24, 1901.

18. "The Old Stone Fort," *Daily Sentinel*, June 24, 1901.

19. A. S. Grant (from Arkansas), "Letter to the Editor," *Houston Daily Post* (Houston, Texas), March 7, 1902.

20 Mrs. W. U. Perkins was a staunch Baptist and forbade her daughter to even walk anywhere close to the Old Stone Fort; she had to walk on the other side of the Square. Louise Perkins, as quoted by Bryan Davis, conversation with the author, April, 2011.

21. Borders, *Hanging*, 40.

22. Editor, *Daily Sentinel* (Nacogdoches, Texas), June 22, 1901.

23. George Ingraham, "Letter to the Editor," *Daily Sentinel,* February 22, 1902.

24. "The Old Stone Fort," (Reprint from *Houston Herald*), *Daily Sentinel*, August 3, 1901.

25. "For Sale," *Daily Sentinel*, February 4, 1902.

26. R. W. Haltom, "Fate of the Old Stone Fort," *Daily Sentinel*, January 14, 1902.

27. Emma B. Shindler, "The Old Stone Fort Letter to the Editor," *Daily Sentinel*, February 14, 1902, and "Club Notes," February 15, 1902, as cited by Spears, "Old Stone Fort."

28. Mrs. C. W. Butts, "Letter to Mrs. Tom Davison, December 1934," Annie Virginia Sanders Research, 1896 – 1973, East Texas Research Center, Steen Library, Stephen F. Austin State University, Nacogdoches, Texas, Collection A-94.

29. Charles Bright, interview with the author, October, 2010.

30. "The Old Stone Fort," *Daily Sentinel*, December 8, 1928.

31. "Successor to the Old Stone Fort," *Daily Sentinel*, September 1, 1902.

32. Virginia Perkins Nelson, interview with the author, 1974.

33. "W. U. Perkins Withdraws from Business in Nacogdoches," *Daily Sentinel*, January 4, 1907.

34. Correspondence in the ETRC from the 1930s shows that Perkins was still smarting from the incident. Would not let the Texas Centennial Committee place a marker on the side of his building.

35. "The Fate of the Old Stone Fort," *Daily Sentinel*, November 17, 1902.

36. Borders, *Hanging*, 42.

37. *Daily Sentinel*, December 8, 1928.

38. Two new historical markers have recently received authorization for the Stone Fort: one for the old building and one for the new Stone Fort Museum, the replica, which is now a historic building in it own right—a monument to lost preservation opportunities. The texts of the new historical markers follow:

OLD STONE FORT

Stones recovered from a razed 18th century structure form the walls of this historic replica building. The stone house stood originally near the intersection of El Camino Real and La Calle del Norte (present Main at Fredonia), and was built by Don Antonio Gil Y'Barbo circa 1788-91. Because he was a military and civic leader, his home also served as an unofficial government building. Y'Barbo sold the property in 1805, and over the next century, owners and tenants used the building as a home, grocery store, restaurant, offices, courthouse, cobbler shop, jail, military barracks, saloon, and as a fortification during three filibustering expeditions and periodic raids by native Americans. Sam Houston had his first law office in Texas in the building in 1833. The building became commonly known as "The Old Stone Fort" by the late 1870s, when proprietors began advertising in the Nacogdoches News a saloon and billiards room at the location.

The landmark structure was demolished in 1902. Citizens used the original stones first in a memorial building on washington square, and again for a historically accurate replica built on the Stephen F. Austin State Teachers College campus in 1936.

Y'barbo's stone house was an important example of 18th century residential architecture, with french and spanish colonial influences—exterior doors for each room, stairs on the gallery porch and fireplaces in each interior room. The stones are from a formation known as Weches Glauconite, a sedimentary rock containing iron clay minerals. Sun-dried adobe blocks formed the interior walls. Window sills, casements and beams were of hand-hewn black walnut. Recorded Texas Historic Landmark – 1962."

STONE FORT MUSEUM

Opening in 1936, the Stone Fort Museum has interpreted the history of East Texas and of the Old Stone Fort while also elevating the local historic preservation ethic. The Old Stone Fort, built in the late 18th century, was an integral part in a wide array of historic changes occurring in East Texas. The razing of the original building in 1902 caused consternation throughout the state and encouraged organizations to preserve other historic structures.

In 1908, the Cum Concilio Club, a local women's organization, opened a Memorial Building dedicated to the razed structure. By the 1930s, the Texas Centennial Advisory Board of Nacogdoches, along with the Nacogdoches Historical Society, proposed that the monument be replaced by a structure that more closely replicated the original building. A renewed interest in history, spurred by the upcoming Centennial of Texas Independence, aided the realization of the project. The Texas Centennial Commission approved the construction of the building on the campus of Stephen F. Austin State Teachers College (now Stephen F. Austin State University). Architect Hal B. Tucker designed the structure, and construction was completed by October 1936. Since then, museum staff have worked to interpret the history of the Old Stone Fort and of East Texas, with particular emphasis on the periods of Spanish and Mexican rule.

In 1992, work was completed on renovations to the museum building, meant to restore a higher degree of authenticity. Today, the Stone Fort Museum continues to serve Texas by interpreting East Texas history through exhibits, programs and its housing in a replica of an important early Texas structure.

39. Borders, *Hanging*, 40.

40. *Daily Sentinel*, June 27, 1902.

41. *Daily Sentinel*, June 28, 1902. Borders, *Hanging*, 49.

42. Partin, *Nacogdoches*, 124.

43. Borders, *Hanging*, 50. See *Daily Sentinel*, October 20, 1902; *Texas Almanac*, 1904 edition, 334.

44. Borders, *Hanging*, 39. The only photograph available (See FIGURE 7.8) of this short-lived building (five years) dictates that the building must be viewed in the background of one of this most unfortunate moment in modern Nacogdoches history. Some books, wanting not to remember the incident, do not even mention the hanging.

45. Borders, *Hanging*, 54.

46. One of Haltom's most racist columns appeared in the *Daily Sentinel*, March 5, 1900:

"Whites vs Negroes.

D. E. Clifton is erecting a nice residence on Houston street opposite the residence of R. A. Hall. The negro shanties of that section of the city are being torn down and replaced with nice cottages to be rented to white people. The day will be welcomed when Dick Hall, Dan Clifton and others clean the negroes all off of North Mound street and make room for the white people that are seeking homes here. A number of lots in that vicinity have been sold to new comers who desire to build homes upon them, but who are delaying building to see what is to be done about breaking up the 'coons' in that quarter. It is to be hoped that the owners of negro houses up there will not retard the growth of that section of the city by continuing to rent houses to the negroes."

47. While not really needed for this book, suspiciously, this special edition is now missing from the archives of the newspaper. We know of this edition only through references.

48. Borders, *Hanging*, 141.

49. Borders, *Hanging*, 141. The process of "whitecapping," or harassing black families, is discussed extensively. To illustrate the breakdown of civility, Borders writes: "Just after Valentine's Day, Sheriff Spradley, in front of Dial's Saloon, walloped editor Haltom about the head with a heavy stick."

50. "Nacogdoches Grocery Company," Business Records [B-48], ETRC, http://libweb.sfasu.edu/proser/etrc/collections/manuscript/corporate/nacgroceryco/index.htmlhttp://libweb.sfasu.edu/proser/etrc/collections/manuscript/corporate/nacgroceryco/index.html. "The Nacogdoches Grocery Company was

founded in May of 1902 by a group of successful Nacogdoches businessmen including John Schmidt, E. A. Blount, B. S. Wettermark, B. F. Hardeman, Oscar Mathews, and S. T. King." This list cited by the ETRC is different from the ones listed by the *Daily Sentinel* on April 24, 1908, at the annual stockholders meeting: John Schmidt, president, E. A. Blount, B. F. Hardeman, C. W. Butt, R. L. Hardeman, J. F. Schmidt, Oscar Matthews.

51. Borders, *Hanging*, 141-142. See Partin, *et al, Nacogdoches*, 116. A. Wettermark & Son was a privately chartered bank founded in Henderson by a Norwegian immigrant, apparently in the I870s. A Nacogdoches branch opened in 1883 with Colonel B. S. Wettermark, son of the founder, as the president. The town's first publicly chartered bank, Commercial National Bank, opened in 1901, but a considerable number of local businessmen and investors stayed with Wettermark's bank because it was not subject to regulation; the state did not begin issuing charters until 1905.

52. "Ponzi Scheme is a swindle in which a quick return, made up of money from new investors, on an initial investment lures the victim into much bigger risks." [Origin: after Charles Ponzi (died 1949), the organizer of such a scheme in the U. S., 1919–20.] Dictionary.com [Online], http://dictionary.reference.com/browse/Ponzi+Scheme.

53. *Daily Sentinel*, January 10, 1903. For other coverage, see January 13; January 21, 1903.

54. *Daily Sentinel*, January 21, 1903.

55. The most comprehensive account, from the *Shreveport Times*, appeared in the *Daily Sentinel*, February 9, 1903.

56. *Daily Sentinel*, January 12, 1903. For coverage of these fires, see Ericson, *Fires and Firemen*, 42-50; Partin, et al, *Nacogdoches*, 122.

57. "A 37,000 Blaze. Nacogdoches has Another Narrow Escape from fatal destruction," *Daily Sentinel*, February 16, 1903.

58. *Daily Sentinel*, April 14, 1903.

59. *Daily Sentinel*, December 24, 1906. Covered also in Ericson, *Fires and Firemen*, 51-52.

60. Ericson, *Fires and Firemen*, 4.

61. Mayer & Schmidt quickly leased another Davidson Building (now the City Offices) until they could rebuild.

62. Partin, *et al, Nacogdoches*, 123. The quote comes from the collected work, but the research by Ericson first appeared in her work *Fires and Firemen*, 4-5; 56-58.

63. *Daily Sentinel*, July 2, 1906. See also, Partin, *et al, Nacogdoches*, 175. R. T. Shindler was Mayor.

64. Robert F. Bruner and Sean D. Carr, *The Panic of 1907: Lessons Learned from the Market's Perfect Storm* (Hoboken, New Jersey: John Wiley & Sons, 2007), 141-143.

65. *Daily Sentinel*, Oct. 12, 1906.

66. *Daily Sentinel*, October 22, 1906.

67. *Daily Sentinel*, October 23, 1906.

"The Carpenters Side

An Open Statement to the Public Concerning their Demands

Nacogdoches, Texas, October 23 – A statement to The People of Nacogdoches: --

We, the members of the Local Union of Carpenters of Nacogdoches, wish to put ourselves square and plain before the good citizens of this unavoidable circumstance that has transpired between ourselves and the contractors of the town. The whole secret of the cause is the high price of groceries, high priced dry goods, and the high price of every other conceivable thing that one has to have to sustain life, and the cheapness of labor. It is a well known fact that no reasonable man would attempt to dispute that the price of living has in the last three years increased at least one third, and it is also a fact that the carpenters of Nacogdoches are working for the same wages that they received three or four years ago, and some are even working for less.

It is also a fact that we cannot take our wives and children to church or any other public gathering in Nacogdoches, and it is all because we cannot dress them in such a manner that any lady would feel at ease in good society. Now, why can't we do this any sane man can answer. It is because we do not wish them to go? No, a thousand times no. For they are just as dear to us in their cheap clothing as if they were dressed in the finest apparel that money could buy, but the cause is this. We don't get enough for our labor to be in such a condition as to enable us to have the real necessaries of life, much less any luxuries. Our troubles are these: The carpenters have been working in Nacogdoches for $2.50 per day, and we have asked for $3 per day and have been refused.

We want to ask this much of the public. Don't you think we deserve it? There is hardly one of us that does not owe some debt that was due six or maybe twelve months ago, and it looks as though we can never pay and no doubt the man had been stamped as a rascal, when it has been impossible to pay him and get something to live on.

We feel we are entitled to $3 per day and are going to get it if we have to leave Nacogdoches ot get it. Nacogdoches is about the only town in the state that pays less than $3 and the scale of wages in most towns is $3 to $3.50. We have no ill towards any of the contractors. If they can't pay it, we lay no blame on them. This is strictly a live and let live proposition for us. We ask the good will of the public, and all who have work to be done, we will make it to your interest if you will please call on some union man.

E. D. Moorer, W. S. Chadwick, Committee"

68. "Work Suspended," *Daily Sentinel*, Oct. 23, 1906.

69. "Strike Settled," *Daily Sentinel*, October 25, 1906.

"Nacogdoches, Texas, Oct. 25, 1906 – To the Union Carpenters and the Contractors of the City of Nacogdoches, Texas: We, the Arbitrating Committee selected by you to arbitrate the differences that have recently arisen between you on account of an increase in the Union scale of wages for the Carpenters of Nacogdoches, beg leave to submit the following:

"We recommend that work be resumed by the carpenters on all contracts now under construction and that the scale of wages on all said uncompleted jobs be $2.05 per day until same have been completed we further recommend that in the future the Union adopt and prepare a regular annual scale of wages to be signed by all the contractors for future work, which said scale shall be binding on both the Union and the contractors during the year.

Respectfully submitted,

E. C. Branch and H. F. Marr

We approve the above recommendations and herby obligate ourselves to abide by same.

D. Rulfs and W. Rulfs, Contractors

Carpenters Union of Nacogdoches, Texas by

R. D. Oliver and T. E. Strickland

A. B. Rusche, Committee."

70. Partin, *et al, Nacogdoches*, 126.

71. Tom McKinney, "The Stone Fort Rifles," an unpublished manuscript submitted to the *East Texas Historical Journal* for an upcoming publication, March, 2012.

72. Joe Ericson, "Nacogdoches Banks and Bankers," *Bicentennial History of Nacogdoches*, 194. See McDonald, *Stone Fort Bank*.

73. "Doctors of Nacogdoches County," Ericson, *Nacogdoches County Families*, 102-124.

74. *Daily Sentinel*, October 20, 1902. Davis, the roommate in college of Alton Birdwell, the first President of Stephen F. Austin State Teachers College, became a key person in the recruitment of SFA to Nacogdoches.

75. Peggy Wright, *A History of the Cum Concilio Club, 1894-1996* (Nacogdoches, Texas, Privately Printed, 1996), 13-15.

76. Partin *et al, Nacogdoches*, 140-141.

77. Sarah Jackso*n, Baker*, 11-14.

78. *Daily Sentinel*, February 18, 1907.

79. Sarah Jackso*n, Baker*, 13.

80. E. A. and Eugene Blount and John Schmidt at Commercial Bank; Sturdevant, Hayter, W. U. Perkins, and Hoya at Stone Fort Bank; Whitaker, Hollis and Blum Mast, and Ingraham at Farmers and Merchant Bank. Even the scoundrel Wettermark lived in a house designed and built by Rulfs. Most of the medical doctors lived in houses by the architect. The first modern hospital opened in a building designed by Rulfs, as did the first Fire Department and City Hall.

Chapter VIII: Downtown After 1900

1. *Daily Sentinel*, February 22, 1900. For another example, see *Daily Sentinel*, May 15, 1902.

2. *Houston Daily Post*, May 3, 1899.

3. *Daily Sentinel*, January 27, 1900.

4. *Daily Sentinel*, June 11, 1900.

5. *Houston Daily Post*, May 3, 1899.

6. Contract, May 4, 1899, Bennett Blake Papers, Box 9, Folder 24, ETRC, SFA.

7. ETRC, http://digital.sfasu.edu/cdm4/document.php?CISOROOT=/EastTexRC&CISOPTR=2103&REC=1. For a recent discussion of the property by the heirs, see "Hoya descendant plans restoration of downtown building," *Daily Sentinel*, November 9, 2010

8. *Daily Sentinel*, May 8 and 9, 1900.

9. *Daily Sentinel*, February 19, 1900.

10. *Daily Sentinel*, March 6, 1900. For information on Fritz Hoya (1839-1923), an unmarried merchant, and his younger brother Charles Hoya (1848-1926), who was a surveyor, see Ericson, *Gateway* III, 420. The documents for the National Register Nomination of this building can be found at, Nacogdoches Sites Survey Online, http://www.sfasu.edu/heritagecenter/1174.asp.

11. *Daily Sentinel*, July 28, 1900.

12. Letter from D. Rulfs to Tony Rulfs, September 14, 1921, shown to the author by Anna Katherine Holbrook (granddaughter), in July 1974.

13. Sanborn Maps, UT, *Nacogdoches*, 1900 through 1922; For the 1929 and 1929-46 maps, only in black and white, see http://sanborn.umi.com/tx/8670/dateid-000009.htm?CCSI=894n.

14. Jere Jackson, "The Hoya Buildings," Heritage Club Markers. The National Register application for Downtown Nacogdoches has also reviewed this building, but their coverage has some careless mistakes, as when they reverse the brick colors and say the building originally had a suspended awning. My own earlier mistake was to assume that the more prominent Hoya, Charles, was the one in charge, whereas it was Fritz Hoya.

15. Later in 1901, the Cason, Richardson, & Co. bought out the Hazle Furniture company and were in the process of consolidating their furniture departments in the Hazle Building. *Daily Sentinel*, July, 10, 1901.

16. *Daily Sentinel*, July 28-29, 1900.

17. Jere Jackson, "The John H. Cox Tobacco Warehouse," (111 North Pecan) Heritage Club Marker Project, 2003. Based on a date on a door facing and testimony, the original 1975 THC survey placed the date of this building at 1891. The 1891 Sanborn Map does show a wooden building at the location. The Victor & Victor Survey, Site No. 226, repeated this information. It was under construction at the time the Sanborn Map of 1900; 1906 just repeats this information, calling the building one story. The 1912 map gives the clearest assessment of the building, probably because of the 1909 remodeling and the fact that it was a highly flammable cigar factory.

18. "Specifications and Contract for a Building on Pecan Street", Cason Estate Papers, ETRC. Only the first part of the contract exists and is titled "Specifications. Of a two story Brick Building to be erected [~~by D. Rulfs~~ *struck through*] for Cason Richardson & Co. on Pecan Street in the town of Nacogdoches, Texas, according to the plans prepared by D. Rulfs, Architect, Nacogdoches, Texas." The person who typed the contract assumed that D. Rulfs would be named contractor, but in cases like this, it was always William Henry Rulfs who would have signed the construction contracts, not D. Rulfs. For other examples, see the contract for Cason's private home in the same collection; see also footnote 6 for reference to the contract on Main Street signed by W. H. Rulfs.

19. Sanborn Maps, UT, *Nacogdoches*, (1912). The Sanborn Maps seem to indicate that the elevators were added about the time of the 1909 remodeling.

20. Dr. Robert Gruebel and his wife Diane Ford began the process of renovation and preservation of the Main and Pecan Street property in 1988. For current property information, see NCAD, Property 22929, http://www.nacocad.org/ accessed February 13, 2011. See also, "Buildings Given Historical Designations," *Daily Sentinel*, March 1, 1990.

21. *Daily Sentinel*, March 26, 1901.

22. *Daily Sentinel*, May 4, 1901.

23. "New Drug Store," *Daily Sentinel*, May 17, 1901. See also, *Daily Sentinel*, March 4, 1902.

24. "Another Building for Blount on North Square," *Daily Sentinel*, May 12, 1902. See also, *Daily Sentinel*, July 2, 1902; August 20, 1902; August 23, 1902.

25. *Daily Sentinel*, August 30, 1902. "It will be but a few days until the Blount and Schmidt building adjoining the Perkins block on Fredonia Street will be complete, and when the rubbish is all cleared away things will look wonderfully improved in that vicinity."

26. Joe Ericson, "Nacogdoches Banks and Bankers," *Bicentennial History.*

27. See Chapter III.

28. *Daily Sentinel*, September 24, 1901.

29. *Ibid.*

30. *Daily Sentinel*, February 14, 1903.

31. The Stone Fort Bank was chartered on February 14, 1903 and opened its doors for business on June 20. E. S. Woodfin was the president at the time of the charter, but Charles Hoya was president at the time it opened. Link Sturdevant rather quickly, however, became the long-serving president of the bank. Archie P. McDonald, *Sentinel of Service: Stone Fort National Bank* (Nacogdoches: Privately Printed by Regions Bank, 2003), 3-4.

32. *Daily Sentinel*, October 21, 1903. The *Houston Daily Post*, February 4, 1903, listed the officers of Commercial bank as: E. A. Blount, President, George C. Ingraham, vice president; Eugene H. Blount, cashier. The directors were John Schmidt, V. E. Simpson, Thomas E. Baker, T. J. Williams, Eugene H. Blount.

33. *Daily Sentinel*, May 9, 1902; May 16, 1902; July 3, 1902; August 15, 1902; August 28, 1902.

34. "Successor to the Old Stone Fort," *Daily Sentinel*, September 1, 1902.

35. *Daily Sentinel,* October 15, 1902.

36. *Daily Sentinel*, February 11, 1905.

37. *Daily Sentinel*, January 4, 1907.

38. *Daily Sentinel*, Special Edition, November, 1906.

39. *Ibid.*

40. "Dissolution of Old Mercantile Firm Mayer & Schmidt," *Daily Sentinel.* January 5, 1903. "Firm of Mayer & Schmidt Reorganized," *Daily Sentinel*, January 9, 1903.

41. Mayer & Schmidt provided a job for Tony Rulfs, Diedrich's son, at their business. *Daily Sentinel*, June 11, 1900. Tony Boeschen, the architect's nephew, also worked for Mayer & Schmidt.

42. Texas Historic Sites Atlas, "Historic and Architectural Resources of Nacogdoches: Community Planning and Development in Nacogdoches: 1830-1940," historic context submitted for the National Register of Historic Places, 1989, http://atlas.thc.state.tx.us/index.asp, October 18, 2010. The markers on the building were written by the author: Jere Jackson, "The Old Cotton Exchange Building, Mast Office Building," Heritage Club Msrkers, 2003.

43. May 30, 1854, *Deed Records,* L: 210-211; W: 320-321; X: 504-505.

44. Jackson, "The Old Cotton Exchange Building, Mast Office Building," Heritage Club Markers, 2003. For pictures and the National Register citation of this building, see Nacogdoches Sites Survey Online, http://www.sfasu.edu/heritagecenter/1279.asp.

45. See *Daily Sentinel*, June 11, 1900. The Sanborn Map of 1900, which was done in October, shows the brick two-story building on the corner of Fredonia and Commerce. *Daily Sentinel*, June 12, 1902. Possibly the man was Will Henry Hartgraves (1870-1846). Ericson, *Gateway* III, 382.

46. Mary Stewart Duncan, interview with the author, March, 1974. At the time the National Register review was done on the background of the Cotton Exchange Building, the survey simply says that the building is reported to be Rulfs building. The citations from the newspaper and the architect's niece and the close associations of Rulfs and Schmidt make it certain that Rulfs did the building. The architectural progressions do also. For a summary of the cotton industry, however, the National Register account is correct, as are most of their descriptions. See Nacogdoches Sites Survey Online, http://www.sfasu.edu/heritagecenter/images/NR_Individual_-_Cotton_Exchange_Building_Old(1).pdf.

47. See, *Daily Sentinel*, May 11, 1934. The other owners besides Schmidt were: H. S. Wettermark, Herman Loeb, G. H. Davidson, E. A. Blount, W. U. Perkins, and Capt. I. L. Sturdevant as the general manager for many years. The plant was sold to Roland Jones in 1907. The plant was destroyed by fire in 1909 and then rebuilt.

48. *Daily Sentinel*, May 9, 1902.

49. *Daily Sentinel*, March 1, 1902. Also see, *Daily Sentinel*, August 30, 1902; October 3, 1902.

50. *Daily Sentinel*, May 23, 1901.

51. In colonial times, this small square in the north east corner of the intersection of North and Main, was known as the old Ecclesiastical Square. The town's horse-watering trough sat there. The hotel occupied the space where the parking lot now exists, immediately north of the small square. There was a small wooden hotel on the plat in the 1900 Sanborn, a two-story building, called the Camp House.

52. "Hoisted a Pine Top," *Daily Sentinel,* January 18, 1902. See also, *Daily Sentinel,* February 14, 1902. The new hotel's name as the "The Plaza Hotel" appeared in the *Daily Sentinel,* February 23, 1902,

53. *Daily Sentinel,* August 19, 1902.

54. *Daily Sentinel*, July 7, 1902.

55. Nacogdoches Grocery Company, ETRC, [B-48]. Wettermark did not abscond with his bank's funds until January of 1903.

56. *Daily Sentinel,* April 24, 1908. Jacob F. Schmidt was born in Germany in 1867, became a US Citizen October 18, 1888, and worked in the Grocery Business. Jacob is not to be confused with John's Schmidt's other nephew, Henry Phillip Schmidt, whose sons Henry and John Louis owned the modern establishment "Schmidt's" in downtown Nacogdoches. Ericson, *Gateway* III, 807.

57. *Daily Sentinel*, August 27, 1906.

58. Special Edition of *Daily Sentinel*, December, 1906.

59. Partin, *et al, Nacogdoches,* 115-117. "The effect of having access to these two railroad lines was literally to make the whole world reachable to persons living in the Nacogdoches area. Naturally, they helped to attract business and industry to the community and gave its farmers a much wider marker for their products."

60. *Daily Sentinel,* November 22, 1904.

61. Sanborn Maps, UT, *Nacogdoches,* (1906).

62. Special Edition, *Daily Sentinel*, November, 1906.

63. Nacogdoches Sites Survey Online, http://www.sfasu.edu/heritagecenter/1171.asp. The 1986 description in the Victor & Victor Survey, Site No. 1414, estimated the building's date at 1900. The comments by the National Register, which date this building to 1920, are most definitely incorrect. The buildings date to 1904-1905; the first pictures and map date to 1906.

64. "Cason, Monk & Company. Incorporated With a Capital Stock of $75,000 to Start With," *Daily Sentinel,* August 27, 1906.

65. Mayer & Schmidt were undergoing a major reorganization of their assets in the summer of 1906.) After the founding of the Nacogdoches Wholesale Grocery Company, Schmidt decided to get out of the retail business in groceries altogether. His decision to sell the hardware business was partial; he kept a major stock interest in Cason, Monk & Company. He divested himself of the management of his firm's furniture business by turning the stock over to a new corporation, Burk-Crain Furniture Company, which was made up of Ed Burk, John Schmidt, and H. D. Crain as incorporators. They set up business, as soon as Cason vacated the premises, at the corner of Pecan and Main (the John H. Cox Building). See *Daily Sentinel*, August 29, 1906.

66. The old Seal & Dunegan Building and the one next door owned by Link Sturdevant were joined. (He designed similar mergers between the buildings he unified to make the Redland Hotel treatment and between the first floor of the John H. Cox building and the building to the west.)

67. *Daily Sentinel,* August 27, 1906.

68. *Daily Sentinel,* Aug 27, 1906. The contractor was a man by the name Fleshman.

69. "Building Boom," *Daily Sentinel*, May 6, 1901.

70. *Daily Sentinel,* July, 10, 1901. The article also discussed the merger of the Hazle Furniture Company and Cason, Richardson & Co. to form "Nacogdoches has the Biggest Furniture Establishment in East Texas."

71. Sanborn Maps, UT, *Nacogdoches,* (1900). By 1905, the *Sentinel* moved again by buying into the Bailey Block.

72. Bailey to Branch, March 23, 1900, *Deed Records*, 39: 400.

73. Sanborn Maps, UT, *Nacogdoches,* (1906).

74. *Daily Sentinel,* August 14, 1909.

75. Branch sold the property to N. D. Naman in 1913 [*Deed Records*, Vol. 81:109]. Later owners included Sam Hayter and his daughter Elizabeth Hayter Montgomery, who sold it to Reese and Lucille Kennedys in 1967 [*Deed Records*, 346:33]. Victor & Victor Survey, Site No. 102. For the modern owners, see NCAD, Property ID 22989, http://www.nacocad.org/.

76. *Daily Sentinel*, May 6, 1901; August 2, 1901; August 7, 1901. Victor & Victor Survey, Site No. 169.

77. *Daily Sentinel*, August 2 and 7, 1901. The roof was finished on August 7.

78. *Daily Sentinel*, August 10, 1904. Blount estimated the proposed hall would be "fifty by eighty feet."

79. NCAD, Property ID 22884, http://www.nacocad.org/.

80. *Daily Sentinel*, May 6, 1901. Harris and Lindsey advertised the property for rent or sale in the *Daily Sentinel*, September 19, 1901.

81. For modern records on these properties, see NCAD, Property ID 22988 and 22985, http://www.nacocad.org/. For older records, see the Harris purchase of the property on October 10, 1899, *Deed Records*, 38: 336-337; Harris sold it to E. D. Williams [May 21, 1900. *Deed Records*, 39: 492-493]. For more pictures, but flawed information, see http://www.sfasu.edu/heritagecenter/1230.asp. *See also,* Sanborn Maps, UT, *Nacogdoches,* (1900 and 1906).

82. *Daily Sentinel,* October 3, 1904. See also, *Daily Sentinel*, February 16, 1905.

83. Gladys Hardeman, niece of B. F. Hardeman, interview with the author, May, 1974.

84. *Daily Sentinel*, October 5, 1904. As to the size and placement of the Hardeman Building, the newspaper said it was "half the space formerly occupied by the Tucker-Hardeman building" which was burned and "extended thirty feet over the ground formerly occupied by the old wooden buildings." This means the new Hardeman Building was shifted thirty feet to the west. On November 11, 1904, Haltom reported on the iron and glass, which would comprise the first floor front. Again on November 24, Haltom reported: The Hardeman Building cost $5,000.The contractor was S. T. Fleshman of Center. The specifications called for Garrison brick throughout most of the structure, with Corsicana pressed brick for the façade.

85. *Daily Sentinel*, January 13, 1905.

86. "New Hotel Building," *Daily Sentinel*, 12 July 1906.

87. *Daily Sentinel,* July 12, 1906.

88. "The Contract Let," *Daily Sentinel*, August 2 and 3, 1906.

89. *Daily Sentinel*, October 12, 22, 23, 25, 1906.

90. One amusing advertisement appeared in the newspaper just days before the opening of the Redland. The old brick warehouse across South Church Street, which at some earlier time had received updating and turned into a hotel, ran this: "THE CITY HOTEL. One Block South of Opera House. Everything New and Up-to-Date. The only First Class Dollar per day House. The only Up Town Hotel. The Only Brick Hotel in the City. C. S. SOUTHERN, PROP." Needless to say, the Redland's opening devalued the City Hotel's claims days later. *Daily Sentinel*, February 23, 1907.

91. *Daily Sentinel*, March 15, 1907

92. *Daily Sentinel*, March 15, 1907. The American Radiator Company installed the system, and the Barron and Bonneville company with representatives out of Dallas did all of the plumbing.

93. *Daily Sentinel*, March 15, 1907.

94. January 3, 1908. "Colonel Bryan Here; The Average Man Will Be His Subject at the Auditorium," *Daily Sentinel*, January 3, 1908.

95. Kulhavy, Pamela Aronson. "A Survey of Nacogdoches Hotels 1830 - 1910", Research Paper, East Texas Research Center, Steen Library, Stephen F. Austin State University, Nacogdoches, Texas, 33 - 34. The Sanborn Map of 1921 is the first to show this additional floor.

96. Tom McKinney, "The Redland Hotel, Lots 9 and 9a, Block 15, 330 and 322 East Main," research assignment paper, Center for East Texas Studies, 1996-98. A. T. Mast, Jr., son of Redland owner A. T. Mast, Sr. of Nacogdoches, interview with Tom McKinney, October 22, 1996, tape recording in author's collections, Nacogdoches.

97. "Rotary Celebrates 100 Years of Fellowship," *Daily Sentinel*, February 24, 2005.

98. Mast to Flany, November 2, 1937, *Deed Records*, 145: 424. Charles Bright bought the building in 1982 (*Deed Records*, 479: 575) and sold it to Richard and Linda Greer in 1997 (December 31, 1997, *Deed Records*, 1172: 73). See also, NCAD, Property 22978, http://www.nacocad.org/. There are some additional pictures and survey material at the Nacogdoches Sites Survey Online, http://www.sfasu.edu/heritagecenter/1213.asp.

99. "Groundbreaking for new GODTEL shelter," *Daily Sentinel*, March 14, 2009.

100. *Daily Sentinel*, 1906, Special Edition, December, 1906. [B97]. List of Rulfs buildings pictured in the 1906 Special Edition: the West and East End Schools; Mayer & Schmidt (1888); Nacogdoches Wholesale Grocery; Tucher, Zeve & Dotson; John P. Davidson Building; the First Brick Block; Main Street Presbyterian Church; Burk-Crain Furniture (Cox Building); Cason-Monk Hardware; Tucher, Zeve & Dotson; H. T. Burk Buildings on Main; J. M. Weeks Building; Banita Hotel; G. H. King building on Main at Church; Hazle Building; First Baptist Church; and the residences of Frank Summers, Roland Jones, E. A. Blount, and C. W. Butt.

101. *Daily Sentinel*, December 26, 1906. There newspaper was full of ads and requests for space. Mayer & Schmidt went to the Davidson Building on the south side of the Square; Perkins, Kleas & Mast moved into the remodeled Hardeman Building which was being made part of the new Redland Hotel; dentist, lawyers, timbermen, and others who had office upstairs in the burnt building had to find new quarters. The Hazle Building once again became fully leased; W. T. Wilson moved back into his former quarters in the Hazel building. Stripling, Haselwood & Co. secured the building next door to the Racket Store on the north side of East Main. The Commercial National bank secured room in the Nacogdoches Land Company building.

102. *Daily Sentinel*, January 17, 1907. For the beginning of these changes, see *Daily Sentinel*, July 2, 1906. Included in the changes were that all buildings had to be provided with gutter and down spouts, and in addition, all privies had to be connected to the new sewer lines. The Redland Hotel received special attention. The City let the bonds for the new $50,000 city water works in May; *Daily Sentinel*, May 3, 1907.

103. "A Mooted Question," *Daily Sentinel*, January 19, 1907.

104 "Passing of a Landmark," *Daily Sentinel*, February 16, 1907. The kickoff date for starting the project of beautification would be Arbor Day, February 22, 1907.

105. *Palestine Daily Herald*, December 26, 1906.

106. *Daily Sentinel*, March 13, 1907.

107. *Daily Sentinel*, March 4, 1907; March 13, 1907; March 27, 1907.

108. *Daily Sentinel*, June 25, 1907. The pine top celebrations attracted more people after the prohibition of liquor and beer sales in 1905.

109. *Daily Sentinel*, March 19, 1907. The lead contractor who got the bid was Shearer out of Lufkin who had worked with Rulfs on the Christ Episcopal Church.

110. *Daily Sentinel*, April 16 and 17, 1907.

111. Farmers and Merchants Bank merged with Stone Fort Bank in 1919. Rulfs remodeled the old 1891 Cox Building at that time.

112. Edward (Jerry) Baker, great grandson of E. A. Blount, helped to guide the author through the many transformation of the Commercial National Bank.

113. J. W. Kennedy bought the bought the Shindler Drug and Jewelry business in 1915. He sold it in 1933 to his sons Leroy and George. By 1944,

the business was solely a jewelry store. In 1952, when George opened a store in Longview, the Jewelry business passed into the sole ownership of Leroy Kennedy. Leroy and Jamie Kennedy purchased the building in 1975. (*Deed Records*, 401: 767) In 1979, Leroy's daughter, Jean, inherited the property, and along with her husband David Stephens, took over the business. Information provided by Jean Kennedy Stephens, interview with the author, March 18, 2012. For modern pictures, see Nacogdoches Sites Survey Online, http://www.sfasu.edu/heritagecenter/1194.asp.

114. NCAD, Property 22923, http://www.nacocad.org/ accessed March 15, 2012. For modern pictures, see Nacogdoches Sites Survey Online, http://www.sfasu.edu/heritagecenter/2092.asp.

115. Ericson, *Fires and Firemen*, 76.

116. For the Sanders Building , see NCAD, Property 22924, http://www.nacocad.org/; for details on the architecture, see Nacogdoches Sites Survey Online, http://www.sfasu.edu/heritagecenter/1198.asp. For the Joe Reindl Building ownership, see NCAD, Property 22926, http://www.nacocad.org/; for more pictures, see Nacogdoches Sites Survey Online, http://www.sfasu.edu/heritagecenter/2094.asp.

117. *Daily Sentinel*, January 4, 1908.

118. *Daily Sentinel*, January 8, 1908.

119. *Daily Sentinel*, January 9, 1908.

120. *Daily Sentinel*, January 15, 1908. On February 21, 1908, Haltom reviewed the plans. On April 17, 1908, he announced that the brick laying had commenced. "The plans were drawn by Mr. D. Rulfs, the well-known contractor of this city, and they are strictly up to date in every particular."

121. *Daily Sentinel*, April 17, 1908, announced that the brick laying had commenced.

122. *Daily Sentinel*, August 6, 1909.

123. *Daily Sentinel*, December 20, 1928.

124. NCAD, Property 22903, http://www.nacocad.org/.

125. *Daily Sentinel*, January 4 and 6, 1908.

126. Victor & Victor Survey, Site No. 157. The survey in 1986 did not think the Palladian windows worth mentioning. Perhaps by that time, the overly bland white paint treatment given the façade in the 1980s had washed away all architectural interest.

127. NCAD, Property 22906, http://www.nacocad.org/.

Chapter IX: Churches and Civic Buildings

1. Carolyn Ericson, "Sacred Heart Parish at Nacogdoches," 50-51.

2. Carolyn Ericson, *Sesquicentennial History of First United Methodist Church, Nacogdoches, Texas, 1837-1987* (Nacogdoches: Ericson Books, 1987), 7, 16-17. Ericson chronicles how the Methodist congregation fluctuated in parallel with the town's population.

3. *Deed Records*, Nacogdoches University to Methodist Episcopal Church South, November 23, 1860, O: 477.

4. Ericson, *Methodist History*, 16-17. Sanborn Maps, UT, *Nacogdoches,* (1885). See also, James Nichols, Jr., "First United Methodist Church of Nacogdoches." Ericson, *Nacogdoches County Families,* 38-39. F

5. Methodist Church Archives, consulted April 7, 2011. The lot was purchased from John A. Binford and T. A. Binford (minor, John Binford, guardian) in transactions of March 12 and April 12, 1887; *Deed Records*, Binford to Methodist Episcopal Church South, April 26, 1887, Y: 14, and Y: 15. G. D. Boger, who purchased the old church to move it across the street, signed these deeds as a "Trustees of the Methodist Episcopal Church South." See, Ericson, *Methodist History*, 207.

6. *Nacogdoches Star-News*, May 13, 1887.

7. "D. Rulfs. Architect, Carpenter, and Contractor of Buildings. Nacogdoches, Texas," *Nacogdoches Star,* March 9, 1888.

8. Sanborn Maps, UT, *Nacogdoches,* (1891, 1896, 1906). The 1891 map shows the sanctuary without the chancel or the enlarged porch; the 1896 and 1906 are identical and show both the new chancel and porch with 45' tower.

9. Lucille Fain, "Westminster Church's History is Traced," *Daily Sentinel* November 11, 1990.

10. Jere Jackson, "Westminster Presbyterian Church, Nacogdoches, Texas," Application for a Texas Historical Marker, Texas Historical Commission, Vertical Files (2008), Austin, Texas. On the schism in the Presbyterian Church, see John R. "Pete" Hendrick in *Handbook of Texas Online*, s.v. "Presbyterian Church," http://www.tshaonline.org/handbook/online/articles/PP/ipp1.html. See also, "Old School-New School Controversy," *Wikipedia*, http://en.wikipedia.org/w/index.php?title=Old_School-New_School_Controversy&oldid=391512211.

11. Sanborn Maps, UT, *Nacogdoches,* 1891, 1900, 1906. The church's changed facade and tower appears for the first time on the 1906 map.

12. Willie Earl Woods Tindall, "Religion: Recollections & Reckonings," *Bicentennial History,* 90.

13. James Partin, "The First Baptist Church, Nacogdoches, Texas," Application for a Texas Historical Marker, Vertical Files (2009), Austin, Texas. Partin is citing Minutes of the Mount Zion Baptist Association of Missionary Baptist Churches in Eastern Texas, 1884, 5; W. T. Parmer, *Seventy-Five Years in Nacogdoches: A History of the First Baptist Church, 1884-1959* (Dallas, Texas: The Dorsey Company, 1959), 56-57.

14. James G. Partin, *Advancing the Kingdom Since 1884: A Pictorial History of the First Baptist Church of Nacogdoches, Texas* (Virginia Beach, Va: Donning Company, 2009), 19 [hereafter Partin, *Pictorial History.*]

15. *Houston Daily Post*, May 3, 1899.

16. Partin, *Pictorial History*, 29. James Partin, correspondence with the author, November 1-7, 2010. Partin referenced the pastor who delivered the dedication sermon for the Rulfs building in 1901; Rev. A. J. Holt, *Pioneering in the Southwest,* (Nashville: The Sunday School Board of the Southern Baptist Convention 1923), 261; and W. T. Parmer, *Seventy-Five Years in Nacogdoches,* 76-77.

17. Partin, *Pictorial History*, 29.

18. Sanborn Maps, UT, *Nacogdoches,* 1900 and 1906.

19. He emphasized the overhanging eaves with decorative brackets; he included horizontal boards that run under the bottom of the windows; the continuous brick facing for the whole basement level, being elevated considerably above ground level, provided a major horizontal element.

20. Sanborn Maps, UT, *Nacogdoches,* 1900.

21. Sanborn Maps, UT, *Nacogdoches,* 1900.

22. See Figure 9.7 for a view of the chimneys which vented the stoves.

23. Sanborn Maps, UT, *Nacogdoches,* 1906. James Partin, correspondence with the author, October 6-8, 2011. The 1906 map shows the wide opening between the auditorium and the west end of the building. Similar flexibility was built into the Methodist Church in 1910 and Zion Hill Baptist Church in 1914. A later Sanborn Map, 1929, shows the space behind the pulpit sectioned off into two spaces, presumably to provide an office for the minister. The new sanctuary in 1941, which replaced the Rulfs building, kept this same working pattern.

24. Partin, *Pictorial History*, 44.

25. The various Christ Church brochures are at odds with one another. One notes Crocket came in 1888 and another uses 1898. Based on his papers, the date 1888 seems correct. His appointment was not full-time at first. George Louis Crocket Papers, A-12, ETRC, SFASU. At the time of the dedication of the historical marker for Christ Church, there is material on Crocket; *Daily Sentinel*, June 17, 1973.

26. *Daily Sentinel*, June 17, 1973, at the 125th anniversary of the congregation. In his own history of recent events leading to the building of the new church building, Crocket hints at the same conclusions. *Daily Sentinel*, February 9, 1901.

27. Vestry Records, Mar. 1893 - Sept. 1901, Christ Episcopal Church Collection, 1844-2004 (B-119), ETRC [hereafter Christ Church Archive].

28. *Daily Sentinel*, January 29, 1900, reported that the tearing the old building down "started today." The review of the church's history in 1973 mistakenly states the congregation continued to worship in the original church until 1902. The wood frame building was torn down by Houston King in 1900, according to the newspaper; the lot was being readied for the new Bailey Block along Church Street. Houston King bought the old Episcopal Church building and tore it down to build a residence on South Pecan Street. *Daily Sentinel*, January 31, 1900. There are other articles on the church: *Daily Sentinel*, January 29, 1900; January 31; February 1, 1900; and February 9, 1900. In the February 9 edition, Crocket gives his own history of the recent tribulations of the preceding years. He ended with words to launch the congregation into a new era, "in the earnest hope that her new home, when it is built, may be truly the presence chamber of God as well as the old one."

29. Their first offer of an alternative place to meet came on January 31. The Presbyterians, the next street over on Fredonia Street, offered their facilities until the new church could be completed. *Daily Sentinel*, February 1, 1900.

30. Vestry Minutes, January 26, 1900, and February 20, 1900, Christ Church Archive. (Incidentally, Jones was originally from Shreveport.)

31. Vestry Minutes, March 2, 1900, Christ Church Archive. Meeting with the Vestry during these sessions were Roland Jones (Secretary), George Crocket (Rector), Dr. Henry Rulfs, Ascot Mathews, Eugene E. Smith, R. C. and R. T. Shindler, Oscar Matthews, and occasionally G. H. Matthews and E. A. Blount (both visitors), and D. Rulfs (architect).

32. Vestry Minutes, April 23, 1900, Christ Church Archive.

33. Vestry Minutes, May 5, 1900, Christ Church Archive.

34. "Memorandum of Agreement," October 29, 1900, Christ Church Archive. One of the Church's histories incorrectly asserts that the bricks came from the Herrin Brick Company; this is refuted by the contract and the Vestry Minutes.

35. *Ibid.*

36. *Ibid.*

37. *Daily Sentinel*, June 17, 1973. See also, Ericson, *Nacogdoches County Families*, 580-581.

38. Vestry Minutes, July 24, 1901, Christ Church Archive.

39. *Daily Sentinel*, September 9, 1901.

40. *Daily Sentinel*, June 17, 1973. The 1973 account did use the Vestry minutes, but not carefully. The date of the contract was correct, but the start date for the building is incorrect. Both the completion date and the occupation date are omitted. The account lumps the purchase of the furniture in April of 1902 with the consecration by Bishop Gregg, which might have been just speculation. Bishop George Herbert Kinsolving (1849-1928) became the assistant bishop of Texas in 1892 and bishop a year later. See William James Battle, "Kinsolving, George Herbert," *Handbook of Texas Online* [Texas State Historical Association], http://www.tshaonline.org/handbook/online/articles/fki30.

41. Quoted in the *Daily Sentinel,* Special Insert, June 17, 1973.

42. The author's efforts have included interviews with current members of the Vestry, searches of the church's basement and archive of blueprints and plans in the company of architect Jerry Sutton (a member of the church), and even contact with the bishop's office.

43. *Daily Sentinel,* June 17, 1973.

44. Jere Jackson, "Westminster Presbyterian Church, Nacogdoches, Texas," Marker Application, 2008. Among the sources used for this application were: Lucille Fain, "Westminster Church's History is Traced," *Sunday Sentinel,* March 7, 1982; another version of this article appears in Ericson, *Nacogdoches County Families*, 53-54. Gerald W. Gillette [Research Historian, Presbyterian Historical Society, Philadelphia, PA] to Rev. Charles L. Pullen [Westminster Presbyterian Church, Nacogdoches], dated September 12, 1973, Westminster Presbyterian Church Archives. The Delegate to the Texas Presbytery was A. J. Murphy; see Texas, Presbytery [Cumberland Presbyterian Church], Minutes, July 8, 1893, photocopy, Westminster Presbyterian Church Archives.

45. *Daily Sentinel,* May 4, 1907; May 18, 1907. In 1906, the Cumberland Denomination reunited with the Presbyterian Church in the United States. Under the new organization, the church became listed in denominational nomenclature as the "Nacogdoches" Presbyterian Church (a name which persisted in records until 1931), but locally the name remained the Main Street Presbyterian Church. Attempts to merge the two Presbyterian congregations came to nothing. The First Presbyterian Church disbanded in 1940 due to declining membership, and most of its members joined the Main Street Presbyterian Church, by then under their new name Westminster Presbyterian Church, at a new location on North Street at Power Street.

46. The lot was part of the old Raguet homestead. *Deed Records*, 43:259.

47. *Galveston Daily News*, July 13, 1902. "Half a block further east is the newly completed Cumberland Presbyterian Church building, also fronting north on the same street, a charming site and a gem of an edifice, upon a corner of the old Raguet home premises, bought from Dr. Mayfield. On this same block and same side of the street, the fine and spacious new home of Miss Fannie Nelson is nearly complete."

48. Sanborn Maps, UT, *Nacogdoches,* 1900 and 1906. The church does not appear on the 1900 maps, but it does appear on the 1906 edition. The church and the steeple remain the same on the 1912, 1921, and 1922 Sanborn Maps.

49. Mrs. William B. Bates, as quoted by Lucille Fain, "Westminster Church's History is Traced," March 7, 1982.

50. For a picture of St. Mary Church in Atens, Germany see Figure 2.16. The northern origins of this architecture can also be seen in the tower of the Old Church in Flam, Norway: Flicker site, http://www.flickr.com/photos/marcel-more/233654714/in/pool-19976275@N00/.

51. Jere Jackson, "Westminster Presbyterian Church, Nacogdoches, Texas," Marker Application, 2008, Vertical Files, Texas Historical Commission, Austin.

52. Mary Stewart Duncan, interview with the author, March, 1974.

53. Sanborn Maps, UT, *Nacogdoches,* 1885-1922. The Catholic Church appears on all of the Sanborn Maps of Nacogdoches. The early maps, depending on the mapper, show approximately the same parameters of the building; some say the eaves were 18 feet and others say 20. Some of the maps before 1906 show a roof mounted belfry. The 1906 map and subsequent maps, however, show an external porch and a two-story tower.

54. Historic American Buildings Survey/Historic American Engineering Record/Historic American Landscapes Survey, Library of Congress, http://www.loc.gov/pictures/collection/hh/item/TX0239/. The supplemental notes accompanying the picture refer to the building after it was moved to become St. Anne's on Fern Lake and ultimately the Church of the Divine Infant on Cotton Ford Road. Other buildings in Nacogdoches County covered in the HABs sweep included the Adolphus Sterne House, the Old University Building, the Peter Ellis Bean House,

the Halfway House in Chireno, and a "Ybarbo Ranch House" (Antonio Gil Y'Barbo) and said to be located on the Stephen F. Austin State Teachers College campus. This reference, which is unclear, refers to the 1936 Replica of the Old Stone Fort.

55. Ericson, *Fires and Firemen*, 57-58.

56. James L. Nichols, Jr., "History of the First United Methodist Church of Nacogdoches, Texas," Pamphlet written in 1987, Methodist Church Archives.

57. *Daily Sentinel*, July 20, 1909.

58. *Daily Sentinel*, June 23, 1910. Ericson, *Methodist History*, 20.

59. A discussion of the Akron Plan churches is available online at the following addresses: Gloria Ferris *The Akron Plan*, http://www.timferris.net/the-akron-plan/. For a discussion of the plan, see United Methodist Churches, The Akron Plan, http://www.flickr.com/groups/umethodist/discuss/72157605185062202/.

60. "Richardsonian Romanesque," Wikipedia, http://en.wikipedia.org/w/index.php?title=Richardsonian_Romanesque&oldid=458049217. "Trinity Church (Boston)," Wikipedia, The Free Encyclopedia, http://en.wikipedia.org/w/index.php?title=Trinity_Church_(Boston)&oldid=446196428.

61. Rulfs first used pivoting windows in his home in 1869 in Stollhammerwisch, Germany. He used them again in the First Baptist Church, the First Methodist Church, and, finally, in the Zion Hill Baptist Church. Sometimes the windows twisted vertically as in those in the Methodist Church and the Hollis Mast House built in the same year. Others, as those in the Baptist Church and the Zion Hill building, pivoted in the middle like those in his home in Stollhammerwisch. The Methodist windows were stained-glass, and when restored in their present building's tower, the restoration removed their functionality.

62. This distribution of materials is even noted on the 1912 Sanborn Map. Sanborn Maps, UT, *Nacogdoches*, 1912.

63. The complete National Registry nomination documents for the Zion Hill Historic District may now be found at the following address: Nacogdoches Sites Survey Online, http://www.sfasu.edu/heritagecenter/627.asp. The National Registry survey is also available through the *Texas Historic Sites Atlas*, http://atlas.thc.state.tx.us/shell-desig.htm, Marker 9403. The 1975 initial survey of Nacogdoches, which the author and Charles Philips conducted, is incorporated in the Victor & Victor Survey (1986), Site No. 854, and subsequently in the National Registry survey.

64. Jere Jackson, "Some History of the Zion Hill First Baptist Church," Application to the Texas Historical Commission for Recorded Texas Landmark Status for Zion Hill Baptist Church, 1976, Texas Historical Commission Vertical Files, Austin, Texas [hereafter Jackson, Zion Hill Marker Application]. Sources for this document included: *Deed Records*, Zion Church Vertical Files, and interviews with Zion Hill Baptist Church families. In particular, Mrs. Ernestine McNeil (granddaughter of Founder Lawson Reed), "A History of Zion Hill First Baptist Church," (a pamphlet periodically reprinted by the church on its anniversaries), Church Vertical Files. For information on Reverend Lawson Reid [Reed], see Ericson, *Gateway* III, 757; for the church, Ericson, *Nacogdoches County Families*, 54-55. Also, Alwyn Barr, *Black Texans: A History of Negros in Texas, 1528-1971* (Austin: Jenkins Publishing Co., 1973), 22, 68. See also, Lawrence D. Rice, *The Negro in Texas, 1874-1900* (Baton Rouge: Louisiana State University Press, 1971), 271-272. Here is an additional passage from the application:

> In 1878, when Reverend Lawson Reed (circa 1840 - April 11, 1924) first came to Nacogdoches from Shreveport, he found no organized Baptist Church serving the black community. After leaving the white church, the black members of the Baptist denomination worshipped with the Presbyterian and the Methodist brethren at the Union Church, located next to the St. Paul Cemetery plot in the southeast part of Nacogdoches. At first, Rev. Reed joined his fellow Baptists in worship at the Union Church and led in services there. His goal, however, was the formation of a separate Baptist church in Nacogdoches. Under his inspired leadership in 1879, those of Baptist persuasion began to worship regularly under a brush arbor between what are Mound and Logansport Streets. When the approach of winter forced the group to look for other accommodations, two of the members of the little group, Frank and Ellen Walton, gave two acres of land for the erection of a building. The Zion Hill congregation's first home was a one-room frame structure, located immediately west of the present Old Baptist Cemetery on Park Street. The year 1879, therefore, saw the establishment of the first organized Baptist Church for blacks in Nacogdoches County. From this original congregation at least two other Baptist Churches in the city, little Zion and the Sunset Galilee, were to take their beginning. The charter members of the group in 1879 were Frank and Ellen Walton, Annie K. McClain, Jim and Annie Rigsby, Harriet Moore, Hattoe Vaughns, Velma Williams McCullough, and the Reeds.

65. H. W. Rusche to D. K. Cason, October 19, 1910, as reported on the Plat Map, D. K. Cason Papers, ETRC.

66. "John Schmidt and Abraham Meyer (heirs) to Zion Hill Baptist Church (Colored), March 16, 1914," *Deed Records*, 82: 299.

67. Jackson, Zion Hill Marker Application (1976).

68. The controversy surrounding the Clay House can be followed in the *Daily Sentinel*, from March through May of 2009. For summaries, see *Daily Sentinel*, May 2 and May 5, 2009. The Texas Historical Commission became involved and wrote an important summary of its conclusions on the house: Stan Graves, Director of the Architecture Division to Bryan Bray, Historic Preservation Officer, March 31, 2009, Texas Historical Commission Vertical Files, Austin, Texas. (Copy sent to Dr. Jere Jackson, Chairman, Nacogdoches County Historical Commission.) "State Historical Commission Visits Disputed Building," *Daily Sentinel*, May 21, 2009. For the resolution, see *Daily Sentinel*, June 13, 2009.

69. "J. P. Popp to Meyer and Schmidt, September 12, 1901," *Deed Records*, 43: 630.

70. This is indicated in the National Registry survey, but the author has received independent confirmation in discussions with Architect Jerry Sutton, July, 2011. The Sanborn Maps did not include the Zion Hill area until 1922; the Clay House is shown and faced east, not towards the church. Sanborn Maps, UT, *Nacogdoches*, 1922.

71. Ancestry.com. *1910 United States Federal Census* [database on-line]. *Nacogdoches, Texas*; Roll: *T624_1581*; Page: *14A*; Enumeration District: *0095*; Image: *172*; FHL Number: *1375594*. In this census, Clay (30) is listed with his wife Ella (27), and five children, ranging in age from 2 to 8. Ten years later, the same people lived there, plus twin boys who were 8 by 1920. [*1920 United States Federal Census, Nacogdoches, Texas,* Roll: T625_1835; Page: 1B; Enumeration District: 124; Image: 716.] See also, Ericson, *Gateway* III, 174.

72. Sharon Rulfs Kerr (great-granddaughter of D. Rulfs), correspondence with the author, July 20, 2003.

73. Birdie Wade, interview with the author, June, 2002.

74. Jackson, Zion Hill Marker Application (1976).

75. Jere Jackson, "Zion Hill Baptist Church: Its History and Legacy," East Texas Historical Association, Fall Meeting, September, 1980, evening session held in the Zion Hill Sanctuary.

76. Jere Jackson, "Zion Hill: An Endangered Species," *Daily Sentinel*, October, 1999.

77. Mike Bay (President of the Nacogdoches County Historical Foundation

starting in 2000), correspondence with the author, June 16-17, 2011.

78. "The History of Public Education in Texas," Texas Education Agency (TEA), http://ritter.tea.state.tx.us/tea/historyoverview.html. For schools in Nacogdoches County, see "Pioneer Women Teachers," Ericson, *Nacogdoches County Families*, 12-14; "School Stories and Pictures," 16-27.

79. Gary Borders, *A Hanging in Nacogdoches: Murder, Race, Politics, and Polemics in Texas' Oldest Town, 1870-1916* (Austin: University of Texas Press, 2006), 50.

80. *Daily Sentinel*, October 20, 1902.

81. Lois Foster Blount, "Some Leaves from the Treasurer's Register of Property and Claims Belonging to the Trustees of the Nacogdoches University and of Debts Due by the Trustees," The Bulletin of The Stephen F. Austin State Teachers College, Historical Number, Bulletin No. 38, January, 1932, 32- 48. An unpublished, slightly different version of this paper "Some Notes on Nacogdoches University, 1845-1900" is located in the Lois Foster Blount Papers, ETRC.

82. *Galveston Daily News*, June 22, 1904.

83. *Galveston Daily News*, January 2, 1904; January 3, 1904. *Palestine Herald*, January 4, 1904. It is interesting that the newspapers did not agree on the amount of the bond election. Galveston got the news out earlier, but had the figure wrong.

84. "Trustees in Session," *Daily Sentinel*, March 21, 1904. "The following architects are here and each has submitted plans: D. Rulfs, of Nacogdoches; J. Overton Parr, representing Taylor & Parr, Greenville, Texas; O. H. P. Rudisell, of Houston; C. H. Page of Austin; Sam P. Herbert, of Waco; John A. Ettler of Beaumont; Malcomb Moore, representing Smith & Moore of Fort Worth." Although it included less detail, the *Galveston Daily News*, March 24, 1904, also reported the meeting.

85. Roxanne Williamson, "PAGE, CHARLES HENRY," *Handbook of Texas Online* (http://www.tshaonline.org/handbook/online/articles/fpa76).

86. *Shiner Gazette* (Shiner, Texas), May 18, 1904. The highest of the six bids was $26,000.

87. *Galveston Daily News*, January 4, 1905. The Central School Building, later known as the Nacogdoches Grammar School after 1915, was torn down in 1956. The East End School by Rulfs, the least expensive of the three schools built in 1904, is still standing, albeit modified by additions.

88. "In her high school building, Nacogdoches has the most imposing structure of the kind in East Texas, for its location, nature has provided a most admirable place." *Daily Sentinel*, January 5, 1905.

89. Mary Stewart Duncan, interview with the author, July 1974.

90. *Daily Sentinel*, November 1, 1904.

91. Sanborn Maps UT, *Nacogdoches*, 1906. http://www.lib.utexas.edu/maps/sanborn/m-o/txu-sanborn-nacogdoches-1906-8.jpg.

92. Ericson, *Fires and Firemen*, 209-211.

93. *Daily Sentinel*, October 20, 1902, and *Daily Sentinel*, November *22*, 1904. Victor & Victor Survey, Site No. 1129. The *Galveston Daily News* gave good coverage of the school issue (see June 22, 25, 1904, and January 5, 1905), but often with incorrect figures. For instance, they said the East and West End Schools cost the same: $5,000 (*Galveston Daily News*, March 24, 1904). The *Palestine Daily Herald* also gave coverage: January 4 and April 11, 1904.

94. The colorized Sanborn Maps at the University of Texas do not include the years 1929 and 1929-1946 for Nacogdoches (the first maps to include the Shawnee Street school). For the later maps, see the ETRC website at SFASU: Digital Sanborn Maps, *Texas*, *Nacogdoches*, 1929 and 1929-1946, http://libweb.sfasu.edu/proser/etrc/collections/maps/.

95. "Clipping gives a look at 1906 Nacogdoches," *Daily Sentinel*, March 3, 1985. See also, Partin, *et al*, *Nacogdoches*, 119.

96. Francis Abernethy, "Campbell, E. J.," in Ericson, *Nacogdoches County Families*, 196-197. For biographical data on Campbell, see Ericson, *Gateway* III, 137.

97. Interviews collected by the Center for East Texas Studies, which sponsored the African American Heritage Project from its inception to 2007. These interviews and others are housed in the Birdie Wade Collection, [A-202] in the ETRC at SFASU, http://libweb.sfasu.edu/proser/etrc/collections/manuscript/personal/aahp/index.html. In particular see the interviews with Mrs. C. L. Simon (January 12, 1998) and C. L. Simon (January 7, 1999) by Tom McKinney. Marion Upshaw, interviews with the author, was published as "An East Texas African-American Dynasty," *Daily Sentinel*, June 17-18-19, 2008.

98. Will Godwin, "E. J. Campbell alumni have strong attachments to old school," *Daily Sentinel*, October 5, 2010.

99. See Figure 9.57 for the only picture extant of the building. Rulfs used the same fanlight windows on the Fanny Nelson House in 1902 and the Catholic Church steeple in 1905.

100. *Daily Sentinel*, January 2, 1905.

101. The dates and the chronology used in the National Registry document "Community Planning and Development in Nacogdoches: 1830-1940" are incorrect. This document is available under the name, "1990 NRHP Multiple Property Documentation Form: Historic and Architectural resources of Nacogdoches Texas," at Nacogdoches Sites Survey Online, http://www.sfasu.edu/heritagecenter/622.asp.

102. For the schools, see NISD, Carpenter Elementary School, http://nacogdoches.tx.schoolwebpages.com/education/school/school-history.php?sectiondetailid=96&; and "Nacogdoches High School," Wikipedia, The Free Encyclopedia, //en.wikipedia.org/w/index.php?title=Nacogdoches_High_School&oldid=451521734.

103. Ericson, *Fires and Firemen*, 9; Ericson *Gateway*, III, 791.

104. *Fire Department Minute Book* (1907-1935), Box 2, Teutsch Collection [A-218], ETRC.

105. *Ibid.*

106. For the passage of the water system, see *Daily Sentinel*, March 16, May 3, 1907. The water system, specifically the hydrant system for fire protection appears on the Sanborn Maps for the first time in 1912. Sanborn Maps, UT, *Nacogdoches,* (1912).

107. Ericson, *Nacogdoches County Families*, 112-113. For biographical information, see Ericson, *Gateway* III, 859.

108. October 5, 1897, *Deed Records,* 34: 528 and 560; see also, November 28, 1898, 38: 79.

109. *Galveston Daily News*, May 4, 1909. The footprint of the Sanitarium appears on the map; Sanborn Maps, UT, *Nacogdoches* (1912).

110. Ericson, *Fires and Firemen*, 66.

111. "1909 . . . Nacogdoches, Texas," Jubilee Pamphlets No.15, July, 1994, Printed by Old Town Printing, provided to the author by Mr. Charles Bright. [Notes supplied by Sally Batchelor, ETRC, M. M. Stripling, Noel Pack Thompson, and from Ericson, *Nacogdoches County Families*.]

112. Sanborn Maps, UT, *Nacogdoches,* 1912, 1921, 1922, 1929, 1929-1946.

113. *Daily Sentinel*, February 22, 1902. Borders, *Hanging*, 50. Partin, *et al*, *Nacogdoches,* 120-121.

114. *Daily Sentinel*, June 11, 1907.

115. *Daily Sentinel*, January 26, 1911, quoted in Partin, et al, *Nacogdoches*, 121.

116. Daily Sentinel, May 1, April 7, 1911.

117. "Architects vs. Construction Company," *Daily Sentinel*, June 9, 1911. The *Daily Sentinel* on July 4, 1911, reported the architects who submitted plans were A. J. Armstrong and Claibe Johnson of Shreveport; A. O. Watson, of Austin; A. D. Phillips of San Antonio; Green & Glover of Houston; W. Chamberlain of Birmingham; Lang & Weichel of Dallas, and A. M. Ponder of Dallas.

118. *Daily Sentinel*, July 12, Sept. 12, 1911. Minutes Commissioners Court Nacogdoches County, I: 9 and 14.

119. Otto H. Lang, (1864–1947) was born in Freiburg, Germany. Heather Watkins, "LANG, OTTO H., Handbook of Texas Online (Texas State Historical Association), http://www.tshaonline.org/handbook/online/articles/fla69.

120. December 9, 1912, *Minutes Commissioners Court, Nacogdoches County*, I: 148-153.

Chapter X: North Street After 1900

1. *Daily Sentinel*, Special Edition, November, 1906. List of pictures of Rulfs buildings in the 1906 Special Edition include: West End School; Mayer & Schmidt Building; Main Street Presbyterian Church; Burk-Crain Furniture; Kaplan Building; Cason-Monk Hardware; Tucker, Zeve & Dotson; H. T. Burk Buildings; J. M. Weeks and E. M Weeks; Banita Hotel; the G. H. King Building; the First Baptist Church; Frank Summers House, Roland Jones House, and C. W. Butt House; Commercial Bank; Nacogdoches Grocery Company; John P. Davidson Building; First Brick Block (North Square).

2. Charles M. Raguet to Joseph E. Mayfield, May 27, 1880, *Deed Records*, V: 261-62. See also, Ancestry.com, *1880 United States Census* [database on-line] *Nacogdoches, Texas*; Roll: 1320; Family History Film: 1255320; Page: 163A; Enumeration District: 47. Ancestry.com. 1900 *United States Census* [database on-line] *Nacogdoches, Texas*; Roll: T623_1661; Page: 9B; Enumeration District: 41.

3. Several circumstances may have occasioned Mayfield's move to the east side of town. His first wife Winfrey Orton Mayfield committed suicide in 1895. He married Kate, his second wife, in 1897. [Bryan Davis, interview with the author, April, 2011.] Mayfield was a director of the First National Bank (West Square) before it closed, and for a while took up offices in the abandoned building, but according to the *Daily Sentinel* of March 5, 1900, he was looking for new office space. He temporally leased a house on Mound Street in 1900, according to the 1900 Census Records. [Ancestry.com. *1900 United States Census* [database on-line] Nacogdoches, Texas; Roll: T623_1661; Page: 9B; Enumeration District: 41.] In 1909, Dr. Mayfield and his wife moved to San Antonio where he died in 1924. Ericson, *Gateway* III, 561. "Doctors of Nacogdoches County," C97, in Ericson, *Nacogdoches County Families,* 111.

4. *Daily Sentinel,* May 6, 1901. The Mayfield House did not appear on the Sanborn Maps until 1906. The Sanborn Maps never show the house as a 2 story house, consistently labeling the house 1-story. The Victor & Victory Survey, Site #186, more correctly classifies the house as 1-1/2 stories. A recent survey has the confusing and incorrect tag, "At some point after 1929, there was a second story added to the original structure." Nacogdoches Site Survey Online, http://www.sfasu.edu/heritagecenter/1314.asp.

5. His papers, especially the columns for the *Daily Sentinel*, are housed in the "Joseph E. Mayfield Collection," A-88, ETRC.

6. Mary Stewart Duncan, interview with the author, March, 1974. Mrs. Duncan was very familiar with the house as owned by first Mayfield and later by Reid., She lived a few houses east on Main Street. See Victor &Victor Survey, Site No. 186.

7. Hans-Rudolf Mengers (Stollhamm, Germany), correspondence with the author, August 4, 2010. Herr Mengers sent a series of historic postcards from the 1870s and 1880s.

8. Ericson, *Gateway* III, 758.

9. Charles Thompson died in 1977; Florence Thompson died in 1980. [Source Information: Ancestry.com. *Texas Death Index, 1903-2000* [database on-line], Original data: Texas Department of Health. *Texas Death Indexes, 1903-2000.* Austin, TX, USA: Texas Department of Health, State Vital Statistics Unit.] Virginia Nelson, conversations with the author, 1974-1976. [The Nelsons and the Thompsons almost always had lunch at the Fredonia Hotel on Sundays. On several occasions, they talked about old houses with the author.)

10. Paul Davis and Helen Davis Daniel, conversations with the author, 2004 and Spring, 2011.

11. *Galveston Daily News*, July 13, 1902. There is no documentation for the claim, in a recent brochure, that the house dates to the 1890s. ["The Nelson-Davis House, 552 East Main Street, Nacogdoches, Texas," (a handout, with no publisher, author, or date.)] The Nelsons did not own the property in the 1890s. (*Deed Records*, April 18, 1902, 49: 32.) The deed was not recorded until September 28. 1903. The house first appears on the map in 1906. Sanborn Maps, UT, *Nacogdoches,* 1906.

12. Dr. James G. Dickson, "A. A. Nelson," Ericson, *Nacogdoches County Families*, F744, 492-493.

13. Nolan Boles, "Report on the History of Nelson-Davis House, 522 E. Main, Nacogdoches, Texas," Research Paper in Dr. Jere Jackson's Local History Class, May 9, 2005. Paper based on interviews with Paul Davis, Helen Davis, and Dr. Robert W. Gruebel.

14. *Daily Sentinel*, April 12, 1902. "Miss Fannie Nelson purchased D. J. E. Mayfield lot fronting on Main Street $1500."

15. Bryan Holt Davis, interview with author, March 14, 2011.

16. *Daily Sentinel*, August 19, 1903.

17. Mary Stewart Duncan, interview with the author, March 1974.

18. Rulfs used the paired windows on the Wilson, Dr. A. A. Nelson, and Mayfield houses. He frequently used front gable with chamfered bay room underneath. The architect used a slip-head window on the front; the full length window gave access to the porch from the front room. The fanlight windows with shingle texturing around them were used on the East and West End Ward Schools and in such houses as the Stephen Blount home. This house appears as Site No. 189 on the Victor & Victor Survey, 522 Main St. East, City Block 17, Lot 4

19. For the recent property history, see Nacogdoches Central Appraisal District, Property ID 22993, http://www.nacocad.org/. Dr. Robert W. Grubel and his wife Jo Ellen Carlson purchased the house on May 19, 1995. For additional pictures of the house today, see Nacogdoches Sites Survey Online, http://www.sfasu.edu/heritagecenter/1315.asp.

20. John B. Nelson purchased the lot in 1890 for $250 from the Raguet heirs [*Deed Records*, November 28, 1890, 28: 7]; he transferred it to his wife in 1892 [*Deed Records*, September 12, 1892, 30: 115]. The value placed on the structure was $1400.

21. For material on Dr. A. A. Nelson, see the section on "Doctors," C97, Ericson, *Nacogdoches County Families*, 101-118. Dr. Albert Aldrich Nelson's son, Albert Langston Nelson, followed his father into the practice of medicine and surgery in Nacogdoches. *See also*, Ericson, *Gateway* III, 651-652.

22. There are two interview sources of information on this house: Mary Stewart Duncan and Dr. Langston Nelson. The interviews with Mrs. Duncan took place in Spring 1974. The conversations with Dr. Langston and Virginia Perkins Nelson, on which the author recorded notes, took place between 1972 and 1976. These memories have received recent confirmation in interviews with close friends of the Nelsons. Bryan and Caroline Davis, interviews with the author, April, 2011. For published biographical information on Langston and Virginia Nelson, see Perkins, *Perkins,* 379 *ff.*

23. The Nelson House is not on the 1891 map, but clearly appears on both the 1896 and 1900 maps as a small three-room house; the 1906 and 1912 maps show the house as remodeled, but without the carport which does not appear until the 1922 map. Sanborn Maps, UT, *Nacogdoches,* (1891 to 1922). Victor & Victor Survey, Site No. 222.

24. Ericson, *Nacogdoches County Families,* C97, 101-118. A. A. Nelson (1814-1892), the surveyor, was the grandfather, not the great grandfather, of A. A. Nelson the medical doctor. The surveyor's son was John Brooks, (1847-1929), and A. A. Nelson was J. B. Nelson's son. A. A. Nelson (the surveyor), therefore, was Langston's great-grandfather. See Ericson, *Gateway* III, 651-652; also Dr. James G. Dickson, "A. A. Nelson," in Ericson, *Nacogdoches County Families*, F744, 492-493.

25. March 20, 1973, *Deed Records*, 381: 417. May 22, 1981, *Deed Records*, 206: 302. For the property history from 1991, see NCAD, Property ID 22866, http://www.nacocad.org/.

26. "C. W. Butts," *Daily Sentinel*, Special Edition, November 1906. James Butts (unmarried) lived with Charles and his wife. Ancestry.com, *1910 United States Census* [database on-line] *Nacogdoches, Texas*; Roll: *T624_1581*; Page: *18A*; Enumeration District: *0093*; Image: *80*; FHL Number: *1375594.*

27. *Daily Sentinel,* April 14, 1903.

28. *Daily Sentinel*, May 8, 1908; July 29, 1909.

29. Peggy Wright, "A History of The Cum Concilio Club, 1894-1996," (Nacogdoches, Texas: Privately Printed, 1996).

30. *Daily Sentinel*, October 24, 1929. See also, Ericson, *Fires and Firemen, 104-105.*

31. Ericson, *Fires and Firemen*, 89-90. The fire was on April 14, 1924.

32. A copy of the holograph map by Karle Wilson Baker of North Street, with additions by her daughter Charlotte Baker Montgomery, was given to the author by Edward "Jerry" Baker. The original is in the Baker-Montgomery Private Archives.

33. Ericson, *Gateway* III, 899-900; Ericson, *Nacogdoches County Families*, 659-660. Although both were called "Frank," John Franklin Summers (1850-1921) is not to be confused with Jesse's son, his nephew, William Franklin Summers (1875-1956).

34. September 4, 1896, *Deed Records*, 33: 529-531. January 22, 1901, but not recorded until February 11, 1915; *Deed Records*, 86: 6. For the advertisement, see *Daily Sentinel*, September 19, 1901.

35. For the Jesse Summers House, see Chapter IV; for the William Frank Summers House (1906) and the Tom Summers House (1913), see later in the present chapter.

36. Sanborn Maps, UT, *Nacogdoches,* 1912. The 1912 Sanborn Map was the first to extend this far up North Street.

37. Ericson, *Gateway* III, 1034.

38. E. Whitaker to Woodall, January 18, 1900, *Deed Records*, 40: 12. Woodall to Power, August 11, 1904, *Deed Records*, 54: 232. For information on Power, see Ericson, *Gateway* III, 727.

39. The Tilfords did not move into the house until sometime during or immediately after World War I; they are listed there in the 1920 census records; father & mother were aged 43 and Gillette was 17. Ancestry.com. *1920 United States Census* [Database online] *Nacogdoches, Nacogdoches, Texas,* Roll: T625_1835; Page: 1A, Enumeration District: 123, Image: 701.

40. "Tildon Tilford Papers," A-114, ETRC.

41. *Daily Sentinel*, March 4, 1902.

42. Ericson, *Gateway* III, 893.

43. Dennis Michael Bradford, "The House That Sam Built: The Stripling Family and Stripling's Drugstore" (Master of Arts Thesis, SFASU, 2000), 36 [hereafter cited as Bradford, "Stripling"].

44. See Chapter VIII. "New Drug Store," *Daily Sentinel,* May 17, 1901.

45. Perkins Drugstore in the First Brick Block (1884), M&S Building (1888), Perkins ("Steamboat") House (1898), Haselwood House (1912), "Tanglewood" (1902), Stripling House on North Street (1905), Crouch-Stripling House (1898).

46. *Daily Sentinel*, January 3, 1905.

47. Craig Stripling, conversations with the author, Spring and Summer of 2011. Photographs from the family collection are used by permission of Craig Stripling.

48. Ericson, *Fires and Firemen*, 51-52. *Daily Sentinel*, December 24, 1906. In the article on the north square deduction, the Stripling loss was listed: "Stripling, Hazelwood & Co., druggests, stock and fixtures $40,000; insurance $15,000."

49. Ericson, *Fires and Firemen,* 53-54; *Daily Sentinel,* May 16,1907.

50. In an earlier advertisement, E. A. Blount described the Laura Blount House this way: "I have for rent . . . a nice six room cottage near my home. E. A. Blount." *Daily Sentinel*, September 9, 1903. For a description of the Laura Blount Chapman House, see Chapter IV.

51. For the dissolution of the Crouch-Simpson Insurance Agency, see *Daily Sentinel*, November 26, 1906. For information on T. J. Williams, see the section on "Commercial National Bank" in the *Daily Sentinel*, Special Edition, November 1906. See also, Maurine Crouch McKinney, "Crouch, William Hill, Sr.," in Ericson, ed, *Nacogdoches County Families,* 246-247. There is an early picture of the house on page 246.

52. For a good account of the Crouch-Stripling House's story, see "Another Landmark to Disappear From Scene," *Daily Sentinel*, October 25, 1960.

53. Sam Black, Jr., b. 20 June 1907 in the Laura Chapman Blount House; William Benjamin (1910), Jane (1911), Morgan Malcom [Mack] (1913), Elizabeth (1916) were all born in the Crouch-Williams-Stripling House. See Ericson, *Gateway* III, 893. Mrs. Elizabeth Stripling, known as Lizzie, died in 1917 shortly after the birth of her daughter Elizabeth. According to the *Daily Sentinel*, she was " a prominent and useful" citizen who was "universally popular." *Daily Sentinel*, November 9, 1917. See also, Bradford, "Stripling," 23.

54. See more texts, *Nacogdoches Star*, July 22, 1892; *Daily Sentinel*, April 26, 1910.

55. Ancestry.com. *1900 US Census* [database on-line], *Nacogdoches, Nacogdoc hes, Texas*; Roll: T623_1661; Page: 17A; Enumeration District: 41. In the Census, his name is spelled with one "t", but most frequently it is spelled with two "tt" as done in the *Daily Sentinel* and Ericson, *Gateway* III, 555-556. In 1910, the family is shown next door to the First Baptist Church. Ancestry.com. *1910 United States Census* [database on-line] *Nacogdoches, Texas*; Roll: *T624_1581*; Page: *3A*; Enumeration District: *0095*; Image: *150*; FHL Number: *1375594.*

56. Sanborn Maps, UT, *Nacogdoches,* 1906. Designated on the 1900 Sanborn Map, there is a street on the lot that Matthews would purchase in 1905. Sanborn Maps, UT, *Nacogdoches,* 1900.

57. Partin, *A Pictorial History,* 49 and 67.

58. *Daily Sentinel*, April 9, 1963. The Sanborn Insurance Maps do not cover the section of North Street where Tipton Ford Motor Company now stands until the 1929 editions. Sanborn Maps, UT, *Nacogdoches*, 1929.

59. Bryan Holt and Carolyn Davis, interview with the author, April 14, 2011.

60. Memoirs of Bill Wilson, December 16, 1992, as reported in Perkins, *Perkins*, 263-264.

61. The author has a post-Victorian image of this house, but it is not good enough to print.

62. Perkins, *Perkins,* 162-164. According to Dorothy Perkins, John and his mother and baby sister went to live with Hardeman, Elizabeth and their family in Rusk County after Richard Crump Perkins (W. U.'s Brother) died. John went to school in Rusk County and to a private school "Summer Hill Select School." He moved to Nacogdoches about 1894. He attended the University of Texas School of Pharmacy and received his PHG in 1898. In 1905, John married Lucy Alice Turner. He and Charles Perkins, his uncle, sold their shares in Perkins Brothers in the period from 1905-07. John later went into the insurance business after his health failed. He died in 1937.

63. The first Sanborn Map to show houses north of Starr Avenue was 1929. In 1966, when Chuck and Ann Phillips purchased the John Hardeman Perkins House, the house had already been pulled down the hill to Pearl Street to make room for commercial development on North Street.

64. Victor & Victor Survey, Site No. 1145. The 1986 survey incorrectly estimated the date of this house as 1915-1925. The 1910 and 1920 census records show John Perkins at this address. Dorothy Perkins is also mistaken about their residence on North Street; it is consistent with 1910 and 1920 Census records. Ancestry.com. *1910 United States Census* [database on-line], Justice Precinct 1, *Nacogdoches, Texas*; Roll: T624_1581; Page: 1A; Enumeration District: 0095; Image: 146; FHL Number: 1375594. 1920 *United States Census* [database on-line]. *Nacogdoc hes, Nacogdoches, Texas*; Roll: T625_1835; Page: 1A; Enumeration District: 123; Image: 701.

65. *Daily Sentinel,* August 1, 1911.

66. Ericson, *Gateway* III, 84. In the 1910 Census, the Guy Blounts were living on the corner of North and Power Streets, possibly in the Laura Blount Chapman House. [Ancestry.com. *1910 United States Federal Census* [database on-line]. *Nacogdoches, Texas*; Roll: T624_1581; Page: 2B; Enumeration District: 0095; Image: 149; FHL Number: 1375594.]

67. There is a wonderful photograph of the Pontifical Field Mass held to side of this house when the 1936 Texas Centennial Committee placed a marker on the property for the site of Mission Guadalupe. See, McDonald, *Pictorial History,* 100.

68. Information and clarification of the family businesses supplied by Edward "Jerry" Baker, in correspondence and conversations with the author, Fall, 2010.

69. The Wettermark House, where the Hayters lived, had a *porte-cachere.* The family would have known the advantages of a covered exit from a vehicle. Carports came into use in the Midwest by 1909; they were in general used by Prairie School architects by 1913. "Carport," Wikipedia, The Free Encyclopedia, http://en.wikipedia.org/w/index.php?title=Carport&oldid=395374564, accessed December 17, 2010.

70. Judy Buckingham, interview with the author, December 3, 2010. *Daily Sentinel,* Haltom in 1928.

71. *Affidavit,* dated June 3, 1935, testified by Jas. N. Thomas and W. U Perkins, *Deed Records,* 139: 123. For the deed see, William P. Fears and wife to J. Hayter, October 9, 1886, *Deed Records,* X: 495. Giles Haltom confirmed these records in a speech he gave on August 25, 1926; the speech was later published under the title "Nacogdoches 50 Years Ago Was Small Compared to Present," *Daily Sentinel,* December 8, 1928. See also, NCAD, Property ID 23727, http://www.nacocad.org/.

72. Ancestry.com. *1920 United States Census* [database on-line], *Nacogdoches, Nacogdoches, Texas*; Roll: *T625_1835*; *1A*; Enumeration District: *123*; Image: *701*. Listed in the household at the time of this 1920 Census were: head of household, Mary Hayter (60), head of the household; her son Sam (40), his wife Penelope (26), daughter Martha (2), and daughter Penelope (10 months) [Sam and Penelope's daughter Mary Elizabeth was born later in 1920, and Sam, Jr. in 1924.]; Mary's unmarried son Robert Hayter (33); her brother William W. Hall (54); and finally, servants Ida Childress (39) and Clifford Hayter (21).

73. Victor & Victor, Site No. 1055, at 1411 North Street. The house is also discussed in the National Register survey of the town's architectural assets. NCAD, Property ID 23727, http://www.nacocad.org/. The Hayters acquired the property in 1886 and did not sell it until 2010.

74. "Hayter House closes doors," *Daily Sentinel,* August 23, 2005; "Farechild's doors closing for good," *Daily Sentinel,* May 27, 2008.

75. Eric Jakimier, interview with the author, April 21, 2011.

76. Marie Leonard, "Student Apartments to Feature Hayter House," *Daily Sentinel,* May 6, 2011. See also Erin McKeon, "New student housing will blend old with new," *Daily Sentinel,* September 13, 2010; *Daily Sentinel,* August 10, 2011; Erin McKeon, "Bringing the old in with the new," *Daily Sentinel,* November 9, 2011.

77. Ericson, *Gateway* III, 407.

78. Sarah A. Carraway (widow of T. J. Carraway) to C. A. Hodges, *Deed Records,* 77: 372. For earlier deeds, see Voight to Weaver, *Deed Records,* U: 34; Weaver to T. J. Caraway, *Deed Records,* 30: 512.

79. The original house can be seen on the Sanborn Map of 1912; the remodeled footprint does not appear until the thorough revision of the maps in 1929. Sanborn Maps, UT, *Nacogdoches,* 1912, 1929.

80. The Hodges House, as it existed on North Street, was familiar to the author because of its identification by Mary Stewart Duncan. Because of the moves and the extensive revisions to the exterior appearance, however, its whereabouts was not known until the Windhams approached the author at the opening of the remodeled Rulfs Office in December 2010.

Chapter XI: Washington Square After 1900

1.The W. H. Whited House (1929) now occupies the property. The structure, originally by architect Shirley Simons, was later remodeled in the 1970s by architect Rayford Stripling. See also, Nacogdoches Sites Survey Online, 711 North Mound, http://www.sfasu.edu/heritagecenter/889.asp, accessed September 15, 2011 [Victor & Victor Survey, No. 1016].

2.Sarah Jacks*on, Baker,* 6-7. Ericson, *Gateway* III, 1022-1026. Kate Floy (Kate Florence Montgomery) was W. T. Wilson's wife. Only two of the Wilson's five children survived: Karle (1878-1960) and Ben T. (1881-1961).

3. Wilson originally purchased the land in two parts from G. A. and Lollie King and J. E. and Kate Gaston [March 16, 1901, *Deed Records,* 41: 281 and March 21, 1901, 42: 549], but there was a mistake in the actual tracts of land being transferred, and both tracts had to be recertified two years later [November 17, 1903, *Deed Records,* 53: 24].

4. Quoted in Sarah Jacks*on, Baker,* 40.

5. In 1927, the Bakers built a new house on North Street and named it "West Windows." In the same year, Baker became the president of Commercial Guarantee Bank. Sarah Jacks*on, Baker,* 63.

6. Karle Wilson Baker, *The Birds of Tanglewood* (College Station: Texas A & M University Press, 2006), 177. The Center for East Texas Studies at Stephen F. Austin State University edited this reprint of Mrs. Baker's work; the edition has comments by Sarah Jackson.

7. Sarah Jacks*on, Baker,* 177.

8. Ericson, *Nacogdoches County Families,* 110.

9. *Daily Sentinel,* January 8, 1908. After the 1908 fire, Dr. Hyde first moved to the new Weeks building and then in 1911 moved his offices to the Blount building. Dr. Carl Henry Rulfs moved his practice first to Lufkin and then eventually to San Augustine. Anna Kathryn Holbrook (his daughter), Ericson, *Nacogdoches County Families,* 580. In 1907, Carl Rulfs was the last Captain of the Stone Fort Rifles.

10. Ericson, *Gateway* III, 292.

11. *Daily Sentinel*, Special Edition, November, 1906.

12. *Daily Sentinel*, Special Edition, November, 1906.

13. Emily Harris (granddaughter of Frank Summers) and Florence Patton (granddaughter of Tom Summers), e-mail correspondence and interviews with the author, October 10, 22, 25, 2010. Ericson, *Nacogdoches County Families*, 660

14. Ancestry.com, *1910 United States Census* [Database Online] *Nacogdoches, Texas*; Roll: T624_1581; Page: 3A; Enumeration District: 0096; Image: 178; FHL Number: 1375594.

15. Zachary T. Mast (father) to Hollis Mast, *Deed Records*, June 1, 1910, Vol. 68, 536. Ericson, *Gateway* III, 552.

16. Hollis Mast Barron, interview with author, May, 1976. Ericson, *Gateway* III, 384. The Victor & Victor Survey, Site No. 785, incorrectly states that the house was built for Hollis Mast's second wife Prudie; it was built for Kate Mast. Hollis and his second wife Prudie later had two children: Henry Wilson, born in 1916, who lived only a week, and Travis, who was born in 1918 just before Hollis died. Ericson, *Gateway* III, 551.

17. Hollis Mast Barron, interview with author, May, 1976.

18. Ancestry.com, *1920 United States Census* [Database Online], *Nacogdoches, Texas*, Roll: T625_1835; Page: 5B; Enumeration District: 124; Image: 724.

19. November 15, 1918. Ancestry.com, *Texas Death Index, 1903-2000* [Database Online], Texas Department of Health, State Vital Statistics Unit. "The pandemic lasted from June 1918 to December 1920, spreading even to the Arctic and remote Pacific islands. Between 50 and 100 million died, making it one of the deadliest natural disasters in human history." Wikipedia contributors, "1918 flu pandemic," Wikipedia, The Free Encyclopedia, http://en.wikipedia.org/w/index.php?title=1918_flu_pandemic&oldid=435995304.

20. Hollis Mast Barron, interview with author, May, 1976.

21. NCAD, Property 22790, http://www.nacocad.org/.

22. *Daily Sentinel*, August 2, 1901. *See also*,, Ancestry.com, *1920 United States Census* [Database Online], *Nacogdoches, Nacogdoches, Texas;* Roll: T625_1835; Page: 5B; Enumeration District: 124; Image: 724.

23. The original house was probably built by John H. Burford. Burford and his wife Libby purchased the property from R. A. Hall in 1902 for $1000 [May 22, 1922, *Deed Records*, 45: 540.] When Burford sold the lot to Haselwood in 1904, the value was $2,500 [January 14, 1904, *Deed Records*, 49: 241].

24. Ancestry.com, *1910 United States Census* [Database Online]. *Nacogdoches, Texas*; Roll: *T624_1581*; Page: *6B*; Enumeration District: *0096*; Image: *185*; FHL Number: *1375594*. Richard A. Hall, who speculated in houses and owned many rental properties, purchased the property as part of a plan to develop lots in the area. He sold the lot to John and Libby Burford in 1902 for $1000. [R. A. Hall and Effie A. Hall to Jno. H. Burford and Libby Burford, May 22, 1902. *Deed Records,* 45: 540.] When the Burfords sold the property to the Haselwoods in 1904, the price was $2500. [*Deed Records*, 49: 241.]

25. Gladys Hardeman, conversations with the author, 1970s. Mrs. Mary Stewart Duncan also confirmed her uncle's design.

26. Archives of the First United Methodist Church, examined by the author in May of 2011. There are photographs of the house and a bronze plaque, which adorned the front of the house at one time.

27. Paint analysis, undertaken in 1980 when house was remodeled as an antique shop, revealed the original paint colors; medium gray with light gray trim. Electricity existed in the house prior to the 1912 remodeling. The author replaced the rotten wood front steps with the present brick steps. The handrails and the finials date from that time, also. *See also,* information on siding patterns at this web site: Western Wood Products Association, "Standard Patterns," http://www.wwpa.org/patterns/sections/g16.pdf.

28. The author owned the house from 1972 to 1992. NCAD, [Database Online] Property No. 22757, http://www.nacocad.org. *See also,* Victor & Victor Survey, Site No 1018. Although the city no longer uses the V&V site numbers, both the 1986 and 1990 survey material, including some new pictures, can be found at Nacogdoches Sites Survey Online, http://www.sfasu.edu/heritagecenter/892.asp.

29. Miss Gladys Hardeman, conversations with the author, 1970s.

30. Ericson, *Gateway* III, 900.

31. Florence Patton, conversations with the author, in 1970 and more recently in 2010. For an affidavit on this property, taken by F. I. Tucker, with Gladys Hardeman, see May 11, 1970, *Deed Records*, 361: 1646.

32. Nacogdoches Sites Survey Online, http://www.sfasu.edu/heritage-center/821.asp. The recent survey of the area (Summer, 2011), as reported, is inaccurate or at minimum misleading. (It is more correctly reported in the earlier surveys by Victor & Victor, Site No. 445.) First, no Sanborn Maps included this part of Nacogdoches, above Hospital Street, until 1906, even though a few of the larger houses on Mound Street appeared in a special section in 1900. Second, the house at 304 North Church, contrary to the statement, does appear on the 1906 map and again on the 1912 map—admittedly, as the one-story Sarah Bagley House. On both the 1921 and 1922 maps, the Bagley House, not the remodeled Summers House, is still shown. All of the houses on Church Street are correctly shown on the 1929 Sanborn Map.

33. Gladys Hardeman (the author's next door neighbor), interview and conversations with the author, early 1970s. Jimmy Sanders (grandson of the Haralsons), interview with the author, June, 1980. Ancestry.com, *1910 United States Census* [Database Online]. *Nacogdoches, Texas*; Roll: T624_1581; Page: 6A; Enumeration District: 0096; Image: 184; FHL Number: 1375594. *1920 United States Census* [Database Online]. *Nacogdoches, Nacogdoches, Texas*; Roll: T625_1835; Page: 7B; Enumeration District: 124; Image: 728. *1930 United States Census* [Database Online]. *Nacogdoches, Nacogdoches, Texas*; Roll: *2379*; Page: *24A*; Enumeration District: *3*; Image: 119. The text on the Richardson house in the Victor & Victor Survey, Site No. 447, contains a number of mistakes. The author can find no records that indicate Charles or W. U. Perkins ever lived in this house. They did build or at least supervised the house's construction for their older sister, Sarah Alice Perkins Richardson, but according to census records, Sarah Alice, her son, Charles, and daughter, Elizabeth were the ones who lived in the house: Alice until her death in 1922; Charles until the late 1920s; and daughter, Elizabeth Richardson Seale, and her family throughout the 1930s. In the 1930 Census, Charles had moved to a boarding house on Main Street. In 1944, the Richardson family sold the house to William Haralson.

34. Sanborn Maps, UT, *Nacogdoches,* (1906, 1912 1921, 1929). The problem with the Sanborn Maps on Church Street is that the company did not consider this part of Nacogdoches important until the building of the new Central School in 1904. While the houses on Church Street were all built by the mid-1890s, the Sanborn Maps do not reach the areas north of Hospital Street until 1906, with the exception of a few houses on Mound Street. The 1906 and 1912 maps show this house to be a one-story house, but it was always 1½ stories; the 1921 map finally showed it as being 1½ stories, which ironically, it had ceased to be; no doubt, the dormer finally convinced the mapper that it was 1½ stories. Finally, in 1929, the footprint of the house is shown with straight lines.

35. Jere Jackson, "The SFA Story," an online history of the university, http://cets.sfasu.edu/story/founders/Sept6/PineTreeHymn.html.

36. Alice Richardson died in 1922 and Charles E. Richardson died in 1942. Ancestry.com, *Texas Death Index, 1903-2000* [Database Online] Austin, TX, USA: Texas Department of Health, State Vital Statistics Unit.

37. Mary (Haralson) and Eugene Sanders, conversations with the author, June, 1974. *See*, NCAD, [Database Online] Property ID, 22754, http://www.nacocad.org.

38. Sanborn Maps, UT, *Nacogdoches,* 1922. There were several houses along the road, for instance the J. P. Suthpen House, close to the point where the road split into the Martinsville Road, but the Richard Orton family who had owned the land did nothing to develop the area. They tried to sell the land to Fannie Starr Nelson, but she preferred the city lot along East Main. The first Sanborn Map to include the area was 1922.

39. Ericson, *Gateway* III, 149.

40. Dianne House, "Imaginative renovation," *Daily Sentinel*, March 13, 1977. For pictures see, Nacogdoches Sites Survey Online, http://www.sfasu.edu/heritagecenter/861.asp.

41. Nacogdoches Sites Survey Online, http://www.sfasu.edu/heritagecenter/861.asp. [Victor & Victor Survey, Site No. 889].

42. The Cason children, while still living at home, were mature, if not yet married. Ancestry.com, 1920 *United States Census* [Database Online] *Nacogdoches, Texas* Roll: *T625_1835*; Page: *11A*; Enumeration District: *124*; Image 735.

43. Diane House, "Imaginative Renovation," *Daily Sentinel*, March 13, 1977. For the modern owners, see NCAD, [Database Online] Property No. 23129, http://www.nacocad.org/. The Stone heirs sold the house to the William N. Thornhills in 1971; John and Linda McKinney purchased it in 1976; Matt Lowe purchased the house in 1983. For pictures see, Nacogdoches Sites Survey Online, http://www.sfasu.edu/heritagecenter/861.asp.

44. Ericson, *Gateway* III, 552.

45. J. Roy Gray Collection, (A-152), ETRC. "J. Roy Gray Dies Today," *Daily Sentinel,* March 30, 1966. Charles Hoya Land Office Dedication Scrapbook. Sterne-Hoya House Museum and Library http://digital.sfasu.edu/cdm/compoundobject/collection/Stern-Hoya/id/210. *See also*, Nacogdoches Sites Survey Online, http://www.sfasu.edu/heritagecenter/852.asp.

46. Sanborn Maps, UT, *Nacogdoches,* (1922).

47. "Craftsman Perspective: A Guide to the History, Aesthetics, and Architecture of the Arts and Crafts Style," http://www.craftsmanperspective.com/history/america.html. *See also:* Paul E. Sprague. "Prairie school," *Grove Art Online*; *Oxford Art Online*, http://www.oxfordartonline.com/subscriber/article/grove/art/T069238; "Bungalow," Wikipedia, http://en.wikipedia.org/w/index.php?title=Bungalow&oldid=483888217; "Prairie School," Wikipedia, http://en.wikipedia.org/w/index.php?title=Prairie_School&oldid=458990811; Virginia and Lee McAlester, *A Field Guide to American Houses* (New York: Knopf, 1995); and Tony P. Wrenn, and Elizabeth D. Mulloy, *America's Forgotten Architecture* (New York: Pantheon Books, 1976).

48. Hollis T. Mast to Henry R. Mast, July 19· 1913, *Deed Records* 8: 388 ($750.00). Hollis Mast would probably not have sold this lot to anyone but his brother; the lot was only 90 feet wide, unusual for the time.

49. Tom Middlebrook, discussion with the author, November 6, 2010. The drawings provided have no elevation of the front façade or sides, just the foundation, roof, and floor plan. The plans have the following legend: "RESIDENCE FOR MR. HENRY R. MAST, NACOGDOCHES, TEXAS. EDWARD A. GEORGE, ARCHICTECT. SHREVEPORT, LOUSINANA. PLAN NO. 255. Date: 11/16/16."

50. Hollis Jean Mast, interview with the author, May, 1976.

51. *Ibid.*

52. NCAD, [Database Online] Property ID, 22791, http://www.nacocad.org. While the Methodist Church owned the house from 1941 to 1953, it was never their parsonage as stated in the National Register documents. From 1936 to 1973, the Haselwood House further up Mound Street was the Methodist Parsonage. See, Ericson, *Methodist History*, 23.

Chapter XII: Designs after 1917

1. Letter by Karle Wilson [Baker], *Daily Sentinel*, February 18, 1907.

2. Germany went into a military dictatorship, Russia went into two revolutions, and the United States left her isolation by entering World War I; all of these events changed the twentieth century.

3. Frederick Eby, *The Development of Education in Texas* (New York: Macmillan, 1925), 193-213. Sam Houston State University History, http://www.shsu.edu/~pin_www/history.html.

4. "EAST TEXAS NORMAL SCHOOL WANTED HERE," *Daily Sentinel,* March 13, 1915 . This meeting elected John Schmidt president, J. Thomas Hall secretary, and W. T. Wilson treasurer. *See also*, Jere Jackson, "The Citizens Committees," http://cets.sfasu.edu/story/founders/Aug16/CitizensCttees.html.

5. "Three New Normal Colleges Created," *Daily Sentinel,* March 17, 1915.

6. "Mass Meeting Held," *Daily Sentinel*, March 22, 1915.

7. *Daily Sentinel,* March 22, 1915.

8. "East Texas Normal Lost," *Daily Sentinel*, April 15 and 17, 1915.

9. "Mass Meeting Called for Tuesday Night," *Daily Sentinel,* March 17, 1917.

10. *Daily Sentinel*, March 21, 1917.

11. *Daily Sentinel,* April 6, 1917.

12. Bettye Herrington Craddock, *The Golden Years: [the First Half Century of Stephen F. Austin State University]* (Waco, Texas: Texian Press, 1973), 5-6.

13. Jackson, *The SFA Story,* "The Nacogdoches Case: The Twenty Three Reasons Why," http://cets.sfasu.edu/story/founders/23Reasons.html.

14. "NACOGDOCHES GETS THE NORMAL SCHOOL," *Daily Sentinel,* July 16, 1917.

15. Jackson, "Reactions in East Texas," http://cets.sfasu.edu/story/founders/Aug16/ET_Reacts.html.

16. Jackson, "The Charter Saved; Funding Lost," http://cets.sfasu.edu/story/founders/Aug16/Delay.html.

17. Jackson, "The Impact of SFA on Nacogdoches," 100th Anniversary Special Edition, *Daily Sentinel*, 1999. See also, *The SFA Story*, http://cets.sfasu.edu/story/campus/impact.html.

18. Jackson, "The Citizens Committees," http://cets.sfasu.edu/story/founders/Aug16/CitizensCttees.html.

19. Resolution, clipping from the *Daily Sentinel,* shared with the author by Anna Kathryn Holbrook in May of 1976.

20. Wilhemina Rulfs Thompson and Mary Stewart Duncan, interviews with the author, 1973-74.

21. John D. Rulfs, Jr. (grandson of William Henry Rulfs), interview with the author, July 12 and July 25, 2012. John's father's middle name, like his own, was "Diedrich," named after the architect. This next generation of the family has continued to have the same spelling problems D. Rulfs did. John D., Jr. said when he went to first grade, the teacher misspelled his name, and he never corrected her. Subsequently, both he and his father gave into the Anglicization by changing the internal "d" to a "t" and changing the "ie" to "ei."

22. For basic information, see Ericson, *Gateway* III, 791. Ancestry.com. *1900 United States Census* [Database Online] *Nacogdoches, Nacogdoches, Texas*; Roll: *1661*; Page: *6B*; Enumeration District: *41*; FHL microfilm: *1241661*. *1910 United States Census* [Datebase Online] Nacogdoches, Texas Roll: *T624_1581*; Page: *13A*; Enumeration District: *0096*; Image: *198*; FHL microfilm: *1375594*. For Bessie Rulfs, see *1920 United States Census* [Datebase Online] *Nacogdoches, Nacogdoches, Texas*; Roll: *T625_1835*; Page: *7A*; Enumeration District: *122*; Image: *681*.

23. Nacogdoches County to T. E. Baker and E. H. Blount, February 24, 1913, *Deed Records*, Vol. 79, 295.

24. Tom McKinney, "SFA's First Benefactor: Frank S. Aikman," *The SFA Story*, http://cets.sfasu.edu/story/founders/Sept6/Aikman.html.

25. "F. S. Aikman, Gym Donor, Succumbs; Death Ends Life, Love Charity for F. S. Aikman," *The Pine Log*, June 24, 1939. Lucille Fain, "A History of the Mahdeen Company," *Daily Sentinel*, 1985, copies in ETRC, Mahdeen Company Papers, B-35, Box 3, Folder 19.

26. "1907...Nacogdoches: The Mahdeen Company," Jubilee Pamphlets (Nacogdoches, Printed by Old Town Printing, nd [1990s]), provided to the author by Mr. Charles Bright.

27. Ruth Fouts Pochman to Victor B. Fain, July 15, 1985, ETRC, Corporate Records B-35, Box 3, Folder 18. (Mrs. Pochman was in one of the early graduating classes from SFASTC.)

28. ETRC, Mahdeen Company Papers, B-35, Box 3, Folder 19.

29. Baker, *et al* to John S. Wyatt, March 16, 1971, *Deed Records*, Vol. 366: 84. *See also,* NCAD, Property No. 23063, http://www.nacocad.org/.

30. Nacogdoches Sites Survey Online, http://www.sfasu.edu/heritagecenter/1157.asp, accessed April 4, 2012.

31. *Daily Sentinel*, April 24, 1908.

32. Both the Cox Building and the building to the east are on the map in 1891; Sanborn Maps, UT, *Nacogdoches, (1891).*

33. McDonald, *Stone Fort National Bank*, 30.

34. April 12, 1919, *Deed Records*, 97: 404. For information on the Woodmen of the World, see "History," http://www.woodmen.com/inside.cfm?main_menu_id=1&sub_menu_id=3&Page_Id=126. For a photograph of the Woodmen's float in the 1902 parade, see McDonald, *Nacogdoches: A Pictorial History*, 81.

35. "Specifications of a Three Story Brick Building 60 X 100, To be Erected on East Main Street in The Town Of Nacogdoches, Texas, For The Woodmen of the World, Liberty Elm Camp No, 210, According to the Plans Prepared by D. Rulfs, Architect," Public Notice No. 1876, September, 21, 1922, *Deed Records,* 105: 544-560. *See also*, Jackson, *"Woodmen of the World Building, 1922,"* Heritage Club Markers. Victor & Victor Survey (1986), Site 176, mistakenly estimated the date to 1915; the Jubilee Pamphlet, *"1923 . . . Nacogdoches"* dates the building to 1926. The building first appear on the Sanborn Maps, UT, *Nacogdoches,* (1929).

36. A wide variety of notes, mechanic's liens, and material liens on the building exist in the deed records of the Frank S. Aikman's Papers. He lent money to the Woodmen in the following amounts: $1770, $1725, $1680, $3090. ETRC, Corporate Archives, Mahdeen Company, 1912-1985, B53.

37. "Specifications," *Deed Records,* 105: 544-560.

38. NCAD, Property No. 22983, http://www.nacocad.org/.

39. Jackson, "SFA Moves to the North Street Campus," *The SFA Story*, http://cets.sfasu.edu/story/founders/Sept6.html.

40. The Davidson Building, in the Second Brick Block on East Main (1885, enlarged in 1889); First National Bank Building (1891); the original two-story brick commercial building at the corner of Pilar and Pecan, which now houses the Nacogdoches Municipal Offices (1891); a private home on North Street, south of the First Baptist Church (ca. 1900); the rebuilding of the Davidson Building on East Main after the fire which also destroyed the Mayer & Schmidt Building (1908-09).

41. Ancestry.com. *1910 United States Census* [Database Online] *Nacogoches, Texas*: Roll: T624_1581; Page: 6A; Enumeration District: 0095; Image: 156. Sanborn Map, UT, *Nacogdoches*, (1912).

42. Mary Stewart Duncan (niece of D. Rulfs), interview with the author, March, 1974. For the property records, see: May to Davidson, September, 26, 1904, *Deed Records*, 52: 537; W. H. Rulfs to Davidson, *Deed Records*, March 30, 1916, 87: 488; Blount and Baker to Davidson, February 7, 1917, *Deed Records*, 90: 64; Hamblin to Davidson, October 20, 1927, *Deed Records*, 119: 127. The Davidson Estate sold the property to R. G. Muckleroy July 13, 1936, *Deed Records*, 140: 607-615.

43. The Maria Davidson Apartment building appeared on the original listing in 1992 and has recently appeared on the Downtown National Register update. The four parts of the application are available online: http://www.sfasu.edu/heritagecenter/624.asp. The latest comments on the Davidson Apartments are Property No. 96, Section 8, Page 64, http://www.sfasu.edu/heritagecenter/documents/Downtown_NR_Section_8_pp_51-80.pdf.

44. *Ibid.*

45. Ancestry.com, *1920 United States Census* [Database Online], *Nacogdoches, Texas*, Roll: T625_1835; Page: 5B; Enumeration District: 124; Image: 724.

46. This statement would apply to the houses for Guy Blount, Mary Hayter, J. Roy Gray, Blum Mast, and Henry Mast.

47. Adlai Mast, Jr., conversations with the author, 1972-1975.

48. Brian Bray, Nacogdoches Historic Preservation Officer, correspondence with the author, November 15, 2010.

49. *Daily Sentinel*, April 30, 1962.

50. Gladys Hardeman and A. T. Mast, Jr., conversations with the author, 1972-1976.

51. Ericson, *Gateway* III, 355.

52. Jackson, "The Campus Property," *The SFA Story*, http://cets.sfasu.edu/story/campus/Index.html, accessed April 5, 2012. The Halls, evidently, continued to live in the house until the early 1920s. See Ancestry.com, [Database Online] *1920 US Census*, Nacogdoches, Texas: Roll: T625_1835; Page: 11B; Enumeration District: 124; Image: 736.

53. See the illustration in Chapter II, Figure 2.31.

54. "Building Plan . . . D. Rulfs, Architect,"D. K. Cason Estate Papers, ETRC.

55. Ericson, *Gateway* III, 56. Baxley, who began as a young man as an accountant with Mayer & Schmidt's department store, was employed at the Nacogdoches Wholesale Grocery Company by the time the house was built.

56. Ancestry.com, [database on-line], *1910 United States Census, Nacogdoches, Texas*; Roll: *T624_1581*; Page: *11B*; Enumeration District: *0096*; Image: *195*; FHL microfilm: *1375594*. *1920 United States Census, Nacogdoches, Nacogdoches,* Texas; Roll: T625_1835; Page: 5A; Enumeration District: 124; Image: 723. *1930 US Census, Nacogdoches, Nacogdoches, Texas*; Roll: 2379; Page: 7A; Enumeration District: 2; Image: 41.

57. D. K. Cason to Robert Cason, May 30, 1923, *Deed Records*, No. 7587, 146: 402. (This deed was not recorded until March 31,1938!) D. K. Cason to Willie Maud Cason Baxley, July 10, 1924, *Deed Records,* No. 426, 112: 414.

58. Mrs. Robert Cason, "Dick Kendall Cason," and "Robert Nance Cason," in Ericson, *Nacogdoches County Families*, 203-204. Willie Maud married Austin Weldon Baxley on 12 April 1917 and had 2 children: Emily Baxley, born 30 January 1922, and Maudell Baxley, born 18 November 1923. Robert Nance Cason married Nellie Mae Ballard on 10 November 1921 and had two children: Winell, born 4 October 1925, and John Robert, born 29 June 1927. *See also*, Ericson, *Gateway* III, 56, and 149.

59. Digital Sanborn Maps, 1929, *Texas: Nacogdoches*, Sheet 8.

60. Nacogdoches Historic Sites Online, http://www.sfasu.edu/heritagecenter/854.asp.

61. NCAD, Property No. 23131, http://www.nacocad.org/.

62. Ericson, *Gateway* III, *821.*

63. Ancestry.com, [database on-line]. *1910 United States Census, Nacogdoches, Texas:* Roll: T624_1581; Page: 1B; Enumeration District: 0096; Image: 175; FHL Number: 1375594. *1920 United States Census, Nacogdoches, Nacogdoches,* Texas; Roll: T625_1835; Page: 5A; Enumeration District: 124; Image: 723. *1930 United States Census, Nacogdoches, Nacogdoches, Texas*; Roll: 2379; Page: 7A; Enumeration District: 2; Image: 41.

64. Sanborn Maps, UT, *Nacogdoches,* (1929).

65. *1920 Census, op. cit.*

66. Ericson, *Gateway* III, 821. *See also*, Stephen B. Tucker, "Stephen B. Tucker," Ericson, *Nacogdoches County Families*, F1094, 678. Stephen Tucker's marriage to two of the Sharp daughters, Rosine and Lucille, makes for a confusing family tree. Stephen and Rosine had three children: Stephen B., Frank Sharp, and Anna Mary Tucker. Lucille, the second wife, was the divorced wife of Stephen Tucker's cousin, Fred F. Tucker and had one son, Fred F. Tucker, III, at the time he moved into his grandmother's house.

67.Ancestry.com. *1930 United States Census* [database on-line]; *Nacogdoches, Nacogdoches, Texas*; Roll: 2379; Page: 19A; Enumeration District: 2; Image: 65.0.

68. Susan Shindler, correspondence with the author, November 18, 2010. Lucette Sharp died in 2010. Confirmed by Senator Kay Bailey Hutchison in correspondence with the author, July 26, 2013.

69. October 1, 1943, *Deed Records*, 159: 379. [Frank Sharp had died *intestate,* leaving the house to Mamie Shindler Sharp.] Dr. Stephen B. Tucker died in 1977; Lucille Tucker died in 1990. [Oak Grove Cemetery Records, information supplied by Carolyn Ericson to the author.]

70. December 16, 2004, *Deed records*, 2176:183.

71. Ericson, *Gateway* III, 821. *See also*, "Kay Bailey Hutchison," Wikipedia, The Free Encyclopedia, http://en.wikipedia.org/w/index.php?title=Kay_Bailey_Hutchison&oldid=468833084; William Addams Reitwiesner, "The Ancestors of Kay Bailey Hutchison," http://www.wargs.com/political/bailey.html.

72. See Chapter IV for the R. C. Shindler House, the E. A. Blount House, and the Laura Blount Chapman House on North Street; Chapter V for the Stephen W. Blount House; Chapter X for his brother Guy Blount's home; and this chapter for the Mamie Shindler Sharp House; Chapter VIII for Blount commercial properties.

73. Ericson, *Nacogdoches County Families*, F99, 171; and Ericson, *Gateway* III, 83-84. See also, "Eugene H. Blount," [Legislative Reference Library of Texas] *Texas Legislators: Past & Present*, http://www.lrl.state.tx.us/legeLeaders/members/memberDisplay.cfm?memberID=2299&searchparams=chamber%3 Note%3D%26leg%3D%26party%3D%26roleDesc%3D%26Committee%3D.

74. Turner, *Nacogdoches in the Jazz Age*, 88-89.

75. "Historic and Architectural Resources of Nacogdoches," *Texas Historic Sites Atlas*, National Register Listing, "Eugene H. Blount House," http://atlas.thc.state.tx.us/shell-county.htm, accessed April 5, 2012. For additional information on this house, *see*, Nacogdoches Sites Survey Online, http://www.sfasu.edu/heritagecenter/2066.asp.

76. The houses along the Gartenstrasse and districts west of the palace where Rulfs worked had these windows everywhere. The palace tower and guard house even had this window treatment. For an example, see the very good tour of Oldenburg photographs on the web at http://www.flickr.com/photos/62765694@N07/6026520762/in/photostream/.

77. Jean Baker, interview with the author, April, 1976.

78. "Eugene Harmon Blount." *Daily Sentinel*, November 25, 1927. "Funeral For Eugene H. Blount Today 2 to 4 O'clock. Episcopal Service," *Daily Sentinel*, November 26, 1927.

79. Turner, *Nacogdoches in the Jazz Age*, 90.

80. NCAD, Property No. 35885, http://www.nacocad.org/.

81. See, Chapter V for information on the Schmidt-Price House. *See also*, April 18, 1896, *Deed Records*, 33:320.

82. Sanborn Maps, UT, *Nacogdoches,* (1906, 1912, 1921, 1922)

83. *Daily Sentinel*, January 17, 1925. Gladys Hardeman, conversations with the author, 1972-1976.

84. The earliest surveys of Nacogdoches architecture (Victor & Victor, 1986) estimate the date of the house, but they miss it by ten years. The survey labels the architecture "folk Victorian." Having access to the Price Papers in the East Texas Research Center, the nomination to the National Register names Rulfs as the architect, unlike the earlier surveys, but the survey still dates the house to 1900-1910 and accepts the ETRC's vague dating of the remodeling to "the 1920s." *See*, Victor & Victor Survey, Site No. 1006; ETRC, Missouri Garrett Price Papers (A 27), Bundle 1.

85. Missoura Garrett Price Papers, 1884-1947, ETRC (A-27), Bundle 1. The archive has the hand-drawn plans by Rulfs for the first floor, second floor, southern and front elevations, specifications for rebuilding the burned residence of W. F. Price, and a map of the Price & Sturdevant Addition which is behind the Price House.

86. Milton Pitts, conversation with the author, November, 2011. See also, NCAD, Property No. 32122, http://www.nacocad.org/.

Chapter XIII: Reflections & Legacy

1. Mary Rulfs, born 27 September 1882 in Nacogdoches, died 5 April 1953; she Married Junius Charles Neyland (1883-1926). Mary had named her son Diedrich after her father. D. Neyland became an architect. See Margaret Arnold's article, "Neyland Plans to Pursue 'New Career,' Old Love," *Daily Sentinel*, August 26, 1980.

2. Ancestry.com. *Louisiana Statewide Death Index, 1900-1949* [database on-line]; Original data: State of Louisiana, Secretary of State, Division of Archives, Records Management, and History: *Vital Records Indices* (Baton Rouge, LA, USA.) At the time the *Daily Sentinel* announced his funeral plans, his age was just estimated.

3. *Daily Sentinel*, February 15, 1926.

4. *Ibid.* At the time of Johanne's death, the Pythians called Diedrich "one of the most active and consistent members of Knighthood in Nacogdoches and has long been cherished by his Brother Knights for his fidelity to the order he so much loves, and in this hour of great trouble and bereavement in the loss of the companion of his bosom." "Resolution of Sympathy, LaNanna Lodge No. 106," *Daily Sentinel*, 1918.

5. *Daily Sentinel*, February 16, 1926. On February 25, 1926, the *San Augustine Tribune*, repeated this quotation from the *Sentinel;* this news clipping, in the possession of Anna Kathryn Holbrook (granddaughter of D. Rulfs), was shared with the author in 1974.

6. There are numerous family members buried in Oak Grove Cemetery: Diedrich Anton Wilhelm Rulfs (1848-1926); his wife Johanne Böschen Rulfs (1849-1918); son Carl Henry Rulfs (1878-1955), son's wife, Anna Taylor Rulfs; their children: Lawrence D. Rulfs, Sr. (1912-1965), Diedrich Anton Rulfs (1913-1988), Infant (1907), Infant (1916), Milam Irion Rulfs (1922-1943 in WWII); granddaughter, Anna Kathryn Hollbrook (1917-2009). The family of half-brother William H. Rulfs (1860-1919): his wife Bessie Snell Rulfs (1873-1934); their children: Anita Rulfs (1897-1903); Gerhardt N. Rulfs (1894-1956); Lewis William Rulfs (1892-1963) and wife Gladys Sallie Evans (1899-1970); Audrey O. Rulfs (1906-1993); Arthur August Rulfs (1903-1986). The family of half-sister Sophia Rebecca Rulfs Wilkens (1862-1940); her husband John Wilken

(1858-1916), and their daughter, Annie Wilken (1899-1977). Many members of the family of Mrs. Johanna Rulfs rest in Oak Grove Cemetery: her mother Conradine Sophie Böschen-Stewart (1818-1887), her brother William Henry (Böschen) Stewart, and his daughter Mary Stewart Duncan (1883-1986), and others.

7. Houses known to be missing: Heitman, Davidson, Barham on North; W. H. Williams House on East Main [mentioned in the *Daily Sentinel*, October 3, 1905]. Rulfs designed numerous houses in adjacent towns, too.

8. Encyclopædia Britannica Online, s. v. "Architecture," accessed accessed January 8, 2012, http://www.britannica.com/EBchecked/topic/32876/architecture. See also, "Architecture," Wikipedia, The Free Encyclopedia, http://en.wikipedia.org/w/index.php?title=Architecture&oldid=469467977. "Marcus Vitruvius Pollio (born c. 80–70 BC, died after ca. 15 BC) was a Roman writer, architect and engineer, active in the 1st century BC. He is best known as the author of the multi-volume work *De Architectura* ("On Architecture"). See also, Wikipedia contributors, "Vitruvius," Wikipedia, The Free Encyclopedia, http://en.wikipedia.org/w/index.php?title=Vitruvius&oldid=468886886.

9. The Cason Estate gave their papers to the author and the Center for East Texas Studies which he heads. The author passed the papers on to the East Texas Research Center as the proper long range depository for the important collection.

10. Center for Palladian Studies in America, "Palladio and Architectural Patternbooks in Colonial America," http://www.palladiancenter.org/patternbooks.html, accessed May 20,, 2012. See also, Allison Frew and Charles Brownell, "Palladio in the Attic: 'Palladian' Motifs Retains Flexibilty Through Millennia of Varied Use," *Palladiana,* Vol. 4, No.1 (Fall, 2009).

11. Brent Hull, "Porch Details by the Book: Old catalogs yield clues to appropriate styles of columns and other millwork," http://www.oldhousejournal.com/Porch_Details_by_the_Book/magazine/1391.

12. James Stevens Curl, "Tuscan Order," [from *A Dictionary of Architecture and Landscape Architecture*, 2000] Encyclopedia.com, http://www.encyclopedia.com/doc/1O1-TuscanOrder.html.

13. "Also known as Archimedes' Constant." *See*, "Pi," Wikipedia, The Free Encyclopedia, http://en.wikipedia.org/w/index.php?title=Pi&oldid=469157922.

14. Masonic affiliations gleaned from Ericson, *Gateway* III.

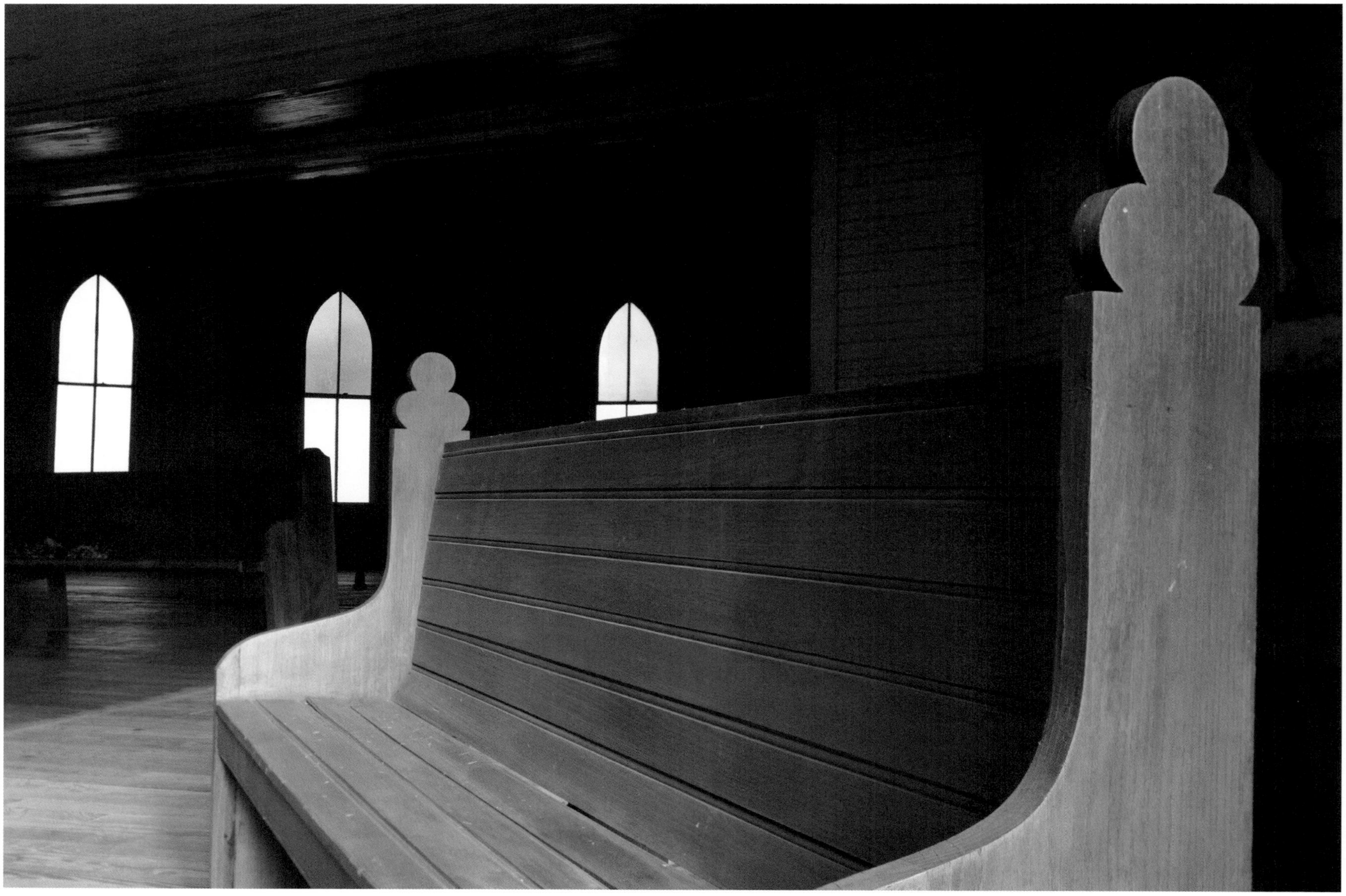

FIGURE 14.02 Pew designed and built by the Rulfs brothers for Zion Hill Baptist Church, 1914. This is one of the few remaining original pews left in the church after the congregation installed new pews after World War II. The gothic windows around the back of the narthex are in the background.

BIBLIOGRAPHY

Newspapers

Daily Sentinel, Nacogdoches, Texas

Dallas Morning News, Dallas, Texas

Fort Worth Gazette, Fort Worth, Texas

Galveston Daily News, Galveston, Texas

Houston Daily Post, Houston, Texas

Nacogdoches Chronicle, Nacogdoches, Texas

Nacogdoches News, Nacogdoches, Texas

Nacogdoches Plaindealer, Nacogdoches, Texas

Nacogdoches Star-News, Nacogdoches, Texas

Nacogdoches Star, Nacogdoches, Texas

Palestine Herald, Palestine, Texas

Shiner Gazette, Shiner, Texas

Archives and Collections

Ancestry.Com [Databases On-Line]. *Texas Death and Birth Records. United States Census Records:* 1880, 1900, 1910, 1920, 1930. *New Orleans Passenger Lists,* 1820-1945.

Baker, Edward Blount (Jerry). Private Photographic and Document Collection.

Baker-Montgomery Archive. Nacogdoches.

Bright, Charles. Private Photographic and Document Collection.

City of Nacogdoches, Historic Sites Survey [Online: http://www.sfasu.edu/heritagecenter/622.asp]:

- Downtown Historic District
- Sterne-Hoya District
- Virginia Avenue District
- Washington Square
- Zion Hill, Individual Properties
- Victor & Victor Survey (1986), Nacogdoches Historic Site Survey [Online: http://www.sfasu.edu/heritagecenter/2079.asp, accessed July 7, 2012].

Cox, Campbell. Private Photographic Collection

East Texas Research Center, Steen Library, Stephen F. Austin State University, Nacogdoches, Texas:

- Baker, Karle Wilson - Papers, 1800s-1963
- Blake, R. B. - Collection, 1628-1941
- Blount Family Papers, 1792-1967
- Blount, Lois Foster - Papers, 1750-1980
- Cason, D. K. - Estate Papers
- Christ Episcopal Church Collection, 1844-2004; Vestry Records, 1893 - Sept. 1901
- Colonial Dames XVII Century, James Haggard Chapter, Nacogdoches Records
- Crocket, George Louis - Papers, 1787-1960
- Gray, J. Roy - Collection
- Hardeman, Gladys - Research Collection, 1957-1965
- Index to Naturalization Records: 1851 – 1915
- Lindsey, Emily Virginia Willis - Papers, 1887-1958
- Mahdeen Company Papers
- Map Collection
- Mayfield, Joseph E. - Collection
- Nacogdoches Grocery Company Business Records
- Nacogdoches County Historical Records
- Newspapers
- Price, Missoura Garrett - Papers, 1884-1947
- Sanders, Vergie - Scrapbook
- Teutsch Early Nacogdoches Documents, 1800-1973
- Tilford, Tildon - Papers.

Handbook of Texas Online. [http://www.tshaonline.org/handbook/online].

Historic American Buildings Survey (HABS), Library of Congress. [Online: http://memory.loc.gov/ammem/collections/habs_haer/].

Methodist Church Archives, First United. Nacogdoches.

Nacogdoches Central Appraisal District. [Online Database: http://www.nacocad.org/default.htm]

Nacogdoches County Deed Records. Nacogdoches County Courthouse.

Nacogdoches County Land Records. [Online Database: https://www.texaslandrecords.com/txlr/TxlrApp/index.jsp].

Newspaper Archive Online. [http://newspaperarchive.com]

Historische Fotos zur Geschichte Oldenburgs (Historical Photographs on the History of Oldenburg). Alt Oldenburg ... endecken! (Old Oldenburg...Join us!). [http://www.alt-oldenburg.de/index.html].

Oldenburg State Archives, Oldenburg, Germany.

Sanborn Fire Insurance Maps – Nacogdoches 1885-1922 [Online: http://www.lib.utexas.edu/maps/sanborn/n.html].

Sanborn Digital Fire Maps, http://sanborn.umi.com/.

Sanborn Fire Insurance Maps - Texas (1877-1922), Perry-Castañeda Library Map Collection, University of Texas [Online: http://www.lib.utexas.edu/maps/sanborn/texas.html].

Sparks, Cecil. Private Phtographic Collection.

Stollhamm Church Records, Book 1832-1861, 503. [Consulted in the Church Rectory; now in the Oldenburg State Archives in Oldenburg, Germany.

Thorstensen, Pam. Private Photographic and Document Collection.

Texas Historical Sites Atlas. Texas Historical Commission [Online: http://atlas.thc.state.tx.us/].

Books

Alexander, D. B. , *Texas Homes of the Nineteenth Century.* Austin: University of Texas Press, 1966.

Andrews, Wayne. *American Gothic: Its Origins, its Trials, its Triumph.* New York: Vintage Books, 1975.

Baker, Edward B. (Jerry), ed. *The Bicentennial Commemorative History of Nacogdoches.* Nacogdoches: Nacogdoches Jaycees, 1976.

Baker, Karle Wilson. *The Birds of Tanglewood.* College Station: Texas A & M University Press, 2006.

Barber, George F. *Victorian Cottage Architecture: An American Catalog of Designs, 1891.* New York: Dover Publications, Inc., 1982. [Originally published by George Barber, *The Cottage Souvenir no. 2.* Knoxville, Tenn: S. B. Newman & Co, 1891.]

Barker, D. W. C. *A Texas Scrap-Book: Made Up of the History, Biography, and Miscellany of Texas and Its People.* New York: A. S. Barnes & Company, 1875.

Barr, Alwyn. *Black Texans: A History of Negros in Texas, 1528-1971.* Austin, Texas: Jenkins Publishing Co., 1973.

Bicknell, A. J. *Victorian Architectural Details.* New York: Dover Publications, 2005.

Bishop, Henry Halsall. *Architecture: Especially in Relation to Our Parish Churches.* New York and London: Society for Promoting Christian Knowledge, 1886.

Borders, Gary. *A Hanging in Nacogdoches: Murder, Race, Politics, and Polemics in Texas' Oldest Town, 1870-1916.* Austin: University of Texas Press, 2006.

Braun, Hermann and Michael Newmann. *Die Oldenburger Newstadtquartiere: Dobben und Haarenesch.* Oldenburg, Germany: Heinz Holzberg Verlag, 1978.

Bruner, Robert F. and Sean D. Carr. *The Panic of 1907: Lessons Learned from the Market's Perfect Storm.* Hoboken, New Jersey: John Wiley & Sons, 2007.

Bryant's Texas Almanac and Railway Guide: All About Texas, As It Was, As It Is!, and As It Will Be! (Dallas, Texas: W. N. Bryant, Editor and Publisher, 1879.

Burke's Texas Almanac and Immigrant's Handbook for 1883. Houston, Texas: J. Burke, 1883.

Butterfield, W. H. and H. W. Tuttle. *A Book of House Plans, Floor Plans and Cost Data of Original Designers of Various Architectural Titles, of Which Full Working Drawings and Specifications are Available.* New York: McBride, Nast & Company, 1912.

City of Nacogdoches, Nacogdoches County. Nacogdoches: Spradley & Hutt, Printers, 1895.

Brown, Nugent. *The Book of Nacogdoches County, July 1, 1927.* Nacogdoches, Texas: Nugent Brown Publisher, 1927. [Republished Nacogdoches: Ericson Press, 1986.]

Bruner, Robert F. and Sean D. Carr. *The Panic of 1907: Lessons Learned from the Market's Perfect Storm.* Hoboken, New Jersey: John Wiley & Sons, 2007.

Cording, Herman. *Als Oldenburg Noch Residenzstadt War: Stadtenwicklung and Stadtleben von der Grafenzeit bis zum Ende de grossherzoglichen Residenz im Jahre 1918.* Oldenburg: Ostendorp Verlag, 1985.

Comstock, William T. *Turn-of-the-Century House Designs: Details of 24 Residences* (New York: Dover Publications, 1994).

——. *Victorian Domestic Architectural Plans and Details: 734 Scale Drawings* (New York: Dover Publications, 1987.

Craddock, Bettye Herrington. *The Golden Years: the First Half Century of Stephen F. Austin State University.* Waco, Texas.: Printed by Texian Press, 1973.

Culbertson, Margaret. *Texas Houses Built by the Book.* College Station, Texas: Texas A&M Press, 1999.

Dede, Klaus. *Butjadingen: Landschaft, Kulturgeschichte, Information.* Bremen, Germany: Verlag Atelier im Bauernhaus, 1998.

Eby, Frederick. *The Development of Education in Texas.* New York: The Macmillan Company, 1925.

Ericson, Carolyn Reeves. *Fires and Firemen of Nacogdoches, Texas.* Nacogdoches: Pineywood Printing, 1976.

——. *Nacogdoches—Gateway to Texas: A Biographical Directory, 1881-1920,* Vol. III [CD, Computer File: LC 20100113]. Nacogdoches: Ericson Books, 2002.

——. *Sesquicentennial History of First United Methodist Church Nacogdoches, Texas 1837-1987.* Nacogdoches, Texas: Ericson Books, 1987.

——. Editor, *Nacogdoches County Families.* Dallas, Texas: Curtis Media Corp., 1985.

——, and Kathryn Hooper Davis. *1900 Census Nacogdoches County, Texas.* Nacogdoches, Texas: Ericson Books, 1989.

Fifield, James Clark. *The American Bar; Contemporary Lawyers of The United States and Canada.* Minneapolis, Minnesota: The James C. Fifield Company, 1918.

Fox, Stephen. *The Country Houses of John F. Staub.* College Station: Texas A&M University Press, 2007.

Francaviglia, Richard V. *Main Street Revisited: Time, Space, and Image Building in Small-Town America.* Iowa City: University of Iowa Press, 1996.

Goodrich, S. G. *A Pictorial Geography of the World.* Boston, Mass.: Charles D. Strong, 1856.

Hammer, Claus. *Oldenburg: Bilder Einer Stadt.* Oldenburg, Germany: Isensee Verlag, 2007.

Haltom, Richard W. *A History and Description of Nacogdoches County Texas* Nacogdoches, Texas, 1880. [Republished Austin: Jenkins Press, 1976.]

Hardeman, Nicholas P. *Wilderness Calling: The Hardeman Family in the American Westward Movement, 1750–1900.* Knoxville: University of Tennessee Press, 1977.

Hodgson, Fred. T. *Practical Bungalows and Cottages for Town and Country.* Chicago, Frederick Drake & Co, 1916.

Hopp, Michael P. *Straßen un Plätze in Oldenburg: Bilder und Fotos von Früher bis Heute.* Oldenburg, Germany: Isensee Verlag, 2008.

Jackson, Jere. *The SFA Story.* Online History of Stephen F. Austin State University. [http://cets.sfasu.edu/story/].

Jackson, Sarah Ragland. *Texas Woman of Letters: Karle Wilson Baker.* College Station: Texas A&M Press, 2005.

Jefferies, Matthew. *Politics and Culture in Wilhelmine Germany: The Case of Industrial Architecture.* Oxford: Berg Publishers, 1995.

Johnson, Frank White. *A History of Texas and Texans*, Vol. 4, Edited and Updated by Eugene C. Barker. Chicago and New York: American Historical Society, 1914.

Johnson, Frank White. *A History of Texas and Texans*, Vol. 5, Edited and Updated by Eugene C. Barker. Chicago and New York; American Historical Society, 1916.

Longhery, Mrs. E. M. *A Pen Picture of the City of Nacogdoches and Nacogdoches County: Their Present and Future.* Nacogdoches: Spradley and Hutt, Printers, 1895.

Longstreth, Richard. *The Buildings of Main Street: A Guide to American Commercial Architecture.* Updated Edition. Walnut Creek: AltaMira Press, 2000.

Loth, Calder and J. T. Sadler, Jr.: *The Only Proper Style: Gothic Architecture in America.* New York Graphic Society, 1975.

Lübbling, Hermann und Heinrich Kunst. *Das Oldenburgerland in Hundert Bildern von Gestern und Heute.* Oldenburg, Germany: Heinz Holzberg Verlag, 1977.

Mahony, Johnson and Cathey Searls, *Eugene Thomas Heiner: 19th Century Texas Architect.* Charleston, S.C.: Johnson Mahony, 2001.

McAlester, Virginia and Lee. *A Field Guide to American Houses.* New York: Knopf, 1995.

McDonald, Archie P. *Nacogdoches, Texas: A Pictorial History.* Virginia Beach, VA: Donning Company, 1996.

——. Editor. *Hurrah for Texas! The Diary of Adolphus Sterne, 1838-1851.* Waco, Texas: Texian Press, 1969.

——. *Sentinel of Service: Stone Fort National Bank.* Nacogdoches: Privately Printed by Regions Bank, 2003.

——, and Hardy Meredith. *Nacogdoches* (Images of America Series). Charleston, South Carolina: Arcadia, 2009.

——. Editor. *Nacogdoches: Wilderness Outpost to Modern City, 1779-1979.* Burnet, Texas: Eakin Press, 1980.

Martel, Gordon. Editor. *Modern Germany Reconsidered, 1870-1945.* London: Routledge, 1992.

Maxwell, Robert. *Whistle in the Piney Woods: Paul Bremond and the Houston, East and West Texas Railway.* Houston: Texas Gulf Coast Historical Association, 1963. [Reprinted Nacogdoches, Texas: East Texas Historical Association, 1998.]

Muchison, Bill, *Nacogdoches Past and Present: A Legacy of Texas Pride; a Photographic Documentary.* Odessa, Texas: B&C Publishing, 1986.

Palliser. *New Cottage Homes and Details.* New York: Palliser, Palliser & Co., 1887.

Palliser, Palliser & Co.'s *American Victorian Cottage Homes.* New York: Dover Publiations, 1990.

Palmer, W. T. *Seventy-Five Years in Nacogdoches: A History of the First Baptist Church, 1884-1959.* Dallas, Texas: The Dorsey Company, 1959.

Partin, James G. *Advancing the Kingdom Since 1884: A Pictorial History of the First Baptist Church of Nacogdoches, Texas.* Virginia Beach, VA: Donning Company, 2009.

Partin, James G. and Carolyn Reeves Ericson, Joe E. Ericson, Archie P. McDonald. *Nacogdoches: The History of Texas Oldest City.* Lufkin, Texas: Best of East Texas Publishers, 1995.

Perkins, Dorothy Neblett. *Descendants of Samuel, James, and Martha Perkins.* Rancho Santa Fe, California: Neblett Press, 1999.

Pierson, W. H., Jr. *American Buildings and their Architects: Technology and the Picturesque: Corporate and Early Gothic Styles.* Garden City, NY: Oxford University Press, 1978.

Reiff, Daniel D. *Houses from Books: Treatises, Pattern Books, and Catalogues in American Architecture, 1738-1950: A History and Guide.* University Park, Pa.: Pennsylvania State University Press, 2000.

Reinders-Düselder, Christoph and Elerd Udo. *Geschichte der Stadt Oldenburg.* v2. 1830-1995. Oldenburg, Germany: Isensee, 1996.

Rice, Lawrence D. *The Negro in Texas, 1874-1900.* Baton Rouge: Louisiana State University Press, 1971.

Rulfs Name in History ("Our Name in History Series" by Ancestry.com). Provo, Utah: Generations Network, 2007.

Runge, Wolfgang. *Die St. Nikolai Kirche in Stollhamm.* Oldenburg, Germany: Isensee, 1981.

Shoppell, R. W. et al. *Turn-of-the-Century Houses, Cottages, and Villas.* New York: Dover Publications, 1983.

Stanton, Phoebe B. *The Gothic Revival and American Church Architecture: An Episode in Taste, 1840–1856.* Baltimore: Johns Hopkins University Press, 1968.

Talbot, Christopher. *Nacogdoches: Then and Now.* Nacogdoches: Stephen F. Austin University Press, 2010.

Turner, Martha Ann. *Old Nacogdoches in the Jazz Age.* Austin, Texas: Madrona Press, 1976.

Turner, Suzanne and Joanne Seale Wilson. *Houston's Silent Garden: Greenwood Cemetery, 1871-2009.* College Station: Texas A&M University Press, 2010.

Victor, Sally S. et al, *Nacogdoches Historic Site Survey and Preservation Feasibility Study, 1986.* Austin, Texas: Victor and Victor Consultants, Inc., 1986.

Williamson, David G. "The Financial Crisis of 1873 and the Great Depression," *Bismarck and Germany, 1862-1890,* 2nd Edition. New York: Longman, 1998.

Wilson, Francis W. *The Hardeman Impact on Early East Texas.* Privately published, January, 1986.

Wrenn, Tony P. and Elizabeth D. Mulloy, *America's Forgotten Architecture.* New York: Pantheon Books, 1976.

Wright, Peggy. *A History of the Cum Concilio Club, 1894-1996.* Nacogdoches, Texas: Privately Printed, 1996.

Published Articles

"1896 . . . Nacogdoches, Texas." Jubilee Pamphlets. Printed by Old Town Printing, nd [1990s]. Provided to the author by Mr. Charles Bright. [The Historical Notes provided by Sally Batchelor (ETRC), *Daily Sentinel*, Ericson, *Nacogdoches County Families,* Mrs. & Mrs. Jack R. McKinney, Campbell Cox, Mrs. Delbert (Pyrtle) Teutsch.]

"1923 ... Nacogdoches, Texas." Jubilee Pamphlets (Printed by Old Town Printing, nd [ca. 1990s]. Provided to the author by Mr. Charles Bright.

"Prairie School," Wikipedia, The Free Encyclopedia, http://en.wikipedia.org/w/index.php?title=Prairie_School&oldid=458990811.

Alexander, D. B. "Influences in Texas Architecture," in *Historic Preservation in Texas: The Comprehensive Statewide Historic Preservation Plan for Texas,* Vol. I. Austin: Texas Historical Commission, 1973.

Battle, William James. "Kinsolving, George Herbert." *Handbook of Texas Online* [Texas State Historical Association], http://www.tshaonline.org/handbook/online/articles/fki30.

Blount, Lois Foster. "The Old Red House," *The Bicentennial Commemorative History of Nacogdoches*, 85-106. Nacogdoches, 1976.

Bright, Charles. "Nacogdoches Downtown Buildings," Notes by Charles Bright, 2003, made available to the author, Fall, 2010.

Brooks, H. 'The Early Work of the Prairie Architects", *Journal of the Society of Architectural Historians*, XIX (1960), 2–10.

Bucek, David C. , "The Architecture of Eugene T. Heiner (1852-1901)," unpublished study, cited on the Texas Historical Commission's site: Texas Historic Sites Atlas, Texas Historical Commission [Online Database].

"The Cultural Entities of Niedersachsen: Butjadingen." http://www.lancewadplan.org/Cultural%20atlas/LS/Butjadingen/butjadingen.htm.

Deaton, Charles. "The Post Offices and Postmasters of Nacogdoches County" *The Bicentennial Commemorative History of Nacogdoches,* 164-176. Nacogdoches, 1976.

Diner, Hasia. "Immigration and U.S. History." http://www.america.gov/st/peopleplace-english/2008/February/20080307112004ebyessedo0.1716272.html.

Ericson, Carolyn Reeves. "German Immigrants the Nacogdoches." *Yesterdays*, Nacogdoches Genealogical Society, Issue XXIV-2, September, 2004, 39-43.

Ericson, Carolyn Reeves. "Sacred Heart Parish at Nacogdoches." Ericson, *Nacogdoches County Families*, 50-51.

Ericson, Joe. "Nacogdoches Banks and Bankers." *The Bicentennial Commemorative History of Nacogdoches,* 191-194. Nacogdoches, 1976.

Evans, Elliot. "The East Texas House," *Journal of the Society of Architectural Historians,* Vol. XI, No.4, pp. 1-2.

Fain, Lucille. "The Old Nacogdoches University" *The Bicentennial Commemorative History of Nacogdoches*, 119-122. Nacogdoches, 1976.

Fox, Stephen. "HEINER, EUGENE T.," *Handbook of Texas Online* [Published by the Texas State Historical Association] http://www.tshaonline.org/handbook/online/articles/fhe48. Johnny Stucco, "The Courthouses of Eugene Heiner (1852-1901)," http://www.texasescapes.com/TexasCourthouses/Courthouses-of-Eugene-T-Heiner.htm.

Frew, Allison and Brownell, Charles. "Palladio in the Attic: 'Palladian' Motifs Retains Flexibilty Through Millennia of Varied Use," *Palladiana*, Vol. 4, No.1 (Fall, 2009).

"Grand Duchy of Oldenburg, 11th edition of *Encyclopaedia Britannica,* [Online Resource; Google Books], http://1911encyclopedia.org/Oldenburg,_Germany_(Grand-Duchy).

Holbrook, Anna Kathryn. Granddaughter of D. Rulfs. Ericson, Carolyn, *Nacogdoches County Families* (Dallas, Texas: Curtis Media Corp., 1985), F909.

Ivy, Melinda Ann Crain. "History of Nacogdoches Newspapers." *The Bicentennial Commemorative History of Nacogdoches*, 195-198. Nacogdoches, 1976.

Jackson, Jere Langdon. "A Case for the Landmark Committee." *Daily Sentinel*, January 27, 2011.

——. "The Daily Sentinel at 100: The Impact of SFA on Nacogdoches." *Daily Sentinel*, July 1, 1999.

——. "Nacogdoches' Visible Past: A Review Of Some Of Our Architectural Heritage." *The Bicentennial Commemorative History of Nacogdoches*,199-23. Nacogdoches: Nacogdoches Jaycees, 1976.

——. "The Important Year of 1917." *Daily Sentinel*, August 9, 1998.

——. "The Nacogdoches Case: The Twenty-Three Reasons Why." *Daily Sentinel*, August 16, 1998.

——. "SFA Opens on Washington Square," *Daily Sentinel*, August 30, 1998.

——. "The Transformation of Nacogdoches between 1890 and 1923: The Legacy of Architect D. Rulfs." *Daily Sentinel.* September, 1999.

——. "Zion Hill: An Endangered Species," *Daily Sentinel*, October, 1999.

Jeffrey, Jonathan. "The Stephen William Blount House." *Daily Sentinel*, July 3, 1988.

"Jones, Roland, House." Texas Historic Sites Atlas, Nacogdoches: National Register Properties Application. [http://www.sfasu.edu/heritagecenter/documents/NR_Individual_-_Jones_Roland_House.pdf.

King, Anthony D. "Bungalow," *Grove Art Online* (Oxford Art Online). http://www.oxfordartonline.com:80/subscriber/article/grove/art/T012273.

Kemp, L. W. "Blount, Stephen W." *Handbook of Texas Online* (http://www.tshaonline.org/handbook/online/articles/fbl31).

Maxwell, Robert S. "Nacogdoches and the Railroads." *The Bicentennial Commemorative History of Nacogdoches.* Nacogdoches: Nacogdoches Jaycees, 1976.

McKinney, Tom. "The Stone Fort Rifles." *East Texas Historical Journal*, March, 2013.

"Oldenburg," *The Encyclopaedia Britannica: A Dictionary of the Arts, Sciences, and General Literature*, Vol. XVII. Chicago: Peale Company, 1891.

"Oldenburg," Wikipedia, The Free Encyclopedia, http://en.wikipedia.org/w/index.php?title=Oldenburg&oldid=367712025 (accessed June 17, 2010).

"Peter II, Grand Duke of Oldenburg," Wikipedia, The Free Encyclopedia, http://en.wikipedia.org/w/index.php?title=Peter_II,_Grand_Duke_of_Oldenburg&oldid=360604368.

Sprague, Paul E. "Prairie school." In Grove Art Online. *Oxford Art Online,* http://www.oxfordartonline.com/subscriber/article/grove/art/T069238.

"Stadtgeschichte (Nordenham History)", http://www.nordenham.de/en/tourismus-und-freizeit/stadtgeschichte.html.

Tindall, Willie Earl. "Religion: Recollections & Reckonings." *The Bicentennial Commemorative History of Nacogdoches*, 85. Nacogdoches, 1976.

Texas. General Land Office. 1881. *Map of Nacogdoches County.* [Austin, Tex.]. General Land Office, c1881. Library of Congress Geography and Map Division Land Use Maps.

"Washington Square Historic District," *National Register of Historic Places,* 1989. Accessed through the *Texas Historic Sites Atlas* on the Texas Historical Commission website (http://atlas.thc.state.tx.us/index.asp).

"Wilhelmshaven," Wikipedia, The Free Encyclopedia, http://en.wikipedia.org/w/index.php?title=Wilhelmshaven&oldid=376732892.

United States Department of the Interior, National Park Service, National Register, "Historic and Architectural Resources of Nacogdoches, Texas" and "Community Planning and Development in Nacogdoches: 1830-1940," http://pdfhost.focus.nps.gov/docs/NRHP/Text/64500647.pdf.

Zucker, Paul. "Architectural Education in Nineteenth Century Germany." *The Journal of the American Society of Architectural Historians.* Vol. 2, No. 3 (Jul., 1942), 6-13.

Unpublished Sources

Boles, Nolan. "Report on the History of Nelson-Davis House, 522 E. Main, Nacogdoches, Texas," Research Paper in Dr. Jere Jackson's Local History Class, May 9, 2005. Paper based on interviews with Paul Davis, Helen Davis, and Dr. Robert W. Gruebel.

Bradford, Dennis Michael. "The House That Sam Built: The Stripling Family and Stripling's Drugstore." Master of Arts Thesis, SFASU, 2000.

Devine, Joe. "Original Site of Sacred Heart Catholic Church, 1847-1936, Nacogdoches, Texas." Application for a Texas Historical Marker #09NA06. Texas Historical Commission, Vertical Files (2009), Austin, Texas.

Dickey, Susan Jean, "F. E. and Oscar Ruffini: Texas Architects," PhD Dissertation. Lubbock, Texas: Texas Tech University, 1993, 17-42.

Hardeman, Gladys , "The History of Melrose," Gladys Hardeman Collection A-69, East Texas Research Center, Ralph Steen Library, Stephen F. Austin State University.

Jackson, Jere Langdon. "D. Rulfs: Master Architect of Nacogdoches." Opening Session (Held in Zion Hill Baptist Church), East Texas Historical Association. Fall Meeting, Nacogdoches, 1980.

——. "From Wood to Brick: Nacogdoches at the Turn of the 20th Century." Lectures on Downtown Nacogdoches to Promote Texas Preservation Week, May 3, 2004.

——. "Photographic Survey of Downtown Nacogdoches," Application for National Endowment for the Arts, 1981. Unfunded Project, Photographic Survey 1-003715.

——. "The Roland Jones House: A Texas State Historical Landmark." Dedication Program with History, December 29, 1973. Nacogdoches County Historical Survey Committee: Privately Printed.

——. "Walking Tours of Downtown Nacogdoches." Nacogdoches: Privately Printed, 1973, 1980-1985.

Kulhavy, Pamela Aronson. "A Survey of Nacogdoches Hotels 1830 – 1910." Unpublished Research Paper, December, 1980. Jackson Local History Seminar. Vertical Files. East Texas Research Center, Steen Library, Stephen F. Austin State University, Nacogdoches, Texas.

Mengers, Hans-Rudolf. "Genealogy of Gerhard Wilhelm Rulfs, Meister in Stollhammerwisch," sent to the author in correspondence, June, 2010.

McKinney, Tom. "SFA's First Benefactor: Frank S. Aikman." The SFA Story, http://cets.sfasu.edu/story/founders/Sept6/Aikman.html.

——. "The George F. Ingraham Building." Application to the Texas Historical Commission for Recorded Texas Historic Landmark, 1998, Marker No. 12099.

——. "The Redland Hotel." Unpublished Research Paper. Center for East Texas Studies, 1996-98.

Nichols, Jr., James L. "History of the First United Methodist Church Of Nacogdoches, Texas." Pamphlet written in 1987, Methodist Church Archives.

Partin, James. "The First Baptist Church, Nacogdoches, Texas." Application for a Texas Historical Marker, Vertical Files (2009), Austin, Texas.

——. "A History of Nacogdoches and Nacogdoches County, Texas to 1877." Master of Arts Thesis. Austin: University of Texas, 1968.

Phillips, Charles ("Chuck"). "The Roland Jones House." Application to the Texas Historical Commission for Texas State Historical Landmark Status." Verticle Files. 1972.

Spears, Carolyn. "The Old Stone Fort and The Stone Fort Museum." Application for Recorded Texas Historic Landmark Marker (Renewal), Texas Historical Commission, January, 2008.

"Specifications for Residence of Roland Jones, Nacogdoches, Texas, 1896-7," Texas Historical Commission Archives, File No. 3822-A, Austin, Texas.

Historical Marker Research by the Author

Jackson, Jere Langdon. Applications for Texas Historical Markers. Approved by the Texas Historical Commission. Applications on File in Austin Texas.

——. "Alton W. Birdwell," THC Marker #12097, 1999.

——. "Austin Building," THC Marker #9245, 1993.

——. "Battle of Nacogdoches (August 2, 1832)," THC Marker #9252, 1979.

——. "Birdwell Field, Aikman Gym and the Women's Recreation Center," THC Marker #15425, 2009.

——. "Burrows - Millard House," THC Marker #9256, 1976.

____. "Diedrich Anton Wilhelm Rulfs," THC Marker #14540, 2008.

——. "Durst - Taylor House," THC Marker #9270, 1994.

——. "First United Methodist Church," THC Marker #9273, 1977.

——. "Karle Wilson Baker," THC Marker #13945, 2007.

——. "Los Ojos de Padre Margil (The Eyes of Father Margil)," THC Marker #9283, 1978.

——. "Milam Lodge #2, Ancient Free and Accepted Masons of Texas," THC Marker #14133, 2008.

——. "Millard - Lee House," THC Marker #9285, 1974.

____. "Nacogdoches *Daily Sentinel,"* THC Marker #12NA04, 2012.

——. "Nacogdoches Federal Building," THC Marker #12101, 1999.

——. "Nicholas Adolphus Sterne," THC Marker #9357, 1976.

——. "Nine Flags of Nacogdoches," THC Marker #14312, 2008.

——. "Oak Grove Cemetery," THC Marker #12102, 1999.

——. "Old Nacogdoches University Building," THC Marker #16000, 2008.

——. "Old North Church Cemetery," THC Marker #12103, 1998.

——. "Original Location of Sacred Heart Catholic Church," THC Marker #16002, 2009.

——. "Pioneering Higher Education in East Texas," THC Marker #12104, 1999.

——. "Rusk Building," THC Marker #12106, 1998.

——. "Sam Houston's First Home in Texas," THC Marker #15904, 2009.

——. "Sparks House," THC Marker #9353, 1976.

——. "Stephen Fuller Austin," THC Marker #9246, 1993.

——. "Sterne House," THC Marker #14549, 1977.

——. "Stone Fort Museum," THC Marker #14842, 2008.

——. "Thomas Jefferson Rusk," THC Marker #12105, 1998.

——. "Thomas Jefferson Rusk" THC Marker #14491, 1998.

——. "Tol Barret House," THC Marker #9249, 1981.

——. "University Tradition in Nacogdoches," THC Marker #12108, 1999.

——. "Washington Square," THC Marker #12109, 1986.

——. "Washington Square: First Home of SFASTC," THC Marker #9401, 1999.

——. "Westminster Presbyterian Church," THC Marker #15980, 2009.

——. "Zion Hill Baptist Church Cemetery," THC Marker #12110, 1999.

——. "Zion Hill First Baptist Church," THC Marker #9403, 1976.

Jackson, Jere Langdon. Research and Markers Written for the Nacogdoches Heritage Club and the Texas Historical Commission. Grant, 2003.

——. "Cason, Monk & Company (1906)."

——. "Church Street."

——. "Commerce Street."

——. "Cotton Exchange Building (1898)."

——. "Cox Building: Branch-Patton Hardware (1888)."

——. "Cox Building: Stone Fort Bank (1891)."

——. "Cox-Cason Building: Tobacco Warehouse (1900)."

——. "D. Rulfs: Master Architect of Nacogdoches (1848-1926)."

——. "*Daily Sentinel's* First Home (1900)."

——. "Davidson Building (1908)."

——. "First National Bank of Nacogdoches (1890)."

——. "Hoya Buildings (1900),"

——. "Jenkins Seed Store."

——. "Johnson Furniture (1899-1900)."

——. "M. G. Hazle Building (1901)."

——. "Mayer & Schmidt Building (1908)."

——. "Old Wettermark Bank Building (1896)."

——. "Opera House (1889 and 1923)."

——. "Plaza Place: Original Mayer & Schmidt Location."

——. "Rebuilding the North Square (1907)."

——. "Redland Hotel (1906-1907)."

——. "Walking Tour of the Square: Old Liberty Hotel."

——. "West Side of the Square."

——. "Woodmen of the World Building (1922)."

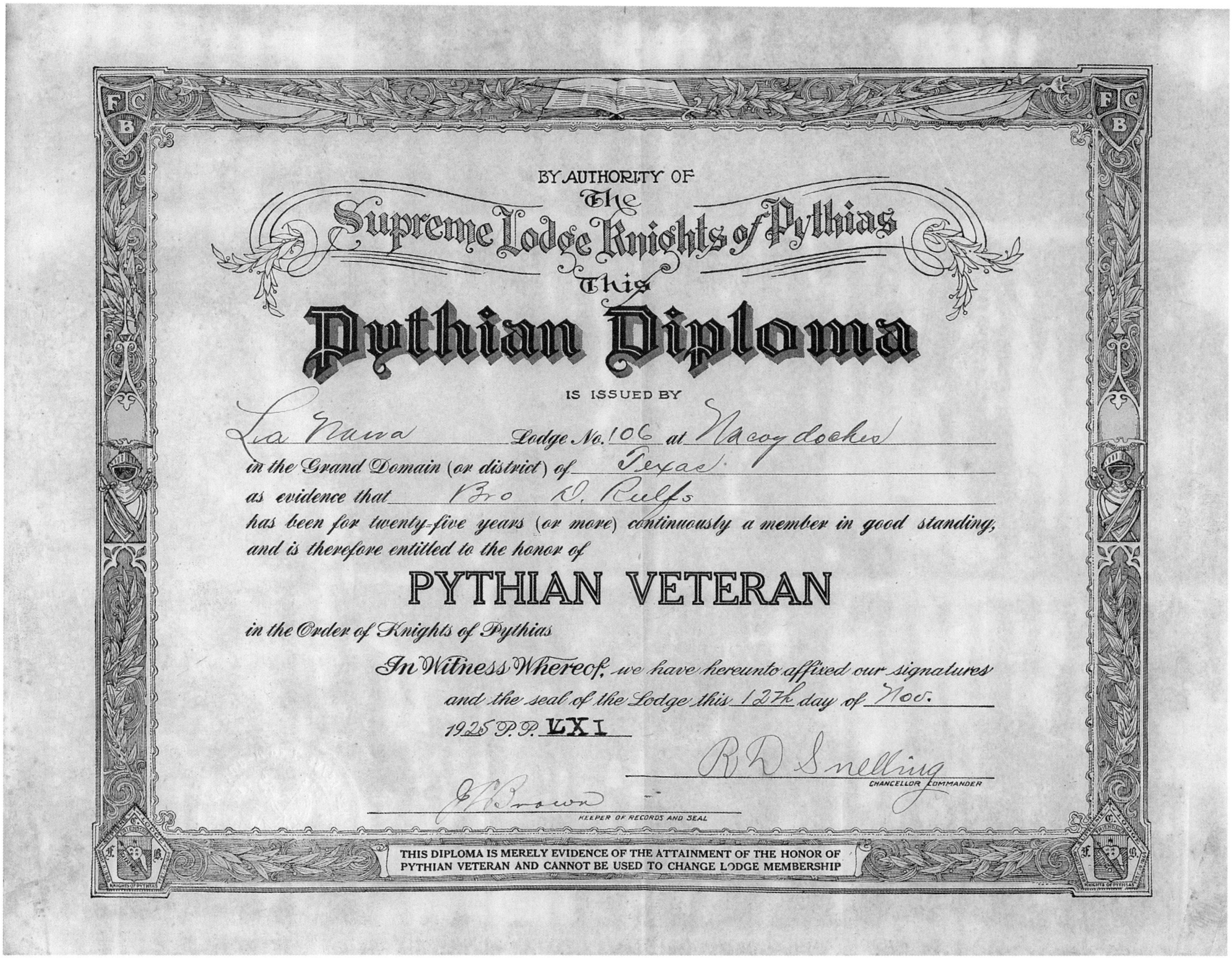

BY AUTHORITY OF

The

Supreme Lodge Knights of Pythias

This

Pythian Diploma

IS ISSUED BY

La Nana Lodge No. 106 at Nacogdoches

in the Grand Domain (or district) of Texas

as evidence that Bro D. Rulfs

has been for twenty-five years (or more) continuously a member in good standing, and is therefore entitled to the honor of

PYTHIAN VETERAN

in the Order of Knights of Pythias

In Witness Whereof, we have hereunto affixed our signatures and the seal of the Lodge this 12th day of Nov.

1925 P.P. LXI

R D Snelling

CHANCELLOR COMMANDER

Brown

KEEPER OF RECORDS AND SEAL

THIS DIPLOMA IS MERELY EVIDENCE OF THE ATTAINMENT OF THE HONOR OF PYTHIAN VETERAN AND CANNOT BE USED TO CHANGE LODGE MEMBERSHIP

FIGURE 14. 03. Pythian Diploma for "Bro. D. Rulfs," 12 November 1925.

Even on an important document such as this, notice that his fellow veterans in the Knights of Pythias used the initial "D" for the architect's first name instead of Diedrich.

This is the type of documentation which only exists in private hands unless families make the item available through deposit in the archive at Stephen F. Austin State University – The East Texas Research Center. Family collections are kept together, indexed, and placed in protective covers and acid-free boxes. This image shown above, scanned by the author in 1976, was lent to the author by Anna Kathryn Hollbrook, the granddaughter of D. Rulfs.

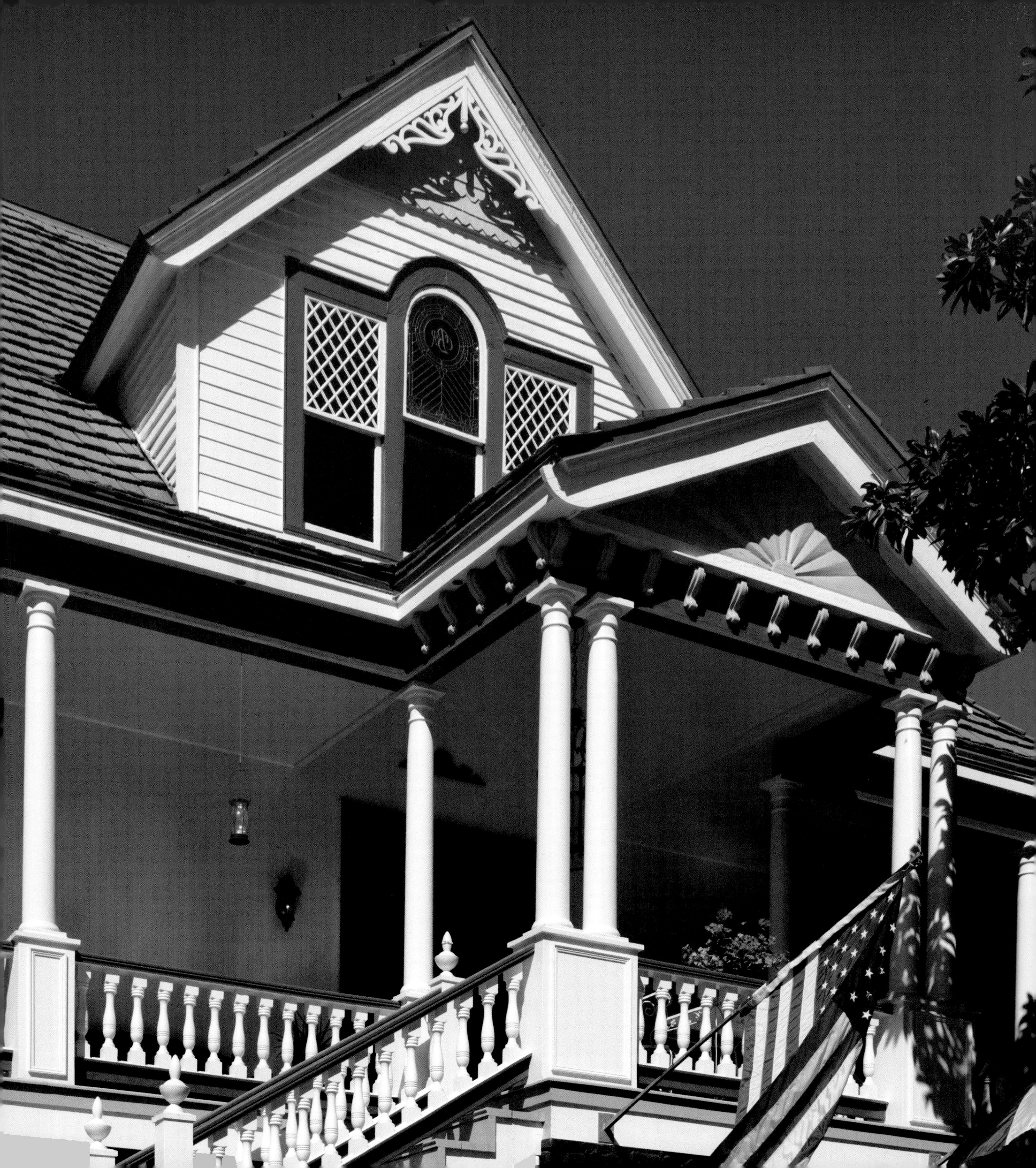

INDEX

*Entries in **bold type** refer to illustrations.

A

B

C

D

E

F

G

H

I

J

K

L

M

N

O

P

Q

R

S

T

U, V

W

X, Y, Z

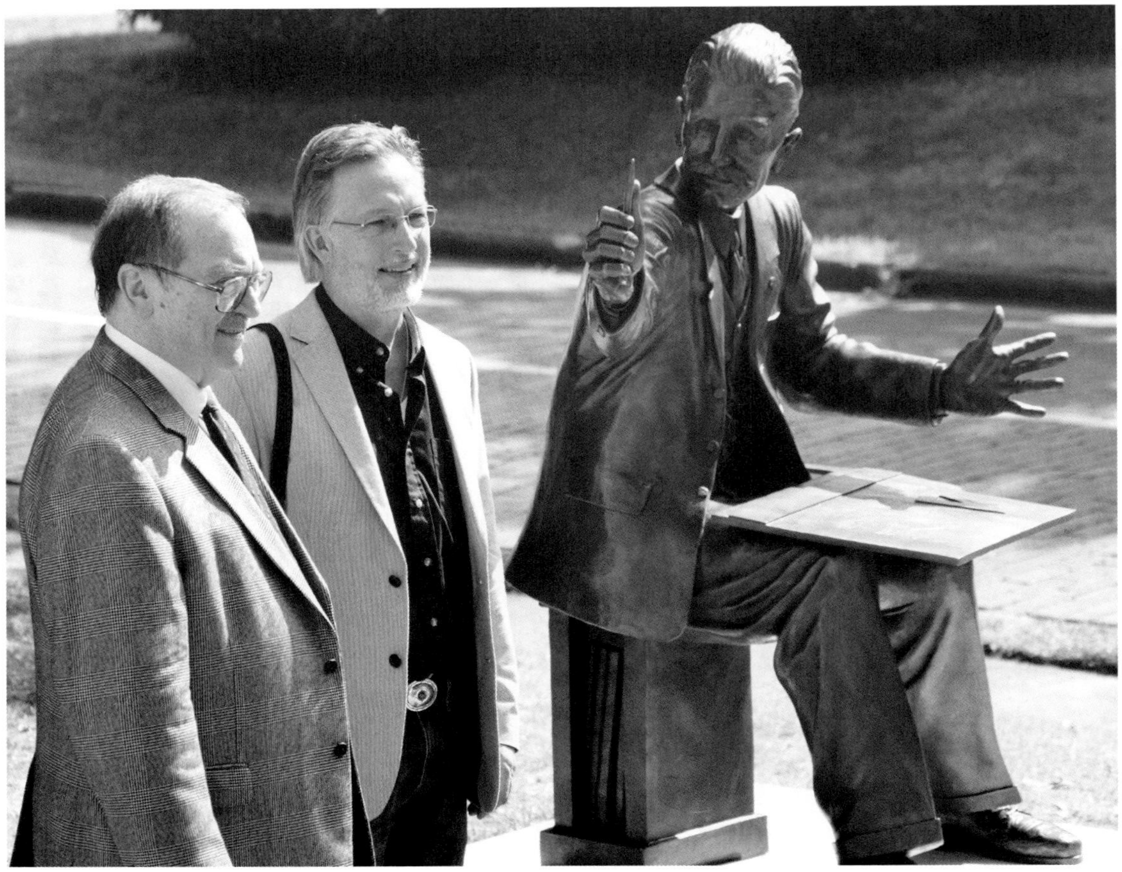

FIGURE 15.2 (Left) Dedication of the D. Rulfs Statue

On August 29, 2013, a statue of Diedrich Rulfs by sculptor Michael Pavolsky of Fort Worth, was dedicated in front of the Roland Jones House at 141 North Church Street. The house, designed and built by Rulfs in 1896-97, is one of the architect's most celebrated works; today is owned by Karen and John Mast. In the photograph, the sculptor Michael Pavlosky and dedication speaker Dr. Jere Jackson are shown by this latest tribute to the architect. Also on the property, along Hospital Street, is the Texas State Historical Marker celebrating the architect's life work. *(See FIGURE 14.02 on page 416.)*

Extract - speech of dedication:

Since history is a living context, every day we make decisions that will either enhance or degrade the history for future generations. There must be some middle ground between the reactionaries who want to return to the past, even if they cannot decide which modern convenience to abandon, and the hypocrisy of the modernists who sanction the destruction of everything old, yet want to exploit being "historic" and advocate historical theme parks. We needs to avoid the sophistry of constantly lamenting lost treasures while ignoring steps to protect those that are still around.

The statue we dedicate today is a another step in correcting the lapse in collective memory about something his contemporaries knew: D. Rulfs designed modern Nacogdoches. His indelible legacy can be enjoyed today in more than 100 architectural structures still standing, many on Plaza Principal. His creations, such as the Roland Jones House, form the core of the city's extensive National Registry Districts.

......

I am a frequent and resolute tourist. I sincerely hope that visitors to Nacogdoches appreciate the markers, the statues, and the history of Nacogdoches. As a tribute to D. Rulfs, the corner of Hospital and Church Streets will now forever stand out, but his works are everywhere. At Sir Christopher Wren's tomb in Saint Paul's Cathedral in London, the inscription is written, "If you seek his monument, look around you." Every brochure on Nacogdoches should paraphrase this inscription: if you seek a monument to D. Rulfs, look around the city of Nacogdoches.

Jere Jackson
August 29, 2013

FIGURE 15.3 (Opposite) The Liberty Bell Wine Bar

The building at 422 East Main Street, designed by Rulfs in 1901 for the Harris-Lindsey Real Estate Partnership and purchased by E. D. Williams shortly thereafter, has recently undergone another transformation in 2013. In recent years, the building was the home of Wrap-It-Up, owned and run by David Welch. John Sloan purchased and stabilized the property by restoring the exterior windows on the second floor and adding a tasteful brick entryway. The historic property now is the home of the Liberty Bell Wine Bar, a new addition to downtown Nacogdoches, owned an operated by Kati Harris.

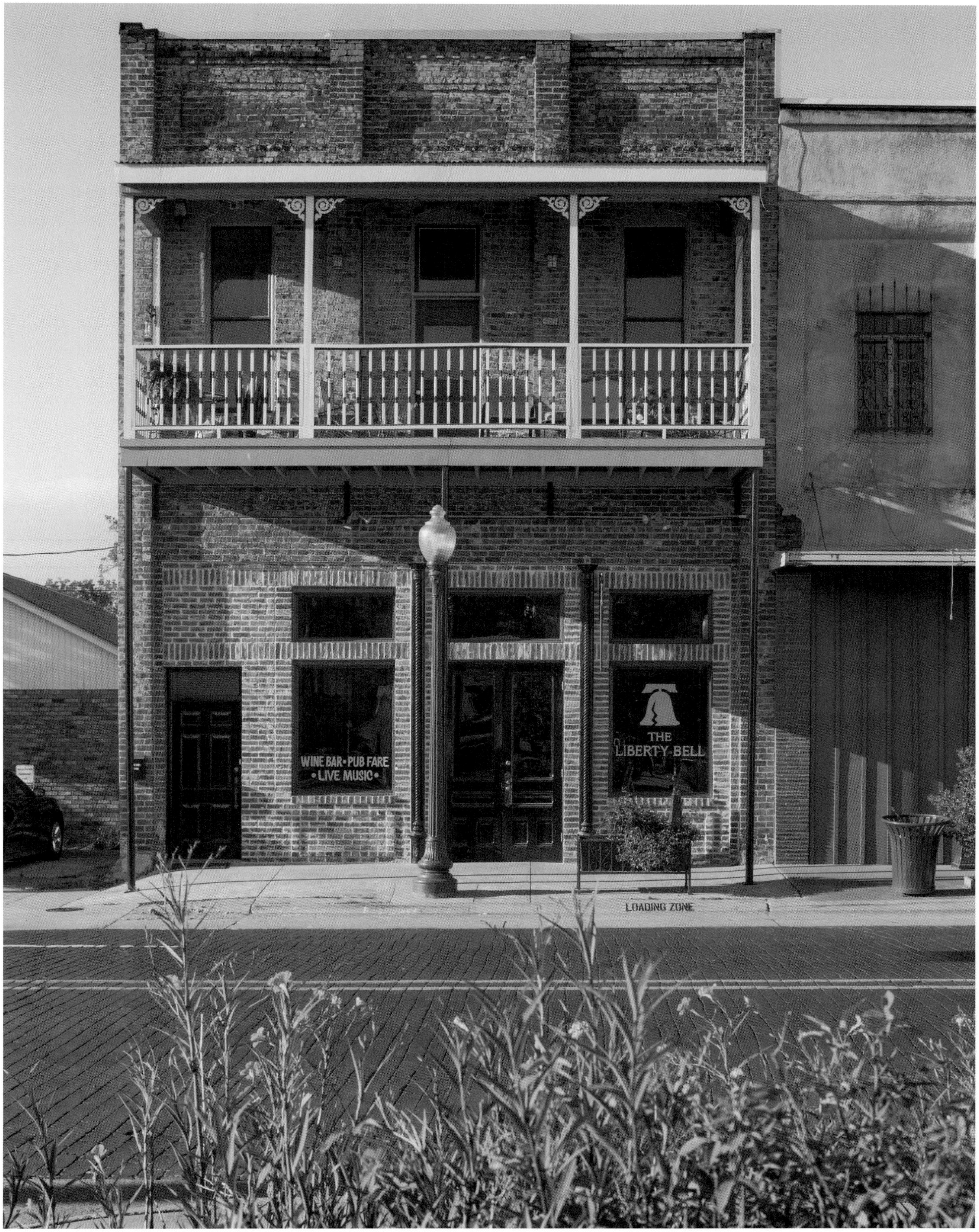
WINE BAR • PUB FARE
• LIVE MUSIC •
THE
LIBERTY BELL
LOADING ZONE

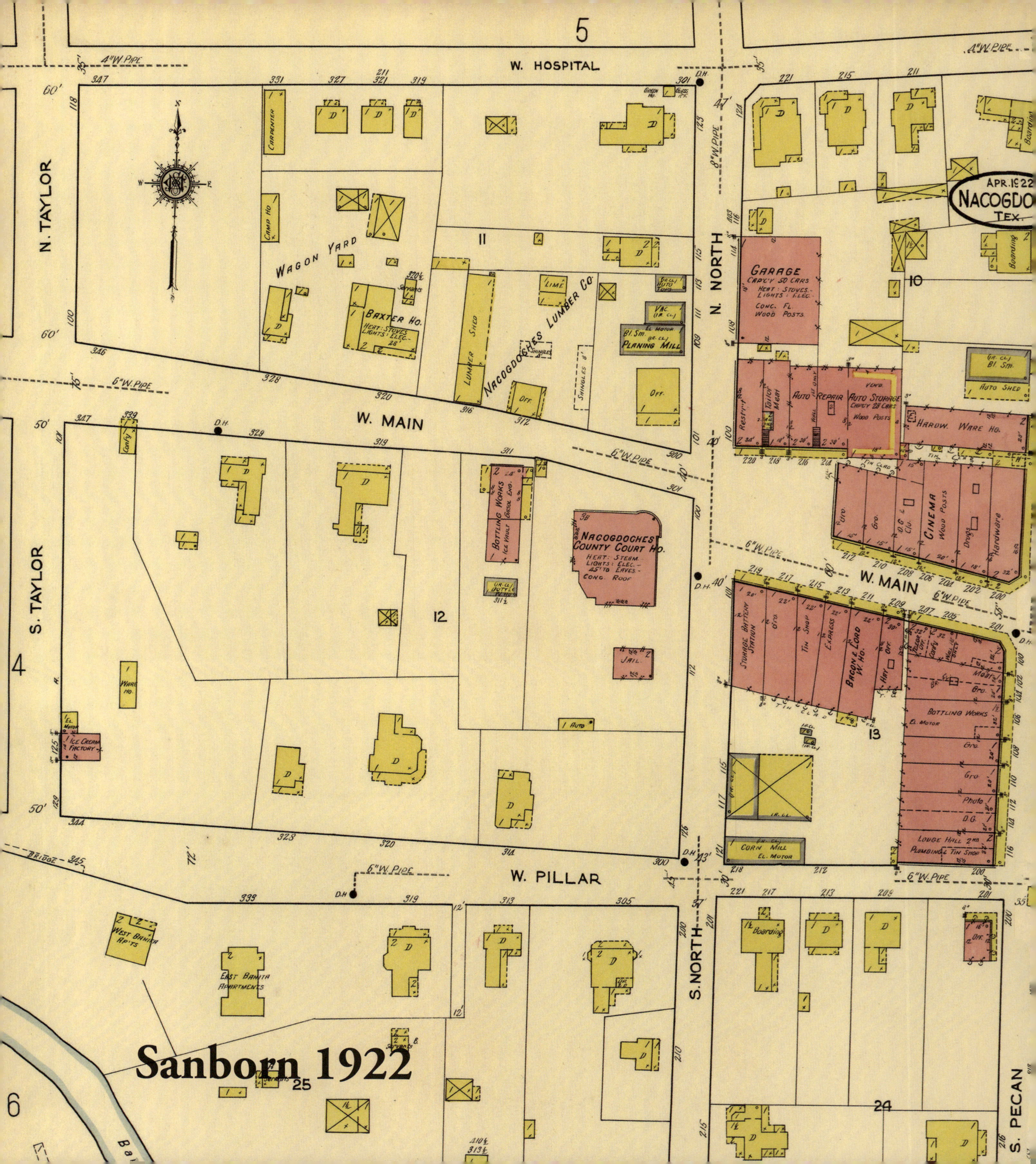

W. HOSPITAL
N. TAYLOR
S. TAYLOR
N. NORTH
S. NORTH
W. MAIN
W. PILLAR
S. PECAN
APR. 1922
NACOGDOCHES TEX.
WAGON YARD
BAXTER HO.
NACOGDOCHES LUMBER CO.
LUMBER SHED
PLANING MILL
GARAGE
AUTO REPAIR
AUTO STORAGE
HARDW. WARE HO.
CINEMA
NACOGDOCHES COUNTY COURT HO.
JAIL
BOTTLING WORKS
ICE CREAM FACTORY
STORAGE BATTERY STATION
TIN SHOP
EXPRESS
BACON & LOAD W. HO.
CORN MILL
LODGE HALL
PLUMBING & TIN SHOP
WEST BANITA AP'TS
EAST BANITA APARTMENTS
Boarding
Sanborn 1922